Psychology

BPS Textbooks in Psychology

BPS Wiley presents a comprehensive and authoritative series covering everything a student needs in order to complete an undergraduate degree in psychology. Refreshingly written to consider more than North American research, this series is the first to give a truly international perspective. Written by the very best names in the field, the series offers an extensive range of titles from introductory level through to final-year optional modules, and every text fully complies with the BPS syllabus in the topic. No other series bears the BPS seal of approval!

Many of the books are supported by a companion website, featuring additional resource materials for both instructors and students, designed to encourage critical thinking and providing for all your course lecturing and testing needs.

For other titles in this series, please go to **http://psychsource.bps.org.uk.**

Psychology

EDITED BY

GRAHAM DAVEY

The British
Psychological Society

This edition first published 2019
© 2019 John Wiley and Sons Ltd

Registered office
John Wiley and Sons Ltd, The Atrium, Southern Gate, Chichester, West Sussex, PO19 8SQ,
United Kingdom

For details of our global editorial offices, for customer services and for information about how to apply
for permission to reuse the copyright material in this book please see our website at www.wiley.com.

Wiley publishes in a variety of print and digital formats and by print-on-demand. Some material
included with standard print versions may not be included in digital versions, secondhand editions
or in print-on-demand. If this product refers to digital ancillaries, you may find information and
instruction on how to access them within this product. Items for some products may be available via
http://booksupport.wiley.com. For more information about Wiley products, visit www.wiley.com.

Designations used by companies to distinguish their products are often claimed as trademarks. All
brand names and product names used in this book and on its cover are trade names, service marks,
trademark or registered trademarks of their respective owners. The publisher and the book are not
associated with any product or vendor mentioned in this book. None of the companies referenced
within the book have endorsed the book.

Limit of Liability/Disclaimer of Warranty: While the publisher and author have used their best efforts
in preparing this book, they make no representations or warranties with respect to the accuracy
or completeness of the contents of this book and specifically disclaim any implied warranties of
merchantability or fitness for a particular purpose. It is sold on the understanding that the publisher is
not engaged in rendering professional services and neither the publisher nor the authors shall be liable
for damages arising herefrom. If professional advice or other expert assistance is required, the services
of a competent professional should be sought.

Library of Congress Cataloging-in-Publication Data
Names: Davey, Graham, editor.
Title: Psychology / Edited by Graham Davey.
Description: Hoboken : Wiley, [2018] | Series: BPS textbooks in psychology |
    Includes bibliographical references and index. |
Identifiers: LCCN 2017054463 (print) | LCCN 2017055954 (ebook) | ISBN
    9781118935606 (pdf) | ISBN 9781118935590 (epub) | ISBN 9781119465799
    (print)
Subjects: LCSH: Psychology.
Classification: LCC BF121 (ebook) | LCC BF121 .P79587 2018 (print) | DDC
    150—dc23
LC record available at https://lccn.loc.gov/2017054463

Set in 11/12.5pt Dante MT by Aptara Inc., New Delhi, India
Printed and bound in Singapore by Markono Print Media Pte Ltd

Cover image: ©hxdbzxy/Shutterstock

Brief Contents

Contents

Chapter 4   **Neuroscience, the Brain, and Behaviour**   **157**

Jamie Ward and Sarah King

Chapter 15   Mental Health and Psychopathology   750

Frances Meeten and Graham Davey

List of Contributors

Abbye Andrews, University of Worcester, UK

Robin Banerjee, University of Sussex, UK

Andy Bremner, Goldsmith's College, UK

Kate Cavanagh, University of Sussex, UK

Mark Conner, University of Leeds, UK

Lucie Corbin, Université de Bourgogne, France

Graham Davey, University of Sussex, UK

Lucy Davies, University College London, UK

Zoltan Dienes, University of Sussex, UK

Tom Farsides, University of Sussex, UK

Alan Garnham, University of Sussex, UK

Mark Haselgrove, University of Nottingham, UK

Graham Hole, University of Sussex, UK

Russell Hutter, University of Leeds , UK

Sarah King, University of Sussex, UK

George Mather, University of Lincoln, UK

Frances Meeten, Institute of Psychiatry, London, UK

Chris Moulin, Université de Bourgogne, France

Daniel Nettle, University of Newcastle, UK

Brian Parkinson, University of Oxford, UK

Felicity Penn, University of Worcester, UK

Anil Seth, University of Sussex, UK

Lance Slade, Canterbury Christ Church University, UK

Charlotte Taylor, University of Worcester, UK

Rhiannon N. Turner, Queen's University Belfast, UK

Dominic Upton, University of Canberra, Australia

Sophie von Stumm, Goldsmith's College, UK

Jamie Ward, University of Sussex, UK

Chantelle Wood, University of Sheffield, UK

Mark Wright, University of Brighton, UK

Preface

Psychology is still one of the most popular disciplines for undergraduate study worldwide. Its attraction for students includes the potential for learning about how and why people do the things they do and learning about a range of approaches to understanding behaviour. Students can also acquire skills that will prove useful in later careers, and studying psychology provides an opportunity to become a professional psychologist working in the applied sector.

But psychology isn't just common sense. It requires a sound basis in biological and social sciences and covers topics as wide ranging as how a nerve impulse is transmitted, how visual illusions are experienced, how babies learn to speak, and how people behave in groups. To understand these very different aspects of human behaviour, we need to learn about processes that occur at many different levels of explanation, including biology, cognition, and the dynamics of social interaction and development. This is what makes the study of psychology fascinating but also intensive in the range of topics that need to be covered.

Taking into account this background, this new introductory book is designed to provide a rich and comprehensive introduction to psychology. It consists of 19 detailed chapters covering all the core areas of psychology, from conceptual and historical issues (Chapter 1) to methodologies (Chapter 2), biological processes (Chapters 3 and 4), individual differences (Chapters 5, 10, and 13–16), cognitive psychology (Chapters 6–9 and 12), developmental psychology (Chapters 11 and 17), and social psychology (Chapters 18 and 19). The chapters are detailed and thorough in the coverage of their topics, and each chapter is written by one or more experts with considerable research and teaching experience in those individual areas. The chapters are also structured into sections that allow the student to learn with the help of numerous interactive features and then test their knowledge of that section before moving on progressively to other potentially more complex material. As such, *Psychology* is significant in the detail with which it covers core psychological knowledge, the range of interactivities it offers instructors and students, and the structured way it organizes material to enable progressive learning.

The table below provides an overview of the structure and content of *Psychology*, together with related levels of analysis and how these topics map onto the core knowledge areas of psychology.

Chapter	Title	Levels of Analysis	Core Knowledge Area
1	The Science of Psychology	Conceptual Issues	Conceptual and Historical
2	Research Methods in Psychology	Methodology	Research Methods
3	Evolutionary and Genetic Foundations of Psychology	Biological Processes	Biological Psychology
4	Neuroscience, the Brain, and Behaviour	Biological Processes	Biological Psychology

(Continued)

(Continued)

Chapter	Title	Levels of Analysis	Core Knowledge Area
5	Motivation	Biological and Cognitive Processes	Individual Differences
6	Consciousness: Conscious Versus Unconscious Processes	Biological and Cognitive Processes	Cognitive Psychology
7	Sensation and Perception	Biological and Cognitive Processes	Cognitive Psychology
8	Learning	Biological and Cognitive Processes	Cognitive Psychology
9	Memory	Biological and Cognitive Processes	Cognitive Psychology
10	Emotion	Biological and Cognitive Processes	Individual Differences
11	Cognitive Development	Biological and Cognitive Processes	Developmental Psychology
12	Language and Thought	Biological and Cognitive Processes	Cognitive Psychology
13	Intelligence	Biological and Cognitive Processes	Individual Differences
14	Personality	Biological, Cognitive and Group Processes	Individual Differences
15	Mental Health and Psychopathology	Biological, Cognitive and Group Processes	Individual Differences
16	The Treatment of Mental Health Problems	Biological, Cognitive and Group Processes	Individual Differences
17	Social Development	Cognitive and Group Processes	Developmental Psychology
18	Social Cognition and Attitudes	Cognitive and Group Processes	Social Psychology
19	Interpersonal, Group, and Intergroup Processes	Cognitive and Group Processes	Social Psychology

TEACHING AND LEARNING FEATURES

As well as being extensively supported with tables, figures, photographic illustrations, video clips, and full glossaries, *Psychology* is supplemented by a range of other features designed to facilitate effective teaching and learning.

Focus points

These provide more in depth discussion of particular topics that are conceptually important, controversial, or simply of contemporary interest. Whenever possible these are linked to everyday examples that allow the reader to consider the issues in a contemporary, everyday context.

Activities

Activities offer the reader an opportunity to engage in active learning about a topic by completing a task or activity. Examples of such activities include simple experiments designed to demonstrate a particular phenomenon, opportunities for further reading and research, and topics and questions suitable for small group discussion. The instructor or teacher may want to make use of these activities when structuring their class teaching.

Research methods

These features contain detailed descriptions of methods utilised in psychology research, and describe the pros and cons of individual methods and their potential uses. These examples supplement the general material provided on research methods in Chapter 2.

Self-test questions

Throughout each chapter the reader will encounter self-test questions. These are designed to test the reader's absorption of basic factual and conceptual knowledge. Instructors and teachers can also use these questions as a basis for discussing key material in class or in small group discussions.

Summaries

The main sections within each chapter end with summaries of the key knowledge covered in that section.

Future directions

Psychology is not a static discipline, and so many chapters end with a future directions section in which the contributors look ahead to describe some of the potentially exciting future developments occurring in their specific areas. This will allow the student to understand the dynamic nature of psychological science and how the subject matter is developing, and will provide a taste of what is to come.

Further resources

All chapters have an extensive bibliography of further reading for the interested reader or the student who requires further detail on specific topics, either to research greater detail for module assignments or simply out of motivated curiosity. A list is provided of relevant articles and books that offer reviews of specific topics, seminal discussion of critical conceptual and theoretical issues, or studies describing important research in an area. Nowadays, students in higher education regularly have free electronic access to many journal articles via their higher-educational institution, and this was one of the main reasons for including a full and extensive list of articles and other resources for students to pursue.

EDITORIAL BOARD

Apart from those psychologists who have contributed directly to the writing of individual chapters, *Psychology* also has the backing and support of an editorial board of experienced psychologists of international reputation. Their role has been to advise on the strategic development of the text and to advise and comment on content and format. I am extremely grateful to the members of this board for their continuing support and guidance. The members of this editorial board are:

Nicola Brace (The Open University, UK)

Holly Branigan (University of Edinburgh, UK)

Rupert Brown (University of Sussex, UK)

Geoff Bunn (Manchester Metropolitan University, UK)

Axel Cleeremans (Free University of Brussels, Belgium)

Pete Clifton (University of Sussex, UK)

Alan Collins (Lancaster University, UK)

Colin Cooper (Queen's University Belfast, UK)

Philip Corr (City, University of London, UK)

Michelle Craske (University of California, Los Angeles, USA)

Richard Crisp (University of Durham, UK)

Tony Dickinson (University of Cambridge, UK)

Robin Dunbar (University of Oxford, UK)

Anna Franklin (University of Sussex, UK)

Adrian Furnham (University College London, UK)

Mark Georgeson (Aston University, UK)

Patrick Haggard (University College London, UK)

Geoff Hall (University of York, UK)

Gordon Hodson (Brock University, Canada)

Tim Hollins (University of Plymouth, UK)

Richard Kemp (University of New South Wales, Australia)

Lia Kvavilashvili (University of Hertfordshire, UK)

Peter Lamont (University of Edinburgh, UK)

Greg Maio (University of Bath, UK)

Tony Manstead (Cardiff University, UK)

Olivier Pascalis (University of Grenoble, France)

Ian Penton-Voak (University of Bristol, UK)

Martin Pickering (University of Edinburgh, UK)

Jane Raymond (University of Birmingham, UK)

Peter Rogers (University of Bristol, UK)

Paul Salkovskis (University of Bath, UK)

Alan Slater (University of Exeter, UK)

Fred Toates (The Open University, UK)

Adrian Wells (University of Manchester, UK)

Fred Westbrook (University of New South Wales, Australia)

Andrew Wickens (University of Central Lancashire, UK)

HAPPY READING AND HAPPY LEARNING!

Finally, I would like to thank everyone involved in developing this learning resource that is *Psychology*. That includes the chapter authors, who have provided detailed, engaging, and accessible contributions; the members of the editorial board for their advice and guidance during the writing of the book; the reviewers for their insightful comments; and in particular the staff at Wiley Blackwell, many of whom have been deeply involved in many different ways in the development of this book.

To the reader and student, I hope you find this a readable, accessible, and enlightening introduction to the wonderful subject that is psychology. I hope it will enable teachers to teach and learners to learn – and that the experience will be an enjoyable one!

Graham Davey
Brighton, February 2018

1   The Science of Psychology

DOMINIC UPTON, CHARLOTTE TAYLOR, FELICITY PENN,
AND ABBYE ANDREWS

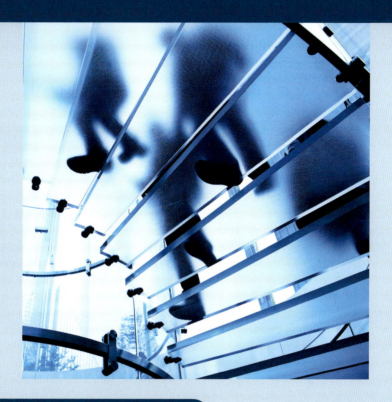

WHAT IS PSYCHOLOGY?

LEARNING OBJECTIVE 1.1

Describe the evolution of psychology from early philosophy to contemporary sociocultural perspectives.

'Psychology – it's all obvious really. It's just common sense!' As a student of psychology, you will also be familiar with the quip, 'So, you're studying psychology – can you read my mind and tell me what I'm thinking?' Studying psychology will not enable you to become proficient in mind reading and it is important to remember that psychology *is* a scientific discipline. So, how do we define psychology? Psychology can be defined as the scientific study of the mind and behaviour. Some authors regard psychology as simply a science of behaviour; however, while this definition does have some merit (psychologists are, of course, interested in observing and measuring behaviour), psychologists also want to understand how and why people think, feel, act and interact with other people in the way that they do. For this reason, psychology is more than a science of behaviour; it is a science of the mind and the processes that shape our behaviour. Psychology is also more than common sense. In fact, there are many examples of psychological research in which the findings are very different from what most people expected. A classic example of counterintuitive findings can be seen in Milgram's (1974) study of obedience (see BBC, 2011). In this study, a teacher was instructed to administer an electric shock to a learner each time they made a mistake on a memory task, slowly increasing the intensity of the shock until it reached an agonizing 450 volts. How many people do you think progressed to administer the full 450-volt shock? If you are familiar with Milgram's study then you may already know the answer. Milgram canvassed the opinions of 40 psychiatrists from a medical school who predicted that approximately 4% of participants would administer the 450-volt shock, a similar figure to that predicted by non-experts. In fact, 65% of participants administered the full shock. People's everyday beliefs are therefore not a good foundation for psychological science, and many currently popular beliefs are false (Kohn, 1990).

To take another example, what makes ill-feeling between work colleagues shift faster? An instance of personal conflict with a colleague can create feelings of anger that are slow to fade. Paradoxically, when a stressful day in the office also involves a specific work-related dispute, bad feelings don't linger so long. According to Meier, Gross, Spector, and Semmer (2013), this counterintuitive finding may reflect our willingness to seek a non-harmful explanation for unpleasant situations, blaming the context rather than the person.

Is it really the case that movie goers enjoy and are emotionally engaged in films shown in 3D compared with 2D (Rooney, Benson, & Hennessy, 2012)? See the discussion point below for more on this topic.

One reason why people may view psychological findings as 'obvious' and 'common-sensical' can be explained by **hindsight bias**, the tendency to view an event as predictable after it becomes known. We will explore hindsight bias in more depth later in this chapter. As you read through this book, you will become familiar with research methodology and the types of evidence used to validate claims about human behaviour. It is important that you adopt a critical and evaluative stance, and not take the evidence at face value. This will help you to develop your critical-thinking skills, important skills for any student of psychology.

DISCUSSION POINT

Read **this article**[1] on the British Psychological Society's website and discuss whether 3D films are more psychologically powerful than 2D.

Basic and applied research

Psychological research can be thought of as either basic or applied in nature. **Basic research** aims to seek knowledge for its own sake. Basic research examines how and why people think and behave in the way they do and may be conducted in a laboratory or real-world setting, with human participants or animals. In contrast, **applied research** is designed to solve practical, real-world problems. As you explore this book, you will find many examples of both basic and applied research that have addressed the complexities of human behaviour. Many psychologists hold the view that all research should have an applied focus, not only making a contribution to scientific knowledge but also having an impact on people, policy, and practice. However, basic and applied research should not be thought of as separate entities; psychologists use basic scientific knowledge to solve real-world, practical problems. Consider the example in Focus Point 1.1, which describes how behaviourist principles of rewards and incentives can be used to motivate students in the classroom. We will explore the behaviourist approach later on in this chapter.

FOCUS POINT 1.1

VIVO MILES: AN ONLINE SCHOOL REWARD SYSTEM

Motivating students to learn is an important goal of education. In order for students to learn effectively, they must be engaged with their learning on a cognitive, emotional, and behavioural level. Vivo is an online school reward system, based upon behaviourist principles designed to improve student engagement, raise attendance, improve grades, and help achieve school values. The programme provides a framework that actively supports a positive behaviour policy and all aspects of 'every child matters', including economic well-being.

Vivos are electronic points, similar to those found in the credit or merit systems that are commonplace in schools, and can be redeemed for a variety of rewards from a customizable catalogue. Students are awarded Vivos for achievements (e.g. excellent classwork or homework) and/or behaviour (e.g. 100% attendance, healthy lunch choices), and they are credited to each pupil's Vivo card. Students can log in online or via their smartphone to check their Vivo Miles balance and exchange their points for items such as cinema tickets, high-street gift vouchers, charity donations, sports equipment, and mobile phone top-ups.

The programme has received praise from students, teachers and parents:

It immediately sold itself as a system that would appeal to students motivated by both immediate and deferred gratification. It was win–win from day one.

(Deputy Head Teacher)

I love using the reward system. In classes it's had a massive effect on the learning, it's increased interest and it certainly motivates children to perform to their very best.

(Teacher)

Feedback from one secondary school implementing the programme found that 95% of students were happier with Vivo Miles than the 'credits and merits' scheme previously in place and 60% of students quickly learned about real-world finances by saving their Vivo currency. A version of the programme for primary schools, Vivo Stars, was launched in 2011 to recognize and celebrate pupils' achievements. The programme enables teachers to award students Vivo points and stickers, which they can use to unlock items for their personal Avatar character.

Find out more about Vivo: https://www.vivomiles.com/index.php.

TEST YOURSELF

1. How can we define psychology?
2. How does psychology differ from common sense?
3. What is the difference between basic research and applied research?

SECTION SUMMARY

- Psychology can be defined as the scientific study of the mind and behaviour.
- Psychology is more than a science of behaviour; it is a science of the mind and the processes that shape our behaviour.
- It is important that you adopt a critical and evaluative stance, and do not take the evidence at face value.
- Basic research examines how and why people think and behave in the way they do. It may be conducted in a laboratory or real-world setting, with human participants or animals.
- Applied research is designed to solve practical, real-world problems.
- Psychologists use basic scientific knowledge to solve practical problems.

PSYCHOLOGY'S ROOTS: THE PATH TO A SCIENCE OF MIND AND BEHAVIOUR

LEARNING OBJECTIVE 1.2

Discuss the main issues and debates that have dominated the history of psychology.

Why do I have to take the Conceptual and Historical Issues in Psychology module? What can I learn from things that happened a long time ago? These are questions that many a psychology student may ask! While the thought of studying the history of psychology may fill you with dread, causing you to fall asleep in the lecture theatre or imagine musty-smelling books in the university library, understanding psychology's roots and its path to a science of mind and behaviour is essential in understanding psychology today and the psychology of tomorrow. The scientific developments in psychology have shaped our understanding of our world, from what we know about philosophical ideas such as the nature of consciousness to our understanding of 'shell-shock' (as it was known in World War I) to the development of treatments for those suffering with post-traumatic stress disorder the design of the 20 pence and £1 coins, and much more. As a student of psychology, you need to be able to reflect not only on how psychology has contributed to philosophical, social and technological change but also on how psychology has been constructed as part of this change (see Focus Point 1.2).

FOCUS POINT 1.2

WHY THE HISTORY OF PSYCHOLOGY IS GOING GLOBAL

In 2008, *The Psychologist* (the official monthly publication of the British Psychological Society) began a feature entitled 'Looking Back', a space for stories and lessons from the history of psychology. In 2011, Dr Adrian Brock discussed why studying psychology's past is actually becoming a global phenomenon:

> Recently I was moaning to a colleague about the fact that a new edition of the textbook that I use in my history of psychology course had appeared and that the university library had ordered only one copy of it for the entire class. When the previous edition appeared in 2002, it had ordered 10. My colleague looked at me with surprise and said: 'Surely the history of psychology hasn't changed all that much since 2002!'
>
> *(Brock, 2011, p. 150, reproduced with permission)*

As Brock argues, the history of psychology is, to some extent, a story, an unfolding narrative aiding our understanding of the human mind and behaviour. It is a well-known story and one that has been recounted in many textbooks (like this one!) for decades. However, the history of psychology is not static; it continues to change and evolve as new cutting-edge research is published that changes what we know about the human mind and behaviour. If what we know about human behaviour is already known then why do researchers continue to seek to understand the human mind and behaviour?

Brock suggests that, in order to answer this question, we first need to understand the difference between psychology's history and its past. The content of many textbooks is a fraction of psychology's past; it serves as what some sociologists and psychologists have termed 'collective memory' (Danziger, 2008). It consists of the things that a particular community at a particular point in history considers worth remembering. In this way, the history of psychology can be rewritten from generation to generation. Indeed, some of the more interesting changes in the history of our discipline have occurred in recent years – for example, an increased emphasis on sociocultural perspectives in psychology.

Most importantly, any advance in our understanding of the history of psychology is also an advance in psychology's object of study itself – ourselves.

Read more in **_The Psychologist's_ archives**[2].

Earlier in the chapter, we learned that psychology is the science of the mind and behaviour. In studying human behaviour, psychologists are interested in exploring the biological, psychological, and environmental factors that influence how and why we behave in the way that we do. This is not new; in fact, it has been an integral part of psychology's history. How did the scope of psychology become so broad? Psychology has roots in philosophy and medicine, in addition to the biological and physical sciences; as a result, there are a number of different perspectives on psychology – that is, different ways in which we can view people's behaviour. The major perspectives in psychology discussed in the following sections of this chapter all help us to understand human nature and have important theoretical and practical applications.

Early philosophy

One of the longest-running debates in psychology is the mind–body problem, as we will explore later in this chapter. Is the mind part of the body or is it a separate spiritual entity? Early philosophers held diverse opinions on the relationship between the mind and the body, and the notion of science itself. Plato (427–347 BCE) was not convinced by the value of science and believed that knowledge is attained by thought. On the other hand, Aristotle (384–322 BCE) argued that there is an intimate relationship between the soul and the body. Aristotle made many contributions to psychology, including the idea that mental health is dependent on both the body and the mind. Despite the excitement created by the ancient Greeks, philosophy and psychology went into a period of decline until the French philosopher, mathematician, and scientist René Descartes (1596–1650) reinstated the mind–body debate. However, Descartes' contributions to psychology were not so positive and were described by Hearnshaw (1987) as leading psychology down a metaphorical cul-de-sac. Descartes claimed that the soul or the mind is the key part of being human, and that to understand human behaviour we first need to understand the workings of the human mind. However, since the mind is not a biological entity, it cannot be studied using objective, scientific methods. As a result, psychology cannot be viewed as a science.

The emergence of psychology as a science

In the mid-1800s, German scientists Ernst Weber (1795–1878) and Gustav Fechner (1801–1887) began to explore the relationship between the mental and physical realms and established a new field called **psychophysics**: the study of how psychologically experienced sensations are dependent on characteristics of physical stimuli.

The beginnings of psychology as a science can be attributed to Wilhelm Wundt (1832–1920), who founded the first experimental psychology laboratory at the University of Leipzig in 1879. Wundt believed that the human mind could be studied by viewing it as separate components, in the same way that a chemist would study a chemical compound. Wundt's approach to the study of the mind is known as **structuralism**: the analysis of the mind in terms of its basic elements. Structuralists used **introspection** to study sensations by exposing participants to various sensory stimuli (e.g. lights, sounds, and tastes) and asking them to report their experiences. Despite the criticisms levelled at this approach, structuralism had an important impact on the development of the scientific study of cognitive processes. In the United States, an alternative perspective on the human mind emerged, known as **functionalism**. In contrast to structuralism, functionalism aimed to study the functions of consciousness rather than its structure and was greatly influence by Charles Darwin's evolutionary theory. William James (1842–1910) was a major proponent of functionalism and his book *Principles of Psychology* greatly enhanced psychology's scope, emphasizing biological and mental processes.

Although, like structuralism, functionalism is not part of modern-day psychology, its legacy is evident in both cognitive psychology, which studies mental processes, and evolutionary psychology, which explores how psychological traits have evolved and adapted over time.

The psychodynamic perspective

The **psychodynamic perspective** seeks to understand the causes of behaviour by examining the internal, inner workings of the human mind, emphasizing the role of unconscious processes. Sigmund Freud (1856–1939) is perhaps the most well-known psychodynamic theorist and developed influential theories of personality and psychosexual development. In the late 19th century, Freud, a young physician in Vienna, began treating patients who exhibited a range of physical symptoms but with no apparent medical cause. Freud also treated patients who had phobias and other conditions. In the absence of a medical explanation, Freud believed that the cause must be psychological, more specifically that the causes were unconscious, hidden from awareness. Freud used free association, a technique that required his patients to verbalize any thoughts that came to mind. Freud developed a form of therapy called **psychoanalysis**, which concerned the examination of unconscious psychological forces. He also proposed that we have innate sexual and aggressive drives that are punished in childhood, resulting in fear and anxiety when we become aware of their presence. This causes us to develop **defence mechanisms**, which are psychological techniques to help us cope with anxiety regarding traumatic experiences.

Freud proposed grand and far-reaching theories of human psychology, and his thinking was developed by a number of individuals, including Melanie Klein (1882–1960), whose contribution to developmental psychology is still evident today in the form of play therapy. Freud's ideas also perpetuated interest in the study of dreams, memory, and mental disorders. While Freud's theories are mostly rejected by contemporary psychological science, his views on the unconscious still support the idea that behaviour can be determined by non-conscious thoughts.

The behaviourist perspective

The **behaviourist perspective** emphasizes the role of the environment in our behaviour. A primary concern of the behaviourists was that psychology was becoming too subjective, using unscientific methods. In 1913, John B. Watson (1878–1958) led a new movement that directly opposed the structuralist, functionalist, and psychodynamic approaches. In Watson's mind, the focus of psychology should be on directly observable behaviour, not unconscious processes. Watson famously commented:

> Give me a dozen healthy infants, well-formed, and my own specified world to bring them up in and I'll guarantee to take any one at random and train him to become any type of specialist I might select – doctor, lawyer, artist, merchant-chief, and, yes, even beggar-man and thief – regardless of his talents, penchants, tendencies, abilities, vocations, and race of his ancestors. I am going beyond my facts and I admit it, but so have the advocates of the contrary and they have been doing it for many thousands of years. (Watson, 1930, p. 82)

Was Watson correct? Or was he indeed 'going beyond his facts'? While behaviour can be shaped by our environment, proponents of the humanistic and cognitive perspectives would challenge this view, as you will see later in this chapter.

B. F. Skinner (1904–1990) also made a significant contribution to modern-day behaviourism. Skinner's research largely involved experimentation on rats to determine how behaviour can be shaped through the processes of reinforcement and punishment. Skinner's approach is known as **radical behaviourism**, which emphasizes that society can utilize the environment to modify behaviour in beneficial ways; the main challenge to this is the concept that human beings are 'free agents'. Behaviourism inspired a collection of techniques known as 'behaviour modification', which manipulate environmental factors to increase positive behaviours and decrease problem behaviours. In the 1950s, Skinner developed 'programmed learning', a concept which suggests that learning is achieved through small, incremental steps, with immediate reinforcement for the student. Behaviourism dominated research on learning in the 1960s, challenging the psychodynamic perspective. However, the rise of the cognitive approach and the study of mental processes caused the interest in behaviourism to wane. Despite this, behaviourism had a significant impact on our understanding of human learning and its principles are clearly evident in many of the behaviour policies in the Western education system today. For example, see Focus Point 1.1, which describes how behaviourist principles of rewards and incentives can be used to motivate students in the classroom. According to the behavioural approach, student motivation is influenced by the use of rewards and incentives by teachers (Pintrich & Schunk, 2002). A reward is defined as an appealing object or event given to a student as a consequence of behaviour – for example, a student is rewarded with a trip to a theme park for 100% attendance over the past term. An incentive is an object or event that can be used to either encourage or discourage behaviour. For example, the promise of the visit to the theme park for 100% attendance is an incentive; actually going on the trip is the reward. Incentives may also be used to discourage negative behaviours – the threat of red marks in the student's planner or detention for not completing homework, for example. Rewards and incentives are useful for short-term involvement in tasks but may not be effective in the long term.

THE EVOLUTION AND IMPACT OF PSYCHOLOGICAL SCIENCE

Origins is a web-based, multimedia timeline developed by the British Psychological Society showcasing the history of psychological science and its contributions to society today. Visit **BPS Origins**[3] and explore the major milestones and discoveries; see how research in psychology has shaped the present and find out how cutting-edge discoveries may influence the future of our discipline.

The humanistic perspective

By the mid-19th century, a new perspective began to emerge to challenge the dominant approaches of psychoanalysis and behaviourism. Humanists disagreed with the focus of the psychodynamic approach that behaviour is guided by unconscious forces. They also rejected the behaviourist view, which proposed that behaviour is determined in response to environmental stimuli. In contrast, the humanistic perspective, or **humanism**, emphasized free will, personal growth, and finding meaning and value in life. Abraham Maslow (1908–1970) was a key figure in the development of humanism and created the **hierarchy of needs**, one of the most influential humanistic explanations of motivation. Maslow proposed a five-tier model of human needs, from basic physiological and safety needs to **self-actualization**. According to Maslow, self-actualization is reached through realization and fulfilment of an individual's potential. Humanists also emphasize the importance of free choice, responsibility, personal growth, and self-worth. From a humanistic perspective, the meaning of our existence rests in our hands. While humanism had a relatively limited impact on psychological science, it still had important applications. For example, Carl Rogers (1902–1987) applied humanist principles to psychotherapy. Maslow's theory also has important implications for education, highlighting the importance of the whole child, including their physical, social, and emotional well-being.

The humanistic emphasis on self-actualization has also emerged in the growing **positive psychology** movement. In contrast to many approaches in psychology that emphasize what is wrong in the world, positive psychology emphasizes how life can be made more fulfilling and how we can nurture the best in ourselves. Positive psychology is primarily concerned with using psychological theory, research, and intervention techniques to understand the positive, adaptive, creative, and emotionally fulfilling aspects of human behaviour (Seligman, 1998).

The cognitive perspective

The **cognitive perspective** seeks to explain human behaviour by examining mental processes. According to cognitivists, humans are essentially information processors whose actions are determined by thought. In the 1950s, psychologists showed a renewed enthusiasm for the study of consciousness and mental processes – a marked shift away from the dominant behaviourist perspective. This is sometimes referred to as the **cognitive revolution** and marked a series of exciting developments in the history of psychology. The rise of computer technology contributed to a new interest in how we understood mental processes, which was influential in the study of memory and attention (Broadbent, 1958). The human mind was now viewed as a system that processes, restores, and retrieves information, which had important implications for how psychologists viewed the structure of memory. The 1950s also witnessed fierce debate between the behaviourists and linguists about how children acquire language. The behaviourists, led by B. F. Skinner, argued that language is acquired through learning. However, the linguist camp, led by Noam Chomsky (b. 1928), claimed that this was far too simplistic. In fact, human beings are preprogrammed to acquire language. In this way, language is innate and cannot necessarily be learned.

The modern-day cognitive perspective encompasses **cognitive psychology**, **cognitive neuroscience**, and **social constructivism**. Cognitive psychologists study the processes that explain how people reason, make decisions, problem solve, remember, form perceptions, and use language. Cognitive psychologists are also interested in the nature of consciousness and how non-conscious processes affect behaviour. Cognitive neuroscience uses brain-imaging techniques to examine brain activity when a person is engaged in a cognitive task. Cognitive neuroscientists are interested in (for example) how the brain acquires knowledge, forms memories, and learns language. In contrast to these very structural approaches to psychology, social constructivism emphasizes that our sense of reality is socially constructed – that is, it is the product of our own way of thinking as members of social groups rather than directly observable. It is evident that the cognitive perspective has developed and diverged over the years but still has a fundamental part to play in psychological approaches to the person.

The biological perspective

The **biological perspective** examines how the processes of the brain influence behaviour. It encompasses the physiological basis of behaviour, behavioural genetics, hormones and behaviour, neuroimaging, neuropsychology, and evolutionary psychology. Recent discoveries in biology have contributed to the dramatic growth in this field in recent years, enabling fascinating insight into the links between the structures of the brain, the human mind, and behaviour. What enables us to feel hungry, sad, happy, or afraid? These are all questions that behavioural neuroscientists seek to understand. **Behavioural neuroscience** examines the brain processes and other physiological functions that influence our behaviour, emotions, and thoughts (Robinson, Rennie, Rowe, O'Connor, & Gordon, 2005). Karl Lashley (1890–1958) and Donald O. Hebb (1904–1985) were two pioneers of the behavioural neuroscience approach. Lashley measured how damage to various parts of the brain affected rats' learning and memory, while Hebb (1949) suggested that connections between nerve cells in the brain are the basis for learning, memory, and perception. Behavioural neuroscientists use brain-imaging techniques, including positron emission tomography and magnetic resonance imaging, to measure brain activity (see Figure 1.1).

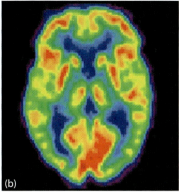

FIGURE 1.1 *Positron emission tomography (PET). (a) PET scanners have a flat bed with a large, circular scanner at one end. (b) Each image of the PET scan shows a horizontal slice of the brain. The parts of the brain illuminated in yellow and red (in this image, around the edges and towards the bottom) indicate those areas of the brain of greatest activity.*

Source: (a) Image copyright Levent Konuk, used under licence from Shutterstock.com; (b) National Institute on Aging / Science Photo Library.

Evolutionary psychology is a recent movement that seeks to explain how evolution has shaped human behaviour. Evolutionary psychologists argue that our mental abilities and behaviour have evolved through the process of natural selection. In 1859, Charles Darwin published the influential yet controversial title *On the Origin of Species*. Undoubtedly, Darwin has shaped the development of modern science, including its attitudes and values, and he is heralded by many as the creator and father of evolutionary theory and the principles of natural selection. Although principally a biologist, Darwin arguably had an overwhelming and lasting impact upon the development of psychology (Sahaklan, 1975).

The sociocultural perspective

The **sociocultural perspective** emphasizes the role of our social environment and culture in how we think, feel, and behave. As humans, we are embedded within a **culture** that shapes our values, beliefs, and our identity. Culture refers to the knowledge, values, customs, and attitudes that guide our behaviour. It is in essence the way of life of a particular group of people. These groups can be defined in many ways – culture may be based on religion, spirituality, ethnicity, occupation, geographic location, educational background, or a combination of these or other factors. All cultural groups possess their own set of **norms**, which are unwritten rules that state what behaviour is accepted and expected (e.g. how to dress and how to introduce yourself to a person in authority). Norms are transmitted to new members of the group through the process of **socialization**.

Psychologists have begun to explore diverse ethnic and cultural groups, leading to the development of **cultural psychology** and **cross-cultural psychology**, explored in more depth later in this chapter. These approaches explore how culture is passed down to its members and examine the commonalities and differences between people from diverse cultures.

DISCUSSION POINTS

1. Why is studying the history of psychology important?
2. How does the humanistic view of behaviour differ from a behaviourist perspective?
3. Describe the origins of the cognitive perspective on behaviour.

SECTION SUMMARY

- Understanding psychology's roots and its path to becoming a science of mind and behaviour is essential in understanding psychology today and the psychology of tomorrow.

- In studying human behaviour, psychologists are interested in exploring the biological, psychological, and environmental factors that influence how and why we behave in the way that we do.

- One of the longest-running debates in psychology is the mind–body problem. Early philosophers, including Plato and Aristotle, contributed to this debate, as did the French philosopher René Descartes.

- In the mid-1800s, German scientists Ernst Weber and Gustav Fechner established a new field called psychophysics, the study of how psychologically experienced sensations are dependent on characteristics of physical stimuli.

- The beginnings of psychology as a science can be attributed to Wilhelm Wundt, who founded the first experimental psychology laboratory at the University of Leipzig in 1879. Wundt's approach is known as structuralism. Structuralists used introspection to study sensations.

- The psychodynamic perspective seeks to understand the causes of behaviour by examining the inner working of the human mind. Sigmund Freud is perhaps the most well-known psychodynamic theorist and developed a form of therapy called psychoanalysis.

- The behaviourist perspective emphasizes the role of the environment in our behaviour. John B. Watson and B. F. Skinner led a new movement that directly opposed the structuralism, functionalism, and psychodynamic approaches.

- Humanism emphasized free will, personal growth, and finding meaning and value in life. Abraham Maslow was a key figure in the development of humanism and developed the five-tier hierarchy of needs.

- The cognitive perspective seeks to explain human behaviour by examining mental processes. The modern-day cognitive perspective encompasses cognitive psychology, cognitive neuroscience, and social constructivism.

- The biological perspective examines how the processes of the brain influence behaviour. It encompasses the physiological basis of behaviour, behavioural genetics, hormones and behaviour, neuroimaging, neuropsychology, and evolutionary psychology. Karl Lashley and Donald O. Hebb were two pioneers of the behavioural neuroscience approach.

- Evolutionary psychology is a recent movement that seeks to explain how evolution has shaped human behaviour.

- The sociocultural perspective emphasizes the role of our social environment and culture in how we think, feel, and behave.

LEVELS OF ANALYSIS: TYPES OF PSYCHOLOGY AND THEIR CONTRIBUTION TO UNDERSTANDING

LEARNING OBJECTIVE 1.3

Describe how psychology can be applied: to you personally, to your studies, and to societal problems.

Human behaviour, and its causes, can be understood at a biological level (e.g. genetic factors and brain processes), a psychological level (e.g. thoughts, feelings, and attitudes), and an environmental level (e.g. our physical and social environments). This is known as **levels of analysis**, a conceptual framework that can be used to help us understand human behaviour. Each of the perspectives discussed earlier in this chapter provide us with different conceptions of human behaviour (see Table 1.1). However, a full understanding of human nature requires us to move between these three levels of analysis. For example, the stress that you feel as you are about to sit an exam or test may be triggered by environmental cues, such as seeing tables arranged in rows, the presence of the invigilators, and so on; however, your feelings of stress and anxiety can also be triggered by chemical changes in the brain, representing a move to psychological and biological explanations of behaviour. To help understand how the levels of analysis framework can help us understand behaviour, let us look at social anxiety disorder (SAD), an excessive emotional discomfort, fear, or worry about social situations and in situations that involve being judged or evaluated by others.

Understanding social anxiety using the levels of analysis framework

Social anxiety can be triggered by public performance situations (e.g. giving a presentation, reading aloud in class) or social situations (e.g. meeting new people starting a new school) (Morris, 2004) and can be explained by biological and biochemical, psychological (e.g. personality), and environmental (e.g. negative life events) factors.

Biological and biochemical factors

Rapee and Spence (2004) suggested that 'genetic factors play a modest but significant role in the development of social anxiety, in both children and adults' (p. 744). Twin studies have found that the heritability estimates for SAD can range from 30% to 50% (Hirshfeld-Becker 2010). However, one recent twin study found only non-shared environment (influences that happen within and outside the family that make siblings from one family different from each other) had a significant influence on SAD in early childhood, whereas genes and shared environment were non-significant influences (Eley, Rijsdijk, Perrin, O'Connor, & Bolton, 2008); this is in contrast to some other studies suggesting the importance of non-shared environmental influences on SAD. More recently, in a longitudinal study of 3,500 twin pairs, Trzaskowski, Zavos,

TABLE 1.1 *Types of psychology and their contribution to understanding.*

	How is human behaviour understood?	What are the causes of human behaviour?	What is the main focus? What methods are used?
Psychodynamic	Controlled by inner forces and conflicts	• Unconscious motives, conflicts, and defences • Early childhood experiences • Unresolved conflicts	• Observations of personality processes in clinical settings • Laboratory research
Behavioural	Responds to the environment	• Past learning experiences • Stimuli and behavioural consequences that exist in the current environment	• Study of learning processes in the laboratory and real-world settings with an emphasis on the measurement of the stimuli–response relationship
Humanistic	Free agent, seeking self-actualization	• Free will, choice, and innate drive towards self-actualization • Search for personal meaning	• Study of meaning, values, and purpose in life • Study of the self-concept
Cognitive	Thinker	• Thoughts, planning, perceptions, attention, and memory processes	• Study of cognitive processes, usually in a laboratory setting
Sociocultural	Social being, embedded in culture	• Norms, social interactions, and group processes in one's culture and social environment	• Study of behavioural and mental processes of people in different cultures • Experiments examining responses to social stimuli
Biological	The human animal	• Genetic and evolutionary factors • Brain and biochemical factors	• Study of the relationship between the brain and behaviour • Role of hormones and biochemical factors in behaviour • Behaviour genetics research

Haworth, Plomin, and Eley (2012) found that genetic factors explained 68% of the continuation of one specific type of anxiety over time.

Psychological factors

Children who are withdrawn, shy, or timid when confronted with a new situation are thought to be more prone to developing SAD. Behavioural inhibition in the second year of life is a hypothesized predictor for social anxiety in later childhood, adolescence, and even adulthood (Moehler et al., 2008). Behaviour inhibition refers to a pattern of behaviour involving withdrawal, avoidance, fear of the unfamiliar, and overarousal of the sympathetic nervous system. Children with behaviour inhibition are cautious, quiet, introverted, and shy in unfamiliar situations (Rosenbaum et al., 2000). In adolescence, inhibition (in addition to social comparison and peer attachment quality) can also predict social anxiety (Cunha, Soares, & Pinto-Gouveia, 2008).

Environmental factors

Parental psychopathology may increase the risk of an individual developing SAD; however, it is the interaction with other factors (e.g. family environment) that appears to be pivotal in the development of SAD. Affected parents may have difficulties modelling appropriate coping strategies and may instead react to their child's fears negatively or become extremely concerned about the level of their child's anxiety, which may result in overprotective behaviours (Ollendick & Hirshfeld-Becker, 2002). Parental rearing styles of overprotection, rejection, and lack of emotional warmth have also been associated with offspring SAD (Knappe et al., 2009).

There is also substantial evidence that negative life events during childhood increase the risk for SAD later in life. Family violence in early childhood has been identified as a risk factor for social anxiety (Binelli et al., 2012) and there may be gender-specific differences in how the disorder affects adult life situations (e.g. men with social anxiety reported greater problems at work and in close personal relationships than controls; Marteinsdottir, Svensson, Svedberg, Anderberg, & von Knorring, 2007). Therefore, while genetic factors have a role to play in the development of social anxiety, psychological and environmental factors are also important influences. In this way, human development can be described as multidimensional – an intricate blend of biological, psychological, and social forces. This forms part of the lifespan view of development.

ACTIVITY 1.1

COMPLETE YOUR OWN LEVELS OF ANALYSIS FRAMEWORK

How could you apply the levels of analysis framework to another developmental or psychological disorder?

1. Create a table with three headings: 'Biological', 'Psychological', and 'Environmental'.

2. Choose one of the terms below and then complete your own levels of analysis framework using each heading as a guide:

   - personality disorders
   - eating disorders (e.g. anorexia nervosa, bulimia nervosa, binge-eating disorder)
   - depression and mood disorders
   - psychosis
   - substance abuse
   - neurological disorders
   - specific learning disabilities (e.g. dyslexia, dyscalculia, dyspraxia
   - childhood anxiety and depression

You may wish to conduct a literature search using electronic databases such as Academic Search Complete, PsycARTICLES or PsycSource to find evidence to support your answers.

TEST YOURSELF

TEST YOURSELF

1. What is meant by the term 'levels of analysis'?
2. How can the levels of analysis framework be used to help understand human behaviour?

SECTION SUMMARY

- Human behaviour, and its causes, can be understood at biological, psychological, and environmental levels.
- This conceptual framework is known as levels of analysis.
- A full understanding of human nature requires us to move between these three levels of analysis.

ISSUES AND DEBATES IN PSYCHOLOGY

LEARNING OBJECTIVE 1.4

Demonstrate knowledge of the recent and possible future developments in the discipline of psychology.

Is psychology a science? What predicts our behaviour: our genes or how we were brought up? These are two classic debates in psychology, and they will be explored in this section, though they are but two of many issues and debates in psychology. Indeed, psychology, being a young science, is resplendent with such debates – this is what makes it such an exciting area of study.

Psychology as a science

A long-running debate within psychology concerns the extent to which it can be called a science. As we outlined at the outset of this chapter (and hopefully refuted!), a common claim from those not studying it is that psychology is just 'common sense' and not a science. In this section we will explore whether psychology can be described as a science. For instance, features of a scientific approach are that there is a definable subject matter, that it involves theory construction, that it involves hypothesis testing, and that it uses empirical methods for data collection. However, what these points fail to tell us is how the scientific process takes place, the sequence of events involved, and the relationship between theory construction, hypothesis testing, and data collection.

If science is concerned with aspects of the real world, then biology is the science of the living world, physics is the science of the physical world, and chemistry is the science of the chemical world. Similarly, psychology would be the science of mind and behaviour (Gross, 2001).

Traditional views of science are concerned with **falsifiability**, which was proposed by Karl Popper (1902–1994) (1957), where a **hypothesis** needs to be fully tested to be a science. Science also needs to be **objective**, where we can see things for what they really are, and not subjective. Science additionally requires understanding, prediction, and control.

Contemporary views of science account for the fact that objectivity may not be achievable and that true objectivity may actually be impossible. Furthermore, contemporary views propose that a single explanation may not fully account for a phenomenon; that is, a number of theories (i.e. psychodynamic, behavioural, humanistic, biological, and cultural) can contribute to the explanation of one behaviour (see the section 'Levels of Analysis' earlier in this chapter).

Nature–nurture debate (heredity versus environment)

Another debate within psychology is the nature–nurture debate. This debate (sometimes referred to as heredity versus environment) is concerned with the extent to which we are determined by our genes (nature) or are the products of our environment (nurture).

There are two extreme views: those of **nativists** and **empiricists**. Nativists adopt an extreme heredity position and the assumption that humans as a whole are a product of evolution. For example, Plato believed that children are born with some innate knowledge and, rather than learning anything new, recollect knowledge that lies dormant in their minds. Empiricists, however, believe that, at birth, the human mind is a **tabula rasa** (a blank slate) and that knowledge comes from experiences and perception. For example, John Locke (1632–1704) believed that all behaviour is learned and that the environment makes people behave in certain ways. However, in practice neither of these two extreme positions is usually adopted, as there are too many facets to the argument to support an all-or-nothing view. So, the question is, how do nature and nurture interact?

This question was first proposed by Francis Galton (1822–1911) in the 19th century, and contemporary beliefs argue that it is in fact an interaction of both nature and nurture that determines behaviour (e.g. Handel, Handunnetthi, Giovannoni, Ebers, & Ramagopalan, 2010). This is known as an **interactionist** view. In Freud's and Jean Piaget's (1896–1980) theories, experience is just as important as underlying mechanisms – therefore, both are interactionists. This is the view that is now generally accepted: genes do not act alone; they always act with experience and this experience determines how genetic material is expressed.

Scientists now recognize that both genetics and the environment work together to enhance an organism's ability to adapt successfully to its environment (Gottesman & Hanson, 2005). In recent years, the interactionist view has been given increasing attention in explaining a range of complex human disorders, such as autism (Meek, Lemery-Chalfant, Jahromi, & Valien, 2013), asthma (Rava et al., 2013), and heart disease (Mi, Eskridge, George, & Wang, 2011). However, not all accept this view, and some argue that genetics can in fact outweigh environmental influences in areas such as school achievement (see Focus Point 1.3). One way the nature–nurture debate is usually studied is by looking at **concordance** rates in identical twins who share exactly the same genetic make-up but have been reared apart and thus have different environmental inputs.

FOCUS POINT 1.3

THE NATURE–NURTURE DEBATE: SHOULD GENETICS HAVE A PLACE IN SCHOOLS?

Can all children achieve academically irrespective of their background? Not so, according to Professor Robert Plomin, a behavioural geneticist. In the summer of 2013, Professor Plomin gave a series of talks at the Department of Education that led to a public outcry when Education Secretary Michael Gove later revealed that he believed genetics outweighs teaching when it comes to how well children perform at school.

In a groundbreaking book, *G Is for Genes*, co-written with Dr Kathryn Asbury, Professor Plomin argues that the idea that children are 'blank slates' is, essentially, wrong. In contrast, children's ability to learn is influenced far more by genetics than by experience. What we should be aiming for, suggests Plomin, is 'a genetically sensitive school'. Asbury and Plomin further stress that genetics is important for policy decision making. Cognitive skills such as learning to read, doing maths, and understanding science are 'some of the most heritable, the most genetically influenced traits that we have, far more than personality or mental illness, and yet not a word is said about genetics in education. For a while, people were quite hostile to it' (Asbury & Plomin, 2013, p. 8).

The authors continue:

If we really do equalize educational opportunity for all children, we get rid of a lot of the environmental variability, so what's left is the genetic variability. You don't get rid of the genetic differences between the children, so, proportionally, more of the individual differences in school achievement will be due to genetic differences. It may be that's why a national curriculum, to the extent that it's successful, actually does increase heritability. (Asbury & Plomin, 2013, p. 10)

DISCUSSION POINT

In **this episode**[4] of *BBC Inside Science*, Dr Adam Rutherford talks to Professor Robert Plomin, King's College London, and Professor Steve Jones, University College London, about the controversies around education and genetics.

Listen to the episode (the discussion starts at 2:18) and discuss some of the issues raised.

Mind–body relationship

Another key debate in psychology is the mind–body relationship. Is the mind part of the body or is the body part of the mind? How do they interact with each other, or are they distinct?

As mentioned earlier in this chapter, René Descartes argued that the mind and body are separate and only interact via the pineal gland in the brain. Although Descartes placed the mind in the brain, he stated that it is a spiritual entity and that the mind and body can in fact exist without each other. This proposal proved to be incorrect, as we now know that the pineal gland is not only used for muscle movement but also plays an important part in the production of hormones. Descartes did, however, introduce the concept of reflexes – the automatic, involuntary actions of the body to environmental events – which are an important feature of survival.

Theories of the mind–body relationship are either **monistic** or **dualistic**:

- Monistic theories suggest that the mind and body are one, and that the mind is not a spiritual entity.

- Dualistic theories suggest that the mind and body are separate (e.g. as Descartes proposed).

Descartes' dualistic theory was challenged by Thomas Hobbes (1588–1674) and by Locke, who had monistic views, and these views are much more in tune with contemporary thinking. For example, Spiegel (2013) identified that stress and social support can affect the course of cancer progression. This shows that the mind and body are not separate, and that one affects the other.

Free will versus determinism

Free will versus determinism is another classic debate within psychology. The debate questions the extent to which our behaviour is under our own control. Free will relates to the notions that people have the ability to choose their own course of action, that they have the freedom to choose their behaviour, and that they have responsibility for their actions. On the other hand, determinism relates to behaviour that we cannot control – that is being influenced by internal or external forces – and argues that free will is just an illusion. Between these two extremes is 'soft determinism', an idea formed by William James, who believed that we do have some choice in our behaviours but that we also have brain mechanisms that control or determine this choice. This suggests that we are free to choose our behaviour but that our choices are drawn from a limited repertoire of predetermined responses. For example, we may have chosen to apply to X University but there are factors that may have determined this, such as our previous experience or our academic ability, which has to some extent been inherited.

The free will versus determinism debate can be applied to almost all human behaviour, including aggression, addiction, eating, psychopathology, and atypical behaviour. Your belief in free will can even influence your behaviour in a predictable way! For example, Baumeister, Masicampo, and DeWall (2009) found that a disbelief in free will reduces helping and increases aggression. Similarly, Vohs and Baumeister (2009) identified that experimentally weakening free-will beliefs led to cheating, stealing, aggression, and reducing helping.

DISCUSSION POINT

How can the free will and determinism debate be applied to explanations of depression, aggression, and relationships?

It is not surprising that many of us believe that we have free will as it matches our subjective experiences. However, despite our desire to assume that we have free will, we must accept some form of determinism.

Psychology and ethics

Ethics are an essential element of all research practice (and, of course, professional practice as well). When carrying out any type of research, it is important to adhere to an ethical code of practice, especially when our research is using people or animals. As researchers we have a moral responsibility to protect our participants from harm.

However, before formal ethical processes were introduced, a number of unethical studies were conducted on both animals and humans (for instance, consider the ethical issues in the Milgram studies described earlier). Animals have been used for a number of different experiments, some of which included maternal deprivation (Harlow, 1958) and drug addiction (Johanson & Balster, 1978). These experiments were carried out with animals because it was felt that it was important to study these topics but that doing so would cause too much harm if the studies were carried out with humans. However, some people believe that it is also unethical to carry out experiments with nonhuman animals, given they cannot consent, cannot be debriefed, and may experience physical or psychological harm. However, others believe that animal experiments are justifiable when the animal has minimal levels of distress and when the experiment will benefit the animal involved or benefit their species (see Festing & Wilkinson, 2007).

In the past, some less-than-ethical studies have also been carried out with humans, for example Watson and Rayner's (1920) study of 'Little Albert', a child of unknown age but probably under 1 year. In this experiment, 'Little Albert' was shown a white rat of which he had no fear, but, when the rat was then shown again, Watson made a loud noise. After the rat was repeatedly presented with the noise, 'Little Albert' developed an emotional response every time he saw an object with a similar property to that of the rat (something white). This experiment would not be approved by today's ethics committees because of a number of ethical problems. There are many other studies that you can probably think of that, again, would also not conform to our ethical standards today, such as Milgram's (1963) obedience study and Zimbardo's Stanford prison study (Haney, Banks, & Zimbardo, 1973). This does not mean that these studies cannot be replicated. Indeed, it is important that these results are replicated so that they can be verified and reinterpreted. Instead these studies can be partially replicated, where a study is replicated as far as possible and specific elements that are unethical today are either removed or modified. Following are some ethical issues arising in early studies:

- Watson and Rayner's 'Little Albert' study (Watson & Rayner, 1920)
  - *Psychological harm*, as the study was designed to produce fear.
  - *No informed consent* – there was no permission from Little Albert's parents.
  - Little Albert was taken from the hospital before the last tests were completed; therefore, it was not possible to remove the conditional emotional response, and therefore there was *no debriefing*.
- Milgram's obedience study (Milgram, 1963)
  - *Deception* – participants actually believed they were shocking real people.
  - *Protection of participants* – participants were exposed to extremely stressful situations, which may have caused psychological harm.
- Zimbardo's Stanford prison study (Haney, Banks, & Zimbardo, 1973)
  - Lack of fully *informed consent*.
  - *Humiliation and distress* were experienced by those acting as prisoners.
  - Participants were not protected from *psychological or physical harm*.

The British Psychological Society (BPS)'s *Code of Ethics and Conduct* (2009) in psychology provides guidelines that discuss several issues relating to research with human participants. These include informed consent, debriefing, deception, confidentiality, and withdrawal. There are a number of other ethical guidelines that may differ in some way; however, the fundamental ethical standards they follow will be very similar. Furthermore, it is now common for research institutions to have their own ethics committee, which will review research proposals and consider the ethical issues raised by them. These committees follow strict ethical guidelines and scrutinize research proposals for ethical issues, making suggestions for areas that may need to be altered. An ethics committee can delay a research project until any ethical issues have been resolved.

TEST YOURSELF

1. What is the difference between the nativist and empiricist perspectives on human development?
2. Why is it important to have ethics in psychology?

SECTION SUMMARY

- Psychology is a young discipline and works hard to engage with key debates, such as answering the question of whether or not psychology is a science.

- Karl Popper proposed that science is founded on the principle of falsifiability, where a hypothesis can and must be fully tested. Science also needs to be objective, to see things for what they really are.

- Psychology can be considered to be the science of mind and behaviour.

- A classic debate in psychology is that of whether our genes or our environment predict our behaviour. Within this nature–nurture debate, nativists adopt an extreme heredity position and the assumption that humans as a whole are a product of evolution. Empiricists believe that the human mind is a blank slate and that knowledge comes from experiences and perception.

- One way the nature–nurture debate is usually studied is by looking at concordance rates in identical twins who share exactly same genetic make-up but have been reared apart and thus have different environmental inputs.

- Another key debate in psychology is the mind–body relationship. Theories of the mind–body relationship are either monistic (mind and body are one) or dualistic (mind and body are separate).

- The free will versus determinism debate is another classic debate within psychology. The debate questions the extent to which our behaviour is under our own control or dictated by external factors.

- Ethics are an essential element of all research practice and professional practice. Studies such as Milgram's obedience study can be partially replicated, with specific elements that are unethical today either removed or modified.

- The BPS's (2009) *Code of Ethics and Conduct* in psychology provides guidelines on issues relating to research with human participants.

BIAS IN PSYCHOLOGICAL RESEARCH

LEARNING OBJECTIVE 1.5

Discuss the main potential biases that can influence the ways that psychological research is conducted and the results interpreted, and examine the potential methods of tackling bias in psychological research.

When studying human behaviour in particular, it is important to be aware of a number of potential biases that might influence the way we conduct our research or the way we interpret our research. You may want to consider some of these when conducting your own research. Research biases include experimenter bias and sampling bias. There are many other types of research bias, some of which will be discussed briefly in this section.

Research bias

Research bias may occur by selecting or encouraging one outcome or answer rather than another. This can happen at any time during the research process, including how the study design or method of data collection are selected, and even affecting data analysis, drawing conclusions, and publication (Pannucci & Wilkins, 2011).

One type of research bias is **experimenter bias** (sometimes called experimenter expectancy effects or observer expectancy effects), which refers to the way in which the results of a study are affected by the experimenter. The experimenter may unintentionally influence the participants in the experiment in order to get the desired results.

Sampling bias exists when a sample is not representative of the population from which it was drawn. Historically, psychologists have under-represented women, ethnic minorities, and non-Westernized cultures and a lot of research is based upon white middle- and upper-class students (Arnett, 2008), typically undergraduate psychology students.

Gender bias refers to the way in which research might be influenced by the gender of the participants, and can be defined as a preference, or prejudice, towards one gender over the other (e.g. one gender is either exaggerated or downplayed). In research, this type of prejudice is known as **androcentrism** – taking male thinking as 'normal' and female thinking as 'abnormal or inferior' (Ritchie, 2009). For example, Bowlby (1944) studied 44 child thieves focusing only on the mother's relationship with the child because the father was considered to be merely the economic and emotional support for the child's mother. Bowlby concluded that maternal deprivation can severely affect a child's mental health, ignoring the potential impact of the father's relationship with the child on the child's well-being. Hare-Mustin and Marecek (1988) proposed two types of gender bias:

- **Alpha bias** – a tendency to exaggerate differences between men and women. An example of an alpha-biased theory is Freud's theory of personality. Freud assumed that a child's superego develops when they identify with their parent of the same sex, with boys developing the stronger superego.

- **Beta bias** – a tendency to exaggerate the similarity between men and women. Kohlberg's (1976) theory of moral development exhibits beta bias as his stages of moral development were based on male moral reasoning, making an inappropriate generalization to women.

Research can often contain a number of gender biases, which include:

- not recording or reporting the sex of the participants involved
- studying more men than women
- studying one pattern of behaviour more so in one sex (e.g. aggression in men)
- researching only one sex.

In psychological history, it comes as no surprise that females have been seen as less important, although this is also true of many other academic disciplines. When psychological research was first conducted, it was difficult for women to become involved, and, when they were, it was assumed that their work was somewhat less important than that of their male counterparts. However, in recent years this has slowly changed as more women take up the discipline (Cynkar, 2007). Other, more contemporary gender biases that may affect research include gay, lesbian, and bisexual biases. This may be by the researcher's selection of research questions and the language used in them, as well as in aspects such as sampling, research design and procedures, protection of participants, and the dissemination of results (Garnets & Kimmel, 2003; Herek, Kimmel, Amaro, & Melton, 1991).

Cultural bias refers to the tendency to ignore differences between different cultures and impose a view taken from one culture on other cultures. There are two types of cultural bias: **ethnocentrism**, the belief that your own culture is superior to another, and **Eurocentrism**, which places an emphasis on Western ideas and then applies these to other cultures to create a universal view of human behaviour.

Cultural bias is evident across many psychological studies (see Activity 1.2) and can also particularly be found in many standardized tests. For example, a number of researchers have unsuccessfully tried to construct culture-free intelligence tests, including Cattell's Culture-Fair Intelligence Test, Goodenough's Draw-a-Person Test, and Williams' Black Intelligence Test of Cultural Homogeneity. Each of these tests has been shown to lack validity across cultures. For instance, Cattell's and Goodenough's tests required participants to draw using pencils and blocks. However, this task would be difficult for children from cultures that are not familiar with such materials. Consequently, these children may score lower than those from cultures to which these materials are familiar. This could lead to children being incorrectly classified in schools (e.g. very bright children placed in a lower set/group).

There are also a number of issues with conducting research with different cultures; these issues are discussed in more detail later on in the chapter.

PERSPECTIVES IN MODERN PSYCHOLOGY

Conduct some research on each of the following classic studies in psychology:

- Bartlett's memory study
- Asch's conformity study
- Milgram's obedience study
- Loftus and Palmer's eyewitness testimony study
- Zimbardo's prison study
- Piaget's three mountains test

For each study:

1. Identify what cultures the participants came from.

2. Identify any methodological issues relating to cultural bias.

3. Suggest some changes that could have been made to the methodology to make it more culturally relevant, looking at it from an objective stance.

4. Finally, ask yourself: How difficult was it to think of changes to make the study more culturally relevant? How might the changes have affected the results?

Tackling bias in psychology

From what has been discussed so far, it is easy to see how biases can be introduced into psychology and psychological research. Although bias is almost always present in every published piece of research, it is mainly up to the reader to consider how bias might influence a study (Gerhard, 2008). However, some biases can be eliminated through careful study design, such as ensuring samples are representative, using objective measures, and employing standardized procedures. Researchers also help to tackle bias by being critical about their results, looking for similarities and differences, and considering effect sizes so that others can see how meaningful the results are.

TEST YOURSELF

1. What are the two types of cultural bias?
2. Historically, why has psychology been gender biased?

SECTION SUMMARY

- When studying human behaviour, it is important to be aware of a number of potential biases that might influence the way we conduct our research or the way we interpret our research.

- There are many types of research bias, including experimenter bias and sampling bias.

- Research bias may occur by selecting or encouraging one outcome or answer rather than another. An example of this is where the experimenter may unintentionally influence the participants in the experiment in order to get the desired results.

- Other biases include sampling bias, gender bias, and gay, lesbian, and bisexual biases.

- Cultural bias refers to the tendency to ignore differences between different cultures and impose a view taken from one culture on other cultures. There are two types of cultural bias: ethnocentrism and Eurocentrism.

- Cultural bias is evident across many psychological studies and can also particularly be found in many standardized tests.

- Although bias is almost always present in every published piece of research, it is mainly up to the reader to consider how bias might influence a study. Researchers also help to tackle bias by evaluating their results critically and objectively.

PSYCHOLOGY AT THE CULTURAL LEVEL

LEARNING OBJECTIVE 1.6

Understand and describe the distinction between cultural psychology and cross-cultural psychology and the research into and implications of these two areas of psychology.

Although an understanding of cultural psychology is essential to be able to study cross-cultural psychology, it is important to make a distinction between the two (Ratner, 2006).

Cultural psychology

Culture refers to the values, traditions, and beliefs that are shared by a particular group of people. Although culture is often associated with nationality and ethnicity, culture can also be defined by age group, sexual orientation, religion, and occupation. Cultural psychologists seek to understand the links underlying cultural influences and behaviour. They focus not only on the interaction of behaviour with the environment but also on the relationship between behaviour and the sociocultural context in which the behaviour occurs.

Culture remains an important factor that shapes individual behaviour through sets of attitudes, beliefs, and values shared by a large population or region (Shiraev & Levy, 2010). For example, in Western culture, handshakes should be firm as weak handshakes are considered limp and cold, but in some Muslim countries (such as Turkey and the Arabic-speaking Middle East) a grip that is too firm is considered to be rude.

Cross-cultural psychology

In contrast to cultural psychology, cross-cultural psychology seeks to understand universality rather than focusing on how local cultural practices influence psychological phenomena. According to Shiraev and Levy (2010), cross-cultural psychology is defined as the 'critical and comparative study of cultural effects on human psychology' (p. 2). Cross-cultural psychology places an emphasis on the critical-thinking and comparative aspects of study, demonstrating the ways in which human activity is influenced by cultural forces (Shiraev & Levy, 2010). Research around cross-cultural psychology requires data from two or more cultures in order to draw comparisons between their data. Thus, cross-cultural psychologists try to explain the vast psychological diversity between differing cultures.

Cross-cultural psychology is an important feature of psychological enquiry because it helps to reduce ethnocentrism. Ethnocentrism is the tendency to see the world from our own point of view; to be judgemental, suspicious, or misunderstand other groups; and to believe in the intrinsic superiority of our own group. For example, in an interesting research study, Whittaker and Whittaker (1972) gave students 10 minutes to draw a map of the world, adding as much detail as possible. The researchers found that, in almost all cases, the students' own country was disproportionately larger (geocentrism), potentially indicating thoughts of grandeur or superiority for their own country.

Approaches: Etic–emic distinction

Research has to begin somewhere, and this usually involves techniques rooted in the researcher's own culture (Berry, 1989). In this instance, cross-cultural psychologists may pick one of two approaches: **etic** or **emic**. The etic approach refers to examining how cultures are similar – that is, examining only one culture using criteria relevant to the internal characteristics of that culture. The emic approach refers to the differences between cultures, revealed by examining many cultures and making comparisons using criteria that are considered to be absolute or universal.

Many attempts have been made to replicate studies originally conducted in the United States in other parts of the world, with researchers assuming that the situation being studied had the same meaning in other cultures as it did in the original culture (Smith & Bond, 1998). For instance, Arnett (2008) found that many prestigious journals of the American Psychological Association were 'based not on a broad cross cultural section of humanity but on a small corner of the population with mainly those living in the United States' (p. 602). Similarly, Webster, Nichols, and Schember (2009) pointed out that a large percentage of psychological research has been conducted predominantly in Western and English-speaking universities and as a result has focused on a relatively small selection of the world's population. Although this research cannot be generalized to the whole population, it is assumed that all populations are similar and is therefore said to be 'imposed etics'.

Individualism versus collectivism

Individualism and **collectivism** are two ways in which we can understand the relationships between individuals in a group. Individualism refers to individuals making their own choices and the extent to which they interact as individuals with the rest of a group. The people in individualistic societies typically view themselves as independent and are usually considered to be represented by Western cultures, such as

Australia, France, the United Kingdom, and the United States. On the other hand, collectivism relates to the views of the group as an entity, a social pattern consisting of closely linked individuals who view themselves as part of one or more collectives and where individuals are mostly concerned with pleasing the social group in which they live (e.g. an individual's family or their group of friends). Collectivistic societies are usually considered to include countries such as China, India, and Japan.

It is important to distinguish between individualistic and collectivistic cultures in psychological study because the ways in which people behave in these two types of culture are likely to differ – especially when it comes to social group behaviour and the psychological beliefs that drive individual behaviour.

Difficulties researching within cross-cultural psychology

There are a number of issues that may arise when conducting cross-cultural research in psychology. A few of these research considerations are listed below:

- Research materials (e.g. apparatus, tests, stimuli) need to be familiar to the participants and valid within each culture.
- There is a need to have high levels of internal consistency as well as external validity (Chen, 2008).
- The participants need to be clearly representative of the culture being studied.
- Will all the participants understand the concept of 'consent' in the same way? In some cultures women are not allowed to give consent; in other cultures consent is frowned upon; and in others the term 'consent' has a completely different meaning.
- The influence of a 'researcher' in different cultures may differ, with participants in some cultures feeling compelled to participate because of the researcher's perceived status.
- Discussing sensitive topics – such as sexuality and human rights, which may not be talked about openly and freely in certain cultures – needs to be considered carefully.
- Conclusions should be drawn from data with a full understanding of what they might mean within a particular cultural context.

Examples of cross-cultural differences in psychological research

Below are a few examples from important areas of psychology of the ways in which culture influences emotion, personality, and health and well-being.

Emotion

There are many examples of cross-cultural differences in the recognition of emotional facial expressions. For instance, Izard (1971) found that North American and European groups correctly identified 75–83% of facial expressions, whereas a Japanese group scored 65% and an African group 50%. Similarly, Jack, Garrod, Yu, Caldara, and Schyns (2012) identified that facial expressions of emotion are not culturally universal. Through the use of a computer graphics system, 30 individuals from Western and Eastern cultures were asked to identify six different basic emotions. The authors found that

Westerners identified each of the six basic emotions with a distinct set of facial movements common to their group. However, those from Eastern cultures did not, their representations showing considerable overlap between emotion categories, particularly for surprise, fear, disgust, and anger.

One way that this can be explained is the fact that emotions are social constructs as a function of the cultural system in which we grow up. For example, the similarities across cultures in emotional expression may be universal across all cultures, while there may be some cultural variation among others.

Personality

Can personality traits be generalized across people from different cultures? Can traits developed by a US psychologist be generalized to people from different countries? For example, Costa and McCrae (1992) developed the Big Five personality traits – a theory which assumes that personality can be described based on just five major important dimensions. However, of these five traits, it has been identified since that *extraversion*, *agreeableness*, and *conscientiousness* are consistently found whereas *openness* and *neuroticism* do not seem to be important within certain cultures. It is therefore difficult to determine whether these latter traits do appear or indeed exist within certain cultures. This is a contemporary issue of debate within psychology.

Health and well-being

People from different cultural backgrounds will have differing opinions on ideal levels of subjective health and well-being. For example, there are a variety of factors that differ across cultures that may influence when and how people present with mental health problems and what type of treatment they seek (Eshun & Gurung, 2009).

Health and well-being can be understood either from a Western evidence-based medical approach or from within traditional indigenous approaches (Prasadarao, 2009). For example, in traditional Chinese medicine, health is regarded as the balance of yin and yang, the two complementary forces in the universe. The balances of yin and yang (hot and cold) are a critical element of many different cultures (e.g. Chinese, Indian, and Mexican) and even affect food choices. In addition, mental health problems are conceived of very differently across different cultures. For example, in Indian Hindu populations, many believe that mental illness is caused by possession by the 'evil eye' (Periyakoil & Dara, 2010); in Japan, mental illness is seen as a weakness in character rather than a treatable illness (Nakane et al., 2005); and in Vietnam, mental illness is considered shameful and often associated with wrongdoing in a previous life (Allotey, Manderson, Nikles, Reidpath, & Sauvarin, 1998). There are many other examples of cultural differences in health beliefs, such as decision making around surgical procedures and treatment (Yosef, 2008), the gender of the health professional a person may see (Periyakoil & Dara, 2010), and the use of a spiritual healer or sorcerer (Allotey et al., 1998; Macfarlane, 2005).

TEST YOURSELF

1. What are the differences between cultural psychology and cross-cultural psychology?
2. How does cross-cultural psychology address bias?
3. What is meant by individualism and collectivism? How do they interact with each other?

SECTION SUMMARY

- Culture refers to the values, traditions, and beliefs that are shared by a particular group of people.

- In contrast to cultural psychology, cross-cultural psychology seeks to understand universality rather than focusing on how local cultural practices influence psychological phenomena.

- The etic approach refers to examining how cultures are similar. The emic approach refers to the differences between cultures.

- A large percentage of psychological research has been conducted predominantly in Western and English-speaking universities and as a result has focused on a relatively small selection of the world's population.

- Individualism and collectivism are two ways in which we can understand the relationship between individuals in a group. It is important to distinguish between individual and collectivist cultures in psychological study because the way in which people behave in these two different types of culture is likely to differ.

- There are a number of issues that may arise when conducting cross-cultural research in psychology. Research considerations include appropriateness of research materials, representativeness of participants, experimenter influence, and topic sensitivity.

- There are many examples of cross-cultural differences in emotion, personality, and health and well-being.

PSYCHOLOGY TODAY

LEARNING OBJECTIVE 1.7

Demonstrate understanding of the applications of psychology as an academic subject and some of the governing and professional bodies in psychology as a career and subject area.

As we have seen earlier in this chapter, the discipline of psychology has grown enormously since the laboratory experiments of William Wundt in 1879, and psychology has emerged from the scientific lab to have a genuine real-world influence. Over the years since the founding of the British Psychological Society in 1901, the expertise of psychologists has begun to have an influence across many areas of society. As we will see later when we explore the psychological professions, psychologists today can be found almost anywhere – even in areas such as traffic management and aviation safety. However, let us first look at psychology as an academic discipline.

Psychology as an academic subject

Psychology is one of the most popular degree subjects, with 66,120 full-time and 28,090 part-time students enrolled on psychology courses across the UK in 2014–2015 (Higher Education Statistics Agency, 2015; most recent national statistics available);

TABLE 1.2 *Areas of academic psychology.*

Area	Description
Biological psychology	The physiological basis of behaviour, behavioural genetics, hormones and behaviour, neuroimaging, neuropsychology, and evolutionary psychology.
Cognitive psychology	Cognitive processes, including memory, learning, thinking, reasoning, perception, language, attention, and consciousness.
Developmental psychology	Physical, cognitive, social, and emotional human development across the lifespan, from the prenatal period through to late adulthood.
Social psychology	Social cognition, attribution, group behaviour and intergroup processes, relationships, prejudice and discrimination, attraction, prosocial behaviour, and aggression.
Individual differences	Personality, intelligence, motivation, emotional intelligence, psychological testing, and cognitive style.
Research methods	Quantitative and qualitative methods, research design, data collection, analysis, and interpretation.
Conceptual and historical issues	Examines the 'big picture' of psychology through key issues and debates that have informed its development, from the origins of the discipline to the present day.

More careers information is available from the British Psychological Society (www.bps.org.uk/careers).

overall, the number of students has grown by some 40% since 2010. People have many different ideas about psychology. One of the main things that surprises people about psychology is the breadth of the topics that are covered during an undergraduate degree. But what does the subject actually involve? The areas in Table 1.2 are strands underpinning the academic subject of psychology that you will study throughout your undergraduate degree.

Since psychology as a discipline is extensive, it is impossible to cover everything during the three (or sometimes four) years of a psychology undergraduate degree. However, students usually get the opportunity to study modules in areas that they find particularly interesting, especially in the final year of study. For example, you might choose to study a forensic psychology module, exploring the psychology of criminal behaviour and offenders.

The skills that are developed while studying psychology are broad and wide ranging. As you can see from the various areas of psychology in Table 1.2, a psychology student will have the opportunity to develop skills in many areas. However, it is important to recognize that psychology at an undergraduate level is just the starting point. In order to become a psychologist or to become professionally skilled in a certain area, you will need to carry out further study and engage in relevant work experience. We will look at the professions and how you can work towards these careers a little later on.

Governing and professional bodies in psychology

The discipline of psychology in the UK is represented by the British Psychological Society (BPS). This is a professional body that aims to promote excellence in the field of psychology through the sharing of scientific knowledge, research, and guidelines for good practice. The BPS also monitors the standard of university courses and training programmes in psychology, including undergraduate and postgraduate degrees and specific training courses. Those courses that meet certain criteria then achieve BPS-accredited status.

Students who successfully complete a BPS-accredited undergraduate degree are eligible for Graduate Basis for Chartered Membership (GBC), which is a requirement for most psychology positions and for a career as a chartered psychologist. The BPS also accredits postgraduate courses that lead to **chartered** status. If you are applying to take an undergraduate psychology degree in the UK, you might like to consider whether or not the course is accredited by the BPS and whether this is important to you or your career. However, it is possible to undertake conversion courses at a later date if you require GBC.

Depending on the area that you specialize in, and your personal interests, you might also be a member of another professional body, such as the UK Council for Psychotherapy, the British Association for Counselling & Psychotherapy, or the Experimental Psychology Society. Other bodies include the Psychological Society of Ireland, the Association of German Professional Psychologists, and the European Health Psychology Society.

Another organization relevant to psychology is the **Health and Care Professions Council (HCPC),** which will be of significance if you plan to have a career in an area of professional psychology. Unlike the BPS, the HCPC is a regulatory or governing body, which means that this organization monitors professional practice and has the power to prevent people from practising. Once you are qualified and practising as a psychologist, you are required to keep a record of your professional activity and development. Professionals are randomly selected for audits and also have to renew their membership every 2 years.

DISCUSSION POINTS

1. What areas of psychology might you expect to study during an undergraduate psychology degree?
2. Which body sets the standards for entry onto the professional register of all practitioner psychologists?

SECTION SUMMARY

- Psychology is one of the most popular degree subjects. In 2014–2015, there were 66,120 full-time and 28,090 part-time students enrolled on psychology courses across the UK.

- The breadth of the topics that are covered during an undergraduate degree surprises most people and the skills that are developed while studying psychology are wide ranging.

- In order to become a psychologist or to become professionally skilled in a certain area, you will need to carry out further study and engage in relevant work experience.

- The discipline of psychology is represented in the UK by the BPS.

- Students who successfully complete a BPS-accredited undergraduate degree are eligible for Graduate Basis for Chartered Membership, which is a requirement for most psychology positions and for a career as a chartered psychologist.

- Depending on the area in which you specialize, and your personal interests, you might also be a member of another professional body.

- An organization relevant to psychology is the Health and Care Professions Council, which will be of significance if you plan to have a career in any area of professional psychology.

PSYCHOLOGY IN ACTION: APPLYING PSYCHOLOGICAL SCIENCE

LEARNING OBJECTIVE 1.8

Demonstrate knowledge of the wide variety of professional careers in psychology and other occupations where a psychological science background is advantageous.

Psychology is a very diverse subject and we have briefly touched upon the key strands underpinning the academic discipline. But how does this translate into the real world? What does psychology have to offer on everyday issues? Understanding psychological theory and research can also have an impact on our own lives and how we act or respond in certain situations (see Research Methods 1.1).

RESEARCH METHODS 1.1

THE SMOKE-FILLED ROOM AND 'THE BYSTANDER EFFECT'

A study in the 1960s revealed an interesting finding about how we act differently when we are in the presence of others compared with when we are alone (Latane & Darley, 1968). Participants were asked to sit in a waiting room, either by themselves or in the presence of two other people. The two others were either real participants or confederates who were aware of the aims of the study.

When the room began to fill with smoke, the researchers measured how long it took each participant to report the smoke. Interestingly, although participants reported the smoke very quickly when they were alone (75% reported it), only 10% of participants reported it at all when they were sat with two confederates who did not respond to the smoke. In fact, even in the presence of two real participants, still only 38% reported the smoke!

This study was part of a series of studies that led to the coining of the term 'the bystander effect'. According to Latane and Darley (1968), people are less likely to react or offer help in an emergency if there are other people around. This appears to be due to a number of factors, including 'pluralistic ignorance', which is the idea that people look at how others react to help them to know what to do, and 'the audience inhibition effect', which is the idea that people don't respond in case they look stupid or appear to be overreacting.

Latane and Darley also referred to 'diffusion of responsibility'. This is the idea that, when others are around, we believe we are less responsible. Additionally, if others are nearby but not visible, we tend to assume that another person will be responding and that our help is not needed. More recent research has shown that this may extend to everyday non-emergency situations as well. For example, people may be more likely to respond to an email requesting help with something when the email is addressed solely to them and not to a number of recipients. One study found that these responses also tended to be lengthier and more helpful (Barron & Yechiam, 2002).

DISCUSSION POINT

Experiments such as Latane and Darley's (1968) with the smoke-filled room provide insight into social behaviour and force us to take some responsibility.

What would you do if you were driving home and saw a large fire in a field as you passed by? Would you think that it must be being dealt with – after all, someone else must have seen it? And would your reaction be affected by the number of people passing by without stopping? Or, knowing what you now know about social behaviour, would you report it, just in case nobody else has?

Similar issues were explored in the 2013 UK Channel 4 TV series *Eye Spy*, narrated by Stephen Fry. This series involved a number of hidden-camera experiments to see how the public would react in certain situations. For example, would anyone speak up when a waiter repeatedly expressed comments of a racist or homosexual nature to a couple in a restaurant? Surprisingly, it seemed that a lot of people did not speak up in these situations.

Although the programme may not have undertaken these experiments in a scientifically rigorous way, it did highlight the social and psychological processes and pressures that people face. *Eye Spy* was presented as a light-hearted look at the morals of people in Britain, with the underlying message that most people are essentially good ('heroes') – but was it really *morals* that were being tested? Was it poor morals that stopped people speaking up when a couple received racist abuse in a restaurant? Or was it in fact psychosocial processes at work, such as the bystander effect (i.e. 'If no one else is saying anything, it must not be necessary for me to speak up')?

A meta-analysis of the research into the bystander effect suggested that this non-intervention is greatest when situations are perceived as dangerous, when perpetrators are present, and when the costs of intervening are potentially physical (Fischer et al., 2011). Although it is unlikely that the people in the *Eye Spy* series felt physically threatened by the person dishing out verbal abuse, it is possible that their behaviour was affected by what other people were doing (or, rather, not doing) as well as concerns about personal repercussions due to the presence of the 'perpetrator'.

The psychological professions

What do psychologists do?

Careers in psychology are just as broad ranging as the subject itself. Psychologists work in many different areas and their roles involve completing a variety of duties on a daily basis. Psychologists apply evidence and theory to human problems; this may be through direct work with individuals or through research and sharing information.

While psychologists cannot 'solve' human problems, they work in collaboration with people to help them develop and utilize coping strategies for the future and to help them change the way they think or behave when their current strategies are not working for them. They use observations, assessments, and scientific research to inform how they work with people and which 'interventions' may be useful. There are a number of types of psychologist; however, it is important to remember that, despite the different titles, the roles of psychologists often overlap due to the core skills that all psychologists develop during their education and training. Also, remember that there are a wide range of careers that psychology graduates might go into, as we will explore later in this chapter. A fuller description of applied and professional psychology can be found in Davey (2011).

Counselling psychologists

Counselling psychologists meet with individuals, couples, or groups who have mental health problems, such as depression or anxiety, or other issues that they are struggling with, such as bereavement, domestic violence, or relationship problems. They may also work with people to promote personal growth. Counselling psychologists work together with individuals to help reduce distress. This usually involves talking therapies, although counselling psychologists might also draw upon other methods of engagement, such as art, music, or play therapy. Counselling psychologists work in a variety of places; these include hospitals, GP surgeries and other healthcare establishments, mental health teams, educational settings, the workplace, and private practice. More information about counselling psychology can be found in the *Handbook of Counselling Psychology* (Woolfe, Strawbridge, Douglas, & Dryden, 2010).

Clinical psychologists

Like counselling psychologists, clinical psychologists work with individuals, couples, and groups with mental health problems. They might also work with people with learning disabilities, brain injury, or physical health problems, and they work across the age span, with children, adults, and older adults. Clinical psychologists carry out assessments to better understand individuals. This might be through observations or the use of questionnaires and **psychometric tests**. Clinical psychologists then use this information to think about how a problem has developed and how it might be managed so as to reduce distress and improve well-being. Clinical psychologists often work in teams and their roles can be very broad. They might work indirectly to support individuals, through working closely with carers and giving advice, or through delivering training to staff teams, for example. They might also provide one-to-one therapy with individuals. Clinical psychologists usually work in healthcare settings such as mental health teams and hospitals, often in the NHS but sometimes for private companies. They might also work independently in private practice. The 'Short Introductions to the Therapy Professions' series provides a useful introduction to this profession (Cheshire & Pilgrim, 2004; Davey, 2011; Davey, Lake, & Whittington, 2014).

Educational psychologists

Educational psychologists work with children and adolescents in schools and other educational settings. They aim to support the development of each young person towards their potential by working with parents, families, and teachers, as well as the child, to find ways of supporting the individual's learning and participation in education. Educational psychologists support young people with a variety of issues, including learning difficulties and behavioural, emotional, and social difficulties. Like clinical psychologists, educational psychologists use various forms of assessment to inform their work with young people. For example, these assessments may be measures of cognitive functioning, which indicate the person's strengths and areas of need. Educational psychologists tend to work in schools, nurseries, and other facilities for young people. Some work privately, providing consultation to people who seek professional support. See Alexander and Winne (2006) and Davey (2011) for introductions to this field.

Health psychologists

Health psychologists are concerned with the psychology of health and well-being. They use their knowledge of behaviour change to advise others (e.g. the media or government) on the best ways to get messages across about health and lifestyle behaviours, such as alcohol use, fruit and vegetable consumption, and use of contraception. Health psychologists also apply their knowledge to physical illness and support people with the psychological impact of illness. They may work in healthcare settings, academic institutions, or private practice. See Davey (2011) and Ogden (2012) for more detailed introductions to health psychology.

Occupational psychologists

Occupational psychologists support people in the workplace by working with employers. They are able to draw on their knowledge of psychology to advise organizations on things like how to keep staff motivated and how to prevent and manage stress in their employees. Occupational psychologists use a range of assessment tools to inform their work, including psychometric tests. Their knowledge and skills are useful for promoting the effectiveness of companies and their workforces. Occupational psychologists work in organizations such as the civil service, the prison service, and government departments, as well as universities.

Forensic psychologists

Forensic psychologists assess people who have committed criminal offences, provide intervention programmes, and give their expert opinions in court. They apply psychological theory, research, and formulation to understand the behaviour of these individuals. Forensic psychologists might also develop interventions for supporting prison staff and promoting well-being and rehabilitation in people who are in prison. They usually work in the prison service, secure hospitals for people with mental health problems, social services, universities, or private practice. See Canter (2010) and Davey (2011) for introductions to the field.

Clinical neuropsychologists

Neuropsychology is an expert field involving the science of the brain and neuropsychological function. Once qualified as a clinical or educational psychologist, you can undertake further study to specialize in neuropsychology. Neuropsychologists work with people who have experienced brain injury, tumours, strokes, and neurodegenerative disorders, providing assessment and support. They tend to work in healthcare settings and rehabilitation centres, as well as academic institutions. Ogden (2005) presents an introductory text with case studies to illustrate the work of a clinical neuropsychologist.

Sport and exercise psychologists

Sports and exercise psychologists provide advice to athletes, coaches, and the general public on all psychological aspects of performance. For example, they might support others to promote team spirit, motivation, and goal setting, or they may help athletes to manage stress. These psychologists work in any settings where people are involved in sports and exercise. See Davey (2011) and Weinberg and Gould (2011) for introductions to this field.

Academic, research, and teaching psychologists

Psychologists also work in research and teaching, usually in educational facilities such as universities (see earlier in this chapter for information about psychological research). Researchers communicate this information to others through presentations at conferences, through teaching, and by publishing their work as journal articles and books. Academics work in teaching or lecturing and usually engage in research activities as well. Read more about teaching in psychology in Upton and Trapp (2010).

 Look through the BPS Media Centre **playlist**[5] from the British Psychological Society for more insights into careers in psychology.

How do I become a professional psychologist?

Every area of professional psychology has a different route. Table 1.3 gives an indication of the qualifications and work experience needed in order to become a chartered psychologist in the UK in any of the areas outlined above. For most of these routes, you will need to have obtained an upper second (2:1) or a first-class degree in addition to voluntary or paid work experience. If you obtain a 2:2 degree, you may need to study for a postgraduate qualification (e.g. an MSc) in addition to voluntary or paid work experience.

All psychologists have a responsibility to work ethically and to ensure their work is centred on promoting well-being and preventing harm. For example, they must always consider whether or not their intervention is wanted or needed and whether or not it would be useful. The HCPC monitors the practice of chartered psychologists throughout their career to ensure they are adhering to the HCPC's standards. Psychologists should also take note of the BPS's Code of Conduct and guidelines for ethical practice, and they must use government legislation and guidance to inform their practice.

TABLE 1.3 *Pathways to becoming a chartered psychologist in the UK.*

Specialism	Postgraduate qualifications and work experience
Counselling psychologist	• Relevant paid or voluntary work experience in mental health • Basic qualifications/training in counselling skills are preferred • Doctorate in counselling psychology, accredited by the BPS and approved by the HCPC or the BPS's Qualification in Counselling Psychology
Clinical psychologist	• Doctoral training in clinical psychology, accredited by the BPS and approved by the HCPC – a 3-year course involving study and work placements • Competition for places on the doctorate course is very high so most candidates will have completed a number of years of work experience before being accepted onto the course (a minimum of 1 year); this might be anything involving working with people, such as the roles of assistant psychologist, research assistant, or support worker
Educational psychologist	• Relevant work experience with children (1 to 2 years minimum) • A doctorate in educational psychology, accredited by the BPS and approved by the HCPC, or, if in Scotland, an accredited master's in educational psychology followed by the BPS's Award in Educational Psychology
Health psychologist	• Voluntary or paid work experience in healthcare settings • A master's in health psychology accredited by the BPS • Stage 2 of the BPS Qualification in Health Psychology, approved by the HCPC (which involves 2 years of supervised practice) or a doctorate programme in health psychology
Occupational psychologist	• A master's in occupational psychology accredited by the BPS • Stage 2 of the BPS's Qualification in Occupational Psychology (which is approved by the HCPC); this involves 2 years of supervised practice
Forensic psychologist	• A master's in forensic psychology accredited by the BPS • Stage 2 of the BPS's Qualification in Forensic Psychology (which is approved by the HCPC and involves 2 years of supervised practice) or a doctorate programme in forensic psychology approved by the HCPC (instead of the master's stage 2 qualification)
Clinical neuropsychologist	• Postgraduate training in clinical or educational psychology accredited by the BPS (see above for clinical and educational routes) • The BPS's Qualification in Clinical Neuropsychology (QiCN)
Sport and exercise psychologist	• A master's in sport and exercise psychology accredited by the BPS • Stage 2 of the BPS's Qualification in Sport and Exercise Psychology (which is approved by the HCPC and involves 2 years of supervised practice)
Academic, research, and teaching psychologist	• To be a chartered psychologist in teaching or research, you will need to complete 5 or more years of professional work experience that is supervised and assessed • To work in research, you will need to complete a doctorate and/or carry out relevant work experience

Note: BPS: British Psychological Society; HCPC: Health and Care Professions Council.

What if these careers don't appeal? What else can I do with a psychology degree?

It is estimated that between 15% and 20% of psychology graduates go on to become professional psychologists (Quality Assurance Agency for Higher Education, 2007). However, this does not mean that the other 80–85% of psychology graduates do not use their knowledge and skills in this area. A background in psychology is not only useful for the above professions; knowledge and skills in this area are invaluable to a wide range of employers. Indeed, the Higher Education Careers Service Unit (2013) has found that graduates with a degree in psychology are highly likely to find employment after graduation, and this appears to be due to the transferrable skills they have gained from their degree. Psychological knowledge is useful for any job or company that involves people (and that is pretty much everywhere!).

However, it is not just this emphasis on people that makes psychologists great employees; they also have a number of skills in research, scientific and critical thinking, statistics, and areas such as biology. Human resources, media, teaching, police, and public services are all examples of areas that might benefit from a background in psychology.

Earlier we touched upon the fact that psychologists might also work in other unusual and diverse areas, such as traffic, aviation, and design. If we take traffic, for example, psychologists have explored concepts such as pedestrian road-crossing behaviour (Harrell, 1991; Rosenbloom, 2009) and indeed psychologists have a lot more to offer on similar issues. One example is ongoing research into the effects of mobile phone use for drivers (e.g. Collet, Guillot, & Petit, 2010) and pedestrians (Schwebel et al., 2012) and the impact that this can have on concentration levels and safety.

Go to the **BPS Careers website**[6] for an interactive look at your journey into psychology.

TEST YOURSELF

1. What are the nine main psychology professions? See whether you can briefly describe the type of work that each psychologist carries out.
2. Why do you need to study for an accredited undergraduate degree programme to progress on to professional training in psychology?

WHO DOES WHAT IN PSYCHOLOGY?

COUNSELLING PSYCHOLOGISTS

- Work with individuals, couples, or groups who have mental health problems, such as depression or anxiety.
- Methods usually involve talking therapies as well as art, music, or play therapy.
- Relevant paid or voluntary work experience in mental health is required.

CLINICAL PSYCHOLOGISTS

- Work with individuals, couples, or groups who have mental health problems, such as depression or anxiety.
- Usually work in healthcare settings such as mental health teams and hospitals.
- A number of years of work experience is usually required before being accepted onto a highly competitive training course.

EDUCATIONAL PSYCHOLOGISTS

- Work with children and adolescents in schools and other educational settings.
- Support young people with a variety of issues, including learning difficulties and behavioural, emotional, and social difficulties.
- Relevant work experience with children is required.

HEALTH PSYCHOLOGISTS

- Use their knowledge of behaviour change to advise others.
- May apply their knowledge to physical illness and support people with the psychological impact of illness.
- An accredited master's degree in health psychology is required.

OCCUPATIONAL PSYCHOLOGISTS

- Support people in the workplace by working with employers.
- May work in organizations such as the civil service, the prison service, or government departments, as well as universities.
- An accredited master's degree in occupational psychology is required.

FORENSIC PSYCHOLOGISTS

- Assess people who have committed criminal offences, provide intervention programmes, and give their expert opinions in court.
- A doctoral programme in forensic psychology is required.

CLINICAL NEUROPSYCHOLOGISTS

- Work with people who have experienced brain injury, tumours, or strokes.
- Postgraduate training in clinical or educational psychology is required.

SPORT AND EXERCISE PSYCHOLOGISTS

- Provide advice to athletes, coaches, and the general public on all psychological aspects of performance.
- An accredited master's in sport and exercise psychology is required.

ACADEMIC, RESEARCH, AND TEACHING PSYCHOLOGISTS

- Communicate research to others through presentations at conferences, through teaching, and by publishing work as journal articles and books.
- Completion of 5 or more years of supervised and assessed professional work experience is required.

SECTION SUMMARY

- Psychologists work in many different areas and their roles involve completing a variety of duties on a daily basis. Psychologists apply evidence and theory to human problems through working directly with individuals or through research and sharing information.

- There are many types of psychologist. However, it is important to remember that, despite the different titles, the roles of psychologists often overlap because of the broad range of core skills that all psychologists develop during their education and training.

- There is a wide variety of careers into which psychology graduates might go, including counselling psychology, clinical psychology, educational psychology, health psychology, occupational psychology, forensic psychology, clinical neuropsychology, sport and exercise psychology, and academic, research, and teaching psychology.

- Every area of professional psychology has a different career path.

- A psychology degree offers a range of transferable skills, meaning that psychology graduates are highly likely to find employment after graduation.

FUTURE DEVELOPMENTS

LEARNING OBJECTIVE 1.9

Discuss possible future developments in psychological research and practice and the implications of these developments for the profession and society at large.

We have seen throughout this chapter how psychology has evolved enormously since Wundt's experiments in 1879. As psychology is a science, it is essential that it continues to develop and that it never remains static. So, what might the future look like for psychology? And in which areas might we see the key changes?

Future developments in academic psychology and research

Future research in psychology will need to be clearer about its potential impact on society. Under the new UK national Research Excellence Framework (REF) (which involves the assessment of a university's research outputs over the previous 6 years), researchers will have to demonstrate that their research has an impact on society. The most recent outcomes were presented in 2014 and a new exercise is planned for 2019–2020. For more information on the REF **visit its website**[7].

Future developments in the psychology professions and the impact on society

In line with the applied emphasis in research, there is also increasing focus on evidence-based practice for professional psychologists. In other words, psychologists in the future will need to ensure that their interventions are supported with research findings. This relates to the growing focus on providing value for money; psychologists can be expensive professionals to employ, and there are now a higher number of professionals who offer similar services for lower salaries. One example is the 'psychological well-being practitioner', who may be able to deliver psychological therapies to individuals with common mental health problems at a lower cost than a clinical psychologist. Psychologists therefore need to ensure they are providing a high-quality service and they need to sell themselves more so that it is clear what they have to offer and why they are worth the extra cost.

In recent times, there has also been more emphasis on service-user involvement or participation, both in research and in the development of services. People who use psychology services have a lot to offer to service development since they are the people who use the services and have the 'lived experience' of dealing with particular issues. When working in collaboration with professionals, service users can create a fuller picture and provide insight into what is needed from services. In the past, the idea that people with mental health problems or other difficulties could actually have an input into what services they received might have been scoffed at; after all, if they're not coping and need the help of a psychologist, how can they tell you what they need? Recently, however, it has become clear that service users *do* have a lot to offer, and who better to ask about a condition or service than a person who has actually experienced it? For example, **INVOLVE**[8], the national advisory body funded by the Department of Health, aims to actively involve members of the public, patients, and users in NHS research, service evaluation, and clinical audit.

There is an increasing role for psychologists in society, along with an increasing recognition of psychology's value. This increase can be seen within the 'traditional' areas of psychology, such as health, clinical, educational, and occupational psychology, but psychologists will also become more apparent in other areas. These may include responding to mass disasters (such as Typhoon Haiyan in the Philippines), traffic, economics, and sports, to name a few. Additionally, psychologists in the future are likely to have greater involvement in informing policies and working with the government. The BPS works with the UK parliaments and assemblies, non-governmental organizations, and international bodies to ensure it has an effective voice. One example is the involvement of the BPS in the consultation process leading to the publication of new regulations for child performers by the Department for Education (2014).

As well as having government involvement, psychologists will need to have more of a role in society in general. As stated by Davey (2007), psychologists surely have more to offer in terms of real-world issues for the public, and there are many social issues that may require psychological knowledge. One example where psychological knowledge is vital is within dementia care. This is an important issue and will become even more so as life expectancy increases. Psychologists may help to provide early diagnoses and assessment, and improve current psychological interventions. Furthermore, an increase in life expectancy may also mean there may be many more individuals who will be left caring for those with dementia or an elderly relative. This can have a considerable impact on a carer's health and well-being, including increased levels of depression, exhaustion, stress, and social isolation (Princess Royal Trust for Carers, 2011). Psychologists will be needed to give support, provide information, and research novel interventions to help improve these issues for carers. Psychologists may also provide carers with access to a range of psychological therapies, such as cognitive behavioural therapy, which are accessible and convenient for carers.

DISCUSSION POINT

How might the future of psychology be different? Name three areas that have been mentioned and then see whether you can think of another area that hasn't been discussed in this chapter.

SECTION SUMMARY

- Future research in psychology will need to be clearer about its potential impact on society.
- In line with the emphasis on applied research, there is also increasing focus on evidence-based practice for professional psychologists and a growing requirement to provide value for money.
- There has also been greater involvement and participation of service users, both in research and in the development of services.
- There is an increasing role for psychologists in society, along with an increasing recognition of the value of psychology as a discipline. Psychologists have more to offer in terms of real-world issues for the public, and there are many social issues that may require psychological knowledge.

CHAPTER SUMMARY

This chapter has considered the ways in which psychology has developed as a discipline from its early philosophical roots to contemporary perspectives on the mind and behaviour. We did this by first exploring the fundamental question of what exactly psychology 'is' and moved on to outline the roots of the discipline by examining the path that the subject has taken through early philosophy to contemporary sociocultural perspectives. We then looked at the discipline through a level of analysis framework and moved on to an evaluation of key issues and debates in psychology as well as an exploration of bias and cross-cultural approaches. The chapter concluded with some thoughts on how the science of psychology is applied at a practical level, with particular emphasis on service-user involvement and participation in the co-design and co-development of services and real-world solutions to social issues.

ESSAY QUESTIONS

1. To what extent did functionalism serve to widen the focus of psychology beyond that of the individual?
2. Discuss some of the key challenges involved in research in cross-cultural psychology.
3. How might public interest in psychology affect the development of our discipline?

KEY TERMS

- **alpha bias:** A tendency to exaggerate differences between men and women.
- **androcentrism:** A type of prejudice that takes male thinking as normal and female thinking as abnormal or inferior.
- **applied research:** Research designed to solve practical, real-world problems.
- **basic research:** Research that aims to seek knowledge for its own sake. Basic research examines how and why people think and behave in the way they do and may be conducted in a laboratory or real-world setting, with human participants or animals.
- **behavioural neuroscience:** Examines the brain processes and other physiological functions that influence our behaviour, emotions, and thoughts.
- **behaviourist perspective:** Emphasizes the role of the environment in our behaviour.
- **beta bias:** The tendency to minimize the differences between men and women.
- **biological perspective:** Examines how the processes of the brain influence behaviour.
- **chartered:** A chartered psychologist is someone who is considered competent (and therefore qualified to practice) in their area of psychology due to having completed the necessary training, study, and work experience.
- **cognitive neuroscience:** Uses brain-imaging techniques to examine brain activity when a person is engaged in a cognitive task.
- **cognitive perspective:** Seeks to explain human behaviour by examining mental processes.
- **cognitive psychology:** The study of the processes that explain how people reason, make decisions, problem solve, remember, form perceptions, and use language.
- **cognitive revolution:** An intellectual movement in the 1950s that marked a shift in emphasis from the behaviourist perspective to the cognitive perspective.
- **collectivism:** A culture that focuses more on the needs of the group and less on individual desire.
- **concordance:** the presence of the same trait in both members of a pair of twins.
- **cross-cultural psychology:** Possible universal behaviours and mental processes. Cross-cultural psychology places an emphasis on the critical-thinking and comparative aspects of study, demonstrating the ways human activity is impacted by cultural forces.
- **cultural bias:** The tendency to ignore differences between cultures and impose an understanding of one culture on other cultures.
- **cultural psychology:** A branch of psychology which identifies that human behaviour is influenced by cultural differences, meaning that psychological phenomena can only be compared in individuals across cultures to a limited extent.
- **culture:** The knowledge, values, customs, and attitudes that guide our behaviour.
- **defence mechanisms:** Psychological techniques to help us cope with anxiety regarding traumatic experiences.
- **dualistic:** A theory which suggests that the mind and body are one and that the mind is not a spiritual entity.
- **emic:** Refers to the differences between cultures and to examinations of multiple cultures using criteria that are considered to be absolute or universal.
- **empiricists:** People who hold to a theory which states that knowledge comes from sensory experience.
- **ethnocentrism:** The use of your own cultural group to make judgements about other groups.
- **etic:** Refers to examining how cultures are similar and to examinations of one culture using criteria relevant to its internal characteristics.
- **Eurocentrism:** An emphasis on Western ideas and the application of those ideas to other cultures in a way that may not be true of the other cultures.
- **evolutionary psychology:** A recent movement that seeks to explain how evolution has shaped human behaviour. Evolutionary psychologists argue that our mental abilities and behaviour have evolved through the process of natural selection.

- **experimenter bias:** The way the results of an experiment are affected by the experimenter.
- **falsifiability:** The notion that a hypothesis can be tested and proved wrong.
- **functionalism:** The study of the functions of consciousness rather than its structure.
- **gender bias:** A preference or prejudice towards one gender over another.
- **Health and Care Professions Council (HCPC):** A body that sets the standards for entry onto the professional register of all practitioner psychologists in the UK and determines an individual's fitness to practice. This includes training, professional skills, behaviour, and health. Anyone who wishes to use the title 'educational psychologist' must be registered with the HCPC.
- **hierarchy of needs:** An approach to motivation proposed by Abraham Maslow. A five-tier model of human needs, from basic physiological and safety needs to self-actualization.
- **hindsight bias:** The tendency for individuals to view events as more predictable than they actually are.
- **humanism (humanistic perspective):** Emphasizes free will, personal growth, and finding meaning and value in life.
- **hypothesis:** A proposed explanation for a phenomenon.
- **individualism:** A culture in which individuals tend to make their own choices and interact less with the rest of the group.
- **interactionist:** A person who believes that both nature and nurture determine a person's behaviour.
- **introspection:** Looking within.
- **levels of analysis:** A conceptual framework that can be used to help us understand human behaviour.
- **monistic:** A theory which suggests that the mind and body are separate.
- **nativists:** People who hold an extreme heredity position, which is the assumption that humans as a whole are a product of evolution.
- **norms:** Unwritten rules that state what behaviour is accepted and expected, (e.g. how to dress and how to introduce yourself to a person in authority).
- **objective:** Refers to seeing things for what they really are and not subjectively.
- **positive psychology:** Emphasizes how life can be made more fulfilling and how we can nurture the best in ourselves. Positive psychology is primarily concerned with using psychological theory, research, and intervention techniques to understand the positive, adaptive, creative, and emotionally fulfilling aspects of human behaviour.
- **psychoanalysis:** A form of therapy that involves the examination of unconscious psychological forces.
- **psychodynamic perspective:** Seeks to understand the causes of behaviour by examining the internal, inner workings of the human mind, emphasizing the role of unconscious processes.
- **psychometric test:** A test used by psychologists (and other professionals) to measure particular things about people, such as personality traits, intelligence, and attitudes. A psychometric test is usually in the form of a questionnaire or a similar paper-based or electronic test.
- **psychophysics:** The study of how psychologically experienced sensations are dependent on characteristics of physical stimuli.
- **radical behaviourism:** Emphasizes that society can utilize the environment to modify behaviour in beneficial ways.
- **research bias:** Occurs by selecting or encouraging one outcome or answer rather than another. This can happen at any time in the research process, including when choosing the study design or method of data collection, and even during data analysis, drawing conclusions, and publication.
- **sampling bias:** Exists when a sample is not representative of the population from which it is drawn.
- **self-actualization:** The top-most level of Maslow's hierarchy of needs, which is reached through fulfilling one's potential.

- **social constructivism:** Emphasizes that our sense of reality is socially constructed – that is, it is the product of our own way of thinking as members of social groups rather than directly observable.
- **socialization:** The process in which norms are transmitted to new members of a group.
- **sociocultural perspective:** Emphasizes the role of our social environment and culture in how we think, feel, and behave.
- **structuralism:** The analysis of the mind in terms of its basic elements.
- **tabula rasa:** The idea that the mind at birth is a blank slate.

NOTES

1. https://digest.bps.org.uk/2012/11/06/are-3d-films-more-psychologically-powerful-than-2d/
2. http://www.thepsychologist.org.uk/archive/archive_home.cfm
3. http://origins.bps.org.uk/
4. http://www.bbc.co.uk/programmes/b03ctc1r
5. https://www.youtube.com/playlist?list=PLCkLQOAPOtT2ATuX2Kz0tApFp-UUFwlIZ
6. http://careers.bps.org.uk/
7. http://www.ref.ac.uk
8. http://www.invo.org.uk/

FURTHER RESOURCES

Beck, H. P., & Irons, G. (2011). Looking back: Finding little Albert. *The Psychologist, 24*(5), 392–395.

British Psychological Society. (2009, January 9). Aiming for psychology. *YouTube.* Retrieved 20 November 2017 from https://www.youtube.com/watch?v=SpS8g34vPGQ (A video providing information for people considering a career in psychology.)

British Psychological Society. (2017). Careers: Your journey into psychology. Retrieved 20 November 2017 from http://careers.bps.org.uk

British Psychological Society. (2017). History of Psychology Centre. Retrieved 20 November 2017 from https://www1.bps.org.uk/what-we-do/bps/history-psychology-centre/history-psychology-centre

British Psychological Society. (2017). *Origins: The evolution and impact of psychological science.* Retrieved 20 November 2017 from http://origins.bps.org.uk (A web-based, multimedia timeline of the development of psychological science and its contributions to society today.)

Brysbaert, M., & Rastle, K. (2009). *Historical and conceptual issues in psychology.* Harlow, UK: Pearson.

Bunn, G., Lovie, A. D., & Richards, G. D. (2001). *Psychology in Britain: Historical essays and personal reflections.* Leicester, UK: British Psychological Society.

Classics in the history of psychology. (1997–). Retrieved 20 November 2017 from http://psychclassics.yorku.ca (A collection of historically significant books, articles and special collections from the scholarly literature of psychology and associated disciplines.)

Davis, O. S., Haworth, C. M., Lewis, C. M., & Plomin, R. (2012). Visual analysis of geocoded twin data puts nature and nurture on the map. *Molecular Psychiatry, 17*(9), 867–874.

Fairholm, I. (2012). *Issues, debates and approaches in psychology.* Baisingstoke, UK: Palgrave Macmillan.

Green, C. D. (2012). *This week in the history of psychology.* Retrieved 20 November 2017 from http://www.yorku.ca/christo/podcasts (Podcasts, interviews, discussions, reviews – everything related to the history of psychology.)

Hatfield, G. (2002). Psychology, philosophy, and cognitive science: Reflections on the history and philosophy of experimental psychology. *Mind & Language, 17*(3), 207–317.

Higher Education Academy. (2013). *Employability in psychology: A guide for departments*. Retrieved 20 November 2017 from http://www.heacademy.ac.uk/assets/documents/subjects/psychology/Employability_Guide.pdf

Marsella, A. J. (2009). Some reflections on potential abuses of psychology's knowledge and practices. *Psychological Studies, 54*(1), 23–27.

Shiraev, E. B., & Levy, D. A. (2012). *Cross-cultural psychology: Critical thinking and contemporary applications* (5th ed.). Boston, MA: Pearson.

Tancredi, L. R. (2007). The neuroscience of 'free will'. *Behavioral Sciences & the Law, 25*(2), 295–308.

Waterman, A. S. (2013). The humanistic psychology–positive psychology divide: Contrasts in philosophical foundations. *American Psychologist, 68*(3), 124–133.

Wertheimer, M. (2012). *A brief history of psychology* (5th ed.). New York, NY: Psychology Press.

REFERENCES

Alexander, P. A., & Winne, P. H. (2006). *Handbook of educational psychology*. Hove, UK: Taylor & Francis.

Allotey, P., Manderson, L., Nikles, J., Reidpath, D., & Sauvarin, J. (1998). *Cultural diversity: A guide for health professionals*. Brisbane, QLD: Queensland Government Press.

Arnett, J. J. (2008). The neglected 95%: Why American psychology needs to become less American. *American Psychologist, 63*(7), 602–614. doi:10.1037/0003-066X.63.7.602

Asbury, K., & Plomin, R. (2013). *G is for genes: The impact of genetics on education and achievement*. Chichester, UK: Wiley-Blackwell.

Barron, G., & Yechiam, E. (2002). Private e-mail requests and the diffusion of responsibility. *Computers in Human Behavior, 18*(5), 507–520.

Baumeister, R. F., Masicampo, E. J., & DeWall, N. C. (2009). Prosocial benefits of feeling free: Disbelief in free will increases aggression and reduces helpfulness. *Personality and Social Psychology Bulletin, 35*(2), 260–268.

BBC. (2011). Psychologist Stanley Milgram and the 'Milgram experiment'. Retrieved 20 November 2017 from http://www.bbc.co.uk/programmes/p00jg58j

Berry, J. (1989). Imposed etics, emics, and derived etics: The operationalization of a compelling idea. *International Journal of Psychology, 24*, 721–735.

Binelli, C., Ortiz, A., Muñiz, A., Gelabert, E., Ferraz, L., Filho, A. S., & … Martín-Santos, R. (2012). Social anxiety and negative early life events in university students. *Revista Brasileira de Psiquiatria, 34*(S1), S69–S74.

Bowlby, J. (1944). Forty-four juvenile thieves: Their characters and home life. *International Journal of Psycho-Analysis, 25*, 19–53.

British Psychological Society. (2009). Code of ethics and conduct. Retrieved 20 November 2017 from https://www.bps.org.uk/news-and-policy/bps-code-ethics-and-conduct

Broadbent, D. E. (1958). *Perception and communication*. London, UK: Pergamon Press.

Brock, A. (2011). Looking back: Why the history of psychology is going global. *The Psychologist, 24*(2), 150–151.

Canter, D. (2010). *Forensic psychology: A very short introduction*. Oxford, UK: Oxford University Press.

Chen, F. F. (2008). What happens if we compare chopsticks with forks? The impact of making inappropriate comparisons in cross-cultural research. *Journal of Personality and Social Psychology, 95*, 1005–1018.

Cheshire, K., & Pilgrim, D. (2004). *A short introduction to clinical psychology*. London, UK: SAGE.

Collet, C., Guillot, A., & Petit, C. (2010). Phoning while driving I: A review of epidemiological, psychological, behavioural and physiological studies. *Ergonomics, 53*(5), 589–601.

Costa, P. T., & McCrae, R. R. (1992). *Revised NEO Personality Inventory (NEO-P I-R) and NEO Five-Factor Inventory (NEO-F FI) manual*. Odessa, FL: Psychological Assessment Resources.

Cunha, M., Soares, I., & Pinto-Gouveia, J. (2008). The role of individual temperament, family and peers in social anxiety disorder: A controlled study. *International Journal of Clinical and Health Psychology, 8*(3), 631–655.

Cynkar, A. (2007). The changing gender composition of psychology. *Monitor Staff, 38*(6), 46.

Danziger, K. (2008). *Marking the mind: A history of memory*. Cambridge, UK: Cambridge University Press.

Davey, G. C. L. (2007). Taking psychology to the people and making them listen. *The Psychologist, 20*(6), 368–369.

Davey, G. C. L. (2011). *Applied psychology*. Chichester, UK: BPS Blackwell.

Davey, G., Lake, N., & Whittington, A. (2014). *Clinical psychology* (2nd ed.). Hove, UK: Psychology Press.

Department for Education. (2014). *Educational psychology funded training scheme*. Retrieved 19 November 2013 from http://www.education.gov.uk/schools/careers/careeropportunities/b00201184/educational-psychology

Eley, T. C., Rijsdijk, F. V., Perrin, S., O'Connor, T. G., & Bolton, D. (2008). A multivariate genetic analysis of specific phobia, separation anxiety and social phobia in early childhood. *Journal of Abnormal Child Psychology, 36*, 839–848.

Eshun, S., & Gurung, R. A. R. (Eds.). (2009). *Culture and mental health: Sociocultural influences, theory, and practice*. Malden, MA: Wiley-Blackwell.

Festing, S., & Wilkinson, R. (2007). The ethics of animal research: Talking point on the use of animals in scientific research. *EMBO Reports, 8*(6), 526–530.

Fischer, P., Krueger, J. I., Greitemeyer, T., Vogrincic, C., Kastenmüller, A., Frey, D., … & Kainbacher, M. (2011). The bystander-effect: A meta-analytic review on bystander intervention in dangerous and non-dangerous emergencies. *Psychological Bulletin, 137*(4), 517–537.

Garnets, L. D., & Kimmel, D. C. (2003). *Psychological perspectives on lesbian, gay, and bisexual experiences*. New York, NY: Columbia University Press.

Gerhard, T. (2008). Bias: Considerations for research practice. *American Journal of Health-System Pharmacy, 65*, 2159–2168.

Gottesman, I. I., & Hanson, D. R. (2005). Human development: Biological and genetic processes. *Annual Review of Psychology, 56*, 263–286.

Gross, R. (2001). *Psychology: The science of mind and behaviour*. London, UK: Hodder & Stoughton.

Handel, A. E., Handunnetthi, L., Giovannoni, G., Ebers, G. C., & Ramagopalan, S. V. (2010). Genetic and environmental factors and the distribution of multiple sclerosis in Europe. *European Journal of Neurology, 17*(9), 1210–1214.

Haney, C., Banks, W. C., & Zimbardo, P. G. (1973). A study of prisoners and guards in a simulated prison. *Naval Research Review, 30*, 4–17.

Hare-Mustin, R. T., & Marecek, M. 1988. The meaning of difference: Gender theory, postmodernism, and psychology. *American Psychologist, 43*, 455–464.

Harlow, H. (1958). The nature of love. *American Psychologist, 13*, 573–685.

Harrell, W. A. (1991). Factors influencing pedestrian cautiousness in crossing streets. *Journal of Social Psychology, 131*, 367–372.

Hearnshaw, L. S. (1987). *The shaping of modern psychology*. London, UK: Routledge & Kegan Paul.

Hebb, D. O. (1949). *The organization of behavior: A neuropsychological approach*. New York, NY: Wiley.

Herek, G. M., Kimmel, D. C., Amaro, H., & Melton, G. B. (1991). Avoiding heterosexist bias in psychological research. *American Psychologist, 46*(9), 957–963.

Higher Education Careers Service Unit. (2013). What do graduates do? Retrieved 1 September 2013 from http://www.hecsu.ac.uk/assets/assets/documents/WDGD_Sept_2013.pdf

Higher Education Statistics Agency. (2015). Higher education statistics for the UK 2015/16. Retrieved 20 November 2017 from https://www.hesa.ac.uk/data-and-analysis/publications/higher-education-2015-16

Hirshfeld-Becker, D. R. (2010). Familial and temperamental risk factors for social anxiety disorder. In H. Gazelle & K. H. Rubin (Eds.), *Social anxiety in childhood: Bridging developmental and clinical perspectives – New directions for child and adolescent development* (Vol. *127*, pp. 51–65). San Francisco, CA: Jossey-Bass.

Izard, C. E. (1971). *The face of emotion.* New York, NY: Appleton-Century-Crofts.

Jack, R. E., Garrod, O. G., Yu, H., Caldara, R., & Schyns, G. P. (2012). Facial expressions of emotion are not culturally universal. *Proceedings of the National Academy of Sciences of the United States of America, 109*(19), 7241–7244.

Johanson, C. E., & Balster, R. L. (1978). A summary of the results of self-administration studies using substitution procedures in primates. *Bulletin on Narcotics, 30*, 43–54.

Kohlberg, L. (1976). Moral stages and moralization: The cognitive-development approach. In T. Lickona (Ed.), *Moral development and behavior: Theory research and social issues*, 31–53. New York, NY: Holt, Rinehart and Winston.

Kohn, A. (1990). *You know what they say …: The truth about popular beliefs.* New York, NY: HarperCollins.

Knappe, S., Lieb, R., Beesdo, K., Fehm, L., Low, N. C. P., Gloster, A. T., & Wittchen, H.-U. (2009). The role of parental psychopathology and family environment for social phobia in the first three decades of life. *Depression and Anxiety, 26*(4), 363–370.

Latane, B., & Darley, J. M. (1968). Group inhibition of bystander intervention in emergencies. *Journal of Personality and Social Psychology, 10*(3), 215–221.

Macfarlane, J. (2005). *The relationship between cultural beliefs and treatment seeking behaviour in Papua New Guinea: Implications for the incorporation of traditional medicine into the health system.* Perth, WA: Centre for International Health, Curtin University of Technology.

Marteinsdottir, I., Svensson, A., Svedberg, M., Anderberg, U., & von Knorring, L. (2007). The role of life events in social phobia. *Nordic Journal of Psychiatry, 61*(3), 207–212.

Meek, S. E., Lemery-Chalfant, K., Jahromi, L. B., & Valien, C. (2013). A review of gene–environment correlations and their implications for autism: A conceptual model. *Psychological Review, 120*(3), 497–521.

Meier, L. L., Gross, S., Spector, P. E., & Semmer, N. K. (2013). Relationship and task conflict at work: Interactive short-term effects on angry mood and somatic complaints. *Journal of Occupational Health Psychology, 18*(2), 144–156.

Mi, X., Eskridge, K. M., George, V., & Wang, D. (2011). Structural equation modeling of gene–environment interactions in coronary heart disease. *Annals of Human Genetics, 75*(2), 255–265.

Milgram, S. (1963). Behavioral study of obedience. *Journal of Abnormal and Social Psychology, 67*, 371–378.

Milgram, S. (1974). *Obedience to authority: An experimental view.* London, UK: Tavistock.

Moehler, E., Kagan, J., Oelkers-Ax, R., Brunner, R., Poustka, L., Haffner, J., & Resch, F. (2008). Infant predictors of behavioural inhibition. *British Journal of Developmental Psychology, 26*(1), 145–150.

Morris, T. L. (2004). Social development. In T. L. Morris & J. S. March (Eds.), *Anxiety disorders in children and adolescents* (2nd ed., pp. 59–70). New York, NY: Guilford Press.

Nakane, Y., Jorm, A. F., Yoshioka, K., Christensen, H., Nakane, H., & Griffiths, K. M. (2005). Public beliefs about causes and risk factors for mental disorders: A comparison of Japan and Australia. *BioMed Central Psychiatry, 5*, 5–33.

Ogden, J. (2005). *Fractured minds: A case-study approach to clinical neuropsychology* (2nd ed.). New York, NY: Oxford University Press.

Ogden, J. (2012). *Health psychology: A textbook* (5th ed.). Maidenhead, UK: Open University Press.

Ollendick, T. H., & Hirshfeld-Becker, D. R. (2002). The developmental psychopathology of social anxiety disorder. *Biological Psychiatry, 51*(1), 44–58.

Pannucci, C. J., & Wilkins, E. G. (2011). Identifying and avoiding bias in research. *Plastic and Reconstructive Surgery, 126*(2), 619–625.

Periyakoil, V. J., & Dara, S. (2010). *Health and health care of Asian Indian American older adults.* Stanford, CA: eCampus Geriatrics.

Pintrich, P. R., & Schunk, D. H. (2002). *Motivation in education: Theory, research and applications* (2nd ed.). Upper Saddle River, NJ: Prentice Hall.

Popper, K. R. (1957). The aim of science. *Ratio, 1*(1), 24–35.

Prasadarao, P. S. D. V. (2009). Culture and mental health: An international perspective. In S. Eshun & R. A. R. Gurung (Eds.), *Culture and mental health: Sociocultural influences, theory, and practice* (pp. 149–178). Malden, MA: Wiley-Blackwell.

Princess Royal Trust for Carers. (2011). *Always on call, always concerned: A survey of the experiences of older carers.* Woodford Green, UK: Princess Royal Trust for Carers.

Quality Assurance Agency for Higher Education. (2007). *Subject benchmark statement: Psychology* (2nd ed.). Gloucester, UK: Quality Assurance Agency for Higher Education. Retrieved 9 November 2013 from http://www.qaa.ac.uk/en/Publications/Documents/Subject-benchmark-statement-Psychology.pdf

Rapee, R. M., & Spence, S. (2004). The etiology of social phobia: Empirical evidence and an initial model. *Clinical Psychology Review, 24*, 737–767.

Ratner, C. (2006). *Cultural psychology: A perspective on psychological functioning and social reform.* Hove, UK: Psychology Press.

Rava, M., Ahmed, I., Demenais, F., Sanchez, M., Tubert-Bitter, P., & Nadif, R. (2013). Selection of genes for gene–environment interaction studies: A candidate pathway-based strategy using asthma as an example. *Environmental Health, 12*(1), 1–5.

Ritchie, T. D. (2009). Gender bias in research. In J. O'Brien, J. Fields, & E. Shapiro (Eds.), *Encyclopedia of gender and society* (pp. 713–715). Thousand Oaks, CA: SAGE.

Robinson, P. A., Rennie, C. J., Rowe, D. L., O'Connor, S. C., & Gordon, E. (2005). Multiscale brain modelling. *Philosophical Transactions of the Royal Society, 360*(1457), 1043–1050.

Rooney, B., Benson, C., & Hennessy, E. (2012). The apparent reality of movies and emotional arousal: A study using physiological and self-report measures. *Poetics, 40*(5), 405–422.

Rooney, B., & Hennessy, E. (2013). Actually in the cinema: A field study comparing real 3D and 2D movie patrons' attention, emotion and film satisfaction. *Media Psychology, 16*(4), 441–460.

Rosenbaum, J., Biederman, J., Hirshfeld-Becker, D., Kagan, J., Snidman, N., Friedman, D., & … Faraone, S. (2000). A controlled study of behavioral inhibition in children of parents with panic disorder and depression. *American Journal of Psychiatry, 157*(12), 2002–2010.

Rosenbloom, T. (2009). Crossing at a red light: Behaviour of individuals and groups. *Transportation Research Part F: Traffic Psychology and Behaviour, 12*(5), 389–394.

Sahaklan, W. S. (1975). *History and systems of psychology.* New York, NY: Wiley.

Schwebel, D. C., Stavrinos, D., Byington, K. W., Davis, T., O'Neal, E., & de Jong, D. (2012). Distraction and pedestrian safety: How talking on the phone, texting, and listening to music impact crossing the street. *Accident Analysis & Prevention, 45*, 266–271.

Seligman, M. E. P. (1998). *Learned optimism* (2nd ed.). New York, NY: Pocket Books.

Shiraev, E. B., & Levy, D. A. (2010). *Cross-cultural psychology: Critical thinking and contemporary applications* (4th ed.). Boston: Pearson/Allyn Bacon.

Smith, P. B., & Bond, M. H. (1998). *Social psychology across cultures: Analysis and perspectives*. Hemel Hempstead, UK: Harvester Wheatsheaf.

Spiegel, D. (2013). Minding the body: Psychotherapy and cancer survival. *British Journal of Health Psychology*, *19*(3), 465–485. doi:10.1111/bjhp.12061

Trzaskowski, M., Zavos, H., Haworth, C., Plomin, R., & Eley, T. (2012). Stable genetic influence on anxiety-related behaviours across middle childhood. *Journal of Abnormal Child Psychology*, *40*(1), 85–94.

Upton, D., & Trapp, A. (2010). *Teaching psychology in higher education*. Oxford, UK: BPS Blackwell.

Vohs, K. D., & Baumeister, R. F. (2009). Addiction and free will. *Addiction Research & Theory*, *17*(3), 231–235.

Watson, J. B. (1930). *Behaviorism* (Rev. ed.). Chicago, IL: University of Chicago Press.

Watson, J. B., & Rayner, R. (1920). Conditioned emotional reactions. *Journal of Experimental Psychology*, *3*(1), 1–14.

Webster, G. D., Nichols, A. L., & Schember, T. O. (2009). American psychology is becoming more international. *American Psychologist*, *64*(6), 566–568.

Weinberg, R. S., & Gould, D. (2011). *Foundations of sport and exercise psychology* (5th ed.). Champaign, IL: Human Kinetics.

Whittaker, J., & Whittaker, S. (1972). A cross-cultural study of geocentrism. *Journal of Cross-Cultural Psychology*, *3*(4), 417–421.

Woolfe, R., Strawbridge, S., Douglas, B., & Dryden, W. (2010). *Handbook of counselling psychology* (3rd ed.). London, UK: SAGE.

Yosef, A. R. O. (2008). Health beliefs, practice, and priorities for health care of Arab Muslims in the United States: Implications for nursing care. *Journal of Transcultural Nursing*, *19*, 284–291.

2 Research Methods in Psychology

GRAHAM HOLE

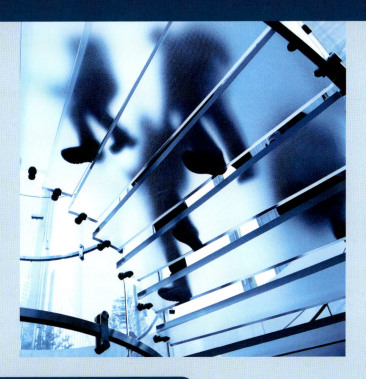

THE SCIENTIFIC METHOD

LEARNING OBJECTIVE 2.1

Demonstrate a good understanding of what makes psychological research 'scientific'.

Non-psychologists often seem surprised that psychologists might think of themselves as being 'scientists'. This chapter could engage in a long philosophical discussion about the definition of science, but essentially psychology is a 'science' because its practitioners generally adopt the following process (see Figure 2.1):

1. Come up with a clearly defined, *testable* question. So, 'does watching *Strictly Come Dancing* rot your brain?' is a question that can be addressed scientifically because we can look at brains and obtain evidence to settle the question one way or the other. 'Can Justin Bieber turn himself into a fridge-freezer, but only when no one is looking at him or filming him?' is not a scientific question because there is no way to obtain any empirical data on the matter.

2. Obtain data on this issue that are open to independent scrutiny by other people. Science is essentially an empirical enterprise, involving the collection of data

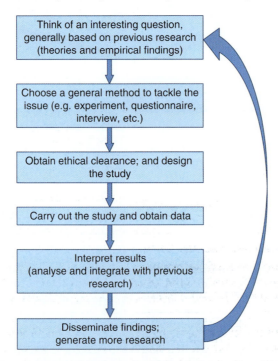

FIGURE 2.1 *Stages in the process of conducting psychological research.*

Psychology, First Edition. Edited by Graham Davey.
© 2019 John Wiley & Sons, Ltd. Published 2019 by John Wiley & Sons, Ltd.

about phenomena. These data are usually **quantitative** measurements, but **qualitative** descriptions of behaviour can also be a valid source of data.

3. Do this using methods designed to rule out as many competing explanations for the data as possible.

Whether or not something is 'scientific' has nothing to do with the subject matter and it's not about whether or not you do experiments: it's the approach that matters. At its heart, science is based on openness and scepticism: I tell you exactly how I obtained my findings so that you don't have to take my word for anything. This is such an important idea in science that *nullius in verba* (take no one's word for it) is the motto of the Royal Society of London. You should be able to replicate my study in all its important details and see if you get the same outcome.

This scepticism should extend to your own findings and theories as well as other people's. As Skinner (1953) put it, science entails having a 'willingness to accept facts even when they are opposed to wishes' (p. 12). Lilienfeld (2010) suggests that science is a set of procedures that protect us against our natural tendency to have a 'confirmation bias' – a bias that leads us to seek evidence that fits in with our pre-existing beliefs.

Perhaps you don't dispute my findings but instead disagree with my theoretical interpretation of them. Most scientific findings are interpreted within the context of a **theory**, a framework for organizing ideas and findings. Actually, most findings originate from a scientist testing a specific testable prediction (a **hypothesis**) that is generated from a theory. So, if you're sceptical about whether my particular theory is correct, you can do two things: you can formulate predictions that follow logically from my theory and test to see whether they hold up in practice. Or you might come up with an alternative theory that explains my data better than my own theory does.

An example of a scientific question

Here's a question that can be answered scientifically. Does **chocolate** make children hyperactive? Non-scientific approaches include decisions based on intuition, anecdote, or an appeal to authority. None of these approaches is a valid way to tackle the question. Many psychological phenomena are quite counterintuitive, anecdotes may be unreliable, and authority figures can be as wrong as anyone else.

Using a scientific approach, firstly we need to think carefully about what would be required in order to answer our question satisfactorily. Before we start, we need detailed and unambiguous definitions of everything, so that we can be sure everyone is talking about the same phenomena. What do we mean by 'children'? Perhaps chocolate affects older children (who have better inhibitory control over their behaviour) less than younger ones, so, at least initially, it would be prudent to restrict our investigations to a reasonably specific age group: say 7- to 8-year-olds.

Next, how much chocolate are we talking about? The effects of chocolate might well be dosage dependent. One Malteser probably wouldn't make much difference to a child, but a whole packet might. So, to begin with, we could start with a certain fixed amount of chocolate, perhaps in line with what children normally get to eat.

What do we mean by 'hyperactive'? We need a clear definition. We could determine the baseline level of activity for children in this age group so that we have something against which to compare their post-chocolate activity levels. It would make sense to measure their activity levels in the same environment, such as the school playground, before and after eating chocolate. Activity might also be affected by children's circadian rhythms, so it would be best to measure activity at the same time each day. (All these precautions are designed to reduce the possibility of extraneous variables producing 'confounds' in our data – more on this later.)

So, we are now asking a very specific question:

> Does eating chocolate [one bag of Maltesers] make 7- to 8-year-olds more active in the school playground at midday than they would otherwise be, where 'more active' is defined as a measurable increase in the amount of running around by each child?

Our reason for asking this question would usually stem from some theory about activity levels in children and the factors that affect them. It might be that we have a theory that children are abnormally susceptible to caffeine. Chocolate contains theobromine, an alkaloid that is chemically similar to caffeine. Consequently, we might expect chocolate to have similar effects to caffeine. Another prediction arising from our theory is that dark chocolate should produce stronger effects than milk chocolate, because it contains more theobromine.

Hopefully, you can see from this example how a theory can both generate testable hypotheses and help to interpret the results of studies. Note also that this theory is potentially falsifiable, something that is vital to the scientific method. It predicts that chocolate will produce hyperactivity, so, if a study shows that it doesn't, then the theory needs to be revised to accommodate these findings. Theories that do not have the potential to be disproved are not scientific.

DISCUSSION POINTS

1. Can the scientific approach be used with phenomena that occur only once, or sporadically and unpredictably (e.g. UFO abductions, poltergeist activity, or extrasensory perception)?
2. How could you try to study these kinds of phenomena?

ACTIVITY 2.1

THE SCIENTIFIC APPROACH

Browse the BBC's ***All in the Mind***[1] archive to listen to examples of psychological science in action.

SECTION SUMMARY

- Scientists come up with a clearly defined, *testable* question.
- Scientists obtain data on this issue that are open to independent scrutiny by other people.
- Scientists do this using methods designed to rule out as many competing explanations for the data as possible.

- Whether or not something is 'scientific' has nothing to do with the subject matter, and it is not about whether or not you do experiments.

- A healthy scepticism should extend to your own findings and theories, as well as other people's.

- Most findings originate from a scientist testing a hypothesis that is generated from a theory.

- A population is a complete set of things and a sample is a limited subset of them. For practical reasons, psychologists can only ever hope to investigate the behaviour of a sample of participants, but they still want their conclusions to have wide generality.

THE DISSEMINATION OF SCIENTIFIC IDEAS

LEARNING OBJECTIVE 2.2

Describe the methods by which scientific findings and research can be disseminated.

Scientific findings are shared in a number of ways. Psychologists often attend conferences, where they might give a talk about their research and then field questions and comments from an audience of their peers. Conferences are good for sharing ideas and finding out about what researchers in a field are doing right now.

To reach a wider audience, psychologists generally publish their findings in a paper in a scientific journal. All reputable journals engage in a process of **peer review**: each paper submitted to the journal is first assessed by the journal's editor. If the editor doesn't think it's complete tosh, they send it to a couple of academics who are experts in that particular field. They each write an independent review of the paper, identifying its strengths and weaknesses and suggesting what should be done with the paper (whether it should be accepted for publication in the journal, generally with some revision, or rejected as unfit for publication). The editor then provides the author with a decision, based on their assessment of the reviews. If invited to resubmit the paper, the author produces a new version that tries to accommodate any alterations required by the editor.

Published papers have therefore been vetted by independent experts in that field. However, it is still important to read them with a sceptical mindset, because even published papers can be flawed: peer review is an imperfect process, conducted by fallible time-pressured academics who may have read the original paper in a rush or overlooked some errors.

Psychologists' findings can also be disseminated in textbooks or by talking to the media. However, these sources are prone to distortion and inaccuracy. Books are generally out of date by the time they appear in print, and authors can sometimes misrepresent findings. The media often oversimplify findings to the point where they bear little relation to their original form. 'High levels of chocolate consumption may lead to slightly heightened activity levels in 8-year-old children' becomes 'kids go psycho after chocolate', all caveats attached to the original findings being ditched in favour of producing a newsworthy story. So, although it may often be difficult to read, you can't beat going back to a researcher's original journal article if you really want to know what they found.

TEST YOURSELF

1. What distinguishes scientific and non-scientific approaches to studying psychological processes?
2. What are the advantages of scientific methods for understanding human behaviour, compared to non-scientific approaches?

SECTION SUMMARY

- Psychologists can disseminate the results of their work by presenting their findings at a conference. Conferences provide a good forum for sharing ideas and learning about current research themes.

- Findings published in scientific journals will reach a wider audience and peer review of submitted papers ensures that high quality is maintained. However, even published papers might be flawed and caution must be exercised when the results are being followed up.

- Publishing work in books is another means of dissemination but has the disadvantage of the results appearing dated because of the lengthy prepublication period.

- Broad exposure can come from talking to the media. However, the media are prone to oversimplification and may distort the findings to create a more dramatic story.

QUANTITATIVE RESEARCH METHODS

LEARNING OBJECTIVE 2.3

Demonstrate understanding of some of the quantitative methods used by psychologists.

Psychologists use a wide variety of methods in order to study behaviour scientifically. Each has its own strengths and weaknesses, as outlined in the discussion below. In many cases, a psychological phenomenon will most fully be understood by tackling it with a variety of methods, a process known as 'converging operations'.

Most psychologists use 'quantitative' methods, investigating behaviour with procedures modelled on those used by the natural sciences. Typically they will use experiments and **observational methods** to obtain numerical data that are subjected to statistical analyses. A sizeable minority of psychologists use 'qualitative' methods, rejecting these quantitative methodologies in favour of more interpretative techniques such as in-depth interviewing and textual analysis.

What constitutes 'good' research? Reliability, validity, and importance

Good research has three attributes: reliability, validity, and importance. **Reliability** simply refers to how reproducible the results are. If you did the study more than once, would you get similar results each time? **Validity** refers to whether or not you are actually measuring what you think you are measuring. For example, if you are interested in measuring surgical patients' assessments of their pain, you need to be careful that you aren't inadvertently measuring something else instead, such as their anxiety level. Importance is a much more subjective attribute. Generally, important findings will be of interest to other researchers and may ultimately lead to lots of further research being generated.

It is important to realize that these three attributes are conceptually independent of each other. A finding can be highly reliable but not valid (although it cannot be valid without also being reliable). It may be both reliable and valid but utterly unimportant (see Focus Point 2.1).

FOCUS POINT 2.1

RELIABILITY WITHOUT VALIDITY

A good example of how reliability and validity do not necessarily go hand in hand comes from the early 19th-century craze for phrenology. Phrenologists thought that different parts of the brain were responsible for different mental 'faculties', such as conscientiousness, benevolence, and acquisitiveness. They also believed that highly developed mental 'faculties' led to larger brain regions, which in turn were reflected in the shape of the skull. As a result, devices were produced to accurately measure the bumps on a person's head.

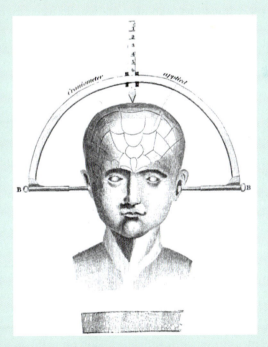

Craniometry measuring tools, used by phrenologists to measure bumps on the skull.

Source: Combe (1846).

These measurements were quite reliable, in the sense that the equipment would produce similar measurements each time it was used on the same head. However, we now know that the bumps on the skull bear no relation to the underlying shape of the brain, and the size of brain regions has little relationship to their function. Thus, phrenological measurements are potentially reliable, in the sense of being reproducible, but totally lacking in validity as a measure of individual differences in cognitive abilities.

Assessing reliability

There are various ways to determine whether a finding is reliable. At the start of this chapter, we said that science depends on healthy scepticism, and ideally findings should be checked by other researchers trying to replicate them. Unfortunately, straight replications of psychology studies are rarely performed because journals tend to prefer to publish new research rather than direct replications of existing studies. One consequence of this trend is the 'file-drawer problem': after a novel finding is reported, other researchers may try to replicate it and fail. The non-replications are consigned to those researchers' filing cabinets, never to see the light of day again. The novel finding exists largely unchallenged, eventually gets cited in textbooks, and takes on a life of its own as a well-established phenomenon. Some apparently well-established psychological phenomena may actually have less empirical support than you might expect.

Reliability is influenced by a number of factors. One is the *size of your sample* (generally, larger samples provide better estimates of the characteristics of the population from which the sample was taken). Another is the *timescale* over which measurements of behaviour take place: the longer the time interval between them, the more likely it is that the individuals concerned have changed, due to factors such as life events and maturation. Reliability also depends on the inherent *stability* of the phenomenon being measured. Measurements of trait anxiety (the extent to which a person is naturally anxious) are likely to be more reliable than measurements of state anxiety (anxiety in response to a particular situation, such as following an earthquake).

Reliability is also affected by the *precision* with which you can measure: the more precise the measurements, the more reliable they are likely to be. You can think of any measurement as consisting of two things: a 'true' measure of the phenomenon of interest, plus random 'noise' or 'error'. Exam performance is a good example. Ideally a statistics exam should be a 'pure' measure of a student's knowledge of statistics. In practice, exam performance on the day is a mixture of the student's knowledge plus random extraneous factors. These might include the student's anxiety level, their amount of luck in revising the right topics, how much sleep they have had recently, and so on. These extraneous factors mean that exam performance is actually an imperfect measure of statistics knowledge. Consequently, if you repeatedly tested a given student on their knowledge of statistics, you would probably find that their exam performance varied somewhat, even if their underlying knowledge of statistics remained totally constant over time.

This idea of a measurement consisting of 'true score plus error' applies even to relatively low-level measures such as simple reaction time. If you repeatedly measure how quickly someone can press a button in response to the onset of a light or the sound of a buzzer, you will find that their reaction time varies somewhat from trial to trial. This variation is presumably due to the random contribution of extraneous factors to each response time score. On each trial, there will be variations in how much attention the participant is paying to the task, and even variations in the speed of nervous conduction between finger and brain.

All this variability has a number of methodological implications. Firstly, it implies that any given score is not *the* score, in a definitive sense, but just one of many possible scores that could have been obtained. The more reliable the measurements, the more similar all these possible scores are likely to be. However, the obtained score will always be an imperfect estimate of some 'true' score for the property in question.

Secondly, it explains why averages crop up so often in quantitative psychological research, whether these are averages of individual performance (e.g. mean response time, mean number of errors) or averages of group performance (e.g. mean anxiety score for a group of soldiers who have been on a tour of Afghanistan versus mean anxiety score for a group of non-combatants). At both levels of analysis, averaging represents an attempt to increase the reliability of measurements by trying to average away the random contributions of extraneous factors.

Many psychologists use formal tests as part of their research – for example, personality tests, IQ tests, and so on. Assessing their reliability poses a problem. Sometimes you can give the same test repeatedly and see whether individuals produce the same results each time. However, this is often impossible: you can't give a person the same IQ test twice because they are likely to remember their answers to some of the questions from the first time they tried it! One solution is to use alternative forms of the test, though it may be tricky to devise different versions that are highly comparable. Another remedy is to use a **split-half reliability** measure. For each participant, the researcher calculates two separate scores, one using only the even-numbered items in the test and the other using only the odd-numbered items. If the test is reliable, these two measures should correlate strongly with each other.

Assessing validity

To determine whether a finding is valid, we need to know whether we have actually measured what we set out to measure. Various types of validity need to be considered. A broad distinction can be made between internal validity and external or ecological validity. **Internal validity** refers to the extent to which a study has been well designed – that is, the extent to which it has successfully measured what it sought to measure. There are many factors that can affect a study's internal validity. Campbell and Stanley's (1966) review remains the definitive discussion of these issues. **External validity** refers to the extent to which the study and its findings can be generalized to other situations, in particular the extent to which they have any relevance to the 'real' world.

How do we assess validity? **Face validity** is the weakest way. It consists of subjectively deciding whether a measure looks like it ought to be measuring what we think it is measuring. **Content validity** involves an assessment of whether a measurement tool contains items that appear to relate to the phenomenon being investigated. So, if you wanted to measure statistical abilities, you would expect a test to contain items related to statistics, not history.

Criterion validity addresses the issue of whether a measure correlates with other known indicators of the attribute. There are two kinds. If a measure has 'concurrent' criterion validity, it should correlate with other indicators at that time. If it has 'predictive' criterion validity, it should correlate with other indicators in the future. Suppose we devise a new IQ test for children. If it has high **concurrent criterion validity**, then children's scores on it should correlate highly with other current IQ test results for those children, at that time. If it has **predictive criterion validity**, it should correlate with measures of the children's future academic attainment, IQ test results at maturity, and so on.

If a measure has high **construct validity**, it correlates with other measures relating to the same theoretical construct. For example, if we have a measure of 'happiness', then people who score highly on our measure should also score highly on other indicators of the same theoretical construct. They should also score differently on measures of other theoretical constructs that we believe are unrelated to happiness, such as depression.

Ecological validity is synonymous with external validity: does the measure have any real-world relevance? Many experimental studies can involve tasks that are rather artificial and unnatural. The results may be reliable (in the sense of reproducible) but not particularly generalizable to real-life situations. This is a long-standing problem. As far back as the 1970s, the developmental psychologist Urie Bronfenbrenner pointed out that 'much of contemporary developmental psychology is *the science of the strange behavior of children in strange situations with strange adults for the briefest possible periods of time*' (Bronfenbrenner, 1977, p. 513, original emphasis). Similar criticisms apply to experiments on adults.

Methods for studying behaviour

This section describes some of the principal methods used by psychologists to investigate behaviour, ranging from observational techniques and interviews through to complex **experimental designs**. It also covers **correlational design** and **quasi-experimental design**: these are often used in more naturalistic situations, where researchers have less control over what happens during the study and what can be measured. The main strengths and weaknesses of each approach are discussed.

Observational methods

One way to find out about a phenomenon is simply to observe it: to watch and systematically record what happens. Observations can take various forms. They can be performed as part of a quantitative study. Researchers might perform event sampling, recording all instances of certain preselected behaviours (a task made much easier with the advent of video recording) or they might use a **time-sampling** technique, for example making a note of whatever behaviour is occurring every 15 seconds during a given observation period. Alternatively, observations can be made as part of a more qualitative study, with data taking the form of detailed notes or descriptions of the behaviour that is being observed.

The strengths of this approach are that observations can be non-intrusive, and so observational methods can be useful for finding out about animals' and people's natural behaviour. The data obtained from observational studies can be less tied to a particular theory than data obtained using experimental methods. However, observational data are by no means theory-free: the researcher's decisions about what to measure may often be dictated by their theoretical preconceptions. Observing behaviour can be very good for generating hypotheses, which can then be tested using experimental methods.

In terms of weaknesses, observational methods can be very time consuming. If the phenomenon that you are interested in rarely occurs spontaneously, you could spend a lot of time waiting for it to happen. Another limitation is that, because you are merely recording behaviours as and when they occur, it can be difficult to establish cause-and-effect relationships. For example, if you watch young rats or rabbits, you'll find that they play mostly at dusk and dawn; but what *causes* them to play at these times? Is it due to a change in ambient light, or temperature, or the consequence of some internal circadian rhythm? Without directly manipulating any of these factors, it's impossible to tell.

An essential part of using observational methods is to employ checks on observer reliability. This is important for two reasons. Firstly, there is the danger of observer bias: the observer's own preconceptions or expectations might unconsciously distort their observations. Secondly, over time, observers can become more familiar with the behaviour that they are recording, and this may lead to changes in their observations. This is especially problematic for developmental studies, where genuine changes over time in the behaviour of interest may easily be confounded with changes in the observer's scoring of that behaviour.

Observer reliability is usually assessed by measuring interobserver agreement: a film of the behaviour of interest is independently scored by the principal observer and a second observer, ideally someone who is naive about the hypotheses being investigated. Checks on interobserver agreement should be done before the main body of observations take place (to ensure that the behaviour categories being scored are reliable) and preferably also at various later points during the study, to ensure that the observer's recordings remain stable over time.

Longitudinal versus cross-sectional designs

Researchers sometimes want to track developmental changes over prolonged periods. Suppose we were interested in the long-term effects of unemployment on psychological well-being. We could perform a longitudinal study. The same individuals could be measured repeatedly, with the measurements spaced far apart in time, perhaps spanning months or years in the case of the long-term unemployed. **Longitudinal designs** can provide rich information about developmental change, especially on an individual level. The problems with longitudinal studies are primarily the time and expense involved in running them, and participant attrition: individuals tend to drop out of these studies over time, especially if they run for years. This can lead to the sample size ending up much smaller than when the study started, and there is the problem of knowing what differentiates those who remain in the study from those who dropped out: are the ones who remain truly representative of the original sample?

An alternative approach is to use a **cross-sectional design**: we could study different groups of individuals, with each group having been unemployed for a different length of time. In most cases, a cross-sectional design is more feasible because it is quicker and cheaper. However, one disadvantage of a cross-sectional design is the risk of **cohort effects**: the groups may differ systematically in terms of life experiences other than the ones of interest to the researcher.

Questionnaires and surveys

Questionnaires can be used for various purposes. They can be used to find out about people's *behaviours*, such as how many road accidents they have had, whether or not they smoke, or how often they have been on political demonstrations. Questionnaires can be used to investigate people's *attitudes*, such as how they feel about immigration, homosexuality, or out-of-town supermarket developments. Standardized questionnaires can also be used as a tool for measuring *personality attributes* such as extraversion, neuroticism, or sensation seeking.

A strength of questionnaires is that they are potentially a straightforward means of obtaining information from other humans. Most humans have language, so why not capitalize on that in order to obtain information from them? Questionnaires have the potential to obtain a great deal of useful information about behaviour. They also remain the principal method for measuring personality attributes.

In terms of weaknesses, questionnaires are susceptible to various kinds of biases that may distort the data obtained (see the review in Bowling, 2005). For example, they are prone to **sampling biases**: the respondents to the questionnaire may not be truly representative of the population that you want to make statements about. Most postal questionnaires tend to have a poor response rate: only about 30% of the questionnaires are returned. What differentiates the 30% who respond from the 70% who don't? This is an important issue, but one for which we can seldom have a definite answer. If the 30% are representative of the non-responders, then things aren't too bad: we may have ended up with a smaller sample than we would have wished, but, if we sent the questionnaire to enough people in the first place, we might still be left with a reasonable sample size.

However, it might be that the 30% who responded differ in important ways from the silent majority. Perhaps only those people who feel really strongly about the topics covered in the questionnaire bother to respond. This might deceive us into thinking that views on an issue are highly polarized, when in truth most people are quite apathetic or indifferent. Actual evidence on this issue is mixed and probably depends to a large extent on the topic being surveyed. However, some public health surveys have found that non-respondents tend to have less healthy lifestyles than respondents, being more likely to smoke and binge drink, and less likely to take exercise (e.g. Hill, Roberts, Ewings, & Gunnell, 1997; Meiklejohn, Connor, & Kypri, 2012). Potentially, if not invariably, poor response rates can pose serious problems of interpretation for the data obtained (Groves & Couper, 1998).

Edwards and colleagues (2002) reviewed 292 studies using postal questionnaires. They evaluated 75 different strategies for increasing response rates. Effective strategies included offering a monetary incentive, sending the questionnaire by recorded delivery, keeping the questionnaire short, and making the questionnaire personalized to the recipient (rather than just saying something like 'Dear householder'). Contacting the recipient beforehand and sending follow-up reminders to non-respondents both increased response rates. Questionnaires from universities were more likely to be returned than questionnaires from other institutions.

These days, questionnaires can be delivered by other means, such as by telephone or the internet (see Focus Point 2.2). Each method has its own strengths and weaknesses. The importance of these will depend on the study. (See deLeeuw, 2012, for a discussion of these issues in relation to web-based questionnaires.) Administering a questionnaire by telephone excludes the deaf and hard of hearing from taking part in a study, while administering it via the internet rules out people who are too poor to own a computer and those who are not computer literate. Postal, telephone, and internet questionnaires would all be pretty useless for finding out about homeless people, migrant workers, or anyone else who doesn't have a fixed address. For these groups, it might be better to take the questionnaire to the respondents in person.

DESIGNING AN ONLINE STUDY

To perform an experiment over the internet is technically tricky, especially if you want to collect reaction-time data. However, creating an online questionnaire or survey is far simpler. The easiest way is to use a company that specializes in providing the tools for people to create online surveys, such as **SurveyMonkey**[2] or **Qualtrics**[3]. A free 'basic' account enables you to create a survey from scratch or use one of a number of pre-existing templates. You can also use or modify pre-existing questions and response options, determine the order in which questions are presented, and highlight inadvertently unanswered questions.

These companies also provide ways by which you can recruit respondents, such as creating a web link to put on a website, displaying the survey in a pop-up window on your website, or emailing invitations to people and tracking who responds to them. They even provide you with basic data-analysis tools for handling the responses once you've obtained them.

Be aware that online questionnaires are subject to ethical considerations as much as any other research, so look at the 'Ethical Principles in Research' section of this chapter before you start. In particular, you need to consider the questions of **informed consent**, confidentiality, and **debriefing**, as these can be especially problematic issues with online studies.

One big disadvantage of postal questionnaires is that the researcher has no control over how the questionnaire is administered. For example, the researcher has no way of knowing in which order the respondent tackled the questions. Administering a questionnaire in person enables the researcher to develop a rapport with the respondent, perhaps building up trust by starting off with more innocuous questions before asking about contentious themes. (This can also be done, to some extent, by administering the questionnaire via the internet, with the respondent forced to answer questions in a set order.) A problem with both postal and internet questionnaires is that it is impossible to know for certain who really completed the questionnaire or the conditions under which it was completed.

Another problem with questionnaires is that respondents are very sensitive to the way in which questions are phrased: even minor phrasing alterations can markedly affect response rates (Schuman & Presser, 1981).

Perhaps the biggest difficulty that besets questionnaire studies is the problem of **self-presentational biases**. Unless respondents can be convinced that their responses are wholly anonymous, they will tend to respond in a way that puts them in a good light. They will tend to downplay 'undesirable' activities and may overemphasize 'admirable' ones. The purpose of many of the items on personality questionnaires is fairly transparent: for example, in an extraversion/introversion questionnaire, it is fairly obvious that the correct answer to a question such as 'How much do you like going to parties?' is 'a lot' if you want to appear extraverted and 'not much' if you want to appear introverted.

Self-presentational biases are especially problematic for face-to-face surveys, where an additional complication may be the characteristics of the interviewer themselves. Faced with questions about immigration, respondents might well give different responses depending on the colour of the interviewer's skin. For postal and internet questionnaires, this is less of a problem because the responses can often be given more anonymously and the respondent has little idea of the researcher's personal characteristics.

Another limitation of questionnaire techniques is that not all phenomena are open to introspection and self-report. People find it particularly difficult to reliably recall information about what has happened to them in the past. Henry, Moffitt, Caspi, Langley, and Silva (1994) investigated how well 18-year-olds could recall information about themselves. These people had been involved in a long-term longitudinal study for their entire lives, so it was possible to compare each participant's retrospective account to earlier records of what had actually happened to them and their subjective experiences at that time. There were only weak correlations between retrospective estimates of 'psychosocial' states such as depression and how the participants had actually reported feeling when they were children.

Cohen and Java (1995) asked people to keep a diary of health-related events for 3 months (e.g. symptoms, medication, and visits to doctors or hospitals). When tested at the end of this period, the diarists could recall only 47% of the events that they had recorded. Similarly, Chapman and Underwood (2000) found that, after just a fortnight, car drivers recalled only about 20% of the accidents and near-misses that they had originally recorded experiencing during that time.

DISCUSSION POINT

Discuss what problems arise when using questionnaires to find out about people's attitudes, personality, or past behaviours. How can this affect the outcome of research based on these questionnaires?

Experiments

In a true experiment, a researcher has complete control over one or more variables. The state of these variables is manipulated, keeping all other variables as constant as possible, and the effects on some outcome variable are observed. A variable that is manipulated by the experimenter is known as an **independent variable** (IV). The outcome variable (the thing the experimenter measures) is called the **dependent variable** (DV).

Let's return to our hypothetical experiment on the effects of chocolate on children. We could assign children randomly to one of two groups (we'll return to the importance of randomization later). We give chocolate to the children in one group and nothing to the other group. Our IV here is 'amount of chocolate consumed', with two 'levels': chocolate versus no chocolate. We have complete control (during the experiment, at least!) of each child's chocolate consumption. We measure the effects of this manipulation on activity levels, specifically the length of time that each child runs around during their midday break. 'Activity level' is our DV.

In short, we manipulate the IV (amount of chocolate consumed) and measure the effects of this manipulation on the DV (activity level). If the experiment has been well designed, then if there are any differences in activity level between the two groups, we can be reasonably sure that they stem from our manipulation of the IV, and not from any other causes.

The experimental method is the best way to unequivocally establish **causal relationships** between variables. Here, we ensure that the only *consistent* difference between the two groups of children is in terms of their chocolate consumption; if activity levels differ between the two groups afterwards, this difference must stem from the differences in chocolate consumption.

However, experiments can be rather artificial and intrusive; they tend to be good for finding out what people *can* do but not necessarily how they behave naturally. As mentioned earlier, experiments may lack ecological validity, meaning that their findings might be reproducible in the laboratory but have dubious relevance to the real world. There are also many phenomena that don't seem to lend themselves to an experimental approach (for examples, see the section later in this chapter on 'Qualitative Research Methods').

How to produce a well-designed experiment

In devising an experiment, the aim is to make sure the *only* thing that affects the DV is the experimenter's manipulations of the IV. In our chocolate experiment, we want to ensure that the *only* thing that affects children's activity levels is the amount of chocolate that we feed them; only then can we be certain that we have established a clear causal relationship between chocolate consumption and activity levels.

Humans (and animals) are inconveniently variable from one to another. If we simply took two children and gave chocolate to one but not the other, we could not logically conclude that any differences between them were due to chocolate. The children might differ in activity levels for all sorts of other reasons, such as how much sleep they had the night before the study took place, natural differences in physiology, how much they ate for breakfast, and so on. We need to eliminate the influence of these 'extraneous variables' as potential explanations for the children's activity levels.

How can we do this? The most commonly used method is to use a number of participants and randomly allocate them to different conditions in an experiment. Each participant will differ in many respects from the others, but these differences will probably be random and inconsistent. Therefore, if we randomly place each participant in different groups, we should end up with two groups that are initially not *consistently* different from one another.

Consider the chocolate experiment again. We randomly allocate children to the 'chocolate' or 'no chocolate' groups. Because the allocation is random, each group will contain children who are hyperactive, inactive, extravert, introvert, tall, short, cheerful, miserable, and so on, but these characteristics will not be consistently different between the two groups – a hyperactive child is just as likely to be in one group as in the other. Now we give chocolate to *all* of the children in the 'chocolate' group and to *none* of the children in the 'no chocolate' group. We have introduced *one* systematic difference between the two groups. If they now differ in activity level, it is highly likely to be due to our manipulation because that is the *only* consistent difference between the two groups.

So this is the fundamental basis of the experimental method in psychology. At its simplest, an experiment involves the following process:

1. Randomly allocate participants to group X or group Y.
2. Then do something to everyone in group X that isn't done to everyone in group Y.
3. See if the two groups now differ from each other. If they do, the difference has probably arisen from your differential treatment of the two groups. This is the 'experimental/control group, post-test only' design (see Figure 2.2): the experimenter measures behaviour after some differential manipulation of an IV has been performed on two groups.

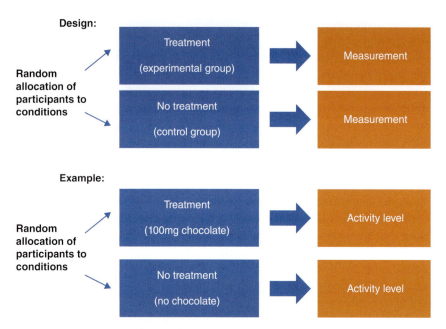

FIGURE 2.2 *Basic 'experimental/control group, post-test only' design.*

More complex experimental designs

The basic two-group experiment is fine, but there are a number of good reasons for sometimes using a more complex design.

Firstly, we can *extend our knowledge of a phenomenon by adding more conditions to the study.* By adding more conditions to a study, we can look at the effects of varying the nature of the IV, rather than simply comparing its presence to its absence. If we added more groups to our chocolate study, with each group receiving a different amount of chocolate, we would be able to find out much more about how chocolate affects behaviour. Does chocolate have an all-or-nothing effect on behaviour? Or is there a fairly systematic dose–response relationship, so that the more chocolate children consume, the more hyperactive they become?

In this example, the different conditions vary *quantitatively* from each other: they differ in how much chocolate is consumed. The different dosages of chocolate represent different points on a common scale. On other occasions it might be interesting to compare conditions that differ *qualitatively* from each other. There is some evidence that, in the United States at least, from an early age white children consume more caffeine than black children (Ahuja & Perloff, 2001). Assuming that tolerance to caffeine can develop, this might produce racial differences in susceptibility to theobromine in chocolate. It might therefore be interesting to compare children of different races, perhaps having groups of white, black, and Asian children.

A second reason to use a more complex design concerns *factorial designs and interactions.* Adding more conditions to an experiment enables us to look at possible **interactions** between variables. Instead of having just one IV in a study, we can have two, three, or more (having more than three IVs is not recommended because the results can become very difficult to interpret).

For example, as well as looking at the effects of chocolate or no chocolate on hyperactivity (IV1), we could manipulate the age of the children (IV2). To do this, we

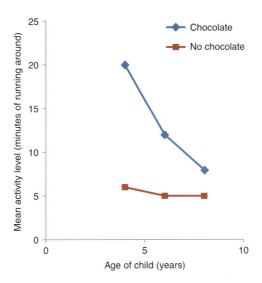

FIGURE 2.3 *Factorial design. The results of an experiment with two independent variables (chocolate consumption and age of child).*

would need to have a separate group of participants for each permutation of the two IVs: thus we might have groups of 4-, 6-, and 8-year-old children. For each of these ages, we could have two groups, one of which would eat chocolate and one of which would not. This would be a '2 × 3 factorial' design (see Figure 2.3).

From this, we could examine the effects of each IV in isolation. Overall, ignoring age, does chocolate produce hyperactivity? Overall, ignoring chocolate consumption, are there age differences in hyperactivity? We could also see whether the two IVs show an interaction with each other: one possibility is that the effects of chocolate on hyperactivity might decrease with age.

Independent measures versus repeated measures designs

So far we've discussed experimental designs in which each participant contributes to only one condition in the study. In our hypothetical chocolate study, a given participant is in either the chocolate group or the no-chocolate group. This is an **independent measures design**. If possible, it is often better to use a **repeated measures design**, in which each participant is used more than once and thus supplies more than one measurement to the study (see Table 2.1).

From a practical point of view, reusing participants means you have to recruit, test, and debrief (and maybe pay!) fewer people than if you used each participant only once. This can produce big savings in terms of time, effort, and cost. From a statistical standpoint, repeated measures designs are advantageous because they tend to reduce the amount of variability in the data. This can make the study more sensitive (better at finding a difference between the conditions in the study, if one exists). In an independent measures experiment, although group members might not be consistently different from each other, they will still differ randomly in all sorts of ways. This will add noise to the data. In a repeated measures design, the people in one condition are remarkably similar to those in the other condition – because they are the same people! The amount of random variation between the conditions is thus greatly reduced; the data contain less noise as a result, and so it becomes easier to detect any differences between the groups due to what the experimenter did.

TABLE 2.1 *Advantages and disadvantages of independent measures and repeated measures designs.*

	Independent measures (between groups)	Repeated measures (within subjects)
Ease of design	Straightforward	Can be more complicated
Number of participants required	More	Fewer
Carry-over effects between conditions	No	Possible
Sensitivity to experimental manipulations	Lower	Higher
Reversibility of conditions	Unimportant	Essential

Repeated measures designs are more sensitive than independent measures designs but they are prone to **carry-over effects**. Completing one condition of a study can often have irreversible effects on a participant. This can cause major problems for interpreting their performance in another condition.

Suppose you are interested in how mood affects memory for words. You want to see how many words people remember when they are happy compared to when they are sad. Ideally you would want to use the same people in both conditions: you could use happy music to induce a happy mood in them on one occasion and then sad music to put them in a miserable mood on a second occasion. However, when it comes to performing the sad condition, participants are likely to remember some of the words from when they encountered them before, in the happy condition. Why is this a problem? Remember that, in a well-designed experiment, the *only* things that vary systematically between conditions are the differences in the IV that have been introduced by the experimenter. Here, we now have a number of other factors (confounding variables) that vary between the conditions. After performing the happy condition, participants may come to the sad condition more practiced at remembering word lists; more fatigued or bored; and, in this instance, perhaps still influenced by the happy state that we induced in them in the first condition.

Because all these confounding variables vary *systematically* between the first and second conditions, we cannot tell how much of the difference between the conditions is due to our mood manipulations and how much is due to these other factors. All these systematic differences are inextricably tied together, making any differences between the conditions uninterpretable.

Sometimes these order effects can be ameliorated by either randomizing the order in which the conditions are performed or **counterbalancing** them. In the present example, we could randomly assign participants to performing the conditions either in one order (happy then sad) or the opposite (sad then happy). This often reduces the effects of confounding variables by preventing them from varying systematically along with the changes in the experimenter's IV. A better strategy, however, would be to employ counterbalancing (see Figure 2.4): half of the participants perform the conditions in one order and half perform them in the other. This is preferable to randomization because we could then specifically check to see whether the order

Random allocation of participants to order 1 or order 2

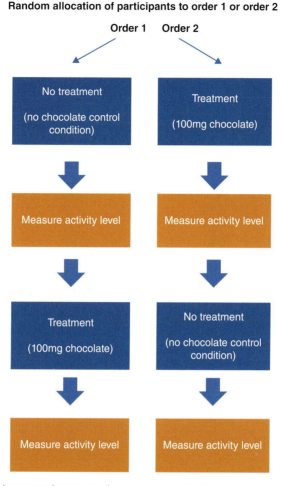

FIGURE 2.4 *A simple repeated measures design, using counterbalancing.*

in which the conditions were performed made any differences to the results of the mood manipulations.

Unfortunately, counterbalancing can get quite complex if you have lots of conditions. With three conditions, A, B, and C, you need seven groups of participants, one for each of the following permutations: ABC, CBA, ACB, BCA, BAC, ACB, and CAB. With four conditions, you need 24 permutations. Each group would also need a separate word list, which raises problems of establishing that the lists are comparably memorable. Sometimes it is easier to use an independent measures design, even if it means spending more time recruiting and running participants.

Finally, there are situations where a repeated measures design simply cannot be used. In our mood and memory experiment, a repeated measures design might be feasible because mood can change from one state to another, and back again. As long as we left enough time between the different mood-induction conditions, the effects of being in one condition would probably wear off, so that we could reuse the participants in another condition. However, in many experiments, the effects of being

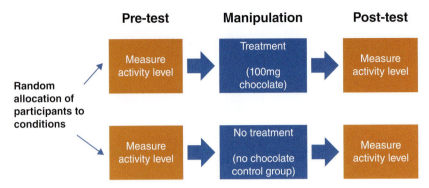

FIGURE 2.5 *A pre-test/post-test experimental design.*

in one condition might be completely irreversible. Suppose we induced a happy mood, showed participants a word list, and then gave them a surprise memory test. It would be unwise to reuse these participants in a sad mood condition because on the second occasion the memory test would no longer be unexpected. Participants' performance in the sad mood condition would be affected not only by the mood induction procedure but also by any strategies that they adopted in anticipation of another memory test.

Pre-test/post-test designs

Post-test-only designs have the disadvantage that they only *assume* that randomization has rendered the two groups comparable before the manipulations of the IV take place. Sometimes randomization can produce some very non-random-looking effects. By using a pre-test/post-test design (see Figure 2.5), it is possible to check that the groups are indeed initially comparable. Participants are randomly allocated to the different conditions and then given a pre-test to ensure that they are comparable at this stage. Then the experimental manipulation occurs, with one of the groups receiving a different treatment from the other. If the groups now differ, we can be reasonably sure that the differences arose because of our experimental treatments.

Solomon four-group design

A disadvantage of having a pre-test is that the pre-test itself might affect performance. Solomon (1949) devised an experimental design to check for this possibility (see Figure 2.6). There are at least four groups: two experimental groups and two control groups. One of the experimental groups and one of the control groups receive a pre-test; the other two groups do not. All groups receive the post-test. It is then possible to see whether the experimental manipulation has affected performance (by comparing the two experimental groups to the two control groups) and also to see whether there were any effects of using a pre-test (by comparing the two experimental groups to each other, and the two control groups to each other). This is an excellent design, but it is rarely used because of the time, effort, and cost involved in producing the four groups.

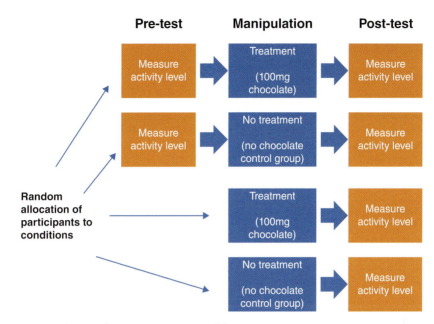

FIGURE 2.6 *Solomon's four-group experimental design.*
Source: Solomon (1949). American Psychological Association. Adapted with permission.

Correlational designs

In a correlational study, the researcher takes measurements on two variables and looks at the relationship between them. The measurements could come from naturalistic observations, survey data, or archival data. There is no attempt to introduce any experimental manipulations. For example, Forgeard, Winner, Norton, and Schlaug (2008) wanted to know whether instrumental music training enhances children's cognitive abilities. Since children can't be *forced* to practise or not practise playing an instrument, all the authors could do was to take various measures from a group of children and see whether there were correlations between them. Musical training was weakly but positively correlated with auditory discrimination, fine motor skills, vocabulary, and nonverbal reasoning: as the amount of musical training increased, so too did scores on these other measures, to some extent.

Sometimes this is the only kind of study that is feasible. An experiment may not be possible, for ethical reasons. In many cases, correlational studies have the advantage of being highly non-intrusive.

However, the main problem with **correlational designs** is that it is often impossible to establish causal relationships between the variables concerned. If two variables (X and Y) are correlated, it might be that X causes change in Y, Y causes change in X, or even that a third variable Z (or set of variables) gives rise to the change in both X and Y. A good example is the length of your two arms. There is a high correlation between the lengths of people's right and left arms. It is obvious that this correlation does not arise because the right arm is *causing* the growth of the left arm, or vice versa: in this instance, a third variable (or set of variables – the combination of genetic and experiential factors that determines growth in general) controls the growth of both arms.

ACTIVITY 2.2

CORRELATION AND CAUSE

The following table shows historical, country-by-country data comparing the incidence of deaths from breast cancer with the intake of fat. The table seems to show that there is a positive correlation between dietary intake of fat and deaths from breast cancer. It is therefore tempting to interpret these data as showing a *causal* relationship (i.e. that a high-fat diet causes breast cancer). However, there are at least six possible explanations. What might they be?

Death rates per 100,000 population per day	Daily dietary fat intake (g) per day			
	Below 40	**41–80**	**81–120**	**121–160**
Up to 5	El Salvador Philippines Thailand	Japan Mexico Sri Lanka Taiwan		
6–10		Bulgaria Chile Hong Kong Romania Venezuela	Greece Spain	
11–15		Portugal	Finland Hungary Poland Slovakia	
16–20			Austria Italy	Australia France Germany Norway Sweden
21–25				Belgium Canada Denmark Ireland Netherlands United Kingdom United States

Adapted from Carroll (1975).

Quasi-experimental designs

In a quasi-experimental design, the researcher does not have complete control over the IVs. This is often the case in 'applied' research, which frequently relies on 'natural experiments'. There are various types of quasi-experimental design.

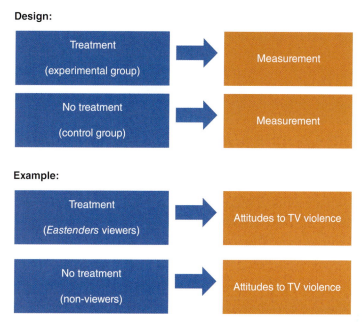

FIGURE 2.7 *The static group comparison design.*

Static group comparison design

A static group comparison design can be used in situations where the researcher would ideally like to conduct a standard experimental versus control group/post-test experiment but cannot assign participants randomly to the experimental and control groups. Two pre-existing groups are used instead. A treatment is given to one group (the experimental group) but not the other (the control group), and the two groups are then tested (see Figure 2.7).

Suppose you are interested in measuring the effectiveness of a new treatment for depression. You get access to a group of depressed people who are starting a programme of the new treatment for 6 months and another group of depressed people who are sticking with conventional treatment methods. Each participant rates their level of depression after their 6 months of treatment.

The overriding problem with this design is that, whatever the outcome of the researcher's manipulations, we don't know whether or not the two groups were truly comparable beforehand. This design is also susceptible to sample selection biases. If patients have been allocated to the new treatment because other treatments have already proved ineffective for them, the chances of the new treatment being effective might be reduced. Alternatively, if the experimental group is full of individuals who signed up for the new treatment because they were extremely enthusiastic about it, this might *increase* the chances of it working. **Regression towards the mean** could also affect the results. If someone scores very high (or very low) on a test, they are more likely to obtain a more average score when tested a second time. Thus, if one group scores particularly low on the measure of interest initially, there is a good chance that their performance will *appear* to have improved on the second test. The change due to regression towards the mean can be confused with genuine change produced by the researcher's intervention.

Interrupted time-series design

In an **interrupted time-series design**, the researcher takes a series of measurements from a group of participants over a period of time. At some point in this sequence, some treatment is given to the group. If the treatment has had an effect, the measurements before and after the treatment should differ.

Suppose we are interested in whether CCTV reduces crime. We could take a monthly count of how many crimes take place in a particular area for 6 months before a CCTV camera is installed and for 6 months afterwards. If there is a noticeable (and preferably persistent) drop in crime rates in the 6 months after camera installation compared with the 6 months before, then it is likely that the drop is related to the introduction of CCTV.

Interrupted time-series designs suffer from the problem that it may be difficult to disentangle the results of the intervention from the effects of other events occurring at the same time. In our example (see Figure 2.8), CCTV installation might be part of a package of actions to reduce crime. There might also be an increased police

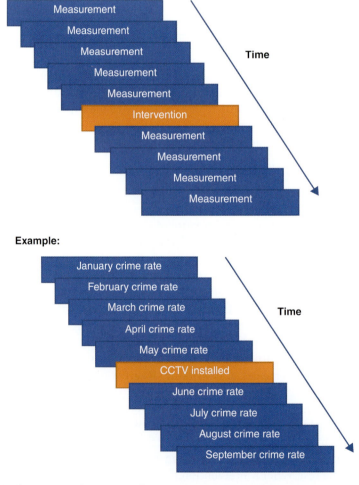

FIGURE 2.8 *The interrupted time-series design.*

presence in the area. Publicity about the CCTV itself might make people more wary of criminals in that area. Perhaps national TV showed some programs about violent crime around that time that raised awareness of crime in everyone's minds, not just that community. Any reduction in crime might be due to any or all of these factors. These problems can sometimes be circumvented by having more than one set of observations, with multiple interventions occurring in a staggered pattern. If crime rates in one neighbourhood show a drop after CCTV is introduced in June and crime rates in another neighbourhood show a drop after CCTV is introduced in September, then we at least know the drop probably wasn't related to any events that coincided with the time at which the interventions were introduced.

The results of interrupted time-series designs are most clear-cut when there is a stable pattern of measurements before the intervention that differs from an equally stable pattern of measurements afterwards. Figure 2.9 shows the number of prescriptions for antibiotics at a hospital in each month over a period of 4 years (Ansari et al., 2003). For the first 24 months there was a steady increase in prescribing antibiotics. An intervention was then introduced to discourage over-prescription. During the second 24 months of the study, the number of prescriptions decreased. Since the intervention coincided with these changes in prescribing, the implication is that the intervention was successful in its aim. The pattern of results is quite clear-cut. However we need to keep in mind that other things may have changed at the same time as the intervention was introduced (e.g. a reduction in funding, increases in the cost of antibiotics, or greater awareness of the dangers of indiscriminate antibiotics use). Since any or all of these may have contributed in whole or in part to the change in the pattern of prescribing, we cannot firmly conclude that the intervention was the prime cause of the change in prescribing behaviour.

Unfortunately, the data are not always as clear-cut as this, and the effect of the intervention can often be difficult to disentangle from random fluctuations in the set of measurements.

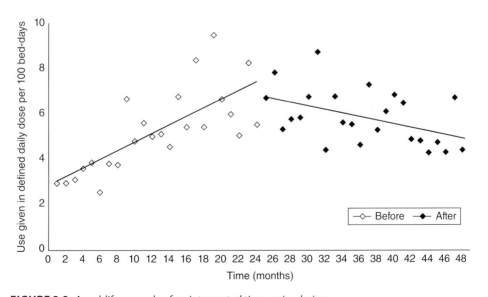

FIGURE 2.9 *A real-life example of an interrupted time-series design.*

Source: Ansari et al. (2003). The British Society for Antimicrobial Chemotherapy. By permission of Oxford University Press.

In terms of their strengths, quasi-experimental studies may often have more eco-logical validity than pure experimental studies. For ethical reasons, they may be the only type of study that can be performed in some situations.

However, the lack of control over the independent variables in the study may often lead to ambiguity in interpreting the results. To investigate the effects of alcohol on driving, the ideal approach would be to take a group of drivers and manipulate the independent variable of 'alcohol consumption': half of the drivers would be randomly selected to never drink before driving, while the other half would be forced to do so. A comparison of the accident rates for the two groups would give unequivocal data on the effects of alcohol on driving performance. In practice, this is impossible to do, for ethical reasons. Therefore, the best we can do is to compare the accident rates of drink-drivers to those of non-drinkers.

If we find a difference between the two groups, it may be due to their different drinking behaviours. However, this interpretation is complicated by the fact that these two group may differ in many other respects: the drinkers and non-drinkers might be different in personality, education, attitudes to risk, differential exposure to risk (because of the time of day at which they typically drive), and so on.

Cohort effects like these affect any experiment using groups that differ in pre-existing ways (e.g. studies looking at age, gender, or personality differences in behaviour): the participants are likely to differ systematically in many ways other than the one by which they have been grouped by the experimenter. Strictly speaking, therefore, many studies that purport to be 'proper' experiments are using a quasi-experimental design, with all the ensuing complications of interpretation.

TEST YOURSELF

1. What is the distinction between reliability and validity?

2. What problems arise in using questionnaires and interviews in order to find out about people's attitudes, personality, or past behaviours?

3. What is the principal difference between a true experiment and a quasi-experimental design, and why is this important?

4. What are the limitations of correlational approaches?

SECTION SUMMARY

- There are a wide variety of methods that psychologists can use to study behaviour quantitatively.

- For determining causal relationships between variables, the experiment is the tool of choice.

- However, experiments can be rather artificial, and they cannot always be used, for ethical or practical reasons.

- In those situations, observational techniques and quasi-experimental methods can be very useful, as long as their limitations are kept in mind – principally, that their lack of control over the variables being investigated means that it may be difficult to rule out competing explanations for the study's results.

ANALYSING AND INTERPRETING QUANTITATIVE DATA

LEARNING OBJECTIVE 2.4

Describe the various statistical techniques used to analyse and interpret quantitative data.

Most psychologists attempt to obtain quantitative data on the phenomena they are studying and then use statistical techniques to help them draw conclusions from them. There are essentially two types of statistics that go hand in hand: *descriptive* statistics (such as averages) and *inferential* statistics (various tests that enable us to determine whether our observed results have occurred merely by chance). This section gives an overview of statistical methods: for more details, consult one of the many psychology statistics textbooks on the market, such as Field (2017).

Descriptive statistics

As the name implies, descriptive statistics describe the phenomenon in question in a quantitative way. The simplest descriptive statistic is merely a count of how often something has occurred, which enables us to obtain a frequency. This can be reported either as an absolute value (e.g. '55 out of 60 participants managed to escape from our shark-infested swimming pool') or as a percentage ('36% of our 120 participants reported feeling nauseous after fairground rides').

Alternatively, we can report a single-number summary of typical performance (an 'average', such as the mean, median, or mode). Most people are familiar with this concept: the media discuss the 'average wage' or the 'average temperature for this time of year'. Fewer people are familiar with an equally important concept: a measure of 'dispersion' or 'spread', which shows how well the average reflects performance in the group of scores that it is intended to summarize. Measures of dispersion include the range (the difference between the highest and lowest scores) and the **standard deviation** (SD) (a kind of 'average difference of scores from the mean').

The SD is a particularly important statistical concept to grasp, as it provides a good indication of how well a mean actually represents the set of scores that it has been calculated from. The smaller the SD, the more closely the scores are bunched around the mean. Here's a set of six scores: 5, 5, 6, 6, 6, and 6. Here's another set: 1, 2, 4, 5, 10, and 12. The mean of both sets is exactly the same (5.67) but this mean is much more similar to all the scores in the first set than it is to the scores in the second set. If I just told you the mean without also telling you the SD, you would have no way of knowing this. However, the SD for the first group is 0.52 whereas for the second group it is 4.41 – almost as big as the mean itself.

The SD shows how much scores are spread out around the mean. There is a special kind of SD called the **standard error of the mean** (SEM) that is also frequently mentioned in scientific reports. The SEM is an estimate of how much a sample mean might vary if the study were repeated many times over. If you perform a study and obtain a mean score for a group of participants, it is tempting to think of that mean as being *the* mean for that group. However, it is more appropriate to think of this mean as merely being a spot estimate, the figure for that particular group of participants on that particular day: if you ran the study repeatedly, you would be highly unlikely to get exactly the same results each time. The SEM is just an estimate of how much the mean would be likely to vary from one occasion to another. Effectively, it's an estimate of how reliable your mean is. If the SEM is large compared to the mean, it suggests that the mean would be likely to vary quite a lot if you repeated the study. If the SEM is relatively small, it suggests that you would be likely to get similar results on another occasion.

Inferential statistics

Often, we want to know whether our results are 'real' or have merely occurred by chance. In the case of our experiment on the effects of chocolate, suppose we found some evidence of a difference between the average activity level of children who have just eaten chocolate and the average for those who haven't. This difference might be due to the effects of the chocolate, but it might have arisen merely due to random variations in activity levels between the two groups. (The groups contain different children, all varying naturally in activity level, so it would be surprising if the average activity levels of the two groups were absolutely identical.)

How can we tell which of these two interpretations is correct? This is where inferential statistics come in. There is a wide variety of statistical tests that can help us to decide how likely it is that the effects we observe are due to chance. Each test is most appropriate in a specific set of circumstances, and most tests generally have a set of conditions attached to them that must be met for the test's results to be valid. A full discussion of these tests and how to use them is outside the scope of this chapter but they all share a broadly similar rationale: null hypothesis significance testing.

Null hypothesis significance testing

For decades, by far the most popular approach in psychology for analysing data has been to engage in **null hypothesis significance testing** (NHST). In essence, it works like this.

- Take two groups of participants from the same population.[i]
- Do something to one group (the 'experimental group') that you don't do to the other (the 'control group').
- The **null hypothesis** is that, after your manipulation, they remain two groups from the same population. In other words, your manipulation has had no effect.

---

[i] In statistics, the term 'population' has a special meaning: it is a complete set of things. Here, our population might be 'British schoolchildren'.

- The **alternative hypothesis** is that your manipulation has affected the experimental group. It has changed them so that they are now effectively a sample from a *different* population than the one to which they originally belonged.

For example, in our hypothetical experiment, we began with two samples from a single population – 'schoolchildren with normal activity levels'. As a result of force-feeding chocolate to one of the groups, we suspect that group has now become a representative sample from a *different* population, the population of 'children with chocolate-induced hyperactivity'.

All we actually *have* is a mean score for each group. These two means will differ somewhat. The question is, what gave rise to that difference? There are two possibilities. If the null hypothesis is true, the difference between the two means will usually (but not always) be small. If the alternative hypothesis is true, the difference between the two means will hopefully be large.

In practice, the difference is often ambiguously moderate in size and it is hard to know which of these two interpretations is the more plausible. The use of an appropriate statistical test can tell us how likely it is that our observed difference between means occurred purely by chance.

FOCUS POINT 2.3

DECIDING BETWEEN THE NULL AND ALTERNATIVE HYPOTHESES

Suppose we perform our experiment on chocolate consumption and find that children who ate chocolate ran around for 10 minutes on average, whereas children who didn't eat chocolate ran around for only 5 minutes. The fundamental question is, did this difference occur merely by chance or does it represent a real difference between activity levels in the two groups?

We can never know for certain what the correct answer is, so we need to make a trade-off between two extremes. We could be really cautious and only accept huge differences as being 'real'. If we do that, we will miss many effects that are small but nevertheless real. We will tend to make many 'false negative' errors (known as 'Type II errors'). Conversely, if we are too eager to decide that even small differences between conditions represent 'real' effects, we will misinterpret many differences that have actually arisen merely by chance. We will now tend to make many 'false positive' errors (known as 'Type I errors').

We need a compromise between these two extremes, so we adopt an arbitrary convention. Suppose we performed our study many times over: if there is really no difference between our groups (i.e. if the null hypothesis is correct), then how often would we get a difference between our group means as large as the one we have actually obtained? If the observed difference between our groups is likely to arise by chance 5 times or fewer in 100 occasions, then we assume that it has *not* arisen by chance – that it represents a 'real' difference between our groups. If the observed difference is likely to occur by chance more than 5 times in 100, then we assume that it probably *has* arisen by chance. This is the source of the mystical 'p values' that you will see written in the results sections of journal articles. If the statistical test result is followed by '$p < .05$', it means that this result is likely to occur by chance with a probability of less than .05 (i.e. fewer than 5 times in 100 trials).

Fortunately, we don't have to calculate these probabilities for ourselves. Statisticians know a lot about how samples relate to their parent populations. They can calculate how likely it is that various sizes of difference will occur, taking into account the size of the samples and the amount of variability within and between them. The result is a statistical test that we, as psychologists, can simply use as a tool in our research.

The essence of NHST in psychology is as follows. Researchers perform a study and then use statistical tests to make comparisons between the groups or conditions. If a test produces a result that is unlikely to have arisen by chance, it is regarded as probably being a 'real' finding; the experimenter's manipulations of the IV are considered to have caused a change in the nature of the groups. If the result is likely to have arisen by chance, then it is assumed that there is no reason to disbelieve the null hypothesis.

One problem with the NHST approach is that null findings are hard to interpret: have they arisen because there really is no effect of the IV on behaviour or because the effect was too subtle to be detected reliably? Many studies in psychology lack sufficient **power**: they use too small a sample size to have a good chance of detecting an effect, even if one does actually exist. This is because of practical considerations. 'Power' calculators exist that can tell you how large a sample size you might need to detect an effect of a given size. The problem is that, in many cases, the recommended sample size is so large that it becomes impractical to run the study. In those situations, it is tempting to run the study with a smaller sample size and hope that it's big enough to detect an effect anyway.

Statistical significance and effect size

It is important to make a clear distinction between statistical significance and the size of the effect. If a result is highly significant statistically, all this means is that it is very unlikely to have arisen by chance; it says nothing about whether the effect is a large one. It is perfectly possible for a difference between two conditions to be statistically significant even though it is quite small in absolute terms. To try to counter this problem, many psychology journals now require authors to report not just the significance level associated with their results but also an appropriate measure of **effect size**. Different statistical tests have different effect size measures associated with them.

To give an example of the difference between the concepts of significance and effect size, consider the correlation coefficient, Pearson's r. The value of r itself is an indication of the strength of the correlation between two variables. $+1$ is a perfect positive correlation, meaning that an increase in the value of one of the variables is associated with a comparable increase in the value of the other. -1 represents a perfect negative correlation, where an increase in one of the variables is associated with a concomitant decrease in the other. An r of 0 means there is no correlation between the two variables at all.

The traditional approach is to report r together with a p-value that tells the reader how likely it is that this particular value of r might be obtained by chance, if there were really no relationship between the two variables concerned. However, even quite small correlations can be statistically significant if the sample size is large enough. What we need is a measure that gives some indication of the strength of the correlation in practical terms, and this is where effect size comes in. For Pearson's r, the measure of effect size is R^2 (also known as the **coefficient of determination**). R^2 is simply the value of r, squared.

R^2 tells you how much of the variation in one of the variables is accounted for by its relationship with the other variable. Thus a .3 correlation means that only 9% of the variation in one of the variables is accounted for, leaving 81% wholly unexplained. Even a .8 correlation accounts for only 64% of the variation. R^2 is really useful, therefore, because it provides you with a good sense of how strong the relationship between the variables really is, in practical terms.

Measures of effect size exist for many other statistical tests. For the t-test, which is commonly used to decide whether the difference between two group means is statistically significant, the measure of effect size is **Cohen's d**. This is a 'standardized difference between the means', obtained by taking the difference between the two group means and dividing it by the average of the groups' SDs. (The advantage of standardizing in this way is that it allows you to compare effect sizes between studies that have used different raw measures.) The resulting measure is in terms of amount of SDs of difference between the groups. So, if $d = 1$, the two groups' means differ by one SD; if $d = 0.5$, they differ by half an SD, and so on. Cohen (1992) has provided guidelines to help assess d. He suggests that an effect size of 0.2 should be considered a weak effect, an effect size of 0.5 should be considered a moderate effect, and an effect size over 0.8 should be regarded as a strong effect. Cohen has stressed that these are only rough guidelines, but, as with Pearson's r, they provide a way of assessing the size of the difference between two groups, rather than merely assessing how likely it is that the difference arose by chance.

FOCUS POINT 2.4

REPORTING CONVENTIONS IN PSYCHOLOGY RESEARCH PAPERS

Writing up research papers is tightly bound by conventions laid down in the *Publication Manual of the American Psychological Association* (2010, now in its sixth edition). This massive tome tells psychologists everything they need to know in order to prepare a paper for submission to a journal, down to the last comma. Pedantic it may be, but, by helping to standardize reports, it makes them easier to read: once you are familiar with the conventions, you know where to look in a report for certain bits of information, and statistical results all appear in much the same format in most journals.

Details of the American Psychological Association guidelines are beyond the scope of this chapter, but, aside from the manual itself, there are many brief guides on the web, such as Purdue University's excellent **Online Writing Lab**[4].

TEST YOURSELF

1. What is the difference between the standard deviation and the standard error of the mean?
2. Why is it important to know about the size of an effect as well as its statistical significance?
3. How should a psychologist interpret (a) a statistically significant finding and (b) a non-significant finding?

SECTION SUMMARY

- Many psychologists attempt to obtain quantitative data on the phenomena they are studying and then use statistical techniques to help them draw conclusions from them.

- There are essentially two types of statistics and they go hand in hand: descriptive statistics (such as averages) and inferential statistics (various tests that enable us to determine whether our observed results have occurred merely by chance).

- The simplest descriptive statistic is merely a count of how often something has occurred, which enables us to obtain a frequency.

- We can also report a summary of typical performance (mean, median, or mode) or report how well the average reflects performance in the group of scores that it is intended to summarize (standard deviation).

- For decades, by far the most popular approach in psychology for analysing data has been to engage in null hypothesis significance testing.

- It is important to make a clear distinction between statistical significance and the size of the effect.

QUALITATIVE RESEARCH METHODS

LEARNING OBJECTIVE 2.5

Demonstrate an understanding of some of the qualitative methods used by psychologists.

So far this chapter has discussed research methods in the quantitative, 'positivist' tradition, where the aim is to obtain quantitative data on a phenomenon using methods akin to those used in physics and chemistry. However, another school of thought within psychology rejects positivism, arguing that methods borrowed from the physical sciences are often unsatisfactory for understanding the richness and complexity of human experience. Whereas mainstream psychology seeks to establish universal laws of nature that apply to everyone, some advocates of qualitative methods claim that we don't study objective 'reality', but rather interpretations or social constructions of that reality, and that therefore these are all we can comment upon. This is called **social constructivism**.

As Howitt (2010) points out, it is difficult to define exactly what 'qualitative psychology' is. He suggests that there is a range of features shared by qualitative techniques, although any one practitioner may not subscribe to all of them. Many qualitative researchers are interested in collecting detailed descriptive data, generally with an emphasis on the individual's perspective. The researcher is seen as an intrinsic, involved part of the research process, whereas more traditional research paradigms envisage the researcher as a detached and disinterested observer. Qualitative studies tend to have a more **idiographic** approach, focusing on the individual, in contrast to the more traditional **nomothetic** approach, which strives to establish generalities from studying groups. Many qualitative researchers are much more interested than quantitative researchers in investigating how individuals experience their own individual world, in a specific time, place, and social context.

Methods for obtaining qualitative data

Participant observation

In participant observation, the researchers immerse themselves in a group of some kind and attempt to understand it from the standpoint of the group members. This approach was developed in anthropology and sociology and is used more in those disciplines than in psychology.

Interviews

Interviews are the most popular method of obtaining qualitative data. They vary considerably in nature. Structured interviews, which have a fixed set of questions, can sometimes amount to little more than an orally administered questionnaire or survey. Semistructured interviews allow the interviewee freedom to respond and enable the researcher to follow up answers for clarification. Unstructured interviews simply comprise a set of issues that the interviewer wants to cover.

A video or audio recording of the interaction is subsequently transcribed to provide a permanent record that can form the basis for qualitative data analysis.

Focus groups

When focus groups are used, the researcher creates a group of individuals and gets them to discuss the topic of interest. The interaction between the individuals may be of interest in addition to their direct answers to the questions put to them. Again, the conversations can be recorded and transcribed for subsequent analysis.

Textual sources

Qualitative analyses are not confined to data obtained from direct interaction with or between participants. They can also be used with diaries, texts from the media (such as internet material or newspaper extracts), and recorded conversations from other sources.

Qualitative data analysis techniques

To lump researchers together as 'qualitative' ignores the fact that they may use these types of raw data in a wide variety of ways, depending on their theoretical stance and the questions they are interested in addressing. The following outline provides a broad overview of some of these techniques by briefly summarizing one or more illustrative studies in each case.

Content analysis/thematic analysis

This is probably the method of qualitative data analysis that has the most overlap with mainstream quantitative techniques. Material is analysed by first deciding on some important themes and categories, and then identifying these within the given text or texts. Some versions of thematic analysis (usually referred to as **content analysis**) involve measuring how often these themes occur. This can be done descriptively or with the aid of statistical techniques.

Evans, Donelle, and Hume-Loveland (2012) analysed 512 messages posted on the forum of an online postpartum depression support group. Based on previous theory, the researchers analysed the messages in terms of the frequency of expressions of various types of social support. The journal article presents no quantitative data, only the authors' descriptive account of their findings together with selected illustrative quotations from the dataset. The conclusion was that the support group offered emotional, informational, and practical support for depressed mothers, as well as a 'safe haven' for them to express their feelings.

Use of content analysis is not confined to textual material: it can be performed with film, video, and other visual materials. Slater, Tiggemann, Hawkins, and Werchon (2012) performed a content analysis on 631 adverts from 14 websites that were popular with adolescents. Each advert was coded in terms of the category of product advertised and various characteristics of any people appearing in the adverts (such as age, attractiveness, and degree of conformity to idealized notions of body shape). The results showed that adverts on teen websites were mainly for cosmetic and beauty products. More than 60% of the non-text adverts (even for computer games) showed at least one person, who was usually a young, thin, and attractive female.

Grounded theory

Grounded theory has its origins in 1960s sociology and the work of Glaser and Strauss (1967; see also Charmaz, 1995). Its basic rationale is that the researcher obtains a set of data first (generally, texts derived from interview transcripts) and *then* tries to develop a theory from those data in a bottom-up way rather than interpreting the data in terms of a pre-existing theory.

Poteat, German, and Kerrigan (2013) investigated the discrimination experienced by transgender individuals in their interactions with healthcare providers. In-depth interviews were conducted with 55 transgender individuals and 12 medical professionals (mainly doctors). These data were first subjected to 'open coding'. The researchers initially selected a subset of the interviews. Each line of the interview transcripts was labelled according to its apparent theme. This produced over 100 codes that were then grouped into 30 broader codes. These were used as the focus for coding the remaining transcripts. These codes were then grouped into five categories: 'feelings about transgender identities', 'feelings about transgender hormone therapy', 'learning about transgender health', 'clinical interactions with transgender patients', and 'interactions with colleagues' (a category used only for healthcare providers). 'Uncertainty' emerged as a recurrent theme within each of these categories. The analysis then involved a process of comparison within and between texts to identify key processes related to stigma in the medical encounter. This process was repeated with the transcripts until 'data saturation' was reached, meaning that no new themes emerged.

From their findings, Poteat et al. speculated that stigma serves a function for healthcare providers: it reinforces the normal doctor–patient power relationships, which are disrupted because of doctors' uncertainty about how to deal with transgender patients. Poteat et al.'s conclusion was that existing theories of stigma and discrimination need to take more account of power relationships in social interactions between authority figures and stigmatized people.

Interpretative phenomenological analysis

Interpretative phenomenological analysis (IPA) looks at the meanings that particular experiences, events, and objects have for participants, and how individuals make sense of these. It is thus an example of 'phenomenological psychology'. It is idiographic in its approach: the focus is primarily on the *individual's* experiences, using small samples or a case-study approach. Semistructured interviews or diaries are analysed in an attempt to understand the participant's experiential world from their own unique perspective.

Schweitzer, Griffiths, and Yates (2012) used IPA to investigate 11 parents' experiences of having a child with cancer. Two 45–90-minute semistructured interviews were conducted with each parent, spaced a year apart. The analysis consisted of initially searching through the content of each interview for obvious themes and then identifying 'meaning units', each corresponding to a single aspect of the individual's experience. These were grouped into subthemes, which were in turn grouped into five superordinate themes: 'a pivotal moment in time' (how the parent responded to the diagnosis of cancer), 'the experience of adaptation in relation to having a sick child', 'the nature of support', 're-evaluation of values during a critical life experience', and 'the experience of optimism and altruism'. The net outcome was a fine-grained analysis not only of how these parents responded to their child having cancer but also of how their personal 'life-world' was changed in both positive and negative ways.

Discourse analysis

Discourse analysis is concerned with how people 'do things' with language; its exponents are interested in how people use language to construct versions of reality and how language functions as a form of social action that regulates social interactions. Inspired by the work of the French philosopher Michel Foucault, Foucaldian discourse analysts focus on how language reflects power relationships in society and how it is used to construct identity. In contrast to other qualitative approaches, in discourse analysis, language doesn't represent 'experience' but is a tool used to achieve various social ends – such as avoiding blame, accusing others, and constructing 'facts' (see Edwards & Potter, 2001).

To give a simple example, Nevile (2006) analysed transcriptions of conversations between airline pilots while they worked. He shows how using 'and' at the start of sentences serves to emphasize that different actions by different crew members are part of a single sequentially organized chain of behaviour, something that would only be implicit in the formal wordings that pilots are supposed to use. For example, before taxiing begins, each pilot in turn has to look out of their window to check that the way ahead is clear. The formal requirement is for one pilot to say 'clear left' and the other to say 'clear right', but the second pilot actually says 'and clear right'. 'And' serves to 'glue' the two sequential actions into a single unit of behaviour, despite the significant time lag between them. It makes it obvious to everyone that this is a second activity that completes the first one, rather than being the initiation of something new.

Strengths of qualitative approaches

Qualitative analysis can provide a rich account of data, and it can identify themes in a narrative that are not explicitly acknowledged by the interviewees themselves. It often focuses on individuals' experiences and subjective worlds in a way that more mainstream methods cannot. It provides insights into how people use language to mediate their social interactions, over and above the explicit meaning of what they actually say.

As we saw earlier, aspirations to be an 'objective' and detached observer can sometimes lead quantitative researchers to lose sight of the fact that an experiment is a social interaction. In contrast, qualitative researchers often draw attention to their involvement in the research process.

Weaknesses of qualitative approaches

The methodology used in many qualitative studies is sometimes poorly specified. Neuendorf (2011) makes this criticism specifically in connection with content analysis studies of gender, but many of her points apply equally to research performed using other qualitative techniques. Ideally, details of the methods that were used should be included in research reports, but in practice these are often omitted. A basic principle of scientific research (potential replicability) is therefore violated. However, this criticism is also true for many quantitative studies, and it is partly a function of academic journals requiring papers to be relatively short.

Many researchers, both quantitative and qualitative, would take issue with some aspects of the grounded theory approach, especially Glaser and Strauss' (1967) claim that hypotheses emerge from data unaffected by prior expectations. This is naive: observation is always selective and inevitably guided by a researcher's interests and preconceptions.

It is difficult to assess the reliability and validity of some qualitative research. Firstly, many articles provide too little information about their results for validity to be assessed. The Evans et al. (2012) article mentioned earlier is a good example of this. How does the reader know that the data do show what the authors claim? Might it be that the authors have selectively chosen quotations that support their argument while ignoring others that do not? There is simply no way of knowing from the published account, so again this calls into question the *scientific* credentials of the study.

Because they usually focus on in-depth analyses of a few participants' data, generalizability is often a problem with qualitative studies. However, given the philosophical stance of many qualitative researchers (that they are focusing on individuals or particular interactions in a specific time and setting, rather than attempting to generalize to 'humanity'), they may not necessarily agree that this is a problem. There is no reason why the individualistic analyses cannot be followed up by larger-scale, more quantitative studies (as recommended by many researchers using grounded theory or IPA).

Finally, it is often difficult to draw cause-and-effect conclusions from qualitative research; but again, many qualitative researchers would argue that this is not the appropriate way to talk about human behaviour.

TEST YOURSELF

1. What are the principal characteristics of qualitative research?
2. What differentiates qualitative and quantitative approaches to the study of language?
3. What are the strengths and weaknesses of qualitative research methods compared to more mainstream approaches?

SECTION SUMMARY

- Some psychologists reject positivism, arguing that methods borrowed from the physical sciences are often unsatisfactory for understanding the richness and complexity of human experience.

- Qualitative studies tend to have a more idiographic approach, focusing on the individual, in contrast to the more traditional nomothetic approach that strives to establish generalities from studying groups.

- Qualitative methods include participant observation, interviews, focus groups, and analysis of textual sources.

- Researchers may use raw data in a wide variety of ways, depending on their theoretical stance and the questions they are interested in addressing.

- Methods of analysis include content analysis/thematic analysis, grounded theory, interpretative phenomenological analysis, and discourse analysis.

- The methodology used in many qualitative studies is sometimes poorly specified.

- It is often difficult to draw cause-and-effect conclusions from qualitative research, though many qualitative researchers would argue that this is not the appropriate way to talk about human behaviour.

- Qualitative research has strengths and limitations that are complementary to those of more mainstream research methods.

- Qualitative methods provide ways to obtain insights into aspects of human experience that would be difficult or impossible to probe with traditional quantitative techniques.

GOOD AND BAD PRACTICE IN PSYCHOLOGICAL RESEARCH

LEARNING OBJECTIVE 2.6

Demonstrate a clear understanding of how to conduct research in an ethical and unbiased fashion.

Psychology researchers have a duty to ensure their research is as high quality as possible: not only does poorly conducted research waste taxpayers' money and participants' time but it can also have serious social consequences (e.g. the spurious link between MMR vaccination and autism; Godlee, Smith, & Marcovitch, 2011). A good researcher ensures that their studies are well designed and that the results are appropriately analysed and interpreted, but being a good *psychology* researcher goes beyond this, because we are working with humans and animals, and this involves special considerations. First and foremost, we need to behave ethically. This section discusses the ethical principles that researchers should adhere to, the problem of bias in research (and how to avoid it), and the thorny issue of scientific fraud.

Ethical principles in research

Detailed guidelines on ethical issues in conducting research are published by the American Psychological Association and the British Psychological Society and must be complied with by all researchers.

RESEARCH METHODS 2.1

ETHICS AND GUIDELINES

Some major guidelines on ethics are as follows:

- The American Psychological Association's ***Ethical Principles of Psychologists and Code of Conduct***[5].
- The British Psychological Society's ***Code of Ethics and Conduct***[6].
- Other countries have their own ethical guidelines, which are broadly similar to those of the American Psychological Association and the British Psychological Society but not identical. See Leach and Harbin (1997) for a review of cross-cultural differences in what is considered 'ethical'.

The principle of informed consent

Before participating in a study, participants have the right to know what the research is about so they can decide whether or not they wish to take part. They should be told what they will be asked to do, how long it will take, and what (if any) physical or psychological risks it might involve. Figure 2.10 shows an example of a consent form that participants can sign to confirm they are willing to take part in an experiment.

Obtaining informed consent can sometimes be a tricky issue. Many psychology experiments depend on participants being unaware of the specific purpose of the study while they are taking part in it because this knowledge would affect their performance. In these situations, it is considered acceptable to obtain 'semi-informed' consent: the participant agrees to take part in a vaguely defined study (e.g. 'a short memory experiment') on the understanding that the purpose of the study will be explained to them in full after they have completed it.

Another problem is how to conduct research on groups that are incapable of giving their informed consent, such as infants, young children, the mentally ill, and people with intellectual deficits. In these cases, it is acceptable to obtain consent from the participant's guardian initially; however, testing must be terminated at once if the participant shows any reluctance to take part. For example, in studies on infants, the study is stopped if the baby shows excessive 'fussiness' (crying, to you or me) as this is taken as an indication that the participant does not want to continue.

Consideration also has to be given to situations where the perceived power relationship between the researcher and the participant means that the participant might feel pressured to give their consent. Prison inmates may feel that refusal to participate might be construed as hostile or antisocial behaviour. Members of institutions such as the armed forces or police may feel obliged to take part because their superiors are seen to be supporting the researcher's activities. In these situations, it is important

---

CONSENT FORM

Study title: _____

Study approval reference: _____

This study will take approximately 15–20 minutes and consists of listening to music, reading vignettes on a computer screen, and taking part in a short task.

Thank you for agreeing to take part in this study. Your formal consent is required to confirm that your participation is voluntary and that you understand that you have the right to withdraw at any time.

I agree to take part in the above research study. I have had the study explained to me and I have read and understood the Explanatory Statement, which I may keep for my records. I understand that agreeing to take part means that I am willing to:

1. listen to music
2. read vignettes
3. take part in a short task.

I understand that any information I provide is confidential, and that no informational that I disclose will lead to the identification of any individual in the reports on the study, either by the researcher or by any other party.

I consent to the processing of my personal information for the purposes explained to me. I understand that such information will be treated in accordance with the terms of the Data Protection Act 1998.

I understand that my participation is voluntary, that I can choose not to participate in part or all of the study, and that I can withdraw at any stage of the study without being penalised or disadvantaged in any way.

Sign:

Date:

FIGURE 2.10 *Example of a consent form.*

that it is made very clear to the participants that they do have a free choice about whether or not to be involved in the study.

Deception in psychological research

Sometimes it is felt necessary to deceive participants about the real purpose of the research. For example, a participant might be led to think that a study is on the palatability of food, while really it is concerned with how the room's lighting conditions affected the amount of food consumed. In a situation like this, participants' behaviour would be unacceptably distorted if they knew what the study was really about (see the following discussion of demand characteristics in the section on 'Experimenter Bias').

Wherever possible, deception should be avoided. Apart from its dubious ethical status (it certainly violates the principle of informed consent), it causes problems for other psychologists. Participants can tend to become highly suspicious of all psychologists, assuming that there is a 'hidden agenda' to a study even if they have been reassured that there is not. This suspicion can often impair performance.

Debriefing

Whether or not deception is employed, once a participant has completed the study, it should be fully explained to them. They should be told what the researcher is trying to find out in as much detail as they care to know. In the course of debriefing, care should be taken to ensure that the participant leaves feeling okay about themselves. Researchers are often not particularly interested in an individual participant's data: the participant is merely part of a group within the study and their data will be averaged together with those from other members of the group. However, many participants experience **evaluation apprehension**: they feel that they are being personally tested and that their performance in the study is a reflection of their own worth as a person. For example, if your study involves a test of intelligence or personality, an individual participant may worry that they have been assessed and found lacking in some way. Therefore, an important part of the debriefing process is to ensure that all participants are made to feel that they have performed satisfactorily.

One special ethical issue in relation to debriefing arises from studies that involve brain-imaging techniques such as fMRI (functional magnetic resonance imaging). Very occasionally an imaging study might detect a potentially worrying anomaly, such as a brain tumour or arterial malformation. In situations like this, the best course of action is to explain to the participant that the scan seems to show something unusual and that it is probably nothing to worry about but that they should see their doctor to get it checked out.

Protection of participants

The researcher has responsibility for participants' physical safety, and also for their mental well-being. If a study involves any activity that might have side effects – such as taking drugs (even innocuous ones such as caffeine or antihistamines), having a brain scan, or being sleep deprived – then participants should be warned about these activities in advance and thoroughly vetted before the study begins to ensure they won't experience any problems. For example, severely claustrophobic individuals are unlikely to enjoy being enclosed in an fMRI scanner for any length of time. If the experiment involves briefly flashing images on a computer screen, participants should be checked to make sure they are not epileptic, as seizures can sometimes be induced in this way.

Once the study has been completed, the aim should be to ensure that the participant leaves the experiment in a good frame of mind. Consequently, if the participant has been stressed in any way (e.g. by being shown a spider if they are spider-phobic) or made to feel depressed (e.g. by mood induction using sad music), the researcher needs to make sure that these effects have been ameliorated before the participant leaves the laboratory. If the study is on the effects of alcohol or other drugs that might impair performance, then the researcher needs to ensure that the participant is in a safe state before they leave, or else arrange for a responsible adult to remain with them until they have fully recovered.

Confidentiality

Participants' privacy should be respected. Firstly, researchers should collect only the minimum of personal information necessary for the study in question. If personal attributes such as sexual orientation, medical history, and dietary preferences are irrelevant to the study, information on these should not be collected. Wherever possible, participants should not be identifiable and their data should be stored securely. This is especially important if the study involves the collection of sensitive information about the participants, such as details of their sexual behaviour or illicit drug use, but it should also be routine practice even for more innocuous studies. If datasets need to be linked (such as data from separate testing sessions over time), then each participant should be assigned a code number that is used each time.

Right to withdraw

Participants have the right to withdraw from a study at any time, and they can demand that their data are destroyed. However frustrating and annoying this might be, the experimenter should acquiesce without complaining.

The special case of animal research

In the United Kingdom, research on animals is strictly governed by Home Office regulations (Home Office, 2013). It is essential to have a licence to perform experiments on animals, even if these involve relatively innocuous procedures. Where there is the likelihood of the animal experiencing pain or suffering, then a special case has to be made for permission to run the study. The benefits of the research must be considered to outweigh the suffering to the animal. No more suffering must be inflicted than is absolutely necessary for the study's data to be obtained, which means testing the minimum number of participants consistent with obtaining reliable data and exposing each animal to the minimum amount of distress possible. Undergraduates are not allowed to conduct any research on animals without constant supervision from a licensed researcher. The British Psychological Society (BPS) (2012) advises that no student should be obliged to conduct research on animals if they feel it is unethical to do so.

The process of obtaining ethical clearance for a study

To ensure that researchers are behaving ethically, the BPS insists that every study has to be checked for ethical issues before it can be conducted. Each institution has its own procedures for doing this, but they all follow a similar pattern: the researcher submits a proposal outlining what the study is about, how it will be conducted, and what ethical issues it raises. This proposal is then scrutinized by an independent researcher or panel, which sometimes includes non-psychologists. The study can only go ahead if it receives approval. The BPS's position is that *all* psychological research should be vetted for ethical issues, whether the research is done by a schoolchild or an eminent professor. For research with special populations, such as hospital patients or prison inmates, the researcher will also have to go through additional ethical clearance procedures for that institution.

Bias in research

Psychological research is by its nature particularly prone to the operation of various biases in data collection. A good researcher is alert to the existence of these and should take steps to minimize their influence on the data.

Selection/sampling bias

This was discussed earlier in connection with response rates to questionnaires, but the problem of sampling bias is a much more general issue in psychology. A number of studies have drawn attention to the fact that psychological research is based heavily on data from a very small and probably unrepresentative sample of humans – those that Henrich, Heine, and Norenzayan (2013) have described as WEIRD societies: Western, Educated, Industrialized, Rich, and Democratic.

Arnett (2008) investigated the issue of sampling bias by surveying empirical studies in six leading US psychology journals. Between 2003 and 2007, 68% of all participant samples in these journals came from the United States, 14% from other English-speaking countries, and 13% from Europe. Just 5% came from the rest of the world. In the *Journal of Personality and Social Psychology* (a journal that should be especially sensitive to issues of cultural bias), approximately 96% of all participants came from Western industrialized countries (who make up only 12% of the world's population).

How much this is a cause for concern probably depends on the phenomenon under investigation. For studies of low-level cognitive processing, it might be possible to extrapolate from undergraduates to all other humans, but in many domains – developmental, health, clinical, and social psychology – psychology undergraduates are not very representative of the rest of humanity. Using published studies, Henrich et al. (2013) made specific comparisons between WEIRD participants and other groups in a wide variety of psychological domains. They concluded that most researchers' implicit assumptions that their findings are generalizable to 'humanity' are at best unproven and, at worst, false.

Experimenter bias

A researcher's beliefs about the likely outcome of a study may sometimes bias the data obtained, so that the results end up in line with the researcher's expectations (e.g. Rosenthal, 1966). Orne (1962) pointed out that experiments are a social situation and that 'subjects' are not just passive recipients of experimental procedures. They actively try to construe what the study is about and may try to give the experimenter 'good' data in line with what they think the experimenter wants. In short, participants may be highly sensitive to the **demand characteristics** of a study. As a result, experimenters can unwittingly bias a participant's performance by providing subtle cues about how the participant should perform. These experimenter expectancy effects have been actively studied for over 50 years, not only in the context of pure research but also in legal settings, doctor–patient relationships, and classroom settings (where they have become known as the **Pygmalion effect**: Rosenthal & Jacobson, 1968). Sadly, although experimenter effects are as important today as they ever were, interest in the subject has declined since the 1970s. Most published studies fail to mention what steps they took (if any) to prevent **experimenter bias** (Klein et al., 2012).

How can experimenters prevent their expectations from affecting their data? Automating experimental procedures (e.g. by using standardized written instructions or by using a computer to administer the experiment in its entirety) can help to minimize unconscious biases from experimenters. The best way is to use **double-blind procedures**, in which neither the experimenter nor the participant knows which condition the participant is in. One way to do this in practice is to have two researchers: the one who actually interacts with the participant does not know which experimental condition the participant has been assigned to. While double-blind procedures are routinely used in medical research, the cost and inconvenience of having a second researcher involved in running a study mean that double-blind procedures are all too rarely used in psychology.

Scientific fraud

The ultimate 'bad practice' in psychology has to be committing fraud. This can take many forms, from plagiarism (passing off someone else's work as your own) to outright fabrication of entire datasets. Two notorious cases of fraud, one in the 1950s and 1960s and one more recently, raise important issues about how psychological research is conducted (see Focus Point 2.5).

NOTORIOUS FRAUDSTERS IN PSYCHOLOGY

The most famous fraudster in psychology is Cyril Burt. Burt supported his conviction that IQ was largely inherited with data from studies on monozygotic twins who had been reared separately from birth. Soon after his death in 1971, suspicions arose about the legitimacy of these data. Kamin (1974) found a number of problems. In particular, there was a troubling statistical issue. Burt reported using IQ tests on 21 pairs of twins in 1955, 30 pairs in 1958, and 53 pairs in 1966. Despite there being different numbers of twins each time, the correlations between the IQs of the twins in each study were exactly the same: 0.771 for twins reared apart and 0.994 for twins reared together. This is extremely unlikely to occur by chance. Finally, the two research assistants who supposedly helped Burt collect the data could never be traced, leading to doubts that they ever existed.

In 2011, it came to light that Diederik Stapel, a social psychologist, had committed fraud in at least 55 of his journal articles as well as 10 of his PhD students' dissertations. From 2004 onwards, he had designed studies and then simply made up the entire set of results, pretending to have had the study run by (fictitious) research assistants in schools to which he had exclusive access.

A highly detailed investigation by three separate committees (at Amsterdam, Groningen, and Tilburg, the universities Stapel had worked at) concluded that Stapel was principally to blame but that he had worked within 'a culture in which scientific integrity is not held in high esteem' (Levelt Committee, Noort Committee, & Drenth Committee, 2012). His ability to commit fraud for so long stemmed from his personal charisma, his powerful positions at Groningen and Tilburg, and research cultures at these institutions in which there was an excessive reliance on trust. The committees also drew attention to flaws in the wider scientific peer-review process. Stapel's results were often too good to be true, there were tell-tale signs in the statistical analyses that the results were dubious, and his research hypotheses were almost always confirmed. However, journal reviewers had apparently failed to notice any of these points.

Burt and Stapel probably committed fraud for different reasons. Burt was a committed hereditarian and may have faked his correlations in order to support his strongly held beliefs. Stapel's motives seem more complex: a similar impatience with the 'messiness' of real data plus a desire for self-advancement. Whatever the reasons, the root cause of these problems will be difficult to fix. A successful career in psychology, as in all sciences, depends on a researcher being prolific: success and productivity generate funding opportunities, promotion, and esteem from academic colleagues. Hence, there are powerful incentives for researchers to commit fraud – or, at the least, not to be too conscientious in their data acquisition and analysis procedures. Thankfully, most researchers are in the business because they genuinely want to make discoveries, and data fabrication does not fit in with that aim. Also, the self-correcting nature of science ultimately helps to uncover even the most ingenious of fraudsters, albeit at the cost of diverted resources and wasted time while this process occurs.

Few researchers would consider committing blatant fraud on the scale of Burt or Stapel. However, minor transgressions may be common, such as 'massaging' data by selectively removing participants who do not provide the 'right' results, or ignoring the results of experiments that don't support the researcher's hypotheses. The committees investigating Stapel made a number of general recommendations that might help to reduce the prevalence of fraud. These included increased emphasis on replication in psychology; the establishment of permanent, publicly accessible archives of protocols, stimulus materials, and raw data; and clear, detailed indications in publications of the contributions of the various authors.

There are already promising developments in line with these recommendations. In March 2013, the Association for Psychological Science announced that its prestigious journal *Perspectives on Psychological Science* would start publishing articles that attempted to replicate previous research findings in a bid to make replication a more valued activity in psychology. These articles take the form of multiple independent replications at various institutions, compiled into a single report and published regardless of the outcomes (so that failures to replicate will see the light of day). In a similar vein, the Center for Open Science is conducting a 'reproducibility study' for psychology. The plan is for numerous labs to independently replicate a selection of studies that have appeared in three top psychology journals. It is hoped the results will give some indication of the robustness and generalizability not only of these particular studies but also of psychological research in general.

TEST YOURSELF

1. What is informed consent?
2. Why it is important for psychologists to behave ethically?
3. What aspects of the scientific method help to detect and prevent fraud?

SECTION SUMMARY

- Psychology researchers have a duty to ensure that the quality of their research is as high as possible.

- First and foremost, researchers must behave ethically. Detailed guidelines on ethical issues in conducting research are published by the American Psychological Association and the British Psychological Society and must be complied with by all researchers.

- Research participants must provide informed consent. Wherever possible, deception should be avoided. Whether or not deception is employed, once participants have completed the study, it should be fully explained to them.

- The researcher has responsibility for participants' physical safety and also for their mental well-being.

- Participants' privacy should be respected.

- Participants have the right to withdraw from a study at any time and they can demand that their data are destroyed.

- Psychological research is by its nature particularly prone to the operation of various biases in data collection. A good researcher is alert to the existence of these biases and should take steps to minimize their influence on the data.

- Research fraud can take many forms, from plagiarism to outright fabrication of entire datasets. Recommendations are being developed that might help to reduce the prevalence of fraud. These include increased emphasis on replication in psychology; the establishment of permanent, publicly accessible archives of protocols, stimulus materials, and raw data; and clear, detailed indications in publications of the contributions of the various authors.

FUTURE DEVELOPMENTS

LEARNING OBJECTIVE 2.7

Describe some of the possible future directions of psychology research and practice.

Brain imaging versus behavioural measures

'Cognitive neuroscience' and even 'social cognitive neuroscience' are hot topics at present, attracting a lot of funding and also capturing the public imagination. The media often talk simplistically about how brain researchers have found the brain region responsible for 'empathy' or some other relatively high-level function, accompanying their articles with images of brains, colour-coded to show regions of high activity. These reports are compelling: research findings are considered to be more credible if they are accompanied by neuroscience language (Beck 2010; Michael, Newman, Vuorre, Cumming, & Garry, 2013; Weisberg, Keil, Goodstein, Rawson, & Gray, 2008).

Will high-tech research eventually supplant behavioural measures such as reaction times and accuracy rates, measures that have stood psychologists in good stead for well over a century? Or are imaging studies, as one of my more cynical colleagues put it, merely 'expensive neophrenology' that actually tell us little more than that behaviour is associated with brain activity of some kind?

Opinions are mixed. Passingham, Rowe, and Sakai (2013) suggest that imaging techniques have given us genuine new insights into how the brain functions, in particular enabling us to understand how information flows through the cerebral cortex in response to task demands. Henson (2005) has argued that imaging data are just another dependent variable for psychologists to use and that they can potentially be used to help psychologists choose between competing theories. Other researchers are more sceptical, arguing that, so far, imaging techniques have told us little about *psychological* functioning (e.g. Coltheart, 2011; Uttal, 2001).

Behavioural measures still have many advantages for psychological research. They are cheap, quick to record, and easily administered to large numbers of participants. They can also be highly portable: these days, it is very easy to put an experiment on a laptop and take it to the participants, rather than requiring the participants to come to a lab. This makes it easier to access groups who were previously difficult to reach, such as elderly people or schoolchildren. For the foreseeable future, imaging technology is likely to remain extremely expensive and highly non-portable, and this will restrict its usefulness. (In 10 years' time, someone reading this while wearing an fMRI scanner the size of a baseball cap will be laughing derisively at this statement.)

Current imaging techniques have complementary strengths and limitations. fMRI is based on measuring changes in blood flow in the brain: more active neurons have a heavier requirement for oxygen and glucose, which are carried to them by the blood. As a result, fMRI has good spatial resolution (about 3–6 mm², depending on the scanner) but relatively poor temporal resolution (in the order of seconds), because changes in blood flow take time. However, many psychological phenomena occur extremely rapidly. Other techniques, such as electroencephalography (EEG) and magnetoencephalography (MEG), are greatly superior for measuring brain responses to fast-moving events. EEG is based on measuring the brain's electrical activity from surface-mounted electrodes. MEG measures changes in the brain's magnetic field from an array of sensors located around the head. Both EEG and MEG have a temporal resolution of less than 1 ms but their spatial resolution is comparatively poor.

An exciting development is that studies are now being performed that combine fMRI and EEG to get the advantages of both techniques: the EEG provides moment-to-moment data while the fMRI data constrain the possible locations of the EEG response to particular brain structures. So, at present, there is still a place in psychological research for behavioural measures such as reaction time and accuracy, and this is likely to be true for some years yet, but technological advances may well render them obsolete sooner rather than later.

Ambulatory assessment

When the limitations of questionnaires were discussed above, it was concluded that retrospective reports are rather unreliable, due to the fallibility and selectivity of human memory. Smartphones and iPads now offer researchers the opportunity to collect data in real time, rather than retrospectively. Rather than relying on the participant's memory, it is now quite easy to produce an app that prompts a participant to enter responses, so that self-ratings of mood or records of behaviour can be made either periodically (using a time-sampling technique) or whenever they are required (**event sampling**). This is known as **ambulatory assessment**.

Portable event recorders have been around for some years, but their expense limited their usefulness. Now that so many people are routinely carrying around a smartphone or a tablet, studies can be conducted 'in the wild', using relatively large numbers of participants. Ambulatory assessment opens up some exciting possibilities for real-time recording of behaviour in real-world situations. Applications include making ecologically valid and reliable measurements of pain, stress, anxiety, mood, cigarette use, social phobia episodes, and dieting behaviour. (For reviews and detailed descriptions of applications, see Bussmann, Ebner-Priemer, & Fahrenberg, 2009; Carpenter, Wycoff, & Trulli 2016; Fahrenberg, Myrtek, Pawlik, & Perrez, 2007; Trull & Ebner-Priemer 2013, 2014.)

The demise of null hypothesis significance testing?

As mentioned earlier, the dominant quantitative approach in psychology has been null hypothesis significance testing (NHST). We have seen that this approach has been criticized by exponents of qualitative methods. It has also been challenged from within the ranks of researchers who use quantitative methods. NHST has come under attack from advocates of **Bayesian statistics** (e.g. Kruschke, 2010). The prestigious APA journal *Psychological Science* has also expressed its dissatisfaction with NHST (Eich, 2014).

An explanation of Bayesian methods goes way beyond this chapter. Suffice it to say that they involve a very different approach from mainstream statistics. In the traditional NHST approach, the null hypothesis is either accepted or rejected. However, in practice, a researcher considers the results from a single experiment in conjunction with those from other studies: judgements about the likelihood that a hypothesis is correct are made on the basis of numerous separate pieces of evidence, not just the findings of one study. The Bayesian approach makes this process much more explicit. It defines the probability of a hypothesis beforehand and then uses the data to see how this probability should be revised. Essentially, if the experimenter's past experiences gave them a strong belief in a specific hypothesis, and the observed data would be likely to occur given that hypothesis, confidence in that hypothesis should be strengthened. At present, Bayesian methods are the preserve of more mathematically sophisticated psychology researchers. Hopefully, this will change as more accessible accounts of them start to become available.

The editors of *Psychological Science* stop short of advocating that researchers switch to using Bayesian statistics, but they highlight the same problems with NHST (see Cumming, 2014) – essentially, that NHST encourages dichotomous 'significant or non-significant?' thinking. They suggest that researchers abandon the traditional *p*-value in favour of reporting effect sizes, confidence intervals (the limits within which a mean is likely to be 95% of the time if the study is repeated many times over), and meta-analyses (where the results of many studies on the same topic are combined).

Overall, it looks like statistical analyses in psychology are likely to change radically in the next few years, with a shift in focus from how *likely* results are to how *sizeable* and *replicable* they are.

TEST YOURSELF

1. What are the relative strengths and weaknesses of fMRI and EEG measures?
2. What are the advantages of Bayesian statistical methods over traditional 'null hypothesis significance testing' methods?

SECTION SUMMARY

- Enormous progress has been made in brain imaging techniques in recent years. Neuroscientists use data from techniques such as fMRI, EEG, and MEG to make inferences about cognitive, socio-cognitive, and emotional functioning.

- Opinions are mixed about the extent to which these techniques have provided genuine new insights into psychological functioning.

- Traditional behavioural measures retain many advantages: they are cheap and easy to use, and can be used with large numbers of participants.

- Ambulatory assessment makes use of portable event-recording devices (nowadays smartphones and iPads) to obtain data about behaviour in real time rather than retrospectively. Applications include measuring pain, stress, anxiety, mood, cigarette use, social phobia episodes, and dieting behaviour (to name just a few!).

- For decades, null hypothesis significance testing has been the dominant quantitative approach in psychology. Although it remains popular, it is gradually being supplanted by alternative approaches, such as Bayesian statistical methods. There is also a shift in emphasis from how *likely* results are to how *sizeable* and *replicable* they are.

CHAPTER SUMMARY

We are living in an exciting era, as far as research methods in psychology are concerned. There seem to be challenges to the current approach to studying behaviour, which for decades has been dominated mainly by experimental studies in conjunction with quantitative statistical analyses using the NHST model. It remains to be seen whether there will be a paradigm shift in dealing with psychological data, comparable to the change from introspection to behaviourism, or from behaviourism to cognitive approaches.

Whatever happens, the current diversity of methodologies being used to study human behaviour scientifically can only be a good thing, with both quantitative and qualitative approaches having something worthwhile to offer. There is also currently a healthy concern with how replicable and generalizable current psychological findings are. Again, this is something that can only be to the good of the discipline as a whole.

Finally, what *are* the effects of chocolate on children's activity levels? Actually, there is a lot of real research on this topic. For an interesting qualitative study of parents' *beliefs* about how sugary foods affect their children, see Brands et al. (2012). These researchers found that parents in four European countries share the belief that sugar affects their children in a dose-dependent way: too little and they lack energy, too much and they are hyperactive. In contrast to parents' beliefs, well-controlled quantitative studies, comparing the effects of sugar to a placebo, find no evidence that sugary foods produce hyperactivity (see the review in Benton, 2008).

ESSAY QUESTIONS

1. Suppose you were interested in whether men and women differed in their ability to park cars. Compare and contrast experimental and observational approaches to investigating this issue, noting the strengths and weaknesses of each.

2. Bronfenbrenner (1977) suggested that developmental psychology is 'the science of the strange behavior of children in strange situations with strange adults for the briefest possible periods of time' (p. 513). What do you think he meant by this statement, and how might the problems he identifies be overcome by researchers?

KEY TERMS

- **alternative hypothesis:** In an experimental context, the hypothesis that the researcher's manipulations have significantly affected the participants' behaviour (as opposed to the null hypothesis that they have not). Where this is the case, any observed effects in the data have not arisen merely by chance but represent 'real' phenomena.
- **ambulatory assessment:** The use of in-the-field methods to measure behaviour more or less as it happens, using techniques such as event recorders, diaries, and smartphone apps.
- **Bayesian statistics:** A branch of probability theory inspired by a theorem devised by Thomas Bayes and developed by Pierre-Simon Laplace during the 18th century. Bayesian approaches incorporate prior knowledge and beliefs in their assessment of the probability that a hypothesis is true.
- **carry-over effects:** In a repeated measures study, these are undesired lingering effects on participants of having taken part in a previous condition. These may include practice, fatigue, or boredom and are problematic because they constitute confounding variables, whose effects may be difficult to separate from those of the variables manipulated by the researcher.
- **causal relationship:** A relationship between two variables, X and Y, such that changes in X produce changes in Y. The relationship has to be unidirectional. X does not have to be the only cause of Y (i.e. it can be 'sufficient' to cause Y, but not 'necessary'). For example, smoking causes lung cancer; lung cancer does not cause smoking; smoking (alone) is sufficient to cause lung cancer; and things other than smoking cause lung cancer.
- **chocolate:** The *Oxford English Dictionary* defines this as 'a food in the form of a paste or solid block made from roasted and ground cacao seeds, typically sweetened and eaten as confectionery'.
- **coefficient of determination:** In a correlational design, the proportion of variance in one of the variables that is explained by that variable's relationship with the other variable. To calculate it, find Pearson's correlation between the two variables and then square it.
- **Cohen's *d*:** An estimate of effect size (technically, it is a standardized difference between two means, obtained by dividing the difference between the two means by the average of their standard deviations). Roughly speaking, $d = 0.2$ is a small effect size, $d = 0.5$ is a medium effect size, and $d = 0.8$ is a large effect size.
- **cohort effects:** Differences between groups in a study that arise because members of each group share similarities other than those of interest to the researcher. For example, claims of 'sex differences' in behaviour have to take account of the fact that males and females have had different life experiences (and hence form different cohorts of individuals) as well as being different chromosomally.
- **concurrent criterion validity:** The extent to which scores on a test correlate with scores on other relevant measures that were taken at the same time. For example, if scores on Hole's

'patented test of neuroticism' correlate well with other measures of neuroticism administered at the same time, then Hole's test has a high degree of concurrent criterion validity (see also **predictive criterion validity**).

- **construct validity:** The extent to which a measure correlates well with other measures of the same psychological construct. For example, a test of extraversion should correlate well with other measures of the psychological construct of 'extraversion'.
- **content analysis:** A variety of research techniques that involve analysing material (interview transcripts, texts, etc.) in terms of how often certain themes or ideas are expressed within it.
- **content validity:** The extent to which test items match the content to which they are supposed to relate. For example, a statistics test has high content validity if it contains items that adequately cover the statistics course's content.
- **correlation:** A relationship between two variables, X and Y, such that change in one is reliably associated with some change in the other. A correlation may be positive (increase in one variable is associated with increase in the other) or negative (increase in one variable is associated with decrease in the other).
- **correlational design:** A research methodology in which the researcher seeks to establish a relationship between two or more variables without directly manipulating them.
- **counterbalancing:** A method of systematically varying the order in which conditions are performed in a repeated measures design, in an attempt to avoid order effects. If counterbalancing is used with two conditions, A and B, half of the participants perform the conditions in the order A then B, and the other half perform them in the opposite order.
- **criterion validity:** A method of assessing the validity of a measure by correlating it with other measures that are already known to be valid.
- **cross-sectional design:** A research design that investigates a developmental phenomenon by using separate groups of participants to represent different developmental stages. For example, a cross-sectional study of age changes in antisocial behaviour might include separate groups of 15-, 20-, and 30-year-olds, rather than tracking the development of a single group of 15-year-olds for 15 years.
- **debriefing:** The process of providing information to participants after they have completed a study. This should include explaining to them what the study was designed to find out and answering any questions they might have about the study and their part in it.
- **demand characteristics:** Cues within a research setting that are used by a participant in order to infer (possibly incorrectly) what the experiment is about, and to modify their behaviour accordingly (e.g. by producing results to support what the participant perceives to be the researcher's hypothesis).
- **dependent variable:** A variable whose values are affected by a researcher's experimental manipulations. Also known as an 'outcome variable'; in effect, a dependent variable is the measure that a researcher chooses to use in an experiment.
- **discourse analysis:** A diversity of qualitative research methods that focus on how people use language to construct their own versions of 'reality' and on how language functions as a form of social action that regulates social interactions.
- **double-blind procedure:** A method for avoiding experimenter bias. The study is designed so that neither the experimenter nor the participant knows which condition the participant is in until after the study is completed.
- **ecological validity:** The extent to which a study's findings can be generalized satisfactorily to real-world situations.
- **effect size:** A numerical measure of the strength of an observed effect. Examples include Cohen's d and the coefficient of determination, R^2.
- **evaluation apprehension:** In the context of research, this refers to effects on a participant's performance produced by their anxiety about being negatively judged by the experimenter.

- **event sampling:** A method of recording behaviour used in observational research. Specified behaviours are recorded as and when they occur (as opposed to time sampling, where behaviour is recorded at fixed time intervals).
- **experimental design:** A research methodology that involves systematic manipulation of one or more independent variables and measurement of the effects of these manipulations on one or more outcome variables (dependent variables), in a bid to determine cause-and-effect relationships between the independent variable(s) and dependent variable(s).
- **experimenter bias:** Effects on a study's data produced by characteristics of the experimenter rather than by the variables of interest. For example, a participant's behaviour may be influenced by the experimenter's personal characteristics (age, gender, race) and/or by the experimenter's expectations about how the participant should perform.
- **external validity:** Synonymous with **ecological validity**.
- **face validity:** The extent to which measurements look like a valid measure of what the researcher wants to investigate. For example, we would expect a test of mathematical ability to include items dealing with numerical concepts but not items related to knowledge of history or geography.
- **grounded theory:** A qualitative research method devised by the sociologists Glaser and Strauss (1967). It uses a sequence of procedures to derive a theory from a set of data: the aim is that the theory ultimately emerges from a structured process of data coding and analysis.
- **hypothesis:** In the context of research methods, a specific prediction about what is likely to happen – for example, following some experimental manipulation.
- **idiographic:** Psychologists who adopt an idiographic approach are primarily interested in the experiences of the individual rather than in the behaviour of groups (see **nomothetic**).
- **independent measures design:** A design in which each participant is involved in only one of the conditions in the study.
- **independent variable:** A variable manipulated by the experimenter.
- **informed consent:** Permission granted by an individual in full knowledge of the possible consequences of doing so; in the context of psychological research, it refers to a participant agreeing to take part in a study once the procedures (including their risks and benefits) have been explained to them.
- **interaction:** In statistical terms, a situation where the state of one variable is significantly affected by the state of another. Interaction can take many forms, but, to give a couple of examples: if there is an interaction between age and gender on some measure, it might be that there is no gender difference for young people but a large one for older people; or perhaps males show no age changes but females do. In both these cases, it makes no sense to discuss either variable (age or gender) in isolation, because the effects of one depend crucially on the effects of the other.
- **internal validity:** The extent to which a study's conclusions are warranted, given the procedures that were followed. A study has high internal validity if it has been well designed, so that the experimenter can be reasonably sure the obtained results are due to their manipulations rather than to the effects of uncontrolled confounding variables.
- **interpretative phenomenological analysis:** A qualitative research method that focuses on phenomenological experiences. It is strongly idiographic (see **idiographic**) and primarily concerned with how people interpret and make sense of their life experiences, and the meanings these have for the participants.
- **interrupted time-series design:** A quasi-experimental research design that involves making repeated measurements before and after some intervention occurs. For example, to investigate the effectiveness of a new road sign, we could repeatedly measure speeds on a road at several time intervals before and after the sign is erected, and then compare the 'before' and 'after' measurements to see whether the sign is effective.

- **longitudinal design:** A design in which developmental phenomena are studied by repeatedly measuring the behaviour of the same individuals over an extended period of time.
- **nomothetic:** An approach that is primarily concerned with making generalizations about behaviour rather than focusing on individuals per se (see **idiographic**).
- **null hypothesis:** In an experimental context, the hypothesis that the researcher's manipulations have not significantly affected the participants' behaviour (as opposed to the **alternative hypothesis** that they have). If true, there is no reason to believe that any observed effects in the data have not arisen merely by chance.
- **null hypothesis significance testing:** The practice of using statistical tests in an attempt to decide whether the results of a study have occurred by chance (acceptance of the null hypothesis) or represent a 'real' effect (acceptance of the alternative hypothesis). The null hypothesis is rejected in favour of the alternative hypothesis if the statistical test suggests that the outcome of the study is highly unlikely to have occurred by chance.
- **observational methods:** Research procedures that involve the observation and description of participants' behaviour. This may involve relatively unstructured naturalistic observation or the use of formal event-sampling or time-sampling techniques.
- **peer review:** The process by which the quality of a researcher's journal articles or grant applications is assessed by independent academics.
- **power:** The ability of a statistical test to detect an effect when one actually exists – i.e. a measure of a test's sensitivity.
- **predictive criterion validity:** The extent to which scores on a test predict scores on other relevant measures in the future. For example, if children's scores on Hole's 'patented test of neuroticism' correlate well with measures of neuroticism administered to them in adulthood, then Hole's test has a high degree of predictive criterion validity (see also **concurrent criterion validity**).
- **Pygmalion effect:** Rosenthal and Jacobsen's (1968) idea that teachers' expectations influence their students' performance.
- **qualitative:** A loose term covering a diversity of psychological research methods that share a focus on the acquisition and analysis of predominantly non-numerical data about behaviour (e.g. from interviews, written texts, photographs, or videos) rather than **quantitative** data.
- **quantitative:** Psychological research methods that involve the acquisition of numerical data about behaviour (e.g. measures such as reaction times or number of errors on a task), usually accompanied by statistical analysis of those data.
- **quasi-experimental design:** A research design in which the researcher does not have complete control over the allocation of participants to conditions within the study and/or does not have control over the timing of the measurements taken.
- **regression towards the mean:** The statistical phenomenon that, if a behaviour is measured repeatedly, extremely high or low scores tend to be followed by scores that are closer to the mean for that measure.
- **reliability:** The extent to which findings are reproducible if a study is repeated.
- **repeated measures design:** A design in which participants perform more than one condition in a study and hence provide more than one score.
- **sampling bias:** Distortion of the data obtained in a study that arises from problems in the way the data were obtained (e.g. because the sample of participants used in a study were unrepresentative of the population of individuals that the researcher wanted to make statements about).
- **self-presentational bias:** A tendency for participants to try to present themselves to researchers in a good light, emphasizing their good points and playing down their bad ones. Synonymous with 'impression management' or 'social desirability bias'.
- **social constructivism:** The claim that the world we experience is fundamentally the product of our social interactions. Understanding and meaning are not developed by individuals in isolation

but in coordination with other humans, primarily via language. For example, our notions of 'gender' and 'childhood' are not simply biological realities but arise from our interactions with society. Social constructivism is consistent with the idea of cultural and historical relativism – and opposed to mainstream psychology's idea that we can be neutral, disinterested observers of a 'real' world.

- **split-half reliability:** A method of assessing the reliability of a test. For each participant, the items in the test are split into two halves and a score is obtained for each half. The scores on the two halves are then correlated: if there is a good correlation, it suggests that the test is reliable.
- **standard deviation:** A numerical measure of how much a set of scores varies around the mean of those scores – essentially the average spread of scores around the mean.
- **standard error of the mean:** A numerical estimate of how much sample means are likely to vary around the true population mean.
- **theory:** An explanation or model, generally based on observation, reasoning, and experimentation. It is used to explain empirically obtained data and to generate testable hypotheses. For a theory to be scientific, it must be testable and hence potentially open to disproof.
- **time sampling:** A technique used in observational studies of behaviour to obtain a representative sample of the behaviour of interest. Measurements of the behaviour in question are made at set time intervals (e.g. every 10 seconds, every minute, or every hour).
- **validity:** A measure is valid if the researcher has truly measured what they set out to measure.

NOTES

1. http://www.bbc.co.uk/programmes/b006qxx9
2. https://www.surveymonkey.com/
3. http://www.qualtrics.com/
4. https://owl.english.purdue.edu/
5. http://www.apa.org/ethics/code/principles.pdf
6. https://www1.bps.org.uk/system/files/user-files/Division%20of%20Clinical%20Psychology/public/Code%20of%20Ethics%20and%20Conduct%20%282009%29.pdf

FURTHER RESOURCES

Banister, P., Bunn, G., Burman, E., Daniels, J., Duckett, P., Goodley, D., … Whelan, P. (2011). *Qualitative methods in psychology: A research guide* (2nd ed.). Maidenhead, UK: Open University Press/McGraw-Hill.

Breakwell, G. M., Smith, J. A., & Wright, D. B. (2012). *Research methods in psychology* (4th ed.). London, UK: SAGE.

Field, A. (2017). *Discovering statistics using IBM SPSS statistics* (5th ed.). London, UK: SAGE.

Field, A. (2017). *Discovering statistics*. Retrieved 20 November 2017 from http://www.statisticshell.com (Useful, interesting and entertaining statistics resources.)

Field, A., & Hole, G. (2003). *How to design and report experiments.* London, UK: SAGE.

Harris, P. (2008). *Designing and reporting experiments in psychology* (3rd ed.). Maidenhead, UK: Open University Press.

Hole, G. (2015). *Teaching resources for Research Skills One (autumn 2015).* Retrieved 20 November 2017 from http://www.sussex.ac.uk/Users/grahamh/RM1web/teaching08-RS.html (Material on introductory statistics.)

Howitt, D. (2010). *Introduction to qualitative methods in psychology* (2nd ed.). Harlow, UK: Pearson.

Morgan Centre for Research into Everyday Lives. (2017). Retrieved 20 November 2017 from https://www.socialsciences.manchester.ac.uk/morgan-centre

REFERENCES

Ahuja, J. K. C., & Perloff, B. P. (2001). Caffeine and theobromine intakes of children: Results from CSFII 1994–96, 1998. *Family Economics and Nutrition Review, 13*(2), 47.

Ansari, F., Gray, K., Nathwani, D., Phillips, G., Ogston, S., Ramsay, C., & Davey, P. (2003). Outcomes of an intervention to improve hospital antibiotic prescribing: Interrupted time series with segmented regression analysis. *Journal of Antimicrobial Chemotherapy, 52*(5), 842–848. doi:10.1093/jac/dkg459

Arnett, J. (2008). The neglected 95%: Why American psychology needs to become less American. *American Psychologist, 63*(7), 602–614.

Beck, D. M. (2010). The appeal of the brain in the popular press. *Perspectives on Psychological Science, 5*, 762–766. doi:10.1177/1745691610388779

Benton, D. (2008). Sucrose and behavioral problems. *Critical Reviews in Food Science and Nutrition, 48*(5), 385–401. doi:10.1080/10408390701407316

Bowling, A. (2005). Mode of questionnaire administration can have serious effects on data quality. *Journal of Public Health, 27*(3), 281–291. doi:10.1093/pubmed/fdi031

Brands, B., Egan, B., Györei, E., López-Robles, J. C., Gage, H., Campoy, C., ... Raats, M. M. (2012). A qualitative interview study on effects of diet on children's mental state and performance: Evaluation of perceptions, attitudes and beliefs of parents in four European countries. *Appetite, 58*, 739–746.

British Psychological Society. (2012). *Guidelines for psychologists working with animals*. Retrieved 20 November 2017 from https://www.bps.org.uk/news-and-policy/bps-guidelines-psychologists-working-animals-2012

Bronfenbrenner, U. (1977). Toward an experimental ecology of human development. *American Psychologist, 32*(7), 513–531.

Bussmann, J. J., Ebner-Priemer, U. W., & Fahrenberg, J. (2009). Ambulatory activity monitoring. *European Psychologist, 14*(2), 142–152. doi:10.1027/1016-9040.14.2.142

Campbell, D. T., & Stanley, J. C. (1966). *Experimental and quasi-experimental designs for research*. Chicago, IL: Rand McNally.

Carpenter, R. W., Wycoff, A. M., & Trull, T. J. (2016). Ambulatory assessment: New adventures in characterizing dynamic processes. *Assessment, 23*(4), 414–424. doi:10.1177/1073191116632341

Carroll, K. K. (1975). Experimental evidence of dietary factors and hormone-dependent cancers. *Cancer Research, 35*, 3374–3383.

Chapman, P., & Underwood, G. (2000). Forgetting near-accidents: The roles of severity, culpability and experience in the poor recall of dangerous driving situations. *Applied Cognitive Psychology, 14*, 31–44. doi:10.1002/(SICI)1099-0720(200001)14:1<31::AID-A. C.P622>3.0.CO;2-9

Charmaz, K. (1995). Grounded theory. In J. A. Smith, R. Harré, & L. van Langenhove (Eds.), *Rethinking methods in psychology* (pp. 27–49). London, UK: SAGE.

Cohen, G., & Java, R. (1995). Memory for medical history: Accuracy of recall. *Applied Cognitive Psychology, 9*, 273–288.

Cohen, J. (1992). A power primer. *Psychological Bulletin, 112*, 155–159.

Coltheart, M. (2011). What has functional neuroimaging told us about the organization of mind? *Cognitive Neuropsychology, 28*(6), 397–402. doi:10.1080/02643294.2012.666964

Combe, G. (1846). *Elements of phrenology* (5th ed.). Edinburgh, UK: Maclachlan, Stewart & Co.

Cumming, G. (2014). The new statistics: Why and how. *Psychological Science, 25*(1), 7–29. doi:10.1177/0956797613504966

deLeeuw, E. D. (2012). Counting and measuring online: The quality of internet surveys. *Bulletin of Sociological Methodology, 114*, 68–78. doi:10.1177/0759106312437290

Edwards, D., & Potter, J. (2001). Discursive psychology. In A. McHoul & M. Rapley (Eds.), *How to analyse talk in institutional settings: A casebook of methods* (pp. 12–24). London, UK: Continuum.

Edwards, P., Roberts, I., Clarke, M., DiGuiseppi, C., Pratap, S., Wentz, R., & Kwan, I. (2002). Increasing response rates to postal questionnaires: Systematic review. *British Medical Journal, 324*, 1183–1185.

Eich, E. (2014). Business not as usual. *Psychological Science, 25*(1), 3–6. doi:10.1177/0956797613512465

Evans, M., Donelle, L., & Hume-Loveland, L. (2012). Social support and online postpartum depression discussion groups: A content analysis. *Patient Education & Counselling, 897*, 405–410. doi:10.1016/j.pec.2011.09.011

Fahrenberg, J., Myrtek, M., Pawlik, K., & Perrez, M. (2007). Ambulatory assessment: Monitoring behavior in daily life settings – A behavioral-scientific challenge for psychology. *European Journal of Psychological Assessment, 23*(4), 206–213. doi:10.1027/1015-5759.23.4.206

Field, A. (2017). *Discovering statistics using IBM SPSS statistics* (5th ed.). London, UK: SAGE.

Forgeard, M., Winner, E., Norton A., & Schlaug, G. (2008). Practicing a musical instrument in childhood is associated with enhanced verbal ability and nonverbal reasoning. *PLoS ONE, 3*(10), e3566. doi:10.1371/journal.pone.0003566

Glaser, B. G., & Strauss, A. L. (1967). *The discovery of grounded theory.* Chicago, IL: Aldine.

Godlee, F., Smith, J., & Marcovitch, H. (2011). Wakefield's article linking MMR vaccine and autism was fraudulent. *British Medical Journal, 342.* doi:10.1136/bmj.c7452

Groves, R. M., & Couper, M. P. (1998). *Nonresponse in household interview surveys.* New York, NY: Wiley.

Henrich, J., Heine, S. J., & Norenzayan, A. (2013). The weirdest people in the world? *Behavioral and Brain Sciences, 33*(2/3), 1–75. doi:10.1017/S0140525X0999152X

Henson, R. (2005). What can functional neuroimaging tell the experimental psychologist? *Quarterly Journal of Experimental Psychology, 58A*(2), 193–233.

Henry, B., Moffitt, T. E., Caspi, A., Langley, J., & Silva, P. A. (1994). On the 'remembrance of things past': A longitudinal evaluation of the retrospective method. *Psychological Assessment, 6,* 92–101.

Hill, A., Roberts, J., Ewings, P., & Gunnell, D. (1997). Non-response bias in a lifestyle survey. *Journal of Public Health Medicine, 19*(2), 203–207.

Home Office. (2013). *Animal testing and research.* Retrieved 20 November 2017 from https://www.gov.uk/research-and-testing-using-animals

Howitt, D. (2010). *Introduction to qualitative methods in psychology* (2nd ed.). Harlow, UK: Pearson.

Kamin, L. J. (1974). *The science and politics of IQ.* New York, NY: Penguin.

Klein, O., Doyen, S., Leys, C., Magalhães de Saldanha da Gama, P. A., Miller, S., Questienne, L., & Cleeremans, A. (2012). Low hopes, high expectations: Expectancy effects and the replicability of behavioural experiments. *Perspectives on Psychological Science, 7,* 572–584.

Kruschke, J. K. (2010). Bayesian data analysis. *Wiley Interdisciplinary Reviews: Cognitive Science, 1*(5), 658–676. doi:10.1002/wcs.72

Leach, M. M., & Harbin, J. J. (1997). Psychological ethics codes: A comparison of twenty-four countries. *International Journal of Psychology, 32*(3), 181–192.

Levelt Committee, Noort Committee, & Drenth Committee. (2012). *Flawed science: The fraudulent research practices of social psychologist Diederik Stapel.* Retrieved 4 December 2013 from https://www.commissielevelt.nl

Lilienfeld, S. O. (2010). Can psychology become a science? *Personality and Individual Differences, 49,* 281–288.

Meiklejohn, J., Connor, J., & Kypri, K. (2012). The effect of low survey response rates on estimates of alcohol consumption in a general population survey. *PLoS ONE, 7*(4), e35527. doi:10.1371/journal.pone.0035527

Michael, R. B., Newman, E. J., Vuorre, M., Cumming, G., & Garry, M. (2013). On the (non)persuasive power of a brain image. *Psychonomic Bulletin & Review, 20,* 720–725. doi:10.3758/s13423-013-0391-6

Neuendorf, K. A. (2011). Content analysis: A methodological primer for gender research. *Sex Roles, 64,* 276–289. doi:10.1007/s11199-010-9893-0

Nevile, M. (2006). Making sequentiality salient: *And*-prefacing in the talk of airline pilots. *Discourse Studies*, 8(2), 279–302. doi:10.1177/1461445606061797

Orne, M. T. (1962). On the social psychology of the psychological experiment: With particular reference to demand characteristics and their implications. *American Psychologist*, *17*, 776–783.

Passingham, R. E., Rowe, J. B., & Sakai, K. (2013). Has brain imaging discovered anything new about how the brain works? *Neuroimage*, *66*, 142–150. doi:10.1016/j.neuroimage.2012.10.079

Poteat, T., German, D., & Kerrigan, D. (2013). Managing uncertainty: A grounded theory of stigma in transgender health care encounters. *Social Science & Medicine*, *84*, 22–29. doi:10.1016/j.soc-scimed.2013.02.019

Publication Manual of the American Psychological Association. (2010, 6th ed.). Washington, DC: American Psychological Association.

Rosenthal, R. (1966). *Experimenter effects in behavioral research*. New York, NY: Appleton Century Crofts.

Rosenthal, R., & Jacobson, L. (1968). *Pygmalion in the classroom: Teacher expectation and pupils' intellectual development*. New York, NY: Holt, Rinehart, & Winston.

Schuman, H., & Presser, S. (1981). *Questions and answers in attitude surveys*. New York, NY: Academic Press.

Schweitzer, R., Griffiths, M., & Yates, P. (2012). Parental experience of childhood cancer using interpretative phenomenological analysis. *Psychology & Health*, *27*(6), 704–720. doi:10.1080/08870446.2011.622379

Skinner, B. F. (1953). *Science and human behavior*. New York, NY: Macmillan.

Slater, A., Tiggemann, M., Hawkins, K., & Werchon, D. (2012). Just one click: A content analysis of advertisements on teen web sites. *Journal of Adolescent Health*, *50*, 339–345.

Solomon, R. L. (1949). An extension of control group design. *Psychological Bulletin*, *46*, 137–150.

Trull, T. J., & Ebner-Priemer, U. (2013). Ambulatory assessment. *Annual Review of Clinical Psychology*, *9*, 151–176. doi:10.1146/annurev-clinpsy-050212-185510

Trulli, T. J., & Ebner-Priemer, U. (2014). The role of ambulatory assessment in psychological science. *Current Directions in Psychological Science*, *23*(6), 466–470. doi:10.1177/0963721414550706

Uttal, W. R. (2001). *The new phrenology: The limits of localizing cognitive processes in the brain*. Cambridge, MA: MIT Press.

Weisberg, D. S., Keil, F. C., Goodstein, J., Rawson, E., & Gray, J. R. (2008). The seductive allure of neuroscience explanations. *Journal of Cognitive Neuroscience*, *20*, 470–477. doi:10.1162/jocn.2008.20040

ACTIVITY SOLUTIONS

ACTIVITY 2.2: CORRELATION AND CAUSE

1. A diet high in animal fat might cause breast cancer.

2. People in wealthy countries also eat more refined foods, sugar, salt, and so on. Perhaps these cause breast cancer.

3. Women in wealthier countries tend to be more obese. Perhaps obesity causes breast cancer.

4. People in wealthy countries live longer. Hence they are more likely to develop cancer in general, and breast cancer is just an example of this tendency.

5. Genetic factors might be at play – perhaps. Caucasian women are more likely to develop breast cancer than non-Caucasians.

6. Reporting factors might be the explanation. Perhaps there is better cancer diagnosis in wealthy countries.

3 Evolutionary and Genetic Foundations of Psychology

DANIEL NETTLE

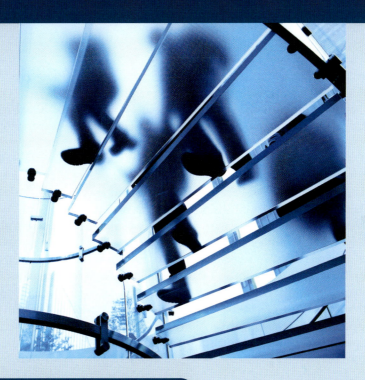

ROUTE MAP OF THE CHAPTER

This chapter sets out the building blocks of evolution and genetics that are required for the study of modern psychology. We humans are the products of an evolutionary history, partly shared with other living animals and partly unique. Over the course of this long history, our genome – the set of genetic information we inherit – has been sculpted by the evolutionary force of natural selection. It is our genome, acting in concert with the environment in which we develop and live, that gives rise to the brains, and hence the psychological characteristics, that we have. The first few sections of the chapter lay out three fundamental principles of genetic evolution – variation, heredity, and differential reproductive success – and illustrate them with examples. We then move on to the consideration of some case studies of how evolutionary and genetic thinking has been useful in psychological research, and we close by examining likely future directions in this area.

INTRODUCTION

LEARNING OBJECTIVE 3.1

Describe the basic principles of genes and their functions

If you have ever taken a long, hot bath, you will notice that your fingers and toes temporarily develop a characteristic pattern of ridges or wrinkles (Figure 3.1). Why do these wrinkles appear? It turns out that, on prolonged contact with water, blood vessels in the fingers and toes constrict, changing the shape of the tissue. The constriction is caused in turn by signals carried from the spinal cord to the peripheries by a system of nerve fibres known as the sympathetic nervous system. We know this because people who have lost function in their sympathetic nervous systems don't show finger wrinkling. This explanation – we wrinkle because of vasoconstriction caused by signals carried by the sympathetic nervous system – is one kind of answer to the question 'Why do our fingers wrinkle on contact with water?'. It is what we call a **mechanistic explanation**; it tells you *how* the body's machinery does it. However, it will probably have struck you that there are other possible types of answer to the question. In particular, we might want to understand *what good it does us* to have fingers that wrinkle like that. Wrinkling is not just something that happens passively; our nervous systems and blood vessels go to a lot of trouble, as it were, to make sure we wrinkle when in contact with water, and it would seem odd if this happened and there was no advantage to it.

An explanation for a phenomenon in terms of the good it does the organism is called an **adaptive explanation**. To give a different example, tuna fish, sharks,

FIGURE 3.1 *Why do fingers wrinkle on contact with water?*
Source: © Afronova / Shutterstock.

dolphins, and seals all have a streamlined body shape. These animals are not closely related. Under the skin, a seal is much more similar to your pet dog than it is to any fish – it gives birth to live young and nurses them. Rather, the different animals have independently evolved the streamlined shape because it is useful for travelling forward through water. Water is much denser than air and thus creates much more resistance, making it energetically very demanding to move through if you are not streamlined. Thus, being streamlined is an adaptive characteristic for a water-living creature.

Why is it that we are able to give adaptive explanations for the characteristics that living creatures have? In other words, why have all living things ended up with many characteristics that are useful for the lives they lead, such as being the right shape for the medium they move through? An answer that may have come to your mind is that, if they didn't have these characteristics, they wouldn't be here. That is, perhaps there were once some seals that were not streamlined, and they had a hard time swimming fast enough to catch their prey, and so they aren't around anymore. This seems a simple answer, but it is exactly right. It is the essence of one of the central ideas of this chapter: adaptation by natural selection (see Focus Point 3.1). It is because of a long process of adaptation by natural selection stretching back into the past that organisms have characteristics that are useful to them in the present. Because any creature alive today is the result of several billion years of evolution, we are justified in asking for adaptive explanations for aspects of their brains and bodies.

FOCUS POINT 3.1

ADAPTATION BY NATURAL SELECTION

Adaptation by natural selection is a central process in evolution. It can be summarized as follows. In each generation, there will be variation between individuals. For example, some ancestral seals will have been slightly more streamlined than others. Those individuals with slightly more useful traits, such as a slightly more streamlined shape in the seal example, will be more likely to survive and leave descendants than others around them. Those descendants will inherit the useful traits of their ancestors. Thus, over many generations, characteristics that are beneficial for the organism in terms of survival and reproduction will become more and more frequent among those currently alive.

Let us return to our wrinkled fingers. We are justified in asking about the adaptive function of finger wrinkling, because a complex mechanism involving sympathetic nerves and peripheral blood vessels would not have become common among our ancestors just by chance. So we can assume that being able to finger-wrinkle provided some kind of benefit to our ancestors. A common objection people make at this point is the following: 'I can think of all kinds of adaptive advantages that finger wrinkling might have had for our ancestors, but it was long ago, we weren't there, and so we will never know which one is right. Speculating about adaptive advantages is thus not science.' It is true that investigating adaptive function is very hard and requires considerable ingenuity, but that's true of lots of other things in science too. The key point is that it is not enough just to come up with adaptive explanations. The real work is in finding ways of testing them.

For finger wrinkling, an adaptive explanation that has been proposed is that wrinkles improve the ability to grip wet objects, possibly by channelling water away from the contact area between the skin and object, much like the rain treads on car tyres (Changizi, Weber, Kotecha, & Palazzo, 2011). This would be useful for any creature needing to move and forage in wet forests, for example. Attempts to test this hypothesis are currently under way, but there is no consensus as yet (see Research Methods 3.1).

RESEARCH METHODS 3.1

DESIGNING AN EXPERIMENT TO TEST AN ADAPTIVE HYPOTHESIS

To test the hypothesis of Changizi et al. (2011) that finger wrinkling improves ability to grip wet objects, Kareklas, Nettle, and Smulders (2013) created a task where participants had to move a series of objects, such as marbles and fishing weights, from one jar to another through a hole in a screen. They had to do this as quickly as possible and were timed. The objects were either wet or dry, and their fingers either were or were not wrinkled. Wrinkling was achieved by the participant sitting with their hands in warm water for 30 minutes. A critical aspect of any experiment is deriving clear predictions from your hypothesis. In the current case, if the adaptive function of finger wrinkling is to improve handling of wet objects (hypothesis), then participants ought to be able to complete the task faster in the wet/wrinkled condition than in the wet/not wrinkled condition (prediction).

Thus, the researchers predicted a time advantage to having wrinkled fingers that would appear only when the objects were wet. This is exactly what they found (see the following figure).

However, Haseleu, Omerbašić, Frenzel, Gross, and Lewin (2014) performed two experiments very similar to that of Kareklas et al. (2013) and observed no time advantage to having wrinkled fingers when objects were wet.

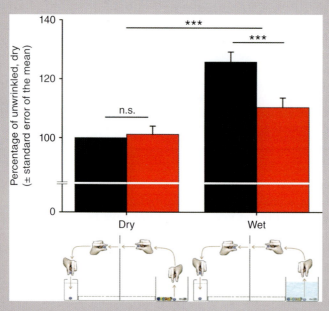

Results from the experiment by Kareklas et al. (2013). The figure shows the time taken to move a set of objects that were either dry (left-hand bars) or wet (right-hand bars) when fingers were either wrinkled (red bars) or not wrinkled) black bars. Asterisks denote a significant difference, whereas 'n.s.' denotes a difference that was not significant.

In view of these discrepant results, we do not yet know whether Changizi et al.'s (2011) hypothesis is correct. This is a normal situation for new hypotheses in psychology. Many experiments by many different groups are usually required before we have a clear picture of whether a hypothesis is robust or not. However, the moral of the story is that adaptive explanations can be testable and falsifiable. These are very important requirements for any empirical science. This shows that adaptive explanations can give rise to empirical research with clear predictions using contemporary humans as participants and employing the standard experimental designs found in psychology. In this respect they are no different from any other class of scientific hypothesis.

This chapter is about adaptive evolutionary explanations and their relevance to modern psychology. Taking an evolutionary perspective is useful across a whole range of different areas of psychology because it gives us tools for thinking about why we have the capacities that we do. Why are humans so good at recognizing certain classes of objects and poor at recognizing others? Why are humans able to learn, rather than just relying on preprogrammed reflexes? Why do humans experience strong motivation to bond to another individual, usually of the opposite sex, starting only in adolescence? These kinds of questions cry out for a way of thinking about what good each of these capacities does for the organism. An evolutionary perspective also reminds us that we are not the only living creatures. How do object recognition, learning, and pair bonding work in other species related to us, such as mice and monkeys? The mechanisms might (or might not) work in similar ways to how they do in ourselves, and so, by studying our living relatives, we gain some understanding both of shared biological systems and of the ways humans are unique.

To understand how evolution works in detail, we also need to cover key aspects of genetics. Genetics is useful to the student of psychology in its own right, since we increasingly appreciate that many psychological disorders, such as autism, as well as normal personality differences have genetic bases. Thus, without an appreciation of genetics, much interesting current psychological research is inaccessible. Note that stressing the importance of evolutionary and genetic principles for psychology does not imply that social, developmental, or cultural factors are unimportant. Social, developmental, and cultural explanations are not, in general, alternatives to evolutionary or genetic ones. Evolutionary explanations involve asking why humans would be susceptible to particular types of social, developmental, and cultural influence. For example, think of language. The language you speak is determined by your culture (i.e. the way people around you speak as you grow up), but your ability to learn language depends on your genes, since all typically developing humans, and no chimpanzees, can learn any human language. We can thus ask the evolutionary question of why humans evolved the genetic capacity to learn a communication system from their surrounding community, while fully appreciating that human languages are cultural systems.

We can break adaptation by natural selection down into three basic principles (which will be discussed in detail in the following sections). The first is **variation**. In every generation and every living creature, individuals are somewhat different from one another. You can verify that this is true just by looking at your friends. Some are tall and some are short, some are dark and some are fair, some are shy and some are bold, some are good at the marathon and others at the sprint. The second principle is **heredity**. That is, traits get passed on from parents to children, at least to some extent. Those of your friends who are very tall probably have tall parents. The third principle is **differential reproduction**. That is, not every individual leaves as many descendants as everyone else. If you put these principles together, as we shall see, you are bound to get adaptive change over the generations.

SECTION SUMMARY

- Adaptation by natural selection is a central process in evolution.
- It is because of a long process of adaptation by natural selection stretching back into the past that organisms have characteristics that are useful to them in the present.
- Adaptive explanations are testable and falsifiable.
- An evolutionary perspective reminds us that we are not the only living creatures.
- To understand how evolution works in detail, we also need to cover key aspects of genetics.
- Adaptation by natural selection can be broken down into three basic principles: variation, heredity, and differential reproduction.

WHAT MAKES YOU UNIQUE? THE ORIGINS OF VARIATION

LEARNING OBJECTIVE 3.2

Describe the basic principles of genetic inheritance.

Biologists refer to the observable characteristics of an individual as that individual's **phenotype**. Your size, your eye colour, your personality, and your love of sweet foods are all components of your phenotype. Psychological traits, as long as they can be objectively measured, are just as much part of the phenotype as physical ones are. Whenever we measure the phenotypes in a population, we find that, even though all individuals are members of the same species, they differ from one another to some extent. Though this is most obvious to us when we look at other humans, it is true in all other species as well (Figure 3.2). You may think that all starlings look the same, but, if you studied them carefully, you would discover that individuals differ measurably. I am prepared to bet that starlings don't all look the same to other starlings!

An individual's phenotype is always the result of the interaction of the information they inherit from their parents with the particular environment in which they develop. Information is inherited principally in the form of genetic material. We refer to individual pieces of functional genetic material as **genes**, and the total set of genetic material you possess as your **genome**. The genome is made of a molecule called

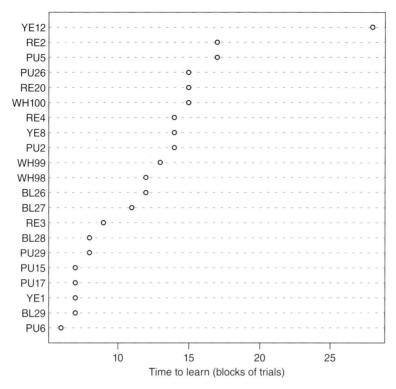

FIGURE 3.2 *Variation in learning speed in a sample of European starlings from Newcastle. Birds were presented with two feeders, one that gave food after a 2 second delay and one that gave food after a 10 second delay. Each row represents a bird, with the code on the left identifying the individual. The data show the number of blocks of trials required before they developed a preference for the short-delay feeder. As you can see, there is marked variation between birds in speed of learning.*

deoxyribonucleic acid, or **DNA**. Your genome is organized into 23 pairs of **chromosomes**. Your genome has been repeatedly copied from the original that was in the single cell that you consisted of at the very beginning of your life. That original was made up of a DNA contribution from your mother, in the form of 23 chromosomes in her egg, and a DNA contribution from your father, in the form of 23 chromosomes in his sperm. To understand why the genome is so important for the phenotype you have, we need to delve a little more into how DNA works, what genes are, and how genes can vary. These are the topics of the next three subsections.

DNA and genes

You have probably read that genes encode the instructions for making your body, but you may be less clear about exactly what genes are or how they act. We will therefore begin with a review of how DNA works. DNA is a remarkable molecule that consists of two strands, each of which has a long backbone made of sugars and phosphates (see Figure 3.3). Along the length of each backbone, arranged like a row of teeth, are sequences of bases, which are compounds known as nucleic acids. There are four types of base: adenine (A), cytosine (C), guanine (G), and thymine (T). The bases can occur in any order along the backbone. Thus, a strand of DNA just five bases long can

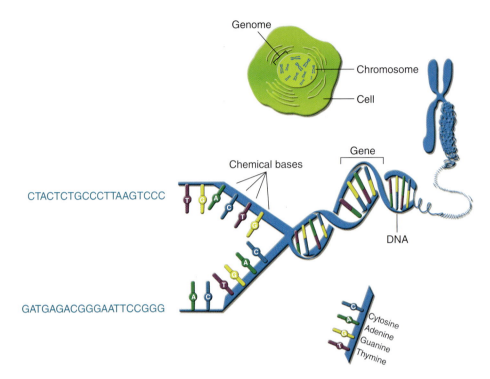

CTACTCTGCCCTTAAGTCCC

GATGAGACGGGAATTCCGGG

FIGURE 3.3 *A representation of the important features of the genome and DNA. Most of the genome resides in the nucleus of each cell, where long sequences of DNA are organized into structures called chromosomes. DNA itself consists of two strands that are twined around each other in a double-helix shape. Along the backbone of each strand is a sequence of chemical bases. These are of four types: adenine (A), cytosine (C), guanine (G), and thymine (T). It is the order of the bases along the backbone that encodes the genetic information. Each base on one strand binds to a particular base on the other strand (e.g. every cytosine on one strand binds to a guanine on the other strand). Thus, each strand is a negative of the other and contains the same information.*

exist in 1024 (4 × 4 × 4 × 4 × 4) different forms, all of which are equally stable (examples are ATAT, ATCG, GGGG, and so on). Your genome consists of something like 6 billion bases in total, which gives you some sense of how many different unique genomes are possible.

When the two strands of DNA pair up, the bases on one strand bond to the bases on the other. An A on one strand will only bond to a T on the other, while a C on one will only bond to a G on the other. This principle is known as **base pairing**. It means that the two strands are a kind of mirror image of one another; you could reconstruct the sequence of bases on either strand from the other strand. One of the great breakthroughs in genetics was understanding that, because of the properties we have described, DNA has the ability to store information. If you wanted to encode, say, the plays of Shakespeare, you could do it using DNA, by setting up a code where every letter of the English alphabet was represented by a particular sequence of three bases, and then synthesizing a DNA molecule with its bases in the order that spells out the text you wanted to represent. Storing information is thus what the genome does. The 'text' represented by the order of bases is not English, of course, but rather sequences of instructions causing particular processes to occur in cells.

What do genes do?

DNA has two functions within living organisms. The first is to make new DNA. That is, nearly every new cell that you grow – and you grow many every day, as cells in your body die and are replaced – has a set of your DNA in it. This DNA is directly copied from the DNA of an ancestor cell. In most cases, the complete set of DNA is copied across from the ancestor to the descendant cell, a process known as **mitosis**. For the particular case of sperm and egg cells, there is a specialized form of DNA replication called **meiosis** that results in just half of the genome being replicated into the new cell. This is because those cells are destined to unite with half a genome from an individual of the other sex to make a new genome and hence a new person.

The second function of DNA is to orchestrate the functioning of your cells. There would be no point in storing information in DNA if the organism could not access that information to use it. Accessing the information stored in DNA happens via a process known as **transcription**. At transcription, the two strands of the DNA molecule are 'unzipped' or split apart. The ends of the bases are now exposed, and a new single-stranded molecule, ribonucleic acid or **RNA**, forms along the exposed bases. RNA also consists of a backbone and a sequence of four bases, and the order of bases on the RNA reflects the order of bases on the DNA on which it forms. Thus, RNA provides a 'readout' of the base order on the DNA.

Once RNA has been formed, it breaks free of the DNA molecule and can be transported elsewhere in the cell. This allows it to influence cellular functions. For example, strands of RNA are transported to structures outside the nucleus called ribosomes and here they cause particular proteins to be synthesized in a process called **translation**. Proteins are essential elements of your body. They account for perhaps 12–18% of your mass and they serve many important functions, such as creating connecting tissue and serving as hormones, antibodies, and enzymes. Proteins are made up of chains of amino acids. The order of DNA bases in the gene that codes for a protein directly determines the order of amino acids in that protein as it is assembled at the ribosome. If the amino acids in a protein in your body are in a different order, then the protein may behave differently and you will end up with cells that have different properties.

The genes that code for all the different proteins you make constitute only a small part of the genome, probably around 1% (this part of the genome is known as the exome). The rest of the genome contains many non-protein-coding genes. These are transcribed into RNA, but the RNA is not translated into protein. Instead, these RNAs are involved in regulating processes within the cell – for example, turning other sets of genes on or off, or increasing or decreasing the rate of some cellular process. What makes humans such complex organisms is not that they make a particularly large number of different proteins. In fact, the number of protein-coding genes is not very different in a human and a roundworm (25,000 versus 19,000). The real difference is that humans have vastly more non-protein-coding genes. This means that in humans a similar sized library of basic proteins can be assembled into more, different combinations that change more in response to inputs from the internal and external environment.

It is a common misunderstanding to think that genes act at the beginning of your life and, thereafter, it is the environment that affects you. It is true that the sequence of bases that you have in your genome stays basically the same your whole life, but your genome is active every second of every day that you are alive. Your genome responds to environmental events in real time. For example, when you eat a meal, you secrete digestive enzymes. For this to happen, genes that produce these enzymes start to be translated and transcribed very rapidly. When you go into a darkened room, genes that encode visual pigments begin to be transcribed. Similarly, when a man sees a woman he is attracted to, genes that control the secretion of testosterone begin to be more active. Thus, the particular genes that you possess are continuously responding to the environmental events that you live through. When you respond to the environment, you respond with your genes.

Genetic variation

Every person's genome is similar but not identical to the genomes of other people. For example, if you looked closely at one copy of chromosome 16 from any particular person, you would find a particular sequence of around 9,000 base pairs called MC1R. MC1R contains the genetic code for making a certain protein: the pigment called melanin that gives your hair its colour. However, if you lined up the 9,000 bases of a copy of MC1R from a redhead against those of a copy of MC1R from a person with black hair, you would realize that the MC1Rs were not quite identical. For 99% of the positions, both individuals would have the same base, but you would find the odd point in the sequence where the redhead had G against the other person's C, or an A against the other person's T. Thus, the redhead and the black-haired person both have MC1R, but the redhead has a slightly different version of MC1R. We call an alternative version of the same gene an **allele**. People often use the terms 'gene' and 'allele' very loosely, and say something like 'redheads carry the MC1R gene', but this is not quite correct. Everyone carries the MC1R gene, but redheads and black-haired people have different *alleles* of MC1R (Figure 3.4). We also use the term **genotype** to refer to which alleles of a particular gene an individual carries (and remember that every person has two copies of almost every gene).

How does having a different sequence of bases at MC1R end up making your hair look different? MC1R is very actively transcribed in cells called melanocytes, which make the pigment for skin and hair. Having a different sequence of DNA bases at MC1R in these cells leads to the making of a different version of the corresponding RNA. The slightly different RNA gets translated into a slightly different version of the protein: redheads make more of a type of melanin called pheomelanin and less of a type called eumelanin. Pheomelanin and eumelanin reflect light differently, hence the different appearance. MC1R is also found in other mammals, and in some other mammals there is allele variation just as there is in humans. For example, American black bears are generally dark but there is a subspecies called the Kermode bear that is ginger (Figure 3.4). These Kermode bears carry a different version of MC1R from other American black bears, very much as in the human case.

MC1R is just one example, but the situation is the same right across the human genome. If you compared the genomes of any two individuals, you would find many sequences that were the same, but other points where one base or even a much longer stretch was different between the two people. Where does this variation come from? There are two main processes that make individuals differ genetically. The first is **recombination**. Recombination refers to the way that DNA from two different parents is combined to make one genome. Recombination is the main function of sex (speaking in evolutionary terms, of course). When two parents reproduce, each of them creates a sample of half of their genome (in a sperm or egg), and that sample is combined with a sample of half of the genome of the other parent. Each sample

FIGURE 3.4 *In humans (a) and in black bears (b) and (c), the difference between dark hair and red hair is due to alleles of the MC1R gene. In each species, there are alleles that cause a shift in the balance of production between two different types of melanin.*

Source: (a) © auremar / Shutterstock; (b) © Tom Middleton / Shutterstock; (c) © Barcroft Media / Getty Images.

is unique. The genome of an offspring is thus not identical to the genome of either parent, and, moreover, successive offspring of the same parents do not have the same genomes as one another, because they draw different samples from the genomes of each parent. The genomes of siblings are, of course, more similar to one another than the genomes of unrelated individuals are (that is what we mean by family relatedness), but they are not exactly the same.

The other process that creates variation is genetic **mutation** (see Focus Point 3.2). The important thing to appreciate is that mutation is random with respect to the functioning of the organism. Genes do not mutate because the phenotypic changes they cause would be useful for the organism. They just mutate for chance reasons. Most mutations that occur either have no detectable effect or are harmful. You can probably appreciate why harmful mutations are much more common than beneficial ones. If you reached into a well-engineered machine such as a computer and randomly swapped some of its parts around, you would be much more likely to break it than you would be to make it run faster. The same is true of genetic mutation. Many of the mutations we know about that do have a measurable effect cause genetic diseases or psychological abnormalities (see Focus Point 3.3). However, the occasional mutation gives rise to a new phenotypic characteristic that is useful in a given environment. These beneficial mutations are the ones that will spread by natural selection. Because mutation occurs every time the genome is replicated, mutation is a diversifying force in populations, constantly introducing phenotypic novelty as the generations go by. You can think of mutation, in consort with recombination, as creating a library of alternative phenotypes each generation, from which natural selection will (metaphorically) choose. We can sum up how the evolutionary process works with the expression 'mutation proposes, selection disposes'.

FOCUS POINT 3.2

GENETIC MUTATION

Whenever mitosis or meiosis occurs, the genome is copied. This is called DNA replication. Replication is in general remarkably accurate, but it is not absolutely perfect, and there are several billion bases to copy. Thus, each time replication occurs, a small number of changes to the genome sequence creep in. These are called genetic mutations, and there are many different types. Some just involve the swapping of one base for another, or one base being deleted. Other types can involve whole strings of bases, sometimes very long, getting deleted or having an extra copy of themselves inserted. Because of large mutations like this, different people's genomes are actually slightly different lengths.

At the extreme, whole extra copies of chromosomes may be replicated in what are called trisomies. Trisomies are the cause of serious genetic disorders such as Down syndrome, which involves an extra copy of chromosome 21. However, not all trisomies lead to problems. About one in a thousand men have an extra copy of the Y chromosome. Apart from being rather tall, they do not differ from other men in any obvious way (although the plots of several novels and the film *Alien 3* would have you believe otherwise!).

Mutations are much more likely to occur at some places in the genome than others. For example, the human genome contains many locations where the sequence CA is repeated many times in a row. These sequences are very prone to mutation, with a significant probability of an extra CA repeat being added or lost every time the DNA is replicated. As a consequence of this high rate of mutation, these CA repeats are very variable from one person to the next; even full siblings look different from one another. These sequences are used in the 'DNA fingerprinting' that has revolutionized forensic science since the late 20th century.

DISCUSSION POINT

This video series[1] from the Royal Institution takes an in-depth look at the human genome and explores the 23 pairs of chromosomes that make up the building blocks of human life. Discuss how genetic mutations can cause individual variation.

FOCUS POINT 3.3

WHEN THE MACHINE BREAKS DOWN:
MAOA AND CONDUCT DISORDER

There is a Dutch extended family where many of the men are, to quote a saying, 'mad, bad and dangerous to know'. The affected men are prone to aggressive outbursts and have been responsible for assaults, arson, attempted rapes, and exhibitionism. The psychiatric diagnosis we would give them is conduct disorder. This is a rare case where there is a single genetic switch that underlies a psychological phenotype. The protein monoamine oxidase A (MAOA) is widely expressed in the brain, and plays a role in the metabolism of the neurotransmitters serotonin, dopamine, and noradrenaline.

You may have heard of these neurotransmitters since they are involved in mood and are the target of action of antidepressant drugs. The allele that the affected men carry has a T instead of a C at the 936th base of the gene. The C that most of us carry would add an amino acid called glutamine to the protein chain. The T that the affected men carry instead ends transcription, meaning that the affected men basically don't make any working MAOA (Brunner, Nelen, Breakefield, Ropers, & Van Oost, 1993). This explains their extremely.poorly regulated moods.

This case raises difficult social questions. Criminals in court have attempted to plead diminished responsibility on the basis that their genes make them offend and therefore they should not be blamed. We should be wary of jumping to any general conclusions about genetic destiny, though. The allele is incredibly rare, and most people with conduct disorder do not carry it. There are common alleles of MAOA with subtler effects (they decrease the activity of MAOA but do not abolish it altogether). These alleles are over-represented in people with conduct disorder, but they only seem to promote violent behaviour where the environment is also violence-promoting – for example, if the people are abused as children (Caspi et al., 2002; McDermott, Dawes, Prom-Wormley, Eaves, & Hatemi, 2013).

Thus, the environment is still crucially important. Moreover, in most cases in psychology where an allele is statistically associated with a disorder, there are many people with the allele but not the disorder, and many with the disorder but not the allele. Even within the Dutch family, the level of actual violent and criminal behaviour is extremely variable across the men. This shows that the link from genotype to phenotype may be statistically strong, but it is not so strong as to constitute destiny. Many environmental inputs and individual decisions can affect how predispositions are actually expressed. Society is responsible for these environmental inputs, and people are responsible for their decisions.

In **this TED Talk from 2009**[2], neuroscientist Jim Fallon talks about his research and personal experience of the MAOA gene.

DISCUSSION POINT

Discuss the varying ways that genetic and environmental factors can have an impact on individual behaviour.

TEST YOURSELF

1. Write down in your own words the differences in meaning between the following terms: genome, chromosome, gene, allele, base.
2. What is the part of the genome that codes for proteins called, and what fraction of the genome does it represent in humans?
3. What is the difference between transcription and translation?

SECTION SUMMARY

- Biologists refer to the observable characteristics of an individual as that individual's phenotype.
- Information is inherited principally in the form of genetic material.
- The total set of genetic material you possess is known as your genome, which is made out of DNA.
- The two strands of DNA pair up through a mechanism known as base pairing.
- In most cases, the complete set of DNA is copied across from the ancestor to the descendant cell, a process known as mitosis.
- Accessing the information stored in DNA happens via a process known as transcription.
- An alternative version of the same gene is called an allele.
- There are two main processes that make individuals differ genetically: recombination and mutation.
- Your genome responds to environmental events in real time.

PASSING IT ON: THE MECHANISMS OF HEREDITY

LEARNING OBJECTIVE 3.3

Demonstrate a clear understanding of the mechanisms of heredity.

The important thing about genetic mutations is not just that they occur but that they can be passed on to subsequent generations. It is because of this ability of novel alleles to be perpetuated into future generations that evolutionary change is possible. In this section, we consider how alleles are passed on, and the related topics of how children resemble their parents and how we find the genes involved in transmitting that resemblance.

Mendelian inheritance

You have two copies of most genes in your genome, one on the chromosome that came from your father and one on the paired chromosome that came from your mother. You might have two copies of the same allele of that gene, in which case your genotype is said to be **homozygous** for that gene, or you might have one copy each of two different alleles, in which case your genotype is said to be **heterozygous**. The principles of how the genotypes of the two parents determine the genotype (and phenotype) of the offspring were first understood by the founder of genetics, Gregor Mendel. For that reason, they are known as Mendel's laws or the principles of Mendelian inheritance.

We will take as an example coat colour in the Egyptian Mau cat. These cats come in two colours, silver and bronze, and which colour an individual has is determined by a single gene. The gene has two alleles, which we will call A and a. The possible genotypes a cat can have are therefore two copies of A (genotype AA), two copies of a (genotype aa), or one copy each of A and a (genotypes Aa and aA). The first two possibilities are homozygous genotypes, while the others are heterozygous. What happens when cats of different genotypes produce kittens together? The way to answer this question is to draw a Punnett square (Figure 3.5). The rows represent all of the different types of egg that the mother could make. For example, if she has genotype Aa, she can produce an egg with an A in, or, with equal probability, an egg with an a in, so one row says A and the other row says a. The columns represent all the types of sperm that the father could make. For example, if he has genotype aa, then both columns will have a at the top, since all his sperm will contain a. Now, to work out

FIGURE 3.5 *Using Punnett squares to predict the genotypes of offspring from the genotypes of their parents. Egyptian Mau cats come in two colours, silver and bronze. Colour is controlled by a single gene with two alleles A and a. To work out the genotypes of offspring from the parents, we draw Punnett squares. The possible eggs that the mother can make are the rows, and the possible sperm the father can make are the columns. Each of the four cells represents a possible (and equally likely) genotype for the offspring. A heterozygous silver female and a homozygous bronze male can produce heterozygous silver and homozygous bronze offspring with equal probability (left-hand square). Two heterozygous silver parents produce offspring with heterozygous genotype or either of the two homozygous genotypes with probabilities of one half, one quarter, and one quarter. This means their kittens will be three quarters silver and one quarter bronze (right-hand square).*

the possible genotypes of their kittens, we just look at all the possible intersections of rows and columns. In the first case (the Punnett square on the left of Figure 3.5), we see that, for this pairing, two kittens from every four (i.e. half) will have heterozygous genotype *Aa*, while the remaining two from every four (the other half) will have homozygous genotype *aa*. The half is an average, since it is a matter of chance which sperm meets with which egg, but, if this mother and this father had a very large number of kittens, you'd expect the proportion of homozygotes to stabilize at around half.

Using Punnett squares, you can quickly arrive at Mendel's principles. These hold not just for the cat example but in general. Mendel's principles are:

- Two homozygotes with the same allele can only produce homozygotes with that allele.
- Two homozygotes with different alleles can only produce heterozygotes.
- Two heterozygotes produce one quarter homozygotes for the first allele, one quarter homozygotes for the second allele, and one half heterozygotes.

The Punnett square allows us to predict the genotype of the kittens, but what about the phenotype, which we might be more interested in? The coat colour the kittens end up with depends on which allele of the gene is **dominant** and which one **recessive**. A dominant allele is one that needs to be present in just one copy in order for the individual to exhibit the associated phenotype, while a recessive allele has to be present in two copies. In the case of Egyptian Maus, silver is dominant and bronze is recessive. This is why we designated the 'silver' allele with a capital *A* and the bronze allele with a lower-case *a*. What this means is that cats of genotype *aa* will be bronze, cats of genotype *AA* will be silver, and cats of heterozygous genotypes *Aa* or *aA* will also be silver. In fact, they will look exactly like cats of genotype *AA*.

However, although heterozygous silver Egyptian Mau cats show no outward evidence of bronzeness, they can produce bronze kittens when mated with the right partner – for this they are known as carriers. If two heterozygous silver cats mate with each other, then on average three quarters of their kittens will be silver and one quarter will be bronze. Looking at the right-hand Punnett square in Figure 3.5, can you see why? One quarter to three quarters is the classic proportion of recessive phenotypes seen when two heterozygotes produce offspring. Mendelian genetics can sometimes become a little more complex than in this example, though, as you will see if you try Activity 3.1.

ACTIVITY 3.1

MENDELIAN GENETICS OF SEX-LINKED TRAITS

In the main text, we looked at how to calculate the expected proportions of different genotypes and phenotypes for genes where an individual inherits one copy from their mother and one from their father. This is the usual situation. However, there are some exceptions. One case that is a bit more complex is where genes reside on the sex chromosomes. You will recall you have 22 pairs of chromosomes with one copy coming from your mum and one from your dad; the genes on these chromosomes are called **autosomal**.

If you are a woman, you also have a twenty-third pair that works in the same way as the autosomal chromosomes: your two X chromosomes. If you are a man, you only have one copy of X, and that copy must come from your mum. You also have another chromosome called Y, and this must come from your dad. Where a gene resides on either X or Y, it will have different patterns of inheritance in children of the two sexes. You can work out the expected patterns by drawing a separate Punnett square for each sex of offspring and shading out the cells that are impossible.

NOW TRY THIS PROBLEM FOR YOURSELF

The gene involved in the most common type of haemophilia (a blood disorder) resides on the X chromosome. It is recessive. This means that having even one copy of the normal-type allele is enough to prevent the disease.

Suppose a woman is a carrier (i.e. she has one copy of the disease allele, but not the disease) and she marries a non-haemophiliac man.

1. What proportion of (a) their daughters and (b) their sons will have haemophilia?

Now suppose the same woman marries a man with haemophilia.

2. What proportions of (c) their daughters and (d) their sons will have haemophilia?

Genetically complex traits

There are some important heritable characteristics that can be understood simply using Mendel's laws. Examples are the **Mendelian diseases**, which are rare but serious heritable conditions underlain by a dysfunctional allele of a single gene. They include cystic fibrosis (recessive allele of a gene called CFTR on chromosome 7) and Huntington's disease (dominant allele of HTT on chromosome 4). However, for the majority of traits, there are many genes involved rather than just a single one. This makes working out the offspring genotype from the genotype of the parents much more complex. A single gene with two alleles has four possible genotypes (*AA*, *Aa*, *aA*, *aa*), two genes with two alleles each produce 16 possible genotypes (*AABB*, *AaBB*, *aaBB*, *AABb*, etc.), and 10 genes with two alleles each produce over a million possible genotypes. That's going to make for a very large Punnett square! Where the number of genes involved in a trait is large, we therefore take a different approach to understanding inheritance. This approach is called **quantitative genetics**.

The idea of quantitative genetics is that there are alleles that increase the value of the phenotypic trait and alleles that decrease it. Take the case of height. Height has a genetic basis, but many dozens of genes are involved. For each of these genes, there are alleles that tend to make people taller, other things being equal, and alleles that tend to make them shorter. If your mother is extremely tall, she probably has lots of the height-increasing ones and few of the height-reducing ones. If your father is of average height, he probably has some of the height-increasing alleles and some of the height-reducing ones. Now, if we want to predict how many height-increasing alleles you are going to inherit, then our best guess will be not as many as your mother, but more than your father. More formally, your genotypic value for height will be approximately the average of your mother's genotypic value and your father's. We can estimate the genotypic values from the phenotypic values of the parents, even if we don't know their genotypes. That is, if the environment remains constant over generations, then people's heights will usually be roughly the average of their two parents' heights.

Estimating heritability

A central concept of quantitative genetics is **heritability**. Heritability refers to the proportion of variation in a characteristic in a given population that is associated with genetic variation. (You will see it expressed either as a proportion or a percentage.) A high heritability for height would mean that, within the population under study, the systematic differences between taller and shorter people were mainly at the genotypic level. A low heritability would suggest that the systematic differences between taller and shorter people were mainly non-genetic (e.g. differences in nutrition or disease exposure). A characteristic being highly heritable does not mean it is 'genetically determined' within the individual. Both genetic and environmental factors are important for every trait. You couldn't grow to a normal height without good nutrition. What a high heritability of height might mean is that, within the group under study, the *differences* in height between people are not due to *variation* in nutrition. This might be, for example, because everyone's nutrition is good, or because everyone's nutrition is bad. Heritability is therefore specific to particular circumstances; if some children experienced a famine, the heritability of height might suddenly plummet.

Heritability is often misunderstood. If heritability is high in one group – for example, affluent students – it does not mean it will be high in a different social group (see Focus Point 3.4). We therefore cannot say anything about the heritability of height in general; it will always depend on which population we are talking about. You also cannot use high within-group heritability to infer that the differences between groups are due to genetics. You are several centimetres taller than your grandparents' generation. Heritability of height is very high within your generation (perhaps as high as 0.9), and it was high within your grandparents' generation too. However, the difference in average heights between your generation and theirs is entirely due to improvements in public health and nutrition.

Heritability cannot be measured directly. It has to be estimated in various ways, all of which have limitations. Most estimates are based on twin studies. Twin studies exploit the fact that human twins come in two kinds. Monozygotic twins are genetically identical, and also tend to experience roughly the same environment. Dizygotic twins also experience roughly the same environment, but they are genetically no more similar than ordinary siblings. Thus, we can use the extent to which monozygotic twins are more similar to one another than dizygotic twins are to provide an estimate of the impact of shared genes on the characteristic under study. If heritability is zero, then we should expect monozygotic twins to be no more similar to each than dizygotic twins are. In practice, monozygotic twins are usually considerably more similar to each other than dizygotic twins are.

Caution is needed in interpreting heritability estimates derived from twin studies. The statistical methods for estimating heritability from phenotypic resemblance of twins make assumptions about the underlying genetics. There could also be non-genetic reasons that monozygotic twins end up more similar to one another than dizygotic twins do. Monozygotic twins share a single placenta, so their in utero experience might be more similar than that of dizygotic twins. Monozygotic twins are also treated more similarly than dizygotic twins are when they are children. Of course, this is ambiguous; they might be treated more similarly because they are more similar, rather than the other way around. Studies of monozygotic twins who were raised apart by different parents tend to support the conclusion that monozygotic twins are substantially more alike in psychological characteristics than dizygotic twins are. Nonetheless, we should remember that twin studies give us only rough and indirect estimates of genetic heritability.

FOCUS POINT 3.4

SOCIOECONOMIC POSITION AND THE HERITABILITY OF INTELLIGENCE

The question of whether variation in intelligence (IQ) is mainly due to variation in genes or variation in the environment has a long and contentious history in psychology. The contention stems from the fact that people have tried to use answers to the question to advance political cases about public expenditures on education. In doing so, they have usually committed basic fallacies, such as arguing that high heritability within one social group (e.g. middle-class Americans) tells you something about the causes of the difference in cognitive performance between that population and a different one (e.g. African Americans living in deprived neighbourhoods).

As it turns out, the heritability of intelligence is itself variable, and that variation is partly explained by social factors. A study by Turkheimer et al. (2003) estimated the heritability of IQ score for 319 pairs of twins of different social backgrounds, represented by a socio-economic status (SES) score varying from 0 (very deprived) to 100 (very advantaged). They found that the heritability – the variation due to genes – was near zero in families with the lowest SES and very large in the highest SES families. By contrast, the proportion of variation in IQ attributable to features of the environment was very large in the lowest SES families and almost zero in the highest SES families.

How can we explain this pattern? A simple way of looking at it is that, in the most affluent social groups, everyone's environment is very good. Nutrition, housing, schooling, and care are all pretty much as good as they can be. Thus, to the extent that there is any variation in IQ performance, the only place it can come from is genetic variation across individuals. Since heritability is the proportion of variation in IQ associated with genetic variation, heritability is therefore high in these groups. By contrast, in more deprived social groups, there is quite a lot of environmental variation too. There are deficiencies in housing, nutrition, schooling, residential stability, and so forth, but not every poor family is affected. Some people are lucky enough to avoid these difficulties despite living in poverty. Thus, the amount of environmental variation relevant to cognitive performance is much higher for deprived groups. This means that the proportionate contribution of genetic variation to the total variation – that is, the heritability – must be much less.

An unusual implication of these remarkable data is that, as a society, we should be wishing for heritabilities of traits such as intelligence to become as high as possible. A high heritability means, effectively, that the environmental cards have been dealt out evenly. Turkheimer et al.'s data show that in contemporary America, this is far from the case.

DISCUSSION POINT

Discuss the following statement:

Given that intelligence is highly heritable, there is little point in spending money on educational facilities for low-achieving groups.

Hunting for the genetic basis of psychological characteristics

Heritability estimates from twin studies suggest that there are genetic factors associated with particular traits, such as personality or vulnerability to psychological disorders. However, these studies can't tell us which genes have alleles that affect these characteristics. To discover this, we need a different kind of study altogether: **association studies**. The principle of association studies is simple. You get a large sample of people who are low or high on the characteristic you are studying and measure their genotype at a number of different sites in the genome. If particular genotypes show up more often in the high group than in the low group, then that gene might be important for the characteristic. When association studies began, genetic technology was primitive and genotype was measured using just a few genetic markers for each participant. More modern studies use several million markers spread over the genome. It is only a matter of time before association studies will sequence every single base of the genome of every participant. This is technically possible at the moment, but still expensive.

Finding the genes involved in particular characteristics is very easy where the number of genes involved is small and each allele has a large effect on the outcome. This is why the genes involved in the Mendelian diseases were identified rapidly. However, the more genes are involved, the more difficult it becomes to identify them, since variation in any particular gene might only change the average value of the phenotype by a very small amount. The current state of knowledge concerning the genetic basis of psychological characteristics is rather perplexing. Twin studies tend to suggest quite high heritability of most characteristics in contemporary populations. However, association studies have in general failed to find the specific genes that account for the heritable effects. This is known as the 'problem of missing heritability'.

There are a number of possible solutions to the problem of missing heritability. The numbers of genes involved in important traits may simply be extremely large, and, moreover, alleles of different genes may interact with one another in complex ways. We may not currently be measuring all of the ways in which genomes can differ. For example, it might not matter so much which base you have at a particular point in a particular gene, but, rather, how many copies of that gene you have. Interactions between genotype and environment may be pervasive (see Focus Point 3.5). Finally, we may have overestimated heritabilities in the first place, because of the simplifications in our methods for doing this. Nonetheless, despite very considerable uncertainties in exactly which genes affect our psychology, the principle remains valid that variation in the genome is related to variation in psychological phenotypes, just as it is to variation in physical phenotypes.

FOCUS POINT 3.5

GENE BY ENVIRONMENT INTERACTIONS

We often speak as if there is variation in a trait due to genetic factors and due to environmental ones, and as if these two sources of influence simply add together. What this ignores, though, is the possibility that which alleles you have might affect how you respond to particular environmental inputs. This type of situation is known as a gene by environment (G × E) interaction.

A famous example of a G × E interaction comes from a study of the predictors of depression (Caspi et al., 2003). Previous studies had implicated the neurotransmitter serotonin in depression. There is a gene called 5-HTT that makes an enzyme important for serotonin function, and this gene has two groups of common alleles, known as 'short' and 'long'. Caspi et al. studied a cohort of around 850 young New Zealanders. They looked at the occurrence of stressful life events between the participants' 21st and 26th birthdays as predictors of a major depressive episode at age 25–26. As you might expect, having more life stressors increased the probability of a depressive episode.

However, breaking the cohort down by genotype revealed different associations for different groups (see the following figure). Bearers of a 'short/short' genotype (two copies of 'short') were much more likely than anyone else to have a major depressive episode, but only if they also had many stressful life events. If they had no life stressors, they were no more likely than other genotypes to experience depression, and in fact possibly a little less likely. The 'short/short' genotype group were thus highly reactive, having a low probability of depression with no life stressors, and a very high probability of depression with numerous life stressors. By contrast, the 'long/long' genotype group were less responsive. Their probability of depression increased only weakly with the number of life stressors. The 'short/long' group were intermediate between the two homozygous genotypes.

There are many other examples of G x E interactions that have been documented since this study appeared. Thus, we cannot conceive of genetic and environmental effects as independent or simply additive. Different alleles affect how we respond to environmental inputs, or, to put it the other way around, different environments affect the consequences of the alleles we bear.

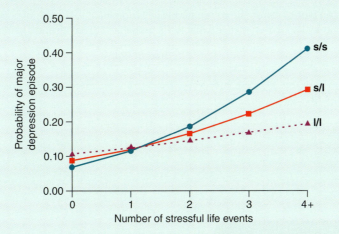

Probability of a major depressive episode as a function of number of stressful life events in a large New Zealand cohort, broken down by 5-HTT genotype. 's/s' represents two copies of the short allele, 'l/l' two copies of the long allele, and 's/l' the heterozygous genotype.
Source: Caspi et al. (2003). Reprinted with permission from AAAS.

TEST YOURSELF

1. In the Manx cat, there is a dominant allele that is lethal when homozygous (the homozygous kittens die in utero and are reabsorbed by the mother). However, when heterozygous, the allele produces healthy cats with no tails. Suppose two tailless Manx cats breed. What proportion of their kittens born will have tails, and what proportion will have no tails?

2. What would a heritability of zero mean, and what would a heritability of 1 (or 100%) mean?

3. Describe in your own words what is meant by a gene × environment interaction.

ACTIVITY 3.2

PUNNETT SQUARES

Answer the following questions.

1. My favourite flower is heterozygous red (*Rr*) and it is crossed with a homozygous white (*rr*) plant. Use a Punnett square to determine the probability of one of their offspring being white.
   a. 100%
   b. 75%
   c. 50%
   d. 25%

2. My dog Fang is heterozygous and long haired (*Ss*) and her mate Snoopy is homozygous and short haired (*ss*). Use a Punnett square to determine the probability of one of their offspring having short hair.
   a. 100%
   b. 75%
   c. 50%
   d. 25%

3. In a certain type of carrot, the colour purple (*P*) is dominant to the colour orange (*p*). According to the Punnett square, what is the probability of an offspring being purple?

		Parent (*Pp*)	
		P	p
Parent (*Pp*)	P	PP	Pp
	p	Pp	pp

   a. 100%
   b. 75%
   c. 50%
   d. 25%

SECTION SUMMARY

- We can use Punnett squares to arrive at Mendel's principles of the production of homozygote and heterozygote genotypes.
- The phenotype depends on which allele of the gene is dominant and which one recessive.
- Mendelian diseases are rare, but serious, heritable conditions underlain by a dysfunctional allele of a single gene.
- Quantitative genetics suggests that there are alleles that increase the value of a phenotypic trait and alleles that decrease it.
- Heritability refers to the proportion of variation in a characteristic in a given population that is associated with genetic variation; it cannot be measured directly.
- The heritability of intelligence is variable and variation is partly explained by social factors.
- Association studies attempt to identify the particular genes that contribute to a phenotype by comparing genetic data from large numbers of people with and without that phenotype.

STAYING ALIVE: THE OPERATION OF NATURAL SELECTION

LEARNING OBJECTIVE 3.4

Describe the basic principles of the interplay of genes and environment.

So far we have established that different individuals have different phenotypes, that those phenotypes are related to their genotypes, and that offspring tend to resemble their parents in phenotype and genotype. Thus, we have nearly all the building blocks for understanding evolution by natural selection. The building block we still need to mention is differential reproductive success. Differential reproductive success refers to the fact that not all individuals leave the same number of surviving offspring. In wild animal populations, this is very obviously true. Given the pressures of disease, predation, and the need to find food and water every day, many individuals die before reaching adulthood, some of those that do reach adulthood don't find mates, and some of those that do reach adulthood and find mates don't manage to successfully rear any young. The principle of differential reproduction is true in humans too. As recently as 100 years ago in Britain, many babies died in the early years of life, and many people were unable to have children due to health problems. Improvements in living standards have eased these forces somewhat, but it is still the case that not everyone has children, and those who do have children don't all have the same number. The next section explores why differential reproductive success is such an important principle.

Consequences of differential reproductive success

The significance of differential reproductive success is that not everyone born becomes an ancestor to members of the next generation. Instead, the ancestors of the next generation are a subset. If they were a random subset, then we would expect them to be no different on average from the wider set of all individuals born. However, what Darwin realized is that the ancestors of the next generation will in general be a very non-random subset of all the individuals born. They will be that subset of individuals who happen to have characteristics that make them good at surviving, finding a mate, and reproducing, in the current environment. They will then pass those characteristics on to their offspring. Thus, because of differential reproductive success, the proportion of individuals bearing characteristics that are beneficial for survival and reproduction will gradually rise from generation to generation. This is the process called natural selection.

We can illustrate the principle of natural selection by returning to our brown and Kermode bears (Figure 3.4b–c). At the moment, Kermode (ginger) bears are very rare, and most bears are brown. We'll estimate that 99% of females are brown and 1% are ginger. To keep things simple, we will assume that brown females have only brown daughters and ginger females only ginger daughters, and we won't consider the colours of the males. Now let us imagine that there is environmental change and North America becomes a sandy desert. Under these conditions, brown females have a 50% chance of surviving long enough to reproduce, and, if they do, they have an average of two daughters. Being ginger makes the bear slightly less conspicuous when hunting for food in the desert, because it blends into the background. This is useful, but doesn't make a very big difference to its survival chances. After all, colour is only one of many things a wild animal needs to survive in a desert. So we will say that ginger females have a 51% chance of surviving to reproduce, and they also have two daughters on average if they do reproduce.

Because of their slightly better survival rate, ginger bears will be slightly overrepresented in the subset of bears that become parents of the next generation, and, since they are ginger, their offspring will also be ginger. This means the proportion of bears that are ginger will fractionally increase every generation. The increase may be small, but the important thing to appreciate is that, when it gets iterated generation after generation, it can make a large difference over time. To illustrate this, Figure 3.6 plots the expected proportions of ginger and brown females in the population as a function of time (assume one generation per year). As the figure shows, in less than 500 years, our population goes from being one mainly composed of brown bears to one mainly composed of ginger bears. A future researcher would come along and see a kind of bear that was well adapted to its desert home by being camouflaged, hardly guessing that the bears had once been dark brown. The adaptation the observer would see is simply the consequence of a tiny historical edge in survival repeated again and again.

In evolutionary biology, relative success at leaving offspring in the next generation is called **fitness**. Note that this is a completely different sense of fitness from the cardiovascular sense. High fitness in the evolutionary sense means an advantage in leaving descendants, and low fitness means a disadvantage. Characteristics associated

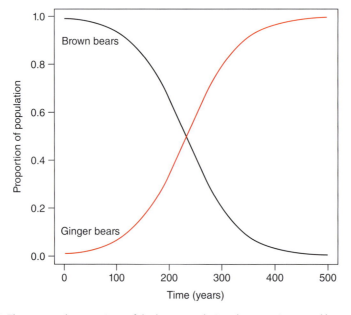

FIGURE 3.6 *The expected proportions of the bear population that are ginger and brown against time, assuming that ginger bears are initially rare but have a very slight survival advantage over brown bears (51% survival versus 50% survival).*

with higher fitness increase in prevalence under the action of natural selection, while characteristics associated with low fitness decreased in prevalence.

Most adaptations are not as simple as a change in coat colour. Complex adaptations such as the vertebrate eye consist of many intricately tailored parts. These complex adaptations have been built up by the same process described in this section, albeit over much longer timescales. The eye has been assembled in various stages, from simple patches of light-sensitive skin to pinhole eyes to lensed eyes to full colour vision. Many of these intermediate stages are still found in nature in some living creature or other. At each stage, mutation and recombination must have created a reservoir of variation in the eye's exact form, on which selection could act. At each stage, the more complex eye must have provided a slight fitness advantage compared to the simpler one. Above all, there needs to have been a truly vast amount of time for the adaptations to have been built up, tiny piece by tiny piece, generation to generation.

Selection at the genetic level

Selection acts on phenotypic characteristics, but its consequence is to change the frequencies of alleles in the population. In our bear example, we know that the ginger colour comes from an allele of MC1R. If the evolutionary trajectory illustrated in Figure 3.6 actually happened, the ginger allele of MC1R, which is currently rare in the bear population, would within 500 years become so common that almost every bear had it. This is because by that time almost every bear alive would be a descendant of one of the small number of starting ancestors who carried that allele. Once an allele has become so common that virtually every living individual in the population has it, it is said to have reached **fixation**.

The allele underlying a characteristic will increase in frequency under natural selection only if the bearers of that allele have, on average, higher fitness than the bearers of alternative alleles of that gene. Thus, to think about which characteristics might be favoured by natural selection, you have to ask yourself whether bearers of an allele for those characteristics would be advantaged or disadvantaged relatively to bearers of alternative alleles. As soon as we think in this way, we see that what natural selection favours is not behaviours that are good for the species, but behaviours that are good for the lineages of individuals practising them. For example, there is a long-standing idea that lemmings commit mass suicide when food resources are short. The idea is that some individuals are programmed to sacrifice themselves so that the species survives. The moment we think about it in terms of the alleles involved, though, we see that this must be nonsense. An allele that caused all of its bearers to commit suicide when there was a bad year would be disadvantaged relative to an allele that did not cause this behaviour. Call the alleles *suicidal* and *non-suicidal*. Let's say that both alleles coexist in the population of lemmings during a period of good years. The moment a bad year comes along, the bearers of *suicidal* all die, and so any animals that do make it through the hard times are bearers of *non-suicidal*. The species survives right enough, but it is now a species composed of non-suicidal lemmings, and so the suicidal behaviour has gone extinct! Accordingly, the supposed suicidal behaviour of lemmings turns out to be a myth, and a famous wildlife documentary that purported to show this behaviour was a shameful fake.

The previous paragraph said that, for an allele to spread under natural selection, its bearers have to have higher fitness *on average* than bearers of alternative alleles. The *on average* is very important. A behaviour that caused some of its bearers to have zero fitness could spread if it also caused the remaining bearers to have extremely high fitness. An example of this principle comes from **eusocial breeding systems**. These are breeding systems in which one class of individuals (e.g. queens) do all the reproducing while other classes (e.g. workers, drones) work to service the reproducing class and its offspring. At first glance, you would think that the alleles for being a worker would die out in a generation, since their fitness is zero. However, these are actually alleles for eusociality. When expressed in workers, the fitness of these alleles is zero, but, when expressed in queens, their fitness is remarkably high. For the alleles for eusociality to spread by natural selection, the *average* fitness of the eusociality alleles, taken across both queens and workers, has to be higher than the fitness of alleles for non-eusociality. There clearly are circumstances where this is the case; eusociality has evolved many times in bees and ants, and once in mammals, in the naked mole rat (Figure 3.7).

The existence of eusociality shows that natural selection does not just favour 'selfish' behaviours. Worker bees labour their whole life for the good of others rather than their personal fitness, with no return at the personal level. For such 'helping' to

FIGURE 3.7 *Evolution of extreme biological altruism in a mammal. In the Palestine mole rat (a), all females reproduce in the normal manner. In the related naked mole rat (b), only the queen within each colony reproduces, and all the other females work to help her raise her pups.*

Source: (a) © Bassem18 at English Wikipedia; (b) GREGORY DIMIJIAN / Science Photo Library.

evolve, genes must be shared between the helper (the worker) and the helped (the queen). We can calculate exactly what the degree of genetic overlap between helper and helped must be for a given level of helping to evolve by natural selection (see Focus Point 3.6).

FOCUS POINT 3.6

HAMILTON'S RULE AND THE EVOLUTION OF ALTRUISM

In the 1960s and 1970s, an English biologist called William Hamilton worked out the mathematics of how natural selection would act on behaviours where one individual helped another, at a cost to its personal fitness and with no personal payback in its lifetime. He showed that such helping behaviour would spread by natural selection as long as a simple condition was satisfied. That condition is known as **Hamilton's rule** and can be expressed as:

$$rb > c$$

Here, b represents the increase in fitness that the helped enjoy as a result of the help, while c represents the decrease in personal fitness that the helper suffers by helping. The r represents the **coefficient of relatedness** between the helper and the helped. The coefficient of relatedness is the degree to which the helper and helped are more or less genetically similar than two randomly chosen members of the population would be. A coefficient of relatedness of 0 means they are just as similar as two randomly chosen individuals, while a coefficient of relatedness of 1 means they are genetic clones. You can see from Hamilton's rule that if r is close to 0, then selection will not favour helping even if that helping would increase the recipient's fitness a great deal and cost the helper rather little. If r is close to 1, then the interests of the two individuals are almost perfectly aligned; selection favours helping as long as the benefit to the helped individual is greater than the cost to the helper.

Hamilton's rule is a powerful explanatory principle for human social life. For example, in all kinds of societies, people favour their kin or clansfolk over non-relatives and take care to channel their resources to those most closely related to them, as Hamilton's rule would predict. However, Hamilton's rule only concerns kinds of helping where there is no personal payback. A great deal of human social behaviour involves doing something for others now and reaping a long-term personal benefit in the future through friendship, reputation, or reciprocity. We do not need to use Hamilton's rule to think about these cases.

Evolutionary biologists reserve the term **altruism** for the cases Hamilton considered, where one individual helps another at a cost to itself and with no personal payback in its lifetime. Psychologists use the term altruism much more broadly, to mean any behaviour in which one individual acts for the good of another. Evolutionary biologists call this broader category **cooperation**. This difference in terminologies has unfortunately led to a great deal of confusion regarding how altruistic humans really are and how their altruistic tendencies might have evolved (West, El Mouden, & Gardner, 2011).

DISCUSSION POINT

Discuss some examples of Hamilton's rule. Remember: Hamilton's rule only concerns kinds of helping where there is no personal payback.

TEST YOURSELF

1. Explain in your own words what the term 'fitness' means in evolutionary biology.

2. Explain why a trait might not be favoured by natural selection even if it is good for the species.

3. Write down Hamilton's rule and explain what each of the three parameters represents.

SECTION SUMMARY

- Differential reproductive success refers to the fact that not all individuals leave the same number of surviving offspring.

- In evolutionary biology, relative success at leaving offspring in the next generation is called fitness. Characteristics associated with higher fitness increase in prevalence under the action of natural selection.

- Most adaptations are complex and emerge over long periods of time.

- Selection acts on phenotypic characteristics, but its consequence is to change the frequencies of alleles in a population. Once an allele has become so common that virtually every living individual in the population has it, it is said to have reached fixation. For an allele to spread under natural selection, its bearers have to have higher fitness on average than bearers of alternative alleles.

- Eusocial breeding systems are those in which one class of individuals do all the reproducing while other classes work to service the queen and her offspring.

- The condition required for natural selection to favour the spread of an allele causing individuals to help another, with no direct benefit to themselves, is known as Hamilton's rule. Normally, it is expressed mathematically as $rb > c$, where r is the coefficient of relatedness, b is the fitness benefit of being helped, and c is the fitness cost of helping.

STAYING ALIVE: SELECTION OF BEHAVIOURS AND ADAPTATION

LEARNING OBJECTIVE 3.5

Describe the basic principles of the genetic basis of psychological traits.

Selection on behaviour

People find natural selection easy to grasp when it comes to physical characteristics. They have no problem with the idea of an allele causing a different fur colour, that fur colour being advantageous, and hence that allele spreading by natural selection.

However, when it comes to behaviour, things seem less clear. Behaviour is constantly changing and is initiated by the environment in a way that is not true for fur colour. Besides, behaviour is something individuals *do* whereas fur colour is something individuals *have*.

When we talk about natural selection acting on behaviour, we are really using a shorthand. What we assume is that a behaviour (e.g. aggression) is underlain by some neurobiological mechanism (e.g. the hormone testosterone). Mutant alleles affect aggression indirectly – for example, by making the effect of testosterone on the brain less potent. The behavioural consequence of bearing an allele that did this might be a reduced tendency to be aggressive across a range of situations, and this might have implications for survival and reproduction. Thus, it is the alleles for making a brain that is less responsive to testosterone that are actually selected for. The consequence is still that aggressive behaviour becomes less prevalent across the generations. Thus, it is acceptable to say that natural selection has acted on aggression, but we should remember that this is a shorthand; natural selection has strictly acted on a neurobiological mechanism that affects the propensity to display aggression. In a few cases, we understand the behaviour, the neurobiological mechanism, and the alleles underlying an evolutionary change (see Focus Point 3.7).

An important corollary of the fact that natural selection acts on neurobiological mechanisms is that it can act on learned behaviours. For example, for some birds, it is useful to have a wide and flexible range of song repertoire, whereas for other birds this is less important. Birdsong is a learned behaviour. Natural selection cannot build a wide and flexible song repertoire directly into the bird. However, it can favour alleles for making certain brain circuits remain responsive to auditory input throughout the bird's life. The consequence is the evolution of what is called open-ended song learning in some bird species. Open-ended learning is what allows certain species (such as mynahs) to pick up human phrases, mobile-phone ring tones, and so on. The ability of mynahs to do this is an evolved capacity, even though 'Who's a pretty boy, then?' is clearly a learned phrase.

FOCUS POINT 3.7

THE PRAIRIE AND MONTANE VOLES

There are rather few cases where we can find an evolved behavioural difference between two species and understand exactly what the mutant alleles were that created the difference, and how they work in the brain to affect behavioural phenotype. One nice case comes from the prairie vole and montane vole. The prairie and montane voles are apparently similar, closely related small rodents. In the montane vole, like many mammals, males provide only sperm to the female. Once they have mated with the female, they disappear. The prairie vole, by contrast, forms long-term pair bonds. Males stay with their females and help to care for the pups. The mechanism that makes males bond in this way is the release into the brain, after mating, of a hormone called arginine vasopressin.

We know this because injecting males with a substance that blocks the action of arginine vasopressin causes pair bonding to fail. It turns out that male montane voles release arginine vasopressin into their brains after mating too. The difference is that prairie voles produce much more of a receptor protein for arginine vasopressin, called *avpr1a*. This means that male prairie voles respond strongly to being injected with arginine vasopressin, by increasingly their affiliative behaviour, whereas male montane voles do not (see the following figure).

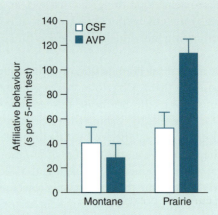

When monogamous prairie voles are injected with arginine vasopressin rather than a control substance, they increase their affiliative behaviour. The related non-monogamous montane vole shows no such pattern. On this graph, AVP represents arginine vasopression and CSF represents the control substance.

Source: Nettle (2009). Reproduced by permission of Oxford University Press.

The prairie vole has a different allele of a gene that regulates production of *avpr1a* than the montane vole does. So far, so good. The difference in behaviour of the prairie vole male can be traced to his responsiveness to a hormone, which can be traced to a variant form of a gene. The really remarkable thing about this particular story is that researchers have been able to genetically engineer a mouse that possesses the prairie vole version of the gene regulating production of *avpr1a* (Young, Nilsen, Waymire, MacGregor, & Insel, 1999). Normal mice behave exactly like montane voles. This engineered mouse responds to arginine vasopressin by increasing his affiliative behaviour, just like a prairie vole does.

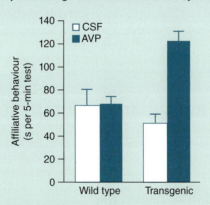

Normal wild-type mice are not monogamous and respond to arginine vasopression injected just like montane voles do. However, a transgenic mouse engineered to contain the prairie vole's version of the gene avpr1a *responds to the injection just like a prairie vole does, by increasing its affiliative behaviour. On this graph, AVP represents arginine vasopression and CSF represents the control substance.*

Data from Young, Nilsen, Waymire, MacGregor, and Insel (1999). *Source:* Nettle (2009). Reproduced by permission of Oxford University Press.

Some caution is needed before extrapolating too far. For example, there are other rodent species that have prairie-vole-like versions of avpr1a and are not monogamous, and many other genes can affect social behaviours. Nonetheless, this is a neat illustration of how a phenotypic difference can be at least partly traced via a brain mechanism to a genotypic one.

Adaptation: The consequence of natural selection

We have seen that natural selection favours alleles that on average increase the fitness of their bearers. We have also seen that, in every generation, mutation offers up a library of new variations for natural selection to select from. All living species have been around for many millions of generations in some form or other, so, although evolutionary change is gradual, there has been plenty of time for it to happen. When you put all these facts together, you arrive at the conclusion that, by now, organisms should be pretty well adapted for the environments they live in. This means that, if they show some measurable characteristic, we are justified in asking why it makes adaptive sense for the characteristic to be like that for the organism, since many alternative 'designs' must have existed over the course of evolution and been selected against in favour of the currently prevalent one.

Of course, there are many constraints on adaptation. Some are physical: it would be great for lions to be able to fly, but basic physics precludes flight in an animal with such large mass. Some are developmental: it might be great for trees to instantly reach 30 metres high, but there is no way of delivering this since they must make their tissues using the energy they can capture from light. Other constraints arise from ecological interactions: it would be great for rabbits to never be predated, but rabbits are coevolving with foxes and every improvement in rabbit defences is met with an improvement in foxes' hunting ability. Because of these constraints, adaptive explanations are most sensible when we compare a characteristic or behaviour that exists with an alternative that plausibly *could* exist, is known to have existed in the past, or currently exists in a related species.

Another important limitation on adaptive explanations is that we should not expect organisms to make appropriate adaptive responses to circumstances that they have not experienced sufficiently often over evolutionary time. When Europeans landed on various remote oceanic islands, they encountered animals so tame that they could simply walk up and take them. This was definitely not adaptive behaviour on the part of the animals, but nothing in those animals' evolutionary history had selected for the ability to respond appropriately to human hunters. We refer to the set of environmental conditions that a species is adapted to as its **environment of evolutionary adaptedness**. The environment of evolutionary adaptedness is not any particular place or time. It is a statistical composite of all the environmental conditions and challenges that an organism has faced, with circumstances that occurred frequently having greater weight than those occurring infrequently, and more recent circumstances having greater weight than more distant ones, other things being equal.

SECTION SUMMARY

- When we talk about natural selection acting on behaviour, we are really using a shorthand. What we assume is that a behaviour is underlain by some neurobiological mechanism.
- There are many constraints on adaptation, including physical, developmental, and ecological ones.
- We refer to the set of environmental conditions that a species is adapted to as its environment of evolutionary adaptedness.

THE VALUE OF EVOLUTION FOR PSYCHOLOGY

LEARNING OBJECTIVE 3.6

Describe the fundamental processes by which natural selection on genes leads to adaptation.

We have now reviewed the general principles of evolution by natural selection and its genetic basis. However, this is a psychology textbook, not a textbook of evolutionary biology. This section is therefore devoted to asking what, specifically, can the principles of evolution do *for psychology*? We will explore this through three case studies, each looking at a psychological question or effect through an evolutionary lens. The first is on negative emotions in birds and humans, the second on infanticide in leopards and humans, and the third on social behaviour and intelligence in apes and humans. In each case study, we will see that an evolutionary perspective brings two useful things to bear on an aspect of human behaviour or cognition. The first is *adaptive thinking*. This, as we have seen, involves asking of each phenomenon, 'Why is it good for the organism for it to work like that, rather than some other way?' The second useful thing is *comparative thinking*. Taking an evolutionary perspective reminds us that there are many other species of animal around that behave and have brains. More importantly, it tells us that we share a great deal of history with these other animals. Processes we see in ourselves may work in similar ways in those other animals. This could mean that the mechanisms we are studying have very ancient origins, arising before the ancestors of humans diverged from those of other animals. Alternatively, the processes may work completely differently in humans from in even our closest relatives. This would suggest that the mechanisms we are studying are specific to the human lineage and have probably evolved relatively recently. Either way, comparison with other species is instructive for understanding ourselves.

Negative emotions and judgement biases

Our first case study comes from the psychology of negative emotions (the kinds of emotions that are extreme in clinical depression and anxiety). Psychologists have known for some time that, when people are in the grip of negative emotions, their judgements are affected. When faced with ambiguous stimuli, depressed or anxious people are prone to give the most negative possible interpretation. This is called 'negative cognitive bias'. A famous experiment showed that, when asked to transcribe spoken words with two possible meanings, anxious people tended to write 'pain' rather than 'pane' and 'die' rather than 'dye' (Eysenck, Mogg, May, Richards, & Mathews, 1991). Similarly, when people have to judge whether an ambiguous face is angry or not, anxious people are more likely to say that it is angry than non-anxious people are. Negative cognitive biases are an important component of how clinical conditions such as depression maintain themselves over time. Since the depressed person is prone to negative judgements about events that happen to them, it is hard for anything to lift their mood. But are negative cognitive biases a specific quirk of certain moods in humans, or are they a more widespread and general principle? There is in fact evidence that negative cognitive biases can be found in other animals and, just as they do in humans, they appear exactly when the individual is in a bad situation.

Bateson and Matheson (2007) devised a task where starlings had to turn over a lid to uncover some food. If the lid was white, the food was edible. If the lid was black, the food had been injected with quinine, which is unpalatable and toxic if consumed in large doses. The birds soon learned to turn over white lids but leave the black ones unturned. In a test, the researchers presented the starlings with grey lids. Would they, optimistically, see the grey lid as close to white, in which case they should turn it over, or would they, pessimistically, see it as nearly back, in which case it should be avoided?

The birds were either housed in bare laboratory cages or in cages enriched with natural features that starlings like – tree branches, water baths, and bark chippings to root around in. Bateson and Matheson found that, when living in the standard cages, the birds were more likely to see the grey lid as close to black and not turn it than they were when living in the enriched cages (see Figure 3.8). The better living conditions made the birds take a more optimistic view about what a grey lid might mean. Similar effects have now been found in many other species, including rats, mice, dogs, sheep, chickens, and even honey bees. When animals are in a good environment or good state, they tend to make more positive judgements about the meaning of ambiguous stimuli than they do when in a bad environment or state.

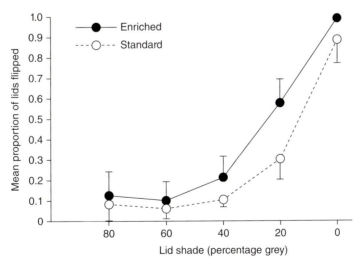

FIGURE 3.8 *Proportions of lids flipped by European starlings who had been trained that a white lid (0% grey) meant a palatable food and a dark lid (80% grey) means food injected with quinine, when they were living in either standard bare cages or enriched cages. The 60%, 40%, and 20% grey lids were ambiguous in the sense that they fell in between the two types of lids the starlings had learned about. Flipping such an ambiguous lid represents optimism that it might mean the same as a white lid; not flipping represents pessimism that it might be like a dark lid.*

Source: Figure 1 from Bateson and Matheson (2007). Reproduced with permission © 2007 Universities Federation for Animal Welfare.

This suggests that negative cognitive biases are not just a quirk of humans and don't just mean that our brains work badly when our mood is low. Instead, the fact that so many different species show similar judgement shifts when conditions are bad suggests that shifting your cognitive bias according to your current situation is a capacity that might have adaptive value, since it has either been retained for many millions of years or has evolved independently many times. The adaptive interpretation of cognitive bias shifts would be something like the following. When we make judgements, we are often deciding whether something is a potentially good opportunity (nice food, a new friend etc.) or else a potential threat (a source of poison, someone who may harm us, etc.). If you are too optimistic in your judgements, you will assume some things are good opportunities when they are actually threats, and, if you are too pessimistic, you will assume some things are threats when they are actually good opportunities. When conditions are bad, you really can't afford to expose yourself to potential threats. It thus makes adaptive sense to reset your judgement threshold so as to assume more things are threats and fewer are opportunities. You may miss a few possible opportunities from thinking they are threats, but, crucially, you won't miss any threats by being too blasé. When conditions improve, you are better buffered against undetected threats, and so you can reset the threshold more towards detecting opportunities with less weight given to the possibility of threatening outcomes.

Viewed in this light, it makes a lot of sense that negative circumstances such as poverty, social isolation, bereavement, and so on lead to low mood, and that low mood leads to negative cognitions. It's not just people being irrational or their brains going wrong, but the playing out in contemporary social environments of a set of evolved mechanisms that are partly shared across many related species. In the clinical extremes of depression and anxiety disorders, these evolved mechanisms may have become dysfunctional, and psychologists need to find ways to counteract their excessive activity. Nonetheless, understanding the evolutionary function of these processes, and the way they work in other animals, may help us to identify strategies to counteract their most severe effects. The brain mechanisms producing judgement shifts are actually quite similar across humans and other mammals. Antidepressant drugs such as fluoxetine that lift negative cognitions in humans have parallel effects on the cognition of nonhuman animals too. Thus, a fully comparative and adaptive approach to negative mood may aid us in understanding low mood, and perhaps eventually mood disorders, in humans.

Infanticide

One of the most appalling of all crimes is the killing of a child by the adults who should care for it. In fact it is so appalling (and rare) that we tend to reserve the label 'unnatural' for it. This means that when it does occur we can only view it as completely inexplicable. However, disturbingly, infanticide is actually not rare in nature. For example, in leopards in South Africa, killing by an adult leopard accounts for nearly half of all cub deaths, and leopards are not an isolated example. How could the killing of the young of a species by members of that species possibly have become so widespread?

Here, we have to remember that natural selection does not act for the good of the species. Instead it favours alleles that give their bearers a fitness advantage over the bearers of alternative alleles. In most mammals, the fitness of males is largely determined by their success at having females bear their offspring and raise them to independence. A male's own offspring contribute to his fitness and he would not be selected to harm them. However, the offspring of other males contribute nothing to his fitness. They may even be a hindrance, since females who are nursing young by another male will not be ready to conceive again. Thus, it could be adaptive for males to kill young that are not their offspring. In particular, they might be selected to do this during the period when the young are still nursing and preventing the female from returning to fertility. Therefore, from an adaptive perspective, we might predict that killing of young might occur in some situations. In such cases, we ought to expect that (1) it would be done by males, (2) it would only happen when those males were unrelated to the offspring, and (3) it would happen when the offspring were very young and delaying the female's return to fertility.

Infanticide by leopards exactly fits this pattern (Balme & Hunter, 2013). Cubs are killed only by males. They are particularly likely to be killed by males that have recently come into the territory and thus are unlikely to be their father. They are generally only killed when very young, aged less than the typical interval between successive births. When they are killed, their mothers conceive and give birth again sooner than if they had lived. Does this have any relevance to humans? Happily, infanticide is not widespread in humans like it is in leopards. However, men are sensitive to whether children are related to them or not. Psychologists have shown that men report a stronger liking of baby faces if those faces are manipulated using computer software to look like them (Platek, Burch, Panyavin, Wasserman, & Gallup, 2002). Their brains even respond more strongly to these stimuli, presumably reflecting deep motivational mechanisms activated by children who look related (Platek et al., 2004).

Occasionally, adults do abuse and even kill children in their care. The perpetrator is almost always a man and almost always unrelated to the child, and the child is almost always very young. An infamous case is that of Peter Connolly ('Baby P'), who was battered to death at the age of 17 months in London in 2007 (BBC News, 2013). In this case, there were not one but two unrelated males in the household (the mother's partner and his brother) and they appear to have been responsible for the bulk of the violence. The two men were later sent to prison, but one of the hard questions for the social services was how they had failed to respond to warning signs: a very young child, living with an unrelated male, having repeated visible injuries.

Figure 3.9 shows the age-specific rates of homicide for children in Canada, for children living with a male who is their father (on the left) and a male who is their stepfather (on the right). As you can see, homicide by the child's biological father basically never happens. When the man is biologically unrelated, homicide is hundreds of times more likely, especially when the child is under two, and the risk rapidly declines as the child exceeds the age at which the mother is likely to be ready to father another child (Daly & Wilson, 1988). Don't be alarmed – the rates in Figure 3.9 are per million children, showing that infanticide is very rare in absolute terms. Most stepfathers are caring and represent no danger to their stepchildren. Nonetheless, it remains the case that the biggest predictor of deliberate harm to a child is the presence of an unrelated male in the household when the child is very young.

What are we to make of this example? Does it mean that men are dangerous and infanticidal by nature, with their urges only kept in check by modern social control? This is clearly not the case, since men in many different societies provide loving care for children who are not their own. Rather, we need to recognize the complex evolved structure of human motivation. People are not leopards. We have a

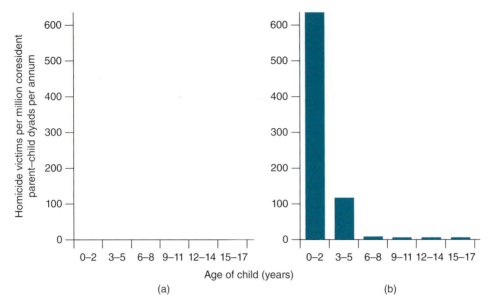

FIGURE 3.9 *Age-specific homicides rate for Canadian children by age who are living with their biological father (a) and with an unrelated male (b).*

Source: Republished with permission of Transaction Aldine from Daly and Wilson (1988); permission conveyed through Copyright Clearance Center, Inc.

completely different family system and a whole host of other social constraints on our behaviour. On the other hand, we do have millions of years of mammalian evolution in our pedigrees. For much of that time there was selection on males to prioritize siring their own offspring over females' investment in their existing offspring. This history has left traces in the psychology of men's responses to children. The harming of children is not in any sense justified or normalized by the fact that infanticide is widespread in other mammals. It does, however, help us to understand in which situations children are at greatest risk of not getting the care they need.

Learning and the lifecycle in humans and chimpanzees

The two species of chimpanzee are our closest living relatives. Genetic evidence reveals that we are really very closely related to the chimpanzees, much more closely related than the chimpanzees are to gorillas. Our ancestors and those of the chimpanzees probably diverged in the period 5–7 million years ago. It seems obvious (e.g. from the fact that I am typing these words on a computer) that some very extraordinary evolutionary developments have occurred in the recent history of the human lineage. Having the living chimpanzees as a comparison allows us to begin to focus on exactly what those developments might have been.

An instructive way of thinking about how human life differs from chimpanzee life is to consider how our production and consumption of food resources changes with age (Kaplan, Hill, Lancaster, & Hurtado, 2000). Chimpanzees begin to forage for themselves in the first year or two of life. They can largely support themselves by the age of 5 and are completely independent before 10. They then provision themselves until they die; other chimpanzees will not feed the elderly. Crucially, adult male chimpanzees never gather more resources than they need for their own immediate consumption (Figure 3.10).

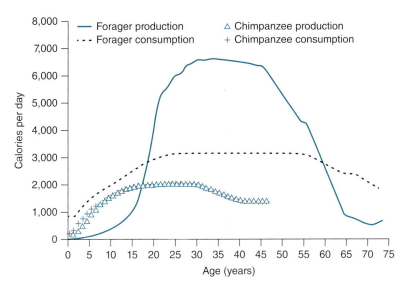

FIGURE 3.10 *Daily production and consumption of resources against age for male chimpanzees and male human hunter-gatherers (foragers).*

Source: Data from Kaplan, Hill, Lancaster, and Hurtado (2000).

In modern societies, very few people are directly involved in food production. If we want human data to compare to the chimpanzees, we need to turn to one of the small groups of hunter-gatherers who still live in various places around the world. Figure 3.10 also shows average production and consumption of food for hunter-gatherer men. As you can see, human children are not able to produce what they need until they are around 20, and before 15 they produce only a tiny fraction of it, even in a society with no schools. Between 20 and 60, they not only produce enough for themselves but also generate a large surplus, often bringing in more than twice what they require. From around 60, their productivity declines, and by 65 they do not produce as much as they consume. It is quite surprising that, in an economic system radically different from our own, the period in which men are economically productive corresponds so closely to the age range that people in developed societies call their career (around 20 to 65).

It is clear from Figure 3.10 what must be happening in humans. The large surplus generated by adults of prime age is being socially redistributed to make up the short-fall of the young and the elderly. Young humans have a long childhood period, and this period is subsidized by adults, who are able to produce surplus to their require-ments. Then, as adults age, their direct productive capacities wane, but again they are subsidized by the prime-age adults.

The prolonged childhood and the adult surplus are linked phenomena, and they tell us a lot about our psychology. Chimpanzees and other apes forage in very straightforward ways. They pick leaves and fruits. They hunt monkeys, and they also crack nuts with stones, probe in holes for termites, and raid bee nests for honey using sticks. Nonetheless, these are all skills that can be learned relatively quickly, which is why chimpanzees can produce most of their food by the time they are aged five. By contrast, even the most technologically basic human society uses complex techniques such as building traps and nets, using arrows or poison darts, fishing with poles and lines, smoking animals out, and so on. Such skills require a great deal of time to learn. Correspondingly, we have evolved the prolonged childhood period, during which the human brain is incredibly plastic, and the child's job is to learn the complex skills prevalent in their environment, through play as much as anything else. Human skills are investments that take a long time to provide a return, but the return is very good when it comes. Human foraging skills are so productive that, once they are acquired, the adults comfortably produce enough to redistribute to the generations above and below them (and the surplus can also be traded, of course, allowing for the basis of the market economy). Adults have an obvious fitness interest in subsidizing their children's learning time, but older adults have an important value too. They are the repository of skills and knowledge, and, across all documented human societies, older adults play an important role as grandparents, providing care and stimulation to their grandchildren.

In terms of how humans live, then, we can highlight some important differences from chimpanzees. A chimpanzee, though living in a social group, is basically self-sufficient for most of its life. Humans are always involved in a cooperative system of social resource transfer, either on the receiving end or on the providing end, or both. Humans are also great learners. However, it's not just that they are better at learning in some general sense than chimpanzees are. Instead, humans seem to be particularly skilled at **social learning**. Social learning is learning from the behaviour of others, rather than just individual trial and error. It is because humans have such highly developed capacities of social learning that every human society produces its own distinctive behavioural traditions, which we call culture. Culture arises as each new generation incorporates the learned behaviours of the previous one into its repertoire. Culture exists in rudimentary form in chimpanzees. For example, different chimpanzee populations have different repertoires of tool use. However, in humans, culture is taken to a new level. In particular, our sophisticated social learning allows for **cumulative cultural evolution**. This refers to the fact that human technologies and institutions become more advanced with every passing generation, until the point where they are so complex that, if they were lost, no single individual would possibly be able to reinvent them in one lifetime. Cumulative cultural evolution can occur because of very rapid, high-fidelity social learning by children, coupled with intelligent elaboration on what is learned.

If we had to characterize the main ways our psychology differs from that of chimpanzees, then, we would focus on the social dimensions of cognition; humans readily form social arrangements for redistribution of resources, adeptly learn socially from others, and, of course, have language, a system for the social transmission of information and the social coordination of behaviour unlike anything seen in other primates. Strong evidence for social cognition being central to human uniqueness comes from a study by Herrmann, Call, Hernandez-Lloreda, Hare, and Tomasello (2007). The researchers tested 106 chimpanzees, 32 orangutans, and 105 human children (2.5 years old) on a large battery of cognitive tasks. Some tasks involved physical cognition, such as using a tool, whereas others were social, such as working out the experimenters' intention. The children were no better than the chimpanzees in the physical cognition tasks. Where they consistently and clearly outperformed all the apes was in the tasks involving a social element (Figure 3.11).

Why did humans evolve a way of life based on difficult foraging techniques, prolonged social learning, and social cooperation, whereas chimpanzees did not? This is not well understood. The home of the common ancestor of chimpanzees and humans is the tropical African forest. The climate has been highly variable in Africa over the

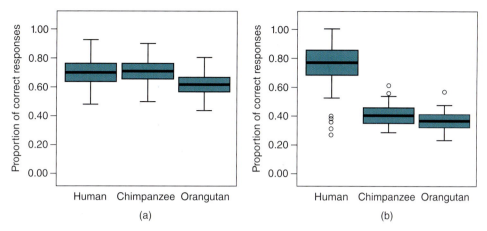

FIGURE 3.11 *Proportion of correct responses on a battery of cognitive tasks in human children, chimpanzees, and orangutans. Panel (a) shows physical tasks, such as using a tool or mentally rotating a shape, while panel (b) shows social tasks, such as inferring the intention of another individual or learning from what someone else is doing.*

Source: Herrmann, Call, Hernandez-Lloreda, Hare, and Tomasello (2007). Reprinted with permission from AAAS.

past few million years. It seems that the chimpanzees stayed in their ancestral habitat, retreating as the forests retreated in periods when Africa was dry. Humans, by contrast, came out of the forests into more open and varied habitats. They may have effectively become specialists at coping with environmental variation and change, becoming good at acquiring different techniques as circumstances or their location changed. For a long period, this was only marginally successful; the human population remained extremely small. However, in the past 2 million years, they began to spread beyond Africa. More decisively, in the past 100,000 years, they were able to use their flexible abilities to colonize every continent, including many environments radically different from the tropical savannahs whence they came.

DISCUSSION POINT

Discuss the following statement:

The fact that humans have cumulative culture means that genetics is less important for understanding human behaviour than it is for understanding the behaviour of other animals.

TEST YOURSELF

1. In the experiment by Bateson and Matheson (2007), why was birds' flipping a grey lid taken as an indication of 'optimism'?

2. Why would it be adaptive for male leopards to kill cubs?

3. How do human infants manage to have such a long period of inability to provide for themselves and still survive?

ACTIVITY 3.3

TRUE OR FALSE?

Indicate whether each statement is true or false.

- When faced with ambiguous stimuli, depressed or anxious people are prone to give the most negative possible interpretation.
- Negative cognitive biases are not found in other animals.
- Infanticide is rare in nature.
- Bateson and Matheson (2007) devised a task where starlings had to try and undo a latch on their cage.
- When animals are in a good environment or good state, they tend to make more positive judgements about the meaning of ambiguous stimuli.
- Psychologists have shown that men report a stronger dislike of baby faces if those faces are manipulated using computer software to look like them.
- Natural selection does not act for the good of the species.
- Leopard cubs are killed only by males.
- Social learning is learning from only individual trial and error, rather than the behaviour of others.
- Chimpanzees are completely independent before the age of 10.
- In modern societies, the majority of people are directly involved in food production.
- The capacity of humans for learned behavioural traditions to become more and more complex with each passing generation is known as cumulative cultural evolution.

SECTION SUMMARY

- We can look at a psychological question or effect through an evolutionary lens.
- Negative cognitive biases are an important component of how clinical conditions such as depression maintain themselves over time and are not just a human quirk.
- Shifting your cognitive bias according to your current situation is a capacity that might have adaptive value. Understanding the evolutionary function of these processes, and the way they work in other animals, may help to identify strategies to counteract their most severe effects.
- It is important to remember that natural selection does not act for the good of the species. Thus, from an adaptive perspective, we might predict that killing of young might occur in some situations. In such cases, we ought to expect that (1) it would be done by males, (2) it would only happen when those males were unrelated to the offspring, and (3) it would happen when the offspring were very young and delaying the female's return to fertility. The biggest predictor of deliberate harm to a child is the presence of an unrelated male in the household when the child is very young.
- The two species of chimpanzee are our closest living relatives. Genetic evidence reveals that we are extremely closely related to the chimpanzees, and having the living chimpanzees as a comparison allows us to begin to focus on exactly how we are both the same and different. The ways in which our production and consumption of food resources change with age is one way of doing this.
- Humans seem to be particularly skilled at social learning, which allows for cumulative cultural evolution.

FUTURE DIRECTIONS

LEARNING OBJECTIVE 3.7

Describe examples of how adaptive and comparative thinking can be brought to bear on psychological questions.

The study of evolution and genetics in relation to psychology is a rapidly developing area. In this final section, we review the most active areas of research and likely future directions within them.

Genetics

No field of the life sciences moves as fast as genetics. You can get some sense of the rapidity of technical progress by browsing journals such as ***PLOS Genetics***[3]. Modern sequencing techniques have made it possible to 'read' the complete DNA sequence in different cells in different organisms directly and relatively fast. It is less than 20 years since the first complete sequence of the genome of any organism was produced. We now have complete or near-complete genomes for many dozens of different species, including extinct ones such as Neanderthals. The complete human genome was first sequenced in 2001. The first human genomes to be sequenced cost millions of dollars; the cost now is probably in the thousands but will soon be in the hundreds or less. Thus, the most likely future direction for human genetics is that quite soon we will for the first time have available the complete genome sequences of many thousands of people, perhaps even whole populations: the **1000 Genomes Projects**[4] was one of the first projects in this direction.

This is particularly important for psychological genetics. There has been a sense of slight disappointment recently that, although we believe psychological characteristics such as intelligence, personality, and vulnerability to psychological disorders to be heritable, we have discovered few of the alleles that are actually involved. Those that we have found only explain a tiny proportion of the heritable effects. This was discussed earlier as the problem of missing heritability.

The association studies done to date have not used the complete genome sequence of the participants but instead a series of markers spread over the genome. Having the complete genome sequence will allow much more sophisticated modelling of the ways that human genomes differ. It is also important that researchers are able to sharply increase the sample sizes they work with. If there are many genes involved in a trait, we will only be able to reliably detect them in very large samples. As well as having many participants, it will be important to have participants whose developmental history is well understood. We are coming to appreciate the ubiquity and importance of gene by environment interactions for psychology (see Focus Point 3.5). These mean that knowing people's genotype is not informative for understanding their psychological outcomes without knowing in detail about their environmental histories too. Increasingly, researchers are using longitudinal cohort studies to answer questions about genetic and environmental effects. In these studies, a population of people is recruited, often at birth, and regularly re-contacted as they grow up. Their genotypes are measured, but so too are all the life events that they experience over time, and their psychological outcomes. These study designs allow gene by environment interactions to be detected, and also allow us to understand the very long-term effects of early environmental factors.

Finally, geneticists are becoming more and more interested not just in what DNA sequences people have but also in how their genes are expressed. Gene expression refers to the level of transcriptional activity of particular genes in particular tissues at particular times. Modern technologies allow the expression levels of thousands of genes to be measured simultaneously. People respond to events such as stress with different gene-expression profiles. These different profiles arise from their genotype, but also from their developmental histories and long-term exposure to environmental events. The study of such long-term alterations in gene expression is called **epigenetics**. Epigenetics will doubtless become a major part of psychology as it becomes better understood (Zhang & Meaney, 2010). It may be a key part of understanding how childhood events can increase vulnerability to disorders such as depression.

Comparative psychology

Something we stressed in this chapter was the importance of comparative information on the psychology of other species. The wealth of comparative information continues to grow, and will do so at an accelerating rate as study techniques become more sophisticated. Often, questions about the neurobiological mechanisms, developmental trajectory, or fitness consequences of a behaviour pattern can be more feasibly studied in a shorter-lived animal than in ourselves. A great recent example comes from the genetics of personality in a familiar garden bird, the great tit. In humans, a number of studies have suggested that variation in a gene called DRD4 might be relevant to the personality dimension of extraversion. Bearers of one allele tend to be slightly more outgoing and novelty-seeking than bearers of the other. The corresponding gene also exists in great tits, also has different alleles, and in the birds too those alleles are related to personality. Personality in birds is assessed by measuring their exploratory behaviour in a standardized novel environment. If anything, this allows for more precise measurement of behavioural phenotype than the self-report questionnaires usually used in humans. In great tits, one allele of DRD4 is associated with a tendency to explore the novel more rapidly (Fidler et al., 2007). Researchers of birds have been able to go one step further than researchers of humans can; Fidler et al. (2007) selected for rapid exploration, choosing in each generation the birds that were most exploratory and letting them breed. They selected who was to breed on the basis of phenotype, not genotype. After four generations, the researchers found that they had sharply increased the frequency of the high-exploration allele in the birds.

The other thing that researchers of birds can do that would be difficult in humans is to study the fitness consequences of being fast or slow in exploration in the wild. Dingemanse, Both, Drent, and Tinbergen (2004) did this by marking birds and tracking their survival and reproduction. It turns out that neither fast nor slow explorers have higher fitness overall. Instead, in some years the fast explorers do well and in other years, with other environmental conditions, it is the slow explorers who do best. This presumably is the reason that both types coexist in the population in the long term. Comparable arguments can be made about the range of observed personality variation in humans. Understanding how natural selection sculpts variation in populations is something that is set to increase in the future, and nonhuman animals with shorter lifecycles than ours will provide much of the information.

Evolution in psychology

Since the 1990s, we have seen the rise of an approach called 'evolutionary psychology' that seeks to bring adaptive explanations more centrally into the way we theorize in psychology. The starting point for evolutionary psychology is to use the question 'What good would it do the organism for the system to work this way?' to generate hypotheses that can be tested using psychological experiments (much as we saw with the finger-wrinkling example discussed at the start of the chapter). Evolutionary psychology has produced some very interesting work on, for example, why the two sexes differ psychologically in the particular ways that they do, and on the ways we make social decisions. You can find summaries of this work in evolutionary psychology textbooks such as Buss (2013). You can also browse the online journals **_Evolution & Human Behavior_**[5] or **_Evolutionary Psychology_**[6] to get a feel for the latest research (both require a personal or institutional subscription).

However, although evolutionary psychology is a flourishing area of the discipline, it may, in the fullness of time, disappear as a distinct entity. The reason for this is that people are beginning to appreciate that taking an evolutionary perspective is not an alternative to, for example, taking a social, cognitive, or developmental perspective. The evolutionary perspective means being prepared to think adaptively and comparatively while doing psychological research. This can (indeed should) be done _within_ paradigms such as cognitive, social, or developmental psychology. Having a separate category called evolutionary psychology encourages the view that evolutionary thinking is something you can do if you want to but are free to ignore if you don't. This does not make sense; all biologists agree that evolution occurred and that the human brain has an evolutionary history partly shared with the brains of other animals. In this sense, there is no such thing as _non_-evolutionary psychology. There is just psychology, and one aspect of psychology is comparative and adaptive questions.

By the same token, having a subdiscipline called evolutionary psychology encourages the belief that taking an evolutionary perspective is _sufficient_ for being able to do psychological research. Again, this is wrong. All psychologists need a good understanding of methods, experimental design, and what is already known about psychological mechanisms. Thus, evolutionary psychology must always be connected to the rest of the body of psychological research. Ideally, it would infuse that body so deeply that people would not notice when they were specifically taking an evolutionary perspective.

SECTION SUMMARY

- The field of genetics is incredibly fast-moving and it is important to keep up to date with developments in research by reading and browsing relevant journals.
- We are coming to appreciate the ubiquity and importance of gene by environment interactions for psychology.

- Geneticists are becoming more and more interested not just in what DNA sequences people have but also in how their genes are expressed. Gene expression refers to the level of transcriptional activity of particular genes in particular tissues at particular times. The study of such long-term alterations in gene expression is called epigenetics.

- Understanding how natural selection sculpts variation in populations is something that is set to increase in future, and nonhuman animals with shorter lifecycles than ours will provide much of the information.

- Evolutionary psychology asks the central question 'What good would it do the organism for the system to work this way?' in order to generate hypotheses that can be tested using psychological experiments.

- People are increasingly beginning to appreciate that taking an evolutionary perspective is not an alternative to, for example, taking a social, cognitive, or developmental perspective.

CHAPTER SUMMARY

This chapter has considered the ways in which an understanding of evolution and genetics contributes to the study of modern psychology. We did this by first outlining the fundamental principles of genetic evolution: variation, heredity, and differential reproductive success. We then moved on to a consideration of how evolutionary and genetic thinking has been useful in psychological research and concluded with an examination of likely future directions within this fast-moving field. The evolutionary perspective underlines the importance of adaptive and comparative thinking in our efforts to understand ourselves as a species; we are the products of a shared evolutionary history and the goal of this exciting and rapidly developing research area is to bring adaptive explanations more centrally into the way we theorize in psychology.

ESSAY QUESTIONS

1. Human beings first occupied northern Europe around 40,000 years ago, migrating from Africa. Sometime in the following thousands of years, those living in Europe evolved pale skins, while those who had remained in Africa and other tropical regions retained their dark skins. Give a detailed account of the mechanisms by which these adaptive differences might have evolved, using the terms 'mutation', 'variation', 'heritable', 'fitness', 'environment', 'selection', and 'fixation' in your answer.

2. To what extent do culture and biological evolution provide alternative explanations for human psychological phenomena?

KEY TERMS

- **adaptive explanation:** An explanation for a trait in terms of that trait's value for survival or reproduction.
- **allele:** An alternative form of a gene.

- **altruism:** In evolutionary biology, behaviour that decreases the actor's personal fitness while increasing the fitness of another individual. In psychology, the term is used more broadly to describe behaviours by one individual that benefit another individual.
- **association studies:** Studies that attempt to identify the particular genes that contribute to a phenotype, by comparing genetic data from large numbers of people with and without that phenotype.
- **autosomal:** Relating to genes that reside in the nucleus of a cell and not on the sex chromosomes.
- **base pairing:** The principle whereby every base on one strand of a DNA molecule binds to a specific base on the other strand, so that cytosine always binds to guanine and vice versa, and adenine always binds to thymine and vice versa.
- **chromosome:** A DNA-bearing structure in the nucleus of a cell.
- **coefficient of relatedness:** A measure of how much more genetically similar two individuals are than randomly selected individuals would be.
- **cooperation:** Behaviour by one individual that benefits another individual or individuals.
- **cumulative cultural evolution:** The capacity of humans for learned behavioural traditions to become more and more complex with each passing generation.
- **differential reproduction or differential reproductive success:** The principle that not all individuals born produce the same number of descendants.
- **DNA:** Deoxyribonucleic acid, the molecule from which the genome is made.
- **dominant:** Of an allele, requiring only one copy to be present in an individual for that individual to develop the associated phenotype.
- **environment of evolutionary adaptedness:** The range of environmental conditions that a species has experienced recurrently over evolutionary time.
- **epigenetics:** The study of long-term alterations in gene expression – for example, alterations caused by stress during development or environmental exposures.
- **eusocial breeding systems:** Breeding systems where one subgroup of the population (the queens) do all the reproduction and other subgroups (workers) expend effort in furthering the queen's reproduction.
- **fitness:** The absolute or relative success at leaving descendants of an individual or class of individuals.
- **fixation:** Of an allele, being present in almost every individual in a population.
- **gene:** A stretch of DNA that is transcribed and has some phenotypic function. This may or may not mean being translated into protein.
- **genome:** The total set of DNA that an individual possesses.
- **genotype:** The combination of alleles of a particular gene or set of genes that an individual possesses.
- **Hamilton's rule:** The conditions required for an allele causing one individual to help another at no direct benefit to themselves to spread by natural selection. Normally expressed as $rb > c$, where r is the coefficient of relatedness, b is the fitness benefit of being helped, and c is the fitness cost of helping.
- **heredity:** The principle that characteristics are passed from parents to their offspring.
- **heritability:** The proportion of population variation in a trait that is associated with variation in genes.
- **heterozygous:** Of a genotype, having one copy each of two different alleles.
- **homozygous:** Of a genotype, having two copies of the same allele.
- **mechanistic explanation:** An explanation for a characteristic in terms of how that characteristic comes about rather than what good it does the organism.
- **meiosis:** The specialized form of cell division that produces a sperm or egg rather than a normal body cell.
- **Mendelian diseases:** Diseases, such as cystic fibrosis, that are directly caused by an allele of one gene and where the pattern of inheritance is therefore simple to determine.

- **mitosis:** The normal process of cell division by which a body cell produces daughters that are genetic clones of itself.
- **mutation:** Changes in DNA sequence that arise from copying errors.
- **phenotype:** The set of observable characteristics of individuals resulting from the interaction of their genotype with the environment.
- **quantitative genetics:** The set of methods for studying the inheritance of traits where many genes are involved.
- **recessive:** Of an allele, requiring two copies to be present in an individual for that individual to develop the associated phenotype.
- **recombination:** The exchange of genetic information between two different genomes. In some animals, such as humans, this occurs at meiosis when a sperm fertilizes an egg.
- **RNA:** Ribonucleic acid. A single-stranded molecule similar to DNA and serving important functions in transcription and translation.
- **social learning:** Learning from other members of a population.
- **transcription:** The process by which an RNA 'readout' of a DNA sequence is formed.
- **translation:** The process whereby an RNA sequence is turned into a sequence of amino acids and thence a protein.
- **variation:** The principle that, in each generation, individuals differ from one another in phenotype.

NOTES

1. https://www.youtube.com/playlist?list=PLbnrZHfNEDZzmKKvdLUKVGpaQeg4tVrPi
2. https://www.ted.com/talks/jim_fallon_exploring_the_mind_of_a_killer#t-2593
3. http://www.plosgenetics.org/
4. http://www.internationalgenome.org/
5. http://www.ehbonline.org
6. http://journals.sagepub.com/home/evp

FURTHER RESOURCES

Association for the Study of Animal Behaviour. (2017). Retrieved 20 November 2017 from http://www.asab.org (The main scholarly association for the study of animal behaviour in the United Kingdom and Europe.)

Buss, D. M. 2009. The great struggles of life: Darwin and the emergence of evolutionary psychology. *American Psychologist*, 64, 140–148.

Buss, D. M. (2013). *Evolutionary psychology: The new science of mind* (4th ed.). Harlow, UK: Pearson.

Davies, N. B., Krebs, J. R., & West, S. A. (2012). *An introduction to behavioural ecology* (4th ed.). Chichester, UK: Wiley-Blackwell.

Dawkins, R. (1989). *The selfish gene* (Rev. ed.). Oxford, UK: Oxford University Press.

Eichler, E. E., Flint, J., Gibson, G., Kong, A., Leal, S. M., Moore, J. H., & Nadeau, J. H. 2010. Missing heritability and strategies for finding the underlying causes of complex disease. *Nature Reviews Genetics*, 11, 446–450.

European Human Behaviour and Evolution Association. (2017). Retrieved 20 November 2017 from http://ehbea.com (A European society for the study of human behaviour from an evolutionary perspective.)

Evolution Institute. (2017). *This view of life*. Retrieved 20 November 2017 from http://www.thisviewoflife.com (An online magazine covering anything and everything [including psychology] from an evolutionary perspective.)

Human Behavior and Evolution Society. Retrieved 20 November 2017 from http://www.hbes.com (An international society for the study of human behaviour from an evolutionary perspective.)

Keller, M. C., & Nesse, R. M. 2006. The evolutionary significance of depressive symptoms: Different adverse situations lead to different depressive symptom patterns. *Journal of Personality and Social Psychology*, *91*, 316–330.

Nettle, D. (2006). The evolution of personality variation in humans and other animals. *American Psychologist*, *61*, 622–631.

Nettle, D. (2009). *Evolution and genetics for psychology.* Oxford, UK: Oxford University Press.

Plomin, R., & Daniels, D. 2011. Why are children in the same family so different from one another? *International Journal of Epidemiology*, *40*, 563–582.

Stearns, S. C., Byars, S. G., Govindaraju, D. R., & Ewbank, D. 2010. Measuring selection in contemporary human populations. *Nature Reviews Genetics*, *11*, 611–622.

Tomasello, M., Carpenter, M., Call, J., Behne, T., & Moll, H. 2005. Understanding and sharing intentions: The origins of cultural cognition. *Behavioral and Brain Sciences*, *28*, 675–691.

REFERENCES

Balme, G. A., & Hunter, L. T. B. (2013). Why leopards commit infanticide. *Animal Behaviour*, *86*(4), 791–799.

Bateson, M., & Matheson, S. M. (2007). Performance on a categorisation task suggests that removal of environmental enrichment induces 'pessimism' in captive European starlings (*Sturnus vulgaris*). *Animal Welfare*, *16*, 33–36.

BBC News. (2013, October 8). Timeline of Baby P case. Retrieved 19 March 2018 from http://www.bbc.co.uk/news/uk-11626806

Brunner, H. G., Nelen, M., Breakefield, X. O., Ropers, H. H., & Van Oost, B. A. (1993). Abnormal behavior associated with a point mutation in the structural gene for monoamine oxidase A. *Science*, *262*(5133), 578–580. doi:10.1126/science.8211186

Buss, D. M. (2013). *Evolutionary psychology: The new science of the mind.* Harlow, UK: Pearson Educational.

Caspi, A., McClay, J., Moffitt, T. E., Mill, J., Martin, J., Craig, I. W., … Poulton, R. (2002). Role of genotype in the cycle of violence in maltreated children. *Science*, *297*(5582), 851–854. doi:10.1126/science.1072290

Caspi, A., Sugden, K., Moffitt, T. E., Taylor, A., Craig, I. W., Harrington, H., … Poulton, R. (2003). Influence of life stress on depression: Moderation by a polymorphism in the 5-HTT gene. *Science*, *301*(5631), 386–389. doi:10.1126/science.1083968

Changizi, M., Weber, R., Kotecha, R., & Palazzo, J. (2011). Are wet-induced wrinkled fingers primate rain treads? *Brain, Behavior and Evolution*, *77*(4), 286–290.

Daly, M., & Wilson, M. (1988). Evolutionary social psychology and family homicide. *Science*, *242*, 519–524.

Dingemanse, N. J., Both, C., Drent, P. J., & Tinbergen, J. M. (2004). Fitness consequences of avian personalities in a fluctuating environment. *Proceedings of the Royal Society B: Biological Sciences*, *271*, 847–852.

Eysenck, M. W., Mogg, K., May, J., Richards, A., & Mathews, A. (1991). Bias in interpretation of ambiguous sentences related to threat in anxiety. *Journal of Abnormal Psychology*, *100*(2), 144–150.

Fidler, A. E., Van Oers, K., Drent, P. J., Kuhn, S., Mueller, J. C., & Kempenaers, B. (2007). Drd4 gene polymorphisms are associated with personality variation in a passerine bird. *Proceedings of the Royal Society B: Biological Sciences*, *274*(1619), 1685–1691. doi:10.1098/rspb.2007.0337

Haseleu, J., Omerbašić, D., Frenzel, H., Gross, M., & Lewin, G. R. (2014). Water induced finger wrinkles do not affect touch acuity or dexterity in handling wet objects. *PLoS ONE*, *9*(1), e84949. doi:10.1371/journal.pone.0084949

Herrmann, E., Call, J., Hernandez-Lloreda, M. V., Hare, B., & Tomasello, M. (2007). Humans have evolved specialized skills of social cognition: The cultural intelligence hypothesis. *Science*, *317*(5843), 1360–1366. doi:10.1126/science.1146282

Kaplan, H., Hill, K., Lancaster, J., & Hurtado, A. M. (2000). A theory of human life history evolution: Diet, intelligence, and longevity. *Evolutionary Anthropology*, *9*(4), 156–185.

Kareklas, K., Nettle, D., & Smulders, T. V. (2013). Water-induced finger wrinkles improve handling of wet objects. *Biology Letters*, *9*(2). doi:10.1098/rsbl.2012.0999

McDermott, R., Dawes, C., Prom-Wormley, E., Eaves, L., & Hatemi, P. K. (2013). MAOA and aggression: A gene–environment interaction in two populations. *Journal of Conflict Resolution*, *57*(6), 1043–1064. doi:10.1177/0022002712457746

Nettle, D. (2009). *Evolution and genetics for psychology*. Oxford, UK: Oxford University Press.

Platek, S. M., Burch, R. L., Panyavin, I. S., Wasserman, B. H., & Gallup, G. G. (2002). Reactions to children's faces: Resemblance affects males more than females. *Evolution & Human Behavior*, *23*(3), 159–166.

Platek, S. M., Raines, D. M., Gallup, G. G., Mohamed, F. B., Thomson, J. W., Myers, T. E., … Arigo, D. R. (2004). Reactions to children's faces: Males are more affected by resemblance than females are, and so are their brains. *Evolution & Human Behavior*, *25*(6), 394–405. doi:10.1016/j.evolhumbehav.2004.08.007

Turkheimer, E., Haley, A., D'Onofrio, B., Waldron, M., Emery, R. E., & Gottesman, I. I. (2003). Socioeconomic status modifies heritability of intelligence in young children. *Psychological Science*, *14*(6), 623–628.

West, S. A., El Mouden, C., & Gardner, A. (2011). Sixteen common misconceptions about the evolution of cooperation in humans. *Evolution & Human Behavior*, *32*(4), 231–262. doi:10.1016/j.evolhumbehav.2010.08.001

Young, L. J., Nilsen, R., Waymire, K. G., MacGregor, G. R., & Insel, T. R. (1999). Increased affiliative response to vasopressin in mice expressing the V1a receptor from a monogamous vole. *Nature*, *400*(6746), 766–768.

Zhang, T. Y., & Meaney, M. J. (2010). Epigenetics and the environmental regulation of the genome and its function. *Annual Review of Psychology*, *61*, 439–466.

ACTIVITY SOLUTIONS

ACTIVITY 3.1: MENDELIAN GENETICS OF SEX-LINKED TRAITS

Daughters = 0% affected
Sons = 50% affected

We stated that the mother is a carrier, so her genotype is *Aa*. We first considered the case where she married a non-haemophiliac man. He only has one X chromosome, but, since he does not have haemophilia, he must have an *A* on it, so we will designate his genotype *A0*.

(a) The daughters of this marriage will get either *A* or *a* from their mum with equal probability. However, all of them will get *A* from their dad, since *A* is the only allele of this gene that he has. Therefore, all of the daughters will have at least one copy of *A* and none of them will be affected by haemophilia.

(b) The sons from this marriage will get either *A* or *a* from their mum with equal probability. They won't get any allele at all from their dad, since they will get a Y chromosome from him and not an X. Therefore, their genotype will be *A0* or *a0* with equal probability. Since *a0* means having no copy of the normal-type allele *A*, half of the sons will therefore be affected by haemophilia.

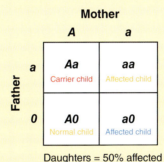

Daughters = 50% affected
Sons = 50% affected

We next considered the case where the same woman marries a man affected by haemophilia. He must have genotype *a0*.

(a) Their daughters will get either *A* or *a* from their mum with equal probability. In all cases they will get *a* from their dad. Their genotypes will therefore be half *Aa* and half *aa*, and so half will be affected by haemophilia.

(b) The genotypes for the sons from this marriage will be the same as for (b). It is immaterial what the dad has on his X chromosome, as he cannot pass this to his sons anyway. Half of the sons will be affected by haemophilia. Counterintuitively, the dad's genotype only matters for the daughters in this example, whereas the mum's genotype is critical to the sons!

ACTIVITY 3.2: PUNNETT SQUARES

1. c: 50%

2. d: 25%

3. b: 75%

ACTIVITY 3.3: TRUE OR FALSE?

True

- When faced with ambiguous stimuli, depressed or anxious people are prone to give the most negative possible interpretation.

- When animals are in a good environment or good state, they tend to make more positive judgements about the meaning of ambiguous stimuli.
- Natural selection does not act for the good of the species.
- Leopard cubs are killed only by males.
- Chimpanzees are completely independent before the age of 10.
- The capacity of humans for learned behavioural traditions to become more and more complex with each passing generation is known as cumulative cultural evolution.

False

- Negative cognitive biases are not found in other animals.
- Bateson and Matheson (2007) devised a task where starlings had to try and undo a latch on their cage.
- Infanticide is rare in nature.
- Psychologists have shown that men report a stronger dislike of baby faces if those faces are manipulated using computer software to look like them.
- In modern societies, the majority of people are directly involved in food production.
- Social learning is learning from only individual trial and error, rather than the behaviour of others.

4 Neuroscience, the Brain, and Behaviour

JAMIE WARD AND SARAH KING

INTRODUCTION

LEARNING OBJECTIVE 4.1

Demonstrate an awareness of the beginnings of modern brain research.

On 13 September 1848, a man called Phineas Gage (Figure 4.1) was working on the Rutland and Burlington railroad in the northeastern United States. He was using a large metal rod (a tamping iron) to pack explosive charges into the ground when a charge accidentally exploded. This pushed the tamping iron up through the top of his skull and it landed about 30 metres behind him. Despite experiencing such a horrific brain injury, Gage was still capable of performing quite complex functions. He was able to walk back to his hotel, sign himself absent from work, and contact a doctor to come and attend to him (Harlow, 1993; Macmillan, 1986). Despite having much of his intellect preserved, he was 'no longer Gage' (Macmillan, 1986, p. 85). Selective damage to parts of his frontal lobe had affected his personality such that he was indifferent to other people, impatient and impulsive, and unable to make and stick to

FIGURE 4.1 *Phineas Gage after his accident.*

plans. After various temporary jobs, including a stint in Barnum's Museum, he died of epilepsy (a secondary consequence of his injury) in San Francisco some 12 years after his accident.

The brain, and the complex network of neurons in it, is what makes you who you are: how you react to others, the decisions that you make, and the risks you take. It dictates not only our personality but also all aspects of our thoughts and behaviour: our actions, language, memories, perceptions, and emotions. Despite the brain having such a central importance to our lives, virtually all of our knowledge of it stems from the past 150 years. For instance, around the time of Phineas Gage's accident, it was still undecided whether different parts of the brain serve different functions or whether all parts of the brain are functionally equivalent (cases such as Gage clearly favoured the former). One attempt to map different functions to different parts of the brain – termed 'phrenology' – had been discredited, and alternative ways of understanding the brain had yet to gain ground. At the time of Gage's accident, neurons had not even been described in terms of their basic structure.

SECTION SUMMARY

- The case of Phineas Gage, who in 1848 experienced a horrific brain injury but was still capable of performing quite complex functions, developed researchers' understanding of whether different parts of the brain serve different functions or whether all parts of the brain are functionally equivalent.

- The brain, and the complex network of neurons in it, is what makes you who you are.

- The brain dictates not only our personality but also all aspects of our thoughts and behaviour: our actions, language, memories, perceptions, and emotions.

- Virtually all of our knowledge of the brain stems from the past 150 years.

NEURONS AND SYNAPTIC TRANSMISSION

LEARNING OBJECTIVE 4.2

Describe the basic structure and functions of the neuron and the role of chemical signalling and neurotransmitters within the functioning of neurons.

All of our behaviour and thoughts are ultimately underpinned by the actions of one particular kind of cell in the body: the **neuron**. Neurons are specialized cells within the brain that provide the communication network that brings sensory information to the brain, processes that information within the brain, and sends motor outputs to the body. Disrupting the function of neurons (e.g. pharmacologically) or losing neurons (e.g. in patients who have dementia) affects behaviour and can be associated with impaired function. This section will start by considering the structure of the neuron and will then consider how neurons communicate both chemically and electrically. Finally, the section will outline how this structure and function can give rise to cognitive skills such as learning and memory, seeing, and hearing.

Structure of the neuron

Like all other cells in the body, neurons contain a nucleus within their cell body, but also specialized processes, the **dendrites**, which receive information from other neurons, and the **axon**, which transmits information from the cell body to a distant location either within the same brain region (an interneuron) or to another brain area (a projection neuron) (see Figure 4.2). Neurons pass information to one another through **synapses**. The synaptic cleft (gap) is located between the axon (presynaptic) and dendrite (postsynaptic). The pre- and postsynaptic terminals of a synapse have specific characteristics that allow the regulated release and detection, respectively, of chemical messengers (termed **neurotransmitters**).

Electrical activity of neurons

Signals are passed within the neuron by electrical activity. Information is transmitted from the cell body (in one brain area) to the synaptic terminal (in another). When a neuron 'fires', it generates an **action potential**, an electrical current (see Figure 4.3), which moves down the axon to the presynaptic terminal, where it causes neurotrans-mitter release (see following section on chemical signalling). The action potential is generated by the movement of positive ions across the membrane (e.g. between the outside and inside of the cell). When at rest, the neuron is not firing, and the membrane potential (e.g. the charge between the inside and outside of the neuron) is negative. This charge difference is maintained by the electrochemical gradient of the membrane and its permeability to different ions. The electrochemical gradient is determined by the many negatively charged proteins that are already present in the neuron, but also by actively pumping sodium ions (Na^+) out of the neuron and potassium ions (K^+) into it. The electrochemical gradient is necessary to allow electrical currents to be generated, and neurons expend a lot of energy maintaining it. Membrane permeability is determined by ion channels (specialized membrane proteins with a central pore), which allow the movement of ions through the membrane.

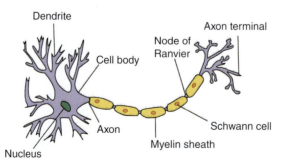

FIGURE 4.2 *The structure of a neuron.*
Source: Wikimedia Commons.

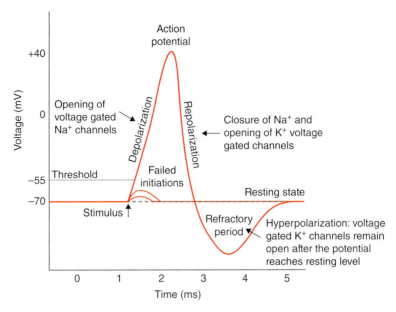

FIGURE 4.3 *Action potential.*

Source: Adapted from Wikimedia Commons.

Ion channels come in various shapes and sizes, and vary in terms of the ions that can move through them and the mechanisms by which they open and close (allowing the flow of ions). Which of these ion channels is open or closed determines the electrical potential of the membrane.

Sodium channels open when the membrane potential becomes positive. They open quickly and cause an inward rush of Na^+, further depolarizing the membrane (making it more positive) and causing an action potential to be generated (or 'fire'). In addition, slower K^+ channels are triggered by the change in voltage; K^+ moves out of the cell, repolarizing the membrane (making it more negative); and the Na^+ channels close. There is a period of hyperpolarization at the end of an action potential when the membrane becomes more negative than during its normal resting state. This refractory period allows a pause between action potentials and keeps them moving in a unidirectional manner. The axons are wrapped in a myelin sheath (fat) to provide insulation, thus speeding the conductance of action potentials down the axon. The properties of the action potential, and the roles of Na^+ and K^+, were first recognized by Hodgkin and Huxley (1952), who did seminal experiments using a squid giant axon for which they were awarded the Nobel Prize in Physiology in 1963. They were able to record the resting membrane potential and explore how the membrane potential varied with changing Na^+ and K^+ concentrations in the extracellular space by pouring beakers of fresh or salt water into the vessel containing the squid giant axon.

Chemical signalling

Information is passed between neurons by chemical signalling. Neurotransmitters are released from the synaptic terminals of one neuron, diffuse across the synaptic cleft, and activate receptors on the postsynaptic terminal. There are relatively few types of neurotransmitter compared to receptors, so much of the selectivity of signalling comes from the receptor that receives the signal.

GABA and glutamate: Stop and go

GABA and **glutamate** are the workhorse neurotransmitters of the brain. Nearly every neuron in the brain produces one or other of these transmitters and thus can be described as **excitatory** (glutamate releasing) or **inhibitory** (GABA releasing). What makes these transmitters excitatory or inhibitory, however, is the receptors that respond to them in the receiving (postsynaptic) neuron. The predominant receptors for both glutamate and GABA are ionotropic – that is, they are ion channels (like the ion channels described in the section above that transmit electrical currents along the axon). Receptor channels differ, however, in that instead of being activated by voltage, they are activated by the binding of a transmitter. The ions that move through the receptor determine whether their effects are excitatory or inhibitory. Glutamate receptors are selective for positive ions, and so, when they open, Na$^+$ rushes into the postsynaptic terminal and causes it to depolarize. On the other hand, GABA receptors are selective for negative ions, so, when the receptor channel opens, it allows the movement of chloride ions (Cl$^-$), which act to buffer the positive ions and maintain the postsynaptic membrane in a hyperpolarized state, effectively preventing it from being excited.

Very often, neurons are in an active state – for example, when they are left to their own devices, they have an intrinsic pattern of firing. Thus the *stop* signal of GABA is as important as the *go* signal of glutamate. Many neurons sit in an inhibited state, being continuously inhibited by GABA, but, when the GABA-releasing neuron itself is inhibited, the GABA signal switches off and the receiving neuron becomes disinhibited and can return to its optimal firing pattern (see Figure 4.4 for an example of this). Alternatively, glutamate release onto the same neuron may cause a depolarization sufficient to overcome the GABA inhibition and thus cause the receiving neuron to fire. There is an optimal balance of these excitatory and inhibitory inputs: too much

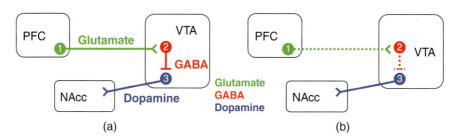

(a)   (b)

FIGURE 4.4 *An example of a GABA/glutamate 'stop' and 'go' network. (a) A network of three cells controls the release of dopamine in the nucleus accumbens (NAcc). With no input, the dopamine projection neuron (blue, 3) would fire spontaneously. However, it is held in an inhibited state due to repetitive firing of a 'stop' GABA interneuron (red, 2) in the ventral tegmental area (VTA). The GABA neuron is being activated by a 'go' glutamate neuron (green, 1) projecting from the prefrontal cortex (PFC). The pattern by which the glutamate neurons fire will determine the firing pattern of the dopamine neuron. (b) In schizophrenia, which is characterized by hypoactivity (less activity) in the PFC, there is less 'go' signal (1), resulting in less 'stop' signal (2), and the spontaneously active dopamine neuron (3) is disinhibited and becomes hyperactive, resulting in elevated dopamine in the nucleus accumbens. This elevated dopamine is thought to mediate some of the symptoms of schizophrenia (e.g. psychosis and paranoia).*

glutamate or GABA can be detrimental or even fatal. Too much glutamate (or too little GABA) can cause a chain reaction of neuronal firing. Such a pattern of firing can lead to epilepsy and seizures (Meldrum, 1995), whereas too much GABA will lead to not enough neurons firing, and vital functions controlled by neural transmission (e.g. respiration, or breathing) will shut down.

There are many receptor subtypes for each neurotransmitter, and their distinct properties and distribution in different brain areas allow for the diverse functions of each neurotransmitter and provide many levels at which neurotransmitter signalling can be controlled. By using genetics to experimentally manipulate different receptor subtypes, we can investigate how glutamate and GABA signalling in different brain areas modulates specific behaviour. $GABA_A$ receptor function has been teased apart in this way. Molecular biologists have established that a single amino acid residue on the extracellular domain of the alpha subunit (see Figure 4.5) is responsible for benzodiazepine binding (Wieland, Luddens, & Seeburg, 1992). They genetically modified mice, switching this amino acid with another to make the specific receptors insensitive to benzodiazepines. Doing this with each alpha subunit in turn and testing the effects of benzodiazepines on mice with these mutations revealed that the alpha1 subunit (expressed throughout the brain) is the one where

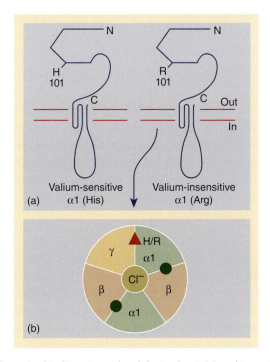

FIGURE 4.5 *Benzodiazepine binding site on the alpha1 subunit (a) and its position in a $GABA_A$ receptor (b). (a) A single amino acid (histidine, H101) in the extracellular domain of $GABA_A$ receptor alpha subunits determines the receptor's ability to bind benzodiazepines; when switched to another amino acid (arginine, R101), they are unable to bind benzodiazepines. (b) Five subunits (two alpha [α1], two beta [β], and one gamma [γ]) join together to form a receptor with a central pore through which chloride (Cl−) moves. The benzodiazepine binding site (red triangle) is positioned at the boundary between the α and γ subunits. The green circles represent the binding sites for GABA.*

Source: Reprinted by permission from Macmillan Publishers Ltd: SCIENCE. Wisden and Stephens (1999), copyright 1999.

benzodiazepines act to cause sedation, whereas the alpha2 subunit, which has more localized expression to the amygdala and striatum, is where benzodiazepines have their anxiety-reducing effects (Rudolph, Crestani, & Mohler, 2001). Understanding the roles of specific subtypes of receptor in different behaviours may in the future allow us to target specific drugs to these receptors and get beneficial behavioural effects without side effects.

Modulators: Acetylcholine, serotonin, dopamine, and noradrenaline

Along with GABA and glutamate, there are a number of other neurotransmitters that play important modulatory roles in the brain, or excitatory roles in the periphery. Acetylcholine, for example, is the glutamate of the periphery, in that it is the excitatory neurotransmitter at the junction between nerves and muscles. Its release from motor neurons excites muscle cells and causes them to contract (through activation of an acetylcholine receptor that fluxes the positive calcium ion, Ca^{2+}). If this transmission is blocked, muscles can't contract. The disease myaesthenia gravis, for example, causes muscle weakness. The mechanism by which this occurs is through an autoimmune reaction: antibodies target and lead to the destruction of acetylcholine receptors at the neuromuscular junction (Conti-Fine, Milani, & Kaminski, 2006). Without those receptors, the muscles do not receive the stimulatory signal from acetylcholine and thus cannot contract. Acetylcholine also acts as a neurotransmitter in the brain. In the central nervous system, it is one of several neurotransmitters that perform modulatory functions. Rather than being distributed throughout the brain, as is the case with GABA and glutamate, the cell bodies of the neurons that release these neurotransmitters tend to be localized to specific brain areas; however, their axonal projections spread diffusely throughout the brain (see Figure 4.6). The cholinergic (acetylcholine-releasing) neurons in the basal forebrain complex have a role in cognition. It is these neurons that are the first to die in the early stages of Alzheimer's disease, and the drugs most commonly used to treat the cognitive deficits associated with Alzheimer's work to boost cholinergic signalling and reverse the cognitive effects of this cell loss (Birks, 2006).

Dopaminergic neurons are located in the midbrain and project forward to the striatum and the prefrontal cortex. Dopamine released from projections from the substantia nigra (midbrain) to the dorsal striatum (caudate putamen) are involved with voluntary movement. Destruction of the dopamine cells in this pathway results in Parkinson's disease (Samii, Nutt, & Ransom, 2004), whereas destruction of the cells receiving the dopamine input in the striatum results in Huntington's disease (Walker, 2007). The most effective pharmacological treatment for Parkinson's disease

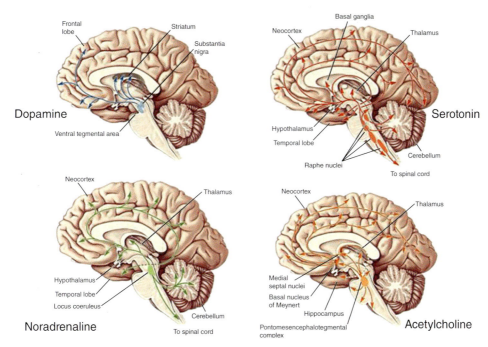

FIGURE 4.6 *The modulatory neurotransmitter systems. The cell bodies for each neurotransmitter are located in discrete parts of the brain, but their projections spread widely. In this way, the activity of a small group of cells can have an impact on a wide range of systems.*

Source: Bear, Connors, and Paradiso (2006).

to date is L-dopa, the chemical precursor to dopamine (Oliver Sachs' book *Awakenings* [1973] and the film of same name provide an excellent description of the discovery of this revolutionary treatment). Directly boosting the production of dopamine in the remaining dopaminergic terminals is sufficient, in the short term, to ameliorate the symptoms of the disease. Dopamine neurons located in the **ventral tegmental area** (next to the substantia nigra) project to the ventral striatum (**nucleus accumbens**) and also the prefrontal cortex. These circuits have been heavily implicated in reward-related behaviour, and dopamine release in the nucleus accumbens occurs in the presence of reward and is integral in training an animal (or human) to repeat behaviours leading to the reward (Schultz, 2002). All drugs of abuse have been shown to increase dopamine release in the nucleus accumbens, and because they do so in a pharmacological manner rather than an indirect manner (as natural rewards do) they hijack the system, biasing behaviour to seek drugs over natural rewards (Everitt, Dickinson, & Robbins, 2001; Robinson & Berridge, 1993; Wise, 2004).

Serotonin is made in the **raphe nuclei** of the brainstem, which have projections throughout the brain as well as down into the brainstem. Serotonin release modulates sleep and wakefulness, appetite, pain, mood, and emotion. The most commonly prescribed antidepressants act to boost serotonergic signalling (Stahl, 1998). The noradrenergic neurons are localized to a very small brain area at the top of the brainstem, the **locus coeruleus**. Although small, the locus coeruleus projects throughout the brain. Noradrenaline has a role in arousal and attention, and noradrenaline neurons fire and release noradrenaline when an animal is alert and attending to the environment (Aston-Jones, Chiang, & Alexinsky, 1991). These neurons are also heavily activated in the fear response, leading to a state of hypervigilance (Bremner, Krystal, Southwick, & Charney, 1996). Outside the brain, noradrenaline and acetylcholine are the primary neurotransmitters of the autonomic nervous system (see the later section 'The Nervous System').

DRUGS AND THE BRAIN

There are many classes of psychoactive drugs (drugs that act in the brain to change mood or behaviour). Most act directly at the receptors for specific neurotransmitters; however, some modulate the activity of the neurotransmitter itself (see the earlier section 'Modulators: Acetylcholine, Serotonin, Dopamine, and Noradrenaline'). Some psychoactive drugs are taken recreationally and some are prescribed to treat specific brain disorders. People have been taking drugs to alter their mental state for time immemorial. Recreational drugs cover legal drugs (such as nicotine and alcohol), illicit drugs (such as cocaine and heroin), and the 'legal highs', a growing number of drugs with modified pharmacology for sale online. Understanding how these drugs act on the brain teaches us about both normal and abnormal functions of the brain and provides new mechanisms to target for therapeutic drugs.

There are a number of drugs that act on either glutamate or GABA receptors. The effects of these drugs on behaviour reflect the importance of these circuits in brain function. Drugs that boost GABA signalling, for example, are beneficial in reducing anxiety (Stephens & King, 2013); however, too much can be a bad thing. The main targets for GABA in the brain are the ionotropic GABA$_A$ receptors, which are made up of a series of subunits that surround the central ion-permeable pore. Drugs that directly activate GABA$_A$ receptors (full agonists) depress the nervous system and in large doses can be fatal. Drugs with this property are not prescribed for anxiety.

However, benzodiazepines, the drugs most often prescribed to treat anxiety, have a more subtle effect. They act as allosteric modulators of GABA$_A$ receptors. That is, they change the properties of how the receptor responds to GABA, but have no effect on their own. Thus, they will increase the inhibition caused by GABA when it is released, but they do not cause a general inhibition themselves. There are pros and cons of boosting or reducing glutamatergic function. Large doses of phencyclidine, which is an NMDA receptor antagonist (a drug that blocks a particular subtype of glutamate receptor; see the next section), cause psychotic symptoms that mimic the symptoms of schizophrenia (Morris, Cochran, & Pratt, 2005). Boosting glutamate receptor function is being investigated as a means to enhance cognitive performance (Lynch, 2004); however, this is likely to be successful through allosteric modulation of the receptors rather than direct activation, as too much glutamate excitation can be bad, causing epileptogenesis or excitotoxic cell death.

Changes in synaptic connectivity as the basis of learning and memory: 'Cells that fire together wire together'

The connections between neurons allow information to be transmitted, processed, and stored. The strength of these connections is constantly changing (neuroplasticity), allowing the brain to encode information and learn and respond to environmental stimuli. Canadian psychologist Donald O. Hebb described a theoretical model in the 1940s that could explain how specific neuronal connections could be strengthened and postulated a cellular basis for learning and memory: 'When an axon of cell A is near enough to excite cell B and repeatedly or persistently takes part in firing it, some growth process or metabolic change takes place in one or both cells such that A's efficiency, as one of the cells firing B, is increased' (Hebb, 1949, p. 62) – or, more simply, 'cells that fire together wire together'. The model has stuck and since the 1940s evidence has been accumulating that fits this model at a molecular and cellular level. In terms of sensory inputs, rather than abstract cells A, B, and C, this model can explain associative learning: learning occurs when two stimuli are linked together – for example, a perfume and a person. Olfactory (smell) information will arrive in the brain at the same time as visual, auditory, and tactile information about the person. The information will be processed through a series of connections from sensory to higher processing neurons. Convergent information will merge onto neurons that integrate the multiple sources of sensory information through individual synapses. Depolarization of the integration neuron sufficient to drive an action potential may normally occur when one stimulus is present (a strong stimulus), leading to a conscious awareness of the other stimuli (e.g. you recognize an elderly woman as your grandmother). The inputs related to the hug (tactile information) and the perfume (olfactory information) might not originally have caused sufficient excitation alone to allow the neuron to fire (weak stimuli), but, after repeated pairing with the stronger stimulus, this will occur. In other words, cells that fire together wire together: after these pairings, the initially weak stimuli alone, the perfume smell, is sufficient to lead to activation of the integration neuron by itself and thus the 'grandmother recognition pathway'. The perfume smell alone will be sufficient to trigger the memory and feelings associated with the grandmother, even in an unrelated context.

The cellular process by which this occurs is **long-term potentiation (LTP)**, a phenomenon first recorded in **electrophysiology** experiments where the extent of depolarization to an input signal was measured before and after an electrical high-frequency stimulation, showing that the response after the stimulation was greater than prior to it (Bliss & Lømo, 1973). Activity at glutamate receptors is the starting point for LTP (Malenka & Bear, 2004). There are two main types of glutamate receptor; they have differing properties and are named after drugs that are specific to them (AMPA and NMDA). AMPA receptors are activated by glutamate and flux Na^+, therefore depolarizing the neuron. NMDA receptors flux Ca^{2+} and Na^+ when bound by glutamate, but can only do so when the neuron is already depolarized. Thus NMDA receptors will only activate at times when a strong depolarization is occurring (lots of AMPA receptor activation) or when neighbouring synapses (different inputs) are coincidentally firing and the summation of their depolarization is sufficient to enable NMDA receptors to respond. As well as this voltage dependency, the other key feature of NMDA receptors is that they flux Ca^{2+} as well as Na^+. The Ca^{2+} entering the cell sets into action a series of intracellular pathways that result in the synapse becoming more sensitive to future inputs – for example, by recruiting more AMPA receptors. As a result, subsequent stimulations at that synapse that previously had a subthreshold response (e.g. a signal relaying the olfactory cue) might now be sufficient to cause the cell to fire and thus activate the 'grandmother recognition pathway' (Figure 4.7).

Although initially discovered in the hippocampus, LTP is now recognized as occurring throughout the brain. All parts of the brain are capable of learning by changing their synaptic connectivity, not just those parts of the brain involved in episodic memory (our store of particular events), such as the hippocampus.

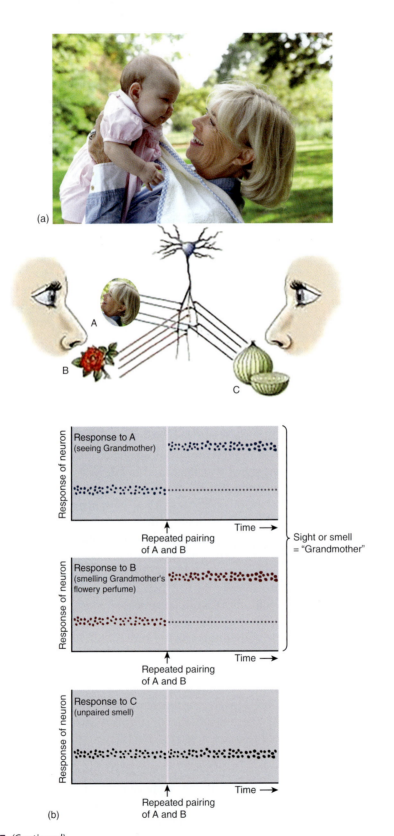

(a)

A

B

C

Response of neuron

Response to A
(seeing Grandmother)

Time →

Repeated pairing
of A and B

Response of neuron

Response to B
(smelling Grandmother's
flowery perfume)

Time →

Repeated pairing
of A and B

Sight or smell
= "Grandmother"

Response of neuron

Response to C
(unpaired smell)

Time →

Repeated pairing
of A and B

(b)

FIGURE 4.7 *(Continued)*

FIGURE 4.7 *Associative learning and long-term potentiation. We receive inputs simultaneously; for example, in (a) there are visual inputs (the sight of Grandmother), tactile inputs (the feel of Grandmother), and olfactory inputs (the smell of Grandmother). The visual information may be strong enough to form a representation of Grandmother alone. However, coincident pairing of these stimuli will lead to the smell bring able to elicit the memory (b). Hence, many years later catching a smell of something may evoke a strong visual memory of another time. This can be explained by neuroplasticity at synapses, which strengthens connections through long-term potentiation.*

Sources: (a) mimagephotography / Shutterstock. (b) adapted from Bear, Connors, and Paradiso (2006).

OPTOGENETICS

Optogenetics is a recently developed technology that seeks to confirm how neurons make and store memories. Sensory neurons translate sensory information into electrical activity that is then processed through the brain. Photoreceptors in the retina are light sensitive; a protein called rhodopsin is activated by light and opens ion channels to activate the neuron. Scientists have taken advantage of this property and invented a new technique, optogenetics (Zhang, Aravanis, Adamantidis, de Lecea, & Deisseroth, 2007). Using genetics, channel-rhodopsins can be targeted and expressed in specific brain cells and pathways. Lasers are then used to focus light into the brain and directly activate the targeted neurons.

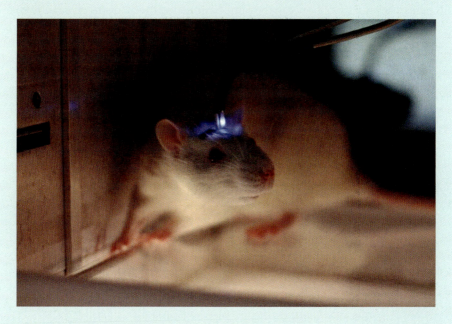

Rat with optogenetic stimulation.

Source: Reproduced with permission of Dr Mike J. F. Robinson.

Optogenetics has revolutionized our ability to determine the function of particular brain cell and circuits, and has recently been used to provide evidence that LTP really is the cellular basis of learning and memory, one of neuroscience's holy grails. Roberto Malinow and colleagues at the University of California, San Diego, first injected viruses designed to express channel-rhodopsin into the amygdalae of rats. They then paired light activation of virus-infected neurons with mild electric shocks (to the rats' paws). Through fear conditioning, the rats learned to associate the shocks with light activation of the amygdala neurons and displayed freezing behaviour to the light pulses alone. The researchers were then able to modify the freezing behaviour (a measure of the learned association) with different frequencies of light stimulation. High-frequency stimulation (LTP-inducing) strengthened the memory (induced more freezing) and low-frequency stimulation reduced freezing (weakened the memory, by a process of long-term depression [LTD]). By using light to directly strengthen and weaken synaptic connections in vivo (using LTP or LTD), and linking this to behavioural outcomes, this work has provided conclusive evidence that LTP is linked to learning and memory (Nabavi et al., 2014).

You can learn more about optogenetics at the **Stanford University optogenetics website**[1].

How neurons code information

As noted before, all neurons have the same basic structure. Moreover, they function in essentially the same manner with regard to electrical transmission and chemical signalling at the synapse (albeit with differences in the actual neurotransmitters and receptors). This raises a key question: how can the same basic neural mechanisms give rise to such a diversity of functions, from hearing and seeing to movement, memory, language, emotion, and personality? The answer, in a nutshell, is that neurons show a high degree of specificity to the kinds of stimuli (and situations) to which they respond (Figure 4.8).

Recall that the magnitude of the action potential does not vary. So this does not offer a way of distinguishing between the functions of different neurons. What does vary, however, is the rate of generation of action potentials (up to an upper limit given by the refractory period), which can be expressed as the number of action potentials generated per second (also called firing rate, or spiking rate). To record

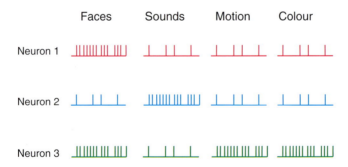

FIGURE 4.8 *The responses of three neurons to four kinds of stimuli (faces, sounds, motion, and colour) are shown: the x-axes of each of the 12 graphs represent time and the y-axes represent 'firing' (presence of an action potential). Neurons can show different 'preferences' for stimuli: neuron 1 responds to faces, neuron 2 responds to sounds, and neuron 3 responds to a wide variety of visual stimuli (faces, motion, and colour). These kinds of preferences are determined by their patterns of connectivity rather than neurochemical properties.*

this, an electrode would need to be inserted in (or very close to) the active neuron. This method is referred to as an electrophysiological technique and, because it is invasive, this tends to be done on nonhuman animals or, less frequently, in humans before undergoing brain surgery. These recordings can be done when the animal or person is awake so that the researcher can observe how the neuron(s) respond to flashes of light, seeing a familiar person, moving a limb, and so on. This method shows that neurons respond (i.e. generate action potentials, or 'fire') only under certain circumstances. For instance, a neuron in the visual cortex may fire when an animal sees a visual stimulus but not when it hears a sound, feels touch, or moves a limb. Moreover, the neuron may respond only to particular visual stimuli rather than all of them. Most sensory neurons only respond to stimuli when they are presented in particular regions of space. This region of space is called a neuron's **receptive field**. In addition to showing spatial selectivity, some neurons in the visual cortex also respond to particular wavelengths of light (associated with different colours) or to lines of particular orientations.

A detailed understanding of how neurons in the visual system code information came from pioneering studies of David Hubel and Torsten Wiesel, who were awarded the Nobel Prize for their work (e.g. Hubel & Wiesel, 1959). The results of their research suggested that there is a hierarchy of processing such that neurons lower down the hierarchy (e.g. a few synapses away from the eyes) code simpler information and that neurons further up the hierarchy (e.g. more synapses away from the eyes) code more complex and detailed information. For instance, cells in one of the first processing points from the eye (called the lateral geniculate nucleus) have relatively small receptive fields such that the neuron fires only when light is in the centre of the receptive field. However, in the next region along (primary visual cortex) many neurons respond not only to points of light but also to bars of light that have a particular orientation (i.e. they have larger receptive fields). These are termed **simple cells** and the idea behind them is that these neurons sum together (through their synaptic connections) activity from several cells lower down the hierarchy. Thus, by adding together point-like receptive fields, it is possible to create line-like receptive fields (Figure 4.9).

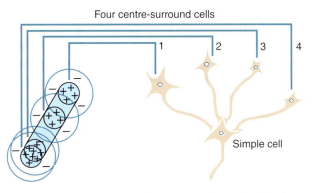

FIGURE 4.9 *Sensory processing of information by neurons is hierarchical. In this example from vision, neurons lower in the hierarchy have small point-like receptive fields (responding to light stimulation in the central region). A neuron higher up in the hierarchy (a so-called simple cell) responds to oriented bars of light as well as points of light. This can be achieved by summing together the outputs of several neurons whose receptive fields are aligned together.*
Source: Zeki (1993).

Similar principles are known to occur elsewhere in the brain. Auditory neurons tend to respond to sounds of a particular frequency (relating to pitch) in addition to having spatial receptive fields. Whereas auditory neurons lower down in the hierarchy tend to respond to a narrowly defined range of tones (e.g. a sound of 200 Hz), ones further up in the hierarchy may respond to a larger frequency band (e.g. 200–400 Hz) or a frequency shift (e.g. a sound shifting from 200 Hz to 300 Hz) (e.g. Kaas, Hackett, & Tramo, 1999). This can be achieved if, for instance, a neuron that responds to sounds in the range 200–400 Hz receives inputs from a set of individual neurons that are selectively responding to 200 Hz, 220 Hz, 240 Hz, and so on (i.e. the equivalent of simple cells in the auditory system). A frequency shift could reflect a neuron that responds to the consecutive activation of two other neurons (one tuned to 200 Hz and the other to 300 Hz). Naturalistic sounds (e.g. speech) tend to involve multiple frequencies changing over time, and this property of speech can be detected by neurons that respond in this way.

If the brain processes incoming information hierarchically then what lies at the top of the hierarchy? (The bottom of the hierarchy is, of course, the sensory organs themselves, and this level is quite well understood.) This question has puzzled neuroscientists for decades without a definitive resolution. To fill the gap in our knowledge, the hypothetical notion of a **grandmother cell** was created (for a historical overview, see Gross, 2002). Grandmother cells are typically defined as neurons that respond to the sight of one thing (e.g. your grandmother) irrespective of incidental changes in the input (e.g. viewing angle, whether she has glasses on or not) but they are also sometimes defined as responding to the concept of the grandmother (e.g. they would also respond to her voice or the thought of her). Further along from the visual cortex, in the inferior temporal lobes, neurons have been observed in the monkey that responded to faces more than objects (e.g. brushes) but these tend to respond to lots of different faces rather than just one (Gross, 1992). More recently, in humans, researchers have recorded even further along the hierarchy and neurons that are akin to grandmother cells have now been observed. For instance, one neuron may respond to Jennifer Aniston and another one may respond to Halle Berry (Quiroga, Reddy, Kreiman, Koch, & Fried, 2005). The neurons respond to lots of different images of that person and often their heard name (Quiroga, Kraskov, Koch, & Fried, 2009). While these findings are intriguing, and potentially the missing link, they do not imply that the neuron is the only neuron in the brain that responds to that person (otherwise it is very unlikely the researchers could ever have found it) and nor do they imply that this is the only stimulus to which the neuron responds (e.g. the 'Jennifer Aniston neuron' also responded to her *Friends* co-star Lisa Kudrow).

Finally, the discussion above has concentrated solely on the notion that information is coded by the rate of firing of neurons. This principle is also termed **rate coding.** However, there is another way in which neurons may code information that has tended to be less studied. This is termed **temporal coding** (where 'temporal' refers to time and is not related to the temporal lobes). In temporal coding, different neurons tend to fire in synchrony with each other and this may be one way for the brain to code the fact that different properties of an object (or different parts of an object) belong together (e.g. Singer, 2009). For instance, neurons in the early visual cortex respond to lines of particular orientations (e.g. the simple cells discussed above). However, several neurons that respond to different regions of space will tend to fire in synchrony with each other if they code the same object (e.g. a single unbroken line) but may fire out of synchrony if they code potentially different objects (e.g. two broken lines) (Engel, Konig, & Singer, 1991).

SECTION SUMMARY

- This section has described the basic structure and function of the neuron.
- The properties of the neuron can act as building blocks to support more complex behaviours.
- Information is transmitted within and between neurons by electrical activity, or the generation of an action potential.
- Information is passed between neurons by chemical signalling. Two of the most important transmitters are GABA and glutamate.
- Along with GABA and glutamate, there are a number of other neurotransmitters that play important modulatory roles in the brain, including acetylcholine, serotonin, dopamine, and noradrenaline.
- The connections between neurons allow information to be transmitted, processed, and stored. The strength of these connections changes constantly, allowing the brain to encode information and learn and respond to environmental stimuli.
- Long-term potentiation is a long-lasting enhancement in signal transmission between two neurons that results from stimulating them synchronously, and occurs throughout the brain.
- Grandmother cells are neurons that respond consistently to the sight or concept of one thing, irrespective of incidental changes in the input.

AN OVERVIEW OF BRAIN STRUCTURES AND THEIR FUNCTIONS

LEARNING OBJECTIVE 4.3

Demonstrate an understanding of the main structures of the brain and the various nervous systems of the human body.

With the preceding sections having considered the actions of individual neurons, and their interactions with connecting neurons, this section starts from the other end of the scale: from the nervous system itself (and its subdivisions) rather than at the cellular level. The section starts by considering different branches of the nervous system (the central and the peripheral) before considering the brain itself and the structures and functions of the various regions of the brain, each of which is likely to consist of billions of neurons working together using the chemical and electrical signalling already described.

The nervous system

The **central nervous system** consists of the brain and the spinal cord. In contrast, the peripheral nervous system consists of nerves sending and receiving signals to other parts of the body. The peripheral nervous system is itself divided into two further systems: the **autonomic nervous system** and the **somatic nervous system**. The somatic nervous system coordinates muscle activity whereas the autonomic nervous system controls and monitors bodily functions such as heart rate, digestion, respiration rate, salivation, perspiration, and pupil diameter. The autonomic nervous system is divided into two complementary divisions. The sympathetic system (noradrenaline) increases arousal (e.g. increased heart rate, breathing, and pupil size) and decreases functions such as digestion. The parasympathetic system (acetylcholine) has a resting effect (decreased heart rate, breathing, and pupil size) and increases functions such as digestion. See Figure 4.10 for a summary.

Most phenomena of interest to psychologists relate to the brain rather than other parts of the nervous system. However, brain–body interactions are an important area within psychology. For instance, responses in the body often serve as a reliable marker of unconscious processing in the brain. Thus, sweating responses (measured by changes in skin conductance) can reflect the processing of risk and emotion (Bechara, Damasio, Tranel, & Damasio, 1997) and we may unconsciously imitate the facial expressions of others (measured by electrical changes in facial muscles) (Dimberg, Thunberg, & Elmehed, 2000).

General architecture of the brain

Neurons are organized within the brain to form **white matter** and **grey matter**. Grey matter is made up of neuronal cell bodies. White matter is made up of axons and support cells (glia). The brain itself consists of a highly convoluted folded sheet

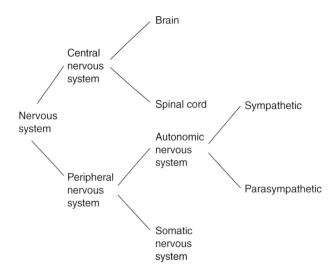

FIGURE 4.10 *The nervous system is organized around several major divisions, the most basic of which is the distinction between the central nervous system (brain and spinal cord) and the peripheral nervous system (for the muscles and bodily organs).*

of grey matter (the **cerebral cortex**), beneath which lies the white matter. In the centre of the brain, buried within the bulk of the white-matter fibres, lies another collection of grey-matter structures (the subcortex). The subcortex includes the **basal ganglia**, the **limbic system**, and the diencephalon. Beneath the subcortex lies the midbrain and, below that, the hindbrain, which connects to the spinal cord and the **cerebellum**.

Functions of the cortical lobes of the brain

The cerebral cortex consists of two folded sheets of grey matter organized into two hemispheres (left and right). The hemispheres are connected together by a massive white-matter tract (the **corpus callosum**) and are also able to communicate with each other via subcortical structures. The surface of the cortex has become increasingly convoluted with evolutionary development. Having a folded structure permits a high surface-area-to-volume ratio and thereby permits efficient packaging. The raised surfaces of the cortex are termed gyri (or gyrus in the singular). The dips or folds are called sulci (or sulcus in the singular).

The cortex is only around 3 mm thick and is organized into different layers that can be seen when viewed in cross-section. The different layers reflect the grouping of different cell types. Different parts of the cortex have different densities in each of the layers. Most of the cortex contains six main cortical layers and this is termed the neocortex (meaning 'new cortex').

The lateral surface of the cortex of each hemisphere is divided into four lobes: the **frontal lobe**, **parietal lobe**, **temporal lobe**, and **occipital lobe**. The divisions between these lobes are shown in Figure 4.11 and a simple summary of their associated functions is given in Table 4.1.

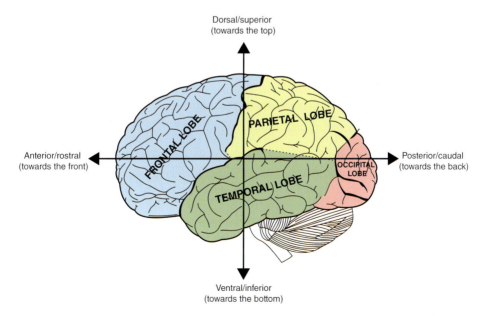

FIGURE 4.11 *The four cortical lobes of each hemisphere of the brain.*
Source: Adapted from Gray (1918).

TABLE 4.1 *The lobes of the brain and their associated functions.*

Cortical lobe	Sensorimotor functions	Higher functions	Common effects of brain damage
Frontal lobe	• Contains the motor cortex (responsible for initiation of voluntary actions)	• Coordinates behaviour • Problem solving • Working memory • Language (Broca's area)	• Disorganized and inflexible behaviour • Impulsivity • Lack of movement on one side of the body (if motor cortex damaged)
Parietal lobe	• Contains the somatosensory cortex (touch and bodily position) • Links perception to action (e.g. hand–eye coordination)	• Literacy and numeracy (particularly on the left) • Spatial cognition and attention (particularly on the right)	• Problems in attending to parts of space • Impaired action • Impaired reading and numeracy
Temporal lobe	• Contains the auditory cortex • Speech recognition • Visual object recognition	• Language and conceptual knowledge • Memory (medial regions)	• Impaired language (aphasia) • Impaired memory (amnesia) • Impaired object recognition (agnosia)
Occipital lobe	• Contains the visual cortex	• Visual imagery	• Impaired visual perception (although not strictly blindness)

Subcortical systems and the midbrain and hindbrain

The basal ganglia

The basal ganglia are large, rounded masses that lie in each hemisphere (Figure 4.12). They surround and overhang the thalamus in the centre of the brain. The main structures comprising the basal ganglia are the caudate nucleus (an elongated tail-like structure), the putamen (lying more laterally), and the globus pallidus (lying more medially). The caudate nucleus and putamen collectively make up an area called the striatum. There are various loops that pass through the basal ganglia connecting them to various regions in the cortex (Alexander & Crutcher, 1990). The basic function of these loops is to modulate activity in these other regions (upwards and downwards), thus both increasing and decreasing the probability of behaviour. For instance, one of these loops passes through the basal ganglia and connects to motor-related regions in the frontal lobes. Disorders of this basal ganglia circuit are characterized as either hypokinetic (poverty of movement) or hyperkinetic (excess of movement); examples of these include Parkinson's disease and Huntington's disease, respectively. Another loop connects different subregions of the basal ganglia (including the nucleus accumbens in the ventral striatum) to a different region of the frontal lobes (orbitofrontal cortex) that is concerned with emotional processing rather than movement or action. This circuit is involved in promoting and preventing risky and rewarding behaviour and is disrupted by addiction.

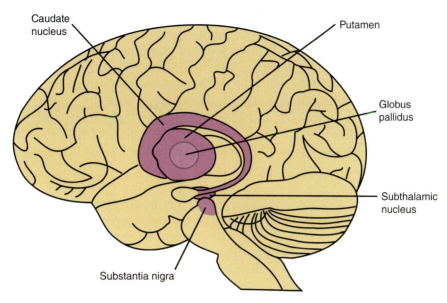

FIGURE 4.12 *The basal ganglia.*
Source: Wikimedia Commons.

The limbic system

The limbic system is important for relating the organism to its environment based on current needs and the present situation, and based on previous experience. It is involved in the detection and expression of emotional responses. For example, the amygdala has been implicated in the detection of fearful or threatening stimuli (e.g. Phelps, 2006) and parts of the cingulate gyrus have been implicated in the detection of emotional and cognitive conflicts (e.g. Botvinick, Braver, Barch, Carter, & Cohen, 2001). Historically, the limbic system has been described as the 'emotional brain' (MacLean, 1949; Papez, 1937). However, this simplification is perhaps as unhelpful as it is inaccurate. Firstly, not all limbic regions have emotion processing as their primary function: the hippocampus is particularly important for learning and memory. Secondly, emotion processing involves a variety of other regions that are not part of the limbic system (e.g. orbital regions of the frontal lobes, and the insular cortex). So, although the limbic system is *important* for emotion, it shouldn't be *equated* with emotion.

The diencephalon

The two main structures that make up the diencephalon are the **thalamus** and the **hypothalamus**. The thalamus consists of two interconnected egg-shaped masses that lie in the centre of the brain and appear prominent in a medial section. The thalamus is the main sensory relay for all senses (except smell) between the sense organs (eyes, ears, etc.) and the cortex. It also contains projections to almost all parts of the cortex and the basal ganglia. The hypothalamus lies beneath the thalamus and consists of a variety of nuclei that are specialized for different functions primarily concerned with homeostatic regulation of the body. These include body temperature, hunger and thirst, and sexual activity.

The midbrain and hindbrain

The midbrain region consists of a number of structures, only a few of which will be considered here. The superior colliculi and inferior colliculi (or colliculus in the singular) are grey-matter nuclei. The superior colliculi integrate information from several senses (vision, hearing, and touch), whereas the inferior colliculi are specialized for auditory processing. These pathways are different from the main cortical sensory pathways and are evolutionarily older. They may provide a fast route that enables rapid orienting to stimuli (flashes or bangs) before the stimulus is consciously seen or heard (e.g. Sparks, 1999). The midbrain also contains a region called the substantia nigra (see Figure 4.12), which is connected to the basal ganglia. Cell loss in this region is associated with the symptoms of Parkinson's disease. The medulla oblongata is in the hindbrain and merges with the spinal cord. It regulates vital functions such as breathing, swallowing, heart rate, and the wake–sleep cycle.

The cerebellum

The cerebellum (literally, 'little brain') is attached to the posterior of the hindbrain. It consists of highly convoluted folds of grey matter and is organized into two inter-connected lobes. The cerebellum is important for dexterity and smooth execution of movement. For instance, it may achieve this by modifying current motor movements as a result of visual feedback about the state of the action (e.g. whether on target).

TEST YOURSELF

Name the four outer lobes of the human cortex and the different functions that they each support.

SECTION SUMMARY

- The nervous system is composed of various branches.
- The central nervous system consists of the brain and the spinal cord.
- The peripheral nervous system consists of nerves that send and receive signals to and from other parts of the body and is divided into two further systems: the autonomic nervous system and the somatic nervous system.
- Neurons are organized within the brain to form white matter and grey matter.
- The brain itself consists of a highly convoluted folded sheet of grey matter (the cerebral cortex).
- Within the brain, the subcortex includes the basal ganglia, the limbic system, and the diencephalon.
- Beneath the subcortex lies the midbrain and, below that, the hindbrain, which connects to the spinal cord and the cerebellum.
- The cerebral cortex consists of two folded sheets of grey matter organized into two hemispheres (left and right).
- The hemispheres are connected together by a massive white-matter tract (the corpus callosum).
- The lateral surface of the cortex of each hemisphere is divided into four lobes: the frontal, parietal, temporal, and occipital lobes.
- The basal ganglia surround and overhang the thalamus in the centre of the brain. Disorders of this circuit are characterized as either hypokinetic or hyperkinetic, leading to Parkinson's disease and Huntington's disease respectively.

- The limbic system is important for relating the organism to its environment based on current needs and previous experience. It is involved in the detection and expression of emotional responses.
- The diencephalon is composed of the thalamus and the hypothalamus.
- The midbrain region consists of a number of structures, including the superior colliculi and inferior colliculi, the substantia nigra, and the medulla oblongata.
- The cerebellum is attached to the posterior of the hindbrain and consists of highly convoluted folds of grey matter. It is organized into two interconnected lobes and is important for dexterity and smooth execution of movement.

ANIMAL NEUROSCIENCE METHODS

LEARNING OBJECTIVE 4.4

Describe the various different neuroscience methods used in animal neuroscience experimentation and demonstrate knowledge of the ethical standards and practices governing such experimentation.

Animal experimentation has proved essential for the study of neuroscience and psychology. It allows connections to be made between neurobiological mechanisms and behaviour in a manner impossible in human studies or alternative systems. Animal experimentation is regulated across the world and legislation is in place to make sure ethical standards and practices are adhered to (e.g. the Animals (Scientific Procedures) Act 1986 in the UK; see Home Office, 2017). Researchers follow the **3Rs**[2], an ethical framework for conducting scientific experiments humanely. The 3Rs refer to replacement, reduction, and refinement:

1. *Replacement* – Animals are only used where necessary and they are replaced with alternatives, such as human studies, computer modelling, or use of lower species (e.g. invertebrates), where possible.
2. *Reduction* – Improvements to experimental designs and analyses are used to minimize or reduce the numbers of animals used.
3. *Refinement* – Where possible, procedures are refined to minimize harm and improve animal welfare.

Neuroscientists work across model systems: in silico, using computers to model how neuronal circuits might work; in vitro, using cell culture to study the structure and function of receptors (for example); ex vivo, using brain slices to look at function in a dish; and in vivo, using living animals to study behaviour. Animal studies have used invertebrates and lower vertebrate species to explore fundamental features of neuronal activity. For instance, the squid giant axon was the preparation used to discover the underlying mechanism and properties of the action potential. Features of simple learning and memory have been explored in snails and sea slugs. To understand how the human brain works to control behaviour, it has been necessary to study function in mammals, all of which have similarly organized brain areas and components. Rodents, mice, and rats are the most commonly used animals in neuroscience research, and methods relating to their use will be described here. These animals share a surprisingly large number of genes with humans (99%, according to the Mouse Genome Sequencing Consortium et al., 2002), and their brains contain homologous regions to those found in humans. The ancestors of the primate lineage, dating back to the extinction of the dinosaurs, came from the rodent family.

TEST YOURSELF

What are the main ethical principles governing the use of animals in neuroscience research?

RESEARCH METHODS 4.1

MODEL SYSTEMS IN NEUROSCIENCE

Four different model systems are used to study neuroscience:

- *In silico* – Computational neuroscientists use computers to try to build models of the neural networks within our brains and test or predict how they might respond in real life. Models of single-cell activity through to whole network activity can allow us to test and develop hypotheses of how the brain might integrate information.

- *In vitro* – Cell culture provides a platform in which to test how cellular components of neurons function. Neurobiologists grow cells in culture and can express specific receptors within them. The cell strain used (whether it is a neuronal culture or other source) will allow the receptors to be studied in isolation or in interaction with other components.

- *Ex vivo* – Brain slices are taken and maintained in an artificial cerebrospinal fluid, and used for electrophysiological recordings. It is in this manner that phenomena such as LTP were first discovered.

- *In vivo* – The only way to truly test behavioural phenomena is in behaving animals. Neuroscientists study the brains and behaviour of many species, ranging from invertebrates (insects and snails) through to lower vertebrates (fish) and mammals (rodents, primates, and humans).

Lesion studies

Lesion studies have been used historically to understand the roles of different brain areas by damaging or inactivating them and studying the impact on behaviour. Unlike human lesion studies, where the lesions arise by happenstance (e.g. in Phineas Gage), in animals lesions can be made selective for discrete brain areas or cell types. Lesions can be made in several ways:

- *physically*, by removing tissue or cutting connections
- *electrolytically*, by stimulating a brain area with an electric current sufficient to cause cell death
- *chemically*, by microinjecting a neurotoxin.

Precise localized lesions are made during stereotactic surgery, where probes or needles are directed to specific brain areas using coordinates relative to the skull. Behaviour is compared to control animals where 'sham' lesions have been made (e.g. the same surgical procedure lacking the chemical or electrical lesion itself). These procedures are performed under anaesthetic to avoid pain or distress to the animal. Although human studies are possible in this area, they occur via 'accidents of nature' (e.g. strokes) and do not provide the anatomical precision of animal models; hence, the replacement ethical criterion is not met for this method.

Electrical stimulation

In the opposite manner to lesion studies, electrical stimulation can be used to stimulate activity in specific brain areas, allowing the behavioural effects of the stimulation to be measured. Using smaller electrical currents than those to make electrolytic lesions, specific brain areas can be stimulated in awake, behaving animals and the effects measured (Olds, 1958; Wise 2002). If stimulation of a brain area is rewarding, then animals can be trained to work (e.g. press a lever) for the stimulation. In this way, neuronal circuits controlling natural (and artificial) rewards can be mapped out.

In vivo electrophysiology, microinjection, or microdialysis

As well as delivering electricity to the brain, probes can be implanted that can record electrical activity within it (electrophysiology), locally deliver drugs (microinjection), or measure local changes in neurotransmitter levels (microdialysis). Electrical activity can be correlated with behaviour and the action of drugs on specific brain regions can be measured in real time. Using microdialysis, the extracellular environment can be probed on a minute-by-minute level for changes in neurotransmitter levels. Components of the extracellular fluid are dialysed into a tube, which is sampled every minute or so and the fluid tested for the presence of neurotransmitters or other molecules (Chefer, Thompson, Zapata, & Shippenberg, 2009). In this way, the release of a neurotransmitter (e.g. dopamine) can be linked to the presentation of a rewarding stimulus (e.g. chocolate) (see Figure 4.13).

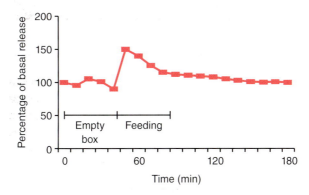

FIGURE 4.13 *In response to a pleasant stimulus, such as food, the level of neurotransmitter is increased.*

Source: Based on Figure 7 of Di Chiara (1999).

As technology develops (e.g. the probes become miniaturized so multiple probes can be implanted), more and more data is being generated to analyse brain function. Computational modelling methodologies are developing in parallel to enable researchers to interpret the vast arrays of data.

Genetic basis of behaviour

Specially bred mouse strains allow the genetic basis of behaviour to be explored. Different strains of mice show different behavioural traits: for example, C57BL/6J mice voluntarily consume large quantities of alcohol whereas another strain, DBA/2J, do not (Yoneyama, Crabbe, Ford, Murillo, & Finn, 2008). Recombinant inbred strains of mice (crosses of C57 and DBA mice that have then been selectively bred to carry identical mixtures of the two strains' genes) can be used to understand the genetic components of this or another behavioural trait (Crabbe, Belknap, Buck, & Metten, 1994). Selecting which inbred strains behave like the parent strains and then comparing which genes they have inherited from which parent allows behavioural traits to be attributed to different genetic loci and individual genes. Inbreeding allows the genetics to be controlled for in a manner not possible in twin and family studies in humans, not to mention the control of environmental factors, which can confound human studies.

Using genetics as a tool

Since the mid-1990s, the field of neuroscience has been revolutionized by the ability to make specific genetic mutations in mice (Picciotto & Wickman, 1998). This has allowed the role of individual genes and proteins in the mouse to be probed for their role in behaviour. There are two main ways in which the modifications can be made to the mouse genome, and these modifications can then be maintained transgenerationally: the genes themselves can be modified so they are switched off (**gene knockout**) or express modified proteins; or new genes (transgenes) can be added that may express a particular gene of interest. Regulatory sequences of DNA can be used to target expression of the transgenes to specific cell populations (Gong et al., 2003; see also the **GENSAT project**[3]. The targeted genes can then activate conditional knockouts (e.g. cell-specific knockouts) or introduce genes with products that can activate or inhibit the cells in which they are expressed (e.g. via optogenetics; see Focus Point 4.2). The above techniques require manipulations to be made and then mice to be bred carrying the mutations. A faster way to introduce new genes to the brain is by stereotactic surgery (under anaesthetic), in which viruses carrying the genetic construct are infused into specific brain areas (Hommel, Sears, Georgescu, Simmons, & DiLeone, 2003). These viral constructs will infect neurons in the local area and introduce the new genetic material, which as above may be a reporter gene (e.g. GFP or channel-rhodopsin) or a construct designed to switch off a specific gene (e.g. by RNA interference) (see Focus Point 4.2).

IMAGING NEURONS

Advances in genetic engineering and cell imaging have allowed huge advances in how we can visualize brain circuits and their activity. In the past, to look at the architecture of a single cell, it needed to be stained using a special stain (termed golgi stain) and then an image traced by hand from multiple serial sections. The most famous pictures describing neuronal structure in this way were those of Santiago Ramón y Cajal in the late 19th century. The 21st-century version of this is represented by the Brainbow mice (Livet et al., 2007), where individual neurons are labelled in such a way that they fluoresce at multiple wavelengths. This allows neighbouring cells to be traced.

A technique developed in 2013, CLARITY, is further revolutionizing the tracing of neurons as it strips out the fat from brains, leaving them translucent, allowing cells to be traced in three dimensions (Chung et al., 2013). And, in 2014, a system was devised that is able to image the activity of multiple cells in three dimensions in real time (Prevedel et al., 2014). At the moment this has been developed to study the simultaneous activity of all 302 neurons in a zebrafish larvae; however, in time it is likely to be possible to image cell activity in the brains of live behaviourally active mice. In this way, the patterns of neuronal activity and cell circuitry can be established in real time and hypotheses about the circuitry mediating specific behaviours can be tested.

SECTION SUMMARY

- Animal experimentation is essential for the study of neuroscience and psychology. Worldwide legislation ensures that ethical standards and practices are adhered to.

- Researchers follow the 3Rs, an ethical framework for conducting scientific experiments humanely. The 3Rs refer to replacement, reduction and refinement.

- Neuroscientists work across model systems: in silico, using computers to model how neuronal circuits might work; in vitro, using cell culture to study the structures and functions of receptors (for example); ex vivo, using brain slices to look at function in a dish; and in vivo, using living animals to study behaviour.

- Lesion studies allow us to understand the roles of different brain areas by damaging or inactivating them and studying the impact on behaviour. In animals, lesions can be made selective for discrete brain areas or cell types. Lesions can be made physically, electrolytically, or chemically.

- Electrical stimulation can be used to stimulate activity in specific brain areas and the behavioural effects of the stimulation can be measured.

- Additionally, probes can be implanted that can record electrical activity within those specific brain areas, locally deliver drugs, or measure local changes in neurotransmitter levels.

- Specially bred mouse strains allow the genetic basis of behaviour to be explored. Neuroscience has been revolutionized by the ability to make specific genetic mutations in mice. This has allowed individual genes and proteins in the mouse to be probed for their roles in behaviour. There are two main ways in which the modifications can be made to the mouse genome: gene knockout or the addition of new genes.

HUMAN NEUROSCIENCE METHODS

LEARNING OBJECTIVE 4.5

Describe the various neuroscience methods used in human neuroscience experimentation and the strengths and weaknesses of employing each method.

Human neuroscience methods typically fall under the umbrella term of **cognitive neuroscience** (whereas the term **behavioural neuroscience** tends to refer to the equivalent enterprise in nonhuman animals). Methods for studying the brains of humans have lagged behind those developed for studying other species because of the need for these methods to be noninvasive. For instance, one of the most commonly used methods, **functional magnetic resonance imaging** (**fMRI**), was not available until as late as the 1990s (Ogawa, Lee, Kay, & Tank, 1990; Figure 4.14).

The methods of cognitive neuroscience can be characterized along several dimensions:

- *Spatial resolution* – The ability of the method to determine *where* neural activity is taking place.

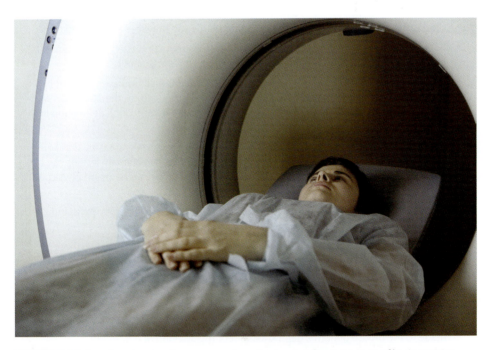

FIGURE 4.14 *Functional magnetic resonance imaging is not a direct measure of brain activity. Instead it measures changes in blood flow and blood oxygenation while the participant's head is placed in a large magnetic field. Changes in blood flow and blood oxygen occur as a result of neural activity and they create localized distortions in the magnetic field that can be measured.*
Source: bikeriderlondon / Shutterstock.

- *Temporal resolution* – The ability of the method to determine *when* neural activity is taking place.
- *Recording/stimulation methods* – Whether brain activity is merely recorded by the equipment or whether it is induced or disrupted.
- *Invasiveness* – Whether a method is purely external to the body (noninvasive) or not (e.g. administering drugs or inserting probes into the brain).

Electrical recording methods

Electroencephalography (EEG) has a relatively long history as a human neuroscience method (Beger, 1929). In EEG, electrodes are placed on the scalp to record electrical brain activity that is conducted through the skull (see Figure 4.15). That is, it is a noninvasive recording method and it is very safe to use. As discussed previously, there are two sources of electrical activity linked to the functioning of neurons. The first relates to active currents linked to the propagation of action potentials along the axon. The second relates to passive currents established in the dendrites of the postsynaptic neuron. An influx of positive ions into the postsynaptic neuron occurs when an excitatory neurotransmitter is released (this leads to a

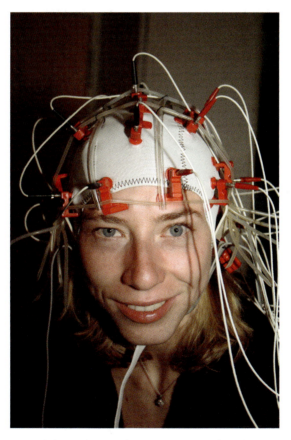

FIGURE 4.15 *Electroencephalography records electrical activity from the brain. The participant wears a cap containing electrodes. The signal from these electrodes is linked to ongoing behaviour (e.g. depending on the task or stimuli the participant is engaged with).*
Source: Daniela Sachsenheimer / Shutterstock.

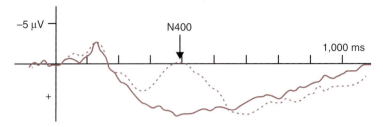

FIGURE 4.16 *Electroencephalography (EEG) in action. EEG can be used to measure electrical brain activity that occurs in response to particular stimuli (e.g. seeing the word 'dog'), which in this context is called an event-related potential. In this example, seeing the word 'dog' out of context (e.g. 'I take my coffee with milk and dog') elicits a negative peak at 400 ms. We can conclude from this that there is a cognitive mechanism that is involved in putting words into context and that it happens about 400 ms after a word is seen. Whether a peak happens to be positive or negative is not relevant: all electrical sources in the brain have positive and negative ends but sometimes only one end is projected up to the scalp.*

Source: Reprinted by permission from Macmillan Publishers Ltd: NATURE REVIEWS NEUROSCIENCE. Lau, Phillips, and Poeppel (2008), copyright 2008.

relative negativity in the extracellular space). This, rather than the action potential, forms the basis for the EEG signal (see Figure 4.16). However, the signal from one neuron is far too weak to detect at the scalp. What is required is a population of neurons to be activated at the same time and also for those neurons to have a similar orientation to each other so that the signal doesn't cancel out. The latter condition is met in the cortical sheet (the pyramidal neurons) but not in many sub-cortical regions. Hence, the EEG signal is not sensitive to all regions of the brain. Moreover, because the measurements are taken at the scalp, it is not always clear where in the brain they originate from because the electrical activity may have been conducted from a distant site. For this reason, EEG is said to have a poor spatial resolution. Given that conduction to the scalp from the source in the brain is rapid, it is said to have an excellent temporal resolution.

In its modern-day usage, the EEG signal is averaged across trials to particular events (e.g. the onset of a stimulus). This is called an **event-related potential (ERP)** and consists of a series of positive and negative peaks and troughs, plotted against time, that correspond to different electrical sources in the brain that contribute at different time points. So, for instance, you could compare the electrical activity in the brain when somebody is reading real words (e.g. 'dog') relative to made-up words (e.g. 'mib', 'proll'). In this example, differences in electrical activity can be detected around 200 milliseconds after the onset of the stimulus (Hauk et al., 2006). You could then establish that this occurred irrespective of whether the word was written in a large or small font size, showing that it doesn't reflect basic visual differences. You could also compare reading words in a sensible context ('I have a pet cat and dog') versus an anomalous one ('I take my coffee with milk and dog'). In this case, the difference in electrical activity between these conditions occurs later, at around 400 ms after the onset of 'dog' (this is termed the 'N400'; Kutas & Federmeier, 2011). Thus, researchers can study the hierarchical nature of information processing using this measure. In this example, there is an early brain mechanism that recognizes words (e.g. 'dog' versus 'mib') and a later mechanism that recognizes whether a word is out of context.

Functional imaging

Functional magnetic resonance imaging is termed a 'haemodynamic method' because it measures changes (i.e. 'dynamic') in blood flow and oxygenation (i.e. 'haemo-'). As such, it does not directly measure the activity of neurons (unlike EEG). When the energy consumption of neurons increases, primarily because of synaptic activity, the neurons extract oxygen from the blood stream. They do this by converting oxyhaemoglobin to deoxyhaemoglobin. In order to ensure that enough oxygen can be provided to the neurons, more blood is pumped into that active region (i.e. the capillaries dilate). Thus, when neurons increase their consumption of oxygen, there is a resulting net increase (not decrease) of oxygen in that region. It is this increase in oxygenation that is measured in fMRI – and it is called the BOLD response (from 'blood oxygen level dependent'). It takes around 6 seconds for the BOLD response to reach its peak and, hence, the temporal resolution of fMRI is quite poor (at least compared to EEG). Oxyhaemoglobin and deoxyhaemoglobin have different magnetic properties, and by placing the participant's head (and brain!) in a large magnetic field it is possible to measure tiny distortions in that magnetic field created by these physiological changes. This can be measured on the scale of a few millimetres and, hence, fMRI is said to have a good spatial resolution (although it is still measuring millions of neurons rather than single neurons). fMRI is noninvasive, and it is generally considered safe unless a person has metal in their body.

Given that the brain is always physiologically active and is always consuming oxygen, it is not possible to simply place someone's brain into the scanner and interpret the signal. Instead it is necessary to compare differences in brain activity (i.e. differences in the BOLD signal) across different experimental conditions. The well-known images of the brain with coloured blobs on them that are generated by fMRI do not show the actual activity of neurons (fMRI doesn't measure that), and nor do they represent the BOLD signal itself, but rather they represent the value of some statistic (normally the p-value from a t-test) that is calculated by comparing the mean activity across conditions. So, to do fMRI research, it is necessary to be a good experimental psychologist with an awareness of what factors to control for and not simply rely on technology alone.

To give one concrete example, one early functional imaging study (using a forerunner of fMRI) examined the specializations of different regions of the visual cortex for different kinds of visual feature (Zeki et al., 1991). In one pair of conditions, an array of moving dots was compared against an equivalent array of static dots. In another condition, an array of coloured squares was compared against an equivalent array of grey-scale squares (Figure 4.17). These pairs of conditions (termed 'contrasts') were well chosen because they are well matched to each other in all aspects except for the aspect of interest (i.e. the presence of movement or colour). One part of the brain was found to be specialized for colour (i.e. it responds to colour minus grey but not moving minus static) and another part of the brain was found to be specialized for motion (i.e. it responds to moving minus static but not colour minus grey).

TEST YOURSELF

What are the main differences between EEG and fMRI?

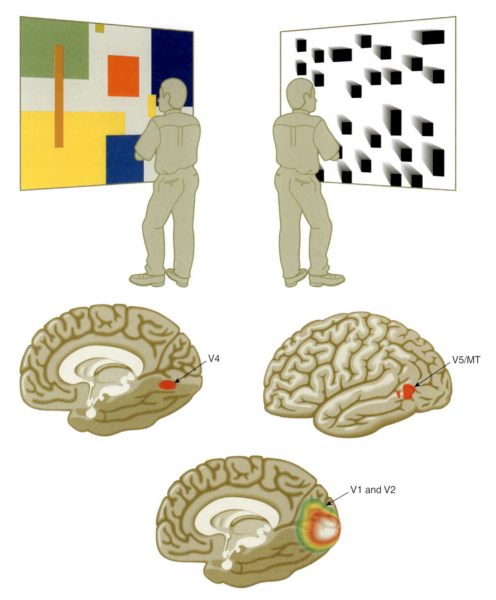

FIGURE 4.17 *Functional imaging is used to reveal what different parts of the brain are specialized for. In this functional imaging study (using a forerunner to fMRI), participants are shown, in the scanner, coloured patterns (relative to grey patterns) or moving dots (relative to static dots). Brain activity can be found in various regions: one region (called V4) responds more to colour than to motion, another region (called V5 or MT) responds to motion more than colour, whereas some regions respond to both (regions V1 and V2).*

Source: Zeki (1992). Reproduced with permission of Jared Schneidman Design.

Neuropsychology

In the 1860s, Paul Broca documented two patients who had sustained brain damage and, as a result, had lost the ability to speak (Broca, 1861). However, in other respects the patients appeared to have good intellectual functioning. On postmortem, it was discovered that both patients had damage to a region of the left frontal lobe (subsequently called **Broca's area**). From this, Broca concluded two things: firstly, that there is a separate faculty of language in the brain, and, secondly, that it may be located in the left frontal lobe. The approach of using patients with brain damage in order to study cognition is typically termed **neuropsychology** and has remained an accepted method in psychology since the time of Broca.

Other important observations followed Broca's discovery. Carl Wernicke (1874) reported a patient who could produce speech but had problems in comprehending speech. He therefore concluded that there are (at least) two language centres in the brain – one involving speech production (linked to Broca's earlier observations) and another involved in comprehension. This line of thinking also leads to the idea that we can draw conclusions about the structure of cognition just from observing the patterns of spared and impaired behaviour. Thus, we could conclude that language comprehension and production draw on separate systems without knowing *where* those systems are (let alone the more difficult question of *how* they are implemented). The term **double dissociation** is used to denote two complementary patterns of behaviour (X is spared, Y is impaired in case A; Y is spared, X is impaired in case B) arising as a result of brain damage or some other manipulation of the brain (see Figure 4.18).

Neuropsychology has tended to operate in two somewhat distinct ways. In one approach, patterns of impairment are used to infer how cognitive processes may be split down into their component parts and thereby understood. This approach has tended to rely on detailed single-case studies (e.g. Caramazza, 1986). In another approach, patterns of impaired behaviour are linked back to the location of damage in the brain (the 'where' question mentioned in the previous paragraph). This approach has benefited greatly from advances in imaging technology that enable lesion locations to be more accurately identified (e.g. Damasio & Damasio, 1989). Thus, the spatial resolution of the method is technically equivalent to that of other MRI techniques. However, human brain lesions are accidents of nature (e.g. caused by stroke) and hence it is rare to get brain damage in circumscribed regions (the situation is very different in animal models, in which lesions are induced). As such, this approach tends to rely on groups of patients who have damage to a shared region (but with the damage varying in size).

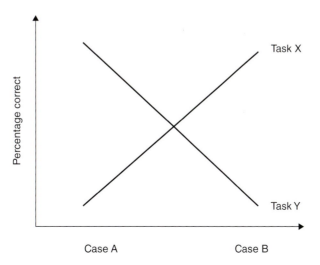

FIGURE 4.18 *Double dissociation.*

You may wonder why the use of brain imaging hasn't made the study of brain-damaged patients to study the brain basis of behaviour obsolete. In fact, the two approaches are complementary to each other (Kosslyn, 1999). In patient-based neuropsychology, it is the brain that is manipulated and the behaviour that is measured; in contrast, in brain imaging of healthy volunteers, it is the behaviour that is manipulated (i.e. the task in the scanner) and the activity in the brain that is measured. Thus, it is often said that brain imaging correlates brain function with behaviour but that direct manipulations of the brain (e.g. by damaging it) can be used to infer causality between brain and behaviour. The same logic can be said to apply to brain stimulation studies and psychopharmacological studies, discussed in the following section.

Brain stimulation

The logic behind brain stimulation studies is that, by stimulating particular parts of the brain, we can understand what functions they serve. This is normally achieved by temporarily disrupting behaviour (e.g. making the participant slower or more error prone). But it can sometimes be achieved by generating reportable symptoms: for instance, eliciting twitches of the finger or flashes of light. Some classic research in this area was performed by Wilder Penfield, who directly stimulated the brain, using electricity, in patients who were undergoing surgery for epilepsy (e.g. Penfield, 1958). The patients reported a variety of symptoms, depending on where was stimulated, including 'a star came down and towards my nose', 'those fingers and my thumb gave a jump', and 'I heard the music again; it is like the radio' (cited in Ward, 2015, p. 1). Penfield's most famous contribution is his mapping of the motor and somatosensory cortices, through which he showed that different regions of the motor cortex and somatosensory cortex represent different parts of the body (Penfield & Rasmussen, 1950). Needless to say, this method is very rarely used due to its invasive nature.

The most commonly used technique for brain stimulation is noninvasive and is termed **transcranial magnetic stimulation (TMS)** (e.g. Walsh & Cowey, 2000). A newer method using noninvasive electrical currents is called transcranial direct current stimulation (e.g. Nitsche et al., 2008). These methods tend to have transient and subtle effects on behaviour (rather than triggering overt symptoms). (Note, again, that the methods of fMRI and EEG do not involve brain stimulation: they are recording methods.)

Transcranial magnetic stimulation consists of a coil that contains a rapidly changing electrical current. This generates a magnetic field that can travel through the skull and generate a secondary electrical current in the underlying neurons. That is, the neurons are activated in response to the applied magnetic field and this means that their ability to respond appropriately to the ongoing task is disrupted (assuming, that is, it is indeed involved in the ongoing task). It is considered to be generally safe provided the intensity and frequency of pulses remain within guidelines and the participant has no history of epilepsy (Rossi, Hallett, Rossini, Pascual-Leone, & Safety, 2009). Each magnetic pulse is very brief (a few milliseconds) although its effects on the brain may last somewhat longer. As such it has a very good temporal resolution, and it can be used to examine the timing of cognition. For instance, TMS over the visual cortex (the occipital pole) disrupts the ability of participants to see a visual stimulus when it is applied at around 100 ms after the visual stimulus but not when it is applied at other post-stimulus time points (Corthout, Uttle, Ziemann, Cowey,

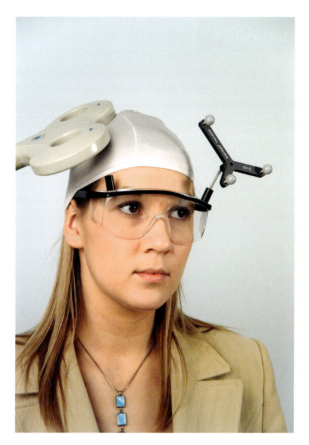

FIGURE 4.19 *Transcranial magnetic stimulation stimulates a region of the brain using a rapidly generated magnetic field. It is sometimes referred to as a 'virtual or reversible lesion' although it is generally considered a safe method.*

Source: University of Durham / Simon Fraser / Science Photo Library.

& Hallett, 1999). TMS is believed to directly affect around 1 cm² of underlying cortex (depending on the stimulating coil) and, hence, has a reasonably good spatial resolution. TMS applied to three different (but nearby) regions of the visual cortex can selectively disrupt either face processing, body processing, or object processing, leaving the remaining two functions unaffected (Pitcher, Charles, Devlin, Walsh, & Duchaine, 2009). However, TMS can only be used to stimulate brain regions that lie close to the skull (see Figure 4.19).

Psychopharmacology

Psychopharmacology is the discipline that studies the effects of drugs on brain and behaviour. Psychopharmacological studies can be incorporated into every level of neuroscience research, from looking at the pharmacological effects of a drug on an animal's behaviour to probing the mechanism of action by testing the drug in mice with mutations in the target receptors of the drug (e.g. the GABA studies described above). In humans, psychopharmacological studies are used to test how drugs influence behaviour for both therapeutic and experimental function.

SECTION SUMMARY

- There are a wide variety of methods in human neuroscience and the list is growing. Although some methods (e.g. fMRI) tend to be particularly in vogue, the reality is that each method has a different profile of strengths and weaknesses and there is not a single method that is fit for all purposes. As such, different methods complement each other.

- Methods such as fMRI have relatively good spatial resolution but poorer temporal resolution, whereas EEG has the complementary profile.

- Single-cell electrophysiology has excellent temporal and spatial resolution but suffers from the drawback of being invasive and does not permit the whole brain to be studied simultaneously.

- Recording methods (including EEG, fMRI, and invasive electrophysiology) enable scientists to correlate brain processes with cognition and behaviour, but stimulation and lesion methods (including neuropsychology, psychopharmacology, and TMS) enable scientists to experimentally change brain functioning and observe effects on behaviour.

HEMISPHERIC LATERALIZATION

LEARNING OBJECTIVE 4.6

Demonstrate knowledge of the function of the two hemispheres of the brain, particularly in relation to handedness.

Although the two hemispheres of the human brain have the same basic architecture, there are subtle structural differences between them (e.g. Galaburda, Lemay, Kemper, & Geschwind, 1978). However, this section is primarily concerned with differences in the functions, rather than the structures, of the two hemispheres.

The sensory and motor systems of the brain are largely crossed. The left hemisphere controls voluntary movements of the right side of the body, and it is involved in the perception of touch to the right side of the body (the right hemisphere deals with the left side). The left hemisphere processes vision from the right side of space, and the right hemisphere processes the left side of space. (Note: it is *not* the case that one eye projects to a single hemisphere; rather it is one side of both eyes that projects to a single hemisphere.) The situation with hearing is a little different: each ear sends signals to both the left and right hemispheres but with more connections ipsilaterally (on the same side) than contralaterally (crossing to the other side). The fact that different parts of space (or the body) project to different hemispheres provides a convenient tool for exploring hemispheric function of more complex skills. For instance, Kimura (1973) summarized results from a set of experiments in which briefly flashed stimuli (e.g. faces or letters) were briefly presented in either left or right space (projecting to the right and left hemispheres). Whereas the left hemisphere showed an

TABLE 4.2 *Identification ratios for different types of visual stimuli presented to either the left or right hemispheres.*

	Left hemisphere	Right hemisphere
Letters	1.2*	1.0
Words	1.5*	1.0
Point localization	1.0	1.2*
Dot enumeration	1.0	1.2*
Depth perception	1.0	1.3*
Faces	1.0	1.2*

Note: The asterisk denotes the hemisphere that has the advantage.

Source: Based on Kimura (1973).

advantage for letters and words, the right hemisphere had an advantage for spatial perception, face perception, and enumeration (see Table 4.2).

Although the information is presented to only one hemisphere, there is nothing to stop that information from travelling within the brain to the other hemisphere via the corpus callosum. However, researchers have studied groups of patients who have undergone surgical damage to the corpus callosum (to prevent the spread of epileptic seizures). These people are called **split-brain patients** and they have been important for understanding the functions of the different hemispheres (Gazzaniga, 2000; Sperry, 1982). In daily life these patients tend to function well. However, in experimental tests in which information is presented to a single hemisphere (e.g. by presenting visual stimuli briefly to one side of space) their difficulties become apparent. Some of the features of these patients are listed below:

- They can name briefly presented objects in the right visual field but not the left visual field (because the left hemisphere tends to be language dominant).
- They can name objects felt in the right but not the left hand (astereognosis).
- They cannot write with the left hand.
- 3D drawings by the right hand can lack depth.

These characteristics are broadly consistent with the notion that the left hemisphere is specialized for language and the right for spatial perception. One important issue is how lateralization of cognitive function is related to handedness. Although there are links between the two, it is not a straightforward relationship (i.e. it is definitely not the case that left-handers are a mirror image of their right-handed counterparts in terms of brain functioning). Before discussing the link, it is important to clarify the concept of handedness. In highly literate cultures, we tend to equate handedness with writing. But using the left or right hand for writing doesn't fully predict the handedness of other skills (e.g. catching or throwing a ball) and psychologists often use detailed questionnaires to measure handedness (Oldfield, 1971). It is also important to recognize that the origins of handedness can't lie in writing because it is too recent an invention in human history. Historical artefacts from tens of thousands of years ago reveal evidence of having been made by predominantly right-handed people (Toth, 1985). Even at the foetus stage, there is a greater tendency to suck the thumb of the right hand (Hepper, Shahidullah, & White, 1991).

ACTIVITY 4.1

ASSESS YOUR HANDEDNESS

The Edinburgh Handedness Inventory (Oldfield, 1971) is widely used as a measure of hand-edness in psychology. Assess your own hand dominance using an **interactive version**[4] of the inventory.

So, how does handedness relate to language laterality? One way in which this has been explored in the past is to use the **Wada test** (e.g. Wada & Rasmussen, 1960). In this test, an anaesthetic is injected into one of the carotid arteries supplying the brain (the left carotid supplies mainly the left hemisphere, and the right carotid the right hemisphere) – so one hemisphere is effectively put to sleep while the other remains awake! The experiment can be repeated in another session with the other hemisphere. The results are summarized in Table 4.3. Most people, whether left or right handed, have language in their left hemisphere. However, left-handers show this tendency more weakly. They are more likely than right-handers to have mixed or right dominance.

One theory that explains the link between right-handedness and left hemispheric language dominance is based on the assumption that the precursor of spoken language may have been gestural language, perhaps akin to a simpler version of modern-day sign languages (Corballis, 2002). There is some indirect evidence for this. Neurons in the primate equivalent of Broca's area respond to specific hand actions, both when seen and when enacted, and this has been likened to a 'vocabulary' of manual gestures (Rizzolatti & Arbib, 1998). So this region, primarily specialized for the hand in our primate ancestors, may have become increasingly specialized for speech during the course of human evolution.

Brain imaging (e.g. using fMRI) reveals a more detailed picture of hemispheric specialization than was previously achievable. One obvious problem with the earlier approaches is that they regarded faculties such as 'language' as essentially monolithic rather than decomposable into various processes, each of which are likely to have their own brain substrates (and which may or may not happen to cluster in the same hemisphere). For instance, the right hemisphere turns out to be dominant for some aspects of language (notably melodic aspects of speech such as intonation; Zatorre, Evans, Meyer, & Gjedde, 1992) and certain aspects of language may be shared between the hemispheres (e.g. our conceptual knowledge, or semantic memory; Mummery et al., 2000). What tends to be more strongly left lateralized (at least in right-handers)

TABLE 4.3 *The relationship between hemispheric language dominance and handedness as measured using the Wada test, in which each hemisphere is 'put to sleep' one at a time.*

Handedness	N	Language dominance (%)		
		Left	Bilateral	Right
Right	140	96	0	4
Left	122	70	15	15

Source: Rasmussen and Milner (1977). Reproduced by permission of Wiley.

is speech production (Dorsaint-Pierre et al., 2006) and this tended to be the aspect of language assessed by earlier methods (e.g. the Wada test).

DISCUSSION POINT

Discuss how the brains of left-handers differ from those of right-handers.

ACTIVITY 4.2

HEMISPHERIC LATERALIZATION: TRUE OR FALSE?

Indicate whether each statement is true or false.

- The two hemispheres of the human brain have very different architectures.
- The left hemisphere controls voluntary movements of the left side of the body.
- Each ear sends signals to both the left and right hemispheres but with more connections contralaterally than ipsilaterally.
- Information travels across the brain via the corpus callosum.
- Split-brain patients are those who are born without a corpus callosum.
- Often, split-brain patients cannot write with their left hand.
- Left-handers are a mirror image of their right-handed counterparts in terms of brain functioning.
- During the Wada test, one hemisphere is put to sleep.
- Broca's area was primarily specialized for the hand in our primate ancestors.
- Speech production tends to be more strongly left lateralized.

SECTION SUMMARY

- Although the two hemispheres of the human brain have the same basic architecture, there are subtle structural differences between them.
- The sensory and motor systems of the brain are largely crossed.
- The situation with hearing is a little different: each ear sends signals to both the left and right hemispheres but with more connections ipsilaterally (on the same side) than contralaterally (crossing to the other side).
- Information travels within the brain to the other hemisphere via the corpus callosum.
- Split-brain patients have undergone surgical damage to the corpus callosum and they have been important for understanding the functions of different hemispheres.
- One important issue is how lateralization of cognitive function is related to handedness.
- However, the origins of handedness cannot lie in what is assumed to be simply writing because it is too recent an invention in human history. The Wada test has been used to explore this more fully.

- One theory that explains the link between right-handedness and left hemispheric language dominance is based on the assumption that the precursor of spoken language may have been gestural language.
- Neurons in the primate equivalent of Broca's area respond to specific hand actions, both when seen and when enacted, and this has been likened to a 'vocabulary' of manual gestures.
- Brain imaging (e.g. using fMRI) reveals a more detailed picture of hemispheric specialization than was previously achievable.

PLASTICITY AND THE BRAIN

LEARNING OBJECTIVE 4.7

Explain the concept of plasticity and the brain in terms of learning a new skill or as a result of a new experience, and describe the effects of brain plasticity as a result of disrupted inputs to the brain or damage to the brain itself.

Plasticity refers to the brain's ability to change as a result of experience. This could be as a result of day-to-day experiences (e.g. encountering a new face, finding food in a different location), as a result of learning new skills (e.g. how to juggle, how to speak French), or as a compensatory mechanism as a result of injury to the brain or the inputs into the brain (e.g. from the sense organs or body). Changes in the brain linked to plasticity occur at multiple levels and operate across various timescales (e.g. Chen, Cohen, & Hallett, 2002). At relatively short timescales, modulations in GABAergic inhibition may enable normally non-functioning synapses to be recruited. This mechanism is believed to happen in short-term sensory deprivation: being in a dark room for days can make the 'visual' cortex more responsive to non-visual inputs. Neurons may also change their responsiveness to new kinds of stimuli (e.g. a neuron that responded to X but not Y may now respond to Y if it has been paired with X). At longer timescales, new structural connections between neurons may be established (Pittenger & Kandel, 2003). Broadly speaking, such changes in the brain can be construed as either functional (using the existing brain architecture in different ways) or structural (changing the brain architecture itself at either the small scale or a larger scale).

One mechanism of change at the neural level may be purely functional. Recall from earlier that neurons become specialized for processing particular kinds of material. This can be quite general (e.g. specialized for vision versus sounds) or very specific (e.g. specialized for this face but not that face). Acquiring a new skill or learning new material will affect the response properties of individual neurons: they may become more selectively tuned to reoccurring or discriminating features in the environment. At the level of the responsiveness of brain regions (recorded in humans using fMRI), it can be shown that differences in literacy expertise predict differences in brain activity in a region of the left inferior temporal lobe specialized for visual word recognition

(Dehaene et al., 2010). Literate people, including those who learned to read as adults, activate this region of the brain when viewing letter strings, but illiterate people do not. A particularly interesting finding is that there is evidence that this region is more tuned to faces in the illiterate group – that is, tuning neurons to respond to written words may mean that they respond less to faces. This may also be one reason why the right hemisphere appears to be more dominant for faces. Moreover, other research has suggested that the reason why this visual word recognition tends to be left lateralized depends on the laterality of speech production (Van der Haegen, Cai, & Brysbaert, 2012).

Plasticity does not only involve functional changes in the brain; it also involves structural changes. These are found not only at the level of the synapse but also in the anatomy of the brain at the millimetre scale (i.e. observable with structural brain images such as MRI). One study trained a group of volunteers with no prior experience in this skill to juggle over a 3 month period (Draganski et al., 2004). After 3 months there was increased density of grey matter in several regions of the brain, including area V5/MT (involved in visual/motion perception) as well as in parietal regions (involved in visuomotor coordination). The increase was still observed, relative to the initial baseline, after a further 3 months of no practice (see Figure 4.20). It is unclear what these grey-matter differences correspond to at the neuronal level, although one suggestion is that they reflect experience-driven synaptogenesis, which strengthens connections within the existing neural architecture.

Thus far, this section has considered plasticity within the normally functioning brain as a result of experience. However, plasticity can occur as a compensatory mechanism after disruption of the nervous system itself. Two examples will be considered here: brain plasticity as a result of disrupted inputs from the periphery (damage to the eyes or limbs) and brain plasticity as a result of damage to a part of the brain itself (reorganization after stroke and other forms of brain injury).

Humans rely heavily on their sense of vision, and one of the lobes of the cortex (occipital lobes) is dedicated almost entirely to the processing of vision. One interesting question is then what happens to the occipital lobes of the brain (structurally

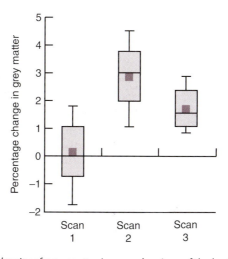

FIGURE 4.20 *Increased density of grey matter in several regions of the brain, including area V5/MT.*

Source: Reprinted by permission from Macmillan Publishers Ltd: NATURE. Draganski et al. (2004), copyright 2004.

or functionally) as a result of blindness either early or late in life. Evidence from brain imaging suggests that blind people activate their 'visual' cortex in response to hearing and touch instead of vision (Noppeney, 2007). The effects tend to be greater after early blindness (during childhood) but are found to a lesser degree in adults who lose their sight. This plasticity appears to be functional insofar as it is associated with better hearing and touch in blind people (Gougoux, Zatorre, Lassonde, Voss, & Lepore, 2005; Sathian, 2005); and disruption of these regions using methods such as TMS affects performance on these tasks (Cohen et al., 1997). Similarly, if a person loses a limb or finger (via amputation) then the part of the somatosensory cortex that responds to touch to that limb does not remain silent but starts to respond to other stimuli. In this case, these parts of the brain now respond to touch on other parts of the body. So neurons that respond to touch on the middle finger will start to respond to touch on other fingers after that finger is amputated (as measured using single-cell electrophysiology in monkeys; Merzenich et al., 1984). In humans, after amputation of an arm, touching the face can activate the 'arm area' of the somatosensory cortex (measured using fMRI) and, moreover, this reorganization is linked to reports of feeling pain in the missing 'phantom' arm (Lotze, Flor, Grodd, Larbig, & Birbaumer, 2001). This is one example in which plasticity may be maladaptive (i.e. leads to more problems than benefits; Flor, Nikolajsen, & Jensen, 2006).

FOCUS POINT 4.4

CAN THE BRAIN REORGANIZE ITSELF AFTER A STROKE?

Strokes are disruptions to the blood supply of the brain that can lead to permanent damage to the brain (i.e. cell death). Although this tissue damage is permanent, the brain can to some degree reorganize the intact regions of itself. This may depend on the age of the individual, with the elderly less able to restore lost functioning. Although strokes tend to be rare in infants and children, they do occur and, in these cases, it is not uncommon for individuals to develop normal intellect and language skills (Ballantyne, Spilkin, Hesselink, & Trauner, 2008). With regard to language acquisition, Liegeois et al. (2004) and others have found that early lesions to the left hemisphere can result in later right-hemisphere language as assessed using fMRI. In this study, even lesions outside 'classical' language areas (e.g. Broca's area) were just as likely to result in right-hemispheric language, which is consistent with the view that functional specialization of regions emerges gradually and in a way that is not completely predetermined. Given that the brain has very limited scope to grow new neurons, it may be wondered whether accommodating language in the right hemisphere would have a detrimental outcome on traditional right-hemispheric functions (e.g. visuospatial skills). There is some evidence for this. Lidzba, Staudt, Wilke, and Krageloh-Mann (2006) report that greater right-hemisphere language (measured with fMRI) following early stroke is associated with poorer visuospatial skills. This suggests that, while early plasticity can aid recovery, this may not be completely without cost.

DISCUSSION POINT

Discuss how the brain can change as a result of learning a new skill or in response to injury.

SECTION SUMMARY

- Plasticity refers to the brain's ability to change as a result of experience.
- Functional and structural changes in the brain linked to plasticity occur at multiple levels and operate across various timescales.
- One mechanism of change at the neural level may be purely functional. Acquiring a new skill or learning new material will affect the response properties of individual neurons.
- Structural changes are found not only at the level of the synapse but also in the anatomy of the brain at the millimetre scale.
- Plasticity can occur as a compensatory mechanism after disruption of the nervous system itself.
- Plasticity can occur as a result of disrupted inputs from the periphery (damage to the eyes or limbs) or as a result of damage to a part of the brain itself (reorganization after stroke and other forms of brain injury).

FUTURE DIRECTIONS

LEARNING OBJECTIVE 4.8

Critically evaluate possible future directions for research in neuroscience.

As technology has rapidly developed, the methods available to the neuroscientist have proliferated. Each method has its own advantages and disadvantages and it is very unlikely that single methods will dominate completely. Significant future advances in this area are likely to come around from a joined-up approach that enables us to, say, link optogenetic methods in animals with human genetic differences that influence behaviour, or to link effects that occur at the small scale (e.g. at the synapse) with the large scale (whole-brain networks). Nor is it the case that the future of neuroscience will sideline psychology and the understanding of behaviour. Even if we were to have a fully detailed map of how all the neurons in a brain are connected, this, by itself, would not explain how we see, think, remember, or interact socially.

SECTION SUMMARY

- As technology has rapidly developed, the methods available to the neuroscientist have proliferated.
- Significant future advances in this area are likely to come from a joined-up approach.
- The future of neuroscience will not sideline psychology and the understanding of behaviour.

CHAPTER SUMMARY

This chapter has considered how your brain makes you who you are. We did this by first examining the structure and functionality of the neuron and moved on to illustrate how drugs affect the fundamental functioning of our neural circuits. We moved on to an outline of the major structures and functions of the brain and nervous system before contrasting the main contemporary neuroscience methods used in animals and humans. The chapter concluded with an evaluation of the importance of hemispheric lateralization and the role of plasticity in learning and brain reorganization. Although virtually all our knowledge about the inner workings of the brainstems from just the past 150 years, innovative and complementary methods are constantly being developed (with a crucial focus on taking a joined-up approach), making neuroscience one of the most technologically exciting fields in contemporary psychology.

ESSAY QUESTIONS

1. How do different neurotransmitters affect synaptic signalling in different ways?
2. Describe three methods for studying the brain and how these relate to principles of neural functioning.
3. How are the brains of left-handers different from those of right-handers?

KEY TERMS

- **action potential:** A short-lasting event change in electrical membrane potential associated with the passage of an impulse along the membrane of a muscle cell or nerve cell.
- **autonomic nervous system:** Part of the peripheral nervous system that controls and monitors bodily functions such as heart rate, digestion, respiration rate, salivation, perspiration, and pupil diameter.
- **axon:** A long, slender projection of a nerve cell or neuron that typically conducts electrical impulses from the cell body to a distant location within the brain. Also known as a nerve fibre.
- **basal ganglia:** Large, rounded masses that lie in each hemisphere and overhang the thalamus and are composed of the caudate nucleus, the putamen, and the globus pallidus. The basal ganglia are implicated in disorders of movement and emotional processing.
- **behavioural neuroscience:** The application of biological principles to the study of physiological, genetic, and developmental mechanisms of behaviour in humans and nonhuman animals.
- **Broca's area:** A region of the left frontal lobe associated with the production of speech.
- **central nervous system:** The body's main processing system, consisting of the brain and the spinal cord. It is responsible for sending, receiving, and interpreting information from all parts of the body.
- **cerebellum:** Meaning 'little brain'; attached to the posterior of the hindbrain and associated with dexterity and smooth execution of movement.
- **cerebral cortex:** The brain's outer layer of neural tissue, consisting of two folded sheets of grey matter organized into two hemispheres (left and right).

- **cognitive neuroscience:** The scientific study of biological substrates underlying cognition, with a specific focus on the neural substrates of mental processes.
- **corpus callosum:** A thick band of nerve fibres that connects the left and right hemispheres of the brain.
- **dendrites:** Tree-like extensions at the beginning of a neuron that help to increase the surface area of the cell body. They receive information from other neurons and transmit electrical stimulation.
- **double dissociation:** The phenomenon by which two cognitive faculties that are believed to be linked in some way can each receive damage while the other remains intact and functioning.
- **electrophysiology:** The study of the electrical properties of biological cells and tissues.
- **event-related potential (ERP):** The measured electrophysiological response resulting from a specific sensory, cognitive, or motor stimulus.
- **excitatory:** Excitatory neurotransmitters stimulate the brain. They include norepinephrine and epinephrine.
- **frontal lobe:** One of four parts of the cerebrum; it controls voluntary movement, verbal expressions, problem solving, willpower, and planning.
- **functional magnetic resonance imaging (fMRI):** A neuroimaging procedure that measures brain activity by detecting associated changes in blood flow.
- **GABA:** GABA (γ-aminobutyric acid) is the brain's main inhibitory neurotransmitter. It is estimated that close to 40% of the synapses in the human brain have GABA receptors.
- **gene knockout:** A genetic technique in which one of an organism's genes is made inoperable.
- **glutamate:** The body's most prominent neurotransmitter and the brain's main excitatory neurotransmitter.
- **grandmother cell:** A neuron that responds consistently to the sight or concept of one thing, irrespective of incidental changes in the input.
- **grey matter:** Grey matter is found on the surface of the cerebral hemispheres and of the cerebellum. It contains most of the brain's neuronal cell bodies.
- **hypothalamus:** A brain region that contains a number of small nuclei with a variety of functions, including the linking of the nervous system to the endocrine system via the pituitary gland.
- **inhibitory:** Inhibitory neurotransmitters balance mood and are easily depleted when excitatory neurotransmitters are overactive. They include serotonin, GABA, and dopamine.
- **limbic system:** A complex set of structures that lies on both sides of the thalamus. It includes the hypothalamus, the hippocampus, and the amygdala. It is heavily implicated in emotional processing and the formation of memories.
- **locus coeruleus:** A small brain area, located at the top of the brainstem, where noradrenergic neurons are localized.
- **long-term potentiation (LTP):** Prolonged synaptic stimulation that results in long-lasting, strengthened synaptic transmission. The mechanisms underlying LTP may contribute to synaptic plasticity during learning.
- **neuron:** An electrically excitable cell that processes and transmits information through electrical and chemical signals.
- **neuropsychology:** The study of the structure and function of the brain as they relate to specific psychological processes and behaviours.
- **neurotransmitters:** Brain neurotransmitters are chemicals that help neurons to communicate with each other and are essential components of the mechanisms that regulate efficient and effective brain functioning.
- **nucleus accumbens:** Located in the midbrain, at the top of the brainstem. It works closely with other brain centres, particularly the ventral tegmental area. These circuits have been heavily implicated in reward-related behaviour.
- **occipital lobe:** One of four major lobes of the mammalian cerebral cortex. The visual processing centre.

- **optogenetics:** Optogenetics uses light to control neurons that have been genetically sensitized to light and is used to confirm how neurons make and store memories.
- **parietal lobe:** One of four major lobes of the mammalian cerebral cortex. It integrates sensory information from various modalities, including spatial sense and navigation, touch, temperature, and pain.
- **plasticity:** The brain's ability to change as a result of experience, skill, or injury.
- **psychopharmacology:** The discipline that studies the effects of drugs on the brain and behaviour.
- **raphe nuclei:** Serotonin is made in the raphe nuclei of the brainstem, which have projections throughout the brain as well as down into the brainstem. Serotonin release modulates sleep and wakefulness, appetite, pain, mood, and emotion.
- **rate coding:** The notion that information is coded by the rate of firing of neurons.
- **receptive field:** Most sensory neurons only respond to stimuli when they are presented in particular regions of space. Such a region of space is called a neuron's receptive field.
- **simple cells:** Cells in the visual cortex that have larger receptive fields because they add together activity from cells lower down the hierarchy of processing.
- **somatic nervous system:** The part of the peripheral nervous system that is responsible for carrying motor and sensory information both to and from the central nervous system.
- **split-brain patients:** Patients who have undergone surgical damage to the corpus callosum to prevent the spread of epileptic seizures. Research with split-brain patients is important for understanding the functions of the two hemispheres.
- **synapses:** Structures that allow a neuron to pass an electrical or chemical signal to another cell.
- **temporal coding:** An alternative to rate coding. The notion that different neurons tend to fire in synchrony with each other and that this may be one way for the brain to code the fact that different properties of an object (or different parts of an object) belong together.
- **temporal lobe:** One of four major lobes of the mammalian cerebral cortex. It is involved in the retention of visual memories, the storage of new memories, the processing of sensory input, and the comprehension of language.
- **thalamus:** Consists of two interconnected egg-shaped masses that lie in the centre of the brain. The thalamus is the main sensory relay for all senses (except smell) between the sense organs and the cortex. It also contains projections to almost all parts of the cortex and the basal ganglia.
- **transcranial magnetic stimulation (TMS):** The most commonly used technique for brain stimulation. Noninvasive, the method uses a magnet to induce weak electrical currents to cause activity in specific or general parts of the brain with little discomfort.
- **ventral tegmental area:** A group of neurons located close in the midbrain (mesencephalon). It is widely implicated in the drug and natural reward circuitry of the brain.
- **Wada test:** A test used to establish cerebral language and memory storage in each hemisphere. Administration of a barbiturate enables each hemisphere to be 'put to sleep' one at a time.
- **white matter:** A component of the central nervous system consisting mostly of glial cells and myelinated axons. It modulates the distribution of action potentials and coordinates communication between different brain regions.

NOTES

1. http://www.optogenetics.org
2. http://www.nc3rs.org.uk/
3. http://www.gensat.org/
4. http://www.brainmapping.org/shared/Edinburgh.php

FURTHER RESOURCES

Bear, M. F., Connors, B. W., & Paradiso, M. A. (2006). *Neuroscience: Exploring the brain* (3rd ed.). Baltimore, MD: Lippincott Williams & Wilkins.

Cooper, J. R., Bloom, F. E., & Roth, R. H. (2003). *Biochemical basis of neuropharmacology* (8th ed.). Oxford, UK: Oxford University Press.

National Centre for the Replacement, Refinement & Reduction of Animals in Research. (2017). 3Rs ethical framework for working with animals. Retrieved 20 November 2017 from https://www.nc3rs.org.uk/the-3rs

Optogenetics Resource Center (2017). Retrieved 20 November 2017 from http://www.stanford.edu/group/dlab/optogenetics/index.html

Quian Quiroga, R., Fried, I., & Koch, C. (2013). Brain cells for grandmother. *Scientific American*, *308*, 30–35.

Ward, J. (2015). *The student's guide to cognitive neuroscience* (3rd ed.). Hove, UK: Psychology Press.

REFERENCES

Alexander, G. E., & Crutcher, M. D. (1990). Functional architecture of basal ganglia circuits: Neural substrates of parallel processing. *Trends in Neurosciences*, *13*, 266–271.

Aston-Jones, G., Chiang, C., & Alexinsky, T. (1991). Discharge of noradrenergic locus-ceruleus neurons in behaving rats and monkeys suggests a role in vigilance. *Progress in Brain Research*, *88*, 501–520.

Ballantyne, A. O., Spilkin, A. M., Hesselink, J., & Trauner, D. A. (2008). Plasticity in the developing brain: Intellectual, language and academic functions in children with ischaemic perinatal stroke. *Brain*, *131*, 2975–2985.

Bear, M. F., Connors, B. W., & Paradiso, M. A. (2006). *Neuroscience: Exploring the brain* (3rd ed.). Baltimore, MD: Lippincott Williams & Wilkins.

Bechara, A., Damasio, H., Tranel, D., & Damasio, A. R. (1997). Deciding advantageously before knowing the advantageous strategy. *Science*, *275*, 1293–1295.

Beger, H. (1929). Uber das elektroenkephalogramm des menschen. *Archiv für Psychiatrie und Nervenkrankheiten*, *87*, 527–570.

Birks, J. (2006). Cholinesterase inhibitors for Alzheimer's disease. *Cochrane Database of Systematic Reviews*, *1*(25 January), CD005593.

Bliss, T. V., & Lomo, T. (1973). Long-lasting potentiation of synaptic transmission in the dentate area of the anaesthetized rabbit following stimulation of the perforant path. *Journal of Physiology*, *232*(2), 331–356.

Botvinick, M. M., Braver, T. S., Barch, D. M., Carter, C. S., & Cohen, J. D. (2001). Conflict monitoring and cognitive control. *Psychological Review*, *108*(3), 624–652. doi:10.1037//0033-295x.108.3.624

Bremner, J. D., Krystal, J. H., Southwick, S. M., & Charney, D. S. (1996). Noradrenergic mechanisms in stress and anxiety. 1: Preclinical studies. *Synapse*, *23*(1), 28–38.

Broca, P. (1861). Remarques sur le siege de la faculte du langage articule, suives d'une observation d'aphemie. *Bulletin et Memoires de la Societe Anatomique de Paris*, *2*, 330–357.

Caramazza, A. (1986). On drawing inferences about the structure of normal cognitive systems from the analysis of patterns of impaired performance: The case for single-patient studies. *Brain and Cognition*, *5*, 41–66.

Chefer, V. I., Thompson, A. C., Zapata, A., & Shippenberg, T. S. (2009). Overview of brain microdialysis. *Current Protocols in Neuroscience*, Unit 7.1. Wiley. doi:10.1002/0471142301 .ns0701s47

Chen, R., Cohen, L. G., & Hallett, M. (2002). Neuroscience: Nervous system reorganization following injury. *Neuroscience*, *111*(4), 761–773.

Chung, K., Wallace, J., Kim, S. Y., Kalyanasundaram, S., Andalman, A. S., Davidson, T. J., … Deisseroth, K. (2013). Structural and molecular interrogation of intact biological systems. *Nature*, *497*(7449), 332–337.

Cohen, L. G., Celnik, P., Pascual-Leone, A., Corwell, B., Faiz, L., Dambrosia, J., … Hallett, M. (1997). Functional relevance of cross-modal plasticity in blind humans. *Nature*, *389*, 180–183.

Conti-Fine, B. M., Milani, M., & Kaminski, H. J. (2006). Myasthenia gravis: Past, present, and future. *Journal of Clinical Investigation*, *116*(11), 2843–2854.

Corballis, M. C. (2002). *From mouth to hand: The origins of language*. Princeton, NJ: Princeton University Press.

Corthout, E., Uttle, B., Ziemann, U., Cowey, A., & Hallett, M. (1999). Two periods of processing in the (circum)striate visual cortex as revealed by transcranial magnetic stimulation. *Neuropsychologia*, *37*, 137–145.

Crabbe, J. C., Belknap, J. K., Buck, K. J., & Metten, P. (1994). Use of recombinant inbred strains for studying genetic determinants of responses to alcohol. *Alcohol and Alcoholism Supplements*, *2*, 67–71.

Damasio, H., & Damasio, A. (1989). *Lesion analysis in neuropsychology*. New York, NY: Oxford University Press.

Dehaene, S., Pegado, F., Braga, L. W., Ventura, P., Nunes, G., Jobert, A., … Cohen, L. (2010). How learning to read changes the cortical networks for vision and language. *Science*, *330*(6009), 1359–1364.

Di Chiara, G. (1999). Drug addiction as dopamine-dependent associative learning disorder. *European Journal of Pharmacology*, *375*, 13–30.

Dimberg, U., Thunberg, M., & Elmehed, K. (2000). Unconscious facial reactions to emotional facial expressions. *Psychological Science*, *11*(1), 86–89.

Dorsaint-Pierre, R., Penhune, V. B., Watkins, K. E., Neelin, P., Lerch, J. P., Bouffard, M., & Zatorre, R. J. (2006). Asymmetries of the planum temporale and Heschl's gyrus: Relationship to language lateralization. *Brain*, *129*, 1164–1176.

Draganski, B., Gaser, C., Busch, V., Schurierer, G., Bogdahn, U., & May, A. (2004). Neuroplasticity: Changes in grey matter induced by training. *Nature*, *427*, 311–312.

Engel, A. K., Konig, P., & Singer, W. (1991). Direct physiological evidence for scene segmentation by temporal encoding. *Proceedings of the National Academy of Sciences of the United States of America*, *88*, 9136–9140.

Everitt, B. J., Dickinson, A., & Robbins, T. W. (2001). The neuropsychological basis of addictive behaviour. *Brain Research Reviews*, *36*(2/3), 129–138.

Flor, H., Nikolajsen, L., & Jensen, T. S. (2006). Phantom limb pain: A case of maladaptive CNS plasticity? *Nature Reviews Neuroscience*, *7*, 873–881.

Galaburda, A. M., Lemay, M., Kemper, T. L., & Geschwind, N. (1978). Right–left asymmetries in brain. *Science*, *199*(4331), 852–856. doi:10.1126/science.341314

Gazzaniga, M. S. (2000). Cerebral specialization and interhemispheric communication: Does the corpus callosum enable the human condition? *Brain*, *123*, 1293–1326.

Gong, S., Zheng, C., Doughty, M. L., Losos, K., Didkovsky, N., Schambra, U. B., … Heintz, N. (2003). A gene expression atlas of the central nervous system based on bacterial artificial chromosomes. *Nature*, *425*(6961), 917–925.

Gougoux, F., Zatorre, R. J., Lassonde, M., Voss, P., & Lepore, F. (2005). A functional neuroimaging study of sound localization: Visual cortex activity predicts performance in early-blind individuals. *PLoS Biology*, *3*, 324–333.

Gray, H. (1918). *Anatomy of the human body*. Philadelphia, PA: Lea & Febiger.

Gross, C. G. (1992). Representation of visual stimuli in inferior temporal cortex. *Philosophical Transactions of the Royal Society B: Biological Sciences, 335*, 3–10.

Gross, C. G. (2002). Genealogy of the 'grandmother cell'. *Neuroscientist, 8*, 512–518.

Harlow, J. M. (1993). Recovery from the passage of an iron bar through the head. *History of Psychiatry, 4*, 271–281. (Reprint of original published in 1848 in *Publications of the Massachusetts Medical Society*.)

Hauk, O., Patterson, K., Woollams, A., Watling, L., Pulvermuller, F., & Rogers, T. T. (2006). Q: When would you prefer a SOSSAGE to a SAUSAGE? A: At about 100 msec. ERP correlates of orthographic typicality and lexicality in written word recognition. *Journal of Cognitive Neuroscience, 18*(5), 818–832. doi:10.1162/jocn.2006.18.5.818

Hebb, D. O. (1949). *The organization of behavior: A neuropsychological theory*. New York, NY: Wiley.

Hepper, P. G., Shahidullah, S., & White, R. (1991). Handedness in the human fetus. *Neuropsychologia, 29*(11), 1107–1111. doi:10.1016/0028-3932(91)90080-r

Hodgkin, A. L., & Huxley, A. F. (1952). A quantitative description of membrane current and its application to conduction and excitation in nerve. *Journal of Physiology, 117*, 500–544.

Home Office. (2017). *Guidance on the operation of the Animals (Scientific Procedures) Act 1986*. Retrieved 20 November 2017 from https://www.gov.uk/guidance/guidance-on-the-operation-of-the-animals-scientific-procedures-act-1986

Hommel, J. D., Sears, R. M., Georgescu, D., Simmons, D. L., & DiLeone, R. J. (2003). Local gene knockdown in the brain using viral-mediated RNA interference. *Nature Medicine, 9*(12), 1539–1544.

Hubel, D. H., & Wiesel, T. N. (1959). Receptive fields of single neurones in the cat's striate cortex. *Journal of Physiology, 148*, 574–591.

Kaas, J. H., Hackett, T. A., & Tramo, M. J. (1999). Auditory processing in primate cerebral cortex. *Current Opinion in Neurobiology, 9*, 164–170.

Kimura, D. (1973). The asymmetry of the human brain. *Scientific American, 228*, 70–78.

Kosslyn, S. M. (1999). If neuroimaging is the answer, what is the question? *Philosophical Transactions of the Royal Society B: Biological Sciences, 354*, 1283–1294.

Kutas, M., & Federmeier, K. D. (2011). Thirty years and counting: Finding meaning in the N400 component of the event-related brain potential (ERP). In S. T. Fiske, D. L. Schacter, & S. E. Taylor (Eds.), *Annual review of psychology* (Vol. *62*, pp. 621–647). Palo Alto, CA: Annual Reviews.

Lau, E. F., Phillips, C., & Poeppel, D. (2008). A cortical network for semantics: (De)constructing the N400. *Nature Reviews Neuroscience, 9*, 920–933.

Lidzba, K., Staudt, M., Wilke, M., & Krageloh-Mann, I. (2006). Visuospatial deficits in patients with early left-hemispheric lesions and functional reorganization of language: Consequence of lesion or reorganization? *Neuropsychologia, 44*, 1088–1094.

Liegeois, F., Connelly, A., Cross, J. H., Boyd, S. G., Gadian, D. G., Vargha-Khadem, F., & Baldeweg, T. (2004). Language reorganization in children with early-onset lesions of the left hemisphere: An fMRI study. *Brain, 127*, 1229–1236.

Livet, J., Weissman, T. A., Kang, H., Draft, R. W., Lu, J., Bennis, R. A., … Lichtman, J. W. (2007). Transgenic strategies for combinatorial expression of fluorescent proteins in the nervous system. *Nature, 450*(7166), 56–62.

Lotze, M., Flor, H., Grodd, W., Larbig, W., & Birbaumer, N. (2001). Phantom movements and pain: An MRI study in upper limb amputees. *Brain, 124*, 2268–2277.

Lynch, G. (2004). AMPA receptor modulators as cognitive enhancers. *Current Opinion in Pharmacology, 4*(1), 4–11.

MacLean, P. D. (1949). Psychosomatic disease and the 'visceral brain': Recent developments bearing on the Papez theory of emotion. *Psychosomatic Medicine, 11*, 338–353.

Macmillan, M. B. (1986). A wonderful journey through skull and brains: The travels of Mr. Gage's tamping iron. *Brain and Cognition, 5,* 67–107.

Malenka, R. C., & Bear, M. F. (2004). LTP and LTD: An embarrassment of riches. *Neuron, 44*(1), 5–21.

Meldrum, B. S. (1995). Excitatory amino acid receptors and their role in epilepsy and cerebral ischemia. *Annals of the New York Academy of Sciences, 757,* 492–505.

Merzenich, M. M., Nelson, R. J., Stryker, M. P., Cynader, M. S., Schoppmann, A., & Zook, J. M. (1984). Somatosensory cortical map changes following digit amputation in adult monkeys. *Journal of Comparative Neurology, 224*(4), 591–605.

Morris, B. J., Cochran, S. M., & Pratt, J. A. (2005). PCP: From pharmacology to modelling schizophrenia. *Current Opinion in Pharmacology, 5*(1), 101–106.

Mouse Genome Sequencing Consortium, Waterston, R. H., Lindblad-Toh, K., Birney, E., Rogers, J., Abril, J. F., … Lander, E. S. (2002). Initial sequencing and comparative analysis of the mouse genome. *Nature, 420*(6915), 520–562.

Mummery, C. J., Patterson, K., Price, C. J., Ashburner, J., Frackowiak, R. S. J., & Hodges, J. R. (2000). A voxel-based morphometry study of semantic dementia: Relationship between temporal lobe atrophy and semantic memory. *Annals of Neurology, 47,* 36–45.

Nabavi, S., Fox, R., Proulx, C. D., Lin, J. Y., Tsien, R. Y., & Malinow, R. (2014). Engineering a memory with LTD and LTP. *Nature, 511*(7509), 348–352. doi:10.1038/nature13294

Nitsche, M. A., Cohen, L. G., Wasserman, E. M., Priori, A., Lang, N., Antal A., … Pascual-Leone, A. (2008). Transcranial direct current stimulation: State of the art 2008. *Brain Stimulation, 1,* 206–223.

Noppeney, U. (2007). The effects of visual deprivation on functional and structural organization of the human brain. *Neuroscience & Biobehavioral Reviews, 31,* 1169–1180.

Ogawa, S., Lee, T. M., Kay, A. R., & Tank, D. W. (1990). Brain magnetic resonance imaging with contrast dependent on blood oxygenation. *Proceedings of the National Academy of Sciences of the United States of America, 87,* 9862–9872.

Oldfield, R. C. (1971). The assessment and analysis of handedness: The Edinburgh Inventory. *Neuropsychologia, 9,* 97–113.

Olds, J. (1958). Self-stimulation of the brain: Its use to study local effects of hunger, sex, and drugs. *Science, 127*(3294), 315–324.

Papez, J. W. (1937). A proposed mechanism of emotion. *Archives of Neurology and Psychiatry, 38*(4), 725–743.

Penfield, W. (1958). Some mechanisms of consciousness discovered during electrical stimulation of the brain. *Proceedings of the National Academy of Sciences of the United States of America, 44,* 51–66.

Penfield, W., & Rasmussen, T. L. (1950). *The cerebral cortex of man: A clinical study of localisation of function.* New York, NY: Macmillan.

Phelps, E. A. (2006). Emotion and cognition: Insights from studies of the human amygdala. *Annual Review of Psychology, 57,* 27–53. doi:10.1146/annurev.psych.56.091103.070234

Picciotto, M. R., & Wickman, K. (1998). Using knockout and transgenic mice to study neurophysiology and behavior. *Physiological Reviews, 78*(4), 1131–1163.

Pitcher, D., Charles, L., Devlin, J. T., Walsh, V., & Duchaine, B. (2009). Triple dissociation of faces, bodies, and objects in extrastriate cortex. *Current Biology, 19*(4), 319–324. doi:10.1016/j.cub.2009.01.007

Pittenger, C., & Kandel, E. R. (2003). In search of general mechanisms for long-lasting plasticity: Aplysia and the hippocampus. *Philosophical Transactions of the Royal Society B: Biological Sciences, 1432,* 757–763.

Prevedel, R., Yoon, Y. G., Hoffmann, M., Pak, N., Wetzstein, G., Kato, S., … Vaziri, A. (2014). Simultaneous whole-animal 3D imaging of neuronal activity using light-field microscopy. *Nature Methods, 11*(7), 727–730.

Quiroga, R. Q., Kraskov, A., Koch, C., & Fried, I. (2009). Explicit encoding of multimodal percepts by single neurons in the human brain. *Current Biology, 19*, 1308–1313.

Quiroga, R. Q., Reddy, L., Kreiman, G., Koch, C., & Fried, I. (2005). Invariant visual representation by single neurons in the human brain. *Nature, 435*, 1102–1107.

Rasmussen, T., & Milner, B. (1977). The role of early left-brain injury in determining lateralization of cerebral speech functions. *Annals of the New York Academy of Sciences, 299*(1), 355–369. doi:10.1111/j.1749-6632.1977.tb41921.x

Rizzolatti, G., & Arbib, M. A. (1998). Language within our grasp. *Trends in Neuroscience, 21*, 188–194.

Robinson, T. E., & Berridge, K. C. (1993). The neural basis of drug craving: An incentive-sensitization theory of addiction. *Brain Research Reviews, 18*(3), 247–291.

Rossi, S., Hallett, M., Rossini, P. M., Pascual-Leone, A., & Safety, T. M. S. C. G. (2009). Safety, ethical considerations, and application guidelines for the use of transcranial magnetic stimulation in clinical practice and research. *Clinical Neurophysiology, 120*(12), 2008–2039. doi:10.1016/j.clinph.2009.08.016

Rudolph, U., Crestani, F., & Mohler, H. (2001). GABA(A) receptor subtypes: Dissecting their pharmacological functions. *Trends in Pharmacological Sciences, 22*(4), 188–194.

Sachs, O. (1973). *Awakenings.* London: Duckworth & Co.

Samii, A., Nutt, J. G., & Ransom, B. R. (2004). Parkinson's disease. *Lancet, 363*(9423), 1783–1793.

Sathian, K. (2005). Visual cortical activity during tactile perception in the sighted and the visually deprived. *Developmental Psychobiology, 46*(3), 279–286.

Schultz, W. (2002). Getting formal with dopamine and reward. *Neuron, 36*(2), 241–263.

Singer, W. (2009). Distributed processing and temporal codes in neuronal networks. *Cognitive Neurodynamics, 3*(3), 189–196. doi:10.1007/s11571-009-9087-z

Sparks, D. L. (1999). Conceptual issues related to the role of the superior colliculus in the control of gaze. *Current Opinion in Neurobiology, 6*(6), 698–707.

Sperry, R. (1982). Some effects of disconnecting the cerebral hemispheres. *Science, 217*(4566), 1223–1226. doi:10.1126/science.7112125

Stahl, S. M. (1998). Mechanism of action of serotonin selective reuptake inhibitors: Serotonin receptors and pathways mediate therapeutic effects and side effects. *Journal of Affective Disorders, 51*(3), 215–235.

Stephens, D. N., & King, S. L. (2013). Neuropharmacology of benzodiazepines. In P. M. Miller, A. W. Blume, D. J. Kavanagh, K. M. Kampman, M. E. Bates M. E. Larimer,…S. A. Ball (Eds.), *Biological research on addiction: Comprehensive addictive behaviors and disorders* (Vol. 2, pp. 605–614). San Diego, CA: Academic Press.

Toth, N. (1985). Archaeological evidence for preferential right-handedness in the Lower Pleistocene, and its possible implications. *Journal of Human Evolution, 14*, 607–614.

Van der Haegen, L., Cai, Q., & Brysbaert, M. (2012). Colateralization of Broca's area and the visual word form area in left-handers: fMRI evidence. *Brain & Language, 122*(3), 171–178. doi:10.1016/j.bandl.2011.11.004

Wada, J., & Rasmussen, T. (1960). Intracarotid injection of sodium amytal for the lateralization of cerebral speech dominance: Experimental and clinical observations. *Journal of Neurosurgery, 17*(2), 266–282. doi:10.3171/jns.1960.17.2.0266

Walker, F. O. (2007). Huntington's disease. *Lancet, 369*(9557), 218–228.

Walsh, V., & Cowey, A. (2000). Transcranial magnetic stimulation and cognitive neuroscience. *Nature Reviews Neuroscience, 1*, 73–79.

Ward, J. (2015). *The student's guide to cognitive neuroscience* (3rd ed.). New York, NY: Psychology Press.

Wernicke, C. (1874). *Der aphasiche symptomenkomplex.* Wrocław, Poland: Cohn and Weigart.

Wieland, H. A., Luddens, H., & Seeburg, P. H. (1992). A single histidine in GABA-A receptors is essential for benzodiazepine agonist binding. *Journal of Biological Chemistry, 267*(3), 1426–1429.

Wisden, W., & Stephens, D. N. (1999). Towards better benzodiazepines. *Nature*, *4016755*, 751–752.

Wise, R. A. (2002). Brain reward circuitry: Insights from unsensed incentives. *Neuron, 36*(2), 229–240.

Wise, R. A. (2004). Dopamine, learning and motivation. *Nature Reviews Neuroscience, 5*(6), 483–494.

Yoneyama, N., Crabbe, J. C., Ford, M. M., Murillo, A., & Finn, D. A. (2008). Voluntary ethanol consumption in 22 inbred mouse strains. *Alcohol, 42*(3), 149–160.

Zatorre, R. J., Evans, A. C., Meyer, E., & Gjedde, A. (1992). Lateralization of phonetic and pitch discrimination in speech processing. *Science, 256*(5058), 846–849. doi:10.1126/science.1589767

Zeki, S. (1992). The visual image in mind and brain. *Scientific American, 267*, 69–76.

Zeki, S. (1993). *A vision of the brain*. Oxford, UK: Blackwell.

Zeki, S., Watson, J. D. G., Lueck, C. J., Friston, K. J., Kennard, C., & Frackowiak, R. S. J. (1991). A direct demonstration of functional specialization in human visual cortex. *Journal of Neuroscience, 11*, 641–649.

Zhang, F., Aravanis, A. M., Adamantidis, A., de Lecea, L., & Deisseroth, K. (2007). Circuit-breakers: Optical technologies for probing neural signals and systems. *Nature Reviews Neuroscience, 8*(8), 577–581.

ACTIVITY SOLUTIONS

ACTIVITY 4.2: HEMISPHERIC LATERALIZATION: TRUE OR FALSE?

True

- Information travels across the brain via the corpus callosum.
- Often, split-brain patients cannot write with their left hand.
- During the Wada test, one hemisphere is put to sleep.
- Broca's area was primarily specialized for the hand in our primate ancestors.
- Speech production tends to be more strongly left lateralized.

False

- The two hemispheres of the human brain have very different architectures.
- The left hemisphere controls voluntary movements of the left side of the body.
- Each ear sends signals to both the left and right hemispheres but with more connections contralaterally than ipsilaterally.
- Split-brain patients are those who are born without a corpus callosum.
- Left-handers are a mirror image of their right-handed counterparts in terms of brain functioning.

5 Motivation

GRAHAM DAVEY

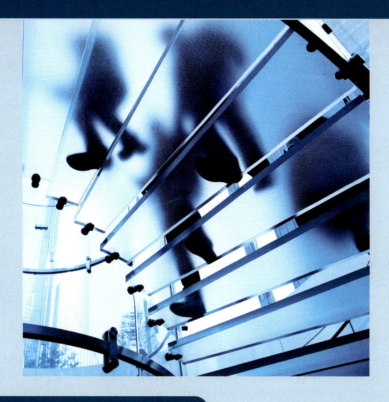

ROUTE MAP OF THE CHAPTER

This chapter describes some of the processes that enable organisms to survive, behave purposefully, and achieve personal and group goals. We begin by describing some of the traditional theories of motivation and then move on to discuss the biological bases of primary motivations such as hunger, drinking, sex, and aggression. We then describe some of the motivational processes that are fundamental to much human behaviour, including intrinsic and extrinsic motivation, and affiliation and achievement motivation. We end the chapter by providing a few examples of how these theories of motivation have been applied in practice.

CHAPTER OUTLINE

THEORIES OF MOTIVATION

LEARNING OBJECTIVE 5.1

Identify and describe the five major theories of motivation.

Researchers across many disciplines – such as psychology, economics, decision making, and sociology – are keen to establish how and why we are motivated to behave in the way we do. For many decades now, researchers have been proposing their own theories of motivation, and we are first going to examine five of the most traditional theories, each of which takes a rather different approach to explaining motivation. But these theories are not necessarily mutually exclusive, and they illustrate ways in which a variety of approaches can be used to try to understand motivation. In this section we will examine in turn:

- **Instinct theory** – This theory proposes that we are motivated primarily by our biological instincts.
- **Drive-reduction theory** – A theory that states we are driven by our desire to keep our physiology in a state of equilibrium.
- **Arousal theory** – This theory argues that we are motivated to behave in a manner that keeps us at a suitable level of arousal.
- The **hierarchy of needs** – The hierarchy of needs argues that there is a predefined order of needs that all people are driven to fulfil. We can only strive to fulfil needs higher up the hierarchy when all of the needs below are met.
- **Incentive theory** – In this approach, rewards are seen as the motivation for our behaviour.

Instinct theory

The concept of instincts has been discussed in the psychological literature for well over 100 years. The instinct theory of motivation proposes that we are biologically programmed to exhibit particular behaviours when we find ourselves in particular circumstances. For example, if you were cooking and you took something out of the oven without using oven gloves, chances are you would be motivated to put the cooking implement down very quickly, or even drop it – even before you realized you'd done it! This kind of response to holding a hot object would not have been taught to you by your parent or caregiver; instead, you were born to respond this way, as it increases the chances of you surviving. There are many instincts; some of the most commonly cited instincts that humans experience are sex, achievement, and aggression (Winston, 2002), all of which will be discussed in further detail later in this chapter.

Psychology, First Edition. Edited by Graham Davey.
© 2019 John Wiley & Sons, Ltd. Published 2019 by John Wiley & Sons, Ltd.

Another example is your reaction to a person sneezing violently in a queue next to you. You would probably move away from them pretty fast! Instinct theory may explain your behaviour by stating that the sneezing has triggered the emotion of disgust in you. Disgust may be a beneficial emotion as it helps to keep us healthy by preventing us from picking up germs and diseases (Davey, 2011), and it has been considered as an emotion that is largely biologically pre-wired (Curtis & Biran, 2001).

Although a popular and well-known theory of motivation, instinct theory has been critiqued widely in the scientific literature. Bernard, Mills, Swenson, and Walsh (2005, p. 131) found that many writers think that instinct theory is overly simplistic because it does not fully consider how our motivations can be affected by our conscious decisions. Many people are motivated to behave in a way that goes against their natural instincts. For example, 1.6 million people in the United Kingdom experience an eating disorder (National Institute of Clinical Excellence, 2004), and eating disorders such as anorexia nervosa are characterized by the individual failing to eat enough to sustain an acceptable body weight. As you know, eating is key for our survival; therefore, instinct theory would not be able to account for these behaviours, which are surprisingly common in many Western societies.

Drive-reduction theory

Drive-reduction theory (see Figure 5.1) argues that we are motivated to keep our bodies in a state of **homeostasis**. Homeostasis is when the conditions inside the human body are at a constant level, which the body's mechanisms will then try to maintain. Examples of homeostasis include maintaining a constant body temperature, fluid level, nutrient level, and blood sugar.

Drive-reduction theory proposes that, when the internal conditions of the body are no longer in balance, we are driven to find a way to bring the body's internal environment back into equilibrium. This occurs, for example, when we lose water from our cells when we consume salty foods. This has the effect of making the body

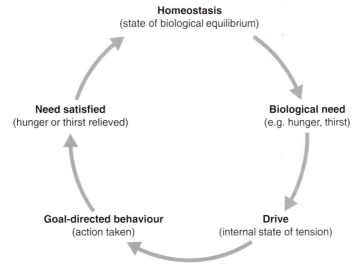

FIGURE 5.1 *Hull's drive-reduction theory.*
Source: Based on Hull (1943).

dehydrated, which acts as a drive to try to increase the body's fluid levels. Our bodies have a set of receptors and mechanisms that detect this water loss and relay this information to the areas of the brain that control our drinking and water conservation; this triggers the motivation to drink, and once water has been consumed our thirst drive is reduced and our body restored to homeostasis. In Africa alone, nearly 1 billion people cannot find clean water to drink and have to resort to drinking dirty water. This means finding clean, safe drinking water is extremely important for the people who live in these areas (Water Project, 2015). Nonetheless, many of these people are aware that drinking dirty water can lead to numerous illnesses and diseases. If we think about this in terms of drive-reduction theory, we might suppose that people may be drinking dirty water in order to reduce the drive for fluids.

If you think about what you have felt motivated to do in the past hour or so, how would drive-reduction theory explain your motivations? From this you might be able to see a problem with drive-reduction theory – the theory does not explain the motivation we feel for the behaviours that we take part in that are not triggered by our homeostatic levels. For example, many people are motivated to go out to a nightclub for a night of dancing. However, this kind of activity often makes us dehydrated, as we get hot and tired, and it often involves a late night including a loss of sleep. We therefore start to move out of homeostatic balance. This example shows that we cannot explain all motivation we experience using the drive-reduction theory of motivation.

Drive-reduction theory also proposes that, when our drives are reduced, we experience this as rewarding (Hull, 1943; see also Berridge, 2000, p. 228) and this then influences our motivation. This has been proposed as one way of attempting to understand **addictive behaviours** (such as drug addiction). In particular, addiction can be conceptualized as the motivation to seek the physiological and neurological pleasures associated with drug taking – many of which stimulate pleasure and reduce pain by influencing the opioid and dopamine systems in the brain. There have been a number of theories that have attempted to explain the way in which rewards influence and motivate behaviour through drive reduction, and these are described below.

Opponent-process theory

In **opponent-process theory**, our biological and neurological systems may respond to stimuli by opposing their initial effects, and this process is illustrated in Figure 5.2. For example, the physiological and psychological effects of a drug may peak soon after it is administered, but this will slowly disperse over time, and as the level of the drug in the system disappears this will lead to an 'after-reaction' that produces physiological effects that are contrary to those of the drug. For instance, after the experience of a pleasurable drug, the after-reaction may be one that is particularly unpleasurable and this process will probably contribute to the aversive effects of withdrawal from an addictive drug.

Learning theory approaches

What is additionally interesting about the rewarding effects of drugs is that they can also be understood in terms of principles associated with associative learning. There are two main processes involved here. The first is the process of **positive reinforcement** and the second is the way in which stimuli associated with positive reinforcement come to act as cues that motivate **craving** for a drug.

Positive reinforcement In many cases, the consequence of taking recreational drugs is that they have short-term pleasurable effects. In learning theory terms, this probably means that they will positively reinforce the behaviours that led to the drug

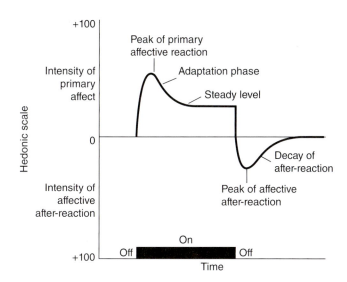

FIGURE 5.2 *A schematic representation of the opposing processes proposed by opponent-process theory.*

Source: Solomon and Corbit (1974). Copyright 1974 by the American Psychological Association. Reprinted with permission.

being taken. Many animals can be taught to make specific responses (such as pressing a lever) to self-administer psychoactive drugs (e.g. Grasing et al., 2003), and these drugs appear to have their reinforcing pleasurable effects through a common brain circuitry in the limbic system (Feltenstein & See, 2008). The drugs achieve their pleasurable effects primarily by influencing the dopamine system, which is a neurotransmitter that regulates movement, emotion, cognition, and feelings of pleasure. This system is known as the brain's reward system, and when it is activated it helps us to learn and remember that something important has happened and to repeat the actions that led to the rewarding effects. Most drugs stimulate this reward system, which enables us to remember the actions (e.g. taking the drug) that led to the feeling of euphoria and pleasure.

Craving Learning theory also helps to explain one particular feature of drug addiction, known as 'craving'. This is when specific situations, sights, and sounds become associated with the pleasurable consequences of drug taking, and so, through a process of associative learning, these sights, sounds, and situations come to elicit a craving for the drug. For example, pubs and clubs will elicit the desire for an alcoholic drink in regular drinkers, and the smell of cigarette smoke will induce cravings for nicotine addicts. Some theories argue that craving or 'wanting' is the primary motivational force in drug addiction, and that the role of the dopamine system is not simply to activate 'pleasurable effects' when a drug is used (**reward pathways**; see Figure 5.3) but also to attribute **incentive salience** to events and stimuli associated with the drug. This makes stimuli associated with the drug more 'attractive' and more 'wanted'. This theory is known as the 'incentive-sensitization theory of addiction' (Robinson & Berridge, 1993, 2003), and in many individuals the repeated use of addictive drugs renders the dopamine system increasingly sensitive to drugs and drug-associated stimuli. Focus Point 5.1 provides you with a more detailed discussion of craving.

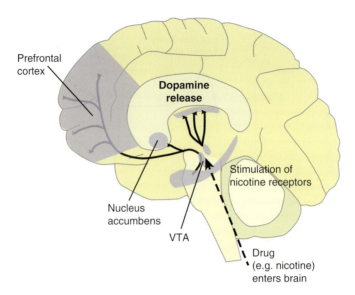

FIGURE 5.3 *The dopamine reward pathway. Most addictive drugs have the ability to stimulate the release of the neurotransmitter dopamine, which induces feelings of euphoria and pleasure and activates the dopamine reward pathway. The important interconnected structures of the reward pathway include the ventral tegmental area (VTA), the **nucleus accumbens**, and the **prefrontal cortex** (the area of the brain responsible for thinking and judgement). The neurons of the VTA contain the neurotransmitter dopamine, which is released in the nucleus accumbens and in the prefrontal cortex.*

Source: Adapted from Wikimedia Commons.

CRAVING

Craving has significant effects on those suffering from substance abuse disorders.

Source: f-f-f-f / Shutterstock.com.

The pleasurable effects of drug use can act as potent stimuli that will generate 'craving' responses to cues associated with the drug. This occurs through a process of conditioning in which the drug acts as a powerful unconditioned stimulus that reinforces conditioned responses to drug cues.

This means that aspects such as the sensory features of the drug (e.g. a white powder), the environment in which it is taken (e.g. a pub), or the people the user socializes with when taking the drug can all become cues that elicit craving for the drug. Cues for a particular drug can actually trigger responses in the user that are very similar to those associated with actual use of the drug, and these include pleasurable feelings, physiological arousal, and activation of brain reward centres (Filbey & DeWitt, 2012). In addition, craving can induce attentional biases that enhance processing of drug cues, as well as drug-anticipatory responses that exacerbate the craving (Field, Mogg, Mann, Bennett, & Bradley, 2013).

Although generated by nonconscious classical conditioning process, craving is often characterized as a conscious state that intervenes between the unconscious cues and consumption (Andrade, May, & Kavanagh, 2012). Craving has significant effects on those suffering substance abuse disorders. People who crave a substance do use that substance more than people who don't crave it (Berkman, Falk, & Lieberman, 2011), and, as you can imagine, craving is a significant obstacle to successful treatment and frequently leads to relapse (Evren, Durkaya, Evren, Dalbudak, & Cetin, 2012; Paliwal, Hyman, & Sinha, 2007).

Arousal theory

Arousal theory proposes that we are motivated to act in a manner that keeps our arousal at a desirable level (Litman, 2005). This desirable level is individual to each person and some people have higher arousal levels than others – this explains why people who are in the same situation can be motivated to behave in different ways. If you have ever been away on a group holiday, you may have witnessed this yourself. Even though everyone in the group is at the same holiday location, some people will want to spend the days sitting on the beach relaxing, while others may want to be off taking part in jet skiing! Arousal theory would suggest that those who want to spend their time on the beach have low arousal levels, while those who want to take part in the water sports have higher levels.

Arousal can also influence our performance levels, and this effect is known as the **Yerkes–Dodson law** (see Udacity, 2013). A diagram of this phenomenon is shown in Figure 5.4. The Yerkes–Dodson law proposes that there is a set level of arousal.

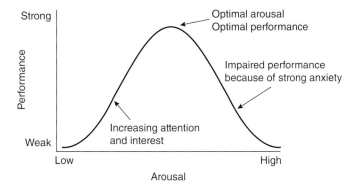

FIGURE 5.4 *The Yerkes–Dodson law.*

Source: Diamond, Campbel, Park, Halonen, and Zoladz (2007).

When we are at this set level, our performance is the highest it can be. However, the further away our arousal levels move from this point, the worse our performance becomes (Cohen, 2011). The Yerkes–Dodson law has been found to apply in many diverse situations. For example, Johnston, Moreno, Regas, Tyler, and Foreyt (2012) studied children aged 11–14 who were taking part in a weight-loss program. They found that those children who had a medium level of dissatisfaction with their weight experienced the greatest weight loss. However, those children with low and high levels of weight dissatisfaction actually increased in weight. The Yerkes–Dodson law has been applied in multiple psychological phenomena and we suggest interested readers consult Teigen (1994) for a review.

Hierarchy of needs

Abraham Maslow is one of psychology's most well-known and well-cited scholars (Haggbloom et al., 2002), and this fame arose because of his theory of motivation known as Maslow's hierarchy of needs. This is one of the oldest theories of motivation, and Maslow began writing about this theory in 1943. A pictorial representation of the theory is shown in Figure 5.5.

Maslow proposed that there are five types of need that we are all motivated to fulfil. However, we cannot try to fulfil all of the needs at the same time; we can only try to fulfil needs that are higher up the pyramid once all of the needs below have been met. Hagerty (1999) tested this prediction from Maslow's theory by collecting data from 88 countries relevant to the five levels of need. He found support for the notion that people can only be motivated by needs higher up the hierarchy once more basic needs have been met.

If we look at the hierarchical structure of these needs, at the bottom of the pyramid are the physiological needs that can be considered as physical requirements for human survival. These include the need for food, water, air, sleep, warmth, and so

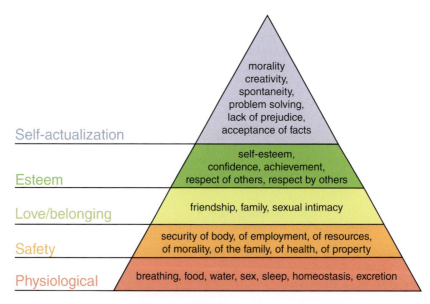

FIGURE 5.5 *Abraham Maslow's hierarchy of needs.*

on. It can be hard for us to think about how it might feel for people who struggle to meet these needs, as the majority of people in developed countries do not have to struggle too much to find food or water. However, if you think carefully, you may be able to think of examples. For example, have you ever seen a homeless person reaching into a dustbin for food? Most of us would struggle to do this ourselves; however, Maslow's theory would propose that, if you were hungry, you would be motivated to find food in any way.

The next stage in the hierarchy focuses on safety needs. These encompass our need to feel secure and sheltered. For example, individuals who are seeking political asylum may be motivated primarily by their safety needs.

Love and belonging needs are focused on people's desire to form social bonds. We will discuss this aspect of motivation later on in this chapter when we discuss motivation for affiliation and review evidence suggesting that having social relationships can be beneficial for our health and well-being. Given that the social media website Facebook had over 2 billion active members as of late 2017, we can probably assume that very many people are motivated to feel connected to other people!

The hierarchy next focuses on esteem needs. This assumes that people are motivated to achieve, feel confident, and be respected. The final level on the hierarchy is **self-actualization**. This means that, when all the previous needs are met, we feel motivated to engage with activities that will make us develop and flourish as individuals. For example, attending university may be an example of you fulfilling your need for self-actualization.

Maslow's hierarchy of needs has been utilized across a wide spectrum of contexts, such as businesses and health practices. It is also very frequently used in the context of education and teaching, and Hutchinson (2003) describes how the hierarchy can be applied in the classroom. For example, she proposes that physiological needs could be met by making sure students get sufficient breaks and ensuring the classroom is at a comfortable temperature, and fulfilling the student's needs for safety could be encouraged by promoting a learning environment that encourages respect in the classroom.

Despite some evidence that appears to support Maslow's hierarchy of needs, it has also received some criticism. For example, sex is placed with other physiological needs at the base of the hierarchy, and some critics believe that this ignores the important emotional and evolutionary implications of sex within many communities (Kenrick, Griskevicius, Neuberg, & Schaller, 2010). In addition, the way in which the hierarchy is constructed is often viewed as ethnocentric, and it does not differentiate between the differing intellectual and social needs found in individualistic societies and collectivist societies (Hofstede, 1984). Wahba and Bridwell (1976) point out that there is only a small body of published research that supports the theory. However, they do note that the theory is difficult to evaluate in a research setting, which is in part due to the fact that many of the terms central to the theory are not clearly operationalized and therefore not easily measurable. This evaluation led Wahba and Bridwell (1976) to deem Maslow's theory as 'almost a nontestable theory' (p. 234).

Incentive theory

When you come to read the section of this chapter on 'Intrinsic versus Extrinsic Motivation', you will see there are two distinctly different types of motivation – one type that is driven by us finding a task or activity interesting and enjoyable (intrinsic motivation) and a further type whereby our behaviour is motivated purely because we reap some kind of benefit from that activity (extrinsic motivation). Incentive theory suggests that it is the second form of motivation that drives much of our behaviour (Bindra, 1959).

Incentives that motivate our behaviour can be divided into two types: primary incentives and secondary incentives. **Primary incentives** are biologically salient to our survival (examples include food and sex). Incentives also include punishments that act as deterrents for behaviour, an example of which is pain.

Secondary incentives and punishments have no inherent value in themselves. They only possess value because we know they are associated with other stimuli and events. For example, designer clothes could be thought of as a secondary incentive as it is the association with living a luxury lifestyle that is rewarding. A secondary punishment could be receiving a demotion at work. The demotion is not harmful in itself – it is the loss of prestige and possible loss of wages that would be punishing.

Incentives are sometimes used by employers in the workplace in the form of bonuses and commissions, which, according to incentive theory, act as secondary incentives. Figure 5.6 shows Bonner and Sprinkle's (2002) model, which would suggest that money influences motivational constructs, which can then affect how much effort people put into a task. This then affects how well someone completes a task (Bonner & Sprinkle, 2002, p. 336).

DISCUSSION POINT

Discuss the differences between primary and secondary incentives and include some examples from your own experience.

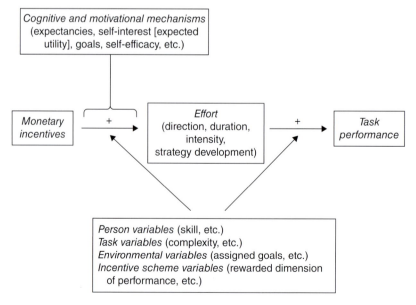

FIGURE 5.6 *A conceptual framework for the effects of performance-contingent monetary incentives on effort and task performance.*

Source: Bonner and Sprinkle (2002).

SECTION SUMMARY

- Five major theories of motivation have been proposed: instinct theory, drive-reduction theory, arousal theory, the hierarchy of needs, and incentive theory.
- Instinct theory proposes that we are motivated primarily by our biological instincts.
- Drive-reduction theory states that we are driven by our desire to keep our physiology in a state of equilibrium.
- Arousal theory argues that we are motivated to behave in a manner that keeps us at a suitable level of arousal. Arousal can also influence our performance levels, and this effect is known as the Yerkes–Dodson law.
- Maslow's hierarchy of needs argues that there is a predefined order of needs that all people are driven to fulfil. We can only strive to fulfil needs higher up the hierarchy when all of the needs below it are met.
- Incentive theory proposes that rewards are seen as the motivation for our behaviour. Incentives that motivate our behaviour can be divided into two types: primary incentives and secondary incentives.

THE BIOLOGICAL BASES OF PRIMARY MOTIVATIONS: HUNGER AND DRINKING

LEARNING OBJECTIVE 5.2

Explain the biological processes that underlie the motivations of hunger and drinking, and name and describe the main disorders associated with eating.

We'll now explore some of the biological processes that are important for our daily survival. Many of these primary motivations form the basis of our behaviour on a day-to-day basis, and they include hunger and thirst (the topics of this section) and sex and aggression (covered in the next main section). Each topic investigates the factors that trigger these motivations and describes some of the biological processes that underlie them.

Hunger

Everyone regularly feels the motivation to eat. For example, it is recommended that men should eat 2,500 calories a day, while it is suggested that women take in 2,000 calories (NHS Choices, 2015). In this section, we will examine the mechanisms that underlie the physiological processes that make us feel hungry and then explore some of the psychological drivers. Finally, we will review why some people experience eating disorders. This includes looking at what happens when people's eating patterns become problematic and also when people simply overeat.

Biological factors involved in hunger

This section will describe the physiology of hunger, including the mechanical signals, chemical signals, and brain signals that motivate us to eat.

Mechanical signals We all have a number of mechanoreceptors in our stomach that can be stimulated by mechanical manipulation. When the stomach is full of food, it stretches out like a balloon. These mechanoreceptors detect the change in the stomach's size and convey this information to the central nervous system (Grundy, 2002). There are a number of different types of mechanoreceptors present in the human body, and it is the tension and stretch receptors that are responsible for relaying information about our feeling full; however, stretch receptors may have a greater role in this process than tension receptors (Carmagnola, Cantu, & Penagini, 2005).

As we will discuss later, obesity is becoming an increasing problem; health services are offering more and more weight-loss interventions for individuals who are overweight, and weight-loss surgery is available that can be used to alter the mechanical signals that trigger hunger. In the United Kingdom, there are two different types of weight loss surgery. The first, a gastric band, decreases the volume of the stomach. Alternatively, people may be offered a gastric bypass, which means the stomach is physically altered so less food is absorbed by the body (NHS, 2011). Both of these procedures lead to stretch receptors becoming activated quickly when someone starts eating. This means they should then stop eating earlier, as the stretch receptors convey the feeling of fullness to the brain. However, although they commonly lead to short-term weight loss, these surgeries can be ineffective in the long term and people can often put weight back on over time (Catalano, Rudic, Anderson, & Chua, 2007; Santoro, 2012). Therefore, along with surgery, the NHS recommends that all patients eat a healthy diet and engage in regular exercise (NHS, 2011). Because influencing the mechanoreceptors does not allow for complete control of an individual's appetite, this implies that there may be other biological mechanisms that also influence our levels of hunger.

Chemical signals When we eat, a number of physiological and chemical processes are involved in the digestion of food. Digestion starts from the time the food is in our mouth right until the food is expelled from the gastrointestinal tract. This process involves the complex molecules in the food being broken down into simple molecules, which the body can use as an energy source. For example, while this conversion is occurring, glucose and lipids are two of the chemicals that are released during digestion that contribute to us feeling satiated.

As well as molecules, the hormones leptin and ghrelin can influence our eating behaviour (Klok, Jakobsdottir, & Drent, 2007). **Leptin** is produced when fat cells increase in size, and the hypothalamus picks up on this increase in leptin and tells the body to stop eating. The stomach releases the second hormone, **ghrelin**, when our bodies require food. Again, the hypothalamus is responsible for monitoring the levels of ghrelin, and, when the hypothalamus detects a threshold level of ghrelin, we begin to feel hunger (Klok et al., 2007).

Brain signals The lateral hypothalamus and the ventromedial hypothalamus relay important information that both stimulates and stops eating. It is the **lateral hypothalamus** that signals to the body that we need to eat. For example, when electrical currents are used to stimulate the lateral hypothalamus in rats, these animals then begin to eat (Wise, 1974). Conversely, damaging the lateral hypothalamus reduces eating behaviour (Teitelbaum & Epstein, 1962). In contrast, the **ventromedial hypothalamus**, which is located next to the lateral hypothalamus, informs the brain when we are full and causes us to stop eating, and lesioning this region leads to obesity in humans and a number of other animals (see King, 2006). It was initially hypothesized that activation of either one of these regions would preclude the other region from being active, and this is known as the **dual-centre theory of motivation**. So, activity in the lateral hypothalamus would not only signal hunger; it would also send inhibitory signals to the ventromedial hypothalamus to prevent us from feeling satiated. However, the effects of these brain centres are more complex than this, and we must remember that eating is a complex behaviour that not only involves mechanical and chemical signals to the lateral hypothalamus and ventromedial hypothalamus but also involves the influence of taste cues and previous learning about whether individual foods have been either nutritious or problematic in the past. Add to this the social and cultural aspects of eating, such as the cultural pressures among young women to maintain a slim body shape in many Western societies, and you can see how complex and multilevelled the factors that contribute to hunger may be.

In addition, men's and women's brains may respond differently to food. Del Parigi and colleagues (2002) placed 22 men and 22 women in a positron emission tomography scanner. Scans were conducted after people had fasted and also when they were full. There was some similarity in terms of brain activation; however, men showed more activity in the frontotemporal and paralimbic regions after fasting. Differences also emerged when brain activity was examined when people were full – women showed significantly greater activity in the sensory association areas and in the dorsolateral prefrontal cortex, while men showed more activity in the ventromedial prefrontal cortex. Del Parigi et al. (2002) interpreted this to indicate that men and women exhibit differential emotional and cognitive reactions to eating.

Drawing the biological mechanisms together To summarize, a number of mechanical, chemical, and brain signals convey information that influences our motivation to start and to stop eating. These signals all interact to control our appetite – for example, our brain detects the levels of chemicals that are released when we digest food and the hormones that are released in response to food, and the brain then processes this information in a way that influences our eating behaviours by generating feelings of either hunger or satiety.

Eating as a behaviour

As well as the basic physiological processes that we have just discussed, other factors can also influence our motivation to eat. Figure 5.7 shows some of the basic physiological factors, higher-level psychological processes, and sociocultural influences that affect eating behaviour. For example, at some point in our lives, all of us have had our appetite levels influenced by psychological factors. For instance, have you ever been through a relationship breakup and found yourself eating lots of comfort foods such as crisps, biscuits, and ice cream? Many people can relate to this experience. Psychological research has documented that our mood can have a big influence on our eating – when people are more stressed, they feel more motivated to eat, hungrier, and less able to restrict what they eat (Groesz et al., 2012).

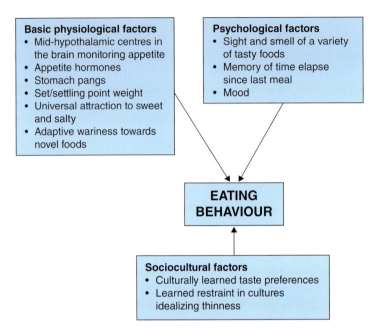

FIGURE 5.7 *Some of the diverse biological, psychological, and sociocultural factors that can influence eating behaviour.*

Eating disorders: What happens when things go wrong with hunger

The obesity epidemic We have just outlined how our mood can make us over-eat. However, there are a number of other factors that can lead to us overeating. If overeating occurs in a situation in which we are not exercising enough to burn off these extra calories, we can become overweight and obese. To be classed as overweight, an individual must have a **body mass index (BMI)** over 25. If the BMI goes above 30, this means an individual is categorized as obese (World Health Organization, 2015). Within Europe, more than half of all adults are overweight or obese and around one third of children are also overweight, and these figures are expected to continue to rise (Irish Medical Organisation & British Medical Association Northern Ireland, 2010). Becoming overweight or obese puts huge pressure on our bodies and can cause a number of health problems, including life-threatening cardiovascular diseases, Type 2 diabetes, and problems with our joints, as well as increasing our risks of experiencing particular types of cancers (World Health Organization, 2015).

Witkos, Uttaburanont, Lang, and Arora (2008) propose that one of the reasons why people are becoming overweight and obese is because in today's modern societies there are more and more highly calorific foods available but we do not exercise enough to burn these calories off. In the past, people ate healthier, home-cooked food and engaged in more exercise. If you speak to older people in your family, they will probably tell you about long walks to school and back and eating freshly cooked food. This type of lifestyle is now much less common than it was over 50 years ago.

One factor that may contribute to our decreasing levels of exercise is an increase in sedentary activities such as television viewing or computer gaming. Because watching television burns very few calories, and we are increasingly viewing more and more television in our free time, it is not hard to see television as a contributor to our increasing waistbands. However, television may also make us more prone to putting on weight for another reason – advertising. When we watch television, we often view a large number of food and drink adverts, and viewing these kinds of adverts has been found to increase eating behaviours in both children and adults (Harris, Bargh, & Brownell, 2009). In one experiment it was found that children who received an educational intervention to reduce their television usage had a lower BMI than those who did not receive the intervention (Robinson, 1999). We must note, however, that this intervention evidence (and other evidence like it) cannot determine whether it was the reduced exposure to adverts that caused the weight loss; increased exercise may have also contributed to this effect.

Another factor is that we are now eating larger and larger food portions (Nielsen & Popkin, 2003); therefore, it is unsurprising that people are putting on weight! Popular documentaries such as *Super Size Me* (2004) and research by Young and Nestle (2007) have pointed out that some fast-food establishments are serving larger portions than they were when they originally opened. However, we are also providing ourselves with larger meals when we are at home (Nielsen & Popkin, 2003), and when we are presented with large food portions it appears most of us are poor at controlling our impulse to eat, and many of us take in more calories than we need when presented with a large plate of food (Ledikwe, Ello-Martin, & Rolls, 2005).

Another factor that appears to influence our weight is one that is probably out of our own control, and this is our genetic make-up. Genetic inheritance plays an important role in determining our weight – in fact around 40–70% of the variation in our weight is accounted for by our genes (reviewed by Herrera, Keildson, & Lindgren, 2011). In some rare cases genetic factors can interfere with the production of leptin molecules (which would normally signal the brain to stop eating), and as a consequence this is a factor that can contribute to obesity (Farooqi & O'Rahilly, 2006).

Bulimia nervosa and anorexia nervosa Many people struggle to manage their eating patterns, and we have already discussed problems of overeating that lead to obesity. One cause of obesity is binge eating, which can give rise to a diagnosis of binge-eating disorder, but eating disorders can also manifest as more complex forms of problematic eating (e.g. bulimia nervosa and anorexia nervosa). Currently, around 1.6 million people in the United Kingdom have an eating disorder (Mental Health Foundation, 2015), and this figure may even underestimate the scale of the problem because people with eating disorders are often secretive about their difficulties and can be reluctant to seek help from professionals. In the following subsections, we will discuss what happens when people experience two particularly distressing eating disorders, namely **anorexia nervosa** and **bulimia nervosa**, which are two of the most common eating disorders (Polivy & Herman, 2002).

Bulimia nervosa Bulimia nervosa is a condition where an individual eats an excessive amount of food and then purge in an attempt to rid themselves of the food they have consumed. People can purge in various ways, but two of the most common methods include sufferers making themselves vomit or taking laxatives. Most people with bulimia engage in this toxic behavioural cycle in a very secretive manner. A binge can be triggered by a variety of factors, such as low mood, experience of stress, or intense hunger. Because the purging behaviours may often bring a sense of relief to people experiencing bulimia, we can begin to see how this harmful behaviour can be reinforced in sufferers (Davey, 2014).

 Professor Janet Treasure discusses the symptoms and impacts of bulimia nervosa in **this video**[1].

Typically, most people who experience bulimia start to experience symptoms between the ages of 16 and 20 years (Stice, Marti, & Rohde, 2013), and, as with the other main eating disorder (anorexia nervosa), the majority of the people who experience bulimia are female (Gotestam & Agras, 1995). Unsurprisingly, therefore, being female has been found to be a risk factor for experiencing an eating disorder. In addition, research by Jacobi, Hayward, de Zwaan, Kraemer, and Agras (2004) has identified a wide range of factors that put someone at risk of an eating disorder. Being concerned about your weight and experiencing trauma, problems with eating as a child, and stomach problems are predictive of later experiences of eating disorders. If you are interested in finding out more about the risk factors for eating disorders, we recommend you read the Jacobi et al. (2004) article for a full list.

Although bulimia may not be as life-threatening as anorexia, the consequences of this illness are still very serious. People who have suffered from bulimia often lose the enamel on their teeth, which can occur after prolonged periods of vomiting, and the parotid glands (otherwise known as the salivary glands), which are located near the mouth and the ears, can become swollen, which gives rise to a puffy face. Irregular menstruation is another side effect of this eating disorder (Davey, 2014).

Treatment guidelines for bulimia nervosa recommend a diverse set of both psychological and pharmacological treatments. Initially, the National Institute of Clinical Excellence (2004) suggested that sufferers could be given help through the use of self-help resources (DeBar et al., 2011); however, for some sufferers, providing self-help is not enough to aid recovery, and psychological interventions such as cognitive behaviour therapy (CBT) can be offered and adapted to the individual needs of the sufferer (National Institute of Clinical Excellence, 2004). Waller et al. (2014) investigated the effectiveness of individual CBT when offered to people experiencing bulimia. After treatment, half of the patients were no longer experiencing an eating disorder and their mood was improved, and they showed healthier thoughts about food and healthier eating patterns.

Other forms of psychological therapy can also be offered. For example, as well as CBT, interpersonal therapy is recommended. Research evidence suggests that this form of psychological therapy can be beneficial, even when offered in a brief format (Arcelus, Whight, Brewin, & McGrain, 2012).

Finally, medication can be beneficial in helping people to recover from bulimia nervosa. Selective serotonin reuptake inhibitors (SSRIs), which are a form of antidepressant drug, can be offered, and the National Institute of Clinical Excellence (2004) explicitly recommends the drug fluoxetine. When offered in a general practice setting, fluoxetine can often be at least as effective as psychological therapies in alleviating bulimia symptoms (Walsh, Fairburn, Mickley, Sysko, & Parides, 2004).

TABLE 5.1 *Commonly used diagnostic criteria for anorexia used by clinicians. For a definitive diagnosis, the following are required.*

DSM-IV TR	ICD-10

• Refusal to maintain body weight at or above a minimally normal weight for age and height (body weight less than 85% of that expected).
 • Intense fear of gaining weight.
 • Disturbance in the way in which the individual's body weight or shape is experienced.
 • In postmenarchal females, amenorrhoea (the absence of three consecutive menstrual cycles).
 • Specifier:
   • restricting type
   • binge-eating/purging type.
	• Body weight is maintained at least 15% below that expected (either lost or never achieved) or BMI ≤ 17.5.
	 • Weight loss is self-induced.
	 • Body-image distortion.
	 • Endocrine disorder – hypothalamic–pituitary–gonadal axis:
	   • in women as amenorrhoea
	   • in men as a loss of sexual interest and potency.
	 • Sequence of pubertal events is delayed or arrested.

Source: Adapted from Goyal, Balhara, and Khandelwal (2012).

Anorexia nervosa People who experience anorexia nervosa become fixated on keeping their body weight down and, as a result, control their food portions to such an extent that they severely restrict the amount of food they eat (see Table 5.1 for a summary of the diagnostic criteria for anorexia nervosa). This means that people with anorexia nervosa will have a significantly low body weight. Davey (2014, drawing on Bryant-Waugh, 2000) notes that anorexia can also cause the following health problems:

> (1) tiredness, cardiac arrhythmias, hypotension, low blood pressure and slow heart-beats resulting from altered levels of body electrolytes, such as sodium and potassium, (2) dry skin and brittle hair, (3) kidney and gastrointestinal problems, (4) the development of lanugo (a soft, downy hair) on the body, (5) the absence of menstrual cycles (amenorrhea), and (6) hypothermia, often resulting in feeling cold even in hot environments.

These health conditions can be extremely serious and, if left untreated, anorexia nervosa can often have life-threatening consequences.

People who experience anorexia typically begin to do so during their teenage years; experiencing anorexia in childhood or after the age of 40 is unusual (Davey, 2014). As with other eating disorders, it is usually women who present to clinical services with anorexia, and Western media may well contribute to this gender bias by portraying female role models who are unnaturally thin (see Figure 5.8). But there may be an increasing number of men experiencing eating disorders; however, they may be less likely than women to come into contact with health services for the condition (National Centre for Eating Disorders, 2015).

As mentioned above, anorexia can be a life-threatening condition; therefore, some individuals may be hospitalized during the course of medical as well as psychological treatment for the disorder (National Institute of Clinical Excellence, 2004). The National Institute of Clinical Excellence (2004) guidelines suggest that a number of psychological interventions could be offered to people experiencing anorexia nervosa.

FIGURE 5.8 *Western media regularly portray female role models as either naturally thin (and therefore representative of only a minority of the female population) or unnaturally thin. Young adolescent females then strive to achieve these relatively unattainable, or simply unhealthy, ideals.*
Source: Olga Ekaterincheva / Shutterstock.

These include CBT, cognitive analytic therapy, interpersonal therapy, and psychodynamic therapy. Finally, a commonly adopted intervention for anorexia is family or systemic therapy, and this is because an adolescent's eating disorder may have its roots in the relationships within the family, and family therapy can help to identify these dysfunctional relationships and to provide a means of managing them (Dallos, 2004).

Drinking

Drinking water is vital for our survival – depending on the outside temperature and our levels of activity, we can normally only survive for around 3 days without fluids (Funston & Wagner, 2010). Many health promotion campaigns are aimed at generally increasing our fluid intake. There are two distinct types of thirst that we experience (Kalat, 2015):

- **Osmotic thirst** occurs when we lose water from inside a cell, which occurs because of increases in salt levels outside the cell.
- **Hypovolaemic thirst** is experienced when we lose fluids from outside the cells. This fluid loss can occur when we sweat, bleed, or experience diarrhoea.

Intracellular fluid and extracellular fluid

The fluid in our body can be divided into two types: the fluid that is found within our cells, which is called **intracellular fluid**, and the fluid that is found outside the cells, which is referred to as **extracellular fluid**. Intracellular fluid is high in potassium and low in sodium, and is largely made up of other types of electrolytes.

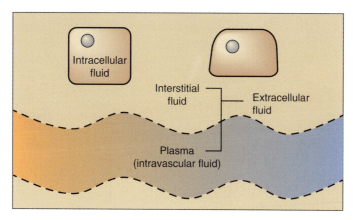

FIGURE 5.9 *Major fluid compartments. Intracellular fluid is fluid within cells. Extracellular fluid is fluid outside cells. The extracellular fluid includes interstitial fluid surrounding the cells, and plasma, the fluid component of blood.*

Extracellular fluid, on the other hand, is found in blood, body cavities, channels in the brain and spinal cord, and muscle and other body tissues, and is generally high in sodium. Extracellular fluid is made up of interstitial fluid and blood plasma (blood plasma is also referred to as intravascular fluid). Figure 5.9 provides a summary of intracellular and extracellular fluid in the body.

Osmotic thirst

When we eat salt, the sodium from the food travels to the extracellular fluid (Kalat, 2015). However, the sodium ions are too large to pass through the semipermeable membrane that surrounds each cell body. This increase in sodium in the extracellular fluid means the concentration of the extracellular fluid is greater than the concentration of the intracellular fluid (Kalat, 2015, p. 302). Because water moves from an area of low solute concentration to areas with high solute concentration – a process known as osmosis – water diffuses through the semipermeable cell membrane from the intracellular compartment to the extracellular compartment (Kalat, 2015; Martin et al., 2010). Receptors in the brain called osmoreceptors register this movement of water. Kalat (2015) identified the organum vasculosum of the lamina terminalis and the subfornical organ as two of the brain regions involved in monitoring osmotic pressure, and the stomach also contains receptors that monitor sodium (Kalat, 2007). All of these receptors convey information to the areas of the brain that influence drinking behaviour (Kalat, 2007, 2015). These receptors also cause the body to increase the levels of a hormone called **vasopressin**, which enables the body to retain water and to increase blood pressure (Kalat, 2007). See Figure 5.10 for a depiction of osmotic thirst.

Hypovolaemic thirst

When we lose blood or sweat, or experience diarrhoea, the volume of our blood plasma drops (Kalat, 2015; Martin et al., 2010). There are a number of receptors that detect this loss of fluid. Firstly there are **baroreceptors**, which are located in the blood vessels (Martin et al., 2010). There are also further receptors located in the kidneys, which cause the production of renin, which then causes a further hormone called angiotensin to be released. Angiotensin is one of the main hormones that motivates drinking, and it also has the effect of stimulating vasopressin – the role of which was discussed earlier – and **aldosterone**, which increases blood pressure and makes the body retain both salt and water (Epstein et al., 1970; Rolls, Jones, & Fallows, 1972). See Figure 5.10 for a depiction of hypovolaemic thirst.

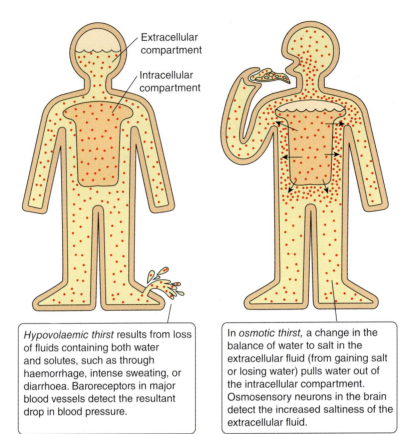

Extracellular compartment

Intracellular compartment

Hypovolaemic thirst results from loss of fluids containing both water and solutes, such as through haemorrhage, intense sweating, or diarrhoea. Baroreceptors in major blood vessels detect the resultant drop in blood pressure.

In *osmotic thirst,* a change in the balance of water to salt in the extracellular fluid (from gaining salt or losing water) pulls water out of the intracellular compartment. Osmosensory neurons in the brain detect the increased saltiness of the extracellular fluid.

FIGURE 5.10 *A diagram summarizing hypovolaemic (left) and osmotic (right) thirst.*

Source: Watson and Breedlove (2012). Reproduced with permission.

FOCUS POINT 5.2

PSYCHOGENIC POLYDIPSIA

Psychogenic polydipsia (PPD) is a condition that causes individuals to experience an extreme thirst, which can lead to them drinking large quantities of fluids (Londrillo, Struglia, & Rossi, 2011; Verghese, de Leon, & Josianssen, 1996). Dundas, Harris, and Narasimhan in 2007 reviewed the evidence surrounding the causes and treatments of PPD and suggested that, although it is probable that there are multiple causes of PPD, problems in the hypothalamus are likely to be involved in causing the condition.

Dundas et al. (2007) also described some of the potentially serious effects psychogenic polydipsia can have on the human body. For instance, when an individual drinks large quantities of water, this causes levels of salt in the blood to drop, which is known as 'hyponatraemia'. The consequences of hyponatraemia can lead to serious physiological and psychological problems and can be fatal if left (Dundas et al., 2007). Managing PPD is challenging as individuals experiencing PPD can have little awareness of their difficulties, and Samaranayake, Arora, Whiting, and Kenedi (2013) describe a case study of a 30-year-old male experiencing schizophrenia and PPD. Cups and receptacles that he could use to drink from had to be removed from his immediate vicinity, and charts were also created to monitor his fluid levels. Staff were educated about the condition and an individualized programme was created to help reduce his drinking. After 4 days, this personalized intervention returned the salt in his blood to normal, healthy levels (Samaranayake et al., 2013).

SECTION SUMMARY

- Everyone regularly feels the motivation to eat.

- A number of mechanical, chemical, and brain signals convey information that influences our motivation to start and to stop eating.

- We all have a number of mechanoreceptors in our stomach that can be stimulated by mechanical manipulation.

- Glucose and lipids are two of the chemicals that are released during digestion that contribute to us feeling satiated.

- The lateral hypothalamus and the ventromedial hypothalamus relay important information that both stimulates and stops eating.

- Within Europe, more than half of all adults are overweight or obese, and around one third of children are also overweight, and these figures are expected to continue to rise.

- Increasing portion sizes and sedentary lifestyles contribute to the increasing levels of overweight and obesity.

- Health services are offering more and more weight-loss interventions for individuals who are overweight.

- All of us have had our appetite levels influenced by psychological factors.

- Eating disorders can also manifest as more complex forms of problematic eating.

- Bulimia nervosa is a condition where an individual eats an excessive amount of food and then purges in an attempt to rid themselves of the food they have consumed.

- People who experience anorexia nervosa become fixated on keeping their body weight down, and, as a result, control their food portions to such an extent that they severely restrict the amount of food they eat.

- Drinking water is vital for our survival – we can normally only survive for around 3 days without fluids.

- There are two distinct types of thirst that we experience: osmotic thirst and hypovolaemic thirst.

- The fluid in our body can be divided into two types: fluid that is found within our cells (intracellular fluid) and fluid that is found outside the cells (extracellular fluid).

- Psychogenic polydipsia is a condition that causes individuals to experience an extreme thirst, which can lead to them drinking large quantities of fluids.

THE BIOLOGICAL BASES OF PRIMARY MOTIVATIONS: SEX AND AGGRESSION

LEARNING OBJECTIVE 5.3

Explain the biological processes that underlie the motivations for sex and aggression and some of the outcomes and consequences of these motivations.

Sex

Searching for a sexual partner is an important focus for many people at some point in their lives. As well as its basic biological purpose of propagating an individual's genes, sex can have a whole host of health benefits, such as improved immune functioning, better cardiac functioning (although this has only been reported in men), and reduced stress. As sex has these personal and societal benefits, it is unsurprising that sex can be such a strong motivator for us (Toates, 2014)!

Evolution of sex

Understanding how and why sex has evolved has been of great interest to scientists (Hartfield & Keightley, 2012) and has been the subject of years of research. As you probably know, sexual reproduction occurs when two organisms come together and combine their genetic material. This then produces an offspring who shares half of its DNA with each of its parents. We can contrast this with asexual reproduction, which is where an organism reproduces by itself and the offspring is therefore genetically identical to the parent organism. It can be argued that sexual reproduction is more costly in evolutionary terms than asexual reproduction because in sexual reproduction it takes two organisms to create an offspring, whereas asexual reproduction involves only one organism but that single organism can produce the same number of offspring (Lehtonen, Jennions, & Kokko, 2012). Further costs of sexual reproduction include the time it takes to find a sexual partner, the energy that is expended in this process, and the risks involved in sex, such as risk of infection and genetic problems that may arise from mixing genetic material (Otto & Lenormand, 2002, p. 252).

In order to overcome this cost, there must be some benefits to encourage humans to engage in sexual reproduction! There are two main theories that have been put forward to explain why sexual reproduction as we know it has evolved. The first of the theories states that sex allows for beneficial traits to be passed around the gene pool (Hurst & Peck, 1996; however, see Otto & Lenormand, 2002, for a critique of this perspective), and the second argues that sex allows for damaging genes to be removed from the gene pool (Hurst & Peck, 1996).

How our environment influences sex

You might not think it, but the environment we are in plays a large role in our sexual motivation and our sexual decision making. For example, the age of sexual consent is not universal, as Table 5.2 illustrates. As well as laws stipulating the age people can have sex, countries also differ in their legal regulations about whom you might be able to choose as a sexual partner. For example, homosexuality is still illegal in some African, Asian, and Middle Eastern countries, and in some countries adultery can still be punishable by death. It may surprise you to know that, globally, one in every two marriages is arranged (Statistic Brain, 2017), and, as a consequence, local laws and cultural practices can play a large role in our decisions about a sexual partner (Davies, 1982).

The biology of sex

In the 1950s and 1960s, William Masters and Virginia Johnson pioneered much of the early laboratory research on sexual behaviour. In fact, they are so well known that there is now a television show called *Masters of Sex* based on their lives! In 1966 the couple published one of the most well-known models of sexual behaviour, which

TABLE 5.2 *Ages of consent across the world.*

Country (continent)	Age of consent
Albania (Europe)	14 for girls and boys, though sex with a girl who 'has not reached sexual maturity' is also illegal.
Angola (Africa)	12, but sex with someone between 12 and 17 may be prosecuted as sexual abuse.
Bolivia (South America)	'The age of puberty'.
Burkina Faso (Africa)	13 for heterosexuals, 21 for homosexuals.
Canada (North America)	16, though exemptions for partners close in age apply. For anal sex, the age of consent is 18, but the act is illegal if more than two people are present or if it takes place in public. Some courts have challenged this.
China (Asia)	14 for all genders and sexual orientations.
Indonesia (Asia)	For heterosexuals, 19 for males and 16 for females. The age of consent for homosexuals is 18.
Japan	13, although individual prefectures can set the age as high as 18.
Mexico (North America)	12 is the federal minimum, but states can set individual restrictions. Some put the age of consent as high as 18.
United Kingdom (Europe)	16 for all genders and sexual orientations.
Venezuela (South America)	16, but sex with a woman up to the age of 21 can be a crime if the woman was 'seduced' and 'known to be honest' beforehand.
Yemen (Asia)	Sex outside marriage is illegal; in 1999 the minimum age for marriage was abolished, and sex with girls as young as 9 is permitted.
Zimbabwe (Africa)	16 for heterosexuals and lesbian women, but male homosexual contact – and, according to some sources, even hand holding between men – is illegal at any age.

they called the sexual response cycle (Masters & Johnson, 1966). This cycle applies to both men and women and proposes that the following physiological stages occur before, during, and after sex:

- *Excitement* – This occurs during the build-up to sex. Blood flow to the male and female sexual organs increases and the heart rate starts to increase.
- *Plateau* – The heart rate continues to increase and the sexual organs continue to change.
- *Orgasm* – During this stage the cardiovascular system is working at its highest level. Muscles begin to contract and spasm and produce an orgasm.
- *Resolution* – The body then returns to normal functioning. During this time women may be able to experience further orgasm(s); however, men experience a refractory period in which they are unable to orgasm.

While this research was groundbreaking, it has also had its critics. For example, Tiefer (2001) questioned their choice of sample, as Masters and Johnson excluded people from their research who were unable to orgasm, so their theory may not be generalizable to people experiencing difficulties with sex. Their sample may also have been very interested in sex – more so than the general public – which again may suggest that the group this theory is based on was not representative. There have also been suggestions that the participants in their research programme may have succumbed to social desirability effects in order to provide the researchers with the results they would like (Tiefer, 2001). Finally, although the laboratory conditions in which the research took place allowed for a great deal of control and accurate measurements from the research team, we can question the ecological validity of laboratory-based research of this kind.

Our hormones play an important role in sexual motivation. The two most well-known female sex hormones, **oestrogen** and **progesterone**, are produced primarily in the ovaries. Men do also produce these hormones but in smaller quantities. Oestrogen causes women to grow sexual features such as breasts, is involved in regulating periods, and has been found to improve mood and memory (Fink, Sumner, Rosie, Grace, & Quinn, 1996). Progesterone is also involved in the menstrual cycle and prepares the body for pregnancy. Research suggests that, while oestrogen increases female sexual motivation, progesterone may decrease it (Pfaus, 2009).

The hormone **testosterone** also affects our sex drive, and we will discuss the importance of testosterone in relation to aggression at a later point in this chapter. Both men and women produce testosterone, with men producing the hormone in the testicles and women producing it in the ovaries. Men and women also produce small amounts of testosterone in the adrenal gland (Eisenegger, Haushofer, & Fehr, 2011). It is known that men produce more testosterone than women, and it has been suggested in the literature that these observed differing testosterone levels explain why men possess a greater sex drive than women (see Van Anders, 2012). In women, the total level of testosterone positively correlates with frequency of sexual intercourse, and so it may well be the case that testosterone levels directly affect a woman's motivation for sex (Morris, Udry, Khan-Dawood, & Dawood, 1987). Low levels of testosterone are also linked to lower sex drive in men, which commonly occurs when they are older (NHS, 2013). Indeed, meta-analyses suggest that testosterone treatments can help men experiencing sexual difficulties (Isidori et al., 2005).

Some studies have identified the importance of the hormone **oxytocin** in sexual behaviour and in particular in feelings of 'love' towards a partner. Oxytocin is a hormone that is produced in the hypothalamus and is then secreted from the pituitary gland at the base of the brain. It also has a significant impact on 'prosocial behaviours' and emotional responses that contribute to relaxation, trust, and psychological stability (Neumann, 2007). Having these effects, it contributes to feelings of love experienced by new lovers. For example, oxytocin levels are significantly higher in new lovers than in single individuals, can trigger in men greater feelings of attraction to their partners than to other women, and can contribute to pair bonding between a pair of new lovers (Schneiderman, Zagoory-Sharon, Leckman, & Feldman, 2012).

What happens in the brain during sex?

There are a number of different areas of the brain that become active when we are sexually aroused; some of these include the amygdala, the insular cortex, and the medial prefrontal cortex – all of which are also active during emotional processing. The ventral striatum is also active, and this area is involved in processing rewards (Karama et al., 2002). However, research has additionally highlighted that there are gender differences in brain activation during sex. Karama et al. (2002) found that,

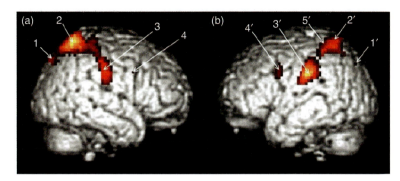

FIGURE 5.11 *Fonteille and Stoléru (2011) reviewed brain-scanning research identifying the areas of the brain active during sexual desire. When healthy male participants were exposed to sexually explicit photographs, the following areas of activation were identified: (1) superior occipital gyrus, (2) superior parietal lobule, (3) inferior parietal lobule, (4) precentral gyrus, and (5) intraparietal sulcus. (a) shows the right side of the brain and (b) shows the left.*
Source: Fonteille and Stoléru (2011).

when viewing sexually arousing videos, men show activation in the thalamus and hypothalamus, which may be areas important in male physiological arousal. However, research since around the late 1990s has shown that there are multiple brain regions that play an important role during sex; see Fonteille and Stoléru (2011) for a review of the regions of the brain involved in sexual desire (Figure 5.11).

Gender differences in sex

As we have seen in the section examining the biology of sex, there are some unique physiological processes that occur for each gender before, during, and after sex. Indeed, popular culture regularly alludes to gender differences in sexual behaviour, as described in the popular book *Men Are From Mars and Women Are From Venus*, written by John Gray (1993). In this section, we will describe some of the common gender differences in sexual desire.

Males and females have been found to be attracted to different characteristics in a sexual partner. Women, for example, have been found to be more concerned than men with non-physical indicators such as intelligence and socioeconomic status, which, from an evolutionary perspective, would suggest that a male could care for the woman and her offspring (Feingold, 1992). In contrast, men have been found to be more interested than women in the sexual desirability of a partner (Regan, Levin, Sprecher, Christopher, & Gate, 2000), and these findings appear to have good cross-cultural reliability (Feingold, 1992).

Sexual fantasies are also considerably different between men and women. Male desires have been found to be visually – and sexually – focused, whereas women focus more on the emotional elements of sexual fantasies (Ellis & Symons, 1990). Men and women also experience feelings of sexual jealousy in response to different cues. Research by Wiederman and Allgeier (1993) found that men become more sexually jealous than women when thinking about a scenario in which a partner goes to a 'pick-up' bar without them, whereas women become more upset than men when thinking about their partner spending more time with another woman than with them. Wiederman and Allgeier (1993) suggest that there are two different types of explanations for these findings. A social learning theory explanation proposes that these differences are explained by the different upbringings experienced by men and women. Alternatively, an evolutionary explanation would suggest that natural selection has selected for men's and women's sexual jealousy to be triggered by different scenarios. In the past, there would have been a reproductive advantage to men having multiple female partners. However, men would not want their female partner also to have multiple sexual partners, as it could result in them spending time, energy, and resources in rearing another man's child. However, from an evolutionary perspective, women would want their male partner to be able to provide for them and their children. Wiederman and Allgeier (1993) conclude that their results were more consistent with the evolutionary approach.

Sexual disorders

Many people experience sexual problems at some point in their lives. For some this problem is short lived, while for others the problems can be ongoing and chronic. People can be reluctant, scared, embarrassed, or nervous to talk to people about their sexual problems. Here we discuss some of the difficulties people can experience with sex.

Sexual dysfunctions Experiencing difficulties with sex is very common; one study found that 34% of men and 41% of women questioned were currently experiencing difficulties with sex (Dunn, Croft, & Hackett, 1998). The most common difficulties among men in England in this study were erectile dysfunction and premature ejaculation, while women were most likely to experience vaginal dryness and infrequent orgasms.

There are a number of factors that contribute to people experiencing difficulties with their sex life. Some of these are psychological. For example, experiencing negative emotions and attentional biases during sexual intimacy can cause problems with sexual performance (Barlow, 1986), and individuals experiencing difficulties with their physical health generally can be more likely to experience sexual difficulties (Basson, 2005). In addition, it is worth noting that changes in sex drive and sexual performance are a common symptom of many mental health problems, especially common mental health problems such as anxiety and depression.

Sexual difficulties are frequently associated with physical illness. Clayton and Ramamurthy (2008) argue that a number of physical conditions (including neurological conditions, heart conditions, cancer, arthritis, and pelvic problems) can cause sexual dysfunction of some kind. However, as Crenshaw and Goldberg (1996) point out, it is not just physical illnesses such as these that can cause sexual dysfunction; so can many of the medications that are provided to help alleviate these physical health conditions (e.g. medications for hypertension or high blood pressure).

There is a range of treatments available for sexual dysfunction. Due to the complex interaction of biopsychosocial factors that can lead to an individual experiencing these difficulties, clinicians have a variety of ways in which they can help sufferers. This may include prescribing medications. The most well-known drug for sexual dysfunction is Viagra, which is used for male impotence; however, drug treatments also exist for female sexual dysfunctions. For example, androgen replacement therapy can be used to increase sexual desire in women (Basson, 1999), while the NHS (2014) also recommends psychological therapies, which may be helpful if people are experiencing difficulties in their relationships or in their personal lives generally.

FOCUS POINT 5.3

PERSISTENT GENITAL AROUSAL DISORDER

Typically, when we think of sexual disorders, we image people who struggle with a low libido or cannot have sex for a physiological reason. However, some people experience a condition called persistent genital arousal disorder, which is also known as restless genital syndrome. People who have this condition have been reported to experience sensations in their genitals that occur in the absence of sexual stimuli and sexual cognitions (Waldinger & Schweitzer, 2009). This can result in the sufferer feeling the need for orgasm or experiencing an orgasm at almost any time.

Persistent genital arousal disorder was only officially documented in the 1980s, and so research investigating the causes and possible treatment options for this condition is ongoing. However, a variety of physical and psychological components may be involved. For example, Goldmeier and Leiblum (2008) identified anxiety as an important risk factor, as are physical factors such as skin disorders and the prolapse of the genitals – which is when part of the bladder, uterus, or vagina begins to move down through the vagina (Kuncharapu, Majeroni, & Johnson, 2010).

Kim Ramsey, who suffers from persistent genital arousal disorder, talks about her illness and the effect it has on her life in **this 2014 article in _The Guardian_**[2].

Paraphillias Individuals diagnosed with a paraphilia usually exhibit sexual feelings and urges towards objects, situations, or people that are not deemed by society as 'normal' or acceptable. Some of the most well-known paraphilias are fetishism, paedophilia, exhibitionism, and sexual sadism. There are a number of different treatments for paraphilias, including drug treatments such as antiandrogens or SSRIs (Thibaut, 2012), and psychological therapies such as CBT (Kaplan & Krueger, 2012). Further information on the aetiology and treatment of paraphilias can be found in Davey (2014).

Risks associated with sex Sex, although fun, can lead to a number of problems if not enjoyed with safety. There are a host of sexually transmitted infections (STIs), such as chlamydia, gonorrhoea, herpes, and HIV, the last of which can develop into AIDS if not treated adequately. In the United Kingdom, people under the age of 25 are one of the groups at the greatest risk of developing an STI (Public Health England, 2014), with the transmission of STIs on the increase (Gilson & Mindel, 2001). As well as infections, there is a risk of pregnancy among heterosexual couples during unprotected sex, and research indicates that young people may often perceive condoms to be stigmatizing and indicative of distrust of the sexual partner (Marston & King, 2006). Nevertheless, condoms can provide effective protection from STIs (Holmes, Levine, & Weaver, 2004), and many health professionals have therefore created sexual education interventions that are aimed specifically at young people and that promote the use of condoms or other contraceptives. Unfortunately, while these interventions are all designed and implemented with the best of intentions, there is little evidence to suggest that they are significantly effective in changing either the sexual attitudes of young people or their sexual behaviour (Oakley et al., 1995).

Aggression

Almost on a daily basis, we witness or hear news of aggression. Nonetheless, feeling aggressive does not necessarily make someone dangerous or pathological; indeed, aggression is a common human emotion (Haller & Kruk, 2006).

Biological causes of aggression

There are a number of biological factors that have been found to influence aggressive behaviour. Listed here are some of the most well-known physiological causes of aggression as identified by Toates (2011).

Hormones Testosterone is one of the most well-researched hormones known to influence aggression. Eisenegger et al. (2011) reviewed the evidence surrounding testosterone and aggression in humans, and found significant associations between testosterone levels and violent behaviour. Testosterone appears to directly increase hostile behaviours, how we process threatening information, and our attention to anger-related stimuli (Dabbs, Karpas, Dyomina, Juechter, & Roberts, 2002; Van Honk et al., 1999)

Neural mechanisms The **amygdala** is a part of the brain that has been identified as an important contributor to aggression in both humans and nonhuman animals, and this may be because the amygdala is a significant brain centre dealing with the immediate processing of emotion-relevant stimuli. Interestingly, electrical stimulation of the amygdala can cause aggressive behaviour in humans, but people are often able to control this anger, which suggests that the amygdala's main role may be in identifying potentially threatening stimuli rather than generating aggressive behaviour itself (Moyer, 1986).

Neurotransmitters Brian neurotransmitters are also important in the initiation and strength of aggressive responses, and dopamine and serotonin have been specifically identified in this respect. **Acetylcholine** is another neurotransmitter that plays an important role in aggression, and, when substances that mimic acetylcholine are injected into the amygdalae of cats, this elicits aggressive behaviour (Grossman, 1963).

Affective aggression

There are various types of aggression. One of the most researched types is **affective aggression**. Affective aggression occurs rapidly, without thought, and produces violent behaviour. It is the most commonly observed form of violent aggression (Nehrenberg, Sheikh, & Ghashghaei, 2013, p. 1033). Anderson and his team (Lindsay & Anderson, 2000) have produced a theoretical model of affective aggression titled the general affective aggression model, which is shown in Figure 5.12. This model was created by integrating factors associated with individual differences with factors associated with situational variables that influence cognitions, emotions, and physiological arousal; the outcome of these interactions determines whether we choose to behave in an aggressive manner or not.

Impulse control

When people try to control an impulse to be aggressive, they must inhibit the short-term urge to behave aggressively in order to pursue a longer-term goal (e.g. it is not helpful

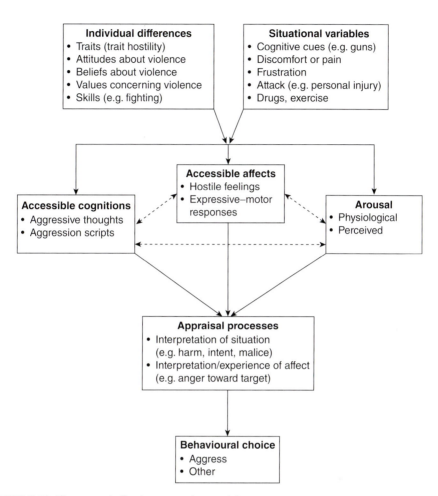

FIGURE 5.12 *The general affective aggression model.*

Source: Lindsay and Anderson (2000). © Sage Publications.

to be aggressive towards an unhelpful nightclub doorman if your aim is to get into the nightclub!). To do this an individual must avoid responding merely to the immediate threat-relevant stimuli in the environment in order to pursue longer-term strategies that will ultimately produce significant (but delayed) benefits (Tice, Bratslavasky, & Baumeister, 2001). For example, aggressive behaviour in most societies can lead to punishments from police authorities, including arrests, criminal prosecutions, and antisocial behavioural orders – so why do we still see so much aggressive behaviour on the streets? Why does it seem so difficult to control the impulse to be aggressive?

Firstly, there is evidence to suggest that there may be innate factors that play a role in how well we can control our urges to be aggressive. Research suggests that males who are generally low in self-control and who also often experience negative emotions may especially struggle to exhibit **impulse control** and are more likely to behave in an impulsive, aggressive manner (Struber, Luck, & Roth, 2008), and this also means they are more likely to become involved in crime. In their paper, Struber and colleagues argued that environmental and psychosocial factors influence the neuronal structures, the neurophysiology, and the personality factors that affect impulse control.

There are also certain cognitive patterns that are characteristic of individuals who are high in impulsivity. Often impulsive people are focused on the present moment.

Commitments in the past or the future are not viewed to be as important as satisfying their current needs (Barratt & Patton, 1983). Impulsive people also self-report rapid thought processing and often judge time to have passed more quickly than it actually has. However, despite these trait characteristics of impulsive individuals, we all have the potential to become aggressive in certain situations. Although cultural norms will usually help us to regulate our behaviour, if we deplete our capacity to self-regulate (by having recently self-regulated in other situations), we are more likely to respond aggressively, especially after having been provoked (DeWall, Baumeister, Stillman, & Gailliot, 2007).

TEST YOURSELF

Why is impulse control important in understanding aggression?

Dealing with challenges

So far we have established that there are a number of biological and psychological processes involved in influencing aggression. In this section we will now examine some of the strategies identified by Baron and Byrne (1997), Baron, Byrne, and Branscombe (2007), and Aronson, Wilson, and Akert (1997) that can be used to de-escalate aggressive situations.

Apologies Cross-culturally, laboratory research suggests that apologizing can reduce aggression (Frederickson, 2010), and apologies that include more verbal material may be more likely to lead to forgiveness (Kirchhoff, Wagner, & Strack, 2012). In contrast, refusing to give an apology can have the opposite effect by benefiting the levels of self-esteem and power of the aggressor (Okimoto, Wenzel, & Hedrick, 2013).

However, we could question the ecological validity of much of the laboratory research that has investigated the effects of apologies. Do you think you would receive an apology the same way if you were in a psychology experiment as you would if you had been a victim of crime? Nevertheless, contrary to what we might expect, when a criminal act has been committed, apologies from the criminal have also been found to be psychologically beneficial for the victim of the crime (Petrucci, 2002).

Mindfulness Mindfulness (NHS, 2017) is a topic found with increasing frequency across many different areas in the psychological literature. Mindfulness has been defined as 'paying attention in a particular way; on purpose, in the present moment, and non-judgmentally' (Kabat-Zinn, 1994, p. 4). Possessing the ability to respond non-judgementally to what is going on around us may be of benefit as it may make us less likely to behave in an aggressive manner, and those people who naturally are high in levels of mindfulness are less likely to report aggressive tendencies (Kelley & Lambert, 2012). Preliminary evidence suggests that mindfulness influences our ability to exert self-control (Friese, Messner, & Schaffner, 2012), and, based on what we discussed previously about the influence of self-control on aggression, we might hypothesize that this is one possible mechanism to explain the observed benefits of mindfulness on aggression (Friese et al., 2012).

Psychological interventions It is probably obvious that people who find it difficult to control their emotions may be less able to manage their aggression (Aronson et al., 1997; Roberton, Daffern, & Bucks, 2014). Therefore, targeting affective regulation strategies in a psychological intervention could be beneficial in reducing levels of aggression (Aronson et al., 1997; Baron & Byrne, 1997; Roberton et al., 2014). Indeed, students who are taught about emotional intelligence are less angry and aggressive than those who do not receive such training (Castillo, Salguero, Fernández-Berrocal, & Balluerka, 2013). Psychological interventions may also be beneficial for those people who display high levels of aggression and may help to reduce violent behaviour generally (McGuire, 2008).

SECTION SUMMARY

- Sex has a basic biological purpose but can have a whole host of health benefits, such as improved immune functioning, better cardiac functioning, and reduced stress.
- Our environment plays a large role in our sexual motivation and our sexual decision making; the age of consent in the country we live in is an example of this.
- William Masters and Virginia Johnson pioneered much of the early laboratory research on sexual behaviour and published a model of sexual behaviour called the sexual response cycle, which consists of excitement, plateau, orgasm, and resolution.
- Our hormones (oestrogen, progesterone, testosterone, and oxytocin) play an important role in sexual motivation.
- A number of areas of the brain become active when we are sexually aroused: the amygdala, the insular cortex, and the medial prefrontal cortex.
- There are some unique physiological processes that occur for each gender before, during, and after sex; for example, males and females have been found to be attracted to different characteristics in a sexual partner.
- Many people experience sexual problems at some point in their lives.
- The most common difficulties among men in England are erectile dysfunction and premature ejaculation, while women are most likely to experience vaginal dryness and infrequent orgasms.
- A paraphilia is the experience of intense sexual arousal to atypical objects, situations, or individuals. Paraphilias include fetishism, paedophilia, exhibitionism, and sexual sadism.
- There are a number of biological factors that have been found to influence aggressive behaviour, including hormones, neural mechanisms, and neurotransmitters.
- Affective aggression is the most researched type of aggression; it occurs rapidly, without thought, and produces violent behaviour.
- Anderson (Lindsay & Anderson, 2000) produced a theoretical model of affective aggression titled the general affective aggression model.
- When people try to control an impulse to be aggressive, they must inhibit the short-term urge to behave aggressively in order to pursue a longer-term goal. This can be harder for some people than for others.
- Evidence-based ways to deal with challenges include apologizing, mindfulness, and psychological intervention.

INTRINSIC VERSUS EXTRINSIC MOTIVATION

LEARNING OBJECTIVE 5.4

Compare and contrast intrinsic and extrinsic motivation.

Imagine it is a sunny day and you feel the urge to go and sit outside. Now think about how you feel when you have to clean the kitchen in your house. Are the two activities driven by the same type of motivation? The likely answer to that question is no! You go outside in the sun because the activity is enjoyable; however, you clean the kitchen not because it is a fun activity but because you need a clean home. From this example, we can begin to get some insight into the two types of motivation that are described in the psychological literature. One type of motivation is called **intrinsic motivation**, and the other type is called **extrinsic motivation** (Figure 5.13). We can define these types of motivation as follows:

- *Extrinsic motivation* is when we participate in an activity in order to attain an external desired reward or outcome that itself may be independent of the activity (e.g. to earn money for washing a car).
- *Intrinsic motivation* is when we do something merely because the activity itself makes us feel good and there is no need for an external reward for engaging in that activity (e.g. sitting in the sun because that activity is accompanied by a warm, relaxing feeling).

FIGURE 5.13 *Motivation can be divided into intrinsic and extrinsic types.*
Source: www.planetofsuccess.com/blog.

In earlier parts of the chapter we have described various forms of extrinsic motivation, in which an external reward helps to motivate the behaviour concerned. In this section of the chapter, we will look more closely at some intrinsic forms of motivation, and in particular how we can establish the kinds of conditions that will motivate behaviours required to achieve longer-term goals for which there are no immediate obvious rewards.

Long-term goals and how to stay focused

In daily life, many of us are tempted to give in to our immediate desires. However, often these temptations are not good for us (Magen & Gross, 2007), and they may prevent us reaching long-term goals we have set (Magen & Gross, 2007). In today's society, when people are increasingly becoming more and more health conscious, growing numbers of people are trying to live a healthy life (Baumeister, Vohs, & Tice, 2007), and to live a truly healthy life an individual would have to overcome desires for fatty and greasy foods, which we are exposed to in adverts and food establishments, often on a regular basis. We would also have to resist the urge to go out drinking on a regular basis, which may be challenging as more and more bars, pubs, and clubs are offering promotions for alcoholic beverages. Finally, we may have to choose to exercise over other enjoyable activities. Overcoming the motivation to engage with these kind of behaviours, which are focused on short-term gratification (Magen & Gross, 2007), would therefore be necessary for someone to reach their goal of living a healthy life.

We can now see how important long-term goals can be in the behavioural choices we make in everyday life. In the psychological literature, a goal has been defined as 'a future valued outcome … It implies discontent with one's present condition and the desire to attain an object or outcome' (Locke & Latham, 2006, p. 265). Locke and Latham have created a theory called goal-setting theory, which describes a number of variables that affect whether or not a goal is achieved:

- *Commitment* – We need to want to reach the goal. The goal must also be seen as worthwhile and a target that can be met.
- *Feedback* – We need to be aware of how we are performing. Locke and Latham (2002) say that, without this, 'it is difficult or impossible for [individuals] to adjust the level or direction of their effort or to adjust their performance strategies to match what the goal requires' (p. 708).
- *Task complexity* – To stay motivating, a goal needs to be challenging in order to stretch us. However, we must be able to meet the goal (Locke & Latham, 2002, 2006).

By applying what we have learned from goal-setting research, we can take steps to try to change our behaviours. This could have an important impact on our lives. For example, a set of behaviours that has huge ramifications for the well-being of society is our health behaviours. Ng et al. (2012) noted that many of the health problems seen today in modern societies could be reduced by people trying to live healthier lives by 'abstaining from tobacco, eating a healthy diet, engaging in more physical activity and taking recommended medications' (p. 325). Therefore, Ng and colleagues argue that we need to be able to motivate people to behave more healthily.

If you were a health psychologist, how would you use the principles of **goal setting** to encourage someone to lose weight? Let's suppose they had a goal of losing three pounds a week. First off, this person would have to want to lose weight. *Commitment* to the goal could be encouraged by asking the person to read about the harmful effects obesity can have. In order to avoid this challenge feeling too *complex*, you could provide the person with diet plans and healthy-eating tips. *Feedback* could be gained through regular weigh-ins. Shilts, Horowitz, and Townsend (2004) have reviewed the effects of goal setting on diet and exercise and found 'moderate evidence' to suggest that goal-setting techniques have a positive influence on diet and exercise. Consequently, the authors suggested that health professionals should use these techniques to encourage healthy living.

Self-determination theory

One of the most well-known theories of motivation, **self-determination theory**, was created by Edward Deci and Richard Ryan, two psychologists from the United States (Figure 5.14). The theory states that there are three universal needs – competence, autonomy, and relatedness – that are experienced by everyone. When these needs are met, a person becomes intrinsically motivated and experiences psychological well-being (Chirkov, Ryan, Kim, & Kaplan, 2003; Ryan & Deci, 2000).

Weinstein and Ryan (2011) suggest that our social surroundings influence whether or not we become self-determined. Being in an environment that promotes the fulfilment of these basic needs (e.g. when a person has important people in their life who support their needs) means that a person's well-being increases and they experience 'autonomous motivation' (Weinstein & Ryan, 2011, p. 5). A cycle then occurs, whereby they then behave in a way where they continue to satisfy their needs for competence, autonomy, and relatedness. However, environments that prevent people meeting their needs lead to individuals experiencing 'controlled motivation' (Weinstein & Ryan, 2011, p. 5) and little well-being. When someone becomes caught in this situation, they struggle to find a location that can meet their needs and can actually put themselves in stressful environments (Weinstein & Ryan, 2011, p. 5).

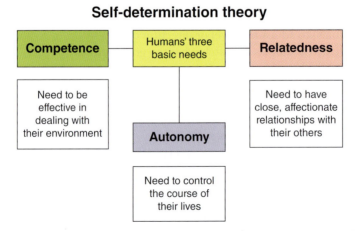

FIGURE 5.14 *The dimensions of Deci and Ryan's self-determination theory.*
Source: Ryan and Deci (2000).

Indeed, Milyavskaya and Koestner (2011) found that the more likely people were to have their psychological needs met, the more likely they were to experience autonomous motivation and well-being.

To recap, we have learned that there are two types of motivation: intrinsic and extrinsic. Deci and Ryan proposed that, if we feel competence, autonomy, and relatedness, we will experience intrinsic motivation and will also experience psychological benefits. However, our environment is key in determining whether we meet these needs or not. We also discussed how in life we need to be able to overcome our short-term desires to be able to achieve long-term goals. By considering goal commitment, goal feedback, and task complexity, we may be able to set goals that we will meet.

SECTION SUMMARY

- There are two types of motivation: intrinsic and extrinsic.
- Extrinsic motivation is when we participate in an activity in order to attain an external desired reward or outcome.
- Intrinsic motivation is when we do something merely because the activity itself makes us feel good.
- Deci and Ryan proposed that, if we feel competence, autonomy, and relatedness, we will experience intrinsic motivation and will also experience psychological benefits. However, our environment is key in determining whether we meet these needs or not. We also need to be able to overcome our short-term desires to be able to achieve long-term goals. By considering goal commitment, goal feedback, and task complexity, we may be able to set goals that we will meet.

AFFILIATION AND ACHIEVEMENT MOTIVATION

LEARNING OBJECTIVE 5.5

Describe the roles of affiliation and achievement in influencing motivation.

When thinking about what drives our behaviours, many people forget about social and personal motivators. However, we are motivated to be socially involved with others (Hill, 1987) and to be seen as able to achieve by others (De Castella, Byrne, & Covington, 2013), and these have been deemed as important forms of motivation (McClelland, 1961). In this section we will look at the importance of affiliation and what can happen if we do not feel affiliated. We will then turn to achievement and look at the psychological processes involved in achievement and how these may be different across the world.

Affiliation

Aristotle was once quoted as saying 'man is by nature a social animal' and researchers today still subscribe to this view. All of us are part of multiple social groups – this could be as part of a family, a university, a workplace, a club, and so on. Indeed, the dynamics of group formation can confer reproductive advantages to primates (Silk, 2007), and these complicated social relationships have led to the evolution of larger brains (Dunbar & Shultz, 2007), facts which suggest that humans are biologically programmed to form social relationships.

However, being in a social group is not just a matter of evolutionary benefit; being part of a social group has benefits to individuals on a day-to-day basis. For example, people with poor social bonds experience poorer health-related outcomes, and Thoits (2011) has proposed up to seven mechanisms by which social relationships may benefit our physical and mental health (listed in Focus Point 5.4).

FOCUS POINT 5.4

SEVEN MECHANISMS BY WHICH SOCIAL RELATIONSHIPS MAY BENEFIT OUR PHYSICAL AND MENTAL HEALTH

Thoits (2011) has argued that social relationships can benefit not only our emotional health but also our physical health. Although this knowledge is well known, she noted that there is currently little understanding as to why this may be. Thoits (2011, pp. 147–149) provides the following suggestions as to how **social support** may benefit us:

1. *Social influence comparison* – Through social contact, we evaluate how our own cognitions and behaviours compare to others, and people generally adjust their behaviours to fall in line with the group.

2. *Social control* – People with whom we spend time can also try to encourage us to engage in healthy and beneficial behaviours.

3. *Behavioural guidance, purpose, and meaning* – Thoits proposes that having a social role (i.e. son or daughter, girlfriend or boyfriend, brother or sister) provides people with an identity and people behave in a way that matches this role. These social roles may also mean people feel that they have an increased sense of being important to others. This is then beneficial for our health.

4. *Self-esteem* – If we see ourselves as having a positive identity through our relationships with others, we are likely to experience greater self-esteem, which has a beneficial effect on our mental health.

5. *Sense of control or mastery* – Perceiving ourselves as fulfilling a social role well may mean that we perceive ourselves to be in control. Feeling in control may make us less likely to experience stress, anxiety, or depression.

6. *Belonging and companionship* – Being part of a social group increases positive feelings. This then increases our well-being.

7. *Perceived social support* – In this increasingly technological era, recent research has begun to investigate whether we need to be with people to experience the benefits of affiliation. With modern technology linking us up to people across the world, including with people we have never met before, it is possible that virtual social support could be beneficial for us. Indeed, it has been found that using online social media, specifically Facebook, is positively correlated with social capital (Ellison, Steinfield, & Lampe, 2007).

Isolation and exclusion

What happens to people when they are not part of a social group or are effectively excluded from society and social interaction? As humans are social creatures, the result of not feeling part of a group can be painful – research suggests feeling socially isolated activates similar regions of the brain to feeling physical pain (Eisenberger & Liberman, 2004). As well as eliciting biological reactions to social exclusion, isolation can affect our emotions, cognitive abilities, and behaviours (Baumeister, Brewer, Tice, & Twenge, 2007). Research has indicated that we do not even have to be in the same room as other people to feel excluded – if we perceive ourselves as being ostracized in interactions with other people online, this can affect our emotions and sense of belonging (Williams, Cheung, & Choi, 2000).

In 2007, Baumeister et al. reviewed the literature on the effects of exclusion. Their review found that, when they are rejected, people behave in an antisocial and aggressive manner and are less prosocial. People can also start to feel physically and emotionally numb. Baumeister and colleagues argued that this numbness might explain why excluded individuals struggle to be sensitive to others. Finally, after being excluded, people seem to be less able to exhibit intelligent behaviour and less able to control their own impulses.

Achievement

Achievement motivation is the drive that people feel to succeed. For example, if you are a university student reading this, you probably experienced achievement motivation in order to pass your exams and reach university. There are many factors that affect our motivation to achieve. For example, Mega, Ronconi, and De Beni (2014, p. 128) found that experiencing positive emotions could increase how prepared, positive, and reflective students were. Positive emotions also increased learning motivation, which subsequently benefited their achievement. The people around us can also influence our motivation. For example, Wentzel (1998) found that, when children aged 11–12 years had supportive relations with parents, teachers, and peers, this had a very positive effect on their motivation at school.

Self-determination theory

In the section on intrinsic and extrinsic motivation in this chapter, we examined self-determination theory. To briefly recap, self-determination theory states that we all require competence, autonomy, and relatedness to feel intrinsically motivated and to experience well-being (Ryan & Deci, 2000), and these three needs are thought to be relatively universal across cultures. For example, in a cross-cultural study spanning eight different countries, research found that students from collectivist cultures (e.g. some Asian cultures) see social goals as motivating, whereas people from individualistic cultures (such as many Western cultures) are focused on their own personal aims (Markus & Kitayama, 1991; Church et al., 2013). In this study, participants were asked to complete a complex battery of measures assessing their needs, well-being, and personality, as well as a questionnaire relating to culture. Although some countries were found to value certain needs from self-determination theory less than other countries, the study provided evidence to support the notion that the constructs identified in self-determination theory do in fact influence well-being across various cultures.

The role of incentives

Earlier in the chapter we discussed incentive theory. Recall that there is evidence that people perform better when they are intrinsically motivated and less well when they are extrinsically motivated (Lepper, Corpus, & Iyengar, 2005; Lepper, Greene, & Nisbett, 1973). However, it is important to note that Ryan and Deci (2000), the creators of self-determination theory, have proposed that four forms of extrinsic motivation can significantly influence self-determination (see Figure 5.15).

As we have discussed at other points in this chapter, overcoming our short-term urges is a useful skill to possess as it can help us get closer to reaching long-term goals (Magen & Gross, 2007; Mischel, Shoda, & Rodriguez, 1989). This has been termed 'delayed gratification' and has been of interest to researchers for many years. Examples of delayed gratification include turning down a drink when you are out with your friends because you have an early morning lecture the next day, or resisting buying something as you are currently saving. In the above section 'Long-Term Goals and How to Stay Focused' we examine how we can use strategies to promote the achievement of long-term goals.

Our ability to delay gratification, even at a young age, can have a number of important influences on what we achieve over the course of our lifetime. For example, in the 1960s and 1970s, a number of researchers measured delayed gratification in 4-year-old children in laboratory settings. Some of these children then took part in further research when they were teenagers. Those individuals who possessed greater delayed-gratification skills as children possessed greater cognitive, social, and coping skills as adolescents (Mischel et al., 1989) and had lower BMIs when they were in their 30s (Schlam, Wilson, Shoda, Mischel, & Ayduk, 2013). Many factors may contribute to our likelihood to engage in this form of self-control, with some being our personality style (Funder, Block, & Block, 1983), our mood (Moore, Clyburn, & Underwood, 1976), and the way in which we were parented (Mauro & Harris, 2000).

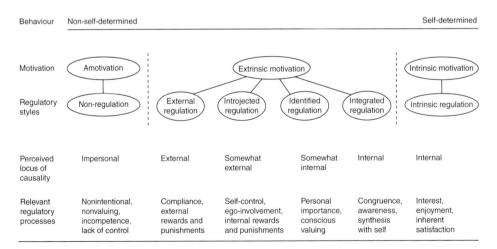

FIGURE 5.15 *The self-determination continuum showing types of motivation with their regulatory styles, loci of causality, and corresponding processes.*

Source: Ryan and Deci (2000).

Cultural differences

The culture we are bought up in has long been thought to influence how motivated we feel to achieve. For example, most cultures can be divided into collectivist or individualistic types, and these different types can significantly influence how important we believe achievement to be, as well as influencing how social relationships affect our motivation to achieve (Trumbull & Rothstein-Fisch, 2011). In particular, collectivist cultures (such as many Asian cultures) tend to influence individuals to view achievement as something that should be accomplished in cooperative groups, while individualistic cultures (such as Western European and North American cultures) place great emphasis on individual achievements.

SECTION SUMMARY

- We are motivated to be socially involved with others and to be seen as able to achieve by others.
- All of us are part of multiple social groups, and humans are biologically programmed to form social relationships.
- Social relationships can benefit not only our emotional health but also our physical health.
- In this increasingly technological era, even virtual social support could be beneficial for us.
- Achievement motivation is the drive that people feel to succeed.
- Self-determination theory states that we all require competence, autonomy, and relatedness to feel intrinsically motivated and to experience well-being.
- Our ability to delay gratification, even at a young age, can have a number of important influences on what we achieve over the course of our lifetime.
- Most cultures can be divided into collectivist or individualistic types, and these different types can significantly influence how important we believe achievement to be, as well as influencing how social relationships affect our motivation to achieve.

APPLICATIONS OF THEORIES OF MOTIVATION

LEARNING OBJECTIVE 5.6

Describe the ways in which theories of motivation can be used in everyday situations.

We have learned about several theories of motivation and reviewed research into motivation. We are now going to draw this knowledge together and think about how we can apply it in several everyday situations.

Performance

It goes without saying that motivation plays a big role in how well we perform tasks, and much research has been conducted on the ways in which intrinsic and extrinsic motivation affect performance. In one particular study, Lepper et al. (1973) utilized a task that the children in their study found enjoyable and intrinsically motivating – namely drawing. Children were allocated to one of three groups. One group was told they would be given a reward for drawing, one group was given an award unexpectedly after their drawing, and the final group were not told about a reward and were not given one. Children who were told about the reward and were then given the reward were less likely than children in the other groups to want to draw when there was no reward offered at a later time. This finding suggests that, when we are extrinsically motivated to complete a task, this reduces our intrinsic motivation to complete the task, which is known as the **overjustification effect** (Lepper et al., 1973; Sansone & Harackiewicz, 2000). This effect does not just occur in children; a meta-analytic review suggests that it occurs across all age groups (Tang & Hall, 1995).

However, upon reviewing this phenomenon, Sansone and Harackiewicz (2000) found that the overjustification effect might not be quite as simple as it seems. For example, they highlight the role of competency: the effect does not seem to occur when people believe they are receiving a reward because they performed well at a task; in this situation, when people receive large rewards they actually become more intrinsically motivated (Rosenfeld, Folger, & Adelman, 1980). The mood you are in can also have an important influence on how susceptible you are to this effect. If you are in a positive mood, extrinsic rewards do not cause you to feel less intrinsically motivated later on (Pretty & Seligman, 1984). These are all factors that we need to take into account when we are attempting to motivate people to do well on a task.

Leadership

Many managers and coaches of sports teams use a variety of motivational techniques to try to generate a winning team, and attempting to get a team of individuals to perform well requires good leadership. One of the most well-known forms of leadership is called **transformational leadership**, and transformational leaders try to boost the motivation and spirits of their team (Bass, 1999, p. 9). Bass and Avolio (1995) propose that transformational leadership consists of the following elements (see also Bass, 1999; Gumusluoglu & Islev, 2009, p. 9):

- *Idealized influence (sometimes referred to as charismatic role modelling or charisma)* – Being charismatic means the leader is liked by their workforce and encourages the workforce to work as a team.
- *Individualized consideration* – The leader possesses an understanding of each member of the team.
- *Inspiration* – Inspirational motivation is a term that describes the leader setting positive goals and offering support to the team in order to reach these goals.
- *Intellectual consideration* – The leader uses techniques to enable their team to become more engaged in their work.

By being a transformational leader, a manager can increase the intrinsic motivation felt by the team (Tierney, Farmer, & Graen 1999). There is particular interest in transformational leadership models in work organizations generally, which is unsurprising given that this form of leadership is correlated with creativity and innovation in the workplace (Gumusluoglu & Islev, 2009).

DISCUSSION POINT

Discuss transformational leadership and the effects it can have. Have you ever had a transformational leader? What was it about their behaviour that led you to see them as a transformational leader?

Saving for a rainy day

Worrying about money can have a huge impact on our daily lives, and people experiencing money-related stress often experience physical and psychological health complaints also (American Psychological Association, 2015). Most of us can think of times when we have not been able to control our spending – indeed the psychological literature has found that **self-regulation** failure may lead to unplanned spending (Baumeister, 2002). However, can our knowledge of motivation help us to save money? Here are some ideas from the motivation literature:

- *Controlling our spending* – In order to be able to overcome our short-term desires to spend money, we can use our knowledge of what we require to self-regulate. By setting a standard, monitoring our behaviour, and exerting willpower and motivation (Baumeister, 2002; Baumeister & Vohs, 2007), we may be able to avoid rash purchases.
- *Setting sensible money-saving goals* – We have discussed some of the components Locke and Latham (2006) propose that may increase our likelihood of achieving our goals. These include being committed to our money-saving goal, seeking feedback on how our saving is going, and setting a saving goal that is challenging but within our abilities to meet.
- *Treating ourselves* – Remember what we have just discussed in the performance section? Receiving a reward when we have performed well and met our savings target may make us feel more intrinsically motivated to continue saving.
- *Meeting our basic needs* – Most us have been warned not to go food shopping when we are hungry, as we end up buying more than we intended. We could use Maslow's theory of motivation to explain this finding; when basic needs are unmet, we cannot achieve needs higher up the hierarchy, such as saving.

SECTION SUMMARY

- Various theories of motivation can be applied to real-life scenarios.
- Motivation plays a big role in how well we perform tasks, and much research has been conducted on the ways in which intrinsic and extrinsic motivation affect performance.

- When we are extrinsically motivated to complete a task, this reduces our intrinsic motivation to complete the task, which is known as the overjustification effect.
- Managers and coaches of sports teams use a variety of motivational techniques.
- Transformational leaders try to boost the motivation and spirits of their team through a combination of idealized influence, individualized consideration, inspiration, and intellectual consideration.
- It is important to develop appropriate self-regulation, particularly when it comes to managing our spending habits.

CHAPTER SUMMARY

This chapter has introduced you to a wide-ranging selection of theories of motivation – processes that motivate us to behave in ways that will maximize our survival, enable us to behave purposefully, and pursue goals. The motivation underlying basic physiological processes such as eating, drinking, sex, and aggression were discussed, and then we moved on to more complex forms of motivation behaviour. These include the factors that determine intrinsic and extrinsic motivation, the need to affiliate and to socialize with others, and the need to achieve. We ended the chapter by providing a few simple examples of how these theories of motivation have been applied in practice.

ESSAY QUESTIONS

1. Compare and contrast any two theories of motivation.
2. Using examples, describe and explain how intrinsic and extrinsic motivation differ.
3. If you wanted to motivate a group of students to study for an exam, what would you suggest they do? Use theories of motivation in your answer.

KEY TERMS

- **acetylcholine:** A neurotransmitter found in the brain and body of many types of animals, including humans. It is a chemical released by nerve cells to send signals to other cells.
- **addictive behaviour:** A behaviour, or a stimulus related to a behaviour (e.g. sex or food), that is both rewarding and reinforcing, and is associated with the development of an addiction (a substance or a behaviour that a person becomes unhealthily obsessed with).
- **affective aggression:** Aggression that involves intense autonomic activation with sympathetic and adrenal stimulation.
- **aldosterone:** A steroid hormone produced by the outer section (zona glomerulosa) of the adrenal cortex in the adrenal gland that plays an important role in regulating blood pressure.
- **amygdala:** The region of the brain responsible for coordinating and initiating responses to fear.

- **anorexia nervosa:** An eating disorder, the main features of which include a refusal to maintain a minimally healthy body weight, a pathological fear of gaining weight, and a distorted body image in which sufferers continue to insist they are overweight.
- **arousal theory:** A theory that argues that we are motivated to behave in a manner that keeps us at a suitable level of arousal.
- **baroreceptors:** Receptors located in the blood vessels. Their function is to sense blood-pressure changes and relay this information to the brain so that appropriate blood-pressure levels can be maintained.
- **body mass index (BMI):** A way of measuring a healthy weight range, derived by using both height and weight measurements.
- **bulimia nervosa:** An eating disorder, the main features of which are recurrent episodes of binge eating followed by periods of purging or fasting.
- **craving:** When specific situations, sights, and sounds become associated with the pleasurable consequences of drug taking; through a process of associative learning, these sights, sounds, and situations come to elicit a 'craving' for the drug.
- **drive-reduction theory:** A theory that states that we are driven by our desire to keep our physiology in a state of equilibrium.
- **dual-centre theory of motivation:** A theory that states that the activation of either one of the lateral hypothalamus or the ventromedial hypothalamus precludes the other region from being active.
- **extracellular fluid:** All bodily fluid outside the cells.
- **extrinsic motivation:** A basis for engaging in behaviour because of the influence of factors outside ourselves.
- **ghrelin:** A peptide hormone produced in the ghrelinergic cells in the gastrointestinal tract that regulates appetite and energy.
- **goal setting:** The process of setting future goals to provide motivation for behaviour.
- **hierarchy of needs:** A model that argues that there is a predefined order of needs that all people are driven to fulfil. We can only strive to fulfil needs higher up the hierarchy when all of the needs below are met.
- **homeostasis:** A tendency of the body to maintain itself in a state of balance or equilibrium.
- **hypovolaemic thirst:** A type of thirst experienced when we lose fluids from outside the cells. This fluid loss can occur when we sweat, bleed, or experience diarrhoea.
- **impulse control:** The inhibition of a short-term urge in order to pursue a longer-term goal.
- **incentive salience:** A motivational 'wanting' attribute given by the brain to reward-predicting stimuli.
- **incentive theory:** A theory that states that much of our behaviour is driven by extrinsic motivation – that is, purely because we reap some kind of benefit from that activity.
- **instinct theory:** A theory that proposes that we are motivated primarily by our biological instincts.
- **intracellular fluid:** Bodily fluids found within the cells of the body.
- **intrinsic motivation:** A basis for engaging in behaviour simply for the satisfaction that is part of doing it.
- **lateral hypothalamus:** The part of the hypothalamus that signals to the body that we need to eat.
- **leptin:** A hormone that is produced within the body when fat cells increase in size.
- **nucleus accumbens:** Part of the limbic forebrain and dopamine system; sometimes known as the brain's 'reward centre'.
- **oestrogen:** Any of a group of steroid hormones that promote the development and maintenance of female characteristics in the body.
- **opponent-process theory:** A theory that proposes that our biological and neurological systems may respond to stimuli by opposing their initial effects.
- **osmotic thirst:** A type of thirst that occurs when we lose water from inside a cell, which occurs because of increases in salt levels outside the cell.

- **overjustification effect:** When we are extrinsically motivated to complete a task, this reduces our intrinsic motivation to complete the task.
- **oxytocin:** A peptide hormone that acts as a neurotransmitter in the brain. It regulates social interaction and sexual reproduction, playing a role in behaviours from maternal–infant bonding and milk release to empathy, generosity, and orgasm.
- **positive reinforcement:** The presentation of a pleasant consequence following a behaviour.
- **prefrontal cortex:** An area of the brain that is important in maintaining representations of goals and the means to achieve them.
- **primary incentives:** Incentives biologically salient to our survival (such as food and sex).
- **progesterone:** An endogenous steroid hormone involved in pregnancy and the menstrual cycle.
- **psychogenic polydipsia (PPD):** A condition that causes individuals to experience an extreme thirst, which can lead to them drinking large quantities of fluids.
- **reward pathways:** The brain neurocircuitries that make something pleasurable.
- **secondary incentives:** These have no inherent value in themselves. They only possess value because we know they are associated with other stimuli and events.
- **self-actualization:** The final level on the hierarchy of needs. This means that, when all the previous needs are met, we feel motivated to engage with activities that will make us develop and flourish as individuals.
- **self-determination theory:** This theory states that there are three universal needs – competence, autonomy, and relatedness – that are experienced by everyone. When these needs are met, a person becomes intrinsically motivated and experiences psychological well-being.
- **self-regulation:** A skill necessary for reliable emotional well-being.
- **social support:** Assistance and care provided by other people within a social network.
- **testosterone:** A steroid hormone that stimulates the development of male secondary sexual characteristics.
- **transformational leadership:** A leadership style in which the leader, through their example and interactions with individuals, attempts to boost the motivation and spirits of their team.
- **vasopressin:** A hormone that enables the body to retain water and increase blood pressure.
- **ventromedial hypothalamus:** The part of the hypothalamus that informs the brain when we are full and causes us to stop eating.
- **Yerkes–Dodson law:** The idea that arousal can influence our performance levels.

NOTES

1. http://www.nhs.uk/video/pages/c_bulimia.aspx
2. http://www.theguardian.com/lifeandstyle/2014/apr/14/women-persistent-genital-arousal-disorder-orgasm-pgad-pain

FURTHER RESOURCES

Anderson, C. A., & Bushman, B. J. (2002). Human aggression. *Annual Review of Psychology, 52*, 27–51.

Arai, S., Stotts, N., & Puntillo, K. (2013). Thirst in critically ill patients: From physiology to sensation. *American Journal of Critical Care, 22*(4), 328–335.

Archer, J., & Coyne, S. M. (2005). An integrated review of indirect, relational and social aggression. *Personality and Social Psychology Review, 9*(3), 212–230.

Deci, E. L., & Ryan, R. M. (2008). Self-determination theory: A macrotheory of human motivation, development and health. *Canadian Psychology, 49*(3), 182–185.

Deckers, L. (2009). *Motivation: Biological, psychological, and environmental.* Boston, MA: Allyn & Bacon.

Locke, E., & Latham, G. P. (2002). Building a practically useful theory of goal setting and task motivation: A 35-year odyssey. *American Psychologist, 57*(9), 705–717.

Locke, E. A., & Latham, G. P. (Eds.). (2013). *New developments in goal setting and task performance.* New York, NY: Routledge.

Miczek, K. A., & Meyer-Lindenberg, A. (Eds.). (2014). *Neuroscience of aggression.* Berlin, Germany: Springer.

Petri, H., & Govern, J. (2013). *Motivation: Theory, research and application* (6th ed.). Boston, MA: Wadsworth.

Robinson, K. C., & Berridge K C. (2003). Addiction. *Annual Review of Psychology, 54,* 25–53.

Ryan, R. M., & Deci, E. L. (2000). Intrinsic and extrinsic motivations: Classic definitions and new directions. *Contemporary Educational Psychology, 25*(1), 54–67.

Sheth, J. N., & Gross, B. L. (1991). Why we buy what we buy: A theory of consumption values. *Journal of Business Research, 22*(2), 159–170.

Thornton, S. N. (2013). Regulation of thirst. *Nutrition Today, 48*(4), S4–S6.

Toates, F. (2011). *Biological psychology* (2nd ed.). Harlow, UK: Prentice Hall.

REFERENCES

Andrade, J., May, J., & Kavanagh, D. J. (2012). Sensory imagery in craving: From cognitive psychology to new treatments for addiction. *Journal of Experimental Psychopathology, 3*(2), 127–145.

American Psychological Association. (2015). *Stress in America: Paying with our health.* Retrieved 15 January 2018 from https://www.apa.org/news/press/releases/stress/2014/stress-report.pdf

Arcelus, J., Whight, D., Brewin, N., & McGrain, L. (2012). A brief form of interpersonal psychotherapy for adult patients with bulimic disorders: A pilot study. *European Eating Disorders Review, 20,* 326–330.

Aronson, E., Wilson, T. D., & Akert, R. M. (1997). *Social psychology* (2nd ed.). New York, NY: Longman.

Barlow, D. H. (1986). Unraveling the mysteries of anxiety and its disorders from the perspective of emotion theory. *American Psychologist, 55*(11), 1247–1263.

Baron, R. A., & Byrne, D. R. (1997). *Social psychology* (8th ed.). Boston, MA: Allyn & Bacon.

Baron, R. A., Byrne, D. R., & Branscombe, N. R. (2007). *Social psychology* (12th ed.). Upper Saddle River, NJ: Pearson.

Barratt, E. S., & Patton, J. H. (1983). Impulsivity: Cognitive, behavioral, and psychophysiological correlates. In M. Zuckerman (Ed.), *Biological bases of sensation seeking, impulsivity, and anxiety* (pp. 77–122). Hillsdale, NJ: Lawrence Erlbaum Associates.

Bass, B. M. (1999). Two decades of research and development in transformational leadership. *European Journal of Work & Organizational Psychology, 8,* 9–32.

Bass, B. M., & Avolio, B. J. (1995). *The multifactor leadership questionnaire: 5x short form.* Redwood, CA: Mind Garden.

Basson, R. (1999). Androgen replacement for women. *Canadian Family Physician, 45,* 2100–2107.

Basson, R. (2005). Women's sexual dysfunction: Revised and expanded definitions. *Canadian Medical Association Journal, 172*(10), 1327–1333.

Baumeister, R. F. (2002). Yielding to temptation: Self-control failure, impulsive purchasing and consumer behaviour. *Journal of Consumer Research, 28*(4), 670–676.

Baumeister, R. F. Brewer, L. E., Tice, D. M., & Twenge, J. M. (2007). Thwarting the need to belong: Understanding the interpersonal and inner effects of social exclusion. *Social and Personality Psychology Compass, 1*(1), 506–520.

Baumeister, R. F., & Vohs, K. D. (2007). Self-regulation, ego depletion, and motivation. *Social and Personality Psychology Compass*, *1*(1), 115–128.

Baumeister, R. F., Vohs, K. D., & Tice, D. M. (2007). The strength model of self-control. *Current Directions in Psychological Science*, *16*(6), 351–355.

Berkman, E. T., Falk, E. B., & Lieberman, M. D. (2011). In the trenches of real-world self-control: Neural correlates of breaking the link between craving and smoking. *Psychological Science*, *22*(4), 498–506.

Bernard, L. C., Mills, M., Swenson, L., & Walsh, R. P. (2005). An evolutionary theory of human motivation. *Genetic, Social, and General Psychology Monographs*, *131*(2), 129–184.

Berridge, K. C. (2000). Reward learning: Reinforcement, incentives and expectations. In D. L. Medin (Ed.), *Psychology of learning and motivation* (Vol. 40, 223–278). San Diego, CA: Academic Press.

Bindra, D. (1959). *Motivation: A systematic reinterpretation*. New York, NY: Ronald Press.

Bonner, S. E., & Sprinkle, G. E. (2002). The effects of monetary incentives on effort and task performance: Theories, evidence, and a framework for research. *Accounting, Organizations and Society*, *27*(4/5), 303–345.

Bryant-Waugh, R. (2000). Overview of the eating disorders. In B. Lask & R. Bryant-Waugh (Eds.), *Anorexia nervosa and related eating disorders in childhood and adolescence* (2nd ed., pp. 27–40). Hove, UK: Psychology Press.

Carmagnola, S., Cantu, P., & Penagini, R. (2005). Mechanoreceptors of the proximal stomach and perception of gastric distension. *American Journal of Gastroenterology*, *100*(8), 1704–1710.

Castillo, R., Salguero, J. M., Fernández-Berrocal, P., & Balluerka, N. (2013). Effects of an emotional intelligence intervention on aggression and empathy among adolescents. *Journal of Adolescence*, *36*(5), 883–892.

Catalano, M. F., Rudic, G., Anderson, A. J., & Chua, T. Y. (2007). Weight gain after bariatric surgery as a result of a large gastric stoma: Endotherapy with sodium morrhuate may prevent the need for surgical revision. *Gastrointestinal Endoscopy*, *66*(2), 240–245.

Chirkov, V., Ryan, R. M., Kim, Y., & Kaplan, U. (2003). Differentiating autonomy from individualism and independence: A self-determination theory perspective on internalization of cultural orientations and well-being. *Journal of Personality and Social Psychology*, *84*(1), 97–110.

Church, A. T., Katigbak, M. S., Locke, K. D., Zhang, H., Shen, J., Vargas-Flores, J., … Ching, C. M. (2013). Need satisfaction and well-being: Testing self-determination theory. *Journal of Cross-Cultural Psychology*, *44*, 507–534.

Clayton, A., & Ramamurthy, S. (2008). The impact of physical illness on sexual dysfunction. *Sexual Dysfunction*, *29*, 70–88.

Cohen, R. A. (2011). Yerkes–Dodson law. In J. S. Kreutzer, J. DeLuca, & B. Caplan (Eds.), *Encyclopedia of clinical neuropsychology* (pp. 2737–2738). New York, NY: Springer.

Crenshaw, T. L., & Goldberg, J. P. (1996). *Sexual pharmacology: Drugs that affect sexual function*. New York, NY: W. W. Norton.

Curtis, V., & Biran, A. (2001). Dirt, disgust, and disease: Is hygiene in our genes? *Perspectives in Biology and Medicine*, *44*(1), 17–31.

Dabbs, J. M., Jr., Karpas, A. E., Dyomina, N., Juechter, J., & Roberts, A. (2002). Experimental raising or lowering of testosterone level affects mood in normal men and women. *Social Behavior and Personality*, *30*(8), 795–806.

Dallos, R. (2004). Attachment narrative therapy: Integrating ideas from narrative and attachment theory in systemic family therapy with eating disorders. *Journal of Family Therapy*, *26*(1), 40–65.

Davey, G. L. (2011). Disgust: The disease-avoidance emotion and its dysfunctions. *Philosophical Transactions of the Royal Society B: Biological Sciences*, *366*(1583), 3453–3465.

Davey, G. L. (2014). *Psychopathology* (2nd ed.). Chichester, UK: Wiley.

Davies, C. (1982). Sexual taboos and social boundaries. *American Journal of Sociology*, *87*, 1032–1063.

DeBar, L. L., Striegel-Moore, R. H., Wilson, G. T., Perrin, N., Yarborough, B. J., Dickerson, J., … Kraemer, H. C. (2011). Guided self-help treatment for recurrent binge eating: Replication and extension. *Psychiatric Services, 62*, 367–373.

De Castella, K., Byrne, D., & Covington, M. (2013). Unmotivated or motivated to fail? A cross-cultural study of achievement motivation, fear of failure, and student disengagement. *Journal of Educational Psychology, 105*(3), 861–880.

Del Parigi, A., Gautier, J. F., Chen, K., Salbe, A. D., Ravussin, E., Reiman, E., & Tataranni, P. A. (2002). Neuroimaging and obesity: Mapping the brain responses to hunger and satiation in humans using positron emission tomography. *Annals of the New York Academy of Sciences, 967*, 389–397.

DeWall, C. N., Baumeister, R. F., Stillman, T. F., & Gailliot, M. T. (2007). Violence restrained: Effects of self-regulation and its depletion on aggression. *Journal of Experimental Social Psychology, 43*, 62–76.

Diamond, D. M., Campbel, A. M., Park, C. R., Halonen, J., & Zoladz, P. R. (2007). The temporal dynamics model of emotional memory processing: A synthesis on the neurobiological basis of stress-induced amnesia, flashbulb and traumatic memories, and the Yerkes–Dodson Law. *Neural Plasticity*, Art. 60803. doi:10.1155/2007/60803

Dunbar, R. I., & Shultz, S. (2007). Evolution in the social brain. *Science, 317*(5843), 1344–1347.

Dundas, B., Harris, M., & Narasimhan, M. (2007). Psychogenic polydipsia review: Etiology, differential, and treatment. *Current Psychiatry Reports, 9*(3), 236–241.

Dunn, K. M., Croft, P. R., & Hackett, G. I. (1998). Sexual problems: A study of the prevalence and need for health care in the general population. *Family Practice, 15*(6), 519–524.

Eisenberger, N. I., & Liberman, M. D. (2004). Why rejection hurts: A common neural alarm system for physical and social pain. *Trends in Cognitive Sciences, 8*(7), 294–300.

Eisenegger, C., Haushofer, J., & Fehr, E. (2011). The role of testosterone in social interaction. *Trends in Cognitive Sciences, 15*(6), 263–271.

Ellis, B., & Symons, D. (1990). Sex differences in sexual fantasy: An evolutionary psychological approach. *Journal of Sex Research, 27*(4), 527–555.

Ellison, N. B., Steinfield, C., & Lampe, C. (2007). The benefits of Facebook 'friends': Social capital and college students' use of online social network sites. *Journal of Computer-Mediated Communication, 12*, 1143–1168.

Epstein, M., Berk, D. P., Hollenberg, N. K., Adams, D. F., Chalmers, T. C., Abrams, H. L., & Merrill, J. P. (1970). Renal failure in the patient with cirrhosis: The role of active vasoconstriction. *American Journal of Medicine, 49*, 175–185.

Evren, C., Durkaya, M., Evren, B., Dalbudak, E., & Cetin, R. (2012). Relationship of relapse with impulsivity, novelty seeking and craving in male alcohol-dependent inpatients. *Drug and Alcohol Review, 31*(1), 81–90.

Farooqi, S., & O'Rahilly, S. (2006). Genetics of obesity in humans. *Endocrine Reviews, 27*(7), 710–718.

Feingold, A. (1992). Good-looking people are not what we think. *Psychological Bulletin, 111*, 304–341.

Feltenstein, M. W., & See, R. E. (2008). The neurocircuitry of addiction: An overview. *British Journal of Pharmacology, 154*(2), 261–274.

Field, M., Mogg, K., Mann, B., Bennett, G. A., & Bradley, B. P. (2013). Attentional biases in abstinent alcoholics and their association with craving. *Psychology of Addictive Behaviors, 27*(1), 71–80.

Filbey, F. M., & DeWitt, S. D. (2012). Cannabis cue-elicited craving and the reward neurocircuitry. *Progress in Neuro-psychopharmacology & Biological Psychiatry, 38*(1), 30–35.

Fink, G., Sumner, B. E., Rosie, R., Grace, O., & Quinn, J. P. (1996). Estrogen control of central neurotransmission: Effect on mood, mental state, and memory. *Cellular and Molecular Neurobiology, 16*(3), 325–344.

Fonteille, V., & Stoléru, S. (2011). The cerebral correlates of sexual desire: Functional neuroimaging approach. *Sexologies, 20*(3), 142–148.

Frederickson, J. D. (2010). 'I'm sorry, please don't hurt me': Effectiveness of apologies on aggression control. *Journal of Social Psychology*, *150*(6), 579–581.

Friese, M., Messner, C., & Schaffner, Y. (2012). Mindfulness meditation counteracts self-control depletion. *Consciousness and Cognition*, *21*(2), 1016–1022.

Funder, D. C., Block, J. H., & Block, J. (1983). Delay of gratification: Some longitudinal personality correlates. *Journal of Personality and Social Psychology*, *44*(6), 1198–1213.

Funston, F., & Wagner, S. (2010). *Surviving and thriving in uncertainty*. Hoboken, NJ: Wiley.

Gilson, R. J., & Mindel, A. (2001). Recent advances: Sexually transmitted infections. *BMJ*, *322*(7295), 1160–1164.

Goldmeier, D., & Leiblum, S. (2008). Interaction of organic and psychological factors in persistent genital arousal disorder in women: A report of six cases. *International Journal of STD and AIDS*, *19*(7), 488–490.

Gotestam, K. G., & Agras, W. S. (1995). General population-based epidemiological study of eating disorders in Norway. *International Journal of Eating Disorders*, *18*(2), 119–126.

Goyal, S., Balhara, Y. S., & Khandelwal, S. K. (2012). Revisiting classification of eating disorders: Toward Diagnostic and Statistical Manual of Mental Disorders-5 and International Statistical Classification of Diseases and Related Health Problems-11. *Indian Journal of Psychological Medicine*, *34*, 290–296.

Grasing, K., Li, N., He, S., Parrish, C., Delich, J., & Glowa, J. (2003). A new progressive ratio schedule for support of morphine self-administration in opiate dependent rats. *Psychopharmacology (Berlin)*, *168*, 387–396.

Gray, J. (1993). *Men are from Mars and women are from Venus*. New York, NY: HarperCollins.

Groesz, L., McCoy, S., Carl, J., Salow, L., Stewart, J., Adler, N., … Epel, E. (2012). What is eating you? Stress and the drive to eat. *Appetite*, *58*(2), 717–721.

Grossman, S. P. (1963). Chemically induced epileptiform seizures in the cat. *Science*, *142*(3590), 409–411.

Grundy, D. (2002). Neuroanatomy of visceral nociception: Vagal and splanchnic afferent. *Gut*, *51*(Suppl. 1), I2–I5.

Gumusluoglu, L., & Islev, A. (2009). Transformational leadership, creativity and organizational innovation. *Journal of Business Research*, *62*, 461–473.

Hagerty, M. (1999). Testing Maslow's hierarchy of needs: National quality-of-life across time. *Social Indicators Research*, *46*, 249–271.

Haggbloom, S. J., Warnick, R., Warnick, J. E., Jones, V. K., Yarbrough, G. L., Russel, T. M., … Monte, E. (2002). The 100 most eminent psychologists of the 20th century. *Review of General Psychology*, *6*, 139–152.

Haller, J., & Kruk, M. R. (2006). Normal and abnormal aggression: Human disorders and novel laboratory models. *Neuroscience & Biobehavioral Reviews*, *30*(3), 292–303.

Harris, J. L., Bargh, J. A., & Brownell, K. D. (2009). Priming effects of television food advertising on eating behavior. *Health Psychology*, *28*(4), 404–413.

Hartfield, M., & Keightley, P. D. (2012). Current hypotheses for the evolution of sex and recombination. *Integrative Zoology*, *7*, 192–209.

Herrera, B. M., Keildson, S., & Lindgren, C. M. (2011). Genetics and epigenetics of obesity. *Maturitas*, *69*(1), 41–49.

Hill, C. A. (1987). Affiliation motivation: People who need people … but in different ways. *Journal of Personality and Social Psychology*, *52*(5), 1008–1018.

Hofstede, G. (1984). The cultural relativity of the quality of life concept. *Academy of Management Review*, *9*, 389–398.

Holmes, K. K., Levine, R., & Weaver, M. (2004). Effectiveness of condoms in preventing sexually transmitted infections. *Bulletin of the World Health Organization*, *82*(6), 454–461.

Hull, C. L. (1943). *Principles of behavior: An introduction to behavior theory*. Oxford, UK: Appleton-Century-Crofts.

Hurst, L. D., & Peck, J. R. (1996). Recent advances in understanding of the evolution and maintenance of sex. *Trends in Ecology & Evolution, 11*(2), 46–52.

Hutchinson, L. (2003). Educational environment. *BMJ, 332*(7556), 1502–1504.

Irish Medical Organisation & British Medical Association Northern Ireland. (2010). *Obesity in Europe*. Retrieved 24 July 2015 from www.imo.ie/policy-international-affair/documents/policy-archive/Obesity-in-Europe_-JP-IMO_BMA.pdf

Isidori, A. M., Giannetta, E., Gianfrilli, D., Greco, E. A., Bonifacio, V., Aversa, A., … Lenzi, A. (2005). Effects of testosterone on sexual function in men: Results of a meta-analysis. *Clinical Endocrinology, 63*(4), 681–694.

Jacobi, C., Hayward, C., de Zwaan, M., Kraemer, H. C., & Agras W. S. (2004). Coming to terms with risk factors for eating disorders: Application of risk terminology and suggestions for a general taxonomy. *Psychological Bulletin, 130*(1), 19–65.

Johnston, C. A., Moreno, J. P., Regas, K., Tyler, C., & Foreyt, J. P. (2012). The application of the Yerkes–Dodson law in a childhood weight management program: Examining weight dissatisfaction. *Journal of Pediatric Psychology 37*(6), 674–679.

Kabat-Zinn, J. (1994). *Wherever you go, there you are*. New York, NY: Hachette Books.

Kalat, J. W. (2007). *Biological psychology* (9th ed.). Belmount, CA: Cengage.

Kalat, J. W. (2015). *Biological psychology* (12th ed.). Belmount, CA: Cengage.

Kaplan, M. S., & Krueger, R. B. (2012). Cognitive–behavioral treatment of the paraphilias. *Israel Journal of Psychiatry, 49*(4), 291–296.

Karama, S., Lecours, A. R., Leroux, J. M., Bourgouin P., Beaudoin, G., Joubert, S., & Beauregard, M. (2002). Areas of brain activation in males and females during viewing of erotic film excerpts. *Human Brain Mapping, 16*(1), 1–13.

Kelley, T. M., & Lambert, E. G. (2012). Mindfulness as a potential means of attenuating anger and aggression for prospective criminal justice professionals. *Mindfulness, 3*(4), 261–274.

Kenrick, D. T., Griskevicius, V., Neuberg, S. L., & Schaller, M. (2010). Renovating the pyramid of needs: Contemporary extensions built upon ancient foundations. *Perspectives on Psychological Science, 5*(3), 292–314.

King, J. C. (2006). Maternal obesity, metabolism, and pregnancy outcomes. *Annual Review of Nutrition, 26*, 271–291.

Kirchhoff, J., Wagner, U., & Strack, M. (2012). Apologies: Words of magic? The role of verbal components, anger reduction and offence severity. *Peace and Conflict, 18*, 109–130.

Klok, M. D., Jakobsdottir, S., & Drent, M. L. (2007). The role of leptin and ghrelin in the regulation of food intake and body weight in humans: A review. *Obesity Reviews, 8*(1), 21–34.

Kuncharapu, I., Majeroni, B. A., & Johnson, D. W. (2010). Pelvic organ prolapse. *American Family Physician, 81*(9), 1111–1117.

Ledikwe, J. H., Ello-Martin, J. A., & Rolls, B. J. (2005). Portion sizes and the obesity epidemic. *Journal of Nutrition, 135*(4), 905–909.

Lehtonen, J., Jennions, M. D., & Kokko, H. (2012). The many costs of sex. *Trends in Ecology & Evolution, 27*(3), 172–178.

Lepper, M. R., Corpus, J. H., & Iyengar, S. S. (2005). Intrinsic and extrinsic motivational orientations in the classroom: Age differences and academic correlates. *Journal of Educational Psychology, 97*(2), 184–196.

Lepper, M. R., Greene, D., & Nisbett, R. E. (1973). Undermining children's intrinsic interest with extrinsic reward: A test of the 'overjustification' hypothesis. *Journal of Personality and Social Psychology, 28*(1), 129–137.

Lindsay, J. J., & Anderson, C. A. (2000). From antecedent conditions to violent actions: A general affective aggression model. *Personality and Social Psychology Bulletin, 26*, 533–547.

Litman, J. A. (2005). Curiosity and the pleasures of learning: Wanting and liking new information. *Cognition and Emotion, 19*, 793–814.

Locke, E. A., & Latham, G. P. (2002). Building a practically useful theory of goal setting and task motivation. *American Psychologist, 57*(9), 705–717.

Locke, E. A., & Latham, G. P. (2006). New directions in goal-setting theory. *Current Directions in Psychological Science, 15*(5), 265–268.

Londrillo, F., Struglia F., & Rossi A. (2011). Psychogenic polydipsia: A mini review with three case-reports. *Journal of Psychopathology, 17*, 445–449.

Magen, E., & Gross, J. J. (2007). Harnessing the need for immediate gratification: Cognitive reconstrual modulates the reward value of temptations. *Emotion, 7*(2), 415–428.

Markus, H. R., & Kitayama, S. (1991). Culture and the self: Implications for cognition, emotion, and motivation. *Psychological Review, 98*(2), 224–253.

Marston, C., & King, E. (2006). Factors that shape young people's sexual behaviour: A systematic review. *Lancet, 368*(9547), 1581–1586.

Masters, W. H., & Johnson, V. E. (1966). *Human sexual response.* Boston, MA: Little, Brown.

Martin, S., Sollner, C., Charoensawan, V., Adryan, B., Thisse, B., Thisse, C., … Wright, G. J. (2010). Construction of a large extracellular protein interaction network and its resolution by spatiotemporal expression profiling. *Molecular & Cellular Proteomics, 9*, 2654–2665.

Mauro, C. F., & Harris, Y. R. (2000). The influence of maternal child-rearing attitudes and teaching behaviors on preschoolers' delay of gratification. *Journal of Genetic Psychology, 161*(3), 292–306.

McClelland, D. C. (1961). *The achieving society.* New York, NY: Free Press.

McGuire, J. (2008). A review of effective interventions for reducing aggression and violence. *Philosophical Transactions of the Royal Society B: Biological Sciences, 363*(1503), 2577–2597.

Mega, C., Ronconi, L., & De Beni, R. (2014). What makes a good student? How emotions, self-regulated learning, and motivation contribute to academic achievement. *Journal of Educational Psychology, 106*(1), 121–131.

Mental Health Foundation. (2015). *Eating disorders.* Retrieved 15 January 2018 from https://www.mentalhealth.org.uk/a-to-z/e/eating-disorders

Milyavskaya, M., & Koestner, R. (2011). Psychological needs, motivation, and well-being: A test of self-determination theory across multiple domains. *Personality and Individual Differences, 50*, 387–391.

Mischel, W., Shoda, Y., & Rodriguez, M. I. (1989). Delay of gratification in children. *Science, 244*(4907), 933–938.

Moore, B. S., Clyburn, A., & Underwood, B. (1976). The role of affect in delay of gratification. *Child Development, 47*(1), 273–276.

Morris, N. M., Udry, J. R., Khan-Dawood, F., & Dawood, M. Y. (1987). Marital sex frequency and midcycle female testosterone. *Archives of Sexual Behavior, 16*, 27–37.

Moyer, K. E. (1986). Biological bases of aggressive behavior. In R. Plutchik & H. Kellerman (Eds.), *Emotion: Theory research and experience* (Vol. 3, pp. 219–236). New York, NY: Academic Press.

National Centre for Eating Disorders. (2015). *Eating disorders in males.* Retrieved 20 November 2017 from http://eating-disorders.org.uk/information/eating-disorders-in-males

National Institute of Clinical Excellence. (2004). *Eating disorders: Recognition and treatment.* Retrieved 15 January 2018 from https://www.nice.org.uk/guidance/ng69

Nehrenberg, D. L., Sheikh, A., & Ghashghaei, H. T. (2013). Identification of neuronal loci involved with displays of affective aggression in NC900 mice. *Brain Structure and Function, 218*(4), 1033–1049.

Neumann, I. D. (2007). Oxytocin: The neuropeptide of love reveals some of its secrets. *Cell Metabolism, 5*(4), 231–233.

Ng, J. Y. Y., Ntoumanis, N., Thogersen-Ntoumani, C., Deci, E. L., Ryan, R. M., Duda, J. L., & Williams, G. C. (2012). Self-determination theory applied to health contexts: A meta-analysis. *Perspectives on Psychological Science, 7*, 325–340.

NHS. (2011). *Weight loss surgery*. Available at http://www.nhs.uk/Livewell/loseweight/Pages/weight-loss-surgery.aspx (accessed 24 July 2015).

NHS. (2013). *The male menopause*. Retrieved 24 July 2015 from http://www.nhs.uk/conditions/male-menopause/Pages/Introduction.aspx

NHS. (2014). *Female sexual problems*. Retrieved 15 January 2018 from https://www.nhs.uk/Livewell/Goodsex/Pages/Femalesexualdysfunction.aspx

NHS. (2017). *Mindfulness*. Retrieved 20 November 2017 from http://www.nhs.uk/conditions/stress-anxiety-depression/pages/mindfulness.aspx

NHS Choices. (2015). Cut down on your calories. Retrieved 20 November 2017 from https://www.nhs.uk/Livewell/Goodfood/Pages/eat-less.aspx

Nielsen, S. J., & Popkin, B. M. (2003). Patterns and trends in food portion sizes, 1977–1998. *JAMA*, *289*(4), 450–453.

Oakley, A., Fullerton, D., Holland, J., Arnold, S., France-Dawson, M., Kelley, P., & McGrellis, S. (1995). Sexual health education interventions for young people: A methodological review. *BMJ*, *310*(6973), 158–162.

Okimoto, T. G., Wenzel, M., & Hedrick, K. (2013). Refusing to apologize can have psychological benefits (and we issue no mea culpa for this research finding). *European Journal of Social Psychology*, *43*(1), 22–31.

Otto, S. P., & Lenormand, T. (2002). Resolving the paradox of sex and recombination. *Nature Reviews Genetics*, *3*(4), 252–261.

Paliwal, P., Hyman, S. M., & Sinha, R. (2007). Craving predicts time to cocaine relapse: Further validation of the Now and Brief versions of the Cocaine Craving Questionnaire. *Drug and Alcohol Dependence*, *93*(3), 252–259.

Petrucci, C. J. (2002). Apology in the criminal justice setting: Evidence for including apology as an additional component in the legal system. *Behavioral Sciences & the Law*, *20*(4), 337–362.

Pfaus, J. G. (2009). Pathways of sexual desire. *Journal of Sexual Medicine*, *6*(6), 1506–1533.

Polivy, J., & Herman, C. P. (2002). Causes of eating disorders. *Annual Review of Psychology*, *53*, 187–213.

Pretty, G. H., & Seligman, C. (1984). Affect and the overjustification effect. *Journal of Personality and Social Psychology*, *46*(6), 1241–1253.

Public Health England. (2014). *Sexually transmitted infections (STIs): Annual data tables*. Retrieved 24 July 2015 from https://www.gov.uk/government/statistics/sexually-transmitted-infections-stis-annual-data-tables

Regan, P. C., Levin, L., Sprecher, S., Christopher, F. S., & Gate, R. (2000). Partner preferences: What characteristics do men and women desire in their short-term sexual and long-term romantic partners? *Journal of Psychology and Human Sexuality*, *12*, 1–21.

Roberton, T., Daffern, M., & Bucks, R. S. (2014). Maladaptive emotion regulation and aggression in adult offenders. *Psychology, Crime & Law*, *20*(10), 933–954.

Robinson, T. E., & Berridge, K. C. (1993). The neural basis of drug craving: An incentive-sensitization theory of addiction. *Brain Research Reviews*, *18*, 247–291.

Robinson, T. E., & Berridge, K. C. (2003). Addiction. *Annual Review of Psychology*, *54*, 25–53.

Robinson, T. N. (1999). Reducing children's television viewing to prevent obesity. *JAMA*, *282*(16), 1561–1567.

Rolls, B. J., Jones, B. P., & Fallows, D. J. (1972). A comparison of the motivational properties of thirst induced by intracranial angiotensin and ester deprivation. *Physiology & Behaviour*, *80*, 26–29.

Rosenfield, D., Folger, R., & Adelman, H. F. (1980). When rewards reflect competence: A qualification of the overjustification effect. *Journal of Personality and Social Psychology*, *39*, 368–376.

Ryan, R. M., & Deci, E. L. (2000). Self-determination theory and the facilitation of intrinsic motivation, social development, and well-being. *American Psychologist*, *55*(1), 68–78.

Samaranayake, C. B., Arora, B., Whiting, J., & Kenedi, C. (2013). Management of psychogenic polydipsia and hyponatremia in an acute mental health unit. *Australian & New Zealand Journal of Psychiatry*, *47*(4), 395–396.

Sansone, C., & Harackiewicz, J. (Eds.). (2000). *Intrinsic and extrinsic motivation.* San Diego, CA: Elsevier.

Santoro, S. (2012). Stomachs: Does the size matter? Aspects of intestinal satiety, gastric satiety, hunger and gluttony. *Clinics (San Paulo)*, *67*(4), 301–303.

Schlam, T. R., Wilson, N. L., Shoda, Y., Mischel, W., & Ayduk, O. (2013). Preschoolers' delay of gratification predicts their body mass 30 years later. *Journal of Pediatrics*, *162*(1), 90–93.

Schneiderman, I., Zagoory-Sharon, O., Leckman, J. F., & Feldman, R. (2012). Oxytocin during the initial stages of romantic attachment: Relations to couples' interactive reciprocity. *Psychoneuroendocrinology*, *37*(8), 1277–1285.

Shilts, M. K., Horowitz, M., & Townsend, M. S. (2004). Goal setting as a strategy for dietary and physical activity behavior change: A review of the literature. *American Journal of Health Promotion*, *19*(2), 81–93.

Silk, J. B. (2007). Social components of fitness in primate groups. *Science*, *317*(5843), 1347–1351.

Solomon, R. L., & Corbit, J. D. (1974). An opponent-process theory of motivation: I. Temporal dynamics of affect. *Psychological Review*, *81*, 119–145.

Statistic Brain. (2017). Arranged/forced marriage statistics. Retrieved 15 January 2017 from https://www.statisticbrain.com/arranged-marriage-statistics

Stice, E., Marti, C. N., & Rohde, P. (2013). Prevalence, incidence, impairment, and course of the proposed DSM-5 eating disorder diagnoses in an 8-year prospective community study of young women. *Journal of Abnormal Psychology*, *122*(2), 445–457.

Struber, D., Luck, M., & Roth, G. (2008). Sex, aggression and impulse control: An integrative account. *Neurocase*, *14*(1), 93–121.

Tang, S.-H., & Hall, V. C. (1995). The overjustification effect: A meta-analysis. *Applied Cognitive Psychology*, *9*(5), 365–404.

Teigen, K. (1994). Yerkes–Dodson: A law for all seasons. *Theory & Psychology*, *4*, 525–547.

Teitelbaum, P., & Epstein, A. N. (1962). The lateral hypothalamic syndrome: Recovery of feeding and drinking after lateral hypothalamic lesions. *Psychological Review*, *69*, 74–90.

Thibaut, F. (2012). Pharmacological treatment of paraphilias. *Israel Journal of Psychiatry*, *49*(4), 297–305.

Thoits, P. A. (2011). Mechanisms linking social ties and support to physical and mental health. *Journal of Health and Social Behavior*, *52*(2), 145–161.

Tice, D. M., Bratslavasky, E., & Baumeister, R. F. (2001). Emotional distress regulation takes precedence over impulse control: If you feel bad, do it! *Journal of Personality and Social Psychology*, *80*(1), 53–67.

Tiefer, L. (2001). Arriving at a 'new view' of women's sexual problems: Background, theory and activism. In L. Kaschak & L. Tiefer (Eds.), *A new view of women's sexual problems* (pp. 63–98). Binghamton, NY: Haworth.

Tierney, P., Farmer, S. M., & Graen, G. B. (1999). An examination of leadership and employee creativity: The relevance of traits and relationships. *Personnel Psychology*, *52*(3), 591–620.

Toates, F. (2011). *Biological psychology* (3rd ed.). London, UK: Prentice Hall.

Toates, F. (2014). *How sexual desire works: The enigmatic urge.* Cambridge, UK: Cambridge University Press.

Trumbull, E., & Rothstein-Fisch, C. (2011). The intersection of culture and achievement motivation. *School Community Journal*, *21*(2), 25–54.

Udacity. (2013). Yerkes–Dodson law: Intro to psychology. *YouTube.* Retrieved 20 November 2017 from https://www.youtube.com/watch?v=8CA6Di3ix0k

Van Anders, S. M. (2012). Testosterone and sexual desire in healthy women and men. *Archives of Sexual Behavior*, *41*, 1471–1484.

Van Honk, J., Tuiten, A., Verbaten, R., Van den Hout, M., Koppeschaar, H., Thijssen, J., & de Haan, E. (1999). Correlations among salivary testosterone, mood, and selective attention to threat in humans. *Hormones and Behavior, 36*(1), 17–24.

Verghese, C., de Leon, J., & Josianssen, R. C. (1996). Problems and progress in the diagnosis and treatment of polydipsia and hyponatremia. *Schizophrenia Bulletin, 22*(3), 455–464.

Wahba, M. A., & Bridwell, L. G. (1976). Maslow reconsidered: A review of research on the need hierarchy theory. *Organizational Behavior and Human Performance, 15*(2), 212–240.

Waldinger, M. D., & Schweitzer, D. H. (2009). Persistent genital arousal disorder in 18 Dutch women: Part I. MRI, EEG, & transvaginal ultrasonography investigations. *Journal of Sexual Medicine, 6*(2), 474–481.

Waller, G., Gray, E., Hinrichsen, H., Mountford, V., Lawson, R., & Patient, E. (2014). Cognitive-behavioral therapy for bulimia nervosa and atypical bulimia nervosa: Effectiveness in clinical settings. *International Journal of Eating Disorders, 47*, 13–17

Walsh, B. T., Fairburn, C. G., Mickley, D., Sysko, R., & Parides, M. K. (2004). Treatment of bulimia nervosa in a primary care setting. *American Journal of Psychiatry, 161*(3), 556–561.

Water Project. (2015). 2015 water projects. Retrieved 15 January 2018 from https://thewaterproject.org/2015-water-projects

Watson, N. V., & Breedlove, S. M. (2012). *The mind's machine: Foundations of brain and behavior.* Sunderland, MA: Sinauer Associates.

Weinstein, N., & Ryan, R. M. (2011). A motivational approach to stress response and adaptation. *Stress & Health, 27*(1), 4–17.

Wentzel, K. R. (1998). Social relationships and motivation in middle school: The role of parents, teachers, and peers. *Journal of Educational Psychology, 90*(2), 202–209.

Wiederman, M. W., & Allgeier, E. R. (1993). Gender differences in sexual jealousy: Adaptionist or social learning explanation. *Ethology and Sociobiology, 14*, 115–140.

Williams, K. D., Cheung, C. K., & Choi, W. (2000). Cyberostracism: Effects of being ignored over the internet. *Journal of Personality and Social Psychology, 79*(5), 748–762.

Winston, R. (2002). *Human instinct: How our primeval impulses shape our modern lives.* London, UK: Bantam Press.

Wise, R. A. (1974). Lateral hypothalamic electrical stimulation: Does it make animals 'hungry'? *Brain Research, 67*(2), 187–209.

Witkos, M., Uttaburanont, M., Lang, C. D., & Arora, R. (2008). Costs of and reasons for obesity. *Journal of the CardioMetabolic Syndrome, 3*(3), 173–176.

World Health Organization. (2015). *Obesity and overweight.* Retrieved 24 July 2015 from www.who.int/mediacentre/factsheets/fs311/en

Young, L. R., & Nestle, M. (2007). Portion sizes and obesity: Responses of fast-food companies. *Journal of Public Health, 28*, 238–248.

6 Consciousness: Conscious Versus Unconscious Processes

ZOLTAN DIENES AND ANIL SETH

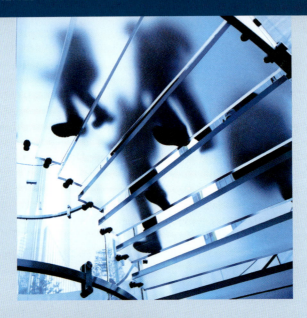

INTRODUCTION

> ### LEARNING OBJECTIVE 6.1
>
> Demonstrate an understanding of the different meanings of the word 'conscious'.

Consciousness has been defined as the presence of any kind of subjective experience at all. When you are conscious, there is 'something-it-is-like' to be you. This 'something-it-is-likeness' goes away when you are unconscious (e.g. during dreamless sleep) and is never there at all for things like tables and chairs. That is, you have conscious experiences; tables do not. Our lives would mean nothing to us if our experiences were not conscious. But how can we be conscious at all? Why are some mental states conscious? Can mental states be unconscious? Can we have unconscious perceptions, memories, learning, intentions, or emotions? And what does this tell us about the function of consciousness? These are the questions we will consider in turn. Firstly we will define different uses of the term 'conscious' (there is little agreement here, even among 'experts') and then we will consider theories of consciousness.

When psychology started as a science in the 19th century, it was the study of conscious experience. Psychologists looked inward to identify what was there. By the middle of the 20th century, behaviourism had rendered mention of the word 'consciousness' taboo. Psychology was strictly about what could be publicly observed: behaviour. Only since about the beginning of the 21st century has that taboo really been broken, with consciousness once more widely recognized as the central problem that it is. Consciousness can be tackled by having subjects look inward, with researchers at the same time using the objective procedures of science to measure the subjects' behaviour and the activity of their brains. We will see how this can be done.

Different uses of the word 'conscious'

In everyday life, sometimes when we use the word 'conscious' we apply it to a creature as a whole; for example, we may say of Tom that he is conscious or unconscious. Call this use of the word **creature consciousness** (a term introduced by the New York philosopher David Rosenthal, 2005). It means roughly that the creature is awake and responsive to the world, rather than asleep or knocked out. We will see later that such consciousness comes in degrees or levels. Tom could be partially conscious. Even if Tom were, as a creature, conscious (he is awake, alert), he might have mental states that were unconscious. According to Freud, he might be acting on desires he does not know that he has. Or he might be flashed an image on the cinema screen that he did not know that he saw (unconscious seeing, or subliminal perception). Conversely, Tom might be asleep while having conscious experiences (maybe dreaming). So individual mental states can be conscious or not independently of whether the creature is conscious or not. Thus, apart from creature consciousness,

Psychology, First Edition. Edited by Graham Davey.

there is also mental state consciousness. Our theories ultimately need to account for consciousness in both senses.

It will be useful to distinguish different types of mental states, so as to be clear about which mental states are claimed to be conscious or unconscious. Seeing a panda eating bamboo is a different mental state from seeing a nightingale on a tree. So mental states differ in what **content** they have. In one case, 'a panda eats bamboo' is the content of the state; in the other, the content is 'a nightingale is on a tree'. (In this chapter, the content of mental states will be indicated in quotation marks.) Different contents mean different mental states. Mental states also differ in how the content is held – that is, what relation we bear to the content. *Seeing* that 'a panda eats bamboo' is a different mental state from *remembering* that 'a panda eats bamboo'. So, even when the content is the same, mental states differ in how that content is held: for the same content, perceiving, thinking, dreaming, and so on are different types of states. In this chapter we will consider the conscious status of perceptions, memories, acquired knowledge, intentions, and emotions. In what follows it will be useful to consider both exactly what the content is and the way it is held, in considering exactly which mental states are conscious or unconscious.

SECTION SUMMARY

- The term 'conscious' has a number of uses; for example, it might apply to a creature or to a mental state. Our theories ultimately need to account for consciousness in both senses.

- By the middle of the 20th century, behaviourism had rendered mention of the word 'consciousness' taboo. Psychology was strictly about what could be publicly observed.

- Consciousness re-emerged as a serious topic in psychology and neuroscience in the 1990s.

THEORIES OF CONSCIOUSNESS: HIGHER-ORDER VERSUS INTEGRATION THEORIES

LEARNING OBJECTIVE 6.2

Demonstrate an understanding of the two main approaches to explaining consciousness.

Theories

What does a theory of consciousness need to explain? We can get some clues from considering some of the characteristics of conscious states. When we consciously perceive a situation, we know how we are perceiving it; for example, you know if you are seeing the situation, hearing it, and so on (Overgaard et al., 2013). When we consciously see a tree, we know that we are specifically *seeing* a tree. (Try it now, if you can.) Consider, by contrast, a person with **blindsight** (Weiskrantz, 1997). These people have had damage (usually due to a stroke) to a part of their visual cortex called V1, the first area of the cortex that visual information reaches. They consider themselves blind in a part of their visual field, the part corresponding to where V1 has been damaged. Nonetheless, they can be persuaded to guess about the properties of objects in their blind field. For example, if they are shown an X or an O, they can be asked to guess 'X' or 'O' (despite the protests they sometimes make that the task is pointless because they do not see anything). And their accuracy can be very good. So they must have seen the shape, because they can discriminate what was there. Yet they may deny seeing at all, and insist that they are completely guessing. That is, the patient sees but there is no corresponding conscious visual experience.

The case of blindsight allows us to compare two popular theories of consciousness: 'higher-order' theories and 'integration' theories. Let's take higher-order theories first (e.g. Rosenthal, 2005). In blindsight there is a visual mental state about the shape of a stimulus. In that minimal sense, the person 'sees' the shape. But the seeing is not conscious seeing. We can characterize the mental state as the person seeing that 'the shape is X'. What is missing, according to higher-order theories, is a mental state that makes the person aware of the seeing itself – that is, a mental state that asserts that 'I am seeing that the shape is X'. This latter mental state would be a mental state about a mental state (because its content is about seeing). A mental state about a mental state is called a higher-order state. Conversely, a state about the world (e.g. a shape being X) is a first-order state. According to higher-order theory, for a mental state to be conscious, there must be a relevant higher-order state. For example, for seeing to be conscious, one needs to represent that one is seeing (and thereby be aware of seeing). According to higher-order theory, in the case of blindsight, it is precisely because the person earnestly and seriously denies seeing that we are justified in regarding the seeing as unconscious. In general, conscious knowledge means you know that you know; if you know without knowing that you know, the knowledge is unconscious.

There are multiple variants of higher-order theory. For example, one variant says that, for a mental state to be conscious, you have to actually have a higher-order state that asserts that you are in the lower-order state (Rosenthal, 2005); a different variant says that you just have to be disposed to have such a state (e.g. you only need to be able to represent that you are seeing if you are asked, or if you wonder about it yourself) (Carruthers, 2000). It has been postulated that there is a region responsible for **higher-order thoughts (HOTs)**, a 'HOT box', in the frontal area of the brain, possibly the dorsolateral prefrontal cortex (Lau & Rosenthal, 2011).

Integration theories of consciousness start from considering other characteristics of conscious states. Conscious information seems to be available to be used in many different ways. For example, if you consciously saw a glass of water you could drink it, leave it where it is, throw it down the sink, put sea monkeys in it, or any other action. On the other hand, a thirsty person with blindsight confronted with a glass of water in their blind field would not spontaneously do anything with the glass. They could only guess that one was there if forced to do so by an experimenter. Unconscious knowledge, like unconscious perceptions, seems to be used in only very specific ways. A child of five uses nouns and verbs appropriately, and so knows of each word whether it should function as a noun or a verb. But, unschooled in grammar, the same child could not perform any arbitrary task, such as hopping on the left leg if a word is a noun and on the right if it is a verb. Unconscious grammatical knowledge is used only for processing language. Some integration theories emphasize this flexibility in the use of conscious information. In some integration theories, in the case of blindsight, it is precisely because the visual information cannot be used flexibly that we are justified in regarding the seeing as unconscious.

The property of flexibility is closely related to the fact that the conscious scene before you this very moment seems unified; you experience it as a whole. Further, even in experiencing it as a whole, you are making many small discriminations – the colours and shapes of different objects, the qualities of different sounds, the pressures on your body, the temperature on your skin – all as part of one experience. In this way of looking at things, your conscious experience can be characterized as highly integrated and yet highly differentiated at the same time. Other integration theories start from this premise.

These two approaches to integration theory (i.e. flexibility versus a unified experience) are best represented by two prominent theories: **global workspace** theory and **information integration** theory. According to global workspace theory (Baars, 1988; Dehaene, Changeux, & Naccache, 2011), the brain consists of many unconscious processors that do their job, make their discriminations, on the information given to them. By themselves, these local processors can only implement very specific functions. The output of each processor competes for access to a 'global workspace'. When some output wins this competition, it is broadcast to many other processors (accounting for flexibility) and at the same time becomes conscious. One way to think of this is that 'winning' information is like an actor on a stage suddenly being picked out by a spotlight. In the brain, the global workspace is often identified with large parts of the frontal and parietal networks.

Information integration theory develops the second view, that conscious experiences are simultaneously integrated and differentiated. Information integration theory – and 'complexity' theories more broadly – are distinguished by proposing explicit mathematical quantities that may correspond with the degree or level of consciousness a creature may have. While the details are complicated, the basic idea is not. Imagine a brain in which all the neurons fired independently of all others. Such a brain would be highly differentiated (i.e. capable of entering many different states) but there would be no integration, and hence no possible unity to any corresponding conscious scene. On the other hand, a brain in which all the neurons fired on and off together, in waves of synchrony, would be highly integrated but not at all differentiated (there would be only two states: all neurons on or all neurons off), meaning that it would incapable of representing the rich space of discriminations needed for consciousness. (In fact, neurons firing simultaneously is characteristic of the brain in seizure, when a person is unconscious.) A conscious brain needs high levels of both integration and differentiation; this is the idea of 'complexity'. Seth, Barrett, and Barnett (2011), Tononi (2008), and Tononi and Edelman (1998) have conjectured relevant 'complexity' measures that are high only when both integration and differentiation are high. Supporting these ideas, it has been found that, if a brain is stimulated by a short magnetic pulse, in an awake brain the pulse produces activation over many parts of the brain, lasting a long time, showing sustained integration between areas; in a sleeping brain, the activation spreads only locally and transiently, showing limited integration (Casali et al., 2013; Massimini et al., 2005).

These different theories of consciousness are compatible in many ways. For example, the architecture of the brain proposed by global workspace theory is well suited for promoting the high integration and differentiation required by information integration theory: information in the workspace should be easily integrated with information in any processor. Also, information in a global workspace is generally available for any processing and so should be available to any mechanism responsible for higher-order thoughts (the HOT box). So the theories may often agree about when a mental state is conscious or unconscious. But the theories are not the same. For example, if information were in the global workspace but blocked from the HOT box, it would be conscious according to global workspace theory yet unconscious according to higher-order theory. (Consider an animal with a global workspace but no HOT box: it would be capable of conscious states according to global workspace theory but not according to higher-order theory.) A bigger difference has to do with which aspects of consciousness the theories try to explain. Higher-order theory and global workspace theory are theories about **conscious content**: they specify whether mental states are conscious or not. They do not specify whether a creature is conscious, or what level of consciousness it might have. Integrated information and complexity theories, on the other hand, are first and foremost theories of **consciousness level**: for example, they would account for the difference between normal waking consciousness and general anaesthesia in terms of levels of integration and differentiation. It is possible to delve further into each theory to find aspects related to both level and content, but this difference in overall aim is worth remembering.

There are other theories of conscious content. One of these, re-entry theory, says that a mental state becomes conscious when it elicits a wave of 'feedback' or 're-entrant' neural processing (Lamme, 2010). That is, activity flows not only forward from simple sensory areas to higher areas of the cortex but also back from higher areas to lower areas, making a loop, where higher and lower areas modify each other's activity. Activation can be sustained by such loops. According to Lamme, these feedback loops (i.e. **re-entrant processing**) produce conscious experience of the content coded by the areas, even if the loop is local to a particular sensory area. This conscious content is only verbally reportable when the re-entrant loop happens to encompass prefrontal and parietal brain regions. According to the theory, activation briefly passing through a bit of brain, and not sustained by recurrent loops, constitutes unconscious processing – even if this activation reaches frontal areas. Such theories explain the phenomenal fact that each individual conscious experience lasts for a period of time, say at least a few hundred milliseconds (a fact also explained by higher-order and integration theories). According to local theories, information can be conscious even when people sincerely and earnestly deny knowing the information and when they cannot use the information in flexible ways (because the loop is local and does not encompass parietal and prefrontal regions). This marks an important distinction with higher-order theory and global workspace theory. There is a lot of evidence for the role of re-entrant processing in conscious states (Lamme, 2010); the question is whether re-entry is sufficient in itself to produce conscious experience or, rather, whether it is just a prerequisite for access to a HOT box or global workspace (for example).

Measuring the conscious status of mental states: Measures and theories

In the United Kingdom, subliminal messages are banned in advertising. Imagine your job is to determine whether a briefly flashed brand name in an advert is perceived consciously or unconsciously in order to determine whether or not the advert should be banned. You could ask people at the end of the advert whether they noticed any words. Let us say that no one mentions the brand name. Does that mean they did not consciously see the brand name in the advert? If the advert lasted a few minutes, maybe they just forgot a brief visual impression by the time the advert was over. Or maybe they were somewhat sure they saw the brand name but not completely sure, and did not want to look silly saying something was there that might not have been there. So we need a more sensitive test. As soon as the word was flashed, we could stop the clip and force people to choose between one of two brand names as the one that was just flashed. Now people would be forced to use whatever knowledge they had, even if they were not completely sure. But, if there was just one trial of this, the test would still be insensitive – one trial is not able to pick up on much. So the procedure could be repeated, using one of two brand names each time, and people would have to guess which one was presented in each trial, for many trials. Now, if people were unable to choose the presented name at above-chance levels, we could conclude that they could not have consciously seen the word. On the other hand, if people could discriminate at above-chance levels which word was shown, would that mean they must have consciously seen the word? Not according to higher-order theory and integration theories of consciousness.

According to higher-order theory, discriminating what word was there requires only a first-order mental state, namely a state whose content is about only the world. For example, the state could represent visual perceptual content about the word 'blitz' that has content that roughly means '"blitz" is displayed'. Such a state could guide a person to choose 'blitz' from another word. But, without a corresponding higher-order state, the seeing would be unconscious. In fact, according to the higher-order account, finding above-chance performance on discriminating what word was there could be the first step to showing there was subliminal perception – and hence banning the advert. To determine whether an appropriate higher-order state was present (i.e. a state that asserts 'I am seeing that the word "blitz" is displayed'), it is necessary to determine whether the person can tell what mental state they are in: can they tell whether they are seeing or guessing? After choosing which word might have been presented in each trial, people could be asked to say whether they 'guessed completely' or 'saw' the word. Or they could be asked to give a confidence rating, saying how confident they were, from a complete guess up through intermediate confidence to completely sure. If, when people said they were completely guessing, they still picked the right word at above-baseline levels, the *guessing criterion* of unconscious knowledge would be satisfied (as with blindsight patients). However, if people could not tell whether they were seeing or guessing, there should be no relation between confidence and accuracy. No relation between confidence and accuracy is called the 'zero correlation criterion' of unconscious knowledge (Dienes, 2008a).

Tests asking people to tell what is in the world (e.g. what word was displayed) are called **objective measures**. Tests asking people to tell what mental state they are in (e.g. a confidence rating) are called **subjective measures**. Higher-order theories motivate the use of subjective measures. Most integration theories do too; when the content of a mental state is widely integrated, it will be available to higher-order thoughts. Thus, in both theories, showing knowledge on objective measures while showing lack of awareness of the knowledge on subjective measures indicates that the knowledge is unconscious. By contrast, in re-entry theories, showing a lack of awareness on subjective measures in no way indicates that the knowledge is unconscious. If people can discriminate which word was there at above-chance levels but they claim they were completely guessing, then the seeing could have been (but need not be) conscious. However, in re-entry theories (as on HOT and global workspace theories), if people are at chance on objective measures, then we can conclude that the knowledge is unconscious.

Integration theories motivate another test of whether knowledge is conscious. If knowledge is conscious, we can flexibly use that knowledge in many ways, according to the theories. That is, we should have control over how the knowledge is used (Jacoby, 1991). So, for example, if a person were asked to pick the word that had *not* just been flashed, conscious seeing would enable them to pick the other brand name, whereas unconscious seeing might draw them to the very word flashed, an impulse they would not know to oppose. In higher-order theory, unconscious knowledge could in principle be used flexibly, just so long as it does not elicit appropriate higher-order states. Indeed, below we will present examples of flexible control over the use of knowledge a person does not know they have.

In sum, the appropriate measure of the conscious status of mental states depends on what theory a researcher presupposes. We need not declare that any of the theories must be the one true theory; an everyday word such as 'consciousness' is bound to have multiple meanings. There may be several natural phenomena that people mean by the word 'conscious'. What we do require of any theory, though, is that it takes part in generating testable, interesting conjectures; then we will be in the business of science (Dienes, 2008b).

TEST YOURSELF

1. What does 'conscious' mean?
2. In what main ways do mental states differ?
3. What are the main theories of consciousness?
4. What are the main ways of measuring whether a mental state is conscious or unconscious?
5. Which measures of consciousness go with which theories?

SECTION SUMMARY

- The case of blindsight allows us to compare two popular theories of consciousness: higher-order theories and integration theories.
- According to higher-order theory, when you have a conscious mental state, you know what that mental state is – by having a mental state about that mental state.

- According to integration theories, your conscious experience can be characterized as highly integrated and yet highly differentiated at the same time.

- Approaches to integration theory are best represented by two prominent theories: global workspace theory and information integration theory.

- There are other theories of conscious content. One of these, re-entry theory, says that a mental state becomes conscious when it elicits a wave of 'feedback' or 're-entrant' neural processing; that is, activity flows not only forward from simple sensory areas to higher areas of the cortex but also back from higher areas to lower areas, making a loop.

- Tests that ask people to tell what state the world is in are called objective measures.

- Tests that ask people to tell what mental state they are in are called subjective measures.

CONSCIOUS VERSUS UNCONSCIOUS MEMORY

LEARNING OBJECTIVE 6.3

Understand the differences between conscious and unconscious memory and the effects of both on the individual.

Unconscious memory occurs when a person uses memory but is not aware of using memory. Warrington and Weiskrantz (1974) provided a demonstration of the phenomenon that inspired much further research in the field of 'implicit memory' – or unconscious memory. (The words 'implicit' and 'explicit' were used presumably because they obviated the need to refer to 'conscious', still virtually a taboo word in experimental psychology at the time.) Warrington and Weiskrantz gave people with amnesia a list of words to remember. As expected, on a later recognition test, people with amnesia did worse than those without (which is how such people were diagnosed with amnesia in the first place). People were also given a stem-completion test. For example, people might be asked to complete the stem PAT__. When people were shown 'patio' as one of the words to be remembered, they completed the stem as 'patio' more often than when they had not been shown 'patio' before. The increase in accuracy or speed in performing a task because the stimulus has been presented before is called **priming**. Both people with and without amnesia showed priming (for a review of relevant studies, see Hayes, Fortier, Levine, Milberg, & McGlinchey, 2012). Because people with amnesia showed priming, there is some form of memory for the word presented earlier (demonstrated in the priming effect) that does not depend on consciously remembering the word. Hence, people with amnesia have a form of unconscious memory. The next sections consider some examples of the role of unconscious memory in everyday life.

Illusion of loudness

Can memory change how we perceive the world? It turns out memories can present themselves as perceptions rather than memories. When people have heard sentences before, those same sentences sound clearer when subsequently heard in noise. Jacoby, Allan, Collins, and Larwill (1988) found that people rated the noise as less loud when listening to old rather than new sentences, even though the noise level was the same. Further, when told about this effect, and asked not to show it, people still thought the noise was quieter for old rather than new sentences. That is, people's memory for the sentences made the sentences appear to be spoken clearly through the noise; people were not aware of using memory, even though it was memory at work. Jacoby argued that unconscious memory expresses itself as 'fluency' (i.e. an ease of processing a stimulus), but the way the fluency is experienced depends on what the person is trying to do. When trying to listen to sentences through noise, the fluency is experienced as the volume of the noise. For an everyday example of memory experienced as perception, consider how, when you have read the lyrics of a song, you can hear them clearly in the music. We will see below other ways unconscious memory can be experienced, such as in liking. The robustness of the illusion of loudness in the face of attempts to overcome it indicates one way in which the unconscious status of memory could be established: by whether the participant can control the effect or not (Jacoby, 1991). People cannot make the illusion of loudness go away when informed of it; thus, Jacoby concludes, the influence is unconscious.

Illusion of truth

Here we explore how familiarity with a claim makes the claim seem true. In a classic experiment, Hovland and Weiss (1951) asked people to read an essay addressing the question 'Can a Practicable Atomic Powered Submarine Be Built at the Present Time?', then an issue of topical concern. After reading, one group was told the author was Robert Oppenheimer, one of the developers of the atomic bomb (who was also a Sanskrit scholar as a hobby; when he first saw the bomb go off, he famously said to himself, 'I am become death, the destroyer of worlds' – his translation from the *Bhagavad Gita*). The participants regarded Oppenheimer as a highly credible source on the topic. Another group was told that the source was a Soviet Union newspaper, a source that had little credibility to the participants. When tested immediately for how much their attitude had changed, the first group (exposed to a credible source) changed their opinions considerably on the topic; the second group (exposed to a non-credible source) changed their opinions scarcely at all. But, after a month's delay, the opinions of the second group had changed and were now very similar to those of the first group. Hovland and Weiss called the increasing influence of the low-credibility source over time the 'sleeper effect'; that is, the low-credibility arguments did not have any influence immediately – it was as if they slept for a time, eventually waking up.

The sleeper effect could be explained along similar lines to Jacoby et al.'s (1988) explanation of the illusion of loudness. Over time, the participants forgot the sources of the arguments, as conscious recollection of the details of the episode in the psychology laboratory faded. Nonetheless, when they were asked about the topic some time later, those arguments may have sprung to mind. Now, with the sources forgotten consciously, the arguments may have seemed like their own – and, therefore, very good ones. Memory for arguments thus presents itself not as memory per se but as our own penetrating insight into a topic.

This phenomenon was explored further by Begg, Anas, and Farinacci (1992). In an initial learning phase, people were presented with obscure statements (such as 'house mice can run at an average of 4 miles per hour') labelled as true or false. In a subsequent test phase, participants were presented with new and old sentences, each categorized as true or false. When people had not been exposed to the sentences before, they thought 45% of them were true. This was the baseline level of believability of the sentences. When a sentence had been labelled 'true' in the learning phase, people thought 66% of such sentences were true in the test phase. The 66% is substantially greater than baseline, which is not surprising. Now the interesting condition was when a sentence had been labelled false. Conscious recollection of the context in which a participant had read this sentence would make them more likely to call it false, so participants should endorse such sentences as true at below-baseline levels. In fact, the participants regarded 59% of such sentences true, substantially above baseline. That is, the familiarity of the sentence made it seem true, even though when it was initially presented it was labelled false! Further, it cannot be that people tried to guess 'true' or 'false' 50% of the time, not being sure which it was; they responded 'true' more than 50% of the time. Familiarity with the sentence made it seem true in a way they could not control. In addition to unconscious memory, there was some conscious memory shown; the 66% for sentences labelled 'true' was higher than the 59% for sentences labelled 'false', a distinction made by consciously recollecting the context.

The illusion-of-truth effect is often used by authoritarian regimes. Dissenting views are suppressed, while the views of the government are repeated endlessly. The repetition of a claim gives it fluency, and fluency gives it credibility. You might think that such an approach would be too obvious to work. Indeed, many people governed by authoritarian regimes may believe their government's tactics to be crass. But that need not stop the tactics from working. As we have just seen, the effects of unconscious memory are those we find difficult to control and overcome. And indeed there is a rational basis to the illusion-of-truth effect. The more independent times we acquire evidence for a claim (such as hearing the claim asserted by unrelated people), the more likely the claim is to be true. Our brains may come to acquire shortcuts to exploit this fact (i.e. we learn to associate fluency with truth). Unfortunately, when manipulative regimes (or companies or religions) take advantage of the shortcut, fluency may no longer be a reliable guide to truth. You can even take advantage of the shortcut yourself in an especially sneaky way – by denying the very facts you want people to eventually believe of you.

FOCUS POINT 6.1

UNCONSCIOUS PLAGIARISM

As we discussed in the case of the illusion of truth, exposure to a new idea can change how people think about a topic. Later, we may not be able to recollect the episode consciously. Nonetheless, when thinking about the topic again, the idea we were exposed to may pop into our head. The idea would feel like our own. Thus, unconscious memory can lead us to plagiarize without knowing it is plagiarism.

For example, George Harrison's melody for 'My Sweet Lord' (1970) was taken from 'He's So Fine' (1963) by the Chiffons. Harrison was fined, but there is no reason to doubt his own claim that he was unaware of the plagiarism that had taken place. Similarly, Wilhelm Fliess suggested to Freud that everyone starts out life bisexual; Freud scorned the idea, only to proclaim it as a new idea – to Fliess himself – 2 years later (see Brown & Murphy, 1989)!

Unconscious plagiarism can be replicated in the lab. Marsh, Landau, and Hicks (1997) asked participants in groups to brainstorm ways to, for instance, improve their university. After a 1 week delay, participants came back and were asked to generate four new ways to address the problem. Participants were specifically told not to repeat ideas from the previous session; nonetheless, about 20% of their 'new' ideas could be shown to come from the initial session. In another study, Stark and Perfect (2007) showed that unconscious plagiarism substantially increased, even when people were very confident that the ideas were their own, if participants had previously been asked to elaborate on other people's ideas so as to improve them. Once you have made an idea your own, it is part of how you think (Popova, n.d.).

The mere exposure effect

The **mere exposure effect** refers to how exposure to a novel stimulus can lead people to like it more (Zajonc, 1968, 1980). For example, if novel shapes are flashed to people quickly, then the more times they are flashed, the more people will like the shapes. You may have had the experience of not being interested in a song when you first heard it but, after hearing it again, and possibly again, you just seemed to start liking it. This is an effect that can be shown in the lab (Szpunar, Schellenberg, & Pliner, 2004; these lab studies on music also show how boredom eventually sets in). Similarly, exposing children to a small piece of food (e.g. a new vegetable) can substantially increase both their liking and their subsequent intake of the food (Wardle, Herrera, Cooke, & Gibson, 2003). Seeing people, even just in the background, can make them seem more attractive. Moreland and Beach (1992) had a group of women sit in lectures, either 0, 5, 10, or 15 times, without interacting with the students. When photos of the women were later rated, there were large increases in rated attractiveness according to the number of times a woman attended a lecture.

What role does conscious memory play in the mere exposure effect? Kunst-Wilson and Zajonc (1980) showed that, when novel shapes were quickly flashed to people, the mere exposure effect occurred even when people could not recognize the old shapes as having previously been displayed. Indeed, Bornstein and D'Agostino (1992) found larger mere exposure effects for shapes that had been displayed subliminally rather than supraliminally (consciously). The converse pattern is also found: Newell and Shanks (2006) found larger effects for supraliminal rather than subliminal stimuli, so there is no necessary relation between conscious memory and the mere exposure effect, one way or the other. Although the mere exposure effect can be impaired by some types of brain damage that also impair conscious memory (e.g. to the right temporal lobe), patients with severe global amnesia can have intact mere exposure effects (Marin-Garcia, Ruiz-Vargas, & Kapur, 2013). In sum, the mere exposure effect does not depend on conscious memory for the exposure episode. It is a form of unconscious memory. Once a stimulus has proven itself safe, because we have survived the encounter with it, we become attracted to that stimulus, whether we consciously remember it or not. The moral is: if you want someone to like you, expose yourself to them.

DISSONANCE REDUCTION

We often change our beliefs and attitudes to make them more consistent with our behaviour, a process called 'dissonance reduction' (Festinger, 1957). For example, once people have made a choice, they come to like the chosen object even more and dislike the rejected items even more (thereby further justifying their choice). Does this effect depend on consciously remembering what choice was made?

Lieberman, Ochsner, Gilbert, and Schacter (2001) asked people to rate art posters for how much they liked them. They were then given a difficult choice between certain posters to take home, with the posters chosen so as to be almost identical in ranked liking. After a distraction, people reranked the posters. As dissonance theory predicts, people's liking increased for the chosen posters and reduced for the rejected ones.

The crucial finding was that this effect was the same for people with amnesia, who when asked to recollect which posters they had chosen were at chance. That is, dissonance reduction does not depend on conscious memory; our attitudes can change without us remembering the cause of that change. Indeed, simply committing to an attitude, especially publicly, can make it stronger, due to dissonance reduction. Do not be too sure that the strength of your opinions on a topic is based just on the cogency of your arguments (Tavris & Aronson, 2007).

General anaesthesia and sleep

What people hear while unconscious because of general anaesthesia can sometimes later influence them (Deeprose & Andrade, 2006). Some studies showed increased recovery rates afterwards if positive suggestions were repeatedly played from headphones during an operation, but these effects have been hard to replicate. Further, these studies did not rigorously measure the depth of anaesthesia. The latter point is important because patients can regain consciousness to varying degrees while under general anaesthesia; the level of anaesthetic needs to be titrated to maintain anaesthetic depth, a procedure that is more rigorously applied these days than it used to be. In fact, analysing the many studies as a whole, evidence remains not for positive suggestions but for the more simple phenomenon of the priming of word-stem completion by those very same words being presented during anaesthesia. This effect holds even when depth of anaesthesia has been ascertained. For example, Iselin-Chaves et al. (2005) found that people completed word stems at above-baseline levels for words presented during deep anaesthesia, even when patients had been instructed to avoid using the words presented during that period.

Deeprose and Andrade (2006) point out that studies controlling awareness have not found evidence of unconscious memory before an incision is made; in studies finding evidence of unconscious memory, stimuli were presented after the first incision. The physiological response to pain may include activation of the amygdala, a structure known to be involved in forming memory traces, especially for fear-relevant material. Future research may yet reveal that positive words or statements may under some conditions be beneficial during an operation; in the meantime it would seem safest for surgeons to try to avoid negative statements during operations.

While general anaesthesia is quite an unusual state to be in, we each fall into dreamless sleep for at least part of each night. Whether we can learn new information during sleep has, however, remained unclear. One study, by Arzi and colleagues (2012), suggests that we can – at least when it comes to smell. Specifically, these authors found that sleeping subjects were able to learn novel associations between particular odours and auditory tones, as shown by 'selective sniffing' the following day. In another study, by Kouider, Andrillon, Barbosa, Goupil, and Bekinschtein (2014), awake participants classified words into categories while transitioning towards sleep. Strikingly, their brains showed task-specific preparatory responses even after sleep onset, as revealed by so-called lateralized readiness potentials. However, even if some forms of simple conditioning and word processing can occur during sleep, that does not mean that sleep is a good way of learning your course material. Wood, Bootzin, Kihlstrom, and Schacter (1992) found no implicit or explicit memory for words played during sleep, unless the person was immediately awakened. The main use of recordings of our lectures played to yourself at night may only be to give yourself a good night's sleep.

Irrational priming

So far the argument that the effects discussed are due to unconscious memory has been that the effects occur despite our intentions (e.g. the illusion of loudness) or because the memory was formed under anaesthesia or under subliminal conditions (e.g. the mere exposure effect), or retrieved under amnesia (e.g. the effects of dissonance reduction). Another argument that could be used for the effect of previous exposure of a stimulus constituting unconscious memory is that the effect would be irrational if produced consciously. Such an argument could be made for the phenomenon of social priming, whereby the way one interacts with people is influenced by a specific previously exposed irrelevant stimulus. For example, Williams and Bargh (2008a) found that, if asked to hold a hot rather than a cold drink briefly, participants later rated other people as being warmer in terms of personality (by 0.5 units on a 1–7 scale). Williams and Bargh (2008b) found that, if asked to plot arbitrary points on a graph close together rather than far apart, people later rated their bond to family members as close rather than far (by 0.75 units on a 1–7 scale). A similar form of behavioural priming was shown by Bargh, Chen, and Burrows (1996), who found that people who read words to do with being elderly walked more slowly when they left the lab (8.3 versus 7.3 seconds to cover the same distance). Similarly, Dijksterhuis and Van Knippenberg (1998) found that people asked to describe attributes of 'professor' rather than 'hooligan' could subsequently answer more general knowledge questions correctly (10% difference). These effects are part of a large number of similar ones explored since around the late 1990s (for a review, see Bargh, Shwader, Hailey, Dyer, & Boothby, 2012). In each case, it would be implausible to claim the effect occurred because of the conscious use of memory; holding a warm cup briefly has no logical bearing on the warmth of people we later meet.

These behavioural priming effects are intriguing and are often cited in popular science. Indeed, minor one-off priming events (such as holding a warm cup for a few seconds) appear to produce large interpersonal effects many minutes later (0.5 units on a 1–7 scale). It would seem that, with some well-thought-out primes, a smooth operator could cynically manipulate romantic dates, business deals, or other interactions. However, attempts to replicate any given effect exactly have met with failure: for example, Lynott et al. (2014), with 861 participants, failed to replicate the warm coffee effect at all; Pashler, Coburn, and Harris (2012) failed to replicate the closeness effect at all; Doyen, Klein, Pichon, and Cleeremans (2012) could only obtain the elderly effect if the experimenter was aware of which participant had been primed; and Shanks et al. (2013) failed to replicate the professor effect at all, with a convincingly sensitive set of experiments. In sum, effects are smaller than many of the studies imply, and likely nonexistent under many conditions. The exact conditions under which behavioural priming may occur remain to be established (e.g. Bargh et al., 2012, suggest that behavioural priming effects may be higher for self-conscious people, though this conjecture needs to be confirmed). Do not be surprised if, after asking your client to sit in a soft chair, they are still a hard negotiator.

Newell and Shanks (2014) point out that there is one form of irrational priming that is frequently replicated: the **anchoring effect** (first investigated by Tversky & Kahneman, 1974; Kahneman was co-awarded the 2002 Nobel Prize for Economics for such work on human judgement). People given a number, for any reason, subsequently bias their estimates of a quantity (date, price, temperature, etc.) towards the given number. For example, if a person is initially asked whether John F. Kennedy was first president before or after 1962 and then is asked to estimate the exact date, the use of 1962 pulls estimates towards that anchor. Even the use of obviously irrelevant numbers can sometimes provide anchors for later estimates. When people were first asked whether they would buy each of a range of products for a dollar figure equal to the last two digits of their social security number, the social security number anchored their later estimates of the most they would be willing to pay for each product (Ariely, Loewenstein, & Prelec, 2003). Similarly, people's estimates of how much they would pay for a meal in a restaurant shown in a photo were higher for a restaurant called Studio97 than for otherwise the same restaurant called Studio17 (Critcher & Gilovich, 2008). Anchoring effects can be overcome to some extent by motivation and by considering arguments to discard the anchor, so long as the person knows the direction in which the anchor is likely to misleadingly pull (Simmons, LeBoeuf, & Nelson, 2010). Thus, when you next go to a restaurant, consider carefully why the most expensive item on the menu may be on the list: not for you to buy it, but to anchor you.

Motivated forgetting of episodes

The phrase 'unconscious memory' may bring to mind the Freudian theory of emotional events being apparently forgotten as a result of the motivation to keep the memories from consciousness, only for them to influence us again later. For example, a painful memory of being told off may be forgotten, but it may make us uncomfortable in similar situations, because the unconscious memory is still active. This Freudian notion is often combined with the therapeutic practice of attempting to bring the memories back to consciousness in order to rob them of their power. Some therapies are based on the conjecture that specific childhood events are responsible for various clinical conditions – for example, a conjecture that specifically sexual abuse, or alien abduction, or satanic ritual abuse, or traumas in previous reincarnations lead to eating disorders or to phobias and so on. The evidence provided for such theories by their proponents is sometimes the fact that, although at the beginning of therapy a client does not recall the right sort of event in any way, by the end of therapy they do, and indeed they have conviction in their recovered memories (see Yapko, 1994, for a survey of psychotherapists regarding their opinions on the reality of the phenomenon). Thus, the conclusion goes, the memory was there all along, unconsciously doing its work.

Unfortunately, the fact that people can be readily led to have convincing memories is not evidence that the events really happened (e.g. Loftus & Ketcham, 1994). Completely false memories can be constructed in the lab in half an hour. Laurence and Perry (1983) asked people to nominate a night of the previous week during which they had slept solidly. They were hypnotically age regressed back to that night and asked whether they remembered any loud bangs that woke them up. After hypnosis, a third of the subjects maintained that the noises had actually happened, and most of these subjects continued to insist the noises had actually happened even after being told the noises had only been suggested. Other procedures, without the use of hypnosis, have been used to create false memories of being lost in a shopping mall when a person was a child (Loftus & Pickrell, 1995). Thus, a client who cannot originally remember being abducted by aliens and spends numerous therapy sessions with a therapist who is themselves convinced the client must have been abducted by aliens may well end up remembering the abduction – whether or not it actually happened.

The clinical evidence for repressed memories may be unconvincing but it can be routinely demonstrated in the lab that some people can forget whole episodes by being motivated to do so, and such memories can continue to exert an influence while apparently forgotten. Specifically, consider a highly hypnotizable person given a post-hypnotic suggestion. The suggestion may be to scratch their eyebrow whenever they hear the word 'experiment', but, it is suggested, they will forget that they have been asked to do so until told otherwise. Highly hypnotizable subjects given such a suggestion will scratch their eyebrow when a hypnotist says 'experiment' and will claim not to remember any instruction to do so (e.g. Orne, Sheehan, & Evans, 1968). (Importantly, in an academic setting, unlike hypnosis on television, there is evidence that subjects rarely fake; that is, if they *claim* to have had compelling subjective experiences, they tend to have *actually* had them: see e.g. Kirsch, Silva, Carone, Johnstone, & Simon, 1989.) The post-hypnotic suggestion is forgotten, yet the forgotten material continues to influence the subject (in a way consistent with the subject's overall goals; Spanos, Menary, Brett, Cross, & Ahmed, 1987). So, there can be motivated forgetting of episodes that remain influential, at least for highly hypnotizable people. This fact has clinical relevance. Normally, hypnotic response furthers the goals of the subject; that is, the hypnotic response is only pursued to the extent that it is appropriate and furthers one's projects (in contrast to, say, the hallucinations and disorders of volition in schizophrenia). But what if one has conflicting goals? The hypnotic response may then work against the subject's other goals. Indeed, hypnotic response appears to involve the same processes as conversion disorders, which may involve amnesia (or blindness, paralysis, or other conditions) with no organic cause – that is, with no physiological brain or neuronal dysfunction known to produce such effects (Oakley & Halligan, 2013). These conversion disorders may fulfil some goal of the patient while apparently contradicting others: they appear to be self-given hypnotic responses gone wrong.

WHAT IS THE UNCONSCIOUS CONTENT?

In the examples given so far, we have considered a range of cases in which memory is involved but the person is not aware of using memory. Thus, in this sense, these can all be described as cases of unconscious memory. But there is another sense in which the use of the term 'unconscious memory' may be misleading. Remember we said of a mental state that it involved some content held in a certain way. In the above examples, was there any content actively being held (used) that was in fact unconscious? In most cases, we do not need to postulate active unconscious content.

Consider the first example of unconscious memory, the illusion of loudness. Initially hearing the sentences builds connections between the representations of the words in the sentences. Thus, when the sentence is heard again, the representations of each word and their connections are accurately activated, and thus heard clearly. There is no need to postulate any content that is actually unconscious; the content that is active is about the words, which are consciously experienced. There is no need to postulate activation of the content 'I studied the sentence for the first time in the lab at 3 o'clock', for example. That is, we do not literally have to postulate a representation of the memory that is unconscious.

This analysis is true for the illusion of truth, unconscious plagiarism, the mere exposure effect, dissonance reduction, and irrational priming. In these cases there *is* a previous external influence that the person is not conscious of as an influence (that is the sense in which there is unconscious memory), but there need be *no* representation of that influencing event that is unconscious (that is the sense in which there is no unconscious memory).

By analogy, consider a fat bee that has eaten a lot of nectar; the bee need not be aware that it is fat *because of* that past nectar (so the past nectar *is* an unconscious influence on its current fatness). But nor does the bee need unconscious representations of having eaten the nectar (there are no unconscious contents!). The bee just needs to have eaten the nectar and hence be fat.

The results regarding general anaesthesia and sleep may necessitate postulating unconscious content – namely, the content of the words perceived during the operation (or while asleep). These examples involve unconscious perception, and a case could be made that there is active unconscious content while a person is perceiving the words (if the person while creature unconscious only had unconscious mental states).

We will explore unconscious perception in the next section and consider further evidence for active unconscious contents. Post-hypnotic suggestion involves conscious perception – and also unconscious contents, but this time operating at the memory stage. The claim for the memories being genuinely unconscious in post-hypnotic suggestion rests on the evidence that, in general, in an academic setting, highly hypnotizable subjects rarely fake (the interested reader might like to pursue that issue further: Kinnunen, Zamansky, & Block, 1994; Kirsch et al., 1989; Oakley & Halligan, 2013; Ward, Oakley, Frackowiak, & Halligan, 2003).

We have seen how past events can influence a person without their awareness: past events can make sentences seem clearer, people and objects more pleasant, and estimates of magnitude more biased. Further, memories can be hidden hypnotically and still influence people. In these cases, the initial events were perceived consciously. We will now consider whether perception itself can be unconscious.

DISCUSSION POINT

Discuss some of the ways in which unconscious memory can express itself.

SECTION SUMMARY

- Unconscious memory occurs when a person uses memory but is not aware of using memory.
- The increase in accuracy or speed in performing a task because the stimulus has been presented before is called priming.
- Memories can present themselves as perceptions rather than memories.
- The sleeper effect is a psychological phenomenon that relates to persuasion. It is a delayed increase of the effect of a message that has been discredited.
- Research has demonstrated that the repetition of a claim gives it fluency, and fluency gives it credibility.
- The mere exposure effect refers to how exposure to a novel stimulus can lead people to like it more.
- We often change our beliefs and attitudes to make them more consistent with our behaviour, a process called dissonance reduction.
- Even conscious exposure to stimuli can result in irrational behavioural effects: for example, anchoring is a cognitive bias that describes the common human tendency to rely too heavily on the first piece of information offered when making decisions.
- The fact that people can be readily led to have convincing memories is not evidence that the events really happened.
- It can be routinely demonstrated in the lab that some people can forget whole episodes by being motivated to do so, and such memories can continue to exert an influence while apparently remaining forgotten.

CONSCIOUS VERSUS UNCONSCIOUS PERCEPTION

LEARNING OBJECTIVE 6.4

Understand the differences between conscious and unconscious perception and the effects of both on individuals.

Methods

For many stimuli, perception involves conscious perception. To make perception unconscious or subliminal, something needs to interfere with normal perceptual processing. We will consider methods for interfering with conscious vision so that only subliminal perception is left. The most common method is **backward masking** (see Figure 6.1). First a word or a picture (the target) is shown on a screen, then a 'pattern mask' is shown. A pattern mask consists of a similar sort of stimulus to the target – for example, a string of letters to mask a word, or one face to mask another face.

The time from the beginning of the target to the beginning of the mask is called the **stimulus onset asynchrony (SOA)**. SOAs are typically measured in milliseconds. For example, if the target is displayed for 48 ms and immediately followed by the mask, the SOA is 48 ms (and the gap between the end of the target and the beginning of the mask, or the 'interstimulus interval', is zero). The mask interrupts the processing of the stimulus, so, for an effective SOA, the participant may perceive only the mask consciously and not the target. (In fact, interference goes in both directions; if a long mask is put before a short target, it can also mask the target, in which case it is called a 'forward mask'. But back masking is the more effective technique.) The SOA is the crucial parameter for a pattern mask; for very long SOAs (e.g. above 100 ms) there is no masking effect. The critical SOA is different for different people; it may be 15 ms for one person and 200 ms for another (e.g. Armstrong & Dienes, 2013).

Pattern masking has been used for decades. However, two new methods have been developed that allow the subliminal stimulus to be displayed for considerably longer than 100 ms: **continuous flash suppression** (Tsuchiya & Koch, 2005) and **gaze-contingent crowding (GCC)** (Faivre, Berthet, & Kouider, 2012). Continuous flash suppression relies on the phenomenon of 'binocular rivalry' (see Figure 6.2). If one image is presented to one eye (e.g. a face) and another image to the other eye (e.g. a house), the person does not see a house-face; rather they see either a house or a face. There is a rivalry between the two images, and the brain decides only one of the objects must really be there. So first the person might consciously see just a house. The conscious experience of the house will last for some seconds, then it will break down at the edges, eaten away by a face, and the face will then come to be consciously seen as the single object there. The face will last for some seconds, before another switch occurs and so on. In continuous flash suppression, this switching between the percepts is prevented by using one image that is very salient. One eye is presented with a random mixture of coloured blocks that are continuously changing. This is the mask. A static target is presented to the other eye. The salient mask captures conscious processing, so the mask remains all the person is conscious of. In this way, the target can be kept masked for an almost indefinite period of time.

Gaze-contingent crowding relies on the fact that stimuli in the periphery can be processed unconsciously. That is, when looking straight ahead, what you focus on for an extended period is likely to be attended to and processed consciously. Stimuli, or changes in stimuli, slightly to one side are often not consciously noticed. In GCC, a peripheral target stimulus is surrounded by masks (i.e. 'crowded'), which means the

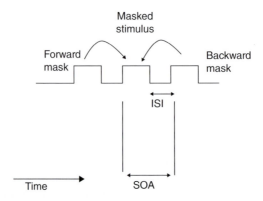

FIGURE 6.1 *Terminology used in masking experiments (see text for explanation). ISI = interstimulus interval; SOA = stimulus onset asynchrony.*

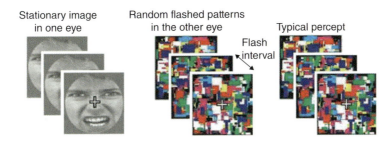

FIGURE 6.2 *Continuous flash suppression. One eye sees the to-be-masked stimulus (here a face) and the other eye sees random colours and motion. The conscious percept is just of random colours and motion.*

Source: Reprinted by permission from Macmillan Publishers Ltd: NATURE NEUROSCIENCE. Tsuchiya and Koch (2005), copyright 2005.

target is not consciously processed – so long as it remains in the periphery. In GCC, an eye tracker is used, which is a device for measuring exactly where the person is focusing (see Figure 6.3). As soon as the participant stops focusing straight ahead, the target disappears, and it reappears when the participant focuses straight ahead again (this is the 'gaze-contingent' part). This way, the participant never gets to focus on the target so that the target can be kept unconscious almost indefinitely.

Thresholds

Cheesman and Merikle (1984, 1986) were the first to distinguish between the **subjective threshold** and the **objective threshold**. In each trial, people were shown one of the four words 'blue', 'yellow', 'green', or 'red'. They had to say which word had been presented. They also gave a confidence rating, anything from 25%, which meant they

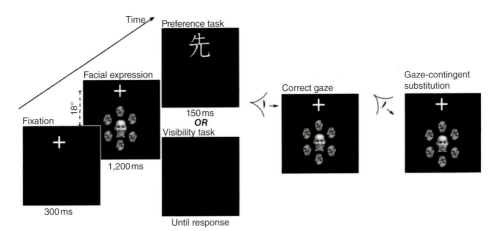

FIGURE 6.3 *Gaze-contingent crowding. The participant is requested to fixate on the cross. In the periphery a prime is shown (here a happy face), flanked by masking stimuli. If the participant moves their eyes to the prime, it is immediately replaced (here by a neutral face), so that the true prime is never consciously perceived.*

Source: Faivre, Berthet, and Kouider (2012). Reproduced by permission of Dr Nathan Faivre.

guessed at chance and they expected that only 25% of their responses were correct (25% because they would be correct one in four times by chance alone, as there were four possibilities), to 100%, which indicated certainty and that they expected 100% of their responses to be correct. For long SOAs between the word and a subsequent pattern mask, a given participant would be very confident and also get most of the answers correct. Perception was clearly conscious. As the SOA was reduced, a point was reached where the person gave a 25% confidence rating (i.e. they believed that they were just guessing). This point is the subjective threshold, because it (subjectively) seems to the person that they are performing at chance. Crucially, at the subjective threshold, people were actually correct 66% of the time, substantially above a chance baseline of 25%. The SOA needed to be reduced further to reach the point where people actually classified the words at 25% (chance); this is the objective threshold, because it is the point where people are objectively at chance. After both thresholds were determined for each participant, the participants performed a Stroop task (see Activity 6.1). That is, they had to say what colour was presented to them while a word was flashed. The word was presented below either the subjective or the objective threshold. In these circumstances, Stroop priming would be shown if people were faster to say the colour when the word was congruent (e.g. the colour was green and the word was 'green') rather than incongruent (e.g. the colour was yellow and the word was 'green'). In fact, Stroop priming was found below the subjective threshold but not below the objective threshold.

What do these results mean? The answer depends on deciding which threshold marks a valid distinction between conscious and unconscious. Sceptics regarding unconscious processing prefer the objective threshold. It is, after all, well, more objective. The subjective threshold may depend on a person's bias in defining at what point they really could not see anything relevant to their choice. On these grounds, Cheesman and Merikle (1984) found no subliminal perception. There was no Stroop priming below the objective threshold. On the other hand, we saw earlier that higher-order theory directly motivates the use of subjective measures – that is, the use of the subjective threshold. Being able to classify what word is there is no guarantee that the perception is conscious; it is only when we know that we see that the perception is conscious. We only need the content 'the word is RED' in order to be influenced towards saying 'red'; first-order contents allow performance on first-order discriminations. Conscious seeing requires the higher-order content 'I see that the word is RED'. Global workspace theory effectively makes the same point: if information is in the global workspace, it is available to higher-order thoughts. Thus, according to these theories, subliminal perception was shown by Cheesman and Merikle in two ways. Firstly, subliminal perception was shown by the fact that, below the subjective threshold, people were still above the objective threshold. They could classify accurately even if they believed they had no knowledge (thus, satisfying the guessing criterion of unconscious knowledge). Second, subliminal perception was shown by the fact that there was Stroop priming below the subjective threshold. Cheesman and Merikle's results illustrate something further. As the SOA was reduced to the objective threshold, subliminal perception was degraded until it was difficult to detect. This means that, if we want to know what subliminal perception can do, it would be a mistake to use the objective threshold, according to higher-order and global workspace theories.

Sceptics regarding subliminal perception might be tempted to endorse local theories of consciousness in order to justify the use of objective thresholds. But we can accept higher-order and integration theories and still accept that the sceptic's point is valid about the potential role of bias in subjective measures. When people in everyday life say 'I guess that…', they mean a range of things. They might even mean they are pretty confident. Leaving subjects free to define 'guess' loosely will surely overestimate the amount of unconscious knowledge. Rather than giving up on subjective measures, another solution is to devise ways of being more rigorous in their use. For example, 'guess' can be precisely defined as being no better than random, with examples (e.g. Cheesman & Merikle, 1984); people's confidence may be elicited by gambling or wagering, so actual rewards are on the line (Dienes & Seth, 2010; Persaud & McLeod, 2008); confidence can be ascertained after every trial rather than after blocks of trials (Kolb & Braun, 1995); and so on. The further crucial argument, provided by Merikle (1992), is that the subjective threshold ultimately proves its worth by showing it qualitatively separates different types of perception. If perception measured to be above and below the subjective threshold behaves like a theory of consciousness says it should, then we are in scientific business. There is something interesting to explain. An example will help to illustrate the argument.

Merikle and Joordens (1997) presented one of two words: 'red' or 'green'. After a variable SOA, a back mask was presented, which was a series of ampersands (&&&&&&) presented in a red or green colour. The task was to name the colour the ampersands were presented in. The trick was that the word and the colour were incongruent 75% of the time and hence congruent only 25% of the time. Thus, if a participant could flexibly use their knowledge of what the word was, they should have been able to predict that the colour would be the opposite, and hence be faster on the *incongruent* rather than the congruent trials; that is, we would expect to get a *reverse* Stroop effect. When the word was presented at above the subjective threshold, this was exactly what was found: a reverse Stroop effect. But, for words below the subjective threshold, the results were the opposite: a normal Stroop effect was found. The results indicate that the subjective threshold is not just a curiosity concerning at what point people happen to define themselves as guessing; rather, it has real consequences for perception and behaviour. Further, the consequences are as predicted by a theory of consciousness: if higher-order thoughts are available only when information is in a global workspace, then perception above rather than below the subjective threshold should involve more flexible use of the information.

In general, it has been easy to obtain priming effects below a subjective threshold, and difficult below an objective threshold. However, using sensitive methods, it has been possible to obtain evidence of processing below an objective threshold as well. For example, Naccache et al. (2005) tested patients undergoing brain surgery. The patients categorized back-masked and unmasked words as threatening or neutral, and could not do so at above-chance levels for masked words: the objective threshold was reached. Nonetheless, electric field potentials recorded directly in the amygdala were different for threatening versus neutral words for both masked and unmasked conditions. That is, the meaning of the word was processed in emotion-relevant parts of the brain. In another example, Faivre et al. (2012) masked faces using gaze-contingent priming. The faces could have neutral, happy, or angry expressions. Participants were at chance at indicating which expression the faces were showing, so the objective threshold was reached. Despite even unconscious knowledge being degraded by the use of an objective threshold, because the primes could be displayed for over a second (unlike with pattern masking), there was sufficient information build-up to obtain priming. The target was a Chinese character, which was rated as pleasant or unpleasant. Smiling faces made the character look more pleasant than the other faces. We will find more examples of priming below the objective threshold in what follows.

ACTIVITY 6.1

THE STROOP EFFECT TEST

Go to http://opencoglab.org/stroop to try the Stroop test. You will be shown words in red, green, blue, orange, or purple. In each instance, you must press the key of the first initial of the colour you see. So, for instance, if the word is printed in red, you would press the r key.

Process dissociation, awareness, and control

When we find a threshold by adjusting SOA, a common logic is that we have found conditions under which the stimulus is never consciously perceived. Having found the threshold, any effects subsequently produced by a prime must have been due to unconscious processing. But what if the threshold fluctuates over time? Then claims for subliminal perception may be undermined. Jacoby, Toth, Lindsay, and Debner (1992) illustrated how, to show subliminal perception, it is not necessary to find conditions in which a stimulus is never consciously perceived. That is, the tasks did not have to reflect purely conscious or purely unconsciously processes; there is a procedure by which we can dissociate the processes for impure tasks – that is, tasks involving both conscious and unconscious processing. Hence, the procedure has been called the **process dissociation procedure (PDP)** (see Jacoby, 2009).

In Jacoby et al.'s (1992) experiment, three words were presented in succession; for example, one trial might have been 'glove', then 'patch', then 'flare'. The first and last words were presented for 500 ms (i.e. half a second) and were hence clearly visible; they acted as forward and backward masks, respectively, for the middle word. The middle word was presented for 50 ms. Finally, a stem was given to the participants to complete, which in half of the trials was the stem of the middle word (e.g. PAT__). In what the researchers called an 'exclusion test', the instruction was to 'complete the stem with a word that comes to mind but not any you just saw displayed'. In the exclusion test, conscious perception of the word would lead a participant to make sure they did not use it; thus, any tendency to use the presented word at above baseline levels must have been due to unconscious perception. In exclusion, conscious and unconscious perception act in opposition. By contrast, in the 'inclusion test', the instruction was to 'complete the stem with one of the words flashed or, if unable to do so, with the first word that comes to mind'. In inclusion performance, conscious and unconscious perception act in concert; they both lead a participant to complete the stem with the displayed word. Having both exclusion and inclusion tests allows a researcher to estimate the relative contributions of both conscious and unconscious perception.

When people completed a stem without having just seen the word, stems were completed 36% of the time with the words used in the experiment. This defined the baseline, the level of stem completion without priming. In the inclusion test the completion rate for the presented words was 63%, which was above baseline. There was priming. But we cannot tell from this alone whether it was conscious or unconscious. The clever innovation was to combine the inclusion and exclusion tests in one experiment. In the exclusion test, subjects completed 50% of the stems with the word that had just been displayed. Inclusion was significantly greater than exclusion; so, people had some control over the use of the information – they could give or withhold the response to some degree. Only conscious perception can allow this, according to Jacoby et al. (1992). In fact, the proportion of trials in which the word was consciously perceived can be estimated as the difference between inclusion and exclusion:

$$(\text{inclusion} - \text{exclusion}) = 0.63 - 0.50 = 13\%$$

Was there any unconscious perception? Performance on the exclusion task (50%) was significantly greater than baseline (36%), showing a lack of control. Conscious perception would result in performance being below baseline. People must have often seen the word in exclusion because it was above baseline, but they cannot have consciously seen the word. So the exclusion performance is evidence for unconscious perception. Thus, for the same tasks and conditions, Jacoby et al. demonstrated a mix of conscious and unconscious perception.

In general, Jacoby's method, the PDP, takes flexible control to be the functional criterion for consciousness. Flexible control as a function of consciousness aligns with global workspace theory. In this particular case, the use of the PDP also aligns with higher-order theory. The exclusion task was another way of testing for the subjective threshold: the instruction was to exclude a word *if participants thought they saw it* – that is, if they had a relevant higher-order thought. Can we make control (the PDP) and subjective measures give different answers to whether perception is conscious or not? Armstrong and Dienes (2013) presented an instruction to exclude (e.g. 'not cat') or include (e.g. 'pick cat') at below the subjective threshold. Following the subliminal instruction, participants were presented with two words (e.g. 'cat' and 'dog'), perceived consciously, and were asked to follow the subliminal instruction by guessing one of the words. For the inclusion instruction, people picked the named word 60% of the time, significantly greater than for the exclusion instruction (45%), which in turn was significantly below baseline (50%). So, people exerted control, and the PDP therefore takes the words as being consciously perceived. But this was precisely what people denied; they said they were purely guessing, so perception was below the subjective threshold. By higher-order theory, perception was unconscious, yet it allowed some control. Further, the words cannot have been in the global workspace as they were not available to the HOT box. So, the PDP does not always produce answers that match the main theories.

Does the unconscious control found by Armstrong and Dienes (2013) challenge global workspace theory? When perception was above subjective threshold in the Armstrong and Dienes study, there was extensive control, with the named word picked close to 100% of the time for inclusion trials and close to 0% of the time for exclusion trials. Thus, conscious perception greatly facilitates control, which is consistent with the idea that the global workspace promotes flexible control. Some flexible control can occur unconsciously, though – a point we will return to in discussing implicit learning and hypnosis (see also Van Gaal, de Lange, & Cohen, 2012).

Just as the PDP can allow conscious and unconscious processes to be dissociated in impure tasks, confidence ratings and other subjective measures can also be used to provide trial-by-trial classifications of whether perception or knowledge is conscious or unconscious, without assuming the task is always purely one or the other. For example, for a given SOA, the trials in which people say they are purely guessing can be taken as involving unconscious perception, and the trials in which people say they saw, or have some confidence, can be taken as conscious perception (e.g. Lau & Passingham, 2006). As long as subjective measures are taken trial by trial, there is no need to assume a task is performed purely consciously or purely unconsciously.

SUBLIMINAL ADVERTISING AND SELF-HELP

In 1957, James Vicary, a private market researcher, claimed to have increased sales of drinks and popcorn in a movie theatre by subliminally flashing messages such as 'Eat popcorn'. However, the study was never published and appears to have been a hoax. Surprisingly, the first authors to address whether subliminal advertising might actually work in the scientific literature are Karremans, Stroebe, and Claus (2006). A single threshold was used for all participants: the trade name 'Lipton Ice' was flashed for 23 ms, with a row of x's presented just before and afterwards for 500 ms, to act as forward and backward masks. A group of people were asked to guess what had been flashed; none could. In the main experiment, one group had 'Lipton Ice' flashed under similar conditions and another group was flashed 'Npeic Tol', an anagram of 'Lipton Ice'. Next people were asked how thirsty they were, and they were then offered a choice of three drinks, one of which was Lipton Ice. For people who were thirsty, there was a large effect; only 20% of people selected a Lipton Ice after exposure to the control prime, but more than 80% did after subliminal priming of the brand name. That is, it is quite possible for subliminal advertising to be effective, though it still needs to be properly tested outside the lab.

Subliminal self-help tapes are often sold with claims that they can improve self-esteem or memory. In a double-blind trial, Greenwald, Spangenberg, Pratkanis, and Eskenazi (1991) tested subliminal audiotapes claimed to improve memory and self-esteem. Half the participants received the memory tape and half the self-esteem tape, and half of each of those were told they received the memory tape and half the self-esteem. Participants believed they had improved on the tape according to the label it had on it, not according to the manufacturer's claimed content. However, on standard tests, participants did not improve on either memory or self-esteem in any of the groups. Improving one's memory may need more than suggestions that it is getting better, subliminal or otherwise. (What's more, careful analysis of the content of such commercial tapes has revealed some brands have no subliminal content at all!)

CONSCIOUSNESS AND ATTENTION

What is the relationship between consciousness and attention? The two are closely related, in that we consciously perceive in detail the objects we selectively attend to, and we have only a dim conscious awareness of objects in the periphery of our attention. But attention and consciousness can be dissociated, as subliminal perception research shows.

Jiang, Costello, Fang, Huang, and He (2006) used continuous flash suppression to present a picture of a naked body on either the left-hand or right-hand side of a screen for 800 ms. People were at chance at indicating which side the naked figure was on, meaning that the figure was presented below the objective threshold. In the main task, people had to make a further difficult perceptual discrimination, about whether some lines were slightly pointing in one direction or another (these stimuli were not masked). The discrimination occurred randomly on either the left- or right-hand side of the screen.

The question is, did the naked figure draw attention to itself even though it was not consciously perceived? If it did, people would find the line discrimination easier if it occurred on the same side of the screen as the figure. In fact, such a priming effect was obtained. Straight men found the line discrimination easier when it was on the same side as a naked female, and harder when it was on the same side as a naked man. Conversely, women found the task easier when it was on the same side as a naked man. Further, lesbian, gay, and bisexual people obtained priming consistent with their stated sexual preferences.

Thus, our attention is drawn to or repelled from objects we cannot consciously see, in ways consistent with our sexual preferences. In sum, we can attend to the very same object that is not consciously perceived, so attention and consciousness are not the same (see Koch & Tsuchiya, 2006). The function of attention is to select a region of space or an object for further detailed processing.

Neural correlates of consciousness

What is the difference between conscious and unconscious perception at the level of neural functioning? What processes in the brain are correlated with conscious awareness? That is, what are the **neural correlates of consciousness**? One strategy for answering this question is to compare conscious and unconscious perception of the same stimulus. Dehaene et al. (2001) presented words either at the objective threshold or else clearly visible (see Figure 6.4). Brain scanning with fMRI while people were looking at the words indicated that both conscious and unconscious words activated an area of the brain involved in word processing, the left fusiform area. However, conscious words led to more extensive brain activity, over the parietal and frontal cortices, whereas processing of the subliminal words was localized. The results allow at least two interpretations. Firstly, conscious awareness may depend on information being widely broadcast in the brain, as per integration theories. Secondly, conscious awareness may instead depend on information reaching a certain area, specifically the HOT box, in the prefrontal cortex, as per higher-order theories.

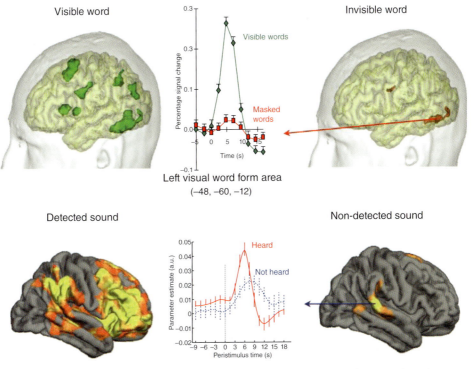

FIGURE 6.4 *Neural correlates of perception I. Conscious perception of words or sounds is often associated with widespread activation of the brain, whereas unconscious perception is associated with local activation in specialist processing areas. a.u.: activation units.*
Source: Dehaene and Changeux (2011).

Lau and Passingham (2006) pointed out that, when we compare clear conscious perception with perception below an objective threshold, there is a confound: the two conditions differ not only in being conscious versus unconscious but also in the overall level of perception being very good versus degraded. Maybe very good perception leads to more activation around the brain than very poor perception. What we need to do is equate objective performance between conscious and unconscious conditions so that only subjective experiences differ. Lau and Passingham asked people to discriminate whether a diamond or a square had been presented; after the discrimination, people said whether they had just guessed or had seen the shape. The researchers found two backward masking conditions in which the actual ability to discriminate was the same yet the proportion of 'guess' versus 'seen' responses differed. That is, first-order perception (as indicated by ability to indicate what the world is like) was the same, but conscious experience differed. In the same study, brain scanning with fMRI showed that the activation difference between conscious and unconscious conditions was very specific. It was apparently localized in the left mid-dorsolateral prefrontal cortex (see Figure 6.5). One interpretation is that this area is the HOT box responsible for creating accurate higher-order thoughts. However, the evidence is not yet clear. Hesselmann, Hebart, and Malach (2011) equated objective performance between consciously seen and unseen trials using continuous flash suppression, and found differences in activation of the higher visual areas of the cortex using fMRI. One problem with interpreting any of these studies is that any area that brain imaging shows to have a difference between conscious and unconscious conditions may not be the neural correlate of consciousness but rather of a precursor to, or a consequence of, consciousness (Aru, Bachmann, Singer, & Melloni, 2012; de Graaf, Hsieh, & Sack, 2012). For example, perhaps extensive processing is required in higher visual areas before a HOT box (or a global workspace) can be reached by a visual stimulus, or perhaps, after a HOT box has been reached, further planning and elaboration happen in the left mid-dorsolateral prefrontal cortex. The jury is still out.

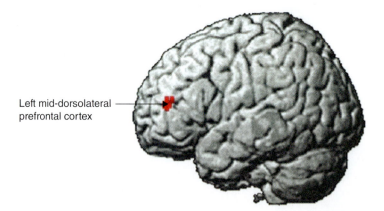

Left mid-dorsolateral prefrontal cortex

FIGURE 6.5 *Neural correlates of perception II. When conscious and unconscious perception are the same when measured by first-order performance (i.e. when people perceiving consciously and unconsciously are just as good at indicating what stimulus is in the world) and differ only in the extent to which the person is aware of perceiving, conscious perception is associated not with widespread activation but with specific activity in the left mid-dorsolateral prefrontal cortex.*

Source: Lau and Passingham (2006). Copyright (2006) National Academy of Sciences, USA.

PHENOMENAL CONSCIOUSNESS AND PERCEPTUAL OVERFLOW

Having a conscious experience is one thing; being able to report it might seem to be another. Maybe you have had an experience but did not know how to express it in words: you might have asked yourself just how to describe that taste, or smell, or colour, or emotional feeling. You had a conscious experience yet did not know how to put it into words. Yet, in the studies described so far, the existence of a conscious experience is measured by the participant being able to report it.

The problem was at least partly dealt with in these experiments by using clearly describable stimuli: words, simple shapes, and so on. But, even for such stimuli, it can be argued that we could be consciously aware of more than we can report. And, if that is true, why accept any of the putative demonstrations of subliminal perception as showing there is anything subliminal going on?

Block (2011) argued that our conscious experience outstrips the contents that are actually accessed and hence reported on. Consider, for example, Sperling's (1960) partial report paradigm, in which people are briefly flashed a grid of letters, three rows of four letters each. People have the impression of clearly seeing the whole display. Yet, when asked to report what letters were there, they can only report about four of them, until, people say, their image of the letters has gone and they can remember no more.

We know there is something to people's impression of clearly seeing all of the letters: if, after the display has disappeared, we indicate soon enough which row to report (top, middle, or bottom), people can indeed report most of that row. That is, almost all of the display is in principle accurately accessible to people for a short period. In sum, the argument goes, people have a rich conscious experience of the whole display, but they can only report a fraction of that experience. Block thus distinguishes between 'phenomenal consciousness' (of the whole visual display) and 'access consciousness' (of what ends up in working memory and can be reported) (see also Lamme, 2010).

The argument that people have phenomenal consciousness of the whole display is based on their report that that is what they experienced. So, interestingly, the content of conscious experience, even for phenomenal consciousness, is still based on people's reports about that experience. One strategy is to take people as having a conscious experience with the content of what they claim to be experiencing. That is, people may be experiencing the world as being a display of distinct letters. But one thing we should not in addition do is to presume that our representation of a thing has the same properties as that thing itself (Dennett, 1992).

For example, we can represent there being five objects without there actually being five representations. Or consider that the representation of an absence is not the same thing as the absence of representation. Although there being distinct letters means there must have been some specific letters, we can represent there being distinct letters without there being representations of specific letters. In fact, the visual system is constructed as a hierarchy of levels of abstraction; one level of abstraction may indicate 'R', while a higher level indicates 'letter'. Top-down influences could lead a higher level to indicate 'letter' even before a lower level has indicated *which* letter, even as a yet lower level has indicated sharp lines (see Hohwy, 2013). The experience could then have content specifying that there is a distinct letter without specifying what that distinct letter is.

Indeed, in Sperling's experiments, he found that, despite the sense of clearly seeing the stimuli, people could not report them (e.g. even just four digits in a display of letters), which is consistent with the precise identities not being consciously perceived. In a neat twist, de Gardelle, Sackur, and Kouider (2009) presented one item in the display that was not a letter but a pseudo-letter; people still often felt that they had clearly seen a display of letters. Whether or not our conscious experiences are indeed richer than our moment-to-moment ability to report them is still an active and much debated area of research.

Vision for action

Goodale and Milner (1992, 2013) argued that the visual system contains two functionally different streams (see Chen, 2013): the ventral stream (from the early visual cortex to the temporal lobe) and the dorsal stream (from the early visual cortex to the parietal lobe). The function of the ventral stream is to support the identification and recognition of objects; the function of the dorsal stream is to enable rapid interaction with the environment. The subliminal processing we have considered so far has involved processing in the ventral stream, as this processing involved recognition of words and shapes. However, unconscious processing may be more characteristic of the dorsal than the ventral stream. Goodale and Milner found that patients with damage to the ventral stream had difficulty verbally recognizing or describing the very same shapes that they could act on effectively. For example, when one participant was asked to reach for objects, she showed appropriate preshaping of her hand according to the size of the object, yet, if she was asked to simply look and judge the size, she could not do it (see Whitwell & Buckingham, 2013, for a critical discussion).

Stottinger and Perner (2006) showed a similar dissociation in normal people (i.e. people without damage to the ventral stream). In Figure 6.6, the diagonal line in the left image looks larger than that in the right image; in fact, it is smaller. When people reached for the diagonals to grab the objects shaped as in the figure, their grip opened during the reach appropriately, being larger for the larger diagonal. However, when people were asked to shape their hand to manually indicate the size, the illusion was shown, with the grip being larger for the smaller object. Thus, it seems there are visual representations that can control action, but they are not globally accessible. Interestingly, global accessibility of a representation is no guarantee that every processor will use it (a feature of a processor called 'cognitive impenetrability'); consciously thinking that the diagonal on the left is larger does not mean the action system will use that information – and just as well, too, as the unconscious knowledge is the more accurate!

We now consider another example of where unconscious knowledge is better than conscious knowledge. Imagine a ballistic object, such as a cricket ball, flying towards someone; they have to run forward, run backward, or stay where they are in order to intercept the object. For a flight of several seconds, in about half a second a person will start running in the right direction, with speed modulated so that they arrive at the right place at the right time. How is this achieved? McLeod and Dienes (1993) showed that people use a strategy involving the angle of gaze (see Figure 6.7). The line of sight from the eye to the ball makes an angle to the horizontal: this is

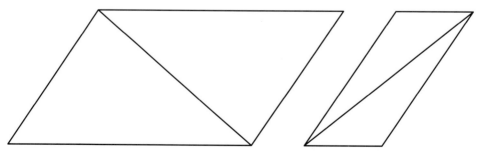

FIGURE 6.6 *The hand is not deceived. The diagonal on the left looks larger than that on the right; in fact it is smaller. If the eye is fooled, what about the hand? (See the text for an explanation.)*
Source: Stottinger and Perner (2006).

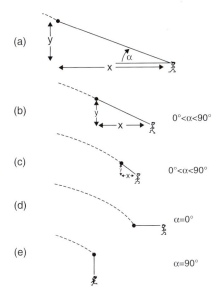

FIGURE 6.7 *How to catch a ball. (a) The angle of gaze to the ball is the angle between the line of sight to the ball and the horizontal. (b–c) If this angle is kept between 0 and 90°, you will arrive at the same place as the ball lands, just as it lands. (d–e) This is because there are only two ways to miss the ball: it falls in front of you, in which case the angle becomes 0°; or it goes over your head, in which case the angle becomes 90°. So any angle between 0 and 90° will ensure interception. In fact, the most efficient way to catch the ball involves letting the angle increase but never to 90°. This can be achieved by letting the tangent of the angle increase at a constant rate. The only thing you need to know about tangents is that they become infinity as angle becomes 90°. So, if the tangent is increasing at a constant rate, the angle will never reach 90° but will be above 0°, and so interception is guaranteed!*

Source: McLeod and Dienes (1996). American Psychological Association. Reprinted with permission.

the angle of gaze. As shown in Figure 6.7, when the tangent of the angle of gaze is increased at a constant rate, interception is guaranteed.

Further, when people are filmed catching balls, they kept the tangent increasing at a remarkably constant rate: people use a simple strategy that efficiently guarantees interception. People's conscious theories of what they do are rather different, however. Reed, McLeod, and Dienes (2010) showed that people believed in rules that did not describe their behaviour and would in fact guarantee failure if they were to be followed. A common theory stated by participants was that they waited until the ball had reached its highest point in its flight and then ran, as their angle of gaze declined from that halfway point. In fact, their angle of gaze increased steadily through the flight until at least the last 200 ms for a successful catch. If people had let the angle of gaze decline from halfway through the flight, they would have failed to get to the ball at the right time. People still believed their incorrect theories even just after running to successfully catch a ball with instructions to notice what their angle of gaze did, and people were every bit as confident in their incorrect beliefs as their correct ones (about what the angle becomes if, for example, the ball is missed and falls in front of them). So here, people's unconscious knowledge, guiding the specific action of intercepting a ballistic object, was more accurate than their conscious beliefs about what they saw, based on general theories. The moral may be that, where there is a clear and simple solution to an ecologically important problem, it is safer to keep performance shielded from flexible conscious knowledge. If you want to catch a ball, just keep your eye on it and run!

TEST YOURSELF

1. What are the ways in which visual stimuli can be made subliminal?
2. How can we tell that perception really was subliminal?
3. What is the relationship between attention and consciousness?

SECTION SUMMARY

- For many stimuli, perception involves conscious perception.
- To make perception unconscious or subliminal, something needs to interfere with normal perceptual processing. The most common method is the use of a backward mask, which interferes with conscious vision so that only subliminal perception is left.
- Continuous flash suppression and gaze-contingent crowding are two new methods of blocking conscious perception.
- Continuous flash suppression relies on the phenomenon of binocular rivalry.
- Gaze-contingent crowding relies on the fact that stimuli in the periphery can be processed unconsciously.
- Cheesman and Merikle (1984, 1986) were the first to distinguish between the subjective threshold and the objective threshold. Sceptics regarding unconscious processing typically prefer the objective threshold.
- The process dissociation procedure is a procedure outlined by Jacoby et al. (1992) that measures the amount of conscious information by the ability to control its use.
- One strategy for discerning the neural correlates of consciousness is to compare conscious and unconscious perception of the same stimulus.
- Goodale and Milner (1992, 2013) argued that the visual system contains two functionally different streams: the ventral stream (from the early visual cortex to the temporal lobe) and the dorsal stream (from the early visual cortex to the parietal lobe).
- The function of the ventral stream is to support the identification and recognition of objects; the function of the dorsal stream is to enable rapid interaction with the environment. Consciousness seems to be associated more with the former than with the latter.

CONSCIOUS VERSUS UNCONSCIOUS LEARNING

LEARNING OBJECTIVE 6.5

Understand the differences between conscious and unconscious learning and the effects of both on individuals.

Implicit learning is the acquisition of unconscious knowledge about the structure of the environment. The term was coined by Arthur Reber in 1967. An everyday example that particularly impressed Reber was natural language. By the age of 5 years, children have learned the major grammatical constructions of their native language environment, but children do not know that they are learning grammar and can describe little if any of the rules of grammar. Not even linguists have a complete grammar of any natural language. But somehow we soak up the structure of our language so we can use it to understand or produce sentences without having explicit or conscious knowledge of what the rules are that we are using. You might think you consciously know some grammar rules. But they are just some simplistic summaries, not the real rules you use. Maybe you have tried to explain to a person learning your native language why their sentence is not as good as your alternative offering. But, if you come up with a rule explaining why, chances are within minutes you have thought of a number of exceptions to your own rule: your own explicit rule cannot have been the real grammatical basis of your own language use. But these observations are anecdotal. Can we rigorously show that knowledge of grammars is unconscious in the lab?

We learn more than just about grammars via implicit learning. Anecdotally it seems we intuitively come to discern patterns in many domains. Consider the rules of our social environment. While your parents may have explicitly taught you some rules (e.g. 'If you have a runny nose, do not wipe it on your clothes'), there are more subtle nuances to polite human interaction that can confound people exposed to a new culture. The anthropologist Kate Fox (2004) describes various rules of being English that many English people would recognize yet never think of articulating. For example, while buying a drink at a pub, we can help the bartender to remember who is next in the queue by subtly indicating, perhaps with our hand or a glass, but we should never, ever lift our elbow off the bar to make a larger motion. That would just be crass. Or consider the learning of musical structure. You can rapidly tell what style of music a piece belongs to (e.g. Bach, the Beatles, or free-form jazz) even before you know how you do it. You might know you like a type of music before you know why, but you must have intuitively determined the structure of the music to know it was the sort of structure you liked. Or consider sporting skills; often thinking about what you are doing makes your performance (i.e. your use of your skills) worse. Often your performance goes up or down for reasons you cannot put your finger on. Often the best athletes find it hard to say what it is they are doing in order to coach others. In all these cases, does the difficulty in articulation arise because the knowledge is genuinely unconscious? Determining the conscious or unconscious status of knowledge requires more than anecdote. Let us see whether we can produce implicit learning in the lab and explore it carefully in the test tube.

Conditioning

The simplest form of structural learning is conditioning, where we learn about a simple association or reinforcement contingency. Early work argued that unconscious conditioning was easy to demonstrate. For example, Greenspoon (1955) asked participants to produce words freely. Whenever participants said a plural noun, they were reinforced with a warm 'Um-hmm'. On average, people produced more plural nouns as a result; yet, on questioning, people did not mention that they were being reinforced for saying plurals. It seems as if people were unconsciously conditioned to use plurals.

Dulany (1963) shows how, in this and other paradigms of the time, people's behaviour can be explained by their conscious hypotheses. In the Greenspoon case, many people claimed in debriefing afterwards that they were being reinforced for saying words in the same semantic category. For example, having been reinforced for saying 'diamonds', the participant continued by saying 'rubies', 'pearls', and so on. In giving semantic associates, the participant happened to continue using the same grammatical form as a side effect. The participant had a 'correlated hypothesis', as Dulany puts it, meaning they had not inferred the experimenter's exact rule; instead they inferred a different one, but one that would tend to give answers the experimenter wanted more often than not. The fact that, upon being asked, the participant did not state the experimenter's rule did not mean the participant unconsciously knew the experimenter's rule; the participant consciously inferred a different yet correlated rule.

Since those early days, demonstrating unconscious conditioning has remained difficult (Hogarth & Duka, 2006; Lovibond & Shanks, 2002). Conditioning experiments typically use only a few salient stimuli; as soon as any unconscious conditioning has happened, attention will naturally be drawn to the key relationship, enabling conscious knowledge of the contingency. One solution is to present the stimuli subliminally. For example, Raio, Carmel, Carrasco, and Phelps (2012) used continuous flash suppression to present one of two faces in a series of trials. Presentation was subliminal according to both objective and subjective thresholds. One of the faces was followed by a shock on the wrist. This face, although it was only ever presented subliminally, rapidly led to a large physiological fear response, as indicated by skin conductance, which increases as a person sweats.

Another way to allow unconscious conditioning to show itself is to use stimuli that misdirect people's conscious hypotheses. People are susceptible to the 'gambler's fallacy', meaning that, after a fair coin has produced a run of heads, people think it is 'about time' a tail came up and rate the probability of a tail as increasing the longer the run of heads. In fact, the probability of a tail is always 0.5 for a fair coin, no matter how the coin previously happened to land. Perruchet (1985) used this effect in a clever way. After hearing a tone, people received a puff of air to their eye 50% of the time. Perruchet measured how strongly the tone made people blink after different numbers of runs, runs of the tone alone, or runs of the tone followed by a puff. The longer the run of a tone followed by a puff, the less people said they expected a puff on the next trial – but the more strongly they blinked. Conversely, the longer the run of a tone alone, the more people said they expected a puff on the next trial – but the less strongly they blinked. That is, the conditioned response (blinking) and conscious expectancy went in opposite directions. Even though the set-up was simple, people were consciously fooled, and unconscious conditioning showed itself. In everyday life, stimuli are rarely presented subliminally or with carefully arranged runs. Implicit learning in everyday life may be more likely for structures more complex than simple conditioning: the richness of the environment may throw off people's conscious hypothesis testing. We will now consider paradigms involving more complex structures.

Implicit learning in the test tube: Grammars

The **artificial grammar learning** paradigm, introduced by Reber (1967, 1989), was inspired by natural language as an example of implicit learning (a type of structural learning too complex to be explained by conditioning; Chomksy, 1957). A grammar, most basically, is a way of sequencing elements. Reber used grammars ('finite state grammars'), which are rich yet still far simpler than those needed for natural language (these were suitable because, if a researcher is going to study a process in the lab, it is best to start from the beginning). To make a finite state grammar, we draw a finite number of states, or circles. We then connect the circles with arrows as we please, as shown in Figure 6.8. Now we follow the arrows through the diagram, producing a sequence of elements along each transition. So, in the figure, the string of letters VTTVM is grammatical according to the grammar. Reber asked people in an initial training phase to memorize or simply look at a number of grammatical letter strings, but without telling people they were structured in any way. After 10 minutes of exposure to the letter strings, people were informed that actually the strings they saw obeyed a complex set of rules; they were then asked to classify new strings as rule governed or not in the subsequent test phase. People could classify the new strings with about 65–70% accuracy, depending on the grammar used, even though in free report afterwards they found it difficult to say what the rules were, and many apologized for mucking the experiment up because they didn't know what they were doing. Reber, Kassin, Lewis, and Cantor (1980) found that, when people were informed of the existence of rules prior to the training phase, their subsequent test performance was either impaired (for complex grammars) or at least not improved. Reber concluded that the learning could not have been a conscious hypothesis-testing processing. Rather, people incidentally absorbed the structure they were exposed to. The artificial grammar-learning paradigm has remained a well-used paradigm for exploring implicit learning.

In many of the original studies, the key evidence for the knowledge being unconscious was that participants did not freely report the structure when asked at the end of the experiment, or, what is better, on a trial-by-trial basis. Often participants could report some things about the letter strings. Reber (1989) indicates, for example, that people could often report which letters could start or finish a string, or which letters could immediately repeat. He speculated that people may have learned the allowable 'bigrams' of the grammar. A bigram is a sequence of two letters; for instance, in VTTVM, the bigrams are VT, TT, TV, and VM. Reber argued that only some of this knowledge was available to report; the rest was unconscious.

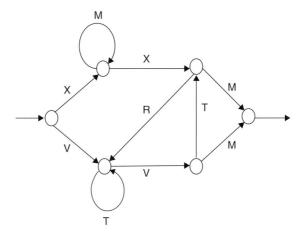

FIGURE 6.8 *A finite state grammar. Any pathway following the arrows is grammatical; for example, XMMXRVM is grammatical.*

Source: Reber (1989). American Psychological Association. Reprinted with permission.

Free report is not a very sensitive test of conscious knowledge, as we saw earlier. As we mentioned, people may not say something simply because they momentarily forgot it. Or they may not say something because they are not quite confident enough to risk saying something that might be wrong, thereby putting their credibility on the line. Finally, if people think the experimenter is interested in one sort of answer, they may indicate ignorance if they did not have knowledge of that type (e.g. if the experimenter is interested in plurals, the participant may truthfully say they had no idea about plurals; Dulany, 1963). One solution is to take confidence ratings in every trial; then the problems just mentioned are sidestepped. If people classify above chance when they believe they are purely guessing, the guessing criterion of unconscious knowledge is satisfied, and, if there is no relation between confidence and accuracy, the zero correlation criterion is also satisfied (Dienes, 2008a). As we have seen, satisfying these two criteria can indicate the presence and amount of unconscious knowledge. As in the case of subliminal perception, subjective measures can be criticized as depending on a participant's decisions as to how to use a confidence scale. Ultimately, no measure proves its worth just by itself; it needs to behave sensibly in testing theoretical predictions (see Focus Point 6.7).

FOCUS POINT 6.7

JUDGEMENT VERSUS STRUCTURAL KNOWLEDGE

We mentioned in Focus Point 6.3 the importance of specifying what content defines the mental state that is conscious or unconscious. When confidence ratings are used, exactly what knowledge can be claimed to be conscious or unconscious? To examine this question, let's look at the sorts of knowledge content people acquire in artificial grammar learning.

In the training phase, people acquire knowledge of the structure of the strings. This knowledge may consist in part of, for example, bigrams and other chunks, or which letters can start a string. Call this structural knowledge. In the test phase, the participant makes a judgement that, for example, a certain string is grammatical. The content of the judgement is something the participant knows about; let's call this 'judgement knowledge'. The structural knowledge is the knowledge that enabled the judgement, but the two have different contents (e.g. 'M cannot start a string' versus 'MTTVT does not have the right structure').

Confidence ratings are indications of confidence in a judgement. Thus, they reflect higher-order thoughts specifically about judgement knowledge. That is, confidence ratings do not directly measure the conscious status of structural knowledge.

Presumably, conscious structural knowledge leads to conscious judgement knowledge. But, if structural knowledge is unconscious, judgement knowledge could be conscious or unconscious. Consider natural language: if shown a sentence, we can know it is grammatical and consciously know that it is grammatical, but not know at all *why* it is grammatical. If both structural knowledge and judgement knowledge are unconscious, then it feels like we are just guessing. If structural knowledge is unconscious but judgement knowledge is conscious, then it feels like we are using intuition. In both cases, we have unconscious structural knowledge. But, in the second case, criteria based on confidence ratings (such as the zero correlation and guessing criteria) might show all knowledge is conscious – because those criteria only assess judgement knowledge.

Dienes and Scott (2005) asked participants in the test phase of an artificial grammar learning experiment to indicate the basis of a judgement. Participants could say 'guess' (the judgement had no basis whatsoever – they may as well have flipped a coin); 'intuition' (the participant had some confidence in the judgement but no idea why it was right);

'rules' (the judgement was based on rules acquired from the training phase that could be stated if asked); or, finally, 'memory' (the judgement was based on recollections of the training strings or parts of them).

The first two attributions (guess and intuition) reflect unconscious structural knowledge and the second two (rules and memory) reflect conscious structural knowledge. People used unconscious structural knowledge attributions about two thirds of the time. For all attributions, people classified significantly above chance, indicating both conscious and unconscious judgement knowledge, and conscious and unconscious structural knowledge. But, taking a sceptical stance, we can ask: why should we believe that when participants give these structural knowledge attributions they are actually picking out real differences in their minds?

A scientific measure can only ever prove itself by showing its sensitivity to theoretical predictions. Evidence is emerging that the attributions show such sensitivity. For example, the accuracy of unconscious structural knowledge was unaffected by whether people were forewarned about rules in the training phase or whether people were consciously distracted by a demanding secondary task; conversely, the accuracy of conscious structural knowledge was harmed by being distracted while searching for rules (Dienes & Scott, 2005). The structural knowledge attributions may pick out real divisions in the mind. An important question for any conjectured measure is under what conditions the measure picks out real differences, and this remains a matter for future research.

Finally, we will consider how flexibly people can use the knowledge they acquire of artificial grammars. Jacoby (1991) argued that unconscious knowledge is inflexible and so not responsive to our intentions regarding whether to use it or not. Wan, Dienes, and Fu (2008) exposed people to sequences from two grammars in two separate 5 minute intervals. The test phase showed sequences from both grammars but participants were asked to pick from just one of the grammars. Can people strategically choose which grammar to use?

The answer is that people can, and for every type of attribution. That is, whether or not judgement knowledge is conscious or not, or structural knowledge is conscious or not, a person can decide to use one grammar and effectively use it. Your intuition can be quite flexible, and it can be based on useful knowledge, whether or not you know what that knowledge is.

Implicit learning in the test tube: Perceptual motor skills

Implicit learning involves not only coming to judge accurately how well formed things feel but also being able to make quick responses in the right situations. In an early study, Nissen and Bullermer (1987) designed a **serial reaction time task** to investigate the expression of implicit knowledge in the timing of motor responses. In this task, a stimulus can appear in one of four locations; for whatever location it appears in a trial, the participant has to press a corresponding button as quickly as possible. To the participant this appears to be just a reaction time task. In fact, the sequence of locations is structured. There might be a long sequence of a single location (e.g. a sequence 12 locations long), or the sequence might follow a finite state grammar, with paths along the grammar randomly chosen each time. In these cases, people become quicker at responding; however, if the sequence is switched for a different sequence, or a random one, people become slow, speeding up again when the original sequence is reinstated. So, people have learned the sequence, yet, often at the end of the experiment, they are surprised to hear there even was a sequence.

The knowledge used in the serial reaction time task has been subjected to extensive testing regarding its conscious status. Objective tests have been used, with participants asked to recognize the sequence, or fragments of it, after training. Sometimes participants fail to recognize the sequence as a whole, seeming to satisfy requirements for the knowledge being unconscious by objective measures. But we always have to ask: what is the content of the knowledge that is claimed to be conscious or unconscious? For example, if people have unconsciously learned only some fragments of the sequence, this may speed their reaction times but not necessarily allow recognition of the full sequence (Perruchet & Amorim, 1992); that is, the participants may have consciously known fragments. When tested with sequence fragments, people often classify them at above-chance levels. But, of course, that does not mean the knowledge is conscious according to the main theories of consciousness. So we need more than objective measures. Destrebecqz and Cleeremans (2001) trained people on an serial reaction time task and then asked them to generate a sequence. In the inclusion condition, people were asked to generate the same sequence they were trained on; in the exclusion condition, they were asked to generate a sequence different from the one they were trained on. In the inclusion condition, people generated correct sequence fragments at above-chance levels. That is, by objective measures, people were performing at above-chance levels. Conscious knowledge would allow this. But so would unconscious knowledge. Crucially, on the exclusion task, people generated fragments from the sequence at above-chance levels. This is opposite to what conscious knowledge would do. So the knowledge was unconscious. What knowledge does this procedure measure the conscious status of? The answer is judgement knowledge (i.e. the knowledge that an item is in the right place in a sequence). If we confidently judge that a production of an item is grammatical, we can include or exclude it. But we do not have to know why a production is grammatical. However, given that at least some of the judgement knowledge is unconscious, we can infer that some structural knowledge is too (see Fu, Dienes, & Fu, 2010, for a direct demonstration of this claim).

In sum, implicit learning can be demonstrated in the lab, which shows that we can make accurate decisions even when we do not know that we know anything – or when we know that we know, but we do not know what we know!

WHEN YOU DO NOT CONSCIOUSLY KNOW YOUR OWN PASSWORD

One problem with passwords or electronic keys for entering a secure site or building is that an attacker can force you to reveal the password, or hand over the hardware key, even when you are far from the building. Bojinov, Sanchez, Reber, Boneh, and Lincoln (2014) came up with a clever solution: you learn the password implicitly so that, as you do not consciously know it, you can never reveal it.

In the current version of this system, participants are initially trained for 45 minutes on a 'serial interception sequence learning' (SISL) task. Training is done using a computer game to implicitly learn a random password. The game consists of circles gradually falling down the screen in seven columns. The goal of the player is to intercept every circle before it hits the bottom; the speed of the circles is adjusted to keep each player just within their ability. The circles follow a fixed long sequence of letters, which can be unique for each person. Bojinov et al. showed that, after training, participants could not deliberately reconstruct the trained sequence: thus, it cannot be deliberately revealed to anyone else.

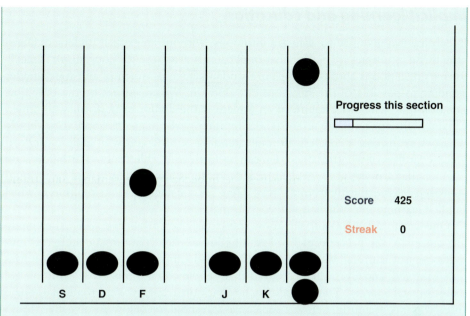

Progress this section

Score   425

Streak   0

The serial interception sequence learning task. Participants have to intercept each circle before it reaches the bottom. In fact, the sequence of circles is fixed.

Source: Bojinov, Sanchez, Reber, Boneh, and Lincoln (2014).

Once they are trained, participants are ready to use their implicit knowledge of their personal sequence as their identification. Over about 6 minutes, people again perform a version of the SISL task that has a mixture of random combinations of letters and parts of the trained sequence. By performing better on the old rather than random pieces of sequence, the participant validates their identity. While the current system is too time consuming for, say, getting money out of a cash machine, it could be used for entering a high-security site in which a person is going to work for an extended period. Or imagine you are a spy in a distant country and one thing you must not do is allow a double agent to extract the ability from you to enter your headquarters back home.

IMPLICIT LEARNING AND SUBLIMINAL PERCEPTION

Implicit learning typically involves seeing a stimulus consciously and acquiring structural relations unconsciously. So implicit learning and subliminal perception are conceptually different. However, in one sense, in implicit learning, we learn to see the structural relations subliminally. Further, a powerful way of showing that unconscious knowledge of structure can be acquired is by presenting stimuli subliminally. Earlier methods of making stimuli subliminal with back masking were not successful because they did not allow enough time for the learning process to occur. Thus, Atas, Faivre, Timmermans, Cleermans, and Kouider (2014) presented two sequences rendered below an objective threshold using gaze-contingent crowding, which allows presentation of stimuli for much longer than back masking. One sequence was rewarded; the other punished. While people's choices to opt out of receiving the reward or punishment were not sensitive to whether they were about to get a punishment or reward, the speed with which they made the choice was. Clearly the knowledge acquired here was degraded compared with when stimuli are consciously seen, as in the above paradigms, where the implicit learning allowed accurate choices. To develop accurate intuition, it is best to consciously experience the relevant stimuli.

Implicit learning and education

If learning can give rise to accurate intuitions, without an explicit understanding of why those intuitions are right, what implications are there for education? Typically formal education is about making sure students have as much of an explicit understanding as possible of the structure of a domain. This need not be the only goal. For example, what we require of an athlete is the ability to perform well athletically, whether or not they understand why their performance is good. (Conversely, what we require of a coach is an understanding of how and why athletes perform well, regardless of whether the coach can perform well athletically.) Further, it is not obvious that arriving at an explicit understanding is always best served by trying to approach a task explicitly from the start. Here we consider various situations in which implicit learning may play a useful educational role.

One way to acquire a skill is to know consciously how to do every step, then gradually automate the procedure. The resulting knowledge is automatic and conscious. With implicit learning, the acquired knowledge is unconscious from the start. Masters, Maxwell, and Eves (2009) showed that people could implicitly learn to hit golf balls to reach a target. To train people, feedback on accuracy was provided in one of three ways: consciously, below a subjective threshold, or below an objective threshold. When feedback was below the objective threshold, no learning occurred. When feedback was below the subjective threshold, people became progressively more accurate (though learning was not as fast as when feedback was conscious). So learning can be implicit in a sporting context – that is, involving unconscious knowledge. Is there any benefit to learning sporting skills implicitly? Maxwell, Masters, and Eves (2003) showed that, when the learning of golf putting was implicit (so that people acquired few verbally reportable rules compared to in explicit learning), it was more resistant to a secondary task. Stressing people with a secondary task especially interfered with performance when people had learned explicitly. Further, if one has conscious knowledge of a sporting skill, put under pressure one might be more likely to 'choke' (think too much about what one is doing so that it disrupts performance) than if the knowledge is implicit. Good coaching will involve encouraging a balance of the implicit and explicit, according to the individual (Masters & Maxwell, 2008). (Interested readers might like to read more in Timothy Gallwey's 1974 book *The Inner Game of Tennis*.)

FOCUS POINT 6.10

INTUITION AND LEARNING MATHEMATICS

It might seem obvious that sporting moves and complex language structures can be learned implicitly, but what about knowledge of mathematics? Surely mathematics can only be learned explicitly? However, mathematicians often have the experience of answers just coming to them; the next stage after arriving at the answer is working out why it is the right answer (e.g. Poincare, 1913). Indeed, Zoltan P. Dienes (e.g. 1960) developed an approach to teaching mathematics to children that is based on building an intuitive understanding of mathematics before making the structures explicit.

According to this method, children first play freely with structured materials that can embody a mathematical concept or structure. For example, the materials could involve coloured blocks of different sizes; you can view some examples of the games **here**[1]. Children are then given progressively more constrained games with the same materials until their choices in the games mean they are following a given mathematical structure.

Next the process is repeated for the same structure but with a completely different sensorimotor embodiment (e.g. dance steps or song; Dienes, 1973). After the child has experienced a few such embodiments of the same structure, they can play the 'meta-game', which is the game of finding the correspondences between the games. When this has been achieved, the child is finally ready to appreciate the structure explicitly. Thus, in this approach, a process of building up an intuitive understanding in several different concrete situations always precedes even the attempt to teach an explicit and fully abstract understanding of mathematics.

The role of unconscious knowledge in this process has yet to be properly explored, but, anecdotally, children sometimes guess accurately in these games without being able to say why they gave the responses they did (for pedagogical evaluation, see Klein, 1987; Sriraman, 2008). So, asking people to work out the structure consciously from the beginning might not be optimal, even for learning mathematics. First it might make sense to hone our intuitions – and then use those intuitions to guide an explicit understanding. Further research is needed into how developing unconscious knowledge may or may not be useful in the classroom (see Sætrevik, Reber, & Sannum, 2006).

DISCUSSION POINT

Discuss some everyday situations where implicit learning might play a role.

Finally, consider learning a second language as an adult. To what extent should we be memorizing explicit grammatical rules or, rather, be immersed in the language environment to soak up the rules unconsciously? Can we acquire the rules of a second language unconsciously – or must we first always consciously notice them? There is evidence that adults can learn aspects of a second language unconsciously. Rebuschat and Williams (2012) presented English participants with sentences composed with English words but German syntax (grammar) determining word order. Thus, the sentences were understandable to the participants, even if they sounded funny (e.g. 'Since his parents groceries needed, purchased David everything necessary'). On a later test with the structural knowledge attributions of Dienes and Scott (2005), when people gave unconscious structural knowledge attributions, they were sensitive to the rules of German syntax. Further, people did not freely state any understanding of the key rules, despite being sensitive to them. That is, the rules could be acquired unconsciously. In a similar way, Chen et al. (2011) and Leung and Williams (2011) showed that people could learn to use various made-up words (e.g. 'chu', 'yu') to mean 'that' depending on whether the noun was living or non-living (e.g. 'chu dog' versus 'yu bag') – and structural knowledge attributions, among other measures, indicated that people made their choices without consciously realizing that the choice was based on the noun being living or non-living.

If syntax can be learned implicitly, learning word meanings might seem to be something that can be learned explicitly quite readily, via dictionary definitions or translations. However, words can have subtle conditions on their use not captured by dictionary definitions. For example, the word 'cause' may seem to have the simple meaning 'to bring about'. But the word is in fact largely used in contexts in which a negative rather than positive event has been brought about (one may 'cause grief' but it sounds slightly odd to 'cause happiness'): we say 'cause' has a 'negative semantic prosody'. This aspect of meaning is subtle and hence may not be noticed explicitly. Indeed, Guo et al. (2011), using structural knowledge attributions, showed people could learn to use certain made-up words in positive or negative contexts, without participants realizing they were choosing the word because of the context being positive or negative. That is, people gained unconscious structural knowledge of semantic prosody.

DISCUSSION POINT

You can read more about unconscious language learning **on the University of Cambridge's website**[2]. Discuss some other examples you can think of where a word has taken on a meaning or condition that is not reflected by the definition in the dictionary.

In sum, various regularities in a second language, from syntax to semantic prosody, can be learned unconsciously, as indicated by subjective measures. When learning a second language, make sure you listen to and repeat sentences in real, concrete contexts so that you soak up all the subtleties, even those that are not in grammar books, in dictionaries, or even consciously noticed by you.

TEST YOURSELF

1. What is implicit learning?
2. In which everyday situations might implicit learning play a role?
3. How can implicit learning be shown in the lab?
4. How can subjective measures be applied to testing implicit learning?

SECTION SUMMARY

- Implicit learning is the acquisition of unconscious knowledge about the structure of the environment.
- Implicit learning typically involves seeing stimuli consciously and acquiring structural relations unconsciously.
- The artificial grammar learning paradigm introduced by Reber (1967, 1989) was inspired by natural language as an example of implicit learning. It often makes use of finite state grammars.
- Nissen and Bullermer (1987) designed the serial reaction time task to investigate the expression of implicit knowledge in the timing of motor responses. The knowledge used in the serial reaction time task, as in artificial grammar learning, has been subjected to extensive testing regarding its conscious status.

- Implicit knowledge can give rise to accurate intuitions when a person knows they have knowledge but not what that knowledge is; implicit knowledge can also give rise to accurate guesses when a person is not aware of even having any knowledge at all.

- Typically, formal education is about making sure students have as much of an explicit understanding as possible of the structure of a domain. However, what we require of an athlete, for example, is the ability to perform well, whether or not they understand why their performance is so good. The coach needs an understanding of how and why athletes perform well, regardless of whether the coach can perform well.

- Many aspects of a second language can be acquired unconsciously.

CONSCIOUS VERSUS UNCONSCIOUS INTENTIONS: VOLITION AND HYPNOTIC RESPONSE

LEARNING OBJECTIVE 6.6

Understand the concept and implications of unconscious intentions.

So far we have considered how memory, perception, and knowledge can be unconscious. What about other mental states – how about intentions? Can a person intend to perform an action but think that they have no such intention? In such a case we would end up doing things we did not consciously intend. Such a notion may seem to strike deeply at a conception of ourselves as in charge of our 'selves' – and it may have relevance to certain psychiatric conditions, such as schizophrenia, where people may do things that they do not experience themselves as having intended to do.

Choice blindness

Johansson, Hall, Sikström, and Olsson (2005) showed people pairs of pictures of female faces and asked them to choose which one they found most attractive. That sounds straightforward, but the experimenters were trained conjurors and on some trials they secretly swapped one face for the other. In these trials, the outcome of the choice became the opposite of what the person intended. Nonetheless, in only a quarter of the trials did people notice the swap. In the remaining trials people were perfectly willing to give justifications for their 'choices'. The authors called this phenomenon 'choice blindness'. (Interestingly, people in the long run come to prefer the choices they believe they have made, even when they did not really make those choices [Hall et al., 2013]; remember Focus Point 6.2, on dissonance reduction, where this effect is predicted by dissonance theory.) Hall, Johansson, Tärning, Sikström, and Deutgen (2010) showed the same effect with tasting foods: they invited shoppers at a supermarket to try different varieties of jam and tea and indicate their preference. When the choice had been swapped, and even for other tastes such as cinnamon apple versus bitter grapefruit, on a majority of occasions people did not notice and were quite willing to give justifications for their 'choice'. Amazingly, people are also often prepared to justify political views they think they have indicated as their own but have actually rejected (Hall et al., 2013; see also Explorable.com, 2010).

These examples indicate how the reasons we give for our actions cannot always be the actual basis of our actions. We may well believe the explanations we provide to the world, but in many cases the justifications are post hoc rationalizations for actions whose actual bases we are no longer aware of – if we ever knew them in the first place. This does not mean we never act on prior conscious intentions: people were not choice blind in all trials. But it does mean we can easily fool ourselves. In choice blindness, we are aware of intentionally making a choice; it is just that we actually made one choice and believe we made another. Next we consider whether we can intentionally perform an action while believing it was not intentional at all.

Ideomotor action and hypnotic response

Tie your keys to a piece of string to make a pendulum, and hold the string between thumb and forefinger, with the keys free to swing. Imagine the keys going around and around. After some seconds of such imagining, many people will find the keys begin moving around, as if by themselves. You can tell that it is you making the motion, though, because, if you imagine the keys circling in the opposite direction, or in a straight rather than a circular motion, you will likely find the keys moving in just that way. This effect of imagination on movement is known as **ideomotor action**, and a pendulum used to illustrate this effect is known as Chevreul's pendulum (after the French chemist Michel Chevreul [1786–1889], who first showed that the pendulum's movement is governed by psychological and not supernatural principles; see Wegner, 2002).

Ideomotor action is partly based on the fact that, when we imagine actions, small contractions of the corresponding muscles happen. The pendulum can magnify these small movements. Such magnification could also be produced by, for example, a dowsing rod, or the combination of several people gently pushing on a cup on a Ouija board. The effects of these magnifiers of small motions can be so compelling that many lay people throughout history have thought a supernatural explanation was necessary, attributing the effects to something other than purely the effect of imagination. (A fourth-century Roman called Hilarius used a version of Chevreul's pendulum and was as a consequence tortured on the emperor's orders for using magic [Wegner, 2002]. Next time someone tells you that the direction of a pendulum you hold indicates your allergies or the gender of your baby, just know that they are being Hilarius.) However, we still need to say more about some ideomotor actions that are too large or complex to be simply accounted for by small muscular movements.

On every continent, and throughout human history, people have had the experience of being possessed by spirits. When possessed, the person can engage in complex tasks or arguments, while it seems to them that it was not them doing it – it was the spirit. Nonetheless, the outcomes are often favourable to the possessed person in terms of gaining goods or status (Lewis, 2003). That is, spirit possession often seems to be a goal-directed activity where a person is not aware of the intentional nature of their own actions. As possession often seems beneficial, it is possible we evolved a mechanism that allowed it to happen – a mechanism that allowed us to convince others of there being a spirit possessing us by first convincing ourselves with self-deception (Dienes & Perner, 2007). The phenomenon comes to us in several forms. For a contemporary case of spirit possession, consider the State Oracle of Tibet, a monk who channels a protector deity that gives important advice of state to the Tibetan government (now in exile), which the monk experiences as not being produced by himself. The same phenomenon appears as people being influenced by inner energy or ch'i being projected at a distance, throwing people around or knocking them out. Consider also people talking in tongues, possessed by the Holy Spirit in Evangelical churches. These experiences are typically subjectively compelling to those who have them. But can we study them in the lab to investigate what is really going on?

Fortunately, one version of the phenomenon comes to us in an easily reproducible way. In the 18th century, when possessions and exorcisms were common in Europe, the convulsions that typically accompanied them apparently became the model for how people thought they should behave during treatment by Anton Mesmer (1734–1815), who developed the idea that he could manipulate magnetic fields around people (by 'mesmerizing' them) (Lynn & Kirsch, 2006). Later, one of Mesmer's pupils mesmerized a peasant on his estate, Victor Race, but Race was not part of high society and did not know that convulsing was the thing to do. Instead, for reasons known only to himself, Race decided that the proper thing to do was to act like he was somehow asleep. The idea caught on. And hence hypnosis was born: the notion of a sleep-like state in which one performs actions one did not intend to do (for summaries of recent research on hypnosis, see the website **Hypnosis and Suggestion**³). In fact, hypnosis has nothing to do with sleep; physiologically speaking, the person is not in any way in a sleep-like state, and people can respond to hypnotic suggestions just as effectively while riding a stationary bike as when feeling drowsy (Banyai & Hilgard, 1976). But hypnotic response does involve experiencing actions as if they were involuntary, just as in spirit possession.

Hypnotic actions can be as complex as one wishes to suggest, given only that the voluntary version of the action is within the normal repertoire of the subject: from an arm rising by itself to automatic writing. As many as 90% of people can experience the easier hypnotic suggestions, and about 10% of people are highly hypnotizable. This means that hypnotic response can be easily studied in the lab (see Dienes, 2015a, 2015b, 2015c, 2015d; Willmarth, 2012). Why does it seem to people that the hypnotic action is involuntary? One type of theory is that hypnotic actions feel involuntary because they *are* involuntary; that is, they are not produced by normal intentional processes (Kirsch, 1985; Woody & Sadler, 2008; see also Dienes, 2015e, 2015f). For example, according to response expectancy theory (Kirsch, 1985), strongly expecting an action to happen (e.g. your arm rising by itself) is sufficient to make the action happen. You do not need to intend to lift your arm; there can just be the expectation of it lifting. In effect, hypnosis is a type of placebo. The theory is elegant in being simple but, unfortunately, hypnotic response is not completely accounted for by expectations (e.g. Benham, Woody, Wilson, & Nash, 2006). Another type of theory argues that hypnotic actions are produced intentionally but feel involuntary because we are not aware of those intentions (e.g. Hilgard, 1977; Spanos, 1986). Dienes and Perner (2007) called the common component of the latter type of theory 'cold control', and suggested considering it as the single mechanism of hypnotic response. That is, according to the theory, hypnotic response involves executive control (the intentional performance of a cognitive or motor action) without accurate higher-order thoughts (HOTs) of intending – indeed, with inaccurate HOTs (e.g. 'I am not intending this action'). Hypnotic response is control without accurate HOTs – cold control (Dienes, 2015g).

Hilgard (1977) and Spanos (1986) provided evidence for the strategic and intentional nature of hypnotic response (for a counterargument that hypnosis can involve automatization, see Lifshitz, Aubert-Bonn, Fischer, Kashem, & Raz, 2013). In one example, Spanos et al. (1987) gave highly hypnotizable subjects ('highs') the post-hypnotic suggestion that they would rub their eyebrow whenever they heard the word 'experiment' over the next 48 hours. Indeed, highs almost without exception rubbed their eyebrow at the end of the first session when told that the experiment was over, and again in 2 days when they came back to the hypnosis lab for the next experiment. However, in between, a confederate with photos of the subjects managed to find each subject and bump into them on campus, asking for the way to 'professor Smith's physics experiment'. None of the subjects rubbed their eyebrow. That is, they only responded to the suggestion when it served a personal purpose. This does not mean highs were faking when they did respond; it means a response that genuinely felt involuntary was constructed to occur so as to fit in with the subject's overall goals. In one sense, then, the person responding hypnotically is still in charge of themselves, even if it feels to them like they are not.

In sum, while there is not yet a consensus about the mechanism of hypnotic response, a common type of theory is that hypnotic response involves a person having intentions they are not aware of having. The person feels their actions and experiences have a cause other than themselves. This may have been useful in a historical, and perhaps evolutionary, context for people to convince themselves and hence others that they were in contact with a higher power. In modern times, this phenomenon has surfaced as hypnosis – and the higher power is often presented as 'the unconscious'. In a therapeutic setting, being convinced that we are in touch with special powers, and that the therapy will therefore be very effective, may increase the effectiveness of the therapy (Kirsch, Montgomery, & Sapirstein, 1995).

SECTION SUMMARY

- The idea that we can do things we do not consciously intend to do conflicts with the concept that we are in charge of ourselves.
- This idea may have relevance to certain psychiatric conditions, such as schizophrenia, where people may do things that they do not experience themselves as having intended to do.
- The reasons we give for our actions cannot always be the actual basis of our actions.
- Sometimes we think we want A but, when we are mistakenly led to believe that we have actually chosen B, we make up all kinds of reasons why B is a much better alternative and why we actually wanted it all along. This is called choice blindness.
- The effect of imagination on movement is known as ideomotor action.
- Ideomotor action is partly based on the fact that, when we imagine actions, small contractions of the corresponding muscles happen.

- Some ideomotor actions that are too large or complex to be simply accounted for by small muscular movements can be explained by the fact that the outcomes are often favourable to the possessed person.

- When responding hypnotically, we perform actions that it seems as if we did not intend. As many as 90% of people can experience the easier hypnotic suggestions, and about 10% of people are highly hypnotizable.

- Theories of hypnosis can be divided into those that postulate that the subject did not intend the hypnotic action and those that postulate that the subject did intend, but was not aware of, the intention. The latter sort of theory is called cold control.

- According to response expectancy theory, the strong expectation of an involuntary action is sufficient to make the action happen, with no intentions needed.

- According to cold control theory, hypnotic response involves more than response expectancies; it also involves executive control.

- In a therapeutic setting, being convinced that we are in touch with special powers, and that the therapy will therefore be very effective, may increase the effectiveness of the therapy.

CONSCIOUS VERSUS UNCONSCIOUS ATTITUDES AND EMOTIONS

LEARNING OBJECTIVE 6.7

Understand the concept and implications of unconscious attitudes and emotions and some of the means of researching these attitudes and emotions.

If you have attitude, must you know it?

To a social psychologist, an 'attitude' is a positive or negative evaluation. We saw previously how subliminal presentation of a stimulus can make someone like that stimulus more – the mere exposure effect (Bornstein & D'Agostino, 1992). In that case, the initial perception was unconscious and the consequent liking was conscious. Could the liking, or attitude, itself be unconscious? Some evidence for this was provided by Adams, Wright, and Lohr (1996). They divided heterosexual men into groups according to a questionnaire that measured homophobia. All participants were exposed to sexually explicit erotic films, and changes in penile circumference were monitored (with a device called a penile plethysmograph) to provide an objective measure of the extent of any erection. Both homophobic and non-homophobic men obtained erections looking at film clips involving sex with women. But the homophobic men were considerably more aroused by male homosexual clips than the non-homophobic men. One plausible theory is that homophobes have unconscious positive feelings about gay sex. Or maybe homophobes are reacting to their purely conscious feelings, feelings they just didn't want to explicitly tell people about. Further research is needed.

To obtain evidence for an unconscious attitude, we need a way of measuring attitude that is not based on self-report; indeed, we need a measure that can contradict self-report in order to show that an attitude is unconscious. The implicit association test (IAT) provides one possibility (see Banaji & Greenwald, 2013, for a popular summary). In this test, a sequence of words appears on a screen. The aim is to classify the words by pressing a left or right button – the left button for pleasant words ('gentle', 'enjoy', etc.) and the right button for unpleasant words ('poison', 'death', etc.). The trick is that in addition the participant makes another classification using the same keys – for example, names of black people with the left button and names of white people with the right button. The task is repeated with all possible combinations of responses (e.g. black and unpleasant on the right and white and pleasant on the left). The question is, is a person faster when white rather than black is paired with pleasant rather than unpleasant? If so, that would indicate prejudice for white people and against black people. And the prejudice would be implicit if people explicitly believed in racial equality. The task can be used to measure prejudice for all sorts of groups – for example, old versus young, fat versus slim, and so on.

An initial key finding was that a greater proportion of people were measured as prejudiced by the IAT than by their explicit reports for many types of prejudice (Banaji & Greenwald, 2013). But does this mean that people's negative attitudes to certain groups are unconscious? Maybe; or perhaps, like having homosexual desires, people explicitly under-report socially difficult attitudes they are nonetheless aware of. Or the IAT may indeed measure automatic tendencies – that a person is aware of. According to Gawronski and Bodenhausen (2006), attitudes as measured by the IAT reflect spontaneous reactions, regardless of whether the person thinks that these reactions are valid or invalid. Conversely, self-reported attitudes result from a person working out their beliefs based on consistency with any other relevant belief (e.g. that all people should be treated equally, regardless of race). Thus, a person might decide that their initial reaction to a person of a different race is inconsistent with their general values and commitments – and thus give different explicit reports than their IAT indicates. A person could be entirely aware of their implicit attitude but quite rightly and honestly not report it as an explicit attitude. Hahn, Judd, Hirsh, and Blair (2014) directly tested this idea by asking people to predict their IAT scores for a range of groups they could be prejudiced towards; their predictions correlated about 0.6 with their actual scores. That is, people seemed quite aware of what their automatic attitudes were. This occurred despite explicit reports of prejudice having a small correlation with the IAT – that is, a person's considered opinion need not be the same as their immediate reaction. The IAT may measure automatic evaluative associations, but that doesn't mean the attitudes are unconscious. Whether the IAT, or similar measures, can pick up on unconscious attitudes in some contexts remains a tantalizing topic for future research.

Berridge and Robinson (1995) argued that liking and wanting are separate; in particular, a drug addict comes to crave – to want – their fix more and more even as they come to like its effects less and less. Further, these authors argued that this wanting could be unconscious. For example, heroin addicts asked to press a lever to obtain solutions of morphine rated a very small dose of morphine as worthless and containing no drug, but still worked very hard to get it by lever pressing – in fact, they worked as hard as they did for moderate doses that they explicitly rated as worthwhile (Lamb et al., 1991). Further, addicts given a certain drug, desipramine, said the drug took away all their craving for cocaine – but they continued to work for cocaine just as hard (Fischman & Foltin, 1992). In these cases, unconscious wanting exerted just as powerful an effect on people as conscious wanting. In sum, the evidence for unconscious liking is not yet substantial. The evidence for unconscious wanting is intriguing – we will see whether these effects can be replicated. In both cases, conscious liking and wanting are measured with subjective measures – expressions of higher-order thoughts of liking or wanting.

Unconscious emotions

It might seem strange to conjecture that emotion can be unconscious. Is not the whole point of an emotion how we consciously feel? Could we really be happy and not know it? But the issues are just the same as for perception. Normally, when we say that Bill saw a dog we mean that he consciously saw it. But such everyday usage of 'see' does not mean that subliminal perception does not exist. Similarly, we can disentangle those aspects of an emotion that could be unconscious from our conscious experience. An emotion involves an appraisal of a situation: fear would not be fear if it did not involve expecting something bad to happen imminently; anger would not be anger if we did not believe an insult or injustice had been committed; and so on. Emotion also involves systematic cognitive changes (e.g. narrowing of attention, focus on certain sorts of information), physiological changes (in heart rate, blood pressure, breathing, and hormone levels), and behavioural changes (e.g. acting out revenge in the case of anger, changes in facial expressions, etc.). There is no logical reason why the appraisals and cognitive, physiological, and behavioural changes need be conscious as such (for reviews from various perspectives, see Barrett, Niedenthal, & Winkielman, 2005). Indeed, reports of people realizing that they had been in love all along, or that they had not been in love for some time, or that they were anxious, or no longer anxious, or noticing they had a spring in their step are not uncommon in literature and biographies.

A strategy for demonstrating unconscious emotion is to induce in people behavioural or other objectively measurable changes associated with the emotion under conditions in which the person reports no change in their emotion. The area has not been thoroughly investigated but there are some promising results (for a discussion, see Winkielman, Berridge, & Sher, 2011). According to Winkielman, Berridge, and Wilbarger (2005), when in a positive rather than a negative mood, people will value and consume more of, for example, a (nonalcoholic) beverage. Consumption can then be used as one index of mood – even if the mood was unconscious. Winkielman, Berridge, and Wilbarger exposed participants to several subliminal emotional facial expressions (happy, neutral, or angry). Exposure to a given emotional expression did not significantly change participants' rated emotion. However, people exposed to the happy rather than the angry face consumed more of a novel beverage and rated it more highly. Further, Tong, Tan, and Tan (2013) found that the subliminal prime of 'unfair' rather than 'fair' produced a more angry facial expression – without a significant change in rated emotion.

In sum, the body of evidence for unconscious emotion is not yet substantial, but, as in the previous section, the evidence is intriguing. Note that, also as in the previous section, the conscious status of the mental state (in this case, emotion) is measured with subjective measures – expressions of higher-order thoughts of being in a certain state.

TEST YOURSELF

1. What is the implicit association test? Does it measure unconscious attitudes?
2. What sort of evidence could show that an emotion was unconscious?

SECTION SUMMARY

- To obtain evidence for an unconscious attitude, we need a way of measuring attitude that is not based on self-report.

- One way of doing this is by using the implicit association test.

- An initial key finding from the use of the implicit association test was that a greater proportion of people were measured as prejudiced than by their explicit reports for many types of prejudice (Banaji & Greenwald, 2013).

- According to Gawronski and Bodenhausen (2006), attitudes as measured by the implicit association test reflect spontaneous reactions, regardless of whether we think that these reactions are valid or invalid.

- Berridge and Robinson (1995) argued that liking and wanting are separate; in particular, a drug addict comes to crave – to want – their fix more and more even as they come to like its effects less and less. Further, they argued that this wanting could be unconscious.

- It might seem strange to conjecture that emotion can be unconscious. However, reports of people realizing that they had been in love all along, or that they were no longer anxious, are not uncommon in literature, so it is conceptually possible to not be aware of what emotion one is in. Further, there is beginning to be evidence for the existence of unconscious emotions.

FUNCTIONS OF CONSCIOUSNESS AND FUTURE DIRECTIONS

LEARNING OBJECTIVE 6.8

Demonstrate an understanding of the current view of the functions of consciousness and possible future research and directions within the field.

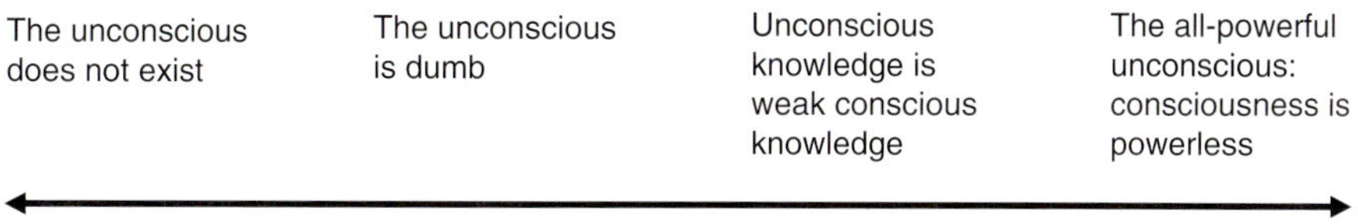

| The unconscious does not exist | The unconscious is dumb | Unconscious knowledge is weak conscious knowledge | The all-powerful unconscious: consciousness is powerless |

FIGURE 6.9 *The functions of consciousness.*

Expert opinion on the function or functions of consciousness spans the full spectrum of possibilities illustrated in Figure 6.9. On one end is the view that the unconscious does not exist; any mental state is conscious and therefore consciousness is required for any mental functioning (e.g. Dulany, 1991). This view requires us to dismiss the evidence we have reviewed for the existence of unconscious memories, perceptions, knowledge, intentions, desires, and emotions. (As the evidence has largely relied on subjective measures, the sceptic is often drawn to denying the validity of subjective measures.) At the other end of the spectrum are those who deny consciousness has a function, or maybe say that it just has the function of post hoc rationalization (e.g. Wegner, 2002). This view requires us to dismiss evidence for differences found between conscious and unconscious processing, particularly the findings that conscious states are often especially effective.

The main theories of consciousness suggest various sorts of functions (Seth, 2009). According to higher-order theory, in principle anything that can be achieved by mental states that have content only about the world can be achieved unconsciously. For example, detecting that things are present, picking them up, retrieving information about the past, and intending to perform actions can all be achieved unconsciously. Thus, the higher-order view tends to put the function of consciousness towards the right of Figure 6.9. Nonetheless, higher-order theories require conscious mental states for any control or regulation that is dependent on knowing we are in a certain state. For example, fear might be best dealt with by running as fast as we can, or by judging that the fear was irrational and that we should confront or reappraise the situation to overcome the fear. Conscious emotion enables this judgement. Integration theory associates consciousness with the process of efficiently combining integration and differentiation; thus, conscious decisions will be more optimal than unconscious decisions when there are many discriminations to be integrated (Seth et al., 2011). On this account, we can perceive unconsciously but conscious perception will be richer. Thus, the integration view tends to put the function of consciousness towards the left of Figure 6.9.

And what does the evidence say? With not enough evidence to draw firm conclusions, we leave you to draw your own – and invite you to read the revised version of this chapter in 10 years' time to find the answer!

Future directions

Research into conscious versus unconscious processes is an increasingly active area, involving researchers from disciplines from neuroscience to social psychology. Multidisciplinary work is in progress motivated by both main approaches to consciousness (integration and higher order theories). A key issue for integration theories is refining measures of how the brain jointly integrates and differentiates information. Current work on such measures is proving promising in distinguishing between different levels of consciousness (e.g. Fecchio et al., 2015), although difficulties remain in putting the various measures into practice and properly testing them. Can we come up with measures that would indicate when an unresponsive or paralysed person is still having conscious mental states? Or measures that would indicate when a baby is conscious? Or an animal? A key issue for higher-order theories is also developing better ways of measuring mental states about mental states, so as to ascertain which animals can have higher-order thoughts (e.g. Couchman, Beran, Coutinho, Boomer, & Smith, 2012) or when mental states are conscious or unconscious (Sherman, Barrett, & Kanai, 2015). Current developments in neuroscience (under the name of 'the Bayesian brain' or 'predictive coding') are modelling the way the brain works in terms of predictions or expectations from the centre forming the basis of perceptions (Clark, 2016; Seth, 2014). Such models involve feedback loops (top-down and back again; or perhaps, better phrased, inside from the centre out and back again) of the sort that could potentially link to higher-order, integration, or re-entry theories of consciousness. Work still needs to be done on understanding the neural bases of both integration and higher-order states (which, we speculate, will involve understanding how those processes involve the Bayesian brain). Once we begin to understand the physiological processes underlying consciousness, both in terms of well-integrated first-order states and the higher-order states about them, implementing those processes in artificial intelligence should prove a useful test bed of theories.

SECTION SUMMARY

- There remains a debate concerning what, if anything, is the function of consciousness.
- One answer is that whatever can be done consciously can be done unconsciously because first-order content is effective in itself, so consciousness has no function.
- Another answer is that consciousness appears to be involved in effective integration and differentiation of information and so is essential for complex tasks.
- Further work is needed to establish the function of consciousness, and this may help to illuminate the possible role of consciousness in animals and AI devices.

CHAPTER SUMMARY

This chapter has considered how we can define the notion of consciousness. We did this by first outlining the major theories of consciousness: higher-order theories and integration theories. We then moved on to a consideration of the evidence for unconscious mental states. We started by examining unconscious memory and the role it plays in perception, liking, and controlling our behaviour. We moved on to explore subliminal perception and how it can shed light on attention, advertising, the neural correlates of consciousness, and control. We then discussed implicit learning and concluded with a consideration of how intentions, desires, and emotions can be unconscious and the impact of this on theories about the function of consciousness.

ESSAY QUESTIONS

1. What would count as evidence for subliminal perception in integration theories of consciousness? How strong is such evidence for subliminal perception?

2. What role do unconscious processes play in learning?

3. Advanced (for final-year students): Consider the findings in an empirical paper published in the journals *Consciousness and Cognition*, *Frontiers in Psychology: Consciousness Research*, *Neuroscience of Consciousness*, or *Psychology of Consciousness: Theory, Research, and Practice* that establish whether a mental state is conscious or unconscious, and discuss how these findings would be explained by (a) a higher-order theory of consciousness and (b) a global integration theory of consciousness.

KEY TERMS

- **anchoring effect:** A form of irrational priming in which people given a number, for any reason, subsequently bias their estimates of a quantity (date, price, temperature, etc.) towards the given number.
- **artificial grammar learning:** A method of exploring implicit learning in the lab inspired by natural language as a prominent everyday case of acquiring unconscious knowledge. An artificial grammar is a set of rules for sequencing items.
- **backward masking:** A technique in which a masking stimulus is shown very shortly after the target stimulus; the mask may interfere with conscious processing so that the resulting perception is subliminal.
- **blindsight:** People with blindsight have had damage (usually due to a stroke) to a part of their visual cortex called V1, the first area of the cortex that visual information reaches. They consider themselves blind in that part of their visual field but can be persuaded to guess about the properties of objects in their blind field.
- **conscious content:** What a conscious mental state is about. For example, if you consciously feel an itch, the conscious content is the itching.
- **consciousness level:** The degree of consciousness you have, from the lowest level of being in a coma though sleep to being fully alert and having a rich, complex experience.
- **content:** What a mental state is about. For example, if you are thinking about unicorns, the content is unicorns.
- **continuous flash suppression:** A method for allowing a subliminal stimulus to be displayed for considerably longer than 100 ms, relying on the phenomenon of binocular rivalry to keep one image suppressed.
- **creature consciousness:** A term introduced by the New York philosopher David Rosenthal, corresponding roughly to one everyday definition of consciousness, namely that 'the creature' (or person) is awake and responsive to the world, rather than asleep or knocked out.
- **gaze-contingent crowding (GCC):** A method for exploring subliminal perception that relies on the fact that stimuli in the periphery can be processed unconsciously.
- **global workspace:** A processing space that makes all information within it available to any processor that might use that information. That is, the contents of the workspace are broadcast globally to be used in any way the system knows how.
- **higher-order thoughts (HOTs):** A thought that asserts that you have a (lower-order) mental state, thereby making you aware of having that mental state. The higher-order thought 'I see the grass is yellow' makes you aware of seeing that 'the grass is yellow'.

- **ideomotor action:** The effect of imagination on movement.
- **implicit learning:** A term coined by Arthur Reber in 1967 to describe the acquisition of unconscious knowledge about the structure of the environment.
- **information integration:** A process by which various elements of a system (e.g. neurons in the brain) come to share information, thereby unifying the processing that all the elements do. In a system complex enough to support consciousness, elements will both share information and contribute their own unique information.
- **mere exposure effect:** A term coined by Zajonc (1968, 1980) that refers to how exposure to a novel stimulus can lead people to like it more.
- **neural correlates of consciousness:** Processes in the brain that are correlated with conscious awareness.
- **objective measures:** Measures that involve asking a person to discriminate what state the world is in. See also **subjective measures**.
- **objective threshold:** The point where people are objectively at chance.
- **priming:** An increase in accuracy or speed in performing a task because the stimulus has been presented before.
- **process dissociation procedure (PDP):** A procedure first outlined by Jacoby, Toth, Lindsay, and Debner (1992) that attempts to separate consciously controlled and automatic processes by asking participants either to choose the same response as would be automatically produced or to choose the opposite response as would be automatically produced. The question is the degree to which people can overcome their automatic habits.
- **re-entrant processing:** A theory of conscious content that says that a mental state becomes conscious when it elicits a wave of 'feedback' or 're-entrant' neural processing (Lamme, 2010).
- **serial reaction time task:** A structured reaction time task designed to investigate the expression of implicit knowledge in the timing of motor responses.
- **stimulus onset asynchrony (SOA):** In empirical research exploring conscious versus unconscious perception, the SOA is the time from the beginning of the target to the beginning of the pattern mask. Typically measured in milliseconds (thousandths of a second), the critical SOA is different for different people.
- **subjective measures:** Measures that involve a person determining what mental state they are in. See also **objective measures**.
- **subjective threshold:** The point at which a person believes that they are performing at chance.

NOTES

1. http://www.zoltandienes.com/math-games
2. http://www.cam.ac.uk/research/news/unconscious-language-learning
3. https://hypnosisandsuggestion.org//

FURTHER RESOURCES

Articles on disorders of consciousness

Bayne, T., & Hohwy, J. (2013). Global disorders of consciousness. *Wiley Interdisciplinary Reviews: Cognitive Science, 5*(2), 129–138.

Bell, V., Oakley, D. A., Halligan, P. W., & Deeley, Q. (2011). Dissociation in hysteria and hypnosis: Evidence from cognitive neuroscience. *Journal of Neurology, Neurosurgery & Psychiatry, 82*, 332–339.

Prominent research groups in consciousness science

Association for the Scientific Study of Consciousness. (2017). Retrieved 20 November 2017 from http://theassc.org

Azrieli Programme in Brain, Mind and Consciousness. (2017). Retrieved 20 November 2017 from https://www.cifar.ca/research/brain-mind-consciousness

Centre for Sleep and Consciousness, University of Wisconsin, Madison. (2017). Retrieved 20 November 2017 from http://centerforsleepandconsciousness.med.wisc.edu

Cognitive Neuroimaging Lab. (2017). Retrieved 20 November 2017 from http://www.unicog.org

Consciousness and Metacognition Lab, University of California, Los Angeles. (2017). Retrieved 20 November 2017 from https://sites.google.com/view/hakwan-lau-lab

Disorders of Consciousness Lab, Western University, Ontario. (2017). Retrieved 20 November 2017 from http://www.owenlab.uwo.ca

Sackler Centre for Consciousness Science, University of Sussex. (2017). Retrieved 20 November 2017 from http://www.sussex.ac.uk/sackler

Other resources on consciousness

Bayne, T., Cleeremans, A., & Wilken, P. (Eds.). (2009). *Oxford companion to consciousness*. Oxford, UK: Oxford University Press.

Category: Consciousness. (2017). *Scholarpedia*. Retrieved 20 November 2017 from http://www.scholarpedia.org/article/Category:Consciousness

Clark, A. (2013). Whatever next? Predictive brains, situated agents, and the future of cognitive science. *Behavioral and Brain Sciences*, *36*(3), 181–204.

Consciousness: The what, why and how. (2017). *New Scientist*. Retrieved 20 November 2017 from http://www.newscientist.com/special/consciousness

Dienes, Z. (2012). Conscious versus unconscious learning of structure. In P. Rebuschat & J. Williams (Eds.), *Statistical learning and language acquisition* (pp. 337–364). Boston, MA: Mouton de Gruyter.

Dienes, Z. (2012). Is hypnotic responding the strategic relinquishment of metacognition? In M. Beran, J. L. Brandl, J. Perner, & J. Proust (Eds.), *The foundations of metacognition* (pp. 267–278). Oxford, UK: Oxford University Press.

Dienes, Z., & Seth, A. (2010). The conscious and the unconscious. In G. Koob, R. F. Thompson, & M. Le Moal (Eds.), *Encyclopedia of behavioral neuroscience* (pp. 322–327). Amsterdam, Netherlands: Elsevier.

Jacoby, L. L., Toth, J. P., Lindsay, D. S., & Debner, J. A. (1992). Lectures for a layperson: Methods for revealing unconscious processes. In R. F. Bornstein & T. S. Pittman (Eds.), *Perception without awareness: Cognitive, clinical, and social perspectives* (pp. 81–120). New York, NY: Guilford Press.

Koch, C., Massimini, M., Boly, M., & Tononi, G. (2016). Neural correlates of consciousness: Progress and problems. *Nature Reviews: Neuroscience*, *17*(5), 307–321.

Merikle, P. (2007). Preconscious processing. In M. Velmans & S. Schneider (Eds.), *The Blackwell companion to consciousness* (pp. 512–524). Oxford, UK: Blackwell.

Neurobanter. (2014–). Retrieved 20 November 2017 from http://www.neurobanter.com

Oakley, D. A., & Halligan, P. W. (2013). Hypnotic suggestion: Opportunities for cognitive neuroscience. *Nature Reviews Neuroscience*, *14*, 565–576. doi:10.1038/nrn3538

Seth, A. K. (2009). Functions of consciousness. In W. P. Banks (Ed.), *Encyclopedia of consciousness* (Vol. 1, pp. 279–293). Amsterdam, Netherlands: Elsevier.

Seth, A. K. (2016). The real problem. *Aeon*. Retrieved 9 March 2018 from https://aeon.co/essays/the-hard-problem-of-consciousness-is-a-distraction-from-the-real-one

Seth, A. K. (2017). The fall and rise of consciousness science. In A. Haag (Ed.), *The return of consciousness* (pp. 13–41). Riga, Latvia: Ax:son Johnson Foundation.

Shanks, D. R. (2005). Implicit learning. In K. Lamberts & R. Goldstone (Eds.), *Handbook of cognition* (pp. 202–220). London, UK: SAGE.

Tibboel, H., De Houwer, J., & Van Bockstaele, B. (2015). Implicit measures of 'wanting' and 'liking' in humans. *Neuroscience and Biobehavioral Reviews, 57,* 350–364.

Velmans, M., & Schneider, S. (Eds.). (2007). *The Blackwell companion to consciousness.* Oxford, UK: Blackwell.

Zelazo, P. D., Moscovitch, M., & Thompson, E. (Eds.). (2007). *The Cambridge handbook of consciousness.* Cambridge, UK: Cambridge University Press.

Zeman, A. (2004). *Consciousness: A user's guide.* New Haven, CT: Yale University Press.

REFERENCES

Adams, H. E., Wright, L. W., Jr., & Lohr, B. A. (1996). Is homophobia associated with homosexual arousal? *Journal of Abnormal Psychology, 105*(3), 440–445.

Ariely, D., Loewenstein, G., & Prelec, D. (2003). Coherent arbitrariness: Stable demand curves without stable preferences. *Quarterly Journal of Economics, 118*(1), 73–105.

Armstrong, A. M., & Dienes, Z. (2013). Subliminal understanding of negation: Unconscious control by subliminal processing of word pairs. *Consciousness and Cognition, 22*(3), 1022–1040.

Aru, J., Bachmann, T., Singer, W., & Melloni, L. (2012). Distilling the neural correlates of consciousness. *Neuroscience & Biobehavioral Reviews, 36,* 737–746.

Arzi, A., Shedlesky, L., Ben-Shaul, M., Nasser, K., Oksenberg, A., Hairston, L. S., & Sobel, N. (2012). Humans can learn new information during sleep. *Nature Neuroscience, 15,* 1460–1465.

Atas, A., Faivre, N., Timmermans, B., Cleeremans, A., & Kouider, S. (2014). Nonconscious learning from crowded sequences. *Psychological Science, 25,* 113–119.

Baars, B. (1988). *A cognitive theory of consciousness.* Cambridge, UK: Cambridge University Press.

Banaji, M. R., & Greenwald, A. G. (2013). *Blindspot: Hidden biases of good people.* New York, NY: Delacorte Press.

Banyai, E. I., & Hilgard, E. R. (1976). A comparison of active-alert hypnotic induction with traditional relaxation induction. *Journal of Abnormal Psychology, 85*(2), 218–224.

Bargh, J. A., Chen, M., & Burrows, L. (1996). Automaticity of social behavior: Direct effect of trait construct and stereotype activation on action. *Journal of Personality and Social Psychology, 71,* 230–244.

Bargh, J. A., Schwader, K. L., Hailey, S. E., Dyer, R. L., & Boothby, E. J. (2012). Automaticity in social-cognitive processes. *Trends in Cognitive Science, 16*(12), 593–605.

Barrett, L. F., Niedenthal, P. M., & Winkielman, P. (Eds.). (2005). *Emotion and consciousness.* London, UK: Guilford Press.

Begg, I. M., Anas, A., & Farinacci, S. (1992). Dissociation of processes in belief: Source recollection, statement familiarity, and the illusion of truth. *Journal of Experimental Psychology: General, 121,* 446–458.

Benham, G., Woody, Z., Wilson, K. S., & Nash, M. R. (2006). Expect the unexpected: Ability, attitude, and responsiveness to hypnosis. *Journal of Personality and Social Psychology, 91,* 342–350.

Berridge, K. C., & Robinson, T. E. (1995). The mind of an addicted brain: Neural sensitization of wanting versus liking. *Current Directions in Psychological Science, 4*(3), 71–76.

Block, N. (2011). Perceptual consciousness overflows cognitive access. *Trends in Cognitive Sciences, 12,* 567–575.

Bojinov, H., Sanchez, D., Reber, P., Boneh, D., & Lincoln, P. (2014). Neuroscience meets cryptography: Crypto primitives secure against rubber hose attacks. *Communications of the ACM*, *57*(5), 110–118.

Bornstein, R. F., & D'Agostino, P. R. (1992). Stimulus recognition and the mere exposure effect. *Journal of Personality and Social Psychology*, *63*, 545–552.

Brown, A. S., & Murphy, D. A. (1989). Cryptomnesia: Delineating inadvertent plagiarism. *Journal of Experimental Psychology: Learning, Memory, and Cognition*, *15*, 432–442.

Carruthers, P. (2000). *Phenomenal consciousness: A naturalistic theory*. Cambridge, UK: Cambridge University Press.

Casali, A. G., Gosseries, O., Rosanova, M., Boly, M., Sarasso, S., Casali, K. R, … Massimini, M. (2013). A theoretically based index of consciousness independent of sensory processing and behavior. *Science Translational Medicine*, *5*(198), 198ra105. doi:10.1126/scitranslmed.3006294

Cheesman, J., & Merikle, P. M. (1984). Priming with and without awareness. *Perception & Psychophysics*, *36*, 387–395.

Cheesman, J., & Merikle. P. M. (1986). Distinguishing conscious from unconscious perceptual processes. *Canadian Journal of Psychology*, *40*, 343–367.

Chen, J. (2013). Josh Chen's brain talk 04: Two streams. *YouTube*. Retrieved 20 November 2017 from https://www.youtube.com/watch?v=y8j0MQfGtjE

Chen, W., Guo, X., Tang, J., Zhu, L., Yang, Z., & Dienes, Z. (2011). Unconscious structural knowledge of form–meaning connections. *Consciousness and Cognition*, *20*, 1751–1760.

Chomsky, N. (1957). *Syntactic structures*. The Hague, Netherlands: Mouton.

Clark, A. (2016). *Surfing uncertainty: Prediction, action, and the embodied mind*. Oxford, UK: Oxford University Press.

Couchman, J. J., Beran, M. J. Coutinho, M. V. C., Boomer, J., & Smith, J. D. (2012). Evidence for animal metaminds. In M. Beran, J. L. Brandl, J. Perner, & J. Proust (Eds.), *The foundations of metacognition* (pp. 21–35). Oxford, UK: Oxford University Press.

Critcher, C. R., & Gilovich, T. (2008). Incidental environmental anchors. *Journal of Behavioral Decision Making*, *21*, 241–251.

de Gardelle, V., Sackur, J., & Kouider, S. (2009). Perceptual illusions in brief visual presentations. *Consciousness and Cognition*, *18*, 569–577.

de Graaf, T. A., Hsieh, P. J., & Sack, A. T. (2012). The 'correlates' in neural correlates of consciousness. *Neuroscience & Biobehavioral Reviews*, *36*, 191–197.

Deeprose, C., & Andrade, J. (2006). Is priming during anesthesia unconscious? *Consciousness and Cognition*, *15*(1), 1–23.

Dehaene, S., & Changeux, J.-P. (2011). Experimental and theoretical approaches to conscious processing. *Neuron*, *70*(2), 200–227.

Dehaene, S., Changeux, J.-P., & Naccache, L. (2011). The global neuronal workspace model of conscious access: From neuronal architectures to clinical applications. In S. Dehaene & Y. Christen (Eds.), *Characterizing consciousness: From cognition to the clinic* (pp. 55–84). Dordrecht, Germany: Springer.

Dehaene, S., Naccache, L., Cohen, L., LeBihan, D., Mangin, J. F., Poline, J. B., & Riviere, D. (2001). Cerebral mechanisms of word masking and unconscious repetition priming. *Nature Neuroscience*, *4*, 752–758.

Dennett, D. C. (1992). *Consciousness explained*. New York, NY: Back Bay Books.

Destrebecqz, A., & Cleeremans, A. (2001). Can sequence learning be implicit? New evidence with the process dissociation procedure. *Psychonomic Bulletin & Review*, *8*, 343–350.

Dienes, Z. (2008a). Subjective measures of unconscious knowledge. *Progress in Brain Research*, *168*, 49–64.

Dienes, Z. (2008b). *Understanding psychology as a science: An introduction to scientific and statistical inference*. New York, NY: Palgrave Macmillan

Dienes, Z. (2015a). Hypnosis 1: Is hypnosis real? *YouTube*, 19 March. Retrieved 15 January 2018 from https://www.youtube.com/watch?v=URkCTcUGocY

Dienes, Z. (2015b). Hypnosis 2: Hypnosis as an altered state. *YouTube*, 19 March. Retrieved 15 January 2018 from https://www.youtube.com/watch?v=nBcKmct0I0E&t=18s

Dienes, Z. (2015c). Hypnosis 3: Hypnosis in a historical and clinical context. *YouTube*, 22 March. Retrieved 15 January 2018 from https://www.youtube.com/watch?v=NaEhDGGb_4c&t=18s

Dienes, Z. (2015d). Hypnosis 4: Memory enhancement and suggestibility. *YouTube*, 6 May. Retrieved 15 January 2018 from https://www.youtube.com/watch?v=tBPdxG3uAnA&t=13s

Dienes, Z. (2015e). Theories of hypnosis. *YouTube*, 24 March. Retrieved 15 January 2018 from https://www.youtube.com/watch?v=juujyu3apqk&t=3s

Dienes, Z. (2015f). Phenomena of hypnosis. *YouTube*, 24 March. Retrieved 15 January 2018 from https://www.youtube.com/watch?v=u429zkKqKyU

Dienes, Z. (2015g). The cold control theory of hypnosis. *YouTube*, 31 March. Retrieved 15 January 2018 from https://www.youtube.com/watch?v=2hYna8LR2Y4

Dienes, Z., & Perner, J. (2007). The cold control theory of hypnosis. In G. Jamieson (Ed.), *Hypnosis and conscious states: The cognitive neuroscience perspective* (pp. 293–314). Oxford, UK: Oxford University Press.

Dienes, Z., & Scott, R. (2005). Measuring unconscious knowledge: Distinguishing structural knowledge and judgment knowledge. *Psychological Research, 69*, 338–351.

Dienes, Z., & Seth, A. (2010). Gambling on the unconscious: A comparison of wagering and confidence ratings as measures of awareness in an artificial grammar task. *Consciousness & Cognition, 19*, 674–681.

Dienes, Z. P. (1960). *Building up mathematics*. London, UK: Hutchinson Educational.

Dienes, Z. P. (1973). *Mathematics through the senses, games, dance, and art*. Windsor, UK: NFER Publishing.

Dijksterhuis, A., & Van Knippenberg, A. (1998). The relation between perception and behavior, or how to win a game of *Trivial Pursuit*. *Journal of Personality and Social Psychology, 74*(4), 865–877.

Doyen, S., Klein, O., Pichon, C.-L., & Cleeremans, A. (2012). Behavioral priming: It's all in the mind, but whose mind? *PLoS ONE 7* (1), e29081. doi:10.1371/journal.pone.0029081

Dulany, D. E. (1963). The place of hypotheses and intentions: An analysis of verbal control in verbal conditioning. In C. W. Eriksen (Ed.), *Behaviour and awareness: A symposium of research and interpretation* (pp. 102–129). Duke University Press.

Dulany, D. E. (1991). Conscious representation and thought systems. In R. S. Wyer and T. K. Srull (Eds.), *Advances in social cognition* (pp. 91–120). Hillsdale, NJ: Lawrence Erlbaum Associates.

Explorable.com. (2010). Choice blindness. Retrieved 20 November 2017 from https://explorable.com/choice-blindness

Faivre, N., Berthet, V., & Kouider, S. (2012). Nonconscious influences from emotional faces: A comparison of visual crowding, masking, and continuous flash suppression. *Frontiers in Psychology, 3*, 129.

Fecchio, M., Casarotto, S., Trimarchi, P. D., Casali, A. G., Landi, C., Pigorini, A., … Massimini, M. (2015). Reliability of the perturbational complexity index in discriminating chronic patients with disorders of consciousness. *Clinical Neurophysiology, 126*(1), e1–e2.

Festinger, L. (1957). *A theory of cognitive dissonance*. Stanford, CA: Stanford University Press.

Fischman, M. W., & Foltin, R. W. (1992). Self-administration of cocaine by humans: A laboratory perspective. In G. R. Bock & J. Whelan (Eds.), *Cocaine: Scientific and social dimensions* (pp. 165–180). Chichester, UK: Wiley.

Fox, K. (2004). *Watching the English: The hidden rules of English behaviour*. London, UK: Hodder & Stoughton.

Fu, Q., Dienes, Z., & Fu, X. (2010). Can unconscious knowledge allow control in sequence learning? *Consciousness and Cognition, 19*, 462–475.

Gallwey, T. (1974). *The inner game of tennis*. London, UK: Pan/Cape.

Gawronski, B., & Bodenhausen, G. V. (2006). Associative and propositional processes in evaluation: An integrative review of implicit and explicit attitude change. *Psychological Bulletin, 132*, 692–731.

Goodale, M. A., & Milner, A. D. (1992). Separate visual pathways for perception and action. *Trends in Neurosciences, 15*(1), 20–25.

Goodale, M. A., & Milner, A. D. (2013). *Sight unseen* (2nd ed.). Oxford, UK: Oxford University Press.

Greenspoon, J. (1955). The reinforcing effect of two spoken sounds on the frequency of two responses. *American Journal of Psychology, 68*, 409–416.

Greenwald, A. G., Spangenberg, E. R., Pratkanis, A. R., & Eskenazi, J. (1991). Double blind tests of subliminal self-help audiotapes. *Psychological Science, 2*, 119–122.

Guo, X., Zheng, L., Zhu, L., Yang, Z., Chen, C., Zhang, L., Ma, W., & Dienes, Z. (2011). Acquisition of conscious and unconscious knowledge of semantic prosody. *Consciousness and Cognition, 20*, 417–425.

Hahn, A., Judd, C. M., Hirsh, H. K., & Blair, I. V. (2014). Awareness of implicit attitudes. *Journal of Experimental Psychology: General, 143*, 1369–1392.

Hall, L., Johansson, P., Tärning, B., Sikström, S., & Deutgen, T. (2010). Magic at the marketplace: Choice blindness for the taste of jam and the smell of tea. *Cognition, 117*, 54–61.

Hall, L., Strandberg, T., Pärnamets, P., Lind, A., Tärning, B., & Johansson, P. (2013). How the polls can be both spot on and dead wrong: Using choice blindness to shift political attitudes and voter intentions. *PLoS ONE, 8*(4), e60554. doi:10.1371/journal.pone.0060554

Hayes, S. M., Fortier, C. B., Levine, A., Milberg, W. P., & McGlinchey, R. (2012). Implicit memory in Korsakoff's syndrome: A review of procedural learning and priming studies. *Neuropsychology Review, 22*(2), 132–153.

Hesselmann, G., Hebart, M., & Malach, R. (2011). Differential BOLD activity associated with subjective and objective reports during 'blindsight' in normal observers. *Journal of Neuroscience, 31*(36), 12936–12944.

Hilgard, E. R. (1977). *Divided consciousness: Multiple controls in human thought and action*. New York, NY: Wiley-Interscience.

Hogarth, L., & Duka, T. (2006). Human nicotine conditioning requires explicit contingency knowledge: Is addictive behaviour cognitively mediated? *Psychopharmacology, 184*, 553–566.

Hohwy, J. (2013). *The predictive mind*. Oxford, UK: Oxford University Press.

Hovland, C. I., & Weiss, W. (1951). The influence of source credibility on communication effectiveness. *Public Opinion Quarterly, 15*(4), 635–650.

Iselin-Chaves, I. A., Willems, S. J., Jermann, F. C., Forster, A., Adam, S., & Van der Linden, M. (2005). Investigation of implicit memory during isoflurane anesthesia for elective surgery using the process dissociation procedure. *Anesthesiology, 103*, 925–933.

Jacoby, L. L. (1991). A process dissociation framework: Separating automatic from intentional uses of memory. *Journal of Memory and Language, 30*, 513–541.

Jacoby, L. L. (2009). Memory, process–dissociation procedure. In T. Bayne, A. Cleeremans, & P. Wilken (Eds.), *The Oxford companion to consciousness* (pp. 430–432). Oxford, UK: Oxford University Press.

Jacoby, L. L., Allan, L. G., Collins, J. C., & Larwill, L. K. (1988). Memory influences subjective experience: Noise judgments. *Journal of Experimental Psychology: Learning, Memory, and Cognition, 14*, 240–247.

Jacoby, L. L., Toth, J. P., Lindsay, D. S., & Debner, J. A. (1992). Lectures for a layperson: Methods for revealing unconscious processes. In R. Bornstein & T. S. Pittman (Eds.), *Perception without awareness: Cognitive, clinical, and social perspectives* (pp. 81–120). New York, NY: Guilford Press.

Jiang, Y., Costello, P., Fang, F., Huang, M., & He, S. (2006). A gender- and sexual orientation-dependent spatial attentional effect of invisible images. *Proceedings of the National Academy of Sciences of the United States of America, 103*(45), 17048–17052.

Johansson, P., Hall, L., Sikström, S., & Olsson, A. (2005). Failure to detect mismatches between intention and outcome in a simple decision task. *Science, 310*(5745), 116–119.

Karremans, J. C., Stroebe, W., & Claus, J. (2006). Beyond Vicary's fantasies: The impact of subliminal priming and brand choice. *Journal of Experimental Social Psychology, 42*, 792–798.

Kinnunen, T., Zamansky, H. S., & Block, M. L. (1994). Is the hypnotized subject lying? *Journal of Abnormal Psychology, 103*(2), 184–191.

Kirsch, I. (1985). Response expectancy as a determinant of experience and behaviour. *American Psychologist, 40*, 1189–1202.

Kirsch, I., Montgomery, G., & Sapirstein, G. (1995). Hypnosis as an adjunct to cognitive-behavioral psychotherapy: A meta-analysis. *Journal of Consulting and Clinical Psychology, 63*, 214–220.

Kirsch, I., Silva, C. E., Carone, J. E., Johnstone, J. D., & Simon, B. (1989). The surreptitious observer design: An experimental paradigm for distinguishing artifact from essence in hypnosis. *Journal of Abnormal Psychology, 98*(2), 132–136.

Klein, S. (1987). *The effects of modern mathematics*. Budapest, Hungary: Akadémiai Kiadó.

Koch, C., & Tsuchiya, N. (2006). Attention and consciousness: Two distinct brain processes. *Trends in Cognitive Sciences, 11*, 16–22.

Kolb, F. C., & Braun, J. (1995). Blindsight in normal observers. *Nature, 377*, 336–338.

Kouider, S., Andrillon, T., Barbosa, L. S., Goupil, L., & Bekinschtein, T. A. (2014). Inducing task-relevant responses to speech in the sleeping brain. *Current Biology, 24*(18), 2208–2214.

Kunst-Wilson, W., & Zajonc, R. (1980). Affective discrimination of stimuli that cannot be recognized. *Science, 207*(4430), 557–558.

Lamb, R. J., Preston, K. L., Schindler, C. W., Meisch, R. A., Davis, F., Katz, J. L., Henningfield, J. E., & Goldberg, S. R. (1991). The reinforcing and subjective effects of morphine in post-addicts: A dose-response study. *Journal of Pharmacology and Experimental Therapeutics, 259*, 1165–1173.

Lamme, V. A. F. (2010). How neuroscience will change our view on consciousness. *Cognitive Neuroscience, 1*(3), 204–240.

Lau, H. C., & Passingham, R. E. (2006). Relative blindsight in normal observers and the neural correlate of visual consciousness. *Proceedings of the National Academy of Sciences of the United States of America, 103*(49), 18763–18768.

Lau, H. C., & Rosenthal, D. (2011). Empirical support for higher-order theories of conscious awareness. *Trends in Cognitive Sciences, 15*, 365–373.

Laurence, J. R., & Perry, C. (1983). Hypnotically created memory among highly hypnotizable subjects. *Science, 222*(4623), 523–524.

Leung, J., & Williams, J. N. (2011). The implicit learning of mappings between forms and contextually-derived meanings. *Studies in Second Language Acquisition, 33*, 33–55.

Lewis, I. M. (2003). *Ecstatic religion: A study of shamanism and spirit possession* (3rd ed.). London, UK: Routledge.

Lieberman, M. D., Ochsner, K. N., Gilbert, D. T., & Schacter, D. L. (2001). Do amnesics exhibit cognitive dissonance reduction? The role of explicit memory and attention in attitude change. *Psychological Science, 12*, 135–140.

Lifshitz, M., Aubert-Bonn, N., Fischer, H., Kashem, I. F., & Raz, A. (2013). Using suggestion to modulate automatic processes: From Stroop to McGurk and beyond. *Cortex, 49*(2), 463–473.

Loftus, E. F., & Ketcham, K. (1994). *The myth of repressed memory*. New York, NY: St. Martin's Press.

Loftus, E. F., & Pickrell, J. E. (1995). The formation of false memories. *Psychiatric Annals, 25*, 720–725.

Lovibond, P. F., & Shanks, D. R. (2002). The role of awareness in Pavlovian conditioning: Empirical evidence and theoretical implications. *Journal of Experimental Psychology: Animal Behavior Processes, 28*, 3–26.

Lynn, S. J., & Kirsch, I. (2006). *Essentials of clinical hypnosis: An evidence-based approach (dissociation, trauma, memory, and hypnosis)*. Washington, DC: American Psychological Association.

Lynott, D., Corker, K. S., Wortman, J., Connell, L., Donnellan, M. B., Lucas, R. E., & O'Brien, K. (2014). Replication of 'Experiencing physical warmth promotes interpersonal warmth' by Williams and Bargh (2008). *Social Psychology, 45*(3), 216–222.

Marin-Garcia, E., Ruiz-Vargas, J. M., & Kapur, N. (2013). Mere exposure effect can be elicited in transient global amnesia. *Journal of Clinical and Experimental Neuropsychology, 35*(10), 1007–1014.

Marsh, R. L., Landau, J. D., & Hicks, J. L. (1997). Contributions of inadequate source monitoring to unconscious plagiarism during idea generation. *Journal of Experimental Psychology: Learning, Memory, and Cognition, 23*, 886–897.

Massimini, M., Ferrarelli, F., Huber, R., Esser, S. K., Singh, H., & Tononi, G. (2005). Breakdown of cortical effective connectivity during sleep. *Science, 309*, 2228–2232.

Masters, R. S. W., & Maxwell, J. P. (2008). The theory of reinvestment. *International Review of Sport and Exercise Psychology, 1*, 160–183.

Masters, R. S. W., Maxwell, J. P., & Eves, F. F. (2009). Marginally perceptible outcome feedback, motor learning and implicit processes. *Consciousness and Cognition, 18*, 639–645.

Maxwell, J. P., Masters, R. S. W., & Eves, F. F. (2003). The role of working memory in motor learning and performance. *Consciousness and Cognition, 12*, 376–402.

McLeod, P., & Dienes, Z. (1993). Running to catch the ball. *Nature, 362*, 23.

McLeod, P., & Dienes, Z. (1996). Do fielders know where to go to catch the ball, or only how to get there? *Journal of Experimental Psychology: Human Perception and Performance, 22*, 531–543.

Merikle, P. M. (1992). Perception without awareness: Critical issues. *American Psychologist, 47*, 792–795.

Merikle, P. M., & Joordens, S. (1997). Parallels between perception without attention and perception without awareness. *Consciousness and Cognition, 6*, 219–236.

Moreland, R. L., & Beach, S. R. (1992). Exposure effects in the classroom: The development of affinity among students. *Journal of Experimental Social Psychology, 28*, 255–276.

Naccache, L., Gaillard, R., Adam, C., Hasboun, D., Clémenceau, S., Baulac, M., Dehaene, S., & Cohen, L. (2005). A direct intracranial record of emotions evoked by subliminal words. *Proceedings of the National Academy of Sciences of the United States of America, 102*(21), 7713–7717.

Newell, B. R., & Shanks, D. R. (2006). Recognising what you like: Examining the relation between the mere-exposure effect and recognition. *European Journal of Cognitive Psychology, 19*(1), 103–118.

Newell, B. R., & Shanks, D. R. (2014). Prime numbers: Anchoring and its implications for theories of behavior priming. *Social Cognition, 32*, 88–108.

Nissen, M. J., & Bullermer, P. (1987). Attentional requirements of learning: Evidence from performance measures. *Cognitive Psychology, 19*, 1–32.

Oakley, D. A., & Halligan, P. W. (2013). Hypnotic suggestion: Opportunities for cognitive neuroscience. *Nature Reviews Neuroscience, 14*, 565–576.

Orne, M. T., Sheehan, P. W., & Evans, F. J. (1968). Occurrence of posthypnotic behavior outside the experimental setting. *Journal of Personality and Social Psychology, 9*, 189–196.

Overgaard, M., Lindeløv, J., Svejstrup, S., Døssing, M., Hvid, T., Kauffmann, O., & Mouridsen, K. (2013). Is conscious stimulus identification dependent on knowledge of the perceptual modality? Testing the 'source misidentification hypothesis'. *Frontiers in Psychology, 4*, 116.

Pashler, H., Coburn, N., & Harris, C. (2012). Priming of social distance? Failure to replicate effects on social and food judgements. *PLoS ONE, 7*(8), e42510.

Perruchet, P. (1985). A pitfall for the expectancy theory of human eyelid conditioning. *Pavlovian Journal of Biological Science, 20*(4), 163–170.

Perruchet, P., & Amorim, M. A. (1992). Conscious knowledge and changes in performance in sequence learning: Evidence against dissociation. *Journal of Experimental Psychology: Learning, Memory, and Cognition, 18*(4), 785–800.

Persaud, N., & McLeod, P. (2008). Wagering demonstrates subconscious processing in a binary exclusion task. *Consciousness and Cognition, 17*(3), 565–575.

Poincare, H. (1913). *The foundations of science*. New York, NY: Science House.

Popova, M. (n.d.). The psychology of cryptomnesia: How we unconsciously plagiarize existing ideas. *Brain Pickings*. Retrieved 20 November 2017 from https://www.brainpickings. org/2014/09/26/cryptomnesia-psychology-of-writing

Raio, C. M., Carmel, D., Carrasco, M., & Phelps, E. (2012). Nonconscious fear is quickly acquired but swiftly forgotten. *Current Biology, 22*, R495–R496.

Reber, A. S. (1967). Implicit learning of artificial grammars. *Journal of Verbal Learning and Verbal Behavior, 6*, 317–327.

Reber, A. S. (1989). Implicit learning and tacit knowledge. *Journal of Experimental Psychology: General, 118*(3), 219–235.

Reber, A. S., Kassin S. M., Lewis S., & Cantor G. (1980). On the relationship between implicit and explicit modes in the learning of a complex rule structure. *Journal of Experimental Psychology: Human Learning and Memory, 6*, 492–502.

Rebuschat, P., & Williams, J. N. (2012). Implicit and explicit knowledge in second language acquisition. *Studies in Second Language Acquisition, 33*, 829–856.

Reed, N., McLeod, P., & Dienes, Z. (2010). Implicit knowledge and motor skill: What people who know how to catch don't know. *Consciousness and Cognition, 19*, 63–76.

Rosenthal, D. M. (2005). *Consciousness and mind*. Oxford, UK: Oxford University Press.

Sætrevik, B., Reber, R., & Sannum, P. (2006). The utility of implicit learning in the teaching of rules. *Learning and Instruction, 16*(4), 363–373.

Seth, A. K. (2009). Functions of consciousness. In W. P. Banks (Ed.), *Encyclopedia of consciousness* (Vol. *1*, pp. 279–293). Amsterdam, Netherlands: Elsevier.

Seth, A. K. (2014). A predictive processing theory of sensorimotor contingencies: Explaining the puzzle of perceptual presence and its absence in synaesthesia. *Cognitive Neuroscience, 5*(2), 97–118.

Seth, A. K., Barrett, A. B., & Barnett, L. C. (2011). Causal density and integrated information as measures of conscious level. *Philosophical Transactions of the Royal Society A: Mathematical, Physical and Engineering Sciences, 369*(1952), 3748–3767.

Shanks, D. R., Newell, B. R., Lee, E. H., Balakrishnan, D., Ekelund, L., Cenac, Z., … Moore, C. (2013). Priming intelligent behavior: An elusive phenomenon. *PLoS ONE, 8*(4), e56515.

Sherman, M. T., Barrett, A. B., & Kanai, R. (2015). Inferences about consciousness using subjective reports of confidence. In M. Overgaard (Ed.), *Behavioural methods in consciousness research* (pp. 87–106). Oxford, UK: Oxford University Press.

Simmons, J. P., LeBoeuf, R. A., & Nelson, L. D. (2010). The effect of accuracy motivation on anchoring and adjustment: Do people adjust from provided anchors? *Journal of Personality and Social Psychology, 99*, 917–932.

Spanos, N. (1986). Hypnotic behaviour: A social–psychological interpretation of amnesia, analgesia, and 'trance logic'. *Behavioural and Brain Sciences, 9*, 449–502.

Spanos, N. P., Menary, E., Brett, P. J., Cross, W., & Ahmed, Q. (1987). Failure of posthypnotic responding to occur outside the experimental setting. *Journal of Abnormal Psychology, 96*(1), 52–57.

Sperling, G. (1960). Negative afterimage without prior positive image. *Science, 131*, 1613–1614.

Sriraman, B. (Ed.). (2008). *Mathematics education and the legacy of Zoltan Paul Dienes*. Charlotte, NC: Information Age.

Stark, L.-J., & Perfect, T. J. (2007). Whose idea was that? Source monitoring for idea ownership following elaboration. *Memory, 15*(7), 776–783.

Stottinger, E., & Perner, J. (2006). Dissociating size representation for action and for conscious judgment: Grasping visual illusions without apparent obstacles. *Consciousness and Cognition, 15*, 269–284.

Szpunar, K. K., Schellenberg, E. G., & Pliner, P. (2004). Liking and memory for musical stimuli as a function of exposure. *Journal of Experimental Psychology: Learning, Memory, and Cognition, 30*(2), 370–381.

Tavris, C., & Aronson, E. (2007). *Mistakes were made (but not by me): Why we justify foolish beliefs, bad decisions, and hurtful acts*. New York, NY: Houghton Mifflin Harcourt.

Tong, E. M. W., Tan, D. H., & Tan, Y. L. (2013). Can implicit appraisal concepts produce emotion-specific effects? A focus on unfairness and anger. *Consciousness and Cognition, 22*, 449–460.

Tononi, G. (2008). Consciousness as integrated information: A provisional manifesto. *Biological Bulletin, 215*, 216–242.

Tononi, G., & Edelman, G. M. (1998). Consciousness and complexity. *Science, 282*, 1846–1851.

Tsuchiya, N., & Koch, C. (2005). Continuous flash suppression reduces negative afterimages. *Nature Neuroscience, 8*, 1096–1101.

Tversky, A., & Kahneman, D. (1974). Judgment under uncertainty: Heuristics and biases. *Science, 185*, 1124–1130.

Van Gaal, S., de Lange, F. P., & Cohen, M. X. (2012). The role of consciousness in cognitive control and decision making. *Frontiers in Human Neuroscience, 6*, 121. doi:10.3389/fnhum.2012.00121

Wan, L. L., Dienes, Z., & Fu, X. L. (2008). Intentional control based on familiarity in artificial grammar learning. *Consciousness and Cognition, 17*, 1209–1218.

Ward, N. S., Oakley, D. A., Frackowiak, R. S. J., & Halligan, P. W. (2003). Differential brain activations during intentionally simulated and subjectively experienced paralysis. *Cognitive Neuropsychiatry, 8*, 295–312.

Wardle, J., Herrera, M.-L., Cooke, L., & Gibson, E. L. (2003). Modifying children's food preferences: The effects of exposure and reward on acceptance of an unfamiliar vegetable. *European Journal of Clinical Nutrition, 57*, 341–348.

Warrington, E. K., & Weiskrantz, L. (1974). The effect of prior learning on subsequent retention in amnesic patients. *Neuropsychologia, 12*, 419–428.

Wegner, D. M. (2002). *The illusion of conscious will*. Cambridge, MA: MIT Press.

Weiskrantz, L. (1997). *Consciousness lost and found: A neuropsychological exploration*. Oxford, UK: Oxford University Press.

Whitwell, R., & Buckingham, G. (2013). Reframing the action and perception dissociation in DF: Haptics matters, but how? *Journal of Neurophysiology, 109*, 621–624.

Williams, L. E., & Bargh, J. A. (2008a). Experiencing physical warmth promotes interpersonal warmth. *Science, 322*, 606–607.

Williams, L. E., & Bargh, J. A. (2008b). Keeping one's distance: The influence of spatial distance cues on affect and evaluation. *Psychological Science, 19*, 302–308.

Willmarth, E. (2012). Willmarth hypnosis interviews: Irving Kirsch, Ph.D. *YouTube*. Retrieved 20 November 2017 from https://www.youtube.com/watch?v=BJHgtYTzimQ

Winkielman, P., Berridge, K. C., & Sher, S. (2011). Emotion, consciousness and social behavior. In J. Decety & J. Cacioppo (Eds.), *The Oxford handbook of social neuroscience* (pp. 195–211). Oxford, UK: Oxford University Press.

Winkielman, P., Berridge, K. C., & Wilbarger, J. (2005). Unconscious affective reactions to masked happy versus angry faces influence consumption behavior and judgments of value. *Personality and Social Psychology Bulletin, 1*, 121–135.

Wood, J. M., Bootzin, R. R., Kihlstrom, J. F., & Schacter, D. L. (1992). Implicit and explicit memory for verbal information presented during sleep. *Psychological Science, 3*(4), 236–239.

Woody, E., & Sadler, P. (2008). Dissociation theories of hypnosis. In M. Nash & A. Barnier (Eds.), *The Oxford handbook of hypnosis: Theory, research, and practice* (pp. 81–110). Oxford, UK: Oxford University Press.

Yapko, M. D. (1994). Suggestibility and repressed memories of abuse: A survey of psychotherapists' beliefs. *American Journal of Clinical Hypnosis, 36*(3), 163–171.

Zajonc, R. B. (1968). Attitudinal effects of mere exposure. *Journal of Personality and Social Psychology Monographs, 9*(2, Pt. 2), 1–27.

Zajonc, R. B. (1980). Feeling and thinking: Preferences need no inferences. *American Psychologist, 35*(2), 151–175.

7 Sensation and Perception

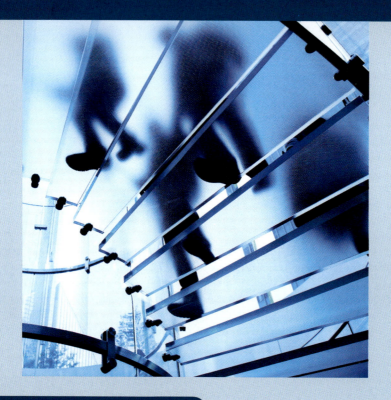

ROUTE MAP OF THE CHAPTER

Research on sensation and perception studies how we acquire, process, and apprehend information from the world around us. Sensations correspond to elementary conscious experiences of sensory stimuli, such as the brightness of a camera flash or the spiciness of a chilli pepper. Perceptions are structured, meaningful understandings of things and events. At a rock festival, for example, you may *sense* the loudness of the amplified sound, the brightness of the spotlights circling the audience, and the wetness of the rain. But you also *perceive* the actions of the band members and the music they are playing. This chapter summarizes our current understanding of how sensations and perceptions are created from the constant barrage of information that arrives at our sense organs. The study of sensation and perception draws on concepts, techniques, and findings across a broad range of scientific fields, so the material in the chapter will help you to appreciate the distinctive contributions that each field makes to our knowledge.

INTRODUCTION   325

THE NEUROSCIENCE OF SENSATION AND PERCEPTION   333

SENSORY QUALIA AND MODALITY   340

AUDITION   347

VISION: PHYSIOLOGY   354

VISION: PERCEIVING OBJECT PROPERTIES   360

MULTIMODAL PERCEPTION   366

FUTURE DIRECTIONS   372

CHAPTER SUMMARY   375

INTRODUCTION

LEARNING OBJECTIVE 7.1

Demonstrate an understanding of the various scientific approaches to studying sensation and perception.

In this section, we introduce some basic principles that underpin the study of sensation and perception. Perception seems easy: when we open our eyes, we see things around us, provided that there is adequate illumination; when a person within earshot speaks, we hear their voice. The apparent simplicity and immediacy of perception hide exquisitely complex processes in the brain that mediate between the various forms of energy arriving from the environment and our understanding of things and events. Clinical cases of brain damage reveal the importance of these processes for normal perceptual functioning. For example, Pallis (1955) reported the case of a man who had a specific difficulty in recognizing faces. The man described his problem as follows:

> I can see the eyes, nose, and mouth quite clearly but they just don't add up. They all seem chalked in, like on a blackboard. I have to tell by the clothes or voice whether it is a man or woman, as the faces are all neutral, a dirty grey colour. The hair may help a lot, or if there is a moustache. All the men appear unshaved. I cannot recognize people in photographs, not even myself. At the club I saw someone strange staring at me and asked the steward who it was. You'll laugh at me. I'd been looking at myself in a mirror. I later went to London and visited several cinemas and theatres. I couldn't make head or tail of the plots. I never knew who was who. (Pallis, 1955, p. 219; reproduced with permission from BMJ Publishing Group Ltd.)

The man had suffered damage to the parts of his brain that specialize in processing faces, caused by a stroke (cerebral embolism) that starved those areas of oxygen. (More about face perception can be found later on in Focus Point 7.5, on social perception.) Rare cases such as this provide dramatic demonstrations of the intimate relationship between brain function and perception. The brain decomposes the sensory world into myriad specific qualities that are processed by separate populations of cells. Damage to a specific population of cells can cause highly selective losses in sensory or perceptual function. Apart from clinical case studies of the consequences of brain injury, a range of other techniques has been used to throw light on how we perceive the world.

Figure 7.1 illustrates the three key elements of perception and the techniques that can be used to study the relationships between them. The process of perception begins with external stimuli arriving at specialized receptor neurons in the nervous system (Box 1). Humans are receptive to a wide range of stimuli, including electromagnetic energy (light), air pressure waves (sound), gravity and acceleration (balance), and

Psychology, First Edition. Edited by Graham Davey.
© 2019 John Wiley & Sons, Ltd. Published 2019 by John Wiley & Sons, Ltd.

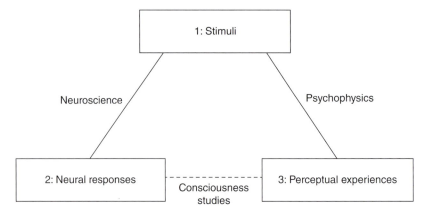

FIGURE 7.1 *The three key elements of perception. External stimuli (Box 1) generate neural responses (Box 2), which lead to perceptual experiences (Box 3). Neuroscience studies the relationship between stimuli and neural responses, while psychophysics studies the relationship between psychological events (perceptions) and physical stimuli. The nature of the relationship between neural activity and perception is still mysterious (dashed line).*

chemical composition (taste and smell). Receptor neurons convert all of these different kinds of energy into the common currency used for all exchanges of information in the nervous system, namely electrical activity (Box 2). This neural activity leads to sensory and perceptual experiences about properties of the external world (Box 3).

Approaches to research in sensation and perception

The relationships between the elements of perception (the lines joining the boxes in Figure 7.1) have been studied for the best part of 200 years. **Psychophysics** focuses on the link between physical stimuli and perception, whereas neuroscience centres on the relationship between stimuli and neural responses. The next two sections will briefly introduce these two approaches to studying perception, and later sections will outline some of the advances that they have made possible. Before moving on, it is worth dwelling briefly on the relationship between neural activity and perception. Notice that the line between these two elements in Figure 7.1 is dashed to indicate that, although almost every researcher accepts that there is a relationship between brain activity and conscious perceptual experiences, there is no agreed account of how the link works or why it exists at all, and there is still some doubt about the proper methods to study it.

Psychophysical methods

Psychophysical research studies the relationship between psychological events (sensations and perceptions) and physical stimuli (light, sound, gravitational force, and so on). The experimental methods employed in psychophysical research were first developed by Ernst Weber and Gustav Fechner at Leipzig University in the middle of the 19th century. Weber carried out experiments to measure the perception of weights held in the hand. He observed that, in order for a participant to reliably judge a 'comparison' weight as heavier than another 'standard' weight (a **just-noticeable difference [JND]**), a fixed amount had to be added to the standard weight. Moreover, when different standard weights were tested, Weber discovered that the added weight had to be a constant fraction of the standard weight. For example, if the JND for a standard weight of 1,000 g was found to be 50 g, then the JND for a standard weight of 2,000 g would be 100 g. So the JND for weight was 1/20. Later observations of a wide range of sensory discriminations, such as brightness and loudness, showed that the JND is nearly always a constant fraction of the standard stimulus (with the value of the constant varying across sensory modalities). This rule became known as Weber's law, and the constant JND became known as Weber's fraction. Fechner extended Weber's findings and identified another law of perception, now known as Fechner's law, that defines how our perception of the magnitude of a sensory stimulus depends on its physical intensity. It follows from Weber's law that, as physical stimulus intensity increases, larger changes are required for an observer to just detect the change; sensory magnitude increases as a nonlinear function of stimulus intensity, as illustrated in Figure 7.2. The equally spaced intervals on the vertical axis indicate equal sensory increments (JNDs), which correspond to unequal increments in stimulus intensity.

Weber's and Fechner's discoveries had a profound impact on the new science of experimental psychology, because they demonstrated for the first time that a highly lawful and consistent relationship exists between mental events and the physical world, at least in terms of relatively simple sensory phenomena such as heaviness, brightness, loudness, and so on. In 1860, Fechner described several 'psychophysical' methods (see Fechner, 1860/1966) that experimenters could use to measure the relationship between sensory stimuli and perceptual responses (in other words, to measure JNDs). In the following 150 years, these methods have been refined and extended to improve their reliability and sensitivity (see Research Methods 7.1).

A huge body of research has grown, furnishing data on many relationships between sensory stimulation and experience, usually based on measuring JNDs. A fundamental working hypothesis in this research is that, when two stimuli produce discriminably different sensations, they *must* produce different patterns of neural activity in the sensory system. Because this kind of hypothesis links together Boxes 2 and 3 in

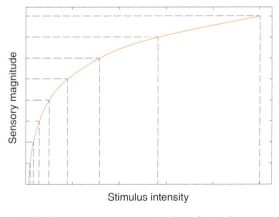

FIGURE 7.2 *The relationship between sensory magnitude and stimulus magnitude is nonlinear. Equal changes in perceived magnitude, shown by the dashed horizontal lines intersecting the vertical axis, correspond to very unequal changes in stimulus intensity; progressively larger physical changes are needed at higher intensities.*

Figure 7.1, it is widely known as a 'psychophysical linking hypothesis'. If we accept such a hypothesis, then the converse must also be true: sufficiently different patterns of neural activity *must* produce discriminably different sensations. This is the theoretical basis for psychophysics, because it means that psychophysical data can be used to draw inferences about underlying neural processes. Although psychophysicists rely heavily on linking hypotheses, they generally do not concern themselves much with how and why the link exists, which is the domain of consciousness research.

RESEARCH METHODS 7.1

SIGNAL DETECTION THEORY

The main text describes a fundamental metric in psychophysical experiments known as the just-noticeable difference, or JND. The JND represents the dividing line or threshold between two sensory experiences, such as 'same' versus 'different' in the example of judging two weights. When the difference between two weights is below the JND, they are judged as the same; when the difference is above the JND, they are judged as different. Unfortunately, the reality of measuring thresholds is more complicated than this. If the difference in stimulus weight (or any other stimulus quantity) is varied in small increments, the observer's response never flicks like a switch from 'same' to 'different' at a certain stimulus level. Instead there is a gradual decrease in 'same' responses and a corresponding increase in 'different' responses over a range of stimulus levels. A graph that plots the percentage of 'different' responses as a function of stimulus level is known as a psychometric function. Since there is no sudden switch in response, what stimulus level can be taken as the threshold or JND? The convention is to take the stimulus level at which the observer is equally disposed towards reporting 'same' and 'different' (i.e. the threshold between mostly saying 'same' and mostly saying 'different'), which corresponds to the 50% point of the psychometric function. Signal detection theory (SDT) offers a framework for understanding why observer responses are so variable and a set of measurement techniques to measure discrimination ability in the face of this variability.

The theory divides the observer's task into two processing stages. In the first stage, a neural response to the stimulus is generated by the sensory system. This response is not constant but fluctuates due to moment-to-moment variations that are nothing to do with the stimulus but reflect variability in the electrical excitability and chemical properties of neurons (internal 'noise'). The second stage is a decision process that compares the magnitude of the neural response to an internally set criterion; if the response exceeds the criterion, then the observer's decision goes one way ('different'); however, if it falls below the criterion, the decision goes the other way ('same'). So observer decisions are influenced both by sensory factors and by decision factors. The observer's criterion can be biased by all sorts of factors that include both the properties of the sensory stimulus and factors such as memory, confidence, cooperativeness, fatigue, expectation, and so on. SDT provides procedures for measuring the observer's ability to discriminate between stimuli, known as d-prime (d'), and their bias, known as beta (β). Note that these two measures cannot distinguish sensory biases from decisional biases (Witt, Taylor, Sugovic, & Wixted, 2015).

To minimize the possible contribution of certain factors to SDT measures, many experimenters use a procedure known as a two-alternative forced-choice task. The observer is given two stimulus intervals, one containing the signal to be detected (e.g. a difference in weight) and the other containing no signal (no difference in weight), and must select the interval that contained the signal. The interval containing the signal varies randomly, of course, and when the observer cannot detect the signal they must resort to guessing (they are not allowed to respond 'don't know'), so the psychometric function varies from 50% (chance) to 100% correct detection. The percentage of correct responses at each stimulus level can be taken as a convenient measure of the observer's ability to discriminate stimuli at that stimulus level.

DISCUSSION POINT

Watch this experiment[1] by Marcus Cheetham and Lutz Jancke of the University of Zurich. Think about ideas for other experiments where using the forced-choice method might be valuable, and discuss.

Neurosciences

The neurosciences are a loosely defined set of scientific disciplines concerned with the scientific study of the nervous system. Two particular disciplines, cognitive neuroscience and computational neuroscience, are fundamentally important for our understanding of sensation and perception.

Cognitive neuroscience focuses on the parts of the nervous system that are involved in cognition, broadly defined to include sensation, perception, learning, memory, attention, language, decision making, and motor control. The discipline has its roots in 19th-century discoveries about the localization of cognitive functions in the brain. Just as in the case of the man described earlier who had lost his ability to recognize faces, many other specific cognitive functions can be compromised by brain injury. One of the earliest discoveries concerned speech deficits following damage to an area of the left frontal lobe of the cortex now known as Broca's speech area.

In the early 20th century, attention began to shift away from examining the function of large brain areas. Researchers became more interested in the structure and function of individual brain cells. Newly developed anatomical staining techniques revealed the structure of single neurons, and later advances in recording techniques allowed neuroscientists to pick up the electrical responses of individual neurons. By the 1950s, researchers such as Horace Barlow at the University of Cambridge and Stephen Kuffler at Johns Hopkins University were able to record the activity of individual neurons in the eye of an awake anaesthetized cat in response to small spots of light. David Hubel and Torsten Weisel extended the technique to record activity in the animal's visual cortex. They discovered (Hubel & Wiesel, 1959) that cortical cells were highly selective for the kinds of visual stimuli to which they responded. For example, some cells only responded to the presence of small lines in just the right part of the visual field, at the correct size and orientation. These discoveries led to theories of perception and recognition based on 'detectors' in the brain that were tuned to respond to simple features such as bars. The idea was that visual objects could be stored and recognized in the brain as collections of features, each of which was initially encoded by a feature detector of the kind described by Hubel and Wiesel (1959).

In the latter half of the 20th century, the focus of neuroscientific research shifted back from microscopic details of single neurons towards the larger-scale structures first identified in the 19th century via clinical cases. The shift was brought about by the advent of **neuroimaging** and neurostimulation techniques, which were first developed as tools for medical diagnosis. Research Methods 7.2 gives a brief description of the most widely used techniques. Each provides particular insights into the brain regions and neural populations associated with specific aspects of sensation and perception.

NEUROIMAGING AND NEUROSTIMULATION

A range of new neuroscientific techniques have been developed over the past 50 years or so for use in therapeutic contexts, as aids for medical diagnosis, or to treat brain dysfunctions. Most of the techniques are noninvasive in that they do not require unpleasant or risky surgical procedures, so neuroscientists have adopted them as scientific techniques that can shed new light on human cognition.

NEUROIMAGING

Neuroimaging techniques can build a highly detailed 3D representation of the structure and function of the living human brain, even while its host is receiving sensory stimuli. Brain scanners usually take the form of a small tunnel just large enough for an experimental participant to lie in. The inner surface of the tunnel contains a ring of emitters and detectors. The emitters send a signal of some kind through the participant's body, and this is picked up by the detectors. Signals pass through the body in many different directions, and sophisticated software builds a picture of the internal structure and function of the body from the signal patterns recorded by the detectors. Computed tomography (CT scanning) was the earliest technique to be developed, and is based on X-rays. CT scans are used to diagnose a wide variety of conditions that alter bodily structure, such as tumours, haemorrhages, and fractures. Some CT scanners can also detect gamma rays emitted by a radioactive tracer ingested by the patient.

Magnetic resonance imaging (MRI) and functional magnetic resonance imaging (fMRI) detect changes in the magnetic properties of molecules in the body, by picking up radio wave signals from hydrogen atoms excited by a strong magnetic field. fMRI scanners can detect changes in neural activity in the brain (the physical correlate of perception), because they pick up changes in blood oxygenation that accompany neural activity (oxygen is the energy source for neural firing). Current fMRI scanners can localize variations in response over a region as small as one millimetre in diameter.

Neuroimaging experiments typically involve comparing brain images produced via different tasks or stimuli, in order to infer the brain structures and pathways activated differentially by them.

NEUROSTIMULATION

Neurostimulation techniques have been developed to stimulate a specific area of the human brain while the experimental participant is performing a sensory or perceptual task. In transcranial magnetic stimulation (TMS), a brief, powerful magnetic pulse is directed at a brain region in an attempt to interfere with the ongoing activity of neurons in that region (Barker, Jalinous, & Freeston, 1985). If the region is important for performing the task, then the participant's data should be affected by the TMS.

Transcranial direct current stimulation (tDCS) uses small electrodes to deliver a low-level current directly to a region of the brain (Utz, Dimova, Oppenländer, & Kerkhoff, 2010). Therapeutically, tDCS has been proven to have beneficial effects for sufferers of Parkinson's disease, tinnitus, and stroke-related motor deficits. It can also be used in a scientific context; tDCS is administered while the experimental participant is performing a cognitive task. As in the case of TMS, the assumption is that, if the relevant brain region is involved in the task, the stimulation will alter performance, either improving or impairing it.

In **this TED Talk**[2] from 2008, neuroscientist and inventor Christopher deCharms demonstrates a new way to use fMRI to show brain activity.

The years since the 1980s have also seen rapid growth in the field of computational neuroscience. The general goal of this discipline in the context of perception is to explain in computational terms how the brain generates perceptions. The concept of computation is useful not just in the more familiar context of mathematical calculations. In an abstract logical sense, *any* process that involves the manipulation of quantities or symbols according to a set of formal rules can be described as a 'computation'. Neurons in the nervous system receive electrical signals from other neurons and produce signals of their own in response, based on a set of well-defined rules governing neural interactions (excitation, inhibition, and so on). So individual neurons and ensembles of neurons can be considered as computational devices. For example, the response of many sensory cells in the nervous system depends on the balance between their excitatory and inhibitory inputs. When excitation exceeds inhibition, a given cell's activity (firing rate) increases; when inhibition exceeds excitation, activity decreases. In an abstract sense, the cell computes the sum of all the excitatory (positive) and inhibitory (negative) signals it receives.

This view of neural processing has its origins in early models of neural function (Hodgkin & Huxley, 1952), but the emergence of the field of computational neuroscience is largely attributed to David Marr's book *Vision* (1982), which outlined a computational framework for theories of visual perception. Marr criticized theories of perception that were inspired directly by neuroscientific discoveries, such as the feature detector theory of object recognition outlined earlier (Hubel & Wiesel, 1959). Neuroscience certainly tells us about the neural structures that are involved in perception, but this information alone is not sufficient for a full understanding of the process. Marr argued that:

> trying to understand perception by studying only neurons is like trying to understand bird flight by studying only feathers: It just cannot be done. In order to understand bird flight, we have to understand aerodynamics; only then do the structure of feathers and the different shapes of birds' wings make sense. (Marr, 1982, p. 27)

Marr argued that theories of perception must consider what information is required for the task in hand, and why this information is useful, in abstract computational terms. Any attempt to build a model of object recognition using individual 'feature-detecting' neurons is, according to Marr, bound to fail. Objects are not just collections of prototypical features. Moreover, an individual neuron in the cortex cannot function as a feature detector because, although its response is quite selective, it is not uniquely driven by one specific feature, such as a line having a specific size, orientation, and position. Each cell responds to a range of features, such as a range of orientations and sizes. More sophisticated models are required, as will be discussed later. The general point is that an adequate theory of sensation and perception should give due consideration to the computational task being performed by the brain. Computational neuroscience thus aims to understand the computations performed by the known neural structures. On the one hand, computational considerations can guide thinking and experimentation in cognitive neuroscience and psychophysics. On the other hand, properties of the neural structures place fundamental constraints on the computations that can be performed. As you will see later on, computational considerations play an important role in enumerating the sensory systems. But for the moment it is important to start with some of the basic facts of sensory neuroscience.

ACTIVITY 7.1

TRUE OR FALSE?

Indicate whether each statement is true or false.

- JND stands for juxtaposed natural difference.
- Psychophysics focuses on the link between physical stimuli and perception.
- Neuroscience centres on the relationship between stimuli and neural responses.
- The rule that the JND is nearly always a constant fraction of the standard stimulus is known as Fechner's law.
- Psychophysical research studies the relationship between psychological events and physical stimuli.
- Hubel and Wiesel (1959) discovered that cortical cells are broadly indiscriminate in the kinds of visual stimuli to which they respond.
- One of the earliest neuroscientific discoveries concerned speech deficits following damage to an area of the left frontal lobe of the cortex now known as Wernicke's speech area.
- Computed tomography is a brain-scanning technique based on X-rays.
- fMRI scanners can detect changes in neural activity in the brain because they pick up changes in blood oxygenation that accompany neural activity.
- A graph that plots the percentage of 'different' responses as a function of stimulus level is known as a psychotropic function.

SECTION SUMMARY

- The apparent simplicity and immediacy of perception hide exquisitely complex processes in the brain that mediate between the various forms of energy arriving from the environment and our understanding of things and events.

- The process of perception begins with external stimuli arriving at specialized receptor neurons in the nervous system. Humans are receptive to a wide range of stimuli, including light, sound, gravity, taste, and smell. Receptor neurons convert all of these kinds of stimuli into electrical activity.

- Psychophysical research studies the relationship between psychological events and physical stimuli. The experimental methods employed in psychophysical research were first developed by Ernst Weber and Gustav Fechner at Leipzig University in the middle of the 19th century.

- Cognitive neuroscience studies the neural structures and processes that serve sensation and perception. Techniques used include clinical case studies, electrical recordings of neurons, neuroimaging, and neurostimulation.

- Computational neuroscience aims to study these neural processes at an abstract computational and mathematical level.

- The emergence of the field of computational neuroscience is largely attributed to David Marr's book *Vision* (1982).

THE NEUROSCIENCE OF SENSATION AND PERCEPTION

LEARNING OBJECTIVE 7.2

Describe the major neural structures involved in human sensation and perception.

Sensory receptors

As mentioned earlier, receptor neurons convert energy arriving at the sense organs from the environment into neural signals. The human nervous system relies on just four types of receptor for all its sensory information. The most ancient and ubiquitous form of receptor is the **mechanoreceptor**, which responds to tissue distortion. The sense of touch is based on five varieties of mechanoreceptor, distributed all over the body just under the skin; they respond to pressure, stretch, and vibration applied to the skin's surface. Sensations of joint position, body movement, and balance also rely on mechanoreceptors. Other animals also possess more exotic sensory receptors. Birds, for example, have receptors that sense the earth's magnetic field (magnetoreceptors).

Perhaps more surprising is the fact that both hearing and balance are also mechanical senses that rely on very similar mechanoreceptors. The inner ear is a series of bony, fluid-filled chambers in the skull. Some chambers contain mechanoreceptors responsible for the sense of balance and others contain the receptors responsible for hearing. In both cases the receptors possess tiny hair-like filaments (stereocilia) that protrude into the fluid. Movement of the fluid caused either by head movements or by fluctuations in air pressure (sounds) deflect the stereocilia and so trigger neural responses. Some of the chambers that house the balance (vestibular) receptors form circular canals that are well suited to detect head rotation. The chamber housing auditory receptors, known as the **cochlea**, is spiral shaped rather than circular, which avoids inadvertent stimulation during head rotation. The receptors are exquisitely sensitive: a displacement of the stereocilia of just 0.3 nanometres (billionths of a metre) – equivalent to the diameters of atoms – is sufficient to produce an auditory sensation.

Vision is served by **photoreceptor** cells in the eye, which each contain light-sensitive pigment molecules. When light strikes these molecules it usually initiates a cascade of biochemical events in the cell that alters its electrical state. The entire process takes just a few milliseconds (thousandths of a second). Human vision can cope with an extremely wide range of light levels; bright daylight is 10 million times more intense than starlight. Such a wide dynamic range is achieved using two different classes of photoreceptor, known as cones and rods. Cones mediate vision between sunrise and dusk, while rods allow us to see in the hours of darkness, at least while there is some light provided by the moon or stars.

Both taste and smell are based on **chemoreceptors**, which respond to chemicals in foodstuffs or carried on the air. However, there are some marked differences between the receptors responsible for taste and smell. There are only five types of taste receptor in the mouth and throat, and these respond selectively to five types of substance: sugars, salts, acids, plant alkaloids, and amino acids. In contrast, there are several hundred types of olfactory receptor in the nasal cavity, and these act as molecule counters for particular kinds of chemical.

The fourth and final type of sensory receptor is the **nociceptor**. These neurons do not have a specialized receptor process but have a 'free nerve ending'. They are spread throughout the body; in the skin, in the oral and nasal cavities, in the eyes, and so on – in fact, in any part of the body that is likely to come into contact with external stimuli (there are none in the brain itself). Nociceptors respond to stimulation that is harmful, such as tissue damage, excessive heat, or high concentrations of certain chemicals. They mediate sensations such as the sting of soap in the eyes, the tingle or burn of chilli in the mouth (or in the eyes after chopping chilli), and the ache felt in tired muscles.

Sensory pathways

You may be wondering why we do not confuse head rotations with sounds, or smells with tastes, given that the sensory receptors mediating these different sensations are so similar, and often so close to each other in the body. The answer lies in the neural processing that occurs after the receptors, in terms of the separation of the fibres carrying receptor signals to the brain (known as afferent fibres) and in terms of the cortical destinations of these fibres. Table 7.1 lists all the receptor types, identifying the nerve fibres and cortical receiving areas associated with each type.

The thousands of fibres carrying signals from receptors are bundled together into sensory nerves. Each nerve is like a large data cable carrying many individual wires. Fibres from different classes of receptor gather together into different nerves, as shown in Table 7.1. It is important to realize that no sensory fibres travel all the way from the receptors to the cortex, with just one synapse or connection between each receptor cell and a corresponding cortical cell. The relationship between the

TABLE 7.1 *Each sensory quality or modality (column 1) is served by a specific type of receptor (column 2). Different afferent fibres carry the receptor signals towards the brain (column 3), where they are received by specialized areas of the cerebral cortex (column 4).*

Modality	Receptor type	Afferent path	Cortex
Balance	Mechano-	Vestibulocochlear nerve, vestibular division	Posterior parietal operculum
Hearing	Mechano-	Vestibulocochlear nerve, cochlear division	Heschl's gyrus
Pain	Noci-	Spinothalamic tract, trigeminal nerve	Primary somatosensory cortex
Smell	Chemo-	Olfactory nerve	Primary olfactory cortex
Taste	Chemo-	Facial, glossopharyngeal, vagus nerves	Primary gustatory cortex
Touch	Mechano-	Lemniscal tract, trigeminal nerve	Primary somatosensory cortex
Vision	Photo-	Optic nerve	Striate cortex

number of receptors and the number of sensory fibres in each nerve varies considerably between the senses. In the case of vision, for example, there are about 130 million photoreceptors in each eye, but only about 1 million optic nerve fibres. In hearing, on the other hand, there are only about 3,500 inner hair cells but 50,000 auditory nerve fibres. So, in vision, many photoreceptors converge onto each optic nerve fibre, but in hearing many auditory nerve fibres converge onto each hair cell. The marked differences in anatomy relate to the different computational tasks performed by the neural structures.

Signals travelling along the sensory pathways to the brain pass through several relaying synapses en route. In all except one of the pathways, the route includes a synapse in a structure known as the **thalamus**, sited in the middle of the brain just above the brainstem. The thalamus contains several large masses of cell bodies that regulate the flow of information around the brain (the thalamus receives extensive projections from the cortex itself). The olfactory pathway is the only one that does not have a synapse in the thalamus, so signals in this modality reach the cortex without the moderating influence of its gatekeeper.

Sensory cortex

Different afferent nerves generally terminate in their own specialized areas of the cortex, known as primary or receiving areas. The only exception is that touch mechanoreceptors and nociceptors terminate in the same cortical area. Figure 7.3 shows the locations of the receiving areas in the left hemisphere of the cortex, with the lateral view on the left and the medial view on the right.

Each primary sensory area makes extensive bidirectional connections to other areas of the cortex involved in sensation and perception, which are known collectively as secondary or association areas. For instance, most of the rear half of the cortex is the secondary visual cortex. Many areas of association cortex retain the specialization of the associated receiving area, such as vision or hearing. But some areas are multisensory in that signals from various sensory systems converge on them.

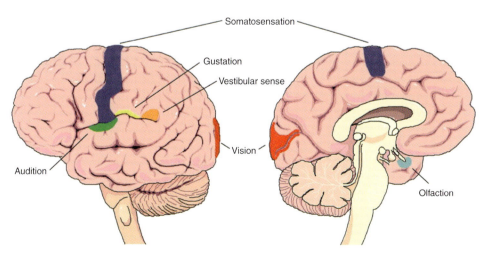

FIGURE 7.3 *Human cortical areas devoted to receiving sensory signals. Information from receptors in each sensory modality arrives at its own specialized receiving area in the cortex.*

For example, the flavour of food is based on an interaction between signals carrying the taste, smell, temperature, touch, sight, sound, and pain of food. An area of the orbitofrontal cortex seems to be involved in processing flavour.

Stimulus tuning in sensory neurons

In all the sensory modalities, individual cortical neurons show a high degree of specialization, in that each cell responds only to a narrow range of stimuli. For example, a specific neuron in the somatosensory cortex may fire strongly only when a very particular part of the body surface is touched. The area may be only a few millimetres in diameter, on a finger or the lips, and it defines the 'receptive field' of the cell. Different cells respond to touch in different body areas; in other words, their receptive fields are at different locations on the body. Selectivity in neural tuning is found for many different stimulus dimensions.

Figure 7.4a shows the tuning of four cells in the visual cortex to the width of stimulus bars in a grating pattern (alternating dark and light bars; the repetition rate of the alternation between dark and light bars is called the 'spatial frequency' of the grating). The left-most (solid) curve represents the tuning of a cell that responds best only to gratings with relatively wide bars (low spatial frequencies). The right-most (dashed) curve shows that another cell responds only to very narrow bars (high spatial frequencies). The bottom graph shows the tuning of 10 cells in the auditory thalamus to the time of arrival of sounds at one ear relative to the other. Sounds that arrive first at the ear on the left side of the head are plotted as having negative time values on the x-axis, and sounds arriving at the right ear first are plotted as having positive times. The left-most cell in the graph responds only to sounds that arrive at the left ear first, whereas the right-most cell responds only to sounds that arrive at the right ear first. Cells in the middle of the plot prefer sounds that arrive at the two ears simultaneously. As described in detail later, sounds that emanate from a source located to the left of the head arrive at the left ear slightly before the right ear (and vice versa for sound sources on the right). So, the cells plotted in Figure 7.4b are in effect tuned to the direction in space from which sounds emanate. Some cells respond to sounds arriving from the left of the head, others to sounds arriving from the right.

Sensory neurons respond more strongly to more intense stimuli, at least over a certain intensity range (sound pressure level, mechanical force, light–dark contrast, and so on). Let's return to one of the cells whose tuning is plotted in Figure 7.4a. The three curves in Figure 7.5 show the visual cell's response as a function of grating spatial frequency at three levels of contrast between the dark and bright bars in the pattern (Albrecht & Hamilton, 1982). Consider first the dotted vertical line, which picks out the cell's response to a pattern at a spatial frequency of six cycles per degree. The line shows that the cell responds strongly to a high-contrast grating (top curve) but weakly to a low-contrast grating at this frequency. Now consider the horizontal dotted line, which picks out a specific response level (firing rate). The line crosses the cell's tuning curves at six places, and each intersection represents a different combination of grating frequency and contrast. So, on the basis of this individual cell's response, it is not possible to infer the precise nature of the stimulus. In other words, if we wish to disentangle this pattern's spatial frequency from its contrast, we can say that the cell responds at the same level to many different combinations of spatial frequency and contrast. This example highlights a fundamental principle of neural

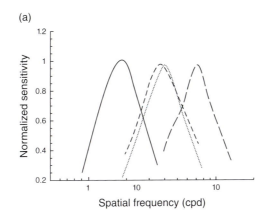

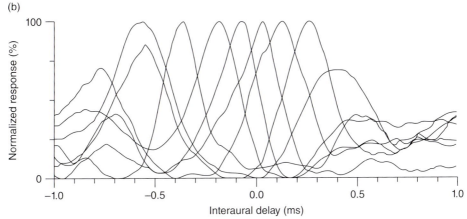

FIGURE 7.4 *Stimulus tuning of sensory neurons in the cortex. (a) Tuning of four cells in the visual cortex to grating patterns of alternating light and dark bars. Each cell responds only to a limited range of bar widths (low frequencies, measured in cycles per degree [cpd], denote wide bars and high frequencies denote narrow bars). (b) The tuning curves of 10 cells in the auditory system to the time of arrival of sounds at the two ears. Some cells respond only when sounds arrive at the left ear first (left of the graph), while others respond only when sounds arrive at the right ear first (right of the graph).*

Source: (a) Based on and reprinted from De Valois, Albrecht, and Thorell (1982), copyright (1982), with permission from Elsevier; (b) Reprinted by permission from Macmillan Publishers Ltd: NATURE. Fitzpatrick, Batra, Stanford, and Kuwada (1997), copyright 1997.

coding known as **univariance**: sensory neurons give only a single output (firing level) so they cannot simultaneously separate out information about different stimulus dimensions (in this case, spatial frequency and contrast). Later on in the chapter, you will read about how the sensory systems get around this limitation in neural coding.

Topographical maps in sensory processing

Topography normally refers to the surface features of an area of terrain, which can be depicted on a map. Each symbol on a map of the terrain specifies a property of the terrain at that location. For example, contour lines specify height above sea level at each location. Neural structures in the sensory systems, such as a layer of cells distributed across the surface of the cortex, or in the thalamus, can be viewed as an area of neural

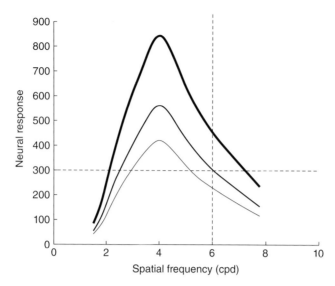

FIGURE 7.5 *The effect of stimulus contrast on the response of one of the visual cells shown in Figure 7.4a. Contrast refers to the difference in luminance between the brighter and darker bars in the grating pattern. The three curves represent response at three contrast levels: high (top curve), medium (middle), and low (bottom). At each grating frequency, such as that shown by the vertical dotted line, the cell responds more strongly at higher contrast than at lower contrast. Many different combinations of frequency (measured in cycles per degree [cpd]) and contrast generate the same level of response; six possible combinations correspond to the intersections of the three curves with the horizontal dotted line.*

'terrain' that can be mapped. Neuroscientists study the tuning properties of individual cells at different locations in the terrain and then create **topographical maps** that summarize how this tuning property is distributed across the surface of the neural structure. The most famous such map shows the distribution of the receptive fields of somatosensory cells across the surface of the somatosensory cortex, as illustrated in Figure 7.6. It shows a sideways cross-section through the right hemisphere of the brain, from the right ear (bottom left) to the top of the head (top right). Cells in the region of cortex near to the top of the head have receptive fields that are located on the legs or feet; they only fire when these body regions are touched. Cells in the region of cortex around the side of the head, near the ear, have receptive fields on the tongue or in the mouth. In fact, the surface of the body is laid out in a very orderly topographical fashion across the surface of the cortex, in terms of receptive field location.

The same general principle applies to many other neural structures in the sensory systems. In the visual cortex, each cell responds only to light arriving at the eyes from a particular region of visual space, known as the cell's visual receptive field, and across the surface of the cortex there is a progressive change in the spatial location of the cells' receptive fields. Many cells in the auditory cortex are selectively tuned to a narrow range of sound frequencies, and there is a progressive change in the preferred sound frequency of cells across successive locations on the cortical surface. Topographical maps are a general feature of sensory processing; neighbouring neurons in a given neural structure have similar, though not identical, stimulus preferences. Close proximity is thought to facilitate interactions between cells that are critical for sensory processing: local interactions can sharpen response selectivity and aid stimulus encoding.

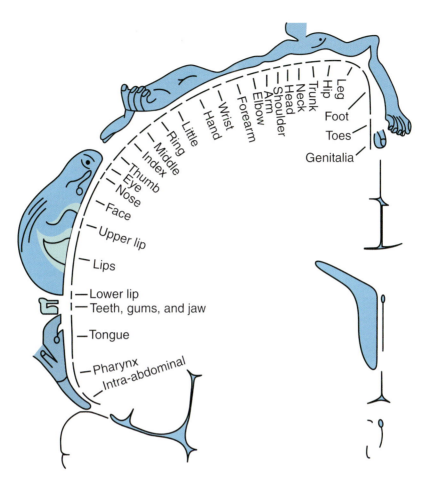

FIGURE 7.6 *A vertical cross-section through the right half of the brain, running sideways from the top of the head (top right) to the right ear (bottom left). This strip of cortex contains cells that respond to tactile stimulation of the body (somatosensory cortex). A topographical map of the body is distributed across the surface of the somatosensory cortex. Each cortical cell responds only to stimulation from a particular region of the body (receptive field of the cell). Neighbouring cells in the cortex respond to neighbouring body regions, and we can build up an entire map of the body across the cortical surface in terms of the receptive field locations of the cells.*

Source: Penfield and Rasmussen (1950). © 1950 Gale, a part of Cengage Learning, Inc. Reproduced by permission. www.cengage.com/permissions.

SECTION SUMMARY

- Receptor neurons convert stimuli arriving at the sense organs from the environment into neural signals. The human nervous system relies on just four types of receptor for all its sensory information: mechanoreceptors, photoreceptors, chemoreceptors, and nociceptors.

- The thousands of fibres that carry signals from receptors are bundled together into sensory nerves, which pass through several relaying synapses en route to the brain. In all except one of the pathways (olfactory), the route includes a synapse in the thalamus, sited in the middle of the brain just above the brainstem.

- Different afferent nerves generally terminate in their own specialized areas of the cortex, known as primary or receiving areas.

- Each primary sensory area makes extensive connections to other areas of the cortex involved in sensation and perception, which are known collectively as secondary or association areas.

- In all the sensory modalities, individual neurons show a high degree of specialization, in that each cell responds only to a narrow range of stimuli. Each neuron also responds more strongly to more intense stimuli than to weaker stimuli, at least over a certain intensity range.

- Neighbouring neurons at each processing site in the brain, such as the thalamus or cortex, tend to have similar though not identical stimulus preferences. So, on a larger scale, the cells are distributed across the neural structure in such a way as to build a map of the sensory domain, such as the surface of the body or locations in visual space.

SENSORY QUALIA AND MODALITY

LEARNING OBJECTIVE 7.3

Describe how sensory qualia are believed to affect conscious mental state, specifically in the areas of olfaction, gustation, somatosensation, and vestibular sense.

Stimulation of sensory receptors usually causes a conscious mental state: awareness of a particular sensory quality, such as colour, loudness, heat, or pressure. These primitive sensory states are known as **qualia**. They are obviously related to the cascade of neural events in the nervous system initiated by the stimulus, though no one has a scientific explanation as to how and why qualia exist. There is a missing link between the physical world (brain states) and the mental world (qualia), as indicated in Figure 7.1. How many sensory modalities do we have? A clear answer to this question lies at the very foundation of the scientific study of perception. For example, investigations into cross-modal interaction and integration in perception are a major focus of contemporary research (discussed later), but they are predicated upon assumptions about distinctions between modalities. Qualia seem to offer an answer because they divide up the sensory world into modes of sensation that are qualitatively different. The sensations evoked by light are qualitatively different from those evoked by sounds, smells, tastes, and touches. Sound *feels* different from light or touch. However, as there is no scientific account of qualia, we cannot legitimately use them as a scientific basis for distinguishing sensory modalities. The issue of how to distinguish between sensory modalities is discussed in Focus Point 7.1.

HOW MANY SENSES DO WE HAVE?

Despite the fundamental nature of this question for the science of sensation and perception, it is given relatively little consideration in the scientific literature. Many textbooks do not even list the sensory modalities. Those that attempt a division usually distinguish six senses, adding the sense of balance to the classic five (seeing, hearing, smelling, tasting, touching). Sometimes the sense of limb position and movement (proprioception) is classed as a separate sense, though it is mostly combined with touch as the 'body sense'. The scientific basis for these divisions is rarely discussed, except perhaps by philosophers (e.g. Gray, 2005; Keeley, 2002). Three particular criteria seem to be important for grouping qualia into different modalities. Each on its own is insufficient for defining a modality, but in combination they can provide a scientific basis for definitions.

1. *Physical* – Different modalities should be based on physically different forms of environmental energy.

2. *Biological* – Different modalities should employ distinct neural pathways in the central nervous system.

3. *Computational* – Different modalities should serve different functions for the organism, and therefore perform different computations.

Table 7.2 evaluates each putative sensory modality in terms of the three criteria. The distinctive *physical* properties of light, sound, mechanical force and motive force certainly allow us to distinguish between vision, audition, somatosensation and the **vestibular sense** respectively. Olfaction and gustation share the same kind of physical stimulus, namely chemical compounds, so there is no basis for classifying them as separate modalities according to this criterion.

TABLE 7.2 *Three criteria for enumerating the sensory modalities: the nature of the physical stimulus, neural pathways, and the computations performed by each system. Vision, audition, olfaction, gustation, and the vestibular sense are clearly distinct modalities. However, given the physical and biological overlap between somatosensation and proprioception, it is appropriate to subsume proprioception under somatosensation, making a grand total of six sensory modalities.*

	Physical	Biology	Computation
Vision	Electromagnetic radiation	Visual pathway	• Visual object segregation, location, and recognition • Self-motion • Scene layout • Orienting
Audition	Air pressure waves	Auditory pathway	• Auditory object segregation, location, and recognition • Orienting • Social communication
Olfaction	Chemical compounds	Olfactory pathway	• Stimulus approach and avoidance • Substance edibility
Gustation	Chemical compounds	Gustatory pathway	• Substance edibility and nutrition

(Continued)

TABLE 7.2 (*Continued*)

	Physical	Biology	Computation
Somatosensation	Mechanical force	Somatosensory pathway	• Haptic object segregation and recognition • Withdrawal • Orienting
Proprioception	Mechanical force	Somatosensory pathway	• Limb position and movement
Vestibular sense	Motive force	Vestibular pathway	• Head position and acceleration • Visual stability • Body posture and equilibrium

Proprioception does not have an external stimulus at all. The source of stimulation is inside the body, in terms of mechanical forces on the joints and limbs, both statically and dynamically. So, according to this criterion, it does not really qualify as a sensory modality that is distinct from somatosensation.

Turning to the second criterion, vision, audition, olfaction, gustation, and the vestibular sense are unquestionably distinct modalities since they have anatomically separate neural pathways. On the other hand, somatosensation and proprioception share a common pathway involving the spinal cord and trigeminal nerve.

According to the final criterion of computation, all seven putative senses have at least some distinctive functions, but they also share others. Vision, audition, and somatosensation all contribute to our ability to recognize objects, while olfaction and gustation are both involved in the assessment of edible substances. The overlap in the functions of the different senses provides a computational basis for multimodal processing.

Vision, audition, olfaction, gustation, and the vestibular sense seem to be distinctively different modalities, so these five modalities are not in dispute. In contrast, the senses of touch, limb position, and limb movement share a physical stimulus (mechanical force) as well as a neural pathway, so it is arguably most parsimonious to group them together as a single, sixth sensory modality called the body sense, or somatosensation. The following sections survey the current state of our knowledge about each of the six sensory modalities, beginning with those that are often considered to be the most simple or primitive.

Olfaction

Humans are astonishingly good at detecting odours. Ethyl mercaptan is often added to domestic gas to aid the detection of leaks, with good reason. If three drops were added to one of two Olympic-sized swimming pools, a human could detect by smell which pool contained the odorant (Yeshurun & Sobel, 2010). Our odour discrimination ability is on a par with the discrimination abilities of our other sensory systems: the JND for odour concentration is around 5–7% (Cain, 1977). Paradoxically, although our discrimination of odour intensity is very good, we are rather poor at identifying specific odours. Less than 50% of household items in daily use can be identified by smell alone (Cain, 1982). Moreover, we often have only a minimal conscious awareness of smells (Sela & Sobel, 2010) and find it difficult to describe them (Jönsson, Tchekhova, Lönner, & Olsson, 2005).

Nevertheless, as you read earlier, the olfactory system is equipped with a very large number of distinct receptor types and a highly organized sensory pathway. It seems that this sophisticated neural system is not best suited to the identification of specific odorants. Unlike in vision and audition, in olfaction there is no agreed mapping of physical stimulus attributes onto perception. So there is no way of predicting the smell evoked by a novel molecule (Khan et al., 2007). However, systematic statistical analyses of the perceptual dimensions people use to evaluate a wide range of odours reveal a highly consistent picture (e.g. Khan et al., 2007; Zarzo, 2008): odour perception has two dominant dimensions. The first dimension relates to the pleasantness–unpleasantness scale, sometimes called hedonic tone. Some smells are judged as, say, pleasantly 'fruity' or 'flowery', while others are perceived as unpleasantly 'musty' or 'animal'. The second dimension relates to the edible–inedible scale. Smells associated with bakery and spice products evoke 'edible' percepts, for example, while smells associated with cleaning and cosmetic products evoke 'inedible' percepts.

So the sense of smell seems to serve as an early warning system for classifying stimuli in terms of two rudimentary but important attributes and leaves the job of identification to other sensory modalities. First, it computes approach versus avoidance: should we get closer to the smell or retreat from it? Second, it computes edibility: should we eat the substance or not? Olfaction is phylogenetically ancient and seems to serve these functions in many other animals; it gives them the minimum amount of information that they need to know about a substance, even if that substance has never been encountered before. Indeed the size of the neural structures in the olfactory system scales directly with its importance for these functions in different animals (Jacobs, 2012).

DISCUSSION POINT

In this video[3], Dr. Stuart Firestein of Columbia University discusses the mysterious connections between taste, smell, and memory. Think about and discuss some of your own sensory memories.

Gustation

Psychophysical research since the late 19th century has identified five primary taste dimensions: sweetness, sourness, saltiness, bitterness, and savouriness. The first four dimensions match those identified in early research on the stimulus preferences of afferent fibres in animals such as cats, rabbits, and rats (Nowlis & Frank, 1977; Pfaffmann, 1955). The fifth dimension was found only relatively recently and is called **umami** after the Japanese word for 'good taste' or 'yummy' (Chaudhari, Landin, & Roper, 2000; Nelson et al., 2002).

The perceptual dimensions of taste indicate quite clearly that the function of the gustatory system is to signal the edibility and nutritional value of foods that have been placed in the mouth (perhaps after screening by the olfactory system). Sourness warns against the acidity of spoiled or unripe foods. Bitter-tasting substances include hydrolyzed proteins, rancid fats, alkaloids, and poisons, which are all potentially harmful, so bitterness is another danger signal. On the other hand, sweetness signals sugar content, and natural sugars are a valuable source of energy, so sweetness encourages consumption. Saltiness relates to the presence of sodium chloride, which is essential for proper neural function, so this taste also tends to encourage consumption. Savouriness or umami relates to the presence of amino acids, particularly monosodium glutamate (MSG).

Amino acids are the building blocks of proteins and are also precursors for important small molecules, as well as metabolic fuel. MSG is found in such foods as parmesan cheese, tomatoes, mushrooms, peas, and walnuts. So, the detection of MSG by gustatory receptors is another trigger for increased consumption. Many snack manufacturers add sugar, salt, and/or MSG to their products in order to increase consumption, and all three are commonly used cooking ingredients in powdered form. MSG is often added to Asian dishes and is made from fermented sugar beet or sugar cane molasses in a way that is quite similar to the way soy sauce (another MSG-rich food) is made.

The gustatory system has very close links with olfaction and somatosensation, to such an extent that the flavour of foods actually reflects not just taste receptor activity but the combined action of all three modalities. Multimodal flavour perception is discussed later in the chapter.

Somatosensation

Somatosensation (which includes proprioception) serves a number of different functions (as indicated in Table 7.2) that map onto anatomical and physiological divisions in the receptors and their pathways. Haptic object perception refers to our ability to identify objects on the basis of somatosensation. Klatzky, Lederman, and Metzger (1985) conducted an experiment to test the ability of blindfolded participants to identify 100 common objects by active touch alone (**haptics**). The objects included items such as a golf ball, a teabag, scissors, a key, and a screwdriver. Recognition was very accurate (96% correct) and fast (two thirds of responses were made within 3 seconds). The two objects responsible for the majority of errors were rice and T-shirts. Haptic object recognition is mediated by neurons in somatosensory and motor areas of the cortex (Reed, Shoham, & Halgren, 2004). Signals arrive in the somatosensory cortex via the lemniscal tract: mechanoreceptor axons travel all the way up the spinal cord, terminating in the brainstem. Connections are relayed to the thalamus and then on to the primary somatosensory cortex. Axons in this pathway are myelinated (i.e. they have a protective coating), which gives them a relatively fast conduction velocity.

Afferent fibres within the lemniscal tract can be divided into two broad classes. One class is called 'rapidly adapting' (RA) and the other is called 'slowly adapting' (SA), on the basis of their change in response level during stimulation. As their name implies, RA fibres respond only during the initial phase of stimulation. These responses seem to mediate our perception of vibration and texture as the skin comes into contact with a surface. SA fibres maintain their activity throughout the period of stimulation, and these responses are involved in sensations of steady pressure (Ochoa & Torebjork, 1983). In combination, RA and SA fibres tell us about the surface properties of tactile objects. Recognition often requires active tactile exploration of felt objects, which is controlled by the motor cortex and provides information about object shape via proprioceptive feedback from joints and muscles (Lederman & Klatzky, 1987).

Nociceptor signals take a different route from mechanoreceptor signals so that they can be dealt with quickly, in keeping with their special role in initiating rapid withdrawal responses to dangerous stimuli. Their axons terminate as soon as they enter the spinal cord. From there the signals branch in two directions: one branch travels up to the thalamus (via the spinothalamic tract) and then through a thalamic relay on to the primary somatosensory cortex, where it contributes to our conscious awareness of pain. The other branch carries signals straight back out to the muscles, creating a reflex circuit that allows rapid withdrawal from potentially dangerous situations. Unlike those in the lemniscal pathway, axons in the spinothalamic pathway are not myelinated so their conduction velocity is relatively slow. Hence, when a drop of hot water falls on your hand, its impact may be sensed half a second before its temperature is felt.

The importance of somatosensation, and the functional division into the lemniscal and spinothalamic pathways, is dramatically illustrated by rare clinical cases in which neurons in the former route are selectively destroyed by a viral illness (Cole & Paillard, 1995). These unfortunate individuals completely lose their ability to sense touch, body position, and body movement. Everyday acts such as sitting, standing, and walking become either impossible or feasible only with intense concentration and visual feedback. A sneeze or sudden darkness inevitably results in a fall. Nevertheless, sufferers are still able to sense heat and pain through the skin.

Vestibular sense

The vestibular sense allows us walk and run without falling over, and even to manage to read a mobile device held in our hands while doing so (an increasingly common sight on a modern campus). On the negative side, vertigo, motion sickness, and the sensory effects of alcohol intoxication (occasionally sighted on campuses as well) can also be attributed to the vestibular sense.

As mentioned earlier (and as shown in Figure 7.7), the vestibular apparatus of each inner ear includes a system of three tunnels and two chambers. Each is filled with fluid and houses a patch of mechanoreceptors. Vestibular responses are generated by displacement of receptor stereocilia. In combination, the five sensory organs can convey very precise information about head rotation and position. The tunnels are called 'semicircular canals' and are arranged at right angles to each other so that rotational acceleration of the head in any direction in 3D space causes fluid motion in at least one canal, which in turn activates the vestibular receptors. The two chambers (the saccule and utricle) are also arranged roughly at right angles to each other, with the former almost vertical and the latter horizontal. The patch of receptors in each chamber is covered by a gritty, jelly-like membrane that shifts under the force of gravity when the head changes position. Any attitude of the head with respect to gravity can be deduced from the pattern of responses in the two chambers.

In keeping with its multiple functions, signals from the vestibular organ travel to the brain by several routes. The reflexive control of body posture and equilibrium is mediated by projections (via the brainstem) to the cerebellum and to motor neurons in the spinal cord. Reflexive control of eye movements involves projections from the semicircular canals to the eye muscles (via the brainstem). This neural circuit, known as the vestibulo-ocular reflex, allows you to read your mobile device even though

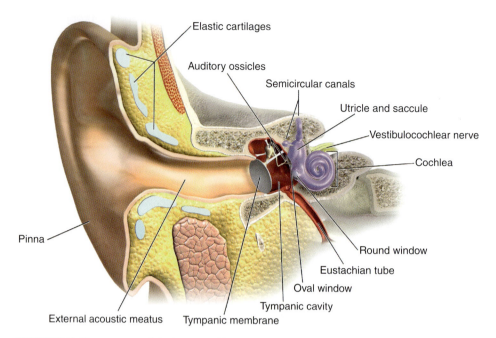

FIGURE 7.7 *The anatomy of the inner ear. The inner ear contains the sense organs for balance and hearing. The vestibular apparatus (balance) consists of three ring-shaped canals (semicircular canals) and two sacs (utricle and saccule); the cochlea (hearing) is spiral shaped. Each of these bony chambers is filled with fluid and also contains a patch of hair cells that respond to movement of the fluid. In the case of balance, fluid movement is caused by head motion and gravitational force. In the case of hearing, air pressure waves cause the eardrum to vibrate, and this movement is transmitted to fluid in the cochlea by tiny bones (ossicles).*
Source: Blausen.com staff (2014).

your head is bobbing up and down as you walk; your eyes rotate by exactly the correct amount to compensate for your head's movements and so maintain visual stability. Conscious experiences of head rotation and bodily movement, such as the feeling of acceleration you experience in a fast-moving vehicle, are mediated by a small projection, via the brainstem and thalamus, from the vestibular organ to the vestibular cortex (Fasold et al., 2002).

Changes in the responses of vestibular receptors are thought to be the cause of some symptoms of alcohol intoxication, particularly nausea, dizziness, and involuntary gaze instability. The hair cells in each semicircular canal are embedded in a gelatinous mass called the cupula, which has the same specific gravity as the surrounding vestibular fluid so that the cupula is not disturbed by changes in head orientation with respect to gravity. But alcohol has a different specific gravity to vestibular fluid and after consumption of a large quantity it diffuses into the fluid and the cupula at different rates. The consequent unnatural buoyancy of the cupula generates responses in the canals in the absence of any actual head rotation, leading to symptoms of intoxication.

For example, when you lie down while intoxicated, the cupula deflects sideways as it tries to float in the fluid, so causing sensations of head spin as well as eye movements that attempt to compensate for the nonexistent head rotation (Fetter, Haslwanter, Bork, & Dichgans, 1999). A standard noninvasive neurological test of brainstem function, known as the caloric reflex test, involves filling the external auditory canal on one side of the head with warm or cold water. The temperature difference with the body creates a convective current in the vestibular fluid of the nearby canal, which should generate reflexive eye rotation either towards or away from the flooded side depending on the temperature of the water (warm or cold respectively) if the brainstem is intact.

SECTION SUMMARY

- Stimulation of sensory receptors usually causes a conscious mental state. These primitive sensory states are known as qualia. However, there is no scientific account of qualia so we cannot legitimately use them as a scientific basis for distinguishing sensory modalities.
- Three particular criteria seem to be important for grouping qualia into different modalities: physical, biological, and computational.
- Although humans' discrimination of odour intensity is very good, we are rather poor at identifying specific odours, have only a minimal conscious awareness of smells, and find it difficult to describe smells. Nevertheless, the neural signalling system is highly sophisticated, with a large number of distinct receptor types.
- Odour perception has two dominant dimensions: pleasantness–unpleasantness (hedonic tone) and edible–inedible.
- Psychophysical research has identified five primary taste dimensions: sweetness, sourness, saltiness, bitterness, and savouriness (also called 'umami').
- These five dimensions indicate that the function of the gustatory system is to signal the edibility and nutritional value of foods that have been placed in the mouth.
- Somatosensation serves a number of different functions, which map onto anatomical and physiological divisions in the receptors and their pathways.
- The lemniscal pathway mediates perception of texture and vibration, and is involved in haptic object recognition. The spinothalamic pathway mediates rapid withdrawal responses to dangerous stimuli, as well as sensations of discomfort and pain.
- The vestibular sense allows us to maintain posture, balance, and gaze stability while keeping still, walking, or running, without the need for conscious control of these actions.
- The vestibular apparatus of each inner ear includes a system of three tunnels and two chambers, each filled with fluid and housing mechanoreceptors. Vestibular signals are generated by displacement of receptor stereocilia by the fluid during head movements.

AUDITION

LEARNING OBJECTIVE 7.4

Demonstrate an understanding of the mechanisms of audition and its effect on perception.

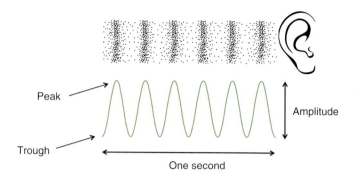

FIGURE 7.8 *Sounds are made up of waves of displacement in air molecules caused by back-and-forth vibration of an object (e.g. a guitar string). The waves contain peaks and troughs in air pressure, which travel away from the object at 335 metres per second. The frequency of the vibration is measured in terms of the number of cycles between maximum and minimum pressure that occur in each second (Hz). In this example, there are six cycles in a 1 second period, so the sound frequency is 6 Hz. The amplitude of the wave (heard as loudness) corresponds to the maximum change in pressure, or difference between the peak and trough of the wave.*

Auditory stimulus

Before considering perceptual aspects of hearing, it is important to establish some basic facts about the physical stimulus upon which it is based. Sound originates from the motion or vibration of an object, which sets up waves of vibration in the surrounding air molecules (Figure 7.8).

The waves travel away from the sound source at about 335 metres per second in air. Most natural sounds are periodic, meaning that they repeat regularly at a specific frequency determined by the vibration of the source, such as a plucked string on a guitar, the beating wing of an insect, or quivering vocal chords. The repetition frequency of the vibration is measured in cycles per second, or hertz (Hz). Subjectively, the repetition frequency of a sound is heard as its pitch. A low-frequency sound of, say, 100 Hz is heard as a deep bass pitch, and a high frequency of, say, 2,000 Hz (2 kHz) is heard as a bright treble pitch. Many sounds have complex cyclical variations in pressure over time.

Figure 7.9a, for example, shows the waveform of a clarinet note. A mathematical technique called Fourier analysis can be used to break the complex waveform down into a set of simpler component sounds called pure tones or sine waves. Figure 7.9b shows the component sine waves making up the clarinet note. Each component can be considered as a pure tone, such as would be produced by a tuning fork. The perceived pitch of the sound is usually determined by the lowest-frequency component in the sound, called the 'fundamental frequency'. The higher frequencies in the sound are always whole multiples of the fundamental frequency, and they give the sound its characteristic timbre. Different musical instruments playing the same note (pitch) sound different because of these higher-frequency components, which are known as harmonics.

Figure 7.10 shows the sound waves produced by different musical instruments playing the same note. Although the frequency of the notes is the same (i.e. the time between repetitions, shown by the T symbols, is the same), the differences in the detailed shapes of the waveforms are due to differences in the higher harmonic frequencies each instrument generates.

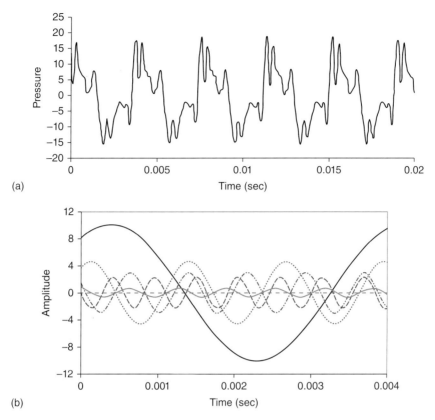

(a)

(b)

FIGURE 7.9 *The complex sound wave produced by a note played on a clarinet, and its component pure tones. (a) Air pressure as a function of time; the note produces cyclical variations in pressure. (b) The component pure tones that make up the note. The largest and lowest-frequency component (known as the fundamental) governs the perceived pitch of the note; the smaller-amplitude, higher-frequency components (known as harmonics) govern the character or timbre of the note.*

Source: Mather (2009). Reproduced with permission of Taylor and Francis.

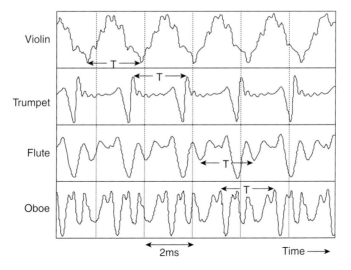

FIGURE 7.10 *Sound pressure waves representing the same musical note played on different instruments.*

Source: Howard and Angus (2009). Reproduced by permission of Taylor and Francis.

The difference in pressure between the peak and the trough of the sound wave is known as its amplitude, and relates to the perceived loudness of the sound. Sound pressure level (SPL) is usually measured on the decibel (dB) scale relative to a fixed reference pressure. The human auditory system can deal with a huge range of sound intensities, and perception of changes in loudness is highly nonlinear (see the earlier discussion of JNDs in the section 'Psychophysical Methods'), so the decibel scale deals in ratios of sound pressure; each doubling of sound pressure adds 6 dB to the SPL. The SPL of normal conversation is about 60 dB, while a loud rock concert has an SPL of 120 dB. Permanent hearing loss is likely when SPL exceeds 140 dB. Such loud sounds destroy the mechanoreceptors mediating audition, and the receptors do not regenerate (unlike taste receptors), so it is advisable to wear ear plugs at loud events to guard against hearing loss.

Auditory physiology

Sounds waves are channelled into the auditory canal by the visible outer ear (pinna), where they hit a thin membrane called the eardrum, which is stretched across the end of the canal. The plots of sound pressure waves in Figures 7.9 and Figure 7.10 also represent the back-and-forth vibration of the eardrum caused by the sounds. The vibration is transmitted to a membrane-covered window in the cochlea by means of a series of tiny bones or ossicles. The spiral-shaped cochlea is filled with fluid, so vibration of the window creates waves in the fluid. The cochlea is divided along its length by a partition that contains the mechanoreceptors for hearing. The receptors are spread out along a membrane called the basilar membrane. Fluid movement creates ripples in the basilar membrane that travel along its length, deflecting the receptor hair cells and so triggering neural responses. As in the cases of all the sensory systems, receptor responses are relayed through a series of neural processing stages before they arrive in the cerebral cortex. Projections from auditory receptors terminate in the brainstem, where they form synapses with large groups of neurons in the cochlear nuclei (one for each ear). From here, neurons connected to both ears send converging projections to another part of the brainstem known as the superior olive. After another two relays in the midbrain and thalamus, projections finally arrive in the receiving area of the cortex, the primary auditory cortex.

Auditory scene analysis

Hearing begins with the arrival of a pair of complex sound pressure waves at the two ears. In a natural environment, these waves are likely to contain a mixture of sound components from many different sources. While you are walking along the street talking with a group of friends, for example, at any one moment each acoustic waveform may contain sounds from several voices mixed in with ambient sounds from passing traffic, nearby conversations, phone ringtones, and so on. The peripheral auditory system encodes the waveform at each ear as a stream of neural impulses travelling along the 50,000 fibres that make up the auditory nerve. In order to fulfil its functions as outlined in Table 7.2, the auditory system must divide up the two signals at the ears into components originating from different sources, and then derive some perceptual meaning from those components. There are several characteristics of sound sources that can be used to separate out their components:

- spatial location
- spectral content
- time or onset.

Spatial location

According to the well-known 'cocktail party effect', our ability to attend to one person's voice against a background of many other voices and sound sources is at least partly based on our ability to separate out the different locations of the sound sources (Hawley, Litovsky, & Culling, 2004). Source direction can vary along three dimensions: left–right dimension (horizontal or 'azimuth'), up–down dimension (vertical or 'elevation'), and near–far dimension ('range'). Physical cues in the sound wave arriving at the two ears allow the auditory system to compute the direction of each sound source along all three dimensions. Azimuth (left–right) localization is based on two binaural (between the ears) cues, one of which was mentioned earlier (see Figure 7.4b). The ears are approximately 14 cm apart horizontally on either side of the head. Consequently, when a sound source is located to one side of the head, the sound emanating from it arrives at the nearer ear slightly before the further ear, creating an interaural time difference (ITD). Furthermore, the sound wave arriving at the further ear is slightly attenuated relative to the wave reaching the nearer ear because it has to pass around the head, so creating an interaural level difference (ILD).

ITDs are incredibly small, amounting to less than a millisecond at most (a thousandth of a second). Different neurons in the brainstem are tuned to different ITDs (as shown in Figure 7.4b). ILDs are detected by a different population of neurons in the brainstem. So, auditory localization in the horizontal plane is thought to be served by two complementary cues. This theory of localization is known as Rayleigh's duplex theory (Yost, 2000).

Judgements of vertical elevation and horizontal range rely on monaural cues (available in each ear individually). Localization in the vertical plane is based on the way that incoming sound waves bounce off the external ear (pinna) on their way to the ear canal. The complex folded structure of the pinna selectively alters high frequencies in the sound wave, boosting some components relative to others in a way that depends on the wave's direction. A good example of the importance of the pinna for localization comes from the familiar experience that sounds heard via headphones (which bypass the pinna) appear to be coming from inside the head.

Distance judgements are based on several cues. Sound intensity halves with each doubling of distance, so in general quieter sounds are likely to be further away. But distance also alters the spectral content of sounds; more distant sounds appear muffled, or lacking in high-frequency detail, because air molecules preferentially absorb energy at these frequencies. Consequently, nearby thunder has a loud crack, while distant thunder is a quiet rumble.

Spectral content

Spectral properties also allow the auditory system to group parts of a complex auditory waveform into discrete auditory objects. One important cue is pitch, determined by a complex sound's fundamental frequency (as described in the section 'Auditory Stimulus'). For example, men tend to speak at a lower pitch than women, so when two people are talking simultaneously it may be possible to separate out the two voices on the basis of their pitch. The fundamental frequency is so important because, as mentioned earlier, all the higher harmonics in a sound are whole multiples of its fundamental. So, if two complex sounds have different fundamentals, their harmonics can be divided into different harmonic series. Indeed, harmonicity itself is a cue for segregating complex sounds into different auditory objects.

Another form of auditory grouping based on spectral content is known as 'streaming'. Consider a sound consisting of a train of pulses at two different frequencies, *a* and *b* (i.e. the sequence of pulses goes *a-b-a-b-a-b*... like a two-tone siren). If the two frequencies are quite similar and the alternation rate is not too high, the listener hears a melody, a single sound of alternating high and low notes. If the frequencies are very dissimilar, or the rate of alternation is very high, the listener hears two separate sounds: *a-a-a*... and *b-b-b*.... Grouping seems to reflect the probability that the two components could be emitted by a single source (Bregman, 1990).

Time or onset

Sounds from different sources in a complex environment often start and stop at different times. Thus, all of the spectral components of the different sounds will necessarily also start and stop at different times. Common onset and offset is a powerful cue for dividing up a complex sound wave into components from different sound sources, even when the components are otherwise very similar (Darwin & Ciocca, 1992). The way that a sound starts (its attack) and stops (its decay) also has a major impact on its perceived timbre, a fact that is well known to makers of music synthesizers. For example, notes played on a guitar or cymbals have a sudden onset and very gradual decay, while a trombone note has a much more gradual attack.

Pitch perception

Pitch plays a crucial role in several auditory functions, including sound source segregation, identification, and speech prosody (perception of stress and intonation). Accordingly, pitch perception has been the subject of extensive research. The pitch of complex natural sounds depends mainly on their fundamental frequency, as described earlier. However, several findings in pitch perception indicate that the computation of pitch by the auditory system is far from simple. Natural sounds almost always contain many harmonics, which convey information about pitch, and evidence indicates that the auditory system does not simply rely on fundamental frequency but combines information from across a sound's spectrum in order to determine its pitch. Complex sounds with different frequency spectra can seem to have the same pitch, and conversely sounds with similar spectra can have different pitches (Plack, Barker, & Hall, 2014). Indeed, listeners can hear the pitch corresponding to a sound's fundamental frequency even when that component is not present at all (though the higher harmonics are preserved), a phenomenon known as the 'missing fundamental'. For example, you can still perceive the pitch of a male friend's voice over the telephone, despite the fact that the fundamental frequency of his voice is around 150 Hz and the small audio speaker in the handset cannot generate frequencies below 300 Hz.

Explanations of pitch perception begin by considering the detailed properties of the cochlea and the firing patterns of auditory nerve fibres. As mentioned earlier, vibrations of the ossicles in the middle ear create travelling waves of displacement along the cochlea's basilar membrane, similar to the waves created by tapping the side of a cup or glass full of liquid. The waves stimulate hair cells spread out along the membrane. The place of maximum displacement, and therefore maximum hair cell response, depends on sound frequency (frequency-to-place conversion). Sound frequency can thus be coded in terms of the place of maximum excitation on the basilar membrane.

The rate of firing of auditory mechanoreceptors fluctuates in time with the peaks and troughs of the wave travelling along the basilar membrane, which in turn depend on vibration frequency, so these fluctuations carry information about pitch; the higher the frequency of the sound impinging on the eardrum, the higher the rate of fluctuation in hair cell activity (within the electrical limits of neural firing). So the cochlea appears to encode pitch-related information in two ways. Firstly, sound frequency is coded in terms of the place of maximum excitation in the receptor array (frequency-to-place conversion). Secondly, frequency is coded in terms of the firing patterns of the auditory nerve fibres. On balance, evidence from studies of pitch perception indicates that temporal patterns of firing in the auditory nerve are more important for pitch perception, though place coding does play a role (Meddis & O'Mard, 1997; Moore, Glasberg, & Shailer, 1984; Plack, Barker, & Hall, 2014).

Neurons in the auditory cortex are selectively tuned to sound frequency, though it is not clear how this frequency tuning is derived from the temporal code provided by the auditory nerve. The primate auditory cortex is mapped topographically (or 'tonotopically'), so that cells with similar frequency preferences lie close together on the auditory surface (Kaas & Hackett, 2000). Such cells are likely to play a central role in pitch perception, and recent neuroimaging studies have sought to identify a 'pitch centre' in the human auditory cortex, which is specialized for pitch perception. The best estimate according to available evidence is a region of the secondary auditory cortex lying adjacent to the primary auditory cortex (Penagos, Melcher, & Oxenham, 2004).

SECTION SUMMARY

- Sound originates from the motion or vibration of an object, which sets up corresponding pressure waves in the surrounding air molecules. The amplitude of the vibration relates to the perceived loudness of the sound and its frequency relates to the sound's pitch.

- Sounds waves set up vibrations of the eardrum, which are transmitted by a series of small bones (ossicles) to a fluid-filled organ (cochlea) that houses auditory mechanoreceptors. Signals from the receptors travel to the brainstem and then on to the thalamus and cortex.

- Auditory analysis of complex sound pressure waves arriving at the two ears divides them up into contributions from different sound sources on the basis of spatial location, spectral content, and time or onset.

- Location cues are partly responsible for the cocktail party effect, which allows you to attend to one person's voice against a background of many other voices and sound sources. Location cues are divided into binaural cues, which allow localization in the horizontal plane, and monaural cues, which allow localization in the vertical plane. Spectral content and timing (onset and offset) allow the auditory system to group parts of a complex auditory waveform into discrete auditory objects.

- Pitch is important for sound source segregation, identification, and speech prosody. Pitch perception is mediated partly by the rate of firing in auditory receptors and partly by the location of the receptors in the cochlea (place coding).

VISION: PHYSIOLOGY

LEARNING OBJECTIVE 7.5

Demonstrate an understanding of the physiological mechanisms of vision.

Visual stimulus

The ancient Greeks believed that vision was based on a 'fire' emitted by the eyes as well as by the sun. But we now know that light is a form of radiant energy, which is emitted, transmitted, or reflected by objects, not by eyes. Light propagates from a source as vibrating electrical and magnetic fields, or waves. Most light sources emit a mixture of different vibration frequencies or wavelengths. Visual sensations are evoked only by wavelengths between about 400 and 700 nm (billionths of a metre). Colour sensations are associated with the wavelength properties of light, as will become clear below (though light rays are not actually coloured, of course). As well as having wave-like properties, light travels in straight lines, or rays, from a light source at such a high speed that it can be considered as instantaneous. However, its speed varies slightly depending on the medium through which it passes.

For example, the speed of light is higher through air than through water or glass. If light rays strike an interface between different media at an oblique angle, the change in speed causes the rays that cross the interface to change direction, rather like a road vehicle veering to one side as it runs onto a verge at the side of the road and slows down. The change in the direction of transmitted light rays (termed 'refraction') is the basis of image formation by lenses. Rays emanating from a point on an external surface enter the human eye via an entrance pupil. The diameter of the pupil varies to regulate the amount of light that enters the eye, though other factors also affect pupil size (see Focus Point 7.2). After the light rays have been admitted through the pupil, they pass through a lens whose shape brings them back together to form an image on the inside back surface of the eye. Rays from many points on an extended surface will create an extended image of the surface in the eye, as illustrated in Figure 7.11.

Visual physiology

Figure 7.12 illustrates the visual pathway. The inner surface of each eye is called the retina and is lined with a network of cells containing over 100 million photoreceptors. Signals from the photoreceptors pass through the network before reaching a neural layer containing ganglion cells. The fibres of these cells form the optic nerve, which emerges from the back of each eye and travels to several structures in the middle of the brain. In humans, most optic nerve fibres terminate in the thalamus, at cell nuclei called the lateral geniculate nuclei (LGN). From here, LGN fibres project to the receiving area of the cortex, known as the 'primary visual cortex' or V1. Cortical cells in V1 then send projections to a host of secondary visual areas in the cortex. Several aspects of visual physiology are especially important for understanding visual sensations and perceptions.

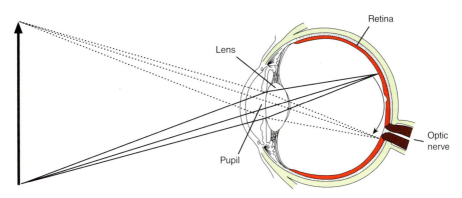

FIGURE 7.11 *Image formation in the human eye. Light rays emanating from each point on an object (just two points are shown) pass through the pupil and are brought into focus on the inner back surface of the eye (the retina). The arrangement of the points on the retina recreates the spatial arrangement of the points on the object, forming a compete image of it.*

Source: Adapted by permission from Macmillan Publishers Ltd: NATURE REVIEWS NEUROSCIENCE. Tamietto and de Gelder (2010), copyright 2010.

FOCUS POINT 7.2

THE PUPIL: WINDOW TO THE SOUL

In the classic science-fiction film *Blade Runner* (1982), the central character's job is to detect 'replicants', escaped androids who are a danger to humans but superficially indistinguishable from them. One of his tests measures pupillary dilation in response to emotional stimuli. Could such a simple physical response really reveal emotional states?

The entrance pupil of the eye varies in diameter to regulate the amount of light reaching the retina but its effectiveness is quite limited; light levels during daytime are millions of times brighter than during night-time, but variations in pupil diameter can only produce a 16-fold variation in retinal illumination. Research has indeed found that pupil size varies with cognitive and emotional state. For instance, Bradley, Miccoli, Escrig, and Lang (2008) monitored pupil diameter while participants viewed emotionally arousing or neutral images, and found that pupils dilated more while participants viewed arousing images.

Large pupils do indicate emotional arousal, and they can influence sexual attraction. Tombs and Silverman (2004) found that both male and female participants rated photographs of a member of the opposite sex as more attractive when they had larger pupils. A drug derived from the deadly nightshade plant causes pupil to dilate and has been used since ancient times to make women appear more seductive (the plant is also known as belladonna, from 'beautiful women').

Photoreceptor properties

Natural light levels vary over a huge 10 million-fold range between starlight and midday sun. Two different types of photoreceptor cell, called **rods** and **cones**, respond over different ranges of light level. Cones are over 30 times less sensitive to light than rods and respond effectively only during bright daylight. Rods operate only after dusk. The transition from cone to rod vision (dark adaptation) takes about 20 minutes, a timescale that is well matched to the time of natural sunrise or sunset, but not to artificial light. This slow dark-adaptation process explains why your vision is severely compromised for a while after moving directly from a brightly lit environment such as midday sunlight into a dark environment such as a cinema.

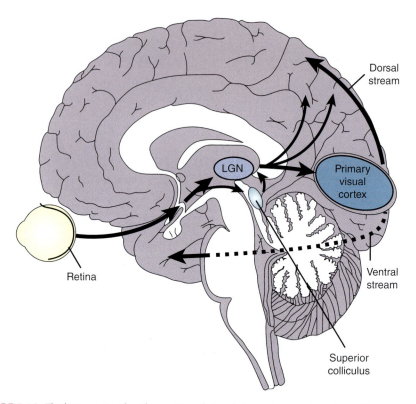

FIGURE 7.12 *The human visual pathway. Neural signals leave the eye along the optic nerve and travel along two routes. A minor route sends the signals to the superior colliculus and a major route sends them to the primary visual cortex via the lateral geniculate nucleus (LGN). Signals are relayed from here along two major streams of cortical processing: one is termed 'dorsal' (over the back of the cortex) and the other is called 'ventral' (around the lower part of the cortex).*

Natural light contains a mixture of many different wavelengths, but different surfaces preferentially reflect only certain wavelengths. Vegetation (grass, leaves, etc.) reflects medium wavelengths, whereas ripe berries reflect longer wavelengths. Reflected wavelengths thus carry information about object properties, such as edibility, and to exploit this fact the visual system uses cone photoreceptor responses to encode wavelength. Cones can be subdivided into three classes based on their response to light wavelength. The three classes respond optimally to different (though overlapping) regions of the visible spectrum: S-cones cover the shortest (bluish) wavelengths, M-cones cover medium (greenish) wavelengths, and L-cones cover the longest (reddish) wavelengths. The latter two classes form the majority of cones; only about 6% of cones are S-cones. The three different cone classes allow us to discriminate the redness of berries against green-coloured leaves. The primary task of rod photoreceptors is to respond to any light that is present in dim conditions, so all rods contain the same kind of photopigment. Consequently, we cannot perceive colour in starlight (but at least we can see the stars).

Rods and cones are distributed in a roughly complementary manner across the retina. Cones are found everywhere on the retina, but they are packed very tightly into an area at the centre of the retina near the optical axis of the lens, which is called the fovea. The high packing density of the cones in the fovea means that this area is responsible for high-acuity vision in bright conditions. Rods, on the other hand, are entirely absent from the fovea but are distributed fairly evenly across the rest of the retina. So, in dim conditions it is best to look slightly away from a target, such as a dim star, in order to direct its image onto a rod-rich area away from the fovea.

Stimulus encoding

The concept of univariance (see the earlier section 'Stimulus Tuning in Sensory neurons') also applies to photoreceptor responses. Each receptor's response level depends on both light wavelength and light intensity, so different combinations of the two stimulus attributes can evoke the same response. The only way to disentangle them and so infer light wavelength is to compare the responses of different receptors to the same light. For example, when stimulated with red light, L-cones will respond more strongly than M-cones, and S-cones will not respond at all. This *relative* level of activity across the cone classes will hold regardless of the absolute intensity level of the light. The process of comparing the relative activity levels of different cone classes can be described mathematically as a computation of the ratios of cone responses. The activity of ganglion cells in the retina can be described quite well in these terms. Each cell combines the signals it receives from a number of photoreceptors. Some of the signals excite the cell and others inhibit it. A cell that receives excitation from L-cones and inhibition from M-cones would be excited by red light and inhibited by green light. Many ganglion cells behave in exactly this way. Others have the opposite response (excited by green and inhibited by red) or respond to the pairing of blue versus a combination of green and red (in other words, yellow). Figure 7.13a shows the receptive field properties of the three largest ganglion cell classes (called midget, parasol, and bistratified ganglion cells). All of the cells receive activity from receptors only within a small, roughly circular area of the retina, which defines each ganglion cell's 'receptive field': namely, the retinal area in which light must fall in order to influence the cell's response (with L, M, and S referring to the three cone classes). In the majority of cells, the excitatory and inhibitory regions of the receptive field are arranged concentrically, with one input in the centre and the opposing input in the surround. As you can see in the figure, different combinations of photoreceptors provide the inputs to the ganglion cells, making them selectively responsive to red versus green, or blue versus yellow, or black versus white.

So, the signals travelling up the optic nerve from the ganglion cells to the LGN have already begun the process of encoding the lightness and colour properties of the image. Cells in the LGN have similar receptive field properties to ganglion cells, but neurons in the visual cortex have more sophisticated stimulus preferences, typically responding selectively to an extended line or edge at a specific orientation and size, and perhaps moving in a particular direction, or with particular wavelength composition, or at a particular binocular depth (mediated by slight differences between the images in each eye, as you experience with stereo TV and cinema). Figure 7.13b shows the percentage of cells in different areas of visual cortex that are selectively responsive to these stimulus attributes (data taken from Lennie, 1998). V1 is the primary visual cortex; the other areas are secondary visual association areas.

Even in the case of highly selective cortical cells, individual responses are ambiguous due to univariance. A particular cell may vary its response according to, for example, the orientation and width of a bar, as well as the difference in light level between the brighter and darker parts of the bar (luminance contrast). Looking

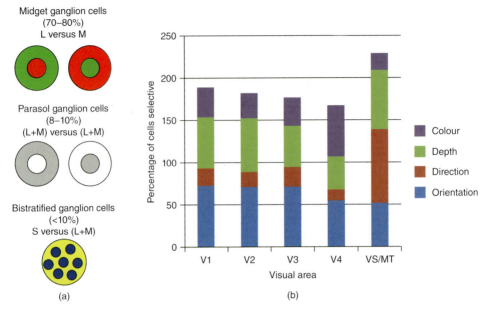

Midget ganglion cells
(70–80%)
L versus M

Parasol ganglion cells
(8–10%)
(L+M) versus (L+M)

Bistratified ganglion cells
(<10%)
S versus (L+M)

(a)

(b)

FIGURE 7.13 *(a) Receptor inputs to several classes of ganglion cell in the retina. Each receives signals from receptors in a roughly circular area of the retina, known as the cell's receptive field. In two of the three ganglion cell classes, receptors in the centre of the receptive field excite the cell, and those in the surround inhibit it (or vice versa). One cell class (midget) receives opposing inputs from M-cones and L-cones, so this class signals redness versus greenness. The second cell class (parasol) receives both excitatory and inhibitory inputs from all three cone types, so it signals brightness versus darkness by virtue of the opposing inputs to the centre and surround of the receptive field (e.g. light in the centre stimulates the cell, while light falling in the surround inhibits it). The third ganglion cell class (bistratified) receives opposing inputs from S-cones and a combination of M- and L-cones (which equates roughly to the yellow part of the spectrum). (b) Stimulus selectivity in the visual cortex. Each bar represents the percentage of cells in each visual cortical area that are selectively responsive to colour, depth, motion direction, or contour orientation. The bars sum to a value greater than 100% because each cortical cell is tuned to more than one stimulus attribute.*
Source: Mather (2009). Reproduced with permission of Taylor and Francis.

at Figure 7.13b, you will notice that the percentages in each column sum to far in excess of 100%. Cells are double-counted because each is selective for at least two stimulus attributes. Three or four stimulus dimensions are confounded in the single response value that each individual cell can provide. So, to encode, say, motion direction, the visual system must compare responses across a population of cells that vary in terms of the stimulus direction that produces the best response. For example, when you view a cascade at a waterfall, cells tuned to downward motion respond much more strongly than those tuned to upward, rightward, leftward, or any other direction, and so you perceive (the visual system computes) downward motion.

The encoding strategy just described is called **population coding** for obvious reasons. All sensory modalities make use of population coding. For example, sound source direction is encoded by a population of cells that vary in their preferred interaural time difference, and visual stimulus width is encoded by a population of width-tuned cells (see Figure 7.4). Population coding is necessary to deal with the ambiguities that are prevalent in univariant cell responses.

Dorsal and ventral processing streams

It is generally agreed that the flow of connections between cells in the visual cortex divides into two distinct streams, known as the **dorsal stream** and the **ventral stream** on the basis of the cortical areas involved. Both streams spring from the primary visual cortex in the occipital lobe, and they run in parallel across the cortex. The ventral stream follows a lower route into the temporal lobe, while the dorsal stream follows a higher route into the parietal lobe. The dorsal versus ventral distinction was first proposed by Ungerleider and Mishkin (1982), who investigated the consequences of cortical lesions in monkeys. They proposed that the two streams serve different functions:

- *What* – The ventral stream specializes in visual discrimination of fine details and object identification.
- *Where* – The dorsal stream specializes in visuospatial processing, including motion analysis and visually guided reaching.

Over the intervening years, the dorsal/ventral distinction has become firmly established as an organizing principle in the visual system, but there has been a great deal of debate, particularly about the functions of the dorsal stream. On the basis of human clinical cases, Goodale and Milner (1992) preferred to describe the dorsal stream as a 'How' stream that specializes in unconscious control of action. There is currently no universal agreement on the best way to characterize the different functions of the dorsal and ventral streams (e.g. Kravitz, Saleem, Baker, & Mishkin, 2011). But for the time being we can tentatively assign some of the computations listed in Table 7.2 to one or the other of the two streams as follows. Object processing is associated with the ventral stream. Scene layout and action guidance computations are performed by the dorsal stream. Self-motion (walking, running) is also computed in the dorsal stream (Orban et al., 1992).

SECTION SUMMARY

- Visual sensations are evoked only by light wavelengths between about 400 and 700 nm (billionths of a metre). Light travels in straight lines, or rays, from a light source at extremely high speed. However, its speed varies slightly depending on the medium through which it passes and this allows optical devices such as eyes to produce images.

- The inner surface of each human eye is called the retina and is lined with a network of over 100 million photoreceptor cells. Two different types of photoreceptor cell in the retina respond over different ranges of light level: cones respond at high light levels; rods respond at low light levels.

- Rods and cones are distributed in a roughly complementary manner across the retina. Cones are found everywhere on the retina, but they are packed very tightly into an area at the centre of the retina near the optical axis of the lens, which is called the fovea.

- Signals from the photoreceptors travel to the lateral geniculate nucleus in the thalamus, from where they are relayed to the visual cortex.

- At each point in the pathway, cells respond selectively; cone photoreceptors respond to some wavelengths more reliably than to others, while lateral geniculate nucleus and cortical cells respond selectively to particular spatial patterns, luminance, or colour. The response of any one cell is nevertheless ambiguous, so the visual system encodes stimulus properties in terms of patterns of response across large ensembles of cells (population coding).

- It is generally agreed that the pathways of processing in the visual cortex are organized into two streams: the dorsal stream (encoding *where* things are and how to reach them) and the ventral stream (encoding *what* things are).

VISION: PERCEIVING OBJECT PROPERTIES

LEARNING OBJECTIVE 7.6

Critically evaluate explanations for perceptual illusions and after-effects, in the context of the structure and function of the sensory systems.

After-effects and illusions

The preceding sections have demonstrated that our perceptions can be described as computations performed by huge populations of neurons in the brain. When you perceive a particular sensory attribute, such as sound direction or surface texture, it represents the outcome of a complex encoding process involving many thousands of cells. It is vital for these computations to be very fast and accurate. Imagine trying to run fast through a dense forest, perhaps fleeing from the roars of a predator, without being able to accurately sense the unpredictable level of the terrain below your feet, or obstructive low-hanging branches ahead, or the direction from which the roars are emanating. Most of the time, of course, the computations underlying these sensations are completed quickly and accurately; otherwise our ancestors would have long since become another meal. But sensation and perception are not totally accurate and reliable. Very occasionally, problems do arise in the form of perceptual experiences that are erroneous or unreliable in some way. Perceptual psychologists usually distinguish two broad categories of such phenomena, known as **after-effects** and **illusions**. Although captivating and compelling in themselves, these effects are scientifically important because they are conscious expressions of the hidden computations underlying perceptual experience. By studying after-effects and illusions, we can gain new insights into the nature and function of the computations.

After-effects

A common scenario involves prolonged exposure to unchanging sensory stimulation. In these circumstances our perception of the stimulus can change in a dramatic way to generate an after-effect. You will already have first-hand experience of sensory adaptation in all of your sensory modalities. Cooking smells lingering in your house tend to fade after a short while. If you leave the house and return later, the smell may also reappear. The pink tinge created by your sunglasses fades away remarkably swiftly, but when you remove the sunglasses the world may appear tinged with a complementary greenish hue for a short while. If you stare at a moving pattern for a while, such as a water cascade (keeping your eyes fixed in position), then any stationary pattern that you view afterwards, such as nearby rocks, will appear to move in the opposite direction. This well-known after-effect is known as the 'motion after-effect'.

All of these after-effects can be explained by population coding. Recall from earlier that perceptual encoding involves population-wide comparisons between the outputs of neurons tuned to different stimuli. In the case of motion, if all direction-selective cells are equally active, we see no motion. We perceive downward motion in the water cascade when cells tuned to this direction are more active than cells tuned to other directions. Prolonged exposure to the cascade selectively fatigues or adapts the cells that respond strongly to it. So, when you view a stationary pattern afterwards, cells tuned to downwards motion are less active than cells sensitive to other directions. As a result, our perception of movement is biased away from the adapted direction; we see motion in the opposite direction.

Many after-effects can be explained by the fact that, after adaptation, population responses in the relevant neurons are distorted by the reduction in the activity of the adapted cells, leading to shifts in perception. A great deal of psychophysical research on motion adaptation is consistent with this explanation of the motion after-effect, for example, and also indicates that there are several distinct populations of motion-sensitive cells that contribute to the after-effect (Mather, Pavan, Campana, & Casco, 2008). Similarly, the colour adaptation you experience when wearing tinted sunglasses is caused by changes in the relative responsiveness of cells tuned to different parts of the colour spectrum. A predominance of red light causes adaptation in cells tuned to these wavelengths, so that white light appears to have the complementary tinge.

Illusions

Even without prolonged exposure, we are sometimes aware that perceptual experience does not always accord with reality; objects, patterns, and surfaces may appear distorted in shape, size, texture, structure, and so on. Figure 7.14 shows three geometrical illusions in which lines appear to be tilted or bent with respect to other lines. They can be explained on the basis of interactions between neurons selectively responsive to line orientation, as follows. Many cells in the visual cortex are selectively tuned to orientation and our perception of contour tilt is based on a comparison of their outputs. We perceive the orientation given by the tuning of the most active cells. Nearby cells in the cortex that are tuned to similar orientations are thought to inhibit each other, which has the effect of magnifying differences in the signalled orientation of nearby lines. Hence lines appear to repel each other in the illusions shown in the figure; acute angles appear larger than they really are (Tolhurst & Thompson, 1975). Many other illusions can also be explained by mutual inhibition between cells in the cortex. Like adaptation, inhibition serves a useful function in that both serve to reduce neural activity that is relatively uninformative (many cells responding to very similar stimulus properties).

Perceptual constancies

Illusions and after-effects of the kind discussed in the previous section shed light on how the visual system estimates relatively simple local properties of the retinal image,

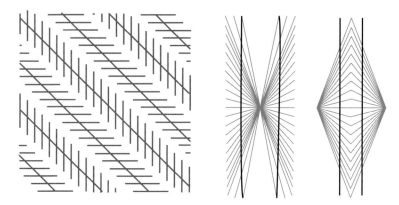

FIGURE 7.14 *Three geometrical visual illusions in which lines appear tilted or bent with respect to other lines. The left-most pattern is known as the Zöllner illusion; the middle and right-hand patterns are known as the Hering and Wundt illusions respectively.*

Source: Mather (2009). Reproduced with permission of Taylor and Francis.

such as contour orientation and movement direction. But the main task of the visual system is to compute the distinctive properties of objects, such as their size, shape, and identity, which are not tied directly to simple image properties. For example, a pen can be recognized regardless of how small or large it is in an image (the pen's retinal image size depends on its distance away from you) or what its orientation is (which depends on the angle from which you are viewing it). The visual system is able to build relatively stable, constant representations of objects despite variations in simple image properties such as retinal size and orientation. Perceptual experience reflects these stable representations to produce effects known collectively as **perceptual constancies**.

Figure 7.15 shows several examples. In the left-most photograph, the figures appear constant in objective size because the depth cues from the corridor allow the visual system to compensate for the greater viewing distance of the smaller figure. When the latter is moved out of its correct position (as in the other photograph), constancy cannot be applied appropriately, meaning one figure seems minified even though it is the same size in the two images. In Figure 7.15b, the two tabletops appear to be different in shape, yet they are actually the same size; depth cues are again used to adjust retinal dimensions and compute object shape, once more leading to a difference between image and object properties. Similarly, the two labelled tiles are actually equal in image lightness, but the visual system takes account of shading information when computing the lightness of the tiles.

These and other examples of perceptual constancy show that the visual system uses contextual cues to infer constant object properties. In the case of size and shape constancy, for example, surrounding contours provide clues as to the depth arrangement of the scene, which are used to adjust the estimation of object size and shape. Perception is a process of inference that goes beyond simple image properties to estimate object properties.

Ambiguity in perception

Cases of ambiguity also reveal that perception involves unconscious inferences or conclusions. Figure 7.16 shows the trapezoidal silhouette of a simple geometrical object. The visual system's task when presented with this silhouette or shadow is

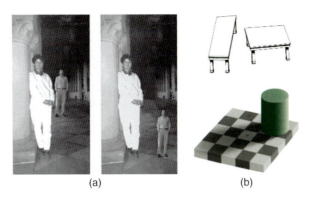

(a)   (b)

FIGURE 7.15 *Examples of perceptual constancy. (a) Size constancy: the two standing figures appear similar in objective size in the left-hand photograph, but their size in the image is very different, as is clear in the other photograph. (b) Shape constancy: the two tabletops appear very different in objective shape, but their shape in the image is identical. Lightness constancy: the tiles labelled A and B appear different in lightness, but they are the same lightness in the image.*

Source: (a) Perdreau and Cavanagh (2011), reproduced by permission of Florian Perdreau; (b) 'Grey square optical illusion', original by Edward H. Adelson, this file by Gustavb, file created by Adrian Pingstone, based on the original created by Adelson (1993), via Wikimedia Commons.

to infer the shape of the object that cast it. In principle a great many different shapes could all give rise to the same silhouette, if they are viewed from particular angles. Some of the possible shapes are shown in the figure. Hence, the image is inherently ambiguous; there is insufficient visual information to specify the shape of the object that created the silhouette. Nevertheless, observers generally agree on what the shape is: a rectangle (e.g. a window) seen from an oblique angle. Why is this interpretation so common, given the multiple possible interpretations available, all equally consistent with the shadow?

Ambiguities of the kind shown in Figure 7.16 can be resolved by bringing in additional information in the form of assumptions based on the properties of the real world, either learned from experience or built into the brain during evolution. The assumptions are combined with information in the image. We tend to assume, for example, that object shapes are regular, balanced, and symmetrical, so the image in Figure 7.16 is interpreted as the outline of a rectangular object, such as a window viewed from an oblique angle. Ambiguities such as the one illustrated in the figure are thought to be widespread in visual images, so inferences are an essential element of sensory processing in perception.

Figure 7.17 shows another kind of ambiguity. In this case, two alternative interpretations are equally plausible. You may not be able to see any meaningful structure in the image, but once you know that it contains a human face then a meaningful interpretation may well emerge. High-level information about the presence of a face leads to a reinterpretation of the incoming sensory data. On the other hand, if you are informed that the image represents a man playing a saxophone, a different interpretation may become apparent. Once these two alternative interpretations have been planted in your head, you may be able to switch between them almost at will (Intaitė, Noreika, Šoliūnas, & Falter, 2013). So far, perceptual inferences have been described in fairly general, vague terms, but it is possible to construct rigorous, testable theories based on perceptual inferences. Since around the turn of the 21st century, theories of perceptual inference have begun to use a mathematical formula called Bayes' theorem. You can read more about the application of Bayes' theorem to perception in Focus Point 7.3.

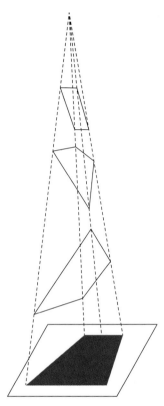

FIGURE 7.16 *The ambiguities of visual images. Any shadow silhouette could be created by a large number of different object shapes. In this example, the trapezoidal shadow can be cast by an infinite variety of four-sided objects, three of which are shown. However, we tend to perceive the object as a tilted rectangle (top-most object).*

FIGURE 7.17 *An ambiguous visual image that can be interpreted in two entirely different ways (see the text for details).*

FOCUS POINT 7.3

BAYESIAN MODELS OF PERCEPTION

Thomas Bayes was an 18th-century Presbyterian minister and mathematician who devised a formula for calculating the probability that an event has occurred based on combining prior knowledge of its probability with new evidence about the event. Bayes' theorem can be applied to all sorts of hypotheses about events and has proven itself to be very useful for modelling perception (Knill & Pouget, 2004).

A medical example may help to give an initial understanding of how Bayesian inference works. During medical diagnosis, a doctor may want to determine the probability that a patient is suffering from each of a range of possible diseases, given a specific symptom. Let's assume that the symptom is indigestion and that one of the possible diseases is a stomach ulcer. So the doctor must estimate the probability that the patient is suffering from an ulcer, given the symptom of indigestion. According to Bayes' theorem, this probability is calculated by combining two sources of information (actually multiplying together two probabilities): first, prior knowledge of the prevalence of ulcers in the patient population, and, second, the likelihood of having indigestion while suffering from a stomach ulcer. If both of these probabilities are high, then it is very likely that the patient has an ulcer. But, if one or the other is very low (say, indigestion is not consistent with an ulcer), then the diagnosis is very unlikely.

Bayesian inference can be applied to visual perception, if we recast 'symptoms' and 'diseases' as follows. A specific visual stimulus is equivalent to a 'symptom' that is consistent with various possible causes (objects or 'diseases'). Let's assume that your retinal image contains the silhouette shown in Figure 7.16. Your visual system must infer the object's shape given only its visual silhouette. The image could have been created by a range of different objects, some of which are shown in the figure. There is insufficient visual information to select the correct object (all the candidate objects are equally likely to have created the image). But prior knowledge may tell you that regular, symmetrical objects are the most commonly encountered objects in the world (most of us live in a built environment; natural forces such as erosion tend to create smooth, symmetrical shapes; creatures tend to be symmetrical). When the equal likelihoods are multiplied by the 'prior' for each object (based on knowledge), one interpretation stands out as most likely.

Bayesian approaches have been applied quite successfully to a range of perceptual decisions. For instance, many illusions of movement can be understood on the basis that the visual system has a prior preference for slowly moving objects over fast-moving objects (Weiss, Simoncelli, & Adelson, 2002). However, Bayesian models are not universally accepted as the best way forward for modelling perception (Bowers & Davis, 2012).

Modern theories to explain how information from different sensory modalities is combined rely heavily on Bayesian approaches. Each sensory modality offers its own likelihood estimate of a particular object property or identity, and the goal is to produce the most reliable single estimate from the multiple estimates that are available. Bayes' theory selects the optimal combination of cues given the information available. Research on multisensory integration is consistent with Bayesian approaches (Ernst & Banks, 2002).

DISCUSSION POINT

Look at these two examples of optical illusions:

1. **the spinning silhouette illusion**[4]
2. **the spiral pinwheel illusion**[5]

What do you see when you look at each illusion?

SECTION SUMMARY

- Prolonged exposure to unchanging sensory stimulation (adaptation) causes changes in the appearance of and sensitivity to stimuli that are similar to the adapting stimuli (after-effects). These changes can be explained by distortions in population responses caused by selective reduction in the activity of adapted cells.

- Changes or distortions in stimulus appearance can also occur even without adaptation; these effects are known as illusions. Many illusions can be explained by inhibition between cells in the cortex that are tuned to similar stimuli, such as similar contour orientations; the mutual inhibition has the effect of magnifying apparent differences between nearby stimuli.

- The perceptual systems are able to build relatively stable, constant representations of objects despite variations in simple sensory properties such as retinal size and orientation. These stable representations are known collectively as 'perceptual constancies'.

- Perception also involves unconscious inferences, as revealed by examples of visual ambiguities that can be resolved by bringing in additional information, such as assumptions based on the properties of the real world, either learned from experience or built into the brain during evolution. A mathematical framework known as Bayes' theorem can help to explain how perceptual ambiguities are resolved.

MULTIMODAL PERCEPTION

LEARNING OBJECTIVE 7.7

Demonstrate an understanding of how different neural systems' mechanisms overlap in the overall make-up of perception.

Looking back at Table 7.2, you will notice that there is considerable overlap between the computations performed by the neural systems serving different sensory modalities:

- Vision, audition, and somatosensation all serve to orient attention to external events.
- Both olfaction and gustation provide information about the edibility and flavour of substances.
- Vision, audition, and somatosensation all serve object processing.
- Vision and the vestibular sense provide information about body motion.

That is, representations of external stimuli, such as edibility and object identity, can be generated via multiple modes of input. When you inspect an apple, for example, you may face a decision as to whether to eat it or not. As you hold and perhaps bite into the apple, vision tells you about its size, shape, and colour; somatosensation tells you about its weight and surface texture; and olfaction and gustation tell you about its characteristic taste and smell. Your knowledge of the apple and its edibility is multimodal. In order to construct a single representation of the apple and its edibility, the brain must combine information from the different modality-specific systems. There is plenty of evidence for this kind of information sharing in the sensory systems, some of which is outlined in the following sections.

Orienting

Orienting refers to the process of directing our attention towards a new sensory input. A simple way to study orienting in the laboratory is to measure a participant's reaction time (RT) to the sudden onset of a sensory stimulus. For example, Diederich and Colonius (2004) measured RTs to a brief flash of light, to the onset of a pure tone, or to tactile vibration delivered to the toe. They found that the fastest reactions to unimodal presentation (only one sensory modality) were to auditory stimuli (mean RT = 132 ms), followed by visual stimuli (mean RT = 163 ms) and then tactile stimuli (mean RT = 177 ms). The interesting question in the present context is what happened when stimuli from two or three modalities were presented together. Diederich and Colonius (2004) found that RTs speeded up by about 20–30 ms under bimodal presentation (two modalities) and by a further 10–20 ms under trimodal presentation (all three modalities). Other studies have found that sensitivity to faint stimuli is also enhanced under multimodal stimulation (McDonald, Teder-Sälejärvi, & Hillyard, 2000). The enhanced ability to orient towards multisensory stimuli can be explained in two ways:

1. *Parallel activation* – According to this explanation, unimodal stimulation excites neural activity, which builds up to a level that is sufficient to trigger a response by the participant. Multimodal stimulation excites two or more systems in parallel, and activity builds up independently in each system until it is high enough in at least one of them to trigger a response by the participant. If we assume some statistical variability in the processing time of each system, parallel activation by multimodal presentation predicts faster mean RTs and more reliable detection simply on statistical grounds ('statistical facilitation'); there are multiple chances to detect the stimulus, as opposed to just one chance under unimodal presentation.

2. *Co-activation* – Unimodal activations are added together to create a combined response that is stronger and more reliable than the activation produced by unimodal stimulation, so performance using multimodal stimulation should again be better. Co-activation could involve direct neural connections between lower-level modality-specific processing areas, which enhance excitation, or the convergence of outputs from multiple modality-specific areas onto high-level multimodal processing areas.

Diederich and Colonius (2004) and others have estimated the amount of statistical facilitation that would be expected from parallel activation, and have concluded that it is not sufficiently high to account for the magnitude of multimodal effects they observed. The inference, therefore, is that modality-specific responses are combined somewhere in the brain to create multimodal activation.

Flavour

The sensation of eating transcends individual sensory modalities, because it combines elements of taste, smell, temperature, touch, sight, sound, and pain. Olfactory and gustatory components are essential to create a sensation complex that is perceived as a **flavour**, but all the components of flavour can signal food edibility. The chemical signals from olfactory and gustatory receptors are well understood and were discussed in the earlier section 'Sensory Receptors', but heat sensations and painful touch can signal that a substance would be harmful to the digestive system if swallowed. The importance of components such as colour and texture should not be underestimated – a point that is well understood by the food industry. Artificial colouring and thickeners are often added to foods such as yogurts and sauces in order to enhance their perceived edibility. The impact of vision, or the lack of it, on flavour can be experienced first-hand in one of the many 'dark dining' restaurants that have become popular worldwide (a truly blind date).

DISCUSSION POINT

In an experiment, Simona Manescu, Johannes Frasnelli, Franco Lepore, and Jelena Djordjevic of the University of Montreal investigated whether odour is judged differently depending on whether it is accompanied by a positive or negative description.

Read the account of the experiment (Manescu, Frasnelli, Lepore, & Djordjevic, 2014) and then discuss some examples from everyday life where external factors, such as packaging or advertisements, can change people's judgement of foods.

Objects

The objects that we perceive through the senses include both concrete entities, such as furniture and animals, and abstract entities, such as spoken words. Most objects offer multimodal information. The combination of vision and speech offers some good examples of multimodal audiovisual object perception. You may be familiar with the experience of listening to a conversation in a crowded bar, watching television in a busy house, or listening to mumbled speech in an art-house movie. It is much easier to comprehend muffled speech while watching the speaker's lip movements. If you look away, it is much more difficult to 'hear' what they are saying. Even when there are no intrusions from background noise, the speech sounds heard can be influenced by visual cues from lip movements. For example, if the sound is 'baa' but the lip movements are consistent with saying 'gaa', then the observer hears 'daa' while they are watching the lips but 'baa' when they are not. This phenomenon is known as the McGurk effect (McGurk & McDonald, 1976). Ventriloquism demonstrates another form of interaction between visual and auditory speech cues: the ventriloquist's speech sounds appear to come from the mouth of the dummy.

Body motion

Body motion is signalled both by the visual system and by the vestibular system. If you sway from side to side, the image projected onto each retina will normally slide back and forth, giving you direct visual confirmation of your body sway (self-motion, mentioned in Table 7.2). The hair cells in your vestibular system will also be deflected by the fluid currents flowing through the chambers of the vestibular labyrinth, giving an additional source of information about your motion. Psychophysical data indicate that humans' perception of body motion does indeed rely upon a combination of visual and vestibular information (Butler, Smith, Campos, & Bülthoff, 2010). You may think that your ability to stand on one leg is due to your sense of balance, but try it with your eyes closed. It becomes much more difficult in the absence of subtle visual cues caused by body sway, which are combined with vestibular cues.

Motion sickness is a common complaint among passengers travelling in cars, aeroplanes, boats, and spacecraft (see Figure 7.18). Symptoms usually include nausea, sweating, and light-headedness. The condition is thought to be caused either by conflicts between the visual and vestibular cues to body motion or by conflicts between different vestibular cues. For example:

- If you are inside a cabin in a moving vessel, with no view of the outside world, movements will be sensed by the vestibular system without any corresponding motion signals from the visual system. The mismatch between visual and vestibular cues tends to cause motion sickness. The condition can be minimized by ensuring that you have a good view out of a window.

- When you tilt your head, separate signals are triggered in different parts of the vestibular organ; rotational acceleration of the head is sensed by the semicircular canals and a change in the direction of gravitational force caused by the change in tilt angle is sensed by the utricle and saccule. The two signals should and do normally match. But, while turning at high speed (e.g. cornering in a fast car or banking in an aeroplane), the resulting *g*-force combines with gravity to alter the tilt signal, so introducing a mismatch with the rotational signal. A common consequence is a feeling of dizziness and disorientation. It is best to avoid making tilting movements of your head while you are a passenger in a vehicle unless the vehicle is moving in a straight line at a constant speed.

- Flight and driving simulators, and IMAX films, contain vivid visual cues about body motion (optic flow) in the absence of vestibular signals (because you are sitting still looking at a screen). The sensation of body motion is often diminished due to the lack of vestibular stimulation. But particularly powerful visual images may cause viewers to experience motion sickness due to the mismatch between their visual and vestibular responses. It is best to use a simulator equipped with hydraulic rams to generate some vestibular signals.

Alterations to vestibular signals can occur when the composition of the vestibular fluid changes, as you may recall from the earlier discussion of the consequences of excessive alcohol consumption. Other potentially harmful substances may also affect the composition of the vestibular fluid, so nausea and sickness may be an evolved response that rids the body of ingested toxins.

FIGURE 7.18 *Motion sickness frequently occurs during space flight because of the lack of gravitational force acting on the vestibular system. The mismatch between the abnormal vestibular signals and visual feedback causes nausea.*
Source: © Mopic / Shutterstock.com.

Explanations of multimodal effects in perception

Psychophysical results clearly indicate that perceptual processing is influenced in various ways by interactions between signals in different sensory modalities. What route do the neural signals follow to achieve this convergence? Unsurprisingly, given the diversity of multimodal effects, a number of different routes seem to be involved:

- The superior colliculus in the midbrain is known to receive projections from several sensory pathways and is thought to integrate responses across the modalities, perhaps under the influence of cortical neurons (Jiang, Jiang, & Stein, 2002). This structure could mediate multimodal orienting effects.

- Neurons in the orbitofrontal cortex of macaque monkeys are multimodal, responding to a combination of smell and taste, or smell and vision, or taste and vision (Rolls & Baylis, 1994). So, this cortical area is a likely neural substrate for multimodal flavour perception.

- Functional neuroimaging studies indicate that cross-modal audiovisual object representations are formed in the lateral temporal cortex, at sites where unimodal visual and auditory signals converge. Cross-modal integration of visual and tactile object perception appears to take place in another higher-order area of the cortex at the border between the occipital and parietal regions, which is normally considered to be part of the ventral visual pathway (Amedi, Malach, Hendler, Peled, & Zohary, 2001).

- Physiological research shows that bimodal neurons in the superior temporal cortex (part of the dorsal stream) are the likely neural substrate of integration between visual and vestibular signals about body motion (Gu, Angelaki, & DeAngelis, 2008).

- Anatomical studies of the primate cortex have found direct connections between the auditory cortex, visual cortex, and somatosensory cortex (Schroeder & Foxe, 2002).

Bayesian theories of multimodal integration have also had some success in explaining data obtained from psychophysical experiments (as explained in Focus Point 7.3).

Figure 7.19 summarizes the processing architecture that serves human sensation and perception. All of the sensory information we receive from the external world is picked up by four different types of sensory receptor (bottom). Signals from the receptors are relayed to the cortex via the thalamus (except for olfactory signals, as mentioned earlier in the section 'Sensory Pathways') and also travel to the superior colliculus. The latter structure is responsible for fast orienting responses to new stimuli across the sensory modalities, while cortical destinations are responsible for analysing the sensory and perceptual attributes of the stimuli. Six qualitatively distinct modalities of *sensation* correspond to the six specialized receiving areas in the cortex: vision, audition, somatosensation, vestibular sensation, olfaction, and gustation (second line). Higher-level cortical areas combine information across the modalities to produce multimodal representations of *perceptual* objects (top).

Notice in Figure 7.19 that signals flow back and forth between different cortical areas as well as between the cortex and subcortical structures (superior colliculus and thalamus). Top-down information flow can prioritize and guide lower-level processing and so help to resolve the ambiguities that are a recurring feature of sensory processing. Information is combined from multiple sources, including various sensory attributes and modalities as well as assumptions based on experience.

The end results of all of this processing are internal representations of the world, which constitute the brain's best guesses as to what is out there. These representations correspond to your sensations and perceptions. Most of the time these guesses are correct, of course, otherwise you would not survive long in a world full of natural hazards.

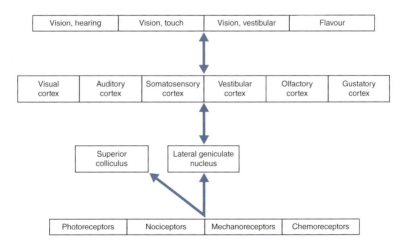

FIGURE 7.19 *Processing architecture of sensation and perception. Most signals from sensory receptors pass through the lateral geniculate nucleus on the way to modality-specific receiving areas in the cortex. There is also a small subcortical projection to the superior colliculus. Higher-level cortical areas compute multimodal object representations, which combine information from multiple modality-specific areas.*

SECTION SUMMARY

- There is considerable overlap between the computations performed by the neural systems serving different sensory modalities, and research has revealed extensive connections between the neural systems serving different modalities, leading to multimodal perception.

- Orienting towards new stimulus events is faster and more reliable when the events involve multiple sensory modalities, consistent with the combination of responses across modalities.

- The flavour of food is an inherently multisensory experience because it has been shown to involve a combination of taste, smell, temperature, touch, sight, sound, and pain.

- Object perception is also multisensory. For example, it is much easier to comprehend speech while watching the speaker's lip movements.

- Human perception of body motion relies upon a combination of visual and vestibular information, as revealed by motion sickness and dizziness during body motions.

- Interactions between signals in different sensory modalities involve a number of different neural routes, involving both cortical and subcortical structures.

FUTURE DIRECTIONS

LEARNING OBJECTIVE 7.8

Demonstrate an understanding of the traditional research undertaken in perception and possible future research and directions within the field.

Perceptual research has traditionally focused particularly on how the sensory systems process simple attributes such as loudness, luminance contrast, sourness, tactile vibration, and so on. Most research has studied each sensory modality in isolation from other modalities, with measures such as the procedures outlined by signal detection theory taken to gauge the role of other aspects of cognition (memory, attention, and so on). There are sound reasons behind this research strategy; when aiming to establish the basic principles of perceptual processing, it is important to begin with the simplest possible stimuli and tasks, which will offer the greatest amount of control of the experimental variables. But a great deal is now known about low-level processing, so the focus of research is shifting towards more complex scenarios involving contributions from multiple modalities, or interactions between perception, memory, and attention. For example, research on sensory substitution is exploring new ways in which a sensory deficit in one sensory modality can be compensated for by using another modality (see Focus Point 7.4).

SENSORY SUBSTITUTION AND CORTICAL PLASTICITY

Sensory substitution devices compensate for loss in one modality (such as vision) by substituting it with information supplied by an artificial receptor to another sensory modality. For example, a blind person can be trained to recognize visual patterns using information presented on the tongue via a tongue display device (TDU; Bach-y-Rita & Kercel, 2003). A device shaped like a lollipop is placed on the tongue, and a flexible array of electrodes on the surface of the device converts simple visual images into patterns of electrotactile stimulation. Another device that has been used in sensory substitution research converts visual information into sounds; as the scene is scanned from left to right, height in the visual field is represented by pitch, and brightness by loudness.

The conventional view of modality specialization in the sensory cortex is that it is fixed. The auditory cortex processes sounds, and only sounds, while the visual cortex processes only images, and so on. But what happens to these specialized areas of cortex when sensory substitution devices are used? Kupers et al. (2006) trained congenitally blind participants to recognize patterns using a TDU. Neuroimaging results indicated that the *visual* cortex of blind participants was activated by the TDU, even though the stimulation was tactile. Furthermore, transcranial magnetic stimulation applied to the visual cortex of these participants induced tactile sensations apparently located on the tongue (in sighted individuals such stimulation would produce flashes of light).

How could a tactile stimulus give rise to a visual sensation, at least in terms of activating the visual cortex, given that tactile responses arrive in the somatosensory cortex (one cannot, of course, ask a blind person whether they are experiencing visual sensations)? One route discussed in this chapter (see the earlier section 'Explanations of Multimodal Effects in Perception') for sharing information between areas serving different modalities involves direct connections between specialist cortical areas. Perhaps training with sensory substitution devices activates and strengthens these links between modality-specific areas, breaking down the barriers between the modalities. A TDU, for instance, may reinforce a pathway linking the somatosensory cortex to the visual cortex.

New research on sensory substitution promises not only new discoveries about the plasticity of the sensory systems but also improvements in the quality of life for recipients of this new technology.

DISCUSSION POINT

Here are some examples of sensory substitution devices and the research behind them. Discuss some ways that you think sensory substitution devices might develop in the future.

- **This video**[6] shows Erik Weihenmayer using the BrainPort TDU technology while climbing Utah's formidable Castleton Tower.
- The vOICe is a sensory substitution device designed to help blind people to use sounds to build an image in their minds of the things around them. **In this 2014 TED Talk**[7], Michael Proulx, from the University of Bath, explains how The vOICe works.
- **In this 2012 TED Talk**[8], Dr. Amir Amedi explains how he uses music and sounds to make blind people 'see' their environment.

Recent research has also begun to focus on the extent to which perceptual processing is optimized for handling human faces and bodies (see Focus Point 7.5).

SOCIAL PERCEPTION

Humans are highly social creatures, generally living in close proximity to others, so social interactions dominate much of human behaviour. These interactions depend on the ability to recognize individuals rapidly and reliably, and to perceive the moods, intentions, and actions of others. Visual perception is especially important in terms of the richness of the information it can provide. For instance, facial movements, gestures, and body actions can communicate gender, sexual orientation, attractiveness, openess, social dominance, vulnerability, threat, and deceptive intent (see Shiffrar, 2008; Van Boxtel & Lu, 2012).

The visual system of the human brain is traditionally considered to be a general-purpose system; it uses the same operations to capture all visual images regardless of their content (Marr, 1982). However, a growing body of research in the area of social perception indicates that many of the brain's neural structures and functions are actually optimized for processing social information, and this research will have fundamental implications for our understanding of how the brain mediates human social interactions (the 'social brain'; Adolphs, 2009). Early visual processing of basic sensory features, such as contour orientation and motion direction, is known to take place in the occipital lobe. Several populations of cells in the temporal lobe seem to specialize in processing socially relevant stimuli, namely faces and bodies.

We can spot a face in a scene, and recognize a familiar face, incredibly quickly (Jacques & Rossion, 2006). In keeping with this expertise, Haxby, Hoffman, and Gobbini (2000) proposed a neural model of face processing that subdivides face perception into two specialized components. The first component processes the invariant aspects of faces, allowing us to recognize faces despite changes in viewpoint, expression, and so on. This process is located in the fusiform face area of the temporal lobe. The second component processes changeable aspects of faces, such as facial expressions of emotion and the direction of eye gaze (highly significant in a social context). This component is located in the superior temporal sulcus.

Naive observers can detect a moving human body in a scene in a fraction of a second, even when the information available is minimal. Johansson (1973) filmed actors in such a way that only 12 isolated points of light were visible, placed on their body at the major joints. Observers can reliably judge gender, identity, mood, and so on from these so-called biological motion displays (see the review in Blake & Shiffrar, 2007). Psychophysical and physiological studies have found evidence for temporal-lobe mechanisms that specialize in the detection of human body motion. As in the case of face perception, there are at least two cortical areas that specialize in body processing; these are known as the extrastriate body area and the fusiform body area. Interestingly, these areas lie adjacent to face-processing areas (Taylor, Wiggett, & Downing, 2007). The picture emerging from recent research is of an extensive network of visual processing areas in the cortex that are specialized for social perception.

Experimental techniques are likely to become yet more sophisticated and complex. Previous research on human sensation and perception has relied heavily on psychophysical techniques; participants make simple judgements about qualities such as loudness, brightness, or bitterness, and the experimenter draws inferences from the results about underlying neural structures. Neuroimaging research now offers new ways to examine how the brain processes sensory stimuli, and it has had a major impact in recent years. Researchers are developing new experimental protocols to push the technique in new directions. Other neuroscientific techniques are also coming to the fore and offer the prospect of new discoveries about the neural processes underpinning perception (see Research Methods 7.2). Nevertheless, psychophysics will continue to play a valuable role in research because only psychophysical data can tell us directly what experimental participants actually perceive during an experiment.

SECTION SUMMARY

- Future research is likely to focus more on interactions between different sensory modalities and interactions between perception, memory, and attention.
- It will also focus on new ways to compensate for a deficit in one sensory modality using another modality; the ways in which the sensory systems are optimised for processing social information; and new, more powerful ways to resolve issues in perception by combining multiple neuroscientific and psychophysical techniques.

CHAPTER SUMMARY

This chapter has considered the ways in which research on sensation and perception examines how we acquire, process, and apprehend information from the world around us. We did this by first exploring some basic principles and key approaches that underpin the study of sensation and perception, namely those of the psychophysical and neuroscientific disciplines. We then specifically examined how neuroscience has contributed to the field, considered some of the difficulties raised by the issue of sensory qualia, and explored specific modalities in greater depth. The chapter next moved on to an exploration of multimodal interaction in perception and how representations of external stimuli, such as edibility and object identity, can be generated via multiple modes of input. Perceptual research is becoming increasingly sophisticated and complex in its efforts to understand how our sensory systems process complex scenarios involving contributions from multiple modalities.

ESSAY QUESTIONS

1. Critically assess the various experimental techniques that can be used to study sensation and perception.
2. Summarize the major neural pathways supporting human perception, and discuss how they can be used to distinguish between the sensory modalities.
3. Assess the evidence that human perception involves the use of inferences to resolve ambiguities.

KEY TERMS

- **after-effects:** A dramatically altered perception of a stimulus resulting from prolonged exposure to unchanging sensory stimulation.
- **chemoreceptor:** Receptor neurons convert energy arriving at the sense organs from the environment into neural signals; taste and smell are based on chemoreceptors, which respond to chemicals in foodstuffs or carried on the air.
- **cochlea:** The auditory portion of the inner ear, a core component of which is the sensory organ of hearing, which lies along a partition separating the cochlea's fluid chambers.

- **cones:** A type of photoreceptor cell (see also **rods**). Rods and cones respond over different ranges of light level. Cones are over 30 times less sensitive to light than rods and operate effectively only during daylight.
- **dorsal stream:** Connections between cells in the visual cortex are organized into two distinct streams on the basis of the cortical areas involved. The dorsal stream follows a higher route into the parietal lobe and specializes in visuospatial processing, including motion analysis and visually guided reaching. See also **ventral stream**.
- **flavour:** The sensation of eating transcends individual sensory modalities. Olfactory and gustatory components are essential to create a sensation complex that is perceived as a flavour.
- **haptics:** Perception and manipulation of objects through touch.
- **illusions:** Experiences of perception not matching reality; in illusions, objects, patterns, and surfaces may appear distorted in shape, size, texture, or structure.
- **just-noticeable difference (JND):** A fundamental metric in psychophysical experiments. It is the smallest change in a stimulus that a participant can reliably detect.
- **mechanoreceptor:** The oldest form of receptor; it responds to mechanical distortion or fluid movement.
- **neuroimaging:** Techniques, such as computed tomography scanning and functional magnetic resonance imaging, that can build a highly detailed 3D representation of the structure and function of the living human brain, even while its host is receiving sensory stimuli.
- **nociceptor:** A receptor with no specialized receptor process but that is spread throughout the body and responds to stimulation that is harmful, such as tissue damage and excessive heat.
- **perceptual constancy:** The ability of the sensory systems to build relatively stable, constant representations of objects despite variations in simple stimulus properties such as retinal size and orientation.
- **photoreceptors:** Receptors in the eye that serve vision. There are two types, called rods and cones, each of which contain light-sensitive pigment molecules. Receptor neurons convert energy arriving at the sense organs from the environment into neural signals.
- **population coding:** The process in which different values of a stimulus attribute, such as direction or tilt, are coded by different patterns of activity in a population of neurons.
- **psychophysics:** A discipline that studies the link between physical stimuli and perception.
- **qualia:** A philosophical term used to refer to primitive conscious mental states, such as colour or heat.
- **rods:** A type of photoreceptor cell (see also **cones**). Rods and cones respond over different ranges of light level. Rods operate only after dusk.
- **thalamus:** A neural structure situated between the vertebrate cerebral cortex and the midbrain that regulates the flow of information around the brain. The olfactory pathway is the only one that does not have a synapse in the thalamus.
- **topographical map:** An ordered spatial distribution of the tuning properties of individual cells at different locations within neural structures such as the surface of the cortex, or in the thalamus.
- **umami:** The fifth primary taste dimension, which was found only relatively recently and is named after the Japanese word for 'good taste' or 'yummy'. Also called 'savouriness'. The other four taste dimensions identified by psychophysical research are sweetness, sourness, saltiness, and bitterness.
- **univariance:** A fundamental principle of neural coding in which sensory neurons give only a single output (firing level) so they cannot simultaneously separate out information about different stimulus dimensions.
- **ventral stream:** Connections between cells in the visual cortex are organized into two distinct streams on the basis of the cortical areas involved. The ventral or 'what' stream follows a lower route into the temporal lobe and specializes in the visual discrimination of fine details and object identification. See also **dorsal stream**.
- **vestibular sense:** A sense that signals rotation of the head as well as the head's position with respect to gravity. It is used to stabilize eye position and body posture. It is also responsible for vertigo, motion sickness, and the sensory effects of alcohol intoxication.

NOTES

....

1. http://www.jove.com/video/4375/perceptual-category-processing-uncanny-valley-hypothesis-dimension
2. https://www.ted.com/talks/christopher_decharms_scans_the_brain_in_real_time
3. http://bigthink.com/videos/unlocking-the-mysterious-connection-between-taste-smell-and-memory
4. http://www.echalk.co.uk/amusements/OpticalIllusions/silhouette/silhouette.html
5. http://www.echalk.co.uk/amusements/OpticalIllusions/pinwheel/pinwheel.html
6. http://www.bbc.co.uk/news/health-13358608
7. https://www.youtube.com/watch?v=2_EA6hHuUSA
8. https://www.youtube.com/watch?v=jVBp2nDmg7E

FURTHER RESOURCES

....

Bermeitinger, C., Goelz, R., Johr, N., Neumann, M., Ecker, U. K., & Doerr, R. (2009). The hidden persuaders break into the tired brain. *Journal of Experimental Social Psychology, 45*(2), 320–326.

Driver, J., & Noesselt, T. (2008). Multisensory interplay reveals crossmodal influences on 'sensory-specific' brain regions, neural responses, and judgments. *Neuron, 57*(1), 11–23.

Greenwald, A. G., Spangenberg, E. R., Pratkanis, A. R., & Eskenazi, J. (1991). Double-blind tests of subliminal self-help audiotapes. *Psychological Science, 2*(2), 119–122.

Hodgkin, A. L., & Huxley, A. F. (1952). A quantitative description of membrane current and its application to conduction and excitation in nerve. *Journal of Physiology, 117*(4), 500.

Intaitė, M., Noreika, V., Šoliūnas, A., & Falter, C. M. (2013). Interaction of bottom-up and top-down processes in the perception of ambiguous figures. *Vision Research, 89*, 24–31.

Kaas, J. H., & Hackett, T. A. (2000). Subdivisions of auditory cortex and processing streams in primates. *Proceedings of the National Academy of Sciences of the United States of America, 97*(22), 11793–11799.

Karremans, J. C., Stroebe, W., & Claus, J. (2006). Beyond Vicary's fantasies: The impact of subliminal priming and brand choice. *Journal of Experimental Social Psychology, 42*(6), 792–798.

Kluender, K. R., Levi, D. M., Bartoshuk, L. M., Herz, R. S., Klatzky, R. L., & Lederman, S. J. (2012). *Sensation and perception* (3rd ed.). Sunderland, MA: Sinauer Associates.

Knill, D. C., & Pouget, A. (2004). The Bayesian brain: The role of uncertainty in neural coding and computation. *Trends in Neurosciences, 27*(12), 712–719.

Kravitz, D. J., Saleem, K. S., Baker, C. I., & Mishkin, M. (2011). A new neural framework for visuospatial processing. *Nature Reviews Neuroscience, 12*(4), 217–230.

Lennie, P. (1998). Single units and visual cortical organization. *Perception, 27*, 889–936.

Marr, D. (1982). *Vision*. San Francisco, CA: Freeman & Co.

Mather, G. (2011). *Essentials of sensation and perception*. Hove, UK: Routledge.

Mather, G. (2016). *Foundations of sensation and perception* (3rd ed.). Abingdon, UK: Routledge.

Nassi, J. J., & Callaway, E. M. (2009). Parallel processing strategies of the primate visual system. *Nature Reviews Neuroscience, 10*(5), 360–372.

Sterzer, P., & Kleinschmidt, A. (2007). A neural basis for inference in perceptual ambiguity. *Proceedings of the National Academy of Sciences of the United States of America, 104*(1), 323–328.

Yeshurun, Y., & Sobel, N. (2010). An odor is not worth a thousand words: From multidimensional odors to unidimensional odor objects. *Annual Review of Psychology, 61*, 219–241.

Zajonc, R. B. (2001). Mere exposure: A gateway to the subliminal. *Current Directions in Psychological Science, 10*(6), 224–228.

REFERENCES

Adelson, E. H. (1993). Perceptual organization and the judgment of brightness. *Science, 262,* 2042–2044.

Adolphs, R. (2009). The social brain: Neural basis of social knowledge. *Annual Review of Psychology, 60,* 693–716.

Albrecht, D. G., & Hamilton, D. B. (1982). Striate cortex of monkey and cat: Contrast response function. *Journal of Neurophysiology, 48*(1), 217–237.

Amedi, A., Malach, R., Hendler, T., Peled, S., & Zohary, E. (2001). Visuo-haptic object-related activation in the ventral visual pathway. *Nature Neuroscience, 4*(3), 324–330.

Bach-y-Rita, P., & Kercel, S. W. (2003). Sensory substitution and the human–machine interface. *Trends in Cognitive Sciences, 7*(12), 541–546.

Barker, A. T., Jalinous, R., & Freeston, I. L. (1985). Non-invasive magnetic stimulation of human motor cortex. *Lancet, 325*(8437), 1106–1107.

Blake, R., & Shiffrar, M. (2007). Perception of human motion. *Annual Review of Psychology, 58,* 47–73.

Blausen.com staff. (2014). Medical gallery of Blausen Medical 2014. *WikiJournal of Medicine, 1*(2). doi:10.15347/wjm/2014.010

Bowers, J. S., & Davis, C. J. (2012). Bayesian just-so stories in psychology and neuroscience. *Psychological Bulletin, 138*(3), 389–414.

Bradley, M. M., Miccoli, L., Escrig, M. A., & Lang, P. J. (2008). The pupil as a measure of emotional arousal and autonomic activation. *Psychophysiology, 45*(4), 602–607.

Bregman, A. S. (1990). *Auditory scene analysis: The perceptual organization of sound.* Cambridge, MA: MIT Press.

Butler, J. S., Smith, S. T., Campos, J. L., & Bülthoff, H. H. (2010). Bayesian integration of visual and vestibular signals for heading. *Journal of Vision, 10*(11), 23.

Cain, W. S. (1977). Differential sensitivity for smell: 'Noise' at the nose. *Science, 195*(4280), 796–798.

Cain, W. S. (1982). Odor identification by males and females: Predictions vs performance. *Chemical Senses, 7*(2), 129–142.

Chaudhari, N., Landin, A. M., & Roper, S. D. (2000). A metabotropic glutamate receptor variant functions as a taste receptor. *Nature Neuroscience, 3*(2), 113–119.

Cole, J., & Paillard, J. (1995). Living without touch and peripheral information about body position and movement: Studies with deafferented subjects. In J. L. Bermudez, A. J. Marcel, & N. M. Eilan (Eds.), *The body and the self* (pp. 245–266) Cambridge, MA: MIT Press.

Darwin, C. J., & Ciocca, V. (1992). Grouping in pitch perception: Effects of onset asynchrony and ear of presentation of a mistuned component. *Journal of the Acoustical Society of America, 91,* 3381–3390.

De Valois, R., Albrecht, D., & Thorell, L. (1982). Spatial frequency selectivity of cells in macaque visual cortex. *Vision Research, 22,* 545–559.

Diederich, A., & Colonius, H. (2004). Bimodal and trimodal multisensory enhancement: Effects of stimulus onset and intensity on reaction time. *Perception & Psychophysics, 66*(8), 1388–1404.

Ernst, M. O., & Banks, M. S. (2002). Humans integrate visual and haptic information in a statistically optimal fashion. *Nature, 415*(6870), 429–433.

Fasold, O., von Brevern, M., Kuhberg, M., Ploner, C. J., Villringer, A., Lempert, T., & Wenzel, R. (2002). Human vestibular cortex as identified with caloric stimulation in functional magnetic resonance imaging. *Neuroimage, 17*(3), 1384–1393.

Fechner, G. T. (1860/1966). *Elements of psychophysics* (trans. H. E. Adler). New York, NY: Holt, Rinehart and Winston.

Fetter, M., Haslwanter, T., Bork, M., & Dichgans, J. (1999). New insights into positional alcohol nystagmus using three-dimensional eye-movement analysis. *Annals of Neurology, 45*(2), 216–223.

Fitzpatrick, D. C., Batra, R., Stanford, T. R., & Kuwada, S. (1997). A neuronal population code for sound localization. *Nature, 388,* 871–874.

Goodale, M. A., & Milner, A. D. (1992). Separate visual pathways for perception and action. *Trends in Neurosciences*, *15*(1), 20–25.

Gray, R. (2005). On the concept of a sense. *Synthese*, *147*(3), 461–475.

Gu, Y., Angelaki, D. E., & DeAngelis, G. C. (2008). Neural correlates of multisensory cue integration in macaque MSTd. *Nature Neuroscience*, *11*(10), 1201–1210.

Hawley, M. L., Litovsky, R. Y., & Culling, J. F. (2004). The benefit of binaural hearing in a cocktail party: Effect of location and type of interferer. *Journal of the Acoustical Society of America*, *115*, 833–843.

Haxby, J. V., Hoffman, E. A., & Gobbini, M. I. (2000). The distributed human neural system for face perception. *Trends in Cognitive Sciences*, *4*(6), 223–233.

Hodgkin, A. L., & Huxley, A. F. (1952). A quantitative description of membrane current and its application to conduction and excitation in nerve. *Journal of Physiology*, *117*(4), 500–544.

Howard, A., & Angus, J. (2009) *Acoustics and psychoacoustics* (4th ed.). Amsterdam, Netherlands: Focus Press.

Hubel, D. H., & Wiesel, T. N. (1959). Receptive fields of single neurones in the cat's striate cortex. *Journal of Physiology*, *148*(3), 574–591.

Intaitė, M., Noreika, V., Šoliūnas, A., & Falter, C. M. (2013). Interaction of bottom-up and top-down processes in the perception of ambiguous figures. *Vision Research*, *89*, 24–31.

Jacobs, L. F. (2012). From chemotaxis to the cognitive map: The function of olfaction. *Proceedings of the National Academy of Sciences of the United States of America*, *109*(Suppl. 1), 10693–10700.

Jacques, C., & Rossion, B. (2006). The speed of individual face categorization. *Psychological Science*, *17*(6), 485–492.

Jiang, W., Jiang, H., & Stein, B. E. (2002). Two corticotectal areas facilitate multisensory orientation behavior. *Journal of Cognitive Neuroscience*, *14*(8), 1240–1255.

Johansson, G. (1973). Visual perception of biological motion and a model for its analysis. *Perception & Psychophysics*, *14*(2), 202–211.

Jönsson, F. U., Tchekhova, A., Lönner, P., & Olsson, M. J. (2005). A metamemory perspective on odor naming and identification. *Chemical Senses*, *30*(4), 353–365.

Kaas, J. H., & Hackett, T. A. (2000). Subdivisions of auditory cortex and processing streams in primates. *Proceedings of the National Academy of Sciences of the United States of America*, *97*(22), 11793–11799.

Keeley, B. L. (2002). Making sense of the senses: Individuating modalities in humans and other animals. *Journal of Philosophy*, *99*(1), 5–28.

Khan, R. M., Luk, C. H., Flinker, A., Aggarwal, A., Lapid, H., Haddad, R., & Sobel, N. (2007). Predicting odor pleasantness from odorant structure: Pleasantness as a reflection of the physical world. *Journal of Neuroscience*, *27*(37), 10015–10023.

Klatzky, R. L., Lederman, S. J., & Metzger, V. A. (1985). Identifying objects by touch: An 'expert system'. *Perception & Psychophysics*, *37*(4), 299–302.

Knill, D. C., & Pouget, A. (2004). The Bayesian brain: The role of uncertainty in neural coding and computation. *Trends in Neurosciences*, *27*(12), 712–719.

Kravitz, D. J., Saleem, K. S., Baker, C. I., & Mishkin, M. (2011). A new neural framework for visuospatial processing. *Nature Reviews Neuroscience*, *12*(4), 217–230.

Kupers, R., Fumal, A., de Noordhout, A. M., Gjedde, A., Schoenen, J., & Ptito, M. (2006). Transcranial magnetic stimulation of the visual cortex induces somatotopically organized qualia in blind subjects. *Proceedings of the National Academy of Sciences of the United States of America*, *103*(35), 13256–13260.

Lederman, S. J., & Klatzky, R. L. (1987). Hand movements: A window into haptic object recognition. *Cognitive Psychology*, *19*(3), 342–368.

Lennie, P. (1998). Single units and visual cortical organization. *Perception*, *27*, 889–936.

Manescu, S., Frasnelli, J., Lepore, F., & Djordjevic, J. (2014). Now you like me, now you don't: Impact of labels on odor perception. *Chemical Senses*, *39*(2), 167–175. doi:10.1093/chemse/bjt066

Marr, D. (1982). *Vision*. San Francisco, CA: Freeman & Co.

Mather, G. (2009). *Foundations of sensation and perception* (2nd ed.). Hove, UK: Psychology Press.

Mather, G., Pavan, A., Campana, G., & Casco, C. (2008). The motion aftereffect reloaded. *Trends in Cognitive Sciences, 12*(12), 481–487.

McDonald, J. J., Teder-Sälejärvi, W. A., & Hillyard, S. A. (2000). Involuntary orienting to sound improves visual perception. *Nature, 407*(6806), 906–908.

McGurk, H., & MacDonald, J. (1976). Hearing lips and seeing voices. *Nature, 264*, 746–748.

Meddis, R., & O'Mard, L. (1997). A unitary model of pitch perception. *Journal of the Acoustical Society of America, 102*, 1811–1820.

Mooney, C. (1957). Age in the development of closure ability in children. *Canadian Journal of Psychology, 11*, 219–226.

Moore, B. C., Glasberg, B. R., & Shailer, M. J. (1984). Frequency and intensity difference limens for harmonics within complex tones. *Journal of the Acoustical Society of America, 75*, 550–561.

Nelson, G., Chandrashekar, J., Hoon, M. A., Feng, L., Zhao, G., Ryba, N. J., & Zuker, C. S. (2002). An amino-acid taste receptor. *Nature, 416*(6877), 199–202.

Nowlis, G. H., & Frank, M. E. (1977). Qualities in hamster taste: Behavioral and neural evidence. In J. L. Magnen & P. MacLeod (Eds.), *Olfaction and taste symposium VI: Information retrieval* (pp. 241–248). London, UK: Information Retrieval.

Ochoa, J., & Torebjork, E. (1983). Sensations evoked by intraneural microstimulation of single mechanoreceptor units innervating the human hand. *Journal of Physiology, 342*, 633–654.

Orban, G. A., Lagae, L., Verri, A., Raiguel, S., Xiao, D., Maes, H., & Torre, V. (1992). First-order analysis of optical flow in monkey brain. *Proceedings of the National Academy of Sciences, 89*(7), 2595–2599.

Pallis, C. A. (1955). Impaired identification of faces and places with agnosia for colours: Report of a case due to cerebral embolism. *Journal of Neurology, Neurosurgery, and Psychiatry, 18*(3), 218–224.

Penagos, H., Melcher, J. R., & Oxenham, A. J. (2004). A neural representation of pitch salience in nonprimary human auditory cortex revealed with functional magnetic resonance imaging. *Journal of Neuroscience, 24*(30), 6810–6815.

Penfield, W., & Rasmussen, T. (1950). *The cerebral cortex of man*. New York, NY: Gale.

Perdreau, F., & Cavanagh, P. (2011). Do artists see their retinas? *Frontiers in Human Neuroscience, 5*(171). doi:10.3389/fnhum.2011.00171

Pfaffmann, C. (1955). Gustatory nerve impulses in rat, cat and rabbit. *Journal of Neurophysiology, 18*(5), 429–440.

Plack, C. J., Barker, D., & Hall, D. A. (2014). Pitch coding and pitch processing in the human brain. *Hearing Research, 307*, 53–64.

Reed, C. L., Shoham, S., & Halgren, E. (2004). Neural substrates of tactile object recognition: An fMRI study. *Human Brain Mapping, 21*(4), 236–246.

Rolls, E. T., & Baylis, L. L. (1994). Gustatory, olfactory, and visual convergence within the primate orbitofrontal cortex. *Journal of Neuroscience, 14*(9), 5437–5452.

Schroeder, C. E., & Foxe, J. J. (2002). The timing and laminar profile of converging inputs to multisensory areas of the macaque neocortex. *Cognitive Brain Research, 14*(1), 187–198.

Sela, L., & Sobel, N. (2010). Human olfaction: A constant state of change-blindness. *Experimental Brain Research, 205*(1), 13–29.

Shiffrar, M. (2008). The visual perception of dynamic body language. In I. Wachsmuth, M. Lenzen, & G. Knoblich (Eds.), *Embodied communication in humans and machines* (pp. 95–110). Oxford, UK: Oxford University Press.

Tamietto, M., & de Gelder, B. (2010). Neural bases of the non-conscious perception of emotional signals. *Nature Reviews Neuroscience, 11*, 697–708.

Taylor, J. C., Wiggett, A. J., & Downing, P. E. (2007). Functional MRI analysis of body and body part representations in the extrastriate and fusiform body areas. *Journal of Neurophysiology, 98*(3), 1626–1633.

Tolhurst, D. J., & Thompson, P. G. (1975). Orientation illusions and after-effects: Inhibition between channels. *Vision Research*, *15*(8), 967–972.

Tombs, S., & Silverman, I. (2004). Pupillometry: A sexual selection approach. *Evolution & Human Behavior*, *25*(4), 221–228.

Ungerleider, L. G., & Mishkin, M. (1982). Two cortical visual systems. In D. J. Ingle, M. A. Goodale, & R. J. W. Mansfield (Eds.), *Analysis of visual behavior* (pp. 549–586). Cambridge, MA: MIT Press.

Utz, K. S., Dimova, V., Oppenländer, K., & Kerkhoff, G. (2010). Electrified minds: transcranial direct current stimulation (tDCS) and galvanic vestibular stimulation (GVS) as methods of non-invasive brain stimulation in neuropsychology – A review of current data and future implications. *Neuropsychologia*, *48*(10), 2789–2810.

Van Boxtel, J. J. A., & Lu, H. (2012). Signature movements lead to efficient search for threatening actions. *PLoS ONE*, *7*, 1–6.

Weiss, Y., Simoncelli, E. P., & Adelson, E. H. (2002). Motion illusions as optimal percepts. *Nature Neuroscience*, *5*(6), 598–604.

Witt, J. K., Taylor, J. E. T., Sugovic, M., & Wixted, J. T. (2015). Signal detection measures cannot distinguish perceptual biases from response biases. *Perception*, *44*(3), 289–300.

Yeshurun, Y., & Sobel, N. (2010). An odor is not worth a thousand words: From multidimensional odors to unidimensional odor objects. *Annual Review of Psychology*, *61*, 219–241.

Yost, W. A. (2000). *Fundamentals of hearing*. San Diego, CA: Academic Press.

Zarzo, M. (2008). Psychologic dimensions in the perception of everyday odors: Pleasantness and edibility. *Journal of Sensory Studies*, *23*(3), 354–376.

ACTIVITY SOLUTIONS

ACTIVITY 7.1: TRUE OR FALSE?

TRUE

- Psychophysics focuses on the link between physical stimuli and perception.
- Neuroscience centres on the relationship between stimuli and neural responses.
- Psychophysical research studies the relationship between psychological events and physical stimuli.
- Computed tomography is a brain-scanning technique based on X-rays.
- fMRI scanners can detect changes in neural activity in the brain because they pick up changes in blood oxygenation that accompany neural activity.

FALSE

- JND stands for juxtaposed natural difference.
- A graph that plots the percentage of 'different' responses as a function of stimulus level is known as a psychotropic function.
- The rule that the JND is nearly always a constant fraction of the standard stimulus is known as Fechner's law.
- One of the earliest neuroscientific discoveries concerned speech deficits following damage to an area of the left frontal lobe of the cortex now known as Wernicke's speech area.
- Hubel and Wiesel (1959) discovered that cortical cells are broadly indiscriminate in the kinds of visual stimuli to which they respond.

8 Learning

MARK HASELGROVE

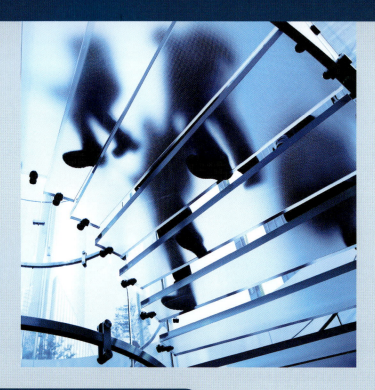

INTRODUCTION: WHAT IS LEARNING AND WHY DOES IT HAPPEN?

LEARNING OBJECTIVE 8.1

Critically evaluate the definition and purpose of learning in humans and other animals.

Learning is something that humans and other animals do almost all of the time. If you read this chapter and manage to remember some of the information that is contained within it to pass an exam, then you will have demonstrated your capacity to learn. If you have a cat or a dog as a pet, then you will have probably observed their ability to suddenly become very attentive towards you once you begin the process of making them a meal. I am reasonably confident that my dog, for example, was not born with a tendency to follow my wife around the kitchen just before his dinner time. I therefore suspect that he has learned this behaviour. Learning is not restricted to your waking hours either; you are even learning about the outside world when you are asleep. Arzi and colleagues (2012) showed that people could learn to change the amount that they sniffed to different sounds when the sounds were established as signals for either nice or nasty smells! And finally, learning is not restricted to relatively complex organisms either; as we shall see soon, learning can be observed even in single-celled organisms (Jennings, 1906).

Defining learning

Despite the numerous examples of learning that can easily be generated from the animal kingdom, it is relatively difficult to pin down an entirely satisfactory definition of the phenomenon. One intuitive definition of learning might be to suggest that it is in some way related to *the acquisition of information*. However, a moment's reflection reveals that this definition is unsuitable: a library acquires information, yet it could hardly be thought to have learned. Perhaps then we need to further qualify this statement: learning is *the acquisition of information by a biological organism*. This definition is better, but it is rather restrictive. It prevents the possibility that learning can occur in machines or computers, when, in everyday life, we know this is possible (think of the ability of Google or your phone to predict what you are going to type). As Domjan (1993) notes, there is no universally accepted definition of learning. However, many of the crucial aspects of learning can be understood as *relatively permanent changes in behaviour as a consequence of experience* (Domjan, 1993, pp. 12–15; Pearce, 2008, p. 13). This definition places an emphasis on the relationship between experience (such as experience based on the environment) and behaviour. However, by defining learning in terms of a change in behaviour, we are still being restrictive. For example, you may read this chapter, remember all of the information within in it, and then never do anything about it. We can refer to this as **behaviourally silent learning** (Dickinson, 1980) because in this case learning has not expressed itself in terms of behaviour. Does this mean that the information that has been acquired has not been learned? From the perspective of the scientific study of learning, we might have to say *yes*, because, no matter how convinced you are that you have acquired the information in this chapter just by reading it, you are relying on **introspection** to make this judgement – and, as we know from the history of psychology, introspection can be a poor method for establishing psychological principles. It is far better, instead, to rely on the measurement of something quantifiable from the organism – and that is why incorporating behaviour into our definition of learning is so important. Responses can be measured and linked to differences in environmental experience and, so long as we have designed our experiments properly, we can make some kind of inference about the underlying properties of learning.

The purpose of learning

Evolution has provided organisms with an impressive collection of reflexes that are present in the neonate from birth and that are expressed, it seems, without the necessity of learning. For example, human infants will demonstrate the rooting reflex, in which the child will turn their head towards an object that gently stimulates their cheek or mouth, and circle around in smaller and smaller arcs until they locate the object. This reflex aids breastfeeding and has obvious survival advantages to the newborn: if the infant had to learn to navigate towards its mother's nipple then it might well starve before acquiring a route to their meal. Reflexes can also be automatic, and fast. For example, in a **reflex arc**, a sensory neuron synapses at the spinal cord and from there onto a spinal motor neuron without having to pass through the brain. This permits sensory input (such as the perception of burning in the hand) to be acted upon quickly (withdrawing the hand from fire) to limit damage.

Reflexive behaviour, clearly, has its benefits then. However, it also has its limitations, for most organisms inhabit environments that have predictive relationships between events. For example, fire is typically bright, often has a smoky smell, and gets progressively warmer the closer you get to it. By learning to link these features of fire with a burn, an organism can avoid ever having to rely on the withdrawal reflex again, by simply learning to avoid stimuli that are associated with fire – and thus avoid being burnt. This being said, the predictive relationships between events in the world may not be permanent, as environments may change with time. For example, the cues for finding food in the spring may be rather different from the cues that are needed to find food during the autumn. Thus, to avoid starving in certain seasons, organisms must be able to modify their behaviour as a consequence of their experiences with the environment. You will recall, of course, that this is the very definition of learning that was provided just a moment ago.

TEST YOURSELF

How would you define learning? Why is learning useful?

SECTION SUMMARY

- Learning is something that humans and other animals do almost all of the time but it is relatively difficult to pin down an entirely satisfactory definition of the phenomenon.

- One intuitive (but incomplete) definition of learning might be to suggest that it is in some way related to *the acquisition of information*, but this is unduly restrictive.

- Many of the crucial aspects of learning can be understood as relatively permanent changes in behaviour as a consequence of experience.

- Evolution has provided organisms with an impressive collection of beneficial reflexes that are present in the neonate from birth; however, these are only beneficial in an environment that remains predictable.

TYPES OF LEARNING

LEARNING OBJECTIVE 8.2

Demonstrate an understanding of examples of fundamental forms of learning – including habituation, sensitization, classical conditioning, and instrumental conditioning – and the factors that influence them.

Habituation and sensitization

Perhaps the most basic form of learning that can be observed is the one in which the simple repetition of a stimulus results in a corresponding change in behaviour. **Habituation** and **sensitization** are both examples of this simple form of learning. In fact, you can very easily demonstrate habituation yourself, with the help of a friend – see Activity 8.1. Habituation refers to a reduction in the vigour, or likelihood, of a response being produced by repeated presentation of a stimulus.

ACTIVITY 8.1

DEMONSTRATION OF HABITUATION

Have a friend stand behind you and instruct them to clap their hands five or six times behind your head at unpredictable times over the period of about a minute. The first time that you hear the hand clap, you may well notice that you feel startled – depending on how loudly your friend clapped, perhaps you even jumped. However, by the time of the fifth or sixth clap, your startle response will have diminished. The effect that you have just experienced is called 'habituation'.

As you might imagine, habituation does not only take place to responses that are evoked by auditory stimuli, or indeed in humans. Kaye and Pearce (1987), for example, showed that the amount of time that a rat would spend orienting towards an illuminated light decreased when the light was repeatedly turned on. In fact, habituation is present across the animal kingdom, and is even demonstrable in single-celled organisms. Jennings (1906) showed that paramecia will contract upon being touched. However, after repeated touching, the number of touches that were required to make the paramecia contract increased to between 20 and 30. Despite its simple nature, habituation provides a way in which an organism can act in seemingly complex ways, such as change its preference to music – which, we might imagine, is the type of behaviour to be expected of intelligent creatures like humans, but not rats. However, Cross, Halcomb, and Matter (1967) showed that musically naive rats, if given a choice, avoided music by Schoenberg relative to music by Mozart. Following this initial test, the rats were exposed to music by Schoenberg for 12 hours a day for 52 days. Following exposure, the rats were given an opportunity to once again determine whether they would prefer to hear music by Mozart or Schoenberg. Now, a slight preference for the music by Schoenberg over Mozart was evident. Despite this behaviour appearing complex, it is little more than a demonstration of habituation. The initial test revealed the rats would avoid music by Schoenberg if given the choice – and this avoidance response could be based upon a very simple feature of the music, such as a preponderance of a particular note that rats find unpleasant. With repeated exposure to the music, this response diminished so that, upon final testing, the avoidance response to music by Schoenberg was comparable in magnitude to that for music by Mozart.

Most studies of habituation in animals do not use classical music as stimuli, which is a great pity. Instead, many studies have instead focused on habituation of rats' neophobic responses to novel flavours (i.e. their reluctance to consume new foods). For example, Domjan (1976) showed that rats, upon encountering a flavour for the first time, would drink very little of it (about 5 ml) – even if they were thirsty and the flavour was sweetened. After repeated exposure to the flavour over 10 days, however, this avoidance response was reduced through habituation, and consumption of the flavour increased (to around 15–20 ml). Habituation of neophobia is a good demonstration of the functional utility of the interaction between learned and innate behaviour. The initial, parsimonious, reaction to novel foods displayed by rats serves a functional role of limiting the possibility of being poisoned by unfamiliar, and potentially deadly, items. The reduction of this avoidance with repeated experience, however, allows the animal to learn to widen its diet to other foods. Habituation can be overcome, however; Groves and Thompson (1970) gave rats 14 presentations of a tone. After an initial short-lived increase in the startle response to the tone (an effect to which we will turn our attention in just a moment), responding to the tone gradually habituated. However, if a light was presented to the rat, then, on the next trial with the tone, responding was restored to the tone. This recovery of responding to a habituated stimulus is called 'dishabituation'.

However, repeated exposure to a stimulus does not always result in the weakening of the response that it evokes; sometimes the opposite may occur, and this is called 'sensitization', which is where simple exposure to a stimulus results in a *strengthening* of the response that it evokes. Cases of sensitization often occur with rather intense stimuli, they can be short lived, and they are considered to be the effect of a more general arousal process. For example, while watching a horror film, the

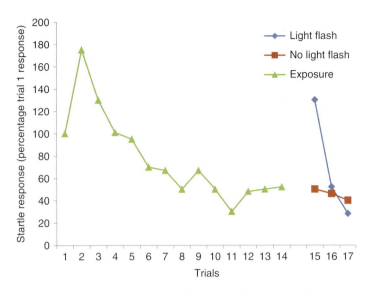

FIGURE 8.1 *Sensitization, habituation, and dishabituation of the rats' startle response.*

Source: Groves and Thompson (1970). American Psychological Association. Adapted with permission.

repeated exposure to, say, mildly scary scenes may build up tension so that, when something very scary happens, your fear response is strengthened. Here we have the sensitization of a response with repeated exposure to scary stimuli, rather than the habituation of a response. Sensitization, habituation, and dishabituation can all be observed in the results of the startle response experiment reported by Groves and Thompson (1970) shown in Figure 8.1. Behaviour is expressed as a percentage of the startle response in trial 1. In trials 2 and 3, the rats were more startled than they were in trial 1 (*sensitization*); however, with further exposure between trials 4 and 14, the startle response gradually weakened (*habituation*). Rats that had a light flash between trials 14 and 15 showed a sudden restoration of the startle response to the tone, relative to control rats who did not receive exposure to the light (*dishabituation*).

 Watch this video[1] of an experiment that investigates habituation and prepulse inhibition of acoustic startle response in rodents. The experiment is based on a paper by Valsamis and Schmid (2011) from the University of Western Ontario.

Sensitization is important for another effect, called 'pseudo-conditioning'. In the next section, we will discuss a type of learning called **classical conditioning**, in which a stimulus that is at first relatively boring to the animal comes to acquire a response by being paired with another, more motivationally significant, stimulus. Under these circumstances it is tempting to conclude that the initially boring stimulus elicited the response because of its relationship with the more motivationally significant stimulus. However, it is possible that the initially boring stimulus may have come to acquire an ability to evoke a response just through the effects of simple exposure – sensitization. In order to be confident that classical conditioning has actually occurred, appropriate control groups must be put in place that rule out this possibility.

Classical conditioning

What is classical conditioning?

If asked 'what is classical conditioning?', many people will be able to describe an experiment performed some time ago by Ivan Pavlov, in which dogs salivated whenever a bell was rung. For the most part, this description is correct; however, this will tend to be about as far as most people's knowledge of conditioning extends. What will not be appreciated, in all likelihood, is that Pavlov's experiment was just one of many conducted by him and his colleagues, and one of many more experiments that have been conducted by other researchers since then to investigate conditioning using different techniques and species in order to gain a better understanding of learning. It is perhaps not surprising that most of these researchers have not followed Pavlov's (1927) lead by studying drooling dogs; however, many researchers have used experimental designs that were first developed by Pavlov, and also continue to use a terminology that Pavlov developed. In order to gain a better understanding of what classical conditioning actually is, we will introduce four key terms that Pavlov himself used. These four terms allow psychologists to describe the stimuli and responses of *any* classical conditioning experiment in a relatively neutral manner. At first sight, it might seem confusing and unnecessary to use four abstract terms instead of describing the actual stimuli and responses from a conditioning experiment. However, as we will see now and later on in this chapter, using these terms has the advantage of allowing psychologists to quickly identify the key components of a conditioning experiment, as well as allowing them to compare and contrast different conditioning procedures with a common terminology.

To describe these four terms, we will refer to Pavlov's original conditioning experiment, the most important component of which was arguably the **unconditioned stimulus (US)**. This was a stimulus that had intrinsic biological significance to the animal, and in Pavlov's experiments was often food, delivered into the dog's mouth. This stimulus was called the unconditioned stimulus because it was able to *unconditionally* elicit a response; that is to say, it elicited a response in the animal without the need for learning. The response that the unconditioned stimulus was itself able to elicit was called the **unconditioned response (UR)**, which in Pavlov's experiments was salivation. In his experiments, Pavlov sounded a bell just before giving food to the dogs on a number of occasions (trials). At first, the bell elicited hardly any responding in the dogs – little more than the turn of a head, perhaps. Pavlov's crucial discovery, however, was that, after a number of trials in which the bell was paired with the food, the bell itself became capable of eliciting salivation in the dogs – even in the absence of any food (see Figure 8.2). Pavlov referred to the response that was elicited by the bell as a **conditioned response (CR)** because its presence was conditional upon the bell being trained with the US (food). Finally, the bell itself was termed, by Pavlov, the **conditioned stimulus (CS)** to identify it as a stimulus that could elicit a response on the basis of its training with the US. Hopefully, by understanding the way in which Pavlov classified stimuli and responses in his experiment, it can be appreciated how classical conditioning is an example of learning, at least as far as it was defined earlier in this chapter – the behaviour of Pavlov's dogs changed in a relatively permanent fashion (i.e. a CR was acquired) as a consequence of experience (pairing the CS with the US).

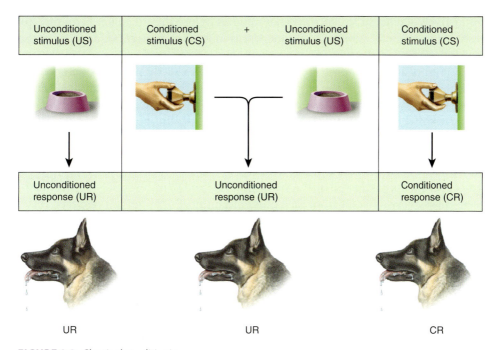

FIGURE 8.2 *Classical conditioning.*

Source: Comer, Ogden, & Furnam et al. (2013). Wiley. Reproduced with permission.

Classical conditioning in slugs and humans

Since Pavlov's discovery of the CR, many thousands of experiments have catalogued the existence of classical conditioning in a whole variety of species, from simple organisms such as the sea slug *Aplysia californica* (Carew, Hawkins, & Kandel, 1983) to rather more complex species such as adult humans (e.g. Bernstein & Webster, 1980). Now, neither the experiment conducted by Carew et al. nor Bernstein and Webster's experiment measured drips of saliva from the mouths of slugs or humans during the ringing of bells. Entirely different measures of conditioned responding were taken to entirely different stimuli. However, because of the terminology provided to us by Pavlov, we can quickly identify the key components of these experiments and understand their experimental designs. For example, in Carew et al.'s study, the experimenters paired the slight touch of a sea slug's siphon (the CS) with a mild electric shock that was delivered 0.5 seconds later to the slug's tail (the US). Before the first conditioning trial, the light touch to the slug's siphon had little effect – it resulted in the siphon withdrawing into the animal's body for only a short amount of time (about 10 seconds). However, after a number of trials in which the light touch was paired with the shock, the light touch came to elicit a withdrawal response that lasted much longer (about 50 seconds) even when the tail shock was not presented. We can identify this withdrawal response that came to be elicited by touching the slug's siphon as the CR.

Bernstein and Webster's experiment was very different. They were interested in understanding whether the food aversions that are often experienced by people undergoing treatment for cancer are a consequence of classical conditioning. To investigate this, Bernstein and Webster asked outpatients at a cancer clinic to eat a distinctively flavoured ice cream 15–60 minutes before their regular chemotherapy session. The logic behind the experiment was that the unpleasant side effects of the chemotherapy (e.g. nausea and vomiting) would serve as the US and support the acquisition of a CR to the ice cream (the CS). This is exactly what was observed by Bernstein and Webster. After only a single pairing of the ice cream with the chemotherapy, patients subsequently expressed an aversion to the ice cream (the CR) by eating less of it than a control group, who had also eaten the ice cream previously but who were not undergoing chemotherapy.

Appetitive and aversive conditioning

The experiments conducted by Carew et al. (1983) and Bernstein and Webster (1980) were clearly very different from each other in a number of important respects. However, they did have a significant feature in common. In both experiments, the motivational significance of the US was negative: that is to say it was an unpleasant event – a shock to the sea slug's tail in Carew et al.'s experiment, and nausea and vomiting in Bernstein and Webster's experiment with humans. Pavlov's experiment, in contrast, used a US that had a positive motivational significance – a pleasant event: food. We can use this distinction between the types of US as a way in which to classify different types of classical conditioning experiment. On the one hand we can have **appetitive conditioning**, in which the motivational significance of the US is positive. Pavlov's experiment is an obvious example of appetitive conditioning, as it uses food as the US in dogs, but appetitive conditioning is also commonly demonstrated in rats (e.g. Zamble, 1967) and pigeons (e.g. Brown & Jenkins, 1968) using food as the US. However, appetitive conditioning is not limited to experiments in which food is the US; water can also be used as a US to elicit a CR of licking in thirsty rats (e.g. Boice & Denny, 1965). Interestingly, sex can also serve as a US (although in this case the CR measured was, perhaps surprisingly, neither drooling nor licking). Domjan, Lyons, North, and Bruell (1986) illuminated a red light (honestly!) to male Japanese quail before allowing them to copulate with a female that was subsequently released into the cage. After only a few pairings of the red light (the CS) with copulation (the US), the quail began to spend more time near the red light during its illumination (a CR). They also grabbed and mounted the female quicker than a control group (who had also been exposed to the red light and female quail, but never together). Domjan, Blesbois, and Williams (1998) also showed that males released more sperm during copulation after being presented with a CS for sex, revealing the adaptive significance of conditioning.

However, not all USs are pleasant. On the other hand, we have **aversive conditioning**, in which the motivational significance of the US is negative. We have already encountered examples of aversive USs in the experiments that were described earlier by Carew et al. (1983) and Bernstein and Webster (1980), where an electric shock or vomiting/nausea served as the USs respectively. In fact, for many years a mild electric shock was commonly used as the US in studies of conditioning with rabbits and rats. In the former case (e.g. Gibbs, Latham, & Gormezano, 1978), the CS (e.g. a tone) may be followed by a brief, mild shock to the rabbit's cheek just strong enough to elicit an eye blink (the US). After a number of pairings of the CS with the US, the tone itself becomes able to elicit a blink in the eye of the rabbit. This is known as 'eye-blink conditioning'. In the latter case, with rats, a CS (e.g. a light) may be paired with the delivery of a mild shock delivered to the grid bars on the floor of a conditioning chamber (see Figure 8.3). After a number of pairings of the CS with the US, the light itself is capable

FIGURE 8.3 *A laboratory rat in a conditioning chamber. Speakers and lights on the walls can serve as conditioned stimuli. The grid floor can be electrified for aversive conditioning. For appetitive conditioning, food can be delivered from the pellet dispenser (top right) through a tube into the area of the box where the rat is poking his nose.*
Source: Mark Haselgrove / Peter Jones.

of eliciting a conditioned fear response in the rat – often measured by video recording how long the animal 'freezes' (remains motionless) during the CS, or by how much the CS interferes with other behaviour being recorded by the experimenter (e.g. Annau & Kamin, 1961). This is known as 'fear conditioning'. Freezing in fear has a significant adaptive value, as remaining motionless in the presence of a predator will result in the animal being much less likely to be detected, and hence attacked. Furthermore, a CS for a painful US has an analgesic (pain-killing) effect, with rats being less sensitive to pain having just been frightened by an aversive CS (Fanselow, 1980).

We have already encountered one example of aversive conditioning produced by a US of vomiting/nausea (Bernstein & Webster, 1980), and you yourself may have acquired an aversion to a particular alcoholic drink due to overindulgence (I certainly have, and am no longer able to tolerate the taste of brown ale after overindulgence during a school field trip!). The study of this effect, in humans, was motivated by the observation of taste-aversion conditioning in rats, in which a flavour (the CS) is paired with a drug (the US) that makes the rat feel nauseous. Upon subsequently encountering the flavour, rats will either avoid it completely after their first taste or consume very little of it (e.g. Garcia, Ervin, & Koelling, 1966). This is called 'taste-aversion learning', and it has a number of properties that have led some to suggest that it may in some way be a special form of learning (e.g. Rozin & Kalat, 1971). For example, it is particularly quick to be acquired (often in just one trial), whereas other CRs (such as appetitive conditioning in rats) are only acquired after many pairings of the CS and US. Perhaps even more impressively, conditioned taste aversions can still be detected when a long interval (sometimes many hours) separates the CS and US, far longer than most other conditioning procedures use. That said, taste-aversion conditioning displays a number of the properties of conditioning that seem to be widespread, both in terms of the particular type of conditioning procedure being used and the species being tested. In the final two sections of this discussion of classical conditioning, we will describe three of these properties: **extinction**, **latent inhibition**, and cue competition (e.g. **blocking**).

Extinction

We have focused so far on examples of the acquisition of conditioned responding, in which an animal learns to elicit a response to a stimulus. However, it is also important to consider how conditioned responding might be lost once it has been acquired. Consider, for instance, the example of taste-aversion conditioning; it makes good sense for humans and other animals to be able to learn to avoid a particular food, if it is paired with some kind of illness, as they will be less likely to consume this food in future – and thus avoid being poisoned. But it also makes sense for humans and animals to be able to modify their behaviour should the food no longer be followed by illness, such as is the case for a chemotherapy patient who is no longer receiving treatment. Learning needs to be sensitive enough to reflect environmental change. This is precisely what happens in extinction.

In this context, extinction does not refer to the death of an entire species. Instead it refers to the gradual disappearance of the CR when the US no longer follows the CS. As is so often the case for the facets of classical conditioning, the basic discovery of extinction was first made by Pavlov (1927). He discovered that the amount of saliva that was drooled by his dogs in response to a bell gradually reduced if the bell was repeatedly presented in the absence of food. Extinction is reliably observed across all of the examples of appetitive and aversive conditioning that were described in the previous section. Indeed, it seems as if the extinction of conditioned responding is just as prevalent as its acquisition. For example, fear conditioning in rats will extinguish if the CS is repeatedly presented in the absence of the shock US (Annau & Kamin, 1961); similarly, the taste aversion conditioned to a flavour paired with illness will extinguish if the flavour is repeatedly presented in the absence of illness (e.g. Garcia, Ervin, & Koelling, 1966). However, extinction could be said to be rather more fragile than acquisition. If a period of time is permitted to pass after conditioning has been extinguished, then the CR can make a **spontaneous recovery** (Pavlov, 1927). Furthermore, if conditioned responding is acquired in one context and then extinguished in a different context, responding will be renewed if the animal is returned to the original context of conditioning (Bouton & King, 1983).

Nonetheless, extinction is an important effect to psychotherapists for, as we shall see later, it is exploited in exposure therapy to reduce the incidence of unwanted behaviours that might have been acquired through classical conditioning. For example, a person might have a phobia of dogs (the CS) as a consequence of being bitten or scared by one (the US) as a child. By providing the phobic client with an opportunity to experience dogs in the absence of being bitten or scared, the phobia should extinguish. However, exposure therapy is not always successful in the long term; clients may relapse into their original phobic ways, and for this reason it is important for psychologists to have a better understanding of extinction and the conditions under which extinguished responding might recover or be renewed.

Preventing conditioning: Latent inhibition and cue competition

Given how widespread conditioning is in the animal kingdom, and how often organisms encounter biologically significant events, it seems as if animals (including humans) should be quivering wrecks or rapturous hedonists – conditioned to fear or be delighted by all manner of things in the world that just so happened to have been followed by some unpleasant or desirable event. Why is this not the case? The answer to this question lies in the selectivity of conditioning. In contrast to the predictions of some early theories of learning (e.g. Hebb, 1949), simply pairing a CS with a US will not necessarily result in the acquisition of a CR, and we can see this principle in operation by understanding two effects that have been extremely influential in the study of classical conditioning: latent inhibition and cue competition.

The first of these effects, latent inhibition, is rather like extinction in reverse. The CS is presented multiple times without the US. However, unlike in extinction, this is done before conditioning, not after. For example, in an experiment by Lubow and Moore (1959), goats were first given 10 presentations of a flashing light. In the second stage of the experiment, the flashing light was paired with a mild electric shock to the goat's foreleg (the US), as was a novel stimulus (the sight of a moving rotor) on other trials. Lubow and Moore found that the CR (leg flexion in this case) was acquired significantly more rapidly to the rotor than to the flashing light. This general observation – more rapid learning to novel than to familiar stimuli – has considerable generality, being demonstrated in a variety of species, including humans, across various conditioning procedures (for a review see Lubow & Weiner, 2010). A number of explanations of latent inhibition have been proposed, but a popular explanation is that conditioning is not successful to the pre-exposed stimulus because pre-exposure reduces the amount of attention that the CS can capture – thus slowing its ability to acquire a CR (e.g. Pearce & Hall, 1980).

The second of these effects, cue competition, is a little more complex but again involves only two CSs. Cue competition occurs when one stimulus influences the ability of another stimulus to evoke a CR, and one of the most influential examples of cue completion is known as 'blocking'. In the first stage of a blocking experiment, a CS (let's call it 'A') is paired with a US on a number of trials until it reliably evokes a CR (you can think of this training as A → US trials). In the second stage of the experiment, a novel stimulus (let's call it 'X') is presented at the same time as A, and this pair of stimuli are followed by the US, again for a number of trials (you can think of this training as AX → US trials). At the end of the experiment, X is presented on its own (that is to say, in the absence of A and the US). What is often observed under these circumstances is that X is very poor at evoking a CR – despite the fact that it has been paired with the US on a number of trials. Blocking is observed in a variety of species, including honeybees (Blaser, Couvillon, & Bitterman, 2004), rats (e.g. Kamin, 1968; see Table 8.1), and humans (Shanks, 1985). A theory of learning that provides an explanation of blocking will be described later in the chapter. For the time being, however, it is sufficient to be aware of this phenomenon, as well as the fact that it shows that

TABLE 8.1 *The design of a typical blocking experiment (e.g. Kamin, 1968). The blocking and control groups both receive pairings of CS X with the US, but only the control group demonstrates a CR.*

Experimental group	Stage 1	Stage 2	Test (and result)
Blocking group	A → US (e.g. tone → shock)	AX → US (e.g. tone & light → shock)	X (weak CR) (e.g. light)
Control group	Nothing	AX → US (e.g. tone & light → shock)	X (stronger CR) (e.g. light)

simply pairing a CS with a US does not always result in the acquisition of a CR. Blocking (as well as latent inhibition) therefore prevents stimuli from becoming indiscriminately conditioned, and therefore stops learning from running away with itself.

Instrumental conditioning

What is instrumental conditioning?

In classical conditioning, the US is delivered to the animal irrespective of its behaviour. Thus it didn't matter whether Pavlov's dogs drooled or not; food would be delivered to them after the CS. A rather different procedure for studying learning, however, makes the delivery of food (for example) dependent on the behaviour of the animal. This type of learning is referred to as **instrumental (or operant) conditioning**.

Thorndike (1898) was the first to systematically investigate how behaviour may change as a consequence of its relationship to environmental events. He placed a cat into a box outside of which was a bowl of food (see Figure 8.4). In order to escape the box and eat the food, the cat had to perform a particular response – such as pull a lever in order to raise a door. At first, the cat would take quite a long time before it made the correct response – perhaps scratching at the floor instead. Once it did make the correct response, however, it was rewarded with a few moments of access to the food, before being placed back into the box. What Thorndike observed was a gradual reduction in the time it took the cat to escape from the box. At first, the cat may have taken between 60 and 120 seconds to escape, but, after a dozen or so trials, it was escaping in around 10 to 20 seconds. Because the time taken by the cat to escape from the box reduced gradually, and not abruptly, Thorndike (1911) argued that the learning that was taking place was a gradual, incremental process rather than, for example, a moment of insight. In fact Thorndike proposed a specific law of conditioning, the 'law of effect': 'Of several responses made to the same situation, those which are accompanied or closely followed by satisfaction to the animal will, other things being equal, be more firmly connected with the situation' (p. 244).

What Thorndike is proposing here is that, in his experiment with cats, the food serves to strengthen a connection (or association) between the animal's environmental stimuli and the response that it makes. Thus, the learning that takes

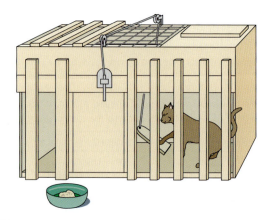

FIGURE 8.4 *Thorndike's apparatus.*

Source: Comer, Ogden, & Furnam (2013). Wiley. Reproduced with permission.

place is between a stimulus and a response (so-called **S–R learning**). According to Thorndike the food only serves to bolster the connection between a stimulus and a response; hence events that increase the probability of a response when presented after it are called 'reinforcers' (see Activity 8.2). Other animals can, of course, also demonstrate instrumental conditioning, and a vast variety of animals – including rats, pigeons, fish, and a variety of invertebrates – can be trained to press levers, pull chains, peck upon keys, swim through hoops, or dig in sand when such responses are followed by reinforcement (for a review, see Mackintosh, 1974). Even humans will acquire a response if it is followed by a reward, as anybody who is paid to turn up for work will know.

ACTIVITY 8.2

REINFORCEMENT AND PUNISHMENT

Reinforcers increase the probability of responses. However, the flip side to reinforcement is punishment, which decreases the probability of responses. Reinforcement and punishment can be either positive or negative. Positivity and negativity, in this context, refer to whether an event is added or removed following the response.

The following table should clarify this (with examples of applications to behaviour of my daughter, Ellie).

	Positive	Negative
Reinforcement (responding increases)	*Add* an appetitive event when the response is made (Ellie receives a sweet for doing her homework)	*Remove* an aversive event when the response is made (Ellie leaves the house early for school to avoid being told off for being late)
Punishment (responding decreases)	*Add* an aversive event when the response is made (Ellie is placed on the naughty step for being mean to her brother)	*Remove* an appetitive event when the response is made (Ellie is not allowed to play football because she said a swear word)

Now create your own list with examples relating to your own behaviour. Think about events that occur during a normal day when your behaviour has been influenced by reinforcement or punishment.

What is learned during instrumental conditioning?

Although instrumental conditioning is widespread in the animal kingdom, we might question Thorndike's (1911) S–R analysis of it. Is it really the case that motivationally significant events in the world (such as food) serve only to strengthen the connection between, for example, the sight of a lever and the response of the cat pulling it? This implies that cats (and, by generalization, other animals) make no connection between the response and the reinforcer. According to this view, then, after pulling a lever and getting food for the umpteenth time, upon escaping from their box, Thorndike's cats will have been entirely surprised by the presence of food.

This prediction, which can be derived from Thorndike's law of effect, was tested by Colwill and Rescorla (1985). They gave rats the opportunity to make two different responses, either the pressing of a lever or the pulling of a chain. Lever presses resulted in the delivery of liquid sucrose, and chain pulls resulted in the delivery of a food pellet. According to the S–R analysis of instrumental conditioning, this training would result in the sucrose reinforcer simply strengthening the sight of the lever with the response of pressing it, and the food reinforcer strengthening the sight of the chain with the response of pulling it. In order to test this, Colwill and Rescorla subsequently devalued sucrose by pairing it with a drug that made the rat feel ill. After this training, they gave the rats an opportunity to make a choice between lever pressing and chain pulling in a final test. Importantly, this choice was conducted in extinction; thus, neither of the reinforcers was presented after the two responses. Colwill and Rescorla observed that the rats made significantly fewer lever presses than chain pulls. This result is not consistent with the S–R analysis of instrumental conditioning proposed by Thorndike, which stipulates that events such as food and sucrose simply strengthen, or reinforce, associations between stimuli and responses (**associative theory**). In Colwill and Rescorla's experiment, the sight of the lever was never paired with the actual performance of lever pressing during the time at which sucrose had been devalued, and so the theory proposed by Thorndike struggles to explain why Colwill and Rescorla's rats would prefer to pull the chain than press the lever. These results can be understood, however, if it is assumed that instrumental conditioning allows animals to learn to connect, or associate, their responses with the consequence of that response. Under these circumstances, during the final test, the rats should avoid pressing the lever because it was associated with the (now unattractive) sucrose, which is precisely what was observed.

In actual fact, instrumental conditioning looks as if it results in the acquisition of more than just one type of associative connection between events: animals may acquire an association between a stimulus and response, as well as between a response and the reinforcer. Which of these two types of associations influences behaviour, it seems, is determined by the amount of training that takes place. In an influential series of experiments, Adams and Dickinson (1981) gave rats training in which presses on a lever resulted in the delivery of food. After this training, food was devalued in a manner similar to that used by Colwill and Rescorla (1985); thus the rats were allowed to eat food (from a dish in their home cage) and then made ill by drug injection. Adams and Dickinson observed that if only a modest amount of lever press training was given to the rats in the first stage of the experiment (100 presses) then, like Colwill and Rescorla's rats, their rats would avoid pressing the lever during the test relative to a control group that had a different substance paired with illness (sucrose). However, if a lot of lever press training was given to the rats in the initial stage of the experiment (500 presses) then the devaluation procedure was, seemingly, without effect (see Figure 8.5).

Adams and Dickinson suggested that instrumental training initially results in behaviour being goal directed – that is to say, performed in order to obtain a reinforcer. However, with extended training, there is a transition from goal-directed behaviour to habit-based stimulus–response behaviour, which is under the control of environmental stimuli and ignorant of the current value of the reinforcer. You might have experienced a similar transition from goal-directed to habit-based behaviour yourself. Consider, for example, the circumstances under which you wipe your feet upon entering your house. In all likelihood, you acquired this response as a child when you were told off by one or both of your parents for not wiping your feet when you had mud on your shoes, or because you were praised for

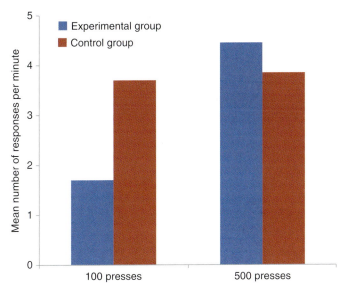

FIGURE 8.5 *The results of Adams and Dickinson's (1981) test stage.*

Source: Adapted with permission of Taylor and Francis from Figure 5.4, p. 153, of Adams and Dickinson (1981). Permission conveyed through Copyright Clearance Center, Inc.

remembering to do it upon walking through the door. However, many years later, you will undoubtedly still find yourself wiping your feet upon entering your home. Do you do this in order to avoid a rollicking or in order to seek praise? I certainly don't. The simple act of wiping your feet upon entering your house – many times – seems to have eventually resulted in stimuli such as the sight of the door mat or the coats near the front door becoming associated with the response of feet wiping. In Adams and Dickinson's terminology, a habit has been acquired. As we shall see later in this chapter, the notion of habitual behaviour has been particularly important to our understanding of other habits, such as habitual drug use. But, as far as the current discussion is concerned, the results of Adams and Dickinson's experiment show that Thorndike's proposal, although at first sight seemingly implausible, may not be entirely without merit.

Factors affecting instrumental conditioning

You may recall from our discussion of classical conditioning that conditioned responding is more successfully acquired if the interval between the CS and the US is relatively short. You may also recall that a CR will extinguish if the CS is presented in the absence of the US. It is a natural question to ask, therefore, whether the sorts of factors that influence classical conditioning also influence instrumental conditioning. In general, the answer to this question appears to be yes: if an interval separates the performance of the response from the delivery of reinforcement, then the acquisition of instrumental conditioning is less successful. Dickinson, Watt, and Griffiths (1992), for example, interposed a variety of delays between the performance of a lever press and the delivery of food to rats and found the rate of responding on the lever progressively declined as the interval between response and reinforcer increased – a so-called gradient of delay. A comparable effect can be observed in humans (Shanks, Pearson, & Dickinson, 1989). Like classical conditioning, instrumental conditioning will extinguish if an animal presses a lever that no longer results in the delivery of reinforcement. B. F. Skinner, an influential figure in the history of instrumental conditioning, was particularly taken by the presence of extinction in instrumental conditioning. In fact, Skinner happened upon the extinction of instrumental conditioning by chance when he was alone in his laboratory one Friday afternoon and the dispenser that delivered food to his rats jammed during a conditioning session. Because of this jam, the number of responses made by the rats gradually diminished. So taken was Skinner by this observation of a gradual extinction curve in his laboratory that he took 'particular care and avoided all unnecessary risks' over the weekend to protect his discovery from loss through his death before he could tell other lab members of his finding (Skinner, 1979, p. 95).

However, we should not labour under the impression that animals will only perform instrumental actions if they are followed by an outcome that has some intrinsic biological significance – such as a food pellet or sucrose solution. Instrumental responding can also be sustained if responses are followed by events that themselves have acquired significance. For example, Hyde (1976) demonstrated that rats would press a lever if it was followed by a brief tone, so long as the brief tone had previously been established as a CS for food. This effect is called **conditioned reinforcement** and is applied widely to train domestic and working animals, such as dogs. In this case, the trainer first establishes the sound of a clicker (normally) as a CS for food. Once this training is complete, any desired behaviour that the dog may perform by chance (such as sitting) is followed immediately by a click to reinforce the behaviour. Conditioned reinforcement is similar to an effect observed in classical conditioning, in which a CR can be established to a neutral stimulus (e.g. a light) by pairing it with another stimulus (such as a tone) that has itself in the past signalled a US. When the effect is observed in classical conditioning, it is referred to as **second-order conditioning** (e.g. Rescorla, 1980).

You may recall from our discussion of classical conditioning that we asked the question of why animals are not quivering wrecks. What is to stop them from indiscriminately forming CRs to all manner of stimuli in the world that happen to be followed by some form of aversive US? We can ask a comparable question of instrumental conditioning. Why do people not perform all manner of strange, perhaps arbitrary responses given that we live in a world full of all manner of potentially reinforcing events? One potential answer to this question is to point out that, in actual fact, people *do* perform all sorts of arbitrary behaviours. Sportspeople often admit to having a 'lucky' pair of socks (for example) that they will regularly wear as a consequence of having once worn them during a victorious sporting event. Furthermore, I am sure I am not alone in having a friend who reserves a pair of 'lucky' underpants to wear on nights out, having once triumphed in them. This sort of superstitious behaviour has also been observed in the humble laboratory pigeon (although, in this case, the pigeon did not come to wear lucky socks or underpants). Skinner (1948) reported an experiment in which pigeons were placed into a cage and food was delivered to them at regular intervals – independently of their behaviour. What Skinner observed in six out of eight pigeons was the acquisition of idiosyncratic behaviours such as hopping from one leg to the other, or rotating counterclockwise two or three times. Skinner reported that the process by which these 'superstitious' behaviours were acquired by the pigeons was obvious: that they were often first performed, by chance, just prior to the delivery of food, and, as a consequence of the reinforcing ability of food, they were subsequently repeated.

Despite being a relatively common phenomenon, superstition does not typically dominate people's lives in the way that we might expect from an application of the principles of instrumental conditioning to human behaviour. We can gain an understanding of why instrumental conditioning might not always be successful from an experiment conducted by Hammond (1980). He trained groups of thirsty rats to make a lever press in order to gain access to water. The first group served as the control group, and for these rats water was only delivered when it was preceded by a response. Not surprisingly, these rats came to press the lever very frequently. An experimental group of rats also received water upon pressing the lever, but they additionally received water independently of lever pressing – during periods when they had not made a response. The results showed that rats in the experimental group lever-pressed far less frequently than the control group. For some reason, gaining reinforcers, independent of behaviour, interfered with the acquisition of instrumental conditioning. It doesn't take too long to imagine a comparable effect in everyday human life. Most people are happy to work reasonably hard, so long as they receive some reward for doing so (such as a salary). However, if your salary were paid irrespective of whether you did any work, there would seem little justification in turning up for work at all.

DISCUSSION POINT

Discuss how instrumental conditioning differs from classical conditioning and suggest some examples from your own experience.

Social learning

Classical and instrumental conditioning have a number of features in common, but a particularly salient feature, at least in the context of the topic that we are about to discuss, is that they are both instances of learning in which the animal is acquiring information in isolation. However, many animals, including humans, are rather sociable beings and spend much of their time in groups. It is therefore particularly important to understand whether and how information might be acquired from other organisms – that is to say, how does **social learning** take place, and what are the sorts of factors that influence it?

As is so often the case when considering learning, it is first important to clarify some terminology. Two terms that will be relied upon while discussing the topic of social learning are 'observer' and 'demonstrator'. The *observer* is the animal that is receiving information in the social situation. This animal is therefore, typically, the focus of any behavioural measurement that is used to detect learning. The *demonstrator*, in contrast, is the animal that is (intentionally or otherwise) providing information to the observer (see Figure 8.6). Obviously, these two roles are not necessarily fixed – the very nature of social interactions means that an animal may take on both roles at any one time. However, these are useful terms to be familiar with, in order to ease the understanding of the flow of information from provider to recipient.

FIGURE 8.6 *The demonstrator rat (on the left) has been trained to press a lever to one side in order to obtain food. The observer rat (on the right) is watching the demonstrator rat perform this response.*

Source: Adapted from Heyes and Dawson (1990). Taylor & Francis. www.tandfonline.com.

Socially learned diet choice

A moment's reflection will reveal a number of instances in which learning in a non-social manner may be detrimental to an organism. For example, in order to learn which foods are safe and nutritious, and which are harmful, an animal places itself in a potentially disastrous situation, as eating a very toxic plant provides the animal with no opportunity to later express its learning about the relationship between the sight or taste of the food and its ultimately lethal consequences. The adaptive significance of being able to observe the consequences of diet choice in other animals is therefore substantial. Galef and colleagues have provided a number of examples of food choice in an observer rat being influenced by the presence of a demonstrator rat. For example, McQuoid and Galef (1992) showed that observer Burmese jungle fowl expressed a preference for eating out of a bowl that they had previously watched demonstrator fowl eating from. Furthermore, Galef (1988) describes an experiment in which a demonstrator rat was first allowed to eat a distinctive and (for the rat) novel food (e.g. cinnamon). Observer rats were then permitted to interact with the demonstrator rat for 30 minutes (in the absence of any food), before the observers were given a choice between cocoa and cinnamon in the absence of the demonstrator. The observers selected the food that had been consumed by the demonstrator.

How might these demonstrations of social learning have arisen? One possibility is through **stimulus enhancement.** Here, the presence of the demonstrator draws the observer's attention to the object or food, encouraging the observer animal to interact with it later. Alternatively, the effect may be a consequence of habituation, which we encountered earlier. Here, mere exposure to the food, for example, could be expected to result in the habituation of the animal's initial neophobic response – causing it to choose the food previously consumed by the demonstrator. Both of these explanations have been rendered unlikely by further experiments by Galef (1988), who showed that observer rats did not show as substantial a preference for cinnamon in a choice test if they had previously experienced the cinnamon dusted over cotton wool or over the rear end of the demonstrator rat, relative to a condition where cinnamon had been dusted over the mouth of the demonstrator. Explanations of social learning of diet choice that appeal to habituation seem to encounter difficulty with these results as the food that the observer would subsequently choose was experienced equally often in the different conditions. Something other than mere exposure seems to be required to explain these results.

Is social learning an example of classical conditioning?

In order to explain the results of socially mediated diet choice, Galef and Durlach (1993) suggested that the acquired preference for the cinnamon could be thought of as a CR, in which the food itself (or the food cup in the case of the experiment by McQuoid & Galef, 1992) acquired the role of a CS that was paired with an appetitive US (in this case, the demonstrator). This potential explanation encounters difficulty, however, with the observation that socially mediated food choice does not seem to be susceptible to the detrimental effects of either cue competition or latent inhibition, both of which, as you will recall, are hallmarks of classical conditioning. Despite these problems, studies of the social acquisition of fear in monkeys have also placed an emphasis on the role of classical conditioning processes.

Mineka and Cook (1988) report that, unlike wild monkeys, monkeys that had been reared in the laboratory did not show a fear response when looking at a snake. Mineka and Cook explored whether this difference was a learned difference that was socially mediated. They showed that lab-reared observer monkeys would acquire a fear response to snakes (e.g. alarm calls, agitation) themselves if they were permitted to simply observe a wild-reared demonstrator monkey's fear response while in the presence of the snake. Mineka and Cook suggested that the snake served as a CS which was associated with the US of the sight of fear in the demonstrator monkey, and called this form of learning **observational conditioning**. In support of this analysis, Mineka and Cook noted that observational conditioning was more successful if the fear response by the demonstrator monkey was stronger. This is in keeping with studies of classical conditioning, which have shown that conditioning is more successful with a stronger US.

Mimicry and imitation

One problem for explanations of social learning that emphasize classical conditioning comes from demonstrations of **mimicry and imitation**, in which an animal acquires a new form of response as a consequence of observation of another animal. In the case of mimicry, observation of a demonstrator's response influences behaviour in the observer, even when there is no immediate reward or punishment, and the classic example of mimicry comes from the ability of some birds to copy the vocalizations that come from other animals, including their owners. Moore (1992), for example, demonstrated that an African grey parrot would come to mimic both the actions made and the words spoken by a demonstrator human who simply entered the room and then left. It is difficult to identify a tangible US in this instance, and therefore equally difficult to accept that this behaviour was acquired through observational conditioning.

Imitation is subtly different from mimicry. According to Heyes (1994), imitation refers to the acquisition of a novel response as a consequence of observing a demonstrator, but, crucially, involves a goal-directed mechanism. An example of imitation in budgerigars was provided by Galef, Manzig, and Field (1986), in which observer budgies watched a demonstrator gain access to food by lifting a flap either with its feet or with its beak. Observer birds that had watched the demonstrator lift the flap with its feet performed this response more frequently than lifting it with their beak, and vice versa for observer birds that had watched the demonstrator bird accessing food with its beak.

Instances of mimicry and imitation are difficult to explain with a theory of social learning that emphasizes the role of classical conditioning because a new form of response is acquired. Recall that in classical conditioning the UR – which is already established in the animal – comes to be evoked by the CS as a consequence of the pairing of these two stimuli. In the case of mimicry and imitation, the response that is acquired is entirely novel. It is perhaps not surprising, therefore, that some have argued that imitation is underpinned by instrumental conditioning, which also permits the acquisition of a novel response (e.g. Heyes & Ray, 2000).

Social learning in humans

One of the most famous studies of social learning in human psychology is the seminal work on social (or observational) learning conducted by Albert Bandura, whose early work suggested that social learning can influence aggressive behaviour in young children. Bandura, Ross, and Ross (1963) asked 4- and 5-year-old children to watch an adult demonstrator play with an inflatable doll (a so-called Bobo doll). Different groups of children watched the adult behave aggressively towards the doll (1) live, (2) on videotape, (3) dressed in a cartoon cat uniform, or (4) not at all. When the children were subsequently given the opportunity to play with the doll themselves, children in groups 1 to 3 displayed significantly more aggressive acts than did children in group 4, the control group.

Despite the fame of Bandura's work, most research into social learning in humans does not, these days, focus on the acquisition of socially undesirable behaviours such as aggression. One particular focus of research has been into a subtle problem that has come to be known as the 'correspondence problem'. In order to understand the problem, consider the following example. You are dancing with a friend and, almost without noticing it, begin to imitate their dance movements – hands and legs moving in synchrony. How is this achieved? Your dance movements are controlled by muscles and tendons, and yet you cannot observe the movements of another person's muscles and tendons; you can only observe the consequences of their activation. How then do you translate what you see somebody else do into your own movement when the two have no correspondence in terms of what you, as an observer, can actually see? A complete answer to this question has yet to be provided, but Brass and Heyes (2005) suggest that viewing another person's actions automatically activates existing motor, or response, representations.

Although they did not set out to solve the correspondence problem, studies of the cognitive neuroscience of action observation are beginning to provide a more complete answer to this question by revealing a network of neurons in the premotor cortex that are activated both when an action is made by an observer and when it is observed being made by a demonstrator. These so-called mirror neurons were first noted, quite unexpectedly, by Di Pellegrino, Fadiga, Fogassi, Gallese, and Rizzolatti (1992), who were measuring the activation of neurons in the premotor region of the brain of macaques in response to the monkey making hand and mouth movements (see Focus Point 8.1). Di Pellegrino et al. noticed that some of these neurons not only fired when the monkey was making a hand movement but also when it observed the experimenter also make a hand movement. Since this discovery, human cognitive neuroscience studies using functional magnetic resonance imaging (fMRI) have revealed parts of the brain (e.g. the inferior frontal cortex and parts of the parietal lobe) that are also strongly activated on occasions when an action is both performed and observed (e.g. Iacoboni et al., 1999).

FOCUS POINT 8.1

MIRROR NEURONS

The precise mechanism that supports the development of mirror neurons has yet to be determined. That said, Press et al. (2012) have shown, using fMRI in humans, that regions of the premotor cortex and parietal lobule will activate both to the sight of abstract stimuli (e.g. coloured shapes) and the responses that people have learned to make to them. Press et al. suggest that mirror neurons are not a form of special adaptation that has evolved solely for imitation but are in fact the consequence of a more general process of associative learning. For a review of mirror neurons, see Kilner and Lemon (2013).

ACTIVITY 8.3

DO AS I DO

Choose two actions (e.g. clapping your hands and clicking your fingers). Ask a friend to 'do as I do' (e.g. clap when I clap, click when I click). Afterwards, ask your friend to 'do the opposite of what I do' (e.g. clap when you click, click when you clap). Ask which of the two tasks was harder – it was probably the second task. This effect is called automatic imitation and is seen not only in humans but also in animals, such as budgerigars (Mui, Haselgrove, Pearce, & Heyes, 2008).

SECTION SUMMARY

- The simplest form of learning that can be observed is the one in which the simple repetition of a stimulus results in a corresponding change in behaviour.

- Habituation, sensitization, and classical conditioning are all examples of learning that result from simple exposure to stimuli in the environment. They are prevalent in a variety of species and are observable in a wide variety of stimuli and response systems.

- Phenomena such as extinction, latent inhibition, and blocking all reveal that learned behaviour may be lost, or not acquired in the first place, depending on the relationship that the CS has with other stimuli in the environment.

- Instrumental conditioning permits animals to take control of their environment. It allows desired environmental events to be obtained and aversive events be avoided. It shares a number of characteristics with classical conditioning; however, it is a matter for future research to determine whether instrumental and classical conditioning are underpinned by a common mechanism.

- Social learning results in a change in behaviour as a consequence of experience. It therefore conforms with the definition of learning that we provided at the outset of this chapter. However, the nature of this experience is subtly different – it is the experience of observing another animal.

HUMAN CAUSAL LEARNING

LEARNING OBJECTIVE 8.3

Demonstrate an understanding of how the principles of simple forms of learning can generate more complex behaviour.

Our discussion thus far has revealed that a popular explanation for learning emphasizes the formation of simple connections, or associations, between events (e.g. Dickinson, 1980). For example, classical conditioning is argued to be the consequence of the formation of an association between the CS and US, and instrumental conditioning is proposed to be a consequence of the formation of associations between a response and a reinforcer (or between a stimulus and a response). Heyes (2001) has suggested that social learning phenomena such as imitation may be the consequence of associative processes, comparable to those observed in instrumental conditioning. And, although we did not discuss the theoretical mechanisms of habituation earlier in this chapter, even habituation has been suggested to be the consequence of an associative process. Wagner (1981), for example, has argued that responding to a stimulus will progressively diminish if it is signalled by another stimulus (e.g. the experimental context). These various proposals beg the question of whether all learning can be understood in terms of the acquisition (or extinction) of associative connections between events (or, to be more accurate, the mental representations of events). From a biological perspective, this proposition makes good sense, as brains are composed (in the case of humans) of billions of neurons, each of which is simply connected by synapses to other neurons. Thus the conceptual architecture of the learning process, as envisioned by associative learning theories, is not dissimilar to the physical architecture of the organ that is responsible for permitting learning to actually take place. Indeed, as we shall see later, certain neurons in the brains of macaques respond in a manner that is consistent with the assumptions of associative theories of learning, lending them a measure of biological plausibility. That said, however, humans and other animals are capable of demonstrating a wide range of seemingly complex behaviours that would appear to be beyond the explanation of theories that propose that learning is no more than changes in connections between things such as tones, lights, responses, and food! It is beyond the scope of this chapter to provide a complete description of the various types of seemingly complex behaviours that seem, at first sight, beyond the explanation of associative theories of learning. In this section we will concentrate on one behaviour in particular. It continues to be the focus of scientific debate about whether it constitutes a challenge for associative theories of learning. It is 'causal learning'.

Human beings encounter an enormous array of paired events every day: some will be the pairing of two rather long-lasting stimuli, such as a television news broadcast followed by a weather report, or two rather more brief events, such as lightning followed by thunder. Other events that human beings encounter every day are pairings of their responses and a stimulus, such as pressing a key on a keyboard resulting in a letter being presented on screen. It is not particularly easy to identify any of these events as a US for classical conditioning, or a reinforcer for instrumental conditioning. However, this does not necessarily mean that learning about the relationship between these pairs of events is not acquired in the same way as instrumentally or classically conditioned responses; it merely means that the second event in the pair is not some form of biologically significant event.

This point is made very clearly in a series of experiments by Dickinson, Shanks, and Evenden (1984), who showed that the properties of animal conditioning are present in people's judgements of causality. In their first experiment, human participants were required to play a computer game in which a military tank was shown to be progressing across a minefield on screen. On each trial, participants could press the spacebar on the keyboard to fire a shell at the tank. On some trials the tank exploded as it passed across the screen, and on other trials it did not. In this way, Dickinson et al. could manipulate the contingency (or correlation) between the participant's responses and the outcome of the trial (explosion) in the same way that, for example, Hammond (1980) did with rats' lever pressing and food. On some blocks of trials in Dickinson et al.'s study, the chance of the tank exploding without the participant making a response was rather low (.25), while on other blocks of trials the chance was rather higher (.75). Following a particular block of trials, participants were asked to make a judgement about the effectiveness of the tank's shells in the game. The results of the experiment showed that occurrences of tank explosions in the absence of a response by the participant reduced their judgements of the causal relationship between their response and its consequence. This result is comparable to the experiment with rats conducted by Hammond, in which presentations of a reinforcer, in the absence of responding, interfered with the acquisition of rats' instrumental responses. Where it differs of course is that, in the case of humans, the response being measured was a *judgement of causality*. The judgement of causality was about the effect of a shell causing an explosion in a game, which is hardly a biologically significant event, and yet here we see it being influenced in a manner comparable to lever pressing in a rat. One explanation offered for the results of Hammond's instrumental conditioning experiment was that rats could be sensitive to the overall correlation between responses and reinforcers. A similar suggestion was considered by Dickinson et al.; however, they rejected this possibility by conducting a second experiment. In this experiment they kept the correlation between participants' responses and the trial outcome fixed between experimental groups, but still observed differences in participants' judgements of causality. This was achieved by setting up an experimental design that was similar to Kamin's (1968) blocking experiment with rats. In this experiment participants simply observed the tank exploding in the minefield before having the opportunity to make responses to shoot it with their shells. This observational training resulted in a reduction of participants' judgements of the causal relationship between firing the shell and the explosion. Dickinson argued that that minefield → explosion association established in the initial stage of the experiment blocked learning about the shell → explosion association when the tank was still within the minefield and continued to explode.

Since Dickinson et al.'s (1984) demonstration that people's judgements of causality are susceptible to blocking, there have been a substantial number of studies demonstrating similar effects of contingency and cue competition under other causality-judgement scenarios (including, perhaps worryingly, people's medical judgements about the relationship between symptoms and illness; e.g. Kruschke & Blair, 2000). We might be tempted to conclude, on this basis, that people's ability to learn about the contingency between events is underpinned by a mechanism that is also responsible for producing conditioning in animals (e.g. Dickinson, 2001). This conclusion has not gone unchallenged. Other researchers have, for example, suggested that human learning is underpinned by more effortful, rational processes. Beckers, Miller, De Houwer, and Urushihara (2006), for example, describe how people could use deductive logic in order to produce a blocking effect. Recall that, in a blocking experiment, a CS is paired with a US (A → US) in stage 1 before the same CS is joined by another CS in stage 2 (AX → US). At the end of the experiment, test trials with X reveal that little has been learned about X – in the terminology of a causal learning experiment, it is said that the animal (or participant) has not learned that X caused the outcome. Beckers et al. suggested that blocking, instead of reflecting a conditioning-like process, is a consequence of the use of deductive logic. This logical deduction is called 'modus tollens' and has the following structure: *if p then q, not q, therefore not p*. An example of the use of modus tollens is: *if* I am an Olympic gymnast *then* I am very fit (*if p then q*); I am *not* very fit (*not q*); *therefore* I am *not* an Olympic gymnast (*therefore not p*). When this is applied to a blocking experiment, we can see how modus tollens might work:

- *If p then q* – If potential causes A and X are both effective causes of a particular outcome, then the outcome should be stronger when both are present than when only one is present.

- *Not q* – The outcome is not stronger when A and X are both present than when only A is present.

- *Therefore, not p* – Thus, A and X are not both effective causes of the outcome.

Given that the training in stage 1 of a blocking experiment establishes quite clearly that A is a cause of an outcome, it follows from the deductive reasoning above that X is certainly not. Although the reasoning here is complex, it can be seen (perhaps after reading it a couple of times) how blocking should be observed through deductive reasoning. Evidence that supports the deductive reasoning analysis of blocking has come from experiments that show that if human participants are given instructions or training prior to blocking that contradicts the *if p then q* statement then blocking is undermined (e.g. Beckers, De Houwer, Pineno, & Miller, 2005). Blocking, however, has been observed in humans under circumstances when higher-order processes are unlikely to be used, such as when time constraints are high. This has led some authors to conclude that human learning is the consequence of both effortful reasoning process and conditioning-like processes (for a review, see McLaren et al., 2014).

SECTION SUMMARY

- Our discussion has revealed that a popular explanation for learning emphasizes the formation of simple connections, or associations, between events.

- An important question in the study of learning asks whether all learning can be understood in terms of the acquisition (or extinction) of associative connections between events.

- However, humans and other animals are capable of demonstrating a wide range of seemingly complex behaviours that would appear to be beyond the explanation of theories that propose that learning is no more than changes in connections between things such as tones, lights, responses, and food.

- As a result, there is much scientific debate about whether causal learning constitutes a challenge for associative theories of learning.
- Dickinson et al.'s (1984) experiment demonstrated that the properties of animal conditioning are also present in people's judgements of causality and that judgements of causality are susceptible to blocking.
- Some have suggested that people's ability to learn about the contingency between events is underpinned by a mechanism that is also responsible for producing conditioning in animals.
- However, other researchers have suggested that human learning is underpinned by more effortful, rational processes.
- This has led some authors to conclude that human learning is the consequence of both effortful reasoning process and conditioning-like processes.

THE THEORETICAL BASIS OF LEARNING

LEARNING OBJECTIVE 8.4

Demonstrate an understanding of the theoretical models that are considered to underpin learning, in particular the Rescorla–Wagner model.

Associative learning

One of the most successful explanations for how learning takes place is provided by associative theories of learning. These theories are based upon the assumption that, when things are paired together, they have an opportunity to be connected together – or associated. Thus, in classical conditioning, when a CS is paired with a US, the two may become associated. In instrumental conditioning, when a response is paired with a stimulus, or a reinforcer, these events may become associated. In fact some authors have focused so much on the importance of the association between events in the world that they have dispensed with distinguishing between stimuli, responses, and reinforcers at all, and instead have just referred to the pair of items that are associated as event 1 and event 2 (Dickinson, 1980). An association is no more than a link, a connection between two events – or, to be more accurate, the representations of events; the association conveys no information in and of itself. The sole consequence of having an associative connection between two events is that if one of these events is activated, then so too will its associate. For example, in the case of Pavlov's dogs, we can say that repeatedly pairing the bell with food resulted in the establishment of an association between the bell and food. Consequently, when a bell is rung in the absence of food, the associative connection between the bell and food will enable the bell to activate the animal's representation of food, and the animal will perform the response ordinarily made in response to food (e.g. drool), as if it were actually presented. In this section we will describe the mechanisms of associative learning.

As in any scientific field, the state of play is constantly changing, and specific theories of associative learning will continue to be tested within the scientific literature and on the basis of these tests either discarded entirely or (more usually) modified in some manner to permit them to explain novel results. However, one theory in particular has had a significant influence across the field of associative learning and contains within it a core idea that has dominated our understanding of how learning takes place. Once we have described this theory and its successes (and some of its limitations), we will investigate whether learning, from this kind of perspective, is realistic at the neural level.

The Rescorla–Wagner model

In 1972, Robert Rescorla and Allan Wagner proposed an influential theory of learning. It was originally developed as a theory to explain how the association between the CS and US forms during classical conditioning; however, it can also be applied to instances of instrumental conditioning. Furthermore, 'connectionist' (or 'neural network') models of many different types of behaviour often have at their centre a learning algorithm that is similar to the proposals of Rescorla and Wagner. The theory, therefore, has applications across the breadth of psychology. The basic idea behind the theory is that learning is simply a change in the strength of the association, or connection, between things. Rescorla and Wagner described the model in terms of classical conditioning, and for the sake of simplicity we will continue to do so here. Thus, in terms of classical conditioning, an association is formed between the CS and US and, according to Rescorla and Wagner (1972), three factors determine how much the strength of the association between the CS and US changes on any conditioning trial. These three factors are:

1. the perceived intensity of the CS
2. the perceived intensity of the US
3. the surprisingness of the US.

The first two factors in this list are perhaps to be expected, and simply state the relatively sensible idea that you will learn more about stimuli when they are perceived to be more intense – thus, animals are more likely to learn about a CS (for example) if it is quite intense compared to if it is not. Quiet or dim stimuli, in comparison, are unlikely to be detected and therefore associated. The third factor on this list requires more attention as it is the most important feature of the **Rescorla–Wagner model**. According to Rescorla and Wagner, learning is influenced by how surprised an animal is by the occurrence of a US. If the US is presented and is entirely expected then, according to Rescorla and Wagner, the strength of the association between it and the CS will not change. In contrast, however, should the presented US be surprising, then it will be associated with the CS. To make this last point more concrete, consider how you might respond to being awarded a grade for an exam. Imagine you get an A+. If you expected to do very well, perhaps because of the many hours of studying that you put in, then you will not be surprised by the A+, in which case you are unlikely to change your method of study – in other words, there is no change in your behaviour as a consequence of experience (i.e. the absence of surprise has resulted in no learning). However, if you were expecting to do well and you got an F instead, perhaps because you thought you understood a topic but clearly missed the point, then you may well change the way in which you study the topic in future – in other words, you have changed your behaviour as a consequence of this experience (i.e. you have learned). Rescorla and Wagner defined surprise as the difference between what you expect to happen and what actually does happen. When this difference in large, then surprise is large and learning will be substantial; when this difference is zero, then there is no surprise and no learning.

Rescorla and Wagner (1972) expressed their theory in mathematical terms. This allows precise predictions to be derived from the theory, which can then be experimentally tested in order to assess its validity. In essence, the theory takes the three factors from the list above and multiplies them together to determine how much the association between the CS and US will change:

$$\text{Learning} = \frac{\text{Perceived intensity}}{\text{of the CS}} \times \frac{\text{Perceived intensity}}{\text{of the US}} \times \frac{\text{Surprisingness}}{\text{of the US}}$$

The reason for multiplying these three factors together is so that, should any one of them be absent, it can be assigned a value of zero. Of course, anything multiplied by zero equals zero. Thus, should the CS or US not be perceived, or should the US not be surprising, then learning will not take place. As we shall see, this last assumption is one of the great strengths of the theory.

Successes of the Rescorla–Wagner model

One of the fundamental predictions of the Rescorla–Wagner model is that learning should progress relatively quickly at first when the CS is followed, surprisingly, by the US; however, later, when these two events become associated, learning will slow down and eventually halt. Rescorla (2001) himself confirmed this prediction of the Rescorla–Wagner model in a series of ingenious experiments with rats and pigeons showing that the change in conditioned responding was indeed greater earlier on in classical conditioning than later. It follows from this observation that if, after many conditioning trials, a new stimulus is added to a CS and the pair are followed by the US, then no learning should take place as a result of the added stimulus. This is because the added stimulus is paired with the US at a time when the US is not at all surprising and therefore will not support any learning. This effect has been confirmed on a number of occasions and has already been described in this chapter in the section on blocking (e.g. Kamin, 1968). The Rescorla–Wagner model also provides a reasonably good explanation for the effects of omitting a US when one is otherwise expected. Under these circumstances the difference between what is expected (e.g. food) and what is actually delivered (nothing) will be negative. Consequently, the strength of the association between the CS and the US should weaken – this is Rescorla and Wagner's explanation for extinction. Should a novel stimulus be added to a CS while it is undergoing extinction then it should acquire an association with the US that is negative – that is to say, it predicts the *absence* of the US. This effect, called 'conditioned inhibition', is well documented in the conditioning literature (e.g. Rescorla, 1969).

Limitations of the Rescorla–Wagner model

The Rescorla–Wagner (1972) model does, however, have its shortcomings. We saw earlier (in the section on latent inhibition) how conditioning proceeds more slowly to a familiar CS than a novel one, (e.g. Lubow & Moore, 1959). The Rescorla–Wagner model cannot explain this result because, at the time of pre-exposure, there is no surprising event – the US has no reason to be expected, and is indeed not presented.

Therefore no learning should take place. Phenomena such as latent inhibition have led some psychologists to propose that theories of conditioning need to acknowledge the importance of the relationship between attention and learning (e.g. Mackintosh, 1975; Pearce & Hall, 1980).

ATTENTIONAL THEORIES OF LEARNING

According to theories of attention and learning, attention to the CS can vary depending on how good a predictor it is of the US. One of the current drives in the study of attention and learning is to understand how learning and attention interact (Mitchell & Le Pelley, 2010). Rather bizarrely, the Pearce–Hall (1980) theory and Mackintosh's (1975) theory explain the relationship between attention and learning in opposite ways. One suggests that animals pay attention to stimuli that are good predictors of outcomes (Mackintosh); Pearce and Hall essentially say the opposite.

Yet recent evidence, collected in the same species and under very similar circumstances, can be shown to support both of these theories (e.g. Haselgrove, Esber, Pearce, & Jones, 2010). To resolve this conundrum, psychologists are trying to determine whether we need to distinguish between two types of attention in learning (e.g. Le Pelley, 2004) or whether in fact we can resolve the problem with just one type of attention (e.g. Esber & Haselgrove, 2011). Once this matter is resolved, we will be in a better position to apply this knowledge to instances of disrupted learning and attention – such as that which occurs in schizophrenia (e.g. Lubow & Weiner, 2010).

The Rescorla–Wagner model also encounters difficulty when trying to explain some instances of **discrimination learning**, in which different stimuli signal different outcomes. For example, one type of discrimination learning task is called 'negative patterning'. Here, two stimuli (e.g. a light and a tone) are presented on their own in some trials and together (simultaneously) on others. When they are presented in isolation, the light and the tone are followed by a US. When they are presented at the same time, however, they are followed by the absence of a US. Although animals are able to solve this discrimination learning task – showing more conditioned responding to the stimuli when the stimuli are presented on their own than when they are presented together (e.g. Woodbury, 1943) – the Rescorla–Wagner model predicts a rather different outcome. This model treats a compound of two stimuli (in this case the conjunction of the tone and light) as nothing more than the sum of its parts. Thus, in the case of negative patterning, the CR to the tone–light compound should be equal to the CR to the strength of the tone and light separately (i.e. twice as strong). However, Woodbury's results clearly showed the opposite pattern. Eventually, the CR to the compound was weaker than that to the individual stimuli. In order to explain effects such as negative patterning, some psychologists have suggested that animals represent stimuli holistically – as a complete configuration – so that a tone and a light are a qualitatively different event when presented together compared to when they are presented separately (e.g. Pearce, 1987).

DISCUSSION POINT

Discuss some of the limitations of the Rescorla–Wagner model.

SECTION SUMMARY

- The Rescorla–Wagner model continues to be an influential theory of how organisms learn.

- It proposes that learning is the product of three variables: the perceived intensity of the CS, the perceived intensity of the US, and the surprisingness of the US.

- These assumptions permit the theory to successfully explain (and indeed predict) a number of phenomena that are observed in conditioning and learning, such as extinction, blocking, and conditioned inhibition.

- Although the Rescorla–Wagner model has its limitations (notably the contribution of attention and configuration to learning), it seems likely that it will continue to form the basis of many future developments in associative learning.

THE ADAPTIVE BRAIN: LEARNING THROUGH CONNECTIONS

LEARNING OBJECTIVE 8.5

Demonstrate an understanding of the neural mechanisms involved in learning.

In the introduction to the above section on human causal learning, it was noted that the theoretical architecture of associative learning makes good sense, because it mirrors the structure of the brain – a collection of interconnected neurons. If this statement has any merit, however, then we should be able to observe phenomena and principles of associative learning at the point of the neural connection; that is to say, at the synapse.

Long-term potentiation and depression

A phenomenon called **long-term potentiation (LTP)** provides evidence for a correspondence between the conceptual architecture of associative learning theories and the underlying neural systems. Bliss and Lømo (1973) reported an enormously influential experiment in which a low-intensity electrical pulse was sent along neurons that form the perforant path (the major neural input into a part of the brain called the hippocampus). The response of neurons that were synapsed upon was measured in the dentate gyrus of the hippocampus itself. Naturally, the stimulation resulted in a population spike, which is a measure of postsynaptic potential (i.e. firing of the neurons in the dentate gyrus). However, Bliss and Lømo's important discovery was that the amplitude of the population spike in the dentate gyrus in response to the low-intensity pulse could be increased through experience. After establishing this baseline population spike, they passed high-intensity (and high-frequency) stimulation along the perforant path. The result of this stimulation was that later – sometimes months later – the population spike in the dentate gyrus was greater in magnitude in response to the weak pulse. This is the phenomenon of LTP. In terms of the language that we have used throughout this chapter, there had been a relatively long-lasting change in behaviour (in this case neural behaviour) as a consequence of experience (high-intensity and high-frequency electrical stimulation) – that is to say, learning.

LTP is not limited to regions of the hippocampus; it occurs in many other parts of the brain (Malenka & Bear, 2004) and, as we have seen, can last for many months. It can be demonstrated in the brains of living animals, as well as slices of the brain that have been taken from an animal and preserved in temperature- and fluid-controlled conditions (Carlson, 2010). The opposite of LTP is **long-term depression** (**LTD**), and this refers to a *reduction* in the population spike at the postsynaptic neuron, caused by low frequency (less than 10 Hz) rather than high-frequency stimulation (Dudek & Bear, 1992).

Of more importance for the current discussion, however, is the existence of 'associative LTP' (e.g. Levy & Steward, 1983). In this case, two neurons (let's call them A and B) both synapse onto a third neuron (let's call this neuron X). If neuron A is only weakly stimulated, on its own, then it may not cause neuron X to fire. However, if we subsequently arrange for neuron A to be weakly stimulated *at the same time* that neuron B is strongly stimulated (which does result in neuron X firing), then something rather interesting happens. If neuron A is now weakly stimulated again, on its own, then now neuron X *does* fire. Thus, if it is arranged for the synapses of two neurons (A and X) to activate at the same time, the neuron that previously could not elicit a response (A) now can. This sounds an awful lot like classical conditioning, in which a relatively neutral stimulus (e.g. a bell) is at first unable to evoke a response (in this case an overt behavioural response) but, after being paired with a stimulus that *is* able to evoke a response (e.g. food), comes to evoke its own, conditioned response. There is now evidence that links LTP with learning. Rogan, Stäubli, and LeDoux (1997b), for example, showed that, while a mild electric shock delivered to the foot will elicit a strong response in the lateral amygdala of rats, a tone will ordinarily not. However, if the rat undergoes a fear conditioning procedure in which the tone is paired with the shock, then the tone itself becomes able to activate the lateral amygdala. Furthermore, if a chemical compound that is known to enhance LTP is injected into rats, then it improves their performance on a variety of learning procedures, including spatial navigation and fear conditioning (Rogan, Stäubli, & LeDoux, 1997a).

The neural basis of surprise

LTP, in its various guises, provides a convincing neural analogue of learning. To take another example, if only the presynaptic or only the postsynaptic neurons fire, then LTP is not observed (Bi & Poo, 2001). This is comparable to saying that, if either the CS or US has a perceived intensity of zero, then no learning should occur, which is precisely one of the predictions of the Rescorla–Wagner model. However, as we noted earlier, the core assumption of the Rescorla–Wagner model is that learning will only take place if the US is surprising. Is this also true at the neural level? Evidence that is consistent with this idea was provided by Waelti, Dickinson, and Schultz (2001). They gave macaque monkeys a blocking procedure in which during the first stage of the experiment a visual stimulus (A) signalled the delivery of juice to the monkey. Following this training, in stage 2, A was accompanied by a novel stimulus (X), and this simultaneous compound of A and X also signalled juice. In keeping with Kamin's (1968) study, at the end of the experiment, Waelti et al. presented X on its own and found that X was rather poor at evoking a CR, relative to a control stimulus. Interestingly, however, blocking was observed not only at the behavioural level but also at the neural level. By the end of the first stage of training, the firing rate of midbrain dopamine neurons was substantial when A was presented, as it was when the compound of A and X was presented in stage 2. However, during the test, when X and a control stimulus were presented in isolation, Waelti et al. observed that the neural response to X was significantly weaker than to the control stimulus. Thus the neural response to the blocked stimulus mirrored the animal's behavioural response – that is to say, in keeping with the predictions of the Rescorla–Wagner model, the neurons in Waelti et al.'s study seemed sensitive to the effect of surprise on learning.

FOCUS POINT 8.3

NEURAL SURPRISE

An experiment by Steinberg et al. (2013) takes the results of Waelti et al. (2001) one step further. Steinberg et al. wanted to establish a causal link between surprise in dopamine neurons and blocking measured at the behavioural level. To do this, they artificially induced surprise in dopamine neurons using a procedure that permits these neurons to fire as if there actually were a discrepancy between what the animals expected and what the animals actually received (when in fact there was not).

Crucially, they did this during the second stage of the blocking procedure with the AX compound when, ordinarily, the animal is fully expecting food as a consequence of the preceding trials (in which A signalled the US) and therefore is not surprised. The results indicated that the blocking effect was significantly weakened. That is to say, by generating surprise at the neural level, Steinberg et al. were able to stimulate learning at the behavioural level, when ordinarily it would not be observed.

SECTION SUMMARY

- Our understandings of the conceptual basis of learning and its neural underpinnings are converging and now inform one another.

- We have described here the neural basis of learning in relation to the Rescorla–Wagner model, but there are also neural circuits that seem to be responsible for the interaction of learning and attention.

- Neuroscience is able to inform psychologists of where (and perhaps how) these different systems interact. This will permit psychologists to refine their theories and make better-specified predictions about learning.

PRACTICAL AND CLINICAL APPLICATIONS OF LEARNING

LEARNING OBJECTIVE 8.6

Understand and apply the principles of learning to real-world examples of behaviour, in particular instances of psychopathology (e.g. phobias, substance abuse).

We have encountered a number of examples within this chapter of how human behaviour can be understood by appreciating learning, in particular through an analysis of the relationship between stimuli in the environment, or the relationship between people's responses and their outcomes. We have seen, for example, how superstitions might have their basis in instrumental conditioning; how food aversions in cancer patients demonstrate, under some circumstances, the properties of classical conditioning; and even how our everyday representation of the causal structure of the world is built, perhaps, on the basis of associative principles. Given how widely the principles of learning have been applied, it is perhaps not surprising that they have also been applied to understanding the causes of a number of clinical conditions and, helpfully, their treatment. We shall consider in this section two classes of unwanted behaviours. First we will examine the acquisition of phobias. Second we will consider the development of drug addiction.

FOCUS POINT 8.4

NUDGE NUDGE

Nudge theory is a relatively modern application of the principles of instrumental reinforcement. Often attributed to the work of Thaler and Sunstein (2008), its application uses a variety of methods to motivate groups and individuals to comply with government, business, or other institutional objectives.

For example, in 2010, a team of 13 individuals with backgrounds in a variety of disciples, including the behavioural sciences, was set up within the cabinet office of the UK government and called the Behavioural Insights Team (more commonly known as the 'The Nudge Unit'). One of the responsibilities of the team was to apply behavioural science techniques to assist with the delivery of governmental policy.

One project was to apply 'behavioural insights' (nudges) to increase people's charitable giving. The methods were varied and included many common-sense ideas (such as attracting people's attention to the cause, making the behaviour that is desired simple to achieve, and so forth) but also the principles of reinforcement – so that desirable behaviour is encouraged. In this case, charitable donations were rewarded by, for example, matching funding, publicizing the names of contributors, or providing small gifts.

Interestingly, one of the behavioural insights of this team was that attention can be attracted to the act of giving to charity by rewarding it (Behavioural Insights Team, 2013). We have already encountered the idea that attention can be enhanced to stimuli (and responses) in our discussion of alternative theories to the Rescorla–Wagner model (e.g. Mackintosh, 1975).

Phobias

A **phobia** is a form of anxiety disorder that is characterized as a persistent fear of an object or a situation that is often out of all proportion to the actual danger that is posed by that object or situation. For example, I have a fear of spiders. I do not like the look of them, and I will not pick them up, much to my children's amusement. Even the thought of having one of the hairy beasts upon me – perhaps on my shoulder – makes my palms clammy and my heartbeat increase. This is despite the fact that I know wild spiders in the UK are harmless creatures that, in the frosty winter months, treat us to the most spectacular-looking webs. People who suffer from a phobia will often go to great lengths to avoid their phobic stimulus, sometimes to the degree that it will interrupt the normal functioning of their daily lives. For example, a person who suffers agoraphobia has a fear of leaving a particular safe place, such as their home. It is a response that prevents them from going outdoors and engaging in everyday activities such as shopping, seeing their friends, or going to work.

The analysis of phobias that is provided by classical conditioning suggests that the phobic stimulus is usually something that is objectively neutral but that has come to acquire a fear response (a CR) as a consequence of being paired with an unpleasant or noxious event in the real world (the US). Consequently, subsequent exposure to the phobic stimulus (the CS) will evoke a CR of fear. As a concrete example, consider the case of a postgraduate student in my department – the School of Psychology – at the University of Nottingham. She reports a fear of Smurfs – the fictional blue creatures from books, television cartoons, and films. The student once demonstrated this fear upon going to the cinema, where she encountered a large cardboard cut-out of a Smurf that was advertising a new movie about the Smurfs. Upon seeing the Smurf, she could feel an anxiety response building and an increase in her heart rate, and she quickly moved away from the cardboard Smurf for fear of having a panic attack. How might such a response to such an innocuous blue cartoon creature have been acquired? Our (23-year-old) student reports that she had not encountered a Smurf since the age of about seven. However, at this age she had been watching a television cartoon with the Smurfs in it, and during this cartoon she had been informed that her pet cat had died.

The explanation of this phobia in terms of classical conditioning seems straightforward. The previously innocuous and neutral Smurf was paired with a traumatic US (news of the death of the family pet). Because the US was entirely surprising, the conditions were optimal for the Smurf to become associated with the traumatic response to the news, and consequently, subsequent exposure to the Smurf, 16 years later, would evoke a CR of anxiety. However, we should be rightly suspicious of this analysis. It is, after all, a case study – a case study based upon an anecdote told to me by a student in a university common room. There is no control condition against which to compare the anxiety response of the student. We therefore have no idea whether the Smurf anxiety that the student experienced was a consequence of the Smurf being paired with the traumatic event or whether it would have developed, perhaps spontaneously, without this pairing. Arguments similar to these have been proposed by a number of critics of the conditioning analysis of phobias. Menzies and Clarke (1995), for example, suggest that many fears may actually be innate and serve the purpose of protecting us from dangerous situations. Phobias of heights and water are obvious examples here, as just one fall from a great height will have disastrous consequences – in this instance one learning trial is one learning trial too many. Other critics of the conditioning analysis of phobia acquisition (e.g. Rachman, 1977) have pointed out that not all stimuli that are paired with unpleasant events go on to become phobic stimuli, and people might also have phobias of stimuli that have never been paired with unpleasant events. Some of these criticisms can be dealt with on the basis of our knowledge of associative learning (Davey, 1989; Field & Purkis, 2012). For example, there are very good reasons why an innocuous stimulus might not go on to become a phobic stimulus even though it has been paired with a traumatic event – the phobic stimulus might have been very familiar to the sufferer before the traumatic event. You will recall from our discussion of the properties of classical conditioning that conditioning proceeds slowly to familiar stimuli – latent inhibition (Lubow & Moore, 1959). Alternatively, the (non)phobic stimulus might have been accompanied by another event that blocked it, if the other event had a history of signalling unpleasant events (Kamin, 1968).

In order to determine whether phobias have some form of conditioning-like event as their basis, it is important to examine the sorts of experiences that people who have phobias have been through and, ideally, see whether these experiences are different from those encountered in a control group of people who do not have a phobia. An example of such a study was provided by Doogan and Thomas (1992), who compared the experiences of participants who did (and who did not) have a fear of dogs. The results of this study provided good support for the conditioning analysis of phobia acquisition. They showed that significantly more adults reported having being frightened by a dog at least once if they were in a high-dog-fear group than if they were in a low-dog-fear group – suggesting that the experiences of dog fearers and dog non-fearers were different. Interestingly, this effect was particularly pronounced in participants whose frightening encounter with a dog was their *first* direct encounter with a dog. That is to say, participants were more likely to suffer a fear of dogs as a consequence of being frightened by a dog if it was novel at the point of the trauma. This effect is highly reminiscent of latent inhibition (see also Davey, 1989, for a similar discussion of the role of latent inhibition in dental phobia).

The debate about the causes of phobias continues. On the one hand, proponents of the nonassociative analysis continue to advocate the influence of inherited fears and provide evidence to support this claim (e.g. Poulton & Menzies, 2002). On the other hand, other researchers maintain a conditioning analysis of phobia acquisition (e.g. Mineka & Zinbarg, 2006). It is almost certainly the case that learning is involved in the *loss* of fears and phobias, as therapies such as systematic desensitization (which is based upon extinction) continue to successfully serve as treatments for phobias. Ultimately, it seems likely that both associative and nonassociative analyses will provide a complete analysis of the acquisition of fears and phobias. However, such a concession would not necessarily be at variance with the principles of classical conditioning, which, after all, acknowledges the existence of both CRs and URs.

ACTIVITY 8.4

BE AFRAID; BE VERY AFRAID

Form a focus group of your friends and family and ask them to describe any fears or phobias that they may have. Once they have done this, ask them whether they can identify any traumatic experiences that surrounded the time at which they first acquired their fear, or, instead, whether they have always had the fear. See whether the experiences of people with specific fears differ from those without those fears.

Drug addiction

Not only am I afraid of spiders but also, for a number of years, I was a drug addict. I was a smoker since I first smoked a cigarette as an undergraduate at the age of 18, and it is only in recent years that I have managed to quit the habit. Throughout my time as a smoker, I was fully aware of the dangers that my habit posed: I knew that it drastically increased my chances of developing lung cancer, as well as the chances of the others around me who were passively inhaling smoke. Why would I do such an irrational and selfish thing?

Similarly, why would an individual who is addicted to cocaine steal money to buy their drug? Why would they risk an overdose and also, potentially, risk losing the support of their friends and family?

The answers to these questions are complex and certainly involve the interaction of a number of variables, including sociodemographic status and the attitudes of peers and family members, to name just two. However, here we will consider the psychological mechanisms at play in the individual addict, in particular from the perspective of associative learning.

 Click here[2] to watch a real-life account of heroin addiction in 'James Recovery Story'.

The role of instrumental conditioning

We have already seen how an organism will come to increase the frequency with which it performs a response if the response is correlated with a reinforcing event. What could be more reinforcing than a hit of cocaine, or the inhalation of nicotine or the drinking of alcohol? The analysis of addiction from the perspective of instrumental conditioning argues that drug-seeking behaviour, and ultimately the response that administers the drug, are maintained through the establishment of an association between these responses, environmental stimuli, and the reinforcing properties of the drug. These reinforcing properties may be either positive (such as the euphoric effects of the drug) or negative (such as the alleviation of withdrawal symptoms).

You may recall from our discussion of instrumental conditioning in animals that the role of the association between a response and a reinforcer can be revealed by devaluing the reinforcer once the response–reinforcer has been established, and examining whether this manipulation influenced subsequent instrumental behaviour (e.g. Colwill & Rescorla, 1985).

Hogarth and Chase (2011) exploited this procedure in an experiment with human smokers who were first trained to press two different keys on a computer keyboard for either chocolate or cigarettes. Not surprisingly, participants' preference for pressing the cigarette key correlated with a variety of measures of tobacco dependence (such as the number of cigarettes smoked per day). Following this instrumental training, participants were asked to smoke freely until they felt satiated – the argument being that the value of the reinforcer would be reduced following this procedure. In a final test, participants were given the opportunity to press the chocolate- or tobacco-associated keys, but in the absence of either of these rewards. The results revealed that all participants selectively reduced their choice of the tobacco key following the devaluation procedure. It seems that, for cigarette smokers at least, performance of a response that acquires a cigarette (i.e. drug-seeking behaviour) is under the control of a response–reinforcer association.

However, you may also recall from the study described by Adams and Dickinson (1981) that not all instrumental behaviour is so easily explained in terms of response–reinforcer (or goal-directed) behaviour. These authors revealed that, with lots of exposure to instrumental conditioning, behaviour becomes insensitive to reinforcer devaluation; instead, behaviour is maintained under these circumstances by an association between the environmental stimuli and the response – a habit. Is there any evidence for a similar transition in drug addiction? In animals, it certainly seems so. Nelson and Killcross (2006) gave rats chronic exposure to a drug by injecting them with amphetamine every day for a week. Following this treatment, the rats were trained to press a lever for sucrose reinforcement before undergoing a reinforcer devaluation procedure in which sucrose was paired with illness. In a final test, in which the rats were given the opportunity to lever press (in the absence of sucrose), Nelson and Killcross observed that the amphetamine rats showed no sensitivity to reinforcer devaluation. However, control rats – who had initially learned to lever press, but in the absence of prior exposure to amphetamine – did show a sensitivity to reinforcer devaluation. The implication of these results is substantial. Simple exposure to a drug, in this case amphetamine, can have a drastic influence on the manner in which behaviour is maintained. Under the conditions of amphetamine addiction, it seems animals are less able to appreciate the consequences of their responses. This result therefore goes some way to understanding (1) why drug addictions are maintained even when a significant tolerance has been acquired to the drug (presumably reducing its value) and (2) why drug addiction results in such irrational behaviour. It remains to be determined whether a similar result is true in human participants. Hogarth and Chase (2012) review the literature on habit-based behaviour in humans, and find some evidence for a comparable effect in smokers. We point the reader who is interested in learning more about the role of habits in addiction to this discussion.

The role of classical conditioning

Drug addicts will frequently report instances of cravings and the onset of withdrawal symptoms when they are not taking drugs. Examples of the sorts of stimuli that can elicit these symptoms of drug addiction are the sight of drug paraphernalia (e.g. the sight of a bag of heroin, a dealer, or somebody injecting), movies about drugs (e.g. *Trainspotting*), or even just talking about drugs (O'Brien, Ehrman, & Ternes, 1986). The fact that objectively neutral stimuli (such as a film) can induce such a significant response in addicts lends itself to the suggestion that such stimuli control the behaviour of addicted individuals through a process of classical conditioning. Neutral stimuli such as the sight of a dealer will be paired with the US of the drug (e.g. heroin, cocaine). A CR of craving, for example, is then elicited by the neutral stimulus, at which point we can identify the sight of the dealer (for example) as a CS. Foltin and Haney (2000) demonstrated that a variety of CRs could be acquired to neutral stimuli that were paired with cocaine in individuals who were habitual cocaine smokers. They paired neutral stimuli (e.g. different smells or visual stimuli) with either cocaine or a placebo. After 15 days of this training, the stimulus associated with cocaine elicited various physiological responses, such as changes in heart rate and skin temperature, as well as changes in subjectively recorded measures of craving (such as participants' ratings of being stimulated or wanting cocaine). As compelling as this result is, however, a weakness of this study is that it was conducted in individuals who had already established a drug habit. It does not tell us whether a similar effect would be present in people who do not have a drug habit. If it wasn't present, then it would simply permit us to conclude that CRs to stimuli associated with drugs only serve to *maintain* cravings and withdrawal symptoms, rather than underlying their acquisition in the first place. Fortunately, a study similar to that conducted by Foltin and Haney has been reported that describes the acquisition of CRs of changes in skin conductance and heart rate to the colour of a liquid that is paired with the consumption of alcohol (Glautier, Drummond, & Remington, 1994). Importantly, these CRs were observed in individuals who reported no history of drinking problems prior to the experiment.

As we saw in our description of classical conditioning earlier in the chapter, as much as CRs can be acquired to neutral stimuli, so too can they be extinguished by simply presenting the CS in the absence of the US. This observation forms the basis of **cue-exposure therapy**, in which the client (in this case a drug addict) is given the opportunity to experience drug-associated stimuli but in the absence of the drug itself, in the hope that the CRs elicited by drug-associated stimuli will extinguish. There have been a number of studies that have examined the efficacy of cue-exposure therapy in drug addiction, some of which suggest an effect of the treatment, other suggesting no effect at all. Conklin and Tiffany (2002) reviewed these in a meta-analysis of cue-exposure studies that employed controlled (i.e. non-case-study-based) experiments that included, as part of their measurement of success, a post-treatment follow-up meeting with the clients. They found that the overall size of the effect (d) of the therapy was 0.08, which was far from statistical significance.

It seems surprising, on the one hand, that cue-exposure therapy is so ineffective in treating drug addiction as we know that extinction works so well in studies of animal conditioning. However, on the other hand, recall that the extinction of conditioned responding is a fragile phenomenon exhibiting spontaneous recovery, and also **renewal**. It is the latter phenomenon that is of particular relevance to the current discussion for it provides a way in which to understand why exposure therapy may not be successful. Renewal refers to a situation in which conditioned responding is established in one context, extinguished in a second context, and then shown to re-emerge if the animal is tested in the original conditioning context. Cue-exposure therapy is rarely conducted in the same context in which the original drug addiction was acquired. Consequently, even though a drug addict may seemingly be clear of their habit following a series of therapy sessions and can tolerate the sight (for example) of drug-associated paraphernalia, should they be exposed to the same stimuli in the context in which they originally acquired their habit, then our understanding of the phenomenon of renewal suggests that they will relapse, which unfortunately frequently happens (Bouton, Winterbauer, & Vurbic, 2012).

ACTIVITY 8.5

A-B-C ANALYSIS

The next time you fancy opening a bottle of wine or, if you are a smoker, lighting a cigarette, have a think about the sorts of environmental stimuli that were present just before and during your craving. Are these drug-associated stimuli? Alternatively, have a think about how you feel before and after drinking or smoking. If you do not drink or smoke, ask one of your classmates who does about their own experiences.

Write down these experiences in a diary and try to identify the antecedents and consequences of your drug-taking behaviour (this is called 'A-B-C analysis'). Should you want to quit your habit, this may help you to identify the sorts of stimuli that are maintaining it.

TEST YOURSELF

Why might a person not acquire a phobia of something that is paired with a scary event?

SECTION SUMMARY

- The principles of learning have been applied to understanding the causes of a number of clinical conditions and their treatment.

- A phobia is a persistent fear of an object or a situation that is often out of all proportion to the actual danger that is posed by that object or situation.

- The explanation of phobia in terms of classical conditioning seems straightforward. However, without a control condition, we cannot be confident that a phobia has arisen as a result of being paired with the traumatic event, or whether it would have developed, perhaps spontaneously, without this pairing.

- Many fears may actually be innate and serve the purpose of protecting us from dangerous situations. Additionally, not all stimuli that are paired with unpleasant events go on to become phobic stimuli, and people also have phobias of stimuli that have never been paired with unpleasant events.

- It is important to examine the sorts of experiences that people who have phobias have been through and, ideally, see whether these experiences are different from those encountered in a control group of people who do not have a phobia.

- Ultimately, it seems likely that both associative and nonassociative analyses will provide a complete analysis of the acquisition of fears and phobias.

- The analysis of addiction from the perspective of instrumental conditioning argues that drug-seeking behaviours are maintained through the establishment of an association between these responses, environmental stimuli, and the reinforcing properties of the drug.

- Simple exposure to a drug can have a drastic influence on the manner in which behaviour is maintained. Under the conditions of drug addiction, it seems humans and animals are less able to appreciate the consequences of their responses.

- The fact that objectively neutral stimuli (such as a film) can induce such a significant response in addicts lends itself to the suggestion that such stimuli control the behaviour of addicted individuals through a process of classical conditioning.

- As we saw in our description of classical conditioning earlier in the chapter, as much as CRs can be acquired to neutral stimuli, so too can they be extinguished by simply presenting the CS in the absence of the US. This observation forms the basis of cue-exposure therapy.

- However, cue-exposure therapy is often ineffective in treating drug addiction despite our awareness that extinction works well in studies of animal conditioning. It is important to bear in mind that extinction of conditioned responding is a fragile phenomenon exhibiting spontaneous recovery and renewal; additionally, cue-exposure therapy is rarely conducted in the same context in which the original drug addiction was acquired.

CONCLUSIONS AND FUTURE DIRECTIONS

LEARNING OBJECTIVE 8.7

Critically evaluate possible future directions for research in learning.

In this chapter we have aimed to achieve two things. First, we have attempted to provide you with an introduction to the properties and principles of learning in humans and nonhuman animals. We have described classical, instrumental, and social learning; some of the factors that influence these phenomena; and a theory and the neural mechanisms that underpin them. We have described examples of learning that have been thought to challenge the simple, associative analysis of learning, and have provided examples of how our understanding of learning has permitted psychologists to acquire a better understanding of how phobias and drug addictions develop.

A second aim was to present a theoretical position, one that suggests that a simple psychological system, which mirrors the architecture of the brain, underpins learning in human and nonhuman animals. Critics of this theoretical position exist, of course – that is the nature of scientific debate – and we have encountered counterpoints to associative learning in the study of human causal learning, and also in the study of the mechanisms of phobia acquisition.

These theoretical differences, of course, do not end here. In the field of animal cognition, a number of authors have attributed a variety of higher-order cognitive functions to the humble laboratory rat (e.g. reasoning: Beckers et al., 2006; empathy: Bartal, Decety, & Mason, 2011). Furthermore, there has been a growth in learning theories that apply statistical (Bayesian) principles to human and animal behaviour (e.g. Jacobs & Kruschke, 2011). These theories are often computationally very complex and have been argued to be biologically implausible (e.g. Bowers & Davis, 2012; Wilson, Nassar, & Gold, 2013), but they do have the ability to explain many phenomena. Whether they will ultimately trump associative theories remains to be determined. In any case, the future of the study of learning will most likely reflect its past – the systematic assessment of different theories of behaviour through well-designed and well-conducted experiments.

Where the future of the study of learning may differ from its past, however, is with a reduction in the use of animals in this research, at least for purely behavioural research. Ethically, this is certainly desirable, but it is important for us not to lose sight of the advances that the study of behaviour in animals has provided for our understanding of learning, and its disorders.

SECTION SUMMARY

- The nature of scientific discovery and debate means that alternatives to the associative analysis of learning exist.
- Future studies of learning will benefit from looking to its past and applying a rigorous approach to the study of the relationship between behaviour and cognition.

CHAPTER SUMMARY

This chapter has considered the fundamental principles of learning in humans and nonhuman animals and how they have been investigated in experimental psychology. We did this by first outlining the properties of simple forms of learning and then moved on to a discussion of more complex learning, in the form of social learning and human causal judgement. We then provided an evaluation of the neural basis of learned behaviour and concluded with a discussion of how the study of learning has been applied successfully in the understanding and treatment of real-life problems, such as phobia and addiction.

ESSAY QUESTIONS

1. Describe some examples of classical conditioning. What are the factors that promote it?
2. What is learned during instrumental conditioning and how do scientists assess this learning?
3. Describe a psychological disorder from the perspective of classical or instrumental conditioning. How convinced are you that associative processes underlie its aetiology?

KEY TERMS

- **appetitive conditioning:** A form of classical conditioning in which the motivational significance of the unconditioned stimulus is positive (e.g. food, water, sex).
- **associative theory:** An explanation of learning which proposes that conditioned behaviour is the consequence of the acquisition and extinction of connections (associations) between events, including stimuli and responses.
- **aversive conditioning:** A form of classical conditioning in which the motivational significance of the unconditioned stimulus is negative (e.g. pain, illness).
- **behaviourally silent learning:** Learning that is not expressed in any change in behaviour.
- **blocking:** The attenuation of conditioned responding to a CS that results from conditioning the CS in compound with a second stimulus that has already been established as a CS.
- **classical conditioning:** A form of learning that involves the pairing of an initially neutral stimulus with a biologically significant stimulus. This training results in a change in responding to the neutral stimulus.
- **conditioned reinforcement:** A stimulus (e.g. a tone) that has acquired the ability to reinforce instrumental behaviour by being paired with a biologically significant stimulus (e.g. food).
- **conditioned response (CR):** The response that is acquired by the conditioned stimulus.
- **conditioned stimulus (CS):** An initially neutral stimulus that comes to acquire a response as a consequence of training with the unconditioned stimulus.
- **cue-exposure therapy:** A psychological treatment given to clients with the aim of reducing the frequency or vigour of an unwanted behaviour (e.g. a phobia, a substance addiction). Cues associated with the unwanted behaviour are presented in isolation or in conjunction with relaxation techniques in order to extinguish the association that established the unwanted behaviour.
- **discrimination learning:** A form of learning in which an animal comes to acquires different responses to different stimuli, or combinations of stimuli.

- **extinction:** A procedure in which a conditioned stimulus is presented in the absence of the unconditioned stimulus, following prior CS–US pairings. As a consequence of this training, the conditioned response will weaken.
- **habituation:** A reduction in the vigour, or likelihood, of a response produced by repeated presentation of a stimulus.
- **instrumental (or operant) conditioning:** A form of learning in which a biologically significant stimulus is presented to an animal upon performance of a response. The relationship between the response and the stimulus is seen to change the animal's behaviour.
- **introspection:** Self-examination or observation of one's own emotions or mental processes.
- **latent inhibition:** The attenuation of conditioned responding by exposure to the CS prior to conditioning.
- **long-term depression (LTD):** A reduction in neural firing as a consequence of low-frequency neural stimulation.
- **long-term potentiation (LTP):** An enhancement in neural firing as a consequence of high-frequency neural stimulation.
- **mimicry and imitation:** Forms of social learning in which a novel response is acquired as a consequence of observing a demonstrator animal. Imitation is assumed to be a goal-directed form of social learning.
- **observational conditioning:** A form of social learning in which a demonstrator animal serves as the US for conditioning to an initially neutral stimulus.
- **phobia:** An irrational fear of an objectively harmless stimulus (e.g. a house spider).
- **reflex arc:** A nerve pathway from a sensory neuron to a spinal motor neuron that does not pass through the brain, allowing quick (reflex) action in response to a potentially damaging stimulus.
- **renewal:** The re-emergence of a conditioned response to a CS when it is presented in the conditioning context, following extinction in a different context.
- **Rescorla–Wagner model:** An influential theory of associative learning, the central assumption of which is that learning is a function of how surprising the US is.
- **second-order conditioning:** A training procedure in which a CS comes to acquire a conditioned response by being paired with another CS, which itself has already been paired with a US (e.g. tone → food, light → tone).
- **sensitization:** A strengthening of a response produced by repeated exposure to a stimulus.
- **social learning:** A change in an animal's behaviour that results from exposure to another animal, or another animal's behaviour.
- **spontaneous recovery:** The re-emergence of a conditioned response to a CS following extinction as a consequence of the simple passage of time.
- **S–R learning:** A theoretical explanation for instrumental conditioning. Environmental stimuli (S) become connected with a response (R) if they are followed by a reinforcer.
- **stimulus enhancement:** An increase in attention to an object brought about by another animal's interaction with the object.
- **unconditioned response (UR):** The response elicited by an unconditioned stimulus.
- **unconditioned stimulus (US):** A biologically significant stimulus (such as food or pain) that is able to elicit a response without training.

NOTES

1. http://www.jove.com/video/3446/habituation-and-prepulse-inhibition-of-acoustic-startle-in-rodents
2. http://link.brightcove.com/services/player/bcpid982198451001?bckey=AQ~~,AAAAkPubc Zk~,_5wRjVEP-2Sma1whESEDFKmqjWi9oghp&bctid=3365398089001

FURTHER RESOURCES

Bouton, M. E. (2007). *Learning and behavior: A contemporary Synthesis.* Sunderland, MA: Sinauer.

Dickinson, A. (1985). Actions and habits: The development of behavioural autonomy. *Philosophical Transactions of the Royal Society B: Biological Sciences, 308,* 67–78.

Dickinson, A. (2001). Causal learning: An associative analysis. *Quarterly Journal of Experimental Psychology, 54*(B), 3–25.

Domjan, M. (2010). *The principles of learning and behavior.* Belmont, CA: Wadsworth.

Haselgrove, M., & Hogarth, L. (2012). *Clinical applications of learning theory.* Hove, UK: Psychology Press.

Heyes, C. (2012). What's social about social learning? *Journal of Comparative Psychology, 126,* 193–202.

Journal of Experimental Psychology: Animal Learning and Cognition. (2017). Retrieved 20 November 2017 from http://www.apa.org/pubs/journals/xan/index.aspx

NHS. (2016). Phobias. Retrieved 20 November 2017 from http://www.nhs.uk/Conditions/Phobias/Pages/Introduction.aspx

NHS. (2017). Overcoming addiction. Retrieved 20 November 2017 from http://www.nhs.uk/conditions/addictions/Pages/Introduction.aspx

Pearce, J. M. (2008). *Animal learning and cognition: An introduction.* Hove, UK: Psychology Press.

Pearce, J. M., & Bouton, M. E. (2001). Theories of associative learning in animals. *Annual Review of Psychology, 52,* 111–139.

Rescorla, R. A. (1988). Pavlovian conditioning: It's not what you think it is. *American Psychologist, 43,* 151–160.

REFERENCES

Adams, C., & Dickinson, A. (1981). Actions and habits: Variations in associative representations during instrumental learning. In N. E. Spear & R. R. Miller (Eds.), *Information processing in animals: Memory mechanisms* (pp. 143–166). Hillsdale, NJ: Lawrence Erlbaum Associates.

Annau, Z., & Kamin, L. J. (1961). The conditioned emotional response as a function of intensity of the US. *Journal of Comparative and Physiological Psychology, 54*(4), 428–432.

Arzi, A., Shedlesky, L., Ben-Shaul, M., Nasser, K., Oksenberg, A., Hairston, I. S., & Sobel, N. (2012). Humans can learn new information during sleep. *Nature Neuroscience, 15*(10), 1460–1467.

Bandura, A., Ross, D., & Ross, S. A. (1963). Imitation of film-mediated aggressive models. *Journal of Abnormal and Social Psychology, 66*(1), 3–11.

Bartal, I. B. A., Decety, J., & Mason, P. (2011). Empathy and pro-social behavior in rats. *Science, 334*(6061), 1427–1430.

Beckers, T., De Houwer, J., Pineno, O., & Miller, R. R. (2005). Outcome additivity and outcome maximality influence cue competition in human causal learning. *Journal of Experimental Psychology: Learning, Memory, and Cognition, 31*(2), 238–249.

Beckers, T., Miller, R. R., De Houwer, J., & Urushihara, K. (2006). Reasoning rats: Forward blocking in Pavlovian animal conditioning is sensitive to constraints of causal inference. *Journal of Experimental Psychology: General, 135*(1), 92–102.

Behavioural Insights Team. (2013). *Applying behavioural insights to charitable giving.* Retrieved 20 November 2017 from https://www.gov.uk/government/uploads/system/uploads/attachment_data/file/203286/BIT_Charitable_Giving_Paper.pdf

Bernstein, I. L., & Webster, M. M. (1980). Learned taste aversions in humans. *Physiology & Behavior, 25,* 363–366.

Bi, G. Q., & Poo, M. M. (2001). Synaptic modification by correlated activity: Hebb's postulate revisited. *Annual Review of Neuroscience, 24*(1), 139–166.

Blaser, R. E., Couvillon, P. A., & Bitterman, M. E. (2004). Backward blocking in honeybees. *Quarterly Journal of Experimental Psychology B: Comparative and Physiological Psychology, 57*(4), 349–360.

Bliss, T. V., & Lømo, T. (1973). Long-lasting potentiation of synaptic transmission in the dentate area of the anaesthetized rabbit following stimulation of the perforant path. *Journal of Physiology*, *232*(2), 331–356.

Boice, R., & Denny, M. (1965). The conditioned licking response in rats as a function of the CS–UCS interval. *Psychonomic Science*, *3*(3), 93–94.

Bouton, M. E., & King, D. A. (1983). Contextual control of the extinction of conditioned fear: Tests for the associative value of the context. *Journal of Experimental Psychology: Animal Behavior Processes*, *9*, 248–265.

Bouton, M. E., Winterbauer, N. E., & Vurbic, D. (2012). Context and extinction: Mechanisms of relapse in drug self-administration. In M. Haselgrove & L. Hogarth (Eds.), *Clinical applications of learning theory* (pp. 103–134). Hove, UK: Psychology Press.

Bowers, J. S., & Davis, C. J. (2012). Bayesian just-so stories in psychology and neuroscience. *Psychological Bulletin*, *138*(3), 389–414.

Brass, M., & Heyes, C. (2005). Imitation: Is cognitive neuroscience solving the correspondence problem? *Trends in Cognitive Sciences*, *9*(10), 489–495.

Brown, P. L., & Jenkins, H. M. (1968). Autoshaping of the pigeon's key-peck. *Journal of the Experimental Analysis of Behavior*, *11*(1), 1–8.

Carew, T. J., Hawkins, R. D., & Kandel, E. R. (1983). Differential classical conditioning of a defensive withdrawal reflex in *Aplysia californica*. *Science*, *219*, 397–400.

Carlson, N. R. (2010). *Physiology of behavior*. Harlow, UK: Allyn & Bacon.

Colwill, R. M., & Rescorla, R. A. (1985). Postconditioning devaluation of a reinforcer affects instrumental responding. *Journal of Experimental Psychology: Animal Behavior Processes*, *11*(1), 120–132.

Comer, R., Ogden, N., & Furnam, A. (2013). *Psychology*. Hoboken, NJ: Wiley.

Conklin, C. A., & Tiffany, S. T. (2002). Applying extinction research and theory to cue-exposure addiction treatments. *Addiction*, *97*(2), 155–167.

Cross, H. A., Halcomb, C. G., & Matter, W. W. (1967). Imprinting or exposure learning in rats given early auditory stimulation. *Psychonomic Science*, *7*, 233–234.

Davey, G. C. (1989). UCS revaluation and conditioning models of acquired fears. *Behaviour Research and Therapy*, *27*(5), 521–528.

Di Pellegrino, G., Fadiga, L., Fogassi, L., Gallese, V., & Rizzolatti, G. (1992). Understanding motor events: A neurophysiological study. *Experimental Brain Research*, *91*(1), 176–180.

Dickinson, A. (1980). *Contemporary animal learning theory*. Cambridge, UK: Cambridge University Press.

Dickinson, A. (2001). The 28th Bartlett memorial lecture. Causal learning: An associative analysis. *Quarterly Journal of Experimental Psychology B: Comparative and Physiological Psychology*, *54*(1), 3–25.

Dickinson, A., Shanks, D., & Evenden, J. (1984). Judgement of act-outcome contingency: The role of selective attribution. *Quarterly Journal of Experimental Psychology B: Comparative and Physiological Psychology*, *36*(1), 29–50.

Dickinson, A., Watt, A., & Griffiths, W. J. H. (1992). Free-operant acquisition with delayed reinforcement. *Quarterly Journal of Experimental Psychology B: Comparative and Physiological Psychology*, *45*(3), 241–258.

Domjan, M. (1976). Determinants of the enhancement of flavored water intake by prior exposure. *Journal of Experimental Psychology: Animal Behavior Processes*, *2*, 17–27.

Domjan, M. (1993). *The principles of learning and behavior*. Pacific Grove, CA: Brooks/Cole.

Domjan, M., Blesbois, E., & Williams, J. (1998). The adaptive significance of sexual conditioning: Pavlovian control of sperm release. *Psychological Science*, *9*(5), 411–415.

Domjan, M., Lyons, R., North, N. C., & Bruell, J. (1986). Sexual Pavlovian conditioned approach behavior in male Japanese quail (*Coturnix coturnix japonica*). *Journal of Comparative Psychology*, *100*(4), 413–421.

Doogan, S., & Thomas, G. V. (1992). Origins of fear of dogs in adults and children: The role of conditioning processes and prior familiarity with dogs. *Behaviour Research and Therapy*, *30*(4), 387–394.

Dudek, S. M., & Bear, M. F. (1992). Homosynaptic long-term depression in area CA1 of hippocampus and effects of N-methyl-D-aspartate receptor blockade. *Proceedings of the National Academy of Sciences of the United States of America*, 89(10), 4363–4367.

Esber, G. R., & Haselgrove, M. (2011). Reconciling the influence of predictiveness and uncertainty on stimulus salience: A model of attention in associative learning. *Proceedings of the Royal Society B: Biological Sciences*, 278, 2553–2561.

Fanselow, M. S. (1980). Conditional and unconditional components of post-shock freezing. *Pavlovian Journal of Biological Science*, October–November, 177–182.

Field, A. P., & Purkis, H. M. (2012). Associative learning and phobias. In M. Haselgrove & L. Hogarth (Eds.), *Clinical applications of learning theory* (pp. 49–74). Hove, UK: Psychology Press.

Foltin, R. W., & Haney, M. (2000). Conditioned effects of environmental stimuli paired with smoked cocaine in humans. *Psychopharmacology*, 149(1), 24–33.

Galef, B. G. (1988). Communication of information concerning distant diets in a social, central-place foraging species 'Rattus norvegicus'. In T. R. Zentall & B. G. Galef (Eds.), *Social learning: Psychological and biological perspectives*. Hillsdale, NJ: Lawrence Erlbaum Associates.

Galef, B. G., & Durlach, P. J. (1993). Absence of blocking, overshadowing, and latent inhibition in social enhancement of food preferences. *Animal Learning & Behavior*, 21(3), 214–220.

Galef, B. G., Manzig, L. A., & Field, R. M. (1986). Imitation learning in budgerigars: Dawson and Foss (1965) revisited. *Behavioural Processes*, 13(1), 191–202.

Garcia, J., Ervin, F. R., & Koelling, R. A. (1966). Learning with prolonged delay of reinforcement. *Psychonomic Science*, 5, 121–122.

Gibbs, C. M., Latham, S. B., & Gormezano, I. (1978). Classical conditioning of the rabbit nictitating membrane response: Effects of reinforcement schedule on response maintenance and resistance to extinction. *Animal Learning & Behavior*, 6(2), 209–215.

Glautier, S., Drummond, C., & Remington, B. (1994). Alcohol as an unconditioned stimulus in human classical conditioning. *Psychopharmacology*, 116(3), 360–368.

Groves, P. M., & Thompson, R. F. (1970). Habituation: A dual-process theory. *Psychological Review*, 77(5), 419–450.

Hammond, L. J. (1980). The effect of contingency upon the appetitive conditioning of free-operant behavior. *Journal of the Experimental Analysis of Behavior*, 34(3), 297–304.

Haselgrove, M., Esber, G. R., Pearce, J. M., & Jones, P. M. (2010). Two kinds of attention in Pavlovian conditioning: Evidence for a hybrid model of learning. *Journal of Experimental Psychology: Animal Behavior Processes*, 36, 456–470.

Hebb, D. (1949). *The organization of behavior*. New York, NY: Wiley.

Heyes, C. (2001). Causes and consequences of imitation. *Trends in Cognitive Sciences*, 5(6), 253–261.

Heyes, C. M. (1994). Social learning in animals: Categories and mechanisms. *Biological Reviews*, 69(2), 207–231.

Heyes, C. M., & Dawson, G. R. (1990). A demonstration of observational learning in rats using a bidirectional control. *Quarterly Journal of Experimental Psychology B: Comparative and Physiological Psychology*, 42, 59–71.

Heyes, C. M., & Ray, E. D. (2000). What is the significance of imitation in animals? *Advances in the Study of Behavior*, 29, 215–245.

Hogarth, L., & Chase, H. W. (2011). Parallel goal-directed and habitual control of human drug-seeking: Implications for dependence vulnerability. *Journal of Experimental Psychology: Animal Behavior Processes*, 37(3), 261–276.

Hogarth, L., & Chase, H. W. (2012). Vulnerabilities underlying human drug dependence: Goal valuation versus habit learning. In M. Haselgrove & L. Hogarth (Eds.), *Clinical applications of learning theory* (pp. 75–102). Hove, UK: Psychology Press.

Hyde, T. S. (1976). The effect of Pavlovian stimuli on the acquisition of a new response. *Learning and Motivation*, 7, 223–239. doi:10.1016/0023-9690(76)90030-8

Iacoboni, M., Woods, R. P., Brass, M., Bekkering, H., Mazziotta, J. C., & Rizzolatti, G. (1999). Cortical mechanisms of human imitation. *Science*, 28, 2526–2528.

Jacobs, R. A., & Kruschke, J. K. (2011). Bayesian learning theory applied to human cognition. *Wiley Interdisciplinary Reviews: Cognitive Science, 2*(1), 8–21.

Jennings, S. (1906). *Behaviour of the lower organisms.* New York, NY: Colombia University Press.

Kamin, L. J. (1968). 'Attention-like' processes in classical conditioning. In M. R. Jones (Ed.), *Miami Symposium on the Prediction of Behavior, 1967: Aversive stimulation* (pp. 9–31). Coral Gables, FA: University of Miami Press.

Kaye, H., & Pearce, J. M. (1987). Hippocampal lesions attenuate latent inhibition and the decline of the orienting response in rats. *Quarterly Journal of Experimental Psychology, 39*(2), 107–125.

Kilner, J. M., & Lemon, R. N. (2013). What we currently know about mirror neurons. *Current Biology, 23*(23), R1057–R1062.

Kruschke, J. K., & Blair, N. J. (2000). Blocking and backward blocking involve learned inattention. *Psychonomic Bulletin & Review, 7*(4), 636–645.

Le Pelley, M. E. (2004). The role of associative history in models of associative learning: A selective review and a hybrid model. *Quarterly Journal of Experimental Psychology B: Comparative and Physiological Psychology, 57*(3), 193–243.

Levy, W. B., & Steward, O. (1983). Temporal contiguity requirements for long-term associative potentiation/depression in the hippocampus. *Neuroscience, 8*(4), 791–797.

Lubow, R. E., & Moore, A. U. (1959). Latent inhibition: The effect of nonreinforced pre-exposure to the conditional stimulus. *Journal of Comparative and Physiological Psychology, 52*, 415–419.

Lubow, R., & Weiner, I. (2010). *Latent inhibition: Cognition, neuroscience and applications to schizophrenia.* Cambridge, UK: Cambridge University Press.

Mackintosh, N. J. (1974). *The psychology of animal learning.* London, UK: Academic Press.

Mackintosh, N. J. (1975). A theory of attention: Variations in the associability of stimuli with reinforcement. *Psychological Review, 82*(4), 276–298.

Malenka, R. C., & Bear, M. F. (2004). LTP and LTD: An embarrassment of riches. *Neuron, 44*(1), 5–21.

McLaren, I. P. L., Forrest, C. L. D., McLaren, R. P., Jones, F. W., Aitken, M. R. F., & Mackintosh, N. J. (2014). Associations and propositions: The case for a dual-process account of learning in humans. *Neurobiology of Learning and Memory, 108*, 185–195.

McQuoid, L. M., & Galef, B. G. (1992). Social influences on feeding site selection by Burmese fowl (*Gallus gallus*). *Journal of Comparative Psychology, 106*(2), 137–141.

Menzies, R. G., & Clarke, J. C. (1995). The etiology of phobias: A nonassociative account. *Clinical Psychology Review, 15*(1), 23–48.

Mineka, S., & Cook, M. (1988). Social learning and the acquisition of snake fear in monkeys. In T. R. Zentall & B. G. Galef (Eds.), *Social learning: Psychological and biological perspectives* (pp. 51–74). Hillsdale, NJ: Lawrence Erlbaum Associates.

Mineka, S., & Zinbarg, R. (2006). A contemporary learning theory perspective on the etiology of anxiety disorders: It's not what you thought it was. *American Psychologist, 61*(1), 10–26.

Mitchell, C. J., & Le Pelley, M. E. (2010). *Attention and associative learning: From brain to behaviour.* Oxford, UK: Oxford University Press.

Mui, R., Haselgrove, M., Pearce, J. M., & Heyes, C. (2008). Automatic imitation in budgerigars. *Proceedings of the Royal Society B, 275*, 2547–2553.

Moore, B. R. (1992). Avian movement imitation and a new form of mimicry: Tracing the evolution of a complex form of learning. *Behaviour, 122*, 231–263.

Nelson, A., & Killcross, S. (2006). Amphetamine exposure enhances habit formation. *Journal of Neuroscience, 26*(14), 3805–3812.

O'Brien, C. P., Ehrman, R. N., & Ternes, J. W. (1986). Classical conditioning in human opioid dependence. In S. R. Goldberg & I. P. Stolerman (Eds.), *Behavioral analysis of drug dependence* (pp. 329–356). New York, NY: Academic Press.

Pavlov, I. P. (1927). *Conditioned reflexes (Trans. G. V. Anrep).* London, UK: Oxford University Press.

Pearce, J. M. (1987). A model for stimulus generalization in Pavlovian conditioning. *Psychological Review, 94*, 61–73.

Pearce, J. M. (2008). *Animal learning and cognition: An introduction.* Hove, UK: Psychology Press.

Pearce, J. M., & Hall, G. (1980). A model for Pavlovian learning: Variations in the effectiveness of conditioned but not of unconditioned stimuli. *Psychological Review, 87*(6), 532–552.

Poulton, R., & Menzies, R. G. (2002). Non-associative fear acquisition: A review of the evidence from retrospective and longitudinal research. *Behaviour Research and Therapy, 40*(2), 127–149.

Press, C., Catmur, C., Cook, R., Widman, H., Heyes, C., & Bird, G. (2012). fMRI evidence of 'mirror' responses to geometric shapes. *PLoS ONE, 7*(12), e51934.

Rachman, S. (1977). The conditioning theory of fear acquisition: A critical examination. *Behaviour Research and Therapy, 15*(5), 375–387.

Rescorla, R. A. (1969). Pavlovian conditioned inhibition. *Psychological Bulletin, 72*(2), 77–94.

Rescorla, R. A. (1980). *Pavlovian second-order conditioning: Studies in associative learning.* Hillside, NJ: Lawrence Erlbaum Associates.

Rescorla, R. A. (2001). Are associative changes in acquisition and extinction negatively accelerated? *Journal of Experimental Psychology: Animal Behavior Processes, 27*(4), 307–315.

Rescorla, R. A., & Wagner, A. R. (1972). A theory of Pavlovian conditioning: Variations in the effectiveness of reinforcement and nonreinforcement. In A. H. Black & W. F. Prokasy (Eds.), *Classical conditioning II: Current research and theory* (pp. 64–99). New York, NY: Appleton-Century-Crofts.

Rogan, M. T., Stäubli, U. V., & LeDoux, J. E. (1997a). AMPA receptor facilitation accelerates fear learning without altering the level of conditioned fear acquired. *Journal of Neuroscience, 17*(15), 5928–5935.

Rogan, M. T., Stäubli, U. V., & LeDoux, J. E. (1997b). Fear conditioning induces associative long-term potentiation in the amygdala. *Nature, 390*, 604–607.

Rozin, P., & Kalat, J. W. (1971). Specific hungers and poison avoidance as adaptive specializations of learning. *Psychological Review, 78*(6), 459–486.

Shanks, D. R. (1985). Forward and backward blocking in human contingency judgement. *Quarterly Journal of Experimental Psychology B: Comparative and Physiological Psychology, 37*(1), 1–21.

Shanks, D. R., Pearson, S. M., & Dickinson, A. (1989). Temporal contiguity and the judgment of causality by human subjects. *Quarterly Journal of Experimental Psychology B: Comparative and Physiological Psychology, 41*(2), 139–159.

Skinner, B. F. (1948). 'Superstition' in the pigeon. *Journal of Experimental Psychology, 38*(2), 168–172.

Skinner, B. F. (1979). *The shaping of a behaviorist: Part two of an autobiography.* New York, NY: Knopf.

Steinberg, E. E., Keiflin, R., Boivin, J. R., Witten, I. B., Deisseroth, K., & Janak, P. H. (2013). A causal link between prediction errors, dopamine neurons and learning. *Nature Neuroscience, 16*, 966–973. doi:10.1038/nn.3413

Thaler, R. H., & Sunstein, C. R. (2008). *Nudge: Improving decisions about health, wealth, and happiness.* New Haven, CT: Yale University Press.

Thorndike, E. L. (1898). Animal intelligence: An experimental study of the associative processes in animals. *Psychological Monographs: General and Applied, 2*(4), 1–109.

Thorndike, E. L. (1911). *Animal intelligence.* New York, NY: Macmillan.

Valsamis, B., & Schmid, S. (2011). Habituation and prepulse inhibition of acoustic startle in rodents. *Journal of Visualized Experiments, 55*, e3446. doi:10.3791/3446

Waelti, P., Dickinson, A., & Schultz, W. (2001). Dopamine responses comply with basic assumptions of formal learning theory. *Nature, 412*, 43–48.

Wagner, A. R. (1981). SOP: A model of automatic memory processing in animal behavior. In N. E. Spears & R. R. Miller (Eds.), *Information processing in animals: Memory mechanisms* (pp. 5–48). Hillsdale, NJ: Lawrence Erlbaum Associates.

Wilson, R. C., Nassar, M. R., & Gold, J. I. (2013). A mixture of delta-rules approximation to Bayesian inference in change-point problems. *PLoS Computational Biology, 9*(7), e1003150.

Woodbury, C. B. (1943). The learning of stimulus patterns by dogs. *Journal of Comparative Psychology, 35*, 29–40.

Zamble, E. (1967). Classical conditioning of excitement anticipatory to food reward. *Journal of Comparative and Physiological Psychology, 63*, 526–529.

9 Memory

CHRIS MOULIN AND LUCIE CORBIN

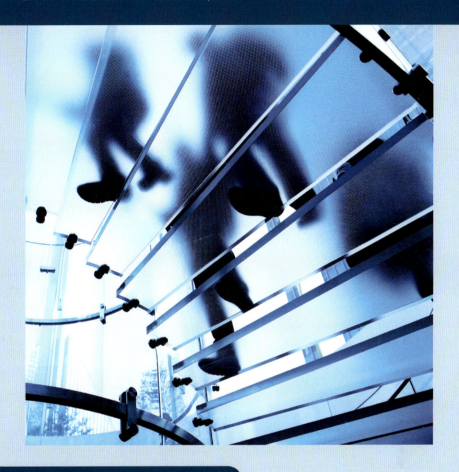

ROUTE MAP OF THE CHAPTER

In this chapter you will learn that memory is composed of many interacting subsystems. It is a complex part of cognition, based on the interactions of various neural regions. Although memory is easily impaired with damage to the brain, much of what we have learned about how memory works comes from the study of brain damage. First the chapter gives an overview of what memory is, then it addresses some common misconceptions, and finally it runs through the main subsystems at work in human memory. The fundamental point is that memory is a dynamic and reconstructive process, not the regurgitation of information from some passive store, such as a notebook.

WHAT IS MEMORY?

LEARNING OBJECTIVE 9.1

Demonstrate an understanding of the functions of memory and the concept of life without memory.

Memory is a fundamental psychological entity, a key cognitive process. It is a building block for many explanations of more complicated entities both theoretical and applied, such as language acquisition, psychopathology, decision making, the self, and even education. To really understand how children develop cognitively, how people look back on their lives, how we learn new skills, and how we come to understand ourselves, we need to understand how memory works.

If you think of any aspect of human endeavour and reflect on how it represents a relatively permanent change in the individual, this must be down to some form of storage in the brain. How that storage works, and what its limitations and features are, is the topic of this chapter. Along the way, we will consider dry topics (such as how we can come to learn a route in a new city), light topics (such as how we remember certain birthdays but not others), and critical and important applied issues (such as how we might be able to report the events of a serious crime we witnessed).

What is memory for?

Memory allows us to have a relationship with our past. Most obviously, it helps us to incorporate new events and abilities into the things we have encountered before. Since humans first walked the plains in search of food, they have used memory to help them find things to eat and to remember where they have previously encountered dangers, for instance (Nairne & Pandeirada, 2008). Memory also lets us have a relationship with our past. Consider a routine but stressful event, such as making a presentation to the rest of your class. How does that feel? What sorts of information could you retrieve to help you get through it with minimal stress? Of course, we've long known that we can use memory techniques to help us learn the content of presentations, but what about reflections on our past experiences?

This was the research focus of Pezdek and Salim (2011), who looked at undergraduates using the Trier Social Stress Test, whereby the reactions to making a presentation are measured – most people find this very stressful so it is an ideal way of ethically inducing stress in the laboratory. Pezdek and Salim told half of their participants that they had had a positive public presentation experience in early childhood. They were then asked to dwell on this experience and generate some details about it – to *reminisce*. In a control condition, another group were told that they had had some experience of overcoming phobias. Following this, all participants prepared a 5 minute presentation – of the kind that might be required during an interview to get into university – which they gave to an experimenter who evaluated the presentation. Pezdek and Salim found that the instruction to dwell on positive experiences of making a presentation gave better performances in the presentation test, and they found less of an increase in anxiety in this group than in the control group. Strikingly, a physiological measure of stress, cortical levels in saliva, showed less of an increase when people had retrieved some positive experiences. This is one example of how memory may sustain us and have consequences beyond the recall of facts. Thinking about yourself in the past influences how you feel and act in the present.

What memory is not

It helps to cast aside a few common misconceptions of memory. As a reader of this book, you will have an interest in the human mind and behaviour. You will also have achieved a certain level of success in the educational system. Along the way, you will have thought about your memory, and how to best get through exams, for instance. Perhaps through the mass media, or just rules of thumb, you will have encountered helpful and unhelpful ideas about how memory functions. But misconceptions about memory are a major stumbling block for memory experts working in courtrooms and clinical settings.

Table 9.1 presents a list of common memory myths, taken from Simon and Chabris (2012). Which of these do you think are true? The actual rates of endorsement of the statements are given later in Table 9.2. In the 1980s, Loftus and colleagues carried out pioneering research with the view of promoting a scientifically informed view of memory (e.g. Loftus & Loftus, 1980). Loftus and Loftus, like Simons and Chabris more recently, felt it was important to understand what people thought about their memories. For instance, despite there being little or no evidence for this idea, many people think of their memory as being relatively permanent: once they've witnessed an event, they believe the representation of it will be relatively stable. In their survey, Loftus and Loftus found that even 84% of people with psychological training thought that memory was permanent, although things could become occasionally inaccessible.

TABLE 9.1 *Myths about human memory.*

Amnesia	People suffering from amnesia typically cannot recall their own name or identity.
Confident testimony	The testimony of one confident eyewitness should be enough evidence to convict a defendant of a crime.
Video memory	Human memory works like a video camera, accurately recording the events we see and hear so that we can review and inspect them later.
Hypnosis	Hypnosis is useful in helping witnesses accurately recall details of crimes.
Permanent memory	Once you have experienced an event and formed a memory, that memory does not change.

Source: Simons and Chabris (2011). Distributed under Creative Commons Attribution 2.5 Generic License (http://creativecommons.org/licenses/by/2.5).

In particular, Wilder Penfield, a brilliant scientist and neurosurgeon, receives a lot of criticism from Loftus and Loftus (among others) for his claim that all memories are stored somewhere permanently. He artificially produced the retrieval of memories by directly stimulating the human brain, producing feelings that he described as 'the stream of a former consciousness flowing again' (Penfield, 1969, p. 152). Penfield's work is overlooked in many textbooks, probably because of this one idea, which is now contrary to all modern theories of memory. But Penfield's original work is fascinating. He was a pioneer in directly applying electrical current to a person with epilepsy's conscious brain and recording their responses. It was in this very artificial context that he observed flashbacks and memories stimulated by an electrical probe on the surface of the exposed brain, and from these observations he came to think that all experience was stored permanently and was retrieved in the manner of a playback of the feelings and perceptions witnessed at the time. Penfield's incredible observations were often cited by psychologists as evidence that no memory is ever lost. As Loftus and Loftus pointed out, this idea that no memory is ever lost had some important (and dangerous) implications: it suggested that there should be a means to retrieve any previous occurrence in a true-to-life form. We'll return to this question later on.

Alas, memory is not as perfect a store as a videotape, but it is not as passive, either. It is a store dedicated to your own interests and goals, and to a large extent what you do and do not remember is guided by what you need to – and want to – retrieve. So, as you read this chapter, you will see that memory is not a notepad or a video recording. It is not an immutable record that is dumped passively into the brain like information onto a hard drive. Memory is an active process that involves reconstruction. As will be shown, memories, even when they are vivid, can actually be false. They are very fragile, and susceptible to suggestion and manipulation. Therefore, memory is not a mere copy of previous experience carved into the brain. It is much more interesting than that.

When memory goes wrong

A good place to start in understanding memory is to think about life without it. We get a window into such experiences through people with severe **amnesia** (memory loss). PJM (the people in case studies are usually referred to by their initials) had a cycling accident while on holiday in France, and as a result spent several weeks in a coma and 6 months in hospital. She described it like this: 'I remember my life up until a couple of years ago… It's weird that the accident just sort of knocked out the two years before it' (Rathbone, Moulin, & Conway, 2009, p. 408). The period of amnesia 'knocked out' several key events, such as the decision to have a second child and the birth of that child, as well as moving to a new house: 'We must have chosen to move here, because we needed more space. But I have no memory of choosing to move here' (p. 408). Imagine having no memory for such important things but having to reason with yourself, and work out the facts of your current existence like a detective.

Consider everything that memory facilitates. There are the everyday tasks: tests, handing in coursework on time, and remembering a friend's birthday. There are also things memory lets you do that you take for granted. If you know how to drive or how to swim, it is because you can 'remember' how to – you have retained this skill. Because of memory, you can have favourite foods, favourite bands, and favourite movies. Not only can you remember friends' birthdays but you can also remember their characteristics and tastes and predict what they might want for their birthday.

Without memory, you would be unable to link the present to the past. It is our memory that stops us from being continually stuck in the present moment, which is why people with very bad memory impairment are often described as 'prisoners of consciousness' (Wilson & Wearing, 1995). Hollywood loves the idea of being stuck – in a day, in a moment – due to memory loss. The film *50 First Dates*, for instance, features the comic creation of 'Ten Second Tom', who is stuck in a loop of 10 seconds, forced to repeat himself and continually reacquaint himself with people as if for the first time. In *50 First Dates*, Lucy (played by Drew Barrymore) is the victim of a debilitating and strange memory disorder. She can adequately store the contents of one day, but, when she sleeps, everything is wiped from her memory and she starts each day anew. *50 First Dates* is an enjoyable film – but to what extent does it misrepresent memory loss? The relationship between representations of memory loss in film and how they really are is very complex.

DISCUSSION POINT

In **this 2012 *Psychology Today* blog post**[1], Wind Goodfried analyses the film *50 First Dates* and asks 'How much of this movie is Hollywood hogwash?' Discuss some of the differences between the movie portrayal of the condition and the real-life account given in the blog post.

In 2010, Smith et al. reported the case of FL, who, following a road traffic accident, much like Lucy, had difficulty in retaining information between one day and the next. To test her problem, the researchers used memory tests where information learned the previous day was presented to her. When FL was told that she had encountered the information the day before, her memory was very poor indeed. However, if the materials from the same day and the day after were intermingled, or if, for instance, she saw a picture on two consecutive days, her memory for materials seen the day before was as good as controls. The authors suggest that, rather than damage to the brain, FL had an amnesia that was influenced by knowledge of how amnesia was depicted in *50 First Dates*. Those who worked with FL felt she really believed she had the problem she described. Interestingly, FL said she had not seen the film before her accident (although it was released some time before) but she did report that Drew Barrymore was her favourite actress.

There is a prominent connection between memory loss and identity. The Alzheimer's Society (UK) has used the idea to underline the impact of memory loss. In July 2010, it ran an advertising campaign with a picture of an empty, unstylish double bed (as we might imagine in an older adult's home) with the tagline 'I wake up with someone new every day.' Simons and Chabris (2011) found that 83% of the general public in their study agreed with the statement 'people suffering from amnesia typically cannot recall their own name or identity' (p. 3; see Table 9.2). Expert opinion, in the same study, was unanimous in its disagreement with this statement. Thus, whereas Hollywood depicts the loss of identity as a black-and-white issue with otherwise intellectually intact people running about solving complex crimes in search of themselves, such as in the *Bourne* films, the reality can be of hospitalized and depressed people with patchy and inconsistent memories who struggle for independence.

TABLE 9.2 *Endorsement of statements about memory from experts and the general public.*

	Percentage who 'strongly' or 'mostly' agree	
	General public	Memory experts
People suffering from amnesia typically cannot recall their own name or identity.	82.7	0.0
The testimony of one confident eyewitness should be enough evidence to convict a defendant of a crime.	27.1	0.0
Human memory works like a video camera, accurately recording the events we see and hear so that we can review and inspect them later.	63.0	0.0
Hypnosis is useful in helping witnesses accurately recall details of crimes.	54.6	0.0
Once you have experienced an event and formed a memory, that memory does not change.	47.6	0.0

Source: Simons and Chabris (2011). Distributed under Creative Commons Attribution 2.5 Generic License (http://creativecommons.org/licenses/by/2.5).

The history of memory research

Memory research has a rich history, beginning with the ancient Greeks, who developed sophisticated ways of remembering complex sets of information without recourse to the written word. They saw memory as like a tablet of wax, which could be carved into. Many of these early metaphors of memory imply some true representation of current experience being registered in its entirety for future interrogation, but it does not work like that. Moreover, memory is not any one 'thing'. There is not one form of memory but many different forms – you can see an overview in Table 9.3.

TABLE 9.3 *Types of memory: a quick-reference guide.*

Autobiographical memory	Memory for our own life's events and facts. Not to be confused with episodic memory.
Episodic memory	Memory for specific events and experiences.
Working memory	The simultaneous storage and manipulation of material in the short term.
Short-term memory	A fragile memory system with a limited capacity store of recent information.
Prospective memory	Memory for actions and events to be completed in the future.
Implicit memory	Memory that is implied in behaviours and feelings, or that is 'non-conscious'.
Semantic memory	Memory for facts and general information.
Declarative memory	Memory that can be reported to another person – typically episodic and semantic memory.
Nondeclarative memory	Also known as procedural memory and broadly synonymous with implicit memory: memory for skills, actions, and procedures.

TABLE 9.4 *Major dichotomies in human memory.*

Explicit memory	Implicit memory
Short-term memory	Long-term memory
Episodic memory	Semantic memory

As you will learn in this chapter, there are experiments and reports of findings in cases such as that of PJM which show that the memory system is composed of separate systems each with a specific task to carry out and a particular set of properties.

As soon as scientists understood that there might be different types of memory, they considered how they interacted. Early memory scientists presented a linear view of memory. According to these views of memory, information progresses through the mind and the brain in set fashion, from original experience through ever more long-term and permanent stores. This idea is logical but it is not true: memory doesn't always work in such a linear fashion, and the modern evidence indicates a series of separable systems and stores that can be integrated into a whole. Thus, human memory is seen as a hierarchy of different types of memory (see Figure 9.7 later) that can be split into a series of dichotomies (Table 9.4). By examining the dichotomies and mastering the differences between them, you will understand how memory varies according to a series of critical factors. The ways in which all the different forms of memory interact, and the evidence for the separate types, remain hotly contested and the subject of much research.

TEST YOURSELF

1. Why is memory not like a videotape?
2. Why might memory be useful in a survival context?
3. Why do memory researchers study issues such as 'the self' and identity?

SECTION SUMMARY

- This section introduced a critical idea: we are our memory. Our tastes, preferences, and perhaps selfhood are all stored in memory.

- It also considered what lay people's beliefs about memory are. Not all of these widely held beliefs are true: most researchers think that memory is not a copy of a previous experience but a reconstruction.

- You will have been thinking about what life is like without memory. Much of what we have learned about human memory comes from neuropsychological evidence examining what life is like for people with amnesia.

MEMORY FOR BEGINNERS: THE COGNITIVE PSYCHOLOGY OF REMEMBERING

LEARNING OBJECTIVE 9.2

Demonstrate an understanding of the cognitive psychology of remembering.

Much of what we will present in this chapter has come about from experiments on memory. In large part, this means that scientists have been interested in measuring what can be remembered, and how, and looking at the factors that influence memory. At the most basic level, we can experimentally present materials to be remembered and measure what can be retrieved at a later date. There are interesting questions, such as how much can we remember after 10 seconds, 10 minutes, or 10 years? And does making associations improve your memory? We can compare people with and without brain injury, or younger and older people. From such experiments, we have learned about a few basics in human memory, which are quickly reviewed below. You might like to think about how factors such as time or the ageing process might influence the patterns described below. If you conduct a search on the internet or read a little further into the subject, you will find many interesting recent discoveries, not just the examples below.

Forgetting and the forgetting curve

One of the pioneers of modern memory theory was Hermann Ebbinghaus, a German born in 1850. He is well known for his observations on forgetting, and in particular for plotting forgetting curves (see Figure 9.1). A forgetting curve describes the decline

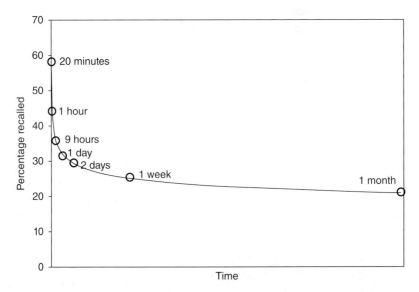

FIGURE 9.1 *A hypothetical forgetting curve, based on Ebbinghaus's ideas and findings. A large amount of information is lost initially, and at the fastest rate. Then, over time, the amount lost is less.*

over time in information that was once available. The elegant curves that are produced when we plot forgetting are the result of most information being lost over a short delay, with the retention of some information being considered almost permanent. If we learn a list of 20 words, for example, we will lose most of the list in the first 20 minutes and continue to forget during the first hour, but, between that hour and a day, we will suffer very little loss of information. Such a fundamental finding (first published in 1885; see Ebbinghaus, 1885 / 1964) has been a building block for many theories of memory. Much of what you read in this chapter will be lost relatively quickly, but you can expect some of these facts to stay with you for the rest of your life!

For the student starting psychology, there are two possible interpretations of forgetting. One, inspired by the shape of the inverse power function – which is like many natural and physical processes, such as the transfer of heat – is that a form of energy drains from the information and it is simply lost. In this way, we might think of information in memory having a 'half-life', and this decay theory describes a passive process. A different view is that forgetting arises from interference – that one new memory might interfere with an old one. This theory can be traced back to Hugo Münsterberg, born just a few years after Ebbinghaus and also from Germany. He observed that, having kept a pocket watch in one pocket for a long time, when he got a new jacket with a different place for his watch, the two locations of watches interfered with each other, leading to difficulty – momentarily – in remembering which pocket his watch was in. In your daily life, you will regularly have had the experience of not being able to retrieve one piece of information but instead being able to remember something else – like trying to recall the album before last of your favourite band but being able only to retrieve the latest one.

It is difficult to imagine how interference may contribute to something as mundane as learning a list of words, but the idea of competition between associations and representations in the mind is now a hot topic in cognition. One contemporary view of forgetting is that it is an active process based on the deliberate **inhibition** of information in the mind. The act of repeatedly bringing to mind one piece of information actively reduces the chances of retrieving other, related information (Anderson, Bjork, & Bjork, 1994).

Ebbinghaus is well known for his forgetting curve, but his general approach to memory is equally important for psychology students. In the late 19th century, at the dawn of psychology as a topic in its own right, Ebbinghaus was bold enough to suggest that higher-order processes such as memory could actually be measured by scientific means. Some of his methods were a little peculiar, in that he used himself as his own subject (and didn't test anyone else), but the methods and materials inspired modern paradigms. We now have no qualms about using scientific methods to tackle higher-order mental processes such as memory. Of the methods Ebbinghaus used, one is notable: he used nonsense materials, such as meaningless strings of letters (e.g. BHT, MVQ, RZK). Ebbinghaus argued that such materials have very little pre-existing meaning and thus can yield a pure measure of memory. The strings of consonants have almost certainly not been encountered before, have very little association with anything else, and therefore require a considerable amount of encoding. The same argument and approach hold today – as will be shown shortly.

Cues and contexts

Research Methods 9.1 considers how to run basic experiments on **recall** and **recognition** – and it uses the same basic tools that memory researchers use. Here, we see that recall memory is always superior to recognition memory; you can recognize what you cannot recall. You should be beginning to think 'why?'. The idea of information being in your head for recognition but not for recall is something of fascination for memory researchers: how come the information is there but we cannot access it unless prompted? The answer is probably obvious to you already – an MCQ test feels easier than reproducing short answers from memory. We will be unable to retrieve the name of a famous actor when we want to, but we will easily be able to pick it out from a list when we search for the film they were in on Wikipedia. In memory disorders, we often find disproportionate deficits in recall. People with damage to the frontal lobes of the brain, can, for instance, recognize information in tests such as the one in Research Methods 9.1, but not recall it. Some researchers describe the difference between recall and recognition as boiling down to an issue of consciousness – and understanding consciousness is one of the most ambitious goals of all scientific enquiry. In recognition, we can somehow access information that we were not conscious of earlier.

RESEARCH METHODS 9.1

MEASURING MEMORY

Students should start running experiments and developing research questions and methods as early as possible. Comparing recall and recognition is a good place to start. The difference between material recalled and recognised is one of the most robust and measurable phenomena in memory. Like many aspects of human memory, it is easiest to explain this idea using an experiment that uses words as stimuli, but we do get the same effects with other kinds of materials: pictures, faces, sounds, and the like.

Produce a list of 30 words. Try to use everyday objects that are easy to imagine, such as 'chair', 'apple', and 'mouse'. Avoid any very distinctive words, such as 'perforation' or 'salamander', because we know that if a word sticks out on your list it'll produce unstable and exaggerated effects. You could write this list on a piece of paper, but to produce an experiment closer to real research you could make a PowerPoint presentation with one word per slide, where the participant has 2 seconds to study each word, with the presentation moving on automatically.

Now produce a second list of words, which will be your recognition test. This will have all the original list of words and an equal number (i.e. 30) of new words. You can again present these words using PowerPoint (but leave enough time for the person to respond) or list the words all on one sheet of paper with a tick box next to each. Mix these words up randomly, so that there is no discernible pattern between old and new words.

Find a participant and ask them whether they'd be happy to try to learn a list of words. (Or write the words down, prepare the materials, and come back to them yourself a few days later in the style of Ebbinghaus.) Give the participant the materials to learn. Then after a little delay – you may engage them in conversation or give them a puzzle to do in order to introduce a little interference – ask them to recall as many words as possible. Give them a sheet of paper and tell them to write down as many words as they can from the list in any order.

This is a test of free recall because the participant can give whichever items they like in any order. If you were to ask them to retrieve the items in the order you gave them, this would be serial recall, which is a cornerstone of short-term memory. But, with 30 items and an interference task between presentation (encoding) and test (retrieval), serial recall would be very difficult! You could also give them the first parts of the words – such as CH_ _ _, AP_ _ _, and MO_ _ _ – and ask them to complete the 'stem' with a word that they studied. This would be (stem) cued recall.

After the participant has had a go at retrieving as much as they can (you can give a time limit, but most people will tell you for themselves that they can't retrieve any more words), give them the recognition test. In this test, the task is to detect the old words from the original list, disregarding the new distracter words. You can ask the participant to say 'yes' or 'no' to each word (as in 'yes I saw it before') or 'old' or 'new' (as in 'it was an old word I have seen before'). If the participant is unsure, encourage them to have a guess. You could even ask them to report how confident they are as a percentage once they have answered yes or no.

Count up the number of words recalled and the number of yes responses. You will find that, even though many words could not be recalled, plenty of words could nonetheless be recognized. Mandler, Pearlstone, and Koopmans (1969) found that, whereas people could only recall 38% of all presented items, they could correctly recognize 96%. The number of words recognized should be higher than the number of words recalled. Of course, a particularly devious, clever, uncooperative participant could just say 'yes' to everything on the recognition test and, moreover, people could just guess.

If someone did the test who never saw the original list, we would expect them to get 50% correct (because there are 30 old words and 30 new words). To account for the possibility of a participant just saying yes to everything or guessing, one formula that is commonly applied is to subtract the number of false positives (the 'yes' responses given to new words) from the hits (the 'yes' responses given to old words). With this correction, if someone is entirely random, they should score zero. And, if they say yes to everything, they will also score zero. Even after this correction, the score for recognition should be much higher than the score for recall. You should find that people make very few false positive errors.

Implicit memory can also be measured with these verbal materials. You could change the test so that you ask people to complete fragments such as the following with the first word that comes into their head: C_ _IR, _IGH_, _OU_E, CH_R_ _, you can measure their 'memory without awareness'. Even when people think they are just guessing, they will be likely to use words they saw earlier, even if they cannot recall or recognize them. That is, they will solve these word fragments as 'chair' and 'mouse' rather than using other possibilities. We add in distracter words such as 'light' and 'church' in order that people do not guess the goal of the experiment and use explicit memory to recall what the items were.

There are many different ways of explaining these recall–recognition data and they have inspired many theories and approaches. One way of thinking about the difference is with Craik's notion of environmental support (Craik & Bialystok, 2008; see Figure 9.2). In brief, bottom-up processing in recognition, where the information is available in the environment (i.e. we can see it or read it), yields a higher level of performance than in recall, where no such cues exist. Early ideas about the difference between recall and recognition focused on the cues used – cued recall performance is usually superior to

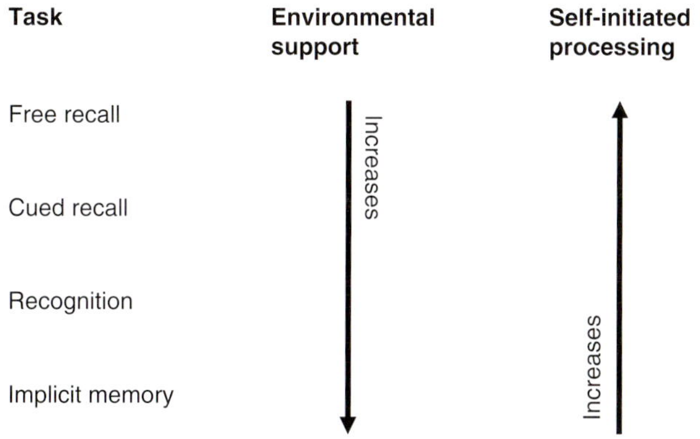

Task	Environmental support	Self-initiated processing
Free recall		
Cued recall	Increases	
Recognition		Increases
Implicit memory		

FIGURE 9.2 *Craik's environmental support framework.*

TABLE 9.5 *Godden and Baddeley's results: mean recall of words (number of words recalled) on dry land and underwater.*

		Recall environment	
		Dry	Wet
Learning environment	**Dry**	13.5	8.6
	Wet	8.4	11.4

Source: Adapted from Godden and Baddeley (1975).

free recall performance. The major explanation concerns the overlap between encoding and retrieval and the effect of context. This is often taught with reference to Godden and Baddeley's (1975) study on deep-sea divers and context-dependent memory. Baddeley and colleagues had been researching the effects of underwater environments on cognition when he noticed that material learned underwater was poorly recalled on land, even though recognition was not similarly affected. In their 1975 paper, the authors cite this as their starting point – and also briefly summarize other, bizarre experiments where, for example, people are strapped to boards and given material while flat or upright, or with their head stuck in a gaudy box with flashing lights. The fact that recall and not recognition is affected suggests some role of a cue. Godden and Baddeley suggested that the context of being underwater acts as a cue, such that things learned underwater should be better recalled underwater. This is the basic idea of context-dependent memory. The numbers from their famous experiment are shown in Table 9.5: material learned and retrieved in the same context yields better performance, even though overall being on dry land or underwater does not affect memory.

There are other examples of this phenomenon where recall and recognition rates vary according not only to external environments or contexts but also internal states and thoughts. When these variations are internal or mood driven, they produce what is referred to as **state-dependent memory**. A perennial student favourite is the idea that you retrieve information better drunk that you encountered while drunk (e.g. see Duka, Weissenborn, & Dienes, 2001). There are jokes to be made here about the conditions under which you study for and take an exam. However, the serious issue might be about how state-dependent memory influences the behaviour of chronic alcoholics. Goodwin, Crane, and Guze (1969) interviewed 100 hospitalized alcoholics, 64 of whom reported memory loss. Among other things, 61% of these 64 had experienced having hidden money or alcohol while drinking, only to forget about it when they were sober and finally have their memory return when they were drinking. In fact, some alcoholics expressed that they drank specifically to facilitate their recall.

TEST YOURSELF

1. What is the effect of context on memory?
2. Why did Ebbinghaus use nonsense syllables in his research?
3. When do we lose information most rapidly from memory – right after learning or a long time after?
4. What is inhibition?

ACTIVITY 9.1

LEARNING AND MEMORY

You should be able to apply what you have learned here to your own studies. It is no surprise that memory experts, who all work in universities and teach students, have occasionally turned their attention to improving student learning. Among these, Robert Bjork is possibly the best known, urging students to 'learn how to learn' (e.g. Bjork, 2001). He also makes points about learning that you can only understand once you have grasped some basics of human memory: 'Elaborate on what you study. Connect it to what you already know. Incorporate it into your general knowledge. Make it rich and semantic (you won't have a fragment-completion test)' (Bjork, 2001, p. 9).

Here are some other memory tricks you could make use of. Think about what you could now explain to your student friends who are not studying psychology. What would you recommend?

1. The testing effect (e.g. McDaniel, Anderson, Derbish, & Morrisette, 2007)

Numerous scientific studies of memory have pointed to the fact that taking a test on studied material enhances subsequent retrieval of that information in a final test. McDaniel et al. (2007) demonstrated the effect in a real classroom situation. Taking a test led to superior final recall than suggestions for extra reading. On top of that, short-answer quizzes promote better retention than multiple-choice questions.

2. Personalized review (e.g. Lindsey, Shroyer, Pashler, & Mozer, 2014)

It is undoubtedly best to review your learning over time. It is no surprise that you may need to relearn more difficult parts of your course (even the most experienced researcher may need to look over the assumptions of the analysis of variance every now and then, for instance). These ideas are encapsulated in retrieval practice: the act of trying to retrieve things that have been learned. Like the testing effect, it is important to practice retrieving information to make sure it is well learned. Lindsey et al. (2014) have shown that it is individualized learning and review that is based on the results of previous retrieval practice that is most efficacious. 'One size fits all' does not apply to human learning, it seems.

3. Close your eyes (e.g. Perfect et al., 2008)

This one needs a little closer examination in educational settings, but it is a fascinating effect. Perfect et al. (2008) showed that memory was enhanced if people closed their eyes while attempting recall. They showed this in cued recall tests for material learned from videos and live interactions – that is, not classroom-style facts and materials – and their results are therefore probably most applicable to eyewitness situations. But, when you're struggling to recall a fact in an exam, it probably won't hurt to close your eyes for a few seconds.

4. Do not cram for an exam (e.g. Cepeda, Pashler, Vul, Wixted, & Rohrer, 2006)

It has long been known (since Ebbinghaus, in fact) that there is a difference between distributed and massed practice, which is the difference between spacing out the repeated presentations of materials and studying them all at once. In general, there is a strong effect of distributed practice, which leads to better retention in the long term. But, when you think about this, it is worth considering your goal. In some of the earliest work in the 1960s, it was shown that massed learning of spellings of new words was actually better earlier on than distributed practice. It was not until 10–20 days later that the distributed practice delivered its value (Fishman, Keller, & Atkinson, 1968).

5. Aim to 'know', not to 'remember' (e.g. Conway, Gardiner, Perfect, Anderson, & Cohen, 1997)

Conway and colleagues aimed to investigate the acquisition of knowledge among a whole year group of psychology undergraduates. During their routine exams, students were encouraged to report their subjective experience: how it was they retrieved the answer. Did they *remember* something about the encoding of the information, did they just *know* it, was it merely *familiar*, or was it a *guess*? Conway et al. (1997) found that, early on in the course, the better-performing students reported that they 'remembered' the answers – they could retrieve some information from the time at which they learned the material. That is, they had an episodic memory of the information. However, when tested later, in the final exam, after some delay, the better students had now shifted to reporting a higher proportion of 'know' responses. They had successfully turned their episodic memories into a form of knowledge. They could no longer report the circumstances of learning the event, but just knew the answer.

6. Classic mnemonics

Since the ancient Greeks, we have been aware of making stories and routes that can enhance our memory. For instance, you can try to link a list of objects together with a story, such as 'Pavlov's dogs were classically trained musicians', in order to remember that his dogs showed classical conditioning. Or you could remember the sequence of famous psychologists in different rooms of your house, or along a familiar route. You could also use rhymes and other tricks, such as a mnemonic using the first letters of words. In school I learned OIL RIG in chemistry, which stands for 'oxidization is loss and reduction is gain', and I have retained it well, although I have no idea where it applies or *what* is lost or gained.

SECTION SUMMARY

- This section has focused on the important issue of forgetting, and you should now have a good grasp of the differences between recall and recognition.

- Most importantly, using Research Methods 9.1, you will be thinking about measurement, and how using experiments with different conditions can lead to better or worse memory, and more or less forgetting.

- Key issues that come from the above are the notions of **availability** and **accessibility**. If information is forgotten completely, it is no longer available. However, in recall, material is not accessible, although a test of recognition tells us it was nonetheless available had we been able to access it. This is one of the frustrating aspects of being human – information does not stay as accessible at all times as we would like it to (see Activity 9.1 for some things you can do about this).

- **Metamemory** research considers just this sort of idea: we may actually be aware of the availability of a piece of information – an actor's name, for instance – even though it is currently inaccessible. This is a description of the commonplace 'tip-of-the-tongue' experience – we know that we know something, but we cannot access it. This act of 'knowing about knowing' is called 'metamemory'.

- The very idea of information being available but not accessible speaks to the idea of the permanence of memory. What might be the best measure to use when investigating whether memory is permanent – recall or recognition (see Research Methods 9.1)? Might the information have been learned, but with insufficient cues to retrieve it?

THINKING ABOUT MEMORY: MODELS AND FRAMEWORKS

LEARNING OBJECTIVE 9.3

Critically evaluate the models and frameworks used to understand and study memory, particularly the multistore model and the levels of processing framework.

Scientists refine their ideas by building and testing models. At their most basic, models summarize patterns of data and provide an intuitive way to understand a complex cognitive system. Because these models summarize vast sets of data and explain how a series of complex processes interact, they are an essential part of learning about memory. A basic three-stage flow chart of memory is shown in Figure 9.3 – you will understand the idea (but perhaps not the terminology) straight away. This is a model of how memory works – a linear sequence from encoding to storage to retrieval. It predicts that you can never recall something without having first encoded it. In this section we give a few ways in which you can think about memory: the idea of it being organized as separate stores, and the idea that it may be a process and not a store.

The multistore model

One of the first models of memory was little more than an elaboration of the three-stage model. The multistore model (Atkinson & Shiffrin, 1968; see Figure 9.4) suggested that human memory is organized around different stores according to the permanence of storage. Sensory details are only retained for the very briefest periods, and memory transfers into successively more durable and long-term stores. Many of these ideas are intuitive and you can support them from your experience of daily life. If you saw a film last night, you would remember the story well today, but it would be unlikely you would remember any dialogue. If, during the film, it was paused, you would undoubtedly be able to repeat the most recent segments of dialogue, possibly even word for word. A year later, unless you'd seen or thought about similar stories, films, or books, you might remember very little about the film – you might even find it possible to enjoy watching it for a second time. These real-world observations point to the idea that memory has various stores, which are more or less fragile.

The multistore model holds that information must pass through three stages in order to become a firmly implanted memory. These three stages are **sensory memory**, short-term memory (STM), and long-term memory (LTM). When we first come across a stimulus, we retain a sensory image – or 'sensory memory' – of it

Encoding ⟶ Storage ⟶ Retrieval

FIGURE 9.3 *The three basic stages of memory function.*

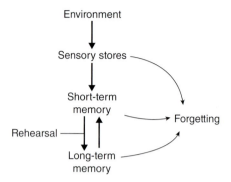

FIGURE 9.4 *The multistore model. Information passes from the environment into a brief sensory store, then into short-term memory. The passage of information from short-term memory into long-term memory is considered to be reliant on use – if information is repeatedly used, or rehearsed, it will pass into long-term memory. Of course, at each stage, there is loss of information from the system: forgetting. This occurs when, due to a lack of attention or a lack of use, information does not transfer from one store to the next.*

Source: Reprinted from Atkinson and Shiffrin (1968), with permission from Elsevier.

for less than a second. Sensory memory is brief, low-level, and fragile; like an after-image, it helps us to keep alive items that we have experienced briefly a bit longer, so that we can – if we chose to – process them more deeply. If, for example, we are copying from one piece of text while typing, we will store a brief sketch of where in the document we are looking, before turning to the computer and turning back again. The sensory information stores the place where we were looking long enough to switch our attention from one thing to another. In the 1960s, George Sperling (see Figure 9.5) ran experiments that showed people could remember the line of a nonsense grid of information if tested immediately, but, after a second had passed, could not do so. If we turn our attention to something else, or just wait a moment, the material will be gone.

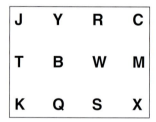

FIGURE 9.5 *A grid of letters for sensory memory experiments. Show this page to someone and then remove it from view – as quickly as you can. How many letters can they report? What if you tell them just to report the top, middle, or bottom lines? Sperling (1960) showed that sensory memory has a limited capacity: you can 'see' all these items at once, but you can pretty much only report one line at a time if the image is presented very quickly (Sperling reports an average capacity of four letters for durations of between 15 and 500 ms). In fact, if you are able to report one line (especially if you didn't know which line to focus on when presented with the items), you are pretty good at this test. Sperling also played around with a delay between the brief flash of this grid and the participants' reports. At a delay of 1 second, the brief store of four items or so had decayed. Sensory memory has a limited capacity and is really very short.*

Some material passes beyond this very short buffer into STM. A key feature of this transition from sensory memory to STM is attention. If we are attending to something, we will be able to process it in a way that means it can be refreshed and maintained a little longer. Atkinson and Shiffrin (1968) proposed that the longer information remains in a short-term store (perhaps the more it is dwelt upon or used), the more likely it is to be transferred into a long-term store. Their claim was that the act of holding information in STM means it should be transferred into a more permanent store: holding material in STM enables learning. For instance, we can help ourselves to retain material by repeating it over and over (especially if it's verbal information, such as an email address we've got printed out on paper to be entered into a computer). Atkinson and Shiffrin argued that all material must be passed from one store to another to be retained for longer and longer intervals. There is filtering according to meaning at each stage, and only meaningful, important information that can be incorporated into existing stores is retained in the long term.

Atkinson and Shiffrin's model was influential in the 1960s, but by the 1970s, according to Baddeley (2004), the model began to struggle to explain all of the data. First, the mere act of holding information in STM was found not to be a guarantee that it would be learned. In part, the type rather than the amount of processing seemed to be critical (this was one idea behind the formation of the **levels of processing** framework, reviewed below). This is clear in daily life: repeated use does not necessarily mean you take the information in. There will be phone numbers, people's names, and facts that you've constantly accessed, repeated, looked up, and promptly forgotten again. In last night's film you may well have registered who the character Lena was for a period of nearly 2 hours. The next day, however, when asked the name of the witch in *Beautiful Creatures*, you may be none the wiser.

Second, neuropsychological reports of people with memory difficulties suggested an intriguing capacity to have LTM without STM abilities. The multistore model does not predict this at all: according to the model, memory should be built up in a linear fashion from the accumulation of information into progressively longer stores. It is relatively common for patients to have intact STM but impaired LTM. For instance, in Alzheimer's disease, people will be very able to repeat a series of five digits presented to them, so long as they are tested immediately. However, if you ask them to repeat the same digits later, they may well have forgotten they were even presented with the test. Thus, the memory deficit in Alzheimer's disease is greater for LTM than for STM (Green, Baddeley, & Hodges, 1996). In fact, this pattern *could* be predicted by Atkinson and Shiffrin's model. We could just argue that, in Alzheimer's disease, there is an inability to transfer information from a short-term store into a long-term store.

However, there are people with brain damage who show the opposite pattern, suggesting that the memory system can't be laid out in a linear fashion as Atkinson and Shiffrin suggested. There are patients, for instance, who can remember long-term information and indeed learn new facts but who cannot retain information in short-term memory. The beginning of this line of reasoning was an important article by Warrington and Shallice (1969), although it doesn't refer directly to Atkinson and Shiffrin's model. Warrington and Shallice describe the case of KF, a 28-year-old who had had a motorbike accident at the age of 17 and had been unconscious for 10 weeks. At first, he could not speak very well at all, but over several years he recovered good speech. His IQ, when measured using verbal tests, was 79, but when tested without verbal tests it was 113. Strikingly, he was unable to *repeat* stimuli: if you gave him two letters to remember, at the rate of one letter per second, he could only remember the correct sequence of two letters on 9 attempts out of 60. Atkinson and Shiffrin's model predicts that this would mean that he should not be able to learn any new information at all. Not so: when given a list of 10 words to learn by heart, KF was able to master the list after seven trials. Control participants achieved the same after an average of nine trials, if at all (four control participants failed to ever learn all the items after 20 trials). Moreover, when tested 2 months later, KF could still remember 7 of the 10 words – without relearning. That KF was able to learn information but not be able to repeat it, even over a very short delay, suggests that LTM is not the mere accumulation of short-term memories. Memories do not pass on a journey from one store to the next as was once thought. You might like to think that your STM and LTM systems are both active and operating on the same material at once.

The levels of processing framework: Memory as a process

The multistore model considered different stores of information according to the duration of storage and the meaningfulness of the information, with an emphasis on what is stored where and for how long. An alternative to this view is to think of memory as a process. The finest example of this idea is the 'levels of processing' effect (e.g. Craik & Lockhart, 1972). This is the finding that, when you study words with a deep level of processing (i.e. when you think hard about the words' meanings, significance, and so on), you remember them much better than when you just think about something relatively shallow or easy to process, such as whether the word is written in capitals or lower case. This is critical, because it says what you *do* with the information is more important than how many times you repeat it in your head. Amazingly, we find the levels of processing effect even when the test is unexpected and people don't wilfully memorize the information. This is an effect of **incidental memory**. In an incidental test, we do not ask people to deliberately remember the materials (most eyewitness situations involve incidental memory – you do not know what was happening until it was too late, and nobody says 'watch really carefully and learn what is about to take place'). We can ask participants just to give ratings of a long list of words, without telling them that we will actually test their memory. Even so, the way in which they encounter the information at encoding affects their later retrieval. This is even the case in the brain. In a review of brain areas that were used to encode verbal materials, Nyberg, Cabeza, and Tulving (1996) found that in any task where there were materials that could be later remembered, no matter whether there was the instruction to encode or not, there was the same activation in the left frontal lobe – which is arguably involved in the encoding of information. Our memory is permanently switched on.

The idea that memory is the result of a process has been put to the test with experiments to test some very big ideas indeed, concerning the self, our very person-hood, and our evolutionary history. In these examples, the experiments are set up like levels of processing experiments. In the first, the **self-reference effect** (e.g. Klein & Kihlstrom, 1986), a whole list of adjectives are processed according to your view of yourself. Am I *generous*? Or, am I *moody*? In a control condition, similar materials are processed with reference to someone else. It is routinely found that, when we judge the words against ourselves, our later memory for the words (e.g. *moody, generous*) is significantly better. Researchers (see Figure 9.6) have even found that we remember the dates of birthdays which are close to our own. In turn, the self-reference effect

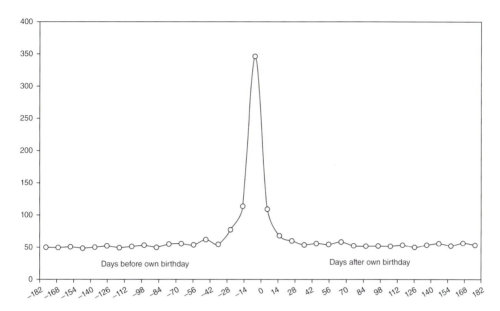

FIGURE 9.6 *I was always on my mind. Recall of other people's birthdays plotted in relation to one's own birthday.*

Source: Adapted from Rathbone and Moulin (2010).

has been turned to the research of what selfhood is, and how it can be disrupted. For instance, people with autism show a reduced self-reference effect compared to people without autism (Lombardo, Barnes, Wheelright, & Baron-Cohen, 2007). These data – results from a relatively simple memory test – have been used to argue that self-processes are impaired in autism: people with autism have a less strongly held view of their self. The study of memory, or the measure of it, is about more than just the retention of information.

A type of levels of processing effect that relates to an even more fundamental issue is found in work on the **survival processing effect** (Nairne & Pandeirada, 2008). Again, the methodology draws upon procedures used in levels of processing experiments. Participants imagine themselves in a hostile natural environment, such as a savannah, and judge how useful a set of items would be for their survival (see Focus Point 9.1 for example instructions). Against a set of various control conditions, it is regularly found that survival processing leads to high levels of recall. This is taken as evidence of the importance of survival in our evolutionary history – we have evolved to quickly and efficiently process things that will ensure our survival, and the extent to which an object can help us survive is a very deep level of processing indeed. At its most specific, researchers who carry out this kind of research use 'ancestral' stimuli, such as grasslands and predators, to emphasize the long-held evolutionary advantage of such evolutionary relevant stimuli. Some researchers have argued against this specific ancestral view of the effect: for example, processing items in relation to their value for surviving against zombies in a city shows the same effect (Soderstrom & McCabe, 2011; Focus Point 9.1). Because we have never actually encountered zombies in our evolutionary past, the effect must derive from something about survival rather than the choice of evolutionarily relevant locations and items.

SURVIVAL INSTRUCTIONS

Soderstrom and McCabe (2011) used different threats (predators or zombies) and environments (city or grasslands) and just changed those words in the instructions below. Recall was highest for the city–zombies condition, by about 10%.

> In this task we would like you to imagine that you are stranded in the *city* of a foreign land, without any basic survival materials. Over the next few months, you'll need to find steady supplies of food and water and protect yourself from *zombies*. We are going to show you a list of words, and we would like you to rate how relevant each of these words would be for you in this survival situation. Some of the words may be relevant and other[s] may not – it is up to you to decide. (Soderstrom & McCabe, 2011, p. 565)

The 30 words that were given to be remembered included 'snow', 'carbon', 'catfish', 'screwdriver', 'whiskey', and 'sword'. Clearly, some of these objects are more useful than others, but that's not the point. The mere fact of judging them for their survival value is what makes them memorable.

DISCUSSION POINTS

1. Why do we need to have scientific models?
2. Which will lead to better memory – referring information you learn to how your lecturer looks, or referring it to what you think and feel?
3. What is a deep level of processing?
4. Can you think of some things you have encountered many times in your life but cannot remember? If so, why can't you remember them?

SECTION SUMMARY

- The multistore model has many failings, but it is nonetheless a good first place to think about how memory is organized into different types and forms. In fact, the model is still cited by scientists today, because, although it has shortcomings, the idea of not being able to transfer information from short-term to long-term memory has currency in explaining many neurological disorders, the effect of a lack of attention, the effects of alcohol, and so on. However, the idea of passive transfer from one system into another is defunct. If we want to make sure information is retained, we have to do something with it.

- Possibly the most important idea in this section is that memory is the result of a process. A deep level of processing will ensure the formation of a strong memory, even if that was not the intention.

- People can also help to ensure that information is retained by artificially adding meaning to it or by wilfully elaborating on the meaning of the information, with mnemonic devices (as we saw in Activity 9.1). These are techniques that impose additional or intensified meaning to improve memory. You might like to think of the things you do to improve your memory. How do they involve deep processing or elaboration? Are they about the cues used to get the information back or about the depth of processing? These are critical issues for educators and students, but, in fact, we've been a little slow to implement them. In Activity 9.1, you can read a few pointers for improving memory in educational settings based on the science of memory.

THREE DICHOTOMIES IN HUMAN MEMORY

LEARNING OBJECTIVE 9.4

Demonstrate an understanding of and the distinction between the three dichotomies in human memory, which pertain to conscious awareness, duration of memory, and general knowledge.

The contemporary view of human memory was shaped by Endel Tulving, starting with an article titled 'How Many Memory Systems Are There?' (Tulving, 1985). Tulving produced a framework by which we can understand the various subsystems of memory, often drawing upon neuropsychological evidence, as we saw with KF. It is Tulving's view of memory that forms the backbone of this chapter and of most modern research. The field of human memory has also drawn upon Squire's (1992) classification of memory, particularly the schematic shown in Figure 9.7. Squire drew up a rough hierarchy of how the various aspects of memory can be related, and referred to a 'biologically real' division of various subsystems, based on his research on patients with damage to the brain. Squire's hierarchy should be your roadmap for understanding memory. Take a look at Figure 9.7 and familiarize yourself with the terms and how they relate to each other. If there is something overlooked in Squire's diagram, it is STM, but, as you will see, the interaction between STM and LTM is taken care of in Baddeley's (2000) working memory model. In this section we run through each of the dichotomies present in Squire's subdivisions of the memory system, which map neatly onto Tulving's conceptualizations of memory.

Implicit versus explicit memory

The main issue in this dichotomy is awareness. To what extent are we aware of the contents of our memory? Can we control and manipulate our memory? Can we report the contents of our memory? Tulving's major contribution was to consider how memories feel and their inherent nature, and this is summed up in this section. He wrote: 'It is difficult to imagine, for instance, that perceptual motor adaptations to distorting lenses and their after effects (e.g. Kohler, 1962) are mediated by the same memory system that enables an individual to answer affirmatively when asked whether Abraham Lincoln is dead' (Tulving, 1985, p. 386).

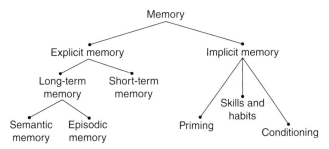

FIGURE 9.7 *Memory is not a monolithic entity. A hierarchy of the various memory systems.*
Source: Adapted from Squire (1992).

Anything that is stored in the brain is 'in memory'. That means knowing the past participle of 'to write' is 'wrote' is in some way a memory. It also means that, if we spend a long summer getting grazes and bruises learning to ride a bike at the age of six and we are still able to ride the bike 10 years later, the ability to ride a bike is in some way a memory. Both of these are examples of implicit memory. They are implicit in that encoding, storage, and retrieval are *implied* in our behaviours and competencies. Implicit memory is grouped together with procedural memory, and, although there are subtle differences in how the terms are used, they can be thought of as synonymous. Certainly, both are safe to be described as nondeclarative memories – that is, memories for actions, skills, and changes in performance that are not verbalizable. Figure 9.7 points to there being rather a lot of different forms of this type of memory, and we briefly run through them here. Explicit memory is covered later on. It is a term that covers a range of types of memory, the key idea being the retrieval of information from memory, such as 'Big Ben is in London' or what you ate for breakfast yesterday.

Skills and habits: Procedural memory

Procedural memory is our memory for skills and physical acts, such as riding a bike. It can be thought of as a library of competencies that have been required and retained, often referred to as 'knowing how'. These are often physical, such as swimming or driving, but can also be applied to habits acquired, such as learning how to do mental arithmetic (e.g. long division). Squire's (1992) primary evidence for this separate subsystem was the learning of new skills at an entirely normal rate in amnesic patients (e.g. Cohen & Squire, 1980; but see also Focus Point 9.2). If you give amnesiacs a new task to learn, such as tracing shapes in a mirror while they can only see the reflection of their hand, they can learn this new skill at entirely the same rate as people without memory impairment. It is a difficult task, but they master it adequately and, in fact, they may not even remember they have done the task before, but still do it perfectly well when encouraged to do it. Real-world examples of this type of memory thus include knowing how to drive a car, knowing how to play the piano, and being able to remember your PIN number at a cash point only by the sequence of finger movements on the pad. Human behaviours are complex, and we are normally very reflective and strategic in what we learn and how. As such, when we learn to drive a car, for instance, we may start with facts and declarative knowledge about the car: this is the brake, this is the steering wheel, when the engine pitch is too high you should change gear, depress the clutch when you change gear, and so on. But the goal is to have a smooth and automatic process, and this undoubtedly relies on the acquisition of new motor skills, and automatic procedures such as are described in this section. It is based on practice and not knowledge – learning by doing.

FOCUS POINT 9.2

THE CASE OF HM

One of the most famous case studies in psychology, HM, was amnesic. In December 2008, a ripple was sent through the memory community at the news of his death. Memory scientists appreciated that much of modern theory had stemmed from his injuries and his willingness to patiently endure so many memory tests. When he died, we could finally learn some more about the man behind the science, and his name: Henry Gustav Molaison. His full life story, including what he contributed to the science of memory, is covered by Corkin (2013).

HM had severe epilepsy as a boy in the 1940s and did not respond well to standard treatment. In 1953, he underwent a temporal lobotomy, which removed part of his temporal lobe – the area around (and including) the hippocampus. This procedure was carried out in order to reduce his epileptic symptoms; surgeons had recently discovered that removing part of the brain involved in epileptic seizures reduced the symptoms – this was actually work in part pioneered by Wilder Penfield (see the section above 'What Is Memory?'). HM's epileptic symptoms were reduced by the procedure, but he was left with a profound memory deficit. He became a one-man focus for research into memory. This was partly because he had a pure and well-defined lesion within the brain (unlike head injury amnesiacs), but it must also partly be due to his generous nature and the dedication of the scientists who worked with him.

HM had, for the most part, anterograde amnesia, where he could not acquire new memories, even though he could remember some events prior to his surgery. He was not, however, impaired generally: his language and intellectual function were above average, and actually better after surgery than before. At the time, the two most interesting facts about HM's memory impairment were that his STM seemed intact (he could repeat a series of digits immediately) but his long-term retention was virtually nil, and also that he could not recall instances of previous test sessions but he could 'learn' new procedural tasks, such as mirror drawing. As such, he showed intact procedural memory but impaired declarative memory, supporting the notion of two distinct memory systems and the role of the hippocampus in raising memory to conscious awareness (see Corkin, 2002).

You can learn more about the case of HM **in this TED Ed lesson**[2] by Sam Kean from 2014. Watch the video then think about the ethical controversies surrounding this case.

Priming

Priming is the action one piece of information can have on another (e.g. Tulving, Schacter, & Stark, 1982). Because information is linked together in a network of associations, we can think of a rich network of associations becoming activated automatically according to whatever is being perceived or thought about (e.g. Ramponi, Richardson-Klavehn, & Gardiner, 2007). The term 'priming' comes from the idea of making ready for action – in the way that a pump is primed ready to produce water by the first few movements of the handle filling the pump with water before it is actually produced.

There are various varieties of priming, all with memory at the centre. In **semantic priming**, there is a benefit (e.g. faster reaction time) in subsequent processing due to the prior processing of something that is related semantically – in *meaning*. Making a decision about whether 'horse' is an animal or not is faster when a person is primed with the word 'pony' compared with when 'horse' is preceded by an unrelated word. In phonological priming, people are quicker to produce the word 'horse', for example, if they have just been primed with the rhyming word 'course' (e.g. Rastle & Coltheart, 1999). Such experimental findings suggest that information is organized in the mind on the basis of language sounds and semantic information.

Repetition priming is the behavioural change associated with the repeated processing of a stimulus. In this case, the idea that we can process information more quickly because we have merely encountered it before, no matter how superficially, implicates memory in many automatic and low-level behaviours (see Figure 9.8). There is the storage of information implied in even the most basic of behaviours. This may be the mechanism behind the **mere exposure effect** (Zajonc, 1968), where we find things attractive, or more pleasant, when we have already been exposed to them: the 'mere repeated exposure of the individual to a stimulus object enhances his attitude toward it' (Zajonc, 1968, p. 1). Mere exposure is something that is exploited

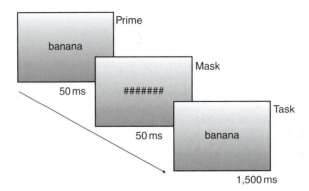

FIGURE 9.8 *A repetition priming experiment. Such experiments are often depicted as a series of screenshots, as the participant would see the words. In this experiment, participants are flashed a word, 'banana', for 50 ms. It is then replaced by a 'mask'. This mask stops an after-image of the word existing in sensory memory. Finally, a third screen presents a word where the participant has to make a response. In this task, the participant could be asked whether the word is real or not, or whether it is a fruit. In either case, repetition priming would be shown – participants would be quicker to make a decision about 'banana' as a consequence of having already been presented with the information (albeit subliminally – without awareness).*

in advertising and in product placement, and it even works for attractiveness: faces that you have seen more frequently, in general, are rated as more attractive.

Priming has often been used subliminally, where people can be given cues that affect future performance that they are not consciously aware of. Subliminal perception refers to occasions where a stimulus (usually visual) is processed but the perceiver has no awareness of it. For example, in subliminal priming experiments, a cue word can be presented very briefly (typically for less than 50 ms), and, although the participant has no awareness that they have seen the word, they will show benefits in processing a subsequent target (e.g. Marcel, 1983).

Conditioning and behaviourism: 'Learning'

The remainder of nondeclarative memory consists of associative and nonassociative forms of learning. Learning is a major facet of human behaviour, often discussed separately from memory, and it led to a whole approach to psychology – behaviourism. In the history of psychology, early behaviourist studies on learning paved the way for later studies of memory function. In fact, for the experimental approach to understanding how we store and retrieve information, we are indebted to early learning theorists. To give a brief overview of the area and its relation to the contemporary understanding of memory function, we concentrate on a few classic studies from the discipline.

Most people will be aware of Pavlov's famous experiments (e.g. Pavlov, 1927), where dogs learned to salivate to a bell because it was paired with the arrival of their food. At first, Pavlov's dogs naturally and automatically salivated to the presentation of their food alone, but, after encountering the bell at the same time as the arrival of the food, they *learned* a new response to the stimulus. The fact that there was a modification in their behaviour over time suggests that a memory was formed for the bell, but, of course, it being with dogs, who can't verbalize or share their experiences, this learning was nondeclarative. In fact, such associations do not need to be wilfully set up; they can just be learned. In humans, such **classical conditioning** can be demonstrated using the eye-blink reflex. In experiments, participants are sat in front of an apparatus that gives little puffs of air that can be presented with another stimulus, such as a red dot on a screen. Humans learn to blink or wince at the onset of a particular stimulus, just like dogs with the bell: they retain a pre-existing behaviour (the eye-blink reflex) but pair it with a new stimulus (e.g. Perruchet, 1985). Because people with amnesia nonetheless retain this ability to form new associations, it would appear to be a different part of memory.

A further learning phenomenon is **nonassociative learning** (a separate box in Squire's schema but left out of Figure 9.7), which refers to other forms of changes in behaviour that are not associative, such as **habituation**. In habituation, we learn not to respond to an ever-present stimulus. An example of this is filtering out the sound of a noisy air-conditioning unit in a lecture theatre, even though it may have been very loud and apparent when you arrived. You may have visited the flats and houses of friends who have become habituated to the noisy trains that roar past in their home: they will not notice, but for you it will be a momentarily terrifying intrusion on your thoughts. They will even sleep through it.

Although many of these learning theories and approaches are old and largely based on research on animal behaviour, they do continue to have a major influence on clinical psychology. For instance, low-level learning processes can be harnessed to stop alcoholics from drinking. An emetic (a drug that makes you nauseous) can be presented at the same time as a drink, so that drinking is associated with the feeling of sickness, and the person 'learns' not to like alcohol. Even 'common-sense' interventions (e.g. where people with arachnophobia are treated by gradually being introduced to spiders) have a sound rationale in learning theory (e.g. Ost, Salkovskis, & Hellstrom, 1991). As people unlearn negative associations between a stimulus (spider) and response (fear), they habituate to the stimulus.

Short-term versus long-term memory

Atkinson and Shiffrin's (1968) breakthrough model (described above) considered the break-down of memory based on how long material is retained, and this has remained a major dichotomy in memory research. Apart from a very few early pioneers, such as Alan Baddeley, the people who work on research into STM rarely work on LTM, and vice versa. Each domain has grown up around its own set of methods and theories. A first issue to deal with is the lay conception of STM. STM is very brief – probably only the order of a minute or so. As such, most people would not think of it as memory at all. In contrast, for many, including medical professionals working with people with memory impairment, STM refers to *recent* events and information – what happened yesterday, at breakfast, or on the last family holiday. In this way, psychologists and medical professionals differ in their description of STM. There are two useful synonyms of STM – 'primary memory' and 'immediate memory' – but unfortunately these do not get used much. In any case, it is better to think about STM in terms of its capacity and its fragility, rather than its duration. A defining characteristic of STM is its limited capacity. George Miller gave us the famous 'magical number seven' (Miller, 1956): STM can only store around seven items. This is often expressed as seven plus-or-minus two, meaning that a STM capacity of five to nine items is considered normal.

You will probably be thinking something like this: 'But I can record more than seven units of information – syllables, numbers – in my mind for temporary use!'

And indeed, we are all able – thankfully – to use STM to briefly register information that is longer than seven units. The main way we do this is through the process of 'chunking'. As an example of chunking, consider your ability to remember a sequence such as 50100898110920017. That is a difficult string of numbers. It is much easier to recall as: 50-10-0898-11-09-2001-7, or easier still if you think of meanings for the chunks: *50 First Dates*, Ten Second Tom, a premium rate phone number code, 11 September 2001, George Miller's magic number. These chunks demonstrate the interchange between LTM, meaning, and STM. We can use knowledge and the breaking down of information into manageable chunks in order to surpass the seven-items rule.

The workings of STM can be easily demonstrated by explaining a classic STM experimental procedure (serial recall) and a related test (the digit **span**). Serial recall measures how many items – in the order that they were presented – people can immediately recall from a short list. A digit span – widely used in intelligence and memory testing in clinical settings – measures the number of digits that can be correctly repeated back in the order that they were presented. Both digit span tasks and serial recall tests (for instance with words) can be used to plot serial position curves (see Figure 9.9).

In a serial recall test, people are given a short list of items at regular intervals and asked to repeat them back in the order they heard or saw them. This can be done with words or digits, and has also been done with faces and pictures (which require different types of tests), but the results are broadly the same. Taking words, Figure 9.9 shows the mean recall performance for a set of participants for 15 words; in the case of the first word (at serial position 1), 70% of the participants recalled the word. Each of the other serial positions in the curve relates to the other words' positions in the list. Serial position curves typically show this 'tick' shape. The high performance for the first item (or perhaps the first few) is called the **primacy effect**, referring to the increased memory for the first part of the list. The tick part for the latter items at the end – usually for the last three or so – is called the **recency effect** – it is the superior memory for the last few items.

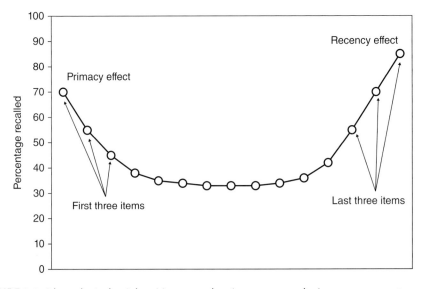

FIGURE 9.9 *A hypothetical serial position curve showing recency and primacy components.*

Primacy and recency effects are robustly found on tests of serial recall – it is something worth trying for yourself in a mock experiment. The primacy effect is proposed to be due to LTM and/or the fact that you can repeat the first few items mentally in your head more times than the other items. For example, if you are asked about the list after half an hour, although the recency effect will have disappeared, the primacy effect will still hold. The process of repeating an item to keep it refreshed in STM is called **rehearsal**. You will be quite aware of rehearsal when you are given some important information but have no means to write it down – repeating the information under your breath, or out loud, will keep the information refreshed. The recency portion of the graph is what we will consider here, because it is proposed to be due to STM: it is the brief register of the last few items that have been read to you – the sort of brief and fragile store that typifies STM. In fact, the recency effect is very susceptible to interference: if you read a list of words and add a meaningless words, or even play a computer beep at the end of it, this addition will interfere with your memory for the last few items – this is called the 'suffix effect'. Likewise, if you repeat 'the', 'the', 'the' over and over again, or some other meaningless sound, it will likewise impair your STM, and this will show up in a reduced recency portion of the serial position curve. The idea of maintenance – such as constantly updating and refreshing material at the same time as listening to new stuff coming in – and the effects of interference were both inspirations behind the idea of working memory, which is what we consider in the next section.

Working memory

The chief difference between STM and working memory is that working memory describes an active process: the simultaneous storage and manipulation of information over short periods of time. In fact, many people use the terms interchangeably, but technically working memory is far more sophisticated and complex than STM. Working memory can be thought of as a system that is responsible for managing and coordinating the lower-level activities being carried out in STM. There is a part–whole relationship between the two: STM is part of, but not all of, working memory.

Working memory is thought of as supporting all cognition in the real world, from simple activities such as copying text or listening while taking notes to the support of more complex cognitive processing such as reasoning, problem solving, and mental arithmetic. Descriptions of working memory range from a useful 'desktop' (such as on your computer, where all information is temporarily stored) to the idea of a 'homunculus' (a little person in your head that can control the contents of your brain and manage all the different streams of information). It is clear that, for most cognitive activity, it is useful to be able to hold some information in mind while accessing related information or performing some action upon it. In your head, solve the sum: 18 + 45. You need to add 8 and 5 to make 13, hold that in your mind while adding 10 and 40, and finally bring together the stored product (13) and 50 to give the solution of 63. This gives you a grasp of what working memory is for, how it works, and how fragile it is. If you are asked a question while in the middle of the sum, chances are you will lose what it is you were holding in mind.

The most frequently encountered model of working memory (Baddeley & Hitch, 1974) is shown in Figure 9.10. It shows three components. Auditory and visual information are processed separately in different 'slave' systems and these are controlled by a central processor, known as the central executive. The phonological loop is responsible for maintaining and manipulating speech while the visuospatial

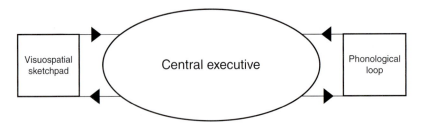

FIGURE 9.10 *Baddeley and Hitch's original working memory model.*

Source: Reprinted from Baddeley and Hitch (1974), with permission from Elsevier.

sketchpad carries out the same for visual and spatial information. This separation of working memory into speech and visuospatial components is supported by selective interference in experiments. In these, people are given two tasks to carry out at the same time. If there is a decrement in performance (i.e. interference) for tasks carried out together, it suggests the tasks rely on the same underlying mechanism. Such experiments are carried out on visual and verbal information: a secondary visual task interferes with memory for visual but not verbal information, and vice versa. Support for these separable verbal and visual components of working memory is provided by neuroimaging studies which indicate that anatomically and functionally different systems are used for the temporary storage and manipulation of verbal and visuospatial material (Smith & Jonides, 1997), as well as studies on neuropsychological case studies who have damage to one and not the other. A development of the working memory model has seen the addition of a fourth component, the episodic buffer, proposed to be controlled by the central executive (Baddeley, 2000; see Figure 9.11).

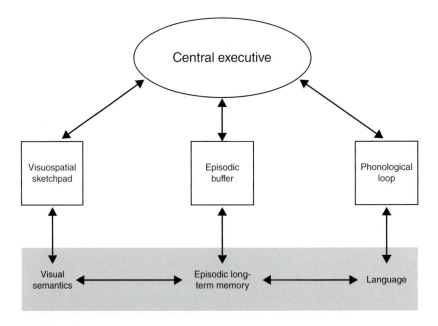

FIGURE 9.11 *Baddeley's updated working memory model. This shows the interaction between long-term and short-term memory, and the episodic buffer.*

Source: Reprinted from Baddeley (2000), with permission from Elsevier.

The episodic buffer is assumed to be a temporary storage system that brings together information from the slave systems and from LTM into a single temporary representation. This fourth component is proposed to play an important part in the process of chunking and in language comprehension.

Baddeley's model is not the only model of working memory – there are others that emphasize different aspects of working memory function and make different predictions about different types of experimental tasks (these are covered in Shah & Miyake, 1999). The interested reader will want to explore models where storage and processing are not separated (meaning that there is a trade-off between the two, rather than there being separate subsystems) (Conway & Engle, 1996). Cowan (1995) does not consider working memory to be a separate system from LTM or STM, but the temporary activation of representations in LTM. The limited capacity of working memory arises because of a limited amount of attention we can pay to the activated items. Other researchers subscribe to a 'time-based resource sharing' model (e.g. Barrouillet & Camos, 2007). This view of working memory emphasizes the need to keep 'refreshing' temporary representations held in the mind.

The utility of working memory is its applicability to real-world situations. For instance, the phonological loop, a component of working memory that allows the temporary storage of sounds over very brief periods, is thought to play a crucial role in learning new words (Baddeley, Gathercole, Papagno, & Degli, 1998). Working memory also plays a role in spatial abilities. For example, Garden, Cornoldi, and Logie (2002) examined the relationship between navigation and working memory. They carried out an experiment in which they asked volunteers to find their way around Padova, Italy. They examined the influence of verbal and visuospatial interference on the ability to learn the city's layout. Participants followed the experimenter on a route through the city. While they were following the experimenter, either the phonological or the visuospatial component of working memory was occupied. To engage phonological processes, participants repeated the same word over and over again into a microphone connected to a portable tape recorder on their back. To engage the visuospatial part of working memory, the participants walked through the streets while tapping out a sequence on a keyboard connected to a computer strapped to their back. Having learned the route under these conditions, participants had to complete the same route again, on their own. Route learning and navigation were impaired by both of these concurrent tasks, which confirms that we learn a route by generating useful verbal labels and descriptions, as well as by thinking about the route visuospatially. The most interesting aspect of the study was that tapping of a repeated sequence was *more* disruptive for those people who were better at navigation under normal circumstances; it might be imagined that these people were used to using a nonverbal spatial strategy to navigate, but, in this case, with the relevant part of working memory otherwise occupied, they were unable to do so.

Working memory capacity is usually measured using complex memory span tasks in which participants are required to combine memory for sequences of items with other processing activities. The amount of memory and processing activity is increased over successive trials until errors are made. A common complex span task is reading span, in which participants read a series of sentences while attempting to recall the final words of each sentence after the final sentence in the sequence (Daneman & Carpenter, 1980). The number of sentences is increased until the participant starts to make errors, and the longest span at which they make no errors is scored as their reading span. Such measures of working memory are closely associated with children's learning and literacy. In fact, many children recognized by their school as having learning difficulties in the areas of reading and mathematics have marked impairments of working memory (Gathercole & Pickering, 2000).

The emphasis on working memory in the classroom is one of the reasons why scientists are currently looking at whether working memory can be improved. Work in this area is in its infancy, and no clear pattern of results has emerged, but the idea is simple: if we can improve working memory, we will be able to improve other cognitive actions, in the classroom and beyond. A critical idea in this field is 'transfer'. Can the benefits of training on one task transfer to another domain or ability? Jaeggi, Buschkuehl, Jonides, and Perrig (2008) claimed that 19 sessions of training on a difficult working memory task had benefits for general intelligence more generally in the 70 participants that they tested.

Corbin and Camos (2011), on the other hand, found significant effects in the working memory training part of their study but no transfer – not even to another test of working memory. Holmes, Gathercole, and Dunning (2009) tested children and found that working memory training improved mathematical ability 6 months later. Holmes et al. place an emphasis on adaptive training: it is important to have a working memory task that is tailored to each participant, a procedure that continues to challenge and test the person undergoing training. Clearly, the results suggest that working memory training could be beneficial, but there are likely details to be sorted out in the training regime, the task used, and even the population it is aimed at. An important issue is to consider whether the transfer is to other very similar tasks or to less similar, real-world tasks (Melby-Lervåg & Hulme, 2013).

Prospective memory

One instance in which we need to keep information active in the brain is when we need to remember to do something in the future, which is called 'prospective memory' (e.g. Ellis & Kvavilashvili, 2000). This is a routine part of daily life: when I next see Akira, I need to give him £10; on the way home, I need to buy a baguette; I must send Laura an email thanking her for the film recommendation; and so on. Prospective memory is a peculiar sort of memory, because it undoubtedly involves encoding, storage, and retrieval, but it acts forwards and not backwards, and it tends to concern actions and not information. Prospective memory somewhat escapes classification in the dichotomies here, and is notable by its absence in Squire's schematic. Compared with retrospective memory, prospective memory is certainly under-researched. It is, however, a major part of everyday life: remembering to take medicine, attend appointments, adhere to arrangements with friends and colleagues, and so on.

One way to think about prospective memory is to think about an interaction between working memory and LTM. We must presumably keep an intention active in order to act on it when the time comes. In fact, experimental tasks and clinical tests of prospective memory usually involve giving people an instruction to do something at a later point and then set them another ongoing task to do. This has a definite flavour of working memory: the participant must keep something in mind while doing something else, and because of that there are high demands on working memory while trying to keep in mind an intention to do something (Marsh & Hicks, 1998). Experimental work in prospective memory is a little like the levels of processing idea too. For instance, the 'intention superiority effect' (e.g. Dockree & Ellis, 2001) shows that to-be-performed actions are more highly activated in memory than other actions, since they are better remembered than words encoded without reference to a future intention.

General knowledge versus personal events

We now come to the final dichotomy – the difference between general knowledge and personal events. There are separate systems for facts and for personal experiences. We've already talked about several key issues in LTM, such as the effects of context on recall and the differences between recall and recognition. Because these are effects based on the recall of material that is of a longer duration and larger than the capacity of short-term memory, you should now be thinking of those things as long term. Now think about your last holiday. Where was it? What did you pack to take with you? Who did you go with? When did you go? Let's imagine you went on holiday to France. Were you happy? Could you make yourself understood in restaurants? Did you see the Eiffel Tower? If you climbed the Eiffel Tower, did you feel nervous about the height or bored by the queue?

In answering these questions, you are accessing your LTM. Specific personal events and episodes in your life are stored in episodic memory, which is represented well by the 'Where?', 'When?', 'What?', and 'Who?' questions. Episodic memory enables us to locate ourselves in the past – in a specific time and place and in a particular question. It also allows us to access feelings and impressions from the time at which the event was encoded. Some people describe this memory as 'mental time travel' or the ability to relive the past. It is rich and evocative and tied to specific events and happenings. But, in answering these questions (such as 'Did you see the Eiffel Tower?'), you also need to access a different type of information: semantic memory. This concerns memory for facts and information, such as 'Paris is the capital of France', 'In France they speak French', and 'the French for snail is *escargot*'. For a memory to be considered semantic, it must be devoid of all the rich, contextual information retrieved from episodic memory. When you retrieve the information that Paris is the capital of France, you do not have to reminisce about who told you this and when it was; the information is just there to be accessed, free of context. In this section we compare these two different types of memory and finish up by describing how they are integrated in autobiographical memory.

Episodic memory

The retrieval of an episodic memory comes from a dynamic, complex system. It is our memory for what we had for breakfast, the memory by which we can describe the events of a crime we have witnessed, and the capacity to repeat that funny story that our friend told us over drinks last Friday. Episodic memory is for one specific 'episode' in life. In our daily lives, it is the memory for one specific instance ('meeting James on my first day at school'), not a repeated event ('learning to drive'). In clinical tests and experiments, it is also defined as the retrieval of information that was 'learned' at a specific encoding phase – the recall of a list of words from 30 minutes ago. Conway (2009) suggested that there are nine characteristics of episodic memory, which are presented in Table 9.6. These characteristics emphasize the sensory nature of memories. They are brief images and details from previous experiences that are specific, and they are also rather fragile and short lived. Critically, Conway suggests that they are memories of experiences, and he also – especially in his last point – considers how they feel. Like the example of Paris above, episodic memory concerns 'mental time travel' and the feeling that we are 'remembering' and not merely 'knowing'. This idea can be traced back to Tulving, who used such subjective experiences to subdivide memory. He suggested that, whereas episodic memory is based

TABLE 9.6 *Conway's nine characteristics of episodic memory.*

1	They contain summary records of sensory-perceptual-conceptual-affective processing.
2	They retain patterns of activation/inhibition over long periods.
3	They are often presented in the form of visual images.
4	They always have a perspective.
5	They represent short 'time slices' of experience.
6	They are represented on a temporal dimension roughly in order of occurrence.
7	They are subject to rapid forgetting.
8	They make autobiographical remembering specific.
9	They are recollectively experienced when accessed.

Source: Reprinted from Conway (2009), with permission from Elsevier.

on remembering (a form of experience called 'autonoetic consciousness'), semantic information is based on 'knowing', which is devoid of the first-person experiences and imagery described in Conway's characteristics.

Does this mean that anything that feels like a memory is a memory? To an extent, yes. Episodic memory is a mental construction and not an exact copy of a previous experience. Fascinatingly, we probably use the same system to imagine the future as reconstruct the past (e.g. Schacter & Addis, 2007). We will sum up some of the evidence for memory reconstruction below, but note the evolutionary angle: 'our memory systems must be engineered to use the past in the service of the present, or perhaps to predict the likelihood of events occurring in the future' (Nairne & Pandeirada, 2008, p. 240). The fact that memory is geared to help us survive, to predict the future, and to support the present means it's necessarily reconstructive. No event is ever an exact repetition of a previous event, and thus an indelible, verbatim version of a previous event is unlikely to be very useful in interacting with the world.

One area where the reconstructive nature of episodic memory is critical is in **eyewitness testimony**. If our memories are a reconstruction based on our own viewpoint and limited information, there is likely to be injustice, especially if the courts do not fully appreciate the reconstructive nature of memory. It was this idea that motivated Elizabeth Loftus's groundbreaking work on **false memory** and suggestibility. In their seminal article from 1974, 'Reconstruction of Automobile Destruction', Loftus and Palmer investigated how the language used in questions alters people's reports of what they saw. They presented their participants with police training and safety films of car accidents and then asked various questions – similar to those that would be posed by police. Participants then wrote an account of the event and answered a key question: 'About how fast were the cars going when they hit each other?' Loftus and Palmer arranged their experiment so that five groups of nine participants each saw an alternative verb in the place of 'hit' (see Table 9.7). They showed that the estimated speed of the car altered according to the word used to describe the crash in the question, with 'smashed' giving the highest estimate of speed.

In a follow-up experiment reported in the same article, a film was shown and 50 participants answered the 'hit' and 50 participants the 'smashed' question. (A further 50 were not asked the question at all.) Importantly, once again, 'smashed' yielded faster estimates than 'hit'. One week later, and without seeing the film for a second time, the participants were again asked about the car crash. This time, a yes/no

TABLE 9.7 *Loftus and Palmer's mean estimates of speed according to the verb used to describe the car crash.*

Verb	Mean speed estimate (mph)
Smashed	40.5
Collided	39.3
Bumped	38.1
Hit	34.0
Contacted	31.8

Source: Reprinted from Loftus and Palmer (1974), with permission from Elsevier.

question was asked of all participants: 'Did you see any broken glass?' (there was, in fact, no broken glass shown in the film). The critical condition was the 'smashed' condition, which could be compared now with a control condition (no question about speed) and the 'hit' condition. In all three conditions, the majority view was that there was no glass seen in the film, which means people's memory, in general, tallies with events. However, in the 'smashed' condition, 16 people reported seeing glass, whereas only 7 did in the 'hit' condition and 6 in the control condition. Loftus and Palmer's article was one of the first demonstrations of how memory is suggestible; our memory of events can be changed subtly by the questions used. Subsequent work by Loftus showed remarkable effects of the structure of a question: just changing a question from 'Did you see *a* broken headlight?' to 'Did you see *the* broken headlight?' changes people's version of events. The chilling implication is that the way in which police ask about events may bias the reports of what happened.

These subtle distortions of memory are a healthy product of a balanced mind and point to a naturally occurring reconstruction of events. Possibly the greatest demonstration of this idea is with the 'DRM' procedure (the initials refer to the originators of the idea: Deese, 1959; Roediger & McDermott, 1995). The DRM is a simple memory task where participants study a list of related words, with one critical item missing, which all the others converge upon. For example, 'bed', 'rest', 'doze', 'blanket', 'tired', and 'snore' are studied, but not 'sleep'. Later, people come to 'remember' seeing 'sleep' on the list even though it was never there. This points to a reconstruction based on semantic memory (see below) and the meaning of the words given, but the feeling reported during recognition is usually one of a confident, vivid memory. Things can feel like a memory even though they are not, and the constant process of making meaning and summarizing the gist from memories leads to a form of false memory. The DRM procedure has been applied ad nauseam to every corner of psychology and psychological disorder, but perhaps none more so interestingly than in people who claim to have been abducted by aliens (Clancy, McNally, Schacter, Lenzenweger, & Pitman, 2002). People who claim to have been abducted by aliens and have a memory of it show higher than usual rates of false memories in the DRM paradigm. We might therefore argue that they are more susceptible to generating false memories based on thoughts and suggestions.

This process, where imagined events turn into false memories, has been termed 'imagination inflation'. In an elegant demonstration of this phenomenon, Wade, Garry, Read, and Lindsay (2002) used doctored childhood photographs to show just how malleable human memory is. In their study, 20 confederates who were part of the experimental set-up recruited a family member (the participants) who they knew was over 18, had not taken a psychology class, and – most importantly – had not taken a balloon ride. The confederates provided photographs of events where their participant was between the ages of 4 and 8 years. The experimenters then inserted the participant – using Photoshop – into the basket of a hot-air balloon. Wade et al. (2002) then interviewed the participants three times using an interview procedure developed for use in real forensic situations, using the undoctored images, but also the balloon ride. For the events depicted in the photographs, the participants were asked to give a free narrative of everything they could recall, and then answered general and afterwards specific questions. A critical part of this was guided imagery work, where the participants speculated about 'Where?', 'When?', and 'Who?' questions concerning the event. The results showed that, at the first interview, even 35% of participants thought they 'remembered' the balloon ride to some degree. At the end of the third session this had increased to 50%.

The big question, it seems, after acquainting ourselves with the data, is can our memory ever be trusted? Thankfully, people do not spend a lot of time and effort in our daily lives trying to trick us with doctored photographs and videos. Also, people tend not to give us sequences of related information with one obvious item deliberately left out. So the first point is that we have to engineer some pretty artificial situations in order to get such strong evidence for reconstructive memory. However, the main reason that we do not just invent whole sequences of memory is neatly summarized via the notions of 'correspondence' and 'coherence' (e.g. Conway, Singer, & Tagini, 2004). Correspondence concerns how well our memories match up to what actually happened – which, as we have seen, can be pretty approximate. Coherence, on the other hand, considers how well memories form a useful 'whole' – how well they match our own personal goals and the other knowledge we hold. It is the drive for coherence, then, that fills in gaps (e.g. with the DRM task), and it also stops us from generating a set of completely random, irrational memories. So, whereas episodic memories may occasionally be at variance with the truth, they are so in a way that is subtle and not easy to detect.

Finally, we return to the permanence of memory. Are episodic memories permanent? If following hypnotherapy we 'recover' a memory that was once lost, how can we be sure it is a real memory and not just a mental construction that feels like a memory? Loftus and Loftus (1980) point out that the question of permanence is somewhat unanswerable, and we paraphrase their example here. Consider that, with a camera strapped to his head, Gary witnesses a crime. Later, Bob watches the movie captured on Gary's camera and hears a description of the event from Gary, but he can't tell whether Gary's description is of his memory of the event or the film of it. That sounds like evidence in support of the idea that Gary has retrieved a permanent verbatim account of what went on; whatever question Bob generated based on the film, however minor the detail, Gary – perhaps aided by mnemonic techniques, brain stimulation, hypnosis, or vitamin supplements – could retrieve the detail. That would be evidence for permanence. The more realistic scenario is that Gary's report is sketchy, with omissions. If you are convinced that there is a permanent store, this observation is neither here nor there – you can always argue about imperfections in the retrieval mechanisms, the cues used, the limitations of brain stimulation techniques, the inefficacy of vitamin pills, and so on: the memories are there but cannot be reached. Thus, the permanency of memory, once you accept that the only way to measure encoding and storage is through a test of retrieval, seems to be one of psychology's unanswerable questions.

Semantic memory

Semantic memory is our store of factual and lexical (language) information. In contrast to episodic memory, semantic memory needs no rich contextual cues and is devoid of a first-person sense of pastness. Semantic memory is a large part of our declarative memory: the store of language and conceptual information, such as categories of 'things'. It is a vast topic, and one that we can only briefly consider here. Its contents are also vast. If you start thinking about knowledge, it can appear almost limitless. List all you know about cheese, for instance. You can start by reporting more obvious associations, such as curdled milk, dairy products, Cheddar, milk production of cows, and so on, but end up talking about the moon being made of cheese, the adventures of Wallace and Gromit, and so on. In turn, you need to know about the concept of what 'dairy' products are and what the word 'production' means. Thus, there are many overlaps with the study of language – since semantic memory is in part a store of words and their meaning. Therefore, the study of semantic memory has typically concerned language processes and the way in which we classify and categorize the world. Central to the notion of semantic memory is a semantic *network*. This can be thought of as the store of semantic knowledge, and semantic memory as the process that taps this store. This is a major difference between semantic and episodic memory: semantic memory is a hierarchy of organized representations with shared features and concepts. Most theory points to their being a network of ideas, although some early models suggested that we stored a list of features and used features to build up concepts and characteristics; for example, the features 'has four legs', 'has a tail', and 'can be a pet' could be used to organize the representations of rabbits, cats, and dogs (Smith, Shoben, & Rips, 1974).

Semantic memory can be thought of either as a hierarchy of concepts and categories (Figure 9.12) or as a network (Figure 9.13) organized by how similar things are to each other (Collins & Loftus, 1975; Collins & Quillian, 1969). In Figure 9.12, there is a semantic cluster of a few examples of foodstuffs, organized in a hierarchy. In their example, Collins and Quillian used natural categories such as animals and birds, but the principles are the same. In the category of animals, we store birds. Within birds we will have flightless birds, including ostriches and penguins, and more typical birds, such as canaries and sparrows. Reaction times change from one level of the network to another – the less distance between these classifications, the quicker we are (e.g. 'animal–bird' is processed faster than 'animal–sparrow'). The original model of 1969

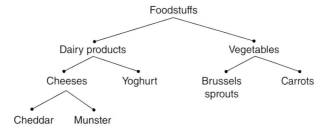

FIGURE 9.12 *A semantic hierarchy of categories, subcategories, and exemplars. Cheeses are a type of dairy product, which in turn is a foodstuff. We can generate exemplars of cheeses, such as Cheddar, Munster, Comté, and Stilton. We can also generate characteristics of these cheeses: hard, soft, smelly, blue, and so on. These are features that may be shared among cheeses, and they help us categorize and organize our factual knowledge.*

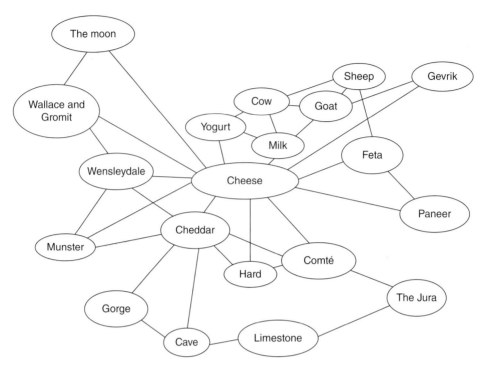

FIGURE 9.13 *A fragment of the semantic network in human memory concerning cheese. The lengths of the links between nodes represent relatedness. A shorter link represents a closer relationship.*

was developed to run as a computer program, and as such was a bit limited regarding human behaviour. Later, Collins and Loftus (1975) reacted to the misconception that semantic memory was necessarily hierarchical. They pointed out that the semantic network is structured somewhat according to typicality. We are quicker to access information about more typical birds than atypical ones, and can verify that a canary is a bird more quickly than we can a penguin. Thus the alternative is that semantic memory is organized as a complex nonhierarchical network, based on the connections between things. An example of this type of network is given in Figure 9.13: because it is not hierarchical and not based on rigid definitions, there can be more fluid and idiosyncratic links, such as between cheese and the moon. The idea that the organization of information in digital systems is like semantic memory continues to be an important idea. For instance, Thompson and Kello (2014) used the presentations of information in Wikipedia to explore how semantic organization works in humans.

In daily life, you can think of semantic memory as being a constantly active network of ideas and concepts that is activated according to your current experience. Augmented reality devices and technological advances such as Google Glass offer to do these sorts of things for us, delivering tailor-made information for each face and place we look at. But, in its own way, the semantic network is quietly and efficiently performing this role. In this way, we can think of semantic memory as exerting a top-down influence, based on knowledge, of the things that we see. For instance, in a park, if we see something moving and something bouncing out of the corner of our eye, we can expect to see a dog chasing a ball, and not a kangaroo. Of course, we do not need to wilfully summon up the generalization that 'dogs chase balls in parks' in order to make this assessment, but we could do that as well, if asked. In fact, we can generate many semantic categories on the fly, such as 'things to take on a picnic', and answer questions based on knowledge and not on experiences (Barsalou, 1985). For instance, we can answer the question 'Does the Queen have toenails?' without ever having given her a pedicure.

Also in daily life, we encounter semantic memory through our scripts and schemas (or, more correctly, schemata). A schema is a plan or outline of behaviour. They are cognitive mental plans that serve as guides for action and that enable us to operate in novel situations. Generally, you can have schemata for how to read a sentence, how to ride a bike, how to order a pint of beer in a bar, and all manner of tasks. They are a way of organizing and summarizing life events, and, although you do not need to regurgitate them word for word as you carry them out, they are declarative, in so far as you can easily output a schema of 'downloading a song from iTunes' to your friend in order that they could do it. A related idea is a 'script'. These are standard sequences of events that have become 'overlearnt' through repeated use. They are plans that are stored and used in certain situations. Consider making your friend a cup of tea: boil the kettle, steep the teabag, add some milk, stir the drink, offer them some sugar. Scripts are a more detailed, less abstract form of schemata, and are more predictable. As with schemata, they are a way of summarizing behaviours in order to keep storage manageable.

Research into semantic memory has offered psychology something of a real breakthrough in the understanding of one form of dementia (Hodges, Patterson, Oxbury, & Funnell, 1992). The structure and function of semantic memory has been researched with reference to semantic dementia (a form of dementia not dissimilar to Alzheimer's disease, but predominantly affecting semantic and not episodic memory). People with semantic dementia find it extremely difficult to name and classify objects (for instance, what certain vegetables are, and even whether they are edible) – so much so that their disorder appears more like a problem of language than of memory.

Autobiographical memory

Autobiographical memory is the store for our life events. It is often thought of as the memory store by which we contain and maintain our sense of identity – who we are as people. A major misconception is that autobiographical memory and episodic memory are one and the same. Episodic memory and autobiographical memory share a part–whole relationship. Autobiographical memory draws on information from individual events and experiences (episodic memory) that are too specific and too personal to be labelled as facts. But, in making sense of these and organizing them, embellishing them even, we draw on information from semantic memory too. They can be thought of as mental constructions. According to Conway (2001), autobiographical knowledge becomes linked to episodic memories in the formation of a specific autobiographical memory. There is not a single system in the brain that gives you autobiographical memory: damage to either the semantic or the episodic memory systems will affect autobiographical memory, albeit in different ways; thus autobiographical memory is not a 'biologically real' type of memory and doesn't feature in Squire's schematic.

Autobiographical memory changes across the lifespan and is depicted in the lifespan retrieval curve (see Figure 9.14), which is observed when people (about 35 years

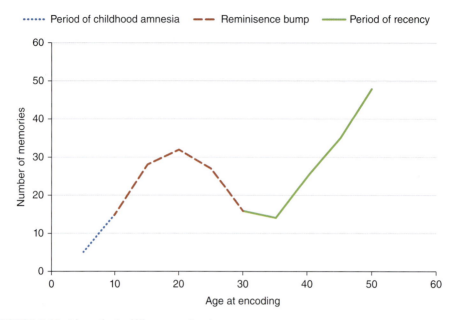

FIGURE 9.14 *A hypothetical lifespan retrieval curve.*

Source: Reprinted from Conway and Williams (2008), with permission from Elsevier.

and older) recall memories from their life (e.g. Rubin, Wetzler, & Nebes, 1986). Memories are plotted in terms of age at the time of the remembered experiences, and the resulting curve usually takes the form in Figure 9.14. The curve consists of three important components: the period of **childhood amnesia** (from birth to approximately five years of age), the period of the reminiscence bump (from about 15 to 30 years), and the period of recency.

What is your earliest memory? It is interesting that we cannot typically remember much before the age of about 4 years. There are many explanations of childhood amnesia. It is peculiar that children appear to have intact memory function at the time but that the memories are not available to them later in life. One explanation is that we lack the vocabulary to understand and encode our life's events when we are young. The evidence that autobiographical memory and language are thus related comes from research using words to cue autobiographical memory: words that we know to be acquired earlier in life, such as 'dragon', cue earlier memories from our own life, in contrast to words acquired later, such as 'cigarette' (Morrison & Conway, 2010). Other researchers suggest that the period of infantile amnesia is due to the fact that the self is not sufficiently well formed to structure the encoding and retrieval of information with reference to the self.

Similarly, the reminiscence bump also has several plausible explanations. One is that this period is permeated by novel experiences and this novelty ensures an enduring representation in the mind. Somewhat counter to this proposal is the finding that, of the experiences recalled from the period of the reminiscence bump, only a small proportion are of novel events. Instead, most are of idiosyncratic events peculiar to the life circumstances and interests of the individual remembered. This suggests an alternative to the novelty hypothesis, which is that the high accessibility of memories from this period may be related to their enduring relation to the self. Possibly, many memories from the period of the reminiscence bump are of 'self-defining' experiences (Singer & Salovey, 1993) and have a powerful effect in binding the self to a specific reality. However, and as with the current understanding of the period of childhood amnesia, there is as yet no generally accepted explanation of the reminiscence portion of the lifespan retrieval curve.

The final part of the lifespan retrieval curve, which has forgetting and recency components, is less contentious: memories recently encoded remain accessible, whereas memories retained over a longer retention interval are subject to decay and/ or interference and so become progressively less accessible.

One interesting form of autobiographical memory is 'flashbulb memory', a particularly vivid memory for a public event of great importance. Typically, people will all have a memory of where they were and what they were doing when they heard about the events of 11 September 2001, the result of the Brexit vote, the Paris attacks in 2016, Michael Jackson's death, and so on. Brown and Kulik (1977) first used the term 'flashbulb' to describe the vividness and detail with which these surprising events are 'burnt' into memory.

The contentious issue in the contemporary **flashbulb memory** literature is whether the memories are special in some way. Brown and Kulik (1977) contended that they are, suggesting that, when an event is highly novel or unexpected, it is more likely to be of biological importance and thus encoding of the memory involves more of the 'lower' brain areas involved in emotion and flight-or-fright mechanisms. We vividly remember the mundane events surrounding our memory of the news event because they are given a particular significance to our well-being. It is presumably evolutionarily important to be able to remember well the circumstances of surprising and emotional events.

Neisser (1982) put forward a strong critique of the concept of flashbulb memories. His argument hinged on the fact that flashbulb memories are prone to distortion, reconstruction, and inconsistencies, just like any other memory. If flashbulb memories are produced by a special encoding mechanism, then they should not be prone to error – we should just catch a snapshot of the actual events occurring at the time. Neisser also suggested that the critical factor in flashbulb memories is rehearsal. These memories for events have particular social value and are likely to be repeatedly retrieved many times, and refreshed by news reports and anniversaries. How many times have you rediscussed the events of 9/11? No one debates that flashbulb memories are particularly persistent, usually vivid memories – they are even intact in sufferers of Alzheimer's disease.

TEST YOURSELF

1. What is the difference between autobiographical memory and episodic memory?
2. What is the difference between short-term memory and working memory?
3. If you are able to retrieve some of the information you have learned from this book in a week's time, what form of memory will you be using?
4. Why don't prospective, autobiographical, and working memory feature in Squire's conceptualization of memory?

SECTION SUMMARY

- This section introduced you to modern views of memory via three key dichotomies. Memory can be classified by conscious awareness (e.g. implicit versus explicit; remembering versus knowing) or by duration (short term versus long term). In each case, there seems to be a biological system responsible for the type of memory in question: short-term memory relies on a different brain system from long-term memory, for instance.

- If you go beyond the contents of this chapter in your reading, you will find that there are researchers who adhere strongly to these dichotomies and others who explain that they are more useful for explaining behaviours than they are scientific fact.

- For instance, because people with brain damage can learn new skills but not remember how, many people argue that these must be separable systems in the brain. Others, however, argue that memory systems are more unified and not separable in such a way (e.g. Shanks & Berry, 2012).

- It is fair to say that human memory is so complex as to need some simplification, and it is down to psychologists to make it clear how and why memory works as it does. Perhaps, though, at some levels, memory will for a long time be difficult to classify and categorize.

FUTURE DIRECTIONS

LEARNING OBJECTIVE 9.5

Critically evaluate possible future directions for research in memory.

We suggest that the future direction of memory research lies in better understanding the brain, better integration of technology into the brain, 'life logging', and – probably most importantly – the better communication of our scientific ideas. First, we tackle a big question: where is memory in the brain? (see Figure 9.15). In fact, we already have a pretty

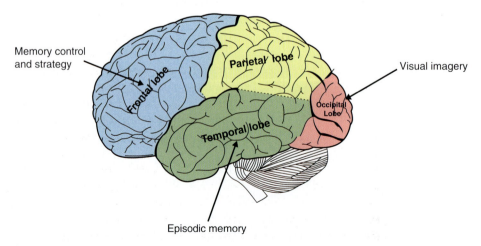

FIGURE 9.15 *The human brain: key regions for memory function.*
Source: Adapted from Gray (1918).

good idea of the crude localization of memory in the brain. The brain has had the starring role in this chapter – much of what we understand about how memory is organized is down to logical inferences about what amnesiacs can and cannot remember, and what and how they learn. Thus, we use brain damage as a sort of 'naturally occurring experiment' that tells us how things must be constructed in the brain. But, of course, as well as doing this we are learning about how to care for and treat memory disorders. Memory research is often neuroanatomically informed too: because we know where the damage is when we work with someone with amnesia or a person with an STM deficit, we can also have a good idea about where in the brain various functions are located.

As we are able to make ever more complex and exciting advances in technology, it will become even more important to understand what a memory is and where. We have started to stimulate parts of the brain artificially in order to treat conditions such as Alzheimer's disease, depression, and Parkinson's disease. In such **deep brain stimulation**, specific parts of the brain are given a mild electrical impulse through a surgically implanted 'brain pacemaker'. We are now beginning to consider how such stimulation might affect memories (Lee, Fell, & Axmacher, 2013). Lee et al. (2013) make the bold proposition that, if we can find the neural 'signature' of encoding and retrieval – that is, the brain waves, their strength, and their frequency – we can artificially boost these oscillations in order to treat memory loss. Like Penfield, Lee et al. base a lot of their reasoning on the fact that direct stimulation of the brain can lead to the vivid recollection of past memories (Jacobs, Kahana, Ekstrom, & Fried, 2007). The future of memory research will need to take on board such ambitious goals.

Lee et al.'s (2013) review of deep brain stimulation focuses on the medial temporal lobe, a region of the surface of the brain folded up inside itself, so it is actually at the very centre of the brain (see Figure 9.16). It has long been known that this is a critical area for memory function, at least since the time of the famous case of HM (see Focus Point 9.2). Figure 9.16 shows the **hippocampus**, thought of as the very heart of most memory tasks, and critically implicated in episodic memory. The hippocampus is thought to be involved in binding together prior experiences to form a rich, detailed representation of the past. As such, it seems to be very well connected – the brain has evolved with the hippocampus being an important junction linking many other regions of the brain. In short, if there is damage to the hippocampus, a profound amnesia results, affecting both new learning (anterograde amnesia) and the retrieval of previously encoded information from before the injury or damage (retrograde amnesia). However, pure damage to the hippocampus alone tends not to lead to deficits in working memory, semantic memory, or implicit memory.

We have also begun to think of memory function relying on a rich network of regions, in particular including the frontal lobe. In his influential 'working with memory' theory, Moscovitch (1992) outlined four regions critical for memory function. First, he stated that the medial temporal lobe is involved in episodic encoding (i.e. retrieval in tests of explicit memory), which is consonant with the traditional view of the hippocampus outlined in the previous paragraph. He also described 'nonfrontal' perceptual and semantic processes that consist of 'modules' dispersed throughout the subcortex (beneath the surface) of the brain, which are responsible for performance on implicit tests of memory, and a basal ganglia component that is involved in sensorimotor, procedural tests of memory. Most critically, he described a 'central' system based in the frontal lobe, which is strategic and can control the other systems. This frontal system does the work and controls the other regions – hence the idea of 'working with memory'. This idea is not far from Baddeley's conception of working memory, although it does not refer to a solely short-term process. The frontal lobes by this view are used to generate strategies, to initiate memory

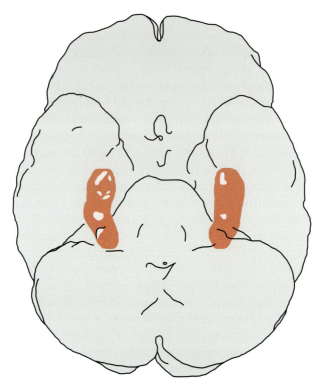

FIGURE 9.16 *The hippocampus in the human brain. This image shows the underside (ventral view) of the brain (the front of the brain is at the top). The blobs show the approximate location of the hippocampus in the temporal lobes of the human brain.*
Source: Wikimedia Commons.

searches, and to check the veracity of what is generated by the other systems. The frontal lobes, so heavily involved in the organization of memory, have therefore unsurprisingly been implicated in working memory – where the role is to manage and control other brain centres involved in perception. Injuries to the frontal lobes often lead to a 'clouding' of memory. People with these types of injuries cannot recall detailed memories (e.g. Wheeler, Stuss, & Tulving, 1997). Similarly, people with damage to posterior regions of the brain (at the back of the head), which contain regions involved in visual processing (the occipital lobes; see Figure 9.15), lose the ability to generate visual images of the past (e.g. Ogden, 1993). When the ability to generate visual images is compromised or lost as a consequence of brain damage, access to specific details of the past held in episodic images is also lost and an amnesia for details of the past results.

One challenge for future research is how to replace or retain this visual imagery, and one obvious solution in this digital age is to use technology to remediate memory – this will be an area of psychology that will be increasingly important. This has been the scientific goal of research with SenseCam, a wearable digital camera developed by Microsoft (see e.g. Berry et al., 2007). This device has a range of sensors for movement, light change, temperature, and so on and uses these sensors to trigger a still image being recorded via a fish-eye lens. It appears that, at least in a series of case studies on people with memory impairment, this system can act as a powerful cue for memory. It has also been shown that people show a generalized benefit to other forms of memory and cognition, not just an effect of using the pictures to reconstruct the past. One idea is that review of SenseCam images might stimulate the hippocampus (Silva, Pinho, Macedo, &

Moulin, 2013). However, much more research is needed on this kind of human–computer interaction and its usefulness in memory impairment.

You will have seen in this chapter just how rich and varied memory function is, and what a broad range of activities it serves. It makes sense, therefore, that there is not any one memory module in the brain, but that storage and retrieval of information are dispersed about the brain in relevant locations for the other sorts of activities that are going on. The understanding of the connections in the brain and the rich complexity of vast networks of millions of neurons is the level on which we now need to consider the brain. But it is a real challenge to look at the workings on a microscopic level in the living brain, and, even if we do succeed in doing this, it will be a huge computational challenge to summarize and store the data from such a complex organ as the human brain. In fact, in understanding the workings of the brain, we are building a model of memory itself – namely, how we can summarize and store the workings of the mind.

As an example, one prominent idea in the field of human ageing was that the ageing process affected human memory through a frontal lobe deficit (see Perfect, 1997, for a review and critique of this view). We know that the frontal lobes are particularly affected by cell loss in healthy ageing, and so this triggered a number of studies comparing healthy older adults with people who had damage to the frontal lobes. The comparison turned out to be a bit crude, but it did lead to new avenues of research and to the idea that older adults struggle with more difficult, strategic memory tasks based on the control of episodic memory, and not so much with those based on the lower-order implicit and semantic subsystems. Of course, the goal of all this neuropsychological and cognitive research into how memory works is to actually help people, and thus these sorts of issues will continue to be of utmost importance with our ageing population. But the most recent view is that it is a network in the whole brain that is responsible for this pattern of deficits (see e.g. Charlton, Barrick, Markus, & Morris, 2010).

A final challenge for the future is to better communicate the findings of our research and measure the impact this will have in schools and hospitals. Return to Table 9.1, which presented common myths about memory. Which of these can you now clarify based on scientific evidence? Which of these now seem illogical? Are there any areas where you need to know more? How could you demonstrate these effects to other people? Human memory is a complex, reflective process based on a rich combination of thoughts and representations being integrated into a meaningful code. Memory is constantly active and a by-product of complex processing. Nothing is processed deeply only to be lost. We need not, therefore, wilfully encode information or 'press save' or take a mental image for later use, like we take a snapshot on our phone of a moment we wish to remember for later. The cognitive view of memory therefore sees it as a set of interrelated stores and processes, and we learn most about these when they go wrong. If you find yourself remembering a previous event, you should best think of this event as a sort of mental construction, based on the synchronization of several brain regions and requiring a careful reconstruction process according to your current thoughts and goals. No memory is an island, but is part of a rich mental life and draws on many different subsystems.

DISCUSSION POINT

How do technological advances challenge the ideas set out by Loftus and Loftus at the beginning of this chapter? Might memory be permanent after all?

SECTION SUMMARY

- The future direction of memory research lies in better understanding the brain, better integration of technology into the brain, and the better communication of our scientific ideas.

- It has never been more important to understand what a memory is and where. Deep brain stimulation might offer one way in which we can achieve this.

- Memory function is rich and varied and it makes sense that there is not any one memory module in the brain, but that storage and retrieval of information are dispersed about the brain.

- We have begun to think of memory function relying on a rich network of regions, in particular including the frontal lobe, as highlighted in Moscovitch's (1992) influential 'working with memory' theory.

- The understanding of the connections in the brain, and the rich complexity of vast networks of millions of neurons, is the challenging level on which we now need to consider the brain.

- A challenge for the future is to better communicate the findings of our research and measure the impact this will have in schools and hospitals.

CHAPTER SUMMARY

This chapter has considered the fundamental nature of memory and has challenged the idea that it is a passive repository of information. We did this by first considering what memory is for and by challenging some of the most prominent memory myths. We then explored the nature of forgetting and the importance of cues and contexts before evaluating contemporary models and frameworks of memory. We moved on to examining the dichotomies in memory research, namely implicit versus explicit memory, short-term versus long-term memory, and general knowledge versus memory for personal events. We concluded by outlining some of the priorities for future memory research, focusing on the importance of understanding the dynamic nature of memory through the sensitive implementation of technological approaches and also the need to communicate research findings effectively in order to dispel myths about memory.

ESSAY QUESTIONS

1. Describe how human memory is subdivided into different systems. How have neuropsychological cases aided our understanding of these systems?

2. Using examples from experimental studies of memory, evaluate the claim that eyewitnesses may be prone to 'remember' events that did not actually happen.

3. What is the difference between episodic memory and autobiographical memory? What form might impairments of autobiographical memory take?

KEY TERMS

- **accessibility:** Whether information in memory can be accessed or not, given that it is available.
- **amnesia:** Memory loss, most often as a result of brain damage. Retrograde amnesia is the inability to recall events in the past: information encountered prior to an accident, injury, or disease. Anterograde amnesia is the inability to form new memories.
- **availability:** Whether or not information has been retained at all in memory in any form.
- **childhood amnesia:** The phenomenon in which we cannot remember any autobiographical memories from early in our life.
- **classical conditioning:** The pairing of a new stimulus with a pre-existing behaviour.
- **deep brain stimulation:** The artificial stimulation of brain regions using electrical probes and a device implanted within the brain.
- **eyewitness testimony:** The memory for events and occurrences in forensic settings – such as the memory for a crime you have witnessed.
- **false memory:** A memory that 'feels' as if it is true but in fact is a mis-recollection of prior events – it is not something intentionally fabricated but a normal part of the memory system.
- **flashbulb memory:** A particularly vivid memory where you can remember your personal circumstances surrounding a particularly distinctive event.
- **habituation:** The decreasing response to a repeatedly present stimulus.
- **hippocampus:** A small brain structure in the medial temporal lobe.
- **incidental memory:** Memory performance where there has not been an explicit instruction to deliberately memorize the information. Not to be confused with implicit memory.
- **inhibition:** The active suppression of information in the mind. A key idea in forgetting.
- **levels of processing:** A framework that allows us to understand how deeply processed information was at encoding. Information that is dwelt upon, transformed, or linked to other information is processed deeply. Superficial processing, such as judging perceptual form and the like, is shallow processing.
- **mere exposure effect:** The effect of familiarity on preference: we like things more that we have encountered more frequently.
- **metamemory:** Our capacity to reflect upon and 'control' our memory system.
- **nonassociative learning:** Learning where no new association is made. As an example, it is a change in response according to repeated exposure to one stimulus, as in habituation.
- **primacy effect:** The tendency to remember well the first items within a set (e.g. a list of words.
- **recall:** The reproduction of material learned at an earlier date.
- **recency effect:** The tendency to remember well the last items of a set – the ones that were presented most recently.
- **recognition:** The capacity to judge whether or not you have encountered a particular piece of information before when it is presented to you.
- **rehearsal:** The active or deliberate process of repetition, which can keep an item – or set of items – in memory.
- **repetition priming:** An improvement in processing as a consequence of having encountered the same material recently.
- **self-reference effect:** The finding that you later remember material better if you have studied with reference to yourself during encoding.
- **semantic priming:** The improvement in processing as a consequence of having recently encountered some other information that was semantically related.
- **sensory memory:** A very brief retention of information in a fragile, limited capacity store – akin to an after-image or echo.

- **span:** A procedure that measures how many items can be held in memory. A span task is one where there is an increase in materials presented with the aim of finding the point at which the participant can remember the most items. It is normal to have a span of about seven items in short-term memory.
- **state-dependent memory:** Memory retrieval that relies on the same internal state (e.g. mood or intoxication) being present at encoding and retrieval.
- **survival processing effect:** The finding that you later remember material better if you have studied it with reference to its usefulness in terms of aiding your survival.

NOTES

1. https://www.psychologytoday.com/blog/psychologist-the-movies/201212/amnesia-in-50-first-dates
2. http://ed.ted.com/lessons/what-happens-when-you-remove-the-hippocampus-sam-kean

FURTHER RESOURCES

Au, J., Sheehan, E., Tsai, N., Duncan, G. J., Buschkuehl, M., & Jaeggi, S. M. (2015). Improving fluid intelligence with training on working memory: A meta-analysis. *Psychonomic Bulletin & Review, 22*(2), 366–377.

Baddeley, A., Eysenck, M. W., & Anderson, M. C. (2009). *Memory*. Hove, UK: Psychology Press.

Corkin, S. (2013). *Permanent present tense: The unforgettable life of the amnesic patient, HM*. New York, NY: Basic Books.

Moscovitch, M., Cabeza, R., Winocur, G., & Nadel, L. (2016). Episodic memory and beyond: The hippocampus and neocortex in transformation. *Annual Review of Psychology, 67*, 105–134.

Omani, H., & Schwartz, B. L. (2018). *Handbook of research methods in human memory*. London, UK: Routledge.

Rathbone, C. J., O'Connor, A. R., & Moulin, C. J. (2017). The tracks of my years: Personal significance contributes to the reminiscence bump. *Memory & Cognition, 45*(1), 137–150.

Rosenbaum, R. S., Gilboa, A., & Moscovitch, M. (2014). Case studies continue to illuminate the cognitive neuroscience of memory. *Annals of the New York Academy of Sciences, 1316*(1), 105–133.

Simons, D. J., & Chabris, C. F. (2011). What people believe about how memory works: A representative survey of the US population. *PloS ONE, 6*(8), e22757.

Thompson, G. W., & Kello, C. (2014). Walking across Wikipedia: A scale-free network model of semantic memory retrieval. *Frontiers in Psychology, 5*, 86.

REFERENCES

Anderson, M. C., Bjork, R. A., & Bjork, E. L. (1994). Remembering can cause forgetting: Retrieval dynamics in long-term memory. *Journal of Experimental Psychology: Learning, Memory, and Cognition, 20*, 1063–1087.

Atkinson, R. C., & Shiffrin, R. M. (1968). Human memory: A proposed system and its control processes. In K. W. Spence & J. T. Spence (Eds.), *The psychology of learning and motivation* (Vol. 2, pp. 89–195). New York, NY: Academic Press.

Baddeley, A. D. (2000). The episodic buffer: A new component of working memory? *Trends in Cognitive Sciences, 4*, 417–423.

Baddeley, A. D. (2004). The psychology of memory. In A. D. Baddeley, M. D. Kopelman, & B. A. Wilson (Eds.), *The essential handbook of memory disorders for clinicians* (pp. 1–14). Chichester, UK: Wiley .

Baddeley, A., Gathercole, S., Papagno, C., & Degli, U. (1998). The phonological loop as a language learning device. *Psychological Review, 105*, 158–173.

Baddeley, A. D., & Hitch, G. (1974). Working memory. In G. A. Bower (Ed.), *Recent advances in learning and motivation* (Vol. 8, pp. 47–90). New York, NY: Academic Press.

Barrouillet, P., & Camos, V. (2007). The time based resource sharing model of working memory. In N. Osaka, R. Logie, & M. D'Esposito (Eds.), *Working memory: Behavioral and neural correlates* (pp. 59–80). Oxford, UK: Oxford University Press.

Barsalou, L. W. (1985). Ideals, central tendency, and frequency of instantiation as determinants of graded structure in categories. *Journal of Experimental Psychology: Learning, Memory, and Cognition, 11*(4), 629–654.

Berry, E., Kapur, N., Williams, L., Hodges, S., Watson, P., Smyth, G., … Wood, K. (2007). The use of a wearable camera, SenseCam, as a pictorial diary to improve autobiographical memory in a patient with limbic encephalitis: A preliminary report. *Neuropsychological Rehabilitation, 17*, 582–601.

Bjork, R. A. (2001). How to succeed in college: Learn how to learn. *APS Observer, 14*(3), 9.

Brown, R., & Kulik, J. (1977). Flashbulb memories. *Cognition, 5*, 73–99.

Cepeda, N. J., Pashler, H., Vul, E., Wixted, J. T., & Rohrer, D. (2006). Distributed practice in verbal recall tasks: A review and quantitative synthesis. *Psychological Bulletin, 132*, 354–380.

Charlton, R. A., Barrick, T. R., Markus, H. S., & Morris R. G. (2010). The relationship between episodic memory and white matter integrity in normal aging. *Neuropsychologia, 48*(1), 114–122.

Clancy, S. A., McNally, R. J., Schacter, D. L., Lenzenweger, M. F., & Pitman, R. K. (2002). Memory distortion in people reporting abduction by aliens. *Journal of Abnormal Psychology, 111*, 455–461.

Cohen, N. J., & Squire, L. R. (1980). Preserved learning and retention of pattern-analyzing skill in amnesia: Dissociation of knowing how and knowing that. *Science, 210*, 207–210.

Collins, A. M., & Loftus, E. (1975). A spreading activation theory of semantic processing. *Psychological Review, 82*(6), 407–428.

Collins, A. M., & Quillian, M. R. (1969). Retrieval time from semantic memory. *Journal of Verbal Learning and Verbal Behavior, 8*, 240–248.

Conway, A. R., & Engle, R. W. (1996). Individual differences in working memory capacity: More evidence for a general capacity theory. *Memory, 4*, 577–590.

Conway, M. A., Gardiner, J. M., Perfect, T. J., Anderson, S. J., & Cohen, G. M. (1997). Changes in memory awareness during learning: The acquisition of knowledge by psychology undergraduates. *Journal of Experimental Psychology: General, 126*, 393–413.

Conway, M. A. (2001). Sensory perceptual episodic memory and its context: Autobiographical memory. *Philosophical Transactions of the Royal Society B: Biological Sciences, 356*, 1297–1306.

Conway, M. A. (2009). Episodic memories. *Neuropsychologia, 47*(11), 2305–2313.

Conway, M. A., Singer, J. A., & Tagini, A. (2004). The self and autobiographical memory: Correspondence and coherence. *Social Cognition, 22*, 491–529.

Conway, M. A., & Williams, H. L. (2008). Autobiographical memory. In J. H. Byrne (Ed.), *Learning and memory: A comprehensive reference* (pp. 893–909). Amsterdam, Netherlands: Elsevier.

Corbin, L., & Camos, V. (2011). Improvement of working memory performance by training is not transferable. *Europe's Journal of Psychology, 7*, 279–294.

Corkin, S. (2002). What's new with the amnesic patient HM? *Nature Reviews Neuroscience, 3*, 153–160.

Corkin, S. (2013). *Permanent present tense: The man with no memory, and what he taught the world.* London, UK: Allen Lane.

Cowan, N. (1995). *Attention and memory: An integrated framework.* New York, NY: Oxford University Press.

Craik, F. I. M., & Bialystok, E. (2008). Lifespan cognitive development: The roles of representation and control. In F. I. M. Craik & T. A. Salthouse (Eds.), *Handbook of aging and cognition* (pp. 557–601). New York, NY: Psychology Press.

Craik, F. I. M., & Lockhart, R. S. (1972). Levels of processing: A framework for memory research. *Journal of Verbal Learning and Verbal Behavior, 11*, 671–684.

Daneman, M., & Carpenter, P. (1980). Individual differences in working memory and reading. *Journal of Verbal Learning and Verbal Behavior, 19*, 450–466.

Deese, J. (1959). On the prediction of occurrence of particular verbal intrusions in immediate recall. *Journal of Experimental Psychology, 58*, 17–22.

Dockree, P. M., & Ellis, J. A. (2001). Forming and canceling everyday intentions: Implications for prospective remembering. *Memory & Cognition, 29*, 1139–1145.

Duka, T., Weissenborn, R., & Dienes, Z. (2001). State-dependent effects of alcohol on recollective experience, familiarity and awareness of memories. *Psychopharmacology, 153*(3), 295–306.

Ebbinghaus, H. (1885/1964). *Memory: A contribution to experimental psychology* (Trans. H. A. Ruger & C. E. Bussenius). New York, NY: Dover.

Ellis, J., & Kvavilashvili, L. (2000). Prospective memory in 2000: Past, present, and future directions. *Applied Cognitive Psychology, 14*, S1–S9.

Fishman, E., Keller, L., & Atkinson, R. C. (1968). Massed versus distributed practice in computerized spelling drills. *Journal of Educational Psychology, 59*(4), 290–296.

Garden, S., Cornoldi, C., & Logie, R. H. (2002). Visuo-spatial working memory in navigation. *Applied Cognitive Psychology, 16*, 35–50.

Gathercole, S. E., & Pickering, S. J. (2000). Working memory deficits in children with low achievements in the national curriculum at 7 years of age. *British Journal of Educational Psychology, 70*, 177–194.

Godden, D. R., & Baddeley, A. D. (1975). Context dependent memory in two natural environments: On land and underwater. *British Journal of Psychology, 66*(3), 325–331.

Goodwin, D. W., Crane, J. B., & Guze, S. B. (1969). Alcoholic blackouts: A review and clinical study of 100 alcoholics. *American Journal of Psychiatry, 126*, 191–198.

Gray, H. (1918). *Anatomy of the human body*. Philadelphia, PA: Lea & Febiger.

Greene, J., Baddeley, A., & Hodges, J. (1996). Analysis of the episodic memory deficit in early Alzheimer's disease: Evidence from the doors and people test. *Neuropsychologia, 34*(6), 537–551.

Hodges, J. R., Patterson, K., Oxbury, S., & Funnell, E. (1992). Semantic dementia: Progressive fluent aphasia with temporal-lobe atrophy. *Brain, 115*, 1783–1806.

Holmes, J., Gathercole, S. E., & Dunning, D. L. (2009). Adaptive training leads to sustained enhancement of poor working memory in children. *Developmental Science, 12*, F1–F7.

Jacobs, J., Kahana, M. J., Ekstrom, A. D., & Fried, I. (2007). Brain oscillations control timing of single-neuron activity in humans. *Journal of Neuroscience, 27*, 3839–3844.

Jaeggi, S. M., Buschkuehl, M., Jonides, J., & Perrig, W. J. (2008). Improving fluid intelligence with training on working memory. *Proceedings of the National Academy of Sciences of the United States of America, 105*, 6829–6833.

Klein, S. B., & Kihlstrom, J. F. (1986). Elaboration, organization, and the self-reference effect in memory. *Journal of Experimental Psychology: General, 115*, 26–38.

Kohler, I. (1962). Experiments with goggles. *Scientific American, 206*, 62–72.

Lee, H., Fell, J., & Axmacher, N. (2013). Electrical engram: How deep brain stimulation affects memory. *Trends in Cognitive Sciences, 17*, 574–584.

Lindsey, R. V., Shroyer, J. D., Pashler, H., & Mozer, M. C. (2014). Improving students' long-term knowledge retention through personalized review. *Psychological Science, 25*, 639–647. doi:10.1177/0956797613504302

Loftus, E. F., & Loftus, G. R. (1980). On the permanence of stored information in the human brain. *American Psychologist, 35*(5), 116–129.

Loftus, E. F., & Palmer, J. C. (1974). Reconstruction of automobile destruction: An example of the interaction between language and memory. *Journal of Verbal Learning and Verbal Behavior, 13*, 585–589.

Lombardo, M. V., Barnes, J. L., Wheelwright, S. J., & Baron-Cohen, S. (2007). Self-referential cognition and empathy in autism. *PloS ONE, 2*(9), e883.

Mandler, G., Pearlstone, Z., & Koopmans, H. S. (1969). Effects of organization and semantic similarity on recall and recognition. *Journal of Verbal Learning and Verbal Behavior, 8,* 410–423.

Marcel, A. (1983). Conscious and unconscious perception: Experiments on visual masking and word recognition. *Cognitive Psychology, 15,* 197–237.

Marsh, R. L., & Hicks, J. L. (1998). Event-based prospective memory and executive control of working memory. *Journal of Experimental Psychology: Learning, Memory, and Cognition, 24,* 336–349.

McDaniel, M. A., Anderson, J. L., Derbish, M. H., & Morrisette, N. (2007). Testing the testing effect in the classroom. *European Journal of Cognitive Psychology, 19,* 494–513.

Melby-Lervåg, M., & Hulme, C. (2013). Is working memory training effective? A meta-analytic review. *Developmental Psychology, 49,* 270–291.

Miller, G. A. (1956). The magical number seven, plus or minus two: Some limits on our capacity for processing information. *Psychological Review, 101*(2), 343–352.

Morrison, C. M., & Conway, M. A. (2010). First words and first memories. *Cognition, 116,* 23–32.

Moscovitch, M. (1992). Memory and working with memory: A component process model based on modules and central systems. *Journal of Cognitive Neuroscience, 4,* 257–267.

Nairne, J. S., & Pandeirada, J. N. S. (2008). Adaptive memory. *Current Directions in Psychological Science, 17*(4), 239–243.

Neisser, U. (1982). Snapshots or benchmarks? In U. Neisser (Ed.), *Memory observed: Remembering in natural contexts* (pp. 68–74). San Francisco, CA: Freeman.

Nyberg, L., Cabeza, R., & Tulving, E. (1996). PET studies of encoding and retrieval: The HERA model. *Psychonomic Bulletin & Review, 3*(2), 135–148.

Ogden, J. A. (1993). Visual object agnosia, prosopagnosia, achromatopsia, loss of visual imagery, and autobiographical amnesia following recovery from cortical blindness: Case MH. *Neuropsychologia, 31*(6), 571–589.

Ost, L. G., Salkovskis, P. M., & Hellstrom, K. (1991). One-session therapist-directed exposure vs self-exposure in the treatment of spider phobia. *Behavior Therapy, 22,* 407–422.

Pavlov, I. P. (1927). *Conditioned reflexes: An investigation of the physiological activity of the cerebral cortex* (Trans. & Ed. G. V. Anrep.) London, UK: Oxford University Press.

Penfield, W. (1969). Consciousness, memory and man's conditioned reflexes. In K. Pribram (Ed.), *On the biology of learning.* New York, NY: Harcourt, Brace and World.

Perfect, T. J. (1997). Memory aging as frontal lobe dysfunction. In M. A. Conway (Ed.), *Cognitive models of memory* (pp. 315–339). Cambridge, MA: MIT Press.

Perfect, T. J., Wagstaff, G. F., Moore, D., Andrews, B., Cleveland, V., Newcombe, S., & Brown, L. (2008). How can we help witnesses to remember more? It's an (eyes) open and shut case. *Law and Human Behavior, 32*(4), 314–324.

Perruchet, P. (1985). A pitfall for the expectancy theory of human eyelid conditioning. *Pavlovian Journal of Biological Sciences, 20,* 163–170.

Pezdek, K., & Salim, R. (2011). Physiological, psychological and behavioral consequences of activating autobiographical memories. *Journal of Experimental Social Psychology, 47*(6), 1214–1218.

Ramponi, C., Richardson-Klavehn, A., & Gardiner, J. M. (2007). Component processes of conceptual priming and associative cued recall: The roles of preexisting representation and depth of processing. *Journal of Experimental Psychology: Learning, Memory, and Cognition, 33,* 843–862.

Rastle, K., & Coltheart, M. (1999). Lexical and nonlexical phonological priming in reading aloud. *Journal of Experimental Psychology: Human Perception and Performance, 25,* 461–481.

Rathbone, C. J., & Moulin, C. J. A. (2010). When's your birthday? The self-reference effect in retrieval of dates. *Applied Cognitive Psychology, 24*(5), 737–743.

Rathbone, C. J., Moulin, C. J. A., & Conway, M. A. (2009). Autobiographical memory and amnesia: Using conceptual knowledge to ground the self. *Neurocase, 15*(5), 405–418.

Roediger, H. L., & McDermott, K. B. (1995). Creating false memories: Remembering words not presented in lists. *Journal of Experimental Psychology: Learning, Memory and Cognition, 24*(4), 803–814.

Rubin, D. C., Wetzler, S. E., & Nebes, R. D. (1986). Autobiographical memory across the adult lifespan. In D. C. Rubin (Ed.), *Autobiographical memory* (pp. 202–221). Cambridge, UK: Cambridge University Press.

Schacter, D. L., & Addis, D. R. (2007). The cognitive neuroscience of constructive memory: Remembering the past and imagining the future. *Philosophical Transactions of the Royal Society B: Biological Sciences, 362,* 773–786.

Shah, P., & Miyake, A. (1999). Models of working memory: An introduction. In A. Miyake & P. Shah (Eds.), *Models of working memory: Mechanisms of active maintenance and executive control* (pp. 1–27). Cambridge, UK: Cambridge University Press.

Shanks, D. R., & Berry, C. J. (2012). EPS Mid-Career Award 2011: Are there multiple memory systems? Tests of models of implicit and explicit memory. *Quarterly Journal of Experimental Psychology, 65,* 1449–1474.

Silva, A. R., Pinho, S., Macedo, L. M., & Moulin, C. J. (2013). Benefits of SenseCam review on neuropsychological test performance. *American Journal of Preventive Medicine, 44,* 302–307.

Simons, D. J., & Chabris, C. F. (2011). What people believe about how memory works: A representative survey of the US population. *PloS ONE, 6*(8), e22757.

Singer, J. A., & Salovey, P. (1993). *The remembered self.* New York, NY: Free Press.

Smith, C. N., Frascino, J. C., Kripke, D. L., McHugh, P. R., Treisman, G. J., & Squire, L. R. (2010). Losing memories overnight: A unique form of human amnesia. *Neuropsychologia, 48*(10), 2833–2840.

Smith, E. E., & Jonides, J. (1997). Working memory: A view from neuroimaging. *Cognitive Psychology, 33,* 5–42.

Smith, E. E., Shoben, E. J., & Rips, L. J. (1974). Comparison processes in semantic memory. *Psychological Review, 81,* 214–241.

Soderstrom, N. C., & McCabe, D. P. (2011). Are survival processing memory advantages based on ancestral priorities? *Psychonomic Bulletin & Review, 18*(3), 564–569.

Sperling, G. (1960). The information available in brief visual presentations. *Psychological Monographs: General and Applied, 74*(11), 1–29.

Squire, L. R. (1992). Declarative and nondeclarative memory: Multiple brain systems supporting learning. *Journal of Cognitive Neuroscience, 4,* 232–243.

Thompson, G. W., & Kello, C. T. (2014). Walking across Wikipedia: A scale-free network model of semantic memory retrieval. *Frontiers in Psychology, 5,* 1–9. doi:10.3389/fpsyg.2014.00086

Tulving, E. (1985). How many memory systems are there? *American Psychologist, 40*(4), 385–398.

Tulving, E., Schacter, D. L., & Stark, H. A. (1982). Priming effects in word-fragment completion are independent of recognition memory. *Journal of Experimental Psychology: Learning, Memory, and Cognition, 8*(4), 336–342.

Wade, K. A., Garry, M., Read, J. D., & Lindsay, D. S. (2002). A picture is worth a thousand lies: Using false photographs to create false childhood memories. *Psychonomic Bulletin & Review, 9,* 597–603.

Warrington, E. K., & Shallice, T. (1969). The selective impairment of auditory verbal short-term memory. *Brain: A Journal of Neurology, 92*(4), 885–896.

Wheeler, M. A., Stuss, D. T., & Tulving, E. (1997). Toward a theory of episodic memory: The frontal lobes and autonoetic consciousness. *Psychological Bulletin, 121*(3), 331–354.

Wilson, B. A., & Wearing, D. (1995). Prisoner of consciousness: A state of just awakening following herpes simplex encephalitis. In R. Campbell & M. Conway (Eds.), *Broken memories: Case studies in memory impairment* (pp. 14–30). Malden, MA: Blackwell.

Zajonc, R. B. (1968). Attitudinal effects of mere exposure. *Journal of Personality and Social Psychology, 9,* 1–27.

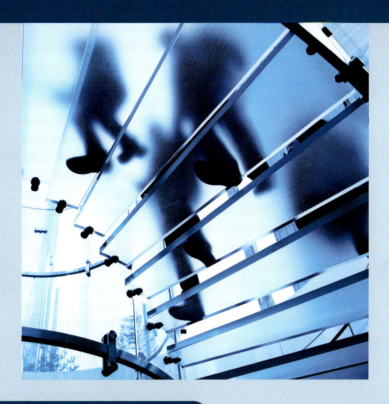

ROUTE MAP OF THE CHAPTER

This chapter addresses two questions: (1) What makes emotion emotional? In other words, how is emotion different from non-emotional experience, and what causal processes determine these differences? (2) What is different about different emotions? In other words, what causes and characteristics distinguish anger from fear and love from happiness? In turn, the chapter discusses three variables that may help to answer these questions: physiological activity of the body and brain, facial expressions, and the individual's person's evaluations and interpretations of the current situation (appraisals). The evidence suggests that there are some differences between emotions across many of these variables but these differences are not always consistent or absolute. The chapter next reviews the implications of this evidence for theories proposing that some 'basic' emotions are innately programmed response syndromes, and considers alternative views.

CHAPTER OUTLINE

INTRODUCTION

LEARNING OBJECTIVE 10.1

Demonstrate an understanding of the basic background to the study of emotions.

It's easy to think of things that can make us emotional: good or bad news; the light at the end of the tunnel or the sealed door preventing any escape; emerging naked from the shower to find unexpected guests on the landing as the bathroom door opens; extreme turbulence at high altitude; wild geese that fly with the moon on their wings; our favourite things, and being without those things.

It's also easy to think of things that we do, think, or feel when we react emotionally to events such as these. We may shout or hide, fight or flee. We may curse under our breath, feel that the whole world is against us, or conclude that we only have ourselves to blame (you do it to yourself … and that's what really hurts). We may be unable to stop replaying events over and over in our heads, or may find ourselves absorbed in the moment, not thinking about anything at all. Our face may flush. Our heart may race. We may smile or frown, turn our nose up, or turn our gaze away. We may stare intently at something or someone, or gaze vaguely into the distance. We may feel hot and bothered or calm and collected, in or out of control. There are pangs, desires, thrills, and chills. It can all get too much.

Clearly, we know a lot about causes and consequences of emotion. So why is it far from easy to get a grip on emotion itself, the thing caused by those causes, that feels like it feels, that makes us do the things that it makes us do? What is the vital ingredient or set of ingredients that makes emotion emotional? The more we reach for its essence, the more it seems to slip through our fingers. Perhaps the separate parts that we know about somehow fit together into the thing itself, like different-shaped Lego pieces without the picture on the box to guide our attempt at construction. Or perhaps we are not asking the right questions in the first place.

This chapter considers evidence that might help us to resolve some of these issues. It focuses particularly on variables that may influence and distinguish emotions and their implications for explanatory theories. Despite several decades of psychological research, big disagreements persist between researchers about how the phenomenon should be conceptualized and investigated and where to look for its causes. The chapter next introduces some of these debates before reviewing research evidence in subsequent sections.

SECTION SUMMARY

- It is common knowledge that various pleasant and unpleasant events can induce emotional reactions.
- Most people are also aware of many of the common symptoms and consequences of emotion, including effects on thoughts, feelings, and actions.
- However, getting a grip on emotion itself seems to require us to go beyond common knowledge.

EMOTION DIFFERENTIATION

LEARNING OBJECTIVE 10.2

Demonstrate an understanding of two general approaches to explaining emotions based on feedback theory and appraisal theory, and of the differences between them.

What makes emotion emotional?

Here's one way to find the emotional part of an emotion. Think of the last time you felt fear, anger, embarrassment, pride, or joy. Now think about which aspects of what was happening you could take away without taking away the emotion too. Probably the specifics of the time and place are not important. Perhaps the precise position or movement of your limbs makes no difference. Keep on taking pieces away one by one until you don't have the emotion any more.

This thought experiment is pretty much the one that William James (1884) attempted when seeking to answer the question 'What is an emotion?'. Whether his conclusion was the correct one is still disputed. However, his way of asking the question had a big influence on the subsequent development of emotion theory. This is what he wrote:

> If we fancy some strong emotion and then try to abstract from our consciousness of it all the feelings of its bodily symptoms, we find we have nothing left behind, no 'mind-stuff' out of which the emotion can be constituted, and that a cold and neutral state of intellectual perception is all that remains. (James, 1884, p. 193)

In other words:

> Without the bodily states following on the perception, the latter would be purely cognitive in form, pale, colourless, destitute of emotional warmth. (p. 190)

James believed that it is the way our bodies react to emotional events that makes our experience an emotional experience. According to him, we register the emotional quality of what we are feeling by sensing these bodily changes. Indeed, for James the bodily reactions come before the emotional experience not afterwards, as we might naively believe.

However, this answer may partly depend on the way that James approached the question in the first place. Because his starting assumption was that emotion is an embodied experience, it is not surprising that this experience stopped seeming emotional once the bodily changes were taken away. Approaching emotion from a different perspective may lead to different conclusions.

In 1960, Magda Arnold based a very similar thought experiment on another, similarly plausible way of thinking about emotions. Instead of focusing on the nature of the internal experience, she was interested in how the world appears to us when we get emotional and how we are disposed to act towards it. For her, emotion involves seeing certain objects as (literally as well as metaphorically) attractive or repulsive, as pulling us towards or away from them. What then makes our perception of these objects an emotional perception? What would you need to take away to stop it being emotional?

Here is what she wrote:

> Both perception and emotion have an object; but in emotion the object is known in a particular way. To perceive or apprehend something means that I know what it is like as a thing, apart from any effect on me. To like it or dislike it means that I know it not only objectively, as it is apart from me, but also that I estimate its relation to me, that I appraise it as desirable or undesirable, valuable or harmful for me, so that I am drawn to it or repelled by it. (Arnold, 1960, p. 170)

For Arnold, what gives emotional quality to our perceptions of the world is the sense that what is happening is *personally significant*. When events matter to us because of their relevance to our current goals and concerns (e.g. when they help or hinder what we are trying to achieve), they lead to emotions and associated impulses to perform actions that bring us closer to or further away from the thing we are emotional about (**action readiness**).

These two thought experiments may make the question of what makes emotion emotional seem like a purely philosophical one – one that psychologists can safely ignore or set aside. However, both James and Arnold developed influential empirical theories based on their conclusions (see Table 10.1). These theories have guided a great deal of important research. James's **feedback theory** argues that the cause of emotion is perceived bodily change (feedback from the body to the brain), meaning that changing the way that the body reacts or the way the body's reaction is perceived also changes emotion. For example, it should be possible to stop someone feeling an emotion by blocking sensations from their body. Arnold's **appraisal theory** argues that the cause of emotion is the perception that an event is personally significant (**appraisal**). This means that changing perceptions and interpretations of events also changes emotional reactions to those events. For example, it should be possible to stop someone feeling an emotion by making the event seem irrelevant to their concerns. This chapter discusses evidence generated by research testing these ideas.

Who was correct, James or Arnold? Do emotions depend on sensing bodily changes or perceiving that events are personally significant? Or do they depend on both? By the end of this chapter, we should be in a better position to tell.

TABLE 10.1 *A comparison of James's and Arnold's theories.*

	James's feedback theory	Arnold's appraisal theory
Nature of emotion	Subjective experience	Action readiness
Cause of emotion	Internally perceived bodily changes	Appraisal of a personally significant event
Differences between emotions	Patterns of bodily change	Patterns of appraisal
How can emotion be manipulated experimentally?	Changing bodily changes or perception of bodily changes	Changing appraisals or appraised events

TEST YOURSELF

What are the main differences between James's feedback theory and Arnold's appraisal theory?

What's different about different emotions?

In addition to disagreeing about how to distinguish emotion from non-emotion, psychologists argue about the distinctions between different kinds of emotion. What gives each distinct emotion its particular quality? What makes fear fearful and joy joyful, for example? Is there a special set of characteristics defining the boundaries between emotion categories?

This question is clearly important to the investigation of emotion. Assuming that emotions genuinely are different from each other, researchers can make no progress in exploring their specific causes and effects unless they know how to tell those emotions apart in the first place. If emotions are seen as distinct subjective experiences, the question also has implications for perceiving our own emotions. For example, James was interested in how someone in an emotional state is able to tell what emotional state it is. What internal signals make the fear experience feel fearful rather than joyful, for example?

Unsurprisingly, James's answer to this question followed the same logic as his answer to the question about what makes emotion emotional. What make different emotions different are the different patterns of bodily changes associated with each of them. Feedback theory therefore makes two claims. The first is that different emotions have characteristic patterns of bodily changes, which occur consistently whenever the emotion occurs and which are different for each different emotion. Let's call this the 'specificity hypothesis'. James presents it as follows:

> The various permutations and combinations of which these organic activities are susceptible make it abstractly possible that no shade of emotion, however slight, should be without a bodily reverberation as unique, when taken in its totality, as is the mental mood itself. (James, 1884, p. 192)

The second claim is that people can tell what emotion they are experiencing by registering these patterns of bodily change. Differentiated emotional experiences are *caused* by the internal perception of differentiated patterns of bodily change: 'every

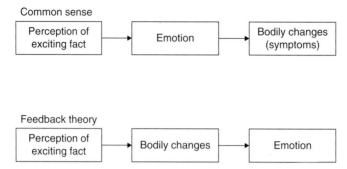

FIGURE 10.1 *James's theory of emotion causation compared with common sense. This figure shows alternative views of the sequence of events characterizing emotional response. According to common sense, emotion immediately follows detection of an emotional object (perception of exciting fact) and emotion in turn produces bodily symptoms. James's alternative idea is that the bodily changes are direct consequences of the perception of the emotional event and the emotion is a subsequent consequence of perceiving these changes.*

one of the bodily changes, whatsoever it be, is *felt*, acutely or obscurely, the moment it occurs' (James, 1884, p. 192). Let's call this the 'feedback hypothesis'.

Taken together, the specificity and feedback hypotheses bring us to the central claim of feedback theory, that common sense gets things the wrong way round in assuming that emotions cause bodily changes (see Figure 10.1). For James, the opposite is true: patterns of bodily change, or perceptions of these patterns, are causes rather than consequences of emotion. They are not symptoms of an emotion that is already present but what activates the emotional experience in the first place:

> Our natural way of thinking … is that the mental perception of some fact excites the mental affection called the emotion, and that this latter state of mind gives rise to the bodily expression. My thesis, on the contrary, is that *the bodily changes follow directly the perception of the exciting fact, and that our feeling of the same changes as they occur IS the emotion.* Common sense says, we lose our fortune, are sorry and weep; we meet a bear, are frightened and run; we are insulted by a rival, are angry and strike. The hypothesis here to be defended says that this order of sequence is incorrect … and that the more rational statement is that we feel sorry because we cry, angry because we strike, afraid because we tremble, and not that we cry, strike, or tremble because we are sorry, angry, fearful, as the case may be. (James, 1884, pp. 189–190)

Again, Arnold's perspective on what is different about different emotions works from different assumptions, which led her to a very different conclusion (see Figure 10.2). For her, it is not the distinctive characteristics of internally perceived experiences that differentiate emotions, but rather the person's differently coloured perceptions of what is happening. These perceptions directly produce emotional impulses to do something about whatever is going right or wrong. When we are angry, we see things as blocking us and have the impulse to remove the blockage. When we are afraid, we see things as threatening and want to escape. These action impulses may be associated with bodily changes of various kinds but these bodily changes do not cause the emotion via feedback processes. Instead the emotion is activated by the appraisal of a personally significant situation (see Figure 10.2). Exactly what kind of personal significance the situation is appraised as having determines the quality of the ensuing emotion.

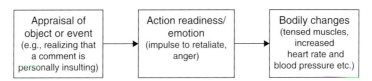

FIGURE 10.2 *Arnold's appraisal theory of emotion causation. This figure shows the sequence of events proposed by appraisal theory. In contrast to Figure 10.1, the appraisal of an object or event rather than the mere perception of an exciting fact initiates the emotion process, and the bodily changes are part of the emotional response rather than prior causes of that response.*

So far, we have considered logical arguments intended to uncover the nature of emotion. But armchair reasoning has its limits. What about the facts? Should we not try to find out what makes emotion emotional and what is different about different emotions by collecting data about actual rather than imagined emotions? Why not use real experiments rather than thought experiments? Over the years, many researchers have attempted to do exactly this, and the following sections review some of their results and conclusions, covering evidence relating to whether emotions differ in associated bodily changes, facial expressions, and appraisals, and whether changes in each kind of variable result in changes in emotion (see Research Methods 10.1).

RESEARCH METHODS 10.1

EMOTION

Emotion research sometimes focuses on directly comparing different emotions to determine what is different about them, and sometimes focuses on manipulating variables that may have a causal influence on emotions (e.g. in making them emotional or making them a particular kind of emotion).

When assessing what's different about different emotions, researchers typically compare them along variables relating to appraisals, facial expressions, and other bodily changes. For example, studies often employ standardized methods intended to induce different emotions in a consistent way and then measure participants' responses on a number of dimensions (e.g. recorded physiological changes, videotaped facial responses, or people's descriptions of their perceptions of events).

To take the additional step of establishing what factors play a causal role in emotion activation and differentiation, researchers manipulate similar variables in controlled experiments in order to assess their effects on emotions. For example, physiological, facial, or appraisal changes can be induced and participants' emotional reactions subsequently measured. If experimental research of this kind can consistently demonstrate that a variable has effects across a wide range of emotions, then conclusions about what makes emotion emotional as well as what makes different emotions different may be possible.

What particular variables have been measured and manipulated in these kinds of research? For most contemporary theorists, emotions are response syndromes consisting of a number of interrelated component processes. As indicated above, the most commonly investigated variables are physiological responses controlled by the autonomic nervous system (e.g. heart rate, blood pressure, and so forth), facial expressions, and appraisals of various kinds. Each of these variables can be measured as a possible index of emotion or manipulated as a possible cause of emotion. For feedback theory, physiological and facial expressions can serve a causal role in producing emotions as measured by appraisals or subjective experiences. For appraisal theory, appraisals are the key causal factor determining physiological, facial, and subjective responses. Testing either theory requires an assessment of how emotional responses change when key variables are manipulated. If making someone appraise someone else's action as blameworthy leads to anger, then this is consistent with the theory that anger depends on appraisal of other-blame (e.g. Lazarus, 1991), and more generally with the idea that emotions depend on appraisal. If manipulating someone's facial movements so that they are more likely to smile increases their happiness (e.g. Strack, Martin, & Stepper, 1988), this is consistent with the idea that happiness is caused (or at least influenced) by feedback (in this case, facial feedback from a smile), and more generally with the idea that emotions depend on bodily feedback.

TEST YOURSELF

1. What makes emotion emotional according to James's feedback theory?
2. What makes emotion emotional according to Arnold's appraisal theory?
3. What is appraisal?

SECTION SUMMARY

- The question of what makes emotion emotional remains highly disputed.

- William James believed that it is the way our bodies react to emotional events that makes our experience an emotional experience. For James the bodily reactions come before the emotional experience, not afterwards.

- James's feedback theory argues that the cause of emotion is perceived bodily change, meaning that changing the way that the body reacts or the way the body's reaction is perceived also changes emotion. We can stop feeling an emotion by blocking bodily sensations.

- Magda Arnold was interested in how the world appears to us when we get emotional, and how we are disposed to act towards it. For Arnold, emotion involves seeing certain objects as attractive or repulsive, as pulling us towards them or pushing us away from them. Personal significance gives emotional quality to our perceptions of the world.

- Arnold's appraisal theory argues that the cause of emotion is the perception that an event is personally significant. Thus, changing perceptions and interpretations of events also changes emotional reactions to those events.

- Psychologists also argue about the distinctions between different kinds of emotion.

- Feedback theory claims that common sense gets things the wrong way round in assuming that emotions cause bodily changes.

- The theory claims that (1) different emotions have characteristic patterns of bodily changes, which occur consistently whenever the emotion occurs and are different for each different emotion (*specificity hypothesis*) and (2) people can tell what emotion they are experiencing by registering these patterns of bodily change (*feedback hypothesis*).

PHYSIOLOGICAL ACTIVITY

LEARNING OBJECTIVE 10.3

Evaluate and synthesize the various sources of evidence concerning differences between emotions that are available to psychologists, including physiological measures and facial expressions.

William James included all kinds of bodily response in his proposal that emotions depend on internal feedback:

> The immense number of parts modified in each emotion is what makes it so difficult for us to reproduce in cold blood the total and integral expression of any one of them. We may catch the trick with the voluntary muscles, but fail with the skin, glands, heart, and other viscera. (James, 1898, p. 1066)

However, James did attach special importance to a set of responses that are apparently difficult to control: 'The *visceral and organic* part of the expression can be suppressed in some men, but not in others, and on this it is probable that the chief part of the felt emotion depends' (James, 1898, p. 1080).

These changes are mostly under the control of the **autonomic nervous system (ANS)** and have been a central focus of much of the research into emotion differentiation since James's time. Many aspects of ANS activity can be measured using electrodes or other transducers attached to the skin, meaning that no invasive procedures are necessary. For example, heart rate and blood pressure measurement are familiar to most of us from visits to the doctor.

Another commonly used ANS measure is skin conductance, which is assessed by passing a small and undetectable electric current between two electrodes attached to the hand (Figure 10.3). One of the main factors affecting skin conductance is how much our palms are sweating, because water is a better conductor of electricity than skin. Recent technological developments mean that it is now possible to take autonomic measurements while people are carrying out their daily activities instead of being kept immobile on a chair or bench (see e.g. Picard, 2010).

Autonomic activity can also be manipulated using drugs or physical exertion. In this section, we will evaluate evidence collected using measurement and manipulation of autonomic activity, respectively, to test the two assumptions of James's theory:

1. *Specificity hypothesis* – Are patterns of autonomic response different for different emotions?

2. *Feedback hypothesis* – Do autonomic responses help to make emotions emotional in the first place? In other words, does autonomic feedback cause or influence emotion, rather than simply being one of its possible consequences?

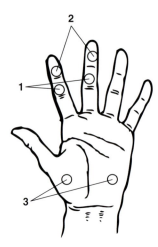

FIGURE 10.3 *Measuring electrodermal activity. Three alternative placements for electrodes (1, 2, or 3) attached to the hand when assessing autonomic activity based on skin conductance.*

Autonomic specificity

In the days before ethics committees, researchers were less reluctant than now to expose participants to potentially disturbing emotion manipulations. One example is a study by Ax (1953) assessing whether anger and fear have different autonomic patterns (**autonomic specificity**).

Ax told his participants that they would be listening to personally selected music while he recorded their physiological responses. He wired them to electrodes before exposing them to two different emotion conditions. In the anger condition, participants were treated roughly by a rude 'relief technician' who accused them of being late and putting his schedule back. In the fear condition, the electrodes delivered mild electric shocks before sparks started to fly from the equipment. The experimenter ran around trying to fix things, shouting in panic about a dangerous high-voltage short-circuit. In postexperimental interviews, participants reported praying and expecting imminent death during the fear manipulation. In the anger condition, a participant reported wanting to punch the technician. Few subsequent studies have used manipulations as powerful as these.

Ax found differences in the measured dimensions of autonomic activity during the fear and anger manipulations. The fear condition involved greater increases in respiration rate and skin conductance, and the overall pattern was similar to that induced by an injection of adrenaline. In the anger condition, there was greater muscle tension, blood pressure increased more, and heart rate decreased to a greater extent. The overall pattern here was similar to that induced by an injection containing both adrenaline and noradrenaline.

Ax's results are consistent with the idea that different patterns of autonomic activity are associated with different emotions. The differences are less dramatic than the apparent subjective differences between the emotions of anger and fear but still detectable using objective measures. The main problem of interpretation concerns the issue of whether autonomic differences depended on the induced emotions rather than other differences between experimental conditions. For example, participants who are warned that they may receive electric shocks may brace themselves for the anticipated pain, and participants being manhandled by a rude technician may try to pull themselves away from him. Neither of these patterns of behaviour are ones that happen every time someone is afraid or angry, and each reflects the particular way in which the emotion was induced in this specific study. How then can we tell whether the active ingredient of the manipulation was the emotion or something to do with the procedure for inducing that emotion? This issue arises because the ANS responds to various kinds of mental and physical activity, and not just to emotion-related responses. Ax's findings might reflect differences in responses to threatened shock and being manhandled rather than fear- and anger-related response more generally.

The best way of checking whether autonomic differences are genuinely related to emotion is to compare responses to the same emotions induced using different techniques. If fear is consistently associated with one response pattern and anger is consistently associated with another response pattern *regardless* of what caused it, then we can be confident that the ANS differences reflect emotions rather than specific induction procedures.

A study reported by Ekman, Levenson, and Friesen (1983) attempted to achieve just this. The researchers compared autonomic responses during six different 'basic' emotions induced using two different methods. One induction technique was based on imagery and involved asking participants to recall and vividly imagine a recent occasion when they had experienced each of the six emotions. The other induction technique was based on the idea that adopting the facial expression corresponding to an emotion also induces the subjective experience of that emotion. According to this **facial feedback hypothesis**, scrunching your nose and pulling back your top lip as if you had smelled something repulsive makes you feel disgusted, and flashing a bright welcoming smile makes you feel happy regardless of how you were feeling before you did it. Ekman and colleagues gave their participants step-by-step instructions intended to induce facial expressions associated with each of the six emotions (see Activity 10.1) and checked that the expressions matched the intended ones before taking the participants' autonomic measurements.

ACTIVITY 10.1

FACIAL FEEDBACK

Here are the instructions Ekman, Levenson, and Friesen (1983) used for putting participants' faces into a 'fear' expression:

A. Raise your brows and pull them together.

B. Now raise your upper eyelids.

C. Now stretch your lips horizontally, back towards your ears.

Here are pictures of an actor following these instructions at the three stages:

Source: Ekman, Levenson, and Friesen (1983). Reprinted with permission from AAAS and Paul Ekman Group LLC.

Try following these steps yourself and check how easily you can produce the required expression in a mirror. Are you feeling the emotion that is intended?

Now try getting a friend to adopt this expression without telling them what the expression is supposed to be or how it is supposed to make them feel. Ask them how they are feeling once you are satisfied that their face matches photo C.

Although the researchers found some autonomic differences between emotions, only one of the six manipulated emotions (anger) showed a wholly distinctive pattern of ANS activity in either task (i.e. one that was significantly different from *all* other sampled emotions). It was possible to distinguish three sets of distinct emotions using ANS data collected in the facial manipulation condition. Anger differed from all other sampled emotions by having either higher skin temperature or higher heart rate, whereas the other emotions fell into two distinguishable groups. One of these groups contained the very different emotions of happiness and disgust.

When autonomic responses were compared across the two induction techniques, the results were even less clear-cut. Only three of the possible differences between emotions were consistently obtained. Similarly, reviews of other research assessing autonomic differentiation suggest that the differences between emotions reported in individual studies do not always replicate in other studies that use different induction techniques (e.g. Cacioppo, Berntson, Larsen, Poehlmann, & Ito, 2000; Kreibig, 2010; Mauss & Robinson, 2009). Thus, reported autonomic differences may depend on techniques used to induce emotions rather than emotions themselves. Because any task involving preparation for action or allocation of attention to different aspects of a situation is likely to induce some autonomic patterning, non-emotional explanations for differences are clearly viable. Indeed, studies using imagery-based techniques such as recollection or mental simulation of emotional episodes tend to find much weaker autonomic differences, perhaps because imagery involves lower levels of preparation for physical activity than more directly involving tasks.

To help interpret the range of findings, Stemmler (1989) distinguished three hypotheses. The **non-specificity hypothesis** is that emotions are not associated with distinctive autonomic patterns. In this case, knowing how someone's ANS is reacting tells us nothing about what emotion they are experiencing. This seems unlikely because of apparent differences between broad classes of emotions associated with tension or excitement (e.g. anger, suspense, fear) and with calmer or more relaxed feelings (e.g. contentment, relief, sadness). Of course, different emotions are also more or less likely in different situations, which themselves induce autonomic changes. The problem of distinguishing emotion-specific ANS patterns from patterns associated with emotions for other reasons again applies here.

The **context-deviation hypothesis** acknowledges this distinction between emotion-specific and context-driven autonomic changes. In this view, each emotion is associated with an autonomic pattern, but the specific demands of any particular emotional situation shift this pattern away from this emotion-specific template. For example, if fear is an adaptive response to threatening situations requiring escape, then fearful situations require the body to prepare itself for escape by mobilizing metabolic resources (autonomic arousal) and, more specifically, delivering energy to the muscles involved in running away. However, in contemporary society, far fewer fear-eliciting events require precisely this form of direct escape and many instead involve quite different forms of activity or muscle movement (e.g. making excuses in order to 'escape' from a commitment that you are anxious about fulfilling). Because these escape goals require different movements from those involved in running away, the autonomic system's activity needs to adjust.

The **absolute specificity hypothesis** specifies that each emotion has a distinctive pattern of autonomic change that occurs *regardless* of the contexts in which it occurs. In other words, the emotion overrides other influences on autonomic activity, leaving a characteristic configuration of bodily change (e.g. James, 1884). Evidence gathered since James's time seems inconsistent with this level of autonomic differentiation (e.g. Levenson, 1994). Instead, many researchers believe that *some* emotions may be loosely associated with certain autonomic response variables in at least some contexts. Measuring autonomic activity can therefore provide important clues about a person's emotional state, especially when the simultaneous effects of extraneous variables on autonomic activity are also known. However, it does not give direct access to emotional differences.

Autonomic feedback hypothesis

In 1927, Walter Cannon published an article roundly criticizing his ex-teacher William James's feedback hypothesis. Cannon did not believe that ANS patterns are what make emotions different from each other. Instead he thought that different emotions involve the *same* pattern of autonomic activity, namely a generalized arousal reaction designed to prepare the body for a wide range of emergency situations. Clearly, if there are no autonomic differences between different emotions, then autonomic differences cannot explain differences between emotions. Further, inducing autonomic arousal by injecting participants with adrenaline does not consistently produce emotional experiences (e.g. Marañon, 1924), suggesting that autonomic activity of the kind associated with emotions is not enough to cause an emotion either.

Four decades later, Schachter (1964) modified feedback theory in response to Cannon's critique and Marañon's evidence. Like Cannon, Schachter believed that very different emotions often involve similar patterns of autonomic activity. Unlike Cannon, Schachter believed that feedback from this undifferentiated autonomic activity still plays a role in causing emotion. In particular, perceptions of arousal can help to explain the intensity of emotional experience. However, for the reasons stated above, undifferentiated arousal (the physiological factor) cannot explain the differentiated quality of an emotional experience, so Schachter believed that a second factor must be combined with arousal to produce specific emotions such as anger and joy.

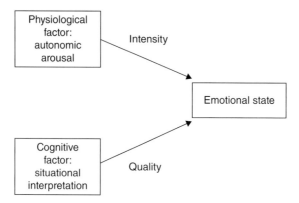

FIGURE 10.4 *Schachter's two-factor theory. According to Schachter's theory, two factors combine to produce an emotion. The intensity of the emotion depends on arousal whereas the quality of the emotion depends on interpretations of the situation.*
Source: Based on Schachter (1964).

If arousal can only tell us how strong our emotion is, what tells us what kind of emotion we are experiencing? According to **Schachter's two-factor theory**, the answer lies in how we interpret our perceived symptoms of arousal (the cognitive factor). If we are experiencing arousal while someone says something irritating, we may conclude that that person's irritating comments are what made us aroused and consequently experience our emotion as irritation or anger. If, on the other hand, we attribute our arousal to the attractiveness of the person with whom we are inter-acting, we may experience love (or at least lust). Finally, if we remember how strong the coffee was that we have just been drinking, we may conclude that our arousal has a non-emotional cause, and thus experience no emotional consequences (see Figure 10.4).

Schachter and Singer (1962) tested these ideas by independently manipulating physiological and cognitive factors in a clever and famous experiment. Participants were told that they would be injected with a new vitamin compound to assess its effects on perceptual performance. In fact, the injection contained either adrenaline (arousal condition) or a saline solution (placebo condition). The cognitive factor was manipulated using two separate procedures. First, the availability of a non-emotional explanation for any experienced arousal was manipulated by warning some of the participants who had been injected with adrenaline about the genuine side effects (non-emotional explanation condition) – for example, that their mouth might feel dry and their heart rate might increase. Other adrenaline-injected participants were misinformed about side effects by being warned of symptoms unrelated to arousal, such as ringing in the ears (misinformed condition), or were told that the injection had no side effects (ignorant condition).

Second, cognitions about possible emotional explanations for experienced arousal were provided by stage-managing two different situations. In both these conditions, participants were left in a waiting room with another supposed participant who was actually an accomplice of the experimenter and had been given instructions about how to act. In the euphoria condition, the accomplice played with objects left in the untidy room and tried to get the real participant to join in the fun and games. For example, he made paper planes and launched them around the room, screwed paper into a ball and tried to improvise a basketball game using the waste bin as a basket, and demonstrated his skills with some conveniently placed hula hoops. In the anger condition, the real and bogus participant both filled out an insulting question-naire containing increasingly personal questions about the bathing habits of family members and their mother's sexual infidelities. While answering the questions, the experimenter's accomplice became increasingly cross, then tore up the questionnaire before storming out of the room.

Schachter and Singer predicted that only participants who were aroused as a con-sequence of the adrenaline injection and did not have a non-emotional explanation for their arousal symptoms would attribute these symptoms to the emotional fea-tures of the situation and thus experience either euphoria or anger. In other words, emotion should depend on experiencing arousal and attributing it to emotional events. In fact, the results were less clear-cut. For example, in the euphoria condi-tion, participants given a placebo injection did not rate themselves as significantly less happy than participants given an adrenaline injection and misinformed about its side effects, suggesting that induced arousal did not increase emotion as intended. Even more problematically, misinformed participants showed moderately positive ratings of their emotional state in both the anger condition and the euphoria condi-tion (Zimbardo, Ebbeson, & Maslach, 1977), apparently undermining Schachter's claim that the same arousal state could be manipulated into widely contrasting emo-tional states.

In sum, Schachter and Singer's (1962) results were inconclusive (Reisenzein, 1983). Subsequent attempts to replicate aspects of the study have also yielded inconsistent findings (e.g. Erdmann & Janke, 1978; Marshall & Zimbardo, 1979; Maslach, 1979). None of the studies disproves Schachter's theory; they simply show how difficult it is to make the cognitive and physiological aspects of emotion vary independently. However, this observation itself might undermine the viability of Schachter's the-ory. The autonomic arousal we experience when emotional usually has an obvious emotional cause that is detected prior to our arousal reaction. Perceiving this cause often provides us with a full explanation for our emotional reaction, including its autonomic aspects, in advance. In other words, it might make more sense to see arousal symptoms as consequences of prior appraisals than as independent influences on emotion.

Central nervous system activity

Cannon (1927) believed that differences between emotions can be found in the brain rather than other parts of the body, but his search for these differences was limited by the technologies available at the time. Unsurprisingly, the development of brain-scanning techniques such as functional magnetic resonance imaging (fMRI; see Figure 10.5) has led to several studies designed to find brain regions that are activated specifically when a particular emotion occurs.

The interpretational problems surrounding such studies are similar to those apply-ing to studies of autonomic differentiation. It is important to establish that any meas-ured activity depends on the induced emotion itself and not simply on the specific method used to induce it. Again, this can be done by showing that the same region is active whenever the emotion occurs regardless of how it is induced.

Reviews of the literature on central nervous system activity during different emo-tions yield similar conclusions to the reviews of ANS activity mentioned above. For

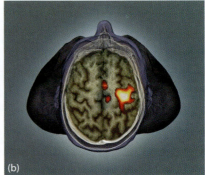

FIGURE 10.5 *Measuring brain activity using a functional magnetic resonance imaging (fMRI) scanner. fMRI measures the distribution of blood flow using a powerful electromagnet to detect movement of iron molecules. This potentially permits localization of brain regions that are active during different tasks (or when experiencing different emotions). (a) shows a scanner and (b) shows a brain scan with the illuminated area indicating activation of part of the motor cortex (the subject is moving their left hand).*
Source: (a) Brand X / Getty Images; (b) ZEPHYR / SCIENCE PHOTO LIBRARY.

example, Lindquist, Wager, Kober, Bliss-Moreau, and Barrett (2012) found little consistency across studies in brain responses associated with particular emotions. When consistency was found, it could often be explained in terms of some other process that relates to the emotion or its causation but is not one of the emotion's essential features.

One brain region that is commonly thought to be associated with emotion is the amygdala (see Figure 10.6). In particular, evidence reviewed by LeDoux (1996) led many researchers to believe that the amygdala is a neural structure responsible for producing the emotion of fear. However, this conclusion is only partly supported by Lindquist et al.'s review. Although amygdala activity was associated with *perceiving* fear in another person's face, it was not consistently associated with *feeling* fear personally. Further, the amygdala was also active when perceiving emotions other than fear from facial expressions. One possible conclusion is that the amygdala performs functions relating to fear (and some other emotions) but does not track this emotion itself. More specifically, several authors argue that amygdala activity relates to the detection of stimuli that are relevant to current goals or the allocation of attention to important objects in the environment (see e.g. Sander, Grafman, & Zalla, 2003; Whalen et al., 2013). Because fear tends to involve monitoring potential threats, amygdala activity often occurs when we are afraid. However, not only can fear occur without amygdala activity but also other emotions may be accompanied by amygdala activity.

According to Lindquist and colleagues, brain system activity does not specifically characterize any particular emotion (or even emotion more generally). A common set of interacting networks distributed around several brain regions generates emotions as well as other kinds of psychological states and processes. If this conclusion is correct, then we will not find differences between emotions simply by checking which part of the brain lights up. However, the evidence does not rule out distinctive but distributed brain circuits (rather than regions) underlying differences between emotions (e.g. Panksepp, 2000).

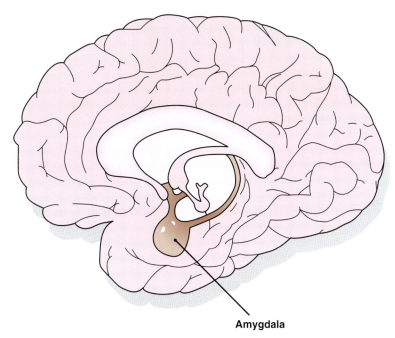

Amygdala

FIGURE 10.6 *The amygdala. This figure shows a sagittal section of the brain indicating the position of the amygdala in the brainstem (in the central lower part of the brain).*
Source: Davey (2014), figure 6.3, p. 154. Reproduced with permission of Wiley.

SECTION SUMMARY

- James posited that emotions depend on internal feedback.

- James acknowledged that bodily responses are not always easy to control, particularly those associated with the ANS.

- ANS activity is not only associated with emotional responses but also responds to changes in attention, activity levels, and so forth.

- The best way of checking whether ANS differences are genuinely related to emotion is to compare responses to the same emotions induced using different techniques.

- Ekman and colleagues (1983) did this by comparing autonomic responses during six different 'basic' emotions induced using two different methods. One induction technique was based on imagery; the other was based on the idea that adopting the facial expression corresponding to an emotion also induces the subjective experience of that emotion. However, these induction techniques did not produce consistent ANS patterns for the same emotions.

- In order to interpret a growing range of findings, Stemmler (1989) distinguished between three hypotheses: the non-specificity hypothesis, the context-deviation hypothesis, and the absolute specificity hypothesis.

- Cannon (1927) was critical of James's feedback hypothesis. Rather than thinking that ANS patterns are what make emotions different from each other, Cannon believed that emotion is associated with a generalized arousal reaction designed to prepare the body for a wide range of emergency situations.

- Schachter (1964) modified feedback theory even further: like Cannon, he believed that different emotions involve similar patterns of autonomic activity. Unlike Cannon, he believed that feedback from this undifferentiated autonomic activity still plays a role in causing emotion.

- According to Schachter's two-factor theory, arousal can tell us how strong our emotion is but it is our cognitive interpretation of arousal that determines which emotion we are experiencing.

- Brain-scanning techniques such as fMRI have led to several studies designed to find brain regions that are activated specifically when a particular emotion occurs.

- One brain region that is commonly thought to be associated with emotion is the amygdala, but the evidence suggests that the amygdala is sometimes active in non-emotional states and sometimes inactive in emotional states. The evidence for other brain regions yields similar conclusions.

FACIAL EXPRESSION

LEARNING OBJECTIVE 10.4

Compare arguments for and against the universality of facial expressions of emotion.

Before Darwin's time, it was widely believed that facial expressions were provided by God for the specific purpose of revealing people's emotions. Since Darwin, it has been widely believed that facial expressions evolved in order to express emotions. Both these views share the assumption that facial expression and emotion have an especially close relationship, and that different expressions characterize different emotions. After all, can't we tell that someone is happy when they give a broad, authentic smile, and can't we see someone's fear in their wide, darting eyes?

In fact, the nature of the association between facial expression and emotion may be less tight and less direct than intuitions might suggest. The present section considers evidence concerning facial differences between different emotions, and whether any such differences are universally found across all human societies. We will also evaluate the 'facial feedback hypothesis', which proposes that smiling is not only *associated* with happiness but can also *cause* it.

Facial differentiation

It seems that researchers can't tell precisely what emotion someone is feeling by measuring their autonomic responses or by checking which part of their brain is active. However, isn't there a quicker and easier way to detect someone's feelings: just by looking at their face? Aren't emotions written into people's expressions for all to see? For example, happy people smile and sad people have long faces. Angry people narrow their eyes and clench their teeth. Embarrassed people blush and look sheepish. Although there probably are some situations where facial movements transparently reveal people's emotional reactions, in fact emotion–expression connections may not always be as direct as we often suppose. This section reviews evidence concerning this issue.

FOCUS POINT 10.1

DISTINCTIVE FACIAL CONFIGURATIONS

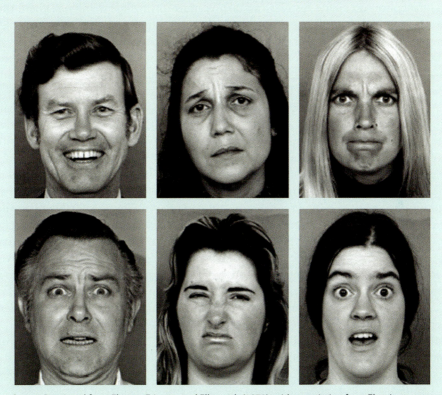

Source: Reprinted from Ekman, Friesen, and Ellsworth (1972), with permission from Elsevier.

The facial expressions shown here are part of a set selected and developed by Ekman and colleagues (see Ekman, Friesen, & Ellsworth, 1972). When asked to choose from the list – happiness, sadness, anger, fear, disgust, and surprise – English speakers consistently agree about which photograph expresses which of these emotions. However, this does not mean that these expressions are commonly associated with these emotions in everyday life. In fact, an emotion may occur without the supposedly characteristic expression and the expression may occur without the supposedly corresponding emotion (e.g. Fernández-Dols & Crivelli, 2013; Reisenzein, Studtmann, & Horstmann, 2013).

It is also unclear whether expressing emotions is the main function of these facial positions. If participants are not told to work out what emotion a face is expressing, their interpretations often refer to situations rather than emotions (e.g. Frijda, 1953). For example, the woman in the centre of the bottom row looks like she has smelled something revolting, and the man in the top-left corner looks like he is offering a friendly greeting. Each of the faces contains features that provide perceivers with information about the person's relationship to what is happening in addition to any emotional meaning. For example, the eyes tell us about attention and alertness and the stretched or relaxed muscles tell us about levels of tension. Faces can certainly be used to convey emotionally relevant information but this does not necessarily mean that they consistently or directly express emotions (see Parkinson, 2005).

Many theorists believe that some distinctive facial expressions are innately associated with emotions for adaptive reasons. For example, Izard (1978) argues that facial positions corresponding roughly to adult expressions of **basic emotions** such as anger, fear, and happiness are shown by infants as soon as muscular coordination is sufficient to permit their production. However, more recent evidence questions whether these infant expressions necessarily reflect the differentiated emotional meanings that they seem to convey. Instead, Camras (1992) suggests that an infant's facial response to generic distress can take various forms depending on where they are directing their attention and how unpleasant the situation is, but does not reflect the particular quality of the current emotional situation (see also Camras, Sullivan, & Michel, 1993). In other words, similar faces might be seen regardless of whether an infant is frustrated, anxious, or in pain, and different faces may occur in the same emotion depending on factors such as emotional intensity and attentional activity.

Another researcher who believes that different facial expressions are universally associated with distinct basic emotions is Ekman (e.g. 1972, 2003). For him, activation of any particular emotion necessarily involves activation of an associated motor program that normally produces its characteristic facial expression. However, he also believes that people learn to control and regulate the facial impulses associated with emotions. Under some circumstances, then, expressions do not reveal a person's true emotions because the tell-tale signals are covered up (see Figure 10.7). **Display rules** are socialized cultural norms about when and where it is appropriate to show or not show a given emotion. They guide people's attempts to suppress or exaggerate their expressions. For example, funeral ceremonies encourage different degrees of overt distress and crying from country to country. In some societies and historical periods, professional mourners wail and shriek in order to encourage others to join in the crying. By contrast, Christian funerals in contemporary Anglo-American contexts tend to encourage the bereaved to hold back their tears.

Ekman's neurocultural theory thus claims that facial expressions resulting from a biologically determined (neural) program shaping facial expression are regulated to meet cultural norms. Fridlund (1994) questions this two-process account by suggesting that facial displays are sensitive to the social context from the moment they are activated (see also Parkinson, Fischer, & Manstead, 2005). Working from evolutionary principles, Fridlund argues that the basic function of facial movements of this kind is to regulate the behaviour of conspecifics by signalling information about social motives. For example, an 'angry' scowl is in fact one of many possible threat displays

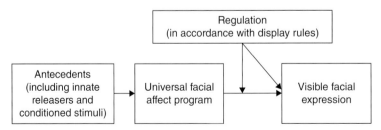

FIGURE 10.7 *Ekman's neurocultural theory. This figure depicts processes contributing to facial expression according to Ekman's neurocultural theory. Emotional events activate neural programs that output motor signals specifying a facial expression characterizing one of the basic emotions. However, facial muscles are also controlled by regulatory processes that can be activated by display rules. What shows on the face may reflect a combination of these two kinds of process.*

that warn another person to back off to avoid being attacked. For Fridlund, a system that automatically expressed subjective internal states to others regardless of social context would not make adaptive sense for at least two reasons. First, the information would not be directly informative about future actions. Second, revealing the information may put the sender at a disadvantage (e.g. by exposing weaknesses to a potential competitor). For this second reason, facial displays need to be sensitive to the identities of other people present to avoid giving away damaging information to those who might exploit it.

For Fridlund, facial expressions do not signify specifically emotional information in the first place. Instead they communicate 'social motives' to others. They are not expressions of some internal state trying to get out into the social world, but displays conveying to others what one is about to do (or wants those others to do). There are also other alternatives to the view that faces directly express emotions. For example, facial configurations might represent action tendencies (Frijda & Tcherkassof, 1997), appraisals (Scherer, 1992; Smith & Scott, 1997), or dimensions of affect such as pleasure or arousal (Russell, 1997; Woodworth & Schlosberg, 1954) rather than distinct emotions. In any of these cases, facial information provides clues that can help us to infer another person's emotional state but do not directly indicate the emotion itself.

Are there universal facial expressions?

Are basic emotions associated with distinctive biologically programmed facial expressions in all humans, as Ekman and Izard suggest? This might seem an easy question to answer. All we need do is observe whether people from different societies show the same expressions for the same emotions. Unfortunately, this turns out to be more difficult than it sounds.

The first problem is finding comparable situations that consistently generate the same emotion in a relatively pure form across all cultures. This is difficult because similar events bring different emotional consequences depending on cultural socialization and learning experiences (as acknowledged by Ekman's neurocultural theory). What makes an English person 'angry' may be quite different from what makes someone from Ifaluk (a Micronesian atoll) experience 'song' (Lutz, 1988). Further, how can we be sure that the words describing these 'emotions' are direct translations in the first place? Perhaps 'song' is not precisely what English speakers mean by 'anger' (Lutz, 1988).

Different display rules operating in different cultures also make it difficult to test whether observed expressions reflect any underlying facial action program. If members of a society have learned to keep their displays of anger in check across a range of social situations, then it will be harder to observe their anger expressions when relevant situations occur.

Partly for these reasons, the most common strategy for testing whether basic emotions are associated with characteristic facial expressions is less direct. Rather than observing facial reactions to emotions, researchers typically show participants from various societies pictures or videos of facial expressions and ask them to make judgements about their emotional meaning (e.g. Jack, Garrod, Yu, Caldara, & Schyns, 2012). The idea is that, if an expression has the same emotional meaning regardless of culture, then this consistent association probably reflects the fact that different cultures actually do express these emotions using these expressions. However, even if the results are positive, this inference may be questionable (Russell & Fernández-Dols, 1997).

Perhaps the most famous studies using the expression–judgement method were conducted by Ekman and colleagues in the 1960s and 1970s (e.g. Ekman & Friesen, 1971). In order to rule out the possibility that members of other cultures had learned to recognize the emotional meaning of Western facial expressions by observing Westerners directly or seeing how they react in films, Ekman's research team visited remote cultures in Borneo and New Guinea that had had very little previous contact with people outside their society.

The investigators showed tribespeople a series of pictures carefully selected to provide clear expressions that American participants consistently allocated to six different emotion categories: anger, sadness, happiness, fear, disgust, and surprise (all so-called basic emotions). The participants' task was to say which of the six possible emotions each facial picture represented using a multiple-choice question. Because there were only six emotion categories provided as possible answers, guessing would give the correct response on a sixth of trials. Participants did significantly better than this for most of the pictured expressions.

At the time of publication, the headline finding was that even members of these remote cultures performed significantly above chance, indicating clearly that there is a universal component to performance at this judgement task. However, the fact that participants were clearly not just guessing when they allocated the faces to emotion categories does not prove that they were able to detect the specific emotional meaning of each presented face directly and perfectly.

Subsequent commentators have emphasized that performance on this task fell short of what we would expect if participants already had clear knowledge of the face's emotional meanings (e.g. Nelson & Russell, 2013; Russell, 1994). Less than half of participants from isolated cultures labelled the intended fear face as 'fear', and less than a third labelled the intended disgust face as 'disgust'. By contrast, more than 90% allocated the smiling face to the happiness category (perhaps because happiness was the only pleasant emotion option available).

Why did participants not perform better if they were familiar with distinctive expressions corresponding to basic emotion categories, as Ekman predicted? The faces were preselected to provide emotional information as clearly and consistently as possible (e.g. to be uncontaminated by display rules) and only one of the six available response options should have been clearly correct if neurocultural theory is true.

Rather than showing that participants universally recognize the same emotions from the same expressions, the results suggest that performance is inconsistent across emotions, expressions, and cultures (see also Jack et al., 2012). Performance on the task clearly depends on participants' cultural background (see Figure 10.8), implying that there are cross-cultural differences even in judgements made about facial expressions selected specifically to exclude socialized display rules (see also Elfenbein & Ambady, 2002).

As Nelson and Russell (2013) and Russell (1994) point out, above-chance performance on this kind of judgement task need not reflect a knowledge of specific emotional meanings of the presented facial expressions. Instead, simply being able to extract some emotion-relevant information from some faces would be sufficient. For example, if we assume that faces universally convey information about experienced pleasure (via upturned or downturned lips; e.g. Russell, 1997), this already allows better-than-chance performance. Because only one face and one emotion word are

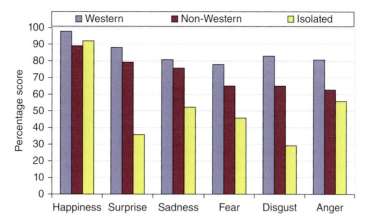

FIGURE 10.8 *Performance on judgement tasks in different cultures. This figure shows the percentage of participants from different cultures who allocate faces intended to express basic emotions to the predicted emotion category. Percentages fall in societies that are progressively more distant from Western culture, except in the case of 'happy' expressions.*

Source: Adapted from Russell (1994). American Psychological Association.

unequivocally positive (the smile and 'happiness'), there are only five instead of six possible emotion options for the other faces. Picking up information about arousal (from eye-widening), muscular tension, and intensity or direction of attention (e.g. from staring or averted eyes) permits further deductions about possible correct and incorrect answers. For example, the fixed forward stare and tensed muscles visible in the 'anger' face make it unlikely that participants will select sadness as the appropriate unpleasant emotion. Something about facial expression clearly is universal, but is this something really to do with distinctive characteristics of categorically different emotions, rather than less directly emotion-relevant information?

Are facial expressions shown consistently in emotional situations?

A further problem is that evidence from judgement studies does not directly address the issue of what faces people actually show when they experience different emotions. To clarify this point, Russell (1994) imagines how someone far from home might try to convey hunger before learning the language of the country they are visiting. One possibility would be to point at your mouth and rub your tummy. It seems highly likely that this strategy would be successful (at above-chance levels) across a wide range of societies. But the fact that the locals might correctly infer that you are hungry does not prove that hungry people typically go around pointing at their mouths and rubbing their tummies. Perhaps, then, some of the photographs of facial expressions used by Ekman's research team depict ways of acting out or otherwise communicating emotional meanings rather than spontaneous expressions of the associated emotions themselves.

Few studies have directly investigated the actual facial expressions occurring during the experience of different emotions across different cultures (see Matsumoto & Wilson, 2008, for an exception). However, emotional situations produce inconsistent facial expressions even within a single culture. Close correspondence between any emotion and any particular pattern of facial movement is rarely found in either naturalistic research (see Fernández-Dols & Crivelli, 2013) or laboratory experiments (see Reisenzein et al., 2013). Even when display rules do not seem to be in operation, there are cases where strong emotions are reported but the predicted facial expression does not occur. This may mean that each emotion is associated with more than one expression or that our emotion categories are too coarsely defined to pick out emotional states that specifically correspond with facial movements. No one believes that facial expressions are wholly independent of emotions. However, there remain questions about whether they directly index emotions themselves or relate to processes that are broadly associated with emotions in certain contexts (e.g. attentional activity and action preparation).

Facial feedback

Cannon's criticisms of James's theory fell squarely on the characteristics of *autonomic* activity that made it an inadequate explanation of differentiated emotions. However, James did not believe that only autonomic responses provide the kind of internal feedback that produces differentiated emotional experiences. Some subsequent theorists have suggested that facial muscles can provide precisely the kind of rapid and differentiated feedback that would be capable of generating distinct emotions (e.g. Tomkins, 1962). Perhaps, then, facial feedback rather than autonomic feedback is what makes different emotions feel different (see Activity 10.1 above).

Laird (1974) conducted one of the first experimental investigations of this facial feedback hypothesis. He told participants that he was interested in the activity of their facial muscles during a perceptual task and attached electrodes to their faces ostensibly in order to measure this activity. Precise electrode placement supposedly required participants to relax or contract certain facial muscles, which the experimenter touched one by one until the resulting facial position approximated that of a smile or an angry frown (although participants were not told that this was the intention). Participants were then shown a series of slides showing pictures of children playing (positive) or members of the Ku Klux Klan (negative). After each picture, participants were asked to rate their current emotional experience (supposedly in order to factor out its confounding effects on facial activity).

Participants reported significantly greater pleasant feelings when their faces had been manipulated into a smile than when they were frowning. Laird argued that interoceptive information provided by the face leads to inferences about the quality of emotional state, just as Schachter had earlier argued that arousal information leads to inferences about the intensity of felt emotion. Consistent with this inferential account was a participant's report of his experience during the experiment:

> When my jaw was clenched and my brows down I tried not to be angry but it just fit the position. … I found my thoughts wandering to things that made me angry which is sort of silly I guess. I knew I was in an experiment and knew I had no reason to feel that way, but I just lost control. (Laird, 1974, p. 480)

Although Laird did not believe that facial feedback typically operates at such a conscious and explicit level, he did endorse the idea that signals from the face contribute to the perception of being emotional – a view that he saw as consistent with James's original formulation of feedback theory (Laird & Bresler, 1990).

Laird's findings suggest that facial feedback has a small but significant effect on emotion. However, they also raise some interpretational issues. First, because only positive and negative expressions were compared, no direct conclusions are possible about the effects of facial feedback on the specific quality of emotion rather than the general dimension of pleasantness. Second, participants were clearly aware that the experimenter was manipulating their facial muscles and may have drawn conclusions about his intentions that in turn affected their emotion ratings. For example, if they recognized that their face had been put into a smiling position, they may have suspected that the experimenter was interested in the effects of smiling on the emotion ratings they were subsequently asked to make. Laird checked for possible demand characteristics of this kind in a postexperimental interview and excluded from his analysis 8 participants (out of 45) who mentioned possible connections between facial position and emotion. It is possible that other participants also considered the same possibility but did not explicitly mention it in the postexperimental interview (perhaps because they did not want to undermine the experimenter's attempt at deception).

Tourangeau and Ellsworth (1979) used a similar facial muscle manipulation to compare two negative expressions ('fear' and 'sadness') with neutral control conditions to establish whether facial feedback can affect the specific quality of unpleasant emotions rather than simply how pleasant participants feel. In this study, facial feedback had no significant effects on participants' emotion reports. However, there was some evidence that holding facial muscles in a fixed position can increase autonomic arousal, suggesting that some apparent effects of facial feedback may be a result of effort or discomfort rather than interoceptive emotion information.

One of the cleverest manipulations of facial feedback was devised by Strack et al. (1988), who tried to minimize participants' awareness that their faces were being manipulated by using a surreptitious procedure. Their study was presented as an investigation of how people cope with disabilities preventing the use of hands for everyday activities. Participants performed a series of tasks including one where they had to write while holding the pen in their mouths. The experimental manipulation involved how they were told to hold the pen, either between their teeth, thus inducing a facial position similar to a smile, or between their lips, thus inducing a more negative facial position (see Figure 10.9).

In Strack et al.'s study 1, cartoons were rated as more funny by participants in the teeth condition than by those in the lips condition. In study 2, a similar effect was found for ratings of amusement but not for ratings of how funny the slides were. Neither effect was large, and statistical reliability depended on adopting a liberal criterion for significance (one-tailed test). Later studies by Andreasson and Dimberg (2008) and Soussignan

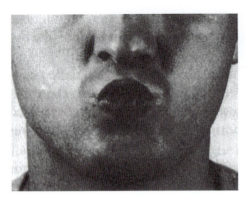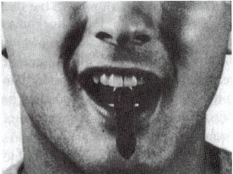

FIGURE 10.9 *Strack, Martin, and Stepper's facial feedback manipulation. This figure shows the manipulation used by Strack and colleagues to test the facial feedback hypothesis. The mouth on the left is holding the pen between the lips, producing an apparently negative facial expression. The mouth on the right is holding the pen between the teeth, producing what appears to be a smile.*

Source: From Strack, Martin, and Stepper (1988). American Psychological Association, reprinted with permission.

(2002) included conditions that replicated Strack and colleagues' original procedure but failed to obtain significant effects. It remains unclear whether the statistical trends apparent in the original research are directly replicable (Wagenmakers et al., 2016).

Other research has assessed the facial feedback hypothesis by examining the responses of people who have been injected with Botox as a cosmetic treatment (see e.g. Davis, Senghas, Brandt, & Ochsner, 2010; Hennenlotter et al., 2009). Botox is a toxin that is targeted at facial muscle activity to give the skin a smoother appearance. The paralysis it induces removes most channels of facial feedback. However, Botox treatment clearly serves emotional needs for those who pay for it, and it is difficult to assess its emotional effects against a directly comparable control group. As in other studies, it is difficult to be sure that any effects on emotion depend specifically on the absence of feedback. The findings of the Botox studies also seem inconsistent across different dependent measures, providing no direct evidence that Botox specifically targets the emotional experiences supposedly corresponding to the muscles that are paralysed.

FOCUS POINT 10.2

EMOTIONAL CONSEQUENCES OF BOTOX TREATMENT

Having your face injected with a toxin that paralyses muscles may seem an extreme measure for smoothing wrinkles, but Botox treatment has become widespread since its introduction in the early 1990s. The visible effects on appearance may bring benefits but some psychologists have worried about more negative consequences. The facial feedback hypothesis implies that the reduction in facial responsiveness induced by Botox will also lead to diminished emotional experience, including a reduction in positive as well as negative emotions. Even negative feelings may serve important functions by informing us about the rewards and costs of particular actions (e.g. Damasio, 1994). For example, feeling anxious about trying something new may encourage appropriate caution. If losing facial feedback reduces the level of this emotional information, then our decisions may be worse. Facial movements also serve interpersonal functions during social interactions. It is more polite to smile when someone tells us their good news than to maintain a fixed expression, for example. It therefore seems likely that people who have had their faces treated with Botox will suffer disruption in their social relationships due to their failure to provide differentiated facial communications.

In sum, studies investigating the facial feedback hypothesis have produced mixed findings. There is little evidence that facial feedback affects the specific quality rather than the intensity of positive or negative emotions. Most studies find small effects on the pleasantness of participants' feelings, but these effects can often be explained by demand characteristics or variables that are confounded with the facial feedback manipulation, such as muscular effort. None of the research supports the idea that facial feedback alone is enough to generate a full-blown emotion. Indeed, if this were possible, why would people often struggle to control their emotions? If all it really took to feel happy was to put on a smile, why wouldn't people do that most of the time?

SECTION SUMMARY

- Since Darwin, it has been widely believed that facial expressions evolved in order to express emotions.
- Emotion–expression connections may not always be as direct as we often suppose.
- According to Ekman (and others), different facial expressions are universally associated with distinct basic emotions.
- In this view, activation of any particular emotion necessarily involves activation of an associated motor program that normally produces its characteristic facial expression, which can be regulated.
- Display rules are socialized cultural norms about when and where it is appropriate to show or not show a given emotion.
- However, according to Fridlund, facial expressions do not signify specifically emotional information in the first place. Instead they communicate social motives to others.
- It is difficult to determine whether or not there are universal facial expressions. The first problem is finding comparable situations that consistently generate the same emotion in a relatively pure form across all cultures. Secondly, evidence from judgement studies does not directly address the issue of what faces people really show when they experience different emotions. Few studies have directly investigated the actual facial expressions occurring during the experience of different emotions across different cultures.
- It has been argued that facial rather than autonomic feedback is what makes different emotions feel different, but studies investigating the facial feedback hypothesis have produced mixed findings.

APPRAISAL

LEARNING OBJECTIVE 10.5

Demonstrate an understanding of how appraisal affects emotion and vice versa.

For many theorists, the key factor that makes emotions emotional and different emotions different from each other is appraisal. But what is appraisal? Most definitions are relatively inclusive. Appraisal means coming to the implicit or explicit conclusion that what is happening is personally significant in a particular way, involving either positive or negative implications for your current goals or concerns.

In other words, appraisal theories propose that people get emotional when they have recognized that something matters to them. The way in which they perceive it as mattering determines what kind of emotional reaction ensues. Appraisal is not a single cognitive process because people may reach conclusions that something matters (and about how it matters) by a variety of routes. Some of these routes involve very low levels of information processing (e.g. perceiving the sudden approach of a looming object or the restrictive tightness of someone's grip), while others involve more deliberative reasoning (e.g. working out that someone's apparently innocuous comment may have been intended as an insult). However the conclusion is reached, its nature is believed to determine the quality of the resulting emotion (Smith & Lazarus, 1993).

For appraisal theorists, emotions depend on extracting information from what is happening in the world around (and relating this information to personal concerns) rather than picking up interoceptive information from inside the body (as feedback theories suggest). This section begins by considering whether different emotions are genuinely characterized by different patterns of appraisal (just as we earlier considered whether they are characterized by different patterns of autonomic activity or facial movement) before moving on to the question of whether appraisal usually or always *causes* emotions.

Appraisal and emotion differentiation

A key assumption of appraisal theory is that different appraisal patterns are what make different emotions different. A number of models have specified which appraised conclusions a person must reach in order to experience different emotions. These models share many similarities, suggesting general agreement about many of the relevant appraisal dimensions (e.g. Ellsworth & Scherer, 2003).

Smith and Lazarus's (1993) model provides a good example. For them, the primary appraisal of **motivational relevance** is necessary for all emotions because people do not feel emotional about events that have no bearing on what they want or do not want to happen. **Motivational congruence** reflects an assessment about whether events are helping or hindering progress towards goals. Appraising events as motivationally congruent produces pleasant emotions whereas appraising events as motivationally incongruent produces unpleasant emotions.

The particular quality of experienced unpleasant or pleasant emotion depends on secondary appraisals concerning options for coping with what is happening. In particular, Smith and Lazarus argue that people appraise the extent to which they are able to deal with the challenges presented by the situation (problem-focused coping potential) and with the emotions that these challenges are likely to induce (emotion-focused coping potential). Further, they appraise whether challenges are likely to persist in future (future expectancy) and who is accountable for what is happening (self-accountability and other-accountability).

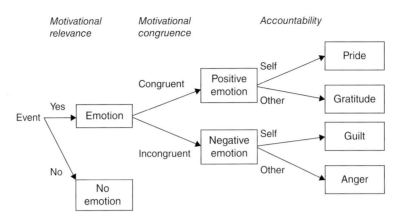

FIGURE 10.10 *Appraisals associated with contrasting emotions. This figure shows how different appraisals of an event are associated with different emotions. If the person appraises an event as motivationally relevant (first column) then there should be some kind of emotional reaction. If the person appraises this event as motivationally congruent (second column), the associated emotion should be positive. If the person appraises themself as personally accountable for this motivationally congruent event, they should experience the specific emotion of pride.*
Source: Based on Smith and Lazarus (1993).

According to this model, knowing a person's appraisal pattern tells you what kind of emotion they are experiencing. For example, events appraised as motivationally relevant, motivationally incongruent, and attributed to someone else's agency (other-accountable) are associated with anger, whereas events appraised as motivationally relevant, motivationally incongruent, and attributed to one's own agency (self-accountable) are associated with guilt (see Figure 10.10).

Smith and Ellsworth (1985) made one of the first systematic attempts to establish that different emotions are characterized by different patterns of appraisal, testing an earlier version of the model presented in Figure 10.10. In their study, participants were asked to recall occasions when they had experienced pure examples of 15 different emotional states (including anger, guilt, sadness, and pride) and describe them in detail. They were then asked to rate these experiences along various appraisal dimensions. For example, participants rated how responsible they thought that 'someone or something other than yourself was for having brought about the events' (Smith & Ellsworth, 1985, p. 822) that had made them feel the emotion (other-accountability), and how personally responsible they thought that they were (self-accountability).

Discriminant analysis suggested that the 15 sampled emotions could be correctly predicted on 40% of occasions using the six measured dimensions of appraisal (see Figure 10.11). Although this is well above the chance level of classification, it does not provide strong evidence that emotions can be *fully* distinguished using appraisal information. In other words, knowing how someone is evaluating and interpreting what is currently happening seems to provide important clues about what kind of emotion they are experiencing but often will not lead you to the correct answer.

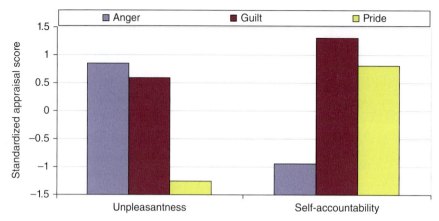

FIGURE 10.11 *Appraisal differences between anger, guilt, and pride. This figure shows reported differences in appraisals associated with three of the emotions sampled by Smith and Ellsworth (1985). Both anger and guilt are associated with high unpleasantness (motivational incongruence) whereas pride is associated with low unpleasantness. Further, both guilt and pride are relatively high in self-accountability, whereas anger is low on self-accountability.*

Source: Based on Smith and Ellsworth (1985).

DESCRIBING EMOTIONS TO MR SPOCK

Smith and Ellsworth's (1985) procedure may have overestimated the strength of association between appraisal profiles and particular emotions. Participants were asked to select 'pure' cases of the emotions and to describe them as if speaking to someone who has never experienced an emotion (such as Mr Spock from *Star Trek*). Participants may therefore have been careful to select 'logical' examples of emotion for the purposes of the study. For example, participants may have decided to report on examples of anger associated with other-blame because it is easier to justify anger when someone else did something blameworthy. Thus, the emotions sampled by Smith and Ellsworth may have included a higher proportion of reasonable cases than might be found in life outside the laboratory.

Parkinson (1999) specifically instructed participants to report on 'unreasonable' as well as 'reasonable' examples of anger and guilt and found that the appraisal patterns characterizing these emotions were less clearly differentiated when unreasonable examples were recalled. Similarly, studies by Kuppens and colleagues (e.g. Kuppens, Van Mechelen, Smits, & de Boeck, 2003; Kuppens, Van Mechelen, Smits, de Boeck, & Ceulemans, 2007) suggest that the appraisal patterns associated with 'anger' can vary across situations and people. Appraisal differences between emotions may be less consistent than previously believed.

A deeper problem concerns the measurement of appraisal and emotion in this kind of research. In particular, participants are often asked to characterize their own experience in emotional terms without any independent confirmation that the correct emotion was actually experienced. Participants also report on their own appraisals in these studies, so the findings actually reflect associations between their reports of emotion and appraisal rather than direct associations between emotions and appraisals themselves. Of course, participants are often in a better position than observers to explain what they are experiencing or have experienced, and it would be surprising if their reports bore no relation to reality. Nevertheless, associations between appraisal and emotion reports may simply confirm that people tend to characterize their emotional experience in appraisal terms, especially when trying to explain or justify it to others.

Despite the shortcomings of the evidence, few researchers deny that there is some association between emotions and appraisals. When angry, we are more likely to feel that something external is to blame for something bad that has happened than when we are experiencing relief or pride, for example. Even if the correspondence between emotions and appraisal patterns is imperfect, emotion carries implications for appraisal, and appraisal carries implications for emotion.

Most theorists would go further by acknowledging that certain kinds of appraisal make it more likely that you will experience a related emotion (e.g. blaming someone else increases the probability of anger). Thus, appraisal is not only associated with emotions but also contributes to their causation under some circumstances. But how central is appraisal's causal role? The next section addresses this question.

Appraisal as a cause of emotion

Evidence that appraisals *can* influence emotions was provided by Lazarus's team in the early 1960s. Participants were shown films selected to induce emotional stress. One of these films was called *Subincision* and depicted a rite of passage into manhood wherein adolescent aboriginal boys in Australia undergo an apparently painful operation on their genitals. Speisman, Lazarus, Mordkoff, and Davison (1964) attempted to manipulate appraisals of the stressful content of this film by changing the film's soundtrack. Some viewers heard that the operation was actually not painful and that the ritual was an occasion for joy (denial condition). Others were encouraged to see the depicted events from a detached anthropological perspective (intellectualization). In a third condition, the voiceover drew viewers' attention to the most painful aspects of the operation (trauma).

Skin conductance was consistently highest in the trauma condition. Participants in the intellectualization soundtrack condition also tended to show lower skin conductance than controls. Thus, the nature of the soundtrack apparently made a difference to the strength of participants' emotional reactions.

For Speisman et al., this and other studies provide support for the notion that appraisals influence emotions causally. However, participants may have responded emotionally to what the voiceover was saying or to the tone of voice in which it was said rather than with altered appraisals of the film's content. The soundtracks also drew the viewers' attention to particular events in the film, meaning that participants probably processed different information in the first place before any appraisal took place. For example, participants in the intellectualization and denial conditions probably paid less attention to the incision made to the boy's penis when the sharpened stone was applied and more attention to the broader social scene, including onlookers' reactions.

Regardless of the specific interpretation of Speisman et al.'s findings, it seems clear that providing people with different information or changing their perspective on events can make a difference to how they react emotionally to those events. Whether these changes depend specifically on appraisals partly depends on how inclusive the concept of appraisal is intended to be.

Subsequent research has extended these findings by assessing effects on the quality as well as the quantity of emotion. A consistent finding is that people can react with different emotions when events are described to them or unfold in different ways (e.g. Roseman & Evdokas, 2004; Smith & Lazarus, 1993). A promising approach to testing causation is to manipulate real-time events that are programmed into video games such as PacMan, where players are represented by moving shapes in a maze that can be chased, blocked, receive rewards, and so on (see e.g. Van Reekum et al., 2004). Such techniques have provided limited evidence that events associated with particular appraisals (such as motivational congruence) affect participants' self-reported emotions or emotion-related responses of the face or autonomic nervous system. However, to date, no published study has systematically manipulated a wide range of appraisals and assessed their differential effects on a variety of emotions. It is also unclear whether the effects of these manipulations are genuinely mediated by appraisals and whether they generalize to directly involving dynamic situations.

FOCUS POINT 10.4

SOCIAL APPRAISALS

In Speisman, Lazarus, Mordkoff, and Davison's film experiments, the events provoking emotional reactions did not directly affect participants themselves but happened to characters shown on a screen. Identifying at some level with another person makes you care about what happens to them so that you appraise events affecting them as personally relevant too. Similar reasoning helps to explain why we have emotional reactions to events affecting other members of a group with which we identify even when we are not directly affected ourselves (Smith, 1993). For instance, sports fans respond emotionally depending on the performance of the team that they support.

Doosje, Branscombe, Spears, and Manstead (1998) showed that group-based appraisals can affect emotional reactions independently of individual appraisals. They found that participants reported higher levels of group-based guilt after hearing that other members of their group had made biased judgements about an out-group even when their own personal judgements were unbiased. These results help to explain why members of national groups can feel guilty about the sins of their ancestors even when they have no personal responsibility for them (e.g. German guilt about Nazi atrocities during World War II; Branscombe & Doosje, 2004). Researchers have also found that group-based rather than individual appraisals affect emotions other than guilt, including fear (Dumont, Yzerbyt, Wigboldus, & Gordijn, 2003), schadenfreude (Leach, Spears, Branscombe, & Doosje, 2003), and anger (Yzerbyt, Dumont, Gordijn, & Wigboldus, 2002).

Interpersonal processes can also shape appraisals (e.g. Manstead & Fischer, 2001; Parkinson, 2001). For example, in social referencing, toddlers use information provided by adult emotional expressions to help them appraise ambiguous events. Sorce, Emde, Campos, and Klinnert (1985) placed a toddler at one side of a glass floor stretching across a small but unbridgeable chasm. At the other side of this 'visual cliff' was the toddler's mother. Toddlers were uncertain whether it was safe to proceed onto the glass, and characteristically looked in turn at the cliff and their mother in order to get further information. When the mother smiled, the toddler almost always crossed the glass. When the mother showed a 'fear' face, the toddler did not cross. In other words, the toddler's appraisal of a potentially dangerous object was negotiated with another person rather than individually computed. Parkinson, Phiri, and Simons (2012) demonstrated similar effects during interactions between adults. Taken together, these findings suggest that appraisals may arise from social as well as individual processes (e.g. Parkinson, 2001). One possible implication is that therapies targeting maladaptive appraisals may need to explore the social–relational context sustaining those appraisals (e.g. family therapy or couples therapy).

Affective primacy

Evidence presented in previous sections suggests that appraisals (or related variables) can play a causal role in determining the intensity and quality of emotions. But how central is appraisal's causal role? For Lazarus (1991), appraisal fully explains emotion (sufficiency), and emotion is impossible without prior appraisal (necessity). In theory, a single case of emotion occurring in the absence of appraisal would disprove the necessity hypothesis. In practice, things are not so simple.

Zajonc (1980) argued that emotion often shapes cognitions such as appraisals rather than vice versa. In his **affective primacy** view, feelings often arise before any kind of cognitive interpretations. For example, you don't need to think about the precise combination of flavours before enjoying a plate of food (see Figure 10.12). More typically, you work out what it is that tastes so good only to explain why you already like it. Does this mean that we can react emotionally before appraising something? Can Lazarus's theory be falsified in such a straightforward way?

The answer partly depends on what we mean by 'emotion' and what we mean by 'appraisal'. If appraisal includes any process involved in registering the pleasant or unpleasant qualities of a stimulus, then the example of enjoying food does not rule out appraisal. Correspondingly, if emotion is restricted to responses to events that involve a deeper appreciation of personal significance, then even the absence of apparent appraisal in food enjoyment does not disprove Lazarus's theory because the response does not count as emotional in the first place.

A published debate between Lazarus (1984) and Zajonc (1984) mainly involved disputes about the interpretation of evidence of this kind. Lazarus rejected Zajonc's examples of apparently appraisal-free emotions by arguing either that they weren't real emotions or that they weren't really appraisal-free. For example, the phenomenon of taste aversion involves animals learning quickly and easily what taste cues are associated with subsequent illness even if the illness occurs long after the taste was originally presented (e.g. Seligman & Hager, 1972). This phenomenon is explained by the adaptive advantage conferred by being able to learn easily which foods might be poisonous (prepared association). Taste aversion can even happen when illness is induced after the animal has been rendered unconscious (e.g. Garcia & Rusiniak, 1980). For Zajonc, this suggests that the emotional reaction to a now disgusting food does not depend on prior appraisal of its qualities. After all, the information concerning its negative aspects was never conscious. Lazarus responds by arguing that taste aversion is a reflex reaction rather than a genuine emotion. However unpleasant the food may now seem to the animal, the fact that it now reacts inflexibly to the food means that the reaction is not an emotional one. Thus, Lazarus implies that the only kinds of response that should count as emotions are those that depend on processes operating at a higher level than mere reflexes, and for him these processes should count as appraisals.

In apparent cases of emotion without appraisal where it is more obvious that the reaction is emotional, Lazarus argues that appraisal is not really absent, just difficult to detect. The fact that someone cannot report on a process explicitly does not rule out unconscious appraisal. How else could an individual's cognitive system know that an emotional reaction needs to be generated except by registering the personal significance of what is happening at some level?

FIGURE 10.12 *Feelings about food. How do you feel about the pictures shown here? What if you could actually smell or taste the food on the plates? What if you are feeling particularly hungry or full up? Do your feelings depend on appraisals?*

Sources: (a) Supot Suebwongsa / Shutterstock; (b) Kelvin Wong / Shutterstock; (c) Irina Meliukh / Shutterstock.

AFFECTIVE PRIMACY AND EMOTION DIFFERENTIATION

Most of the evidence debated by Lazarus and Zajonc addresses the question of what makes emotion emotional. For Zajonc, emotion can occur without cognitive activity (e.g. as a reflex) whereas Lazarus believes that some kind of appraisal is always a necessary precondition. Lazarus's views also have implications for the question of what's different about different emotions. His cognitive primacy position implies not only that emotion always depends on appraisal but also that specific emotions depend on specific patterns of appraisal that give them their distinctive quality. Another way of evaluating Lazarus's arguments, then, is to consider whether specific appraisals are necessary conditions for specific emotions. For example, does anger always depend on prior other-blame appraisals? Focus Point 10.3 considered evidence that anger is not consistently associated with the same appraisals across individuals and situations (e.g. Kuppens et al., 2003; 2007; see also Parkinson, Roper, & Simons, 2009). If this conclusion is correct, then appraisals cannot fully explain the distinctive characteristics of this emotion. But maybe there is some underlying consistency to the appraisal processes producing anger that is not detected by the self-report measures used in these studies. Undetected implicit processes still may have shaped emotional quality outside participants' awareness. Without sufficiently sensitive methods for tracking all varieties of appraisals, it is difficult to be sure how closely associated with different emotions they really are.

Instead of arguing about what counts as 'emotion' and what counts as 'appraisal', Leventhal and Scherer (1987) recommend finer grained distinctions between different kinds of causes and effects. In their view, researchers should seek to understand which specific appraisal-related processes lead to specific emotional consequences. They explicitly distinguish between different levels of appraisal processes, each of which can affect a range of emotion-relevant variables (including autonomic responses and facial expressions). For example, an infant's distressed reaction to arm restraint (Camras, Campos, Oster, Miyake, & Bradshaw, 1992) is induced by *sensorimotor processes* operating at a relatively low level of information processing whereas an adult's indignation on reading about someone's political views is more likely to reflect higher-level *conceptual processes*. Whether both kinds of reaction are equivalently emotional is a question of semantics that can be sidestepped. Correspondingly, whether the sensorimotor and conceptual processes both count as appraisal is irrelevant to our empirical understanding. Having established the specific processes and their effects, it becomes possible to explore their interrelations and develop more integrative theories.

Many appraisal theorists now acknowledge that appraisal is not the sole cause of all emotions (e.g. Roseman, 2013; Scherer & Ellsworth, 2013). Disagreements now mainly relate to its relative centrality and mode of operation. Among appraisal theorists, there is also disagreement about the sequence in which appraisal processes unfold (e.g. Ellsworth & Scherer, 2003; Roseman & Smith, 2001). For theorists such as Smith and Lazarus, appraisal subprocesses may occur simultaneously (in parallel) or in a variety of possible sequences, with emotional consequences simply depending on the resultant pattern of meaning, however it is generated. For Scherer, there is a determinate and logical sequence to appraised meanings, and the process starts with more basic stimulus evaluation checks assessing novelty and intrinsic pleasantness of current events and ends with checks of norm-compatibility and so on. These checks occur in rapid succession and cycle repeatedly like a radar system, detecting events that require emotional response. Scherer's view also raises the possibility that emotional reactions to stimulus evaluation checks consolidate dynamically over time in tandem with the cumulative uptake of environmental information (see also Scherer & Ellworth, 2013; Parkinson, 2001). Instead of simply switching on in response to recognition of the particular personal significance of a transaction, emotions unfold in ongoing attunement to the unfolding structure of the events shaping them.

TEST YOURSELF

What are the theories surrounding appraisal and its role in emotion?

SECTION SUMMARY

- For many theorists, the key factor that makes emotions emotional and different emotions different from each other is appraisal.

- Appraisal means coming to the conclusion that what is happening is personally significant in a particular way, involving either positive or negative implications for your current goals or concerns.

- Appraisal theories propose that people get emotional when they have recognized that something matters to them.

- For appraisal theorists, emotions depend on extracting information from what is happening in the outside world rather than picking up interoceptive information from inside the body.

- A key assumption of appraisal theory is that different appraisal patterns are what make different emotions different.

- A number of models have specified what appraised conclusions a person must reach in order to experience different emotions.

- Smith and Lazarus's (1993) model specifies six appraisal dimensions to account for differences between emotions: motivational congruence, problem-focused coping potential, emotion-focused coping potential, future expectancy, self-accountability, and other-accountability.

- Most theorists would acknowledge that certain kinds of appraisal make it more likely that you will experience a related emotion (e.g. blaming someone else increases the probability of anger).

- Appraisal's causal role is under debate. Speisman et al. (1964) demonstrated that appraisals *can* influence emotions: providing people with different information or changing their perspective on events can make a difference to how they react emotionally to those events.

- Regarding the centrality of appraisal's causal role, Zajonc's (1980) affective primacy view argued that emotion often shapes cognitions such as appraisals rather than vice versa.

- However, Lazarus rejected Zajonc's examples of apparently appraisal-free emotions by arguing either that they weren't real emotions or that they weren't really appraisal-free.

- Many appraisal theorists now acknowledge that appraisal is not the sole cause of all emotions (e.g. Roseman, 2013; Scherer & Ellsworth, 2013). Disagreements now mainly relate to its relative centrality and mode of operation.

WHAT'S DIFFERENT ABOUT DIFFERENT EMOTIONS?

LEARNING OBJECTIVE 10.6

Demonstrate an understanding of basic emotion theories and their implications for response coherence.

This chapter has explored a number of approaches to the question of what makes different emotions different. It is now time to review possible answers to this question. These answers differ in three ways. First, there are disagreements about how to explain associations between different components of the response syndromes thought to characterize emotions (e.g. why do particular appraisals, autonomic responses, and facial expressions tend to go together?). Second, there are disagreements about how closely associated these components are in the first place (e.g. does anger always involve the same pattern of appraisals and facial and autonomic responses?). Finally, there are disagreements about whether perceived differences between emotions really depend on response patterns. Instead, one reason why emotions seem different may be that we have learned to see them as different.

Basic emotions?

According to some psychologists, there are a number of basic emotions (such as anger, fear, sadness, disgust, and joy) that are clearly distinguishable on the basis of consistent patterns of **syndrome components**. For example, Ekman (1972, 2003) believes that each basic emotion is characterized by its own facial expression and a distinctive pattern of autonomic activity (e.g. Ekman et al., 1983), regardless of the cultural background of the person experiencing it. These and other response components are coordinated by an innately specified control program located in the central nervous system. The program is activated by an appraisal that is designed specifically to identify adaptively relevant events requiring immediate response. For example, fear is activated by detection of danger and involves preparing for flight and expressing to others that there is a potential threat (aiding their survival and potentially soliciting assistance in dealing with the threat). Being equipped with such a fear program enabled our ancestors to survive when confronted by wild animals.

Since we do not have access to time machines that allow us to observe what happened when fear and other basic emotions first evolved, evidence for such a theory is necessarily indirect. Finding that similar emotion response syndromes characterized all human societies would be consistent with the basic emotions account. However, as we have seen above, interpretation of the evidence about the universality of emotion–expression links is problematic. The fact that there is some universal component to judgements of facial expressions does not prove that each emotion is directly associated with a corresponding expression for biological reasons. Links between autonomic response patterns and emotion seem to be variable even within a single culture. Even appraisal patterns are not perfectly correlated with emotions. In short, the level of coherence of emotion response syndromes seems to be relatively low (see e.g. Mauss, Levenson, McCarter, Wilhelm, & Gross, 2005; Mauss & Robinson, 2009).

For this reason, many basic emotion theorists now believe that emotion syndromes are loosely coupled systems rather than tightly packaged response patterns that run off in an identical way regardless of context. This provides flexibility that permits more adaptive responses to the specifics of the emotion-provoking situation. However, the open-systems view tends to weaken the idea of a basic emotion, since there is now no fixed structure and components may overlap across different emotions. At what point does a response package become so open that its content simply scatters?

Explaining response coherence

As seen in the previous section, basic emotion theorists often explain associations between emotional response components (e.g. autonomic changes, facial expressions, and appraisals) by reference to evolutionary history. However, there are other possibilities. Camras (1992) suggests that emotional response components are not innately coordinated but become interlinked during the processes of development and socialization. Ortony and Turner (1990) argue that response components occur together because they are simultaneously elicited by different aspects of a structured situation in real time. For example, separate parts of a so-called anger syndrome might intercorrelate simply because anger situations tend to have several concurrent features that independently activate them. In particular, people tend to stare at the object blocking their goals, furrow their brows because they are struggling to overcome that obstacle, and become aroused in preparation for action.

Lewis and Liu (2011) integrate the above alternatives by proposing that the coordination of emotion components depends partly on innate programming, partly on socialization, and partly on real-time influences of environments during ongoing transactions. Thus, some of what holds emotions together may be based on biology, some on learning, and some on how the direct response to the situation is shaped by simultaneous forces.

Perceiving coherence

Do differences between different emotions necessarily depend on the patterning of different components such as autonomic changes, facial expressions, and appraisals? In fact, associations between these components are often loose. Does this mean that different emotions are not really as different as they seem? Perhaps perceived differences between emotions do not reflect their actual distinctive response patterns. Instead they may depend on the way we interpret the responses. Some differences between emotions may be in the eye of the beholder (or mind of the perceiver) rather than in what the beholder perceives.

To help explain this idea, Russell (2003) draws a parallel with the way in which people perceive astral constellations such as the Great Bear (see Figure 10.13). Stars

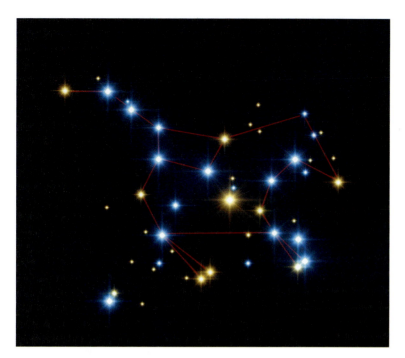

FIGURE 10.13 *The stars making up the constellation of the Great Bear (Ursa Major) and the imaginary lines between them that help you see the stars as part of the bear. What people see when looking at these stars depends not only on the way the stars are patterned in the sky but also on the shapes that people impose on the patterns.*
Source: ROGER HARRIS / SCIENCE PHOTO LIBRARY.

are scattered in overlapping clusters. In principle, these loose clusters could be demarcated in a variety of different ways. Imagining lines connecting them into coherent shapes makes it easier for us to make sense of them. But these shapes are not wholly defined by the star patterns themselves; they also depend on how and where we draw the lines. Maybe something similar happens when people perceive associations between different response components and interpret them as patterned emotions.

According to Russell, people learn to represent experience in emotional terms by acquiring cognitive scripts (Fehr & Russell, 1984). These scripts specify what features should be present (and in what sequence) for an episode to be classified as a clear (prototypical) example of the emotion in question. Just as looking for the Great Bear helps us to perceive a constellation in the night sky, applying a cognitive script of how anger unfolds makes us see connections between response components (e.g. autonomic changes, facial expressions) and link them into a coherent whole. The prototypical script for 'anger' specifies that someone offends you, you react with a characteristic facial scowl or snarl, you feel aroused, you see the other person as to blame for what is happening, and so on. If all these features are present (in the appropriate sequence), then you will almost certainly classify your experience as anger. You may also attribute anger to yourself if a reasonable proportion of the prototypical features are present (e.g. Russell & Fehr, 1994). Thus, the various 'components' of the syndrome are not integrated aspects of a prepackaged basic emotion, coordinated by control programs and activated by appraisals; instead they are responses that sometimes fall together into clear patterns (for a variety of reasons) but at other times are less tightly associated.

Russell's ideas raise questions about the extent to which emotion concepts reflect the underlying nature of 'emotional' phenomena themselves. According to some supporters of the idea of basic emotions, the emotion concepts represented by words such as 'anger' and 'fear' correspond to definite coherent response patterns determined by biology: they carve nature at its joints. According to Russell, the joints are where they are partly because of where we happen to be carving them.

Barrett (2006) developed the **conceptual act theory**, which makes more specific claims about the role of emotion representation in perceiving distinct emotional experiences. She argues that the central phenomenon represented by emotion concepts is **core affect,** consisting of directly perceived levels of pleasure and arousal (see also Russell & Barrett, 1999). Core affect is only experienced as emotional when it is conceptualized in emotional terms by the perceiver. In other words, core affect underlies emotional experience but is not itself emotional until it is categorized (conceptualized) in emotional terms.

Like Schachter, Barrett argues that emotion depends on linking internal perception with interpretations of what is happening. Her extension of feedback theory has become increasingly influential partly because of its ability to cope with evidence concerning limited response coherence, without sacrificing the notion that emotions are experienced as distinct mental states. However, both Barrett's and Schachter's theories seem to focus mainly on explaining how people perceive their own emotions, which may not always be the same thing as emotion itself. Both theories find it harder to explain how people might become emotional without knowing that they are emotional. For example, philosophers have argued that a jealous person is often the last to realize that they are jealous (e.g. Bedford, 1957). Jealousy is evident in someone's reactions to events concerning a relationship even when the jealous person is unaware of reacting in a jealous way. Similarly, someone involved in a disagreement might beat on a table and shout out 'I am *not* angry' in a way that directly contradicts the evidence. What makes someone's orientation to events emotional may not always be their perception of being emotional. For example, anger need not involve believing that you are angry; it may instead reflect the perception that others are behaving in an irritating manner (see e.g. Frijda, 2005; Lambie & Marcel, 2002).

TEST YOURSELF

1. What's different about different emotions?
2. What does it mean for an emotion to be 'basic'?
3. Outline the conceptual act theory of emotion.

SECTION SUMMARY

- Researchers disagree about how to explain associations between different components of the response syndromes thought to characterize emotions, how closely associated these components are in the first place, and whether perceived differences between emotions really depend on response patterns.

- According to some psychologists, there are a number of basic emotions that are clearly distinguishable on the basis of consistent patterns of syndrome components.
- Because evidence suggests that different response components are not always closely associated, many basic emotion theorists have concluded that discrete emotions are flexible systems rather than tightly packaged response syndromes.
- However, this open-systems view tends to weaken the idea of the existence of basic emotions.
- Lewis and Liu (2011) proposed that the coordination of emotion components depends on innate programming, socialization, and real-time influences.
- Alternatively, it has been argued that differences between emotions may be in the eye of the beholder – according to Russell (2003), people learn to represent experience in emotional terms by acquiring cognitive scripts.
- Barrett (2006) developed the conceptual act theory, which argues that the central phenomenon represented by emotion concepts is core affect, consisting of directly perceived levels of pleasure and arousal that are only experienced as emotional when conceptualized in emotional terms by the perceiver.

CONCLUSIONS AND FUTURE DIRECTIONS

LEARNING OBJECTIVE 10.7

Demonstrate an understanding of the theories proposed in relation to emotion historically and of possible future research and directions within the field.

Although different emotions clearly feel different from one another, it turns out that their response profiles are less consistent and less distinctive than is usually assumed. One reason is that we tend to think of prototypical instances when comparing emotions. Although anger that is overtly expressed towards someone you are fighting has different symptoms and expressions from fear of a wild animal chasing you, this does not mean that these differences apply regardless of when, where, and how anger or fear occur. Some theorists conclude that differences between emotions depend on how they are represented or conceptualized rather than on the response components themselves. But what makes anger angry and fear fearful seems to reflect more than how we think about those experiences.

According to appraisal theory, emotions are modes of action readiness designed to deal with adaptive issues identified by appraisals. In this view, emotion differences do not necessarily reflect patterns of autonomic change or facial expression because the same action readiness mode may involve a relatively wide range of internal preparatory responses or physical movements. Perhaps, then, 'anger' involves an attempt to remove various kinds of blockage by whatever means are available. Perhaps 'fear' is the urgent need to escape from something threatening our well-being, regardless of whether this something is physical or mental, and whether it is concrete or abstract, and regardless of whether escape involves running away, hiding, or struggling to escape the clutches of whatever is frightening us. Our bodily changes would be very different in each example of these distinct emotions but our orientation, motivation, and attunement to particular kinds of information would still have a characteristic structure. Thus, autonomic patterning and distinctive facial expressions may be present for pure and prototypical examples of emotion without being necessary features defining emotion differences more generally.

Turning to feedback theory, the evidence discussed above makes it unlikely that all aspects of emotional experience depend on registering bodily changes as James's theory originally implied. At least some aspects of emotion seem to be activated or maintained by processes relating to appraisal and more generally by the management of goal conflicts and priorities during action control (Moors, 2017). However, different aspects of emotional episodes reflect different kinds of process. For example, the sense of embodied engagement with events may contribute to some forms of emotional experience (e.g. Prinz, 2004), as when we find ourselves absorbed in a struggle with someone or something or melt into another person's arms.

One of the differences between emotion theories is that they disagree about what emotion is in the first place. In particular, feedback theories focus on explaining an individual's perception of being in an emotional state whereas appraisal theories are more concerned with accounting for emotional action tendencies or orientations towards objects or events in the environment. Even if we restrict our focus to explaining emotional experience, researchers now believe that this experience can take a variety of forms (Lambie & Marcel, 2002). If we attempt to explain emotional syndromes, we are faced with the challenge that they seem to reflect open systems of loosely coupled component processes rather than tightly packaged basic emotions (e.g. Mauss & Robinson, 2009).

As suggested above, one way forward is to scale down our theoretical ambitions and focus on lower-level processes (Leventhal & Scherer, 1987). For example, it is easier to demonstrate that particular kinds of attention or attribution have effects on specific outcomes relating to facial activity, autonomic response, or implicit associations than it is to show that cognition more broadly is the cause of emotion. Research adopting this kind of approach has already produced promising results (e.g. Moors, 2013; Scherer, 2013) and it seems possible that a broader and deeper understanding may be consolidated from emerging findings.

Another important aspect of this research is its attempt to move beyond an exclusive reliance on self-report as the central measure of emotion. Although people are certainly able to provide researchers with important information about their emotional experiences, their communications are influenced by presentational factors that go beyond simple description. For example, saying that you are angry serves as a strategy for blaming someone and is not just a simple characterization of an internal state. For this reason angry remarks tend to be sensitive to the presence of other people of various kinds. In many circumstances, you are less likely to say that you are angry when the person you are communicating to may treat your statement as an accusation.

A further important development involves investigating emotions as dynamic processes that unfold over time in interaction with the physical and social environment (Cunningham, Dunfield, & Stillman, 2013; Verduyn, Van Mechelen, Tuerlinckx, Meers, & Van Coillie, 2009). Most experiments into emotion have involved either asking people to remember or imagine emotions, or exposing them to stimuli with plausibly emotional effects. Much less work has focused on how people experience and express emotions when directly involved in unfolding transactions. Investigation of variations in emotion-related processes over time in real-life settings using the latest technologies promises to open up important new avenues for research (e.g. Picard, 2010).

Finally, as indicated by the research into group emotions and social appraisals described above, there is increasing interest in the social functions of emotions (Hareli & Rafaeli, 2008; Parkinson et al., 2005; Van Kleef, 2009). Rather than seeing emotions as events located squarely within an individual consciousness, researchers have started to explore how people respond to other people's emotions and how their own emotions are oriented to other people's emotions (e.g. Butler & Randall, 2013). When viewed as unfolding modes of engagement with the social world, emotions and their differences may start to reveal their true meaning and purpose.

SECTION SUMMARY

- Appraisal theories distinguish emotions according to modes of action readiness rather than specific response profiles.

- Differences between appraisal theories and feedback theories partly reflect their different conceptions of emotion, as functionally oriented responses or personal experiences, respectively.

- One way of improving progress in emotion research is to resist explaining integrated emotions and focus on lower-level causal relationships between inputs and outputs (e.g., Leventhal & Scherer, 1987).

- It is also important to triangulate self-report data with other sources of evidence about emotional processes.

- Attention to the dynamic and social aspects of emotion can further extend and advance our understanding of the phenomenon.

CHAPTER SUMMARY

This chapter has considered the fundamental questions of what makes emotion emotional and what differentiates emotions from each other. We did this by discussing the three main variables that may help to answer the pressing questions involved in emotion research: specifically, the roles of physiological activity, facial expressions, and individual appraisal of the context. We moved on to evaluate the evidence suggesting that some basic emotions are innately programmed response syndromes, and we gave consideration to alternative views, such as conceptual act theory. It is argued that disagreements in emotion research stem from a fundamental disagreement about what emotion actually *is*. A priority for future emotion research is to focus on lower-level processes and also to move beyond an exclusive reliance on self-report as the central measure of emotion. Little work in the field has focused on the real-time unfolding of the experience and expression of emotions and their social function between people and within social contexts. An adjusted research focus will undoubtedly help to determine what emotions are really *for*.

ESSAY QUESTIONS

1. Can psychologists tell what emotion someone is feeling (e.g. whether a person is angry, afraid, or happy) by measuring autonomic responses?

2. Do people in all societies show the same facial expressions when experiencing the same emotions?

3. Do all emotions depend on prior appraisals?

4. Compare and contrast the accounts of emotion differentiation offered by basic emotions theorists and their critics.

KEY TERMS

- **absolute specificity hypothesis:** One of three possible positions concerning autonomic specificity distinguished by Stemmler (1989), absolute specificity proposes that every time a particular emotion occurs the same pattern of autonomic response is observed regardless of context.

- **action readiness:** The body and mind's state of preparation for performing an emotion-relevant action. According to Arnold (1960), emotion can be defined as a state of action readiness.

- **affective primacy:** Zajonc's (1980) proposal that emotion (or at least affect) can occur prior to cognitive activity and be independent of it.

- **appraisal theory:** Covers a number of similar but not identical accounts of emotion sharing the assumption that appraisals can explain or at least describe differences between different emotions. Most appraisal theorists propose that appraisals cause emotions some or all of the time.

- **appraisal:** Evaluation and interpretation of what is happening with reference to personal goals or 'concerns'. It can operate at an automatic and unconscious level.

- **autonomic nervous system (ANS):** The division of the nervous system responsible for controlling basic functions that can operate without deliberation. The ANS adjusts heart rate, blood pressure, pupil size, and so on in response to external stimuli and internal needs.

- **autonomic specificity:** The idea that different emotions are characterized by distinctive patterns of autonomic activity. In other words, autonomic specificity implies that measuring autonomic activity allows researchers to determine what emotion a participant is experiencing.

- **basic emotions:** Innately differentiated emotions shared across the human species, often thought to be associated with distinctive facial expressions and autonomic nervous system patterns. Psychologists disagree about whether differences between emotions only occur as a function of individual development and socialization.

- **conceptual act theory:** Developed by Barrett (e.g. 2006), the idea that emotional experience depends on the individual's categorization of states of core affect (consisting of pleasure and arousal).

- **context-deviation hypothesis:** One of three possible positions concerning autonomic specificity distinguished by Stemmler (1989), the context-deviation hypothesis proposes that emotions alter autonomic responses to situations but that the recorded autonomic pattern reflects a combination of emotional and situational responses.

- **core affect:** Proposed by Russell and Barrett (1999) as a combination of pleasure and arousal that is associated with a range of different emotions and non-emotional states. According to Barrett (e.g. 2006), core affect needs to be conceptualized by the individual before it is articulated as a distinctive emotional experience.

- **display rules:** Norms about appropriate expression of emotion in different contexts. According to Ekman (1972), people may exaggerate or minimize their spontaneous facial responses in accordance with these display rules so that they appear to have more or less of a particular emotion than they really feel.
- **Ekman's neurocultural theory:** Ekman's model of how cultural and biological factors contribute to the facial expression of emotion. Antecedents of emotion and display rules may vary from culture to culture depending on socialization. However, the neural program specifying spontaneous expressions for each basic emotion is innate, universal, and unaltered by socialization.
- **facial feedback hypothesis:** The proposal that the internal perception of facial position influences emotion. For example, according to the facial feedback hypothesis, smiling can make you feel happier.
- **feedback theory:** The idea that emotional experience depends on feeling the body react to events. Feedback theory was popularized by William James, who believed that each distinct emotion involves a distinctive configuration of bodily activity and that perceiving this configuration is what induces the feeling of the corresponding emotion.
- **motivational congruence:** According to Smith and Lazarus's (1993) model of appraisal, motivational congruence is the assessment of whether what is happening helps or hinders progress towards currently active goals and determines whether the resulting emotion is pleasant or unpleasant.
- **motivational relevance:** According to Smith and Lazarus's (1993) model of appraisal, motivational relevance is the assessment of whether what is happening relates to currently active goals and determines whether an emotion is activated.
- **non-specificity hypothesis:** One of three possible positions concerning autonomic specificity distinguished by Stemmler (1989), non-specificity proposes that emotions cannot be distinguished by measuring autonomic nervous system activity.
- **Schachter's two-factor theory:** Proposes that emotions depend on internal perceptions of autonomic arousal (physiological factor determining emotional intensity) combined with interpretations of the situation (cognitive factor determining emotional quality).
- **syndrome components:** A term implying that emotions involve responses operating across many separate systems (e.g. autonomic changes, facial expressions, and suchlike). Psychologists disagree about whether these responses are coordinated by top-down processes (e.g. appraisals) and about the degree of association between components.

NOTE

1. https://www.youtube.com/watch?v=wW0PaKOXxQI]

FURTHER RESOURCES

Arvid Kappas Emotion Research. (2010–). Retrieved 20 November 2017 from http://www.arvidkappas.com (A blog and useful links concerning emotion research maintained by the former president [2013–2018] of the International Society for Research on Emotion.)

Barrett, L. F., & Russell, J. A. (Eds.). (2014). *The psychological construction of emotion*. New York, NY: Guilford Press. (An up-to-date compendium of theory and research associated with the psychological constructionist approach to emotion.)

Ellsworth, P. C. (1994). William James and emotion: Is a century of fame worth a century of misunderstanding? *Psychological Review, 101,* 222–229.

Fernandez-Dols, J. M., & Russell, J. A. (Eds.). (2017). *The science of facial expression*. Oxford, UK: Oxford University Press. (A collection of chapters by key thinkers in the study of facial expression.)

Frijda, N. H. (2007). *The laws of emotion*. New York, NY: Psychology Press. (A monograph by one of the most influential thinkers in emotion psychology.)

International Society for Research on Emotion. (n.d.). Retrieved 20 November 2017 from http://isre.org (This site also provides links to the society's regular newsletter, *Emotion Researcher*.)

Keltner, D., Oatley, K., & Jenkins, J. M. (2013). *Understanding emotions* (3rd ed.). Oxford, UK: Wiley-Blackwell. (An accessible, well-written, and well-informed textbook giving wide coverage of emotion theory and research.)

Parkinson, B., Fischer, A. H., & Manstead, A. S. R. (2005). *Emotion in social relations: Cultural, group, and interpersonal processes*. New York, NY: Psychology Press. (Gives detailed coverage of social approaches to emotion including reviews of research concerning cultural factors, group processes, and interpersonal interactions.)

Society for Affective Science. (n.d.). Retrieved 20 November 2017 from http://society-for-affective-science.org (Another international society involved in emotion research.)

Strongman, K. T. (2003). *The psychology of emotion: From everyday life to theory* (5th ed.). Chichester, UK: Wiley . (This textbook approaches the study of emotion by surveying the range of emotion theories that have been proposed over the years.)

REFERENCES

Andreasson, P., & Dimberg, U. (2008). Emotional empathy and facial feedback. *Journal of Nonverbal Behavior, 32*, 215–224.

Arnold, M. B. (1960). *Emotion and personality: Vol. 1. Psychological aspects*. New York, NY: Columbia University Press.

Ax, A. F. (1953). The physiological differentiation between fear and anger in humans. *Psychosomatic Medicine, 15*, 433–442.

Barrett, L. F. (2006). Solving the emotion paradox: Categorization and the experience of emotion. *Personality and Social Psychology Review, 10*, 20–46.

Bedford, E. (1957). Emotions. *Proceedings of the Aristotelian Society, 57*, 281–304.

Branscombe, N. R., & Doosje, B. (Eds.). (2004). *Collective guilt: International perspectives*. New York, NY: Cambridge University Press.

Butler, E. A., & Randall, A. K. (2013). Emotional coregulation in close relationships. *Emotion Review, 5*, 202–210.

Cacioppo, J. T., Berntson, G. G., Larsen, J. T., Poehlmann, K. M., & Ito, T. A. (2000). The psychophysiology of emotion. In M. Lewis & J. M. Haviland-Jones (Eds.), *Handbook of emotions* (2nd ed., pp. 173–191). New York, NY: Guilford Press.

Camras, L. A. (1992). Expressive development and basic emotions. *Cognition and Emotion, 6*, 269–284.

Camras, L. A., Campos, J. J., Oster, H., Miyake, K., & Bradshaw, D. (1992). Japanese and American infants' responses to arm restraint. *Developmental Psychology, 28*, 578–583.

Camras, L. A., Sullivan, J., & Michel, G. (1993). Do infants express discrete emotions? Adult judgments of facial, vocal, and bodily actions. *Journal of Nonverbal Behavior, 17*, 171–186.

Cannon, W. B. (1927). The James–Lange theory of emotions: A critical examination and an alternative theory. *American Journal of Psychology, 39*, 106–124.

Cunningham, W. A., Dunfield, K. A., & Stillman, P. E. (2013). Emotional states from affective dynamics. *Emotion Review, 5*, 344–355.

Damasio, A. R. (1994). *Descartes' error: Emotion, reason, and the human brain*. New York, NY: Avon Books.

Davis, J. I., Senghas, A., Brandt, F., & Ochsner, K. N. (2010). The effects of Botox injections on emotional experience. *Emotion, 10*, 433–440.

Doosje, B., Branscombe, N. R., Spears R., & Manstead, A. S. R. (1998). Guilty by association: When one's group has a negative history. *Journal of Personality and Social Psychology, 75*, 872–886.

Dumont, M., Yzerbyt, V. Y., Wigboldus, D., & Gordijn, E. H. (2003). Social categorization and fear reactions to the September 11th terrorist attacks. *Personality and Social Psychology Bulletin, 29*, 1509–1520.

Ekman, P. (1972). Universals and cultural differences in facial expressions of emotion. *Nebraska Symposium on Motivation, 19*, 207–283.

Ekman, P. (2003). *Emotions revealed: Understanding faces and feeling.* London, UK: Weidenfeld & Nicolson.

Ekman, P., & Friesen, W. V. (1971). Constants across culture in the face and emotion. *Journal of Personality and Social Psychology, 17*, 124–129.

Ekman, P., Friesen, W. V., & Ellsworth, P. C. (1972). *Emotion in the human face: Guidelines for research and an integration of findings.* New York, NY: Pergamon Press.

Ekman, P., Levenson, R. W., & Friesen, W. V. (1983). Autonomic nervous system activity distinguishing among emotions. *Science, 221*, 1208–1210.

Elfenbein, H. A., & Ambady, N. (2002). Is there an in-group advantage in emotion recognition? *Psychological Bulletin, 128*, 243–249.

Ellsworth, P. C., & Scherer, K. (2003). Appraisal processes in emotion. In R. J. Davidson, H. Goldsmith, & K. R. Scherer (Eds.), *Handbook of affective sciences* (pp. 572–595). Oxford, UK: Oxford University Press.

Erdmann, G., & Janke, W. (1978). Interaction between physiological and cognitive determinants of emotions. *Biological Psychology, 6*, 61–74.

Fehr, B., & Russell, J. A. (1984). Concept of emotion viewed from a prototype perspective. *Journal of Experimental Psychology: General, 113*, 464–486.

Fernández-Dols, J.-M., & Crivelli, C. (2013). Emotion and expression: Naturalistic studies. *Emotion Review, 5*, 24–29.

Fridlund, A. J. (1994). *Human facial expression: An evolutionary view.* San Diego, CA: Academic Press.

Frijda, N. H. (1953). The understanding of facial expression of emotion. *Acta Psychologica, 9*, 294–362.

Frijda, N. H. (2005). Emotion experience. *Cognition and Emotion, 19*, 473–497.

Frijda, N. H., & Tcherkassof, A. (1997). Facial expressions as modes of action readiness. In J. A. Russell & J.-M. Fernández-Dols (Eds.), *The psychology of facial expression* (pp. 78–102). New York, NY: Cambridge University Press.

Garcia, J., & Rusiniak, K. W. (1980). What the nose learns from the mouth. In D. Muller-Schwarze & R. M. Silverstein (Eds.), *Chemical signals* (pp. 141–156). New York, NY: Plenum Press.

Hareli, S., & Rafaeli, A. (2008). Emotion cycles: On the social influence of emotion in organizations. *Research in Organizational Behavior, 28*, 35–59.

Hennenlotter, A., Dresel, C., Castrop, F., Ceballos Baumann, A. O., Wohlschläger, A. M., & Haslinger, B. (2009). The link between facial feedback and neural activity within central circuitries of emotion: New insights from Botulinum toxin-induced denervation of frown muscles. *Cerebral Cortex, 19*, 537–542.

Izard, C. E. (1978). On the ontogenesis of emotions and emotion–cognition relationships in infancy. In M. Lewis & L. Rosenblum (Eds.), *The development of affect* (pp. 389–413). New York, NY: Plenum Press.

Jack, R. E., Garrod, O. G. B., Yu, H., Caldara, R, & Schyns, P. G. (2012). Facial expressions of emotion are not culturally universal. *Proceedings of the National Academy of Sciences of the United States of America, 109*, 7241–7244.

James, W. (1884). What is an emotion? *Mind, 9*, 188–205.

James, W. (1898). *The principles of psychology (Vol. 2).* London, UK: Macmillan.

Kreibig, S. D. (2010). Autonomic nervous system activity in emotion: A review. *Biological Psychology, 84*, 394–421.

Kuppens, P., Van Mechelen, I., Smits, D. J. M., & de Boeck, P. (2003). The appraisal basis of anger: Specificity, necessity and sufficiency of components. *Emotion, 3*, 254–269.

Kuppens, P., Van Mechelen, I., Smits, D. J. M., de Boeck, P., & Ceulemans, E. (2007). Individual differences in patterns of appraisal and anger experience. *Cognition and Emotion, 21*, 689–713.

Laird, J. D. (1974). Self-attribution of emotion: The effects of expressive behavior on the quality of emotional experience. *Journal of Personality and Social Psychology, 29*, 473–486.

Laird, J. D., & Bresler, C. (1990). William James and the mechanisms of emotional experience. *Personality and Social Psychology Bulletin, 16*, 636–651.

Lambie, J. A., & Marcel, A. J. (2002). Consciousness and the varieties of emotion experience: A theoretical framework. *Psychological Review, 109*, 219–259.

Lazarus, R. S. (1984). On the primacy of cognition. *American Psychologist, 39*, 124–129.

Lazarus, R. S. (1991). *Emotion and adaptation*. New York, NY: Oxford University Press.

Leach, C. W., Spears, R., Branscombe, N. R., & Doosje, B. (2003). Malicious pleasure: Schadenfreude at the suffering of an outgroup. *Journal of Personality and Social Psychology, 84*, 932–943.

LeDoux, J. E. (1996). *The emotional brain*. New York, NY: Simon & Schuster.

Levenson, R. W. (1994). The search for autonomic specificity. In P. Ekman & R. J. Davidson (Eds.), *The nature of emotion: Fundamental questions* (pp. 252–257). New York, NY: Oxford University Press.

Leventhal, H., & Scherer, K. R. (1987). The relationship of emotion and cognition: A functional approach to a semantic controversy. *Cognition and Emotion, 1*, 3–28.

Lewis, M. D., & Liu, Z. (2011). Three time-scales of neural self-organization underlying human basic and non-basic emotions. *Emotion Review, 3*, 416–423.

Lindquist, K. A., Wager, T. D., Kober, H., Bliss-Moreau, E., & Barrett, L. F. (2012). The brain basis of emotion: A meta-analytic review. *Behavioral and Brain Sciences, 35*, 121–143.

Lutz, C. A. (1988). *Unnatural emotions: Everyday sentiments on a Micronesian atoll and their challenge to western theory*. Chicago, IL: University of Chicago Press.

Manstead, A. S. R., & Fischer, A. H. (2001). Social appraisal: The social world as object of and influence on appraisal processes. In K. R. Scherer, A. Schorr, & T. Johnston (Eds.), *Appraisal processes in emotion: Theory, methods, research* (pp. 221–232). New York, NY: Oxford University Press.

Marañon, G. (1924). Contribution à l'étude de l'action émotive de l'adrenaline. *Revue française d'endocrinologie, 2*, 301–325.

Marshall, G., & Zimbardo, P. G. (1979). Affective consequences of inadequately explained physiological arousal. *Journal of Personality and Social Psychology, 37*, 970–988.

Maslach, C. (1979). Negative emotional biasing of unexplained arousal. *Journal of Personality and Social Psychology, 37*, 953–969.

Matsumoto, D., & Wilson, J. (2008). Culture, emotion, and motivation. In R. M. Sorrentino & S. Yamaguchi (Eds.), *Handbook of motivation and cognition across cultures*. New York, NY: Elsevier.

Mauss, I. B., Levenson, R. W., McCarter, L., Wilhelm, F. L., & Gross, J. J. (2005). The tie that binds? Coherence among emotion experience, behavior, and physiology. *Emotion, 5*, 175–190.

Mauss, I. B., & Robinson, M. D. (2009). Measures of emotion: A review. *Cognition and Emotion, 23*, 209–237.

Moors, A. (2013). On the causal role of appraisal in emotion. *Emotion Review, 5*, 132–140.

Moors, A. (2017). Integration of two skeptical emotion theories: Dimensional appraisal theory and Russell's psychological construction theory. *Psychological Inquiry, 28*, 1–19.

Nelson, N. L., & Russell, J. A. (2013). Universality revisited. *Emotion Review, 5*, 8–15.

Ortony, A., & Turner, T. J. (1990). What's basic about basic emotions? *Psychological Review, 97*, 315–331.

Panksepp, J. (2000). Emotions as natural kinds within the mammalian brain. In M. Lewis & J. M. Haviland-Jones (Eds.), *Handbook of emotions* (2nd ed., pp. 137–156). New York, NY: Guilford Press.

Parkinson, B. (1999). Relations and dissociations between appraisal and emotion ratings in reasonable and unreasonable anger and guilt. *Cognition and Emotion, 13,* 347–385.

Parkinson, B. (2001). Putting appraisal in context. In K. R. Scherer, A. Schorr, & T. Johnstone (Eds.), *Appraisal processes in emotion: Theory, methods, research* (pp. 173–186). New York, NY: Oxford University Press.

Parkinson, B. (2005). Do facial movements express emotions or communicate motives. *Personality and Social Psychology Review, 9,* 278–311.

Parkinson, B., Fischer, A., & Manstead, A. S. R. (2005). *Emotion in social relations: Cultural, group, and interpersonal processes.* Philadelphia, PA: Psychology Press.

Parkinson, B., Phiri, N., & Simons, G. (2012). Bursting with anxiety: Adult social referencing in an interpersonal balloon analogue risk task (BART). *Emotion, 12,* 817–826.

Parkinson, B., Roper, A., & Simons, G. (2009). Appraisal ratings in diary reports of reasonable and unreasonable anger. *European Journal of Social Psychology, 39,* 82–87.

Picard, R. W. (2010). Emotion research by the people, for the people. *Emotion Review, 2,* 250–254.

Prinz, J. J. (2004). *Gut reactions: A perceptual theory of emotion.* Oxford, UK: Oxford University Press.

Reisenzein, R. (1983). The Schachter theory of emotion: Two decades later. *Psychological Bulletin, 94,* 239–264.

Reisenzein, R., Studtmann, M., & Horstmann, G. (2013). Coherence between emotion and facial expression: Evidence from laboratory experiments. *Emotion Review, 5,* 16–23.

Roseman, I. (2013). On the frontiers of appraisal theory. *Emotion Review, 5,* 187–188.

Roseman, I. J., & Evdokas, A. (2004). Appraisals cause experienced emotions: Experimental evidence. *Cognition and Emotion, 18,* 1–28.

Roseman, I. J., & Smith, C. A. (2001). Appraisal theory: Overview, assumptions, varieties, controversies. In K. R. Scherer, A. Schorr, & T. Johnstone (Eds.), *Appraisal processes in emotion* (pp. 3–19). New York, NY: Oxford University Press.

Russell, J. A. (1994). Is there universal recognition of emotion from facial expression? A review of the cross-cultural studies. *Psychological Bulletin, 115,* 102–141.

Russell, J. A. (1997). Reading emotions from and into faces: Resurrecting a dimensional-contextual perspective. In J. A. Russell & J.-M. Fernández-Dols (Eds.), *The psychology of facial expression* (pp. 295–320). New York, NY: Cambridge University Press.

Russell, J. A. (2003). Core affect and the psychological construction of emotion. *Psychological Review, 110,* 145–172.

Russell, J. A., & Barrett, L. F. (1999). Core affect, prototypical emotional episodes, and other things called emotion: Dissecting the elephant. *Journal of Personality and Social Psychology, 76,* 805–819.

Russell, J. A., & Fehr, B. (1994). Fuzzy concepts in a fuzzy hierarchy: Varieties of anger. *Journal of Personality and Social Psychology, 67,* 186–205.

Russell, J. A., & Fernández-Dols, J.-M. (1997). What does a facial expression mean? In J. A. Russell & J.-M. Fernández-Dols (Eds.), *The psychology of facial expression* (pp. 3–30). New York, NY: Cambridge University Press.

Sander, D., Grafman, J., & Zalla, T. (2003). The human amygdala: An evolved system for relevance detection. *Reviews in the Neurosciences, 14,* 303–316.

Schachter, S. (1964). The interaction of cognitive and physiological determinants of emotional state. *Advances in Experimental Social Psychology, 1,* 49–80.

Schachter, S., & Singer, J. E. (1962). Cognitive, social, and physiological determinants of emotional state. *Psychological Review, 69,* 379–399.

Scherer, K. R. (1992). What does facial expression express? In K. T. Strongman (Ed.), *International review of studies in emotion* (Vol. 2, pp. 139–165). Chichester, UK: Wiley .

Scherer, K. R. (2013). The nature and dynamics of relevance and valence appraisals: Theoretical advances and recent evidence. *Emotion Review, 5,* 150–162.

Scherer, K. R., & Ellsworth, P. C. (2013). The unbearable heaviness of feeling. *Emotion Review, 5,* 189–191.

Seligman, M. E. P., & Hager, J. L. (1972). *Biological boundaries of learning.* New York, NY: Appleton-Century-Crofts.

Smith, C. A., & Ellsworth, P. C. (1985). Patterns of cognitive appraisal in emotion. *Journal of Personality and Social Psychology, 48,* 813–838.

Smith, C. A., & Lazarus, R. S. (1993). Appraisal components, core relational themes, and the emotions. *Cognition and Emotion, 7,* 233–269.

Smith, C. A., & Scott, H. S. (1997). A componential approach to the meaning of facial expressions. In J. A. Russell & J.-M. Fernández-Dols (Eds.), *The psychology of facial expression* (pp. 229–254). New York, NY: Cambridge University Press.

Smith, E. R. (1993). Social identity and social emotions: Toward new conceptualizations of prejudice. In D. M. Mackie, D. Hamilton, & D. Lewis (Eds.), *Affect, cognition, and stereotyping: Interactive processes in group perception* (pp. 297–315). San Diego, CA: Academic Press.

Sorce, J. F., Emde, R. N., Campos, J., & Klinnert, M. D. (1985). Maternal emotional signaling: Its effect on the visual cliff behavior of 1 year olds. *Developmental Psychology, 21,* 195–200.

Soussignan, R. (2002). Duchenne smile, emotional experience, and autonomic reactivity: A test of the facial feedback hypothesis. *Emotion, 2,* 52–74.

Speisman, J. C., Lazarus, R. S., Mordkoff, A., & Davison, L. (1964). Experimental reduction of stress based on ego-defense theory. *Journal of Abnormal and Social Psychology, 68,* 367–380.

Stemmler, G. (1989). The autonomic differentiation of emotions revisited: Convergent and discriminant validation. *Psychophysiology, 26,* 617–632.

Strack, F., Martin, L. L., & Stepper, S. (1988). Inhibiting and facilitating conditions of the human smile: A non-obtrusive test of the facial feedback hypothesis. *Journal of Personality and Social Psychology, 54,* 768–777.

Tomkins, S. S. (1962). *Affect, imagery and consciousness: Vol. 1. The positive affects.* New York, NY: Springer.

Tourangeau, R., & Ellsworth, P. C. (1979). The role of facial response in the experience of emotion. *Journal of Personality and Social Psychology, 37,* 1519–1531.

Van Kleef, G. A. (2009). How emotions regulate social life: The emotions as social information (EASI) model. *Current Directions in Psychological Science, 18,* 184–188.

Van Reekum, C. M., Banse, R., Johnstone, T., Etter, A., Wehrle, T., & Scherer, K. R. (2004). Psychophysiological responses to appraisal dimensions in a computer game. *Cognition and Emotion, 18,* 663–688.

Verduyn, P., Van Mechelen, I., Tuerlinckx, F., Meers, K., & Van Coillie, H. (2009). Intensity profiles of emotional experience over time. *Cognition and Emotion, 23,* 1427–1443.

Wagenmakers, E.-J., Beek, T., Dijkhoff, L., Gronau, Q. F., Acosta, A., Adams, R. B., Jr., … Zwaan, R. A. (2016). Registered replication report: Strack, Martin, & Stepper (1988). *Perspectives on Psychological Science, 11,* 917–928.

Whalen, P. J., Raila, H., Bennett, R., Mattek, A., Brown, A., Taylor, J., … Palmer, A. (2013). Neuroscience and facial expressions of emotion: The role of amygdala–prefrontal interactions. *Emotion Review, 5,* 78–83.

Woodworth, R. S., & Schlosberg, H. (1954). *Experimental psychology.* New York, NY: Holt, Rinehart and Winston.

Yzerbyt, V., Dumont, M., Gordijn, E., & Wigboldus, D. (2002). Intergroup emotions and self-categorization: The impact of perspective-taking on reactions to victims of harmful behaviors. In D. M. Mackie & E. R. Smith (Eds.), *From prejudice to intergroup emotions: Differentiated reactions to social groups* (pp. 67–88). Philadelphia, PA: Psychology Press.

Zajonc, R. B. (1980). Feeling and thinking: Preferences need no inferences. *American Psychologist, 35,* 151–175.

Zajonc, R. B. (1984). On the primacy of affect. *American Psychologist, 39,* 117–123.

Zimbardo, P. G., Ebbeson, E. B., & Maslach, C. (1977). *Influencing attitudes and changing behavior* (2nd ed.). Reading, MA: Addison-Wesley.

11 Cognitive Development

ANDY BREMNER

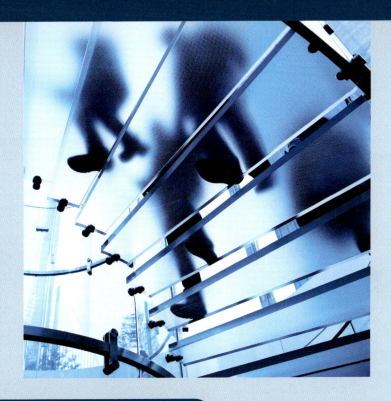

INTRODUCTION

LEARNING OBJECTIVE 11.1

Demonstrate an understanding of the two main aims of developmental psychology.

Albert Einstein once gave advice to an anxious parent who was keen for their child to become a scientist. Einstein is reported to have said, 'First, give him fairy tales; second, give him fairy tales; and third, give him fairy tales!' (Kunitz & Loizeaux, 1963, p. 678).

It's probably fair to say that the anxious parent in question may have been a little disappointed by Einstein's advice. But his suggestion captures a range of the ways in which we think about early life and development. It seems that Einstein identified childhood as a time of imagination. He also thought that particular kinds of experience in early life (in this case those that stimulate the imagination) have an important role to play in development. This example captures the two main aims of developmental psychology: first, to understand the ways in which psychological processes are different across the various stages of our lives (in this case, childhood is identified as being more fanciful and imaginative than adulthood) and, second, to try to understand how it is that we develop from one life stage to the next – how particular experiences, behaviours, and biology give rise to developmental change.

Einstein's view of childhood seems to be that it is a period of fantasy and imagination. A somewhat similar characterization of childhood was captured by the French philosopher Jean-Jacques Rousseau, who regarded it as a period of innocence and play (Rousseau, 1762/1979). This view will be shared by almost anyone you choose to talk to on the street. However, some have argued that our modern conceptions of childhood as a time of innocence and play are social constructions, invented by people like Rousseau. For instance, Philippe Ariés (1962), a social historian, argues on the basis of portrayals of children in paintings that in mediaeval times children were treated like miniature adults rather than being considered different to adults.

Others contend that childhood as a separate 'playful' period of life is a universal phenomenon, and this perhaps seems more likely and is certainly the more accepted view among modern developmental psychologists. The characterization of qualitatively different life periods is a theme that runs throughout developmental psychology. Furthermore, the suggestion that play or imagination is necessary for development and education is also very important in the field. We will discuss these ideas and the scientific support for them, among many others, in this chapter.

Psychology, First Edition. Edited by Graham Davey.
© 2019 John Wiley & Sons, Ltd. Published 2019 by John Wiley & Sons, Ltd.

Why study development?

As just mentioned, the two main questions that developmental psychologists concern themselves with are (1) to understand the ways in which psychological processes are different across the various stages of our lives and (2) to try to understand how it is that we develop from one life stage to the next – how nature and nurture interact to drive development.

But why would we be interested in these issues? When asked this question, some of the first answers that people typically come up with are that understanding development can help us to help people in either clinical or educational settings. This is certainly correct. Research from developmental psychology often informs our understanding of developmental disorders such as **autism spectrum disorder** and **developmental dyslexia**. Although traditional explanations of childhood disorders conceptualized impairments as being static throughout the lifespan, it is now much more commonly agreed that we need to think about the ways in which impairments change across development. Renowned developmental scientist and theorist Annette Karmiloff-Smith summed this up in the title of one of her papers: 'Development itself is the key to understanding developmental disorders' (Karmiloff-Smith, 1998).

Likewise, educational practice is frequently influenced by developmental research. In the UK, **phonics** has been adopted by the Department for Education as the most effective method for teaching reading. The phonics approach to reading is based on teaching children the relationships between letters (or clusters of letters) and sounds as the building blocks that then help them to read whole words and sentences. The current prevalence of this approach is due in no small part to research by developmental psychologists demonstrating that early awareness of speech sounds in young nursery-age children is a strong predictor of later learning ability in primary school (Bradley & Bryant, 1983; Lundberg, Olofsson, & Wall, 1980; Wagner & Torgesen, 1987).

But perhaps the most important answer to the question of why we should study development is that it helps us to better understand human nature. Development is not just restricted to infancy and early childhood. We spend all of our lives developing, right through adulthood and into old age. So to understand development is to understand human nature itself. Even if we were to take a more narrow view of development and consider just infancy and childhood, the study of development is still hugely revealing about ourselves. The question of where we, our personalities, experiences, knowledge, and skills come from is answered in large part by the processes that developmental psychologists study.

SECTION SUMMARY

- The two main questions developmental psychologists concern themselves with are (1) to understand the ways in which psychological processes are different across the various stages of our lives and (2) to try to understand how it is that we develop from one life stage to the next – how nature and nurture interact to drive development.

- The study of development is key to the study of clinical and educational progress, both typical and atypical (e.g. in autism spectrum disorder or developmental dyslexia).

THEORIES OF DEVELOPMENT: HOW NATURE AND NURTURE INTERACT

LEARNING OBJECTIVE 11.2

Compare and contrast some important theories in developmental psychology.

As indicated, one of the main concerns of developmental psychology is to try to understand the processes that cause changes from one developmental stage to the next. This line of enquiry attempts to clarify the relative roles of inheritance and environment (nature and nurture) in development, and is the main consideration on which we will focus in outlining the various theoretical approaches in developmental psychology.

Early theoretical accounts of development

In the first half of the 20th century, the dominant school of thought among early developmental psychologists came from the behaviourist tradition and in consequence placed a very strong emphasis on the role of nurture by the environment. John B. Watson is particularly famous for his assertion that he could tailor an environment in order to shape the development of infants and children in any way he wanted:

> Give me a dozen healthy infants, well-formed, and my own specified world to bring them up in and I'll guarantee to take any one at random and train him to become any type of specialist I might select – doctor, lawyer, artist, merchant-chief and, yes, beggar-man and thief, regardless of his talents, penchants, tendencies, abilities, vocations, and race of his ancestors. (Watson, 1930, p. 82)

This quote seems to dismiss any possibility that development could be at all influenced by characteristics a child might bring with them into the world, and I suspect that most parents reading this (especially those with two or more children who are not identical twins) will find Watson's claim a little strident. However, it is important to acknowledge that Watson was to an extent reacting to equally strong arguments made by prominent figures in the **eugenics** movement around the start of the 20th century. People like Francis Galton (1904) stated that many human traits are inherited and advocated methods (many of which are today considered highly problematic from a moral standpoint) for improving the genetic quality of the human population.

And so the early debates in developmental psychology took on a rather dichotomous flavour, with psychologists adopting theoretical positions that tended to emphasize either nature or nurture at the expense of the other. We can call these extreme theoretical positions either **empiricist**, which emphasizes nurture and the role of experience, or **nativist**, which emphasizes nature and inheritance.

As we have already stated, the dominant empiricist position at the start of the 20th century was **behaviourism**. It is important to remember that the behaviourist approach was not primarily developmental. Indeed, the most important scientific contributions of behaviourism came from laboratory studies of adult animals (especially rats and pigeons). These kinds of studies helped to reveal some of the mechanisms by which learning occurs in animals and humans. The behaviourists were able to shed a lot of light on the simple mechanisms of learning (such as classical and instrumental conditioning) whereby animals and humans learn new behaviours by being exposed to novel combinations of environmental stimuli. However, these accounts of learning were then applied to developmental psychology with very little adaptation. Development was simply seen as an extended process of learning, and so (in contrast to Rousseau's position described earlier) the behaviourists did not characterize early life as being a distinct life stage as such.

Another group of ideas about development that was important in the early 20th century became known as **maturationism**. In contrast to the behaviourists, who tended to think of development in the same way as learning in a mature adult, maturationists (such as Arnold Gesell) carefully considered how our psychological machinery (our bodies and nervous systems) change in early life. Gesell, and other researchers such as Myrtle McGraw (e.g. McGraw, 1943), undertook careful studies of motor development, concluding that the ability to move develops according to fixed schedules.

For instance, Gesell and Ames (1940) argued that the development of motor competency in infancy is characterized by **cephalocaudal** and **proximodistal** trajectories of development in which abilities mature in a specific direction along the body (see Figure 11.1). The cephalocaudal direction implicates development from head to feet, and here Gesell and Ames were describing how the first body movements that infants master involve keeping the head upright on the neck, whereas an ability to control the torso in sitting develops later, and controlling the legs and feet in standing and walking develop later still. The proximodistal direction describes how motor control starts in bodily locations that are close to the core of the body and develops towards the extremities. A good example of this is the development of reaching. Whereas young infants' early reaches tend to be controlled by movements of the whole arm (swiping movements at the object they're reaching for), they gradually gain control of more and more proximal locations (e.g. the wrists and then fingers) to coordinate more sophisticated and accurate reaching and grasping movements (e.g. Berthier, Clifton, McCall, & Robin, 1999). Gesell and Ames (1940) argued that these fixed trajectories are due to a kind of genetic blueprint that sets out the basis for development before it has happened. This is a particularly nativist viewpoint.

Current thinking in developmental psychology tends to be more circumspect in regard to the nature/nurture debate, typically portraying development as a process that unfolds as a consequence of the interaction between nature and nurture rather than as a result of one or the other. In the remainder of this section we will outline approaches that have taken this **interactionist** position.

Jean Piaget's constructionism

The Swiss scientist Jean Piaget (1896–1980) can rightly be credited with having been the single person who has had the most important influence on modern developmental

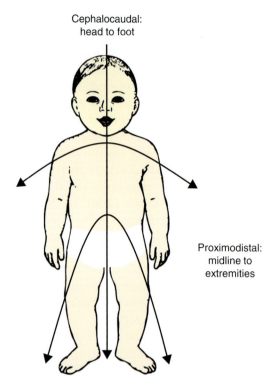

Cephalocaudal:
head to foot

Proximodistal:
midline to
extremities

FIGURE 11.1 *Cephalocaudal and proximodistal directions of motor development as described by Gesell and Ames (1940).*

psychology. Piaget's particular interest was in what he termed 'genetic epistemology' or, put more simply, the origins of knowledge. His argument in a nutshell was that infants and children themselves construct their own knowledge of the world through actively engaging with their own environments. Piaget (1936/1952) argued that children come into the world with a range of reflexes and means of acquiring knowledge. According to his account, the application of these active 'schemas' to the environment yields new experiences for children, which force them to change the ways in which they act on and think about the world. Two important Piagetian concepts here are 'assimilation' and 'accommodation'. Assimilation is the drive to take in new information to form schemas, and accommodation is the means whereby the schema is adapted to make sense of that new information. So, according to Piaget's account, the processes of assimilation and accommodation constantly challenge and modify schemas through development, changing the ways in which infants and, later, children act on and think about the world around them. This description of development as a process in which infants and children construct their own understanding of the world became known as **constructionism** (you'll also sometimes hear it referred to as 'constructivism').

Piaget was certainly of the view that development is made up of qualitatively distinct life periods or stages. There are three main stages of development in Piaget's constructionist theory. The first is the **sensorimotor period** (0–2 years), in which Piaget described infants as gradually mastering an ability to act on the world by developing and honing action schemas (we will return to this later). According to Piaget, this process of sensorimotor development culminates in an ability (at about

2 years) to start to think about the world independently of action, to think about the world in a symbolic way. During the subsequent **concrete operations period** (2–11 years), children progressively hone their ways of thinking about the world – their powers of imagination – such that by 11 years children enter the **formal operations period** (11 years onwards), in which they are able to think in completely abstract hypothetical terms.

Piaget's account of development has encountered many challenges over the years, particularly in terms of the ways in which he stipulates children's abilities at particular developmental stages; many researchers have argued that his stage account typically underestimates children's and infants' cognitive abilities. However, the idea of genetic epistemology, in which knowledge is brought about by the interaction between a set of reflexes and internal motivation to explore the world (either in action or thought), on the one hand, and environmental input, on the other hand, still has many adherents today. More recently, researchers (of a Piagetian bent or otherwise) have begun to attempt to understand the biological processes that underpin the interactions between nature and nurture that give rise to development. This has started to reveal some exciting new advances in our understanding of the role of biological processes in development.

DISCUSSION POINT

Discuss the main ideas articulated in Piaget's constructionist account of cognitive development. What are your thoughts on the challenges that have been proposed in opposition to this approach?

Developmental cognitive neuroscience

What happens in the brain when our cognitive abilities develop? This is a question that has begun to take centre stage in developmental psychology in recent years. But why should we concern ourselves with the brain? Do we really learn anything useful by considering how neurons and regions of nervous tissue underpin our developing abilities? Psychologists, including developmental psychologists, have not always considered biological processes to be very relevant in understanding cognitive abilities (e.g. Mehler, Morton, & Jusczyk, 1984). Perhaps we can understand development simply by considering the interaction between inherited abilities and the environment to which we are exposed, without having to think about how this works in the brain. Activity 11.1 considers this matter.

ACTIVITY 11.1

WHY DO WE NEED TO THINK ABOUT THE BRAIN TO UNDERSTAND COGNITIVE DEVELOPMENT?

In recent times, researchers have argued that, in order to fully solve the puzzle of how development happens, it is going to be crucial to shed light on the biological changes that underpin it (Johnson & de Haan, 2011; Mareschal et al., 2007). Let's think about an example of why this might be the case.

Imagine you are a 7-month-old infant. Over the past months you've been honing your ability to reach for and pick up interesting objects and toys. A classically described difficulty that infants of this age demonstrate is an inability to reach for and retrieve toys that have just been hidden (for instance, under a cloth) in front of their eyes (**object permanence**; Piaget, 1950/1954). To succeed at this task, you have to be able to do a range of things. Before moving on to read the next part of the activity, can you list all of the cognitive functions you need to retrieve the hidden toy? (Hint: think about cognitive functions, perceptual functions, and motor skills.)

In order to retrieve the hidden toy, you will require a range of cognitive functions. Among other abilities you will have to be able to see the toy being hidden, you will have to remember what the toy is and where it has been hidden, you will have to have an understanding that the toy continues to exist when out of sight, you will have to know about how to uncover the toy and pick it up, and you will have to have the requisite motor skills to do this.

Each of the abilities just described is underpinned by a network of brain regions. These networks will be located in various parts of the brain and nervous system. From your knowledge of the functions of different parts of the brain, can you think of some brain regions that will be involved in the functions you've just listed?

Remembering an object and where it is (holding a representation of it in short-term memory), and organizing the actions needed to uncover the object and pick it up are largely underpinned by networks of neurons in the **prefrontal cortex**. Perceiving the object and the hiding event are likely to take place in the occipital and temporal brain regions. As we discussed above, the functions of different parts of the body mature at different rates. This is also the case in the brain. So, if different parts of the brain and nervous system mature at different points in development, the various abilities you need as an infant to retrieve a hidden toy might not all develop at the same time.

The prefrontal cortex, for instance, takes a notoriously long time to develop relative to the rest of the human brain, and so we might expect the short-term memory and action planning aspects of hidden object retrieval to develop much later than the perceptual aspects. And so, perhaps, because of the way the brain develops, even though you can see the toy being hidden and know that it continues to exist, you may, at 7 months of age, still fail to retrieve it because you cannot yet hold a representation of an object in memory and plan actions to retrieve it (e.g. Baillargeon, 2004; Diamond, 1990; Mareschal, 2000; Mareschal & Bremner, 2006). Biologically inspired arguments like this have been put forward by several developmental theorists to explain why particular cognitive abilities emerge at particular points in development. As we shall see later in this chapter, the prolonged maturation of the prefrontal cortex has implications for cognitive development across a wide range of situations and abilities.

We've seen from Activity 11.1 how biological factors can play a role in cognitive development, but how does development actually work in the brain? Johnson and de Haan (2011) propose some alternative ways of explaining developmental changes in brain function. One is called the 'maturational' account of brain development. An extreme version of this account would assume that much of the neural machinery that underlies our abilities comes predescribed in our genetic inheritance, but that the developmental emergence of cognitive abilities is constrained (or held up) by the maturation of relevant parts of the brain. This account therefore implies that the brain areas specialized for particular tasks (e.g. face perception, object perception) mature without the need for a major input from our experience of the environment around us.

Another approach favoured by Johnson and de Haan (2011) is the **interactive specialization** account, which suggests, contrary to the maturationist account, that particular parts of the brain are not predesigned for specific tasks, but rather that the brain becomes gradually differentiated into areas and networks that are specialized for particular tasks. Importantly, interactive specialization argues that this process of specialization occurs to a large extent in response to the environmental stimulation that infants and children experience.

But which approach is the correct one? It is early days in answering this question, and it is important to acknowledge that processes of maturation and interactive specialization could both be going on at once. However, opinion is certainly moving towards the view that maturation cannot be the sole explanation of brain development. As we shall see, there is now much evidence that environmental factors play very important roles in the way brains and networks of neurons develop. Furthermore, evidence showing that the regions involved in particular tasks (e.g. in face perception; Cohen Kadosh, Cohen Kadosh, Dick, & Johnson, 2011; Halit, de Haan, & Johnson, 2003) change substantially over development suggests that the way the brain functions changes a lot in the first years of life. This is certainly consistent with Johnson's (2011) interactive specialization account.

SECTION SUMMARY

- Developmental psychologists are interested in understanding the ways in which psychological processes are different across the various stages of our lives, and understanding how it is that we develop from one life stage to the next.

- Research from developmental psychology often informs our understanding of developmental disorders such as autism spectrum disorder and developmental dyslexia, and influences educational practice.

- The question of where we, our personalities, experiences, knowledge, and skills come from is answered in large part by the processes that developmental psychologists study.

- The dominant empiricist position at the start of the 20th century was behaviourism.

- Another group of ideas about development that was important in the early 20th century became known as maturationism, which argued that the development of motor competency in infancy is characterized by cephalocaudal and proximodistal trajectories of development.

- The Swiss scientist Jean Piaget (1896–1980) is credited with having been the single person who has had the most important influence on modern developmental psychology.

- Piaget's stage theory of development argues that infants and children themselves construct their own knowledge of the world through actively engaging with their own environments.

- The field of developmental cognitive neuroscience has begun to take centre stage in developmental psychology in recent years.

- Two significant theories in this field are the maturational account and the interactive specialization account.

RESEARCH METHODS IN DEVELOPMENTAL PSYCHOLOGY

LEARNING OBJECTIVE 11.3

Discuss the research methods used in the study of developmental psychology and the specific challenges and ethics of working with infants and children.

How do we measure developmental change? What methods allow us to determine whether development is due to inheritance (nature), experience (nurture), or an interaction between these? As in other areas of psychology, most developmental psychologists use scientific methods to investigate the questions they are interested in. Theoretical accounts are formulated, and then hypotheses derived and tested, sometimes in experimental situations (e.g. a child is given a task on a computer and their accuracy and reaction time are measured), and other times in more correlational scenarios (e.g. behaviours in classroom might be correlated to aspects of the home environment). As research methods in psychology more generally are covered elsewhere in this book, we will focus here on aspects of research methods that are of particular importance to studying development. We will highlight two crucial things that set developmental investigations apart from psychological investigations more broadly. The first is that developmental studies try to measure changes in ability over time, and the causes of those changes. The second is that development investigations have to deal with the challenges of studying and comparing different age groups of children. As we will see, the challenges of approaching these matters are not straightforward.

Researching developmental change

Perhaps the simplest way to measure developmental change is to compare individuals of different ages or groups of individuals of different ages. For instance, imagine we are interested in examining improvements in visual recognition of faces between 4 and 6 years of age. To do this we might run an experimental face recognition task on two groups of children, one made up of 4-year-olds and the other comprising 6-year-olds. Let's imagine we presented pictures of celebrities to these groups of children and measured their naming accuracy and their speed at naming the celebrities (i.e. a reaction time measure). This kind of research design is called **cross-sectional**, in that the experimenter looks at a cross-section of performance across age groups. Any difference in the average performance of the two age groups might be taken as an indication of developmental change in face recognition. There are of course some problems with the particular example we have given, which we'll come on to, but the important thing to note at this stage is that cross-sectional studies provide a quick and easy way to compare the performance of different age groups and thus get an idea as to whether developmental change occurs between them.

The most important limitation of the cross-sectional design is that there might be differences other than the one we are interested in (in this case, age) between the two groups we want to compare. If we were testing in a school, it might be that the school changed its admissions policy from one year to the next so that the 6-year-olds would not only be older than the 4-year-old group but might also be from different parts of town or different socioeconomic backgrounds. Perhaps the 6-year-olds perform better than the 4-year-olds because their parents let them watch more television, rather than because of the age difference. **Longitudinal designs** get over this kind of problem by comparing the same children at different stages in their own development. Given this focus on change within the individual rather than changes between groups, longitudinal studies provide much richer information about how developmental change occurs. The obvious problem with longitudinal studies is that they are much more time consuming, requiring us to wait for the child to get older between testing one age and the next. An example of a long-term longitudinal study is the Millennium Cohort Study (Centre for Longitudinal Studies, 2018), which is following the lives of around 19,000 children born in the United Kingdom in 2000–2001.

So far we have discussed measuring changes in ability over development. But how do scientific investigations get at the causes of development? Answering questions about the causes of development is a much more complex challenge. Certainly, developmental psychology studies that simply measure and describe developmental change vastly outnumber those that directly assess the causes of development. It is much more difficult to measure the causes of development because of technical and cost challenges, but also for a number of ethical reasons. The principal ethical concern is that measuring the causes of development often involves intervening in some way. This is difficult to justify with human children or infants unless we have a strong reason to believe that the alterations we make will not be harmful in any way. For this reason many studies of the effects of the environment on development have been carried out with animals. However, this is not to say that there are no studies that examine the effects of altered environments on human development. **Training studies**, in which the effects of a particular training regime on cognitive development are measured, are a case in point; one set of investigations has focused on whether training working memory can lead to improvements in working memory in early childhood (Holmes, Gathercole, & Dunning, 2009; Melby-Lervåg & Hulme, 2013).

Of course, both environment and inheritance play roles in development, so as well as determining the effects of environmental experience on development we also have to consider how environmental and hereditary factors interact. One of the most useful ways of examining the roles of inherited and environmental factors on development comes from twin studies in the field of **behavioural genetics**. By examining whether traits are more commonly shared between identical rather than fraternal twins, we can determine the extent to which genetic inheritance is important in the development of those traits.

Working with infants and children

One of the most challenging aspects of developmental research is working with the participants. Infants do not understand experimental instructions, and so we have to rely on them to behave in an expected manner (the expected behaviours frequently do not play out). Techniques for studying physiological and neural processes (such as electroencephalography [EEG] or functional magnetic resonance imaging [fMRI]) rely on the participants staying still for a certain duration. This is very difficult to ensure with certain age groups. Even at ages at which we can give verbal instructions, toddlers and children are notoriously uncooperative when it comes to following or even listening to an experimenter's instructions. Sitting still seems to be very difficult for young children even when they are trying hard to do so. Furthermore, as we shall see later, even when we think that they have followed our instructions, children often turn out to have interpreted them in a different way to how we expected. Professor Paul Bloom of Yale University discusses these challenges in a video (Bloom, 2012).

Given the different ways in which different age groups behave and respond to task demands, developmental psychologists have had to come up with some particularly clever ways of determining how infants and children perceive, think, and learn. Imagine trying to determine what a newborn baby can see. Coming fresh to this problem, and without knowing much about the literature, it is clear that this is going to be a complicated task. Yet developmental psychologists specializing in infant perception, through careful honing of experimental methods, have been able to find out a great deal about how newborn babies see the world. And so the ways in which we determine cognitive abilities vary depending on the age group we're working with.

Imagine we're interested in determining whether a range of age groups of children understand or perceive object permanence (an ability to recognize that an object continues to exist in a particular place after observing someone hiding it in front of them). If we're trying to do this with a 2-month-old, an 8-month-old, and a 4-year-old, we would likely use very different methods for each participant. We would probably observe eye movements in response to hiding events in the 2-month-olds, and we might see whether the 8-month-old will reach and search by hand (manually) for the hidden object. For the 4-year-old we would be likely to probe their understanding with questions.

This is all well and good, and necessary, but it reveals an important problem for developmental psychology: that we cannot always compare cognitive abilities in different age groups using the same measures. If we cannot compare an ability across age groups using the same measure, how can we be sure that any changes we see are due to changes in the ability we're interested in or due to differences in the ways the ability is measured across age groups? We shall see a few instances of this deep-seated problem for developmental psychology in this chapter. To cut a long story short, the likely solution to this problem is to gather as many measures of ability as possible from each age group. The more agreement we have between measures, the more sure we can be that we're getting an accurate picture about ability.

The ethics of working with children is a crucial concern in developmental psychology. As with research in human adults, it is considered vital that the research does not bring child participants to any harm, and we also have to make special considerations for the ways in which children differ from adults in this regard. Materials that have no impact on an adult might be quite unsuitable for children. The most substantial issue concerning research participation in young children surrounds **informed consent**. The principle of obtaining informed consent from research participants is considered one of the most important aspects of ethical conduct in research, the idea being that agreement to participate in research should be based on a clear understanding of the procedures for the research and the reasons for conducting it in the first place. This clearly presents problems when we're working with young children or preverbal infants. For this reason, research projects with child participants typically gain consent to participate from the child's parent or caregiver. It is also considered important, where possible, to seek positive assent to participate from the child participant.

TEST YOURSELF

1. What are the practical and ethical challenges that are associated with undertaking research with infants and children?
2. What steps would you take to overcome these challenges?

SECTION SUMMARY

- Developmental studies try to measure changes in ability over time, and the causes of those changes. Development research also has to deal with the challenges of studying and comparing different age groups of children.

- Perhaps the simplest way to measure developmental change is to compare individuals of different ages or groups of individuals of different ages. This kind of research design is called cross-sectional research, and the experimenter looks at a cross-section of performance across age groups.

- The most important limitation of the cross-sectional design is that there might be differences other than age between the two groups we compare. Longitudinal studies get over this kind of problem by comparing the same children at different stages in their own development.

- Studies that examine the effects of altered environments on human development are called training studies; here, the effects of a particular training regime on cognitive development are measured.

- Both environment and inheritance play roles in development, so as well as determining the effects of environmental experience on development we also have to consider how environmental and hereditary factors interact. One of the most useful ways of examining the roles of inherited and environmental factors on development comes from twin studies in the field of behavioural genetics.

- One of the most challenging aspects of developmental research is working with the participants. Given the different ways in which different age groups behave and respond to task demands, developmental psychologists have had to come up with some particularly clever ways of determining how infants and children perceive, think, and learn.

- The principle of obtaining informed consent from research participants is considered one of the most important aspects of ethical conduct in research.

DEVELOPMENT OF THE BRAIN AND NERVOUS SYSTEM

LEARNING OBJECTIVE 11.4

Identify and describe the key stages in development of the brain and nervous system from conception to adulthood.

We all start out as a single fertilized egg – a **zygote**. This zygote contains the deoxyribonucleic acid (DNA), the biological code of our inheritance, which will be passed on to every other cell created in development throughout our body, brain, and nervous system. The DNA in our cells contains the code for each cell to create the proteins that help build up our bodies. Perhaps the most amazing aspect of biological development is the means by which the cells in our bodies become differentiated for different purposes, despite containing exactly the same DNA. In a process called gene expression, the environmental (chemical) context in which a cell develops determines which parts of its DNA are decoded and used to create proteins. So, depending on where in the body a cell is, different aspects of our DNA are expressed, and thus different proteins are made. This helps to explain why, despite having exactly the same DNA, one cell in the eye will produce the colours of our iris, whereas another cell in our big toe will produce the proteins needed to manufacture toenails. The developmental biologist C. H. Waddington (1957) captured the complexity of this process of cellular development in what he termed the **epigenetic landscape** (see Figure 11.2).

Waddington's epigenetic landscape is used to illustrate how the context in which a cell develops (the landscape) has a very important role to play in the way it becomes differentiated. The idea of the epigenetic landscape is not just influential in developmental biology. Psychologists such as Piaget have also used it as an analogy for understanding not just the development and differentiation of cells but also the psychological development of an individual human (ontogenetic development). The undulating landscape (see Figure 11.2) illustrates the many paths that ontogenetic development could take; how we develop psychologically as a person is determined by the ways in which the undulations influence our progress from one stage to the next.

At a biological level, then, it is clear that the way in which development occurs is as an interaction between our inheritance (our DNA) and environmental factors.

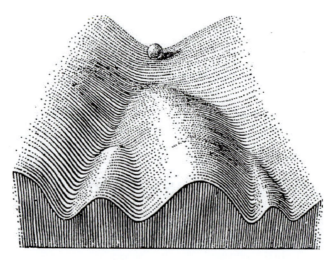

FIGURE 11.2 *Waddington's (1957) epigenetic landscape. Waddington used the epigenetic landscape as an analogy for understanding how the environment in which a cell exists determines the way in which it is expressed (the path it follows in development). The epigenetic landscape can also be used as an analogy for understanding how the environment influences the development of a person or organism.*

Source: Waddington (1957). Routledge. Reproduced by permission of Taylor & Francis Books UK.

The environment in which a cell develops and becomes functionally differentiated determines the ways in which its genetic inheritance is expressed (Plomin, DeFries, Knopik, & Neiderhiser, 2013). It seems reasonable to assume that a similar interactive process is happening in the brain and nervous system, underpinning psychological development in human infants and children. We describe this process in the following sections.

Biological development from conception to birth

Once an ovum has been fertilized by a sperm cell and a zygote has been created, cell division happens rapidly. Around the point at which the ball of cells becomes implanted in the uterine wall, we start to see the first evidence of differentiation of cell types. The collection of cells that will eventually become a mature adult human starts to take on a defined structure (at this point it becomes known as an **embryo**). Different layers of cells emerge, one of which, the **ectoderm**, later becomes the nervous system. As the ectoderm is thus the most interesting aspect of the developing embryo from the point of view of the developmental psychologist, we will focus on it.

The ectoderm folds over on itself to become a tube of cells, the structure of which will later form the central column of the nervous system – the brain and spinal cord. Next, cells start to become differentiated within the **neural tube**. Along its length, the neural tube differentiates into the different structures of the brain and nervous system, with the forebrain (including the cerebral hemispheres), midbrain, and hindbrain at one end and the spinal cord at the other. As the embryo takes shape, the cells along the back of the developing spinal cord and brain differentiate into sensory systems and the cells along the front become the motor systems. In the radial dimension (between the inside and the outside) the neural tube differentiates into layers of cells that have different functions in wiring together the various areas of the nervous system. Figure 11.3 illustrates some of these developing differentiations in the nervous system (particularly those along the length of the neural tube).

Casting our minds back to the process of gene expression described earlier, it is important to remember that all of these differentiations are happening due to environmental factors. All of these cells contain the same DNA. It is the fact that the cells in different parts of the embryo are developing under different environmental conditions that leads them to become specialized in the ways in which they are. The developing differentiation of the anatomy of the nervous system and body which we are describing here forms the basis of the gradual specialization of different parts of the nervous system for different functions, such as perception, memory, language, and movement.

The central role of environmental factors in cellular differentiation means that the developing nervous system is especially vulnerable to perturbations in the environment. If the embryo or **foetus** is exposed to toxins in utero, this can lead to abnormal prenatal development. Such toxins are called **teratogens**, and include a range of chemicals and pathogens such as alcohol, nicotine, rubella, and stress hormones (see Leman, Bremner, Parke, & Gauvain, 2012).

The differentiation of the nervous system we have just described is made possible by the growth (through cellular division) of new cells. The cells that make up the nervous system (largely neurons and glial cells) increase hugely in number during

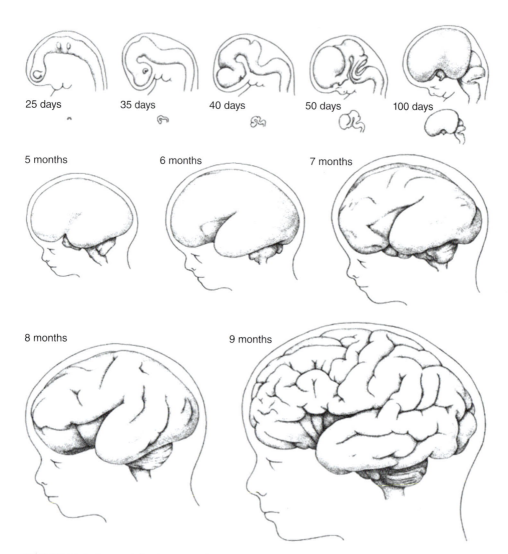

25 days   35 days   40 days   50 days   100 days

5 months   6 months   7 months

8 months   9 months

FIGURE 11.3 *Prenatal development of the central nervous system. The neural tube becomes differentiated into the various structures of the central nervous system, gradually becoming more convoluted such that at the time of birth it no longer resembles a tube. Differentiation along the length of the tube into the forebrain, midbrain, hindbrain, and spinal cord are illustrated here, but further differentiations occur at a finer level of detail, and also in the radial axis and circumference of the neural tube.*

Source: Reproduced with permission. Copyright © 1979 Scientific American, a division of Nature America, Inc. All rights reserved.

prenatal life. The zygote is made up of just one cell. By the time the embryonic period begins (at around 10 days), the ectoderm (the tissue that will later form the nervous system) is made up of several hundred cells (including neurons and glial cells). But by the time we are born there are tens of billions of neurons alone. This large number of neurons (and the correspondingly large number of synapses between neurons) in the newborn infant make up a broad canvas on which postnatal experience can lay down its imprint to shape the brain and nervous system into the complex functioning organs that adults possess.

Biological development from infancy to adulthood

The adult brain contains around 86 billion (86,000,000,000) neurons (Azevedo et al., 2009), and (very) roughly 51,600,000,000,000 connections or synapses between neurons. Via these synapses, the neurons of the central nervous system are arranged into networks that are specialized to carry out particular cognitive functions (e.g. face recognition versus speech processing). But what changes occur between birth and adulthood that give rise to the brain and nervous system in this mature state? According to Johnson & de Haan (2011), the vast majority of neurons are already present at the point of birth. The major changes to the cellular structure of the nervous system following birth involve changes in synaptic connectivity. The number of synapses in the nervous system appears to undergo a rise and fall in postnatal life (see Figure 11.4), which reflects overlapping processes of **synaptic proliferation** (the making of synaptic connections) and **synaptic pruning** (the breaking of synaptic connections), which are ongoing simultaneously in development. Synaptic pruning and differentiation are guided by a number of factors. Some connections appear to be made due to chemical interactions between particular brain regions (e.g. Molnár & Blakemore, 1991). But we also see that the electrical activity of our neurons (itself driven by environmental experience) drives the formation and pruning of synapses (Fox & Wong, 2005; Holtmaat & Svoboda, 2009; Mataga, Mizuguchi, & Hensch, 2004; Shatz, 2008).

Another important change happening in postnatal biological development involves the myelination of neurons. Myelin is a fatty insulating sheath that surrounds the electrical conducting axons of neurons. Myelin increases a great deal during postnatal life, even into early adulthood in certain regions of the brain, and this brings changes

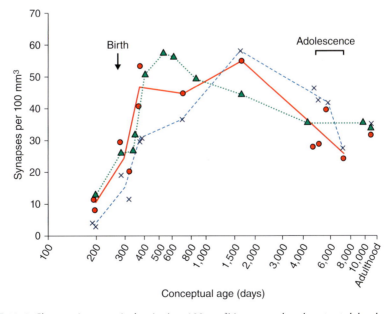

FIGURE 11.4 *Changes in synaptic density (per 100 mm³) in prenatal and postnatal development. The triangles and dotted line represent synaptic density in the visual cortex, the circles and solid line represent the same in the auditory cortex, and the crosses and dashed line represent synaptic density in the prefrontal cortex. Synaptic proliferation and pruning are significantly delayed in development in the prefrontal cortex relative to the rest of the brain.*

Source: Huttenlocher and Dabholkar (1997). John Wiley and Sons.

in the speed of neural processing. Myelin insulation allows neurons to send electrical signals more quickly.

But what do these biological changes mean for psychological development? Although it is quite easy to speculate that changes in the number of synapses, or speed of electrical connectivity (through increased myelination), in the brain should have wide-reaching implications for our cognitive processes, evidence demonstrating that this is the case is somewhat more difficult to come by.

Perhaps the best clues to how biological changes in the brain influence cognitive development come from the different rates of development of particular brain areas. Figure 11.4 shows the rise and fall in the number of synapses across prenatal and post-natal life, mentioned earlier in this section. However, the density of synapses is plotted differently according to different brain regions, and we can see that both synaptic proliferation and pruning occur substantially later in the prefrontal cortex relative to the other brain areas (here, the visual and auditory cortices).

There is plenty of evidence that this relative delay in the development of the pre-frontal cortex has an impact on cognitive development. As we discussed earlier in this chapter, this delay in prefrontal cortex development could explain why young infants take a long time to learn to plan actions appropriately. The prefrontal cortex plays crucial roles in cognitive functions such as inhibition, planning, and short-term memory, and all of these are known to continue to develop substantially throughout childhood and into adolescence. Blakemore (2008), for instance, argues that the delayed development of the prefrontal cortex has an important impact on the development of social understanding in adolescence.

And so this kind of argument demonstrates how the different rates of biological development across the brain can play important roles in the ways our cognitive functions develop. As we shall see throughout this chapter, functions that are sub-served by the prefrontal cortex are often particularly delayed in development relative to functions in earlier-maturing brain regions. Sensory areas that are among the earliest to develop appear to subserve perceptual function from very early in life. As we shall see in the next section, infants are surprisingly sophisticated in their perceptual skills from early in life, and even prenatally.

SECTION SUMMARY

- The developmental biologist C. H. Waddington (1957) captured the complexity of cellular development in what he termed the epigenetic landscape. Waddington's epigenetic landscape is used to illustrate how the context in which a cell develops has a very important role to play in the way it becomes differentiated.

- At a biological level, it is clear that the way in which development occurs is as an interaction between our inheritance (our DNA) and environmental factors.

- Once an ovum has been fertilized by a sperm cell and a zygote has been created, cell division happens rapidly.

- The central role of environmental factors in cellular differentiation means that the developing nervous system is especially vulnerable to toxins known as teratogens.

- The major changes to the cellular structure of the nervous system following birth involve changes in synaptic connectivity. Synaptic proliferation and synaptic pruning are overlapping processes that are guided by a number of factors.

- Another important change happening in postnatal biological development involves the myelination of neurons.

- Perhaps the best clues to how biological changes in the brain influence cognitive development come from the different rates of development of particular brain areas. In particular, there is plenty of evidence that this relative delay in the development of the prefrontal cortex has an impact on cognitive development.

MULTISENSORY PERCEPTUAL DEVELOPMENT

LEARNING OBJECTIVE 11.5

Identify and describe the key stages in the development of multisensory perceptual abilities in prenatal, newborn, and young children.

At the beginning of the 20th century, the commonly held view concerning infants' perceptual abilities was that they were initially very limited. In a famous observational diary, Charles Darwin recorded the development of his son, William Erasmus ('Doddy'). With respect to perceptual development, he observed the following:

> His eyes were fixed on a candle as early as the 9th day, and up to the 45th day nothing else seemed thus to fix them; but on the 49th day his attention was attracted by a bright-coloured tassel, as was shown by his eyes becoming fixed and the movements of his arms ceasing. It was surprising how slowly he acquired the power of following with his eyes an object if swinging at all rapidly; for he could not do this well when seven and a half months old. At the age of 32 days he perceived his mother's bosom when three or four inches from it, as was shown by the protrusion of his lips and his eyes becoming fixed; but I much doubt whether this had any connection with vision; he certainly had not touched the bosom. Whether he was guided through smell or the sensation of warmth or through association with the position in which he was held, I do not at all know. (Darwin, 1877, p. 286)

There are a few interesting things that we can take from Darwin's observation. First, he was clearly of the view that his young son was perceptually naive, especially in the domain of vision. However, as we shall see in this section, despite Darwin's renowned powers of observation, we now know him to have been at least partially incorrect in this regard. Nonetheless, he makes an important observation concerning the difficulty newborns have with tracking moving objects with their eyes. This holds up well to more recent investigations: although newborns can follow moving objects with a series of sudden eye movements (saccades), the smooth-pursuit eye movements that characterize adults' fixations on moving objects do not begin to emerge until around 3 months of age (Aslin, 1981; Richards & Holley, 1999).

However, as Darwin makes it clear, it is difficult to know, just by observing an infant's responses to their perceptual world, which senses they are using to recognize things or people. He points out that it is difficult to determine exactly how Doddy was able to recognize certain objects (in this case his mother's breast). Infants, like adults, have available to them a range of sensory systems, including vision, hearing, smell, taste, and touch, which can all help them to perceive particular objects. For instance, we can recognize particular people through their visual appearance (typically their face), the sound of their voice, and, perhaps particularly pertinent for the newborn infant, their very smell or even the way in which they touch us (Bremner, Lewkowicz, & Spence, 2012).

However, the arrival in the 1960s of experimental methods for assessing perceptual ability in young infants has meant that more recently we have been able to overcome the limitations of purely observational methods such as the ones used by Darwin. As we shall see, clever methods, including fine-grained inspections of infants' visual fixation behaviour, have yielded much more sensitive tests of perceptual ability. Experimental control of the stimuli we present to infants has also allowed us to determine which sense modalities babies use to perceive and recognize their environment.

Work examining perception in adult humans has shown that our senses influence each other throughout our perceptual experience (Stein, 2012), meaning that our perceptions of the world are inherently multisensory. Set in contrast to this, the great majority of research on perceptual development has tended to examine development in just one sense modality at a time (focusing in particular on vision and hearing). By restricting investigations to single modalities, and avoiding questions about how multisensory perception develops, researchers may be missing out on crucial clues to how perception really develops. It is clear that in order to fully understand perceptual development we need to consider not just the development of individual sensory modalities but also the ways in which our senses interact and function together.

The following sections will describe a little of what is known about perceptual development, focusing in particular on prenatal life and infancy, as these are the key life stages at which perceptual development occurs. We will cover some of the large body of work that has investigated how infants perceive their world through single sensory modalities (vision, hearing, smell, etc.). However, we will also dedicate a section to discussing how interactions between the senses change across early life.

Prenatal and newborn perceptual abilities

It might be tempting to think that perception begins once we are born, but actually an ability to sense and respond to sense information begins well before birth in the early stages of prenatal life (see Figure 11.5). Touch is the first sense the foetus responds to. At only 7 weeks' gestation a human foetus will move if its lips are touched (Hooker, 1952; Humphrey, 1964). The foetus shows hand-grasp responses to touches on the palm at 12 weeks' gestation (Humphrey, 1964). Responses to changes in body position (sensed through the vestibular system) are seen very early, at 11–25 weeks' gestation (Gottlieb, 1971). The first evidence of hearing is apparent at 24 weeks' gestation, when the foetus will startle in response to loud sounds outside the uterus (Abrams, Gerhardt, & Peters, 1995). Even though there is very little in the way of visual input in utero, premature infants' eyes will track moving objects from around 28 weeks' gestation and perhaps earlier (Fifer & Moon, 2003).

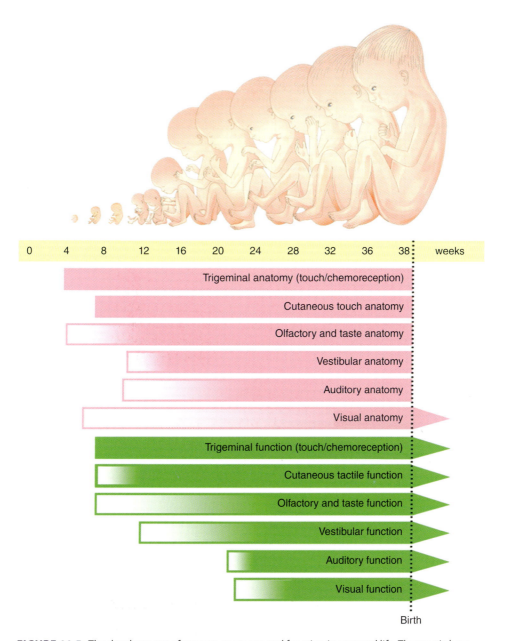

FIGURE 11.5 *The development of sensory anatomy and function in prenatal life. The top six bars indicate the emergence and maturation of sensory anatomy. The bottom six bars indicate the onset of function of the senses.*

Source: Adapted from Bremner, Lewkowicz, and Spence (2012); Moore and Persaud (2008); Occelli, Spence, and Zampini (2011, Fig. 1).

 Watch this 2011 TED Talk[1], in which author Annie Murphy Paul debates when learning begins.

And so, even early in prenatal development, the foetus processes and responds to sensory inputs in some way. But what does it make of these sensory inputs? Is it fair to think of the responses that foetuses make as indicating that they perceive and learn from their sensory environment in anything like the way we do as adults? There are at least some clues that foetuses learn about their perceptual world in a way that prepares them for life in the outside world.

In the 1980s, DeCasper and colleagues asked whether human foetuses can learn in utero about sounds they hear from the outside world. DeCasper and Fifer (1980) pioneered a procedure in which they relied on newborn babies' tendency to vary their patterns of sucking. In these studies, newborn babies could change the way in which they sucked in order to control what they heard on a tape recorder. The authors played newborns a soundtrack of either their mother or a strange woman speaking to them, and they set the study up in such a way that particular patterns of sucking (e.g. short or long bursts) activated one soundtrack or the other. They found that infants changed their patterns of sucking in order to switch on and hear their own mother's voice in preference to that of the stranger. This suggests that, even as early as birth, newborn babies can recognize the sound of their own mother's voice. Do they learn about those sounds in the first few hours of life, or do they recognize their mother's voice from sounds they have heard in utero?

DeCasper and Spence (1986) conducted another study using the same technique, but this time asking whether newborn babies could recognize a particular pattern of speech (rather than the sound of someone's voice). They asked pregnant women to read a passage from a children's book to their foetuses twice a day in the last 7 weeks of pregnancy. Then, once the babies were born, the authors played soundtracks of the mother reading either the same passage of text or a different passage of text from a different book. The newborns preferred, and changed their sucking patterns to keep playing, the soundtrack of the text they had heard in utero.

DeCasper and colleagues' studies seem to show that human foetuses can learn about the sounds of particular voices and speech that they hear when in the womb. Of course, it would be silly to suggest that they fully understand what they are hearing, but certainly we can imagine that what they do learn about might be the first steps in learning to perceive and understand the social auditory world of people and language (Hepper, 1996; Saffran, Werker, & Werner, 2006). Perhaps, for instance, they are learning about the melodic patterns of speech: what is called **prosody**. In fact, there is some evidence that foetuses learn about melodic patterns in music. Hepper (1988) showed that newborn babies could recognize the theme tune of their mother's favourite soap opera, which they had likely heard many times through the uterus wall in the lead-up to birth.

Of course, sound is not the only sensory modality that is stimulated in utero. Odours and tastes, for instance, are presented to the foetus in the amniotic fluid, and we know that chemosensory receptors are among the first to be mature anatomically in prenatal life (at around 11 weeks; Schaal & Durand, 2012). Schaal, Marlier, and Soussignan (2000) showed that, when a mother eats anise during pregnancy, the newborn baby will later show fewer aversive responses to anise odours in the first days of life (Schaal and colleagues presented the anise odours underneath the newborns' noses and examined how much they turned their heads away from the smell). The newborns must have experienced anise odours in utero as a flavour in the amniotic fluid, leading them to habituate to (i.e. learn about) this particular aroma.

And so, there is plenty of evidence to suggest that foetuses learn much from their sensory environments in utero, through several senses. Perhaps the sense that is least likely to receive useful input in the womb is vision. Although some light makes it through the uterine wall, there is unlikely to be enough light in the womb to make out much about the foetus's visual surroundings. However, techniques described in Research Methods 11.1 show that, as soon as a baby arrives in the outside world, their visual systems enable them to differentiate quite complex aspects of their visual environments.

RESEARCH METHODS 11.1

FINDING WINDOWS ONTO VISUAL PERCEPTION IN EARLY LIFE

In 1961, Robert Fantz published a seminal article describing the findings of a new technique for examining perceptual abilities in very young babies: the **visual preference** method. In this procedure, Fantz placed infants on their backs, showed them two or more visual stimuli at the same time, and observed their eyes to record how long they looked at each stimulus. He found that the infants (who were only 2 weeks of age) preferred complex patterns, such as drawings of a human face, over simple patterns and solid colours. The preference that babies showed demonstrates that they can perceive these visual stimuli and differences between them.

The findings that emerged from visual preference studies by Fantz and others following his article give a remarkable account of perceptual competence in early life, which was unavailable to those using less quantitative observational methods (e.g. Darwin). We have found, for instance, that newborn babies (even those who are only 30 minutes old) prefer to look at faces than at scrambled face patterns (Johnson, Dziurawiec, Ellis, & Morton, 1991), that newborns of only a few days of age prefer to look at pictures of faces that are looking directly at them than those whose gaze is averted (Farroni, Csibra, Simion, & Johnson, 2002), and that newborns prefer to look at audiovisual events that are synchronized in time to those that are not synchronized (Lewkowicz, Leo, & Simion, 2010). All of these findings give a striking picture of the newborn baby as being perceptually competent, which is at odds with how people thought about infant perception until the 1960s.

But there is a problem with the visual preference procedure. If babies have no intrinsic preference for one stimulus over the other then they may be able to perceive differences that are not apparent in visual preference behaviour. Fantz (1964) developed another method, which helps to get around this problem: the **visual habituation** technique. The visual habituation technique makes use of the fact that, after some experience of a particular visual stimulus, infants begin to lose interest. They look at the stimulus less and inspect other aspects of their surroundings. They habituate to a specific visual sight. Next, if we present the same baby with a stimulus they have not seen together with the stimulus they have just been habituated to, then they will typically look longer at the novel stimulus. This **novelty preference** means that we can examine perceptual discriminative abilities independently of any intrinsic preference that a baby might have. Crucially, novelty preferences tell us not just about visual perception but also about visual memory; if a newborn shows a preference for looking at novel stimuli over familiar, then we know that they have encoded and remembered the familiar stimulus.

Using the habituation technique and variants on it, researchers have shown that newborns are surprisingly competent at deciphering their visual world. In many cases, they differentiate between objects and events based on their real properties (i.e. their real size, shape, and pattern, not just the sizes and shapes they present from a particular point of view; Slater, Mattock, & Brown, 1990; Slater, Mattock, Brown, & Bremner, 1991; Slater, Morison, & Rose, 1983).

We know from studies of visual preferences and visual habituation that infants can perceive their visual world with a degree of sophistication that would not even have been considered by earlier scientists such as Charles Darwin. But what does this competence tell us? Many researchers, for instance Elizabeth Spelke (*New York Times*, 2012; Spelke, 1998; Spelke, Breinlinger, Macomber, & Jacobson, 1992) have argued on the basis of these findings that babies come into the world ready for perception. According to Spelke (e.g. Spelke & Kinzler, 2007), infants are provided with **core knowledge** of the world, which helps them to decipher the complex visual array they experience when born into it. However, this kind of claim remains controversial. One problem for this kind of argument is that it is difficult to be sure, based on patterns of looking, that babies make perceptual discriminations in the same way that adults or even young children do (Haith, 1998). Furthermore, there are a number of clear ways in which young babies are limited in their perceptual abilities. As we shall see in the next section, it seems likely that experience plays an important role in changing the ways in which babies perceive the world around them in the first year of life.

Perceptual development in the first year of life

As we saw in the previous section, infants have some surprisingly sophisticated perceptual abilities in the first days and weeks of life. They can perceive and recognize voices, speech, and odours experienced in utero. Even with their most recently acquired sensory apparatus (vision), young infants seem to perceive and respond to a world of objects (Slater et al., 1990), patterns (Slater et al., 1991), and colours (Franklin & Davies, 2004). Nonetheless, perceptual studies of development in the first year of life have shown that there are many changes to the ways in which babies perceive their sensory worlds. Perception is progressively tuned to the baby's specific environments. Perceptual experience in the first months of life changes the way the baby perceives their world so that, as they develop, they are more and more provided with the most useful information about the world in which they find themselves.

In the domain of hearing, perhaps the most important developments are in the way babies perceive speech sounds. **Phonemes** (the sounds that make up speech) vary between different languages, such that the speech sound discriminations that might be important to an infant growing up in one language can be different to those of an infant growing up with a different language. Werker and Tees (1984) examined whether the language we grow up listening to in the first year of life (remember that babies do not typically learn to speak until the second year) affects the ways in which we perceive speech sounds. Werker and Tees (1984) tested infants growing up in English-speaking communities, comparing 6-month-olds and 12-month-olds. They examined the infants' ability to discriminate speech sounds in languages they had not heard before (Hindi, and Nlaka'pamux, a native Canadian language). They found that the 6-month-olds were just as good at discriminating between speech sounds in English and the languages they had not heard before. The 12-month-olds, however, were only able to differentiate the English speech sounds. So it seems that we start out being able to make phoneme discriminations across a wide range of languages but gradually narrow the range of phoneme discriminations we can make to just those that are relevant to the language we hear day to day; we become more specialized. This phenomenon is known as **perceptual narrowing**.

Perceptual narrowing is also seen in the way infants perceive their visual environments. In a study of face recognition, Pascalis, de Haan, and Nelson (2002) compared how well 6- and 9-month-old infants could distinguish the faces of different individuals. They compared infants' ability to differentiate monkey faces and human faces. In the experiment they presented the infants with a face and then examined whether they would next show a novelty preference when presented with the familiar face they had just seen, side by side with a novel face. They found that the 9-month-olds were better able to differentiate between the human faces than the monkey faces, whereas the 6-month-olds were equally good at recognizing human and monkey faces. So, whereas early in the first year we can seemingly make discriminations between faces regardless of species, later in the first year we become more specialized to discriminate just faces of our own species, losing the ability to differentiate the faces of a species we do not see day to day. We show perceptual narrowing in face perception across the first year of life.

The development of our perception of touch has been studied less than the development of our other senses (Bremner, Holmes, & Spence, 2012). Why is this? Touch is the earliest sense to develop prenatally (Gottlieb, 1971). It is also the most extensive sense, with receptors spread right across our bodies (by comparison, our hearing, seeing, smelling, and tasting organs are restricted to the head). The neglect of touch therefore seems like an important oversight. So it is not surprising that researchers have now begun to consider the potential importance of touch in development (e.g. Begum Ali, Spence, & Bremner, 2015; Bremner, Mareschal, Lloyd-Fox, & Spence, 2008; Bremner & Spence, 2017; Fairhurst, Löken, & Grossman, 2014; Rigato, Ali, Van Velzen, & Bremner, 2014).

Bremner's recent research has focused on how infants develop a sense of where touches occur on the body and in the outside world. Imagine that you feel a mosquito bite on your arm. Even without seeing the insect, you have a sense of where that touch is on your body, and you quickly look towards it and aim a swipe with your other hand. Bremner and colleagues (Bremner et al., 2008; Rigato et al., 2014) have been examining how infants develop an ability to locate touches in this way across the first year of life (see Figure 11.6).

In their studies, Bremner and colleagues typically attach vibrotactile 'buzzers' to infants' hands and measure their behavioural responses when a tactile stimulus is triggered (typically a hand is moved). They have found that, although infants are good at locating touches by making hand movements from a young age (they move the hand that was touched), between 6 and 10 months of age there are some big improvements in their sense of where touches are. First, whereas 10-month-olds know where to look when they feel a touch, 6-month-olds only very infrequently move their eyes to fixate the location of a touch. They seem to have very little sense of where touches occur in their visual field. Second, even when responding to a touch with a hand movement, they make mistakes when their hands are in unfamiliar positions (e.g. when their arms are crossed; see Figure 11.6). It seems that babies get much better as they get older at updating where touches are in the world across changes in the positions of their limbs.

This study highlights an important message about perceptual development in that it is clear that we have to learn not just how to interpret signals from a single sense modality (e.g. touch) but also how to combine information across modalities to make sense of the information coming in. In this case, to know where a touch is in the visual field, we not only have to know where on our bodies the touch is falling but also have to take into account where our arms are in visual space.

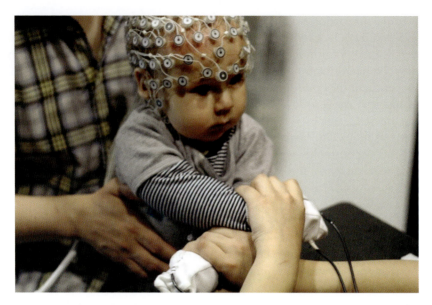

FIGURE 11.6 *An infant taking part in a tactile perception experiment. Vibrotactile stimulators are attached to the hands and held on with gloves. The stimulators deliver a mild tactile buzz to the palms. This experiment (Rigato et al., 2014) also measured electroencephalography brain activity in response to the tactile stimuli, using an electrode sensor net to measure the naturally occurring electrical activity on the scalp; this activity originates in the brain.*

Source: Reprinted from Rigato, Ali, Van Velzen, and Bremner (2014). Copyright (2014), with permission from Elsevier.

How we come to use our senses together

Having multiple senses through which to perceive the world around us brings some important benefits. Multiple senses provide richer and more accurate information about the world around us (see Bremner, Holmes, & Spence, 2012). However, they also pose a problem for the developing infant. How does the infant know which sensations to link together across the senses? This problem is captured by a famous quote from William James, a pioneering psychologist working at the turn of the 19th and 20th centuries: 'The baby, assailed by eye, ear, nose, skin and entrails at once, feels it all as one great blooming, buzzing confusion' (James, 1890, p. 462). In making this statement, James was arguing that, without experience, the infant does not know which sensations from the different senses to bind together with which and so perceives a muddle of information across the senses. But is this the case? Actually, the prevalent view these days among developmental psychologists is that newborn infants are able to make much better sense of the multisensory world than James argues, and without having had much sensory experience to guide them.

The famous American developmental psychologist Eleanor Gibson (1969) argued that infants can perceive correspondences between the senses from birth. For instance, Gibson argued that audiovisual events such as, for instance, a ball bouncing will be perceived as unified events by the newborn baby. Gibson's proposal was that development proceeds through what she called **differentiation**, such that infants gradually learn which aspects of multisensory events belong to one modality (e.g. vision) and which belong to another modality (e.g. audition). So, in our example, the baby will gradually learn that the bouncing ball event is made up of sounds (the thud when it hits the floor) and sights (the motion and changes in direction it is possible to watch).

But was Gibson correct to make this argument? Many investigations appear to confirm her suggestion. Let's take an example that will strike a chord of familiarity with some of the studies we've already been discussing. Lewkowicz and Ghazanfar (2006) were interested in whether infants could match the auditory sounds of speech to the visual sights of someone speaking. Carrying on from the work by Pascalis et al. (2002) discussed above, they examined whether babies could do this when observing monkeys making vocalizations (see Figure 11.7). They presented two videos side by side, one of a monkey making a 'coo' call and the other of the same monkey making a 'grunt'. At the same time, they played the sound of either the coo or the grunt and observed which face the infants looked at. Newborn babies and 4-month-olds were much more likely to look at the face that was making the movements that corresponded to the sounds being played. The 12-month-olds could not make that match, though, and looked equally at both matching and nonmatching vocalizations. So, like in the studies examining the development of speech perception and face perception, we see perceptual narrowing here. Infants lose the ability to make matches between monkey faces and vocalizations as they become older, likely because they do not experience monkeys much in their day-to-day lives.

As well as the fact that the multisensory matches made by infants become narrower as they get older, an important point to take from this study is that we seem to be born with the ability to perceive at least some correspondence between the senses. This seemingly agrees with Gibson's idea of a unity of the senses at birth. But is this always the case? In fact, one study we've already discussed, the investigation of how babies

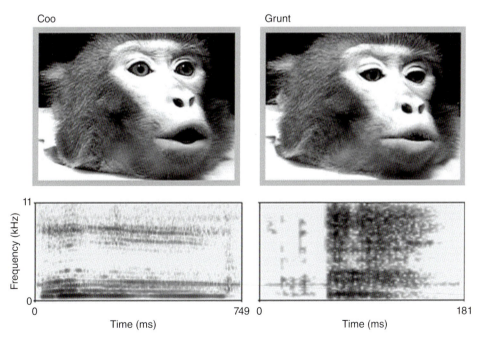

FIGURE 11.7 *Lewkowicz and Ghazanfar's (2006) study of multisensory matching. Infants of several different ages were shown videos of monkeys cooing and grunting presented side by side. At the same time they heard either the coo sound or the grunt sound. Newborns and 4-month-olds looked longer at the face that was making the movements that matched the sound they were hearing. Older infants showed no visual preference. Multisensory perceptual matching narrows as we get older.*
Source: Lewkowicz and Ghazanfar (2006). Copyright (2006) National Academy of Sciences, USA.

localize touch sensations (Bremner et al., 2008), shows that we have to learn how to make some matches across the senses. Remember that in that study the younger infants did not know where to look when they felt a touch on their hands, but the older infants (10 months old) looked to touch sensations quite quickly. In this case it seems that babies have to learn how to link up touches to places in the visual field. Multisensory development is currently a topic of great interest in perceptual development, and debates like this one are ongoing (Bremner, Lewkowicz, & Spence, 2012).

SECTION SUMMARY

- A large body of work has investigated how infants perceive their world through single sensory modalities.

- An ability to sense and respond to sense information begins well before birth, in the early stages of prenatal life.

- There is plenty of evidence to suggest that foetuses learn much from their sensory environments in utero, through several senses.

- DeCasper and Fifer (1980) found that, even as early as birth, newborn babies can recognize the sound of their own mother's voice. Further work by DeCasper and colleagues seems to show that human foetuses can learn about the sounds of particular voices and speech that they hear when in the womb.

- Odours and tastes are presented to the foetus in the amniotic fluid, and we know that chemosensory receptors are among the first to be mature anatomically in prenatal life (at around 11 weeks; Schaal & Durand, 2012).

- In 1961, Robert Fantz published a seminal article describing the findings of a new technique for examining perceptual abilities in very young babies, called the visual preference method. He extended this with the visual habituation technique.

- As a consequence, researchers including Elizabeth Spelke have argued that babies come into the world ready for perception, with core knowledge of the world, which helps them to decipher the complex visual array they experience when born into it.

- The development of our perception of touch is increasingly being studied: research indicates that babies get much better as they get older at updating where touches are in the world across changes in the positions of their limbs.

- We have to learn how to combine information across modalities to make sense of the information coming in.

- American developmental psychologist Eleanor Gibson (1969) argued that infants can perceive correspondences between the senses from birth and that development proceeds through what she called differentiation: infants gradually learn which aspects of multisensory events belong to which modalities.

SENSORIMOTOR DEVELOPMENT

LEARNING OBJECTIVE 11.6

Identify and describe the key stages in sensorimotor development.

We've now covered a little of how babies learn to perceive the world around them. In this section we'll look at how they learn to use that ability to act on the world in useful ways. When you chance to observe a newborn baby, the overwhelming impression is likely to be one of helplessness. Newborns are often quite still and, when they do move, those movements look strange and uncoordinated. As we'll see, however, these early movements are important. They work in ways that allow the newborn baby to survive.

This section will later argue that the most important developments in the ways infants and children move are in terms of the ways perception is used to guide movements. Babies and children have to learn how to link up what they perceive with what they do. This is why this section is titled 'sensorimotor development', rather than just 'motor development'.

Newborn motor reflexes

Human babies arrive in the world with a range of movement capabilities. It is particularly notable that they produce some 'set-piece' movements that appear somewhat stereotyped in nature and usually perform an important function. These movements, traditionally known as **neonatal reflexes**, are easy to elicit at birth but typically wane as the baby gets older. Let's cover a few of them. The **rooting reflex** is a response to tactile (touch) stimulation on the cheek. In this response, the newborn's mouth will typically open and move towards the source of the touch. The **sucking reflex** is a rhythmic sucking of the nipple (or, for instance, a finger) when inserted into the mouth. These reflexes obviously play important roles in gaining food for the newborn baby. Rooting helps them place a source of food (typically their mother's nipple) in their mouth. Sucking stimulates the flow of milk from the breast.

Other reflexes have less clear-cut functions. While the stepping movements that newborns make resemble the steps taken by older children and adults when walking, they certainly do not support walking and some researchers have suggested that they are unrelated to later walking and have a quite different function. Prechtl (1984), for instance, has suggested that neonatal stepping is a hangover from prenatal development, when it would have helped the foetus to turn around in the uterus, preventing it from becoming stuck to the sides of the womb.

A 'reflex' is a movement stimulated by a specific sensory trigger, elicited automatically without conscious control. However, more recent commentaries on neonatal behaviour have tended to dismiss the idea that all the neonatal reflexes are reflexive in the traditional sense. Von Hofsten (2004) argues that many newborn behaviours traditionally described as reflexes are in fact purposeful actions over which the newborn has control. Taking the example of the rooting reflex, Von Hofsten (2004) points out that the newborn does not root when they have recently fed. The rooting response cannot be purely reflex driven if it is modified by motivational states such as hunger. In a slightly different line, Prechtl (1981; see also Bremner, 1994) argues that newborn behaviours are not prewired reflexes but instead adaptive behaviours that have been learned in order to help the infant survive in the womb.

Another way that we can think about neonatal reflexes (whether they are actually reflexes or not) is as the building blocks of later behaviour. As infants develop, they will need to form increasingly complex ways of interacting with their environments. It is difficult to develop the kinds of complex sensorimotor skills that adults possess from nothing. Reflex behaviours almost certainly make this task easier by providing infants with a set of behaviours that can be adapted to new behaviours and can be linked together in increasingly complex ways to form the skills adults possess. As we'll see in the next section, Piaget thought that reflexes not only provide the basis for infants to develop their abilities to move and act but are actually the starting point for the development of thinking about the world.

As already mentioned, after the first few weeks of life, many of the neonatal reflexes begin to wane. The strong responses newborns make to specific stimuli (e.g. grasping when something is placed in their hand; stepping when the soles of their feet are touched) decline. This has led some commentators to argue that, as the infant's brain matures, the infant becomes more able to inhibit reflexive responses. This argument resembles those put forward by the maturationists discussed earlier, as it suggests that motor development proceeds according to some kind of preconceived (inherited) plan. Esther Thelen and colleagues present evidence that gives us reason to doubt this kind of account. In fact, Thelen (1984) has argued that the disappearance of one particular reflex – the **stepping reflex** – is actually illusory. According to Thelen it remains, but in a less obvious form. Let's look at research on the stepping reflex in more detail.

If we place young infants on their back, we often see rhythmic kicking movements in which the legs alternate. Whereas stepping declines substantially in the first months, kicking (in the lying-down posture) stays present or actually increases. Thelen (1984) found that stepping and kicking movements were virtually identical in terms of the movement patterns and the timings at which the leg muscles were activated, and therefore suggested that stepping does continue, but just disappears when the baby is upright. Why might this be? Thelen, Fisher, and Ridley-Johnson (1984) showed that, in babies who had stopped demonstrating the stepping reflex, it could be encouraged once more if they were placed in water. Conversely, adding weights to stepping babies' legs stopped the stepping response. It seems, therefore, that the most important factor in infant stepping is the weight of the legs. Stepping seems to decrease in development not because of the development of cortical inhibition from the brain but because the legs become heavier as babies get older! Kicking continues once stepping has disappeared because weight exerts less of a burden for stepping when the infant is lying down.

Thelen's studies of sensorimotor development in early life have been very important in developmental psychology. Perhaps the most important contribution has been to show that we have to take into account a huge array of different factors, some of them not immediately obvious, for thinking about why development occurs. In the studies of kicking mentioned above, the increasing weight of infants' legs is a case in point. Whereas earlier developmental psychologists had to figure out some complicated brain-based explanations of why reflexes wane in the first months of life, Thelen (1984) pointed out how much more simple physical changes can often play an important role in changing behaviour.

DISCUSSION POINT

Discuss the evidence that is available to support the theory that newborn babies actually intend to product so-called reflex responses.

Learning to link perception to action

As stated at the beginning of this section, the crucial hurdles in developing an ability to manipulate and move around our environments involve learning how to link up movement with perception: sensorimotor development. The earliest forms of sensorimotor behaviours are, of course, the reflexes we have just discussed. These reflex behaviours are typically produced in response to specific sensory stimuli. However, the neonatal reflexes are too inflexible and comprise too narrow a repertoire to help us develop the sensorimotor skills required by a mature adult. We have to learn new ways to link up perception and action. This section will illustrate how sensorimotor development works by considering the development of balance and locomotion (an ability to sit and stand upright and to walk around our environments).

The ability to stand upright without falling over is one of the crowning achievements of early development. How is this achieved? It is tempting to think that all we need to do is keep our feet, legs, and back rigid, and that'll keep us upright. This is entirely wrong, however. How could this work, for instance, on any kind of slope? Our centre of gravity would be shifted relative to the point of fulcrum (our feet) and we'd topple like a tree whose roots have given way. Of course, the answer is that when we stand we are using more than just our muscles to maintain balance. Our brains are constantly monitoring the ways in which our limbs are moving relative to one another, and how our body is moving with respect to the environment. A wide array of sensory information is used by the brain to feed into muscular control. The information we use to control movement (balance included) is multisensory. We use inputs from our muscles and joints (proprioception) to tell us how our body is moving. We use vision and our vestibular sense to tell us how our body is moving relative to the environment around us.

A classic demonstration of the role of role of vision in maintaining balance was conducted with human infants. Lee and Aronson (1974) put babies who had just learned to stand in a **swinging room**. A swinging room is a room in which the ground stays still but the walls and ceiling move (see Figure 11.8). Because we use visual cues concerning the distance of objects (such as walls) in order to stay upright, swinging rooms can interfere with our balancing. Walls that are moving only slightly can cause adults to sway like puppets that are visually tethered to the movements of the room (Lee & Lishman, 1975). For infants who have just learned to stand, the effect is more dramatic: the swinging room induces them to fall over (Lee & Aronson, 1974). What does this show us? It shows that, from the earliest stages of standing, infants use visual information about movements of the body relative to the environment (what is referred to as **optic flow**) to help them keep upright.

Later studies have shown that younger infants use optic flow to sit upright (Butterworth & Hicks, 1977). It even turns out that newborns respond to optic flow by adjusting their head posture (Jouen, Lepecq, Gapenne, & Bertenthal, 2000). Nonetheless, there are some very important developmental changes in the ways in which infants use visual information to maintain their balance.

Let's take the transition between infant and adult standing. In Lee and Aronson's (1974) study, the infants toppled often at even small perturbations of the swinging room. But adults were able to cope a bit better with the swinging room. Even though they were affected by the misleading movement of the walls, and often swayed in response, Lee and his colleagues seldom saw an adult fall over as the infants did. The

FIGURE 11.8 *A newly standing infant in Lee and Aronson's (1974) swinging room. The movements of the walls of the room cause optic flow in patterns of expansion and contraction. Infants, and to some extent adults, rely heavily on these cues to balance, and so the swinging room causes infants to fall over (hence the two experimenters waiting to catch the infant in the picture).*

Source: Lee and Aronson (1974). Copyright © 1974, Psychonomic Society, Inc. With permission of Springer.

likely reason for this is that, whereas the infants were relying all-out on vision to maintain their balance, the adults were maintaining balance using a mixture of visual information and proprioception from their joints. Whereas the visual information from the swinging room told the adults that they were moving, the proprioceptive cues from their ankle joints will have signalled that the floor was actually stationary. This shows how adults use a mixture of sensory cues to balance. The development of many sensorimotor abilities, including standing, walking, and reaching with the hands, involves learning how to juggle information from multiple sensory modalities, rather than just relying on one sensory cue (Nardini & Cowie, 2012). Evidence shows that this process of fine tuning our use of the senses continues to develop well into childhood and even into adolescence (Bremner, Hill, Pratt, Rigato, & Spence, 2013; Cowie, Makin, & Bremner, 2013; Cowie, Sterling, & Bremner, 2016; Nardini, Begus, & Mareschal, 2013; von Hofsten & Rösblad, 1988).

Going back to balancing, it is important to note that there are also some changes in the precise ways in which infants and children use optic flow information to stay upright. Bertenthal and Bai (1989) showed that, whereas infants younger than

9 months relied on optic flow for sitting no matter where that optic flow appeared in their visual field, infants of 9 months of age were more responsive to optic flow in the periphery of their visual fields. Bertenthal and Bai (1989) hypothesized that the greater sensitivity to optic flow in the periphery was due to the greater importance of that information in the standing posture, which 9-month-olds would have been trying out for the first time. Higgins, Campos, and Kermoian (1996) found some evidence to support this idea, as they showed that the more experience with walking infants had, the more likely they would be affected by peripheral optic flow in a swinging room. Thus, our developing behaviours affect the ways in which we have to learn to use perception for action.

The ways in which infants make use of sensory information to control their actions in the world continue to change as they adopt new ways of sitting, standing, and moving around. Each new motor ability brings with it a new set of demands for interpreting the sensory environment (Adolph & Berger, 2006). Moving from the sitting to the standing position means that body movement will be specified by a completely new set of visual cues. This actually provides a good explanation for why, when infants learn to move in a new way (e.g. they begin to walk for the first time), they start to make very bad decisions about when they can safely walk on a certain terrain or not (Adolph & Robinson, 2013). The point at which infants have only just started to walk is a time when parents have to be extra careful to keep their child away from the stairs!

This story about the development of the sensory control of balance and walking is just one illustration of sensorimotor development. The messages you should take away, and that also apply to other domains of sensorimotor development, are: (1) there are multiple sources of sensory information for us to use in the control of action; (2) the kinds of sensory information that we need to control an action depend on the specific action and posture we are in; (3) sensorimotor development is a process of learning from experience about which sensory cues help us control the ways in which we move; and, finally, (4) as infants and children acquire new motor skills (such as crawling and walking), they often have to learn afresh the sensory cues for controlling them.

SECTION SUMMARY

- The crucial hurdles in developing an ability to manipulate and move around our environments involve learning how to link up movement with perception: sensorimotor development.

- Human babies arrive in the world with a range of 'set-piece' movements traditionally known as neonatal reflexes, which usually perform important functions.

- These are building blocks of later behaviour but there is disagreement over whether these reflexes disappear or, according to some researchers, simply lie dormant, as illustrated by the stepping reflex.

- Whereas earlier developmental psychologists had to figure out some complicated brain-based explanations of why reflexes wane in the first months of life, Thelen (1984) pointed out how much more simple physical changes can often play an important role in changing behaviour.

- The ability to stand upright without falling over is one of the crowning achievements of early development. A classic demonstration of the role of vision in maintaining balance was conducted with human infants by Lee and Aronson (1974), who put babies who had just learned to stand in a 'swinging room'.

- The ways in which infants make use of sensory information to control their actions in the world continue to change as they adopt new ways of sitting, standing, and moving around.

COGNITIVE DEVELOPMENT

LEARNING OBJECTIVE 11.7

Identify and describe the key stages in cognitive development from birth to old age.

As adults, we take for granted much of the knowledge that we have of ourselves and the world around us. But the ways in which we behave, think, and speak from moment to moment throughout the day all make many assumptions about the world, which we can describe as knowledge. For instance, when your cat walks out of sight into the next room, you don't typically consider that it may have gone out of existence. You assume that it continues to exist out of sight in another place. We also take for granted our knowledge of other people. Take a look at Figure 11.9 for an illustration of the kinds of assumptions we make about other people's behaviour.

One way of studying cognitive development is to try to understand the origins of the knowledge that people have of the world. This is very much the approach taken by Piaget (see earlier in this chapter). Piaget made very few assumptions about the newborn infant, arguing that they have to construct knowledge of the world around them almost from scratch by actively engaging with it and learning from it. As we'll see, many researchers eventually disagreed with Piaget about this.

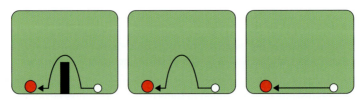

FIGURE 11.9 *In the image on the left, you see a lamb jump over a barrier to get to its mother ewe on the other side. As adults, when we watch events like this we make the assumption that the movement of the lamb is purposeful and rational. If we were to put the lamb back where it was again, but this time took the barrier away, we would not expect the lamb to jump in the same way it did last time (middle picture). We would expect it to run directly to its mother (right-hand picture). Gergely and Csibra (2003) call this the 'teleological stance'.*

Source: Reprinted from Gergely and Csibra (2003). Copyright (2003), with permission from Elsevier.

Another approach to studying cognitive development is from the point of view of cognitive functions such as memory, attention, planning, and so on. This approach to cognitive development takes an important inspiration from what cognitive psychologists have revealed about cognitive processes in mature adults. In this line of enquiry, cognitive developmentalists have tended to pursue not so much the origins of particular kinds of knowledge (as Piaget did) as developmental changes in the ability to process knowledge or information. For this reason, you will often hear this approach being referred to as the **information-processing account of cognitive development**.

The origins of knowledge in infancy

Let's consider sensorimotor development (covered in the previous section) in the context of Piaget's constructionist theory of cognitive development. Piaget was interested in sensorimotor development not so much for the sake of understanding how infants develop an ability to move around and manipulate their environments (though he certainly wrote a lot about this) but more from the point of view of understanding how the development of sensorimotor abilities impacts upon infants' and children's burgeoning understanding of the worlds that they inhabit. In fact, as we've already covered, Piaget labelled the first 2 years of development the 'sensorimotor' period of cognitive development. His idea was that, in the first 2 years of life, infants' intelligence is completely rooted in their practical skills in the world: their ability to move around their environment and manipulate it. According to this view, infants only have a conception of objects and space in terms of what they do with these things.

Piaget argued that infants start out understanding the world in terms of reflexes. They root for the sake of rooting, or suck for the sake of sucking. According to Piaget (but in contrast to some more recent positions already mentioned; e.g. Von Hofsten, 2004), newborns have no comprehension of executing their actions in order to gain something (e.g. food). They just do these things for their own sake.

The beauty of Piaget's account lies in how he argued that infants move beyond this very basic early cognitive existence. Backed up by his observations of infants' behaviour (he studied mostly his own children: Laurent, Lucienne, and Jacqueline), he argued that infants, through actively engaging in the world with these reflexes, arrive at experiences that force them to change the ways in which they act on the world. For instance, they might have learned to grasp objects put in the hand with one sensorimotor scheme, and to look at objects presented to their visual fields with another sensorimotor scheme. A moment of discovery comes when a baby first realizes that they can both grasp and look at the same thing. At this point, according to Piaget, the baby starts to organize their sensorimotor schemes together so that they can both grasp something to look at it and look at something to grasp it. This also leads to important acquisition in terms of knowledge. The infant realizes that the object they can grasp and look at is not something that is just grasped or just looked at; it is something independent from the infant's actions, something that exists in an objective universe out there. This example helps to show how Piaget envisaged sensorimotor experience to give rise to new ways of thinking about the world.

The idea that the foundations of knowledge are based in a mastery of sensorimotor actions has clear implications. Put most simply, the suggestion is that the ways in which babies play with movements and with objects in the first years of life are fundamental to their cognitive development. This approach argues that we need appropriate sensorimotor development in order to develop intellectually. As we shall see next, more recent studies have suggested that this is not always the case.

Perhaps the first problem for Piaget's sensorimotor account of cognitive development comes from the knowledge that there are many instances of children without limbs who manage to develop with typical intelligence. Gouin Décarie (1969) showed that children who were born without limbs in the 1960s as a result of the controversial prescription of the drug thalidomide to their mother during pregnancy were able to progress through and beyond Piaget's sensorimotor period, and to develop with normal intelligence in later life. This certainly waters down the claim that sensorimotor development is necessary for cognitive development.

Second, there have now, since Piaget, been a huge range of studies of infant cognitive abilities that seem to demonstrate that infants understand quite a lot about the world in advance of being able to express that knowledge in their manual behaviour (their behaviour with their hands), and certainly at a much younger age than Piaget originally suggested.

The alternative account to Piaget's is perhaps best articulated by this quote from an article by Spelke and colleagues:

> At 3 and 4 months of age, infants are not able to talk about objects, produce and understand object-directed gestures, locomote around objects, reach for and manipulate objects, or even see objects with high resolution. Nevertheless, such infants can represent an object that has left their view and make inferences about its occluded motion … infants represent objects and reason about object motions. (Spelke et al., 1992, p. 627, American Psychological Association, Inc, reprinted with permission)

So, on the one hand, Piaget argues for a gradual development of knowledge across the first years of life, as a result of sensorimotor development. On the other hand, more recent researchers such as Spelke et al. (1992) say that knowledge of the world is provided by our inheritance (our nature), independent of sensorimotor development. As mentioned earlier in this chapter, this has been called the 'core knowledge' account (Spelke, 1998; Spelke & Kinzler, 2007), and it represents a modern nativist explanation of development. These different opinions have come about largely because of the different methods used by Piaget and more recent researchers; whereas Piaget relied largely on observations of what infants could do with their hands, the predominant approach since the early 1980s has been to use babies' looking behaviour to tell us about what they know. Focus Point 11.1 outlines what we know about the development of object knowledge, and in particular the understanding that objects continue to exist when out of sight.

OBJECT PERMANENCE IN INFANCY

In Piaget's (1936/1952, 1950/1954) account of the sensorimotor period, object permanence, or the understanding that objects continue to exist when out of sight, is a crucial step in gaining a practical understanding of the world. Piaget documented the acquisition of object permanence through observations of infants' manual behaviour (their interactions with objects with their hands). Piaget played games with infants, hiding objects (typically a toy of some kind) and watching to see whether they would look for and recover them. Among his three children, the first attempts to uncover and retrieve objects that had been hidden in full view came at about 8 months of age. At 6 months, for instance, Piaget's children would observe an object they were interested in and wanted to hold being hidden under a cloth in front of their eyes. However, as soon as it had been covered up, manual searching for the object would cease. Piaget concluded that until 8 months infants do not have a conception of the continued availability of objects to action once they are out of sight.

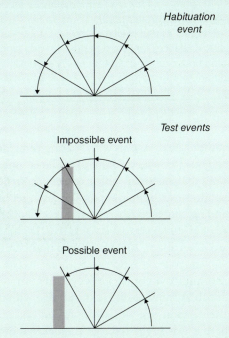

A schematic depiction of the stimuli presented to 5-month-olds in Baillargeon, Spelke, and Wasserman's (1985) 'violation of expectation' test of object permanence. See the text below for a full description.
Reprinted from Baillargeon (1991), with permission from Elsevier.

In the 1980s, however, a new method came along for investigating infants' understanding of the world. Baillargeon, Spelke, and Wasserman (1985) adapted the habituation-of-looking technique to investigate infants' expectations about the world. The authors habituated 5-month-old infants to a drawbridge moving towards and away from them through 180 degrees. After this habituation phase, a block was introduced in full view. The drawbridge was raised again, obscuring the block, and it then went either through 110 degrees to rest against the block (the possible event) or through 180 degrees, apparently passing right through the obscured block (the impossible event). The 5-month-olds looked longer at the impossible than the possible event. The impossible event is a violation of the physical principle of object permanence. Baillargeon et al. (1985) concluded that, because the 5-month-olds looked longer at this event, they had the expectation that the object continued to exist when it was out of sight.

Looking time techniques[2] were first developed to investigate infants' perceptual discriminative abilities rather than their expectations, so one possibility is that the infants didn't look longer at the impossible event because of their expectations, but rather because of some perceptual preference. Indeed, there have been a number of criticisms levelled at the **violation-of-expectation technique** on this basis (Haith, 1998). Nonetheless, the design of Baillargeon et al.'s (1985) experiment attempts to rule out at least some of these perceptual explanations. In the figure in this box, you can see that the impossible event is also the more perceptually familiar event, being a 180-degree rotation as seen in the habituation phase (and by the same token the possible event is more perceptually novel, being a 110-degree rotation). This speaks against the preference for the impossible event being due to its perceptual novelty. However, one of the more substantive criticisms of Baillargeon's study turns the tables on this clever design, pointing out, and demonstrating, that infants prefer to look at the impossible event because of its perceptual familiarity (Rivera, Wakeley, & Langer, 1999).

Nonetheless, Baillargeon et al.'s (1985) violation-of-expectation technique has survived these critiques and has been adapted for use to examine a wide range of questions about infant cognition, including understanding of other physical principles (Baillargeon, 2004), number (including addition and subtraction; Wynn, 1992), and even theory of mind (see the section 'Social Cognitive Development' below; Onishi & Baillargeon, 2005).

Even if we accept that there are problems with looking-time methods such as the violation-of-expectation technique, the sheer weight of evidence coming from looking-time studies clearly demonstrates that infants are able to express knowledge of the world with their eyes before they can do so with their hands. Research seems to show that young infants have an understanding of objects (their permanence, solidity, and constancy; e.g. Baillargeon, 2004; Spelke et al. 1992), spatial layouts (e.g. Bremner, Bryant, Mareschal, & Volein, 2007; Kaufman & Needham, 2011), and even number, mathematics, and people's actions (Onishi & Baillargeon, 2005; Spelke & Kinzler, 2007). This certainly forces us to revise Piaget's sensorimotor account. However, the important question we still have to answer is why, if babies show so much knowledge with their eyes, they cannot demonstrate this with their hands. We already discussed one possible explanation for this in Activity 11.1, where it was suggested that the delayed development of the prefrontal cortex might lead to the later development of manual ability. Another possibility is that looking-time studies may tell us about a different level or kind of knowledge from that shown in the playful behaviour with the hands that Piaget studied (Bremner & Mareschal, 2004; Mareschal, 2000; Munakata, McClelland, Johnson, & Siegler, 1997).

Development of logical thought in childhood

According to Piaget, the culmination of the first 2 years of development (his sensorimotor period) is an ability to think in **symbolic representations**. His argument was that infants emerge from the sensorimotor period being able to think about objects that are not visibly present instead of simply knowing how to act on objects and the world. Under this account, a 2-year-old can for the first time think about ways of doing things with objects in their environment in the absence of the actual actions (i.e. in an imaginary way). Children at this stage move into Piaget's 'concrete operations' period, which spans roughly 2–11 years of age. For Piaget, the central challenge of the concrete operations period is for children to learn to use rules and mental operations to think in a logical way about the world.

At an early stage in the concrete operations period, the **preoperational stage** (2–7 years of age), Piaget characterized children as being unable to manipulate mental representations in a logical way. Let's take the example of 'conservation'. In **conservation tasks** (see Figure 11.10), children are shown transformations in the way objects or substances appear: maybe a row of counters is spread out, or a short, fat glass of water is poured into a tall, thin glass. According to Piaget, when preoperational

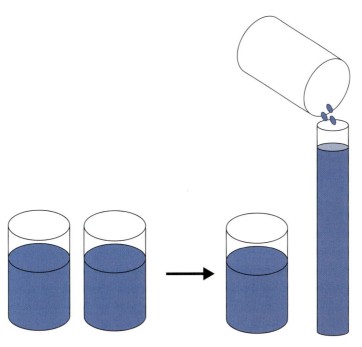

FIGURE 11.10 *Piaget's conservation task. Children are shown two identical beakers with the same amount of liquid in them. One beaker is then poured into a taller, thinner beaker and the children are asked to compare the beakers ('Which has more?'). Preoperational children (children under 7 years) will typically answer that the far-right beaker contains more.*

children are presented with these kinds of scenario, they are deceived into thinking that the objects in question have changed in more fundamental ways (e.g. they would say that the number of counters or the amount of water has increased).

Another classic problem that Piaget gave to preoperational children was his **perspective-taking task**. In this task children are typically shown a 3D scene (Piaget used a mountain scene and so the task is often called the 'three mountains task'). The children are then shown a doll, which is placed at a different vantage point to themselves, and they are asked to pick from a set a photograph of the scene as it appears from the doll's perspective. Preoperational 4-year-olds typically pick their own view rather than that of the doll, which Piaget explained as being due to **egocentrism**, or a difficulty in moving beyond (in Piaget's terms 'decentring' from) their own perspective. As they get older, children typically manage some kind of perspective taking (e.g. picking a photo with a front–back reversal only), but it is not until 7 or 8 years or so that children can pass this task, in this form at least.

One of the fascinating aspects of Piaget's account of the concrete operations period is the way in which he used one framework for interpreting young children's difficulties with a range of different tasks (Gold, 1987). For both conservation and perspective taking, he argued that preoperational children's difficulties are in reversing transformations (imagining the opposite of a perceived change). So, according to this account, attaining an ability to transform mental representations in a reversible way is the crucial step for moving beyond the preoperational stage. This idea of central developments that impact on a range of domains is referred to as a **domain-general account of development**.

Piaget's account of concrete operations has certainly not gone unchallenged. One of the main criticisms is that Piaget did not control the cognitive demands of his tasks very well. For instance, Bryant (1974) has argued rather convincingly that the reason that preoperational children may have failed some of Piaget's tasks was not because they did not understand the concepts or the logic that Piaget was trying to get at, but rather that they had problems in retaining in short-term memory the questions or other vital bits of information needed to do well at the task. Several studies (e.g. Bryant & Trabasso, 1971; Pears & Bryant, 1990) have shown that, once these memory demands are reduced, preoperational children can show logical reasoning that Piaget did not ascribe to children until beyond 7 years of age. We shall cover the development of memory in the next section.

Another important criticism of Piaget's work with children is that the tasks he used to measure children's thinking may have led children into incorrect answers. Margaret Donaldson is one of the leading critics in this regard. She argues (Donaldson, 1978) that Piaget did not fully appreciate the social context of the experiments he conducted. Let's take the conservation task as an example. In the number conservation task, the experimenter typically first shows two evenly spread rows of counters and asks the children whether there is the same number or a different number of counters in each. The experimenter then spreads out one row of counters and asks the child the same question again. The argument goes that the ostentatious spreading action and the repeated questioning actually lead young children into the incorrect response when they would otherwise have answered correctly. So it is possible that supposedly preoperational children may actually be able to conserve number after all.

McGarrigle and Donaldson (1975) set out to test this possibility. They did this by changing the way in which the transformation was made. They reasoned that, if the transformation was made as if by accident, then it would appear to the child to be irrelevant to the task, and they would therefore ignore it and their true conservation abilities would be revealed. The authors managed to make the accidental transformation appear irrelevant by including a 'naughty teddy' (manipulated by the experimenter) into the task. The naughty teddy was mimed as rampaging across the table and in the process accidentally lengthening one of the rows of counters. The experimenter then asked the crucial conservation question of whether the number of counters in the two rows was the same or different. McGarrigle and Donaldson (1975) found that, when the transformation was made seemingly accidentally, the 4-year-olds responded more accurately. They concluded, counter to Piaget, that preoperational children are able to conserve number, but that the way in which Piaget asked the questions led children into responding inaccurately (although a counter to this has also been provided by Moore & Frye, 1986). Donaldson's (1978) point is well taken. It is crucial to take the social context of experiments into account if we are to know exactly what we are measuring when we ask children questions.

The concern that Piaget did not consider social factors in his studies extends far beyond a criticism of his experiments, however. Others have criticized a lack of consideration of the role of the social world in Piaget's theoretical account of development (see Lourenço & Machado, 1996). With all of the emphasis on children constructing their own cognitive development through active assimilation and accommodation, there is indeed little space in Piaget's account for social interactions and culture to play a role in development (Cole, 2006). The foil to Piaget in this respect is the Russian psychologist Lev Vygotsky.

FIGURE 11.11 *A schematic illustration of Vygotsky's zone of proximal development (ZPD). The ZPD is a region of learning and development that is sensitive to the input from other, more experienced people. Given aid that is appropriately tailored to the ZPD, the child can progress.*
Source: Adapted from Wikimedia Commons.

Vygotsky (1978) proposed what has become known as a sociocultural approach to cognitive development, in which development is viewed as largely a result of children's interactions with more experienced people, such as parents, teachers, and older siblings. A helpful illustration of Vygotsky's approach is the concept of the **zone of proximal development (ZPD),** which he proposed. The ZPD (see Figure 11.11) is the difference between a child's actual developmental level and the potential developmental level under guidance or in collaboration with other, more experienced people (e.g. adults). There are several hints that the ZPD is a real phenomenon. Wood (1998), for instance, describes in detail how careful monitoring on the part of a teacher enables them to provide the optimal support for children's learning.

Towards the end of childhood, children enter the final period in Piaget's account, the formal operations period, which lasts from 11 or 12 years through adolescence and into adulthood. Individuals entering this stage supposedly not just become able to think logically about concrete phenomena (such as the three mountains in the perspective-taking task, or the matter involved in the various conservation tasks Piaget designed) but also graduate to thinking and reasoning about hypothetical or abstract scenarios that have no basis in reality. For instance, they are now able to think about problems such as the following: If Adam is taller than Joe and Joe is taller than Luke, who is taller between Luke and Adam? Because the heights of these various people are hypothetical, Piaget argued that this problem was out of the reach of children in the concrete operations period. This of course has implications for what children can do with mathematical algebra, in which symbols stand for hypothetical quantities.

More recently, researchers have questioned whether there is a stage-like shift into formal operational thinking in the way that Piaget argued. Many conducting research on adolescent children are happy to say that hypothetical thinking increases at this age, but fewer adhere to there being a sudden shift in the way that Piaget stipulated (Kuhn & Franklin, 2006). It is clear that some of the abilities that Piaget argued to be part of formal operations are the kind of problems that begin to be mastered in adolescence. Being able to integrate different sources of information in order to solve a problem is one such skill. This is observable in problems such as figuring out how balance works (in balancing a beam, weight and distance from the fulcrum are both variables that need to be considered; Holt et al., 2012; Siegler, 1981). What researchers have questioned is whether these developments occur due to the precise stage-wise shifts that Piaget stipulated (e.g. Siegler, 1996).

Development of cognitive functions: The information-processing approach

In the 1950s and 1960s, the first translations of Piaget's works were starting to gain the attention of developmental psychologists in the English-speaking world. As already discussed above, Piaget's account laid down an important challenge to the behaviourist models of understanding development that were predominant at the time. Whereas behaviourism tended to ignore the role of internal mental processes, Piaget was primarily addressing the origins of such processes in their role in children's thinking. Around the same time, gauntlets were being thrown down at behaviourism from the new field of cognitive psychology, which was investigating how adults encode, manipulate, and store information in internal representations (e.g. Neisser, 1967). Cognitive psychologists were formulating new models of memory, attention, and speech recognition. This 'information-processing' tradition of research in cognitive psychology gained some adherents in developmental psychology, leading to a new way of thinking about cognitive development.

The information-processing account of cognitive development gained prominence in the 1970s and 1980s. Developmentalists working in this new movement focused on developmental changes in the key parameters of the new models of mature cognitive processes such as memory. For instance, one of the key findings of research on short-term memory demonstrated that adults have a restricted short-term memory span; Miller (1956) demonstrated that adults' short-term memory span is limited to around seven items (give or take). Developmental psychologists in the information-processing movement thus considered how changes in the capacity of short-term memory in early life could have an effect on cognitive development (e.g. Pascual-Leone, 1970). And so, information-processing accounts competed directly with Piaget's in explaining cognitive development. Whereas Piaget appealed to changes in the ways children think, information-processing accounts suggested that developmental changes in performance on his tasks could rather be explained by changes in memory capacity (e.g. Bryant & Trabasso, 1971). Of course, as well as laying down a challenge to Piaget, studies of the development of memory are also interesting in their own right. Let's take a look at short-term memory development more closely.

It is abundantly clear from the literature that children's short-term memory improves dramatically as they get older (Gathercole, 1999). Figure 11.12 shows developmental improvements on a number of different tests of short-term (or working) memory. However, researchers came to suggest that changes in capacity were not the best way to explain improvements in short-term memory performance; changes in the way children *use* their memory seemed to be important. First, studies of short-term memory in infants using looking-time tasks (e.g. Ross-Sheehy, Oakes, & Luck, 2003) have shown that capacity limitations (for remembering visual items) are fairly adult-like by the end of the first year of life! Second, researchers began to find that improvements in the use of strategies for using and aiding memory make a good account of improvements in memory. For instance, Hitch and Towse (1995) showed that the speed at which children could rehearse the items they were trying to hold in their mind was an even better prediction of their working memory span than was their age.

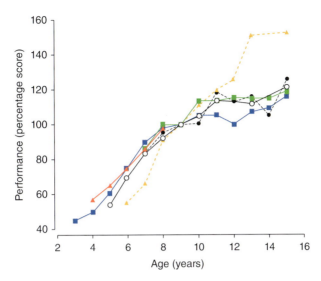

FIGURE 11.12 *Changes in short-term memory performance with age. The y-axis gives the level of performance as a percentage of 9-year-olds' performance on a task. The x-axis gives children's ages. The different lines represent different short-term memory tasks, including digit span, listening span, and spatial span. There are clear increases in short-term memory capacity with age.*

Source: Reprinted and adapted from Gathercole (1999). Copyright (1999), with permission from Elsevier.

Perhaps the cognitive functions that are of most interest at the moment are **executive functions**. Executive functions is an umbrella term to denote various mental processes involved in controlling our thinking and behaviour. Executive functions include things that you may well have heard of before, such as inhibition, planning, means–end coordination, cognitive control, and task switching. But it is not just their involvement in cognitive control that groups executive processes together. They are all to some extent located in a particular area of the brain: the prefrontal cortex. As already mentioned, the prefrontal areas of the brain are typically the slowest to mature, biologically speaking, with anatomical and functional changes ongoing well into adolescence and even adulthood (see Blakemore, 2008). The impact of this more protracted biological developmental process is readily apparent in children's executive abilities, which also tend to emerge slowly.

A classic test of executive function is the **dimensional change card sort (DCCS) task**, developed by Zelazo, Frye, and Rapus (1996). In this task children are asked to sort cards that vary on two dimensions (e.g. red rabbits and blue aeroplanes). The children have to sort the cards in their deck onto targets in which the dimensions are switched (so, in our example, onto blue rabbits and red aeroplanes). For instance, they might have to put all of the blue aeroplanes into a blue stack (on the blue rabbit) and all of the red rabbits into a red stack (onto the red aeroplane). Children of 3 years tend to be quite good at this. What they are not so good at is adapting to a change in the rules of the game. If they suddenly have to start sorting by shape (i.e. putting the blue aeroplanes onto the red aeroplane and the red rabbits onto the blue rabbit) when they were previously sorting by colour, they tend to perseverate with the old game rules, even though they realize that the game rules have changed. It's as if they have the necessary knowledge but don't have full control over what they are doing. By 4 years of age, children have typically sorted this problem out and are able to switch between rules. However, as with the prefrontal cortex, there continue to be developments in executive function throughout childhood and beyond. Some researchers have even claimed that the risky behaviours in which adolescents tend to get involved can to some extent be explained by delayed development of prefrontal areas of the brain and executive functions (e.g. Braams, Van Leijenhorst, & Crone, 2014).

One of the limitations of the information-processing approach to cognitive development is that it advances few ideas about the causes of developmental change. It often describes improvements in some cognitive process (e.g. memory) but does not offer explanations of why or how that change is occurring from one developmental level or stage to the next. Perhaps the most frequent suggestion, however, is related to maturational approaches discussed at the beginning of this chapter. Researchers such as Diamond (1990) and Leslie (2000) have suggested that maturation of brain areas such as the prefrontal cortex independently of experience allow improvements in executive function. As we have seen already, these kinds of maturational changes have been put forward to explain why young infants seem unable to act on early knowledge. This is a way in which information-processing accounts ally to some extent with modern nativist ideas about cognitive development in which core knowledge about the world is provided by our inheritance (Leslie, Friedman, & German, 2004; Spelke & Kinzler, 2007).

Social cognitive development

An aspect of cognitive development that has received perhaps the most attention in recent years is the development of the cognitive abilities and knowledge we use in social contexts. One particular focus in this regard has been the development of the ability to understand mental states: the development of a **theory of mind**. Researchers have examined how children come to understand that other people can have different beliefs about or perspectives on the world from themselves. The origins of this kind of investigation can of course be seen in Piaget's seminal work on perspective taking (e.g. his three mountains task, discussed earlier). However, the classic study in this field was conducted by Wimmer and Perner (1983).

Wimmer and Perner (1983) put together what has become known as a **false-belief task**, in which children were tested for their understanding that a different person could have a different (incorrect) belief about the world than the one they had themselves. This task is illustrated in Figure 11.13. In this task, a scenario is mimed with dolls and props by the experimenter. There are two protagonists (Sally and Ann) and two hiding places (a black box and a white box). Sally places a marble in the black box and goes for a walk. Ann moves the ball from the black box to the white box. Sally returns, and the child is asked whether Sally will look for her ball in the black box or the white box. Knowing that Sally has a false belief about where the ball is (she thinks it is in the black box, whereas we know that Ann has moved it to the white box), we would answer that she will look in the black box. However, up until around 4–5 years of age, children tend to respond to this question by saying that Sally will look for the ball where they themselves know it to be (in the white box). In this task, they appear unable to separate their own and others' knowledge of the world.

Gopnik and Astington (1988) show that improvements in understanding mental states and false beliefs are not limited to understanding other people's minds. They found that an ability to accurately remember and report one's own state of mind

Sally has a black box and **Ann** has a white box.

Sally has a marble. She puts the marble into her box.

Sally goes for a walk.

Ann takes the marble out of Sally's box and puts it into her box.

Sally comes back and wants to play with her marble.

Where will **Sally** look for her marble?

FIGURE 11.13 *A storyboard of the Sally–Ann or location false-belief task (Wimmer & Perner, 1983), used to test attribution of mental states to others in children.*

Source: Byom and Mutlu (2013). Copyright © 2013 Byom and Mutlu.

develops between 3 and 4 years. They designed a task called the **Smarties task**, in which the experimenter shows a child participant a box of Smarties (a brand of sweets). The experimenter asks the child, 'What do you think is in this box?' Usually, 3- to 4-year-olds say, 'Smarties!' The experimenter then reveals, much to the child's disappointment, that the box actually contains pencils. The test of false belief comes next, when the experimenter asks, 'What did you think was in the box when I first showed it to you?' At this point, older children will typically answer correctly ('Smarties'), but 3- to 4-year-olds will typically fail to realize that their past state of mind differed from reality, and will consequently answer 'pencils'. It seems that there is a qualitative change in the way children think about mental states, generally at around 4 to 5 years of age.

But what it is that makes it difficult for young children to perform well on false-belief tasks? A number of researchers have argued that there is a conceptual shift around 3 to 4 years in which children become able to represent and reason about mental states (e.g. Gopnik, 1993; Wimmer & Weichbold, 1994).

 Watch this 2011 TED Talk[3], in which child development psychologist Professor Alison Gopnik discusses her research into intelligence gathering and decision making in babies.

Others have argued that an ability to represent mental states is available much earlier in life, but that there are additional challenges of false-belief tasks that make them difficult for 3- to 4-year-olds. Alan Leslie has put forward the case that we have an inherited system for understanding mental states: a **theory-of-mind module** (Leslie & Thaiss, 1992; Leslie et al., 2004). More specifically, Leslie has argued that an early engagement in pretend play (seen for the first time at around 2 years of age in typically developing children) indicates an ability to keep track of differences between reality and pretend false states of affairs – in other words, an early ability to represent mental states.

Under this kind of account, difficulties with false-belief tasks are thought to an extent to be based in the information-processing characteristics of these tasks, and in particular their executive demands (Leslie, German, & Polizzi, 2005; Roth & Leslie, 1998). False-belief tasks do indeed involve a necessity of switching between different kinds of information, something that resembles the demands of the DCCS test of executive function described in the previous section (Kloo & Perner, 2003). For this reason, it will come as no surprise that success at false-belief tasks and the DCCS task develops at the same age.

Problems for all of these accounts have been raised by the finding that even young infants, in certain situations, can solve false-belief tasks. Onishi and Baillargeon (2005), using looking-time tasks (like those discussed in Focus Point 11.1), have shown that 15-month-old infants spend more time looking when someone searches successfully for an object when they should have had a false belief, than if they search unsuccessfully. Such observations have again raised the question of why it is that infants appear able to succeed in looking-time tasks when young children have such difficulty years later in a verbal or behavioural version of a task (Leslie, 2005; Perner & Ruffman, 2005).

So, as you can see, despite much research, we are still a long way from understanding the origins of an ability to understand mental states. Nonetheless, research into the development of an ability to perceive and understand the social world continues to be a very important theme in cognitive developmental research. One of the reasons for this is obvious. As humans are social animals, our social cognitive abilities are obviously of key importance (e.g. Dunbar, 1993; Dunbar & Shultz, 2007). Another reason for the current emphasis on social cognitive development is that impairments in social perception and understanding appear to be of importance in developmental disorders, particularly autistic spectrum disorders (Baron-Cohen, Leslie, & Frith, 1985; Leslie & Thaiss, 1992). A more recent focus that promises to shed light on the origins of social cognitive abilities and impairments is to investigate the biological processes underlying social cognitive development (see Focus Point 11.2).

TEST YOURSELF

How could you design a test to determine whether a young child has a 'theory of mind'?

FOCUS POINT 11.2

INSIGHTS INTO SOCIAL COGNITIVE DEVELOPMENT FROM NEUROSCIENCE

There is now a large body of work investigating the networks in the brain that process information about the social world (e.g. Adolphs, 2003; Frith, 2007). Several brain regions have been identified as being part of this social brain network, with weird and wonderful names such as the fusiform face area, the orbitofrontal cortex, and the superior temporal sulcus. Developmental cognitive neuroscientists have begun to attempt to understand the development of this social brain network in early life.

One of the main ways researchers have attempted to look at the development of the social brain is by examining the development of neural responses to human faces. Studies with infants have tended to rely on a technique called electroencephalography (EEG), which measures electrical activity from the brain that arises naturally on the surface of the scalp (see Figure 11.6). Researchers typically present faces to the babies and measure brain responses called event-related potentials (ERPs). One of the first studies to use this technique (Halit et al., 2003) found that aspects of this face ERP become more sensitive to features of typical faces as infants get older. For instance, whereas adults' ERPs show a specific kind of response to faces that are in their usual orientation (i.e. upright), 6-month-olds do not yet show specific responses to upright faces. These changes are thought to reflect the developing specialization of the brain for responding to an expert social task: processing human faces.

Researchers have also tracked changes in the social brain in adolescence. We already mentioned that brain changes in adolescence provide a biological explanation for the increases in risk taking, sensation seeking, and aggression shown in this life period (Braams et al., 2014; Steinberg, 2007). It is also known that there are some protracted improvements across adolescence in the ability to reason about mental states (assessed through more complex versions of the theory-of-mind tasks described above; Dumontheil, Apperly, & Blakemore 2010). The ability to recognize facial emotions also continues to develop throughout adolescence (Blakemore, 2008), and several groups have investigated face processing in childhood and adolescence using functional magnetic resonance imaging (fMRI; Cohen Kadosh et al., 2011; Gogtay et al., 2004; Scherf, Behrmann, Humphreys, & Luna, 2007). fMRI is able to provide clearer information than EEG about which brain regions are activated during a given task. For instance, Cohen Kadosh et al. (2011) have demonstrated changes in the ways the different parts of the social brain network interact while processing faces between late childhood and adulthood.

> **Watch this 2012 TED Talk**[4], in which cognitive neuroscientist Professor Sarah-Jayne Blakemore discusses the workings of the adolescent brain, in particular the social brain.

Cognitive development in adulthood and old age

In this chapter so far we have focused on the development of cognitive processes from prenatal life to the beginning of adulthood. However, development continues throughout the lifespan. In this final section of the chapter we'll take a look at some of the changes in cognitive abilities in later life.

Information-processing abilities decline during adulthood, but when these declines occur depends very much on the kind of cognitive ability that we are talking about. For instance, the speed at which we respond to perceptual stimuli begins to decline in the 20s (Salthouse, 2004), continuing through adulthood. It will come as little surprise that memory also declines in later life, although this decline tends to start a little later than perceptual declines, beginning in the late 30s. From this stage on, adults gradually find it harder to remember new information, such as series of numbers and names of new people (Salthouse, 2004).

With these changes in cognitive functions, do we see changes in intelligence as adults age? It turns out that this depends on the distinction between fluid and crystalized intelligence (Horn & Cattell, 1966). **Fluid intelligence** is the ability to perform mental operations efficiently (such as the kinds of abstract reasoning problem that Piaget gave to adolescents in the formal operations period; see above). **Crystallized intelligence** is expressed when we are asked to access verbal and factual knowledge. Schaie, Willis, and Pennak (2005), in a long-term longitudinal study, found that, whereas fluid intelligence begins to decline rather early in adulthood (see Bergland, 2013), crystallized intelligence remains rather stable until the mid- to late 60s.

SECTION SUMMARY

- One way of studying cognitive development is to try to understand the origins of the knowledge people have of the world.

- Supported by his observations of infants' behaviour (he mostly studied his own children), Piaget argued that infants, through actively engaging in the world, arrive at experiences that force them to change the ways in which they act on the world.

- This approach argues that we need appropriate sensorimotor development in order to develop intellectually. It is challenged by the fact that there are many instances of children without limbs who manage to develop with typical intelligence.

- In addition, there have been many studies that demonstrate that infants understand a lot about the world in advance of being able to express that knowledge in their manual behaviour (i.e. with their hands), and certainly at a much younger age than Piaget originally suggested.

- Piaget's stage theory of development has been criticized for its rigidity, its lack of consideration of social factors, and the possibility that the tasks he used to measure children's thinking may have led children to incorrect answers.

- Baillargeon et al. (1985) adapted the habituation-of-looking technique to investigate infants' expectations about the world.

- Even if we accept that there are problems with looking-time methods, the sheer weight of evidence coming from such studies demonstrates that infants are able to express knowledge of the world with their eyes before they can do so with their hands.

- Another approach to studying cognitive development, which gained prominence in the 1970s and 1980s, is from the point of view of cognitive functions such as memory, attention, planning, and so on. In this line of enquiry, cognitive developmentalists have tended to examine developmental changes in the ability to process knowledge or information. This approach is often referred to as the information-processing perspective on cognitive development.

- The cognitive functions that are of most interest at the moment are executive functions.

- Vygotsky (1978) proposed what has become known as a sociocultural approach to cognitive development, underpinned by the concept of the zone of proximal development.

- There has been particular interest in the development of the cognitive abilities and knowledge we use in social contexts. In particular, researchers have sought to understand the development of the ability to understand mental states: the development of a theory of mind, examined by using a false-belief task.

CHAPTER SUMMARY

This chapter has considered the enormous idea that every process or phenomenon you will study in psychology as a discipline has some kind of developmental history. For this reason alone the potential scope of developmental psychology is huge. We did this by covering the very substantial literature on cognitive development in a necessarily sparse fashion but we have highlighted a number of areas that are of current interest in recent scientific publications.

We began with perceptual development, and looked not just at how visual and auditory perception develop but also at some of the less studied senses that are gaining prominence in research, such as touch and olfaction (smell). We also examined how changes in the interactions among the senses develop in early life. Given the crucial role of multisensory interactions in determining how we perceive the world, it is likely that research into multisensory development will continue to grow (Bremner, Lewkowicz, & Spence, 2012). We then examined the contemporary interest in the role of the brain in cognitive development.

At the beginning of the chapter, we outlined how understanding biological changes in the brain and nervous system can shed light on how development works. As technical advances continue, it is likely that more and more information will become available regarding functional brain development. Thus, the role of biology in developmental psychologists' explanations of cognitive development is likely to increase in the coming years. Neuroscientific means of enquiry are already having a particularly important impact on our understanding of the development of social cognitive abilities in early life.

ESSAY QUESTIONS

1. What do we know about the changes that occur in the brain that underlie perceptual and cognitive development in infancy and childhood?

2. Explain the main developmental changes in the ways infants perceive the world around them during the first year of life.

3. How well does the evidence support Piaget's accounts of cognitive development in infancy and childhood?

KEY TERMS

- **autism spectrum disorder:** A developmental disorder that affects social communication, interactions, and behaviours.
- **behavioural genetics:** The study of the role of genetics and environment in human behaviour.
- **behaviourism:** A school of thought in psychology that explains human behaviour via learning from exposure to particular environmental situations.
- **cephalocaudal:** A maturational trajectory in which abilities emerge in order, from head to foot.
- **concrete operations period:** The second period in Piaget's stage theory of cognitive development, spanning 2–11 years, in which children master an ability to think logically about the world.
- **conservation tasks:** A set of classic Piagetian tasks given to children in the concrete operations period to test their ability to 'conserve' invariant properties of objects or substances across certain transformations (e.g. across the squashing or spreading out of a ball of plasticine).
- **constructionism:** An account of cognitive development that owes much to Piaget, in which children actively constructs their own development.
- **core knowledge:** The idea put forward by Elizabeth Spelke that infants possess knowledge of the physical and social world independently of experience.
- **cross-sectional design:** A research design in which, in developmental psychology, different age groups of children are compared at a single point in time.
- **crystallized intelligence:** The ability to express verbal and factual knowledge; this remains stable until old age.
- **developmental dyslexia:** A developmental difficulty with learning to read.
- **differentiation:** An account of development put forward by Eleanor Gibson in which infants gradually learn to produce different responses to distinct aspects of their perceptual environments.
- **dimensional change card sort (DCCS) task:** A task developed by Zelazo and colleagues to assess executive function in young children; it involves switching between card-sorting rules.
- **domain-general account of development:** A theoretical account of development in which one advance is argued to affect ability across a wide range of domains (e.g. mathematical, language, logical, spatial).
- **ectoderm:** One of the three distinct layers of cells that makes up the early embryo and goes on to become the nervous system.
- **egocentrism:** An inability to move beyond one's own perspective on the world, which Piaget ascribed particularly to preoperational children.
- **embryo:** The developing organism between the stage of being a single fertilized egg, and a foetus in which all major organs and structures are fully differentiated.

- **empiricism:** The argument that development results from experience.
- **epigenetic landscape:** An analogical device for understanding how the environmental context of a cell or an individual influences its development.
- **eugenics:** The belief that it is possible to improve the quality of the human race via selective breeding.
- **executive functions:** An umbrella term used to denote various higher cognitive processes involved in controlling behaviour and thinking.
- **false-belief task:** A task developed by Wimmer and Perner to assess young children's ability to represent another person's mental state (belief) when that is different to their own.
- **fluid intelligence:** The ability to perform mental operations efficiently; this declines from early in adulthood.
- **foetus:** The prenatal organism from the point at which all of its major organs and structures are fully differentiated.
- **formal operations period:** The final of the three periods in Piaget's stage theory of cognitive development, during which children are said to master thinking about the world in a hypothetical or abstract way.
- **information-processing account of cognitive development:** A theoretical account of development that emphasizes the importance of changes in cognitive parameters such as short-term memory capacity.
- **informed consent:** An ethical principle that states that research participants should always be fully informed before they are asked to give their consent to participate.
- **interactionism:** The argument that development results from an interaction of inheritance (nature) and experience (nurture).
- **interactive specialization:** An account of brain development that argues that functional specialization of brain regions results from experience-dependent interactions between neural networks.
- **longitudinal design:** A research design in which changes from one point of development to the next are traced within individuals.
- **maturationism:** The argument that our abilities mature according to genetically prespecified timetables.
- **nativism:** The argument that we inherit abilities that then emerge independently of experience.
- **neonatal reflexes:** A range of responses to specific sensory stimulation, made by newborns. There is debate over whether these behaviours are truly reflexive or automatic.
- **neural tube:** The tube of cells in the embryo that goes on to become the central nervous system.
- **novelty preference:** A preference for attending to novel visual information.
- **object permanence:** The ability to appreciate that objects continue to exist when out of sight or reach.
- **optic flow:** The pattern of motion in the visual field specifying self-motion.
- **perceptual narrowing:** A process in which perceptual discriminative abilities that have little relevance to an infant's everyday life disappear as the infant gets older.
- **perspective-taking task:** A classic Piagetian task given to children in the concrete operations period to test ability to understand how a given object or scene can appear differently according to different views or perspectives.
- **phonemes:** Speech sounds that are the smallest units of speech that affect meaning.
- **phonics:** A method for teaching reading and writing by developing phonemic awareness (an awareness of speech sounds).
- **prefrontal cortex:** A part of the cerebral cortex that subserves ability at higher cognitive functions, such as planning, inhibition, and short-term memory, and which has a particularly extended course of development.

- **preoperational stage:** A substage in Piaget's concrete operations period, during which children are unable to succeed in applying logical operations to their thought.
- **prosody:** The rhythmic and intonation patterns in speech.
- **proximodistal:** A maturational trajectory in which abilities emerge in order from the body core to the extremities (i.e. the hands and feet).
- **rooting reflex:** A neonatal reflex in which the newborn's mouth moves towards tactile stimulation on the cheek.
- **sensorimotor period:** The first period in Piaget's stage theory of development, spanning 0–2 years, in which infants master an ability to act on their environment.
- **Smarties task:** A task developed by Gopnik and Astington (1988) to assess young children's ability to represent their own past mental state (belief) when that is different from their current mental state (belief).
- **stepping reflex:** A neonatal reflex in which newborns make a stereotypical stepping motion.
- **sucking reflex:** A neonatal reflex in which newborns rhythmically suck on a nipple when it is inserted into the mouth.
- **swinging room:** Experimental apparatus in which it is possible to create the illusory visual impression of self-movement towards and away from the walls of a room.
- **symbolic representations:** An ability to represent the world independently of one's actions on it. This is the culmination of Piaget's sensorimotor period.
- **synaptic proliferation:** The developmental process by which neurons form new connections (synapses) with other neurons.
- **synaptic pruning:** The developmental process by which connections between neurons are removed.
- **teratogens:** Agents that can upset the development of the embryo or foetus.
- **theory of mind:** An ability to think and reason about mental states.
- **theory-of-mind module:** A cognitive module for thinking about mental states, which has been hypothesized by some researchers to be innate.
- **training studies:** A research design in which the effect of a particular environment (or training regime) on development is assessed.
- **violation-of-expectation technique:** A looking-time technique in which infants are shown events that violate certain physical and/or social principles. If the infant looks longer at the violating event, this is taken as evidence of their understanding of the violated principle.
- **visual habituation:** The process of learning about visual patterns, which leads to the direction of visual attention away from familiar and towards novel visual patterns.
- **visual preference:** A method for examining visual perceptual abilities in infants by relying on their preferences to look at particular visual patterns (e.g. faces).
- **zone of proximal development (ZPD):** The difference between a child's actual developmental level and their potential developmental level under the guidance of a more experienced person.
- **zygote:** A single fertilized egg in which the genes of the parents are combined.

NOTES

1. http://www.ted.com/talks/annie_murphy_paul_what_we_learn_before_we_re_born?language=en
2. https://www.youtube.com/watch?v=uAl3y3zIpuk
3. http://www.ted.com/talks/alison_gopnik_what_do_babies_think?language=en
4. https://www.ted.com/talks/sarah_jayne_blakemore_the_mysterious_workings_of_the_adolescent_brain

FURTHER RESOURCES

Arterberry, M. A., & Kellman, P. J. (2016). *Development of perception in infancy: The cradle of knowledge revisited*. Oxford, UK: Oxford University Press.

Begum Ali, J., Spence, C., & Bremner, A. J. (2015). Human infants' ability to perceive touch in external space develops postnatally. *Current Biology, 25*(20), R978–R979.

Bjorklund, D. F., & Causey, K. B. (2017). *Children's thinking: Cognitive development and individual differences* (6th ed.). Thousand Oaks, CA: Sage.

Blakemore, S.-J. (2008). The social brain in adolescence. *Nature Reviews Neuroscience, 9*, 267–277.

Bremner, A. J., Lewkowicz, D. J., & Spence, C. (Eds.). (2012). *Multisensory development*. Oxford, UK: Oxford University Press.

Bryant, P. E., & Trabasso, T. (1971). Transitive inferences and memory in young children. *Nature, 232*, 456–458.

Hepper, P. (1988). Fetal 'soap' addiction. *Lancet, 331*(8598), 1347–1348.

Johnson, M. H. (2011). Interactive specialization: A domain-general framework for human functional brain development? *Developmental Cognitive Neuroscience, 1*(1), 7–21.

Johnson, M. H., & de Haan, M. (2011). *Developmental cognitive neuroscience* (3rd ed.). Oxford, UK: Wiley-Blackwell.

Leman, P., Bremner, A., Parke, R. D., & Gauvain, M. (2012). *Developmental psychology*. London, UK: McGraw-Hill.

Melby-Lervåg, M., & Hulme, C. (2013). Is working memory training effective? A meta-analytic review. *Developmental Psychology, 49*(2), 270–291.

Slater, A., Mattock, A., & Brown, E. (1990). Size constancy at birth: Newborn infants' responses to retinal and real size. *Journal of Experimental Child Psychology, 49*(2), 314–322.

Von Hofsten, C. (2004). An action perspective on motor development. *Trends in Cognitive Sciences, 8*(6), 266–272.

Werker, J. F., & Tees, R. C. (1984). Cross-language speech perception: Evidence for perceptual reorganization during the first year of life. *Infant Behavior & Development, 7*(1), 49–63.

Wimmer, H., & Perner, J. (1983). Beliefs about beliefs: Representation and constraining function of wrong beliefs in young children's understanding of deception. *Cognition, 13*(1), 103–128.

Zelazo, P. D., Chandler, M., & Crone, E. (Eds.) (2010). *Developmental social cognitive neuroscience*. Abingdon, UK: Taylor & Francis.

REFERENCES

Abrams, R. M., Gerhardt, K. J., & Peters, A. J. M. (1995). Transmission of sound and vibration to the fetus. In J. LeCanuet, W. Fifer, N. Krasnegor, & W. Smotherman (Eds.), *Fetal development: A psychobiological perspective* (pp. 315–330). Hillsdale, NJ: Lawrence Erlbaum Associates.

Adolph, K. E., & Berger, S. E. (2006). Motor development. In W. Damon & R. Lerner (Series Eds.) & D. Kuhn & R. S. Siegler (Vol. Eds.), *Handbook of child psychology. Vol 2. Cognition, perception, and language* (pp. 161–213). Hoboken, NJ: Wiley.

Adolph, K. E., & Robinson, S. R. (2013). The road to walking: What learning to walk tells us about development. In Philip David Zelazo (Ed.), *Oxford handbook of developmental psychology* (Vol. 1, pp. 403–443). New York, NY: Oxford University Press.

Adolphs, R. (2003). Cognitive neuroscience of human social behaviour. *Nature Reviews Neuroscience, 4*(3), 165–178.

Ariés, P. (1962). *Centuries of childhood: A social history of family life* (trans. R. Baldick). London, UK: Jonathan Cape.

Aslin, R. N. (1981). Development of smooth pursuit in human infants. In D. F. Fisher, R. A. Monty, & J. W. Senders (Eds.), *Eye movements: Cognition and visual perception* (pp. 31–51). Hillsdale, NJ: Lawrence Erlbaum Associates.

Azevedo, F. A., Carvalho, L. R., Grinberg, L. T., Farfel, J. M., Ferretti, R. E., Leite, R. E., … Herculano-Houzel, S. (2009). Equal numbers of neuronal and nonneuronal cells make the human brain an isometrically scaled-up primate brain. *Journal of Comparative Neurology*, *513*(5), 532–541.

Baillargeon, R. (1991). Reasoning about the height and location of a hidden object in 4.5- and 6.5-month-old infants. *Cognition*, *38*(1), 13–42.

Baillargeon, R. (2004). Infants' reasoning about hidden objects: Evidence for event-general and event-specific expectations. *Developmental Science*, *7*(4), 391–414.

Baillargeon, R., Spelke, E. S., & Wasserman, S. (1985). Object permanence in five-month-old infants. *Cognition*, *20*(3), 191–208.

Baron-Cohen, S., Leslie, A. M., & Frith, U. (1985). Does the autistic child have a 'theory of mind'? *Cognition*, *21*(1), 37–46.

Begum Ali, J., Spence, C., & Bremner, A. J. (2015). Human infants' ability to perceive touch in external space develops postnatally. *Current Biology*, *25*(20), R978–R979.

Bergland, C. (2013). Too much crystallized thinking lowers fluid intelligence. *Psychology Today*, 26 December. Retrieved 11 January 2018 from https://www.psychologytoday.com/blog/the-athletes-way/201312/too-much-crystallized-thinking-lowers-fluid-intelligence

Bertenthal, B. I., & Bai, D. L. (1989). Infants' sensitivity to optical flow for controlling posture. *Developmental Psychology*, *25*(6), 936–945.

Berthier, N. E., Clifton, R. K., McCall, D. D., & Robin, D. J. (1999). Proximodistal structure of early reaching in human infants. *Experimental Brain Research*, *127*(3), 259–269.

Blakemore, S.-J. (2008). The social brain in adolescence. *Nature Reviews Neuroscience*, *9*, 267–277.

Bloom, P. (2012). Little ones in the lab. *Big Think*. Retrieved 11 January 2018 from http://bigthink.com/videos/little-ones-in-the-lab

Byom, L. J., & Mutlu, B. (2013). Theory of mind: Mechanisms, methods, and new directions. *Frontiers in Human Neuroscience*, *7*, 413. doi:10.3389/fnhum.2013.00413

Braams, B. R., Van Leijenhorst, L., & Crone, E. A. (2014). Risks, rewards, and the developing brain in childhood and adolescence. In V. F. Reyna & V. Zayas (Eds.), *The neuroscience of risky decision making* (pp. 73–91). Washington, DC: American Psychological Association.

Bradley, L., & Bryant, P. E. (1983). Categorizing sounds and learning to read: A causal connection. *Nature*, *301*(5899), 419–421.

Bremner, A. J., Bryant, P. E., Mareschal, D., & Volein, Á. (2007). Recognition of complex object-centred spatial configurations in early infancy. *Visual Cognition*, *15*, 1–31.

Bremner, A. J., Hill, E. L., Pratt, E., Rigato, S., & Spence, C. (2013). Bodily illusions in young children: Developmental change in the contribution of vision to perceived hand position in early childhood. *PLoS ONE*, *8*, e51887.

Bremner, A. J., Holmes, N. P., & Spence, C. (2012). The development of multisensory representations of the body and the space around the body. In A. J. Bremner, D. J. Lewkowicz, & C. Spence (Eds.), *Multisensory development* (pp. 113–136). Oxford, UK: Oxford University Press.

Bremner, A. J., Lewkowicz, D. J., & Spence, C. (Eds.). (2012). *Multisensory development*. Oxford, UK: Oxford University Press.

Bremner, A. J., & Mareschal, D. (2004). Reasoning … what reasoning? *Developmental Science*, *7*, 419–421.

Bremner, A. J., Mareschal, D., Lloyd-Fox, S., & Spence. C. (2008). Spatial localization of touch in the first year of life: Early influence of a visual code, and the development of remapping across changes in limb position. *Journal of Experimental Psychology: General*, *137*, 149–162.

Bremner, A. J., & Spence, C. (2017). The development of tactile perception. *Advances in Child Development and Behavior*, *52*, 227–268.

Bremner, J. G. (1994). *Infancy* (2nd ed.). Oxford, UK: Blackwell.

Bryant, P. (1974). *Perception and understanding in young children: An experimental approach* (Vol. 588). London, UK: Methuen.

Bryant, P. E., & Trabasso, T. (1971). Transitive inferences and memory in young children. *Nature, 232*, 456–458.

Butterworth, G., & Hicks, L. (1977). Visual proprioception and postural stability in infancy: A developmental study. *Perception, 6*(3), 255–262.

Centre for Longitudinal Studies. (2018). Welcome to the Millennium Cohort Study. Retrieved 11 January 2018 from http://www.cls.ioe.ac.uk/page.aspx?sitesectionid=851

Cohen Kadosh, K., Cohen Kadosh, R., Dick, F., & Johnson, M. H. (2011). Developmental changes in effective connectivity in the emerging core face network. *Cerebral Cortex, 21*(6), 1389–1394.

Cole, M. (2006). Culture and cognitive development in phylogenetic, historical and ontogenetic perspective. In W. Damon & R. Lerner (Series Eds.) & D. Kuhn & R. Siegler (Vol. Eds.), *Handbook of child psychology: Vol. 2. Cognition, perception and language* (6th ed., pp. 636–686). New York, NY: John Wiley.

Cowie, D., Makin, T., & Bremner, A. J. (2013). Children's responses to the rubber hand illusion reveal dissociable pathways in body representations. *Psychological Science, 24*, 762–769.

Cowie, D., Sterling, S., & Bremner, A. J. (2016). The development of multisensory body representation and awareness continues to 10 years of age: Evidence from the rubber hand illusion. *Journal of Experimental Child Psychology, 142*, 230–238.

Darwin, C. (1877). A biographical sketch of an infant. *Mind, 7*, 285–294.

DeCasper, A. J., & Fifer, W. P. (1980). Of human bonding: Newborns prefer their mothers' voices. *Science, 208*(4448), 1174–1176.

DeCasper, A. J., & Spence, M. J. (1986). Prenatal maternal speech influences newborns' perception of speech sounds. *Infant Behavior & Development, 9*(2), 133–150.

Diamond, A. (1990). The development and neural bases of memory functions as indexed by the AB and delayed response tasks in human infants and infant monkeys. *Annals of the New York Academy of Sciences, 608*(1), 267–317.

Donaldson, M. (1978). *Children's minds*. New York, NY: Fontana Press.

Dumontheil, I., Apperly, I., & Blakemore, S. J. (2010). Online usage of mental state inference continues to develop in late adolescence. *Developmental Science, 13*(2), 331–338.

Dunbar, R. I. (1993). Coevolution of neocortical size, group size and language in humans. *Behavioral & Brain Sciences, 16*(4), 681–694.

Dunbar, R. I., & Shultz, S. (2007). Evolution in the social brain. *Science, 317*(5843), 1344–1347.

Fairhurst, M. T., Löken, L., & Grossmann, T. (2014). Physiological and behavioral responses reveal 9-month-old infants' sensitivity to pleasant touch. *Psychological Science, 25*(5), 1124–1131.

Fantz, R. L. (1961). The origin of form perception. *Scientific American, 204*, 66–72.

Fantz, R. L. (1964). Visual experience in infants: Decreased attention to familiar patterns relative to novel ones. *Science, 146*(3644), 668–670.

Farroni, T., Csibra, G., Simion, F., & Johnson, M. H. (2002). Eye contact detection in humans from birth. *Proceedings of the National Academy of Sciences of the United States of America, 99*(14), 9602–9605.

Fifer, W. P., & Moon, C. (2003). Prenatal development. In A. Slater & G. Bremner (Eds.), *An introduction to developmental psychology* (pp. 95–114). Oxford, UK: Blackwell.

Fox, K., & Wong, R. O. (2005). A comparison of experience-dependent plasticity in the visual and somatosensory systems. *Neuron, 48*(3), 465–477.

Franklin, A., & Davies, I. R. (2004). New evidence for infant colour categories. *British Journal of Developmental Psychology, 22*(3), 349–377.

Frith, C. D. (2007). The social brain? *Philosophical Transactions of the Royal Society B: Biological Sciences, 362*(1480), 671–678.

Galton, Francis. (1904). Eugenics: Its definition, scope, and aims. *American Journal of Sociology, 10*(1), 1–25.

Gathercole, S. E. (1999). Cognitive approaches to the development of short-term memory. *Trends in Cognitive Sciences, 3*(11), 410–419.

Gergely, G., & Csibra, G. (2003). Teleological reasoning in infancy: The naive theory of rational action. *Trends in Cognitive Sciences, 7*(7), 287–292.

Gesell, A., & Ames, L. B. (1940). The ontogenetic organization of prone behavior in human infancy. *Journal of Genetic Psychology, 56*(2), 247–263.

Gibson, E. J. (1969). *Principles of perceptual learning and development.* New York, NY: Appleton-Century-Crofts.

Gogtay, N., Giedd, J. N., Lusk, L., Hayashi, K. M., Greenstein, D., Vaituzis, A. C., … Thompson, P. M. (2004). Dynamic mapping of human cortical development during childhood through early adulthood. *Proceedings of the National Academy of Sciences of the United States of America, 101*(21), 8174–8179.

Gold, R. (1987). *The description of cognitive development: Three piagetian themes.* Oxford, UK: Clarendon.

Gopnik, A. (1993). How we know our minds: The illusion of first-person knowledge of intentionality. *Behavioral & Brain Sciences, 16*, 1–14.

Gopnik, A., & Astington, J. W. (1988). Children's understanding of representational change and its relation to the understanding of false belief and the appearance–reality distinction. *Child Development, 59*(1), 26–37.

Gottlieb, G. (1971). Ontogenesis of sensory function in birds and mammals. In E. Tobach, L. R. Aronson, & E. Shaw (Eds.), *The biopsychology of development* (pp. 67–128). New York, NY: Academic Press.

Gouin Décarie, T. (1969). A study of the mental and emotional development of the thalidomide child. In B. M. Foss (Ed.), *Determinants of infant behavior* (Vol. 4, pp. 167–187). New York, NY: Barnes and Noble.

Haith, M. M. (1998). Who put the cog in infant cognition? Is rich interpretation too costly? *Infant Behavior & Development, 21*(2), 167–179.

Halit, H., de Haan, M., & Johnson, M. H. (2003). Cortical specialisation for face processing: Face-sensitive event-related potential components in 3- and 12-month-old infants. *Neuroimage, 19*(3), 1180–1193.

Hepper, P. (1988). Fetal 'soap' addiction. *Lancet, 331*(8598), 1347–1348.

Hepper, P. G. (1996). Fetal memory: Does it exist? What does it do? *Acta Paediatrica, 85*(Suppl. 416), 16–20.

Higgins, C. I., Campos, J. J., & Kermoian, R. (1996). Effect of self-produced locomotion on infant postural compensation to optic flow. *Developmental Psychology, 32*(5), 836–841.

Hitch, G. J., & Towse, J. N. (1995). Working memory: What develops. In W. Schneider & F. E. Weinart (Eds.), *Memory performance and competencies: Issues in growth and development* (pp. 3–21). Northvale, NJ: Lawrence Erlbaum Associates.

Holmes, J., Gathercole, S. E., & Dunning, D. L. (2009). Adaptive training leads to sustained enhancement of poor working memory in children. *Developmental Science, 12*(4), F9–F15.

Holt, N., Bremner, A. J., Sutherland, E., Vliek, M., Passer, M., & Smith, R. (2012). *Psychology: The science of mind and behavior* (2nd ed.). London, UK: McGraw-Hill.

Holtmaat, A., & Svoboda, K. (2009). Experience-dependent structural synaptic plasticity in the mammalian brain. *Nature Reviews Neuroscience, 10*(9), 647–658.

Horn, J. L., & Cattell, R. B. (1966). Refinement and test of the theory of fluid and crystallized general intelligences. *Journal of Educational Psychology, 57*(5), 253–270.

Hooker, D. (1952). *The prenatal origin of behavior.* Lawrence, KS: University of Kansas Press.

Humphrey, T. (1964). Some correlations between the appearance of human fetal reflexes and the development of the nervous system. *Progress in Brain Research, 4*, 93–135.

Huttenlocher, P. R., & Dabholkar, A. S. (1997). Regional differences in synaptogenesis in human cerebral cortex. *Journal of Comparative Neurology, 387*, 167–178.

James, W. (1890). *The principles of psychology* (Vol. 1). New York, NY: Holt.

Johnson, M. H. (2011). Interactive specialization: A domain-general framework for human functional brain development? *Developmental Cognitive Neuroscience, 1*(1), 7–21.

Johnson, M. H., & de Haan, M. (2011). *Developmental cognitive neuroscience* (3rd ed.). Oxford, UK: Wiley-Blackwell.

Johnson, M. H., Dziurawiec, S., Ellis, H., & Morton, J. (1991). Newborns' preferential tracking of face-like stimuli and its subsequent decline. *Cognition, 40*(1), 1–19.

Jouen, F., Lepecq, J. C., Gapenne, O., & Bertenthal, B. I. (2000). Optic flow sensitivity in neonates. *Infant Behavior & Development, 23*(3), 271–284.

Karmiloff-Smith, A. (1998). Development itself is the key to understanding developmental disorders. *Trends in Cognitive Sciences, 2*(10), 389–398.

Kaufman, J., & Needham, A. (2011). Spatial expectations of young infants, following passive movement. *Developmental Psychobiology, 53*, 23–36.

Kloo, D., & Perner, J. (2003). Training transfer between card sorting and false belief understanding: Helping children apply conflicting descriptions. *Child Development, 74*(6), 1823–1839.

Kuhn, D., & Franklin, S. (2006). The second decade: What develops (and how). In W. Damon & R. M. Lerner (Eds.), *Child and adolescent development: An advanced course* (doi:10.1002/9780470147658. chpsy0222). Hoboken, NJ: Wiley .

Kunitz, S., & Loizeaux, M. D. (1963). *Wilson Library Bulletin, 37*.

Lee, D. N., & Aronson, E. (1974). Visual proprioceptive control of standing in human infants. *Perception & Psychophysics, 15*(3), 529–532.

Lee, D. N., & Lishman, J. R. (1975). Visual proprioceptive control of stance. *Journal of Human Movement Studies, 12*, 87–95.

Leman, P., Bremner, A. J., Parke, R. D., & Gauvain, M. (2012). *Developmental psychology*. London, UK: McGraw-Hill.

Leslie, A. M. (2000). 'Theory of mind' as a mechanism of selective attention. In M. S. Gazzaniga (Ed.), *The new cognitive neurosciences* (2nd ed., pp. 1235–1248). Cambridge, MA: MIT Press.

Leslie, A. M. (2005). Developmental parallels in understanding minds and bodies. *Trends in Cognitive Sciences, 9*(10), 459–462.

Leslie, A. M., Friedman, O., & German, T. P. (2004). Core mechanisms in 'theory of mind'. *Trends in Cognitive Sciences, 8*, 528–533.

Leslie, A. M., German, T. P., & Polizzi, P. (2005). Belief–desire reasoning as a process of selection. *Cognitive Psychology, 50*(1), 45–85.

Leslie, A. M., & Thaiss, L. (1992). Domain specificity in conceptual development: Neuropsychological evidence from autism. *Cognition, 43*(3), 225–251.

Lewkowicz, D. J., & Ghazanfar, A. A. (2006). The decline of cross-species intersensory perception in human infants. *Proceedings of the National Academy of Sciences of the United States of America, 103*(17), 6771–6774.

Lewkowicz, D. J., Leo, I., & Simion, F. (2010). Intersensory perception at birth: Newborns match nonhuman primate faces and voices. *Infancy, 15*(1), 46–60.

Lourenço, O., & Machado, A. (1996). In defense of Piaget's theory: A reply to 10 common criticisms. *Psychological Review, 103*(1), 143–164.

Lundberg, I., Olofsson, Å., & Wall, S. (1980). Reading and spelling skills in the first school years predicted from phonemic awareness skills in kindergarten. *Scandinavian Journal of Psychology, 21*(1), 159–173.

Mareschal, D. (2000). Object knowledge in infancy: Current controversies and approaches. *Trends in Cognitive Sciences, 4*(11), 408–416.

Mareschal, D., & Bremner, A. J. (2006). When do 4-month-olds remember the 'what' and 'where' of hidden objects? In M. H. Johnson & Y. Munakata (Eds.), *Attention and performance: Vol. 21. Processes of change in brain and cognitive development* (pp. 427–447). Oxford, UK: Oxford University Press.

Mareschal, D., Johnson, M. H., Sirois, S., Spratling, M., Thomas, M. S., & Westermann, G. (2007). *Neuroconstructivism-I: How the brain constructs cognition*. Oxford, UK: Oxford University Press.

Mataga, N., Mizuguchi, Y., & Hensch, T. K. (2004). Experience-dependent pruning of dendritic spines in visual cortex by tissue plasminogen activator. *Neuron, 44*(6), 1031–1041.

McGarrigle, J., & Donaldson, M. (1975). Conservation accidents. *Cognition, 3*(4), 341–350.

McGraw, M. B. (1943). *The neuromuscular maturation of the human infant.* New York, NY: Columbia University Press.

Mehler, J., Morton, J., & Jusczyk, P. W. (1984). On reducing language to biology. *Cognitive Neuropsychology, 1*(1), 83–116.

Melby-Lervåg, M., & Hulme, C. (2013). Is working memory training effective? A meta-analytic review. *Developmental Psychology, 49*(2), 270–291.

Miller, G. A. (1956). The magical number seven, plus or minus two: Some limits on our capacity for processing information. *Psychological Review, 63*(2), 81–97.

Molnár, Z., & Blakemore, C. (1991). Lack of regional specificity for connections formed between thalamus and cortex in coculture. *Nature, 351,* 475–477.

Moore, C., & Frye, D. (1986). The effect of experimenter's intention on the child's understanding of conservation. *Cognition, 22*(3), 283–298.

Moore, K. L., & Persaud, T. V. N. (2008). *The developing human: Clinically oriented embryology* (8th ed.). Philadelphia, PA: Saunders Elsevier.

Munakata, Y., McClelland, J. L., Johnson, M. H., & Siegler, R. S. (1997). Rethinking infant knowledge: Toward an adaptive process account of successes and failures in object permanence tasks. *Psychological Review, 104*(4), 686–713.

Nardini, M., Begus, K., & Mareschal, D. (2013). Multisensory uncertainty reduction for hand localization in children and adults. *Journal of Experimental Psychology: Human Perception & Performance, 39*(3), 773–787.

Nardini, M., & Cowie, D. (2012). The development of multisensory balance, locomotion, orientation and navigation. In A. J. Bremner, D. J. Lewkowicz, & C. Spence (Eds.), *Multisensory development* (pp. 137–158). Oxford, UK: Oxford University Press.

Neisser, U. (1967). *Cognitive psychology.* East Norwalk, CT: Appleton-Century-Crofts.

New York Times. (2012). Science: Elizabeth S. Spelke. *YouTube,* 30 April. Retrieved 11 January 2018 from https://www.youtube.com/watch?v=HnOllgd-8Ao

Occelli, V., Spence, C., & Zampini, M. (2011). Audiotactile interactions in temporal perception. *Psychonomic Bulletin & Review, 18,* 429–454.

Onishi, K. H., & Baillargeon, R. (2005). Do 15-month-old infants understand false beliefs? *Science, 308*(5719), 255–258.

Pascalis, O., de Haan, M., & Nelson, C. A. (2002). Is face processing species-specific during the first year of life? *Science, 296*(5571), 1321–1323.

Pascual-Leone, J. (1970). A mathematical model for the transition rule in Piaget's developmental stages. *Acta Psychologica, 32,* 301–345.

Pears, R., & Bryant, P. (1990). Transitive inferences by young children about spatial position. *British Journal of Psychology, 81*(4), 497–510.

Perner, J., & Ruffman, T. (2005). Infants' insight into the mind: How deep. *Science, 308*(5719), 214–216.

Piaget, J. (1936/1952). *The origin of intelligence in the child.* London, UK: Routledge & Kegan Paul.

Piaget, J. (1950/1954). *The construction of reality in the child.* New York, NY: Basic Books.

Plomin, R., DeFries, J. C., Knopik, V. S., & Neiderhiser, J. (2013). *Behavioral genetics* (6th ed.). New York, NY: Worth.

Prechtl, H. F. (Ed.). (1984). *Continuity of neural functions from prenatal to postnatal life* (Vol. 94). Cambridge, UK: Cambridge University Press.

Prechtl, H. F. R. (1981). The study of neural development as a perspective of clinical problems. In K. J. Connolly & H. R. Prechtl (Eds.), *Maturation and development: Biological and psychological perspectives* (pp. 198–215). Philadelphia, PA: J. B. Lippincott.

Richards, J. E., & Holley, F. B. (1999). Infant attention and the development of smooth pursuit tracking. *Developmental Psychology, 35*(3), 856–867.

Rigato, S., Ali, J. B., Van Velzen, J., & Bremner, A. J. (2014). The neural basis of somatosensory remapping develops in human infancy. *Current Biology, 24*(11), 1222–1226.

Rivera, S. M., Wakeley, A., & Langer, J. (1999). The drawbridge phenomenon: Representational reasoning or perceptual preference? *Developmental Psychology, 35*(2), 427–435.

Ross-Sheehy, S., Oakes, L. M., & Luck, S. J. (2003). The development of visual short-term memory capacity in infants. *Child Development, 74*(6), 1807–1822.

Roth, D., & Leslie, A. M. (1998). Solving belief problems: Toward a task analysis. *Cognition, 66*(1), 1–31.

Rousseau, J.-J. (1762/1979). *Emile, or On education* (trans. A. Bloom). New York, NY: Basic Books.

Saffran, J. R., Werker, J. F., & Werner, L. A. (2006). The infant's auditory world: Hearing, speech, and the beginnings of language. In W. Damon & R. Lerner (Series Eds.) & D. Kuhn & R. S. Siegler (Vol. Eds.), *Handbook of child psychology: Vol 2. Cognition, perception, and language* (pp. 58–108). Hoboken, NJ: Wiley .

Salthouse, T. A. (2004). What and when of cognitive aging. *Current Directions in Psychological Science, 13*(4), 140–144.

Schaal, B., & Durand, K. (2012). The role of olfaction in human multisensory development. In A. J. Bremner, D. J. Lewkowicz, & C. Spence (Eds.), *Multisensory development* (pp. 29–62). Oxford, UK: Oxford University Press.

Schaal, B., Marlier, L., & Soussignan, R. (2000). Human foetuses learn odours from their pregnant mother's diet. *Chemical Senses, 25*(6), 729–737.

Schaie, K. W., Willis, S. L., & Pennak, S. (2005). An historical framework for cohort differences in intelligence. *Research in Human Development, 2*(1/2), 43–67.

Scherf, K. S., Behrmann, M., Humphreys, K., & Luna, B. (2007). Visual category-selectivity for faces, places and objects emerges along different developmental trajectories. *Developmental Science, 10*(4), F15–F30.

Shatz, C. J. (2008). The emergence of order in visual system development. In M. H. Johnson, Y. Munakata, & R. O. Gilmore (Eds.), *Brain development and cognition: A reader* (pp. 231–244). Oxford, UK: Wiley-Blackwell.

Siegler, R. S. (1981). Developmental sequences within and between concepts. *Monographs of the Society for Research in Child Development, 46*, 1–74.

Siegler, R. S. (1996). *Emerging minds.* Oxford, UK: Oxford University Press.

Slater, A., Mattock, A., & Brown, E. (1990). Size constancy at birth: Newborn infants' responses to retinal and real size. *Journal of Experimental Child Psychology, 49*(2), 314–322.

Slater, A., Mattock, A., Brown, E., & Bremner, J. G. (1991). Form perception at birth: Revisited. *Journal of Experimental Child Psychology, 51*(3), 395–406.

Slater, A., Morison, V., & Rose, D. (1983). Perception of shape by the new-born baby. *British Journal of Developmental Psychology, 1*(2), 135–142.

Spelke, E. S. (1998). Nativism, empiricism, and the origins of knowledge. *Infant Behavior and Development, 21*(2), 181–200.

Spelke, E. S., Breinlinger, K., Macomber, J., & Jacobson, K. (1992). Origins of knowledge. *Psychological Review, 99*, 605–632.

Spelke, E. S., & Kinzler, K. D. (2007). Core knowledge. *Developmental Science, 10*, 89–96.

Stein, B. E. (Ed.). (2012). *The new handbook of multisensory processes.* Cambridge, MA: MIT Press.

Steinberg, L. (2007). Risk taking in adolescence: New perspectives from brain and behavioral science. *Current Directions in Psychological Science, 16*(2), 55–59.

Thelen, E. (1984). Learning to walk: Ecological demands and phylogenetic constraints. *Advances in Infancy Research, 3*, 213–250.

Thelen, E., Fisher, D. M., & Ridley-Johnson, R. (1984). The relationship between physical growth and a newborn reflex. *Infant Behavior & Development, 7*(4), 479–493.

Von Hofsten, C. (2004). An action perspective on motor development. *Trends in Cognitive Sciences, 8*(6), 266–272.

Von Hofsten, C., & Rösblad, B. (1988). The integration of sensory information in the development of precise manual pointing. *Neuropsychologia, 26*(6), 805–821.

Vygotsky, L. S. (1978). *Mind in society* (M. Cole, V. John-Steiner, S. Scribner, & E. Souberman, Eds.). Cambridge, MA: Harvard University Press.

Waddington, C. H. (1957). *The strategy of the genes.* London, UK: Allen.

Wagner, R. K., & Torgesen, J. K. (1987). The nature of phonological processing and its causal role in the acquisition of reading skills. *Psychological Bulletin, 101*(2), 192–212.

Watson, J. B. (1930). *Behaviorism* (rev. ed.). Chicago, IL: University of Chicago Press.

Werker, J. F., & Tees, R. C. (1984). Cross-language speech perception: Evidence for perceptual reorganization during the first year of life. *Infant Behavior & Development, 7*(1), 49–63.

Wimmer, H., & Perner, J. (1983). Beliefs about beliefs: Representation and constraining function of wrong beliefs in young children's understanding of deception. *Cognition, 13*(1), 103–128.

Wimmer, H., & Weichbold, V. (1994). Children's theory of mind: Fodor's heuristics examined. *Cognition, 53*(1), 45–57.

Wood, D. (1998). *How children think and learn* (2nd ed.). Oxford, UK: Wiley-Blackwell.

Wynn, K. (1992). Addition and subtraction by human infants. *Nature, 358*(6389), 749–750.

Zelazo, P. D., Frye, D., & Rapus, T. (1996). An age-related dissociation between knowing rules and using them. *Cognitive Development, 11*(1), 37–63.

12 Language and Thought

ALAN GARNHAM

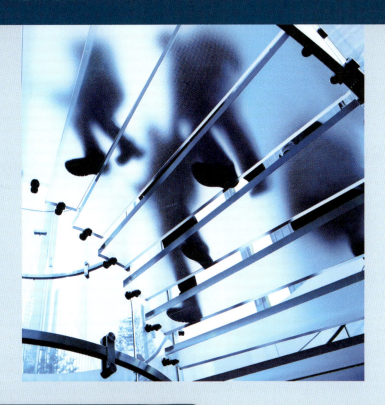

we divide the world into and the concepts that correspond to these categories, as these are the building blocks of many of our thoughts. It continues with a discussion of the three main lines of research on thinking: reasoning, problem solving, and judgement and decision making. All of these suggest that there are two systems for thinking, a fast, intuitive, error-prone one and a slow, effortful one. The chapter then considers creativity; the neuropsychology of thinking; whether thinking might be taught and, if so, how; and how thinking develops. The section ends with a discussion of some broader issues: the role of metacognition in thinking, and expertise, wisdom, and rationality. The chapter closes with a brief look at how language and thought are related to one another.

INTRODUCTION

LEARNING OBJECTIVE 12.1

Set the context for learning about the psychology of language and thought.

Language and higher-level **thinking** pervade human life and make it different from that of other animals. It has sometimes been suggested that there is an absolute divide between humans and other animals in the ability to use language and to engage in higher-level thought. We will touch on these issues later. Meanwhile, here is a riddle, brought to the attention of psychologists by Tony Sanford (1985), which gives us some important insights into the abilities studied in this chapter. Look at the riddle and see whether you can solve it before reading on:

> A man and his son were away for a trip. They were driving along the highway when they had a terrible accident. The man was killed outright but the son was alive, although badly injured. The son was rushed to the hospital and was to have an emergency operation. On entering the operating theatre, the surgeon looked at the boy and said, 'I can't do this operation. This boy is my son.' How can this be? (Sanford, 1985, p. 311)

While some people report no difficulty, the majority are confused by an apparent inconsistency, which results from attributing gender to the characters. The answer to the riddle is that the surgeon is the boy's mother. Gender stereotypes (surgeons are more commonly male than female – in 2016, only 11.1% of consultant surgeons in England were women; Royal College of Surgeons, 2017) and the male aura created by the use of words such as 'father', 'boy', and 'son' make the problem difficult.

So, what does the riddle tell us about language and thinking? A broad conclusion, but one that is only partly misleading, is that language is easy and thinking is hard. When we speak or read a language that we have learned in childhood, it comes naturally to us. Thinking, on the other hand, is often difficult. As the surgeon riddle shows, it can be compromised by preconceptions. And, when we engage in conscious trains of thought, we often experience the cognitive effort of thinking about complex matters in a way that we don't experience when using language.

In this chapter, we will look at language and thinking separately, as there are different traditions in cognitive psychology, which is the discipline in which language and thinking are studied. At the end, we will ask how they are related, since thoughts are often expressed in language and, at least for many people, language is the main medium for thinking.

SECTION SUMMARY

- Language and thinking pervade human life.
- Language is easy to use; thinking can be hard.
- Language and thinking are usually studied separately in psychology – a division followed in this chapter.

LANGUAGE

LEARNING OBJECTIVE 12.2

Describe the evolution and structure of language as a communication tool, how language is acquired by children and used by adults (including bilingual adults), and the role of the brain in language use.

Human and animal communication

Language is primarily a system for communication, in a broad sense of that term. The work of linguists (who study language in general and specific languages, such as English, French, or Swahili, in their own right) and psycholinguists (who study the psychology of language) sometimes fails to emphasize the communicative function of language. The broad sense of communication includes not only the communication of factual information (or information that pretends to be factual) but also social communication, in which language helps to establish and maintain social relations. These functions of language link it to the simpler systems of communication used by other animals. These systems may convey detailed information, but in a very specific domain; the waggle dance of honeybees (Georgia Tech College of Computing, 2011), for example, provides information about sources of nectar – or these systems may convey limited information, for example about a small number of types of approaching predator, as in the alarm calls of vervet monkeys (BBC, 2013).

Linguists tend to focus on structural aspects of language and, indeed, an influential approach to language in the early 20th century was known as 'structuralism'. Languages show structure at many different levels (see Table 12.1). It is generally agreed that, despite the rather obvious superficial differences, which block communication between speakers of different languages, the underlying structures of all human languages are basically the same.

It is also worth mentioning that work since the 1960s, in both linguistics and psycholinguistics, has demonstrated that sign languages, such as British Sign Language and American Sign Language, are languages in their own right (and not, for example,

TABLE 12.1 *Levels of linguistic description.*

Level	Subject matter	Subdivisions
Phonetic	The sounds of speech	Articulatory (how sounds are produced by the vocal system)
		Acoustic (the physical properties of speech sounds)
		Auditory (how sounds are processed by the auditory system)
Phonological	Rules about systems of sounds in particular languages	Phonemic (rules about individual sounds that can distinguish between words in a particular language)
		Suprasegmental (tone, stress, and prosody)
Morphological	Basic meaning-bearing units, such as (noncomplex) words, prefixes, and suffixes	Inflectional (changes to the form of a word depending on its role – e.g. 'eat' versus 'eats' versus 'eating')
		Word formation (derivation and compounding – e.g. 'un-decid-abil-ity' and 'dog catcher')
Lexical	Words	
Syntactic	Rules about how words group into phrases, clauses, and sentences	
Semantic	Meaning (mainly literal meaning)	Lexical (word meaning)
		Structural (how meaning depends on syntax)
Pragmatic	Contextual aspects of meaning	Speech acts
		Presupposition and implicature
		Information structure
		Politeness

parasitic on English as spoken in the surrounding communities). Sign languages form words from finger, hand, and arm configurations and locations, on the left or right of the body (for example), but at higher levels they exhibit similar structural complexity to other human languages. American Sign Language has achieved prominence in language research via attempts to teach it to great apes, such as chimpanzees (Gardner & Gardner, 1969) and gorillas (Patterson, 1978; see also Gorilla Foundation, n.d.), whose vocal apparatus makes it difficult or impossible for them to master spoken language. Apes learn individual signs ('words') reasonably readily, but at nothing like the rate that human children learn words. In addition, both the range of situations in which they use such signs and the complexity of the way they use them are relatively restricted.

One linguistic approach to characterizing human languages is to recognize their 'design features' (Hockett, 1960). Some of these features reflect human languages' structural properties and others reflect their properties as systems for communication. Design features are useful for comparing human languages with systems of **animal communication**, which have only a subset of the features of human languages or have the same features but to a restricted degree. One particular limitation of animal communication systems is that, unlike human languages, they are strongly bound to the here and now. This limitation relates both to the information that animals are able to communicate (e.g. vervet monkeys might signal the immediate presence of a snake [Seyfarth, Cheney, & Marler, 1980], but they cannot indicate that an area looks like it might harbour snakes) and to the link with animals' current emotional states. Human language, on the other hand, allows disengagement from our current location and lets us talk about other places and times; at least in principle, it also allows disengagement from our current emotional state.

The evolution of language

The similarities between animal communication and human language raise questions about the evolution of human language. The evolution of behaviour, as opposed to physical characteristics, is notoriously difficult to study. Indeed, in 1866, the Linguistic Society of Paris banned debates on the **evolution of language**, because of the difficulty of bringing empirical evidence to bear on this issue.

Most complex physical structures, such as eyes, are thought to have evolved gradually over time, capitalizing on variation in populations of organisms and sometimes on 'random' mutations. However, mutations are most often harmful, and are extremely unlikely to produce complex structures out of nothing. Nevertheless, in the case of the evolution of language, there have been suggestions that language appeared suddenly and relatively recently. These ideas, although biologically less plausible than gradualist accounts, have gained credence because of their association with the influential linguist and political commentator Noam Chomsky (e.g. Hauser, Chomsky, & Fitch, 2002). Chomsky argues that language proper (as opposed to animal communication systems) is uniquely human, an idea that is consistent with the notion that language appeared suddenly at some point after our human ancestors separated from the lineages that have become modern apes (maybe 100,000 years ago, according to Chomsky). It also suggests that human language and animal communication systems need not be closely related. See BBC (2015) for a video exploring Noam Chomsky's thoughts on language acquisition.

Despite Chomsky's influence, gradualist theories of the evolution of language are currently in the ascendant, though there is no general agreement as to what the most important precursors of language might be, or how they might have developed into human language. One certain fact is that the human vocal system is uniquely suited to producing the range of vocalizations used in human languages, and to combining vocalization with breathing, even though it compromises our ability to avoid choking while vocalizing. Nevertheless, the descended larynx, or low voice box, which is a crucial part of the human vocal system, is not unique to humans, but is found, for example, in red deer, where it is used to signal body size, sometimes misleadingly (Fitch & Reby, 2001). We can tell from examination of fossil remains that the vocal systems of our ancestors have changed considerably in the past several hundred thousand years (Lieberman, 1998). What is harder to determine is the role, if any, of language in driving those changes. It is possible that our ability to use spoken language is a fortuitous consequence of changes that occurred for other reasons.

One view of the evolution of language is that the crucial precursor of language was the ability to have complex thoughts, in which relations between events, objects, and properties can be represented. However, many other factors have been suggested that might explain the evolution of certain aspects of human language. For example, Robin Dunbar (1996) proposed that vocal grooming, perhaps in the form of something like modern-day gossip, replaced physical grooming, and hence allowed human ancestors to interact closely with many more conspecifics, with the result that social groups became larger and more complex. Dean Falk (2004) has suggested that, because infant 'naked apes' could not cling to their mothers without being held, they often had to be set down, and that vocal communication was a means of reassuring them at a distance.

These ideas are not mutually exclusive, but they all are difficult to prove. Another major issue in the evolution of language is to identify the function of any protolanguage and, hence, how it might have benefited those animals or humans developing so that it could be selected for by standard evolutionary mechanisms, including kin selection and reciprocal altruism.

The structure of language

Levels of description

Although we are not usually aware of it as language users, languages are complex systems, with structure at many levels. The most important aspect of language structuring is what the linguist Charles Hockett (1960) called 'duality of patterning' – patterning at the levels of sound and meaning. Hockett talks about 'sounds' because spoken language is the basic form of human language. Writing is a more recent development; spoken language is prior to this, both historically and for individuals. There are sounds that are specific to language and are different from coughs, grunts, whistles, and other nonlanguage sounds. These language sounds express meaning, and both sounds and meaning have complex structures or patterns. The relations between the sound structures and the meaning structures are what enable us to use language to communicate information. Languages draw on a pool of sounds, called 'phones'. A phone is the smallest unit of sound that can make a difference in meaning, although, in any particular language, some phones will be equivalent because they are never used to make contrasts between different words. Notoriously, for example, Japanese speakers have difficulties with the 'r' versus 'l' distinction in English, because the distinction is not important in their language, and some Indian languages have more or less aspirated ('breathy') 'd' sounds that can signal different words in those languages but would not do so in English. Sounds that signal differences between words in a particular language, such as the 'b' sound and the 'p' sound that distinguish 'bin' and 'pin' in English, are called 'phonemes', and may have different pronunciations in different contexts. For example, the same phoneme in Japanese may sometime be pronounced 'l' and sometimes 'r'. In the first year of life, infants home in on the phonemic distinctions that are important in the language spoken around them (Werker & Tees, 1983). Other distinctions, which they can make earlier in life, become difficult to impossible to make after the first year. In English, phonemes correspond to the most common sounds of certain letters (a, b, c, p, t, etc.) or groups of letters (ch, th, ee, etc.). Phonemes are commonly divided into vowels and consonants, which have different acoustic properties. In all languages there are (phonological) rules that determine what patterns of phonemes are allowed in constructing words. Then there are rules (of syntax or grammar) for how to put words together to make phrases, clauses, and sentences.

Meanings are also structured. We tend to think of meanings being associated with words. Nouns are names of people, animals, plants, inanimate objects, and abstractions. Verbs are names of actions, events, states, and processes. Adjectives and adverbs are names of properties. Then there are various grammatical words – determiners such as 'a' and 'the'; prepositions such as 'in', 'on', and 'to'; auxiliaries such as 'may' and 'would'; and so on – that link the main, content-bearing words in various ways. There are also rules for how the meaning of groups of words depends on the way the words are put together. Consider a verb such as 'put'. An action of putting requires a person who does the putting, something (usually an object) that is put somewhere, and a place where the object is put (e.g. 'Mary put the baked potatoes on the table'). Rules about sentence structure tell us where the verb should go in a sentence about putting (there may be several alternatives – e.g. 'The potatoes were put on the table by Mary') and where the people and things involved in the putting should be mentioned in the sentence.

The whole complex set of rules allows us to use the sounds of our language to express a complex set of meanings, including the ability to describe things that happen at a distance in either time (the past, the future) or space (distant lands) or both. Where such an ability exists in animal communication systems (e.g. in the honeybee dance) it is much more limited in scope than in human language.

Written language differs from spoken language most obviously in the way that words are made up – for example, of letters rather than sounds in a language such as English. The higher-level structure of phrases, clauses, and sentences is basically the same in spoken and written language. Most languages use alphabetical systems in which letters or groups of letters correspond in a more (e.g. Finnish) or less (e.g. English) regular way to phonemes. However, there are other ways of representing words, such as the logographs of traditional Chinese script and the signs standing for syllables used, in a complex mix with logographs, in Japanese.

Psychologists need to know about the structure of languages, because it is important for psychological theories of how language is processed.

Schools of linguistics

Academic interest in describing the structure of human languages goes back at least 3,000 years, to work in India on Sanskrit. Modern linguistics can be traced to the rediscovery of this work by Sir William Jones in the 18th century and to his discovery (using what came to be known as the comparative method) that Sanskrit was related to Latin and Classical Greek, and hence that all three had a common ancestor, known as Proto-Indo European. Another scholar of Sanskrit, the Swiss linguist Ferdinand de Saussure, instigated a more systematic study of linguistic structure that continues to have a profound influence on the more formal approaches to linguistics that were developed in the 20th century, largely by, or in response to, the work of Chomsky.

Impact on psychological research

In the early part of the 20th century, the American linguist Leonard Bloomfield was influenced by Wilhelm Wundt, regarded as the founder of experimental psychology and an early student of the psychology of language. Ironically, Bloomfield became a behaviourist in the 1930s when most of Anglo-Saxon psychology was dominated by behaviourism, but there was virtually no mutual influence between Bloomfield's behaviourism in linguistics and behaviourism in psychology.

More important for psychology was the work of Chomsky, who focused on the biological and cognitive bases of human language. Chomsky (1957; 1965) developed a way of describing language structure, particularly the structure of words within phrases and sentences, that lent itself to being incorporated into a 'machine' that could process structures. Chomsky also developed the psychologically relevant distinction between linguistic *competence* – what people know explicitly or implicitly about their language – and linguistic *performance* – the error-prone, time-constrained use of language in everyday circumstances. In the 1950s and 1960s, Chomsky worked with pioneers of cognitive psychology and artificial intelligence (particularly George Miller), and for a period in the 1960s and 1970s attempts were made to produce psychological theories of language processing that incorporated Chomsky's ideas (Fodor, Bever, & Garrett, 1974). In the end, these attempts were not particularly successful (Garnham, 1983), partly because they were based on a particular version of Chomsky's theory, which was subsequently extensively revised. Later psycholinguists tended to retain only the basic ideas of describing the structure of phrases and sentences in formulating their theories of language processing.

DISCUSSION POINT

Discuss how human language differs from other systems of communication. Does this make it superior to these other systems of communication?

Language acquisition by children

Chomsky believed, quite rightly, that descriptions of language structure are crucial to psychological theories of how language is used by mature speakers. Perhaps more important for Chomsky were the implications, as he saw them, of how languages are structured for how children learn a language or languages in the course of their childhood.

The idea of a Universal Grammar and the Chomskyan legacy

Most children learn a language simply by being in an environment in which language is used to communicate with them, and they, in turn, start to use language as a means of communication. This observation raises questions about what is learned, what the basis of the learning is, and how that learning is possible without much training or correction. One thing that children learn is words – lots of them, probably several new words a day at the peak of vocabulary development. There are controversies about how words are learned, to which we will return below. However, there has probably been more controversy about how the rules for putting words together are learned.

Chomsky argued that children get very poor evidence about the grammatical rules of their language. The evidence is poor for two reasons. First, it is (allegedly) almost all positive evidence – hearing examples of what are supposed to be correct sentences and never being told that other strings of words are not allowed. Second, even the positive evidence is full of errors and incomplete sentences. Chomsky (e.g. 2006) therefore argued that children are born with a Universal Grammar – a set of principles that tells them what kind of rules are found in the grammars of human languages. Given these constraints on what they can learn, the evidence they have becomes sufficient to select among the restricted set of possibilities.

These ideas are related to Chomsky's theory of language evolution – it is the inbuilt Universal Grammar that is supposed to have suddenly appeared – and are disputed for the same reasons. In addition, various aspects of Chomsky's 'poverty of the stimulus' argument have been challenged. Is the information available to the child as poor as Chomsky claims? Do the technical proofs of what can and cannot be learned from positive evidence alone (Gold, 1967) apply directly to real language learning?

Empirical work on learning grammar

Prompted in part by the cognitive revolution of the 1950s, Roger Brown and colleagues embarked on an in-depth empirical investigation of grammar acquisition based on detailed transcripts of the speech of three children known as Adam, Eve, and Sarah. Brown's book *A First Language: The Early Stages* (1973) describes the structure of children's early utterances, up to the point where the mean length of their utterances is about 2.5 words. Brown borrowed ideas from Chomsky about how sentences are structured, though in the early stages structures are simple, and each one is used to convey a variety of meanings. For example, a two-word utterance with a name and a noun can indicate possession ('Kim car' = Kim's car) or an agent plus an action ('Daddy kiss' = Daddy is kissing).

Later empirical work showed that children have mastered most of the structural aspects of their language by the age of 5 or 6, but that some of the more subtle aspects take several more years to acquire – for example, knowing how to interpret structures such as 'John is easy to please', in which it is not John that does the pleasing, in contrast with, say, 'John is eager to please'.

Statistical learning approaches This empirical work did not resolve the debate about whether language is acquired by using a Universal Grammar to analyse what we hear around us, as Chomsky suggests, or whether general learning mechanisms might play a more prominent role in **language acquisition**. One aspect of human learning, overlooked by Chomsky, is our ability to extract statistical patterns from things we encounter, including language. Some things go together more often than others. For example, 'the' comes before 'boy' much more frequently than 'to' comes before 'boy'. And 'a', 'this', and 'that' behave like 'the' in this respect, and not like 'to'. Some recent approaches to language acquisition, particularly those influenced by computer modelling, have claimed a major role for statistical learning in language acquisition. Empirically, Saffran (2003) showed that 8-month-old infants were sensitive to statistical relations among syllables in streams of nonsense speech. They learned which syllables were heard together and which were not. Sensitivity to statistical patterns could also underlie the acquisition of phonology and syntax.

Learning word meanings Since young adults know tens of thousands of words of their native language, they must have learned, on average, several new words each day. Particularly when they are young, children do not have the meanings of words explained to them but pick those meanings up in other ways, relying on both linguistic and nonlinguistic context. Methods of analysing text by computer, such as latent semantic analysis (Landauer, Foltz, & Laham, 1998), attempt to define a word's meaning in terms of other words it typically occurs with. This idea, which is closely related to the notion of statistical learning, could potentially provide children with cues to the meaning of new words, depending on what previously known words a new word appears with.

In addition, Markman (1989) and others have proposed that, when children hear a new word, they use heuristic methods to guess the word's meaning. For example, they prefer to take words to refer to whole objects rather than parts of them, and they prefer to take words to refer to kinds of things that they do not already have labels for (mutual exclusivity), which can cause problems with learning near synonymous words, such as 'bunny' and 'rabbit'. Carey (e.g. Carey & Bartlett, 1978) has suggested that such methods can lead to so-called 'fast mapping' of words onto **concepts**, so that word meanings can be learned in a single exposure. It is true that principles such as mutual exclusivity can lead to correct immediate choices of what a word refers to. A novel word, such as 'blug', will be associated with a novel item, rather than something a child already has a name for – a rabbit, for example. However, nothing more permanent needs to have been learned about the meaning of the novel word by making such a mapping, and, indeed, there is evidence that the meanings are not learned in this way (McMurray, Horst, & Samuelson, 2012). We do not have a complete picture of how children learn so many words.

In **this 2010 TED Talk**[1], Professor Patricia Kuhl discusses her research into how babies learn languages by listening to the humans around them and 'taking statistics' on the sounds they need to know.

Understanding and producing language

The core questions in psycholinguistics are about the mental representations and processes used by ordinary adults in the **production** (speaking and writing) and understanding (listening and **reading**) of their own language. As we have already said, one issue for the student of these issues is that using our own language, in everyday settings, is a natural and almost effortless activity, and it can be hard to realize that complicated mental processes underlie it. Another complication is to understand how the two aspects of language use fit together. First, language unfolds through time – literally, in the case of speech, and to some extent literally in the case of writing and, because of the way we go through texts, reading. So, as we speak or listen or write or read, we are dealing with different bits of a text or conversation at different times. Second, each bit of the conversation or text goes through a series of processing stages, to be described below.

For largely practical reasons, psycholinguists have focused more on understanding than on producing language, and more on written language than on spoken language. It is easier to carry out properly controlled experiments on **comprehension** and with printed materials (often text on a computer screen).

Comprehension

The best way of trying to grasp the questions that scientists ask about language comprehension – questions that do not occur to everyday language users – is to listen to a language you do not know or look at a text in a language with an unfamiliar script (e.g. one of the southern Indian languages, if you are European). If you listen to an unfamiliar language, you will hear language-like sounds, as opposed to coughs or grunts, but you will not understand anything. Furthermore, if you listen carefully, you will notice that there are hardly any breaks in the sound – certainly not between each pair of words. When proficient English speakers listen to English, the breaks between the words are obvious. But they are not there in the sound waves! Written language, even in an unfamiliar script, usually has word breaks. But it does not indicate, for example, whether it is to be read from left to right (as for English) or right to left (as for Arabic and Hebrew).

Thinking of language in this way shows that what initially comes to the ears or the eyes is an auditory or visual stimulus (unfolding through time), and to get from that stimulus to an understanding of the message conveyed, however straightforward, involves complex, though usually unconscious, psychological processes. These processes occur in three main stages, always remembering that processing is applied successively to later and later parts of the input. First come the processes that identify letters (in most scripts) and words. For spoken language, the units corresponding to letters are phonemes, and as mentioned above they typically correspond, often in slightly complicated ways, to letters or small groups of letters. In English, for example, the letter 'c' can have a c-type sound (as in 'can') or an s-type sound (as in 'cent'), and a pair of letters, such as 'ch' or 'sh', may correspond to a single sound. In spoken language, again as indicated above, the process of identifying the words includes finding out where one word begins and another ends. Solving this problem, the so-called segmentation problem, uses both information about which words are in the language and general rules, such as that words do not overlap in the speech stream and don't usually have sounds between them. The segmentation problem was illustrated to comic effect in the famous Two Ronnies hardware store sketch, where Ronnie Corbett gives Ronnie Barker four candles when what he really wanted was fork handles.

Crucial for the task of identifying words is a store of knowledge about the words of the language you are speaking, what they look like, and what they sound like. This store is called the 'mental lexicon'. Identifying a word is the process of deciding which of the words you know (if any) the current visual or acoustic pattern corresponds to. Since about 1990 most people have agreed that this process relies on a set of interconnected detectors, one for each word you know, together with detectors for letters and for subcomponents of letters (see McClelland & Rumelhart, 1981, for the original version of this model). The system works very quickly – too quickly for us to notice it working. But experiments can detect effects of factors such as how long a word is, how common it is, whether it has a regular or irregular spelling, and whether there are many or few other words that are spelled the same or sound the same.

In the second stage of comprehension, words are put together in groups that typically have certain kinds of meanings, but before the particular meaning has been worked out. This stage is called 'syntactic analysis' or 'parsing'. So, for example, in the previous sentence, the two words 'this' and 'stage' form a closely knit group – nouns, or naming words, such as 'stage' are often preceded by determiners such as 'this', 'the', 'a', 'some', or 'these'. Smaller groups then form bigger groups, until a structure is constructed for a whole sentence. This stage of processing deals with longer stretches than the previous stage, and it works on things that we are not currently hearing or reading, but that we have just heard or read in the past few seconds. There can be ambiguities in the way in which words are grouped, which will lead to ambiguities in meaning. If 'the cop saw the man with the telescope', who had the telescope? Compare this with 'the cop saw the man with the revolver' (and see Taraban & McClelland, 1988, for an experimental investigation of this effect). And did the British troops really leave their breakfast in the South Atlantic: 'British left waffles on Falklands'?!

Finally, in the third stage, meaning is computed. That short phrase covers a multitude of sins. The meanings of the words identified in the first stage, and the contribution to meaning of the groupings of the second stage, help to fix the literal meaning of what has been written or said. But its significance in its context, both linguistic and nonlinguistic, also needs to be determined. Might the language be figurative? (Buckets can literally be kicked, but the phrase 'kick the bucket' often has a different meaning.) Is a social message being conveyed? Particularly for these broader aspects of meaning, still larger sections of conversation or text may have to be considered. And all the while the conversation or text may be continuing, with new material to be incorporated with what has gone before. Links have to be made between language and the things in the real or imaginary world that are being discussed. And, in texts or conversations of any length, expressions with different formal properties (e.g. 'the table' and 'it') have to be identified as referring to the same thing (see Garnham, 2001, for some of the factors that affect this process).

Another question that naturally arises is how these three stages are related to one another. In particular, does information just flow forward from one stage to the next – from word identities to the word-grouping stage and then the structures from the grouping stage to the stage that works out meaning? Or can information flow back? If the meaning stage is telling us that the text is about someone with a lighting problem, do we prefer to analyse a bit of speech as 'four candles' rather than 'fork handles', for example? You might think the answer is obvious: of course we use the results of the higher-level (meaning) processing to interpret new inputs. But, in terms of the flow of information in the language-processing system, the answer is not so easy. The reason is that the early stages need not provide definitive answers to the questions they are supposed to answer. What goes forward could be: 'This bit of speech might be "four candles" or "fork handles" but it is definitely not "three nightlights" or "knife blades".' A small number of possibilities can be passed forward, to be accepted or rejected at a later stage. There is a strong argument (Norris, McQueen, & Cutler, 2000) that this 'architecture', to use a rather grand word that is often employed in this context, is the most efficient and the actual one.

Production

Roughly speaking, language production is the mirror of comprehension. It starts with a mental representation of the information to be conveyed. This representation is used to generate the linguistic forms that can be used to convey that information, and eventually a set of commands to the vocal system to produce a sequence of language sounds. As in comprehension, the various processes have to be gone through for successive bits of speech, and there are many empirical questions about what the units of planning are and how the processes are interleaved in time. Furthermore, the notion of a sequence of language sounds is somewhat misleading, since, because of the way the articulatory system works, individual phonemes do not occur one after the other in the stream of speech but are, to use a technical term, co-articulated.

Serial and interactive models As in comprehension, there are two types of model: serial or feedforward only (Roelofs, 1997) and interactive (Dell, 1986). The distinction lies in whether the various processes of language production are applied one after the other with no referring back to previous stages, or whether such referring back is possible. If serial models are allowed to put multiple possibilities forward to the next stage (e.g. for which word to choose to express a particular idea), the two types of model can be difficult to distinguish. At a phenomenological level, different types of process do interact, so, for example, the process of 'blending' (which is a semantic process; for example, someone vacillating between saying 'children' and 'young' might say 'chung') is influenced by phonological factors. However, such phenomenological interactions do not necessarily imply process interactions, as we saw in the case of comprehension.

Speech errors and other experimental evidence Much of the evidence for how speech production works comes from the study of speech errors. The focus in this research is on linguistic properties of such errors, not on Freudian questions about what such errors reveal about people's hidden thoughts. There is no incompatibility between these approaches, even if there is little evidence for the veracity of Freud's ideas. Interestingly, the speech errors reported by Freud have the linguistic properties reported by people who study speech errors from a psycholinguistic point of view. Some types of speech error, such as 'spoonerisms' (e.g. saying 'our queer old dean' instead of 'our dear old queen'), involve two elements, and the maximum distance between the two elements indicates the size of the unit that is planned all at once. The nature of the changes in speech errors gives some indication of the building blocks of the representations of language. More detailed information, for example about the independence or otherwise of sound-based errors and meaning-based errors, can provide information about the relationship between sound-based and meaning-based process in production.

Speech errors can also be induced experimentally, for example in Bernard Baars' SLIP (Spoonerisms of Laboratory-Induced Predisposition) paradigm (Baars, Motley, & McKay, 1975). After saying a series of word pairs, such as 'best rose' and 'bets rode', a significant proportion of people will pronounce 'red bowl' as 'bed roll'. Because such experimentally produced spoonerisms are less frequent when the spoonerism does not produce words (e.g. 'bit rope' to 'rit bope'), Baars argued that there is a late monitoring process in speech production that checks whether what is being said 'makes sense' in the sense that it is made up of real words.

Dialogue

Dialogue involves both comprehension and production. A crucial question is: what else is involved in engaging in dialogue other than the basic processes of comprehension and production? A general model, proposed by Pickering and Garrod (2004), suggests that the participants in a dialogue align their linguistic output at a variety of levels, from low-level factors such as how they pronounce the sounds of their language and how fast they talk, to high-level factors such as the expressions they use to refer to the things they are talking about. Alignment cannot be total, otherwise the speakers would be saying exactly the same thing in exactly the same way, but there is greater similarity than would be expected if alignment processes were not taking place. Older work by Clark shows that, as a dialogue progresses, people agree on short terms to refer to what were originally unfamiliar objects (e.g. Clark & Wilkes-Gibbs, 1986). One question that this, and other, alignment processes raise is to what extent information about one's audience influences how one says what one wants to say: to what extent is 'audience design' an important factor in language production? In one sense, it ought to be, if your goal is to be understood. However, Keysar has shown that there are circumstances in which information about the audience seems to be ignored and speakers behave egocentrically (e.g. Keysar, Barr, & Horton, 1998). Particularly in spoken interactions, the real-time pressures on computing what to say may be too great for all relevant factors to be taken into consideration.

Reading

In much psycholinguistic research, printed texts are used. However, the main focus is not on reading itself but on processes assumed to be common to reading and listening. Indeed, most of this research uses printed material for convenience, and recognizes that spoken language is the primary form of language.

Nevertheless, because reading has certain special properties, and because it is of interest from an educational point of view, there has been a separate tradition of work on reading that has two main lines of research. One investigates the movement of the eyes across the page during reading, and how that relates to the extraction of information from the text. The other concerns language disorders that are specific to reading, namely the **dyslexias**. We will consider these two lines of research in turn.

Eye movements in reading

The initial stages of processing written language are different from those for spoken language. In English we read from left to right and from the top to the bottom of the page. The text is all there, and we move our eyes over it to take it in sequentially, in approximately the same order as if the same words were spoken. We do not have intuitive insight into the way our eyes move across a page of text. The basic pattern must be left to right along the lines and down the lines of the page. However, before they learn about eye movements in reading, many people think their eyes move smoothly along the lines of text. In fact, it is relatively easy to look at another person's eyes when they are reading and to observe a series of small jerky movements, with short pauses between those movements. Starting in the 19th century, ways of taking an accurate record of these movements were developed. For straightforward text, the movements (called 'saccades') cover on average about seven to eight letters, unless the text is very large or very small, and the pauses (called 'fixations') last about a fifth to a quarter of a second (though sometimes considerably longer). Only a small central area of the visual field has clear enough vision to identify individual letters, and, on a particular fixation, upcoming letters receive more attention than previously read letters, not because of any asymmetry in the visual field but because previous letters – to the left of the fixation point for English and other left-to-right languages; to the right for Hebrew and other right-to-left languages – have already been identified. Most movements are forward, but a small number (less than 10% for simple text) go back (called regressions). In addition, there is a backwards sweep at the end of each line. The fixations typically fall on longer words, with short words often missed. For medium-length words the fixation is usually close to the middle, but for longer words it is usually nearer the beginning, and there may be one or more further fixations on the same word (see Figure 12.1). Many of the factors that influence the

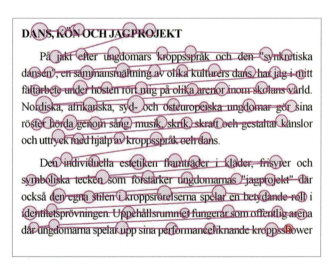

FIGURE 12.1 *A trace of eye movements in reading.*

Source: Wikipedia (author of image: Lucs-kho).

identification of words more generally, such as frequency and regularity of spelling, have effects on how long a fixation lasts.

Theories of eye movement control (oculomotor and cognitive) A more general question is how the overall pattern of fixations and saccades is controlled. We know that these kinds of eye movement are used to look around the world, and that smooth movements are only commonly found when we are tracking single moving objects. Saccades and fixations have been co-opted for the purposes of reading. When the eye stops in a fixation, how long it stops for depends on what it stops on – is the word easy or hard to process, in its context? However, there has been a lively debate about how the pattern of saccades is controlled. Is it primarily by properties of how the eye moves and by low-level visual properties – the basic shapes and sizes of the upcoming words, which can be seen further to the right than the individual letters can be made out (the oculomotor control theory; O'Regan, 1992)? Or is there a relatively small area of peripheral vision where higher-level properties of the upcoming text can be extracted (words and their meanings) in such a way as to influence the extent of the next saccade (e.g. Henderson & Ferreira, 1990)?

Dyslexias: Developmental and acquired

Although reading is a relatively recent development, there are language disorders that appear to be specific to reading – the dyslexias. Dyslexias can be developmental or acquired. Developmental dyslexia is particularly important in the context of learning to read. It is seen in children who have difficulties that are specific to language, rather than other cognitive skills, and also specific to written language rather than spoken language. There is, however, a great deal of controversy about developmental dyslexia. One source of controversy is about how specific to language and to written language the deficits of dyslexics are. One view is that dyslexics have difficulty with information about the order of items in any rapidly presented sequence (Bakker, 1972). Another source of controversy is whether there is any specific deficit in dyslexia other than poor reading ability (Elliott & Gibbs, 2008). Given that reading ability and, say, mathematical ability are not perfectly correlated, there is bound to be a small proportion of children who are good at one but well below average on the other. In a country such as the United Kingdom, this small proportion will turn out to be a relatively large number of children. So, the question is whether the reading abilities of some or all dyslexics are different from those of other poor readers who are also relatively unskilled all round.

In many cases it appears they are not. We have already mentioned the issue of serial order skills and dyslexia. Another, possibly related, problem shown by poor readers, including dyslexics, is poor phonological skills – the relative inability to deal with the sound system of the language (Vellutino, Fletcher, Snowling, & Scanlon, 2004). Poor readers have difficulty picking the odd one out in rhyming sets (e.g. cat, bad, mat, rat) and with other related tasks. In some ways this characteristic of dyslexics is surprising, since the problems that define their condition arise with written language.

Acquired dyslexias result from brain injuries of various kinds – for example, from strokes or closed head injuries (i.e. those in which there is no penetration of the skull). Unlike developmental dyslexias, acquired dyslexias fall into relatively distinct categories, which reflect different ways that written words are processed. The relationship between the visual appearance of a word and its sound can be determined in two ways. The overall appearance can be linked directly to the sound, or rules for how individual letters are pronounced can be used to derive the pronunciation of the word. For regularly spelled words these two methods produce the same results, but for irregular words only the 'direct' method gets it right, For example, most '-int' words in English are pronounced with a short 'i' as in 'mint', so a rule-based system will mispronounce 'pint'. *Surface dyslexics* appear to have lost the direct route for reading, so they regularize the pronunciation of irregular words and hence may fail to identify them properly – if you see 'pint' and think it rhymes with 'mint' you might not realize what word those letters represent. *Phonological dyslexics*, on the other hand, cannot pronounce strings of letters that are not words, and so seem to have lost the rule-based method of reading. The existence of the two types of dyslexic is evidence for the separateness of the two routes of reading (Coltheart, Rastle, Perry, Langdon, & Ziegler, 2001). A further class of acquired dyslexics, which includes deep dyslexics and semantic dyslexics, have difficulty with reading because they have, at least partially, lost the connection between printed word forms and their meanings.

Bilingualism

Bilingualism, or multilingualism more generally, is a complex topic in which there is a growing interest as more people across the world learn second languages (often English). Bilingualism, to take the simplest case, can range from complete native fluency in two languages to native fluency in one and passable competence in another. Psychologists ask questions about whether cognitive resources are shared between the different languages, particularly if they subscribe to the idea that all languages show basic similarities. They also ask questions about how knowing two languages influences other cognitive functions, compared to the case of monolingualism.

Types of bilingualism

There are a number of ways of classifying bilinguals. *Consecutive* versus *sequential* bilingualism refers to whether the languages are learned together or one first and then the other. *Compound* versus *coordinate* bilingualism refers to whether the languages are learned in the same setting or different settings. *Dominant* versus *balanced* bilingualism refers to whether one language is used to a greater extent than the other. Some combinations of these types of bilingualism are more common than others.

One aspect of the shared resources question that psychologists ask about bilingualism is how knowledge of one language affects the learning of another language. This question is perhaps most pertinent in the case of relatively late learning of the second language, when the so-called critical period for language acquisition is past. From everyday knowledge about foreign accents to the intrusion of words and grammatical constructions from the first language into the second, it is not surprising that psychologists have confirmed considerable influences of properties of the first language on the learning of the second.

Cognitive impacts of bilingualism

Another increasingly important question is about the cognitive impacts, beneficial or detrimental, of being bilingual. Despite early claims about problems caused by trying to learn two languages, it now seems that the impact of being bilingual is almost wholly beneficial. Bialystok (e.g. 1988) has shown that knowing more than one language cues young children to the abstract and arbitrary nature of linguistic signs at an earlier age than monolingual children, and gives them greater metalinguistic awareness. Bialystok (e.g. Bialystok & Martin, 2004) also argues that the need to inhibit competing words, from the other language, is related to bilinguals' better performance in executive function tasks, related to problem solving and planning.

 Educator Mia Nacamulli discusses the different types of bilingualism and the cognitive benefits of bilingualism in **this TedEd video**[2].

TEST YOURSELF

What lessons can be learned from the study of bilingualism?

The biological bases of language and language disorders

Psychologists use observations about what happens when systems break down to study their functions. Cognitive systems break down when parts of the brain are damaged. So the study of language disorders provides information about brain structures involved in language processing.

Classic aphasias and the Wernicke–Geschwind model

Although Aristotle's idea that the brain's main function is to cool the blood had already been overturned a few decades after his death (in 322 BCE), concrete ideas about links between the brain and language were not formulated until the 19th century. Franz Josef Gall's phrenology (the study of the shape and protuberances of the skull, based on the now discredited belief that they reveal character and mental capacity) was clearly flawed, but, shortly after Gall, French pioneers Jean-Baptiste Bouillaud (1825) and Marc Dax presented systematic empirical evidence for the location of language functions, with Bouillaud recognizing the importance of the frontal lobes and Dax identifying the asymmetrical localization of language functions, with the left hemisphere playing the major role. These researchers based their ideas on the identification of specific language disorders associated with damage to particular brain areas. Such disorders are known as **aphasias**. Later in the 19th century, Paul Broca (1861) and Carl Wernicke (1874) reported classic cases of expressive and receptive aphasias, associated with damage to different areas of the left hemisphere, now referred to as Broca's area and Wernicke's area.

For various reasons, work on aphasias suffered neglect for over half a century, after which time a model of a brain network for language, tentatively investigated by Wernicke, was revived by Norman Geschwind (1972), who showed that a large number of aphasic patients could be, at least roughly, classified by the model. However, the differences from one case to the next turned out to be somewhat problematic, and this fact was one of the inspirations for a different type of approach to language impairment, and, indeed to cognitive impairment more generally.

Cognitive neuropsychological approaches

Mainstream cognitive psychology from the 1950s to the 1980s showed little interest in locating cognitive functions in different parts of the brain and instead focused on the understanding of those functions at an abstract level. Indeed, its underlying philosophy was called functionalism. The associated cognitive neuropsychological approach, which was particularly prominent in the United Kingdom, studied cognitive function via its breakdown in cases of brain damage, and used, in particular, the phenomenon of double dissociation (deficit in function A without a deficit in function B, and vice versa) to argue for separation of function. It regarded questions about brain localization as of secondary importance. Arguments from pairs of cases that show double dissociation do not suffer from the potential flaws of arguments from association of deficits, which might be mediated by physical proximity in the brain; similarly, in single dissociations, the impaired task might be more difficult than the spared task and not possible with a partly damaged system. This approach had particular successes in the study of various kinds of acquired dyslexia and in the generation of dual-route models of reading, based on the distinction between phonological dyslexia and surface dyslexia.

Cognitive neuroscientific approaches

A somewhat later development was that of cognitive neuroscience. This development was based on the introduction of brain-imaging techniques such as positron emission tomography and functional magnetic resonance imaging, and of other methods of investigating brain activity, such as electroencephalography (EEG) (see Western University, 2011) and transcranial magnetic stimulation (see Neuroboffin, 2010). Brain-imaging techniques, which can identify regions of the brain involved in cognitive tasks, have confirmed the classical findings from the aphasias and have extended them by identifying additional brain areas and circuitry that are activated during language processing.

More important in research on the psychology of language has been the study of event-related potentials (ERPs): changes following specific events in the world, such as beginning to read a particular word in a sentence, that are detected in EEG recordings of electrical activity on the scalp. There are methods of trying to infer brain localization of function from scalp activity, but they are not always reliable. Psycholinguists are more interested in characteristic positive and negative deflections in ERPs. These components have functional interpretations, such as indicating difficulties in integrating the current word into the meaning of the sentence so far, and thus their use has much in common with the approach of cognitive neuropsychology, except that ERP work requires groups of participants, rather than single cases.

Embodiment

Another line of work has looked at a different kind of link between language and the human body – usually not the brain in this case – and the body's interactions with the environment. The claim is that concepts, and maybe more abstract aspects of language, such as grammatical structures, are embodied in or based on the way that the human body interacts with the (rest of) the physical world. For example, people find it easier to make a response to a sentence about opening a drawer when they have to pull a lever towards themselves, and easier to make a response to a sentence about closing a drawer when they have to push a lever away, in both cases reflecting the direction of movement of the drawer if they were performing the action themselves (Glenberg & Kaschak, 2002). This idea provides a basis for the link between language as a mental phenomenon and language as a way of describing the world. It potentially solves the so-called symbol grounding problem (Harnad, 1990).

Future developments

As in the study of cognition in general, there is considerable interest in what can be learned about the psychology of language from the relatively new techniques of cognitive neuroscience. Some of these techniques remain expensive, but all are becoming more accessible to users who no longer need the technical competence of the earlier pioneers. To what extent cognitive neuroscience can answer the open questions in the psychology of language is a moot issue. Arguably, what is needed is not so much more sophisticated methods but a more sophisticated theoretical analysis of what functions cognitive systems perform. Another recent development is the use of crowd-sourcing and related techniques to gather large datasets that are more representative of ordinary language use. Web-based systems, such as Amazon's Mechanical Turk, can be used to collect large set of norms, such as ratings for the age at which words are learned (Kuperman, Stadthagen-Gonzalez, & Brysbaert, 2012), an important factor in how they are processed. Apps for Smartphones can be used to measure reaction times in a way that could only be dreamed of a few years ago. For example, Dufau et al. (2011) report a very large-scale, cross-linguistic lexical decision study. In a lexical decision experiment, people judge, as quickly as possible, whether a string of letters is a real word, and the time they take reflects the difficulty, or otherwise, of identifying the word.

Whatever direction the psychology of language takes, the increasing importance of communication, in many different forms, in modern societies, makes the understanding of this aspect of human life even more necessary.

SECTION SUMMARY

- Language is primarily a system for communication, which helps to establish and maintain social relations.
- Linguists tend to focus on structural aspects of language.
- One linguistic approach to characterizing human languages is to recognize their design features (Hockett, 1960).
- The similarities between animal communication and human language raise questions about the evolution of human language.

- There have been suggestions that language appeared suddenly and relatively recently. These ideas, although biologically less plausible than gradualist accounts, have gained credence because of their association with the influential linguist Noam Chomsky.

- One view of the evolution of language is that the crucial precursor of language was the ability to have complex thoughts, in which relations between events, objects, and properties can be represented.

- Languages are complex systems, with structure at many levels. The most important aspect of language structuring is what the linguist Charles Hockett (1960) called duality of patterning.

- The relations between the sound structures and the meaning structures are what enable us to use language to communicate information. Languages draw on a pool of sounds, called phones.

- Sounds that signal differences between words in a particular language, such as the 'b' sound and the 'p' sound that distinguish 'bin' and 'pin' in English, are called phonemes, and may have different pronunciations in different contexts.

- Academic interest in describing the structure of human languages goes back at least 3,000 years, to work in India on Sanskrit.

- Chomsky developed the psychologically relevant distinction between linguistic competence and linguistic performance.

- Most children learn a language simply by being in an environment in which language is used to communicate with them, and they, in turn, start to use language as a means of communication.

- Chomsky argued that children get very poor evidence about the grammatical rules of their language and argued that children are born with a Universal Grammar.

- In the 1950s, Roger Brown and colleagues embarked on an in-depth empirical investigation of grammar acquisition but did not resolve the debate about whether language is acquired by using a Universal Grammar, or whether general learning mechanisms, including statistical learning, might play a more prominent role in language acquisition.

- Core questions in psycholinguistics concern the mental representations and processes used by ordinary adults in the production and understanding of their own language.

- Listening to a foreign language being spoken aloud shows that getting to an understanding of the message conveyed involves complex, usually unconscious psychological processes.

- These processes occur in three main stages: the processes that identify words, word grouping (parsing), and computation of meaning.

- As in comprehension, there are two models of language production: serial or feedforward only (Roelofs, 1997) and interactive (Dell, 1986).

- Much of the evidence for how speech production works comes from the study of speech errors, such as spoonerisms.

- Dialogue involves both comprehension and production. Pickering and Garrod (2004) suggest that the participants in a dialogue align their linguistic output at a variety of levels, from low-level factors, such as how they pronounce the sounds of their language and how fast they talk, to high-level factors, such as the expressions they use to refer to the things they are talking about.

- In much psycholinguistic research, printed texts are used and the main focus is on processes assumed to be common to reading and listening.

- There are two main lines of reading research: one investigates the movement of the eyes across the page during reading, and the other concerns language disorders that are specific to reading, namely the dyslexias.

- The movements of the eyes across the page while reading are called saccades and cover on average about seven to eight letters. Most movements are forward, but a small number (less than 10% for simple text) go backwards (called regressions).

- Many of the factors that influence the identification of words more generally, such as frequency and regularity of spelling, have effects on how long a fixation lasts. There has been a lively debate about how the pattern of saccades is controlled.

- Language disorders that appear to be specific to reading are known as the dyslexias. Dyslexias can be developmental or acquired.

- Bilingualism, or multilingualism more generally, is a complex topic in which there is a growing interest. There are a number of ways of classifying bilingualism: consecutive versus sequential, compound versus coordinate, and dominant versus balanced.

- Another increasingly important question is about the cognitive impacts, beneficial or detrimental, of being bilingual.

- The study of language disorders provides information about brain structures involved in language processing. Specific language disorders associated with damage to particular brain areas are known as aphasias. Paul Broca (1861) and Karl Wernicke (1874) are key figures in this field.

- The development of brain-imaging techniques has opened up the field of psycholinguistic research to cognitive neuroscience. More important in research on the psychology of language has been the study of event-related potentials: changes following specific events in the world (such as beginning to read a particular word in a sentence) that are detected in EEG recordings of electrical activity on the scalp.

THINKING

LEARNING OBJECTIVE 12.3

Describe and evaluate psychological research on thinking and reasoning, recognize the different strands of work in the psychology of thinking, and consider how they might be related to each other.

The psychology of thinking and reasoning has been approached from a number of different starting points. There are three main strands of research, sometimes addressing the same issues from different perspectives. These strands are usually known as (1) **reasoning**, (2) **problem solving**, and (3) **judgement** and **decision making**. After first considering concepts, out of which many thoughts are built, we will look at these three strands in turn, before turning to other issues in the psychology of thinking. All three strands of work have identified limitations on the power of human thinking but, explicitly or implicitly, they also point to a stark contrast between humans and other animals.

Concepts and categories

Concepts, which correspond to word meanings or possible word meanings, are the building blocks of our thoughts. Through their links to words' meanings, they create a connection between language and thought. Concepts allow us to treat different things as the same. Every chair is different from every other chair, but the basic function of a chair is to be sat on. If we could not think of different things in the same ways – ways that are appropriate to our interactions with them – we would experience the 'blooming buzzing confusion' that James (1890, p. 488) talked about in *The Principles of Psychology*.

Types of concept

Much of the psychological research on concepts has focused on concepts corresponding to nouns (e.g. 'bird', 'robin', 'chair') or more complex phrases based on nouns (e.g. 'red chair'), which correspond to classes of object. The two most important classes of (concrete) object are natural kinds – things that occur naturally in the world (animals, plants, rocks, etc.) – and artefacts – things that we construct (chairs, cars, houses, etc.). Abstract objects, arguably, also fall into these two categories (e.g. happiness versus law). Other categories of words and the corresponding types of concept are equally important in our thinking, even if they have received less attention from psychologists. Corresponding to verbs are actions, events, states, and processes; corresponding to adjectives are properties of objects; and corresponding to adverbs are properties of actions, events, states, and processes.

Psychological theories and their limitations

In the 1960s and early 1970s, two psychological theories of word meanings and concepts were developed. They appeared dissimilar but were different formulations of what is known as the 'classical view of concepts', which can be traced back to Aristotle. The classical view is primarily a theory about concepts based on nouns and it claims that, to belong to the category corresponding to a noun concept (e.g. 'bird' or 'chair'), an object has to have certain properties. If it has all of them it is in the category, but, if there is one or more property it does not have, it is not in the category. The properties are said to form a set of (individually) necessary and (jointly) sufficient conditions for belonging to the category.

The two psychological theories of the 1960s and 1970s were based, in the one case, on the notion of 'features of meaning' (Rips, Shoben, & Smith, 1973) and, in the other case, on the notion of 'hierarchies of concepts' (Collins & Quillian, 1969). The feature notion maps more obviously onto the classical view of concepts, and features are, in fact, also included in the semantic hierarchy view. The latter view recognizes that noun concepts (e.g. animal → mammal → dog → collie) and to some extent other concepts (e.g. cook → fry, boil, roast, poach, etc.) form hierarchies from the general to the specific, and that a member of a category lower in the hierarchy will inherit features from higher up, allowing for economies in the representational system (collies bark because they are dogs, have warm blood because they are mammals, and can move of their own accord because they are animals). See Figure 12.2.

Problems with the classical view of concepts emerge when we take a concept and try to list the features that are necessary and sufficient for it to belong to the corresponding category. The philosopher Ludwig Wittgenstein (1953) challenged people

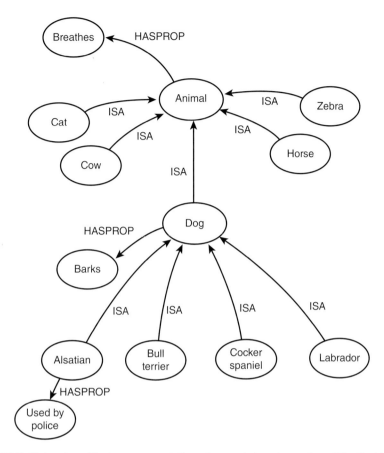

FIGURE 12.2 *Network and feature representation of concepts/word meanings. ISA = 'is a', in the sense of 'is a type of' (e.g. apple is a type of fruit); HASPROP = 'has the property' (e.g. grass has the property of being green).*

Source: Garnham and Oakhill (1994, Fig. 2.1, p. 24). Reproduced with permission of Wiley.

to think about this issue for the concept of a game. As an exercise, you might try to think for yourself what these features could be. Don't forget that there are many different types of game. Wittgenstein concluded that what relates games is not a set of defining features but a series of interlocking similarities that he called 'family resemblances'. Wittgenstein's ideas were part of the inspiration for an alternative psychological theory of concepts, 'prototype theory'. Prototype theory suggests that the mental representation of a concept is centred on a prototypical member of the corresponding category together with the idea that similarity to the prototype determines category membership. The main proponent of prototype theory, Eleanor Rosch (e.g. Rosch & Mervis, 1975), also noted another fact that the classical theory ignores. Concepts can be more or less general, but there is a level of generality, the basic level, that people find easiest to use (Rosch, Mervis, Gray, Johnson, & Boyes-Braem, 1976). For example, we like to classify things as apples, as opposed to bananas or oranges, but we find fruit too abstract a category, and a particular type, such as Gala apples, is often overspecific for our purposes.

Prototype theory is not without its problems. The phenomenon of 'conceptual combination', for example, is difficult for the theory to handle. Concepts do not just exist in isolation but combine together in interesting ways. A prototypical pet might be a cat or a dog, and a prototypical fish might be a cod or a salmon, but a prototypical pet fish is a goldfish. It is difficult to make Rosch's prototype theory account for this fact, though methods have been proposed (e.g. Smith & Osherson, 1984). In addition, apparently similar combinations may have different meanings (e.g. compare the meanings of olive oil and baby oil).

Other problems for prototype theory include the fact that some odd numbers (e.g. 3) are more prototypical than others (e.g. 597) (Armstrong, Gleitman, & Gleitman, 1983), even though there clearly are necessary and sufficient conditions for being an odd number – being like a prototypical odd number is not enough. Ad hoc categories (those made up for a particular purpose, such as things to rescue from your house in case of a fire) also have more or less prototypical members, even though those categories are not, presumably, stored in memory (Barsalou, 1983).

These problems with the classical theory and prototype theory have led to other types of theory being proposed. The two most important ones are 'exemplar-based theories' (Medin & Schaffer, 1978) and 'theory-based theories' (Murphy & Medin, 1985). The first type of theory is partly a reaction to the vagueness of the notion of similarity in prototype theory. It says that concepts are represented by their exemplars, usually arranged according to similarity on a clearly defined set of dimensions. For a new example to be in the set, it must be very close to an existing exemplar. Theory-based theories of concepts hold that the organization of concepts is based on theories – often lay theories – of how the world works. Concepts get their meaning from the roles they play in the theories of which they are part.

DISCUSSION POINT

Discuss the idea of concepts and the different types of concepts and their implications.

Reasoning: Deductive and inductive

One of the three main strands of work on thinking is reasoning research. Historically, it has focused on certain types of reasoning problem, such as conditional reasoning and syllogisms, studied by logicians, and tasks related to hypothesis testing devised by the English psychologist Peter Wason, who was influenced by the philosophical analysis of the scientific method by Karl Popper (1959).

Logic, mental logic, and mental models

Logic, like mathematics, is difficult. It has taken intelligent people a long time to develop systems of logic, and students learning those systems almost always find their task to be a hard one. A core area of logic is deductive argument, in which the conclusion contains no more information than is (hidden in) the premises, but where that information can be more or less difficult to extract. Aristotle described a constrained realm of deductive reasoning – 'syllogisms' – that contains some very easy deductions:

    All the artists are beekeepers.
    All the beekeepers are chemists.
    So, all the artists are chemists.

and some very hard ones:

> All the beekeepers are artists.
> None of the chemists are beekeepers.
> So, some of the artists are not chemists.

One way that logicians explain which deductions are valid (meaning that the conclusion must be true if the premises are true) is to formulate logical rules for working from the premises to the conclusion, by a series of steps called a 'proof'. A corresponding psychological theory about how people try to draw out conclusions that are implicit in the information they have is that a version of the rules of logic is in people's minds. This theory is called the 'doctrine of mental logic' (Rips, 1994). An alternative theory – 'mental models theory' – is that people build models of situations consistent with the premises and try to consider all possible ways of combining them (Johnson-Laird, 1981). Often the two types of theory make different predictions about which problems should be hard and which should be easy; for example, a syllogism might have a short proof but require multiple models, and a great deal of work since the 1980s has attempted to see which theory's predictions most closely match the way people behave.

Belief bias

Another aspect of deductive reasoning is that people are influenced in the conclusions they draw by what they believed prior to trying to draw a conclusion. This fact is not apparent in the example above, because people tend not to have beliefs about arbitrary characteristics or interests (e.g. being artists, beekeepers, or chemists). That is part of the reason for choosing such examples in psychological studies. But, in everyday life, we mostly try to draw conclusions about things we are interested in and hence have beliefs about. For example, French people are typically thought to have an interest in good food. So, if a person sees:

> All the French people are wine drinkers.
> Some of the wine drinkers are gourmets.
> So, some of the French people are gourmets.

they may be inclined to judge that the plausible conclusion follows validly from the information in the premises. However, it does not, because the wine drinkers who are gourmets might all be of another nationality, and that would be consistent with the information in the first two statements. The mental models theory of deductive reasoning makes detailed predictions of the effects of prior beliefs on syllogisms of different levels of difficulty, and these predictions are largely borne out (Oakhill, Johnson-Laird, & Garnham, 1989).

Deduction, induction, and everyday reasoning

An issue facing logicians, and hence also psychologists studying deductive reasoning, is the relationship between deduction as exemplified in syllogisms, and reasoning in everyday life. Much of that reasoning is not deductive but inductive: the premises provide support for the conclusion without guaranteeing it to be true. A typical kind of inductive reasoning is to conclude that things will happen the way they always have happened (e.g. the sun will rise tomorrow). Inductions are not valid in the way deductions are. Deductive conclusions must be true if their premises are true. Inductive conclusions need not be. There has been extensive philosophical discussion about the reasons why we should (or should not) rely on inductive reasoning.

Some of our **everyday reasoning** does seem to take the form of drawing out information that is implicit in the premises we are arguing from. Whether the processes used in everyday reasoning are the same as those used in formal reasoning is a debated point. One person who argues that the two are different is David Perkins (1985). Apart from issues about modifying or supplementing the information from which an argument starts, which, according to Perkins, is possible in everyday reasoning but not in formal reasoning, Perkins points out that everyday reasoning typically involves a number of short lines of argument on either side of an issue, rather than the single, often longish line of argument that comprises a proof in formal reasoning.

Perkins (see Perkins, Farady, & Bushey, 1991, for an overview) and Deanna Kuhn (1991) have studied informal arguments in detail and found them to be biased, with people offering many 'my side' arguments, supporting the conclusion they wish to press and rather few 'other side' arguments. This bias does not go away with educational level or with **expertise** in the domain of the argument. This bias is a version of the confirmation bias discussed in the section on **hypothesis testing** below. The other major problem that Perkins identifies in everyday reasoning is what he calls 'metacognitive shortfall' – lack of ability to recognize problems with and improve one's reasoning strategies.

The work of Perkins looks at abstract argumentation. Another line of work on everyday reasoning shows that, when people solve practical problems in their everyday lives, they reason fluently. Work on mental financial transactions in both adults (Scribner, 1984, on workers packing goods in a milk processing plant and selling goods from delivery trucks) and children (Carraher, Carraher, & Schliemann, 1985, on Brazilian child street vendors calculating the amount to charge in sales of multiple items) shows deft mathematical skills that are often not reproduced when the same people are asked to carry out equivalent calculations as classroom arithmetic.

Hypothesis testing

Related to work on deductive reasoning is research on how people use individual instances to decide whether general hypotheses are true. This research was instigated by Peter Wason and draws on the work of philosopher of science Karl Popper, who emphasized that general statements can be definitively falsified by individual observations, but not proved. A single black swan refutes the statement 'all swans are white', but 3,849 white swans do not prove it is true!

Wason and Johnson-Laird (1972) showed that, nevertheless, people tend to consider confirming or positive instances of a hypothesis when trying to decide whether it is true, rather than falsifying ones. In the Wason selection task (Activity 12.1), people tend to pick cards that could confirm the rule: the even number (because it might have a vowel on the back) and the vowel (because it might have an even number on the back). What they should do is pick the even number (because it might *not* have a vowel on the back) and the consonant (because it might have an even number on the back). That is to say, they should choose cards that might not conform to the rule and hence be the single case that proves it false.

ACTIVITY 12.1

WASON SELECTION TASK

If you are doing this activity in a group, some people should try the first version and some the second version.

VERSION 1

You are given four cards, each with one face showing:

You are told that each card has a letter on one side and a number on the other. Your task is to answer the following question:

Which cards must be turned over to see whether the rule 'If a card has a vowel on one side, it has an even number on the other' applies to all the cards?

Write down your answer now.

VERSION 2

You are given four cards, each with one face showing:

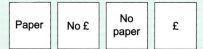

Each card represents a person who passes a newspaper stand with an honesty box. One on side it tells you whether the person took a newspaper. On the other side it tells you whether they put money in the honesty box. Your task is to answer the following question:

Which cards must be turned over to see whether the statement 'If a person takes a paper, they put money in the honesty box' is true?

Write down your answer now. Was the second version easier? Why?

More direct evidence for confirmation bias comes from another Wason task, the 2–4–6 task. People are given the sequence 2–4–6 and are told it fits a rule the experimenter is thinking of. They are asked to try to find out the rule by presenting other sequences of three numbers and being told whether they fit the rule. They also have to write down why they are presenting each sequence. These written protocols provide clear evidence that people present sequences they think conform to the rule that they are currently predicting is in the experimenter's mind.

Problem solving

The second strand of work on thinking looks at problem solving. This work has its origins in the precursors of behaviourism, in Gestalt psychology, and in artificial intelligence. At the end of the 19th century, Edward Thorndike (1898), in the first psychological experiments using animals, investigated how cats learn to escape from 'puzzle boxes'. In a puzzle box, a particular action, such as treading on a lever, opens a door and allows the cat to get out. Thorndike found that cats performed random actions in the box until one such action happened to cause the door to open. Thorndike noted two facts about cats' escapes from puzzle boxes. First, the time to escape reduced gradually. Second, watching other cats try to escape was no help. These facts led Thorndike to characterize the learning (or problem solving) by the cats as trial-and-error learning, and to deny any role for insight.

There is no doubt that trial-and-error learning occurs, but does insight also have a place in human problem solving? The Gestalt psychologists, who were mainly Germans working in the decades after Thorndike, argued that it does. Indeed, one of them, Wolfgang Köhler, suggested that the same is true of chimpanzees. In a famous study reported in his book *The Mentality of Apes* (1921/1925), he described the ingenious methods that chimps used for reaching bananas that were outside their cages, methods that often seemed to come to them suddenly. In human problem solving, one type of case that was studied in detail by the Gestaltists involves the breaking of functional fixedness – the tendency to think of an object as having a particular purpose – as illustrated in Duncker's (1935/1945) candle problem (see Activity 12.2).

ACTIVITY 12.2

DUNCKER'S CANDLE PROBLEM

You are given a candle, a box with some drawing pins (thumb tacks) in it, and a book of matches.

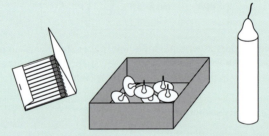

Source: Dunker (1945). Reproduced with permission.

How can you attach the candle to the wall and light it so it burns safely and so that wax does not drip onto the table below the wall?
  Think about the solution before you look up the answer.

The study of problem solving was revitalized by the cognitive revolution of the 1950s, and in particular by the work of Allen Newell and Herb Simon (and their early collaborator John Clifford Shaw). Newell, Simon, and Shaw developed early computer models of complex problem-solving behaviour, such as playing chess (Newell, Shaw, & Simon, 1963); proving theorems in logic (Newell, Shaw, & Simon, 1957); and, in their General Problem Solver program (Newell, Shaw, & Simon, 1959), problem solving more generally. General Problem Solver was the precursor of a general computational architecture or cognition, called Soar, later proposed by Newell (1990).

In their research on human problem solving, summarized in a 1972 book of that name, Newell and Simon combined ideas from computer modelling with the analysis of 'think aloud' protocols collected from people as they were solving problems. The problems that Newell and Simon studied were mostly puzzle-book problems, such as 'missionaries and cannibals' or 'the Tower of Hanoi' (as in Activity 12.3). Such problems lend themselves to computer analysis as they have clearly specified starting states, end states (in which the problem is solved), and operators, or moves that can be made in trying to get from the starting state to the end state. Unfortunately, many of the problems we have in everyday life do not have these properties.

ACTIVITY 12.3

CLASSIC PROBLEMS FROM THE PROBLEM-SOLVING LITERATURE

See whether you can solve the following classic problems. As you do so, try to think about how you are going about finding a solution. If it helps, write down what you are doing, and why, at each step.

MISSIONARIES AND CANNIBALS

Three missionaries and three cannibals must cross a river using a boat that can carry two people at most. At both banks, if there are missionaries present on the bank, they cannot be outnumbered by cannibals (if they were, the cannibals would eat the missionaries). The boat cannot cross the river by itself with no people on board. How do the six people get across safely?

THE TOWER OF HANOI

Four discs of decreasing size are placed on the left-hand peg of a row of three pegs. The discs must be moved to the right-hand peg. The rules are (1) only one disc can be moved at a time and (2) a larger disc can never be put on top of a smaller disc. The middle peg can be used. How can this be achieved?

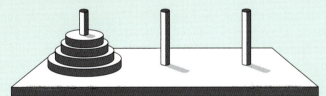

This problem is considered in further detail below.

Source: Garnham and Oakhill (1994, Fig. 11.1, p. 206). Reproduced with permission of Wiley.

Heuristics for problem solving

Two major ideas emerged from this work. One was ways of thinking about and representing problems, with the possibility that such representations are used in the human brain. The other idea was heuristics for problem solving. **Heuristics** are quick and not always reliable methods for trying to solve problems – necessary because most of the problems that Newell and Simon analysed were too difficult to solve by methods that would guarantee a correct solution (called algorithmic methods). A well-known heuristic method is hill climbing, in which, at each stage in attempting to solve a problem, a move is made from the current state to a state that more closely resembles the end state.

In some cases this method works, but in others it is necessary to move away from the solution at one point in order to approach it again later. For example, in missionaries and cannibals problem, some crossings of the river leave fewer people on the far bank.

State-space and problem-reduction methods

The most basic way of representing problems developed by Newell and Simon is the 'state-space approach'. This method is based on the analysis of problems in terms of starting states, end states, and operators. For example, in the Tower of Hanoi problem (see Activity 12.3), the start state is the one in which all the discs are on the left-hand peg, the end state is the one in which all the discs are on the right-hand peg, and the operators are the permitted moves (one disc, from one peg to another, not placing it on a smaller disc). A state-space can then be represented as an upside-down tree, in which (a representation of) the starting state is at the top. Underneath it are the states that can be reached in a single move (by applying a single operator). Then beneath them are states that can be reached in one more move, and so on. Part of a state-space representation of the missionaries and cannibals problem is shown in Figure 12.3. With even a small number of possibilities at each stage, the state-space soon becomes very large. The application of state-spaces to problem solving is that somewhere inside the (upside-down) tree should be at least one representation of the end state. The path from the starting state to the end state shows the sequence of moves necessary to solve the problem. A possible method for solving a problem, but one that is often impractical, is to construct the whole state-space, or a large part of it, and then to search through it for the goal state and, hence, the path to it from the starting state.

Newell and Simon (1972) presented evidence that people think in this way. In the think-aloud protocols they collected, it is often clear that people are talking about states and ways to get from one to another. However, presumably because of working memory limitations, they have great difficulty in keeping anything but a small number of states and transitions between them in mind. If you cannot hold a large number of states in mind, it is difficult or impossible to search through parts of a state-space to find a solution to a complex problem. These facts provide another take on why people need a different approach, using heuristic methods, for solving problems.

Newell and Simon (1972) reported a second, general, method for representing problems, called 'problem reduction'. This method is based on the intuitive idea that complex problems can be solved by splitting them into smaller problems that can be solved more easily. Eventually, 'problems' are reached that are so trivial that they are not problems at all. Although problem reduction is a general method, it is not as general as approaches based on state-space representations, because not all problems have obvious decompositions.

The Tower of Hanoi (see Activity 12.3) is a problem that lends itself to problem reduction. Consider a four-disc version of the Tower of Hanoi. The problem can be decomposed into two three-disc problems and a (trivial) one-disc problem. The two three-disc problems are (1) to transfer the top three discs onto the spare peg and (2) to transfer them from the spare peg to the target peg, onto which the largest disc has, in the meantime, been moved (see Figure 12.4). Newell and Simon (1972) were able to identify, from their verbal protocols, people who were using a problem-reduction approach to the Tower of Hanoi, as opposed to just thinking about states and possible moves from them (state-space approach). They found that people who used problem reduction were more successful both in the (shorter) time taken to solve the problem and the (smaller) number of disc moves used.

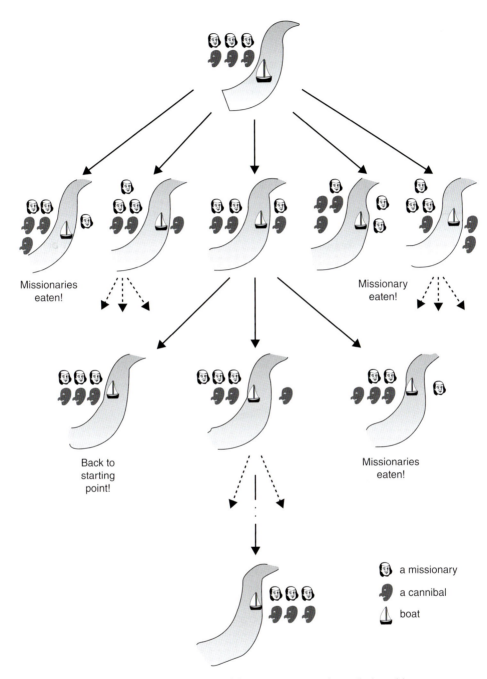

FIGURE 12.3 *A state-space representation of the missionaries and cannibals problem.*
Source: Garnham and Oakhill (1994, Fig. 11.2, p. 209). Reproduced with permission of Wiley.

Analogy

Another approach to solving problems is to try to relate new problems to old ones that you already know how to solve. A particular version of this approach is to use structural analogies between problems in different domains and, hence, with different content. Research on this topic by Mary Gick and Keith Holyoak (1980, 1983) and

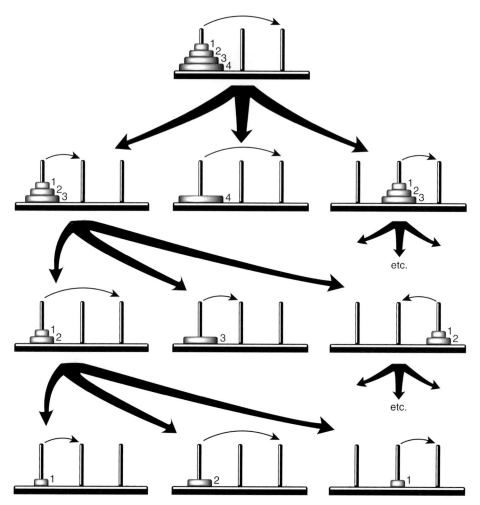

FIGURE 12.4 *A problem-reduction representation of the four-disc Tower of Hanoi.*
Source: Garnham and Oakhill (1994, Fig. 11.4, p. 203). Reproduced with permission of Wiley.

Dedre Gentner (1983) has shown that people can use such analogies, particularly if they are prompted, but they have difficulty in doing so spontaneously. In one well-known example, people solve a problem about how a general can attack a fortress with several roads leading to it, each of which is mined in such a way that, if the whole army marches down the road, the mines will be detonated (smaller groups of soldiers should be sent down different roads and converge at the fortress). They are then asked to solve Duncker's (1935 / 1945) inoperable tumour problem, in which a single beam of radiation directed at a tumour will damage the healthy tissue between the skin and the tumour. The analogy should be obvious, once you have been prompted to look for it: target the tumour with multiple weak beams of radiation that only coalesce in the tumorous tissue.

Judgement and decision making

What we decide to do in everyday life depends on both what we believe or know and what we want. The psychology of decision making is, therefore, also known as belief–desire psychology. You may know that there are bananas in the fruit bowl in the next room, but, if you don't like bananas, you're not likely to go and get one. If you know there aren't any bananas, no matter how much you want one, you can't have one now. Some of the beliefs that govern our behaviour are permanently stored in our memory, but, in more complicated cases, and particularly when our behaviour should be guided by whether something is likely or not, we need to make judgements, to generate the relevant beliefs.

Whether I take my kids to the (nonbookable) public tennis courts depends on how likely it is that there will be a free court. That judgement depends on factors such as the time of day, the weather, and whether tennis is in people's minds, for example because it is Wimbledon fortnight. The best way to make a judgement, though one that is not always possible, is to look at relative frequencies in previous cases of the same kind. To do this properly, I would have to keep a record of times we have been to the tennis courts and what the other factors were at those times (Cool? Hot? Too hot? During Wimbledon? Two months later?). Unless I have a very peculiar compulsion I won't have done this, but I will be able to recall, more or less accurately, some previous times when we have tried to get a court. We will return to this use of recalling examples from memory to make judgements later.

The correct method for making judgements of likelihood requires categorizing things and counting them to calculate real probabilities. Categorizing and counting can be a laborious process, which we only engage in when it really matters. Insurance companies collect this kind of information to help them to decide on premiums for drivers of different ages, or people with homes in different areas of the country. The ages and areas are the categories, and the number and amounts of claims by people in those categories are the things that need to be counted. Medics should, and sometimes do, keep detailed records of their patients' symptoms, treatments, and outcomes. However, most of us, most of the time, and for most purposes, don't. How then do we make the judgements of likelihood that, together with our desires, drive our choices?

Kahneman and Tversky's heuristics for judgement

The idea that we use mental shortcuts – heuristics – to make these judgements was developed in the 1970s by Amos Tversky and Daniel Kahneman (1974), and contributed to Kaheman's 2002 Nobel Prize in Economics. Kahneman and Tversky's notion of a heuristic is related to that of Newell and Simon. In their best-known work, Kahneman and Tversky (1984) identified three heuristic methods for making judgements and showed how the use of these methods could explain a number of systematic biases in the judgements that people make. The three heuristic methods are:

- *availability* – or judging likelihood by how readily examples come to mind from memory
- *representativeness* – or judging whether a person, thing, or event belongs to a certain category by how closely it resembles core or prototypical members of that category
- *anchoring and adjustment* – or judging by starting with a rough idea of the answer (the anchor) and then adjusting that initial estimate on the basis of further considerations.

The first two of these methods rely on fundamental cognitive processes – retrieval from memory and assessment of similarity – and it is, therefore, hard for someone making a judgement to suppress them.

Kahneman and Tversky presented a number of demonstrations of these heuristic methods in action. For availability, they showed, for example, that people claim there are more words starting with the letter R than have R as the third letter, though categorize and count shows that the reverse is true. Words tend to be retrieved from memory by their first letter, not their third letter. So words beginning with R come more easily to mind than those with R as the third letter. Other phenomena attributed to availability include a tendency to overestimate our contribution to domestic chores compared to the contribution of our partner (Ross & Sicoly, 1979). We also overestimate the frequency of causes of death that have wide media coverage – train or passenger aircraft accidents, for example – and underestimate those that do not, for example asthma attacks (Lichtenstein, Slovic, Fischhoff, Layman, & Combs, 1978). You can read an interview with Daniel Kahneman in *The Guardian* (Burkeman, 2011).

The classic studies of representativeness are the 'Tom W' experiments (see Research Methods 12.1). In the best-known example, people are given a description of 'Tom W' that fits a stereotype of computer science students. They are then asked to judge whether the person is likely to be a computer science graduate student or a humanities graduate student. Even though they can judge correctly that there are many more humanities students than computer science students (the base rates of belonging to these categories), their judgements of the likelihood of Tom W belonging to the categories almost exactly match their judgements of how well the description fits the stereotype.

JUDGEMENTS OF REPRESENTATIVENESS

In an experiment published in 1973 (the date is relevant because of the proportions of graduate students in different disciplines at that time), Kahneman and Tversky elicited three types of judgement.

One group of participants was simply asked to estimate the percentage of students in nine different fields of study: business administration, computer science, engineering, humanities and education, law, library science, medicine, physical and life sciences, and social science and social work. Asking this question ascertained the beliefs in the population from which the participants were drawn about the so-called base rates of students in different disciplines.

Two other groups were presented with the following character sketch:

Tom W is of high intelligence although lacking in true creativity. He has a need for order and clarity, and for neat, tidy systems in which every detail fits in the appropriate place. His writing is rather dull and mechanical, occasionally enlivened by corny puns and flashes of the imagination of the sci-fi type. He has a strong drive for competence. He seems to have little feeling or sympathy for other people and does not enjoy interacting with others.

Group 2 was asked to rank the nine fields of study according to how closely the character sketch matched a prototypical student in that field.

Group 3 was told that the sketch was written when Tom W was in high school, using projective tests (i.e. it was fairly old and based on a methodology not regarded as reliable). They were asked to rank the nine fields of study according to how likely Tom W was to be a student in those fields.

> The crucial question was how the results from the three groups of participants compared to one another.
>
> The answer was that groups 2 and 3 gave very similar responses, which were different from those of group 1. When asked how likely a person was to belong to a particular group, judgements were based on the similarity of the person (or at least an old and probably unreliable description of the person!) to a prototypical member of the group, and the participants did not reflect the more general probability of the person being in one group rather than another (base rates).

The classic finding for anchoring and adjustment is that people do not adjust enough from anchors, even if they know those anchors have no bearing on the correct answer. For example, if people are asked to estimate what proportion of states in the United Nations are African states and are given what they take to be randomly generated anchors of 10% or 65%, the final estimates of the two groups are 25% and 45%. The right answer is about 30%.

Prospect theory versus utility theory

As we said before, beliefs (or judgements) have to be combined with desires or preferences in order for us to make decisions. The classic analysis of how decisions should be made comes from economics and is known as '(subjective expected) utility (SEU) theory' (Savage, 1954; von Neumann & Morgenstern, 1944). Utility means the value of a thing or an outcome to a particular person. Different people like different things, and their decisions and choices will be guided by their own preferences. Faced with the same choice, two different people will make different decisions.

If you choose directly between two things – what film to watch or what car to buy – the things from which you are choosing will have a variety of relevant attributes: the price, power, style, colour, and comfort of a car, for example. Each attribute is more or less important to a particular person. Price may be paramount if you are short of cash, but style or power may be of more concern if you are a millionaire. Each option has a value for each attribute. A new BMW might cost £35,000. A 10-year-old Ford might be £800. 'Multi-attribute utility theory', a theory about how to make choices among objects with many properties, says that, in choosing your car, you should weight the attributes according to their importance to you, and make a weighted combination of the values (to you) of each object on each attribute to get an overall utility for each option. Then you chose the one with the highest overall value.

Things are more complicated when you choose between actions, because the same action may have different outcomes. In comparing actions, SEU theory says to judge the probabilities of the different outcomes and use those probabilities to calculate an average value of the outcome of the action. So, for example, if you were thinking about buying a lottery ticket, the possible outcomes would be a total loss of your small stake, or small probabilities of winning a variety of prizes. For a lottery, there are objective ways of calculating the probabilities, but this is not always true in other situations; hence, the probabilities in SEU theory can be subjective, as can the values. SEU theory tells you to choose the action with the highest average outcome. But you may have to prepare for the possibility of a bad outcome. In the lottery example, if you calculated the expected value of buying a ticket in monetary terms, the outcome would be a loss on average, otherwise the lottery company would not make any money. In that sense, you would be better off not buying a ticket. However, the subjective value (utility) to you of winning, say, £10,000 might be more than 5,000 times the (negative) value of 'losing' £2 by buying a ticket. There is also the thrill of playing, which might increase the utility of buying a ticket.

Deviations from utility theory in everyday decisions People do not make these calculations overtly in everyday life. But is utility theory a good approximation of how they actually behave? To avoid one possible misunderstanding, utility should not be identified with monetary value. Different people place different values on money, and the same amount of money has different values to the same person, depending on how much they already have and what they want to buy. Utility theory has difficulty with some of these issues, but not with others. For example, people tend to be loss averse, in the sense that they regard the loss of something – an amount of money, for example – more negatively than they regard (positively) a gain of the same thing (Kahneman & Tversky, 1984). Most people are reluctant to accept evens bets (e.g. heads I give you £100, tails you give me £100). Being loss averse is not incompatible with being risk-seeking for losses. When all possible outcomes involve either likely or certain loss, people prefer choices that give them some chance, even if small, of avoiding a loss, rather than choices that lead to certain losses – in other words, they prefer the options that are only *likely* to lead to loss over options that are *certain* to lead to loss. Conversely, for probable gains, people are, in general, risk-averse. With their own money, they prefer safe investments. With low probabilities, the pattern reverses. People are risk-seeking for large, low-probability gains. They buy lottery tickets rather than keeping the £1 or £2 stake money. But they are risk-averse for large, low-probability losses, and hence they buy insurance.

Because monetary value and utility are not the same thing, SEU theory can, broadly speaking, accommodate these facts. However, consider the following:

> Jack and Jill each have £5 million. Which is happier (i.e. which attributes more utility to the money they have)?

We don't know Jack and Jill's respective attitudes to money, so the best guess is that both are equally happy.

Now consider:

> Yesterday Jack had £1 million and Jill had £9 million. Which of them is happier, given that they both have £5 million today?

Now it is almost certainly Jack who is happier with his £5 million. We tend to judge value not in absolute terms but relative to a reference point, such as the (recent) status quo. Until Kahneman and Tversky starting thinking about facts of this kind, nobody had noticed that everyday decision making deviates substantially from utility theory. The idea of value relative to a reference point, together with some systematic biases in the way people judge probabilities, led Kahneman and Tversky (1984) to formulate a theory of how people actually make decisions, rather than how economists say they should, called 'prospect theory'. The biases in probability judgement arise with probabilities close to 0 or 1 – very small probabilities of something being the case or not, or of something happening or not happening. We tend to magnify small risks in our minds.

There are other aspects of human decision making that do not fit with utility theory. One is the 'endowment effect' (Thaler, 1980) – the effect of personal ownership. Owning something increases its value to the owner. When people name a selling price for something they own, that price is higher than they would have paid to acquire it before they owned it. The endowment effect is not seen in business transactions, because goods are not owned for personal reasons but to be sold.

A second phenomenon that does not fit well with utility theory is mental accounting. For example, people say they are more willing to travel across town to another branch of the same store to save £5 on a £15 calculator than to save £5 on a £125 jacket, even if both items are stocked by both branches of the store and are to be purchased together.

Third, the way a problem is presented or 'framed' can influence the choice that is made. The best-known examples involve presenting options as gains or losses. Kahneman and Tversky's Asian flu problem (an adapted version of which is used in Activity 12.4) is a good example.

ACTIVITY 12.4

THE ASIAN FLU PROBLEM (ADAPTED FROM TVERSKY AND KAHNEMAN, 1981)

Imagine that the United Kingdom is preparing for the outbreak of an unusual Asian disease, which is expected to kill 600 people. Two alternative programmes to combat the disease have been proposed. The exact scientific estimates of the consequences of the programmes are outlined below.

Before you read on, note that there are two versions of the problem, one with Programmes A and B and the other with Programmes C and D. Choose one version or the other and decide which programme you would select if the decision were yours. If you are in a group, get some people to look at one version and some to look at the other.

VERSION 1

In a group of 600 people:

- *Programme A* – 200 people will be saved.
- *Programme B* – There is a one-third probability that 600 people will be saved, and a two-thirds probability that no people will be saved.

Which programme do you prefer?

VERSION 2

In a group of 600 people:

- *Programme C* – 400 people will die.
- *Programme D* – There is a one-third probability that nobody will die, and a two-thirds probability that 600 people will die.

Which programme do you prefer?

ANALYSIS

In the original study, in the first version of the problem, 72% of participants preferred programme A (the remainder, 28%, opting for programme B). In the second version, 78% preferred program D, with the remaining 22% opting for program C. Does this outcome reflect your choice in the version you looked at?

Now, look at the programmes again, and remember that in each case we are referring to 600 people.

- Programme A and programme C are the same: 200 people definitely die; 400 definitely live.
- Programme B and programme D are the same: there is a one-third chance that no one dies/everyone lives, and a two-thirds chance that all 600 die/no one lives.

In each version the choice is the same, but the preferences reverse. When the problem is presented in terms of gains (lives saved; A versus B), people are risk-averse and choose the option with certain outcomes. When the problem is presented in terms of losses (deaths; C versus D), people are risk-seeking (and loss-averse) and choose the option that might allow any loss to be avoided.

Utility theory cannot explain this result, which is usually described as an effect of framing (the way the problem is presented or framed), but prospect theory can.

The effect of framing often gives rise to preference reversals, with no 'proper' (utility-based) factor to explain those reversals. If the outcomes, their utilities, and their probabilities are fixed, SEU theory says that the outcome with the highest utility, or the action with the highest expected utility, must be chosen. So, the way decisions are made by people in their everyday lives is not the same as the way economists believe decisions are made in markets.

Two systems for thinking

In all three of the major strands of work on thinking – reasoning, problem solving, and judgement and decision making – a distinction has been made between *normative theories* (logic, probability, search through complete state-space representations), which specify what people should do if they have certain goals, such as the goal of maximizing their likely gains, and *descriptive theories*, which account for how people actually behave. In addition, many of the so-called descriptive theories are based on things that people can do easily (such as retrieving information from memory), whereas following normative prescriptions can involve hard mental work.

This common theme has crystallized into the idea that there are two systems for thinking: a fast, 'intuitive' system (System 1), based on associations, and a slower, effortful system, based on more complex reasoning (System 2). This distinction can be traced back at least as far as William James's 1890 book *Principles of Psychology*. Kahneman (2011) describes the two systems in depth in his book *Thinking, Fast and Slow*. According to Kahneman, the fast system is always active when we are awake, but the slow system likes to run in a low-effort mode and does not always succeed in its attempts to monitor the fast system, particularly when it is fatigued.

Much of the earlier work focused on errors made by the fast, intuitive system, but recent views are more nuanced, identifying circumstances in which fast judgements can be better than considered ones, for example in cases of well-developed expertise. Malcolm Gladwell (2005) has championed this idea in his book *Blink*, while identifying circumstances in which quick judgements can go badly wrong. For example, under stress, armed police may misinterpret clues as to whether people they are chasing down are armed or not. One of Gladwell's key examples, which he believes shows the power of fast thinking, is in judgements about a supposedly ancient Greek statue bought by the Getty Museum in California in 1985 for $10 million (see Focus Point 12.1). Antiquities experts were dubious about the statue as soon as they saw it, and many of the documents that originally accompanied it have been exposed as crude forgeries (e.g. one had a postcode that did not exist at the time the document was dated). However, controversy about this statue continues, and the case for the fast thinking system remains unproven, at least in this instance. The slow, deliberative system (System 2) is also error prone. But, more importantly, it can become fatigued (because System 2 thinking is effortful), and it may allow System 1 to take back control of judgements and decisions that it is not suited to making. An interesting and thought-provoking case study is based on an analysis of real-world decisions about parole for prisoners (see Focus Point 12.2).

FOCUS POINT 12.1

THE GETTY KOUROS

A kouros is an ancient Greek sculpture of a nude male, facing forward, arms at sides, left leg slightly further forward than right leg. Rather few kourai remain (about 200, including damaged and fragmentary examples, but only 12, including the Getty kouros, that can be described as almost complete). Paul Getty was an oil billionaire, who founded his own museum in California and left a considerable sum of money to the museum at his death in 1976. In the 1980s, the museum was offered a well-preserved kouros for about $10 million. It completed a lengthy investigation, convincing itself (by analytic, type 2 thinking and, some say, wishful thinking) that the statue was probably genuine.

A number of antiquities experts reported that, on first impression (type 1 thinking), something seemed wrong with the statue, though they could not always say what.

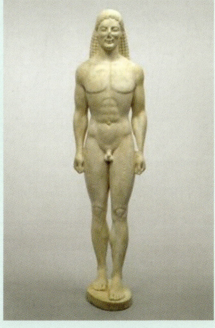

Source: Digital image courtesy of the Getty's Open Content Program.

Much of the 20th-century documentation that the dealer, Gianfranco Becchina, had provided with the statue proved to be fraudulent, and nothing could be established, definitively, about the first (alleged) 2,500 years of its existence. One letter, dated 1955, referred to a bank transaction on an account that was opened only in 1963.

Among antiquities experts, the opinion against the authenticity of the statue has, if anything, grown. However, other types of investigation have failed to prove the statue is modern or to identify a forger.

In the Getty Museum today, the kouros is labelled as 'Greek, about 530 BC, or modern forgery'. This is a difficult case, where neither type 1 nor type 2 thinking has proved conclusive.

Kimmelman (1991) contains more information about the Getty kouros.

PAROLE DECISIONS

System 2 thinking is effortful, and the system is easily fatigued. When it is fatigued it falls back on easy (and perhaps safe) ways to make decisions.

Danziger, Levav, and Avnaim-Pesso (2011) looked at real decisions of eight Israeli parole-board judges over a 10-month period. The judges started their work shortly after breakfast and took two meal breaks (midmorning snack and lunch) during their working day.

A safe decision for a parole board judge is not to grant parole. Such a decision maintains the status quo of keeping the person in prison.

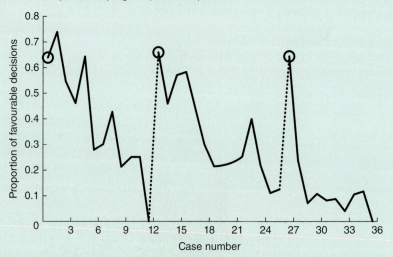

Proportions of rulings in favour of the prisoners by ordinal position. Circled points indicate the first decision in each of the three decision sessions; tick marks on the x-axis denote every third case; a dotted line denotes food break. Because unequal session lengths resulted in a low number of cases for some of the later ordinal positions, the graph is based on the first 95% of the data from each session.

Source: Danziger, Levav, and Avnaim-Pesso (2011). Reproduced with permission.

As the figure shows, the proportion of cases in which parole was granted fell from about 65% just after eating, when the judges were presumably fresh, to a very low figure immediately before the next break.

Because this was a real-world study, there were a number of factors that could not be taken into account. For example, the breaks confounded resting and eating, and there was no direct measure of mental fatigue. Nevertheless, the results indicate the existence of a major influence on judges' decisions that is not related to judicial aspects of the cases they are considering.

The neuropsychology of thinking

Compared with language, there is relatively little work on the neuropsychology of thinking. Goel (2009) looked at a variety of tasks from the domains of problem solving, reasoning, and judgement and decision making, and discovered characteristic patterns of brain activity related to three aspects of the tasks: whether heuristic or algorithmic processes are involved, whether the problem is clearly structured, and whether different systems (heuristic versus analytic; System 1 versus System 2) suggest different answers. He concluded that the brain regions involved and the relations between them are roughly the same in all three domains, which reinforces the suggestion that the division between the three domains is largely one of historical accident. More specifically, Goel identified two brain systems. The first is a left lateralized frontal-temporal system, which includes language-processing regions and which deals with familiar, concrete material. The second is a bilateral parietal visuospatial system, which deals with abstract or unfamiliar material. These two brain systems correspond roughly to the two systems of thinking discussed in the previous section. The distinction between the two (brain) systems is reflected in the classic neuropsychological phenomenon of double dissociation (see the section above on 'The Biological Bases of Language and Language Disorders').

Another recent development is an increasing interest in 'neuroeconomics' (see, e.g., Loewenstein, Rick, & Cohen 2008), which is the application of cognitive neuroscience techniques to the study of judgement and decision making, though results that advance our theoretical understanding are hard to find.

The development of thinking

As with language, there is a separate tradition of studying the development of thinking. Historically, the study of the development of thinking has been central to developmental psychology, largely because of the work of Jean Piaget (see e.g. 1951; 1952; 1954). When working with Alfred Binet, Piaget noticed that children's answers to some IQ test questions were systematically different from those of adults, and this observation led him to his stage theory of cognitive development, in which fairly abrupt changes to children's ways of thinking are thought to occur between four main stages of development: sensorimotor, preoperational, concrete operations, and formal operations (the stage of logical thinking). Piaget's theory became highly elaborated and was based, primarily, on observation of his own children, using a particular technique of posing questions and analysing the answers. The theory is supposed to explain aspects of children's thinking, such as the failure to realize that objects have a permanent existence (e.g. when out of sight) or that quantities, such as volume, are conserved in operations such as pouring water from one container to another of a different shape.

Later theorists have challenged Piaget's interpretation of his observations. Others have been attracted to the ideas of the Russian psychologist Lev Vygotsky (e.g. 1934/1986). Vygotsky saw cognitive development as a less rigid process than Piaget did, and he emphasized the importance of social factors in development. He is famous for his notion of the zone of proximal development, which constrains how far you can go, at a particular moment, beyond what you already know.

The information-processing approach to cognition developed in the 1950s had an obvious application to cognitive development. Given that Piaget tried to provide a detailed formal account of the processes by which children think, one view of the information-processing approach is that it provides a modern take on Piaget's ideas. However, as indicated above, modern theorists prefer observations from more standard empirical techniques than those used by Piaget, and have not always agreed with him on the facts to be explained. They have also argued that Piaget did not pay enough attention to matters such as whether children could remember the details of problems they were supposed to be solving. Furthermore, the information-processing approach does not, of itself, suggest distinct developmental stages of the kind proposed by Piaget, and many more recent developmentalists have eschewed such stages. Nevertheless, neo-Piagetians, such as Juan Pascual-Leone (1970) and Robbie Case (1985), have proposed stage theories within an information-processing framework.

Teaching thinking

Given that our thinking is error prone, an important question is whether we can be taught to think better. Most of our education is content based (e.g. geography, history, French), and when we are taught skills they are often specific skills, such as how to conduct psychology experiments. We are rarely subjected to explicit attempts to teach us how to think. Is this because thinking cannot be taught, or because it is difficult to teach thinking, or because of other factors, such as the way education is conceived?

Researchers who study biases in thinking find that they can readily describe those biases, suggesting that people could be taught to avoid them. Jonathan Baron (2008), in particular, has suggested that 'actively open-minded thinking' (p. 200) can help. To engage in such thinking is to follow guidelines such as 'fairness to other possibilities than the one we initially favor' (p. 200), and to have standards against which to judge particular examples of thinking. However, Baron provides little evidence that people can be taught to follow such a scheme on a moment-to-moment basis. Indeed, Baron's principles are general ones, and it is not clear that people can apply such principles while engaged in complex thinking, or that they can generalize lessons learned in one domain to a different domain.

Thinking skills programmes

A different approach is to try to develop a specific thinking skills programme and to assess its efficacy in a real-life context. In 1985, Nickerson, Perkins, and Smith reviewed a variety of such programmes. Some, such as Feuerstein's (1980) Instrumental Enrichment and the Venezuela Project, report significant improvements in thinking ability, but it is unclear what aspects of these programmes have an effect, or whether they do anything more than providing additional educational opportunities. Whether thinking can be taught or improved, other than by engaging in the activities of thinking, remains an open question.

Creative thinking

An important type of thinking for the advancement of society that does not fit neatly into the three main strands of research is creative thinking. **Creativity** is analysed in terms of originality and usefulness, though a rather broad notion of usefulness is needed to cover both creativity in maths and the sciences, and creativity in the arts. Indeed, there is a question that has not completely been resolved about the relationship between creativity in these two domains. Creativity involves the application of normal thought processes, particularly those of problem solving, to hard cases. But there is also a social dimension to creativity. Whether an idea is creative depends on the intellectual status quo at the time it is proposed. Whether it has an impact also depends on social factors. Ideas, like organisms, struggle for survival, and so concepts from evolutionary theory have been used in the study of creativity.

Cognitive analysis

The study of thinking, reasoning, and decision making is part of cognitive psychology. However, the idea that originality and usefulness are important for creativity poses problems for a purely cognitive approach. Originality and usefulness are both defined by contextual factors, and those factors are not directly reflected in the cognitive processes that lead to a person having ideas that are regarded as creative.

Nevertheless, cognitive psychologists assume that the mental processes that lead to creative thoughts are similar to those that are found in expert problem solving, and no convincing evidence against this view has ever been presented. Of course, there are complications. Too much knowledge of, and expertise in, traditional ways of thinking can hamper creativity. Einstein, for example, was notoriously selective in the physics he studied. Furthermore, creative people solve difficult problems, and often develop new ways of thinking about things (in maths and science) or doing things (in the arts). However, we all, occasionally, solve problems that are hard for us, and we sometimes have the experience of looking at a problem in a novel way.

One interesting feature of hard problems is that, because they take a long time to solve, and we have other things in our lives, we have to set them aside. Sometimes, when we come back to them, obstacles to solving them seem to have disappeared. The period of setting aside is known, in Graham Wallas's (1926) four-stage theory of creativity (see Popova, n.d.), as incubation. Wallas thought that complex unconscious mental processes are at work during periods of incubation. More recently, however, David Perkins (1981) has suggested something simpler: that, in order to solve hard problems, we allow the wrong methods of attacking a problem, which have become highly active through repeated attempts to use them, to become less dominant.

Relationship of creativity with problem solving and expertise

Creativity in maths and sciences usually requires a high level of expert knowledge of the domain in which the creative person works. However, the example of Einstein shows that overfamiliarity with traditional thinking may not be what is required. Expertise itself is not usually equated with creativity. Expertise in the arts has an equally complex relationship with creativity. Leonardo da Vinci, for example, acquired a variety of skills in the workshop of Andrea del Verrocchio, which he then used to refine and extend what was possible with those techniques. Picasso, on the other hand, who showed great skill in classic techniques in his youth, used his knowledge of those techniques to rebel against them. The place of (traditional) expertise in modernist and postmodernist art is different again.

The role of problem solving in creativity is less controversial, though sometimes it can be difficult to formulate the problem that an artist is trying to solve. As mentioned above, the solution to a problem may involve reconceptualization – ideas such as velocity, force, and gravity have different interpretations in Einstein's theory of relativity than in the classical mechanics of Newton. New ideas in the arts are less likely than those in the sciences to be best exploited by their inventors. It was not Haydn or Mozart who invented the symphonic form, but probably one of the lesser known Bachs. The idea that reconceptualization may be necessary for creativity led Maggie Boden (1980) to formulate her 'impossibility theory of creativity' – not the idea that creativity is impossible, but that, after an important creative leap, it is possible, using revised concepts, to have thoughts that were not previously possible.

Social factors

Part of the reason that a purely cognitive idea of creativity is problematic, particularly for high-level creativity, is that creativity is judged by the two features of usefulness and novelty. Both can be difficult to assess, and usefulness in the arts, in maths and science, and in the invention of artefacts are different things. Nevertheless, whether something is novel depends on whether it has been suggested or produced before. In other words, creativity depends on social context. There are some interesting issues that arise around the issue of novelty. Newton and Leibniz invented, at about the same time and largely independently, the mathematical calculus – it was an idea whose time had come, at least for gifted mathematicians. And some Indian mathematicians in the early 20th century (in particular Srinivasa Ramanujan), who had not had much interaction with the mainstream mathematics of the Western world, (re)discovered some difficult theorems of number theory, as well as many new ones.

Dean Simonton (1984) and Mihaly Csikszentmihalyi (1988) have explicitly examined the role of social factors in creative thinking and in the definition of creativity. Csikszentmihalyi argues that, in addition to an individual being creative, two other factors are necessary for creative achievement: a social field that determines whether ideas are retained, and a more global stable cultural domain in which those ideas can flourish. Simonton talks about the persuasive powers of creative people and of their champions, which determine whether those ideas have an impact.

Evolutionary theory and creativity

According to Csikszentmihalyi, the way that the social field selects ideas for retention has parallels to processes, such as natural selection, found in theories of evolution. Other researchers, such as David Perkins (1988) and Phil Johnson-Laird (1993), have also suggested parallels with evolutionary processes in their theories of creativity. Perkins suggests that creative ideas are generated by creative people, and then selected and preserved in a stable domain, as proposed by Csikszentmihalyi. Johnson-Laird has studied two aspects of jazz improvisation. He argues that chord sequences, which are typically developed during rehearsal, evolve according to Darwinian processes, in which many possibilities are generated and many discarded. Bass lines, on the other hand, are improvised during a performance, and their generation has to be severely constrained by a process that bears more resemblance to that proposed by Lamarck, which is not believed to play a major role in biological evolution.

 Mihaly Csikszentmihalyi asks 'What makes life worth living?' in **this 2004 TED Talk**[3].

> **DISCUSSION POINT**
>
> Discuss whether thinking can be taught and whether people can be taught to improve their thinking.

Metacognition

One type of thinking is thinking about thinking. More generally, the term 'metacognition' is used to describe cognition about cognition. Thoughts about thoughts are also known as higher-order thoughts, and one well-known theory of consciousness, David Rosenthal's (2005) higher-order thought theory, claims that, to be conscious of a mental state, you need to be aware of being in that state. However, not all thought processes are open to introspection. So, there may be metacognitive processes that we are unaware of, because they are not associated with thoughts in the everyday sense.

Metacognition is linked to strategies for learning (see the section on 'Teaching Thinking') and to any theory of cognition that proposes a higher-order controller for thought processes. Theories of executive function try to explain how we allocate resources to different processes, depending on current needs. It is widely agreed that the frontal lobes play a crucial role in this process. Phineas Gage, an American railroad worker, had a metal rod blown through his frontal lobes in 1848, and the disruption in his ability to run his life is an indication of the frontal lobes' importance in the planning of behaviour. Recent imaging work has also shown frontal lobe involvement in the solving of IQ test items, where planning and allocation of resources are needed at a much more local level (Duncan et al., 2000). More generally, metacognitive processes play an important role in complex thinking, yet they remain relatively neglected in the psychological literature on thinking.

Knowledge, expertise, and wisdom

Newell and Simon's (1972) work on problem solving, in which they studied puzzle-book puzzles, looked at people who did not regularly solve problems of that kind – novice problem solvers. However, for problems that are more important in people's lives, such as diagnosing illnesses or deciding where to drill for oil, people train to become experts. In addition, there are games, such as chess, bridge, and poker, that have much in common with puzzle-book problems but that are taken very seriously in certain circles, and where expertise is also critical.

Experts versus novices

The classic study of the difference between experts and novices is that of Dutch psychologist and chess master Adriaan de Groot, whose 1946 thesis was published in English translation in 1965 as the book *Thought and Choice in Chess*. De Groot realized that there are a great many possible ways that a game of chess can develop. The equivalent of Newell and Simon's state-space is inconceivably large. For a game like chess, the state-space representation has to take account of the fact that players take turns, so odd layers represent times at which one player can make a move and even layers represent points at which the other player can make a move. In addition, there is no simple equivalent to the idea of looking through the tree for a solution to 'the problem'. Both players are looking for a path to a win for themselves, but they must take account of the fact that, when the other player takes their turn, they will try to choose the best move for them, which should be the worst move for their opponent. Of course, if players could survey the whole state-space in their minds, there would be no interesting game. But players are limited in how much of such a mental space they can think about. To choose the 'best' move, they can only consider a small number of possibilities and they can only look ahead (to see how well those possibilities pan out) for a small number of moves. What de Groot showed was that grand master chess players do not think through the consequences of more moves than club players, but they think through the consequences of what are agreed later to be better possibilities. Good players are also good at remembering configurations of pieces that are important for the development of the game. Simons (2012) discusses this work further. Following de Groot's thesis, later work by Chase and Simon (1973) emphasized that the difference between novices and masters lies in the amount of chess-related knowledge they have and how they are able to apply that knowledge rapidly and directly to analysing game positions.

Acquisition of expertise

These ideas led to a picture of expertise as the possession of easily deployable, specialized knowledge, rather than as the ability to engage in the more complex chains of thought that puzzle-book problem solvers often have to undertake. Anders Ericsson (e.g. 1990), in the United States, and Michael Howe (e.g. Howe, Davidson, & Sloboda, 1998), in the United Kingdom, developed a view of expertise, at least in mental rather than physical domains, as something that anyone can acquire, provided they are prepared to apply themselves to acquiring the knowledge base. For a normal person, with other things to do, such knowledge acquisition, in a domain of any complexity, would take about 10 years – giving rise to the '10-year rule' for becoming an expert. Deeply autistic savants, who find it difficult to engage in other activities, develop exceptional expertise in certain domains (e.g. drawing, piano playing, calendrical calculation) rather more rapidly (Howe, 1989). This view, that application holds dominion over aptitude, has always met with some scepticism, and in more recent writings Ericsson has withdrawn somewhat from his more extreme views.

Wisdom

Wisdom is different from knowledge and expertise, and, according to folklore, tends to increase with age. It has been associated with crystalized intelligence, which Raymond Cattell (see 1971) distinguished from the fluid intelligence of younger people, as two separate components of general intelligence, or g, as measured in IQ tests. More recently, Paul Baltes (e.g. Baltes & Staudinger, 2008) has explicitly linked wisdom with expertise in a particular domain: the conduct and meaning of life. Robert Sternberg's (1998) balance theory of wisdom takes a slightly different, though related, view: wisdom is the use of intelligence to balance competing needs and to seek a common good. Sternberg specifically distinguishes wisdom from analytic (IQ-type) intelligence and suggests that being intelligent in that way may work against the development of wisdom. He claims that analytic intelligence is associated with unwise ways of thinking, which he describes as the fallacies of egocentrism, omniscience, omnipotence, and invulnerability. The idea is that intelligent people tend to think they are always right and so fail to learn from their mistakes. Wisdom, however, has its advantages. In particular, the work of Baltes has shown that wisdom is associated with both physical and mental well-being in old age (Baltes, Smith, & Staudinger, 1992).

 Psychologist Professor Barry Schwartz argues for the importance of wisdom in today's world in **this 2009 TES Talk**[4].

Rationality

We said at the beginning of this chapter that thinking is hard. Many people fail to figure out that the surgeon is the boy's mother. We have also seen that people make other systematic errors in their thinking, and that some of these errors can be difficult to overcome. What, if anything, do these facts tell us about human **rationality**? The philosopher L. Jonathan Cohen (1981) pointed out that it is only because some people have developed notions of what is rational that we can identify things that other people do as wrong or possibly irrational. There is, then, a sense in which people are, or at least can be, rational, even if particular acts by particular people are not. Indeed, within such a framework, it is possible to identify some individuals as irrational much of the time, and all (or most) people as being irrational under some circumstances. A more specific interpretation of Cohen's view is that acting rationally is acting according to the dictates of particular normative theories, such as formal logic in the case of reasoning and probability theory, and utility theory in the case of judgement and decision making.

Types of rationality: Adaptive and analytical

In the mid-20th century it was common to hear people saying, sometimes somewhat despairingly, that intelligence is what IQ tests measure. Since that time there have been many attempts to counter this position, one of which is to contrast adaptive and analytical intelligence. Adaptive intelligence is the ability to function well in one's environment. It is one of the three components in Sternberg's (1996) triarchic theory of intelligence (called, in that context, practical intelligence) and is used to ascribe intelligence to nonhuman animals. A related notion can explain away some instances of apparent irrationality, by claiming that people who behave in certain ways may not be acting according to the dictates of analytical intelligence but are behaving in a way that makes sense in the environment in which they find themselves.

Problems with following normative theories

Another reason for apparently acting irrationally is that there are costs to following normative theories that must be taken into account in decision making. For example, in making probabilistic judgements, the correct thing to do is categorize and count. However, categorization and counting can be difficult and time consuming. Insurance firms may need to know exact risks if they are to set viable but competitive premiums, but you do not need to know exact numbers just to make conversation about how dangerous young male drivers might be, and you cannot justify devoting the time to find out. There is, therefore, a sense in which one kind of apparent irrationality can be explained away. Given that there is a cost in time and effort to calculating the rational choice, that cost must be set against the benefit of having the right answer as opposed to a guesstimate that might be pretty good. As Nobel Laureate Herb Simon (1982) pointed out, our rationality is bounded by limitations on our cognitive resources.

There are, nevertheless, many cases where the ideas of adaptive behaviour and limited resources do not give a compelling account of apparent irrationality. Examples discussed earlier in this chapter include:

- use of confirmation rather than falsification in testing general hypotheses
- ignoring base rates and using representativeness when the base rates are given
- framing and, more generally, preference reversal in decision making
- allowing emotions and prior beliefs to influence judgements.

In all these cases, interest lies in systematic deviations from the dictates of normative theories. Random errors would just indicate poor mental processes. It is also interesting to note that expertise does not necessarily protect against these errors.

Other problematic features of human cognition that might lead to irrational behaviour include:

- the inability to suspend judgement when we have too little information
- having impossible or conflicting goals, such as to live forever, or to save and spend
- not to be clear about our goals
- succumbing to social pressures, as demonstrated in classic social psychology experiments on obedience (Milgram, 1974) and conformity (Asch, 1956)
- failing to discount sunk costs, which by definition cannot be recovered and should not, therefore, influence future decisions
- effects of innumeracy, including failure to grasp statistical concepts
- inability to reason about causes (System 1 often sees causes that are not there)
- overconfidence.

We can be certain that some people behave irrationally some of the time. The challenges are to create a clear and convincing account of what counts as rational, and to determine whether people's lives are better if they can be taught to avoid instances of irrationality.

Future developments

The notion of two systems of thought will be of continued importance and may provide at least one cornerstone for the amalgamation of the various historical strands of work on thinking. Behavioural economics, in which the lessons of work on judgement and decision making are applied, where appropriate, to economic activity, will also continue to grow in importance, particularly given the economic difficulties being experienced in much of the world. For example, the boom-and-bust cycles that have plagued market economies may be explained by inappropriate assessments of, and reactions to, market trends. People who study thinking continue to hope that the lessons they learn about how and when thinking can be poor can be applied to improving thinking under those circumstances. Whether this hope is a vain one remains to be seen.

SECTION SUMMARY

- There are three main strands of research into the psychology of thinking and reasoning, sometimes addressing the same issues from different perspectives. These strands are usually known as reasoning, problem solving, and judgement and decision making.

- Concepts, which correspond to word meanings or possible word meanings, are the building blocks of our thoughts, and they create a connection between language and thought.

- In the 1960s and early 1970s, two psychological theories of word meanings and concepts were developed. They were different formulations of what is known as the classical view of concepts: one based on the notion of features of meaning and the other based on hierarchies of concepts.

- Other theories of concepts, developed in response to problems with the classical theory, include prototype theory, instance-based theories, and theory-based theories.

- The first main strand of work on thinking is reasoning research, which has focused on certain types of reasoning problem, such as conditional reasoning and syllogisms.

- The second strand of work on thinking, problem solving, has its origins in behaviourism, Gestalt psychology, and artificial intelligence.

- An idea that emerged from the work of Allen Newell, John Clifford Shaw, and Herb Simon was that of heuristics – quick and not always reliable methods for trying to solve problems.

- The psychology of decision making is also known as belief–desire psychology.

- We often need to make judgements in order to generate the relevant beliefs.

- The idea that we use heuristics to make these judgements was developed in the 1970s by Amos Tversky and Daniel Kahneman (1974), who identified three heuristic methods for making judgements: availability, representativeness, and anchoring and adjustment.

- The classical analysis of how decisions should be made comes from economics and is known as '(subjective expected) utility theory' (Savage, 1954; von Neumann & Morgenstern, 1944).

- Kahneman and Tversky (1984) went on to formulate a theory of how people actually make decisions, rather than how economists say they should, called prospect theory.

- In all three of the major strands of work on thinking – reasoning, problem solving, and judgement and decision making – a distinction has been made between normative theories and descriptive theories.

- In all three strands, another idea that has emerged is that there are two systems for thinking: a fast, 'intuitive' system, based on associations, and a slower, effortful system, based on more complex reasoning.

- Compared with language, there is relatively little work on the neuropsychology of thinking. Goel (2009) suggests that there are two brain systems: a left lateralized frontal-temporal system, which includes language-processing regions, and a bilateral parietal visuospatial system, which deals with abstract or unfamiliar material.

- Historically, the study of the development of thinking has been central to developmental psychology, largely because of the work of Jean Piaget and Lev Vygotsky.

- The information-processing approach to cognition, developed in the 1950s, had an obvious application to cognitive development, and modern theorists prefer observations from more standard empirical techniques than those used by Piaget.

- Can we be taught to think more effectively?

- Most of our education is fact based and, when we learn skills, they are often specific and applicable to certain contexts.

- Thinking skills programmes report significant improvements in thinking ability, but it is important to consider whether it is aspects of the programmes that have an effect or whether it is simply the exposure to additional educational opportunities.

- Creativity is important for the advancement of society and is analysed in terms of originality and usefulness.

- Creativity involves the application of normal thought processes, particularly those of problem solving, to hard cases. But there is also a social dimension to creativity.

- Cognitive psychologists assume that the mental processes that lead to creative thoughts are similar to those that are found in expert problem solving, and no convincing evidence against this view has ever been presented.

- Expertise, overfamiliarity, and reconceptualization are important factors in both problem solving and creativity.

- Dean Simonton (1984) and Mihalyi Csikszentmihalyi (1988) have examined the role of social factors in creative thinking and in the definition of creativity.

- The term metacognition is used to describe cognition about cognition. Thoughts about thoughts are also known as higher-order thoughts, and higher-order thought theory claims that, to be conscious of a mental state, you need to be aware of being in that state.

- Problem solving can take many forms and requires various degrees of expertise.

- The classic study of the difference between experts and novices is that of Dutch psychologist and chess master Adriaan de Groot (1946/1965).

- De Groot showed that grand master chess players do not think through the consequences of more moves than club players, but they think through the consequences of what are agreed later to be better possibilities. Good players are also good at remembering configurations of pieces that are important for the development of the game.

- These ideas led to a picture of expertise as the possession of easily deployable, specialized knowledge.

- Anders Ericsson (e.g. 1990) and Michael Howe (e.g. Howe, Davidson, & Sloboda, 1998) developed a view of expertise as something that anyone can acquire, provided they are prepared to apply themselves to acquiring the knowledge base; expertise takes about 10 years to acquire.

- Wisdom is associated with crystalized intelligence, which Raymond Cattell (see 1971) distinguished from the fluid intelligence of younger people.

- Paul Baltes (e.g. Baltes & Staudinger, 2008) has explicitly linked wisdom with expertise in the conduct and meaning of life.

- Robert Sternberg's (1998) balance theory of wisdom states that wisdom is the use of intelligence to balance competing needs and to seek a common good.

- Rational behaviour is frequently associated with behaviour that complies with norms, but, for various reasons, norms can be difficult to follow.

LANGUAGE AND THOUGHT

LEARNING OBJECTIVE 12.4

Critically evaluate the ways that language and thought might be related, and assess how empirical evidence might favour one of the various possibilities.

We have discussed language and thought, two cognitive domains in which humans far outstrip other animals and may differ from them in a qualitative way. The two are interlinked. One complication in determining how they are related is that different people give different reports of how they think. Some say their thoughts are entirely verbal. Others give a prominent role to visual imagery. Indeed, these differences were one of the reasons for the failure of introspectionism to produce coherent psychological theories in the early 20th century. Nevertheless, much of our thinking requires linguistic expression. So how are language and thought related? Do we just express our thoughts in language, with languages having to take the forms they do so that they can be used to express the kinds of thought we have? Or do languages shape the nature of those thoughts?

The traditional view

The traditional view, which can be traced back to Aristotle, is that thought is prior to language. Many modern thinkers have subscribed to a version of this view, including the developmental psychologist Jean Piaget and the linguist Noam Chomsky. The Universal Grammar that Chomsky discusses is partly there to ensure that languages can express the kinds of thoughts that people have.

One issue with the traditional view is whether language and thought are always related in the way that view suggests or whether, in individual development, they are initially related in some other way. The Russian psychologist Lev Vygotsky (1934/1986) claimed that the role of language as a vehicle for the direct expression of underlying thoughts has to develop. For example, in young children, Vygotsky observed what appeared to be a much looser connection between language and speech than that seen in adults. A child might say 'don't press' when instructed not to press a rubber bulb, but might nevertheless press the bulb.

The Sapir–Whorf hypothesis (linguistic determinism and linguistic relativity)

A more radical alternative to the traditional view has been suggested a number of times, but most notably in the early to mid-20th century by the American linguist Edward Sapir and his sometime student, the largely self-taught documenter of Native American languages Benjamin Lee Whorf (Carroll, 1956). The so-called **Sapir–Whorf hypothesis** or linguistic relativity hypothesis claims that the way a person thinks is affected by structural aspects of the language(s) they speak. The strongest version of the hypothesis replaces 'affected' by 'determined', which leads to the twin hypotheses of linguistic relativity and linguistic determinism.

Much of the evidence that Whorf put forward in support of these hypotheses comes from his analysis of Native American languages, which he was partly instrumental in recording at a time when they were dying out. However, one famous anecdote is based on an English-language example and claims that, in his professional work as a fire insurance inspector, Whorf noted that a fire had been started because a still-glowing cigarette end had been thrown into an 'empty' gasoline can, which was in fact full of highly flammable gasoline vapour. The vapour, not surprisingly, caught fire as the cigarette was dropped in. The way people thought about the cans appeared to be determined by their use of the label 'empty'.

Many of the arguments that Whorf made from Native American languages have been shown to be suspect or to rely on equivocation. For example, his famous observations (Whorf, 1940) about the number of words for types of snow in Inuit languages as compared with English are suspect factually and also fail to take into account the cultural importance of identifying different types of snow if one lives in the Arctic.

In the 1950s psychologists began investigating basic colour terms (those that are not the names of other things – black, white, red, blue, green, and yellow rather than orange, salmon, rose, lilac, saffron). This work, together with linguistic analyses that began with Berlin and Kay's book *Basic Color Terms* (1969), suggested that major differences in colour vocabulary are not reflected in the way colours are perceived (which might be regarded as one aspect of thinking).

Recent developments

The work on colour led to a period in which the Sapir–Whorf hypothesis was unfashionable and Whorf was viewed unfavourably. Since the mid-1990s, however, a number of researchers, including Steve Levinson (2003) and Lera Boroditsky (see Fausey & Boroditsky, 2011), have identified other domains in which language appears to have an influence on cognition. For example, in some languages, such as Kuuk Thaayorre (a native Australian language spoken in parts of Queensland), all directional terms refer to map directions such as north and south, rather than directions relative to the speaker such as left and right. Speakers of Kuuk Thaayorre have a much better sense of map directions than speakers of English. Similarly, but closer to home for most of us, English speakers are better than Spanish speakers at remembering who caused accidental events to happen (Fausey & Boroditsky, 2011) because English tends to use agentive constructions to describe such events ('John broke the vase') whereas Spanish tend to use impersonal constructions ('Se rompió el florero'; 'The vase broke').

Linguist Steven Pinker discuss what our language habits reveal in **this 2005 TED Talk**[5].

This recent work demonstrates that being a speaker of a particular language can affect the fluency that a person has in thinking in certain ways. However, there is no evidence for the strong linguistic determinism that Whorf is sometimes said to have espoused. Whether he did or not is a moot question, as his writings are often informal and can be interpreted in various ways. Furthermore, an issue that has plagued Whorfian research often remains. Is it the language itself that affects thinking or does culture more generally have an influence – maybe map directions are more important in Kuuk Thaayorre-speaking cultures than in English-speaking cultures. Nevertheless, this recent research shows that well-designed experiments can show clear and interesting effects. The challenge is to interpret those effects correctly.

TEST YOURSELF

What kind of evidence might show linguistic relativity to be true?

SECTION SUMMARY

- Language and thought are interlinked.
- A key question is whether we just express our thoughts in language or whether languages shape the nature of our thoughts.
- The traditional view, which can be traced back to Aristotle, is that thought is prior to language.
- An alternative is the so-called Sapir–Whorf hypothesis or linguistic relativity hypothesis, which claims that the way a person thinks is affected by structural aspects of the language(s) they speak.
- The Sapir–Whorf hypothesis fell out of favour, but contemporary researchers have revived the interest in exploring the connection between language and cognition. This recent work demonstrates that being a speaker of a particular language can affect the fluency that a person has in thinking in certain ways.

CHAPTER SUMMARY

This chapter has examined the faculties of language and thinking and asked some fundamental questions about the interconnectedness and philosophical origins of speech and thought. We began by looking at the evolution of language as a communication system before exploring how language is learned or acquired. We then examined language understanding and production, and the special properties of reading. The next section concluded with an outline of the biological bases of language in the human brain.

The following section introduced thinking and gave an evaluation of how we categorize and conceptualize the world and how this relates to the way we think. We moved on to a discussion of reasoning, problem solving, and judgement and decision making, and the assertion that there are two systems for thinking: a fast, intuitive, error-prone one, and a slow, effortful one. We then considered creativity, the neuropsychology of thinking, whether and how thinking might be taught, and how thinking, expertise, wisdom, and rationality develop. We concluded with a brief look at how language and thought are related to one another.

ESSAY QUESTIONS

1. Describe in detail the two systems of thinking, giving examples of the kinds of thinking that each system is involved in.

2. How are language and thought related to each other?

KEY TERMS

- **animal communication:** The transfer of information from one animal or a group of animals to one or more other animals. Strongly limited to the here and now.
- **aphasia:** A speech disorder resulting in difficulties producing or comprehending speech.
- **bilingualism:** An ability that ranges from complete native fluency in two languages to native fluency in one and passable competence in another.
- **comprehension:** The complex process of deriving meaning from spoken, written, and signed language.
- **concepts:** Ideas of what something is or how it works.
- **creativity:** The generation of an original idea, concept, or physical object.
- **decision making:** The relationship between belief and desire that guides what we decide to do in everyday life.
- **dyslexia:** A language disorder that appears to be specific to reading.
- **everyday reasoning:** The kind of reasoning in which people engage in their ordinary lives. It typically involves a number of short lines of argument on each side of an issue, rather than the single, often longish line of argument that comprises a proof in formal reasoning.
- **evolution of language:** The manner in which language structure and humans' ability to communicate have changed over time. The evolution of language is a hotly debated topic, primarily because of the difficulty of bringing empirical evidence to bear on this issue. Noam Chomsky is a key figure.
- **expertise:** High-level skill or knowledge in a particular field.
- **heuristics:** Mental shortcuts in thinking that produce quick results that are often, but not always, correct.
- **hypothesis testing:** In the case of everyday thinking, how people use individual instances to decide whether general hypotheses are true.
- **judgement:** Forming a belief about whether something is true or how likely it is.
- **language acquisition:** The process by which humans acquire the capacity to perceive and comprehend language, as well as to produce and use words and sentences to communicate.
- **language:** A system for communication.
- **problem solving:** The use of systematic or semi-systematic methods to find a way of getting from a state that is regarded as problematic to a state in which the problem is solved.
- **production:** The speaking and writing of language.
- **rationality:** Thinking or behaving in a way that conforms with accepted norms of correct reasoning.
- **reading:** The complex cognitive process of decoding written or printed symbols in order to construct meaning.
- **reasoning:** The drawing of conclusions that are not explicitly stated from explicit information and, in some cases, other relevant knowledge.

- **Sapir–Whorf hypothesis:** The principle of linguistic relativity, which states that the structure of a person's language influences their world view.
- **thinking:** The process of considering or reasoning about something.
- **wisdom:** The quality of having and employing experience, knowledge, and good judgement.

NOTES

1. https://www.ted.com/talks/patricia_kuhl_the_linguistic_genius_of_babies
2. http://ed.ted.com/lessons/how-speaking-multiple-languages-benefits-the-brain-mia-nacamulli
3. http://www.ted.com/talks/mihaly_csikszentmihalyi_on_flow?language=en]
4. http://www.ted.com/talks/barry_schwartz_on_our_loss_of_wisdom?language=en
5. http://www.ted.com/talks/steven_pinker_on_language_and_thought?language=en
6. http://www.youtube.com/watch?v=laLS8gHzROg
7. https://www.youtube.com/watch?v=5Wn4EboLrMM

FURTHER RESOURCES

Danziger, S., Levav, J., & Avnaim-Pesso, L. (2011). Extraneous factors in judicial decisions. *Proceedings of the National Academy of Sciences of the United States of America*, 108(17), 6889–6892.

Evans, J. St. B. T. (2012). Questions and challenges for the new psychology of reasoning. *Thinking and Reasoning, 18*, 5–31.

Harley, T. A. (2014). *The psychology of language* (4th ed.). Hove, UK: Psychology Press.

Hockett, C. F. (1960). The origin of speech. *Scientific American, 203*, 89–97.

Holyoak, K. J., & Morrison, R. G. (2012). *The Oxford handbook of thinking and reasoning*. Oxford, UK: Oxford University Press.

Kahneman, D. (2011). *Thinking, fast and slow*. London, UK: Penguin.

Kahneman, D., & Tversky, A. (1984). Choices, values, and frames. *American Psychologist, 39*, 341–350.

Traxler, M. J. (2012). *Introduction to psycholinguistics*. Chichester, UK: Wiley-Blackwell.

Tversky, A., & Kahneman, D. (1974). Judgment under uncertainty: Heuristics and biases. *Science, 185*, 1124–1131.

REFERENCES

Armstrong, S., Gleitman, L., & Gleitman, H. (1983). What some concepts might not be. *Cognition, 13*, 263–308.

Asch, S. E. (1956). Studies of independence and conformity: I. A minority of one against a unanimous majority. *Psychological Monographs: General and Applied, 70*(9), 1–70.

Baars, B. J., Motley, M. T., & McKay, D. (1975). Output editing for lexical status from artificially elicited slips of the tongue. *Journal of Verbal Learning and Verbal Behavior, 14*, 382–391.

Bakker, D. J. (1972). *Temporal order in disturbed reading: Developmental and neuropsychological aspects in normal and reading-retarded children*. Rotterdam, Netherlands: Rotterdam University Press.

Baltes, P. B., Smith, J., & Staudinger, U. M. (1992). Wisdom and successful aging. In T. Sonderegger (Ed.), *Nebraska symposium on motivation* (Vol. 39, pp. 123–167). Lincoln, NE: University of Nebraska Press.

Baltes, P. B., & Staudinger, U. M. (2008). Wisdom: A metaheuristic (pragmatic) to orchestrate mind and virtue toward excellence. *American Psychologist, 55*, 122–136.

Baron, J. (2008). *Thinking and deciding* (4th ed.). Cambridge, UK: Cambridge University Press.

Barsalou, L. (1983). Ad hoc categories. *Memory & Cognition*, *11*, 211–227.

BBC. (2013). The varied alarm calls of the vervet monkey. Retrieved 12 January 2018 from http://www.bbc.co.uk/programmes/p016dgw1

BBC. (2015). Noam Chomsky on language acquisition. Retrieved 12 January 2018 from http://www.bbc.co.uk/programmes/p02hdy9f

Berlin, B., & Kay, P. (1969). *Basic color terms: Their universality and evolution*. Berkeley, CA: California University Press.

Bialystok, E. (1988). Levels of bilingualism and levels of linguistic awareness. *Developmental Psychology*, *25*, 560–567.

Bialystok, E., & Martin, M. M. (2004). Attention and inhibition in bilingual children: Evidence from the dimensional change card sort task. *Developmental Science*, *7*, 325–339.

Boden, M. A. (1980). *The creative mind: Myths and mechanisms*. London, UK: Weidenfeld & Nicolson.

Bouillaud, J.-B. (1825). *Traité clinique et physiologique de l'encéphalite, ou inflammation du cerveau*. Paris, France: J.-B. Baillière.

Broca, P. (1861). Remarques sur le siege de la faculté du langage articulé, suivés d'une observation d'aphémie. *Bulletin de la Société Anatomique de Paris*, *36*, 330–357.

Brown, R. (1973). *A first language: The early stages*. Cambridge, MA: Harvard University Press.

Burkeman, O. (2011). Daniel Kahneman: 'We're beautiful devices.' *The Guardian*, 14 November. Retrieved 12 January 2018 from https://www.theguardian.com/science/2011/nov/14/daniel-kahneman-psychologist

Carey, S., & Bartlett, E. (1978). Acquiring a single new word. *Proceedings of the Stanford Child Language Conference*, *15*, 17–29.

Carraher, T. N., Carraher, D. W., & Schliemann, A. D. (1985). Mathematics in the street and in schools. *British Journal of Developmental Psychology*, *3*, 21–29.

Carroll, J. B. (Ed.). (1956). *Language, thought, and reality: Selected writings of Benjamin Lee Whorf*. Cambridge, MA: MIT Press.

Case, R. (1985). *Intellectual development: Birth to adulthood*. Orlando, FL: Academic Press.

Cattell, R. B. (1971). *Abilities: Their structure, growth, and action*. New York, NY: Houghton Mifflin.

Chase, W. G., & Simon, H. A. (1973). Perception in chess. *Cognitive Psychology*, *4*, 55–81.

Chomsky, N. (1957). *Syntactic structures*. The Hague, Netherlands: Mouton.

Chomsky, N. (1965). *Aspects of the theory of syntax*. Cambridge, MA: MIT Press.

Chomsky, N. (2006). *Language and mind* (3rd ed.). Cambridge, UK: Cambridge University Press.

Clark, H. H., & Wilkes-Gibbs, D. (1986). Referring as a collaborative process. *Cognition*, *22*, 1–39.

Cohen, L. J. (1981). Can human irrationality be experimentally demonstrated? *Behavioral and Brain Sciences*, *4*, 317–331.

Collins, A. R., & Quillian, M. R. (1969). Retrieval time from semantic memory. *Journal of Verbal Learning and Verbal Behavior*, *8*, 240–247.

Coltheart, M., Rastle, K., Perry, C., Langdon, R., & Ziegler, J. (2001). DRC: A dual route cascaded model of visual word recognition and reading aloud. *Psychological Review*, *108*, 204–256.

Csikszentmihalyi, M. (1988). Society, culture, and person: A systems view of creativity. In R. J. Sternberg (Ed.), *The nature of creativity: Contemporary psychological perspectives* (pp. 325–339). Cambridge, UK: Cambridge University Press.

Danziger, S., Levav, J., & Avnaim-Pesso, L. (2011). Extraneous factors in judicial decisions. *Proceedings of the National Academy of Sciences of the United States of America*, *108*(17), 6889–6892.

De Groot, A. D. (1946/1965). *Thought and choice in chess*. The Hague, Netherlands: Mouton.

Dell, G. S. (1986). A spreading activation theory of retrieval and sentence production. *Psychological Review*, *93*, 283–321.

Dufau, S., Duñabeitia, J. A., Moret-Tatay, C., McGonigal, A., Peeters, D., Alario, F.-X., … Grainger, J. (2011). Smart phone, smart science: How the use of smartphones can revolutionize research in cognitive science. *PLoS ONE*, *6*, e24974.

Dunbar, R. I. M. (1996). *Grooming, gossip, and the evolution of language*. London, UK: Faber & Faber.

Duncan, J., Seitz, R. J., Kolodny, J., Bor, D., Herzog, H., Ahmed, A., ... Emslie, H. (2000). A neural basis for general intelligence. *Science, 289*(5478), 457–460.

Duncker, K. (1935/1945). On problem solving. *Psychological Monographs, 58*(5), i–113.

Elliott, J. G., & Gibbs, S. (2008). Does dyslexia exist? *Journal of Philosophy of Education, 42,* 475–491.

Ericsson, K. A. (1990). Theoretical issues in the study of exceptional performance. In K. Gilhooly, M. Keane, R. Logie, & G. Erdos (Eds.), *Lines of thinking: Reflections on the psychology of thinking* (Vol. 2, pp. 5–28). Chichester, UK: Wiley .

Falk, D. (2004). Prelinguistic evolution in early hominids: Whence motherese? *Behavioral and Brain Sciences, 27,* 491–503.

Fausey, C. M., & Boroditsky, L. (2011). Who dunnit? Cross-linguistic difference in eye-witness memory. *Psychonomic Bulletin & Review, 18,* 150–157.

Feuerstein, R. (1980). *Instrumental enrichment: An intervention program for cognitive modifiability.* Baltimore, MD: University Park Press.

Fodor, J. A., Bever, T. G., & Garrett, M. F. (1974). *The psychology of language: An introduction to psycholinguistics and generative grammar.* New York, NY: McGraw-Hill.

Fitch, W. T., & Reby, D. (2001). The descended larynx is not uniquely human. *Proceedings of the Royal Society B: Biological Sciences, 268,* 1669–1675.

Gardner, R. A., & Gardner, B. T. (1969). Teaching sign language to a chimpanzee. *Science, 165,* 664–672.

Garnham, A. (1983). Why psycholinguists don't care about DTC: A reply to Berwick and Weinberg. *Cognition, 15,* 263–269.

Garnham, A. (2001). *Mental models and the interpretation of anaphora.* Hove, UK: Psychology Press.

Garnham, A. J. V., and Oakhill, J. (1994). *Thinking and reasoning.* Oxford, UK: Blackwell.

Gentner, D. (1983). Structure-mapping: A theoretical framework for analogy. *Cognitive Psychology, 7,* 155–170.

Georgia Tech College of Computing. (2011). The waggle dance of the honeybee. *YouTube,* 2 February. Retrieved 12 January 2018 from https://www.youtube.com/watch?v=bFDGPgXtK-U#

Geschwind, N. (1972). Language and the brain. *Scientific American, 226*(4), 76–83.

Gick, M. L., & Holyoak, K. J. (1980). Analogical problem solving. *Cognitive Psychology, 12,* 306–355.

Gick, M. L., & Holyoak, K. J. (1983). Schema induction and analogical transfer. *Cognitive Psychology, 15,* 1–38.

Gladwell, M. (2005). *Blink.* London, UK: Penguin.

Glenberg, A. M., & Kaschak, M. P. (2002). Grounding language in action. *Psychonomic Bulletin & Review, 9,* 558–565.

Goel, V. (2009). Cognitive neuroscience of thinking. In G. G. Berntson & J. G. Cacioppo (Eds.), *Handbook of neuroscience for the behavioral sciences* (pp. 417–430). New York, NY: Wiley .

Gold, E. M. (1967). Language identification in the limit. *Information and Control, 10,* 447–474.

Gorilla Foundation. (n.d.). Project Koko. Retrieved 12 January 2018 from http://www.koko.org/project-koko

Harnad, S. (1990). The symbol grounding problem. *Physica D, 42,* 335–346.

Hauser, M. D., Chomsky, N., & Fitch, W. T. (2002). The faculty of language: What is it, who has it, and how did it evolve? *Science, 298,* 1569–1579.

Henderson, J. M., & Ferreira, F. (1990). Effects of foveal processing difficulty on the perceptual span in reading: Implications for attention and eye movement control. *Journal of Experimental Psychology: Learning, Memory, and Cognition, 16,* 417–429.

Hockett, C. F. (1960). The origin of speech. *Scientific American, 203,* 89–97.

Howe, M. J. (1989). *Fragments of genius: The strange feats of idiots savants.* London, UK: Routledge.

Howe, M. J., Davidson, J. W., & Sloboda, J. A. (1998). Innate talents: Reality or myth? *Behavioral and Brain Sciences, 21,* 399–407.

James, W. (1890). *The principles of psychology.* New York, NY: Holt.

Johnson-Laird, P. N. (1981). *Mental models.* Cambridge, UK: Cambridge University Press.

Johnson-Laird, P. N. (1993). *Human and machine thinking*. Hillsdale, NJ: Lawrence Erlbaum Associates.

Kahneman, D. (2011). *Thinking, fast and slow*. London, UK: Penguin.

Kahneman, D., & Tversky, A. (1984). Choices, values, and frames. *American Psychologist, 39*, 341–350.

Keysar, B., Barr, D. J., & Horton, W. S. (1998). The egocentric basis of language use: Insights from a processing approach. *Current Directions in Psychological Sciences, 7*, 46–50.

Kimmelman, M. (1991). Art; absolutely real? Absolutely fake? *New York Times*, 4 August. Retrieved 12 January 2018 from http://www.nytimes.com/1991/08/04/arts/art-absolutely-real-absolutely-fake.html?pagewanted=all

Köhler, W. (1921/1925). *The mentality of apes (trans. Ella Winter)*. London, UK: Kegan Paul, Trench, Trubner.

Kuhn, D. (1991). *The skills of argument*. Cambridge, UK: Cambridge University Press.

Kuperman, V., Stadthagen-Gonzalez, H., & Brysbaert, M. (2012). Age-of-acquisition ratings for 30,000 English words. *Behavior Research Methods, 44*, 978–990.

Landauer, T., Foltz, P. W., & Laham, D. (1998). Introduction to latent semantic analysis. *Discourse Processes, 25*, 259–284.

Levinson, S. C. (2003). *Space in language and cognition: Explorations in cognitive diversity*. Cambridge, UK: Cambridge University Press.

Lichtenstein, S., Slovic, P., Fischhoff, B., Layman, M., & Combs, B. (1978). Judged frequency of lethal events. *Journal of Experimental Psychology: Human Learning and Memory, 4*, 551–578.

Lieberman, P. (1998). *Eve spoke: Human language and human evolution*. New York, NY: W. W. Norton.

Loewenstein, G., Rick, S., & Cohen, J. (2008). Neuroeconomics. *Annual Review of Psychology, 59*, 647–672.

Markman, E. M. (1989). *Categorization and naming in children: Problems of induction*. Cambridge, MA: MIT Press.

McClelland, J., & Rumelhart, D. (1981). An interactive activation model of context effects in letter perception: Part 1. An account of basic findings. *Psychological Review, 88*, 375–407.

McMurray, B., Horst, J. S., & Samuelson, L. K. (2012). Word learning as the interaction of online referent selection and slow associative learning. *Psychological Review, 119*, 831–877.

Medin, D. L., & Schaffer, M. M. (1978). Context theory of classification learning. *Psychological Review, 85*, 207–238.

Milgram, S. (1974). *Obedience to authority: An experimental view*. New York, NY: Harper & Row.

Murphy, G. L., & Medin, D. L. (1985). The role of theories in conceptual coherence. *Psychological Review, 92*, 289–316.

Neuroboffin. (2010). Using TMS to localize brain functions. *YouTube*, 31 March. Retrieved 2 February 2018 from https://www.youtube.com/watch?v=mD34o-sW22A

Newell, A. (1990). *Unified theories of cognition: The 1987 William James lectures*. Cambridge, MA: Harvard University Press.

Newell, A., Shaw, J. C., & Simon, H. A. (1957). Empirical investigations with the logic theory machine. *Proceedings of the Western Joint Computer Conference, 15*, 218–239.

Newell, A., Shaw, J. C., & Simon, H. A. (1959). Report on a general problem-solving program. In *Proceedings of the International Conference on Information Processing* (pp. 256–264). London, UK: UNESCO.

Newell, A., Shaw, J. C., & Simon, H. A. (1963). Chess-playing programs and the problem of complexity. In E. A. Feigenbaum & J. Feldman (Eds.), *Computers and thought* (pp. 39–70). New York, NY: McGraw-Hill.

Newell, A., & Simon, H. A. (1972). *Human problem solving*. Englewood Cliffs, NJ: Prentice-Hall.

Nickerson, R. S., Perkins, D. N., & Smith, E. E. (1985). *The teaching of thinking*. Hillsdale, NJ: Lawrence Erlbaum Associates.

Norris, D., McQueen, J. M., & Cutler, A. (2000). Merging information in speech recognition: Feedback is never necessary. *Behavioral and Brain Sciences, 23*, 299–370.

Oakhill, J. V., Johnson-Laird, P. N., & Garnham, A. (1989). Believability and syllogistic reasoning. *Cognition*, *31*, 117–140.

O'Regan, J. K. (1992). Optimal viewing position in words and the strategy-tactics theory of eye movements in reading. In K. Rayner (Ed.), *Eye movements and visual cognition: Scene perception and reading* (pp. 333–354). New York, NY: Springer.

Pascual-Leone, J. (1970). A mathematical model for the transition rule in Piaget's developmental stages. *Acta Psychologica*, *32*, 301–345.

Patterson, F. G. (1978). The gestures of a gorilla: Language acquisition in another pongid. *Brain and Language*, *5*, 72–97.

Perkins, D. N. (1981). *The mind's best work*. Cambridge, MA: Harvard University Press.

Perkins, D. N. (1985). Reasoning as imagination. *Interchange*, *16*, 14–26.

Perkins, D. N. (1988). The possibility of invention. In R. J. Sternberg (Ed.), *The nature of creativity: Contemporary psychological perspectives* (pp. 362–385). Cambridge, UK: Cambridge University Press.

Perkins, D. N., Farady, M., & Bushey, B. (1991). Everyday reasoning and the roots of intelligence. In J. F. Voss, D. N. Perkins, & J. W. Segal (Eds.), *Informal reasoning and education* (pp. 83–106). Hillsdale, NJ: Lawrence Erlbaum Associates.

Piaget, J. (1951). *Play, dreams and imitation in childhood*. New York, NY: W. W. Norton.

Piaget, J. (1952). *The origins of intelligence in children*. New York, NY: International Universities Press.

Piaget, J. (1954). *The construction of reality in the child*. New York, NY: Basic Books.

Pickering, M., & Garrod, S. (2004). Toward a mechanistic psychology of dialogue. *Behavioral and Brain Sciences*, *27*, 169–190.

Popova, M. (n.d.). The art of thought: A pioneering 1926 model of the four stages of creativity. *Brain Pickings*. Retrieved 12 January 2018 from https://www.brainpickings.org/2013/08/28/the-art-of-thought-graham-wallas-stages

Popper, K. R. (1959). *The logic of scientific discovery*. London, UK: Hutchinson.

Rips, L. J. (1994). *The psychology of proof: Deductive reasoning in human thinking*. Cambridge, MA: MIT Press.

Rips, L. J., Shoben, E. J., & Smith, F. E. (1973). Semantic distance and the verification of semantic relations. *Journal of Verbal Learning and Verbal Behavior*, *14*, 665–681.

Roelofs, A. (1997). The WEAVER model of word-form encoding in speech production. *Cognition*, *64*, 249–284.

Rosch, E., & Mervis, C. B. (1975). Family resemblances: Studies in the internal structure of categories. *Cognitive Psychology*, *7*, 573–605.

Rosch, E. H., Mervis, C. B., Gray, W. D., Johnson, D. M., & Boyes-Braem, P. (1976). Basic objects in natural categories. *Cognitive Psychology*, *8*, 382–439.

Rosenthal, D. M. (2005). *Consciousness and mind*. Oxford, UK: Clarendon Press.

Ross, M., & Sicoly, F. (1979). Egocentric biases in availability and attribution. *Journal of Personality and Social Psychology*, *37*, 322–336.

Royal College of Surgeons. (2017). Women surgeon statistics. Retrieved 2 February 2018 from https://www.rcseng.ac.uk/careers-in-surgery/women-in-surgery/mission-and-goals/women-surgeon-statistics

Saffran, J. R. (2003). Statistical language learning: Mechanisms and constraints. *Current Directions in Psychological Science*, *12*, 110–114.

Sanford, A. J. (1985). *Cognition and cognitive psychology*. London, UK: Weidenfeld & Nicolson.

Savage, L. J. (1954). *The foundations of statistics*. New York, NY: Wiley .

Scribner, S. (1984). Studying working intelligence. In B. Rogoff & J. Lave (Eds.), *Everyday cognition: Its development in social context* (pp. 9–40). Cambridge, MA: Harvard University Press.

Seyfarth, R. M., Cheney, D. L., & Marler, P. (1980). Vervet monkey alarm calls: Semantic communication in a free-ranging primate. *Animal Behaviour*, *28*, 1070–1094.

Simon, H. A. (1982). *Models of bounded rationality*. Cambridge, MA: MIT Press.

Simons, D. (2012). How experts recall chess positions. *The Invisible Gorilla*, 15 February. Retrieved 12 January 2018 from http://theinvisiblegorilla.com/blog/2012/02/15/how-experts-recall-chess-positions

Simonton, D. K. (1984). *Genius, creativity, and leadership*. Cambridge, MA: Harvard University Press.

Smith, E. E., & Osherson, D. N. (1984). Conceptual combination with prototype categories. *Cognitive Science*, 8, 357–361.

Sternberg, R. J. (1996). *Successful intelligence*. New York, NY: Simon & Schuster.

Sternberg, R. J. (1998). A balance theory of wisdom. *Review of General Psychology*, 2, 347–365.

Taraban, R., & McClelland, J. L. (1988). Constituent attachment and thematic role assignment in sentence processing: Influences of content-based expectations. *Journal of Memory & Language*, 27, 597–632.

Thaler, R. (1980). Toward a positive theory of consumer choice. *Journal of Economic Behavior and Organization*, 1, 39–60.

Thorndike, E. L. (1898). Animal intelligence: An experimental study of the associative processes in animals. *Psychological Review Monograph Supplements*, 2(4), i–109.

Tversky, A., & Kahneman, D. (1974). Judgment under uncertainty: Heuristics and biases. *Science*, 185, 1124–1131.

Tversky, A., & Kahneman, D. (1981). The framing of decisions and the psychology of choice. *Science*, 211, 453–458.

Vellutino, F. R., Fletcher, J. M., Snowling, M. J., & Scanlon, D. M. (2004). Specific reading disability (dyslexia): What have we learned in the past four decades? *Journal of Child Psychology and Psychiatry*, 45, 2–40.

von Neumann, J., & Morgenstern, O. (1944). *Games and the theory of economic behaviour*. Princeton, NJ: Princeton University Press.

Vygotsky, L. (1934/1986). *Thought and language* (rev. ed.). Cambridge, MA: MIT Press.

Wallas, G. (1926). *The art of thought*. London, UK: Cape.

Wason, P. C., & Johnson-Laird, P. N. (1972). *Psychology of reasoning: Structure and content*. London, UK: Batsford.

Werker, J. F., & Tees, R. C. (1983). Developmental changes across childhood in the perception of non-native speech sounds. *Canadian Journal of Psychology*, 37, 278–286.

Wernicke, C. (1874). *Der Aphasische Symptomencomplex: Eine Psychologische Studie auf Anatomischer Basis*. Breslau, Poland: Cohn und Weigert.

Western University. (2011). What is electroencephalography (EEG)? *YouTube*, 4 October. Retrieved 2 February 2018 from https://www.youtube.com/watch?v=o6MK60SFK0k

Whorf, B. L. (1940). Science and linguistics. *Technology Review*, 42(6 April), 229–231, 247–248.

Wittgenstein, L. (1953). *Philosophical investigations*. Oxford, UK: Blackwell.

ACTIVITY SOLUTIONS

ACTIVITY 12.1: WASON SELECTION TASK

Version 1

The E card and the 7 card (*not* E and 2) should be turned over. Here is the logic.

If any one card doesn't obey the rule, you know the rule doesn't apply to all four cards. If a card does obey the rule, so what? But maybe one of the others doesn't (*confirmation* doesn't show the rule is true). You need to find out whether any card falsifies the rule but you don't know what's on the back of the cards. So, turn over cards that *might* not obey the rule. Only the E and the 7 fall into this category – E if it has an odd number on the back, 7 if it has a vowel on the back.

Version 2

The 'Paper' card and the 'No £' card should be turned over. The logic is the same as for the first version.

ACTIVITY 12.2: DUNCKER'S CANDLE PROBLEM

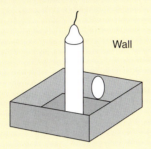

Wall

The problem demonstrates the notion of functional fixity. The box is seen as a container for the drawing pins and not as part of the solution to the problem. If the drawing pins are provided in a pile by themselves, with the box as a separate item, the problem is much easier to solve.

ACTIVITY 12.3: CLASSIC PROBLEMS FROM THE PROBLEM-SOLVING LITERATURE

If you can't work out the solutions to these problems, you can find them online:

- **Missionaries and cannibals**[6]
- **The Tower of Hanoi**[7].

There is more than one way of solving each problem, so, if yours is different from the one in the video, that doesn't mean it is wrong.

13 Intelligence

Sophie von Stumm

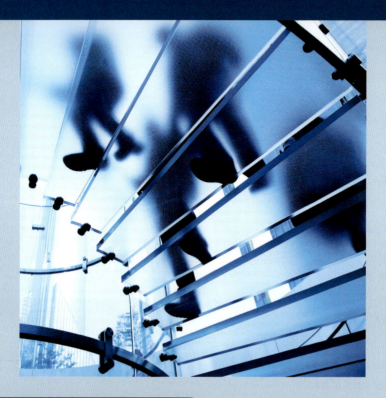

INTRODUCTION AND DEFINING INTELLIGENCE

LEARNING OBJECTIVE 13.1

Describe the theoretical concept of intelligence and its measurement.

Psychological traits that differ *between* and *within* people are referred to as 'dimensions of individual differences'. Essentially, every characteristic that differs between people is a dimension of individual differences, including the length of people's pinkie. Of course, some dimensions of individual differences are more important than others: in principle, individual differences in psychological traits – such as intelligence and personality – are thought to be more relevant in our lives than individual differences in physiological traits – such as pinkie length, or height and weight.

Intelligence is believed to be one of the most important dimensions of individual differences because it affects a wide range of life outcomes, including achievement and health. As a simple example, people with higher intelligence tend to do better in school and gain greater educational qualifications overall. As a result, they often earn higher incomes and live in nicer houses. In line with this, intelligence has been described as 'one of the most central phenomena in all of behavioural science, with broad explanatory powers' (Jensen, 1998, p. xii). Because of its importance for everyday life, intelligence lies at the core of a buzzing and bubbling research field that draws from several scientific disciplines: for example, **psychometrics** is the study of assessments of human intelligence, behavioural geneticists explore the environmental and genetic causes of differences in intelligence, and neuroscientists seek to locate intelligence in the brain. Although intelligence research is truly interdisciplinary and has made substantial progress, our knowledge today about intelligence – specifically its nature, development, and origin – is far from complete. In addition to, or perhaps because of, its many unknowns, intelligence continues to be a very controversial topic, not only in the context of research but everywhere.

Intelligence is neither easily nor unanimously defined. It has been noted, with a smirk, that there are almost as many definitions of intelligence as there are academic experts researching this construct (Jensen, 1998). Likewise, there are numerous terms that are used interchangeably with intelligence in the literature – for example, cognitive ability, mental ability, IQ, intellectual potential, intellectual capacity, the *g*-factor, and simply *g*.

Difficulties in defining intelligence

Researchers have struggled to come up with a comprehensive consensus definition since the first scientific writings on intelligence, which date back to the

Psychology, First Edition. Edited by Graham Davey.
© 2019 John Wiley & Sons, Ltd. Published 2019 by John Wiley & Sons, Ltd.

19th century. It took Raymond Cattell (1905–1998), a prolific and seminal intelligence researcher, six full pages in 1943, when intelligence research was just about to fit into its childhood shoes, to review the 'general muddle' (p. 161) that surrounded the definition of intelligence. Today, such a review would be impossible because of the vast number of publications, theories, and empirical evidence that have been accumulated on intelligence. In other words, intelligence researchers and other scientists and writers use a variety of definitions and ideas when they investigate intelligence. Is it a problem not to have one universal and specific definition of intelligence?

Most interesting things in life tend to be complex, sometimes too complex to fit a static and clear definition. Just think of what is truly interesting in your life – my guess is that you are thinking about other people and how you feel about them (and about your studies, of course). Each person is uniquely different from another in various shades and layers and, likewise, your relationship with another person is unique and different from other relationships that you have. In fact, there are no two people that you feel about and relate to in exactly the same way. If people and our relationships with them cannot be defined unanimously, how could there be an adequate definition of 'one of the most central phenomena in all of behavioural science'?

Indeed, some of the greatest pioneers in intelligence research 'refused to be halted by demands for an exact meaning-style definition, deciding that there was a sufficient corpus of research findings to be described and explained' (Deary, 2001, p. 2). While this is an acceptable, albeit bold, position, it makes a discussion of intelligence and its basic concepts rather difficult.

A consensus definition of intelligence

It seems most appropriate to cite a definition of intelligence that was supported by a consensus of the majority of intelligence researchers at the time. This definition was put together by 52 intelligence research experts in 1994, after the publication of *The Bell Curve: Intelligence and Class Structure in American Life* in the same year by Richard Herrnstein and Charles Murray had raised a lot of controversy about intelligence research. According to this consensus definition, which was first published in the *Wall Street Journal* rather than in a scientific journal, intelligence is:

> A very general mental capability that, among other things, involves the ability to reason, plan, solve problems, think abstractly, comprehend complex ideas, learn quickly and learn from experience. … it reflects a broader and deeper capability for comprehending our surroundings—'catching on', 'making sense' of things, or 'figuring out' what to do. (Gottfredson, 1994)

This definition emphasizes the ability to quickly comprehend and adapt to novel circumstances as a core aspect of intelligence, but it excludes accumulated knowledge, experiences, and information, which have been argued to also constitute important aspects of intelligence (e.g. Ackerman, 1996; Cattell, 1943). As a consequence, the consensus definition of intelligence is neither universal nor exhaustive. To overcome this problem, we can help ourselves in asking what intelligence is by looking at two additional questions: (1) What do we need intelligence for? And (2) where is intelligence located?

FOCUS POINT 13.1

INTELLIGENCE: A CONTROVERSIAL RESEARCH DISCIPLINE?

Controversies in science occur when research findings challenge what is commonly assumed to be true. For example, a study suggesting that going to school lowers intelligence would cause controversy – first, because schools are generally believed to help children develop their intelligence (that is, after all, why we have schools) and, second, because many other studies have shown the opposite: schools increase intelligence (see e.g. Brinch & Galloway, 2012).

In individual differences research, controversies often occur when the causes of people's differences in IQ are discussed. In particular, the statement that intelligence is heritable often divides people. However, heritability itself offers little reason for controversy: it merely implies that there are differences between people that can be attributed to genetic factors. It does not mean that these differences are innate or fixed. This point will be discussed in more detail later on in the chapter.

For now, the important thing to understand is that the concept of heritability is often misinterpreted. As a result of such misinterpretations, the crudest ideas have developed – for example, that people cannot study for an IQ test and improve their IQ test scores, or that children who perform badly in the first year of school will always struggle with academic achievements. Crude ideas tend to elicit strong responses from thinking members of the population, which in turn result in raging controversies. In essence, however, findings from intelligence research are usually far from controversial: they overwhelmingly show that intelligence differences – just like any other phenotypic differences – are a result of the interplay between genes and environments.

A working definition of intelligence

Let's have a go at answering the two questions raised in the previous section. The answer to the first is that we need intelligence for … everything. There is not a single task in the world that people can perform well without intelligence: no matter whether you are ordering coffee, writing an essay, or crossing the street, you always need to figure out how to do it. That is, you need intelligence to *adapt* to whatever challenge presents itself in your day-to-day activities. The answer to the second question (about the location of intelligence) is also straightforward: intelligence is located in the *brain*. Admittedly, some people claim that they think with their gut or that they are guided by their gut feelings but, really, they rely on their brains when it comes to crossing the street or studying for an exam, just like the rest of us. If we add these answers together, we can formulate a working definition of intelligence: the *adaptability of the brain*. This definition is broad and flexible because it is applicable across contexts and environments. Admittedly, it is not a very narrow definition of intelligence but that may be just fine for 'one of the most central phenomena in all of behavioural science'.

ACTIVITY 13.1

INTELLIGENCE IN EVERYDAY LANGUAGE

Think of all the terms that, in your opinion, define intelligence. Use a dictionary, if you want. Eliminate terms that have the same meaning as other words. Order the remaining terms in order of priority. Which term do you think is the most important in describing intelligence? Why?

SECTION SUMMARY

- Psychological traits that differ *between* and *within* people are referred to as 'dimensions of individual differences'.

- Intelligence affects a wide range of life outcomes, including achievement and health.

- Researchers have struggled to come up with a comprehensive consensus definition since the first scientific writings on intelligence, which date back to the 19th century.

- A consensus definition of intelligence was supported by 52 intelligence research experts in 1994. It emphasizes the ability to quickly comprehend and adapt to novel circumstances as a core aspect of intelligence but it excludes accumulated knowledge, experiences, and information.

HISTORY OF INTELLIGENCE

LEARNING OBJECTIVE 13.2

Describe the core advances in the history of intelligence research.

The idea that people differ in their mental abilities pre-dates the Roman Empire, but the first scientific investigation into intelligence is attributed to the Spanish physician Juan Huarte de San Juan, who published *Examen de ingenios para las sciencias* (loosely translated as *Examination of the Abilities for the Sciences*) in 1575 (Fernández-Ballesteros & Colom, 2004). Complete records of Huarte's works no longer exist but his 'examen' are considered to be the earliest scientific writings on intelligence, and in particular on testing intelligence.

The influence of Francis Galton

Intelligence originated as a discipline of scientific study in England. It was inspired by Charles Darwin's seminal publication *On the Origin of Species* (1859), which has formed the basis of our understanding of organisms' natural order and development to the present day. Darwin's work immediately had great influence, and it inspired one man in particular: Francis Galton, Darwin's younger half cousin (Fancher, 2009). On reading Darwin's book, Galton focused his scientific curiosity on 'heredity, talent and character' (Galton, 1865). Initially, he pursued a 'historiometric research' approach (see Research Methods 13.1) to the study of intelligence. He reviewed the family trees of eminent men who had made significant intellectual contributions to society. These genealogical investigations led Galton to conclude that exceptional intellectual achievement runs in families and is genetically transmitted from one generation to the next (Galton, 1869).

FOCUS POINT 13.2

SIR FRANCIS GALTON

Francis Galton was born 1822 in Birmingham to a wealthy and accomplished family. Galton started life as a child prodigy: he learned to read at the age of 2, and by the age of 5 he spoke some Latin and Greek. By the age of 6 he had moved on to reading adult literature, including Shakespeare. Today he is often described as a polymath, a person whose expertise spans a significant number of subject areas. In other words, Galton was a man of many talents (Fancher, 1985). First and foremost, Galton was a geographer and explorer; for example, in 1853 he was awarded the Royal Geographical Society's gold medal in recognition of his studies of Africa.

He subsequently wrote a best-selling travel guide – *The Art of Travel*, a handbook of practical advice for the Victorian on the move – which is still in print today. Galton's interests were not confined to geography, however. He was an adviser to Scotland Yard and suggested using the human fingerprint as a marker of personal identification. He laid the foundation of modern-day statistics by analysing **covariance** and introducing correlation and regression models. He was also interested in meteorology and prepared the first weather map that was published in a newspaper.

You can read more about Francis Galton **here**[1].

RESEARCH METHODS 13.1

HISTORIOMETRY

Historiometry is the statistical analysis of retrospective data. In other words, historiometric studies analyse data that have been extracted from historical accounts of people's lives. It is most commonly used as a method for studying individual differences in achievement across the lifespan. For example, if you wanted to know whether becoming a musical genius is associated with growing up in a musical family, you could look up all famous musicians and check their biographies to find information about the musicality of their families.

The method was first introduced by the Belgian mathematician Adolphe Quetelet (1796–1874), who sought to study the relationship between age and achievement by analysing the biographies of famous French and English playwrights. Historiometry became truly popular after Francis Galton applied it to find the origin of 'genius'. Specifically, he wanted to test whether genius is inherited or not.

In one study, Galton identified seminal British men throughout history using encyclopaedias, and he investigated their family trees. Galton found that these men, who made significant contributions to the development of humanity, often came from the same family dynasties. Based on this observation, Galton concluded that genius runs in families and that it is therefore inherited.

We know today that this is not necessarily true: when something runs in a family, it does not necessarily do so for genetic reasons but perhaps, instead, because of an environment that all family members are exposed to. That said, historiometry is nonetheless an interesting research method for the study of individual differences, and it continues to be used by researchers today.

Intelligence and academic performance

Galton was the first to suggest that there is an association between individual differences in intelligence and in academic performance, notably maths (please consider the quote that follows in the context of Galton's time – a time when few people went to university, when only men were admitted to study at Cambridge, and when men's intelligence was thought to be of a completely different quality from that of women):

> There can hardly be a surer evidence of the enormous difference between the intellectual capacity of men, than the prodigious differences in the numbers of marks obtained by those who gain mathematical honours at Cambridge. (Galton, 1869, p. 16)

Galton's theoretical link between intelligence and academic performance is remarkable because it continues to influence our understanding and measurement of intelligence. As discussed before, intelligence is best defined as the adaptability of the brain. Indeed, because of its generalist nature, this definition of intelligence does not refer to a specific context of adaptability, such as school or work. However, intelligence is often implicitly understood as a much narrower construct, in line with Galton's quote above. As a result, intelligence is frequently mistaken as referring to the adaptability of the brain *to school*. This idea is reflected by the nature of many intelligence tests that assess basic school knowledge and skills, such as primary verbal and numerical ability.

Although Galton was the first to proclaim that intelligence has something to do with mastering academic challenges, his own attempts to measure intelligence shared little resemblance with school-like assignments. Instead of administering exam-type tests, Galton established the Anthropometric Laboratory in London's Science Museum. Here, Galton measured people on all sorts of characteristics – including physical traits such as height and weight, but also reaction time and sensory perception – to find out more about their individual differences. For example, in one test, Galton presented his participants with a box covered on one side with a dark cloth. Participants had to reach into the box underneath the cloth and identify through touch the object inside the box without being able to see it. Over the years, Galton collected a vast amount of data from thousands of people but they were of limited use for his studies of intelligence. Galton did not find systematic associations between his measures and, as a result, his contributions to intelligence research remain largely theoretical. By comparison, his achievements in related disciplines, especially in statistical methodology, behavioural genetics, and twin studies, have found greater practical applications in modern research.

The first intelligence test

The test that later became known as the first intelligence test was developed in France by Professor Alfred Binet and his assistant Théodore Simon. They had been commissioned by the French Department of Education to develop a test that would help to identify children who struggled in school and who had learning difficulties. These children were then to receive extra tutoring to improve their school performance. The fact that children could have learning problems had only been recognized recently, after the introduction of compulsory schooling in the 1880s and 1890s. Prior to that, most people had not attended school, with the exception perhaps of Sunday school. They had also not been required to learn reading, writing, or arithmetic. Only after schools had been established and it was mandatory for everybody to attend did children's differences in academic performance become evident.

Binet and Simon were experts on abnormal child development and they had studied children's cognitive growth and intellectual deficits for many years. Based on their research background, Simon and Binet were ideally suited to the development of a test that would differentiate normally developing children from those who were intellectually challenged. After conducting preliminary studies, they introduced a set of 30 test items that formed the core of their test (Binet & Simon, 1905/1961). The items were matched to children's ages and increased in difficulty. For example, at the age of 3, a test item asked children to point to their own nose. At age 4, children had to recognize and name objects, such as a knife or desk. By the age of 7, the children were asked to describe a scene from a picture that they were shown and to complete sentences so that they were logical and accurate. The children's intellectual level was then judged according to the number of items that they had solved correctly. For example, a child who was aged 6 years and correctly completed all three items for age 6 and two items for age 7 was said to have a mental age of 6.6 years.

The Binet–Simon scale

Binet and Simon's test was a simple but practical measure of children's learning (dis)ability that allowed a quick differentiation of normally developing children from those with cognitive deficits. In line with the test's purpose, the test items corresponded to skills required in the context of school, which Binet and Simon were careful to highlight. For example, one item asked children to draw simple patterns from memory, just as they would draw letters from memory when learning the alphabet. Another example was defining objects in brief sentences, which showed a child's ability to recognize and summarize information. In other words, then, Binet and Simon referred to the test as an intelligence test but understood it as a measure of school-related abilities (i.e. scholastic abilities) rather than of general intelligence.

After publishing the test, Binet and Simon debated whether tests could be standardized to the extent that they could be used for all children, regardless of their educational and cultural background. They authored a vast number of articles together that, among other things, discussed the proposition that children's intelligence development may be too **heterogeneous** for one standardized test to work well. However, they described their intelligence test as a good marker for what French children had learned up to the moment of testing in comparison to their peers. Despite this, Binet and Simon were unsure whether the test could forecast children's future intelligence. They also agreed that the test was probably not accurate for children who were born and raised outside France (i.e. in other cultures). Most of Binet and Simon's careful consideration and caution was soon brushed aside by a series of events. First, Henry Goddard, an ambitious American student who had read Galton's studies on talent and genius, came across the French intelligence test during his travels in Europe. Goddard thought the test was an excellent instrument to test what he called 'innate intelligence' and translated the 'Binet–Simon Scale' into English (see Gould, 1981, for a review). He took the test to the United States, where it was widely used and from where it was eventually sent on to England, the home of Darwin and Galton and, thus, the new discipline of intelligence.

USES OF INTELLIGENCE TESTS

Intelligence tests are used today in a variety of areas. Perhaps the most obvious application is in school and educational settings, the context in which the first intelligence test was developed. Here, intelligence tests are applied to determine children's readiness for school or their suitability for a certain type of school. Also, intelligence tests are used to monitor children's learning and to identify potential learning disabilities. In a similar vein, intelligence tests are used in occupational settings, such as in assessment centres that seek to identify the most suitable candidates for a job.

A second field of application for intelligence tests is in the diagnosis of health problems. For example, specially developed intelligence tests are used to test whether people's cognitive ageing is healthy or whether they may suffer from a form of dementia. Likewise, intelligence tests are administered in psychiatric settings, where they are one of many factors that contribute to formulating a diagnosis.

Finally, intelligence tests are widely used in research settings, and not necessarily in the context of intelligence research. For example, they are typically administered to children in studies that investigate autism and cognitive, social, and psychological development.

TEST YOURSELF

1. What was Francis Galton's role in intelligence research?
2. Describe the first intelligence test in your own words: How and where was it developed? What items did the test include? Who and what was the test for?

SECTION SUMMARY

- The first theories of intelligence and, with that, the foundation of intelligence as a scientific discipline originated in England through the writings of Sir Francis Galton.

- Early on, intelligence was thought to vary between people, to be associated with people's differences in academic performance, and to be genetically influenced.

- The first measurement tool for assessing individual differences in intelligence came from France, where it was used to detect children with learning disabilities. Since then, intelligence tests have been implemented across the globe, in educational settings and a variety of other contexts.

MODERN INTELLIGENCE TESTS

LEARNING OBJECTIVE 13.3

Describe and compare the main types of, and differences between, the commonly used modern intelligence tests.

Since Binet and Simon's first test, a lot of progress has been made in the design of intelligence tests. As a result, a wide range of intelligence tests are in use today. Although modern intelligence tests share many characteristics with their ancestors, they also differ from previous tests, as well as from each other, in some aspects.

Similarities in intelligence tests

First, all intelligence tests differentiate between the people who take the test. In other words, test takers typically obtain a range of different scores on an intelligence test. This occurs because some people solve an item correctly while others provide an incorrect solution. Think of it the other way around: a test item that everybody solves correctly, just like an item that nobody manages to solve correctly, does not discriminate between people because everybody gets the same score. If you had a test that only included items that everybody could solve correctly, everybody would get a perfect score. As a result, there would be no individual differences – the test score would be a constant. This may seem like a self-evident point but it is of great importance: intelligence tests imply finding differences between people. Specifically, they quantify those differences and infer a rank order of people's position according to their different scores.

A second shared characteristic of intelligence tests is that they meet statistical criteria that determine a test's 'construct validity' (see Focus Point 13.4), including reliability and concurrent and predictive validity (Cronbach & Meehl, 1955). Reliability refers to a test score's stability across different assessment occasions and methods. Concurrent validity is the extent to which two or more tests of the same construct overlap or correlate. For example, test scores from two different maths tests should be highly positively correlated if they both measure a person's ability to solve maths problems. Predictive validity refers to the degree to which a test score is associated with an outcome – for example, the degree to which intelligence test scores predict school grades. Reliability and validity are required elements of construct validity but neither is sufficient to confirm a test's quality.

CONSTRUCT VALIDITY

Lee Cronbach (1916–2001), an American educational psychologist (and, yes, the guy who invented Cronbach's alpha) wrote in 1955, together with Paul Meehl (1920–2003), a leading philosopher of science, the most influential article on construct validity: 'Construct Validity in Psychological Tests'. According to this article, construct validity is a summary term that describes a series of statistical tests. These tests are conducted to establish whether a measurement instrument – for example, an intelligence test – is of good quality. The idea of construct validity is best illustrated using an example.

Imagine that we have developed a new intelligence test that presents participants with a series of complex drawings that they have to remember and redraw by hand from memory. For every correctly redrawn drawing, the participant gets a point. To ensure that this new test truly measures intelligence, we need to test a series of hypotheses about the test. If we can confirm these hypotheses, the test will have shown itself to be of good quality as an intelligence test.

A first hypothesis is that the IQ test is reliable. In other words, people should obtain the same scores on this test across different measurement occasions. To check whether this is true, we might administer the same test to a group of people twice, perhaps once today (time 1) and again in 3 weeks (time 2). We can then compare people's scores across time, by correlating the scores at time 1 and time 2. This is known as 'test–retest reliability'. If the test scores correlate highly across two time points, we can be sure that the test measures a stable dimension of individual differences.

A second hypothesis is that the test scores resemble scores from other, previously established intelligence tests. In particular, we would expect a significant positive correlation between the scores from our new test and other measures: after all, each of them is supposed to assess the same thing – intelligence. To test this, we might administer three intelligence tests, including our new one and two others, to a group of people. We could then calculate the correlations between the three test scores. If the correlations are high, our test will have 'concurrent validity'. Concurrent validity marks the extent to which two or more measures of the same construct (i.e. intelligence) overlap.

A third hypothesis is that our new test has 'criterion-related validity' or 'predictive validity'. That is, the IQ scores are expected to predict specific outcomes, such as school grades. To test the predictive validity of our test, we might correlate its scores with the grades that a group of students obtained in their final year of school. If there is a meaningful relationship between the test scores and grades, we will conclude that our test is predictive of scholastic achievement.

There are many more hypotheses that can be tested to establish construct validity. That said, the three hypotheses outlined above are central to establishing construct validity. It is important to remember that construct validity is not a single method or statistic. Instead, it is a scientific process of hypothesis testing. Or, as Cronbach and Meehl (1955) stated, 'in essence the best construct is the one around which we can build the greatest number of inferences, in the most direct fashion' (p. 288).

A third characteristic common to IQ tests is that their scores can be compared. To this end, IQ scores are typically transformed into a normal distribution, also known as a **bell curve**, with a mean of 100 IQ points and a standard deviation of 15 IQ points (Figure 13.1). The majority of people score between plus and minus one standard

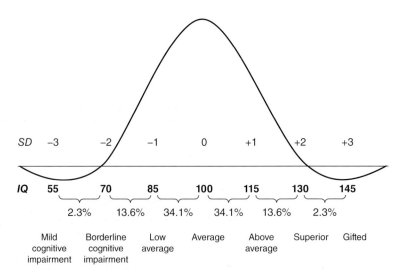

FIGURE 13.1 *A bell curve of IQ scores with standard deviations. It shows the normal distribution of IQ scores, which have a mean of 100 and a standard deviation (SD) of 15. Thus, if your IQ is 100, you have 'average' intelligence, whereas an IQ of 130 shows superior intelligence and an IQ of 70 signals mental disability.*

deviation on an intelligence test. To be exact, that makes 68.2% of people who have an IQ score between 85 and 115 points. Fewer people score at the lower and upper ends of the IQ score distribution. It is important to remember that this bell curve, with a mean of 100 and a standard deviation of 15, is not a naturally occurring score system. Instead, IQ scores from different test batteries are transformed to match this distribution, which allows a comparison of IQ scores across measurement instruments and testing occasions.

Differences in intelligence tests

Notwithstanding their similarities, intelligence tests also differ in important ways. For example, tests differ in their scope, format, length, and complexity. Also, there are various ways of administering intelligence tests: some require a trained tester who examines each test taker individually, and some can be completed by groups of people, usually under supervised exam conditions. Finally, some tests are copyright protected and can only be used on payment of a licensing fee; others are freely available.

The most striking difference between intelligence tests, however, is rooted in the types of items that they are made up of. Some tests consist of multiple-choice knowledge questions, others assess pattern recognition, and some tests present test takers with an adaptation of a real-life problem that they have to solve. In addition, some measurements of intelligence do not require people to fill in a test but, instead, involve biological measures being taken that are thought to signify individual differences in intelligence. An example is reaction time – specifically, the time it takes you to respond to a stimulus. People's differences in reaction time correlate significantly with other intelligence test scores – in other words, smarter people are also faster.

FOCUS POINT 13.5

IQ TESTS

Intelligence tests differ in their content and the nature of their items. Here, we will look at examples of three popular formats of intelligence tests.

1. VERBAL REASONING

Verbal reasoning tests tend to assess people's vocabulary as well as their ability to reason abstractly about the relationships and nature of the terms included in an item. In the following example, the aim is to identify the pair of words that correctly completes the statement. In this case, drink is to water as eat is to bread, so c is the correct answer and is underlined:

	is to water	as eat is to
a	continue	drive
b	foot	enemy
c	drink	bread
d	girl	industry
e	drink	enemy

A very popular verbal reasoning test is the Miller Analogies Test, which predicts academic and job performance (Kuncel, Hezlett, & Ones, 2004). In the next example, the aim is to choose the word that has a relationship with the word 'mason' that is most comparable to the relationship between 'carpenter' and 'wood'. The answer is *c*, which is underlined:

mason/?: carpenter/wood

a   iron

b   chisel

c̲   stone

d   building

2. MATRIX REASONING

Matrix reasoning tests are thought to be one of the best and purest measures of intelligence, because they do not require an understanding of language. Thus, they are thought to be culture-free tests that can be used to assess people from different countries and backgrounds on intelligence.

In a matrix reasoning text, you typically see a 3 x 3 grid with one entry missing. You are then given several answer options and have to choose the one that logically completes the grid.

3. PROCESSING SPEED

Processing speed tests evaluate how quickly people can process a lot of information that is often relatively meaningless. Thus, processing speed tests are not strictly about the ability to reason or to identify the correct solution in a complex task. Instead, they present a bulk of almost unmanageable information and ask test takers to shift through it as quickly as possible.

Here is an example of a processing speed task. Participants see two columns of strings of letters and numbers. Two opposing strings may be the same or differ in one element. Test takers have to mark as quickly as possible the pairs of strings that are identical. The key to processing tests is that they are very strictly timed: typically, test takers only have a few seconds to work through the task, making it almost impossible to get full scores.

Indicate all pairs that are equal	
856592153494	856592153494
QMA3FV2UMPAX	QMA3FV2UMPAX
AE97QUUTC19J	JE97QUUTC19J
P3820KLWGWIK	P3820KLWGW1K
238520682562	238520682562
885951737386	885951737286
MZX5EE01DGIJ	MZX5EE01DGIJ
LC2N1AZQ1GRR	LC2N1AZQ1GR4
280000520610	280000520610
ZIISENDZXV10	ZI1SENDZXV10

Source: Adapted from screen of moo-Q smartphone app.

Considering the diverse nature of intelligence tests, a new question emerges: Do all these different tests measure different kinds of intelligence? Or is it possible to use different tests to measure the same thing? In other words, do all these different tests have sufficient concurrent validity to claim that they measure the same construct (i.e. intelligence)? We will address this question in the next section.

DISCUSSION POINT

Discuss which intelligence tests are considered 'culture-free' and what features make them so.

SECTION SUMMARY

- A wide range of intelligence tests are in use today.
- All intelligence tests aim towards differentiating between the people who take the test.
- Intelligence tests quantify differences between people and infer a rank order of people's positions according to their different scores.
- Reliability and validity are required elements of construct validity but neither is sufficient to confirm a test's quality.
- Scores from different tests can be compared by transforming them into IQ scores, which have a mean of 100 and a standard deviation of 15. Intelligence tests differ substantially in the ways in which they are administered, structured, and compiled.
- In spite of the differences, many tests are considered valid measures of intelligence.

FACTORS OF INTELLIGENCE

LEARNING OBJECTIVE 13.4

Define and describe the latent structure of intelligence and its factors.

Now that we have discussed the definition of intelligence as a theoretical construct and the origin of intelligence tests, an additional question arises: What is the structure of intelligence? Is it one general entity or does it comprise many different kinds of intelligence? Considering that intelligence tests are vastly different, do they also assess different kinds of intelligence? Or are the tests similar enough to tap the same construct? We might also wonder whether intelligence follows a hierarchical structure, with more important intelligences at the top and less valued ones at the lower levels.

Two observations will help us in answering these questions. The first one has already been discussed: people differ between one another in intelligence (i.e. interpersonal **variance**). That is, some score high, some score low, and some score somewhere in between. Two or three people may even have the same score but the same score will never be had by everybody. Thus, there is variance in intelligence test scores. Second, people differ not only from one another in intelligence but also within themselves (i.e. intrapersonal variance): some do better in certain types of tests, such as map reading, and not so well in others, such as solving multiple-choice questions. If you think about your own abilities, you will probably be aware that you do better in some areas and worse in others: for example, many people think of themselves as being either science oriented or language focused. However, very rarely do people report that they excel in both areas or, beyond that, that they are equally skilled across many areas and contexts.

Two logical conclusions follow from the observations that there is inter- and intrapersonal variance in intelligence. First, if the interpersonal variance (differences between people) is greater than the intrapersonal variance (differences within people), then intelligence is one general entity (i.e. general intelligence). In other words, if differences in intelligence are greater between people than within them, then the intelligence scores from different IQ test batteries will be positively correlated. Conversely, if the intrapersonal variance in intelligence is greater than the interpersonal variance, then intelligence comprises several entities (i.e. multiple intelligences). Here, intelligence scores would not be correlated across tests. So, what is greater – the intelligence differences that we observe between people or those that we see within them?

The g-factor

The somewhat counterintuitive answer is that intelligence differences between people are greater than the differences within them. As a result, scores from different intelligence tests – for example, tests of mathematical and verbal intelligence – are positively correlated. That is, people who do well in one test also do well in any other intelligence test relative to the other test takers. Intuitively, this finding seems odd because we often think of our own abilities in terms of weaknesses and strengths. We typically believe that we are good at doing some tests and worse at others. We are wrong: we overestimate our intrapersonal differences and underestimate how much we differ from other people.

The positive **correlations** between intelligence test scores are referred to as **common variance**. Common variance refers to the intelligence differences between people that are common to all tests (Kline, 2000). Common variance in intelligence test scores is labelled as the general factor of intelligence (the g-factor or just g). This name combines the empirical observation that intelligence is general and the statistical method that helps in identifying the common variance, namely **factor analysis**. Factor analysis was pioneered by Charles Spearman (1863–1945), an English psychologist, who had studied under Wilhelm Wundt in Leipzig and was also strongly influenced by Galton's ideas. In his research, Spearman observed a group of schoolboys and found that all their grades and test scores were positively correlated. Specifically, Spearman studied the boys' scholastic performance across different academic subjects, including not only writing, reading, and arithmetic but also sports and music. He also tested the boys on a series of measures that he had developed himself, which assessed individual differences in sensory perception and processing – for example, the boys' ability to spot a stimulus. Spearman found that all the test scores, regardless of whether they had been assessed through school exams or by his own psychological tests, correlated positively with each other. In search of a method that would enable him to quantify the common variance in the test scores, Spearman developed factor analysis. He described factor analysis and the theory of the general intelligence factor (g) in a seminal article published in *The American Journal of Psychology* in 1904.

FOCUS POINT 13.6

PREDICTIVE VALIDITY OF *G*

What things does general intelligence predict? Because intelligence is 'one of the most central phenomena in all of behavioural science, with broad explanatory powers' (Jensen, 1998, p. xii), perhaps a better question is, what does it not predict?

Intelligence has been shown to influence all sorts of life outcomes. Some of these are relatively straightforward and predictable, such as educational attainment, job performance, income, physical and psychological health, health behaviours such as smoking and alcohol consumption, and longevity. But other outcomes under the influence of intelligence are less intuitive, such as marital stability, height, attractiveness, and even sperm quality (see Deary, 2012, for a comprehensive review paper on intelligence's associations). Let's take a look at a specific study on longevity as an example.

The best research about the predictive validity of intelligence is longitudinal in nature. Longitudinal studies test a representative sample of people on intelligence when they are comparatively young, namely in childhood. These children are then observed as they grow up and go through adulthood, and data are recorded about their lives. Using statistical models, we can then test whether and to what extent general intelligence in childhood is associated with later life outcomes.

One famous study of this kind is the Aberdeen Cohort Study from Scotland, whose participants were born in 1921. As part of the Scottish Mental Survey, which is described in detail in the later section 'The Lothian Birth Cohort 1921', they completed an intelligence test when they were 11 years old (in 1932). Six decades later, researchers from the universities of Edinburgh and Aberdeen traced the study participants and recorded their survival status until January 1997, when they were aged 76. Of the participants who were traced, 1,084 had died and 1,101 were alive (Whalley & Deary, 2001). Those who had died by 1997 had had an average IQ of 97.7 points at age 11. By comparison, those alive in 1997 had had an average IQ of 102 when they were children. In other words, smarter kids live longer.

Another way of looking at the relationship between IQ and survival is illustrated by the graphs below. The lighter shapes represent the top quartile of IQ – that is, the 25% of the sample that scored best in the IQ test at age 11. The darker shapes represent the bottom quartile of IQ – that is, the 25% of the sample who performed worst in the IQ test.

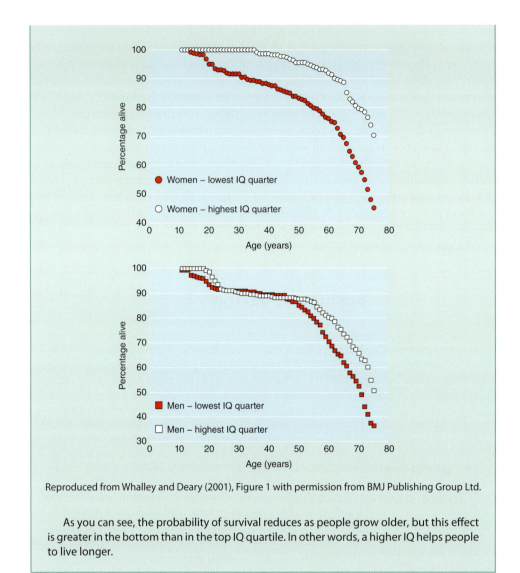

Reproduced from Whalley and Deary (2001), Figure 1 with permission from BMJ Publishing Group Ltd.

As you can see, the probability of survival reduces as people grow older, but this effect is greater in the bottom than in the top IQ quartile. In other words, a higher IQ helps people to live longer.

Latent traits

The *g*-factor is a statistical construct that refers to an entity that cannot be directly observed. It is a so-called **latent trait** that describes an implicit behavioural characteristic (MacCallum & Browne, 1993). Think of it this way: we can observe intelligent behaviour but we cannot observe intelligence per se. In other words, we can record people's intelligence test scores, and based on such records we can make inferences about people's intelligence.

We thereby assume that intelligence drives people's performance in the various intelligence tests and that the test scores' positive correlation reflects this common 'intelligence' driver. Another example of latent traits is personality traits, such as anxiety. Unlike observing hair colour or height, we cannot observe a person's anxiety directly; we can only observe anxious behaviours or demonstrations of anxious performance. For example, depending on your level of anxiety, you might sleep well or not so well the night before an exam. Likewise, depending on your level of anxiety, you may be more or less prepared to quit a job you dislike without having lined up a new one. As psychologists, we can measure the number of hours you slept before an exam and the number of days that passed before you quit your job. Based on these measures we can then draw a conclusion about your latent trait of anxiety, which we cannot observe directly but whose consequences we see in your behaviour.

ACTIVITY 13.2

LINKING LATENT TRAITS AND OBSERVABLE BEHAVIOURS

Think of a latent trait that describes individual differences between people but cannot be directly observed. Come up with various behavioural manifestations of that trait (i.e. behaviours that you could observe) and think of other ways to measure individual differences in this trait. If you cannot think of an example, try this one: curiosity.

Just one factor?

Spearman's work continues to inspire researchers to the present day but it particularly intrigued two men, who subsequently advanced factor analysis and our understanding of intelligence. One was the aforementioned Raymond Cattell, a British-born psychologist and student of Spearman, who worked at several universities including Columbia and Harvard. In 1941, Cattell gave a much noted conference presentation in which he outlined that intelligence is better thought of in terms of two factors rather than one. He labelled these two factors **fluid intelligence** and **crystallized intelligence**, with fluid intelligence referring to pure reasoning power and crystallized intelligence to the information and experiences that an individual accumulates or learns over time (Cattell, 1943). This idea had been summed up even earlier: 'Intelligence, then, involves two factors, – the capacity for knowledge and knowledge possessed' (Hemnon, 1921, p. 195).

Another psychologist who was inspired by Spearman was Louis Thurstone (1887–1955), who worked at the universities of Chicago and North Carolina. Thurstone was a psychometrician and focused on developing new methods of factor analysis. Through this work, Thurstone became convinced that Spearman's unitary conception of intelligence – that is, Spearman's focus on only one factor – was inaccurate. Instead, Thurstone formulated a model of intelligence that built on seven 'primary mental abilities'. He considered these primary mental abilities to be relatively independent factors that exist next to each other (Thurstone, 1938). In other words, Thurstone believed that there are seven equally important factors of intelligence rather than just one. The seven intelligences, or primary factors of ability, according to Thurstone are (1) verbal comprehension, (2) word fluency, (3) number facility, (4) spatial visualization, (5) associative memory, (6) perceptual speed, and (7) reasoning. However, in his later studies, Thurstone could not confirm that the seven primary abilities were entirely separate. Instead, he found that they were all positively correlated because of an underlying latent trait: a general intelligence factor – Spearman's *g*! Thurstone pressed on with his research in statistics to find a mathematical solution for the apparently contradictory findings. He developed new factor-analytic techniques that allowed the modelling of variances with a general intelligence factor as well as with seven specific abilities. In line with this statistical model, Thurstone reformulated his theory of intelligence, introducing for the first time the notion that intelligence had a hierarchical structure. Since then, Thurstone's findings have served many researchers as a starting point for the study of intelligence. To the present day, hierarchical models of intelligence are generally accepted as the most accurate representation of variances in intelligence test scores.

The three-stratum model

The most comprehensive study on the psychometric structure of intelligence to date was conducted by John Bissell Carroll (1916–2003), who was one of the 52 experts in intelligence research who signed the consensus definition first published in 1994 in the *Wall Street Journal*. Starting in the 1960s when he was a professor at Harvard, Carroll aggregated other researchers' datasets that included people's intelligence test scores on a variety of cognitive measures. After his official retirement as director of the Thurstone Psychometric Laboratory at the University of North Carolina in 1979, Carroll began to review more than 1,500 such datasets. He selected the ones with the highest quality, and this resulted in 461 datasets collected from a wide range of samples, including children, college students, adults, ageing populations, the physically disabled, and the cognitively impaired. It took Carroll more than 20 years, and for most of this time he was emeritus professor, to reanalyse this wealth of data and formulate his 'three-stratum theory of intelligence' (Carroll, 1993).

At the core of Carroll's theory is the observation that intelligence is hierarchical, with three levels. The general factor (*g*) sits at the top level, also referred to as the third stratum, of the hierarchy. At the second-stratum level, nine broad factors of cognitive ability are assembled, including fluid and crystallized intelligence but also auditory perception and processing speed (Figure 13.2). At the third level, which is

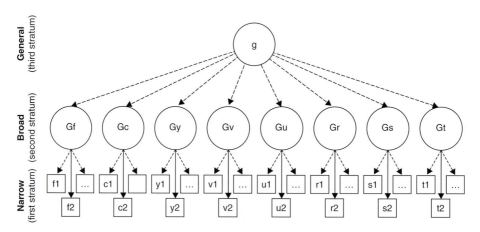

FIGURE 13.2 *The three-stratum model. Second-stratum factors are ordered in correspondence to the decreasing strength of their association with g from left to right. Factors in the first stratum are only indicated by letters and numbers; for example, y1 under Gy might refer to digit recall. g = general factor of intelligence; Gf = fluid intelligence; Gc = crystallized intelligence; Gy = general memory and learning; Gv = broad visual perception; Gu = broad auditory perception; Gr = broad retrieval ability; Gs = broad cognitive speediness; Gt = processing speed.*

Source: Adapted from Carroll (1993).

also referred to as the first stratum, narrow cognitive abilities are listed, for example reading ability and the ability to discriminate sounds.

The three-stratum model of intelligence is thought to be the best representation of variances in intelligence test scores. As such, it refers largely to the structure of intelligence differences that exist between people but less so to intrapersonal variances in intelligence. It is therefore not possible to estimate how much of an individual person's intelligence is explained by general (third-stratum), broad (second-stratum), or narrow (first-stratum) abilities. Instead, these factors refer to proportions of interpersonal variances – in other words, the amount of differences between people – that can be bundled to specific intelligence factors. In general, the three-stratum model implies that intelligence is a domain-general characteristic, with people doing well in one task also doing well in others. However, it never accounts for all intelligence variances and, thus, it is always possible for people to do exceptionally well in one task or IQ test and less so in a different one, even if it occurs rarely.

Recent models of the structure of intelligence

Carroll published his findings in 1993 in a seminal book called *Human Cognitive Abilities: A Survey of Factor-Analytic Studies*. Although no other researcher has since undertaken comparable efforts to identify the structure of human cognitive ability, the topic continues to attract a lot of interest. Most recently, Tom Bouchard, a professor at the University of Minnesota, and his former PhD student Wendy Johnson, who works at the University of Edinburgh, wrote several articles on the structure of intelligence (e.g. Johnson & Bouchard, 2005). In one study, they analysed scores from 436 adult individuals who had completed 42 intelligence tests. The results were only partially in line with Carroll's model of intelligence. In particular, Johnson and Bouchard identified a hierarchical structure with a *g*-factor at the top level, just like Carroll, but their second- and third-stratum factors were different from Carroll's model. Johnson and Bouchard found evidence for only three second-stratum factors, not nine as previously proposed (Carroll, 1993); they labelled the three verbal, perceptual, and image rotation.

Critique of structural models of intelligence

The structure of human cognitive ability is an interesting and important question. However, factor-analytic methods can only contribute so much to finding an answer to this issue. Factor analysis is predominantly a statistical method that summarizes observed information. It is used to group observed variances into different latent factor dimensions – for example, fluid and crystallized intelligence. This grouping depends inevitably on the types of test scores included in the analysis.

Let us go over this point using an example: imagine that we administer three different tests of verbal ability to a group of participants – for example, word recognition, vocabulary, and reading speed. All test scores will be highly positively correlated because they tap the same construct space, namely verbal ability. We then administer two more tests that do not measure verbal ability but instead auditory perception. Let's say one tests individual differences in the ability to rhythmically tap along to a song and the other one measures how quickly people recognize a song when it's played to them. The scores from these tests will correlate positively with the verbal ability scores, as predicted by Spearman's general factor of intelligence, *g*. However, the correlations between auditory scores and verbal scores will be lower than the correlations between just the three verbal test scores. Likewise, the correlation between the two auditory tests will be greater than the correlation between auditory and verbal tests. The reason is that two auditory tests assess very similar abilities and, thus, they share a lot of common variance.

However, an auditory and a verbal test assess somewhat different abilities and so they have less variance in common. In a factor analysis, two latent factors would then emerge: one that captures all common variance between the verbal ability tests and one that captures the common variance within the auditory test scores. While this finding makes perfect sense statistically, it would be a bold claim to conclude that human intelligence is just verbal and auditory. As these are the only two aspects measured, what could we possibly know about other components of intelligence? In short, factor analysis is not a miraculously wise method that helps you to discover a mysterious structure. Instead, it is a very practical tool that summarizes directly observed variables – and what a summary then looks like depends very much on the information that was there to be summarized in the first place. As a consequence, factor analysis will only yield reliable and informative results about the structure of intelligence if a wide range of abilities is observed. Carroll's work followed this approach and his review of abilities and ability test scores is to date the most extensive. We may therefore consider Carroll's findings as particularly informative and of greater importance than other, more limited attempts to explain observed variances in intelligence test scores.

TEST YOURSELF

1. What is the three-stratum model of intelligence?
2. What is the *g*-factor?

SECTION SUMMARY

- Intelligence test scores are positively interrelated: people who do well in one test, such as a vocabulary test, will also do well in another test, such as a memory task.

- The correlations between people's test scores are greater for tests that require similar skills, such as a vocabulary and a word-fluency test.

- People's similarities in test scores are known as common variance.

- Common variance in turn is identified by factor analysis, which produces latent factors.

- Many researchers have asked how many latent factors there are in intelligence but no unanimous answer has been found to date.

- That said, the general research consensus is that there is one general factor of intelligence – factor *g* – that can be identified in any set of IQ scores.

- We can link this finding of a general factor to the theoretical notion that intelligence is 'a very general mental capability' (Gottfredson, 1994, p. 13) or the adaptability of the brain.

INTELLIGENCE DEVELOPMENT

Intelligence can differ within (intrapersonal variance) and between (interpersonal variance) people. Development in intelligence is studied by looking at change and stability in both interpersonal and intrapersonal variance. An example of intrapersonal variance in intelligence is when a person takes the same test twice – for example, today and in 2 years' time – and achieves different scores at each measurement occasion (the same approach as test–retest reliability, described above). Interpersonal or between-person variances occur in groups, not in individuals, when the rank order of intelligence test scores changes across two measurement occasions. Here, the change is relative: a person's absolute score may be the same across both measurement occasions (i.e. zero intrapersonal variance) but the person's rank position relative to the other test takers differs over time. The two core questions that underlie research on intelligence development are: (1) How does intelligence change as a characteristic over time? And (2) do some people become smarter than others as they grow older?

Intrapersonal stability and change: Fluid and crystallized intelligence

Within a person, intelligence is both stable and flexible across the lifespan. The changes that occur over time depend on the type of intelligence, or the factor of intelligence. Earlier in this chapter, we discussed two specific intelligence factors, namely fluid and crystallized intelligence (Cattell, 1943). Fluid intelligence peaks in young adulthood, around the age of 21 years, and declines steadily thereafter. By comparison, crystallized intelligence increases throughout adulthood and reaches its peak at the age of 60 years. Furthermore, crystallized intelligence remains relatively stable at a high level throughout old age (Figure 13.3).

Crystallized intelligence is typically assessed with measures of vocabulary, language skills, and word knowledge. Scores in these measures are representative of the information that a person has learned previously (see the Miller Analogies Test in Focus Point 13.5 as an example). In addition, crystallized intelligence is thought to indicate a person's knowledge and experiences – for example, their academic studies and occupational expertise. As fluid intelligence declines over time and crystallized intelligence increases, intelligence changes occur within the person. The observation of intrapersonal changes in intelligence that correspond to changes in age has informed many developmental theories of intelligence.

In this context, a famous theory is the intelligence-as-process, personality, interests, and intelligence-as-knowledge theory, in short the PPIK theory (Ackerman, 1996) (Figure 13.4). 'Intelligence-as-process' closely resembles fluid intelligence and refers to the intellectual capacity that a person can apply to learning. 'Intelligence-as-knowledge' refers to crystallized intelligence and accumulated knowledge. The PPIK

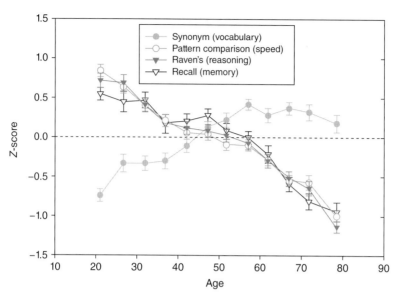

FIGURE 13.3 *Age-related changes in cognitive ability. The fluid intelligence measures of processing speed, reasoning, and memory show substantial, fairly linear declines from the age of 20 onwards. By comparison, vocabulary test scores increase with age, although overall to a lesser extent. 'Raven's' refers to Raven's Matrices, a popular nonverbal reasoning test that asks participants to identify the missing element that completes a pattern or matrix. See 'Matrix Reasoning' in Focus Point 13.5 for more details.*

Source: Adapted from Salthouse (2004).

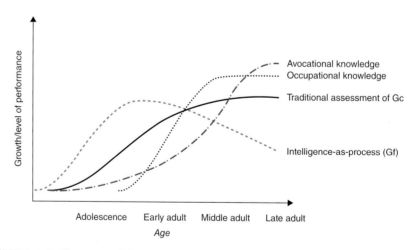

FIGURE 13.4 *An illustration of the development of intelligence according to Ackerman's PPIK (intelligence-as-process, personality, interests, and intelligence-as-knowledge) theory. Intelligence-as-process peaks in early adulthood and declines thereafter. Intelligence-as-knowledge, including crystallized intelligence, occupational knowledge, and avocational knowledge, increases throughout adulthood and only peaks in later life. Gc = crystallized intelligence; Gf = fluid intelligence.*

Source: Adapted from Ackerman (1996), with permission from Elsevier.

theory suggests that intelligence-as-process develops into intelligence-as-knowledge over time. This development is thought to be guided by personality traits and interests (Ackerman, 1996). Specifically, personality and interests are likely to determine where, when, and how people invest in their intelligence and thus accumulate knowledge. Here, the personality trait curiosity plays an important role (von Stumm, Hell, & Chamorro-Premuzic, 2011). Curious people seek out and engage in learning opportunities, because they enjoy cognitive challenges. Furthermore, curious people use their fluid intelligence to access and process new information that in turn helps them to enrich their intelligence-as-knowledge. Therefore, curiosity describes a principal hunger for knowledge and information. By comparison, interests guide the investment of fluid intelligence with regard to specific topic areas. For example, some people are interested in science and technology, and others are more captivated by arts and aesthetics. A person with a particular interest will apply their abilities to a greater extent to pursue knowledge in that area of interest than elsewhere. That is not to say that scientists and artists cannot be equally curious – both are hungry for knowledge, just different kinds of it. As a consequence, artists and scientists will become experts in different knowledge areas and thereby interpersonal differences may arise in addition to the intrapersonal differences.

Interpersonal stability and change

People change within themselves in intelligence over time but they can also change relative to each other. That is, individual differences in intelligence may change over time with some people improving and some people declining relative to others. Interpersonal variance is also known as rank-order (in)stability. Think of a correlation between intelligence test scores from a group of people that were assessed at two different time points – for example, today and in 3 weeks' time. If the correlation is 1, all people in the study sample scored exactly the same relative to one another at both times. Figure 13.5 illustrates this point: all three people change in intelligence over time – they all decline (intrapersonal variance) – but their relationship to one another remains the same at each time point. By contrast, in Figure 13.6, intelligence changes over time within each person and, in addition, each person also changes relative to the others: person 1 (P1) mostly declines, while person 2 (P2) mostly increases in

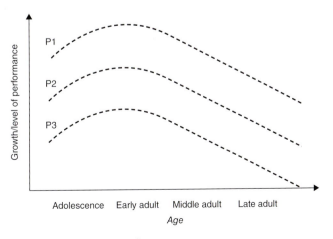

FIGURE 13.5 *Interpersonal stability in intelligence.*

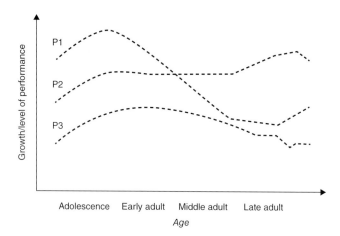

FIGURE 13.6 *Interpersonal change in intelligence.*

intelligence compared with the others. This change between people is then interpersonal variance.

Individual differences in intelligence are thought to be fairly stable across the lifespan (Deary, 2012). In line with this hypothesis, many studies have tested correlations of intelligence test scores at two or more points in time (see Research Methods 13.2). These studies typically find that intelligence scores are strongly, positively correlated over time, suggesting that the rank order of intelligence is largely stable over time. We will next look at a very famous study from Scotland that investigated the stability of intelligence (see also Focus Point 13.6).

RESEARCH METHODS 13.2

CROSS-SECTIONAL AND LONGITUDINAL STUDIES

Change and stability in individual differences are studied using cross-sectional and longitudinal research methods. In a **cross-sectional** study, all data are collected at one point in time. For example, a cross-sectional study on age-related differences in intelligence will test a group of people and assess their intelligence and age. Using the collected data, intelligence test scores and age can then be correlated to test whether a relationship exists between the two variables. For example, we would expect to find a negative correlation between age and fluid intelligence because older people do slightly worse in fluid ability tests than younger people.

In a **longitudinal study**, data are collected across two or more points in time. For example, a longitudinal study on age-related differences in intelligence will test a group of people on intelligence this year and again in 2 years' time. We can then compare whether people did better or worse this year in comparison with the next test in 2 years' time. If they do worse at the later assessment time, we might conclude that age has a negative effect on intelligence test performance. Longitudinal studies can include participants who were all born in the same year (i.e. a cohort study) or participants who have different ages but all are assessed at the same, regular time intervals.

 You can view a collection of videos and podcasts on longitudinal studies **here**[2].

The Lothian Birth Cohort 1921

In 1931, the Scottish government became interested in the intelligence of the Scottish people. To assess intelligence in the Scottish population, the government conducted the 'Scottish Mental Survey' in 1932. In this survey, all 11-year-old children who went to school on 1 June 1932 in Scotland were tested on intelligence. They all completed the Moray House Test, a standardized IQ test at the time that suited 11-year-olds. The tests were distributed and scored by school teachers across the country. Overall, 87,498 children were tested that day on intelligence. However, after some initial government reports, the Scottish Mental Survey was soon forgotten. It was only in the late 1990s that researchers from the universities of Edinburgh and Aberdeen remembered the survey. They located the score sheets that the teachers had completed in 1932, and they started searching for people who had taken part when they were 11 years old. By then, in the 1990s, the Scottish Mental Survey children were all in their 70s.

In 2000, the researchers identified 550 men and women from Edinburgh and the surrounding areas who had taken part in the Scottish Mental Survey at age 11 and who were now (i.e. in 2000) 79 years old. This group of people is known today as the Lothian Birth Cohort 1921. The name results from combining place and time: Lothian is the region of the Scottish Lowlands that includes Edinburgh, and all of the study participants were born in 1921. The Lothian Birth Cohort 1921 has now been followed up many times and on each occasion study participants completed a number of intelligence tests. At the follow-up ages of 79 years, 87 years, and 90 years, they took the Moray House Test that they had also taken in 1932 in school when they were 11 years old. Table 13.1 shows the correlations between the Moray House Test scores over time. The correlations range from .51 to .66, which may be interpreted as medium to large effect sizes.

These data suggest that intelligence is both stable and flexible over time. It is a remarkable observation that about half of people's differences in the Moray House Test scores did not change over the timespan of 68 years and more in the Lothian Birth Cohort of 1921. In other words, people who did well in the IQ test at age 11 years also did well in it when they were almost 80 years old. Likewise, people who did badly at age 11 did not do much better 68 years later compared with the other test takers.

Before we conclude that people's differences in intelligence do not change over time, let's look at some of the limitations of the Scottish study. First, it can tell us nothing about the time between ages 11 and 79 years, or what happened throughout people's adulthood. Second, the study is built around one intelligence test, the Moray House Test, which is a short and simplistic measure of intelligence in school children. It therefore says little about other factors of intelligence, such as the knowledge a person has accumulated throughout adulthood. Finally, the study participants were all born in and around Edinburgh in 1921, and most of them continued to live in this

TABLE 13.1 *Correlations between intelligence test scores on the Moray House Test from age 11 to age 90.*

	IQ at 79	IQ at 87	IQ at 90
IQ at 11	.66	.51	.54
N	548	207	106

Note: Data in this table were adapted from Gow et al. (2011) and Deary, Pattie, and Starr (2013); coefficients are not corrected for range restriction.

area. As a result, they had similar school and life experiences, which may have influenced their intelligence test scores to be more stable than they might have been for people who were exposed to more diverse experiences and environments. In summary, intelligence is stable but also malleable: it changes within and between people over time – sometimes more so, sometimes less. In the next section, we will look at some of the causes that change individual differences in intelligence.

DISCUSSION POINT

Click here[3] to read more about the Lothian Birth Cohorts. Discuss what the longitudinal intelligence data from the Lothian Birth Cohort 1921 shows.

SECTION SUMMARY

- Intelligence can differ within (intrapersonal variance) and between (interpersonal variance) people.
- Within a person, intelligence is both stable and flexible across the lifespan. The changes that occur over time depend on type of intelligence, or the factor of intelligence.
- The observation of intrapersonal changes in intelligence that correspond to changes in age has informed many developmental theories of intelligence.
- People change within themselves in intelligence over time but they can also change relative to each other.
- Interpersonal variance is also known as rank-order (in)stability.
- Individual differences in intelligence, or the rank order of IQ scores, are thought to be fairly stable across the lifespan.
- The study of the Lothian Birth Cohort of 1921 investigated the stability of intelligence, but the study is not without its limitations.

CAUSES OF INDIVIDUAL DIFFERENCES IN INTELLIGENCE

LEARNING OBJECTIVE 13.6

Compare and contrast the different 'causes' that behavioural geneticists study to understand the origin of individual differences in intelligence.

In the previous section of this chapter, we discussed the types of variance that occur in intelligence and how intelligence develops within and between people over time. We have yet to address the question of why people differ in intelligence.

Behavioural genetics is a research discipline concerned with the aetiology (i.e. the origin) of individual differences in characteristics or traits. Behavioural geneticists use methods such as twin and adoption studies to estimate the proportion of variance in a given trait – in our case, intelligence – that can be attributed to genetic influences, as well as the proportion of variance in the same trait that is due to environmental influences. The proportion of variance due to genetic influences is typically referred to as **heritability**. The proportion of variance due to environmental factors is often referred to just as 'environment'. For example, we might say that intelligence has a heritability of 50% and that the environment accounts for the other 50%. This statement seems pretty simple and innocent but it is almost always misinterpreted.

Errors in the interpretation of scientific findings and theories happen frequently but some errors have greater consequences than others. Misunderstanding behavioural genetics and heritability can have dramatic consequences for how we understand and relate to each other, and for how we structure society and its institutions. For example, the widespread but false idea that intelligence is inherited and unchangeable can make people think that only the smart children should go to school, not everybody. However, in truth, all children get smarter when they go to school, regardless of how bright they were to begin with (Brinch & Galloway, 2012). So, school is crucial for everybody to achieve their potential and restricting access to education limits children's opportunities. Because of the far-reaching impact that ideas about scientific evidence can have, it is pivotal to understand what heritability is and what it is not. We will address that next.

Heritability

Heritability is a statistical construct and consequently it has little meaning for your personal development and life. Heritability always refers to differences in a group, not to differences between two individuals. It also makes no inferences about characteristics within an individual. In other words, heritability of 50% does *not* mean that half of your intelligence is genetically determined and the other half is made up by the environment. It also does *not* mean that half of your intelligence is fixed and half of it can be changed. Instead, heritability of 50% means that half of the differences observed between individuals can be explained by genetic differences between those individuals.

Another important point is that heritability is not something that happens in isolation or independently of the environment. The development of any organism is always the result of correlations and interactions between genes and environment. However, we often forget about the gene–environment correlations and interactions when we talk about heritability because heritability estimates appear as if they were an enclosed entity. It is true that we can obtain a value for the statistical construct heritability but it is also true that this statistical construct does not exist as a single, independent factor in real life.

Lastly, it is important to not confuse heritability with **heredity**. As outlined above, heritability is a statistical estimate of a proportion of variance. By contrast, heredity is the passing of traits from the parent to the offspring generation. In other words, one is an estimate of the quantity of genetic influences and the other is the biological process of inheritance.

Genetic influences on intelligence

Many studies have reported on the heritability of intelligence. They often compare the resemblance of monozygotic twins, who share the same **genome**, and dizygotic twins, who are genetically only as similar as other fraternal siblings (see Figure 13.7). The findings from twin studies are very consistent: first, intelligence is heritable and, second, heritability increases with age (Haworth et al., 2010). That is, the heritability of intelligence in children up to the age of 10 years is about 30%, in adolescence it is around 50%, and in adulthood and later life it is about 70%. This means, then, that the amount of differences in intelligence between people can be more and more attributed to genetic differences as the people grow older. Increasing heritability of intelligence does not mean that people become more genetically determined as they grow older. To understand why heritability increases as people grow older, we first need to discuss gene–environment correlations and gene–environment interactions.

Gene–environment correlations

Gene–environment correlations can be summarized as *passive*, *active*, or *evocative*. Passive gene–environment correlations refer to the associations that exist between a person's genetic predisposition and their environment without any direct contribution or action of the person. Think, for example, of a baby boy: the baby shares his genes with his parents, who have created an environment for themselves and the baby. That environment will, to a certain extent, match the parents' genetic predispositions. As a result, the baby's genes will also correlate with the environment that his parents provide. Active gene–environment correlations refer to people seeking out environments that match their genetic predispositions. For example, as

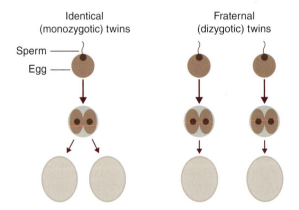

FIGURE 13.7 *Monozygotic and dizygotic twinning. In monozygotic twinning (left), one egg and one sperm meet. The resulting zygote – that is, the fertilized egg – divides into two separate entities that form the basis of the two embryos. Because both embryos result from the same zygote, the emerging twins are monozygotic. In dizygotic twinning (right), two eggs meet two sperms, resulting in two zygotes that develop into two embryos. That is, each zygote resulted from a specific egg–sperm combination. Because each egg and sperm is unique, even if they come from the same parents, these twins are as genetically similar as other siblings.*

Source: Adapted from Wikipedia, "Twin."

the baby grows older, his genetic predisposition may lead him to develop a preference for toy cars. As a result, the boy will pick up toy cars more often than other toys when he is presented with a choice – for example, in the playground, at nursery school, or at home. In turn, parents, carers, aunts, and uncles may react to the baby's toy preference by buying even more toy cars. This is then an evocative gene–environment correlation. Evocative gene–environment correlations occur when a person's genetic predisposition triggers a matching response from the environment. Gene–environment correlations happen throughout development. Over time, they contribute to maximizing the congruency between a person's genetic predisposition and their environment. Let's go over gene–environment correlations one more time focusing on intelligence.

Let's assume there is a baby girl with the genetic predisposition to be smart. The baby girl is born to parents who buy many cognitively stimulating baby toys (passive gene–environment correlation). The baby engages with the wonderful toys, always finding new ways of playing with them (active gene–environment correlation). As a result, the baby's parents buy more cognitively stimulating toys, but this time the toys are more challenging than the previous ones (evocative gene–environment correlation). The little girl is likely to rise to the challenge, thus reinforcing her genetic predisposition for being smart and developing intelligence.

This example is, of course, oversimplified. It does, though, help in understanding how genes and environment work together in development, and why heritability of intelligence may increase with age. That is, we continuously select our environments to match our genetic predispositions. As a result, our genetic differences explain more of the variance between us over time, because our environments are selected to let genetic influences shine. However, the simplicity of the example also has a disadvantage. It suggests that there are specific genes and environments that can be distinctly identified because they contribute to children's cognitive development. But this identification of genes and environments has proven difficult in research.

Gene–environment interactions

Gene–environment interactions happen when the same gene is differently expressed depending on the environment. This is best illustrated by the case of phenylketonuria (PKU), which is a metabolic genetic disorder. PKU is caused by a mutated gene for the enzyme phenylalanine hydroxylase that prevents the amino acid phenylalanine (phe) from being metabolized. As a result, phe accumulates in the brain. While phe in small dosages is harmless and, in fact, indispensable for a human to function, it causes mental retardation when it is in high concentrations. Therefore, children with PKU used to grow up with severe cognitive problems and brain abnormalities. However, the disorder can be treated through regulating dietary patterns. In particular, children who are diagnosed with PKU are put on a phe-free diet; that is, they avoid foods that contain high amounts of phe, such as chicken, fish, and dairy products. If this diet is started early in the child's life and strictly adhered to, then normal brain development takes place. In summary, the gene mutation itself is associated with two very different expressions of **phenotype**: one of normal and one of abnormal development. The difference lies in the environment: for PKU, it is the diet that determines the outcome of a gene mutation.

Identifying genes

Genetic influences on psychological traits exist, and it is very important to understand them. However, the ways in which they influence phenotypic expressions, including intelligence, are extremely complex and not yet well understood. In 2003, scientists announced the completion of the Human Genome Project, which had the aim of decoding the entire human genome. The human genome consists of 3 billion base pairs. Each base pair forms one of the rungs that bridge the other lines of DNA's double-helix structure. It took hundreds of researchers, huge funding resources, and more than 10 years to identify all of the base pairs. However, when the decoded genome was made available for research, geneticists and other scientists across disciplines were enthusiastic that some of the greatest mysteries about human behaviour were about to be solved. Of course, intelligence researchers were also excited: the knowledge of the human genome was a new opportunity to substantiate earlier findings about the heritability of intelligence in twin studies.

Researchers hoped that they could identify the genes that would contribute to explaining individual differences in intelligence. However, the enthusiasm was soon subdued. Only a few units of genetic variation were identified that were significantly associated with intelligence differences. Often, these units were discovered in one study but the next study failed to confirm them. Also, the significant genetic variants explained very little of the observed differences in people's intelligence test scores. In other words, they had very small effect sizes. The previous twin studies had suggested intelligence was heritable at about 70% in adulthood. However, the genetic variants that were significant in the new 'genome-based' studies explained less than 1% of people's differences in intelligence. Researchers then realized that there is not one, or two, or even a hundred genes that influence intelligence. Instead, we assume today that there are thousands and thousands of genetic variants that each have a very small effect size but are associated with intelligence (Plomin & von Stumm, 2018).

The study of the effects of genetic variants on intelligence is difficult for several reasons. First, human DNA is highly complex. Parts of the DNA interact with other parts; some parts 'sleep' and are 'woken up' through unknown mechanisms; and the function of some parts can only be guessed at (indeed, this part of the DNA was until recently referred to as 'junk DNA'). In short, human DNA is tough to crack and, so far, we do not understand it well enough. Researchers will probably spend many more years before we know how the DNA codes for cognitive development and intelligence.

Second, genes interact and correlate with environments, as discussed above. Genes do not operate in a vacuum. They operate in the context of an environment. Think back to earlier, when we discussed PKU and how dietary patterns affect cognitive development. It is plausible that the same principle applies to other genes. For example, some people might have a genetic predisposition to become smart but only if they eat a lot of fish. In other words, genes that influence intelligence will probably only be reliably identified if they are studied in the context of their environment. Because environments are just as complex as genes (see next section), it is so far impossible to design studies that allow for narrowly observing the gene–environment interplay in humans.

Identifying environments

Identifying genetic variants is not the only difficulty when it comes to understanding why people differ in intelligence. Studying environments can be just as messy: just like genetics, environments are complex and interactive. Even worse, many of them are also genetically influenced because of gene–environment correlations and interactions.

The 'environmental' construct that is most commonly studied in research on intelligence is family socioeconomic status, which refers to the wealth and resources that a family has. Socioeconomic status is composed of several variables, including the family's income, the parents' educational level, and the family's principal resources – for example, not only their house and car(s) but also their network of social contacts and support. Therefore, socioeconomic status spans a massive range of variables and aspects, all of which define a child's home environment.

Family socioeconomic status or home environment is associated with intelligence and intelligence development. However, it is difficult to identify specific variables – or environments, if you will – within the nexus of socioeconomic-status factors that affect intelligence because all of them are intertwined. As a result, researchers continue to argue about the influence of specific environmental variables. As an example, a controversial issue in this context is breastfeeding. Does it advance children's intelligence or is it not an important factor in how smart a child will be? Some studies have shown breastfeeding does affect intelligence in children, but others have reported no significant associations (e.g. Der, Batty, & Deary, 2006). Many other environmental variables are hotly debated (e.g. see Focus Point 13.7 for a discussion of the benefits of listening to Mozart for babies' intelligence). Notwithstanding the debates about what the exact variables are that affect children's intelligence and how they do so, a large body of empirical research has shown that a child's home environment in its entirety matters a lot when it comes to IQ.

FOCUS POINT 13.7

THE MOZART EFFECT

The Mozart effect was first observed by Rauscher, Shaw, and Ky (1993), who published their findings in the famous scientific journal *Nature*. The researchers asked university students to complete tests of spatial reasoning after experiencing one of the three following listening conditions.

In the first condition, students listened to the first movement ('Allegro con Spirito') of Mozart's Sonata for Two Pianos in D major (KV 448). In the second condition, they heard verbal instructions that told them to relax. In the final condition, students heard nothing – this was the neutral condition, which is also often referred to as the control condition in an experiment. Rauscher and colleagues found that their participants performed best in spatial reasoning after listening to Mozart. They also observed that this effect did not last beyond 15 minutes after the exposure to Mozart's music.

While the authors never made any claims that listening to Mozart enhances intelligence, the study was widely perceived to have proven exactly that. As a result, an entire industry developed around selling Mozart CDs to pregnant women and new parents, who were told that their babies' intelligence would increase because of the music. There is no evidence that confirms this theory (Pietschnig, Voracek, & Formann, 2010): a baby's intelligence has little to do with listening to Mozart.

You can read more about the study **at the BBC website**[4].

French adoption studies

An important research question in intelligence is to what extent an improvement in home environment is mirrored by children's intelligence development. In other words, is it possible to improve children's IQ by transferring them from bad environments into nicer ones? A team of French researchers set out to tackle exactly that question using an adoption study design (Dyume, Dumaret, & Tomkiewicz, 1999). The researchers looked through official adoption records in France between 1970 and 1978 to identify children who had been adopted between the ages of 4 and 6 years from one family into another. They specifically searched for children who had completed an IQ test before they were adopted, and they identified 65 children out of 5,000 adoption cases. All children in the study had experienced abuse and neglect in their birth homes. In most cases, they had not been given up for adoption but were taken from their biological parent(s) by social services because the children had been raised under conditions that were unacceptable. After being removed from their biological parent(s), the children spent some time in various foster homes before they were adopted into families with whom they would stay until they became adults. In summary, the children included in this study had experienced a great deal of deprivation and suffering in infancy.

Experiences of early life deprivation affect children's development across various domains, including their cognitive development. It is therefore no surprise that the children in this study had an average IQ score of 78 points when they were aged 4 to 6 years, before their adoption. This score is more than 1.5 standard deviations below the population mean of 100 (Figure 13.1), and it signifies that many of the children were at risk of mental retardation. Ten years after the children had been adopted into stable family homes, they completed another set of IQ tests. At this second testing occasion, trained psychologists visited the children's schools and tested their entire school class on IQ. This was done to avoid singling out the adopted children and to ensure that the psychologists, teachers, and children involved were blind to the fact that this was a study about IQ development. The IQ test was age adapted; that is, tests were used that had been validated and normed before in large samples of children who were of the same age as the children in the adoption study. Likewise, children's IQ scores between the ages of 4 and 6 had been assessed with similarly standardized tests that were age adapted. Thus, it was possible to directly compare the children's IQ scores from before and after the adoption. What do you think this comparison showed?

Ten years after being adopted, the children (who originally had an average IQ of 78 points) achieved 91 IQ points on average. This is a gain of 13 IQ points or almost 1 standard deviation. In other words, after being placed and brought up in a nice family environment, the children showed substantial gains in IQ. This finding illustrates how intelligence can be improved through changes in environment. Of course, the French adoption study followed a rare quasi-experimental design that is not always available. For example, for ethical reasons, we cannot try to do the reverse and see whether children from nice families will decline in their intelligence if they are put into impoverished family homes. However, a large number of other quasi-experimental and longitudinal studies support the findings of the French adoption studies. For example, children who go to school for longer are more intelligent than children who attend school for fewer years (Brinch & Galloway, 2012; Protzko, Aronson, & Blair, 2013).

Two more things should be mentioned about the findings of the French adoption study. The first concerns the characteristics of the families that the children were adopted into. Children who had been adopted into families of high socioeconomic status showed the greatest gains in intelligence. As we discussed earlier, socioeconomic status refers to access to resources; for example, high-socioeconomic-status families are likely to provide their children with more toys, books, and other learning opportunities than families of low socioeconomic status. Accordingly, the children adopted into high-socioeconomic-status families gained on average almost 20 IQ points compared with children adopted into low-socioeconomic-status families, who gained on average 8 IQ points. In summary, all children showed significant gains in IQ after adoption but those gains were even greater for children who were placed in families that had better resources.

The second noteworthy finding refers to the rank-order stability of IQ scores in this sample. The correlation between the children's IQ scores at the ages of 4 to 6 years and their IQ scores 10 years later was .67 (corrected for range restriction), which is a relatively high correlation value. This correlation suggests that, even though the children made substantial gains in IQ over time, their rank order of intelligence was relatively stable. In other words, children who did better in the IQ test before their adoption relative to the other children also did better in the IQ test that they completed after the adoption. This goes to show that changing the mean level does not necessarily affect the rank order of scores. Think of it this way: if everybody were to gain 10 IQ points, the mean IQ would go up by 10 IQ points – that is, we'd have a mean of 110 IQ points in the population. However, the amount or extent of individual differences in the population's IQ would not change just because the mean changed.

DISCUSSION POINT

Discuss whether intelligence is heritable and, if so, what this means.

SECTION SUMMARY

- The individual differences in intelligence are caused by the interplay of genetic and environmental variables.
- Both environment and genetics are incredibly complex factors, and each entails an enormous amount of information and parameters.
- To make matters even more complex, the relationship between genes and environment is not simply additive; they correlate and interact.
- Despite the vast progress of scientific discoveries in behavioural genetics, we are still only at the beginning of understanding the gene–environment interplay.
- As a result, we have some principal ideas about factors that drive differences in intelligence but the exact developmental mechanisms involved are as yet unknown.

ALTERNATIVE MODELS OF INTELLIGENCE

LEARNING OBJECTIVE 13.7

Discuss the alternative models of intelligence known as hot intelligence models.

Since the earliest days of intelligence research, scientists have speculated that traditional notions of IQ are too reductionist and narrow to adequately represent intelligence. The core premise of this claim is that there are additional skills or abilities that are not assessed by typical intelligence tests. Mostly, this notion refers to individual differences in the ability to get along with people, or so-called social intelligence. Many believe that these additional skills are in fact more important for real-life outcomes than actual IQ test scores. Accordingly, several theoretical models of intelligence have been developed that contradict Carroll's three-stratum model and the idea of a *g*-factor. These models are commonly described as 'hot intelligences' in contrast to the 'cold' analytical notion of intelligence (Chamorro-Premuzic, 2014). The most prominent hot intelligence models include emotional intelligence, the triarchic theory of intelligence, and the theory of multiple intelligences, each of which is described in some detail below. Historically, hot intelligence models have not been supported by much empirical evidence; this problem is also discussed in this section.

Emotional intelligence

Emotional intelligence is the ability to manage and understand one's own and other people's emotions. It was originally conceived by Salovey and Mayer (1990), who studied individual differences in the ability to correctly identify emotions in portrait photographs. They defined emotional intelligence as an ability or intelligence, just like reasoning or mathematical ability. Accordingly, the first emotional intelligence tests asked participants to identify the *correct* answer to a question (see Figure 13.8). As such, these tests followed the same design as traditional intelligence tests. Many researchers criticized this measurement approach because they thought of emotional intelligence as a more flexible trait that is not adequately measured by IQ-type tests. The debate about how to best measure emotional intelligence continues today. That said, some groundbreaking work in this area has led to the development of more diverse tests for emotional intelligence. In particular, Daniel Goleman published a best-selling book in 1995, *Emotional Intelligence*. In it, Goleman argued that emotional intelligence is more important for success than IQ. He conceptualized emotional intelligence as a set of competencies that can be trained and learned. Following this idea, recent years have witnessed the emergence of a trait perspective on emotional intelligence (Petrides & Furnham, 2001). Thus, emotional intelligence is no longer understood as an ability but instead as a personality trait. Based on this theoretical approach, a new test for emotional intelligence was developed that is more similar to a personality test than an IQ test. In particular, this test asks people to rate themselves on a number of items that assess a person's tendency to be emotionally intelligent.

FIGURE 13.8 *What emotion is the child in the picture experiencing? (a) happiness, (b) sadness, (c) anger, or (d) excitement?*

Source: Orange-studio / Shutterstock.com.

An example item is 'I usually know how my friend is feeling at a given moment'. The test is known as the Trait Emotional Intelligence Questionnaire and it was created by K. V. Petrides and Adrian Furnham (2001). To read more about the trait emotional intelligence research program, go to the **London Psychometric Laboratory site at University College London**[5].

The triarchic theory of intelligence

In 1985, Robert Sternberg published a small but influential book on the triarchic theory of intelligence. According to this book, intelligence comes in three components: analytical, practical, and creative. The three components are thought to be unrelated to one another; that is, people may be high in analytical intelligence and at the same time low in creative intelligence. This notion contradicts the idea of a general intelligence factor, which implies that all of the various measures of intelligence are always positively correlated with one another. Analytic intelligence resembles the cold intelligence that is assessed with traditional IQ tests. Practical intelligence is the ability to figure out what needs to be done in a given situation. It emphasizes a practical rather than an intellectual approach to problem solving. Creative intelligence is the ability to come up with original ideas and to make novel contributions to knowledge. Sternberg illustrated the three components with three psychology PhD students. Emma does excellent literature reviews, is a wizard in statistics, and gets top scores in any exam or test – she scores high on analytic intelligence. Lisa does not get top scores and statistics is a bit of a mystery to her but she has published some of her work and attended conferences, and she networks well. Lisa scores high on practical intelligence, because she figured out what the important things were for her to do to be a successful PhD student. Finally, we have Paula, who has neither top grades nor publications but has something else: Paula has innovative ideas and so she proposes new experimental studies and formulates interesting research questions. Paula, then, scores high on creative intelligence.

Multiple intelligences

A final model that contrasts with the traditional notion of IQ is the theory of multiple intelligences. It was proposed by Howard Gardner in his book *Frames of Mind: The Theory of Multiple Intelligences* (1983). Gardner identified seven criteria that define an intelligence. The criteria include for an intelligence (1) to potentially be isolated through brain damage; (2) to have a history of evolutionary development; (3) to include a series of core operations; (4) to have an encoding system or symbolic expression; (5) to have a distinct developmental progression; (6) to have known prodigies, exceptional talents, or savants; and (7) to have empirical support from experimental psychology and psychometric findings.

Think, for example, of verbal ability: (1) the ability to speak and process language can be lost through brain damage; (2) it is evolutionarily important because it enables humans to communicate; (3) it includes core operations, such as uttering sentences; (4) it is encoded in letters; (5) it develops distinctly in humans, and somewhat independent of other intelligences and skills; (6) some people are exceptionally gifted in language, such as William Shakespeare and Philip Larkin; and (7) verbal ability can be psychometrically measured and experimentally manipulated. Accordingly, Gardner identified verbal ability as an intelligence, together with seven other abilities that met his seven criteria. These intelligences included visual–spatial, logical–mathematical, musical–rhythmic, bodily–kinaesthetic, interpersonal, intrapersonal, and naturalistic abilities. This list is nonexhaustive and other abilities might exist that also qualify as intelligence. Gardner emphasized that intelligence is not hierarchical (cf. Carroll, 1993) and that each person is intelligent in at least one of the many existing multiple intelligences.

ACTIVITY 13.3

WHAT QUALIFIES AS 'INTELLIGENCE'?

Think of an ability and see whether it qualifies by running through Gardner's criteria. If you cannot think of one yourself, try face recognition as an example.

Issues with theories of hot intelligence

Hot intelligence theories clearly have their appeal. First, they widen the construct space of intelligence by suggesting that there is more to it than being 'school smart'. Second, hot intelligence theories offer a more egalitarian idea of ability, including the notion that all people are intelligent in one way or another. Finally, it is plausible that they explain individual differences in behaviour, thought, and affect better than IQ or personality test scores, because hot intelligences are often combinations of both (i.e. traits and abilities).

However, hot intelligence theories also have their problems. First, they are almost impossible to test for. Many people have tried to develop adequate measures for emotional intelligence, for example, as well as for all the other intelligences, but the tests often do not work well. In other words, they fail to achieve construct validity.

Second, scores from hot intelligence tests typically correlate very highly with scores from cold intelligence tests (Visser, Ashton, & Vernon, 2006). For example, Visser and colleagues (2006) showed that actual IQ test scores correlated highly with the test scores from Gardner's multiple intelligences. In fact, the test scores for Gardner's multiple intelligences converged to a single factor of general intelligence. That is basically Spearman's general factor of intelligence. It follows that hot intelligences can be differentiated theoretically but not empirically. In itself, this may not be a problem – after all, we are surrounded by theoretical notions that have little empirical evidence, such as horoscopes and Santa Claus. The lack of empirical evidence for hot intelligences, however, is problematic because it undermines their central premise. In short, there is little scientific support for the importance of hot intelligences for individual differences in behaviour, thought, and affect.

DISCUSSION POINT

Discuss the advantages and disadvantages of 'hot intelligence' theories.

SECTION SUMMARY

- Scientists have long speculated that traditional notions of IQ are too narrow to adequately represent intelligence.
- Alternative models of intelligence are commonly described as hot intelligences.
- The most prominent models include emotional intelligence, the triarchic theory of intelligence, and the theory of multiple intelligences.
- Historically, hot intelligence models have not been supported by much empirical evidence.
- Hot intelligence theories clearly have their appeal: they widen the concept of intelligence and make it more egalitarian.
- However, hot intelligences are limited: they are almost impossible to test for and, crucially, scores from hot intelligence tests typically correlate very highly with scores from cold intelligence tests.

FUTURE DIRECTIONS

LEARNING OBJECTIVE 13.8

Critically evaluate possible future directions for research and study in intelligence.

Because it is 'one of the most central phenomena in all of behavioural science, with broad explanatory powers' (Jensen, 1998, p. xii), intelligence is an important subject of study – perhaps even the most important. Intelligence spans a broad construct space that is dominated by a general factor of intelligence but also includes a wide range of other ability and knowledge domains. Current research focuses largely on investigating the causes of individual differences in intelligence. Much of this work seeks to disentangle genetic and environmental influences on intelligence, as described earlier in this chapter. But behavioural genetics is not the only discipline that is fast-moving and making advances in the understanding of intelligence.

A second research area follows neuroscientific approaches to study intelligence. Of course, the brain has always attracted much interest and played an important role in intelligence research. However, two events have made brain-related research even more relevant for the study of intelligence. One was the announcement of the BRAIN Initiative, which stands for Brain Research through Advancing Innovative Neurotechnologies, or simply the Brain Activity Map Project. The BRAIN Initiative is modelled on the previous Human Genome Project, which resulted in the complete decoding of the human genome in 2003. BRAIN is a collaborative research initiative that was launched by US President Barack Obama on 2 April 2013. The aim of the initiative is to map the activity of every neuron in the human brain. A total of US$3 billion has been made available through to 2023 to fund research that maps the brain.

The other event was also an announcement of a research initiative. This one is known as the Human Brain Project and it is mainly funded by the European Union. The aim of the project is to build a computer model of a functioning brain that will allow the simulation of brain operations across various contexts. The Human Brain Project is backed by a funding package of €1.2 billion that will supports research until 2023. So far, hundreds of researchers from 135 research institutions in 26 countries are involved in the project.

Mapping and modelling the brain are likely to help us to answer important questions in the future. For example, where in the brain does intelligence happen? How do neurons encode different kinds of information? What makes some brains more efficient than others? As we potentially become able to answer these questions, new questions will arise that we cannot even foresee at this moment. It is also likely that the findings obtained through these brain research initiatives will add to what we will learn from other fields, notably from behavioural genetics. In summary, we can reasonably expect to learn a vast amount of new information about individual differences in intelligence over the next years. Watch this space!

SECTION SUMMARY

- Intelligence continues to be at the forefront of psychological and behavioural research.
- The latest research efforts focus on mapping the brain to better understand the functional mechanisms of intelligence.
- Although IQ has been studied since the 19th century, the greatest breakthroughs in understanding individual differences in intelligence are yet to come.

CHAPTER SUMMARY

This chapter has considered the definition, structure, and measurement of intelligence and the ways in which twin and adoption studies have contributed to research in the field. First, we reviewed fundamental difficulties and consensus in the definition of intelligence. Then, we outlined the history of intelligence research and the development of the first intelligence tests. The chapter moved on to discussing contemporary intelligence research, focusing on the latent factor structure of intelligence and the ways in which intelligence might be measured. In addition, stability and change in intelligence over the lifespan were examined, both within and between people. We also discussed the causes of individual differences in intelligence, as well as alternative models of intelligence, namely the hot intelligences. The chapter concluded with a look at future questions and directions in intelligence research.

ESSAY QUESTIONS

1. Does intelligence change across the lifespan and, if so, how?
2. Compare and contrast two different theories of intelligence.
3. What were the core developments in the history of intelligence research?

KEY TERMS

- **behavioural genetics:** The study of genetic and environmental causes of individual differences in behaviour, thought, and affect.
- **bell curve:** The normal distribution curve of individual differences in IQ points in the population. Bell curves of IQ are typically normed to have a mean of 100 and a standard deviation of 15 IQ points.
- **common variance:** The amount of variance (i.e. individual differences) that is shared between several test scores or observations. In other words, common variance is the extent to which test scores co-vary or correlate.
- **correlations:** A correlation is the standardized covariance. Correlations range from –1 to + 1, indicating either a perfectly negative or perfectly positive association between two variables. In other words, a correlation of 1 implies that, as one variable increases by one unit (e.g. age by a year), the other also increases by one unit (e.g. number of wrinkles).
- **covariance:** A statistical value or coefficient that describes the direction and strength of the relationship between two variables.
- **cross-sectional study:** An observational study that collects data from a population or sample at one specific point in time.
- **crystallized intelligence:** The entirety of a person's knowledge that is accumulated through learning experiences across the lifespan.
- **emotional intelligence:** The ability to manage and understand one's own and others' emotions.
- **factor analysis:** A statistical method for extracting common variance from a set of correlated observations or test scores. It is used to reduce the number of observed variables through identifying their underlying latent structure.

- **fluid intelligence:** A person's reasoning capacity, logical thinking, and ability to solve novel problems. It is thought to be little influenced by training or past learning experiences.
- **genome:** The entirety of an organism's genetic information (i.e. its DNA).
- **heredity:** The biological process of inheritance, whereby genetic information is passed on from the parent generation to the offspring generation.
- **heritability:** The amount of trait variance in a population that can be attributed to genetic differences in the same population.
- **heterogeneous:** A term referring to the uniformity of a property or trait. When something is homogeneous, it is uniform in composition or character; conversely, something is heterogeneous if it is varied in its composition or character. Take white yogurt and a stew as examples: white yogurt is homogeneous (same composition), while stew is heterogeneous (different vegetables and meats; with bits, not a smooth purée).
- **latent trait:** An implicit psychological trait that cannot be directly observed. In other words, latent traits are unobserved entities that are inferred from a set of observed test scores.
- **longitudinal studies:** A study involving repeated assessment of the same population or sample over time. Longitudinal studies vary in duration: some span a few weeks (e.g. medical trials), others several centuries (e.g. climate development).
- **phenotype:** An organism's observable traits or characteristics as well as its produced behaviour. By comparison, a genotype is an organism's inherited instructions, which are encoded in units of genetic information (e.g. genes).
- **psychometrics:** Literally, 'measurement of the soul'. It refers to the study of assessment instruments and tests of individual differences in psychological traits.
- **variance:** The amount of difference observed in a population. The term is usually used with reference to differences in one specific trait or measure.

NOTES

1. http://www.sciencemuseum.org.uk/broughttolife/people/francisgalton.aspx
2. http://www.cls.ioe.ac.uk/page.aspx?&sitesectionid=1350&sitesectiontitle=Multimedia
3. http://www.lothianbirthcohort.ed.ac.uk/
4. http://www.bbc.com/future/story/20130107-can-mozart-boost-brainpower
5. http://www.psychometriclab.com/

FURTHER RESOURCES

Ackerman, P. L. (1996). A theory of adult intellectual development: Process, personality, interests, and knowledge. *Intelligence, 22,* 227–257.

Deary, I. J. (2012). Intelligence. *Annual Review of Psychology, 63,* 453–482.

Deary, I. J., Whalley, L. J., & Starr, J. M. (2009). *A lifetime of intelligence.* Washington, DC: American Psychological Association.

Dyume, M., Dumaret, A. M., & Tomkiewicz, S. (1999). How can we boost IQs of 'dull children'? A late adoption study. *Proceedings of the National Academy of Sciences of the United States of America, 96,* 8790–8794.

Human Intelligence. (n.d.). Retrieved 20 November 2017 from http://www.intelltheory.com (This site includes biographical profiles of people who have influenced the development of intelligence theory and testing, in-depth articles exploring current controversies related to human intelligence, and resources for teachers.)

London Psychometric Laboratory. (n.d.). Retrieved 20 November 2017 from http://www.psychometriclab.com (Based at University College London and directed by Dr. K. V. Petrides, the London Psychometric Laboratory is home to the trait emotional intelligence research program.)

Nisbett, R. (2010). *Intelligence and how to get it: Why schools and cultures count*. New York, NY: W. W. Norton & Co.

Nisbett, R. E., Aronson, J., Blair, C., Dickens, W., Flynn, J., Halpern, D. F., & Turkheimer, E. (2012). Intelligence: New findings and theoretical developments. *American Psychologist*, *67*, 130–159. doi:10.1037/a0026699

Plomin, R. (2013). Child development and molecular genetics: 14 years later. *Child Development*, *84*(1), 104–120.

Sternberg, R. J. (1985). *Beyond IQ: A triarchic theory of human intelligence*. New York, NY: Cambridge University Press.

Visser, B. A., Ashton, M. C., & Vernon, P. A. (2006). Beyond *g*: Putting multiple intelligences theory to the test. *Intelligence*, *34*, 487–502.

von Stumm, S., Hell, B., & Chamorro-Premuzic, T. (2011). The hungry mind: Intellectual curiosity is the third pillar of academic performance. *Perspectives on Psychological Science*, *6*, 574–588.

REFERENCES

Ackerman, P. L. (1996). A theory of adult intellectual development: Process, personality, interests, and knowledge. *Intelligence*, *22*, 227–257.

Binet, A., & Simon, T. (1905/1961). New methods for the diagnosis of the intellectual levels of subnormals (trans. E. S. Kite). In J. J. Jenkins & D. G. Paterson (Eds.), *Studies in individual differences: The search for intelligence* (pp. 90–96). New York, NY: Appleton-Century-Crofts.

Brinch, C. N., & Galloway, T. A. (2012). Schooling in adolescence raises IQ scores. *Proceedings of the National Academy of Sciences of the United States of America*, *109*, 425–430.

Carroll, J. B. (1993). *Human cognitive abilities. A survey of factor-analytic studies*. Cambridge, UK: Cambridge University Press.

Cattell, R. B. (1943). The measurement of adult intelligence. *Psychological Bulletin*, *40*, 153–193.

Chamorro-Premuzic, T. (2014). *Personality and individual differences* (3rd ed.). Chichester, UK: Wiley.

Cronbach, L. J., & Meehl, P. E. (1955). Construct validity in psychological tests. *Psychological Bulletin*, *52*, 281–302.

Deary, I. J. (2001). *Looking down on human intelligence*. Oxford, UK: Oxford University Press.

Deary, I. J. (2012). Intelligence. *Annual Review of Psychology*, *63*, 453–482.

Deary, I. J., Pattie, A., & Starr, J. M. (2013). The stability of intelligence from age 11 to age 90 years. *Psychological Science*, *24*(12), 2361–2368.

Der, G., Batty, G. D., & Deary I. J. (2006). Effect of breast feeding on intelligence in children: Prospective study, sibling pairs analysis, and meta-analysis. *British Medical Journal*, *333*(7575), 945–950.

Dyume, M., Dumaret, A. M., & Tomkiewicz, S. (1999). How can we boost IQs of 'dull children'? A late adoption study. *Proceedings of the National Academy of Sciences of the United States of America*, *96*, 8790–8794.

Fancher, R. E. (1985). *The intelligence men: Makers of the IQ controversy*. New York, NY: W. W. Norton.

Fancher, R. E. (2009). Scientific cousins: The relationship between Charles Darwin and Francis Galton. *American Psychologist*, *64*, 84–92.

Fernández-Ballesteros, R., & Colom, R. (2004). The psychology of human intelligence in Spain. In R. Sternberg (Ed.), *International handbook of intelligence* (pp. 79–103). New York, NY: Cambridge University Press.

Galton, F. (1865). Hereditary talent and character. *Macmillans Magazine*, *12*, 157–166, 318–327.

Galton, F. (1869). *Hereditary genius*. London, UK: Macmillan.

Gardner, H. (1983). *Frames of mind: The theory of multiple intelligences*. New York, NY: Basic Books.

Goleman, D. (1995). *Emotional intelligence*. New York, NY: Bantam Books.

Gottfredson, L. (1994). Mainstream science on intelligence. *Wall Street Journal*, 13 December, A-18.

Gould, S. J. (1981). *The mismeasure of man*. New York, NY: W. W. Norton.

Gow, A. J., Johnson, W., Pattie, A., Brett, C. E., Roberts, B., Starr, J. M., & Deary, I. J. (2011). Stability and change in intelligence from age 11 to ages 70, 79 and 87: The Lothian Birth Cohorts of 1921 and 1936. *Psychology and Aging, 26*, 232–240.

Haworth, C. M. A., Wright, M. J., Luciano, M., Martin, N. G., de Geus, E. J. C., Van Beijsterveldt, C. E. M., ... Plomin, R. (2010). The heritability of general cognitive ability increases linearly from childhood to young adulthood. *Molecular Psychiatry, 15*, 1112–1120.

Hemnon, V. A. C. (1921). Intelligence and its measurement: A symposium – VIII. *Journal of Educational Psychology, 12*, 195–198.

Herrnstein, R., & Murray, C. (1994). *The bell curve: Intelligence and class structure in American life*. New York, NY: Free Press.

Jensen, A. R. (1998). *The g factor: The science of mental ability*. Westport, CT: Praeger.

Johnson, W., & Bouchard, T. J., Jr. (2005). Constructive replication of the visual-perceptual-image rotation (VPR) model in Thurstone's (1941) battery of 60 tests of mental ability. *Intelligence, 33*, 417–430.

Kline, P. (2000). *A psychometric primer*. London, UK: Free Association Press.

Kuncel, N. R., Hezlett, S. A., & Ones, D. S. (2004). Academic performance, career potential, creativity, and job performance: Can one construct predict them all? *Journal of Personality and Social Psychology, 86*, 148–161.

MacCallum, R. C., & Browne, M. C. (1993). The use of causal indicators in covariance structure models: Some practical issues. *Psychological Bulletin, 114*, 533–541.

Petrides, K. V., & Furnham, A. (2001). Trait emotional intelligence: Psychometric investigation with reference to established trait taxonomies. *European Journal of Personality, 15*, 425–448.

Pietschnig, J., Voracek, M., & Formann, A. K. (2010). Mozart effect – Shmozart effect: A meta-analysis. *Intelligence, 38*, 314–323.

Plomin, R., & von Stumm, S. (2018). The new genetics of intelligence. *Nature Reviews Genetics*. doi:10.1038/nrg.2017.104.

Protzko, J., Aronson, J., & Blair, C. (2013). How to make a young child smarter: Evidence from the database of raising intelligence. *Perspectives on Psychological Science, 8*, 25–40.

Rauscher, F. H., Shaw G. L., & Ky, K. N. (1993). Music and spatial task performance. *Nature, 365*(6447), 611.

Salovey, P., & Mayer, J. (1990). Emotional intelligence. *Imagination, Cognition, and Personality, 9*, 185–211.

Salthouse, T. A. (2004). What and when of cognitive ageing. *Current Directions in Psychological Science, 13*(4), 140–144.

Spearman, C. E. (1904). General intelligence: Objectively determined and measured. *American Journal of Psychology, 15*, 201–293.

Sternberg, R. J. (1985). *Beyond IQ: A triarchic theory of human intelligence*. New York, NY: Cambridge University Press.

Thurstone, L. L. (1938). *Primary mental abilities*. Chicago, IL: University of Chicago Press.

Visser, B. A., Ashton, M. C., & Vernon, P. A. (2006). Beyond *g*: Putting multiple intelligences theory to the test. *Intelligence, 34*, 487–502.

von Stumm, S., Hell, B., & Chamorro-Premuzic, T. (2011). The hungry mind: Intellectual curiosity is the third pillar of academic performance. *Perspectives on Psychological Science, 6*(6), 574–588.

Whalley, L. J., & Deary, I. J. (2001). Longitudinal cohort study of childhood IQ and survival up to age 76. *British Medical Journal, 322*(7290), 819–822.

14 Personality

TOM FARSIDES

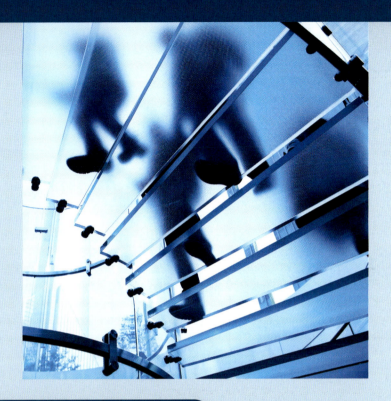

INTRODUCTION TO PERSONALITY

LEARNING OBJECTIVE 14.1

Describe key features of how the word 'personality' can be conceptualized.

Humans: Individuals and types

Students are often attracted to psychology because they want to 'understand people'. This desire has three related but distinct components. First, students want to know 'what makes people tick'. They suspect that all people share some fundamental psychological characteristics that could be understood and perhaps used to predict and control people's behaviour. These students are interested in 'human psychology'. Second, they want to understand specific individuals, often themselves. They want to know what gives particular people the specific characteristics they have and what might make them change, ideally for the better. These students are interested in 'individual psychology'. Finally, some students are interested in potentially distinct types of person (e.g. men or psychopaths). They want to know what, if anything, makes these sorts of people alike and different from other people. These students are interested in taxonomic or 'differential psychology'. **Personality psychology** – the psychology of persons, personalities, and personhood – is the branch of psychology that most directly addresses these issues. Because of its various concerns, aspects of personality psychology sometimes have specific or alternative names, such as 'personology' or 'the psychology of **individual differences**'. Parts of personality psychology also have close links with some aspects of social psychology.

Theories, data, and science

The main thing that differentiates personality psychologists from others who make claims about people is that personality psychologists are **psychologists**. Psychologists are committed to using empirical data to develop their theories. If a theory does not do a good job of describing the way the world seems to be, the theory needs to change. The better a theory captures what seems to go on in the world, the better that theory is.

Many contemporary psychologists are also **scientists**. The most important characteristic of scientists is that they attempt to develop theories empirically by working as a community. This means that part of what scientists do is to evaluate the empirical evidence regarding each other's theories. To be scientifically successful, numbers of people expert in empirical research methods need to agree that a theory does a pretty good job of capturing what goes on in the world.

Psychology, First Edition. Edited by Graham Davey.
© 2019 John Wiley & Sons, Ltd. Published 2019 by John Wiley & Sons, Ltd.

Relativity, conditionality, and statistics

Many descriptions of people's personalities are relative. Characteristics such as 'confidence' often make most sense when they are understood in comparison to alternative ways of being. People tend to think of themselves and others as confident relative to other people or to how they themselves are at other times. Many descriptions of people's personalities are also conditional (i.e. dependent on particular conditions). A person might be sociable with same-sex others but shy with members of the opposite sex. For reasons such as these, many descriptions of people's personality rely on compared averages. People may be described as happy people, for example, if they appear happier than most other people when each individual's happiness is averaged over time, within or across particular types of situation.

Description and explanation

Accurate description can be very useful for prediction and control. If someone is accurately described as 'belligerent when drunk', it is probably wise to avoid spilling their beer. One aspect of accurate description is specification of the situations in which the description holds. Implicit in the description 'this person is belligerent when drunk' is that the person is considerably more belligerent when drunk than when sober. If this were not the case, a less misleading description would be simply to say, 'this person is belligerent'. This latter description has a broader domain of application. It suggests that the person is more belligerent than most people, in most situations, most of the time. Spilling their beer will still most likely trigger their belligerence, but so too will putting too much milk in their tea, failing to let them into traffic, looking at them quizzically, and so on.

Past behaviour is often the best single predictor of future behaviour (although see Franklin, 2013). Explanation nevertheless enables better prediction and control than does mere description. Knowing the reason for observed regularities allows us to understand when they will be replicated and how they might change. A modern meme (originating from Bertrand Russell) tells of an **inductivist** turkey who believes it has nothing to fear from the caring farmer who has consistently nurtured it from the moment it hatched. The turkey's description of the farmer's behaviour is accurate. Its prediction is nevertheless fatally flawed. It has failed to appreciate the reasons for the description's accuracy. Come Christmas, it is stuffed.

Latent and manifest

A person who is belligerent when drunk shows or 'manifests' this aspect of their personality when they are drunk. At other times, this aspect of their personality is hidden or latent. The characteristic of being-belligerent-when-drunk is not apparent when the person is sober. It is nevertheless part of the person's character and will be reliably revealed when the conditions are right. Understanding **latent characteristics** is far more difficult than simply listing **manifest characteristics**. One reason for this is that latent characteristics can manifest themselves in ways that appear different on the surface: a child may have an enduring latent characteristic that manifests itself differently across different situations or as the child gets older, for example. A child urinating on the floor and refusing to share might be manifesting symptoms of the latent characteristic of something like 'disregard for others', as might its adult characteristics of using people solely as sex objects and being a particularly heartless traffic warden.

Just as apparently different manifest behaviours can stem from a single latent characteristic, apparently similar manifest behaviours can stem from different latent characteristics. A person helping a friend to put up a tent may be motivated by a desire to be helpful, a desire to impress witnesses, a desire to humiliate the person they are 'helping', a desire to make the person they are helping feel beholden to them, or any number of other desires. In each case, the manifest behaviour is the same but the underlying reason for it is different.

Stability and change

The factors above complicate what is meant by personality stability and change. If a person is confident with members of the same sex but not with members of the opposite sex, are they 'the same person' in each situation or do they undergo regular 'personality change' depending on who they are talking to? Can stability in manifest behaviour indicate personality change? For example, might using a potty be an indicator of having a 'mature personality' or being 'a mature person' when young but of being 'infantile' later in life? Sensible answers to many such questions can only be given if there is some agreement on what 'personality' is and on how it is revealed.

TEST YOURSELF

1. Is gender a legitimate topic of study for a personality psychologist? Why?
2. What does it mean to describe a person as 'kind'? In your answer, make mention of relativity, conditionality, and the distinction between latent and manifest characteristics.
3. You discover that a new friend has been arrested several times. What do you want to know to feel confident about continuing your friendship?

SECTION SUMMARY

- Personality psychology uses empirical methods to seek consensual descriptions and explanations of human nature, similarities and differences across people, and unique individuality.

- Personality characteristics are often at least implicitly relative, conditional, and statistical. 'Brave', for example, might mean 'braver on average than most in dangerous situations'.

- Endurance is a minimum requirement for a personality characteristic. An account of how or why a characteristic endures is a minimum requirement for an explanation of it.

- Latent characteristics are enduring potentials for manifestation. Someone with latent hostility has a predisposition towards manifest hostility.

- Latent characteristics can manifest in ways that may not be obviously connected. This can make the endurance of latent characteristics difficult to establish.

PSYCHODYNAMIC PERSONALITY THEORY

LEARNING OBJECTIVE 14.2

Discuss the background, claims, and key features of psychodynamic personality theory.

Much modern personality theory has developed as an aid to counselling and psychotherapy. This modern era started with Sigmund Freud challenging the consensus that all psychiatric problems had determinable physical causes and medical solutions. This section reviews Freud's key thoughts as they relate specifically to personality. In brief, Freud came to believe that during infancy and childhood people develop unconscious methods for coping with extreme anxiety and then continue using these defence mechanisms throughout life, even when more mature responses to events would be more functional.

Origins

Sigmund Freud was born half-way through the 19th century, in 1856. He died soon after the start of the World War II, in 1939. Following qualification as a doctor in Austria, Freud became fascinated by **hysteria**. This was a diagnosis given when, for no apparent physical reason, people engaged in strange behaviour without seeming to want to or sometimes even noticing. Freud wondered whether hysteria could be cured verbally, just as hypnotized people can be commanded to stop their often strange and seemingly involuntary behaviours. In the process of coming to believe it could, Freud started to develop what is possibly the most influential ever theory of personality.

Consciousness

Freud believed that there are various levels of consciousness, most often summarized using his metaphorical **topographical model**. This equates consciousness to awareness of what is in one's mind at any given time. If you **introspect** right now, whatever you become aware of is the current content of your **conscious**. As you read the following words, the contents of your consciousness will probably change to include your awareness of your nation's capital city. Awareness of that fact was probably not within your consciousness when you started to read this paragraph, but it is now. That knowledge was **preconscious**, not in your consciousness but easily moved into it, for example by an environmental cue such as words on a screen. The preconscious is anything that can be moved relatively easily into the conscious but that is not currently there. Freud thought that many psychological processes happen unconsciously, alongside and in interaction with conscious psychological processes. The **unconscious** comprises psychological aspects of mind and body that are difficult or impossible to pull into the conscious. Such an unconscious means that people can find it difficult or impossible to become aware of the reasons for much of what they do.

Instincts

Influenced by Darwin's recently published theory of evolution (*On the Origin of Species*, 1859), Freud thought that people biologically inherit motivational mechanisms that support survival. These instincts strongly incline people to engage in a wide range of behaviours, often in reaction to features of situations they encounter. Because they are so important for survival, these behaviours are largely automatic. They do not need people to consciously choose to act as they do. They do not even need people to always be aware of their actions. And they certainly do not need people to be aware of their reasons for acting as they do. In short, many of these motives can operate outside people's conscious awareness and some may be impossible for people to become aware of via introspection.

Freud initially proposed that many behaviours stem from self-preservation **instincts** and that many others stem from species-preserving sexual instincts. Freud (1929/2004) later collapsed both these sets of inclinations into a single category of **life instincts**. At the same time, Freud suggested that in many situations people have various strong inclinations towards things like aggression, violence, and destruction. These inclinations he termed **death instincts**. Although death instincts are often described as being distinct from and antagonistic to life instincts, it is not difficult to conceive that instinctive orientations towards violence and similar behaviour could in some circumstances promote survival.

Stages of development

Freud thought that different parts of the body are particularly important for motivation at different ages. Because the energies associated with life instincts are sometimes referred to as **libido** and **eros**, these parts of the body are sometimes called **erogenous zones**. Such terms emphasize the **sexuality** that was undoubtedly central to Freud's thinking. Within psychodynamic writing, such terminology is, however, rarely best interpreted in its narrow modern sense. Rather, the key significance of such terms is that people seek survival, often by instinctively doing things that are pleasurable and avoiding things that are not.

At birth, many instincts trigger activities involving the mouth, and stimulation of the mouth triggers many instincts. Infants use their mouths a lot, particularly during the deeply nourishing and bonding activity of breastfeeding. Babies also use their mouths to cry out when they have unmet **needs** and desires.

During this **oral stage**, infants start to develop beliefs about themselves, the world around them, and the relationship between the two. Optimal personal development requires an adequate balance between indulgence and frustration. Enough indulgence teaches children that the world is reliable, dependable, and trustworthy. Enough frustration teaches children that they must and can tolerate delayed gratification. The interaction between these things teaches children that they have some control in the world. Too much indulgence and children can become passive, dependent, and egocentric. Too much frustration and children can become distrustful, despairing, or aggressive. As infants become toddlers, toilet training becomes a central issue. How this **anal stage** is handled has a significant influence on infants' developing beliefs and subsequent behaviour. Excessive liberalism again encourages egocentrism and inadequate concern for anything or anyone other than the self. Excessive demands, harshly enforced, foster wariness of a world perceived as being largely hostile.

TABLE 14.1 *Erikson's psychosocial stages.*

Approximate age	Focal issue	Optimal outcome (if not excessive)	Negative outcome
0–1	Is my world predictable and supportive?	Trust	Mistrust
1–3	Can I do it myself?	Autonomy	Shame and doubt
3–6	Am I good?	Initiative	Guilt
6–11	Do I do things well?	Industry	Inferiority
Adolescence	Who am I and where am I going?	Ego identity	Identity diffusion
Young adulthood	Shall I live alone or share my life?	Intimacy	Isolation
Middle adulthood	Can I produce something of value?	Generativity	Stagnation
Old age	Have I led a full life?	Integrity	Despair

As toddlers become children, they become fascinated by sex and gender differences, particularly within the family. How other people respond to children's curiosity and concern during this **phallic stage** makes a lasting impression on many of their important subsequent beliefs and practices. At this time, most children come to identify primarily with their same-sex parent and develop predominantly heterosexual preferences. These become increasingly enacted during the **genital stage** of adolescence onwards.

Erik Erikson modified and extended Freud's developmental theory. He reconceptualized each 'psychosexual' stage as a series of age-specific **crises** or, more appropriately, **tasks**. An infant's first task, for example, during Freud's oral stage, is to unconsciously answer the implicit question, 'Is my world predictable and supportive?' Excessive indulgence of the infant addressing this task leads to an unrealistically affirmative answer and the person becomes too trusting, gullible, and imprudent. Excessive frustration leads to an unrealistically negative answer and the person becomes too untrusting, suspicious, and calculating. Healthy development requires finding a Goldilocks point between these two extremes. Subsequent tasks each culminate in arrival at an answer to another question. As can be seen in Table 14.1, early questions relate to each of Freud's psychosexual stages but Erikson also extended his amended model to capture developmental tasks throughout the lifespan (see Boeree, 2006a, for more details about Erikson's work).

FOCUS POINT 14.1

IDENTITY CRISIS

The key task of adolescence is to establish a clear sense of personal identity: who one is and where one is going. Marcia (1966) suggested that the development of people's identities during this stage depends on two processes. The first is whether or not people have wondered about what to believe and do occupationally and ideologically, as well as in a variety of other life domains, such as sexual relationships. This is the key adolescent 'crisis'. The second identity process identified by Marcia is the extent to which people have made a commitment to various ways of being in each of these life domains. This commitment can be made with or without prior questioning. As illustrated in the table below, the presence or absence of questioning and commitment results in an **identity status**. Four of these are possible.

- Foreclosure occurs when commitment to an identity is made before personally inter-rogating all the options. As a result of a lack of imagination or an inability to think of alternatives, a person accepts an identity that is perhaps expected of them without wondering whether other identities might be available and more personally attractive. Once alternatives are considered – that is, once crisis has occurred – foreclosure is no longer an option.

- Identity diffusion occurs when a person has little, lost, or abandoned interest in explor-ing possible identities and making a commitment to particular ones. A person with identity diffusion does not really know or care who they are and may be listless or accept with neither enthusiasm nor resistance one or more identities suggested for them by others or by circumstances.

- Moratorium occurs when a person is actively seeking an identity but has yet to make commitments to specific ones. People with this status may switch between various possibilities, 'trying on' different identities to see how they feel and fit with other com-mitments they have or are considering.

- Identity achievement occurs after a thorough exploration has left a person able to make commitments to particular identities that they find personally attractive and suitable.

Marcia's four identity stages.

		Identity exploration (crisis)?	
		No	Yes
Identity commitment?	No	Identity diffusion	Moratorium
	Yes	Foreclosure	Identity achievement

Source: Marcia (1966). American Psychological Association. Reproduced with permission.

ACTIVITY 14.1

ARE 'YOU' THERE YET?

What is your identity status in each of the following life domains: occupation, ideology, religion, sexuality, and gender? Are there any other domains in which achieving an identity is important for you? How integrated are your identities across domains and why might this matter? How might the relationship between adolescence and identity in the United States of the 1960s be the same and different in your culture today?

ACTIVITY 14.2

I'M A CELEBRITY – WHO AM I?

Think about actors or musicians who have been in the public eye since childhood. Try to identify when and how each person negotiated their identity crises. If you knew someone famous who was dealing with such issues, what advice or support do you think you could give them?

Id, ego, and superego

Babies are primarily motivated by genetically inherited instincts. They cry when uncomfortable, suckle when hungry, and so on. Prelinguistic and with limited cognitive and emotional development, they are largely unaware of what they are doing and have little tolerance when their needs are not met. Babies may not know what they want or have much awareness of what they are doing or why, but will nevertheless scream loud and long until someone else works out how to make them happy. Babies have no interest in whether their mothers' nipples are sore; if they want to continue feeding, they will do everything within their power to demand that this happens.

Freud named this aspect of personality the **id**. The id is demanding and frustration-averse. It is purely pleasure-seeking: it wants instant gratification of personal hedonic desires. It is impatient, irrational, and intolerant. It wants what it wants and it wants it now. It does not respond well when it does not get it. It is not interested in any reasons why meeting its demands may not be prudent, kind, or even possible.

Infantile instincts serve most babies well, but only to a degree and only for so long. Even the most devoted parents have limits on how much they are able and willing to meet their babies' demands. As babies' capacities to understand and to interact with the world grow, they develop prudence. They develop a sense of self – an **ego** – and learn that instant gratification of the id's demands is not always possible or even in the self's long-term interests. While the id is childishly hedonistic, the ego is realistic. It learns that some demands and the way they are expressed are counterproductive, leading to frustration and pain rather than pleasure.

Part of learning about the world is learning that other people exist and have preferences and demands of their own. Children learn early about the consequences of pleasing or displeasing those with power to make their lives comfortable or otherwise. Over time, children internalize important others' beliefs and expectations, especially those of their same-sex parent. Whereas the id seeks pleasure and the ego seeks to master reality, this **superego** seeks perfection. Depending on the socialization processes leading to the superego's development and the ability of the child to make sense of them, the superego's requirements can be flexible, practical, and tolerant, or they can be every bit as inflexible and unreasonable as the demands of the id. For Freud, these aspects of personality coexist from fairly early childhood throughout life. A mature ego has the job of trying to coordinate and pursue the demands of both the infantile id and the idealistic superego when confronted by the constraints and opportunities of reality.

Psychodynamics

Language and other factors facilitate the impression that our lives have a relatively straightforward narrative. One thing happens and leads to another, which leads to another, and so on, and the whole sequence is relatively open to introspection and explanation. Freud's theories challenge such intuitions. Simultaneous, rapidly changing, and often conflicting **psychodynamic** demands may be being made by each of the id, ego, and superego, many of which are likely to be operating well outside conscious awareness. If you are given an unexpected compliment by a disliked teacher, you may experience rival fleeting impulses to smile or subtly sneer and end up surprising yourself by pulling a rather strange face in your desire to behave appropriately.

Trauma, anxiety, and coping

Instinctive behaviour is driven by the **pleasure principle**. If instinctive behaviour turns out to be pleasurable, all is well; people can happily continue to act instinctively. When instinctive behaviour has distressing consequences, **trauma** and **anxiety** can occur. Remember that instincts are innate because they tend to aid survival. Because of this, experiencing negative effects when behaving instinctively can feel deeply threatening (Focus Point 14.2). The more pronounced the apparent threat to self, the more traumatic the experience will be and the more anxious a person will become about the possibility of repeating such a distressing experience.

THREAT AND ANXIETY

After a person has developed a sense of self, distinct from the world around it, experience, imagination, and socialization can suggest that unbridled pursuit of pleasure may have extremely unpleasant consequences. Babies and infants wanting nourishment and fun often seek pleasure by nuzzling their mothers' breasts, playing with bodily products, stimulating their genitals, and the like, and they sometimes do things like this in public. If children are given or threatened with extremely harsh punishment for such behaviour, they will find this traumatic and are likely to become fearful of even the possibility of repeating the behaviour.

Freud (1929/2004) suggested that because all people live in social groups, frustration of their desires is inevitable and necessary. In society, people simply cannot act on or even unreservedly express their every desire without someone else perceiving that their own pleasures are being thwarted – and then potentially acting very negatively in response. This is why so much of social life is codified and it is also why social living involves a certain amount of discontent and anxiety. Social codes detail which forms of instinct expression or pleasure seeking will be generally deemed acceptable or unacceptable and they also dictate the rewards and punishments that can be expected when they are followed or violated. The curtailed liberty that social codes and their enforcement brings results in citizens living in a constant state of at least unconscious anxiety and discontent.

ACTIVITY 14.3

CODE BREAKING

Think about the social codes in the social groups you inhabit: your family, your school or workplace, your society, and so on. To what extent can those codes be understood as regulating instinct expression to promote harmonious living for all? What do you make of the fact that some codes differ according to people's age, sex, or status? Are some societies' codes better or worse than others, or just different, and why? If people have been traumatized and made anxious by being on the receiving end of harsh discipline as children, what sorts of social codes do you imagine them favouring as adults, and why?

Particularly severe anxiety is primarily handled by avoidance, which can take many forms. People can avoid situations they find potentially traumatic. This can cause **fixation** or **arrested development**. Rather than face the challenges required to grow, people can simply avoid them and stick with what is familiar. By so doing, they become relatively immature. Teenagers afraid (or made afraid) of their developing sexuality might cope with their anxiety by continuing to play relatively childish games, for example.

Freud and his followers listed an impressive array of psychological techniques they thought people could use to cope with anxiety in traumatic situations that cannot be physically avoided. Primary among these **defence mechanisms** is **repression** (Brewin & Andrews, 2000). This involves either failing to consciously acknowledge the existence of whatever is threatening or doing so very fleetingly before pushing it into the unconscious. To use a controversial example, people who have been traumatically abused may later avoid the horror of processing this consciously by remembering only good things about their abuser. Table 14.2 gives brief details for a few specific defence mechanisms.

Keeping threatening things unconscious requires effort and this depletes people's mental capabilities. The more people defend themselves by keeping things unconscious, the more literally simple-minded they become. This can have a cumulative effect. The younger people are when they experience trauma, the earlier they will need to defend themselves against anxieties. This limits their subsequent ability to interact effectively with the world, which increases the likelihood that they will find more things threatening and perhaps experience further trauma. These people will then need to expend further energy defending themselves and so the negative spiral continues. In Freudian terms, problems at an early stage of development leave people

TABLE 14.2 *Defence mechanisms shown in descending order of maturity according to Vaillant's (1977) categorization.*

	Example	Conception: When used as a defence mechanism, this involves...	Other examples
Mature defences	Altruism	Reacting to loss by taking pleasure in helping others (e.g. an ex-drinker becoming a sponsor for Alcoholics Anonymous).	Anticipation Humour Sublimation Suppression
Neurotic defences	Displacement	Redirecting impulses towards less threatening targets (e.g. yelling at the kids when scared to yell at your partner).	Dissociation Intellectualization (including isolation, rationalization, and undoing) Reaction formation
Immature defences	Projection	Seeing and often condemning in others what would be threatening if recognized in the self (e.g. others' 'excessive' violence or promiscuity).	Acting out Fantasy Hypochondria Passive aggression
Pathological defences	Denial	Refusing to acknowledge reality (e.g. a terminal diagnosis).	Delusion Distortion

relatively unprepared to cope effectively with the challenges presented by each subsequent developmental stage.

A final phenomenon that is important here is **regression**. This occurs when people seek relief from a stressful situation by using strategies that brought them comfort at an earlier stage of development. Examples include behaviours such as sucking your thumb, engaging in excessively ordered activities, or being overly eager to please other people. When such behaviours are compulsively used to self-soothe in ways that limit functioning, they are **symptoms** of **neuroses**.

Human nature and variability

Many of Freud's theories concern human nature: characteristics common to all people. Freud suggested that all people are born with commonly inherited instincts, share personality structures and processes, go through the same developmental stages, and so on. Freud's theories also predict individual differences. Freud's thoughts on stages of development, for example, suggest age differences in such things as interests, abilities, and social preferences. Freud's theories also suggest reliable differences across types of people. Perhaps most obviously, they predict various sex differences.

Although biology certainly matters within Freud's theories, experience plays a crucial role. All humans share the same instincts, but how people are treated when they express those instincts will determine how readily or reluctantly they will express them in similar ways in the future. If children's normal instinct expression is responded to in unusual ways, those children's subsequent personality development is also likely to be unusual. Similarly, cultures that reliably differ in how they respond to particular forms of instinct expression may generate or replicate reliable personality differences across those cultures.

FOCUS POINT 14.3

FREUD AND PERSONALITY

According to Freud, babies are mostly alike. Their features are mainly the ones inherited by virtue of them being human beings. They seek pleasure and to avoid discomfort, and the sources of each are universal (e.g. pleasure comes from food when hungry, comfortable temperatures, a balance of security and exploration, and so forth).

Depending on when and where they are born, babies will almost immediately experience varying consequences of engaging in their universally instinctive pleasure-seeking behaviours. Cultures, subcultures, and caregivers have different child-rearing beliefs, abilities, and practices. Different situations can also impact differentially on the quality of childcare provision. Each difference in child rearing has the potential to affect babies' personality development.

A culture or subculture that overly indulges infants will raise citizens with tendencies to be excessively trusting and passive. A culture or subculture that overly frustrates infants' needs will raise citizens with tendencies to be excessively suspicious and exacting. Cross-cultural and between-group personality differences will result.

Boys and girls have different biologies and different developmental paths, although the latter stem as much from psychological as from biological causes. Freud thought that children's recognition of biological sex differences has a profound effect on their gender and sexual development. Broadly speaking, children come to identify with their same-sex parent and develop more sexualized orientations towards members of the opposite sex. The sex differences that result from such events also tend to be exacerbated by the fact that most societies treat children in gender-specific ways. Boys and girls tend to be rewarded and punished for doing different things. This affects how comfortable children are pursuing and expressing pleasure in particular ways and leads to further gender differences. You can learn more about gender roles **here**[1].

Stages of development result in age differences in personality, such as in motivation, cognitive abilities, self-regulation, and the like. These also result in age-specific responses to life events that may themselves affect personality development. A father laughing when his daughter urinates on the carpet will have a different effect on her personality development depending on whether she is a teenager or a tiny baby. A mother breast-feeding her son will have a different impact on his personality development depending on whether he is 6 months or 6 years old.

Freudian theory also suggests that experiential history is important in personality development. A baby repeatedly traumatized at a young age will approach subsequent events in a very different way from one given an optimum balance of indulgence and frustration. Such effects are also likely to be cumulative, with the former baby being increasingly less able than the latter baby to experience situations in ways that promote healthy personality development.

In sum, Freud's theory suggests that all humans share fundamental similarities, some of which reliably lead to individual and group differences in personality (e.g. according to people's age and gender). Moreover, people's experiences further affect their personality development and some of those experiences lead to cross-cultural and between-group personality differences.

Psychoanalytic personality research

Freud's theory suggests that enduring personality characteristics can result from people becoming chronically fixated in or regressing to particular developmental stages. For example, Kline and Storey (1977) devised questionnaire measures of **oral optimism** and **oral pessimism**. Oral optimism, theoretically associated with the oral stage being excessively rewarding, is indicated by self-reports suggesting such things as relatively high optimism, dependence, verbal fluency, and sociability. Oral pessimism, theoretically associated with the oral stage being excessively punishing, is indicated by self-reports suggesting such things as relatively high pessimism, independence, envy, coldness, verbal aggression, hostility, and malice. Subsequent research has found associations between oral pessimism scores and smoking and depression (e.g. Maltby, Lewis, & Hill, 1998).

Related research has investigated personality characteristics interpretable from but not exclusively grounded in a Freudian perspective – for example, Bornstein's (1992) work on the dependent personality, arguably closely related to the oral optimist. Such research typically includes Freud's theories among its influences and, although it may have amendments that include things such as changes to the way things are labelled, is interpretable as being 'generally supportive' of Freud's basic ideas.

Other research derives from the notion that people need to develop healthy egos to cope with the various demands of id, superego, and reality. People with **resilient** egos are able to respond flexibly and effectively to changing and sometimes challenging circumstances. People with less resilient egos tend to be either **overcontrolled**, dominated by their superego's excessive expectations, or **undercontrolled**, dominated by their id's unchecked impulsivity. Ego resilience is associated with a range of beneficial outcomes while being undercontrolled in particular is associated with a range of unfortunate ones, such as poor academic conduct, delinquency, and psychopathology (e.g. Robins, John, Caspi, Moffitt, & Stouthamer-Loeber, 1996).

Related research has focused on the social aspects of personality development. People receiving adequate nurturance are said to develop personalities that facilitate them developing 'secure' interpersonal relationships while those experiencing neglect or abuse have dispositions that tend to lead to various forms of insecure relationships. Wiseman, Mayseless, and Sharbany (2006), for example, found that undergraduates' loneliness at university was predicted by the quality of their remembered early relationships with their parents.

Freud's theories also formed the foundation for research on the authoritarian personality – 'a major landmark in the history of psychology, as well as being the single most important contribution to the study of fascism' (Billig, 1978, p. 36). This work is examined in some detail in the next section to illustrate how Freudian ideas can inform our understanding of crucial real-world events.

The authoritarian personality

The main body of initial research on the **authoritarian personality** was presented in a 1,000-page book of the same name (Adorno, Frenkel-Brunswik, Levinson, & Sanford, 1950). The first 10 pages still provide one of the best available accounts of Freudian personality theory. Here, the authors suggest that personality largely comprises a set of dispositions to react in predictable ways to particular circumstances, significantly shaped by how people were treated when following their natural instincts during childhood. They also note some important implications of this. First, widespread child-rearing practices can produce pronounced commonalities across people. Second, rapid changes in widespread child-rearing practices can produce marked generational and geographical differences in personality. Third, ideologies and propaganda will be attractive to different people according to how well these things promise to meet their personality needs. One main outcome of the authoritarian personality research programme was a measure called the F-scale. High scores on the F-scale identify people who are highly respectful of authority and hostile to anyone who is not. Scores on this scale correlate with a wide range of attitudes and behaviours such that people scoring high or low on the measure can be said to have strongly distinct personalities.

Billig (1978) described the typical highly authoritarian personality as a person

> who had a strict, disciplined upbringing, and has suppressed all feelings of resentment and aggression he might have felt towards his parents. Instead the authoritarian tends to idealize his parents, but at the same time he retains a subconscious hostility towards them. His attitudes toward authority in general parallel his attitudes towards his parents. Outwardly that authoritarian is respectful, and even deferential, towards authority-figures – the inward anger is tightly repressed and is displaced onto those he considers to be his inferiors. Thus the authoritarian has an excessive concern for rank and status. He likes social position to be clearly defined, and in general he is intolerant of ambiguity and is unable to handle his ambivalent feelings. Just as he cannot handle his aggressive feelings, so too does the authoritarian find it difficult to develop a balanced outlook on sexual matters. He is obsessed with sex, but in a puritanical and hypocritical manner. He generally finds personal

intimacy difficult and prefers to follow the 'correct' social roles rather than express his own emotional feelings. The ... authoritarian ... is ... a weakling, who copes with his own inadequacies by excessive reverence to the powers that be and by venting his aggressiveness upon his social inferiors and upon 'inferior' outgroups. (p. 108)

Personality change

Psychoanalytic problems are thought to occur when the ways people use to defend themselves against anxiety are more problematic than they are helpful. Therapists use a variety of techniques to help people realize that this has happened. In large part, this means helping people become consciously aware of an earlier trauma and the feelings it evoked in ways that people – now older and with more resources and support – can deal with less defensively. This **catharsis** and the realization that previously used defences are now neither necessary nor helpful frees people to deal with the world more functionally.

Catharsis may help people with some mental health problems by alleviating their anxieties, ridding them of troubling symptoms, and steering them towards more functional patterns of behaviour, but it is not the only route to personality improvement. Personality development can benefit, for example, from 'appropriate parenting' at any age: that is, receiving from others an optimal balance of consistent indulgence and expectation (Feeney, 2004).

Evaluation

Psychoanalytic theory offers a rich account of all aspects of personality. It provides explanations of human nature, individual differences, development, cultural influences, and psychopathology. There is also evidence of personality types and traits derived from, or at least consistent with, Freudian thought.

The main problem with psychoanalytic theory is that it is not easy to confidently specify or test specific hypotheses derived from it. It is *too* all-encompassing and flexible to be considered scientific. It can explain anything *after* it has happened but its predictions tend to be vague. Many things that can be explained by Freudian theory can be explained just as well using theories that are both more parsimonious and better able to make precise predictions.

Of course, a theory having limitations is not justification enough to abandon it completely. It is also very poor justification for demanding that no one talks seriously about it. It can be fun speculating what Freud would think about the significant number of people who get so extremely agitated when defending or dismissing his theories. Westen (1998) is highly recommended for readers seeking a thorough, clear, and balanced source of further information on Freud's influence on personality psychology.

DISCUSSION POINTS

1. Using Erikson's theory of psychosocial development as a guide, what optimal and suboptimal outcomes are possible from a midlife crisis?
2. What advice would you give parents who wanted to raise a non-authoritarian child, and might there be any risks in them trying to do so?

SECTION SUMMARY

- Much modern personality theory has developed as an aid to counselling and psychotherapy.

- Freud came to believe that, during infancy and childhood, people develop unconscious methods for coping with extreme anxiety and then continue using these defence mechanisms throughout life, even when more mature responses to events would be more functional.

- Freud became fascinated by hysteria and wondered whether it could be cured verbally.

- Freud believed that there are various levels of consciousness, most often summarized using his metaphorical topographical model.

- Influenced by Darwin's recently published theory of evolution (*On the Origin of Species*, 1859), Freud thought that people biologically inherit motivational mechanisms or self-preservation instincts that support survival.

- Freud thought that different parts of the body are particularly important for motivation at different ages. He proposed that children pass through various stages in the process of maturation: the oral, anal, phallic, and genital stages.

- Erik Erikson modified and extended Freud's developmental theory. He reconceptualized each psychosexual stage as a series of age-specific crises or, more appropriately, tasks.

- Freud compartmentalized the human personality into the id, ego, and superego.

- Freud's theory suggests that enduring personality characteristics can result from people becoming chronically fixated in or regressing to particular developmental stages. For example, Kline and Storey (1977) devised questionnaire measures of oral optimism and oral pessimism.

- Other research derives from the notion that people need to develop healthy and resilient egos to cope with the various demands of id, superego, and reality.

- Research into the authoritarian personality states that personality largely comprises a set of dispositions to react in predictable ways to particular circumstances, significantly shaped by how people were treated when following their natural instincts during childhood. The research resulted in the development of the F-scale. High scores on the F-scale identify people who are highly respectful of authority and hostile to anyone who is not.

TRAIT PERSONALITY THEORY

LEARNING OBJECTIVE 14.3

Discuss the background, claims, and key features of trait personality theory.

If psychoanalytic personality theory tends towards being somewhat theory heavy and evidence light, trait theory tends towards the opposite. It is a largely data-driven approach that some argue is often lacking much meaningful theory (Eysenck, 1992).

Qualities of manifest traits

At a minimum, **traits** are adjectives or phrases that can be used to describe regularities in people's manifest behaviour. If a person is said to have a trait of discretion, that person is being described as being *reliably* discrete.

Manifest traits vary in their **consistency**. Consistency describes regularity of behaviour across time. Some degree of consistency is required for people to have manifest traits; otherwise it would not be possible to describe their regularities of behaviour. Nevertheless, the more regularity across time there is in people's behaviour, the more consistent their manifest traits. Some people are somewhat considerate. Others are rarely if ever inconsiderate. The latter have more consistent traits of considerateness.

Manifest traits also vary in their **generality**. Generality describes regularity of behaviour across different sorts of situation. Some manifest traits show high consistency only within rather specific situations. A person might be consistently confident on stage but not be particularly confident in other situations. Other people are consistently confident in more or less any situation. The latter have more general (or broad) traits of confidence.

Manifest traits are **universal** in the sense that everyone can be given a score indicating how strongly they manifest any given regularity of behaviour. Everyone can be scored for how conscientiousness they are, even if their scores may indicate that they are reliably lacking in conscientiousness.

Manifest trait scores are usually calibrated by comparing the extent to which different people manifest regularities of particular behaviours. Typically, a few people will obtain extremely low scores, a few people will obtain extremely high scores, and most people will obtain scores somewhere in the middle. Thus, manifest trait scores are **dimensional** and indicate individual differences. While some sense can be made of claims that people scoring at opposite extremes on given traits are different **types** of people, this can mask the fact that their differences are really a matter of degree and that most people are not extreme types. Most people are not 'introverts' or 'extraverts' but differ in how much of their behaviour is relatively introverted or extraverted.

Organizing trait descriptions

There are potentially as many manifest traits as there are different ways of describing regularities in people's behaviour. Many descriptions, though, are near-synonyms, which means that additional descriptions often add little or no useful information to that given by a well-chosen starter-list. Many trait theories try to describe as much as possible about behavioural regularities using as few as possible distinct descriptive terms.

Eysenck (1947) found that many terms used to describe people correlated with each other but not with other descriptors that themselves correlated among themselves. So, for example, people described as sociable also tended to be described as lively and active, and people described as moody also tended to be described as emotional and irrational, but there was little correlation between people's sociability and their moodiness. Based on such findings, Eysenck proposed that numerous individual differences in people's consistent temperament and behaviour can be

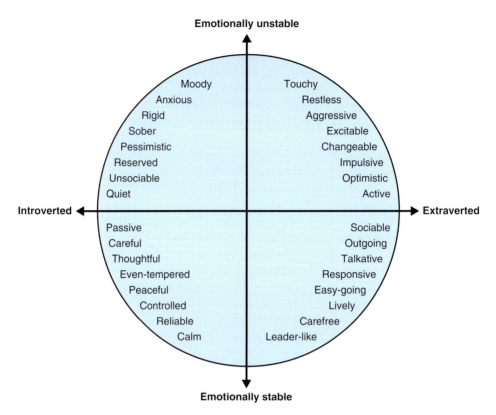

FIGURE 14.1 *Eysenck's Big Two traits of introversion–extraversion (horizontal axis) and emotional stability–instability/neuroticism (vertical axis). Each quadrant shows characteristics associated with being relatively low or high on each trait.*

captured simply by noting their relative positions on two **independent** dimensions: **introversion** versus **extraversion** and **emotional stability** versus **neuroticism**. Knowing how people score on each of these dimensions enables the prediction of a large number of more specific reliable attributes. As can be seen in Figure 14.1, people who are relatively high in both extraversion and neuroticism are likely to be more regularly restless, impulsive, and aggressive than are people obtaining lower scores on either dimension.

Eysenck and Eysenck (1976) came to believe that the **Big Two** model did not capture important traits manifest by people at the margins of society. Adding a third dimension of **psychoticism** versus impulse control allowed them to do this. This **Big Three** theory is often called Eysenck's **PEN model** after the *p*sychoticism, *e*xtraversion, and *n*euroticism extremes of the three traits in it.

It has increasingly been argued that five dimensions are optimal for parsimoniously but comprehensively describing universal regularities in manifest behaviour. In psychology, these are usually described using Costa and McCrae's five factor model of personality traits (FFM) (McCrae & Costa, 2008). The FFM identifies the **Big Five** personality dimensions as openness to experience (O), conscientiousness (C), extraversion (E), agreeableness (A), and neuroticism (N), which handily form the acronym OCEAN. Each trait within the FFM is a relatively broad one that is composed of and indicated by a number of more specific traits, often termed **facets**. Agreeableness, for example, is composed of and indicated by people having a relatively high combination of manifest enduring trust, straightforwardness, altruism, compliance, modesty, and tender-mindedness. Block (1995) provides a fascinating history and critique of this important model's development.

The six-trait **HEXACO model** of personality (see Ashton, Lee, & de Vries, 2014) differs from the FFM mainly by essentially splitting the latter's agreeableness trait into two, one capturing how straightforward people are in social interaction and the other capturing how concerned people are with others' welfare (Ashton & Lee, 2005). The model calls these traits *h*onesty–*h*umility and *a*greeableness, respectively, with the other letters of the model's name coming from *e*motionality (previously called neuroticism), *e*xtraversion, *c*onscientiousness, and *o*penness to experience.

DeYoung, Quilty, and Peterson (2007) found that each of the FFM traits could be meaningfully split into two narrower traits: openness to experience into intellect and openness, conscientiousness into industriousness and orderliness, extraversion into enthusiasm and assertiveness, agreeableness into politeness and compassion, and neuroticism into volatility and withdrawal. This finding suggests that a 10-trait model would be very similar to the FFM other than in sacrificing parsimony for specificity.

Researchers argue about how many traits are optimal. When dealing with manifest traits, there is unlikely ever to be consensus, as people will differ in what they want trait models to do and what characteristics they therefore want them to have. Models with fewer traits tend to be relatively parsimonious but provide only broadbrush descriptors of personality, analogous to models of 'general intelligence' (*g*). Models with larger numbers of traits tend to be relatively complex but provide 'precise' personality descriptions, analogous to models of 'multiple' or 'specific intelligences'. At the extremes are 'single-trait models' of 'general' personality (Musek, 2007) and models of personality that seek to describe behaviour in very specific situations (see the section titled 'Behavioural Signatures' below).

RESEARCH METHODS 14.1

FACTOR ANALYSIS

Factor analysis is a statistical technique that investigates both whether lots of measures are in large part measuring the same things and how many 'things' are being measured.

Try it out for yourself by indicating how well each of the following statements describe you, using a scale running from 1 = 'Does not describe me well' to 5 = 'Describes me very well' (from Davis, 1983):

1. In emergency situations, I feel apprehensive and ill at ease.

2. I sometimes feel helpless when I am in the middle of a very emotional situation.

3. Being in a tense emotional situation scares me.

4. I often have tender, concerned feelings for people less fortunate than me.

5. When I see someone being taken advantage of, I feel protective towards them.

6. I would describe myself as a pretty soft-hearted person.

If the statements were put to a large number of subjects, the responses to the first set of three would positively correlate with each other. The more a person felt that one of these statements described them well, the more they would feel that the other statements in the set also described them well.

Responses to the second set of three statements would also positively correlate with each other. Again, the more a person felt that one of the statements described them well, the more they would feel that the other statements in the set also described them well.

Responses to statements from one set would not correlate as highly with responses to statements from the other set. This is because the first set of statements indicates one thing, the second set indicates another, and those two things do not correlate very highly with each other. Specifically, the first set of statements indicates a trait of finding emotional or emergency situations personally distressing while the second set indicates a trait of feeling concerned about others' welfare, and it is perfectly possible to have one of these traits but not the other.

Two characteristics of factor analysis are particularly important to note. First, results are heavily influenced by the specific measures included in the analysis. If no statements indicating concern for others' welfare are included, factor analysis obviously cannot identify concern for others' welfare as something that various items are measuring. Less obviously, perhaps, researchers can 'rig' factor-analytic results by including (only) measures specifically for what they want to find. This is what Costa and McCrae explicitly did when developing their five factor model of personality traits (FFM). They only included measures if they seemed good indicators of one of the five FFM traits and also seemed 'independent' of the other four. If a particular test item did not indicate one and only one of the traits they sought to measure, Costa and McCrae replaced it with a measure that they hoped would better give them the result they sought.

Second, the factors identified by factor analysis need to be interpreted and given a name. Someone needs to decide what 'thing' each factor indicates. What I have called 'concern for others' welfare' above could instead equally be called 'sympathy', 'compassion', or 'empathy'.

These characteristics of factor analysis explain some of the apparent discrepancies between results obtained by different trait researchers. As Eysenck so clearly demonstrated, researchers can find evidence of either two or three traits simply by selecting which trait indicators to include in their analysis. Similarly, whether a set of test items most indicates 'openness to experience' or 'intellect' will depend, in part, on which specific set of measures is used and how the resultant factor is interpreted.

Traits predict behaviour

Manifest traits typically describe the relative extent to which people behave in particular ways, on average, across a range of situations. A person high in extraversion is high in extraversion *because* they are more extravert than other people, on average, across situations in which manifestations of extraversion vary. Because this is what trait scores are, it would be remarkable if they didn't predict behaviour. But they do (e.g. Paunonen, 2003). Schwartz et al. (2013), for example, found strong and distinctive associations between traits and the sorts of language people routinely use on social media. Their work shows that people high in neuroticism use a lot of words indicative of being upset and people low in neuroticism (and therefore high in emotional stability) use much more positive and celebratory language. This should not surprise anyone. Experiencing and interacting with the world in these distinctive ways is part of what it means that people are relatively neurotic or emotionally stable.

Matching measures with what they are supposed to measure

Prediction of behaviour is most accurate when the behaviour and the measure used to predict it have a similar degree of specificity. Traits are usually broad measures, measuring average behaviour over a range of situations over time. They therefore usually predict similarly broad behaviours better than they do narrower ones. They tend to be better at predicting an average of behaviours over a range of trait-expressive situations than they are at predicting behaviour in any particular single situation. Knowing that a person scores high in the broad trait of agreeableness will usually allow better prediction that the person will be relatively agreeable, on average, across a range of situations than it will of how the person will behave in a specific one-off situation (Epstein, 1980).

Behavioural signatures

In 1995, Mischel and Shoda recommended identification of reliable individual differences in patterns of enduring but highly situation-specific behaviours. These are called **behavioural signatures**. Four children's behavioural signatures in verbal aggression are illustrated in Figure 14.2. The labels on each horizontal axis show five specific situations: being approached by a peer, being teased by a peer, being praised by an adult, and so on. The vertical axis shows how verbally aggressive each child was, on average, in each specific type of situation, relative to other children in the study. A score of zero on the vertical axis would indicate that a child showed an average level of

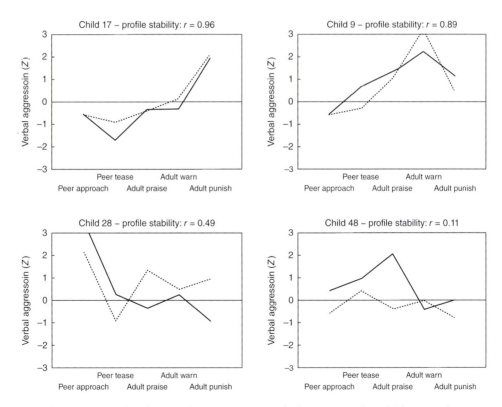

FIGURE 14.2 *Example behavioural signatures. How verbally aggressive four children are relative to other children in each of five situations. For details, see the text.*

Source: Shoda, Mischel, and Wright (1994). American Psychological Association. Reproduced with permission.

verbal aggression that was exactly typical for the children in the study in that particular type of situation. Scoring above zero indicates a higher than typical amount of verbal aggression and scoring a negative number indicates a lower than typical amount of verbal aggression. The solid and dotted lines show each child's level of average verbal aggression according to measures taken during two different periods of time.

Child 17, shown in the top-left graph, reliably reacts with about as much verbal aggression as other kids in the study when praised or warned by an adult or when approached by a peer. They are considerably less verbally aggressive than others when teased by a peer during one of the sampling timeframes (but not the other) and markedly and consistently more verbally aggressive than other kids in response to being punished by adults.

Compare this with Child 9, shown in the top-right graph. Child 9 behaves normally when approached or perhaps even teased by a peer but seems to have issues when interacting with adults. Whether praised, punished, or, especially, warned by adults, this child is reliably exceptionally verbally aggressive in response.

Child 9 and Child 17 both show strong behavioural consistency within a range of particular situations, as indicated by their respective 'profile stability' r coefficients being close to 1. Child 28 and Child 48 show much less behavioural consistency.

Behavioural signatures recognize differences when they occur between people with identical 'general trait' scores in, for example, aggression. A child who is reliably aggressive with peers and reliably passive with adults could easily obtain the same score for 'trait aggression' as both another child with exactly the opposite pattern and a third child who was somewhat erratically aggressive. Knowing each child's behavioural signature in aggression would allow for much better judgements of how aggressive they are likely to be in particular future situations than would their trait aggressiveness scores. This need not be taken as a criticism of general trait measures: they strive to do something different.

Behavioural signatures reverse a trend in trait research. Rather than seeking to describe as much as possible about human behaviour with as few measures as possible, behavioural signatures are used to describe behavioural characteristics in a potentially infinite number of very precise situations – for example, how upset people will be in comparison to each other, on average, when witnessing pets being abused by their owners, or something similar.

Animal traits

Animals' individual differences in average behaviour over time and situations can also be captured using trait measures. Gosling and John (1999) reviewed 19 previous studies investigating 12 sorts of animal and found that all could be rated on measures of four of the Big Five traits. The exception was conscientiousness, which was found to be meaningful only for descriptions of chimpanzees' behaviour. Gosling, Kwan, and John (2003) found that strangers evaluating dogs' traits from their behaviour arrived at similar judgements to the dogs' owners. Indeed, the correspondence between these two ratings of dogs' 'personalities' was at least as strong as has been found between self- and other ratings of human personality (Paulhus & Bruce, 1992). Some researchers speculate that such trait similarity across species is evidence of common evolutionary histories (e.g. Mehta & Gosling, 2008). Maybe, but maybe it means little more than that trait theories provide rather generally useful systems of descriptive terminology.

ACTIVITY 14.4

THE FIVE FACTOR 'MODEL' OF...

Think of a category of objects or things (e.g. nations, cars, household objects, flowers). Now think of an example from your chosen category that you can imagine describing as being particularly low or high in any of the following qualities: openness to experience, conscientiousness, extraversion, agreeableness, and neuroticism.

You might think of 1930s Germany as being particularly low in openness to experience, for example. Now score your exemplar on the remaining four traits. Finally, repeat this exercise with other exemplars from your chosen category until you have examples of both high and low scores on all five traits. What does your success or failure on this task suggest to you about the five factor model of personality traits?

Explaining traits

The phrase 'personality trait' can be used to refer to a pattern of observable behaviour or to something 'about' or 'within' a person that causes them to exhibit that pattern of behaviour. The former is merely a description whereas the latter is an explanation of the description.

Imagine two people who seem very alike. Both are social workers. Both are in stable, long-term relationships and have partners and children who adore them. Both are almost unfailingly polite and kind. Neither has a bad word to say about anyone. It is rare for either of them to lose their temper. Both are trusted and valued by friends and acquaintances alike. Both are manifestly 'nice' people. Or, to put it another way, both have similar sets of 'nice' *manifest* traits.

It is undeniable that these people behave the way they do because of the sorts of people they are. There must be something 'about' or 'within' them that causes them to react in such predictably similar ways.

It is tempting to say that these people both behave so nicely because they *are* nice, that they were born with 'nice' genes, that they are nice 'deep down', or similar, and then to say that it is the niceness 'within' them that *causes* them to be so nice in practice. That is, it is tempting to infer latent 'niceness' traits from manifest 'niceness' traits and then 'explain' the latter with reference to the former. This is circular reasoning. It says that people must be a certain way deep down if they regularly behave that way on the surface – and then 'explains' the surface behaviour by saying it stems from the inferred deep-down characteristics.

The error here is that there can be a variety of underlying reasons for any given set of observed events. This is sometimes called the principle of **equifinality**. While people often veer towards seeking 'the' explanation for any given phenomenon, the principle of equifinality reminds us that this may be an error. Things that appear to have the same cause do not always do so.

To return to our social workers, one is indeed nice by virtue of being born that way. He loves life and everything about it. He likes people and relishes opportunities to make them happier. He's always been this way and no one expects him to change. Unless something remarkable happens to change who this man is, he was literally born and will remain a people person.

This is not the case with the other social worker. He and his analyst know the truth. He has a very dark temperament. Whenever anything upsets him – which happens more than he would like – his instant impulse is aggressive. He automatically blames others and has to fight the urge to lash out. He scares himself. However, he learned long ago the consequences of allowing his impulses free expression. Fed up with seeing fear and hatred in others' eyes and also with his growing sense of self-loathing, he has been determined to become a better person. Over the years, he has learned to keep himself in check. He has discovered how rewarding it can be to ignore or smother his natural inclinations and to find ways of behaving that he and others appreciate. Although his initial impulses tend to be far from nice, indeed because his initial impulses tend to be far from nice, he takes great pride in being just about the nicest person anyone knows – on the surface at least.

Both social workers behave the way they do because of things 'within' them, but different things are involved in each case. The similarities in their surface traits are not good enough evidence to safely infer similarities in their latent trait, still less to infer that the same latent traits cause the similarities in the manifest traits.

Most personality traits are descriptive of coherent sets of manifest characteristics. To say that someone has a particular trait is usually to say no more than that person reliably behaves in particular ways and that this makes them reliably different from people who act in other ways in such situations. It is also common to infer that these differences stem from 'something' within the person but, as we have seen, this is a somewhat questionable practice unless independent evidence exists to corroborate such an inference.

To the limited extent that trait theorists have been seriously interested in explaining where manifest traits come from, most have speculated biological underpinnings. Eysenck, for example, speculated that enduring individual differences in psychoticism, extraversion, and neuroticism derive from chronic differences in people's levels of particular hormones (e.g. androgen), higher brain (i.e. cortical) activity, or lower brain (i.e. limbic) activity, respectively. Empirical investigations of such biological underpinnings of manifest traits have tended at best to provide weak evidence (for a review, see Cooper, 2010). The main reason for this is likely to be that stabilities in broad characteristics such as manifest traits are the result of interactions between many specific biological mechanisms (e.g. instincts) and many situational (e.g. cultural) and experiential (e.g. learning histories; see section 'Social Cognitive Personality Theories' below) factors.

One manifest trait that people have sought to explain is heroic helping. If we can understand why some people are exceptionally willing to incur considerable costs to help others, perhaps we can find ways to make such behaviour less exceptional.

The altruistic personality

The organization Yad Vashem celebrates gentiles (non-Jews) who took substantial personal risks during World War II to help rescue Jews from Nazi persecution. Oliner and Oliner (1992) found that such rescuers typically helped in many ways over an extended period, thus suggesting a broad and enduring manifest trait that differentiated rescuers from others who did little or nothing to help. The Oliners discovered that the differences were much broader and more enduring than this. Forty years after the war, past rescuers relative to past bystanders had more Jewish friends, a greater commitment to egalitarianism, stronger family attachments, broader social commitments, and more personal integrity (honesty, helpfulness, ability to take responsibility, a willingness to stand up for their beliefs), and they also engaged in more community helping (campaigning, volunteering, donating, supporting, helping). Oliner and Oliner (1992) concluded that rescuers' manifest traits must stem from 'enduring internally determined predispositions' (p. 375) and identified this as an **altruistic personality**.

Oliner and Oliner (1992) also thought that rescuers' 'enduring predisposition to act selflessly on behalf of others … develops early in life' (p. 3). Seeking to understand why, they found that rescuers received less ethnocentric parenting than did bystanders. Their parents were more likely to discuss Jews but were more likely to avoid using Jewish stereotypes, especially negative ones. Rescuers were also considerably more likely than bystanders to describe their family as close and to describe themselves as having been very close to both their mother and their father.

The Oliners found that rescuers' wartime activities were overwhelmingly ethically motivated, driven largely by beliefs that non-discriminatory care should be given to the oppressed by anyone able to provide it. Oliner and Oliner (1992) summarized their findings by claiming that rescuers were more able

> to recognize a choice where others perceived only compliance and to believe they could succeed where others foresaw only failure. This, coupled with their significantly greater attachments to people – their stronger feelings of closeness to others, their greater sense of responsibility toward them, and their heightened empathy for pain – predisposed them to altruistic behavior generally. But it was their inclusiveness – their willingness to see different types of people as essentially similar to themselves and their inclination to befriend others on the basis of personal qualities … which helps to explain why they helped Jews. (p. 178)

ACTIVITY 14.5

CAN FREUDIAN THEORY 'EXPLAIN' ANYTHING?

Give a Freudian account of the likely development of altruistic personalities. Make sure to evaluate each of the Oliners' conclusions, in light of what is said in the 'Explaining Traits' section above, and remember that different underlying explanations can be found or suggested for apparently similar surface behaviours.

Interactionism

Even when latent traits are speculated to predispose people to regularities of manifest behaviour, no trait theorist thinks that any 'internal' personality variable is the sole cause of behaviour. **Interactionism** posits that most behaviours result from an interaction of many causal factors, including, perhaps, multiple latent traits.

Evaluation

Regularities of behaviour across situations and across time clearly exist, as do reliable individual differences in those manifest traits. An immense research literature attests to this fact (e.g. Caspi, 2000). Among other things, this literature suggests that – where and when they have been measured – people's broad manifest traits typically do not change very much on average, especially after adolescence. Most relatively extraverted 21st-century North American teenagers are likely to become relatively extraverted adults (Soldz & Vaillant, 1999). How much any of this would be a surprise to non-psychologists is debatable.

Much less research has investigated possible reasons for such regularities. Without knowing these, it is difficult to speculate about the circumstances, if any, in which personality traits will or can be made to change. Knowing that trait scores have tended not to change very much in the samples so far studied does not at all entail that individual trait scores cannot change.

Because they are predominantly descriptive, contemporary trait models also give little guidance about healthy development. If anything, trait theorists have been keen to deny that particular trait scores are better than others. People relatively high in either introversion or extraversion are different from each other but neither is necessarily healthier or better developed. Thus, although various psychiatric conditions can be described in terms of combinations of trait scores (Widiger & Mullins-Sweatt, 2009), those descriptions alone do not provide much guidance for how, if at all, things can be improved.

SECTION SUMMARY

- Trait theory is a largely data-driven approach that some argue is often lacking much meaningful theory.

- Traits are adjectives or phrases that can be used to describe regularities in people's manifest behaviour. The phrase 'personality trait' can be used to refer to a pattern of observable behaviour or to something 'about' or 'within' a person that causes them to exhibit that pattern of behaviour. The former is merely a description whereas the latter is an explanation for the description.

- Manifest traits vary in their consistency. Consistency describes regularity of behaviour across time.

- Manifest traits also vary in their generality. Generality describes regularity of behaviour across different sorts of situation.

- Manifest traits are universal in the sense that everyone can be given a score indicating how strongly they manifest any given regularity of behaviour.

- Manifest trait scores are dimensional and indicate individual differences.

- There are potentially as many manifest traits as there are different ways of describing regularities in people's behaviour. Many trait theories try to describe as much as possible about behavioural regularities using as few as possible distinct descriptive terms.

- Eysenk proposed that numerous individual differences in people's consistent temperament and behaviour can be captured simply by noting their relative positions on two independent dimensions: introversion versus extraversion and emotional stability versus neuroticism. He extended this to form the Big Three theory, often called Eysenck's PEN model after the psychoticism, extraversion, and neuroticism extremes of the three traits in it.

- It has increasingly been argued that five dimensions are optimal for parsimoniously but comprehensively describing universal regularities in manifest behaviour. In psychology, these are usually described using Costa and McCrae's five factor model of personality traits (FFM). The FFM identifies the Big Five personality dimensions as openness to experience (O), conscientiousness (C), extraversion (E), agreeableness (A), and neuroticism (N), which handily form the acronym OCEAN.

- The six-trait HEXACO model of personality differs from the FFM mainly by essentially splitting the latter's agreeableness trait into two.

- DeYoung et al. (2007) found that each of the FFM traits could be meaningfully split into two narrower traits.

- Manifest traits typically describe the relative extent to which people behave in particular ways, on average, across a range of situations.

- Prediction of behaviour is most accurate when the behaviour and the measure used to predict it have a similar degree of specificity.

- A recent development in trait theory has been to identify reliable individual differences in patterns of enduring but highly situation-specific behaviours. These are called behavioural signatures.

- Animals' individual differences in average behaviour over time and situations can also be captured by using trait measures.

HUMANISTIC PERSONALITY THEORY

LEARNING OBJECTIVE 14.4

Discuss the background, claims, and key features of humanistic personality theory.

A critic might argue that traditional Freudian theory pessimistically conceives of people as barely bridled egoists struggling to assert themselves in punishingly constraining societies and that trait theory provides only simplistic descriptions of people equivalent to those that might be given of strangers or pets. As its label suggests, **humanistic personality theory** attempts a third way, conceiving of people not as dark or mysterious but as wondrous creatures full of positive potential.

What people need

Henry Murray (1938) suggested that people have primary and secondary needs. **Primary needs** are those necessary for physical survival and for biological growth. These include needs for such things as food, water, air, sex, and pain avoidance. **Secondary needs** are those Murray thought necessary for psychological growth. At a broad, trait-like level there are secondary needs for things such as ambition, materialism, power, affection, and information. Each of these broad needs encompasses narrower, facet-like needs. Power needs, for example, include needs for dominance, abasement, autonomy, deference, blame avoidance, and aggression. According to Murray, all people have all such needs but for each person some needs have higher priorities than others. Plenty of research supports both the idea that there are some things that all people seek or benefit from and the idea that people differ in some of the things that they personally seek or benefit from. These things are often labelled needs – for instance, needs for achievement, power, and affiliation (McClelland, 1961).

Be yourself

Carl Rogers (e.g. 1961) suggested that people have only one fundamental need: a need for **self-actualization**. Rogers thought that **human nature** confers a natural tendency towards positive growth. People are living things and as such have evolved in ways that support survival and increasing maturity over time. People should therefore trust their natural inclinations and their ability to learn from experience to become ever more adaptive creatures. Rogers called this willingness to trust the self the **organismic valuing** process.

However, Rogers also thought that society pressurizes people into becoming something they are not. Trying to be the sort of person that others seem to want can make us lose touch with our true selves and our natural inclination towards positive growth.

Conditions of worth

Humans are social animals. Other people can provide or withdraw all sorts of physical and psychological support. They can also inflict all sorts of physical and psychological pain. Pleasing others is often smarter than antagonizing them, especially when they have power.

People often try to control each other. Sometimes this is very overt, being implemented with obvious bribes or threats. More often, it is much more subtle. People value others conditionally, judging each other by how each behaves. They impose **conditions of worth** and express conditional regard. **Conditional negative regard** occurs when people show disapproval of others because of what they do, and **conditional positive regard** happens when people express approval of others because of their behaviour. By expressing conditional regard, people imply conditions of worth. People are judged by what they do. Evaluation of people is inseparable from evaluation of their actions and accomplishments.

People face countless messages of this sort. You are only a good child if you please your parents. You are only a real man if you are brave. You are only a good person if you have an appropriate combination of political or religious views. You are only a good student if you work hard or achieve certain grades. You are only attractive if you have a particular body shape, drive the right car, wear the right clothes, behave the right way, listen to the right music, and so on.

When people suspect that important others will remove their support or even become hostile towards those whom they do not consider worthy, and if judgements of worth seem conditional on doing or being certain things, the pressure felt to try to meet such conditions of worth can be immense.

Congruence

Conditional regard undermines organismic valuing. If others make it clear that they want you to do something, even if you were already planning to do it, you may act for reasons that do not support your personal growth. You may act to curry or keep others' favour rather than acting from your heart's desire. If you act in the former way, you risk losing touch a little with your real self. The more you try to fulfil others' desires rather than being true to your own, the more you risk losing your sense of authenticity and integrity and the less healthy your subsequent development is likely to be.

Rogers suggested that people are **congruent** to the extent that they are aware of their true inclinations and reactions. They are able and willing to acknowledge aspects of themselves that they know others might disapprove of and that they may even be a little alarmed about themselves. They recognize and accept things about themselves that might be considered evidence of weakness, deviance, or folly. Having confronted their impulses, they are in a better position to consider and choose from the full range of behavioural options available to them. It is possible to be congruent when giving one's impulses free rein or when overriding them; one simply has to recognize and accept them. People should do what feels right, whether that is acting on their initial impulses or choosing what seems a better option upon reflection. As long as people are in tune with their impulses and do what they want to do, they are congruent and exhibit **self-determination**.

Conditions of worth tend to make people feel anxious whatever they do. Knowing or suspecting that others do not trust us and will judge us harshly if we behave in particular ways makes it difficult to trust ourselves, to trust our organismic valuing process, to be congruent, and to be self-determined. If we conform to others' expectations, we risk feeling increasingly inauthentic and alienated from our true desires. If we do as we want, we risk being thought bad by others whose judgements matter to us and also perhaps having to suffer the consequences of doing so.

People in complex societies typically face multiple, strong, enduring, and conflicting conditions of worth, and for this reason anxiety and alienation are often widespread, severe, and chronic (see Burke, 1991).

 Professor Mihaly Csikszentmihalyi, a positive psychologist, discusses 'What makes a life worth living?' **in this TED Talk from 2004**[2].

Maturity

One of the most distinctive aspects of Rogers' theory is his belief that human nature is such that most people will mature in a positive way unless prevented from doing so.

> I find that man, like the lion, has a nature. My experience is that he is a basically trustworthy member of the human species, whose deepest characteristics tend toward development, differentiation, cooperative relationships; whose life tends fundamentally to move from dependence to independence; whose impulses tend naturally to harmonize into a complex and changing pattern of self-regulation; whose total character is such as to tend to preserve and enhance himself and his species, and perhaps to move it toward its further evolution. (Rogers, 1957, p. 201, reprinted with permission)

Rogers says that as people mature:

- They tend to move away from facades. Pretense, defensiveness, putting up a front, tend to be negatively valued.

- They tend to move away from 'oughts'. The compelling feeling of 'I ought to do or be thus and so' is negatively valued. The client moves away from being what he 'ought to be', no matter who has set that imperative.

- They tend to move away from meeting the expectations of others. Pleasing others, as a goal in itself, is negatively valued.

- Being real is positively valued. The client tends to move toward being himself, being his real feelings, being what he is. This seems to be a very deep preference.

- Self-direction is positively valued. The client discovers an increasing pride and confidence in making his own choices, guiding his own life.

- One's self, one's own feelings come to be positively valued. From a point where he looks upon himself with contempt and despair, the client comes to value himself and his reactions as being of worth.

- Being a process is positively valued. From desiring some fixed goal, clients come to prefer the excitement of being a process of potentialities being born.

- Sensitivity to others and acceptance of others is positively valued. The client comes to appreciate others for what they are, just as he has come to appreciate himself for what he is.

- Deep relationships are positively valued. To achieve a close, intimate, real, fully communicative relationship with another person seems to meet a deep need in every individual, and is very highly valued.

- Perhaps more than all else, the client comes to value an openness to all of his inner and outer experience. To be open to and sensitive to his own *inner* reactions and feelings, the reactions and feelings of others, and the realities of the objective world – this is a direction which he clearly prefers. This openness becomes the client's most valued resource. (Rogers, 1964, p. 166, reprinted with permission)

Congruent people tend to become healthy, happy citizens. Being in touch with and accepting everything they think and feel and doing whatever feels right allows people to develop in ways that are good for them and good for the societies in which they live.

As for the self, so too for others. Trusting and accepting other people allows them to be congruent, to learn from their own mistakes, and to develop into healthy, happy citizens. Controlling or trying to control others, even for their own good, ultimately leads to problems.

Personality change

Conditions of worth and conditional regard influence people's personalities. Once a person learns, for example, that loved ones disapprove of members of particular social categories – Muslims, homosexuals, conservatives, extraverts, whatever – it will be difficult for that person to act on impulses or decisions to befriend one of those sorts of people, let alone to become one of them.

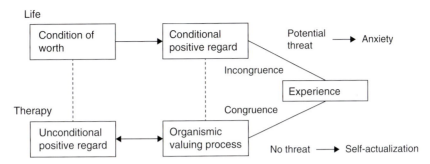

FIGURE 14.3 *A diagrammatic summary of Rogers' theory of personality development. See text for details.*

When people are able to employ organismic valuing, their personality changes in positive ways over time. They learn that acting on impulses can have initially unexpected or unappreciated consequences that they do not like. Next time they are faced with a similar situation, their immediate impulses may be different in the light of experience or they may take a little longer to decide what they really want to do. Learning that long-term consequences can differ from short-term ones brings about the possibility of prudence. Learning that overcoming one's anxieties can have rewarding consequences makes bravery an option. Learning that it can be pleasing in some circumstances to help or to hurt others leads to possibilities for altruism or aggression. As long as people truly want to do so, acting on decisions made after reflection is perfectly consistent with being true to themselves, even if their initial impulses were to act in different ways.

Figure 14.3 illustrates Rogers' view of healthy and unhealthy personality development. The dotted vertical lines show alternatives. Multiple sources in life (the media, family, friends, employers) suggest to people that they will only be of worth and value to the extent they meet certain conditions. As these are often unrealistic and frequently mutually exclusive, people worry about failing and losing the love and respect of others they care about. And, to the extent that people internalize others' expectations, they also find it increasingly difficult to love and respect themselves. In turn, this leads them to want to deny aspects of reality (e.g. their 'failings') and find it difficult to trust themselves (e.g. their desires). Therapeutic relationships provide **unconditional positive regard** and encourage trust in and commitment to people's true selves. This enables people to be guided by desires and mechanisms that lead automatically to personality development so that people become increasingly healthy individuals and better citizens.

Person-centredness

Rogers' ideas have had profound effects on socializing practices such as counselling, education, parenting, employment, and government. If controlling people makes them anxious and alienates them from a process that would otherwise guide them towards development that is good for them and their society, attempting to control people would rarely seem a useful or moral thing to do. And, if setting conditions of worth and giving conditional regard is a form of social control, encouraging others to behave in particular ways runs the risk of being harmful for them and society, no matter how benign or benevolent people's intentions are.

Rogers initially put these ideas into practice by developing **person-centred** counselling (Rogers, 1992). Rather than give clients advice or encouragement to behave in particular ways, Rogers attempted to put them back in touch with their organismic valuing process and have the courage to act on their own preferences. To do so, clients need to recognize that many of their anxieties and much of their personal dissatisfaction stem from trying to please others. They also need to develop unconditional positive regard for themselves. Doing these things allows clients to become congruent and then self-determined, which in turn automatically leads to individually and socially positive personality development.

Unconditional positive regard is the bedrock of person-centred counselling. The counsellor values clients without conditions of worth. This provides a sense of security to clients and enables them to take the risk of valuing themselves. Clients know that their counsellor will value them come what may. Two other skills or characteristics help counsellors help clients. These are empathy and congruence. **Empathy** involves understanding others' thoughts and feelings. This helps counsellors to help clients identify the sources of their anxiety and dissatisfaction and also helps clients to identify their own preferences. Congruence (which can be thought of as a kind of empathy for the self) helps counsellors to identify their own preferences, which in turn helps them to keep their empathy accurate and their positive regard unconditional.

Person-centred approaches have the same bedrock of unconditional positive regard in other domains as they do in counselling. Person-centred education seeks to support students' self-acceptance and self-determination; person-centred employers try to pursue their own goals in ways that benefit from workers being given as much supported autonomy as possible; child-centred parenting seeks to support children learning things for themselves naturally, making their own decisions, and becoming captains of their own fate; and person-centred government attempts to minimally restrict and maximally support citizens' self-determination. In each case, the belief is that trusting people and helping them to trust themselves are ultimately in everyone's best interests.

Abraham Maslow

Abraham Maslow (see e.g. 1968) made two very important contributions to humanistic personality theory. He had well-being as a research focus and he developed his famous hierarchy of needs.

Psychologists often focus on problems and ways to avoid or reduce them. The temptation for them is then to generalize what they have found to theorize about human nature and make universal policy recommendations. This assumes that what works well for people with problems will also be beneficial for people without them.

Partly to avoid such overgeneralization based on biased sampling, Maslow explicitly researched optimal personality development. He selected 21 people whom he thought had unquestionably fulfilled their potential and become all they could be (see Focus Point 14.4). The list included Albert Einstein, Aldous Huxley, William James, Abraham Lincoln, and Eleanor Roosevelt. Using whatever information he could find about such people, Maslow sought characteristics that they tended to have in common and that at the same time differentiated them from everyone else. Boeree (2006b) summarizes Maslow's characteristics, many of which are very similar to the list of mature values Rogers identified (see the section above on 'Maturity').

FULFILLING HUMAN POTENTIAL

Humanistic psychologists are keen to identify both how people can fulfil their potential and how they can find a sense of fulfilment. These are not necessarily the same thing. Finding a sense of fulfilment is also not necessarily the same thing as enjoying yourself.

Philosophers have wondered for centuries about 'the good life'. Psychologists have investigated such matters empirically. Some psychologists have sought to identify the nature of a sense of fulfilment and how it relates to other subjectively positive psychological experiences. Typically, this involves differentiating between a feeling or an emotion often labelled 'happiness' and a deeper sense of satisfaction sometimes called 'eudemonia'.

Psychologists have also sought to understand how people achieve such subjectively positive psychological experiences. This typically involves identifying distinct sources of happiness or satisfaction and seeing which source promotes which outcome. A common expectation and finding among psychologists is that the sources of feeling happy are distinct from the sources of a sense of satisfaction and that pursuing the former can interfere with achieving the latter and, ironically, with achieving the former too. To pursue happiness can be directly self-defeating and it can also distract people from doing things that would lead to deeper feelings of fulfilment.

In a paper titled 'Happiness Is Everything, or Is It?', Ryff (1989) identified and developed measures for six 'key aspects of positive functioning', which in combination she claims comprise psychological well-being and/or the route to it. She labels these as self-acceptance, positive relations with others, autonomy, environmental mastery, purpose in life, and personal growth. The following table describes the characteristics of people likely to obtain high or low scores on each dimension.

Definitions for six dimensions of well-being.

Low scorer	High scorer
Self-acceptance	
• Feels dissatisfied with self. • Is disappointed with what has occurred with past life. • Is troubled about certain personal qualities. • Wishes to be different than what he or she is.	• Possesses a positive attitude towards the self. • Acknowledges and accepts multiple aspects of self, including good and bad qualities. • Feels positive about past life.
Positive relations with others	
• Has few close, trusting relationships with others. • Finds it difficult to be warm, open, and concerned about others. • Is isolated and frustrated in interpersonal relationships. • Is not willing to make compromises to sustain important ties with others.	• Has warm, satisfying, trusting relationships with others. • Is concerned about the welfare of others. • Is capable of strong empathy, affection, and intimacy. • Understands the give-and-take of human relationships.
Autonomy	
• Is concerned about the expectations and evaluations of others. • Relies on judgements of others to make important decisions. • Conforms to social pressures to think and act in certain ways.	• Is self-determining and independent. • Is able to resist social pressures to think and act in certain ways. • Regulates behaviour from within. • Evaluates self by personal standards.

Low scorer	High scorer
Environmental mastery	
• Has difficulty managing everyday affairs. • Feels unable to change or improve surrounding context. • Is unaware of surrounding opportunities. • Lacks a sense of control over the external world.	• Has a sense of mastery and competence in managing the environment. • Controls a complex array of external activities. • Makes effective use of surrounding opportunities. • Is able to choose or create contexts suitable to personal needs and values.
Purpose in life	
• Lacks a sense of meaning in life. • Has few goals or aims; lacks a sense of direction. • Does not see purpose of past life; has no outlook or beliefs that give life meaning.	• Has goals in life and a sense of directedness. • Feels there is meaning to present and past life. • Holds beliefs that give life purpose. • Has aims and objectives for living.
Personal growth	
• Has a sense of personal stagnation. • Lacks a sense of improvement or expansion over time. • Feels bored and uninterested with life. • Feels unable to develop new attitudes or behaviours.	• Has a feeling of continued development. • Sees self as growing and expanding. • Is open to new experiences. • Has a sense of realizing his or her potential. • Sees improvement in self and behaviour over time. • Is changing in ways that reflect more self-knowledge and effectiveness.

Source: Adapted from Ryff and Keyes (1995). American Psychological Association. Reproduced with permission.

TEST YOURSELF

According to Ryff's criteria, how positive is your psychological well-being? Would you say that such well-being is a marker of how much you are fulfilling your human potential, of how fulfilled you *feel*, both, or neither?

Whereas Rogers thought that healthy people are motivated by a constant process of self-actualization throughout their lives, Maslow conceived of self-actualization as an outcome of successful self-development. In 1943, Maslow proposed a five level 'hierarchy of needs' with a need for self-actualization at the top. Below the need for self-actualization are physiological needs, safety needs, affiliation needs, and esteem needs, respectively. Maslow thought that each of these lower **deficiency needs**

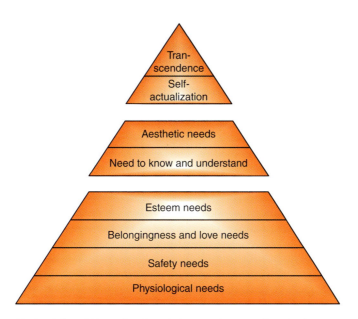

FIGURE 14.4 *Maslow's (later) hierarchy of needs (see text for an explanation).*

requires satisfaction before the next highest need becomes a priority. Thus, safety needs are only a concern after physiological needs are satisfied (and are therefore no longer pressing); safety needs must be satisfied before affiliation needs become salient; and so on. Only when all four deficiency needs are satisfied do people become aware of and motivated by the **growth needs** for self-actualization.

Maslow later differentiated sublevels of self-actualization and placed a need for self-transcendence at the very top of the pyramid (see Figure 14.4; Koltko-Rivera, 2006). In becoming all that they can be, people start to think about making contributions to projects beyond mere self-development. One way of doing this is by voluntarily serving others.

DISCUSSION POINT

Do you think self-actualization is a process or an outcome? What is the evidence for your opinion?

Autonomous service

Colby and Damon (1992) asked 22 moral experts (philosophers, theologians, and the like) to create a list of attributes that someone who exemplifies morality might have. The list suggested characteristics such as having a sustained and non-discriminatory respect for all humanity and consistently acting in accordance with moral principles. The authors then interviewed 84 people identified as satisfying these criteria and their characteristics were examined. Many of these characteristics were those that qualified them as moral exemplars in the first place, so no great surprises there! Most importantly for current purposes was that the exemplars willingly prioritized service. They wanted to serve others' interests. The same was found by Hart and Fegley (1995) among African American and Latin American adolescents nominated by community leaders as having demonstrated unusual commitments to care for others or for the community. Similarly, Lee, Kang, Lee, and Park (2005) interviewed 60 people honoured on a national television programme for having behaved with exceptional altruism over an extended period. In each sample, researchers found that exceptional helpers showed 'a high sense of integrity, high self-esteem, and high autonomy'; their altruism was 'consistent, voluntary, and well self-controlled' (Lee, Kang, Lee, & Park, 2005, p. 151).

Findings such as these suggest that the most impressive among us see little difference between doing what they want to do and being good citizens. Such people want to help others and to have a positive impact on society (Frimer, Walker, Dunlop, Lee, & Riches, 2011). According to humanistic personality theorists, such integration of self-interest and inclusive other-interest is a hallmark of self-actualized or self-actualizing people.

Roth (2008) investigated individual differences in college students' motives to help others. As predicted by humanistic approaches to personality, he found that students who liked to help others remembered their parents supporting their autonomy (and therefore giving them unconditional positive regard) while students who were selective and somewhat mercenary in their helping remembered parents whose regard for them appeared to have been more conditional upon their behaviour. Roth's research suggests that negative or positive conditional regard may be inferior to autonomy support at nurturing a sense of helping being intrinsically fulfilling. This can be illustrated by some of the statements Roth used. Statements measuring parental autonomy support included:

- As a child or adolescent, my [parents] explained to me why [they] thought it was important to help others.
- When my [parents] felt that I wasn't helpful enough to a friend in need, [they] tried to understand why.

Statements measuring parental conditional regard included:

- As a child or adolescent, I often felt that I would lose much of my [parents'] affection if I stopped being helpful and considerate of others.
- As a child or adolescent, I often felt that my [parents] would show me more affection or approval than [they] usually did if (or when) I was helpful and considerate towards others.

Roth's results suggest that providing conditional rewards for helping can make helping itself less satisfying and therefore less likely to be spontaneously repeated. Conditional rewards can undermine people's natural inclinations to be helpful and to derive satisfaction from being so. This is supported by research in which it was found that volunteers who remembered their parents supporting their autonomy were themselves intrinsically altruistic and would support others even when it was personally difficult to do so. People who remembered their parents being less supportive of their autonomy tended to volunteer only when there was clearly something in it for them (Clary & Miller, 1986).

Evaluation

Wicker, Brown, Wiehe, Hagen, and Reed (1993) presented participants with a list of situations that mapped onto Maslow's need hierarchy (e.g. having enough to eat and drink, feeling safe and unafraid, being part of a special group, being recognized by others as an outstanding student, and being mentally healthy and making full use of one's capabilities). Participants were asked to indicate how good they would feel if they were in each of these situations and how bad they would feel if they did not have these things. Negative reactions got stronger at the thought of lower-level needs not being satisfied and positive reactions got stronger when people thought about being in the situations indicative of higher-level needs being met. Consistent both with the idea of a needs hierarchy and with differentiating deficiency needs from growth needs, the thought of having basic needs unmet makes people anticipate being miserable and the thought of attaining higher levels of need satisfaction delights people.

Research supports the idea of a distinction between need-deficit conditions leading to ill health and need-satisfaction conditions facilitating thriving (e.g. Bartholomew, Ntoumanis, Ryan, Bosch, & Thøgersen-Ntoumani, 2011; Vansteenkiste & Ryan, 2013). Bartholemew, Ntoumanis, Ryan, and Thøgersen-Ntoumani (2011), for example, found that the mental and physical health of athletes whose needs were thwarted suffered such that they experienced negative feelings, emotional exhaustion, and burnout. Increasingly satisfying athletes' needs, on the other hand, led to increasingly positive outcomes such as positive emotions and feelings of vitality.

Need research has in the past been plagued by the same sort of 'How many?' and 'Which ones?' questions that have dogged trait research. Rather than trying to settle the matter by seeking consensus on the most useful set of needs, though, need research has begun to seek progress by increasing specificity. The questions asked now tend to be 'Needs for what and when?' and the equivalent 'What happens when particular needs are not met?' Food is clearly necessary for survival but people do not want to eat all the time and will suffer in different ways if they eat too much. Rather than make sweeping and seemingly contradictory claims that people both need to eat and have a need to refrain from eating, it is perhaps more useful to specify what happens when people eat particular things in particular amounts in particular ways in particular circumstances. Increasingly, it is being realized that similar things can be said about many things previously rather sweepingly claimed to be needs.

Like Freud's, Rogers' personality theory offers a rich and thought-provoking account of many aspects of personality, largely based on its founder's beliefs derived from self-examination and attempts to understand and help others. It is, however, a much simpler theory and allows more obvious specification of testable hypotheses. It also offers a more encouraging view of personality development and the conditions needed to facilitate it. Whereas Freud considered that important personality development often requires people to remember and 're-experience' traumatic situations from childhood that they have spent most of their lives actively trying to keep out of their consciousness, Rogers suggests that personality (and societal) improvement is possible merely by supporting people so that they can identify and do what they actually want to do in the present.

TEST YOURSELF

1. How can education meet or thwart students' needs?
2. What role might art play in personality development?

SECTION SUMMARY

- Humanistic personality theory conceives of people not as dark or mysterious but as full of positive potential.

- Henry Murray (1938) suggested that people have primary and secondary needs. Primary needs are those necessary for physical survival and for biological growth, while secondary needs are those Murray thought necessary for psychological growth.

- Carl Rogers (e.g. 1961) suggested that people have only one fundamental need: a need to self-actualize. He thought that human nature confers a natural tendency towards positive growth and that people should therefore trust their natural inclinations. Rogers called this willingness to trust the self the organismic valuing process.

- Rogers proposed that people value others conditionally, judging each other by how each behaves. They impose conditions of worth and express conditional regard. Conditional negative regard occurs when people show disapproval of others because of what they do and conditional positive regard happens when people express approval of others because of their behaviour.

- Congruence is a vital part of Rogers' theory: he suggested that people are congruent to the extent that they are aware of their true inclinations and reactions.

- One of the most distinctive aspects of Rogers' theory is his belief that human nature is such that most people will mature in a positive way unless prevented from doing so.

- Rogers' person-centred ideas have had profound effects on socializing practices such as counselling, education, parenting, employment, and government.

- Maslow made two very important contributions to humanistic personality theory. He had well-being as a research focus and he developed his famous five-level hierarchy of needs.

- At the top of Maslow's original needs hierarchy is a need for self-actualization. Below the need for self-actualization, in ascending order, are physiological needs, safety needs, affiliation needs, and esteem needs.

SOCIAL COGNITIVE PERSONALITY THEORIES

LEARNING OBJECTIVE 14.5

Discuss the background, claims, and key features of social cognitive personality theories.

Social cognitive theories of personality take the foundations of **behaviourism** as their starting point. These foundations are **classical conditioning** and **instrumental conditioning** (or **operant conditioning**), sometimes collectively referred to as forms of **associative learning**. These are methods of exploiting the way animals learn associations (i.e. what goes with what) to encourage or discourage particular forms of behaviour. As the term suggests, social cognitive theories of personality build on basic conditioning theories by taking into account the importance of social and cognitive processes in human learning. Personality development starts by people responding in reliable ways to frequently encountered stimuli, but, as their cognitive abilities increasingly facilitate powers of self-regulation, people increasingly choose for themselves how their personalities develop and are expressed.

Behaviourism

Pavlov's discovery of classical conditioning and Skinner's development of instrumental conditioning are among the most important discoveries in psychology. Their basic principles are simple; they can be flexibly employed to encourage most animals to increase or decrease the frequency with which they engage in more or less any behaviour they are biologically capable of – and, when carefully used, they work with almost infallible reliability.

Classical conditioning

All animals have biological reactions to certain stimuli. Show a hungry dog food and it will salivate. All animals also have an ability to learn associations – things that seem to go together. Ring a bell every time a hungry dog is shown food and it will come to associate ringing bells with food when hungry. Make this association fairly strong by having those things coexist with some regularity and the dog will come to expect all the things when any of them are present. In short, the dog will come to expect food whenever it hears a bell. It will then have the biological reaction that it previously had to food at times of hunger. It will salivate.

Classical conditioning thus involves animals coming to associate things that previously did not elicit a biological reaction with things that do so naturally (or because of prior conditioning). Learning via classical conditioning is therefore limited to being able to make these specific associations.

Instrumental learning

All animals have preferences. They like or dislike some situations more than they like or dislike others. Often it is easy enough to work out how to make a situation better or worse from an animal's point of view – for instance, by introducing or removing something that the animal likes or dislikes in that moment (e.g. food when it is hungry). If a situation is made better from an animal's point of view and this seems to have occurred because of something it did, that behaviour seems to the animal to have been rewarded. Similarly, if a situation is made worse from an animal's point of view and this seems to have occurred because of something it did, that behaviour seems to the animal to have been punished. Instrumental learning occurs when the animal comes to associate particular behaviours with particular rewarding or punishing consequences. And, because animals tend to seek rewards and to avoid punishment, they are likely to repeat behaviours that have previously been rewarding and to avoid those that have previously been punishing. If a trainer administers rewards or punishments conditionally in response to particular behaviours, learners will usually be more or less likely to repeat those behaviours, respectively.

Observational learning

All animals are capable of learning associations by experience. Some animals are also capable of **observational learning**.

Participants in an experiment by Berger (1962) witnessed people seeming to react with pain after hearing a tone. Participants later gave a fear response when they heard the same tone again. One explanation of this is **vicarious (classical) conditioning**. Respondents appeared to have learned to associate the tone and pain, despite not having personal experience of that association. In a study by Mineka, Davidson, Cook, and Kleir (1984), rhesus monkeys similarly learned an intense and enduring fear response to snakes after witnessing intense reactions by their parents to either real or live snakes.

TEST YOURSELF

Provide a *non-vicarious* classical conditioning account for the studies used as examples of vicarious conditioning. Hint: imagine being a participant in Berger's (1962) study. How would you have felt when watching others' pain after the tone sounded?

Humans have some capacities to a much greater extent than any other animal. One set of such superior capacities is cognitive. In comparison to any other animal, people are amazing at thinking.

One thing humans use their cognitive powers for is to learn about the consequences of others' behaviours and think about whether they can use what they learn in personally rewarding ways. Having this capacity for social (instrumental) learning makes humans incredibly versatile students.

Prior to his work on **moral disengagement**, Albert Bandura illustrated the potential and implications of **social learning**. In a study conducted by Bandura in 1965, nursery school children watched a 5 minute film in which a man called Rocky was physically and verbally aggressive towards a large 'Bobo' doll. Some of Rocky's behaviours were rather distinctive, such as when he kicked the doll across the room and shouted 'fly away' or raised the doll up and hit it with a mallet.

The children were split into three groups. The control group watched only the part of the film just described. Children in the other two groups watched a slightly extended version. Children in one group saw Rocky being rewarded for his behaviour by being praised as a strong champion and given fizzy drinks and confectionery. Children in the remaining group saw Rocky being punished by being called a bully, smacked with a rolled-up magazine, and threatened with a harder spanking for any repeat of his cowardly behaviour.

All the children were then allowed to play for 10 minutes in a room full of toys that included a Bobo doll and a mallet. At the end of this session all the children were offered rewards for every one of Rocky's phrases and acts they could copy.

When offered incentives, boys were equally good at copying Rocky's aggressive behaviour whichever experimental condition they were in. So were girls, although on average they imitated Rocky very slightly less than did the boys. This shows that all the children did well at learning Rocky's novel forms of aggression and were willing and able to replicate them when given incentives to do so. Rather than automatically mimicking behaviours they were exposed to, the children acquired an *ability* to behave in novel ways and then largely *chose* whether and when it would be rewarding to enact those behaviours.

Boys copied Rocky almost as much before being offered incentives to do so as after, with one exception. Until offered incentives to do so, boys copied Rocky somewhat less if they had seen him punished for his behaviour.

Across all three conditions, girls copied Rocky much less than boys did until they were offered incentives to do so. They nevertheless copied him a little unless they had seen him punished for his aggression, in which case they copied him hardly at all.

The gender differences in this experiment could be explained in various ways. What is more important here is that both boys and girls copied Rocky relatively infrequently when observing him suggested to them that they might be punished for copying him, although both were able and willing to imitate novel behaviours when they had reasons to think that doing so would be rewarding.

As well as learning potential behaviours by observing others, humans can learn things that help them work out whether and when engaging in those behaviours will or will not be personally rewarding.

Culture and instruction

As well as having exceptional cognitive skills compared with other animals, humans excel linguistically and culturally. As well as learning directly from observing what happens to other people, people can learn from what other people tell them, both directly during instruction and indirectly via the media and the arts. People can be told that great or dire things will happen to them if they engage in various practices. They can also imagine what would happen if they emulated the actions of heroes or villains of history or fiction.

Self-efficacy beliefs

What people learn can be affected by their existing beliefs. Particularly important are **self-efficacy beliefs**. These are beliefs that each person has about what they are able to achieve. Learning that someone else obtained all manner of rewards for behaving in a particular way will not lead to imitation if a person believes that they are incapable of acting in the same way or of obtaining similar rewards for doing so. Similarly, knowing that someone else was punished may not prevent imitation if a person thinks that they can engage in the behaviour while avoiding the same punishment.

Like other beliefs, self-efficacy beliefs are affected by all manner of things, including experience, observation, instruction, and imagination. Self-efficacy beliefs have all sorts of effects that influence people's actions and reactions. People high in self-efficacy select relatively ambitious goals, show greater persistence in pursuit of those goals, are more confident and less anxious about their goal pursuits, are more able to think of potential set-backs as learning opportunities, and are more likely to achieve important tasks, all of which form a positive feedback loop to strengthen self-efficacy beliefs.

Goals and self-regulation

One of the greatest gifts of human cognition is how it makes imagination possible. In particular, people can imagine different possible futures, predict how personally rewarding each might be, and judge how likely it is that they can bring each about by their own actions. Within social cognitive personality theory, it is abilities such as these that enable self-determination. People can imagine various possibilities and choose which they wish to pursue and what sorts of people they want to become.

People also have the ability to reward and punish themselves. They can take pleasure and feel pride in their achievements and feel guilt, shame, or anger when they disappoint themselves. This is because their imagination tells them what might have been had they acted differently. They can congratulate or condemn themselves depending on whether or not they gave in to moments of foolishness or weakness – for example, when immediate temptation clashed with the effective pursuit of important long-term **goals**.

Individual differences in **self-regulation** can have profound consequences. Pre-school children's ability to resist a tasty treat for a time in order to obtain a reward of a second treat predicts a range of positive outcomes 10 or more years later (Eigsti et al., 2006).

Personality problems

Personality problems can be caused by psychological factors that disrupt people's ability to operate effectively in the world. In social cognitive approaches to personality, many such problems stem from enduring dysfunctional beliefs people have acquired about themselves or the world. Therapeutic interventions tend to focus on identifying which beliefs are causing problems and changing those beliefs for more functional ones.

Chronic anxiety, for example, is caused by people believing that the world is more dangerous than it is or that they haven't got the ability to cope effectively when difficult situations arise. Therapy involves challenging such beliefs, such as by having people find out that the situations they fear are less frequent and often less drastic than they believe. Removing people's dysfunctional beliefs increases their ability to appraise the world more realistically, which in turn allows them to better understand and choose among the options available to them. Instead of experiencing uncontrolled, suboptimal, and often unpleasant reactions to situational cues, people increasingly develop self-determination.

Moral commitment

People receive many messages about what it means to be good and what happens when they are or are not – from families, from the media, from various social institutions, and from the feelings people get when they act in certain ways or bring about certain consequences. Social cognitive theories of personality are unique among those considered in this chapter in suggesting that many people reach a level of maturity whereby they can actively choose for themselves what morality means for them and how moral they want to be.

Aquino and Reed (2002) developed a measure of the extent to which people *want* to be like a person who is caring, compassionate, fair, friendly, generous, hardworking, helpful, honest, and kind. (Note that this is an aspiration, not necessarily an achievement.) Subsequent research suggests that, compared with people without a commitment to be moral in this way, people aspiring to have a moral identity of this sort are much more attuned to perceiving situations as morally relevant and thinking that the relevant moral concerns have implications for personal behaviour (Aquino, Freeman, Reed, Felps, & Lim, 2009).

FOCUS POINT 14.5

MORAL COMMITMENTS

Most people have many identities – for example, as a woman, a student, a friend, a Spaniard, and so on. Situations often suggest that certain identities are temporarily particularly relevant and others less appropriate. For instance, being in class tends to activate an 'educational' identity, such as teacher or student, and suppress identities such as 'party animal' or 'son'.

For some people, though, certain identities are so central and important to them that these identities are relatively 'chronically' activated (i.e. less affected by situational cues). Think of someone you know who is particularly earnest or zealous. The chances are that they have a specific and wide-reaching identity that is very dear to their heart. Being religiously observant or artistic or a keen feminist or whatever is so important to them that it is a key aspect of who they are, of their personhood. They rarely if ever 'turn that specific identity off'. There rarely seems to be much downtime from it.

Aquino, Reed, Thau, and Freeman (2007) found that people committed to being moral were less likely than those who were not to support highly punitive military retaliation for the events of 9/11. They were also less likely to let those events blunt their negative feelings about American soldiers abusing Iraqi detainees. Whereas many people allowed themselves to entertain thoughts and feelings of vengeful aggression, people who had dedicated themselves to moral conduct did not.

ACTIVITY 14.6

HISTORIC MORAL COMMITMENT

Think of famous people in history who behaved in exceptional ways. What were their key identities? To what extent were they motivated by a vision of a future they did or did not want to exist? How did this influence how they behaved in and across situations? Did their key commitments enable them to forgo immediate pleasures and accept relatively minor sacrifices?

Now ask the same questions of someone currently in the media for behaving exceptionally. One possibility is Edward Snowden, an American who leaked classified information from the US National Security Agency in 2013. He discusses his actions and motives **here**[3].

Evaluation

Social cognitive theorists build their theories on some of the most demonstrably robust phenomena in psychological science. Arguably, though, the most interesting aspect of the social cognitive theory of personality is the structure built on top of its foundation. The theory suggests that well-functioning mature humans can to a large extent free themselves from mechanistic applications of learning theory. Although influenced by biology, culture, and life experiences, mentally healthy people can prioritize certain rewards and routes to those rewards and can develop plans to overcome temptations in pursuit of their self-selected goals. While there are impressive banks of research supporting such claims, the extent to which people can be self-determined in this way may always be a matter of faith.

Findings such as these point to the importance of people's beliefs about personality *for* personality. Encourage people to believe that they 'are' selfish and lazy (or whatever) and the chances are that they will *become* reliably more selfish and lazy (or whatever).

FOCUS POINT 14.6

IS PERSONALITY DESTINY?

People differ in how much they believe that aspects of personality are fixed or flexible (Church et al., 2003). Believing that aspects of personality are fixed leads to a fatalistic approach to actions and outcomes (Dweck, Chiu, & Hong, 1995; Job, Dweck, & Walton, 2010). If a person believes themselves simply to 'be' shy (Beer, 2002), athletically ungifted (Biddle, Wang, Chatzisarantis, & Spray, 2003), fat (Burnette, 2010), immoral (Chiu, Dweck, Tong, & Fu, 1997), aggressive (Giles & Heyman, 2003), or untrustworthy (Haselhuhn, Schweitzer, & Wood, 2010), there will seem little point in trying to encourage them to be anything other than what they 'are'.

Believing that negatively evaluated aspects of personality are fixed rather than flexible can also promote relatively prejudiced expectations and harsh, discriminatory social practices (Bastian & Haslam, 2007; Baumeister, Masicampo, & DeWall, 2009; Brescoll & LaFrance, 2004; Finkel, Burnette, & Scissors, 2007; Gervey, Chiu, Hong, & Dweck, 1999; Haslam & Levy, 2006; Jayaratne et al., 2006; Kammrath & Dweck, 2006).

It is possible to encourage or undermine people's beliefs about the fixidity or flexibility of aspects of personality (Dweck, 2008). Brescoll and LaFrance (2004) showed that newspaper reports could alter how fixed or flexible people thought gender differences were. Haslam and Ernst (2002) showed that science coverage could do the same for people's beliefs about mental health conditions.

Changing people's views about the fixidity or flexibility of aspects of personality can change their subsequent thoughts, feelings, motivation, behaviours, and achievements. Mueller and Dweck (1998) found that praising students' intelligence rather than their effort fostered beliefs that intellect is relatively fixed rather than flexible and undermined students' academic motivation. Relative to control group participants, students encouraged to think of intelligence as flexible rather than fixed enjoyed and engaged in academic activities more and got better grades (Aronson, Fried, & Good, 2002). Managers encouraged to think of their employees' abilities as flexible rather than fixed became more willing and better able to help struggling employees (Heslin, VandeWalle, & Latham, 2006).

TEST YOURSELF

In what ways, if any, is learning affected by human nature?

SECTION SUMMARY

- Social cognitive theories of personality take the foundations of behaviourism as their starting point: classical conditioning and instrumental (or operant) conditioning.

- Pavlov's discovery of classical conditioning and Skinner's development of instrumental conditioning are among the most important discoveries in psychology.

- Participants in an experiment by Berger (1962) witnessed people seeming to react with pain after hearing a tone. Participants later gave a fear response when they heard the same tone again. One explanation of this is vicarious (classical) conditioning.

- A study by Albert Bandura in 1965 illustrates the potential and implications of social learning. In this study, nursery school children watched a 5 minute film in which a man called Rocky was physically and verbally aggressive towards a large 'Bobo' doll.

- As well as learning directly from observing what happens to other people, people can learn from what other people tell them, both directly during instruction and indirectly via the media and the arts.

- What people learn can be affected by their existing beliefs. Particularly important are self-efficacy beliefs and the way in which these beliefs influence goal setting and the ability to self-regulate in order to achieve a desired outcome.

- Personality problems are caused by psychological factors that disrupt people's ability to operate effectively in the world. Chronic anxiety, for example, is caused by people believing that the world is more dangerous than it is.

- Social cognitive theories of personality suggest many people reach a level of maturity whereby they can actively choose for themselves what morality means for them and how moral they want to be.

CONCLUSIONS AND FUTURE DIRECTIONS

LEARNING OBJECTIVE 14.6

Critically evaluate the models used to understand and study personality and possible future research and directions within the field.

Especially once stripped of idiosyncratic jargon and arguably unnecessary assumptions, there are considerable overlaps across personality theories. They nevertheless differ in various ways. The theories differ in the extent to which they seek to merely describe people or to explain things about them. Trait theories have so far tended merely to describe regularities in psychological characteristics. The other theories covered have sought explanations for such regularities. When asked why people behave the way they do, all the theories considered – other than trait theories – have some sort of an explanation.

Having explanations means that theories can attempt to specify the extent to which people's personalities can change and in what circumstances. Trait theorists tend to approach the question of change the same way they go about identifying traits in the first place – empirically. Rather than give theoretical accounts of when and how personality can change, trait theorists usually simply investigate possible personality changes over the life course. The other theories have things to say about when and why personality will stay the same or change. This may well be why trait theories are also unique in not yet having counselling approaches stemming from, associated with, or closely aligned to their personality theory.

Explanatory theory only confers an advantage if it is persuasively supported by data. Here, Freudian theory faces the biggest challenges, for several reasons. First, the theory is so expansive and nuanced that it is very difficult to confidently identify exactly what it might predict in many circumstances. It is often possible to use the theory to make completely contrary hypotheses. Second, this theory is enormously influenced by the work and thoughts of one man, Sigmund Freud. Although he was admirably able to change his mind in the light of new experiences or new interpretations of old experiences, he was less able to lay out the links between data and theory in ways that persuaded critical others. Third, Freud's theories are often neither intuitively appealing nor attractive. While many aspects of humanistic personality theories share some of the weaknesses just listed of psychoanalytic theory, humanistic theories are much more appealing to many. They seem empowering and liberating while Freudian theory can seem depressing and inescapable.

Social cognitive theories arguably have a considerable explanatory edge over the other approaches to personality reviewed here. Not only are they built on the very strong foundations provided by learning theories but they are also closely aligned to increasingly dominant approaches to mental health intervention (cognitive behaviour therapy) and are also committed to scientific development. This means that cognitive behavioural approaches continually evolve to incorporate state-of-the-art science and also seek to do so in ways that lend themselves to further scientific development.

Not everyone prioritizes science above and to the exclusion of all other concerns. Many people find different aspects of each of the personality approaches particularly attractive for various reasons. This is why some people choose not to choose between personality theories. Many counsellors and therapists believe there is much to be gained by using combinations or blends of approaches. Theories can be helpful in reminding people to ask questions that might otherwise not be thought of. Was this person ever badly let down during childhood by someone who should have been trustworthy? How consistent is this person's behaviour across situations? Where does this person get their sense of worth from? Can this person imagine a future different from their past? Scientists may like testability, prediction, and control. Clinicians often prefer utility.

Theories of personality are not good or bad per se; they are good or bad for specific purposes. Which personality theories most appeal to you and why? What, if anything, does your answer reveal about the sort of person you are?

As to future directions in personality, some will be similar to future directions in other areas of psychology and will depend in part on developments in disciplines aligned to psychology. Neurological and genetic correlates of postulated personality processes will be sought. Ever larger datasets will assist exploration of personality patterns and profiles across time and space. New multivariate statistical analyses will be developed and exploited in attempts to support or challenge particular positions.

Cross-fertilization across specialisms within psychology will also inspire work in new directions. Hierarchical models of personality traits comparable to recent models of intelligence seem likely, as do searches for 'Big n' models of needs or motives (e.g. Sternberg, 1984; Vignoles, Regalia, Manzi, Golledge, & Scabini, 2006).

Finally, while some will continue to seek commonalities across approaches to personality, champions of each particular approach will remain. Although all psychologists value data, especially those aspiring to be scientists, data are rarely decisive. Freud's theories have been scorned and ridiculed for over a century, particularly by scientifically inclined psychologists. At times, this was the case with central planks of Freudian theory that few have any doubts about today (e.g. the existence of unconscious processes and the importance of infant experiences for subsequent personality development). Freud's theories endured *despite* the best efforts of academics and scientists, not because of them. This is not to say that all Freud's theories were correct, although it has to be remembered that he developed his ideas a century ago, when conventions of science, scholarship, and expression were very different from how things are today. As noted by Westen (1998), 'Many aspects of Freudian theory are indeed out of date, and they should be: Freud died in 1939, and he has been slow to undertake further revisions' (p. 333). It is rather to say that future research is unlikely to make many adherents of particular personality approaches change their allegiance – and that may not be a wholly bad thing.

SECTION SUMMARY

- Theories differ in the extent to which they merely describe or additionally attempt to explain people's personalities. Reliance on pure description is probably most marked within trait theories of personality.

- For that reason, relative to the other theories considered, trait theories lack detailed accounts of personality change and any close association with particular approaches to counselling.

- Freud's theories are perhaps the least scientific of those considered in this chapter. They lack both strong foundations in scientific data and the ability to make predictions that can be meaningfully tested using data.

- Social cognitive theories are arguably the most scientifically supported among those considered in this chapter. They are built on scientifically robust foundations and are routinely amended in light of scientific discoveries.

- Theories are evaluated using various criteria. This means that different theories will appeal to different people in different circumstances and for different reasons.

- Science and fashion are likely to play roles in amending the theories reviewed here, albeit to different extents. Long-established and relatively self-contained theories such as Freud's are less likely to substantially change than are more recent theories whose contents have thus far been largely determined by empirical findings, such as trait theories.

CHAPTER SUMMARY

This chapter has considered the nature of personality and has reviewed four of the main approaches taken by psychologists in order to better understand its key aspects. We did this by first exploring the nature of Freud's psychodynamic personality theory before moving on to an evaluation of the trait approach. The third, humanistic, approach emphasizes a person's capacity for personal and social growth and fulfilment. The fourth approach, that of social cognitive personality theory, recognizes that people can develop in a variety of ways, depending upon the influences they are exposed to and their beliefs about what actions and development are possible. Future research into personality theory is likely to become increasingly multidisciplinary and hierarchical in nature, with neurological and genetic correlates of postulated personality processes also sought. Nonetheless, while some will continue to seek commonalities across approaches to personality, champions of each particular approach will remain.

ESSAY QUESTIONS

1. What did children learn in Bandura's (1965) 'learned aggression' study?

2. What does the Schwartz et al. (2013) 'Facebook study' reveal about the nature of traits?

KEY TERMS

- **altruistic personality:** The name given by Oliner and Oliner (1992) to describe the complex of characteristics that gentile rescuers of Jews from Nazi Europe appeared to have in common and that differentiated them from matched non-rescuers.
- **anal stage:** The second of Freud's 'psychosexual' stages of development, occurring between about 1 and 3 years of age. With a particular focus on toilet training, it involves issues of conflict, self- and other-control, and compromise.
- **anxiety:** In Freudian terms, the feeling accompanying memory or anticipation of trauma.
- **arrested development:** The Freudian notion of a person failing to make progress to a later stage of psychosexual development (fixation), with the result that their reactions to and coping with situations become increasingly immature with age.
- **associative learning:** Methods of exploiting the way animals learn associations (i.e. what goes with what) to encourage or discourage particular forms of behaviour.
- **authoritarian personality:** A personality type extensively studied by Adorno et al. (1950), making heavy use of psychoanalytic theory. People of this type are dispositionally attracted to fascistic ideas and practices, are conformist, and are intolerant of difference, ambiguity, and change.
- **behavioural signatures:** Reliable individual differences in patterns of enduring but highly situation-specific behaviours.
- **behaviourism:** An attempt to explain behaviour via a combination of (often only) classical conditioning and instrumental conditioning, collectively sometimes called associative learning.

- **Big Five:** In psychology, often used as an interchangeable term for Costa and McCrae's five factor model of personality traits (FFM), which consists of the traits openness to experience, conscientiousness, extraversion, agreeableness, and neuroticism.
- **Big Three:** Hans Eysenck's three-trait model, in which psychoticism versus impulse control is added to the **Big Two**. Also known as the PEN model.
- **Big Two:** Hans Eysenck's two-trait model, which consists of introversion versus extraversion and emotional stability versus neuroticism.
- **catharsis:** The Freudian notion of relieving neuroses and symptoms by re-experiencing earlier trauma at a more mature stage of development or with more support.
- **classical conditioning:** A process of learning whereby animals come to associate things that previously did not elicit a biological reaction with things that do so either naturally or because of prior conditioning.
- **conditional negative regard:** Judging people negatively on the basis of their behaviour.
- **conditional positive regard:** Judging people positively on the basis of their behaviour.
- **conditions of worth:** A term for when people indicate to others that they are only worthy if they satisfy certain conditions (e.g. being rich and famous, a good citizen, and the like).
- **congruent:** A Rogerian concept that occurs when people are aware of their true inclinations and reactions.
- **conscious:** Freud's term for a metaphorical area of the brain in which knowledge exists or psychological processes occur in ways of which people are aware.
- **consistency:** A quality of traits in which there is regularity of behaviour across time.
- **crises:** A term used by Erik Erikson to describe key tasks people encounter at particular stages of development (e.g. becoming relatively autonomous as a toddler).
- **death instincts:** Instincts speculated by Freud to have been evolutionarily selected and that incline people towards behaviours such as aggression, violence, and destruction.
- **defence mechanisms:** In Freudian thought, ways in which people keep from consciousness thoughts or feelings that they would otherwise find traumatic.
- **deficiency needs:** Needs relatively low in Maslow's hierarchy, each of which must be met before the next highest need becomes pressing and provides motivational force. Lack of satisfaction of such needs has negative outcomes.
- **dimensional:** A quality of traits such that scores of the extent to which people manifest those traits fall along a range from very little to very much.
- **ego:** A Freudian term for a person's sense of self. Develops after the id and operates using the reality principle. It has the job of trying to coordinate and pursue the demands of both the infantile id and the idealistic superego when confronted by the constraints and opportunities of reality.
- **emotional stability:** A trait indicating an absence of neuroticism.
- **empathy:** In Rogerian counselling, an attempt to understand others' thoughts and feelings, perhaps including ones of which they themselves are barely aware.
- **equifinality:** A principle by which different causes can have identical effects.
- **erogenous zones:** A Freudian term for areas of the body sequentially of primary importance during different phases of 'psychosexual' development (e.g. mouth, anus, genitals).
- **eros:** A Freudian term used to refer to an energy associated with life instincts.
- **extraversion:** A trait indicating preference for company.
- **facets:** Subcomponents of traits describing relatively narrow or specific regularities of behaviour.
- **fixation:** In Freudian thinking, a reason for a person failing to make progress to a later stage of psychosexual development (see also **arrested development**).
- **foreclosure:** An identity status (reached during an identity crisis) in which a commitment is made to an identity before all available options have been adequately considered.

- **generality:** A quality of traits in which there is regularity of behaviour across different sorts of situation.
- **genital stage:** The fourth and final of Freud's 'psychosexual' stages of development, occurring from about 11 years of age following a period of little psychosexual activity after resolution of the phallic stage. The focus is again on the genitals, this time expressed as more overt sexual interest and activity.
- **goals:** In social cognitive theories, a goal is an imagined outcome that is thought to be possible and likely to be either positively or negatively valued and is for that reason actively pursued or avoided, respectively.
- **growth needs:** Relatively high in Maslow's hierarchy, these are needs that become pressing and provide motivational force only once the lower, **deficiency needs** have been met. Satisfaction of such needs promotes positive outcomes.
- **HEXACO model:** HEXACO is an acronym of *h*onesty-*h*umility, *e*motionality, *e*xtraversion, *a*greeableness (versus anger), *c*onscientiousness, and *o*penness to experience. See http://hexaco.org for details.
- **human nature:** The set of qualities that people necessarily have by virtue of being human.
- **humanistic personality theory:** An approach to personality and psychology most generally popularized by Carl Rogers and Abraham Maslow. It is based on the belief that people have a nature that will lead to positive outcomes for self and others if people trust themselves rather than comply with actual or perceived social demands.
- **hysteria:** A Freudian diagnosis given when, for no apparent physical reason, people engage in strange behaviour without seeming to want to or sometimes even noticing.
- **id:** A Freudian metaphor for the most infantile part of a person. The id is hedonistic and seeks pleasure. It is demanding, intolerant, unrealistic, and uncompromising, wanting instant gratification of all desires.
- **identity achievement:** An identity status (reached during an identity crisis) in which thorough exploration has left a person able to make commitments to particular identities that they find personally attractive and suitable.
- **identity diffusion:** An identity status (reached during an identity crisis) in which a person has little, lost, or abandoned interest in exploring possible identities and making a commitment to particular ones.
- **identity status:** A term used by Marcia to describe one of four possible situations within an identity crisis (i.e. **foreclosure**, **identity diffusion**, **moratorium**, or **identity achievement**).
- **independent:** If two or more measures are independent, scores on one are not reliably associated with scores on the other(s).
- **individual differences:** Psychological differences between people, often enduring ones.
- **inductivist:** Someone who makes predictions by generalizing from patterns observed in particular instances.
- **instincts:** Inherited processes of automatically responding in certain ways to particular stimuli, sometimes without conscious awareness.
- **instrumental conditioning:** A process of learning that occurs when an animal comes to associate particular behaviours with particular rewarding or punishing consequences and becomes more or less likely to repeat that behaviour, respectively. Also called operant conditioning.
- **interactionism:** In trait theory, this is the belief that factors both internal and external to people (e.g. traits and situations) interact to cause particular effects.
- **introspect:** To examine the contents of one's conscious.
- **introversion:** A trait indicating preference for one's own company.
- **latent characteristics:** Enduring predispositions to manifest particular characteristics when those characteristics are triggered by specific stimuli.
- **libido:** A Freudian term used to refer to an energy associated with life instincts.

- **life instincts:** Instincts speculated by Freud to have been evolutionarily selected because they aid survival.
- **manifest characteristics:** Enduring observable characteristics.
- **moral disengagement:** Albert Bandura's idea that various strategies can be used to allow people to ignore moral principles they allegedly subscribe to, without punishing themselves for doing so.
- **moratorium:** An identity status (reached during an identity crisis) in which a person is actively seeking an identity but has yet to make commitments to specific ones.
- **needs:** Things that are required to obtain or achieve something important to people, such as life or psychological well-being.
- **neuroses:** For Freud, a collection of diagnoses given to people dealing with trauma or anxiety less well than would most other people in similar circumstances, as revealed by diagnostic symptoms.
- **neuroticism:** A trait of emotional instability.
- **observational learning:** A combination of vicarious conditioning and social learning (social instrumental conditioning).
- **operant conditioning:** Another term for **instrumental conditioning**.
- **oral optimism:** A Freudian personality type stemming from a person being overindulged during the oral stage of psychosexual development. Sometimes called oral receptive, this results in a person being excessively trusting.
- **oral pessimism:** A Freudian personality type stemming from a person being overly frustrated during the oral stage of psychosexual development. Sometimes called oral aggressive, this results in a person being excessively mistrustful.
- **oral stage:** The first of Freud's 'psychosexual' stages of development, occurring between birth and 2 years of age. With a particular focus on breastfeeding and weaning, it involves issues of self- and other-awareness, dependability, and trust.
- **organismic valuing:** Carl Rogers' idea that people should listen to and trust their own inclinations about what they want to and should do, as doing so will naturally guide them towards positive personal and social growth.
- **overcontrolled:** A personality type compatible with the Freudian notion that people's actions can sometimes be excessively driven by perceptions of others' expectations. Contrasts with people who are resilient or undercontrolled.
- **PEN model:** Hans Eysenck's three-trait model in which psychoticism is added to the Big Two. Also known as the Big Three.
- **personality psychology:** The psychology of persons, personalities, personhood, and individual differences. Previously sometimes referred to as personology.
- **person-centred:** A Rogerian approach to support that involves helping people to be in touch with, trust, and be guided in their actions by their organismic valuing process.
- **phallic stage:** The third of Freud's 'psychosexual' stages of development, occurring between about 3 and 6 years of age. With a particular focus on sex and gender, its successful resolution involves increasing identification with the same-sex parent and development of attraction towards members of the opposite sex. It is followed by a period of little psychosexual activity prior to the genital stage.
- **pleasure principle:** The instinctive motivational force of the id postulated by Freud, it compels people to pursue hedonic pleasure and avoid pain.
- **preconscious:** Freud's term for a metaphorical area of the brain in which knowledge exists or psychological processes occur without people's awareness, but can easily be brought into consciousness.
- **primary needs:** Things thought by Murray (1938) to be necessary for physical survival and for biological growth (e.g. food, water, air, sex, pain avoidance).
- **psychodynamic:** An approach to personality and psychology most generally popularized by Sigmund Freud based on the belief that multiple conscious and unconscious psychological events can have interactive effects.

- **psychologists:** People committed to using empirical data to develop their theories about people's psychology.
- **psychoticism:** A trait associated with low or high impulse control.
- **regression:** The Freudian term for when people under pressure operate using processes associated with an earlier (i.e. immature) psychosexual stage of development.
- **repression:** In Freudian thought, one of the main defence mechanisms that accompanies all others. It involves keeping, removing, or blocking from consciousness something that a person would find traumatic.
- **resilient:** A personality type compatible with the Freudian notion that people can achieve a level of maturity so that they are able to respond flexibly and effectively to changing and sometimes challenging circumstances. Contrasts with people who are over- or undercontrolled.
- **scientists:** People working within an expert community committed to collaboratively developing empirically justified theories.
- **secondary needs:** Things thought by Murray (1938) to be necessary for psychological growth (e.g. ambition, materialism, power, affection, information).
- **self-actualization:** The humanistic notion of moving towards or achieving one's potential as a person.
- **self-determination:** This occurs when people are congruent and make and act on their own decisions.
- **self-efficacy beliefs:** Beliefs about the possibility of achieving or avoiding certain outcomes by virtue of one's own actions.
- **self-regulation:** When people administer self-rewards and self-punishments in response to perceived satisfactory or unsatisfactory effort or progress towards a selected goal.
- **sexuality:** A Freudian term stressing the motivational importance of pleasure seeking and pain avoidance as instincts supporting survival.
- **social cognitive:** An approach to personality and psychology more generally that incorporates into learning theory insights from social and cognitive psychology.
- **social learning:** The process of learning from observing the actions of others and the consequences that appear to follow from such actions.
- **superego:** A Freudian metaphor for the part of self internalized from the expectations of important others and society. Contains the conscience and seeks perfection.
- **symptoms:** For Freud, relatively unusual and problematic physical or mental manifestations of an unconscious psychological problem.
- **tasks:** An alternative term for what Erik Erikson called **crises**.
- **topographical model:** Freud's metaphorical model of psychological processes occurring on different levels of awareness: unconscious, preconscious, or conscious.
- **traits:** Descriptions of regular behaviours or psychological predispositions that result in regular behaviour.
- **trauma:** In Freudian terms, experience suggesting an imminent and serious threat to the self's continued healthy existence.
- **types:** Categorical differences between people such that a given person either is or is not a member of that type of person.
- **unconditional positive regard:** A Rogerian notion of being warm and approving towards others irrespective of their conduct.
- **unconscious:** Freud's term for a metaphorical area of the brain in which knowledge exists or psychological processes occur without people's awareness and are difficult or impossible to bring into the conscious.
- **undercontrolled:** A personality type compatible with the Freudian notion that people's actions can sometimes be excessively driven by their immediate, egocentric desires. Contrasts with people who are resilient or overcontrolled.

- **universal:** A quality of traits such that everyone can be given a score indicating how strongly they manifest a particular regularity of behaviour.
- **vicarious (classical) conditioning:** A form of learning in which animals observe others reacting in emotionally valenced (i.e. positive or negative) ways to particular stimuli and themselves act later in ways that show similar reactions to the same stimuli.

NOTES

1. https://www.psychologytoday.com/basics/gender
2. https://www.ted.com/talks/mihaly_csikszentmihalyi_on_flow?language=en
3. http://www.theguardian.com/world/video/2013/jun/09/nsa-whistleblower-edward-snowden-interview-video

FURTHER RESOURCES

Altemeyer, R. A. (2006). *The authoritarians*. Retrieved 29 January 2018 from https://theauthoritarians.org/options-for-getting-the-book

Bandura, A. (2006). Towards a psychology of human agency. *Perspectives on Psychological Science*, *1*(2), 164–180.

Block, J. (1995). A contrarian view of the five-factor approach to personality description. *Psychological Bulletin*, *117*, 187–215.

Breland, K., & Breland, M. (1961). The misbehavior of organisms. *American Psychologist*, *16*, 681–684.

Cooper, C. (2010). *Individual differences and personality* (3rd ed.). London, UK: Hodder.

Green, C. (2010). *Classics in the History of Psychology*. Retrieved 20 November 2017 from http://psychclassics.yorku.ca/author.htm

Kirschenbaum, H., & Henderson, V. L. (1990). *The Carl Rogers reader*. London, UK: Constable.

Rogers, C. R. (1992). The necessary and sufficient conditions of therapeutic personality change. *Journal of Consulting and Clinical Psychology*, *60*(6), 827–832.

Westen, D. (1998). The scientific legacy of Sigmund Freud: Towards a psychodynamically informed psychological science. *Psychological Bulletin*, *124*, 333–371.

REFERENCES

Adorno, T. W., Frenkel-Brunswik, E., Levinson, D. J., & Sanford, R. N. (1950). *The authoritarian personality*. New York, NY: Harper.

Aquino, K., Freeman, D., Reed, A., II, Felps, W., & Lim, V. K. G. (2009). Testing a social-cognitive model of moral behavior: The interactive influence of situations and moral identity certainty. *Journal of Personality and Social Psychology*, *97*, 123–141.

Aquino, K., & Reed, A., II. (2002). The self-importance of moral identity. *Journal of Personality and Social Psychology*, *83*, 1423–1440.

Aquino, K., Reed, A., II, Thau, S., & Freeman, D. (2007). A grotesque and dark beauty: How moral identity and mechanisms of moral disengagement influence cognitive and emotional reactions to war. *Journal of Experimental Social Psychology*, *43*(3), 385–392.

Aronson, J., Fried, C. B., & Good, C. (2002). Reducing the effects of stereotype threat on African American college students by shaping theories of intelligence. *Journal of Experimental Social Psychology*, *38*, 113–125.

Ashton, M. C., & Lee, K. (2005). Honesty-humility, the Big Five, and the five factor model. *Journal of Personality, 73*(5), 1321–1353.

Ashton, M. C., Lee, K., & de Vries, R. E. (2014). The HEXACO honesty-humility, agreeableness, and emotionality factors: A review of research and theory. *Personality and Social Psychology Review, 18*, 139–152.

Bandura, A. (1965). Influence of models' reinforcement contingencies on the acquisition of imitative responses. *Journal of Personality and Social Psychology, 1*, 589–595.

Bartholomew, K. J., Ntoumanis, N., Ryan, R. M., Bosch, J. A., & Thøgersen-Ntoumani, C. (2011). Self-determination theory and diminished functioning: The role of interpersonal control and psychological need thwarting. *Personality and Social Psychology Bulletin, 37*(11), 1459–1473.

Bartholomew, K., Ntoumanis, N., Ryan, R. M., & Thøgersen-Ntoumani, C. (2011). Psychological need thwarting in the sport context: Assessing the darker side of athletic experience. *Journal of Sport and Exercise Psychology, 33*(1), 75–102.

Bastian, B., & Haslam, N. (2007). Psychological essentialism and attention allocation: Preferences for stereotype-consistent versus stereotype-inconsistent information. *Journal of Social Psychology, 147*(5), 531–541.

Baumeister, R. F., Masicampo, E. J., & DeWall, C. N. (2009). Prosocial benefits of feeling free: Disbelief in free will increases aggression and reduces helpfulness. *Personality and Social Psychology Bulletin, 35*(2), 260–268.

Beer, J. S. (2002). Implicit theories of shyness. *Journal of Personality and Social Psychology, 83*, 1009–1024.

Berger, S. M. (1962). Conditioning through vicarious instigation. *Psychological Review, 29*, 450–466.

Biddle, S. J. H., Wang, C. K. J., Chatzisarantis, N. D. L., & Spray, C. M. (2003). Motivation for physical activity in young people: Entity and incremental beliefs about athletic ability. *Journal of Sports Sciences, 21*, 973–989.

Billig, M. (1978). *Fascists: A social psychological view of the National Front*. London, UK: Harcourt Brace Jovanovich.

Block, J. (1995). A contrarian view of the five-factor approach to personality description. *Psychological Bulletin, 117*, 187–215.

Boeree, C. G. (2006a). Erik Erikson. Retrieved 20 November 2017 from http://webspace.ship.edu/cgboer/erikson.html

Boeree, C. G. (2006b). Abraham Maslow. Retrieved 20 November 2017 from http://webspace.ship.edu/cgboer/maslow.html

Bornstein, R. F. (1992). *The dependent personality*. New York, NY: Guilford Press.

Brescoll, V., & LaFrance, M. (2004). The correlates and consequences of newspaper reports of research on sex differences. *Psychological Science, 15*, 515–520.

Brewin, C. R., & Andrews, B. (2000). Psychological defence mechanisms: The example of repression. *The Psychologist, 13*, 615–617.

Burke, P. J. (1991). Identity processes and social stress. *American Sociological Review, 56*, 836–849.

Burnette, J. L. (2010). Implicit theories of body weight: Entity beliefs can weigh you down. *Personality and Social Psychology Bulletin, 36*, 410–422.

Caspi, A. (2000). The child is father of the man: Personality continuities from childhood to adulthood. *Journal of Personality and Social Psychology, 78*(1), 158–172.

Chiu, C., Dweck, C. S., Tong, J. Y., & Fu, J. H. (1997). Implicit theories and conceptions of morality. *Journal of Personality and Social Psychology, 73*, 923–940.

Church, A. T., Ortiz, F. A., Katigbak, M. S., Avdeyeva, T. V., Emerson, A. M., Flores, J. J., & Reyes, I. J. (2003). Measuring individual and cultural differences in implicit trait theories. *Journal of Personality and Social Psychology, 85*, 332–347.

Clary, E. G., & Miller, J. (1986). Socialization and situational influences on sustained altruism. *Child Development, 57*, 1358–1369.

Colby, A., & Damon, W. (1992). *Some do care: Contemporary lives of moral commitment*. New York, NY: Free Press.

Cooper, C. (2010). *Individual differences and personality* (3rd ed.). London, UK: Hodder.

Davis, M. H. (1983). Measuring individual differences in empathy: Evidence for a multidimensional approach. *Journal of Personality and Social Psychology*, 44, 113–126.

DeYoung, C. G., Quilty, L. C., & Peterson, J. B. (2007). Between facets and domains: 10 aspects of the Big Five. *Journal of Personality and Social Psychology*, 93(5), 880–896.

Dweck, C. S. (2008). Can personality be changed? The role of beliefs in personality and change. *Current Directions in Psychological Science*, 17(6), 391–394.

Dweck, C. S., Chiu, C., & Hong, Y. (1995). Implicit theories and their role in judgments and reactions: A world from two perspectives. *Psychological Inquiry*, 6, 267–285.

Eigsti, I. M., Zayas, V., Mischel, W., Shoda, Y., Ayduk, O., Dadlani, M. B., … Casey, B. J. (2006). Predicting cognitive control from preschool to late adolescence and young adulthood. *Psychological Science*, 17(6), 478–484.

Epstein, S. (1980). The stability of behavior: II. Implications for psychological research. *American Psychologist*, 35(9), 790–806.

Eysenck, H. J. (1947). *Dimensions of personality*. London, UK: Routledge.

Eysenck, H. J. (1992). Four ways five factors are not basic. *Personality and Individual Differences*, 13(6), 667–673.

Eysenck, H. J., & Eysenck, S. B. G. (1976). *Psychoticism as a dimension of personality*. London, UK: Hodder & Stoughton.

Feeney, B. C. (2004). A secure base: Responsive support of goal strivings and exploration in adult intimate relationships. *Journal of Personality and Social Psychology*, 87, 631–648.

Finkel, E. J., Burnette, J. L., & Scissors, L. E. (2007). Vengefully ever after: Destiny beliefs, state attachment anxiety, and forgiveness. *Journal of Personality and Social Psychology*, 92, 871–886.

Franklin, K. (2013). 'The best predictor of future behavior is … past behavior': Does the popular maxim hold water? *Psychology Today*, 3 January. Retrieved 20 November 2017 from http://www.psychologytoday.com/blog/witness/201301/the-best-predictor-future-behavior-is-past-behavior-0

Freud, S. (1929/2004). *Civilisation and its discontents* (rev. ed.). London, UK: Penguin.

Frimer, J. A., Walker, L. J., Dunlop, W. L., Lee, B. H., & Riches, A. (2011). The integration of agency and communion in moral personality: Evidence of enlightened self-interest. *Journal of Personality and Social Psychology*, 101(1), 149–163.

Gervey, B. M., Chiu, C., Hong, Y., & Dweck, C. S. (1999). Differential use of person information in decisions about guilt versus innocence: The role of implicit theories. *Personality and Social Psychology Bulletin*, 25, 17–27.

Giles, J. W., & Heyman, G. D. (2003). Preschoolers' beliefs about the stability of antisocial behaviour: Implications for navigating social challenges. *Social Development*, 12(2), 182–197.

Gosling, S. D., & John, O. P. (1999). Personality dimensions in nonhuman animals: A cross-species review. *Current Directions in Psychological Science*, 8(3), 69–75.

Gosling, S. D., Kwan, V. S., & John, O. P. (2003). A dog's got personality: A cross-species comparative approach to personality judgments in dogs and humans. *Journal of Personality and Social Psychology*, 85(6), 1161–1169.

Hart, D., & Fegley, S. (1995). Prosocial behavior and caring in adolescence: Relations to moral judgement and self-understanding. *Child Development*, 66, 1346–1359.

Haselhuhn, M. P., Schweitzer, M. E., & Wood, A. M. (2010). Beyond belief: How implicit beliefs influence trust recovery. *Psychological Science*, 21(5), 645–648.

Haslam, N., & Ernst, D. (2002). Essentialist beliefs about mental disorders. *Journal of Social and Clinical Psychology*, 21(6), 628–644.

Haslam, N., & Levy, S. R. (2006). Essentialist beliefs about homosexuality: Structure and implications for prejudice. *Personality and Social Psychology Bulletin*, 32(4), 471–485.

Heslin, P. A., VandeWalle, D., & Latham, G. P. (2006). Keen to help? Managers' implicit person theories and their subsequent employee coaching. *Personnel Psychology, 59,* 871–902.

Jayaratne, T. E., Ybarra, O., Sheldon, J. P., Brown, T. N., Feldbaum, M., Pfeffer, C. A., & Petty, E. M. (2006). White Americans' genetic lay theories of race differences and sexual orientation: Their relationship with prejudice toward blacks, and gay men and lesbians. *Group Processes and Intergroup Relations, 9,* 77–94.

Job, V., Dweck, C. S., & Walton, G. M. (2010). Ego depletion: Is it all in your head? Implicit theories about willpower affect self-regulation. *Psychological Science, 21*(11), 1686–1693.

Kammrath, L., & Dweck, C. S. (2006). Voicing conflict: Preferred conflict strategies among incremental and entity theorists. *Personality and Social Psychology Bulletin, 32*(11), 1497–1508.

Kline, P., & Storey, R. (1977). A factor analytic study of the oral character. *British Journal of Social and Clinical Psychology, 16,* 317–328.

Koltko-Rivera, M. E. (2006). Rediscovering the later version of Maslow's hierarchy of needs: Self-transcendence and opportunities for theory, research, and unification. *Review of General Psychology, 10*(4), 302–317.

Lee, D. Y., Kang, C. H., Lee, J. Y., & Park, S. H. (2005). Characteristics of exemplary altruists. *Journal of Humanistic Psychology, 42,* 146–155.

Maltby, J., Lewis, C. A., & Hill, A. P. (1998). Oral pessimism and depressive symptoms: A comparison with other correlates of depression. *British Journal of Medical Psychology, 71*(2), 195–200.

Marcia, J. E. (1966). Development and validation of ego-identity status. *Journal of Personality and Social Psychology, 3*(5), 551–558.

Maslow, A. H. (1943). A theory of human motivation. *Psychological Review, 50*(4), 370–396.

Maslow, A. H. (1968). *Toward a psychology of being* (2nd ed.). New York, NY: Reinhold.

McClelland, D. C. (1961). *The achieving society.* New York, NY: Free Press.

McCrae, R. R., & Costa, P. T., Jr. (2008). The five-factor theory of personality. In O. P. John, R. W. Robins, & L. A. Pervin (Eds.), *Handbook of personality: Theory and research* (3rd ed., pp. 159–181). New York, NY: Guilford Press.

Mehta, P. H., & Gosling, S. D. (2008). Bridging human and animal research: A comparative approach to studies of personality and health. *Brain, Behavior, and Immunity, 22*(5), 651–661.

Mineka, S., Davidson, M., Cook, M., & Kleir, R. (1984). Observational conditioning of snake fear in rhesus monkeys. *Journal of Abnormal Psychology, 93,* 355–372.

Mischel, W., & Shoda, Y. (1995). A cognitive-affective system theory of personality: Reconceptualizing situations, dispositions, dynamics, and invariance in personality structure. *Psychological Review, 102*(2), 246–268.

Mueller, C. M., & Dweck, C. S. (1998). Intelligence praise can undermine motivation and performance. *Journal of Personality and Social Psychology, 75,* 33–52.

Murray, H. A. (1938). *Explorations in personality.* Oxford, UK: Oxford University Press.

Musek, J. (2007). A general factor of personality: Evidence for the Big One in the five-factor model. *Journal of Research in Personality, 41*(6), 1213–1233.

Oliner, S. P., & Oliner, P. M. (1992). *The altruistic personality: Rescuers of Jews in Nazi Europe.* New York, NY: Free Press.

Paulhus, D. L., & Bruce, M. N. (1992). The effect of acquaintanceship on the validity of personality impressions: A longitudinal study. *Journal of Personality and Social Psychology, 63*(5), 816–824.

Paunonen, S. V. (2003). Big Five factors of personality and replicated predictions of behavior. *Journal of Personality and Social Psychology, 84*(2), 411–422.

Robins, R. W., John, O. P., Caspi, A., Moffitt, T. E., & Stouthamer-Loeber, M. (1996). Resilient, overcontrolled, and undercontrolled boys: Three replicable personality types. *Journal of Personality and Social Psychology, 70*(1), 157–171.

Rogers, C. R. (1957). A note on 'The Nature of Man'. *Journal of Counselling Psychology, 4*(3), 199–203.

Rogers, C. R. (1961). *On becoming a person.* Oxford, UK: Houghton Mifflin.

Rogers, C. R. (1964). Toward a modern approach to values: The valuing process in the mature person. *Journal of Abnormal and Social Psychology, 68*(2), 160–167.

Rogers, C. R. (1992). The necessary and sufficient conditions of therapeutic personality change. *Journal of Consulting and Clinical Psychology, 60*(6), 827–832.

Roth, G. (2008). Perceived parental conditional regard and autonomy as predictors of young adults' self- versus other-oriented prosocial tendencies. *Journal of Personality, 76*(3), 513–533.

Ryff, C. D. (1989). Happiness is everything, or is it? Explorations on the meaning of psychological well-being. *Journal of Personality and Social Psychology, 57*(6), 1069–1081.

Ryff, C. D., & Keyes, C. (1995). The structure of psychological well-being revisited. *Journal of Personality and Social Psychology, 69*(4), 719–727.

Schwartz, H. A., Eichstaedt, J. C., Kern, M. L., Dziurzynski, L., Ramones, S. M., Agrawal, M., … Ungar, L. H. (2013). Personality, gender, and age in the language of social media: The open-vocabulary approach. *PLoS ONE, 8*(9), e73791.

Shoda, Y., Mischel, W., & Wright, J. C. (1994). Intraindividual stability in the organization and patterning of behavior: Incorporating psychological situations into the idiographic analysis of personality. *Journal of Personality and Social Psychology, 67*, 674–687.

Soldz, S., & Vaillant, G. E. (1999). The Big Five personality traits and the life course: A 45-year longitudinal study. *Journal of Research in Personality, 33*(2), 208–232.

Sternberg, R. J. (1984). Toward a triarchic theory of human intelligence. *Behavioral and Brain Sciences, 7*(2), 269–287.

Vaillant, G. E. (1977). *Adaptation to life*. Boston, MA: Little, Brown.

Vansteenkiste, M., & Ryan, R. M. (2013). On psychological growth and vulnerability: Basic psychological need satisfaction and need frustration as a unifying principle. *Journal of Psychotherapy Integration, 23*(3), 263–280.

Vignoles, V. L., Regalia, C., Manzi, C., Golledge, J., & Scabini, E. (2006). Beyond self-esteem: Influence of multiple motives on identity construction. *Journal of Personality and Social Psychology, 90*(2), 308–333.

Westen, D. (1998). The scientific legacy of Sigmund Freud: Towards a psychodynamically informed psychological science. *Psychological Bulletin, 124*, 333–371.

Wicker, F. W., Brown, G., Wiehe, J. A., Hagen, A. S., & Reed, J. L. (1993). On reconsidering Maslow: An examination of the deprivation domination proposition. *Journal of Research in Personality, 27*(2), 118–133.

Widiger, T. A., & Mullins-Sweatt, S. N. (2009). Five-factor model of personality disorder: A proposal for DSM-V. *Annual Review of Clinical Psychology, 5*, 197–220.

Wiseman, H., Mayseless, O., & Sharabany, R. (2006). Why are they lonely? Perceived quality of early relationships with parents, attachment, personality predispositions and loneliness in first-year university students. *Personality and Individual Differences, 40*(2), 237–248.

15 Mental Health and Psychopathology

FRANCES MEETEN AND GRAHAM DAVEY

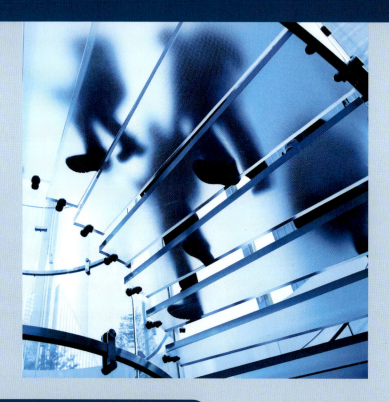

INTRODUCTION TO PSYCHOPATHOLOGY

LEARNING OBJECTIVE 15.1

Provide a basic definition of psychopathology and discuss the prevalence of mental health problems.

Psychopathology is the study of mental health problems. In this chapter we will be looking at how psychology has contributed to the definition of mental health problems, the way in which those problems are conceptualized, how we classify and diagnose them, and what factors cause and maintain the symptoms of some of the more important mental health problems we find in society generally.

Let's begin with a couple of self-reports of people suffering rather different types of mental health problems. In the examples below, Michelle reports suffering from anxiety symptoms, while Sophie describes some of the psychotic experiences she had prior to receiving a diagnosis of schizophrenia.

Michelle's story

I'm 26 years old and experience severe anxiety. I've had on and off panic attacks since I was 17. I've really worked hard to manage it using breathing, daily exercise, and diet. I thought I'd beaten it ... 2 years pretty symptom-free. But shortly after becoming engaged, the panic attacks started and anxiety came back with a vengeance. I can barely manage my days at work, I have little appetite, and I'm terrified of negative thoughts I've been having. My scariest thought in the past was having a heart attack. But knowing I'm in such good physical shape I know this isn't a possibility. My scary thought for the past few weeks has been what if I kill myself ... so scary I try not to be alone. My doctor has given me some medication, but I don't know if it's working. My friends who know about psychology say I'm fine and those thoughts are my anxiety.

Sophie's story

By about October of 1992, I believed that DJs on the radio were talking directly to me. When I told other people this they just laughed. But these DJs started to become very important to me, so I continued to believe it was happening, despite what other people were saying. I just kept it as my secret, until eventually when I was not at work I would listen to the radio 24 hours a day.

I believed that a radio DJ wanted a relationship with me, and throughout the course of our courtship (over the airwaves) the DJ and myself would actually discover the meaning of life. Everything had a meaning and eventually I had a sort of vision: God, he spoke to me and said, 'No matter what happens, I will always love you.' I felt special and chosen and at the same time I thought that other people were telepathic and could read my mind. Then I began to get physical or tactile hallucinations. I thought that I had been shot in the head to remove a blood clot. Then, as I was working with one of my colleagues, I actually felt my brain crack open, then masses of blood came out of one of my ears, then a small trickle from the other. That night, I thought that the devil was after me – I saw him come through one of the speakers of my stereo system. I was also probably hearing voices, but they were mixed in with the talk of the radio DJs. Suddenly, I became frustrated and ran out of the house into the middle of the road and started screaming. My neighbour came out and told me to come inside. He told me he had called the police and I started thumping him thinking he was the devil.

The experiences of the illness left me socially inept, mainly because I couldn't think to speak and engage in interpersonal relationships.

Clearly, the experiences of Michelle and Sophie are very different, but they have two things in common, and these two things are the factors that tend to define mental health problems. First, in both cases their symptoms and experiences caused them considerable distress. Second, their symptoms eventually affected their ability to function on a day-to-day basis: mental health problems can have a considerable negative impact on an individual's ability to do their job, to remain in employment, to deal with family responsibilities, and to interact socially. However, defining what is and is not a mental health problem is a difficult issue. For example, we all worry and we all get depressed at times, but these feelings may not significantly interfere with our everyday living. However, for some other people, their experience of these feelings may be so extreme as to cause them significant distress and to prevent them from undertaking normal daily living. So, before we begin to discuss mental health problems in detail, there is some groundwork we need to do by discussing how the way we define psychopathology has evolved over time, and in what ways we can define and classify mental health problems generally. So we'll continue with a discussion of the prevalence of mental health problems, followed by a brief history of psychopathology, and then move on to a discussion of how we define mental health problems and the explanatory approaches we currently use to understand psychopathology.

The prevalence of mental health problems

According to World Health Organization (2008) figures, in the United Kingdom mental health problems are the single largest cause of disability, contributing up to 22.8% of the total burden (compared with 15.9% for cancer and 16.2% for cardiovascular disease). Of this, depression alone accounts for 7% of the disease burden (World Health Organization, 2008). At least one in four people in the United Kingdom will experience a diagnosable mental health problem in any one year (Office for National Statistics Psychiatry Morbidity Report, 2001), and in most developed countries around one in five people has a diagnosable mental health problem at any one time (Substance Abuse and Mental Health Services Administration, 2011). Common mental health problems that contribute to these figures include anxiety and anxiety disorders (see Michelle's story above) and mood disorders such as depression. More severe mental health problems (such as psychoses) are somewhat less prevalent at around 5% of the population and around 3.7% of the population report having had serious thoughts of suicide in the prior 12 months (Substance Abuse and Mental Health Services Administration, 2011).

As a significant cause of disability, the wider economic cost of mental health problems is immense. This has been estimated at £105 billion each year in England alone (Centre for Mental Health, 2010), including the costs of services, lost productivity at work, and reduced quality of life. As a result, the cost of poor mental health to businesses amounts to £1,000 per employee per year. It is clear that, apart from the personal distress and dysfunction caused by mental health problems, there is also the broader issue of its economic cost to society.

SECTION SUMMARY

- The symptoms and experiences of mental health problems cause individuals considerable distress.
- Symptoms may eventually affect a person's ability to function on a day-to-day basis.
- In the United Kingdom, mental health problems are the single largest cause of disability.
- In most developed countries around one in five people has a diagnosable mental health problem at any one time.
- Common mental health problems that contribute to these figures include anxiety, anxiety disorders, and mood disorders such as depression.
- The wider economic cost of mental health problems is immense and has been estimated at £105 billion each year in England alone.

A BRIEF HISTORY OF PSYCHOPATHOLOGY

LEARNING OBJECTIVE 15.2

Discuss the history of psychopathology, specifically the historic theories of demonic possession and the medical or disease model.

Throughout history, we have been willing to label behaviour as 'mad', 'crazy', or 'insane' if it appears unpredictable, irrational, or harmful, or if it simply deviates from accepted contemporary social norms. But the term 'madness' does not imply a cause – it simply redescribes the behaviour as something that is unusual. A historical perspective on psychopathology and 'madness' is important because it helps us to understand how our views of the causes of mental health problems have changed and developed over time, and it also helps us to understand how approaches to treating and dealing with mental health problems have changed. We will begin by looking at a historical perspective on explaining psychopathology, which is known as **demonic possession**. We will then describe how the **medical model** of psychopathology developed and finish with a discussion of the transition from traditional mental **asylums** to modern-day evidence-based care for people with mental health problems.

Demonic possession

Many forms of psychopathology are accompanied by what appear to be changes in an individual's personality, and these changes in personality or behaviour are some of the first symptoms that are noticed. The fact that an individual's personality seems to have changed (and may do so very suddenly) has historically tended people towards describing those exhibiting symptoms of psychopathology as being 'possessed' in some way. That is, their behaviour has changed in such a way that their personality appears to have been taken over and replaced by the persona of someone or something else.

Explanations of psychopathology in terms of 'possession' have taken various forms over the course of history, and as a result many who have been suffering debilitating and distressing psychological problems have been persecuted and physically abused rather than offered the support and treatment they need. Many ancient civilizations, such as those in Egypt, China, Babylon, and Greece, believed that those exhibiting symptoms of psychopathology were possessed by bad spirits (a practice known as 'demonology') and the only way to exorcise these bad spirits was with elaborate ritualized ceremonies that frequently involved direct physical attacks on the sufferer's body in an attempt to force out the demons (e.g. through torture, flogging, or starvation). Nevertheless, demonic possession is still a common explanation of psychopathology in some less-developed areas of the world – especially where witchcraft and voodoo are still important features of the local culture, such as in Haiti and some areas of Western Africa (Desrosiers & Fleurose, 2002). The continued adoption of demonic possession as an explanation of mental health problems (especially in relation to psychotic symptoms) is often linked to local religious beliefs (Hanwella, de Silva, Yoosuf, Karunaratne, & de Silva, 2012; Ng, 2007) and may often be accompanied by exorcism as an attempted treatment – even in individuals with a known history of diagnosed psychotic symptoms (e.g. Tajima-Pozo et al., 2011). Nye (2012) contains an exploration of the use of 'exorcism' in British Asian communities.

DISCUSSION POINT

Discuss how demonic possession been used to explain mental health problems in the past and present times.

The medical or disease model

As cultures develop, so too do the types of causes to which they attribute behaviour. In particular, as we began to understand some of the biological causes of physical disease and illness, our conception of 'madness' moved very slowly towards treating it as a disease (hence the term 'mental illness').

The medical model of psychopathology was an important development because it introduced scientific thinking into our attempts to understand psychopathology and shifted explanations away from those associated with cultural and religious beliefs. The medical model has given rise to a large body of scientific knowledge about psychopathology that is based on medicine – this profession is known as **psychiatry** – and the primary approach of the medical model is to identify the biological causes of psychopathology and treat them with medication or surgery.

The medical model of psychopathology has some important implications for the way we conceive of mental health problems. First, an obvious implication is that it suggests that medical or biological causes underlie mental health problems. However, while biological factors may play a role in the causes of some mental health problems, biological and medical explanations are not the only way in which psychopathology can be explained, and it is often a person's experiences that may be dysfunctional, not their biological substrates.

Second, the medical model adopts what is basically a reductionist approach by attempting to reduce the complex psychological and emotional features of psychopathology to simple biology. If you look at the personal accounts provided at the beginning of this chapter by Michelle and Sophie, it is arguable whether the phenomenology (i.e. the personal experience of psychopathology) or the complex cognitive factors involved in many psychological problems can be reduced to simple biological descriptions. Biological reductionism cannot easily encapsulate the distress felt by sufferers; nor can it easily explain the dysfunctional beliefs and forms of thinking that are characteristic of many psychopathologies.

Finally, as we have mentioned already, there is an implicit assumption in the medical model that psychopathology is caused by 'something not working properly'. This view of psychopathology is problematic for a number of reasons. First, rather than reflecting a dysfunction, psychopathology might just represent a more extreme form of normal behaviour. We all get anxious, we all worry, and we all get depressed. Yet anxiety, worry, and depression in their extreme forms provide the basis of many of the mental health problems. In this sense, psychopathology can be viewed as being on a dimension rather than being a discrete phenomenon that is separate from normal experience; there is accumulating evidence that important psychopathological symptoms are on a dimension from normal to distressing, rather than being qualitatively distinct (e.g. Haslam, Williams, Kyrios, McKay, & Taylor, 2005; Olatunji, Williams, Haslam, Abramowitz, & Tolin, 2008).

WHAT IS CLINICAL PSYCHOLOGY?

Clinical psychology seeks to identify and define mental health problems, understand the causes of these problems, and provide *evidence-based* psychological therapies and support to help people better manage their problems.

DIFFERENTIATING CLINICAL PSYCHOLOGY AND PSYCHIATRY

Although there is some overlap between the domains of clinical psychology and psychiatry (both seek to identify and define mental health problems and alleviate distress, and both can do research), there are some key differences. Health problems can be understood from a number of different perspectives and the same is true for psychological health. It is common to read in psychology textbooks that mental health problems should be considered from a biopsychosocial (biological, psychological, social) perspective. While taking these multiple perspectives into account, clinical psychology focuses mainly on psychological models to understand mental health, and clinical psychologists are often psychology graduates who have gone on to complete a further 3 years' postgraduate intensive clinical psychology training (in the United Kingdom, this training is completed with the NHS).

Psychiatrists have a medical degree and then go on to further training to specialize in psychiatry. The common focus of psychiatry is using the medical model to understand mental health problems. Psychiatrists (because of their medical training) can prescribe medication. For further information about the role of psychiatrists, see the **Royal College of Psychiatrists' website**[1], and for further information about clinical psychology, see the **British Psychological Society Division of Clinical Psychology website**[2].

PSYCHOLOGICAL AND CLINICAL ASSESSMENTS

One role of clinical psychology is to assess individuals to provide a diagnosis or evaluation of their needs. In making a clinical assessment, psychologists will draw upon their clinical knowledge and expertise and, alongside talking to the individual they are assessing about their experiences, they will often also use validated assessments. Validated assessments are one of a number of tools that a clinician may use in a clinical assessment. There are several different types of assessment and they have been defined and then rigorously tested to make sure they are reliable and valid measures of what is being measured.

One commonly used diagnostic assessment is the SCID, or the 'Structured Clinical Interview' for *Diagnostic and Statistical Manual* (DSM) disorders. The SCID is a semistructured diagnostic interview based on the DSM's classification of Axis I and Axis II disorders. Diagnosis using an interview such as the SCID can be useful, as receiving a diagnosis usually enables people to gain access to specialist services. However, arguably, providing a diagnosis based on DSM classification may not necessarily help individuals better understand their own specific mental health problems and in some cases can lead people to feel stigmatized.

SECTION SUMMARY

- A historical perspective on psychopathology and 'madness' is important because it helps us to understand how our views of the causes of mental health problems have changed and developed over time.

- Historically, people described those exhibiting symptoms of psychopathology as being 'possessed' and the only way to exorcise these 'bad spirits' was deemed to be with ritualized ceremonies that involved physical attacks on the sufferer's body.

- Demonic possession is still a common explanation of psychopathology in some less-developed areas of the world.

- The medical model has given rise to a large body of scientific knowledge about psychopathology that is based on medicine, and this profession is known as psychiatry.

- Many clinical psychologists criticize the medical model's reductionist approach.

DEFINING PSYCHOPATHOLOGY

LEARNING OBJECTIVE 15.3

Describe and evaluate the various ways in which psychopathology has been defined.

The problems reported by Michelle and Sophie at the beginning of this chapter are typical of those reported by people with mental health problems. But how do we define what is a mental health problem and what is not? Unlike in medicine, we can't simply base our definitions on the existence of a pathological cause. This is because, first, as we have already argued, common psychological problems often do not have underlying physical or biological causes and, second, knowledge of the causes of many psychopathologies is still very much in its infancy, so we are not yet in a position to provide a classification of psychopathologies based on causal factors. This leads us to try to define psychopathology in ways that are independent of the possible causes of such problems – and, as we shall see, many attempts to do this have important ethical and practical implications.

Deviation from the statistical norm

We can use statistical definitions to decide whether an activity or a psychological attribute deviates substantially from the **statistical norm**, and in some areas of clinical psychology this has been used as a means of deciding whether a particular disorder meets diagnostic criteria. For example, in the area of intellectual disability, an IQ score significantly below the norm of 100 has been used in the past as one criterion for diagnosing intellectual disability. Figure 15.1 shows the distribution of IQ scores in a standard population, and this indicates that the percentage of individuals with IQ scores below 70 is likely to be relatively rare (i.e. around 2.5–3% of the population). However, there are at least two important problems with using deviations from statistical norms as indications of psychopathology. First, in the intellectual disability case, an IQ of less than 70 may be statistically rare, but, rather than simply forcing the individual into a diagnostic category, a better

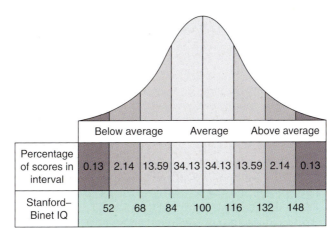

FIGURE 15.1 *This figure represents a normal distribution curve for IQ scores. From this distribution it can be seen that 68.26% of people score between 84 and 116 points, while only 2.27% of people have an IQ score below 68 points. This graph suggests that around 2–3% of the population will have IQs lower than the 70 points that is the diagnostic criterion for intellectual development disorder. However, the problem with basing a definition of psychopathology on scores that deviate substantially from the norm is that high IQ is also very rare: only 2.27% of the population have an IQ score greater than 132 points.*

Source: Davey (2014b, Fig. 1.1, p. 15). Reproduced with permission of Wiley.

approach would be to evaluate the specific needs of individuals with intellectual disabilities in a way that allows us to suggests strategies, services, and supports that will optimize individual functioning. Second, as we can see from Figure 15.1, substantial deviation from the norm does not necessarily imply psychopathology because individuals with exceptionally high IQs are also statistically rare, yet we would not necessarily be willing to consider this group of individuals as candidates for psychological intervention.

FOCUS POINT 15.2

LEARNING, INTELLECTUAL, AND DEVELOPMENTAL DISABILITIES

The term 'learning disability' has a broad coverage. It can to refer to specific learning disabilities (e.g. dyslexia), intellectual disabilities (caused by birth or childhood events, or chromosomal disorders), and pervasive developmental disorders (e.g. autistic disorder).

Dyslexia is an example of a specific learning disability and is used to describe individuals who experience disorders of both reading and written expression. Common symptoms of dyslexia are slow reading, omissions or substitutions of words, poor comprehension and difficulty with written tasks (including spelling errors), difficulty with paragraph organization, and poor handwriting. Dyslexia is often recognized in childhood, and genetic studies show an inherited component to dyslexia, with one study showing that between 23% and 65% of children with dyslexia have a parent with the disorder (Scarborough & Dobrich, 1990).

Intellectual disabilities are characterized by individuals having lower than average intellectual functioning, such as impairments in adaptive functioning (e.g. not developing age-appropriate social and educational skills) that occur before the age of 18 and are not due to injury or illness occurring later in life (Davey, 2014b). Examples of intellectual disabilities include chromosomal disorders such as Down syndrome, where individuals have an extra chromosome; the prevalence rate of Down syndrome is approximately 0.15% (Simonoff, Bolton, & Rutter, 1996).

Intellectual disabilities can also occur while the foetus is developing in the womb. One such example is foetal alcohol syndrome, where alcohol consumed by the mother during pregnancy enters the foetus' blood stream and negatively affects development. Another category of developmental disorders is known as pervasive developmental disorders, of which one example is autistic spectrum disorder (ASD). In ASD, children from an early age may display characteristic behaviours such as appearing withdrawn and not developing age-appropriate verbal and nonverbal communication skills; they may also have difficulty learning new skills.

Other common features of ASD include rigid or stereotyped patterns of behaviour, and individuals with ASD can become very distressed if routine is broken. Furthermore, individuals with ASD may exhibit stereotyped body movements, including clapping, rocking, and swaying (Davey, 2014b). The occurrence of ASDs is now known to have a genetic component, with a study showing approximately a twofold occurrence in ASDs among full siblings as compared with half siblings (Constantino et al., 2013). There is also some evidence that ASD is associated with brain abnormalities, with some implicated areas being the frontal lobes, the limbic system, the cerebellum, and the basal ganglia (Sokol & Edwards-Brown, 2004).

DISRUPTIVE BEHAVIOUR PROBLEMS: ADHD AND CONDUCT DISORDER

One of the most widely recognized disruptive behaviour problems in childhood is attention deficit hyperactivity disorder, or ADHD, also referred to as hyperkinetic disorder. In ADHD, behaviour problems are characterized in terms of two broad categories of inattentiveness and hyperactivity/impulsiveness, and the majority of children in the United Kingdom diagnosed with ADHD experience both of these behaviour types. Arguably, hyperactivity and impulsiveness are typical childhood behaviours, but the National Institute for Health and Care Excellence (2009) indicates that inattentiveness, hyperactivity, and impulsiveness are 'maladaptively high' in ADHD (p. 20). ADHD is more common in boys than girls and a survey of 10,438 children in the United Kingdom found that 3.62% of boys and 0.85% of girls had ADHD (Ford, Goodman, & Meltzer, 2003). As with many common mental health disorders, there is no one identifiable cause of ADHD, but risk factors such as genetics as well as psychosocial and environmental processes that influence biology (such as maternal smoking and drug use during pregnancy) are all thought to play a part in the onset of ADHD.

Deviation from social and political norms

There is often a tendency for the members of a society to label a behaviour or activity as indicative of a mental health problem if it is different from what they consider to be the social norms for that culture. We assume (perhaps quite wrongly) that socially normal and acceptable behaviours have evolved to represent adaptive ways of behaving, and that anyone who deviates from these norms is exhibiting psychopathology. However, it is very difficult to use deviation from social norms, or even violations of social norms, as a way of defining psychopathology.

First, different cultures often differ significantly in what they consider to be socially normal and acceptable. For example, in some non-democratic countries, political dissidents who are active against the government can often be labelled as 'mentally ill' and incarcerated in psychiatric hospitals; for instance, this was one way of controlling dissidents in the former Soviet Union (Goldacre, 2002). Second, it is difficult to use cultural norms to define psychopathology because cultural factors seem to significantly affect how psychopathology manifests itself. For example, culture can produce 'culture-bound' symptoms of psychopathology that seem to be confined to specific cultures and can influence how stress, anxiety, and depression manifest themselves (e.g. Nicolas, DeSilva, Grey, & Gonzalez-Eastep, 2006).

Distress and disability

Later in this chapter we will look at some of the ways in which psychologists and psychiatrists have attempted to classify psychopathology. In order to be diagnosed as a psychological disorder, one of the most common requirements is that the symptoms must cause 'clinically significant distress or impairment in social, academic, or occupational functioning' (American Psychiatric Association, 2013, p. 20). It is clearly the case that many individuals with severe symptoms of psychopathology do suffer considerable personal distress – often to the point of wanting to take their own lives. Defining psychopathology in terms of the degree of distress and impairment expressed by the sufferer is useful in a number of ways. First, it allows people to be the judge of their own symptoms rather than subjecting them to judgements about their 'normality' made by others in society such as psychologists or psychiatrists. Many people who are diagnosed with mental health problems originally present themselves for treatment because of the distress and impairment caused by their symptoms, and to some degree this makes them judges of their own needs. Second, defining psychopathology in terms of the degree of distress and impairment experienced can be independent of the type of lifestyle chosen by the individual. This means we judge whether someone has a mental health problem on the basis of how they are able to cope with their own lifestyle.

TEST YOURSELF

1. What are the problems in using statistical norms to define psychopathology?
2. How might distress and disability be used in defining mental health problems?

SECTION SUMMARY

- The question of how to define what is a mental health problem and what is not is long-standing and complex.
- Common psychological problems often do not have underlying physical or biological causes, and knowledge of the causes of many psychopathologies is still very much in its infancy.
- There is often a tendency for the members of a society to label a behaviour or activity as indicative of a mental health problem if it deviates from statistical, political, or social norms.
- Defining psychopathology in terms of the degree of distress and impairment expressed by the sufferer is increasingly seen as a viable alternative method of definition.
- None of these individual ways of defining psychopathology is ideal.
- In practice, classification schemes tend to use an amalgamation of all these approaches, with emphasis being placed on how distressing the individual's symptoms are, whether they are life-threatening, and whether they cause significant disruption to normal daily living.

EXPLANATORY APPROACHES TO PSYCHOPATHOLOGY

LEARNING OBJECTIVE 15.4

Describe and compare the main explanatory approaches to understanding psychopathology.

Human beings are multifaceted organisms; they consist of a genetically propagated biological substrate that serves as a basis for behaviour and a whole range of psychological processes, such as thinking, learning, remembering, and perceiving. These genetic, biological, behavioural, and psychological processes are interdependent and together make up our conception of the complete thinking and behaving human being. But genetic, biological, behavioural, and psychological processes can also be studied independently, and this view also applies to psychopathology. For example, symptoms of psychosis might be explained genetically (in terms of the inheritance of genes that give rise to a predisposition for these symptoms), biologically (in terms of abnormalities in brain function that generate symptoms), behaviourally (in terms of how symptomatic behaviours are learned through experience), and psychologically (in terms of how symptoms might be generated by dysfunctional ways of thinking). In many cases, a specific psychopathology can be explained at all these different levels. Furthermore, these explanations within different paradigms are not mutually exclusive; they supplement each other and provide a fuller, richer understanding of the psychopathology. The following sections briefly summarize these different explanatory perspectives.

Biological models

Genetics and **neuroscience** are two of the most important biological paradigms through which researchers attempt to understand psychopathology. The discipline of genetics provides us with a variety of techniques that allow an assessment of whether psychopathological symptoms are inherited or not, and neuroscience techniques allow us to determine whether psychopathological symptoms are associated with abnormalities or differences in brain or central nervous system functioning.

Genetics

People are biological organisms who come into the world with a biological substructure that will be significantly determined by the genes they have inherited from their ancestors. It is therefore almost a truism to say that behaviour – and mental health problems too – will have at least some genetic component. However, in the vast majority of psychopathologies we describe in this book, people do not solely inherit a mental health problem through their genes; a mental health problem develops because of an interaction between a genetic predisposition and our interactions with the environment (Shenk, 2010). This is called a **diathesis–stress model** of psychopathology, where 'diathesis' refers to an inherited predisposition and 'stress' refers to a variety of experiences that may trigger the inherited predisposition. This interaction between genes and experiences gives rise to the notion of heritability. **Heritability** is a measure of the degree to which symptoms can be accounted for by genetic factors, and this ranges from 0 to 1; the nearer this figure is to 1, the more important are genetic factors in explaining the symptoms. One new area of genetics highly relevant to psychopathology is **epigenetics**. We know that aspects of psychopathology and mental health can be influenced by genetics and hereditary factors, and we moreover know that personal experiences can also influence psychopathology. However, research in the developing area of epigenetics suggests that the early experiences of an individual may either trigger or inhibit the expression of genes they may possess that make them vulnerable to mental health problems such as anxiety or depression, and in this way there can be a direct interaction between environmental factors and inherited factors. This has important implications for our understanding of how mental health problems develop and the aetiology of those disorders (Kofink, Boks, Timmers, & Kas, 2013).

Neuroscience

The neuroscience paradigm seeks an understanding of psychopathology by identifying aspects of the individual's biology that may contribute to their symptoms. The main focus of this paradigm is on brain structure and function, although the broader activity of the neuroendocrine system has also been implicated in some psychopathological symptoms, especially mood disorders (the neuroendocrine system involves interactions between the brain and the endocrine system, which produces hormone secretions in the body). One example of the way that neuroscience and study of the brain may further our knowledge of psychopathology is when we find abnormalities in specific functional brain areas that are associated with psychopathological symptoms. For example, the **frontal lobes** are especially important and are the areas of the brain that are considered to make us uniquely human. The frontal lobes are known to be important in executive functions such as planning and decision making, error correction and troubleshooting, dealing with novel situations, and inhibiting habitual and impulsive responses. Given these important functions, it is an area of the brain where deficits or abnormalities have been implicated in many types of psychopathology, including attention disorders, perseveration and stereotyped behaviour patterns, lack of drive and motivation, inability to plan ahead, and apathy and emotional blunting. Alternatively, because the frontal lobes also control response inhibition, deficits in this area can also be associated with impulsivity, euphoria, and aggressive behaviour (Brower & Price, 2001; Meyers, Berman, Scheibel, & Hayman, 1992).

Psychological models

Some approaches to understanding and explaining mental health problems do not directly refer to the individual's biology; they refer specifically to psychological factors, such as how that individual thinks, how they process information, how they learn, and the kinds of beliefs they hold, and, in particular, how these psychological factors influence the acquisition and maintenance of mental health problems. In this section we will look briefly at four specific psychological approaches, namely the psychodynamic model, the behavioural model, the cognitive model, and the humanistic–existentialist model.

The psychodynamic model

The psychodynamic approach was first formulated and pioneered by the Viennese neurologist Sigmund Freud (1856–1939). In his influential theory of **psychoanalysis**, Freud attempted to explain both normal and abnormal psychological functioning in terms of how various psychological mechanisms help to defend against anxiety and depression by repressing memories and thoughts that may cause conflict and stress. Freud argued that three psychological forces shape an individual's personality and may also generate psychopathology. These are the id (instinctual needs), the ego (rational thinking), and the superego (moral standards). Freud used the concept of the id to describe innate instinctual needs – especially sexual needs. He noted that, from a very early age, children obtain pleasure from nursing, defecating, masturbating, and other 'sexually' related activities and that many forms of behaviour are driven by satisfying the needs of the id. As we grow up, Freud argued that it becomes apparent to us that the environment itself will not satisfy all our instinctual needs, and we develop a separate part of our psychology known as the ego. This is a rational part of the psyche that attempts to control the impulses of the id, and ego defence mechanisms develop by which the ego attempts to control unacceptable impulses of the id and reduce the anxiety that the id's impulses may arouse. The superego develops out of both the id and the ego, and represents our attempts to integrate 'values' that we learn from our parents or society. Freud argued that we often judge ourselves by these values that we assimilate; if we think our behaviour does not meet the standards implicit in these values, we will feel guilty and stressed.

According to Freud, the id, ego, and superego are often in conflict, and psychological health is maintained only when they are in balance. However, if these three factors are in conflict, then behaviour may begin to exhibit signs of psychopathology. Individuals attempt to control conflict between these factors and also reduce stress and conflict from external events by developing **defence mechanisms**; descriptions of some important defence mechanisms are given in Table 15.1.

Psychoanalysis was arguably the first of the 'talking therapies' and as many as 20% of modern practising clinical psychologists identify themselves at least in part with a psychoanalytical or psychodynamic approach to psychopathology (Prochaska & Norcross, 2003). However, psychoanalytic theory does have many shortcomings. For example, the central concepts in psychoanalytic theory are hard to objectively define and measure, and it is therefore difficult to conduct objective research on them to see whether they are actually related to symptoms of psychopathology in the way that Freud and his associates described (Erdelyi, 1992).

TABLE 15.1 *Defence mechanisms in psychoanalytic theory.*

Denial	Denying the existence of the source of the anxiety (e.g. 'I didn't fail my exam – it must be a mistake').
Repression	Suppressing bad memories, or even current thoughts that cause anxiety (e.g. repressing thoughts about liking someone because you are frightened that you may be rejected if you approach them).
Regression	Moving back to an earlier developmental stage (e.g. when highly stressed, you may abandon normal coping strategies and return to an early developmental stage, for example by smoking if you are fixated at the oral stage).
Reaction formation	Doing or thinking the opposite to how you feel (e.g. if you are angry with your boss, you may go out of your way to be kind and courteous to them).
Projection	Ascribing unwanted impulses to someone else (e.g. an unfaithful husband who is extremely jealous of his wife might always suspect that she is being unfaithful).
Rationalization	Finding a rational explanation for something you've done wrong (e.g. you didn't fail the exam because you didn't study hard enough but because the questions were unfair).
Displacement	Moving an impulse from one object (target) to another (e.g. if you've been told off by your boss at work, you go home and shout at your partner or kick the dog).
Sublimation	Transforming impulses into something constructive (e.g. redecorating your bedroom when you're feeling angry about something).

Note: Each of these Freudian defence mechanisms functions to reduce the amount of stress or conflict that might be caused by specific experiences.

The behavioural model

The behavioural model adopts the broad view that many examples of psychopathology reflect our learned reactions to life experiences. That is, psychopathology can be explained as learned reactions to environmental experiences. This approach was promoted primarily by the behaviourist school of psychology, which argued that many forms of psychopathology are the result of 'faulty learning' brought about through processes of either classical conditioning or operant conditioning. One famous example of the behaviourist approach is the study of 'Little Albert' by Watson and Rayner (1920). Albert was an 11-month-old infant and Watson and Rayner attempted to condition in him a fear of his pet white rat. They did this by pairing the rat – the conditioned stimulus – with the frightening event of a loud noise produced by striking an iron bar – the unconditioned stimulus, which distressed Albert (producing an unconditioned response) (see Figure 15.2). After several pairings of the rat with the noise, Albert began to cry (the conditioned response) whenever the rat was introduced into the room. This type of explanation was popular in the 70 years following the Little Albert studies, and more sophisticated contemporary conditioning models of specific phobias have since been developed (Davey, 1992a, 1992b, 1998).

The behavioural approach led to the development of important behavioural treatment methods, including **behaviour therapy** and **behaviour modification**. For example, if psychopathology develops through normal learning processes, then it should be possible to use those same learning processes to help the individual 'unlearn' any maladaptive behaviours or emotions. This view enabled the development of treatment methods based on classical conditioning principles (such as flooding and systematic desensitization). As influential as the behavioural approach has been over the years, it too has some limitations. For example, learning paradigms may simply not represent the most ideal conceptual framework in which to describe and understand some quite complex psychopathologies. For instance, many psychopathologies are characterized by a range of cognitive factors such as information-processing biases and dysfunctional ways of thinking, and learning theory jargon is probably not the

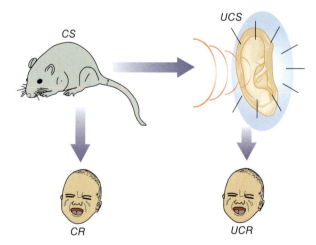

FIGURE 15.2 *The 'Little Albert' classical conditioning study. This study by Watson and Rayner (1920) demonstrated the acquisition of a phobia by pairing Little Albert's pet rat (the conditioned stimulus, CS) with a loud noise (unconditioned stimulus, UCS). His original fearful response to the loud noise (the unconditioned response, UCR) is then transferred to the pet rat (the conditioned response, CR).*
Source: Davey (2014b, Fig. 6.2, p. 152). Reproduced with permission of Wiley.

best framework in which to accurately and inclusively describe these phenomena. The cognitive approaches we will describe next are probably more suited to describing and explaining these aspects of psychopathology.

DISCUSSION POINT

Discuss how classical conditioning might be used to explain the acquisition of psychopathological symptoms.

The cognitive model

Perhaps the most widely adopted current psychological model of psychopathology is the cognitive model, and one in four of all present-day clinical psychologists would describe their approach as cognitive (Prochaska & Norcross, 2003). Primarily, this approach considers psychopathology to be the result of individuals acquiring irrational beliefs, developing dysfunctional ways of thinking, and processing information in biased ways. It was an approach first pioneered by Albert Ellis (1962) and Aaron Beck (1967). For example, Beck argued that depressed individuals have developed unrealistic distortions in the way they perceive themselves, the world, and their future, and these cognitive distortions cause their depressive symptoms. In particular, the cognitive approach argues that depression results from the depressed individual having developed negative beliefs about themselves (e.g. 'I am worthless'), the world (e.g. 'bad things always happen'), and their future (e.g. 'I am never going to achieve anything'), and these beliefs act to maintain depressive thinking. The cognitive approach has also been highly successful in generating an influential approach to treatment. If dysfunctional thoughts and beliefs maintain the symptoms of psychopathology, then these dysfunctional thoughts and beliefs can be identified, challenged, and replaced by more functional cognitions. This has given rise to a broad-ranging therapeutic approach known as **cognitive behaviour therapy**.

The humanistic–existentialist approach

Some approaches to psychopathology are based on the belief that insights into emotional and behavioural problems cannot be achieved unless individuals are able to gain insight into their lives from a broad range of perspectives. People not only acquire psychological conflicts and experience emotional distress; they also have the ability to acquire self-awareness, develop important values and a sense of meaning in life, and pursue freedom of choice. If these latter abilities are positively developed and encouraged, then conflict, emotional distress, and psychopathology can often be resolved. This is the general approach adopted by humanistic and existentialist models of psychopathology, and the aim is to resolve psychological problems through insight, personal development, and self-actualization. An influential example of the humanistic–existential approach is 'client-centred therapy', developed by Carl Rogers (1951, 1987). This approach stresses the goodness of human nature and assumes that, if individuals are unrestricted by fears and conflicts, they will develop into well-adjusted, happy individuals. The client-centred therapist will try to create a supportive climate in which the client is helped to acquire positive self-worth. The therapist will use empathy to help them understand the client's feelings and unconditional positive regard, through which the therapist expresses their willingness to totally accept the client for who they are.

However, approaches such as humanistic and existentialist ones are difficult to evaluate. For example, most controlled studies have indicated that clients undergoing client-centred therapy tend to fare no better than those undergoing non-therapeutic control treatments (Patterson, 2000). In contrast, exponents of existentialist therapies believe that empirical methodologies are inappropriate for estimating the effectiveness of such therapies because such methods either dehumanize the individuals involved or are incapable of measuring the kinds of existential benefits that such approaches claim to bestow (Walsh & McElwain, 2002). Nevertheless, such approaches to treatment are still accepted as having value and are still used at least in part by clinical psychologists, counselling psychologists, and psychotherapists.

SECTION SUMMARY

- Our genetic, biological, behavioural, and psychological processes are interdependent and together make up our conception of the complete thinking and behaving human being.
- Genetics and neuroscience are two of the most important biological paradigms through which researchers attempt to understand psychopathology.
- In the diathesis–stress model of psychopathology – where 'diathesis' refers to an inherited predisposition and 'stress' refers to a variety of experiences that may trigger the inherited predisposition – the interaction between genes and experiences gives rise to the notion of heritability.
- One new area of genetics highly relevant to psychopathology is epigenetics.
- The main focus of the neuroscience paradigm is on brain structure and function.
- Psychological models that try to explain mental health problems include the psychodynamic, behavioural, cognitive, and humanistic–existentialist approaches.

CLASSIFYING MENTAL HEALTH PROBLEMS

LEARNING OBJECTIVE 15.5

Describe and compare the main approaches to classifying psychopathology.

Even though it is difficult to find a good, simple definition of what a mental health problem is, there is still a need to be able to classify different mental health problems. This is important so that we can develop effective treatments for what in practice are often a range of very different mental health problems, with very different symptoms and different causes. In this respect, classification is necessary if we are to effectively organize services and support for sufferers. For example, the needs of individuals with an intellectual disability, major depression, an anxiety-based disorder, or substance dependency are all very different and require different approaches and different means of support and intervention. We need to have some basis for differentiating these different kinds of problems and determining the different kinds of support that each might need, and classification systems provide a common language for reporting and monitoring mental health problems, allowing the world to share and compare data in a consistent way.

The development of classification systems

The first extensive system for classifying psychopathology was developed by the World Health Organization, which added psychological disorders to the **International List of Causes of Death** (**ICD**) in 1939. Despite this development, the mental disorders section in the ICD was not widely accepted, and in 1952 the American Psychiatric Association published its first **Diagnostic and Statistical Manual** (**DSM**). The most recent version of the latter is the DSM-5 (American Psychiatric Association, 2013). The ICD system is currently in its 10th edition (ICD-10), with ICD-11 under development as we write this, and most revisions of the DSM have been coordinated with the ICD to ensure some consistency of diagnosis across the two systems. For convenience and consistency, we will use only the DSM-5 diagnostic system in this chapter when we discuss some individual psychological disorders.

Before attempting to classify psychopathology, it was necessary for the DSM to define what it considers to be a mental health problem. DSM consequently does make some attempt to rule out behaviours that are simply socially deviant as examples of psychopathology and puts the emphasis on *distress* and *disability* as important defining characteristics. Distress relates to the chronic experience of pain or distressing emotions, and disability refers to the fact that distress can lead to impairment in one or more important areas of functioning, such as education, employment, and dealing with family and social responsibilities. Table 15.2 provides a list of the chapters in the DSM-5, which provide the diagnostic criteria for a range of mental health problems.

While classification systems such as the DSM-5 attempt to provide an objective and reliable set of criteria by which mental health problems can be diagnosed, they are in

TABLE 15.2 *Chapters in the DSM-5.*

- Neurodevelopmental Disorders
- Schizophrenia Spectrum and Other Psychotic Disorders
- Bipolar and Related Disorders
- Depressive Disorders
- Anxiety Disorders
- Obsessive–Compulsive and Related Disorders
- Trauma- and Stressor-Related Disorders
- Dissociative Disorders
- Somatic Symptom and Related Disorders
- Feeding and Eating Disorders
- Elimination Disorders
- Sleep–Wake Disorders
- Sexual Dysfunctions
- Gender Dysphoria
- Disruptive, Impulse-Control, and Conduct Disorders
- Substance-Related and Addictive Disorders
- Neurocognitive Disorders
- Personality Disorders
- Paraphilic Disorders
- Other Mental Disorders

Note: The total number of disorders in the DSM-5 did not increase significantly relative to the previous edition, but some disorders had their importance recognized by being allocated separate chapter headings (e.g. obsessive compulsive disorder). The chapter on neurodevelopmental disorders is a new heading containing autism spectrum disorders, intellectual development disorder, and attention deficit hyperactivity disorder. The chapter on substance-related and addictive behaviours now includes gambling disorder.

many senses imperfect. First, as you will see later on in this chapter, the DSM-5 does not classify psychopathology according to its causes but does so merely on the basis of symptoms. This can be problematic in a number of ways. For example, psychopathologies that look the same on the surface may have different causes and as a consequence may require different forms of treatment. Also, diagnosis on the basis of symptoms gives the illusion of explanation when it is nothing more than a redescription of the symptoms (Carson, 1996). So, to say that 'she hears voices because she has schizophrenia' sounds like an explanation, but within the DSM-5 schizophrenia is merely a collective term for the defining symptoms. Second, simply using DSM-5 criteria to label people with a disorder can be stigmatizing and harmful (see next section), as individuals with a mental health diagnosis can be viewed and treated differently within society. Third, the DSM-5's diagnostic classification tends to define disorders as *discrete entities*. That is, after being assessed, you will either be diagnosed with a disorder or you will not, yet the cut-off point where someone is diagnosed with a mental health problem is purely arbitrary. This arbitrary nature of diagnosis is supported by the fact that the symptoms of many common mental health problems, such as anxiety and depression, are on a dimension from mild to severe, with no obvious cut-off point where we can establish that above that line someone has a psychopathology and below it they do not (Krueger & Piasecki, 2002).

TEST YOURSELF

Can you name some of the issues involved in classifying mental health problems?

SECTION SUMMARY

- Even though it is difficult to find a good, simple definition of what a mental health problem is, there is still a need to be able to classify different mental health problems in order to determine effective treatments, services, and support.

- The first extensive system for classifying psychopathology was developed by the World Health Organization, which added psychological disorders to the International List of Causes of Death in 1939.

- In 1952 the American Psychiatric Association published its first *Diagnostic and Statistical Manual* (DSM). The most recent version, the DSM-5, was published in 2013.

- Classification systems are imperfect: they tend to classify psychopathology on the basis of symptoms, they are potentially stigmatizing, and they define disorders as discrete entities.

MENTAL HEALTH AND STIGMA

LEARNING OBJECTIVE 15.6

Discuss the stigma that develop for people with mental health problems and the campaigns undertaken to counteract this stigma.

There are still attitudes within most societies that view mental health problems as threatening and uncomfortable, and these attitudes frequently foster stigma and discrimination towards people with those problems. For example, notice how reactions to Louise changed when she suffered a mental health problem, and how this led to loss of respect and consideration:

> In some cases I became a 'second class citizen'. I could be treated with a briskness and dismissive air that had never been present before. I could be rudely dismissed and ignored on special occasions. My presence was clearly thought to be potentially threatening. Perhaps I wouldn't be happy enough or introduce inappropriate topics. I had laid bare my weakness and others were not about to forget it. These people, like all human beings, probably thought that they were doing the right thing. They were saving others from my presence. They also probably thought that they were treating me as my merits deserved. I had permanently lost the respect and consideration that I had once received.
>
> *Source:* 'A Question of Dignity' from www.mentalhealth.com.

Such reactions are common when people are brave enough to admit they have a mental health problem; this can often lead on to various forms of exclusion or discrimination – either within social circles or within the workplace.

Studies have suggested that stigmatizing attitudes towards people with mental health problems are widespread and commonly held (Crisp, Gelder, Rix, Meltzer, & Rowlands, 2000). In a survey of over 1,700 adults in the United Kingdom, Crisp et al. (2000) found that (1) the most commonly held belief was that people with mental health problems are dangerous – especially those with schizophrenia, alcoholism, or drug dependence; (2) people believed that some mental health problems, such as eating disorders and substance abuse (see the next section, 'Psychological Disorders'), are self-inflicted; and (3) respondents believed that people with mental health problems are generally hard to talk to. People tended to hold these negative beliefs regardless of their age, regardless of what knowledge they had of mental health problems, and regardless of whether they knew someone who had a mental health problem. Perhaps surprisingly, stigmatizing beliefs about individuals with mental health problems are held by a broad range of individuals within society, regardless of whether they know someone with a mental health problem, have a family member with a mental health problem, or have a good knowledge and experience of mental health problems (Moses, 2010; Wallace, 2010).

The social stigma associated with mental health problems almost certainly has multiple causes. We've seen in the section on historical perspectives that throughout history people with mental health problems have been treated differently, excluded, and even brutalized. This treatment may come from the misguided views that people with mental health problems may be more violent or unpredictable than people without such problems, or somehow just 'different', but none of these beliefs has any basis in fact (e.g. Swanson, Holzer, Ganju, & Jono, 1990). The medical model also implies that mental health problems are on a par with physical illnesses and may result from medical or physical dysfunction in some way (in fact, many may not be simply reducible to biological or medical causes). This in itself implies that people with mental health problems are in some way 'different' from 'normally' functioning individuals. It is also important to acknowledge that the media regularly plays a role in perpetuating stigmatizing stereotypes of people with mental health problems. For example, cinematic depictions of schizophrenia are often stereotypical and characterized by misinformation about symptoms, causes, and treatment. Other examples include a national tabloid newspaper in the United Kingdom that ran a front-page news story with the headline '1,200 Killed by Mental Patients' in October 2013.

Mental health stigma matters because it has many negative effects on the lives of people with mental health problems. It encompasses both prejudicial attitudes and discriminating behaviour towards individuals suffering with mental health problems, and the social effects of this include exclusion, poor social support, poorer subjective quality of life, and low self-esteem (Livingston & Boyd, 2010). As well as its effects on people's quality of daily living, stigma has a detrimental effect on treatment outcomes, and so hinders efficient and effective recovery from mental health problems (Perlick et al., 2001).

The fact that such negative attitudes appear to be so entrenched suggests that campaigns to change these beliefs will have to be multifaceted, will have to do more than just impart knowledge about mental health problems, and will need to challenge existing negative stereotypes, especially as they are portrayed in the general media (Pinfold et al., 2003). In the UK, the **Time to Change** campaign is one of the biggest programmes attempting to address mental health stigma and is supported by both charities and mental health service providers. This campaign creates blogs, videos, TV advertisements, and promotional events to help raise awareness of mental health stigma and the detrimental effect this has on sufferers of mental health problems.

DISCUSSION POINT

Discuss how mental health stigma affects the lives of individuals with mental health problems. Research instances of mental health stigma in your country and add your findings to the discussion.

SECTION SUMMARY

- The belief that mental health problems are threatening fosters stigma and discrimination towards people with those problems.
- Studies have suggested that stigmatizing attitudes towards people with mental health problems are widespread and commonly held.
- Many believe that people with mental health problems may be more violent or are somehow just 'different'.
- The media often perpetuates stigmatizing stereotypes about people with mental health problems.
- Experiencing stigma affects people's quality of daily living and has a detrimental effect on treatment outcomes and recovery.
- In the United Kingdom, the Time to Change campaign is one of the biggest programmes attempting to address mental health stigma.

PSYCHOLOGICAL DISORDERS

LEARNING OBJECTIVE 15.7

Describe the important characteristics and possible causes of a range of common mental health problems, namely anxiety and anxiety-related disorders, depression, schizophrenia spectrum disorders, and personality disorders.

In this section we discuss some of the most common mental health problems and their causes – or at least their causes as we currently understand them. We begin with the two most common mental health problems – anxiety and depression – and then go on to discuss less common but more severe mental health problems, such as schizophrenia spectrum disorders and personality disorders.

FOCUS POINT 15.3

POST-TRAUMATIC STRESS DISORDER

Post-traumatic stress disorder (PTSD) is one of the few disorders in the DSM-5 in which the cause of the disorder is a defining factor. Diagnosis of PTSD is considered only if the individual has experienced an extreme trauma prior to their symptoms. They may have:

1. directly experienced the trauma (e.g. been involved in a natural disaster such as an earthquake or fire, or been subjected to life-threatening physical abuse such as rape)

2. witnessed a traumatic event in which others may have suffered (e.g. witnessing the 9/11 terrorist attacks in New York)

3. learned that a severe traumatic event has happened to a close family member or friend

4. been repeatedly subjected to distressing details of trauma (e.g. the kind of regular exposure to details of trauma that might be experienced by police officers or emergency workers).

The symptoms typical of PTSD are grouped into four categories:

1. **intrusive symptoms**, such as flashbacks, intrusive thoughts, or physiological reactions

2. **avoidance responding**, such as active avoidance of thoughts, memories, or reminders of the trauma

3. **negative changes in cognition and mood**, such as persistent fear, horror, anger, guilt, or shame; persistent negative beliefs about themselves, others, or the world (e.g. 'no one can be trusted', 'I've lost my soul forever'); or dissociative feelings of detachment or estrangement from others

4. **increased arousal and reactivity**, such as hypervigilance and exaggerated startle responses.

Studies suggest that PTSD symptoms are developed by up to 90% of rape victims, between 70% and 90% of torture victims, over 50% of prisoners of war, between 20% and 25% of earthquake and flood survivors, and around 15% of motor vehicle accident victims (see Davey, 2014b, ch. 6). The DSM-5 also emphasizes that PTSD symptoms can be acquired in cases where the stressor has not been life-threatening to the sufferer (e.g. watching images of the 9/11 terrorist attacks on television).

The **lifetime prevalence** rate for PTSD is between 1% and 3% (Helzer, Robins, & McEvoy, 1987). However, prevalence rates are significantly higher for groups who are at risk of experiencing severe trauma. These include a 12–33% prevalence rate for civilians living in war zones (Farhood & Dimassi, 2012), a 10% prevalence rate for rescue workers (Berger et al., 2012), and a 13.2% prevalence rate for members of operational infantry in the 21st-century Iraq and Afghanistan conflicts (Kok, Herrell, Thomas, & Hoge, 2012). Around 50% of adults experience at least one event in their lifetime that might qualify as a PTSD-causing trauma (Ozer & Weiss, 2004), which means that many people experience trauma but do *not* develop PTSD. It is understanding these individual differences in susceptibility to PTSD that will give us some insight into the mechanisms that give rise to PTSD.

Anxiety and anxiety-related disorders

We all feel anxious from time to time. In fact, feeling anxious is a normal and adaptive response to stressful situations that threaten our short- and long-term goals in life. For example, feeling anxious before an exam can spur us on to work hard at revision in order to achieve the goal of passing the exam. However, for some people anxiety can become excessive. When anxiety is excessive in relation to a triggering situation, the effects can be long lasting (e.g. feeling anxious every day for a number of months) and distressing to the point that the individual is prevented from going about daily life, and these may be signs that help should be sought to manage the anxiety.

Anxiety: What is it?

The experience of anxiety can be understood from both a physical and a psychological perspective. Common physical symptoms of anxiety include a rapid heartbeat, sweating, a dry mouth, dizziness, shaking, and difficulty swallowing. People who experience more severe and chronic anxiety also report problems such as difficulty getting to sleep or staying asleep, frequent diarrhoea, difficulty urinating, sexual difficulties, headaches, and excessive thirst. Common psychological symptoms of anxiety include feeling keyed up or on edge and restless. The following subsections provide examples of some common anxiety disorders. We have chosen three anxiety-based problems and for each one we will examine symptoms, diagnosis, and aetiology.

FOCUS POINT 15.4

SOMATIC SYMPTOM DISORDERS

Somatic symptom disorders have traditionally been characterized by the experience of physical symptoms (e.g. pain, difficulty breathing, loss of sight), which are suggestive of a medical condition for which there is no diagnosable evidence.

According to the DSM-5, somatic symptom disorders must be accompanied by abnormal thoughts, feelings, and behaviours in relation to the physical symptoms, such as concerns about the medical seriousness of the symptoms, inability to accept the absence of a serious medical complaint, heightened health anxiety and worry, heightened reactions in response to physical symptoms, and excessive time devoted to the problem. However, in the DSM-5, these symptoms may or may not be accompanied by an underlying medical condition, and this is based on the belief that a somatic symptom disorder should not be diagnosed purely on the basis that a medical cause for symptoms cannot be demonstrated. The cause of somatic symptoms can often be hard to identify.

Lind, Delmar, and Nielsen (2014) explored the role of stress in somatic symptom disorders and found that many patients diagnosed with these disorders exhibited low emotional self-awareness and that patients had disconnected their physical awareness from their emotional distress. Because patients showed a lack of ability to identify and express stress-related thoughts and feelings, they were vulnerable to stressors, which had a negative impact on their ability to relax and sleep. This hypothesis by Lind, Delmar, and Nielsen highlights how an inability to manage stress can have not only a negative psychological impact but also a negative physiological impact.

Another prominent view is that individuals with somatic symptom disorders engage in catastrophic thinking about their symptoms (e.g. Witthöft & Hiller, 2010). Here the assumption is that the perception of bodily sensations is interpreted in a catastrophic manner, which in turn increases physiological arousal, which is again interpreted catastrophically and heightens anxiety. Somatization can be difficult to diagnose and patients can find uncertainty around diagnosis stressful. Although it can be hard to find organic causes of symptoms in somatic symptom disorders, these disorders can be distinguished from cases of malingering because the individual is unaware of the process by which the symptoms occur and cannot rid themselves of the symptoms at will.

Generalized anxiety disorder

Generalized anxiety disorder (**GAD**) is a fairly common anxiety disorder with a lifetime prevalence of 4–7% (Hoge, Ivkovic, & Fricchione, 2012). Typical symptoms of GAD include daily anxiety and anxious expectation, and worry about future events to the degree that coping with the ups and downs of daily life becomes difficult to manage and significant distress is experienced.

Causes of generalized anxiety disorder It is important to consider why some people develop this form of excessive and uncontrollable worry while others don't. Like any psychological disorder, the onset of GAD can be understood from a number of different perspectives.

Genetic factors There is evidence to support a genetic account of GAD; first-degree relatives of individuals with GAD have been found to be five times more likely to develop GAD (Noyes, Clarkson, Crowe, Yates, & McChesney, 1987). However, as highlighted in the National Institute for Health and Care Excellence (2011) guidelines for GAD, these genetic markers are linked to anxiety more generally rather than GAD specifically and are also associated with other anxiety disorders, such as panic disorder or agoraphobia. A lot of research on the aetiology and maintenance of GAD has focused on cognitive and psychological processes.

Cognitive factors Another predominant area of research has examined how highly anxious individuals process information. Research suggests that highly anxious individuals have an **attentional bias** towards threatening stimuli, which means that they allocate a greater amount of their attentional resources to threatening information than they do to non-threatening information (MacLeod, Mathews, & Tata, 1986). Individuals with GAD are also known to hold beliefs about the utility of worrying.

For example, individuals with GAD often hold the belief that worry is a useful way of dealing with perceived threats and problems, and this is termed **positive beliefs about worry** (Wells & Papageorgiou, 1998). These beliefs are often maintained when some temporary reduction in anxiety is felt, but this only reinforces the idea that worrying is a useful tool with which to manage anxiety. Finally, individuals with GAD are known to possess a number of psychological constructs that contribute to excessive worrying. Examples of these include experiencing high **intolerance of uncertainty** (Dugas, Gagnon, Ladouceur, & Freeston, 1998); high levels of responsibility for negative outcomes, often termed **inflated responsibility** (Startup & Davey, 2003); and high levels of **perfectionism (clinical perfectionism)** (Pratt, Tallis, & Eysenck, 1997). Research indicates that these psychological constructs, along with the endemic negative mood experienced by many worriers, drive people to persevere with the worry process (Meeten & Davey, 2011).

Specific phobias

Specific phobias are characterized by an individual presenting with fear that is out of proportion to the actual danger posed by the object or situation. The DSM-5 divides specific phobias into five subtypes: animal type (fear caused by animals and insects, such as spider or dog phobia), natural environment type (such as water or height phobia), blood–injection–injury type (such as blood or needle phobia), situational type (such as fear of flying, driving through a tunnel, or driving over a bridge), or other type (this can be fear of a range of stimuli, such as button or cotton wool phobia, or fear of characters, such as clown phobia). A review of specific phobia prevalence rates indicated a lifetime prevalence rate for animal phobias of 3.3–7%; of the natural phobias, height phobia had the highest prevalence rate, at 3.1–5.3%; of the situational phobias, claustrophobia had the highest prevalence rate, at 3.2–3.3%; and lifetime prevalence rates for blood–injection–injury phobia were reported at 3.2–4.5% (LeBeau et al., 2010).

Causes of specific phobias   As discussed above, there are many different types of phobias, including phobias of seemingly benign objects, such as buttons (called koumpounophobia). In seeking to explain why fear responses to these stimuli occur, several different theories concerning the aetiology of specific phobias have been proposed. One theory that has received a lot of attention is the classical conditioning account of phobias. The famous study in which an 11-month-old baby known as 'Little Albert' was trained to be fearful of his pet white rat through classical conditioning methods (Watson & Rayner, 1920) set out to examine whether phobias could be learned. A description of this study can be found above (see Figure 15.2). Classical conditioning studies such as that performed by Watson and Rayner explain how people can learn to fear a benign stimulus if it is associated with a negative event. However, this explanation can be problematic when applied to phobias, as many people cannot remember having a negative experience that could have preceded the onset of their phobia, and not everyone develops a phobia after experiencing a traumatic event. Furthermore, a conditioning account does not explain the fact that phobias are often constrained to specific groups of stimuli, such as animals or environmental phobias.

Another explanation is that we are biologically prepared or predisposed to fear certain stimuli that were threatening to us in our evolutionary past. This theory is called **biological preparedness** (Seligman, 1971) and proposes that fear of certain stimuli would have been an advantage for survival thousands of years ago and thus this explains why people still fear these stimuli now, even though these threats are often removed in modern life. To examine this view, researchers have performed classical conditioning studies with 'classic' fear-relevant stimuli, such as pictures of snakes, and irrelevant stimuli, such as pictures of houses. They found that people developed a fear of the threat-relevant stimuli more quickly than the neutral stimuli and that the fear-relevant stimuli association had greater resistance to **extinction** than the neutral stimuli (e.g. Cook & Mineka, 1990).

An alternative view is that different phobias are acquired though different routes. One alternative pathway that has been proposed to account for the onset of small-animal phobias and blood–injection–injury phobia is the disgust emotion (Davey, 2011; de Jong & Merckelbach, 1998). One of the primary functions of the disgust emotion is to prevent us from consuming contaminated food. Individuals with elevated disgust sensitivity have been shown to display increased avoidance of disgust-relevant objects, and Davey (1992b) proposed that small animals are common phobic stimuli due to the fact that they have high disgust relevance and have often been associated with contamination (e.g. rats, cockroaches, maggots, and the like). A second pathway associated with the onset of some situational phobias is related to panic. Support for this view comes from findings showing high comorbidity between panic disorder and some specific phobias, such as height phobia and claustrophobia (Starcevic & Bogojevic, 1997). In summary, evidence suggests that there are multiple pathways to the development of phobias, and different phobias may have different development routes.

Obsessive compulsive disorder

Obsessive compulsive disorder (OCD) is characterized by **obsessions** and **compulsions**. Obsessions are defined as 'intrusive repetitive thoughts, images or impulses that are unacceptable and/or unwanted and give rise to subjective resistance' (Rachman & Hodgson, 1980, p. 251). Although we all experience thoughts that we find are distressing or inappropriate (for instance, imagining a family member is dead), we rarely perceive these thoughts as being important or that they have real-life consequences. However, individuals with OCD often experience a high frequency of obsessive thoughts and find their obsessive thoughts to be more intense and more disturbing than a non-clinical population (Rachman, 1997). As a result of the distress caused by repetitive and unwanted obsessive thoughts, individuals with OCD develop ritualized compulsions that they perform in order to prevent negative outcomes from occurring. Compulsions can take a number of different forms, with two prevalent types being washing and checking compulsions (Hodgson & Rachman, 1977). In the short term, compulsions serve to reduce anxiety. The compulsion is performed to prevent a perceived negative outcome from occurring, and when the negative outcome does not occur this reinforces the value of performing the compulsion. Examples of compulsive behaviours are turning a light switch off a certain number of times or washing one's hands using a specific routine, with the process being repeated if it is not performed exactly right.

Causes of obsessive compulsive disorder There are a number of pathways through which OCD is thought to occur. We will consider examples of biological and psychological accounts.

First, from a *neurobiological perspective*, some differences in brain structure and function have been observed in people diagnosed with OCD. There is support for the view that OCD has a neurobiological basis, with basal ganglia dysfunction implicated in OCD (Insel, 1992) and a high incidence of OCD and OCD-related disorders (e.g. Tourette syndrome) occurring in those with basal ganglia lesions (Chacko, Corbin, & Harper, 2000). From a biochemical perspective, both **serotonin** and **dopamine** have been highlighted as candidate mechanisms in the development of OCD. One reason that serotonin has received a lot of interest is that serotonin reuptake inhibitors are often prescribed as a treatment for OCD. However, the exact link between OCD and the serotonergic system remains unclear. There is also evidence for a genetic pathway in OCD, with family studies showing that first-degree relatives have an increased risk of developing OCD (Pauls, 2010).

Second, there are several *cognitive factors* thought to be important in the onset and maintenance of OCD. One cognitive theory proposes that individuals with OCD perceive intrusive thoughts as being important due to experiencing inflated levels of responsibility for harm to others (Rachman, 1998; Salkovskis, 1985). This heightened sense of responsibility often signals a need to act and provokes **neutralizing behaviours** in the form of compulsions. Another cognitive construct that is implicated in OCD is perfectionism. Individuals with OCD often report feeling that things are not right and that, in order to try to attain a feeling of rightness, they need to perform an action such as checking that locks are secure or that they have washed their hands properly (Coles, Frost, Heimberg, & Rheaume, 2003). Attaining a feeling of rightness is a subjective experience and often this 'not just right' experience feeds into compulsive behaviours that the individual feels compelled to perform to reduce the feelings of distress. Another factor thought to drive repetitive behaviours in OCD is memory distrust. Initially it was assumed that when individuals with OCD reported feeling uncertain about whether they had completed an action properly they had a memory deficit. More recently, research has indicated that they actually have less confidence in their memory and thus they are more likely to doubt their actions, rather than not remember them (Tolin, Abramowitz, Brigidi, & Foa, 2003; Van den Hout & Kindt, 2003).

TEST YOURSELF

1. What cognitive factors are implicated in the onset of GAD?
2. What are the shortfalls of the classical conditioning account of specific phobias?
3. What neurobiological factors are thought to be important in OCD?

Depression

Everyone occasionally feels sad or blue. Often these types of feelings are a normal response to a negative life event and are fairly short lived. However, people who suffer depressive episodes may find that they have a number of the following symptoms on a daily basis: feelings of sadness and emptiness, feelings of worthlessness, changes in appetite or sleep patterns, loss of interest in sex, slowed thinking and/or body movements, difficulty concentrating, and unexplained physical symptoms such as pain, recurrent thoughts of suicide, or a suicide attempt. These symptoms are common to major depressive disorder, which is discussed in more detail below.

Major depressive disorder

Major depressive disorder (**MDD**) is a fairly common disorder that has a lifetime prevalence rate of approximately 4–10%. However, rates in women are estimated at 1.5–2.5 times higher than those in men (Waraich, Goldner, Somers, & Hsu, 2004). According to the DSM-5 classification, an individual experiencing MDD may experience five or more depressive symptoms over a 2-week period, for most of the day, every day, and find that their daily activities are impaired because of their symptoms. However, an individual can also be diagnosed with persistent depressive disorder (previously called dysthymia), where depressed or low mood must be present for 2 years but is deemed to be less severe than MDD, with individuals presenting with two or more depressive symptoms.

Causes of depression

When seeking to understand how and why depression occurs, it is important to take into account the number of theoretical approaches through which depression can be understood. Depression can develop for a variety of reasons and there is evidence to support a number of different developmental models.

Biological theories of depression Biological theories include genetic accounts of depression, where evidence from twin studies has, for example, demonstrated that 31% of the variance in symptoms of depression can be accounted for by genetic factors (Agrawal, Jacobson, Gardner, Prescott, & Kendler, 2004). Another biological model of depression that has received a lot of interest is the role of neurochemical factors. The **monoamine theory of depression** proposes that depression is associated with low levels of two monoamine neurotransmitters: serotonin (Lapin & Oxenkrug, 1969) and **noradrenaline** (also termed norepinephrine) (Bunny & Davis, 1965). Evidence for this theory comes from usage of antidepressant medications (such as **tricyclic antidepressants** and **monoamine oxidase inhibitors**) that serve to increase the levels of these neurotransmitters in the brain. The evidence for the view that depression is caused by reduced levels of these neurotransmitters is, however, mixed. One problem with this rather simplistic view is that increasing serotonin levels does not have an immediate effect on depressive symptoms (despite the fact that it takes only hours for drugs to affect these neurotransmitters) as antidepressants often take some weeks to have an effect (Delgado et al., 1999). Furthermore, approximately 40% of people with depression do not respond to antidepressant drugs (Wong & Licinio, 2001). One possibility is that changes in brain gene expression that occur after ongoing use of antidepressants may account for the effects of antidepressant medication (Wong & Licinio, 2001). Finally, some argue that the interplay between neurotransmitters such as serotonin and noradrenaline is more complex than previously thought and that there may be an imbalance in levels of neurotransmitters rather than a deficit (Rampello & Nicoletti, 2000). A complete account of the neurochemical mechanisms that underlie depressive symptomatology is still being debated, and some examples of papers that discuss this further are Porcelli et al. (2011) and Willner, Scheel-Krüger, and Belzung (2013).

Cognitive factors There are numerous psychological theories of depression, such as psychodynamic explanations (e.g. Freud, 1917/1963) and behavioural explanations (e.g. Lewinsohn, 1974). One of the most influential models of depression is Beck's

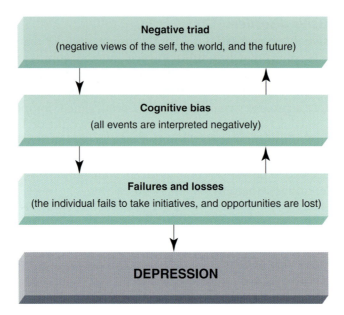

FIGURE 15.3 *Beck's negative schema in depression. This figure shows how the negative biases in the thinking of depressed individuals lead to a vicious cycle in which depression becomes a self-fulfilling prophecy.*

Source: Davey (2014b, Fig. 7.3, p. 207). Reproduced with permission of Wiley.

(1967, 1987) **cognitive model of depression** (Figure 15.3). At the heart of this cognitive explanation is the view that depression is maintained through a number of cognitive distortions or biases that result in the individual thinking about and experiencing the world in a negative way. Beck (1967, 1987) proposed that negative thinking in depression could be viewed in terms of a negative triad composed of negative views of the self (e.g. 'I am worthless'), the world (e.g. 'Everyone hates me because I am worthless'), and the future (e.g. 'I'll never be good at anything'). The negative cognitive triad underpins negative cognitive schema through which depressed individuals interpret the world. By employing a negative cognitive schema, individuals with depression are more likely than others to exhibit negative information-processing biases that ensure that they experience the world in a negative way. Consequently, individuals with depression often start to behave in a way that confirms their negative view of the world; for example, they may believe that it is pointless trying to get a job or socialize, and thus new potentially positive opportunities are missed and the negative schema through which they view the world is reinforced. One time at which individuals may start to experience chronic negative thinking is after a stressful life event. For some people, the experience of a negative, uncontrollable, and stressful event (such as the sudden death of a loved one) can trigger feelings of helplessness and depression.

TEST YOURSELF

1. What is Beck's cognitive model of depression?
2. What is the monoamine theory of depression?

EATING DISORDERS

Eating disorders develop from an interplay of biological, psychological, and sociological factors and can be characterised by undereating, overeating, or both. Alongside difficulty with eating behaviours, individuals who experience an eating disorder often also experience co-morbid difficulties with mood, such as low mood and self-esteem and high levels of anxiety. There are three main categories of eating disorder:

* anorexia nervosa
* bulimia nervosa
* binge-eating disorder.

ANOREXIA NERVOSA

Anorexia nervosa is characterized by a number of key symptoms such as a refusal to maintain a healthy body weight. Individuals with anorexia often hold a distorted image of their body such that when they see themselves in the mirror they do not observe themselves to be underweight. Anorexia has a higher incidence in females, with a lifetime prevalence rate of 0.9% in women compared with 0.3% in men (Kessler et al., 2004; Kessler, Chiu, Dernier, & Walters, 2005; Walters, Zaslavsky, & Zheng, 2004), although anorexia in men may be less likely to be diagnosed than in women. Anorexia is often comorbid with other mood and anxiety disorders, with comorbidity between anorexia and depression reported to be as high as 63% (Herzog, Keller, Sacks, Yeh, & Lavori, 1992).

BULIMIA NERVOSA

Individuals with bulimia nervosa, like those with anorexia, fear weight gain and hold a distorted view of their body shape. However, individuals with bulimia often maintain a normal body weight. Bulimia is often characterized by recurrent episodes of binge eating (excessive intake of food in one sitting) followed by periods of purging, such as by forced vomiting or by periods of fasting. In the *purging subtype*, individuals will often engage in vomiting or laxative use to expel food eaten in a binge episode. In the *nonpurging subtype*, individuals will engage in fasting or excessive exercise as compensatory behaviours for food consumed. Bulimia is often seen as a disease that affects only women.

BINGE-EATING DISORDER

A key feature of binge-eating disorder is recurrent episodes of binge eating. However, unlike in bulimia, in binge-eating disorder there are no episodes of fasting or purging to compensate for binge eating. Consequently, individuals with binge-eating disorder are often overweight. As with other eating disorders, in binge-eating disorder comorbidity with other psychological disorders is common, with one study reporting comorbidity between binge-eating disorder and mood, anxiety, and substance misuse disorders (Grilo, White, & Masheb, 2009).

Schizophrenia spectrum and other psychotic disorders

Psychosis is a collective name given to an extensive range of disparate symptoms characterized by disturbances in thought and language, sensory perception, emotion regulation, and behaviour. Sufferers may experience sensory **hallucinations** and also develop thinking biases that may lead to pervasive false beliefs or **delusions** about themselves and the world around them. Individuals with psychotic symptoms may often withdraw from normal social interaction because of these disturbances of perception and thought, and this can result in poor educational performance, increasing unproductivity, difficulties in interpersonal relationships, neglect of day-to-day activities, and a preoccupation with a personal world to the exclusion of others; the presence of various combinations of these symptoms may lead to a diagnosis of any one of a number of **schizophrenia spectrum disorders**.

The DSM-5 lists five important characteristics for diagnosing schizophrenia spectrum disorders. The first four of these characteristics are traditionally known as **positive symptoms**, because they tend to reflect an excess or distortion of normal functions (e.g. developing inappropriate beliefs or perceiving things that are not there), and the final category represents what are known as **negative symptoms**, and these reflect symptoms characteristic of a diminution or loss of normal functions. We will discuss these various types of symptoms below.

Research psychologist Eleanor Longden describes her experience of being diagnosed with schizophrenia and her journey back to mental health in **this 2013 TED Talk**[3].

Delusions

Delusions are commonly experienced by around 75% of those individuals hospitalized because of their psychotic symptoms (Maher, 2001), and, while some delusions may be clearly bizarre (e.g. the individual may believe that all of their internal organs have been taken out and replaced by those of someone else), others may not (e.g. a paranoid belief that the individual is constantly under surveillance by the police). The main types of delusion found in those experiencing psychosis are persecutory or paranoid delusions, in which the individual believes they are being persecuted, are being spied upon, or are in danger (usually as the result of a conspiracy of some kind).

Hallucinations

People suffering psychotic symptoms regularly report sensory abnormalities across a broad range of sensory modalities, and this is usually manifested as perceiving things that are not there. Hallucinations can occur in any modality (e.g. auditory, olfactory, gustatory, or tactile), but the most common are auditory hallucinations (**hearing voices**), reported by around 70% of sufferers (Cleghorn et al., 1992). Auditory hallucinations can be experienced as external voices commanding the individual to act in certain ways, two or more voices conversing with each other, or a voice commentating on the individual's own thoughts.

Disorganized thinking or disorganized speech

Disorganized thinking will normally be inferred from the individual's speech, and there are several common features displayed by individuals experiencing psychotic symptoms. The most common is **derailment** (or **loose associations**), where the individual may drift quickly from one topic to another during a conversation. Their answers to questions may be tangential rather than relevant (**tangentiality**), and in some cases their speech may be so disorganized that it is neither structured nor comprehensible.

Disorganized and abnormal motor behaviour

A sufferer's behaviour may be unpredictable and agitated. In addition, the person's appearance may be dishevelled and they may well dress in an inappropriate manner (e.g. wearing heavy, thick clothing in hot weather or walking around in public in

FIGURE 15.4 *Catatonic stupor. In some very severe cases of psychosis, the individual may lapse into a catatonic stupor. Those who lapse into this state become withdrawn and inactive for long periods. In extreme cases this may take the form of catatonic rigidity, in which the individual will adopt a rigid, often awkward posture for many hours. Others exhibit what is known as 'waxy flexibility', and will maintain a posture into which they have been placed by someone else.*
Source: Grunnitus Studio / Science Photo Library. Reproduced with permission of Science Photo Library.

only their underwear). Catatonic motor behaviours are characterized by a significant decrease in reactivity to the environment (**catatonic stupor**; see Figure 15.4); maintaining rigid, immobile postures (catatonic rigidity); resisting attempts to be moved (catatonic negativism); or purposeless and excessive motor activity that often consists of simple, stereotyped movements (catatonic excitement or stereotypy).

Negative symptoms

Negative symptoms include diminished emotional expression generally, including reductions in facial expressions of emotion, lack of eye contact, poor voice intonation, and lack of head and hand movements that would normally give rise to emotional expression.

The causes of schizophrenia spectrum disorders

The lifetime prevalence rate for a diagnosis of schizophrenia is around 0.3–0.7%, which is significantly lower than the prevalence rates for the common mental health problems discussed earlier. However, this disorder still afflicts around 24 million people worldwide, mostly in the age group 15–35 years. The World Health Organization (1990) has recognized that schizophrenia is one of the top 10 medical disorders causing disability, and the mortality rate among people with a diagnosis of schizophrenia is around 50% higher than normal, with sufferers tending to die around 10 years earlier than individuals who have never been diagnosed with schizophrenia (Jeste, Gladsjo, Lindamer, & Lacro, 1996).

The overarching approach to understanding psychosis is a diathesis–stress perspective. That is, psychosis is thought to be caused by a combination of a genetically inherited biological diathesis (a biological predisposition to schizophrenia) and environmental stress. This means that even if you have a genetically preprogrammed disposition to psychosis, you may well not develop any symptoms unless you experience certain forms of life stressors. Such stressors might involve early rearing factors (Schiffman et al., 2001), dysfunctional relationships within the family (Bateson, 1978), or an inability to cope with the stresses of normal adolescent development (Harrop & Trower, 2001) or with educational or work demands. In addition, research on the diathesis–stress approach to schizophrenia suggests that stress may worsen symptoms in those with a genetic vulnerability to psychosis through its effect on cortisol production in the body (Jones & Fernyhough, 2007).

Genetic factors   That psychosis has an inherited component has been supported by the results of concordance studies. Table 15.3 shows the probability that, if an individual is diagnosed with schizophrenia, a family member or relative will also develop the disorder. This shows that the probability with which the family member or relative will develop schizophrenia is dependent on how much genetic material the two share in common (Gottesman, McGuffin, & Farmer, 1987). In addition, twin studies have indicated that the heritability estimate for schizophrenia is approximately 80% (Sullivan, Kendler, & Neale, 2003), which makes schizophrenia one of the most heritable psychiatric disorders (Gejman, Sanders, & Kendler, 2011).

Brain neurotransmitters   Many researchers have suspected that the thought disorders, hallucinations, and behaviour problems characteristic of schizophrenia may be caused by malfunctions in brain neurotransmitters. The biochemical theory of schizophrenia that has been most prominent since the mid-20th century is known as the **dopamine hypothesis**, and this account argues that the symptoms of schizophrenia are importantly related to excessive activity of the neurotransmitter dopamine. So, how might dopamine activity be involved in the production of psychotic symptoms? Figure 15.5 illustrates two important dopamine pathways in the brain: the **mesolimbic pathway** and the **mesocortical pathway**. These two pathways begin in the ventral tegmental area of the brain but may have quite different effects on the appearance of psychotic symptoms. First, an excess of dopamine receptors only seems to be related to the positive symptoms associated with schizophrenia (hallucinations, delusions,

TABLE 15.3 *Concordance rates for individuals with a diagnosis of schizophrenia.*

Relationship with proband[a]	Percentage diagnosed with schizophrenia
Spouse	1.00
Grandchildren	2.84
Nieces/nephews	2.65
Children	9.35
Siblings	7.30
Dizygotic (fraternal) twins	12.08
Monozygotic (identical) twins	44.30

[a]A proband is a person serving as the starting point for the genetic study of a family.

Source: Adapted from Gottesman, McGuffin, and Farmer (1987), by permission of Oxford University Press.

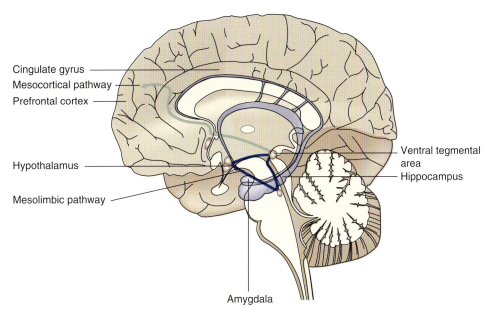

Cingulate gyrus
Mesocortical pathway
Prefrontal cortex

Hypothalamus

Mesolimbic pathway

Ventral tegmental area
Hippocampus

Amygdala

FIGURE 15.5 *Dopamine pathways in the brain. Abnormalities in dopamine activity may be linked to the brain's mesocortical pathway and mesolimbic pathway. Both begin in the ventral tegmental area, but the former projects to the prefrontal cortex and the latter to the hypothalamus, amygdala, and hippocampus. The dopamine neurons in the prefrontal cortex may be underactive (leading to the negative symptoms of schizophrenia), and this underactivity may then fail to inhibit dopamine neurons in the mesolimbic pathway, causing an excess of dopamine activity in this pathway (resulting in positive symptoms) (e.g. Davis et al., 1991).*

Source: Davey (2014b, Fig. 8.1, p. 253). Reproduced with permission of Wiley.

disordered speech), and this effect of excess dopamine appears to be localized in the mesolimbic dopamine pathway (Davis, Kahn, Ko, & Davidson, 1991). However, the mesocortical pathway begins in the ventral tegmental area but projects to the prefrontal cortex, and the dopamine neurons in the prefrontal cortex may be underactive. This has important implications for cognitive activity because the prefrontal cortex is the substrate for important cognitive processes such as working memory, and these cognitive processes contribute to motivated and planned behaviour (Winterer & Weinberger, 2004). In this way, dopamine activity might account for both the positive and the negative symptoms observed in schizophrenia.

Cognitive factors   There has been a resurgence of interest in psychological models of psychosis – especially cognitive models that view psychotic symptoms as the result of cognitive biases in attention, reasoning, and interpretation (Savulich, Shergill, & Yiend, 2012). Of specific interest to cognitive theorists are the delusional beliefs that are regularly developed during psychotic episodes, and over 50% of individuals diagnosed with schizophrenia are diagnosed with paranoid schizophrenia (Guggenheim & Babigian, 1974). First, there is evidence that individuals with delusional disorder have *attentional biases* that lead them to selectively attend to pathology-congruent information. For example, individuals with persecutory delusions exhibit attentional biases towards stimuli that have emotional meaning or are relevant to their paranoia (Fear, Sharp, & Healy, 1996). Second, research has indicated that individuals with delusional beliefs (particularly persecutory beliefs) have an **attributional bias**, which means they tend to attribute negative life events to external causes (Bentall, Corcoran, Howard, Blackwood, & Kinderman, 2001), and this bias will almost certainly act to maintain paranoid beliefs as well as maintaining their delusions that someone or something external is threatening them.

Third, considerable evidence has accrued to suggest that individuals with delusional disorders have a reasoning bias in the form of **jumping to conclusions**. That is, such individuals make a decision about the meaning or importance of an event on the basis of significantly less evidence than someone without a delusional disorder (Westermann, Salzmann, Fuchs, & Lincoln, 2012). This evidence suggests that jumping to conclusions may create a biased reasoning process that leads to the formation and acceptance of delusional beliefs and eventually to delusional symptoms (Savulich et al., 2012).

Finally, accounts of psychotic delusions have been supplemented by findings that a number of other *information-processing biases* may be involved in the development of delusions. For example, Morrison (2001) has argued that many individuals diagnosed with schizophrenia have a bias towards interpreting cognitive intrusions such as *hearing voices* as threatening in some way. Interestingly, hearing voices is not restricted to individuals suffering psychosis, and around 13% of healthy individuals report hearing voices (Bevan, Read, & Cartwright, 2011). However, what characterizes hearing voices in individuals suffering psychosis is the distress that these voices induce. Individuals with a diagnosis of schizophrenia report the voices they hear as more unacceptable, uncontrollable, and distressing than healthy individuals (Morrison, Nothard, Bowe, & Wells, 2004), and interpreting voices as dominating or insulting is associated with distress.

DISCUSSION POINT

Discuss how 'jumping to conclusions' affects the development of delusional thinking in schizophrenia.

Familial factors Another construct that has been closely linked to the appearance and reappearance of psychotic symptoms is known as **expressed emotion**. Expressed emotion refers to high levels of criticism, hostility, and emotional involvement between key members of a family, and this is known to be an important contributor to relapse in individuals suffering psychotic symptoms. One mechanism by which expressed emotion may trigger relapses is through a high sensitivity to stress in psychosis sufferers. The stress caused by expressed emotion may trigger cortisol release in the hypothalamic–pituitary–adrenal system, and this is known to increase dopamine activity and so reactivate symptoms in vulnerable individuals (Walker, Mittal, & Tessner, 2008).

TEST YOURSELF

1. What are the five important characteristics for diagnosing schizophrenia spectrum disorders?
2. What are concordance studies and how do they contribute to an understanding of the causes of schizophrenia?
3. What is the dopamine hypothesis?

Personality disorders

The DSM-5 defines a personality disorder as 'an enduring pattern of inner experience and behaviour that deviates markedly from the expectations of the individual's culture, is pervasive and inflexible, has an onset in adolescence or early adulthood, is stable over time, and leads to distress and impairment' (American Psychiatric Association, 2013, p. 645). Personality disorders are often associated with unusual ways of interpreting events, unpredictable mood swings, or impulsive behaviour.

The DSM-5 lists 10 diagnostically independent personality disorders, and these are organized into the three primary clusters shown in Table 15.4: (1) odd/eccentric personality disorders, (2) dramatic/emotional personality disorders, and (3) anxious/fearful personality disorders. Those personality disorders grouped in Cluster A all have characteristics that resemble many of the symptoms of schizophrenia (see above), but unlike in schizophrenia sufferers there is no apparent loss of touch with reality or the experiencing of sensory hallucinations. Cluster B consists of people diagnosed with dramatic/emotional personality disorders, who tend to be erratic in their behaviour, self-interested to the detriment of others, emotionally labile, and attention-seeking. Finally, as the name suggests, people with an anxious/fearful personality disorder (Cluster C) exhibit anxious and fearful behaviour. However, unlike in the main anxiety disorders, the anxious and fearful behaviour exhibited will have been a stable feature of their behaviour from late childhood into adulthood.

Two of the most well known of these disorders are **borderline personality disorder** (**BDP**), characterized by major and regular shifts in mood, impulsivity and temper tantrums, and an unstable self-image, and **antisocial personality disorder** (**APD**), which is characterized by a chronic indifference to the feelings and rights of others, lack of remorse, impulsivity, and pursuit of the individual's own goals at any cost. Individuals with APD are often labelled as 'sociopaths' or 'psychopaths'.

Borderline personality disorder
The cardinal features of BDP are an enduring pattern of instability in personal relationships, a lack of a well-defined and stable self-image, regular and predictable changes in mood, and impulsive behaviour. In particular, individuals with BPD appear to

TABLE 15.4 *The three clusters of personality disorders in the DSM-5.*

Cluster	Disorders
Cluster A: Odd/eccentric personality disorders	Paranoid personality disorder Schizoid personality disorder Schizotypal personality disorder
Cluster B: Dramatic/emotional personality disorders	Antisocial personality disorder Borderline personality disorder Narcissistic personality disorder Histrionic personality disorder
Cluster C: Anxious/fearful personality disorders	Avoidant personality disorder Dependent personality disorder Obsessive compulsive personality disorder

have a significant fear of abandonment and rejection. The results of this fear of rejection are (1) regular and unpredictable shifts in self-image characterized by changing personal goals, values, and career aspirations; (2) prolonged bouts of depression (Luca, Luca, & Calandra, 2012), deliberate self-harm, suicidal ideation, and actual suicide attempts (Venta, Ross, Schatte, & Sharp, 2012); and (3) impulsive behaviour, such as drug abuse, physical violence, and inappropriate promiscuity (Sansone & Wiederman, 2009).

Antisocial personality disorder

The fundamental feature of APD is an enduring disregard for, and violation of, the rights of others. The behaviour of individuals with APD deviates substantially from what we would consider to be normal standards of social behaviour, morality, and remorse, and is very closely linked with adult criminal behaviour. A survey of prison populations in 12 Western countries found that 47% and 21% of male and female inmates, respectively, met diagnostic criteria for APD, which is around 10 times the prevalence rate found in the general population (Fazel & Danesh, 2002). To be diagnosed with APD, an individual must be at least 18 years of age and display some of the following characteristics: (1) failure to conform to social and legal norms, (2) deceitfulness and impulsivity, (3) irritability and aggressiveness, (4) consistent irresponsibility (e.g. repeated failure to honour obligations), and (5) lack of remorse. Individuals with APD show a disregard for the safety of themselves and others, and this is evidenced by their impulsive, often aggressive behaviour and failure to plan ahead.

ACTIVITY 15.1

PERSONALITY DISORDERS

Determine whether each of the following points should be classified as linked with borderline personality disorder or antisocial personality disorder.

- major and regular shifts in mood
- pursuit of the individual's own goals at any cost
- very closely linked with adult criminal behaviour
- impulsivity
- temper tantrums
- consistent irresponsibility
- unstable self-image
- labelled as 'sociopaths' or 'psychopaths'
- individual must be at least 18 years of age
- enduring pattern of instability in personal relationships
- lack of remorse
- significant fear of abandonment and rejection
- failure to conform to social and legal norms
- prolonged bouts of depression

- irritability and aggressiveness
- deliberate self-harm, suicidal ideation, and actual suicide attempts
- chronic indifference to the feelings and rights of others
- inappropriate promiscuity

SUBSTANCE USE AND DEPENDENCY

The recreational use of substances includes socially acceptable legal substances (such as alcohol) and illegal substances (such as cannabis or cocaine). Use of substances, whether legal or illegal, can result in abuse or psychological and sometimes physiological dependency. Pathological use of substances has traditionally been divided into two categories: substance abuse and substance dependency. Substance abuse is defined as a maladaptive pattern of substance use over a period of 12 months or more and is associated with distress and impairment in tasks of daily living.

Substance dependency includes both behavioural and physiological symptoms. When a person is dependent on a substance, there will be evidence of increased tolerance for the substance such that users will require a high dose of the substance to achieve the same effects. Dependency on a substance can also be characterized by withdrawal symptoms, indicating that the body requires the drug to maintain a state of physiological normality. Individuals dependent on a substance often go to extreme lengths to obtain the substance and may engage in behaviours that they would not normally undertake (e.g. risky behaviours) in order to obtain the drug. In the DSM-5, substance abuse and substance dependency are addressed in one overarching disorder. Substance use disorder in the DSM-5 is measured on a continuum from mild to severe and each substance is a separate disorder with categories such as alcohol use disorder and stimulant use disorder. See Davey (2014b) for an up-to-date explanation of substance use disorder in the DSM-5.

People take substances for a number of reasons, but not everyone who regularly uses a substance develops a dependency or a harmful relationship with the substance. Studies have looked at risk factors for developing substance use problems. In a study examining longitudinal risk and protective factors for substance use and problem use in emerging adulthood (Stone, Becker, Huber, & Catalano, 2012), the authors found that young adults had an increased risk of problems with substances if they were male, had substance-dependent parents, lacked belief in conformity, had low commitment in school, or were early users.

You can watch videos about the effects of common recreational drugs on the brain **here**[4].

TEST YOURSELF

1. What are the three main personality disorder clusters?
2. What are the main characteristics of antisocial personality disorder?

SECTION SUMMARY

- In this section we have examined examples of anxiety and related disorders, namely generalized anxiety disorder, specific phobias, and obsessive compulsive disorder.

- Although each of these disorders has different symptoms, they share in common an extreme anxiety response that often feels uncontrollable.

- We have also seen that the development and maintenance of each of these disorders can be understood from multiple biological and psychological perspectives.

- In this section we have looked at examples of biological and psychological accounts of major depressive disorder (MDD). Neurochemical explanatory accounts of MDD implicate reduced levels of the neurotransmitters serotonin and noradrenaline (nor-epinephrine), although the exact nature of neurochemical causes of depression is still under scrutiny.

- In MDD an influential psychological account is Beck's cognitive model, which emphasizes how negatively biased information processing can maintain a negative view of the self and the world.

- As indicated by the diathesis–stress hypothesis, there are several vulnerability factors for MDD, and stressful life events often contribute to the onset of these disorders along with biological and cognitive predispositions.

- Psychosis is a name given to a collection of disparate symptoms; the DSM-5 redefined the DSM series' diagnostic categories into what are known as schizophrenia spectrum disorders. Symptoms are classified as either positive or negative.

- These combinations of symptoms frequently result in a marked inability to undertake normal social and occupational functioning.

- The prominent approach to explaining the development of psychotic symptoms is a diathesis–stress one.

- There is good evidence that many of the symptoms of psychosis are associated with imbalances in brain neurotransmitters such as dopamine, which may lead to cognitive deficits in important brain areas such as the prefrontal cortex, where attention, memory, and executive functioning are all impaired.

- In addition, cognitive theories of psychotic symptoms suggest that, especially, the development of cognitive biases in attention, attributional processes, reasoning, and ambiguity interpretation may play an important role in developing and maintaining the delusional beliefs often apparent in individuals suffering psychotic symptoms (Savulich et al., 2012).

- Personality disorders represent relatively long-standing, pervasive, and inflexible patterns of behaviour that deviate from acceptable norms within individual cultures.

- They are regularly associated with unusual ways of interpreting events, unpredictable mood swings, or impulsive behaviour.

- Explaining the causes and development of personality disorders is still largely in its infancy. However, many theories of personality disorders look to childhood experiences and developmental factors for the causes of these extreme behaviour patterns (Davey, 2014b, ch. 12).

CONCLUSIONS AND FUTURE DIRECTIONS

LEARNING OBJECTIVE 15.8

Critically evaluate the definitions, classifications, and explanations of mental health problems and possible future research and directions in the field.

Research on the causes of mental health problems continues across a number of important disciplines, including psychology, neuroscience, and genetics. Psychological approaches explore the cognitive and behavioural elements of mental health problems, including the role played by standard psychological processes such as attention, memory, and learning. Very often, the contribution that these processes make to psychopathology can first be investigated in healthy individuals and then extrapolated to clinical populations – an approach known as 'experimental psychopathology' (see Davey, 2014a) – because of the central role that conducting experiments plays in developing these kinds of psychological models (Vervliet & Raes, 2012). This approach has already contributed significantly to our understanding of the causes of psychopathology, one aspect of which is the role that attention and memory biases play in the acquisition and maintenance of common mental health problems such as anxiety and depression (e.g. MacLeod & Mathews, 2012; Mathews & MacLeod, 2005).

Neuroscience research continues to seek biological 'markers' for mental health diagnostic categories – that is, evidence of abnormalities in localized brain functioning that are indicative of specific psychopathological disorders. This was an explicit aim of the team that developed the DSM-5 (Kupfer, Kuhl, & Regier, 2013), although, to date, this approach has not yet revealed much in the way of biological markers that would unambiguously aid the diagnosis of mental health problems. Future research may be able to refine this process to make it more fruitful, but there are others who believe that the true causes of most common mental health problems lie in either psychological processes or the socioeconomic conditions that many people experience, and not in abnormalities in brain or biological functioning (e.g. Pilecki, Clegg, & McKay, 2011).

Approaches such as those being developed in molecular genetics have channelled significant effort into attempting to identify the specific genes through which the risk for mental health problems may be transmitted, the chromosomes on which these genes are located, and how these genes and their possible defects may give rise to psychopathological symptoms. Other techniques, such as genome-wide association studies, allow researchers to identify rare mutations in genes that might give rise to psychopathological symptoms – especially those mutations that give rise to 'copy number variations', a term referring to an abnormal copy of DNA in a gene (either a deletion or a duplication). These methods have so far had variable success in identifying the individual genes that may be responsible for mental health problems, with mutations resulting in DNA deletions (International Schizophrenia Consortium, 2008) as well as mutations causing

DNA duplications (Kirov et al., 2009; Levinson et al., 2011) having been found to be associated with diagnostic disorders such as schizophrenia. However, while many studies have shown associations between individual genes and schizophrenia symptoms, there have also been many failures to replicate these findings (Kim, Zerwas, Trace, & Sullivan, 2011), and this may testify to the heterogeneous nature of many mental health problems. One final exciting development in genetics and psychopathology is the area of epigenetics, where research suggests that the early experiences of an individual may either trigger or inhibit the expression of genes they possess that make them vulnerable to mental health problems such as anxiety or depression, and in this way there can be a direct interaction between environmental factors and inherited factors. For example, early life stress can enable the expression of genes that control the neuroendocrinology of PTSD, which then puts such individuals at higher risk of developing PTSD after highly traumatic life experiences (Yehuda et al., 2010). This has important implications for our understanding of how mental health problems develop and the aetiology of those disorders (Kofink et al., 2013).

Finally, the most recent revision of the DSM – the DSM-5 – is at the time of writing only 4 years old. However, the principles behind its development have sparked considerable debate about the validity of the specific diagnostic categories it describes and whether they represent 'illness' or 'disease' categories – with underlying causes – in the same way that other medical diagnostic criteria do. One rather radical alternative to 'diagnostic categories' that is being developed currently is an approach known as 'network analysis'. This approach maps out the relationships between symptoms in an individual suffering mental health problems and provides something similar to a diagnosis based on the causal relationships between these symptoms (e.g. how insomnia and other symptoms may cause hypervigilance in PTSD). This provides the potential to treat an individual's problems based on how their symptoms causally affect one another, and this enables that individual's problems to be defined as an interactive network of symptoms that define the individual's disorder or problem. This is an approach that does not allude to the symptoms having an 'underlying cause' but views them as being a network of symptoms that maintain each other (Borsboom & Cramer, 2013; Wigman et al., 2015).

SECTION SUMMARY

- Psychological approaches to mental health problems explore the cognitive and behavioural elements of these problems, including the role of normal psychological processes such as attention, memory, and learning.

- Neuroscience research continues to seek biological 'markers' for mental health problems as an aid to diagnosis.

- Advances in molecular genetics have enabled the identification of specific genes through which the risk for mental health problems might be transmitted.

- Genome-wide association studies allow researchers to identify mutations in genes that might give rise to mental health problems.

- The relatively new area of epigenetics suggests that early experiences may either trigger or inhibit the expression of genes that make people vulnerable to mental health problems.

- Network analysis is a new and radical alternative approach to defining mental health diagnostic categories.

CHAPTER SUMMARY

This chapter has considered some of the conceptual issues relevant to mental health, including how we define, classify, and explain mental health problems. We did this by first examining the history of how psychopathology has been explained and exploring some of the important paradigms that have contributed to our understanding of mental health problems. We then looked at individual psychological disorders. Some mental health problems, such as anxiety and depression, are relatively common, but there are many forms that mental health problems can take. Some are quite severe and disabling, while others can have important detrimental effects on everyday functioning and on others. We are continuing to understand how psychological, biological, and genetic mechanisms contribute to mental health problems, and in the future it will be models capable of combining these various explanatory approaches that will provide a full understanding of individual mental health problems and contribute to the development of more effective treatments.

ESSAY QUESTIONS

1. Compare and contrast the various ways in which mental health problems might be defined. How have these various approaches been applied to classifying mental health problems?

2. Describe and evaluate at least two theories of specific phobias.

3. Compare and contrast biological and psychological models of depression.

KEY TERMS

- **antisocial personality disorder** (APD): A personality disorder characterized by a chronic indifference to the feelings and rights of others, lack of remorse, impulsivity, and pursuit of the individual's own goals at any cost. Individuals with APD are often labelled as 'sociopaths' or 'psychopaths'.

- **asylums:** Institutions for the care of people who are mentally ill. Asylums emerged in the 19th century as part of the rise of institutional psychiatry and have gradually been replaced by the modern psychiatric hospital.

- **attentional bias:** The allocation of a greater amount of attentional resources to information related to recurring thoughts. For example, highly anxious individuals have an attentional bias towards threatening stimuli.

- **attributional bias:** A cognitive bias that refers to the errors made when people try to explain their own and others' behaviours. There are many different types of attribution bias. For example, individuals with persecutory beliefs tend to attribute negative life events to external causes.

- **behaviour modification:** The traditional term for the use of behaviour change techniques to increase or decrease the frequency of behaviours.

- **behaviour therapy:** A broad term in which the methods focus on either just specific, learned behaviours or those behaviours in combination with thoughts and feelings that might be causing them.

- **biological preparedness:** A theory that states that we are biologically prepared or predisposed to fear certain stimuli that were threatening to us in our evolutionary past.

- **borderline personality disorder (BPD):** A personality disorder characterized by major and regular shifts in mood, impulsivity and temper tantrums, and an unstable self-image.
- **catatonic stupor:** In some very severe cases of psychosis, the individual may lapse into a catatonic stupor. Those who lapse into this state become withdrawn and inactive for long periods.
- **cognitive behaviour therapy:** A talking therapy that can help you manage your problems by changing the way you think and behave.
- **cognitive model of depression:** A view, developed by Aaron Beck, stating that depression is maintained through a number of cognitive distortions or biases that result in the individual thinking about and experiencing the world in a negative way.
- **compulsions:** Irresistible urges to behave in a certain way.
- **defence mechanisms:** Unconscious coping techniques that reduce anxiety. Not to be confused with conscious coping strategies.
- **delusions:** An idiosyncratic belief maintained despite its being contradicted by reality or rational argument.
- **demonic possession:** The historical belief that personality change was due to an individual's personality being taken over and replaced by the persona of someone or something else.
- **derailment:** A thought disorder where the individual may drift quickly from one topic to another during a conversation, which may consist of a sequence of unrelated or only remotely related ideas. Also called loose associations.
- *Diagnostic and Statistical Manual* (DSM): A psychiatric classification manual first published in 1952 by the American Psychiatric Association. The most recent version, the DSM-5, was published in 2013.
- **diathesis–stress model:** A psychological theory that attempts to explain behaviour as a predispositional vulnerability together with stress from life experiences.
- **dopamine hypothesis:** A prominent biochemical theory of schizophrenia that argues that the symptoms of schizophrenia are importantly related to excessive activity of the neurotransmitter dopamine.
- **dopamine:** A neurotransmitter associated with motor functions and emotional responses.
- **epigenetics:** A developing area of genetics research that looks at heritable changes in gene expression. Epigenetic change can be influenced by several factors including age, lifestyle, and disease state.
- **expressed emotion:** A term that refers to high levels of criticism, hostility, and emotional involvement between key members of a family; known to be an important contributor to relapse in individuals suffering psychotic symptoms.
- **extinction:** In classical conditioning, extinction occurs when a conditioned stimulus is presented alone, so that it no longer predicts the coming of the unconditioned stimulus and conditioned responding gradually stops.
- **frontal lobes:** A brain area considered to make us uniquely human; known to be important in executive functions such as planning and decision making, error correction and troubleshooting, dealing with novel situations, and inhibiting habitual and impulsive responses.
- **generalized anxiety disorder (GAD):** A common anxiety disorder; typical symptoms include daily anxiety and anxious expectation and worry about future events to the degree that coping with the ups and downs of daily life becomes difficult and significant distress is experienced.
- **genetics:** The study of heredity and the variation of inherited characteristics.
- **hallucinations:** Things that are perceived despite not being there. People suffering psychotic symptoms regularly report sensory abnormalities across a broad range of sensory modalities.
- **hearing voices:** A form of auditory hallucination; it can be experienced as external voices commanding the individual to act in certain ways, two or more voices conversing with each other, or a voice commenting on the individual's own thoughts.
- **heritability:** A measure of the degree to which symptoms can be accounted for by genetic factors; it ranges from 0 to 1, and the nearer this figure is to 1, the more important are genetic factors in explaining the symptoms.

- **inflated responsibility:** An important contributor to the onset and maintenance of obsessive compulsive disorder and generalized anxiety disorder. One cognitive theory proposes that individuals experience inflated levels of responsibility for harm to others, which signals a need to act and provokes neutralizing behaviours in the form of compulsions.
- **International List of Causes of Death (ICD):** The global health information standard for mortality and morbidity statistics, which is increasingly used in clinical care and research to define diseases and study disease patterns.
- **intolerance of uncertainty:** A cognitive bias that affects how a person perceives, interprets, and responds to uncertain situations. It is particularly prevalent in sufferers of generalized anxiety disorder. Individuals who are intolerant of uncertainty easily experience stress and cope with stressful situations using repetitive thought, such as worry and rumination.
- **jumping to conclusions:** An attributional bias observed frequently in those experiencing delusions. Individuals make a decision about the meaning or importance of an event on the basis of significantly less evidence than someone without a delusional disorder.
- **lifetime prevalence:** The proportion of a population that at some point in their life (up to the time of assessment) has experienced a particular condition.
- **loose associations:** Another term for **derailment**.
- **major depressive disorder (MDD):** A common depressive disorder that, according to the DSM-5, causes an individual to experience five or more depressive symptoms over a 2-week period, most of the day every day, and to find that their daily activities are impaired because of their symptoms.
- **medical model:** The medical model of abnormal psychology is a reductionist approach that assumes mental disorders simply stem from physical causes.
- **mental health stigma:** Stigma is the extreme disapproval of a person or group on grounds that are perceived to distinguish them from other members of society. Stigmatizing people for their mental health problems often makes their difficulties worse and makes it harder for them to recover.
- **mesocortical pathway:** A dopaminergic pathway in the brain associated with psychotic symptoms. It connects the ventral tegmentum to the cerebral cortex, in particular the frontal lobes.
- **mesolimbic pathway:** A dopaminergic pathway in the brain associated with psychotic symptoms. It begins in the ventral tegmental area of the midbrain and connects to the nucleus accumbens.
- **monoamine oxidase inhibitors:** Chemicals that inhibit the activity of the monoamine oxidase enzyme family and increase the levels of serotonin and noradrenaline in the brain. They have a long history of use as medications prescribed for the treatment of depression.
- **monoamine theory of depression:** A theory that proposes that depression is associated with low levels of two monoamine neurotransmitters: serotonin and noradrenaline.
- **negative symptoms:** Symptoms experienced as part of schizophrenia spectrum disorders and that are characteristic of a diminution or loss of normal functions. They include diminished emotional expression generally, including reductions in facial expressions of emotion and lack of eye contact.
- **neuroscience:** The neuroscience paradigm seeks an understanding of psychopathology by identifying aspects of the individual's brain structure and function that may contribute to symptoms.
- **neutralizing behaviours:** In the context of obsessive compulsive disorder, neutralizing behaviours are compulsions that are performed in order to mitigate or remove the impact of negative intrusive thoughts.
- **noradrenaline:** The hormone and neurotransmitter most responsible for vigilant concentration; often referred to as a 'fight or flight' chemical. Also referred to as norepinephrine.
- **obsessions:** Intrusive and repetitive thoughts, images, or impulses that are unacceptable and/or unwanted.
- **obsessive compulsive disorder (OCD):** A disorder characterized by obsessions and compulsions. As a result of the distress caused by repetitive and unwanted obsessive thoughts, individuals with

OCD develop ritualized compulsions that they perform in order to prevent negative outcomes from occurring.

- **perfectionism (clinical perfectionism):** A cognitive construct that is implicated in obsessive compulsive disorder, in which individuals report feeling that things are not right and that in order to try to attain a feeling of rightness they need to perform an action such as checking that locks are secure or that they have washed their hands properly.
- **positive beliefs about worry:** Beliefs about the utility of worrying, often held by those with anxiety disorders. For example, individuals with generalized anxiety disorder often hold the belief that worry is a useful way of dealing with perceived threats and problems.
- **positive symptoms:** Psychotic symptoms that tend to reflect an excess or distortion of normal functions (e.g. delusions, hallucinations, disorganized thinking, and abnormal motor behaviour).
- **post-traumatic stress disorder (PTSD):** One of the few disorders in the DSM-5 in which the cause of the disorder is a defining factor. Diagnosis of PTSD is considered only if the individual has experienced an extreme trauma prior to their symptoms.
- **psychiatry:** The study and treatment of mental illness, emotional disturbance, and abnormal behaviour, based on the medical model of psychopathology.
- **psychoanalysis:** A Freudian approach that attempts to explain both normal and abnormal psychological functioning in terms of how various psychological mechanisms help to defend against anxiety and depression by repressing memories and thoughts that may cause conflict and stress.
- **psychosis:** A collective name given to an extensive range of disparate symptoms characterized by disturbances in thought and language, sensory perception, and emotion.
- **schizophrenia spectrum disorders:** A spectrum disorder is a mental disorder that includes a range of linked conditions. The presence of different combinations of positive and negative symptoms may lead to a diagnosis of any one of a number of schizophrenia spectrum disorders.
- **serotonin:** A monoamine neurotransmitter popularly thought to be a contributor to feelings of well-being and happiness. Serotonin reuptake inhibitors are often prescribed as a treatment for clinical depression and obsessive compulsive disorder.
- **specific phobias:** Phobias characterized by an individual presenting with fear that is out of proportion to the actual danger posed by the object or situation. The DSM-5 divides specific phobias into five subtypes: animal type, natural environment type, blood–injection–injury type, situational type, and other type.
- **statistical norm:** A statistical concept representing the combined responses of a representative group, against which a subject is compared.
- **tangentiality:** An aspect of disorganized thinking or disorganized speech, observed in those with psychotic symptoms, in which conversation may be tangential rather than relevant.
- **Time to Change:** A widespread UK campaign attempting to address mental health stigma. Supported by both charities and mental health service providers (see http://www.time-to-change.org.uk).
- **trycyclic antidepressants:** Chemical compounds used primarily as antidepressants. They have been largely replaced in clinical use in most parts of the world by newer antidepressants, such as selective serotonin reuptake inhibitors.

NOTES

1. http://www.rcpsych.ac.uk/
2. https://www1.bps.org.uk/networks-and-communities/member-microsite/division-clinical-psychology
3. https://www.ted.com/talks/eleanor_longden_the_voices_in_my_head
4. http://www.talktofrank.com/drugs-on-the-brain

FURTHER RESOURCES

Arboleda-Florez, J., & Sartorius, N. (2008). *Understanding the stigma of mental illness: Theory & interventions*. Hoboken, NJ: Wiley.

Beck, A. T. (2008). The evolution of the cognitive model of depression and its neurobiological correlates. *American Journal of Psychiatry, 165*, 969–977. doi:10.1176/appi.ajp.2008.08050721

British Psychological Society. (2018). Consultation papers. Retrieved 20 November 2017 from http://dcp.bps.org.uk (Information about clinical psychology in the UK.)

Craighead, W. M., & Craighead, L. W. (2008). *Psychopathology: History, diagnosis, and empirical foundations*. Hoboken, NJ: John Wiley.

Davey, G., Lake, N., & Whittington, A. (2014). *Clinical psychology* (2nd ed.). London, UK: Psychology Press.

Davey, G. C. L. (2014). *Psychopathology* (2nd ed.). Chichester, UK: Wiley-Blackwell.

Davey, G. C. L., Dash, S., & Meeten, F. (2014). *Obsessive compulsive disorder*. New York, NY: Palgrave Macmillan.

Davey, G. C. L., & Wells, A. (2006). *Worry and its psychological disorders: Theory, assessment and treatment*. Chichester, UK: Wiley.

Fischer, B. A. K., Keller, W. R., Arango, C., Pearlson, G. D., McMahon, R. P., Meyer, W. A., … Buchanan, R. W. (2012). Cortical abnormalities in deficit versus nondeficit schizophrenia. *Schizophrenia Research, 136*, 51–54.

Gejman, P. V., Sanders AR & Kendler KS. (2011). Genetics of schizophrenia: New findings and challenges. *Annual Review of Genomics & Human Genetics, 12*, 121–144.

Henderson, C., & Thornicroft, G. (2013). Evaluation of the Time to Change programme in England 2008–2011. *British Journal of Psychiatry, 202*(Suppl. 55), 45–48.

Hill, J. (2003). Early identification of individuals at risk for antisocial personality disorder. *British Journal of Psychiatry, 182*, S11–S14.

Lieb, K. Z., Schmahl, C., Linehan, M. M., & Bohus, M. (2004). Borderline personality disorder. *Lancet, 364*, 453–461.

McLaughlin, K. A., & Nolen-Hoeksema, S. (2011). Rumination as a transdiagnostic factor in depression and anxiety. *Behaviour Research and Therapy, 49*(3), 186–193.

Mishara, A. L., & Schwartz, M. A. (1995). Conceptual analysis of psychiatric approaches: Phenomenology, psychopathology, and classification. *Current Opinion in Psychiatry, 8*, 312–316.

NHS Digital. (2009). *Adult psychiatric morbidity in England: 2007 – Results of a household survey*. Retrieved 20 November 2017 from http://www.hscic.gov.uk/pubs/psychiatricmorbidity07 (An adult psychiatric morbidity survey.)

Power, M. (Ed.). (2003). *Mood disorders: A handbook of science and practice*. Chichester, UK: Wiley.

Royal College of Psychiatrists. (n.d.). Retrieved 20 November 2017 from http://www.rcpsych.ac.uk (Information about the role of psychiatrists in mental health services.)

Salkovskis, P. M., Wroe, A., Gledhill, A., Morrison, N., Forrester, E., Richards, C., … Thorpe, S., 2000. Responsibility attitudes and interpretations are characteristic of obsessive compulsive disorder. *Behaviour Research and Therapy, 38*(4), 347–372.

Savulich, G., Shergill, S., & Yiend, J. (2012). Biased cognition in psychosis. *Journal of Experimental Psychopathology, 4*, 514–536.

Shafran, R., & Rachman, S. (2004). Thought action fusion: A review. *Journal of Behavior Therapy and Experimental Psychiatry, 35*, 87–107.

Time to Change. (n.d.). Retrieved 20 November 2017 from http://www.time-to-change.org.uk (A UK campaign to address mental health stigma.)

Wells, A. (1999). A metacognitive model and therapy for generalized anxiety disorder. *Clinical Psychology & Psychotherapy, 6*, 86–95.

REFERENCES

Agrawal, A., Jacobson, K. C., Gardner, C. O., Prescott, C. A., & Kendler, K. S. (2004). A population based twin study of sex differences in depressive symptoms. *Twin Research, 7*(2), 176–181.

American Psychiatric Association. (2013). *Diagnostic and statistical manual of mental disorders* (5th ed.). Washington, DC: American Psychiatric Association.

Bateson, G. (1978). The double-bind theory – misunderstood? *Psychiatric News*, April, 40.

Beck, A. T. (1967). *Depression: Clinical, experimental and theoretical aspects*. New York, NY: Harper & Row.

Beck, A. T. (1987). Cognitive model of depression. *Journal of Cognitive Psychotherapy, 1*, 2–27.

Bentall, R. P., Corcoran, R., Howard, R., Blackwood, N., & Kinderman, P. (2001). Persecutory delusions: A review and theoretical integration. *Clinical Psychology Review, 21*, 1143–1192.

Berger, W., Coutinho, E. S. F., Figueira, I., Marques-Portella, C., Luz, M. P., Neylan, T. C., ... Mendlowicz, M. V. (2012). Rescuers at risk: A systematic review and meta-regression analysis of the worldwide current prevalence and correlates of PTSD in rescue workers. *Social Psychiatry and Psychiatric Epidemiology, 47*, 1001–1011.

Bevan, V., Read, J., & Cartwright, C. (2011). The prevalence of voice-hearers in the general population: A literature review. *Journal of Mental Health, 20*(3), 281–292.

Borsboom, D., & Cramer, A. O. J. (2013). Network analysis: An integrative approach to the structure of psychopathology. *Annual Review of Clinical Psychology, 9*, 91–121.

Brower, M. C., & Price, B. H. (2001). Epilepsy and violence: When is the brain to blame? *Epilepsy & Behavior, 1*, 145–149.

Bunny, W. E., Jr., & Davis, J. M. (1965). Norepinephrine in depressive reactions: A review. *Archives of General Psychiatry, 13*, 483–494.

Carson, R. C. (1996). Aristotle, Galileo, and the DSM taxonomy: The case of schizophrenia. *Journal of Consulting and Clinical Psychology, 64*, 1133–1139.

Centre for Mental Health. (2010). Economic and social costs of mental health problems. Retrieved 8 February 2018 from https://www.centreformentalhealth.org.uk/economic-and-social-costs

Chacko, R. C., Corbin, M. A., & Harper, R. G. (2000). Acquired obsessive-compulsive disorder associated with basal ganglia lesions. *Journal of Neuropsychiatry & Clinical Neurosciences, 12*, 269–272.

Cleghorn, J. M., Franco, S., Szechtman, B., Kaplan, R. D., Szechtman, H., Brown, G. M. ... Garnett, E. S. (1992). Toward a brain map of auditory hallucinations. *American Journal of Psychiatry, 149*(8), 1062–1069.

Coles, M. E., Frost, R. O., Heimberg, R. G., & Rheaume, J. (2003). Not just right experiences: Perfectionism, obsessive-compulsive features and general psychopathology. *Behaviour Research and Therapy, 41*, 681–700.

Constantino, J. N., Todorov, A., Hilton, C., Law, P., Zhang, Y., Molloy, E., ... Geschwind, D. (2013). Autism recurrence in half siblings: Strong support for genetic mechanisms of transmission in ASD. *Molecular Psychiatry, 18*(2), 137–138. doi:10.1038/mp.2012.9

Cook, M., & Mineka, S. (1990). Selective associations in the observational conditioning of fear in rhesus monkeys. *Journal of Experimental Psychology: Animal Behavior Processes, 16*, 372–389.

Crisp, A. H., Gelder, M. G., Rix, S., Meltzer, H. I., & Rowlands, O. J. (2000). Stigmatisation of people with mental illness. *British Journal of Psychiatry, 177*, 4–7.

Davey, G. C. L. (1992a). Classical conditioning and the acquisition of human fears and phobias: A review and synthesis of the literature. *Advances in Behaviour Research and Therapy, 14*, 29–66.

Davey, G. C. L. (1992b). Characteristics of individuals with fear of spiders. *Anxiety Research, 4*, 299–314.

Davey, G. C. L. (1998). Learning theory. In C. E. Walker (Ed.), *Comprehensive clinical psychology: Foundations of clinical psychology* (Vol. 1, pp. 391–421). Amsterdam, Netherlands: Elsevier.

Davey, G. C. L. (2011). Disgust: The disease-avoidance emotion and its dysfunctions. *Philosophical Transactions of the Royal Society B: Biological Sciences, 366*(1583), 3453–3465.

Davey, G. C. L. (2014a). How do we justify doing mental health research on healthy individuals? A 'manual' for experimental psychopathology. *Papers from Sidcup*, 6 June. Retrieved 23 January 2018 from http://www.papersfromsidcup.com/graham-daveys-blog/how-do-we-justify-doing-mental-health-research-on-healthy-individuals-a-manual-for-experimental-psychopathology

Davey, G. C. L. (2014b). *Psychopathology* (2nd ed.). Chichester, UK: Wiley.

Davis, K. L., Kahn, R. S., Ko, G., & Davidson, M. (1991). Dopamine in schizophrenia: A review and reconceptualization. *American Journal of Psychiatry*, *148*(11), 1474–1486.

de Jong, P. J., & Merckelbach, H. (1998). Blood–injection–injury phobia and fear of spiders: Domain specific individual differences in disgust sensitivity. *Personality and Individual Differences*, *24*, 153–158.

Delgado, P. L., Miller, H. L., Salomon, R. M., Licinio, J., Krystal, J. H., Moreno, F. A., … Charney, D. S. (1999). Tryptophan-depletion challenge in depressed patients treated with desipramine or fluoxetine: Implications for the role of serotonin in the mechanism of antidepressant action. *Biological Psychiatry*, *46*, 212–220.

Desrosiers, A., & Fleurose, S. S. (2002). Treating Haitian patients: Key cultural aspects. *American Journal of Psychotherapy*, *56*, 508–521.

Dugas, M. J., Gagnon, F., Ladouceur, R., & Freeston, M. H. (1998). Generalized anxiety disorder: A preliminary test of a conceptual model. *Behaviour Research and Therapy*, *36*, 215–226. doi:10.1016/S0005-7967(97)00070-3

Ellis, A. (1962). *Reason and emotion in psychotherapy*. New York, NY: Lyle Stuart.

Erdelyi, M. H. (1992). Psychodynamics and the unconscious. *American Psychologist*, *47*, 784–787.

Farhood, L. F., & Dimassi, H. (2012). Prevalence and predictors for post-traumatic stress disorder, depression and general health in a population from six villages in South Lebanon. *Social Psychiatry and Psychiatric Epidemiology*, *47*, 639–649.

Fazel, S., & Danesh, J. (2002). Serious mental disorder in 23000 prisoners: A systematic review of 62 surveys. *Lancet*, *359*, 545–550.

Fear, C. F., Sharp, H., & Healy, D. (1996). Cognitive processes in delusional disorder. *British Journal of Psychiatry*, *168*, 61–67.

Ford, T., Goodman, R., & Meltzer, H. (2003). The British Child and Adolescent Mental Health Survey 1999: The prevalence of DSM-IV disorders. *Journal of the American Academy of Child and Adolescent Psychiatry*, *42*, 1203–1211.

Freud, S. (1917/1963). *A general introduction to psychoanalysis*. New York, NY: Liveright.

Gejman, P. V., Sanders, A. R., & Kendler, K. S. (2011). Genetics of schizophrenia: New findings and challenges. *Annual Review of Genomics and Human Genetics*, *12*, 121–144.

Goldacre, B. (2002). When hospital is a prison. *The Guardian*, Retrieved 20 November 2017 from https://www.theguardian.com/society/2002/jul/16/mentalhealth.lifeandhealth

Gottesman, I. I., McGuffin, P., & Farmer, A. E. (1987). Clinical genetics as clues to the real genetics of schizophrenia (a decade of modest gains while playing for time). *Schizophrenia Bulletin*, *13*(1), 23–47.

Grilo, C. M., White, M. A., & Masheb, R. M. (2009). DSM-IV psychiatric disorder comorbidity and its correlates in binge eating disorder. *International Journal of Eating Disorders*, *42*, 228–234.

Guggenheim, F. G., & Babigian, H. M. (1974). Catatonic schizophrenia – epidemiology and clinical course: 7-year register study of 798 cases. *Journal of Nervous and Mental Disease*, *158*(4), 291–305.

Hanwella, R., de Silva, V., Yoosuf, A., Karunaratne, S., & de Silva, P. (2012). Religious beliefs, possession states, and spirits: Three case studies from Sri Lanka. *Case Reports in Psychiatry*, *2012*. doi:10.1155/2012/232740

Harrop, C., & Trower, P. (2001). Why does schizophrenia develop at late adolescence? *Clinical Psychology Review*, *21*, 241–266.

Haslam, N., Williams, B. J., Kyrios, M., McKay, D., & Taylor, S. (2005). Subtyping obsessive-compulsive disorder: A taxometric analysis. *Behavior Therapy*, *36*, 381–391.

Helzer, J. E., Robins, L. N., & McEvoy, L. (1987). Posttraumatic stress disorder in the general population: Findings of the Epidemiologic Catchment-Area Survey. *New England Journal of Medicine, 317*(26), 1630–1634.

Herzog, D. B., Keller, M. B., Sacks, N. R., Yeh, C. J., & Lavori, P. W. (1992). Psychiatric comorbidity in treatment-seeking anorexics and bulimics. *Journal of the American Academy of Child and Adolescent Psychiatry, 31*(5), 810–818.

Hodgson, R., & Rachman, S. (1977). Obsessional-compulsive complaints. *Behaviour Research and Therapy, 15*, 389–395.

Hoge, E. A., Ivkovic, A., & Fricchione, G. L. (2012). Generalized anxiety disorder: Diagnosis and treatment. *British Medical Journal, 345*, e7500.

Insel, T. R. (1992). Toward a neuroanatomy of obsessive compulsive disorder. *Archives of General Psychiatry, 49*, 739–744.

International Schizophrenia Consortium. (2008). Rare chromosomal deletions and duplications increase risk of schizophrenia. *Nature, 455*, 237–241.

Jeste, D. V., Gladsjo, J. A., Lindamer, L. A., & Lacro, J. P. (1996). Medical comorbidity in schizophrenia. *Schizophrenia Bulletin, 22*(3), 413–430.

Jones, S. R., & Fernyhough, C. (2007). A new look at the neural diathesis–stress model of schizophrenia: The primacy of social-evaluative and uncontrollable situations. *Schizophrenia Bulletin, 33*, 1171–1177.

Kessler, R. C., Berglund, P., Chiu, W. T., Demler, O., Heeringa, S., Hiripi, E., … Zheng, H. (2004). The US National Comorbidity Survey Replication (NCS-R): An overview of design and field procedures. *International Journal of Methods in Psychiatric Research, 13*(2), 69–92.

Kessler, R. C., Chiu, W. T., Dernier, O., & Walters, E. E. (2005). Prevalence, severity, and comorbidity of 12-month DSM-IV disorders in the National Comorbidity Survey Replication. *Archives of General Psychiatry, 62*(6), 617–627.

Kim, Y., Zerwas, S., Trace, S. E., & Sullivan, P. F. (2011). Schizophrenia genetics: Where next? *Schizophrenia Bulletin, 37*(3), 456–463.

Kirov, G., Grozeva, D., Norton, N., Ivanov, D., Mantripragada, K. K., Holmans, P., … O'Donovan M. C. (2009). Support for the involvement of large copy number variants in the pathogenesis of schizophrenia. *Human Molecular Genetics, 18*, 1497–1503.

Kofink, D., Boks, M. P. M., Timmers, H. T. M., & Kas, M. J. (2013). Epigenetic dynamics in psychiatric disorders: Environmental programming of neurodevelopmental processes. *Neuroscience & Biobehavioral Reviews, 37*, 831–845.

Kok, B. C., Herrell, R. K., Thomas, J. L., & Hoge, C. W. (2012). Posttraumatic stress disorder associated with combat service in Iraq or Afghanistan: Reconciling prevalence differences between studies. *Journal of Nervous and Mental Disease, 200*, 444–450.

Krueger, R. F., & Piasecki, T. M. (2002). Toward a dimensional and psychometrically-informed approach to conceptualizing psychopathology. *Behaviour Research and Therapy, 40*, 485–499.

Kupfer, D. J., Kuhl, E. A., & Regier, D. A. (2013). DSM-5: The future arrived. *Journal of the American Medical Association, 309*, 1691–1692.

Lapin, I. P., & Oxenkrug, G. F. (1969). Intensification of the central seretogenic processes as a possible determinant of the thymolpetic effect. *Lancet, 1*, 132–136.

LeBeau, R. T., Glenn, D., Liao, B., Wittchen, H. U., Beesdo-Baum, K., Ollendick, T., & Craske, M. G. (2010). Specific phobia: A review of DSM-IV specific phobia and preliminary recommendations for DSM-V. *Depression and Anxiety, 27*, 148–167.

Levinson, D. F., Duan, J., Oh, S., Wang, K., Sanders, A. R., Shi, J., … Gejman, P. V. (2011). Copy number variants in schizophrenia: Confirmation of five previous findings and new evidence for 3q29 microdeletions and VIPR2 duplications. *American Journal of Psychiatry, 168*, 302–316.

Lewinsohn, P. M. (1974). Clinical and theoretical aspects of depression. In K. S. Calhoun, H. E. Adams, & K. M. Mitchell (Eds.), *Innovative treatment methods in psychopathology* (pp. 19–66). New York, NY: Wiley.

Lind, A. B., Delmar, C., & Nielsen, K. (2014). Struggling in an emotional avoidance culture: A qualitative study of stress as a predisposing factor for somatoform disorders. *Journal of Psychosomatic Research*, 76(2), 94–98. doi:10.1016/j.jpsychores.2013.11.019

Livingston, J. D., & Boyd, J. E. (2010). Correlates and consequences of internalized stigma for people living with mental illness: A systematic review and meta-analysis. *Social Science & Medicine*, 71, 2150–2161.

Luca, M., Luca, A., & Calandra, C. (2012). Borderline personality disorder and depression: An update. *Psychiatric Quarterly*, 83(3), 281–292.

MacLeod, C., & Mathews, A. (2012). Cognitive bias modification approaches to anxiety. *Annual Review of Clinical Psychology*, 8, 189–217.

MacLeod, C., Mathews, A., & Tata, P. (1986). Attentional bias in emotional disorders. *Journal of Abnormal Psychology*, 95(1), 15–20.

Maher, B. A. (2001). Delusions. In H. E. Adams & P. B. Sutker (Eds.), *Comprehensive handbook of psychopathology* (3rd ed., 309–340). Hingham, MA: Kluwer Academic.

Mathews, A., & MacLeod, C. (2005). Cognitive vulnerability to emotional disorders. *Annual Review of Clinical Psychology*, 1, 167–195.

Meeten, F., & Davey, G. C. L. (2011). Mood-as-input hypothesis and perseverative psychopathologies. *Clinical Psychology Review*, 31, 1259–1275.

Meyers, C. A., Berman, S. A., Scheibel, R. S., & Hayman, A. (1992). Case report: Acquired antisocial personality disorder associated with unilateral left orbital frontal lobe damage. *Journal of Psychiatry & Neuroscience*, 17(3), 121–125.

Modestin, J., & Villiger, C. (1989). Follow-up-study on borderline versus nonborderline personality disorders. *Comprehensive Psychiatry*, 30(3), 236–244.

Morrison, A. P. (2001). Cognitive therapy for auditory hallucinations as an alternative to antipsychotic medication: A case series. *Clinical Psychology & Psychotherapy*, 8(2), 136–147.

Morrison, A. P., Nothard, S., Bowe, S., & Wells, A. (2004). Interpretations of voices in patients with hallucinations and non-patient controls: A comparison and predictors of distress in patients. *Behaviour Research and Therapy*, 42(11), 1d8872.

Moses, T. (2010). Being treated differently: Stigma experiences with family, peers, and school staff among adolescents with mental health disorders. *Social Science & Medicine*, 70, 985–993.

National Institute for Health and Care Excellence. (2009). *Attention deficit hyperactivity disorder: Diagnosis and management of ADHD in children, young people and adults*. London, UK: National Institute for Health and Care Excellence.

National Institute for Health and Care Excellence. (2011). *Generalised anxiety disorder and panic disorder (with or without agoraphobia) in adults*. London, UK: National Institute for Health and Care Excellence.

Ng, F. (2007). The interface between religion and psychosis. *Australasian Psychiatry*, 15, 62–66.

Nicolas, G., DeSilva, A. M., Grey, K. S., & Gonzalez-Eastep, D. (2006). Using a multicultural lens to understand illness among Haitians living in America. *Professional Psychology: Research and Practice*, 37, 702–707.

Noyes, R., Clarkson, C., Crowe, R. R., Yates, W. R., & McChesney, C. M. (1987). A family study of generalized anxiety disorder. *American Journal of Psychiatry*, 144, 1019–1024.

Nye, C. (2012). Possession, Jinn and Britain's backstreet exorcists. *BBC News*, 19 November. Retrieved 23 January 2018 from http://www.bbc.co.uk/news/uk-20357997

Office for National Statistics Psychiatry Morbidity Report. (2001). *Psychiatric morbidity among adults living in private households, 2000*. London, UK: Stationery Office.

Olatunji, B. O., Williams, B. J., Haslam, N., Abramowitz, J. S., & Tolin, D. F. (2008). The latent structure of obsessive-compulsive symptoms: A taxometric study. *Depression and Anxiety*, 25, 956–968.

Ozer, R. J., & Weiss, D. S. (2004). Who develops posttraumatic stress disorder? *Current Directions in Psychological Science*, 13, 169–172.

Patterson, C. H. (2000). *Person-centered approach and client-centered therapy: Essential readers*. Ross-on-Wye, UK: PCCS Books.

Pauls, D. L. (2010). The genetics of obsessive-compulsive disorder: A review. *Dialogues in Clinical Neuroscience, 12*(2), 149–163.

Perlick, D. A., Rosenheck, R. A., Clarkin, J. F., Sirey, J. A., Salahi, J., Struening, E., & Link, B. (2001). Stigma as a barrier to recovery: Adverse effects of perceived stigma on social adaptation of persons diagnosed with bipolar affective disorder. *Psychiatric Services, 52*, 1627–1632.

Pilecki, B. C., Clegg, J. W., & McKay, D. (2011). The influence of corporate and political interests on models of illness in the evolution of the DSM. *European Psychiatry, 26*, 194–200.

Pinfold, V., Toulmin, H., Thornicroft, G., Huxley, P., Farmer, P., & Graham, T. (2003). Reducing psychiatric stigma and discrimination: Evaluation of educational interventions in UK secondary schools. *British Journal of Psychiatry, 182*, 342–346.

Porcelli, S., Fabbri, C., Drago, A., Gibiino, S., De Ronchi, D., & Serretti, A. (2011). Genetics and antidepressant: Where we are. *Clinical Neuropsychiatry, 8*(2), 99–150.

Pratt, P., Tallis, F., & Eysenck, M. W. (1997). Information-processing, storage characteristics, and worry. *Behaviour Research and Therapy, 35*, 1015–1023.

Prochaska, J. O., & Norcross, J. C. (2003). *Systems of psychotherapy: A transitional analysis* (5th ed.). Pacific Grove, CA: Brookes/Cole.

Rachman, S. (1997). A cognitive theory of obsessions. *Behaviour Research and Therapy, 35*, 793–802.

Rachman, S. (1998). A cognitive theory of obsessions: Elaborations. *Behaviour Research and Therapy, 36*, 385–401.

Rachman, S., & Hodgson, R. (1980). *Obsessions and compulsions*. New York, NY: Prentice Hall.

Rampello, L., & Nicoletti, F. (2000). Dopamine and depression: Therapeutic implications. *CNS Drugs, 13*, 35–45.

Rogers, C. R. (1951). *Client-centered therapy*. Boston, MA: Houghton Mifflin.

Rogers, C. R. (1987). Rogers, Kohut, and Erickson: A personal perspective on some similarities and differences. In J. K. Zeig (Ed.), *The evolution of psychotherapy* (pp. 179–187). New York, NY: Brunner/Mazel.

Salkovskis, P. M. (1985). Obsessional-compulsive problems: A cognitive behavioural analysis. *Behaviour Research and Therapy, 23*, 571–583.

Substance Abuse and Mental Health Services Administration. (2011). *Results from the 2011 National Survey on Drug Use and Health: Summary of national findings*. Washington, DC: US Department of Health & Human Services.

Sansone, R. A., & Wiederman, M. W. (2009). The abuse of prescription medications: Borderline personality patients in psychiatric versus non-psychiatric settings. *International Journal of Psychiatry in Medicine, 39*(2), 147–154.

Savulich, G., Shergill, S., & Yiend, J. (2012). Biased cognition in psychosis. *Journal of Experimental Psychopathology, 3*, 514–536.

Scarborough, H. S., & Dobrich, W. (1990). Development of children with early language delays. *Journal of Speech and Hearing Research, 33*, 70–83.

Schiffman, J., Abrahamson, A., Cannon, T., LaBrie, J., Parnas, J., Schulsinger, F., & Mednick, S. (2001). Early rearing factors in schizophrenia. *International Journal of Mental Health, 30*, 3–16.

Seligman, M. E. P. (1971). Phobias and preparedness. *Behavior Therapy, 2*, 307–320.

Shenk, D. (2010). *The genius in all of us: Why everything you've been told about genetics, talent, and IQ is wrong*. New York, NY: Doubleday.

Simonoff, E., Bolton, P., & Rutter, M. (1996). Mental retardation: Genetic findings, clinical implications, and research. *Journal of Child Psychology and Psychiatry, 37*, 259–280.

Sokol, D. K., & Edwards-Brown, M. (2004). Neuroimaging in autistic spectrum disorder (ASD). *Journal of Neuroimaging, 14*, 8–15.

Starcevic, V., & Bogojevic, G. (1997). Comorbidity of panic disorder with agoraphobia and specific phobia: Relationship with the subtypes of specific phobia. *Comprehensive Psychiatry, 38*, 315–320.

Startup, H. M., & Davey, G. C. L. (2003). Inflated responsibility and the use of stop rules for catastrophic worrying. *Behaviour Research and Therapy, 41*, 495–503.

Stone, A. L., Becker, L. G., Huber, A. M., & Catalano, R. F. (2012). Review of risk and protective factors of substance use and problem use in emerging adulthood. *Addictive Behaviors, 37,* 747–775.

Sullivan, P. F., Kendler, K. S., & Neale, M. C. (2003). Schizophrenia as a complex trait: Evidence from a meta-analysis of twin studies. *Archives of General Psychiatry, 60,* 1187–1192.

Swanson, J. W., Holzer, C. E., III, Ganju, V. K., & Jono, R. T. (1990). Violence and psychiatric disorder in the community: Evidence from the Epidemiologic Catchment Area surveys. *Hospital & Community Psychiatry, 41,* 761–770.

Tajima-Pozo, K., Zambrano-Enriquez, D., de Anta, L., Moron, M. D., Carrasco J. L., Lopez-Ibor, J. J., & Diaz-Marsa, M. (2011). Practicing exorcism in schizophrenia. *BMJ Case Reports, 2011* (feb15 1), bcr1020092350–bcr1020092350. doi:10.1136/bcr.10.2009.2350

Tolin, D. F., Abramowitz, J. S., Brigidi, B., & Foa, E. B. (2003). Intolerance of uncertainty in obsessive-compulsive disorder. *Journal of Anxiety Disorders, 17,* 233–242.

Van den Hout, M. A., & Kindt, M. (2003). Repeated checking causes memory distrust. *Behaviour Research and Therapy, 41,* 301–316.

Venta, A., Ross, E., Schatte, D., & Sharp, C. (2012). Suicide ideation and attempt among inpatient adolescents with borderline personality disorder: Frequency, intensity, and age of onset. *Personality and Mental Health, 6,* 340–351.

Vervliet, B., & Raes, F. (2012). Criteria of validity in experimental psychopathology: Application to models of anxiety and depression. *Psychological Medicine, 12,* 1–4.

Walker, E., Mittal, V., & Tessner, K. (2008). Stress and the hypothalamic pituitary adrenal axis in the developmental course of schizophrenia. *Annual Review of Clinical Psychology, 4,* 189–216.

Wallace, J. E. (2010). Mental health and stigma in the medical profession. *Health, 16,* 3–18.

Walsh, R. A., & McElwain, B. (2002). Existential psychotherapies. In D. J. Cain & J. Seeman (Eds.), *Humanistic psychotherapies: Handbook of research and practice* (pp. 253–278). Washington, DC: American Psychological Association.

Walters, E. E., Zaslavsky, A., & Zheng, H. (2004). The US National Comorbidity Survey Replication (NCS-R): Design and field procedures. *International Journal of Methods in Psychiatric Research, 13*(2), 69–92.

Waraich, P., Goldner, E. M., Somers, J. M., & Hsu, L. (2004). Prevalence and incidence studies of mood disorders: A systematic review of the literature. *Canadian Journal of Psychiatry, 49,* 124–138.

Watson, J. B., & Rayner, R. (1920). Conditioned emotional reactions. *Journal of Experimental Psychology, 3,* 1–14.

Wells, A., & Papageorgiou, C. (1998). Relationships between worry, obsessive-compulsive symptoms and metacognitive beliefs. *Behaviour Research and Therapy, 36,* 899–913.

Westermann, S., Salzmann, S., Fuchs, X., & Lincoln, T. M. (2012). Introducing a social beads task. *Journal of Experimental Psychopathology, 3*(4), 594–611.

Wigman, J. T. W., Van Os, J., Borsboom, D., Wardenaar, K. J., Epskamp, S., Klippel, A., … Wichers, M. (2015). Exploring the underlying structure of mental disorders: Cross-diagnostic differences and similarities from a network perspective using both a top-down and a bottom-up approach. *Psychological Medicine, 45*(11), 2375–2387. doi:10.1017/S0033291715000331

Willner, P., Scheel-Krüger, J., & Belzung, C. (2013). The neurobiology of depression and antidepressant action. *Neuroscience & Biobehavioral Reviews, 37,* 2331–2371. doi:10.1016/j.neubiorev.2012.12.007

Winterer, G., & Weinberger, D. R. (2004). Genes, dopamine and cortical signal-to-noise ratio in schizophrenia. *Trends in Neurosciences, 27*(11), 683–690.

Witthöft, M., & Hiller, W. (2010). Psychological approaches to origins and treatments of somatoform disorders. *Annual Review of Clinical Psychology, 6,* 257–283.

Wong, M. L., & Licinio, J. (2001). Research and treatment approaches to depression. *Nature Reviews Neuroscience, 2,* 343–351.

World Health Organization. (1990). *Schizophrenia and public health*. Geneva, Switzerland: World Health Organization.

World Health Organization. (2008). *The global burden of disease: 2004 update*. Retrieved 8 February 2018 from http://www.who.int/healthinfo/global_burden_disease/GBD_report_2004update_full.pdf

Yehuda, R., Flory, J. D., Pratchett, L. C., Buxbaum, J., Ising, M., & Holsboer, F. (2010). Putative biological mechanisms for the association between early life adversity and the subsequent development of PTSD. *Psychopharmacology, 212*, 405–417.

ACTIVITY SOLUTIONS

ACTIVITY 15.1: PERSONALITY DISORDERS

Borderline personality disorder

- major and regular shifts in mood
- impulsivity
- temper tantrums
- unstable self-image
- enduring pattern of instability in personal relationships
- significant fear of abandonment and rejection
- prolonged bouts of depression
- deliberate self-harm, suicidal ideation, and actual suicide attempts
- inappropriate promiscuity

Antisocial personality disorder

- pursuit of the individual's own goals at any cost
- very closely linked with adult criminal behaviour
- consistent irresponsibility
- labelled as 'sociopaths' or 'psychopaths'
- individual must be at least 18 years of age
- lack of remorse
- failure to conform to social and legal norms
- irritability and aggressiveness
- chronic indifference to the feelings and rights of others

16 The Treatment of Mental Health Problems

KATE CAVANAGH AND GRAHAM DAVEY

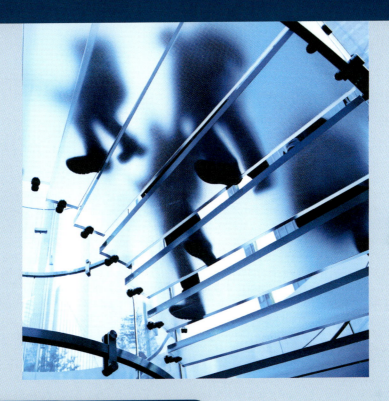

INTRODUCTION

LEARNING OBJECTIVE 16.1

Describe the roles of the three different kinds of mental health professional and the main principles of the 'stepped care' approach.

Joanne's story

Joanne is a 28-year-old teaching assistant who lives with her partner Tom and their 2-year-old daughter Annie. About 12 months ago, Joanne was involved in a car accident while driving home from the local supermarket. No one was hurt, but after the incident Joanne felt very unsettled and anxious, and noticed that she was more jumpy than usual. Annie was in the back of the car at the time of the accident and Joanne thought, 'What if something had happened to her?' She lay awake at night running over the scene of the accident in her mind, wondering what she might have done differently and thinking 'I'm a bad mother.' She avoided driving her car and started asking Tom if he could take Annie to nursery in the mornings. After about 6 months, things hadn't got better – in fact they'd got worse; Joanne felt anxious all the time, she still wasn't driving, and she had started to avoid going anywhere outside the house with Annie, even on foot – worried that something might happen to her. She'd never felt like this before. She agreed with Tom that they should visit her general practitioner (GP) to see what could be done to help. Joanne's GP listened to her current difficulties and recommended that she go for an assessment with the local Improving Access to Psychological Therapies service. Joanne was offered an appointment a few days later and met with a therapist who suggested that she could benefit from a period of guided self-help, supported by a psychological well-being practitioner (PWP) who would help her to understand and overcome her anxiety after the accident and get her back on the road. Over the next 8 weeks, Joanne worked through some exercises specially designed to help people who had developed a fear of driving after an accident, and she spoke to her PWP once a week on the phone. The sessions helped her to understand that her anxiety was a perfectly normal response to the accident, and that with practice she would learn to feel safe again behind the wheel. Each week Joanne was encouraged to explore her thoughts and emotions in relation to driving; check out any unhelpful, unrealistic beliefs she may have developed; and build back up to driving her usual routes again step by step, practising each step for long enough for her anxiety to subside. Joanne started by getting used to sitting in her parked car, being a passenger, and eventually driving short distances until she felt able to get back to the supermarket. It wasn't easy, but weekly phone calls with her PWP helped her to overcome the challenges and stay motivated to reach her goals. Now she's back driving her car as usual, taking Annie to playgroups and picnics, feeling calm (most of the time!), and sleeping normally again.

Mental health problems can take many forms and are often associated with emotional distress and functional impairment. When facing mental health challenges, it is sometimes possible to engage in adaptive coping strategies that help us to negotiate difficult periods in life (e.g. seeking help and support from friends and family or using problem-solving strategies to deal with life problems that may be causing or maintaining symptoms). Alternatively, if people feel unable to cope with the distress and disruption associated with their symptoms, they may seek professional help and support. As we can see from Joanne's story, when she found herself struggling for longer than expected after her car accident, and realized that her anxiety was beginning to interfere with her choices and activities, she decided to seek help.

The first port of call for most people seeking mental health care in the United Kingdom is usually their doctor or GP. It is estimated that people with emotional or psychological conditions make up between a quarter and a third of a GP's work-load. GPs can make an initial assessment of a mental health condition, offer advice, and prescribe medication. Primary care practices, where GPs are typically based, are often also able to offer psychological help and support for mental health difficulties in the form of self-help information, stress management courses, short-term **counselling**, brief psychological therapy, or computer-based interventions such as computerized cognitive behavioural therapy. If necessary, a GP can arrange referrals to other treatments and services, such as **Improving Access to Psychological Therapies (IAPT)** services, specialist clinical psychology, counselling or psychotherapy services, or community mental health teams. IAPT services also accept direct referrals from people seeking help.

This is a fairly standardized route by which individuals suffering from mental health problems come into contact with the treatment methods that may help to alleviate their symptoms and their distress. Others may simply decide to bypass health services available in their community and directly approach an accredited counsellor or psychological therapist who can privately supply the treatment services they require.

Whichever route is followed, the aim is to find the best match of treatment for the person to help them to overcome their current distress and build their resilience against future challenges. Finding the best match of treatment for the person requires the consideration of the evidence base for a range of different potential treatment strategies for the presenting difficulties, including both medication and psychological interventions, but also the individual needs and preferences of the individual with mental health challenges and their family. Good communication between health and social care professionals and service users is essential to allow people to make informed decisions about their care.

In some cases, mental health professionals, such as clinical psychologists, will work directly with people seeking treatment for mental health difficulties on a one-to-one basis or in a group. As well as offering therapies themselves, it is becoming increasingly common for clinical psychologists to support other mental health practitioners. This includes training and supervising psychological therapists (such as cognitive behavioural therapy [CBT] therapists) and teaching and supporting non-therapists (such as community mental health nurses, social workers, and doctors) to use psychological principles in their work. It is important that all mental health professionals regularly update their knowledge and skills over the course of their working lives. This kind of **continuing professional development (CPD)** is essential to retaining their status as legally registered practitioners.

Mental health professionals and health service provision

There are several kinds of mental health professional, each with a particular training route and specialist focus. These are described in Table 16.1.

Modern health service provision often involves a multidisciplinary approach. Doctors, nurses, clinical and counselling psychologists, counsellors, psychotherapists, occupational therapists, social workers, and other specialist workers such as **psychological well-being practitioners** work together in teams to alleviate distress and improve well-being within their local communities. In mental health services, different types of treatment and different ways of working are offered for people presenting with different kinds of problems and differing severities of distress. This approach to delivering services for mental health problems is called 'stepped care'.

TABLE 16.1 *Mental health professionals.*

Clinical psychologists	Clinical psychologists are healthcare professionals who specialize in the assessment, understanding, and treatment of mental health conditions. They are also trained in research, and often evaluate the benefits of different kinds of treatment approaches.
Counselling psychologists	Counselling psychologists are a relatively new breed of professional applied psychologists concerned with the integration of psychological theory and research with therapeutic practice.
Psychiatrists	Psychiatrists are qualified medical doctors who have done further training in treating mental health conditions. Psychiatrists can prescribe medication and are based in hospitals, GP surgeries, and community mental health centres.
Counsellors	Counsellors are trained to provide talking therapies that aim to help people to cope better both with their life and their mental health condition. Many counsellors specialize in a specific type of therapy, such as humanistic therapy or cognitive behavioural therapy.
Psychotherapists	Psychotherapists have a similar role to counsellors, but they usually have more extensive training and are also often qualified psychologists or psychiatrists. Psychotherapy tends to be a longer and more intense process than counselling.
Community mental health nurses	A community mental health nurse, also sometimes known as a community psychiatric nurse, is a registered nurse with specialist training in mental health.
Occupational therapists	Occupational therapists take a client-centred approach to helping people struggling with a physical, mental, or developmental health problem to develop, recover, or maintain daily living and work skills.
Social workers	Social workers are often used to bridge the gap between mental health services and wider social service provision. They can provide advice on a variety of practical issues, such as benefits, housing, day care, and training.
Psychological well-being practitioners	Psychological well-being practitioners work within the Improving Access to Psychological Therapies service in the United Kingdom. They provide high-volume, low-intensity interventions for clients with mild to moderate mental health problems, and their work is usually based on a cognitive behavioural model.

Mental health professionals work in a wide range of locations and provide both inpatient and community services in primary and secondary care. An example is IAPT services, which offer a coordinated approach to primary care for adults with common mental health problems such as anxiety and depression. An initial needs assessment helps to identify what kind of treatment is most likely to be beneficial for the service user, and this might include both a choice of psychological therapies and vocational support (see Focus Point 16.1). In secondary care, **early intervention in psychosis** teams aim at detecting and intervening early and in a holistic manner for young people with psychosis, incorporating a range of psychiatric, psychological, psychosocial, and vocational interventions (see Focus Point 16.2).

FOCUS POINT 16.1

IMPROVING ACCESS TO PSYCHOLOGICAL THERAPIES

One in four adults experience at least one diagnosable mental health problem in any one year, and one in six people in the United Kingdom will be diagnosed with either chronic anxiety or depression (O'Brien, Singleton, Bumpstead, & Office for National Statistics, 2001; Office for National Statistics, 2001). Mental health is the largest single cause of disability in the United Kingdom, with the total loss of economic output due to depression and anxiety estimated to be in excess of £12 billion a year (London School of Economics, 2006). Therefore, not only does it make good therapeutic sense to improve access to mental health treatments but it also makes good economic sense to help people recover from their problems.

Given the evidence-based success of therapies such as cognitive behavioural therapy (CBT) for common mental health problems, many countries are now trying to find ways to increase and improve access to these therapies. This has given rise to large-scale initiatives, commonly known as Improving Access to Psychological Therapies (IAPT), which aspire to significantly increase the availability of **evidence-based interventions**, such as CBT. The initiative aims at meeting these goals by:

1. training significant numbers of practitioners in psychological therapies such as CBT

2. improving access and reducing waiting times for treatment

3. increasing client choice and satisfaction.

A planned consequence of this will be improved social and economic participation as those previously suffering from common mental health problems return to work and normal social and family functioning. As a result, the costs of the IAPT programme are expected to be offset by the increased economic contribution of those who have recovered from their mental health problems (e.g. see Radhakrishnan et al., 2013).

Key successes of the programme in the United Kingdom in the first 3 years include:

1. seeing more than 1 million people in IAPT services

2. recovery rates in excess of 45%

3. over 45,000 people moving off benefits into paid employment (Department of Health, 2012).

Schemes for improving access to psychological therapies are now being rolled out in many countries, including developing countries such as India, Pakistan, and Uganda (Patel, Chowdhary, Rahman, & Verdeli, 2011), where lay and community health workers are being trained in evidence-based practices. However, the challenges of providing access to psychological therapies for those who need them are still immense, with the 'treatment gap' (a term used to describe the shortfall in mental health provision for sufferers) exceeding 75% in most parts of the world (Kohn, Saxena, Levav, & Saraceno, 2004).

IAPT services are currently being expanded to increase service-user choice among the range of evidence-based therapies such as CBT and interpersonal psychotherapy, and to extend the reach of these programmes beyond common mental health problems towards children and young people, chronic physical conditions, medically unexplained symptoms, and severe mental illness.

EARLY INTERVENTION IN PSYCHOSIS SERVICES

Early intervention in psychosis (EIP) services are founded on the basis that a critical period exists in the first 2–3 years following a first psychotic episode, and this critical period determines the long-term trajectory of psychosis. The shorter the duration of untreated psychosis during this critical period, the better the long-term outcome in terms of symptoms and also, importantly, social and vocational functioning. Some have argued that untreated psychosis is toxic, having an impact on brain structure and function, and that early pharmacological interventions can arrest this neurotoxic deterioration.

A strong case has been provided for the psychological impact of early psychosis. Psychosis is most likely to occur in the late teens and early adolescence, often precipitated by stress and an increase in the difficulties of daily life. The onset of psychosis disrupts education and early work opportunities, which has an impact on independence at a key developmental stage, just as young people are leaving home and starting new jobs and relationships. This early critical period is deemed a period of heightened risk and also heightened plasticity, during which the potential for change is at its greatest. EIP services are intended to detect and intervene early, and in a holistic manner, incorporating a range of psychiatric, psychological, psychosocial, and vocational interventions.

Drawing on developmental models, EIP services aspire to promote recovery, social and occupational inclusion, and the return to ordinary lives of young people with psychosis. Early intervention during this critical period leads to increased service-user satisfaction; fewer symptoms, relapses, and hospital admissions; better health, well-being, and social and occupational functioning; and fewer suicides in the medium to long term (Birchwood, Todd, & Jackson, 1998; Marshall, Lockwood, Lewis, & Fiander, 2004; McGorry, Killackey, & Yung, 2008).

Work to promote better engagement of young people in EIP services (the Early Youth Engagement in first episode psychosis – the EYE project) identified the value of hope and goal-focused approaches in promoting youth engagement with EIP services (Greenwood et al., 2015). You can find more about the EYE project **here**[1].

As well as seeking professional help, many people facing mental health challenges seek support from other people experiencing similar difficulties. For example, Self Help Services is a user-led mental health charity providing services across the northwest of England that include self-help groups, support for online CBT (see Focus Point 16.5), and overnight accommodation and support for adults at a crisis point with difficulties such as panic attacks and depression. There are also several national charities that offer information and peer support for people facing mental health challenges and their loved ones: for example, Anxiety UK, Beat, and Mind.

Parents, partners, children, siblings, other relatives, friends, colleagues, and neighbours also often play an important role in promoting recovery. This might include offering emotional, practical, or financial support to people living with mental health challenges. It is estimated that there are up to 1.5 million people in the United Kingdom caring for a relative or friend with a mental health problem (National Co-ordinating Centre for NHS Service Delivery and Organization, 2002). Having a supportive social network that includes at least one close confiding relationship is known to be one of the most protective factors against mental health problems and one of the best promoters of sustained recovery (Brown, Adler, & Bifulco, 1988; Brown & Harris, 1978).

TEST YOURSELF

1. Can you describe the roles of three different kinds of mental health professional?
2. What are the main activities of clinical psychologists working within healthcare services?
3. What does IAPT stand for, and what are the main aims of this initiative?

SECTION SUMMARY

- Mental health problems can take many forms and are often associated with emotional distress and functional impairment.
- If people feel unable to cope with the distress and disruption associated with their symptoms, they may seek professional help and support.
- The first port of call for most people seeking mental healthcare is usually their doctor or general practitioner (GP). If necessary, a GP can arrange referrals to other treatments and services, such as Improving Access to Psychological Therapies services, specialist clinical psychology, counselling or psychotherapy services, or community mental health teams.
- As well as seeking professional help, many people facing mental health challenges seek support from other people experiencing similar difficulties.
- Parents, partners, children, siblings, other relatives, friends, colleagues, and neighbours also often play an important role in promoting recovery.

PSYCHOLOGICAL TREATMENTS FOR MENTAL HEALTH PROBLEMS

LEARNING OBJECTIVE 16.2

Compare and contrast a range of treatment approaches for mental health problems.

Just as there is no one cause of mental health problems, there is no one-size-fits-all treatment strategy. There are several different approaches to treating mental health problems, which include biological, psychological, social, and environmental methods. Sometimes one single approach may be taken; other times complementary approaches from these different perspectives may be integrated to offer a more complex intervention.

The major psychological therapies have been developed from a small number of important theoretical approaches, including psychodynamic, cognitive, behavioural, and systemic approaches. This section continues with a summary of how these theoretical approaches are applied to treat mental health problems.

Psychodynamic treatments

The aim of most **psychodynamic therapies** is to reveal unconscious conflicts that may be causing symptoms of psychopathology. Bringing unconscious material into consciousness is believed to have the effect of lessening psychological disturbance. These approaches assume that unconscious conflicts develop early in life, and therapy is designed to identify life events that may have caused these unconscious conflicts. Once this has happened, the therapist can help the client to acknowledge the existence of these conflicts and bring them into conscious awareness; the therapist can then work with the client to develop strategies for change (Frosh, 2012).

Probably the most well-known form of psychodynamic therapy is **psychoanalysis**, which is based on the theoretical works of Sigmund Freud (1856–1939). In psychoanalysis there are several basic techniques that can be used to help individuals gain a sense of understanding of their symptoms. These include:

- **free association**, in which the client is encouraged to verbalize all thoughts, feelings, and images that come to mind, thereby helping to bring into awareness any unconscious conflicts or associations between thoughts and feelings

- **transference**, when the analyst is a target for emotional responses and the client behaves or feels towards the analyst as they would behave towards an important person in their life

- **dream analysis**, wherein unconscious conflicts are thought to reveal themselves in symbolic forms in dreams

- **interpretation**, the means by which the psychoanalyst interprets information from all of the above sources to enable the client to identify important underlying conflicts.

The two long-term variants of psychoanalysis are long-term psychoanalytic psychotherapy (LTPP) and psychoanalysis. In psychoanalysis, the client lies on a couch and the therapist sits in a chair behind them, and the frequency of sessions ranges from two to five per week. In LTPP the client and therapist sit in chairs opposite each other and meet usually just once or twice a week. Both therapies are designed to last over several years.

Cohort studies of clients completing psychoanalysis indicate improvements in symptoms and personality characteristics over time, but methodological limitations of the available studies raise caution in the interpretation of these findings (de Maat et al., 2013). In studies where the comparative benefits of LTPP have been measured, evidence is mixed and limited. LTPP has been shown to be more effective than control treatments that do not possess a specialized psychotherapy component, but not when compared with other psychotherapies (Smit et al., 2012).

In the second half of the 20th century, a variety of types of briefer, less intensive forms of psychodynamic therapy were developed. Like psychoanalysis, these short-term psychodynamic psychotherapies (STPPs) explore interpersonal relationships alongside unconscious feelings, drives, and conflicts, but are typically more focused on achieving therapeutic change via symptom reduction, decreasing future vulnerability, and increasing long-term resiliency. Blagys and Hilsenroth (2000) described seven distinguishing features of STPP and interpersonal therapies: (1) a focus on affect and the expression of patients' emotions; (2) an exploration of patients' attempts to avoid topics or engage in activities that hinder the progress of therapy; (3) the identification of patterns in patients' actions, thoughts, feelings, experiences, and relationships; (4) an emphasis on past experiences; (5) a focus on patients' interpersonal experiences; (6) an emphasis on the therapeutic relationship; and (7) an exploration of patients' wishes, dreams, or fantasies. STPP has been found to be effective for the treatment of depression in adults, although not more effective than other psychotherapies (Driessen et al., 2010). It is recommended by the **National Institute for Health and Care Excellence (NICE)** (2009; see also Focus Point 16.3) as a treatment option for depression for people who do not want or do not benefit from other forms of psychological intervention, such as CBT.

FOCUS POINT 16.3

THE NATIONAL INSTITUTE FOR HEALTH AND CARE EXCELLENCE

The National Institute for Health and Care Excellence (NICE) is an independent organization in England and Wales that provides evidence-based national guidance on the most effective ways to prevent, diagnose, and treat disease and ill health. NICE guidance is intended to improve health and social care for England and Wales by reducing inequalities and variation in healthcare and promoting person-centred care. NICE guidance supports healthcare professionals and others to make sure that the care they provide is of the best possible quality and offers the best value for money.

NICE has published nearly 100 guidelines relating to mental health, including guidance on the identification, assessment, and treatment of depression, anxiety disorders, eating disorders, psychosis, alcohol dependence, personality disorders, dementia, attention deficit hyperactivity disorder, nocturnal enuresis, and antenatal and postnatal mental health.

Psychodynamic approaches may also be used outside the traditional clinic setting (Lemma & Patrick, 2010) and there is a long history of providing psychotherapeutic services in schools and community clinics. One innovative example that takes psychodynamic therapy 'off the couch' is the Grow2Grow project, described in Focus Point 16.4.

GROW2GROW: AN ALTERNATIVE MENTAL HEALTH PROVISION FOR YOUNG PEOPLE

Reproduced by permission of Commonwork.

Grow2Grow is an innovative project that applies psychodynamic principles away from the clinic setting. Set up by Paula Conway, a clinical psychologist and psychoanalytic psychotherapist, Grow2Grow provides therapeutically supported vocational placements for young people aged between 14 and 24 with complex mental health problems. Grow2Grow is based at Commonwork, an organic dairy farm, market garden, and conference and study centre where young people work in real social enterprises – for example, with the dairy herd or in the market garden growing organic fruit and vegetables to supply the local community.

Young people with complex mental health and emotional and/or behavioural problems attend the project for 2 days per week for up to 2 years. Many have been out of school, college, or employment for years. On the project they work, cook, and eat together and every young person also has weekly individual psychoanalytically informed key working. The key working allows for a more active approach than traditional psychodynamic work.

Grow2Grow has a very active engagement approach, which is essential for young people who struggle to participate in life. As well as phoning, texting, and even going to young people's homes to pick them up, key workers address engagement issues at assessment and then regularly in sessions. The model identifies two parts of the personality that may be in conflict with each other. One part wants to engage, attend, and participate in the project while another part may say, for instance, 'They don't like me; it isn't for me; it's better to stay home.' Addressing this right from the start can overcome anxiety and sustain engagement (see Conway & Ginkell, 2014). Young people attending the project have made significant improvements in mental health and well-being, and over 80% have achieved educational, vocational, or employment outcomes. You can learn more about the work that Grow2Grow does **here**[2].

Arts therapies

Arts therapies are interventions that combine psychotherapeutic techniques, often based on psychodynamic ideas, with activities aimed at promoting creative expression, including art, dance movement therapy, drama therapy, and music therapy. In arts therapy, the artist encourages the client to create something that relates to their feelings or experiences. Arts therapies are used in a range of contexts and are recommended by NICE for both adults (NICE, 2014) and children and young people (NICE, 2012) experiencing psychosis and schizophrenia. The client does not need to have any previous experience or artistic skill. You can find out more about arts therapies by visiting the **British Association of Art Therapists' website**[3].

Interpersonal therapy

Interpersonal psychotherapy (IPT) is a structured, time-limited psychological therapy that was specifically developed for the treatment of major depression (Klerman, Weissman, Rounsaville, & Chevron, 1984). IPT is based on the idea that psychological symptoms, such as depressed mood, can be understood as a response to current difficulties in relationships, which may in turn affect the quality of those relationships. It has sometimes but not always been considered a psychodynamic psychotherapy (Markowitz, Svartberg, & Swartz, 1998). Typically, IPT focuses on current relationship themes, such as conflict with another person, life changes that affect how the person feels about themselves and others, grief and loss, or difficulty in starting or keeping relationships going. During therapy the client works with the therapist to understand the reciprocal relationship between interpersonal factors and depression, and seeks to reduce their symptoms by learning to cope with or resolve interpersonal problem areas.

IPT is at least as effective as other psychological therapies for depression (Cuijpers et al., 2011), and it is recommended as a treatment choice for depression by NICE (2009). You can find out more about IPT at the website of the **International Society of Interpersonal Psychotherapy**[4].

Behaviour therapies

In the 1940s and 1950s, dissatisfactions with psychoanalytic approaches led psychologists to look towards the developing area of experimental psychology for objective knowledge that might be used to inform therapy. The body of knowledge that psychologists turned to was that of **conditioning**, and this gave rise to what came to be known as behaviour therapies. In contrast to psychoanalysis, behaviour therapies stressed the need to treat symptoms of psychopathology as bona fide behavioural problems rather than the mere symptoms of some other, hidden underlying cause or conflict. Many psychologists believed that at least some psychological disorders were the result of what was called **faulty learning**, and that symptoms were acquired through simple conditioning processes. The reasoning for developing therapies based on learning principles was that if psychological problems are acquired through learning, then conditioning principles can be used to develop treatments that effectively help the individual to 'unlearn' those problematic associations. Two distinctive strands of **behaviour therapy** developed from these assumptions. The first is a set of therapies based on the principles of classical conditioning, and the second is based on principles of operant conditioning. While the former group of therapies continues to be known as behaviour therapy, the latter group has also come to be known as **behaviour modification** or **behaviour analysis**.

Therapies based on classical conditioning principles

Behaviour therapy effectively originates in the writings of Joseph Wolpe (1958), who argued that many forms of emotional disorder can be treated using the classical conditioning principle of **extinction**. The assumption was that if emotional problems such as anxiety disorders are learned through classical conditioning, they can be 'unlearned' by disrupting the association between the anxiety-provoking cues or situations and the threat or traumatic outcomes that they have become associated with. In practice, this means ensuring that the anxiety-provoking stimulus, event, or situation is experienced in the absence of accompanying trauma so that the former no longer comes to evoke the latter. The most famous behaviour therapy techniques to apply extinction principles are **flooding**, **counterconditioning**, and **systematic desensitization**, and they have collectively come to be known as **exposure therapies** (Richard & Lauterbach, 2007) because they are all based on the need to expose the client to the events and situations that evoke their distress and anxiety – so that the client can learn that they are no longer threatening (see Davey, 1998).

Graded-exposure therapy is recommended by NICE for the treatment of anxiety disorders including phobias and PTSD. In PTSD, exposure is done in two ways:

- imaginal exposure to the trauma memories
- in vivo exposure to now safe situations that are avoided due to their association with trauma.

Aversion therapy is another treatment based on classical conditioning, but it is different from the preceding therapies because it attempts to condition an aversion to a stimulus or event to which the individual is inappropriately attracted. For example, aversion therapy has most widely been used in the treatment of addictive behaviours such as alcoholism, and in these procedures the taste of alcohol is paired with aversive outcomes (e.g. sickness-inducing drugs) in order to condition an aversive reaction to alcohol. Aversion therapy is no longer considered an acceptable treatment in the United Kingdom (Heather, Raistrick, & Godfrey, 2006).

Therapies based on operant conditioning principles

Operant conditioning is concerned with influencing the frequency of a behaviour by manipulating the consequences of that behaviour. Operant conditioning principles have mainly been used in therapy in three specific ways: (1) to understand what rewarding or reinforcing factors might be maintaining an inappropriate or maladaptive behaviour – this is known as functional analysis (e.g. factors that might be maintaining challenging or aggressive behaviours); (2) to use rewards to try to establish new or appropriate behaviours (e.g. to establish self-help or social behaviours); and (3) to use negative or punishing consequences to try to suppress or eliminate problematic behaviours in need of urgent attention (e.g. to eliminate or suppress self-injurious behaviours).

In **functional analysis** the therapist attempts to identify consistencies between problematic behaviours and their consequences – especially to try to discover whether there might be a consistent consequence that appears to be maintaining the behaviour by rewarding it. Identifying the nature of the consequence allows the therapist to disrupt the reinforcement contingency and to reduce the frequency of problematic behaviour through extinction. Functional analysis has been adopted across a range of clinical settings and has been successfully applied to a wide range of behaviours (Beavers, Iwata, & Lerman, 2013).

Other important interventions based on operant conditioning include the **token economy**, **response shaping**, and **behavioural self-control**. In the psychiatric setting, a token economy involves participants receiving tokens (a generalized reinforcer) for engaging in behaviours defined by the programme; at a later time, these tokens can then be exchanged for a variety of reinforcing or desired items (e.g. access to the hospital grounds, a visit to the cinema, and suchlike). Response shaping is a procedure that can be used to encourage new behaviours that are not already occurring at a reasonable frequency. Here, the therapist will first reinforce an existing behaviour that does occur quite frequently and is an approximation to the specific target response. Once this general response is established, reinforcement is given only for closer and closer approximations to the target response. Finally, the use of operant conditioning principles in therapy does not have to be overseen or administered by a therapist. The principles can be used by any individual to manage their own behaviour. This personal use of operant conditioning principles has come to be known as behavioural self-control (e.g. see Thoresen & Mahoney, 1974) and has since been developed into multifaceted behavioural programmes to deal with a variety of personal problems, including addiction, habits, obsessions, and other behavioural problems (Lutzker & Martin, 1981).

Behavioural activation

Behavioural activation is a psychological therapy based on the principle that, when people become depressed, many of their activities function to enable them to avoid or escape from unpleasant thoughts, feelings, or situations. The behavioural activation approach was developed by Peter Lewinsohn and it focuses on activity scheduling to help clients with depression to re-engage in pleasurable and meaningful personal and social activities so that these can be positively reinforced. Planned timetables of activity are developed that promote engagement with both pleasurable and challenging experiences and reduce behavioural and cognitive avoidance. The client is encouraged to introduce small changes and build up their level of activity gradually towards long-term goals. (To see how this works, you should tackle Activity 16.1.) Meta-analyses had found that behavioural approaches have the same kind of success in treating depression in adults as cognitive therapy (Cuijpers, Van Straten, & Warmerdam, 2007; Ekers, Richards, & Gilbody, 2008) and behavioural activation is recommended by NICE as a treatment choice for depression. Structured group physical activity programmes are also recommended by NICE (2009) as an intervention choice for mild to moderate depression.

ACTIVITY 16.1

MAKING GOOD USE OF YOUR TIME: ACTIVITY SCHEDULING

One of the principles of behavioural activation is that when we feel low, anxious, or stressed, our motivation to do things often decreases. We may find that we give up hobbies or activities that we've previously enjoyed, avoid difficult tasks, and do fewer things that are in line with our goals or values. Activity scheduling is a method used to help people to identify important activities that are missing in their lives and to gradually put these into action, and to notice where too much time may be being spent doing activities that are unrewarding or the longer-term outcomes of which are unwanted. You can make your own activity schedule and work on it over the coming week by following these instructions.

Create the following Activity Diary to make a plan for the week ahead. Start by filling in all the activities that you have to do: for example, going to lectures, preparing and eating meals, doing housework, attending appointments, and so forth. This will show you all the time that you have free. Then you can begin to plan other activities that you would like to do. You may find it helpful to plan in some time for socializing, hobbies and interests, exercise, and time for yourself. Try to include at least one activity that you used to enjoy but haven't done lately – some examples might be visiting a friend you haven't seen in a while, going swimming, climbing a hill, or doing something creative (e.g. painting, drawing, or making something). Try also to include something that you've been avoiding but that is aligned with your goals and values (maybe tidying your desk so you can work more effectively, or going for a run if you haven't been for a while). Don't forget to leave some space to chill out!

ACTIVITY DIARY

Try to plan activities to fill your week – this can help you to make good use of your time.

	Mon	Tue	Wed	Thur	Fri	Sat	Sun
Getting up							
Morning							
Lunch							
Afternoon							
Evening							
Bedtime							

Now, put this plan into action. Keep in mind that a major mistake is to try to tackle everything at once. Introduce small changes, building up gradually towards long-term goals.

It is important to monitor the effect of your scheduled activities on your mood. Did you notice anything in particular about the effect of specific activities on your mood throughout the week? At the end of the week, do you feel better or worse for doing the things you planned?

Behavioural couples therapy

Behavioural couples therapy is based on the principle that in some cases unhelpful patterns of relating within a romantic relationship can cause and maintain depression and other mental health difficulties. This therapy is offered to couples where one of the partners is experiencing mental health problems and there is relationship distress. The intervention, developed by Andrew Christensen and Neil Jacobson, aims to help couples understand how their interactions may affect one another in order to change and develop more helpful interactions that may reduce stress and increase support within the couple. The focus of the treatment is on relieving stress, re-establishing positive activities in the relationship, and improving communication and problem-solving skills. Behavioural couples therapy is a structured, time-limited intervention that involves weekly activities for both partners. For example, one aspect of behavioural couples therapy focuses on increasing positive activities within the relationship. This may involve tasks such as each partner keeping a note of nice things the other person has done over the week (e.g. 'He cooked a delicious dinner', 'He told me he loved me', 'He played with the children on Saturday morning while I went swimming'), planning a shared rewarding activity (or 'date') each week, and making time to actively do nice things for each other. These kinds of activities can improve both relationship quality and mental health.

Randomized controlled trials have shown that behavioural couples therapy can be an effective treatment strategy (Whisman, Johnson, & Li, 2012) and it is recommended by NICE (2009) as a treatment for people with depression in the context of relationship distress.

Cognitive therapies

The origins of cognitive therapy

Since the 1960s it has become clear that cognitive factors play an important role in psychopathology. For example, some symptoms can be caused or maintained by unhelpful 'ways of thinking' – either about the self or the world (e.g. in major depression). In other cases, psychopathologies are characterized by dysfunctional ways of processing and interpreting incoming information. For example, many anxiety disorders are characterized by a bias towards processing threatening or anxiety-relevant information (e.g. generalized anxiety disorder) or towards interpreting ambiguous information negatively (e.g. panic disorder). If these cognitive factors are maintaining psychopathological symptoms, then developing treatments that try to address and change these dysfunctional cognitive features is important. Two early forms of cognitive therapy based on these assumptions were **rational emotive therapy** and **Beck's cognitive therapy**.

The way in which people construe themselves, their life, and the world is likely to be a major determinant of their feelings, and rational emotive therapy, developed by Albert Ellis (1962), was one of the first cognitive therapies to address these factors. In particular, Ellis believed that people carry around with them a set of implicit assumptions that determine how they judge themselves and others, and that many of these implicit assumptions may be irrational and cause emotional distress. For example, two common irrational assumptions are (1) expecting perfection from yourself and from others and (2) expecting approval from others for everything you do. Clearly, there will be many occasions when these goals are not met, and this will cause anxiety, depression, and emotional discomfort. Rational emotive therapy attempts to challenge these irrational beliefs and to persuade the individual to set more attainable life goals. As such, rational emotive therapy is a good example of a group of therapies that attempt to change a set of core beliefs about the world that may be dysfunctional (i.e. either fallacious or acting as a source of conflict and emotional distress).

One of the first cognitive therapies was a cognitive therapy for depression developed by Aaron Beck. He argued that depression results when an individual develops a set of cognitive schemas (or beliefs) that bias the individual towards negative interpretations of the self, the world, and the future, and any therapy for depression must therefore address these schemas, deconstruct them, and replace them with more rational schemas (i.e. ones that do not always lead to negative interpretations). Beck's cognitive therapy does this by engaging depressed individuals in an objective assessment of their

1. Situation	2. Moods	3. Automatic thoughts (images)
Who? What? When? Where?	What did you feel? Rate each mood (0–100%).	What was going through your mind just before you started to feel this way?
At home with Georgia and Archie on Tuesday afternoon. I put them in front of the TV for a couple of hours so I could get on with some housework.	Guilty (80%) Low (70%)	I shouldn't let them watch so much TV. I'm a really bad mum for letting them watch TV. I bet none of my friends would do this.

FIGURE 16.1 *An example of a CBT diary: Three-column thought record.*

beliefs, and requires them to evaluate the validity of their ideas about themselves, the world, and the future.

Out of these early pioneering cognitive therapies developed what is now known as **cognitive behavioural therapy (CBT)**. This is an umbrella term for many different therapies based on the principle that how we think about a situation has a powerful effect on how we feel and how we act, and in turn that what we do can affect our thoughts and feelings. These interventions share the common aim of changing both cognitions and behaviour in order to alleviate distress. In CBT the therapist and client work together to understand the client's experiences and to overcome overwhelming problems by breaking them down into smaller parts. Clients learn to identify unrealistic and unhelpful thinking patterns and processes that may be maintaining their difficulties and are given techniques to challenge and change these habits in daily life. During therapy the client develops more adaptive and helpful ways of thinking about themselves and their world and learns practical ways to improve their state of mind on a daily basis. As well as working with the therapist during therapy sessions, the client is encouraged to engage in learning activities in between therapy sessions. These learning activities might include keeping a diary of significant events and associated feelings, thoughts, and behaviours (see Figure 16.1); practising 'behavioural experiments' to test out whether their beliefs about themselves and the world are accurate; and practising new ways of thinking, behaving, and reacting in situations that are typically associated with distress.

In general, CBT is perceived as an evidence-based and cost-effective form of treatment that can be successfully applied to a very broad range of psychopathologies (Butler, Chapman, Forman, & Beck, 2006). It is thought to be equally as effective as other forms of psychotherapy, and superior to many other forms of psychotherapy when treating anxiety and depressive disorders (Tolin, 2010, although not all studies support this; cf. Cuijpers, Van Straten, Andersson, & Van Oppen, 2008). CBT appears to have an enduring effect in the treatment of depression and the anxiety disorders that reduces risk for subsequent symptom return (Hollon, Stewart, & Strunk, 2006; NICE, 2011). NICE guidelines also suggest that CBT should be considered, alongside medication treatment, for anorexia nervosa (NICE, 2004a) and for all people with psychosis who continue to experience distressing symptoms (NICE, 2014).

'Waves' of cognitive behavioural therapy

CBT has not been a static treatment innovation and, just like any other knowledge-based development, new forms of CBT have evolved out of earlier ones. These progressive developments have come to be known as 'waves', and at the present time we are experiencing what is called the third wave of CBT techniques. Recently developed therapies include mindfulness-based cognitive therapy, and acceptance and commitment therapy.

Mindfulness-based cognitive therapy (**MBCT**) (Segal, Teasdale, Williams, & Gemar, 2002) is a therapy that incorporates mindfulness practice and principles with cognitive therapy. Mindfulness refers to the ability to fully notice our current experiences (thoughts, feelings, bodily sensations) while being kind, accepting, and non-judgemental of these experiences (Bishop et al., 2004; Kabat-Zinn, 2003) (see Activity 16.2).

This therapy differs from traditional cognitive therapy in that, while cognitive therapy is interested in identifying and changing the content of thoughts and beliefs, MBCT is interested in developing a different way of relating to this content. The theory underlying MBCT is that it is not the content of negative thoughts and beliefs that is distressing; rather, it is how we respond to these experiences. Rumination is the tendency to think about negative thoughts, feelings, and their consequences over and over; to get lost in the content; and to be attached to the content (Nolen-Hoeksema, 2000). Getting trapped in the process of rumination can lead to depression. During MBCT people engage in mindfulness meditation practices and learn through practice to take a step back and to observe all experiences (including thoughts) non-judgementally, and to mindfully make decisions about how best to respond rather than responding automatically and in potentially unhelpful ways. In this way, MBCT can help people to let go of ruminative ways of responding to negative thoughts. MBCT was designed as a relapse-prevention intervention for depression for people who are currently well but who are at risk of relapse, at least in part because it is believed that when in dysphoric moods they may be particularly vulnerable to rumination, which may potentiate a negative cycle into depression.

There is evidence from randomized controlled trials that MBCT in comparison to usual care is effective at reducing the risk of relapse for people who are currently well and who have experienced three or more previous episodes of depression (Kuyken et al., 2008; Ma & Teasdale, 2004). NICE (2009) recommends MBCT for use in this group.

ACTIVITY 16.2

DEVELOPING MINDFULNESS

Mindfulness means paying attention, on purpose, in the present-moment and without judgement.

(Kabat-Zinn, 1994, p. 4)

Mindfulness can be developed by paying attention, without judgement, to our present-moment experience through (1) formal mindfulness meditation practices, which may focus, for example, on paying attention to the body, to our breathing, to thoughts, or to challenging situations, and (2) informal practices, where we learn to apply the principles of mindfulness to activities in our daily lives, such as walking, eating, or cleaning our teeth.

One example of a mindfulness practice is mindful breathing. Try this for yourself by following these instructions:

- Sit comfortably and, if it feels okay to do so, close your eyes.
- Direct your attention to your breathing (you don't need to change anything – just notice each breath coming in and going out).
- When thoughts, feelings, or external distractions occur, simply accept them – don't judge or get involved with them.
- When you notice that your attention has drifted away from the breathing, gently bring it back. It's natural for thoughts and feelings to arise and for your attention to follow them, but, each time, simply bring your attention back to the breathing.

NHS Choices (2016) contains more information on mindfulness.

Acceptance and commitment therapy (ACT) is also a third-wave CBT intervention that has grown in popularity over recent years. It is an approach that adopts some aspects of mindfulness but has developed more from the behaviour analysis (or Skinnerian) approach to understanding behaviour. ACT differs from traditional CBT in that, rather than getting individuals to manage and change their thoughts and the way they think, it teaches them to 'just notice', accept, and embrace private events such as thoughts (especially thoughts that may be intrusive, distressing, or unwanted). As such, it aims to help individuals to clarify their personal values, to take action on them, and to increase their psychological flexibility (Hayes, Luoma, Bond, Masuda, & Lillis, 2006).

There is some evidence that ACT may be helpful for a range of difficulties (Hayes et al., 2006; Öst, 2008) but ACT is not recommended by NICE as a specific treatment choice.

Systemic and family therapies

Systemic and family therapies work with the interactional patterns and relationship dynamics between people that may be associated with mental health difficulties (Dallos & Draper, 2005). Family therapy works to nurture and promote change by (1) helping to improve communications between members of the family, especially where communication between individuals might be the cause of psychopathology in one or more family members; (2) helping to resolve specific conflicts – for example, between adolescents and their parents; and (3) applying **systems theory** (attempting to understand the family as a social system) to treatment to gain an understanding of the complex relationships and alliances that exist between family members (Minuchin, 1985).

In **family therapy**, the therapist or family therapy team meets with those members of the family willing to participate in discussion about a topic or problem raised by one or more members of the family. In many cases, family therapists focus on how patterns of interaction within the family maintain the problem (e.g. an eating disorder) rather than trying to identify the cause (the latter possibly being seen as trying to allocate blame for the problem within the family); therapists may also suggest to family members different ways of responding to each other. Family therapists may also draw on cognitive behavioural methods and psychodynamic approaches, depending on the nature of the problem and its underlying causes.

Not all systemic therapies involve all family members – the systemic approach can be used to work with an individual or couple alone, but keeping their wider family in mind. There is good evidence to suggest that these therapies can be helpful ways of working with families in distress where the identified client is either a child or an adult (Retzlaff, von Sydow, Beher, Haun, & Schweitzer, 2013; von Sydow, Beher, Schweitzer, & Retzlaff, 2010). NICE (2014) guidelines recommend that family therapies should be considered, alongside medication treatment, for all people with psychosis who continue to experience distressing symptoms. NICE (2004a) also recommends family therapy for the treatment of anorexia nervosa.

Humanistic psychotherapies

Throughout the 20th century, many psychotherapists felt that psychological therapy was losing sight of both the feelings of the individual and the individual themselves. As a consequence, a number of what are called **humanistic therapies** developed. Arguably the most successful of these is client-centred therapy (Rogers, 1961). These therapies have a number of factors in common: (1) they emphasize the need for the therapist to develop a more personal relationship with the client; (2) they are **holistic therapies**, in emphasizing the need to consider the 'whole' person during therapy, not just their problems; (3) they see therapy as a way of enabling individuals to make their own decisions and solve their own problems; (4) they see the therapist–client relationship as a genuinely reciprocal and empathetic one; and (5) they see increasing emotional awareness as a critical factor in alleviating psychological distress and as necessary before the client can begin to resolve life problems.

Client-centred therapy focuses on the individual's immediate conscious experience, and critical to this form of humanistic therapy is the creation of a therapeutic climate that allows the client to progress towards becoming a person who is independent, self-directed, and pursuing self-growth. For Carl Rogers (1902–1987), **empathy** (putting yourself in someone else's shoes) was the central important feature of any therapist–client relationship and it is this ability that is essential in guiding the client towards resolving their own life problems. Empathy has at least two main components in this context: (1) an ability to understand and experience the client's own feelings and personal meanings and (2) a willingness to demonstrate **unconditional positive regard** for the client. This latter feature involves valuing the client for who they are and refraining from judging them. In addition, most humanistic therapies, such as client-centred therapy, are non-directive. The therapist acts primarily as an understanding listener who assists the client by offering advice only when asked. The general approach attempts to eliminate symptoms by moving clients from one phenomenological state (e.g. a state of anxiety or depression) to another (e.g. one that enables clients to view themselves as worthy and respected individuals).

Research evidence suggests large gains for clients of humanistic and experiential therapies in comparison to those who do not receive treatment, with clinically similar effects to other kinds of psychological therapy (Elliot, Greenberg, Watson, Timulak, & Freire, 2013). In particular these therapies appear to be helpful for populations experiencing depression, relationship or interpersonal problems, and anxiety, and those coping with chronic medical conditions, psychosis, or substance misuse.

SECTION SUMMARY

- Just as there is no one cause of mental health problems, there is no one-size-fits-all treatment strategy. There are a range of approaches to treating mental health problems that include biological, psychological, social, and environmental methods.

- The major psychological therapies have been developed from a small number of important theoretical approaches including psychodynamic, cognitive, behavioural, and systemic approaches.

- Humanistic, holistic therapies evolved out of the way in which many psychotherapists felt that psychological therapy was losing sight of both the feelings of the individuals and the individuals themselves. Arguably the most successful of these is client-centred therapy (Rogers, 1961).

WAYS OF DELIVERING PSYCHOLOGICAL THERAPY

LEARNING OBJECTIVE 16.3

Compare and contrast a range of delivery options for treatment for mental health problems, namely group therapies, teletherapy, e-therapy, and self-help.

Most of the various kinds of psychological therapy described above were developed and are typically offered in a one-to-one therapy model, where the individual client (or, in the case of couples or family therapy, members of an individual family) meets with the therapist on a regular basis for sessions lasting approximately 1 hour. However, this is not the only approach to offering therapy and some therapies are offered in alternative ways – for example, in **group therapy**, teletherapies, **internet interventions**, and guided or unguided self-help formats.

Group therapies

Group therapies can be useful when a group of individuals share similar experiences or challenges. In group therapies people can benefit from their relationship not just with the therapist (or group facilitator) but also with other members of the group. For example, groups may help people to feel less isolated and more supported, to develop social and interpersonal skills through interacting with the other group members, to see how others handle similar problems to their own, and to learn new perspectives.

There are several kinds of group interventions, which include self-help and mutual-support groups (such as Alcoholics Anonymous), as well as manualized psychological interventions such as stress management, group CBT, and MBCT.

There is evidence that group therapies can be just as effective as individual therapies in some contexts. Adapting interventions for groups is likely to be a cost-effective solution for service providers as well as an effective way of helping clients to manage symptoms of psychopathology.

Teletherapy

Most clients telephone their therapists, if only to schedule an appointment, but the telephone can also provide a means of facilitating and conducting treatment. **Teletherapy** can save time and reduce travel costs when clients live in remote or inaccessible areas, and real-time videoconferencing is also used with clients who are unable to attend a clinic. Comparative studies of face-to-face, real-time videoconferencing, and two-way audio therapy suggest that differences in outcomes among the three modes of treatment delivery are surprisingly small (Day & Schneider, 2002; Shore, 2013).

In a review of 65 papers reporting on videoconferencing psychotherapy, Backhaus et al. (2012) conclude that it is feasible, acceptable, and typically associated with similar outcomes to face-to-face therapies. Where it was measured, Backhaus et al. found that the quality of the therapeutic relationships developed through videoconference interactions was also comparable with that in face-to-face interventions.

E-therapy

E-therapy, such as via email or online chat, provides another potential form of communication between therapists and clients. These methods have been demonstrated to be efficacious and cost-effective in a number of well-designed treatment studies (e.g. Hollinghurst et al., 2010; Kessler et al., 2009). However, there are also some limitations to online communication: it relies on the therapist's and client's ability to articulate themselves in written language, and it may increase opportunities for miscommunication in the absence of nonverbal cues (Rochlen, Zack, & Speyer, 2004).

Self-help

NICE (2004b) describes **self-help** as 'a self-administered intervention ... which makes use of a range of books or a self-help manual that is based on an evidence-based intervention and is designed specifically for the purpose' (p. 358). In addition to books and manuals, self-help interventions can be delivered by computer program, via an app, or in other multimedia formats. Most published studies of self-help have explored interventions based on the principles of CBT (see Bennett-Levy, Richards, & Farrand, 2010); however, mindfulness and acceptance approaches have also been explored (Cavanagh, Strauss, Forder, & Jones, 2014).

Self-help resources can be used either without any professional support or with support from a coach or therapist (Coull & Morris, 2011; Newman, Szkodny, Llera, & Przeworski, 2011). There is some evidence that guided self-help is more effective than unguided self-help for common problems such as anxiety and depression (Gellatly et al., 2007; Richards & Richardson, 2012).

NICE currently recommends that self-help interventions based on the principles of CBT should be offered as a treatment choice to people experiencing mild to moderate depression, panic disorder, generalized anxiety disorder, and obsessive compulsive disorder (NICE, 2011). Computerized CBT is also recommended as a treatment choice for people experiencing mild to moderate depression and phobias (see Focus Point 16.5).

COMPUTERIZED COGNITIVE BEHAVIOURAL THERAPY

Computerized cognitive behavioural therapy (CCBT) has been developed as an alternative to therapist-delivered CBT and consists of highly developed software packages that can be delivered online with support available from trained helpers via telephone calls or emails throughout treatment. For example, **Beating the Blues** consists of a 15-minute introductory video and eight 1-hour interactive sessions, and includes homework to be completed between sessions. The program helps clients to identify thinking errors, evaluate negative thoughts, and explore their core beliefs, and it provides help and advice on more adaptive thinking styles. **FearFighter** is a CBT-based package for phobic, panic, and anxiety disorders and is divided into nine steps. The package helps clients to identify specific problems, develop realistic treatment goals, and monitor achievement through graded exposure.

Studies comparing CCBT with other forms of support and intervention suggest that CCBT can be a valuable and effective way of treating individuals with common mental health problems (Grist & Cavanagh, 2013). However, there are still issues surrounding client engagement with CCBT. Clearly, clients need to have an adequate knowledge of computers and they may often view CCBT as both mechanical and impersonal (Beattie, Shaw, Kaur, & Kessler, 2009). CCBT may also lack some of the ingredients of successful therapy that are a function of the therapeutic relationship between therapist and client (Dogg-Helgadottir, Menzies, Onslow, Packman, & O'Brian, 2009). However, there are indications that it may be possible to incorporate these important ingredients of the **therapeutic alliance** into self-help programmes such as CCBT (Barazzone, Cavanagh, & Richards, 2012).

SECTION SUMMARY

- Most of the various kinds of psychological therapy were developed and are typically offered in a one-to-one therapy model.

- However, this is not the only approach to offering therapy; some therapies are offered in alternative ways – for example, in group therapies, teletherapies, internet interventions, and guided or unguided self-help formats.

- Computerized CBT has been established as an alternative to therapist-delivered CBT and consists of highly developed software packages that can be delivered online with support available from trained helpers via telephone calls or emails throughout treatment. Examples include Beating the Blues and FearFighter.

SOCIAL AND ENVIRONMENTAL APPROACHES TO TREATMENT

LEARNING OBJECTIVE 16.4

Compare and contrast a range of social and environmental approaches to the treatment of mental health problems.

Social and environmental approaches to treatment consider the role of people's circumstances in their well-being and draw on social and environmental resources to reduce distress and promote positive change.

Social group interventions

Having a supportive social network is believed to offer important protection against mental health problems, and also to be a powerful promoter of recovery. Conversely, social isolation might be a risk factor for both the onset and the duration of mental health problems (Brown & Harris, 1978; Brown, Adler, & Bifulco, 1988). To counteract these effects, social group interventions may have some positive effects for people with depression who are also socially isolated (e.g. Gater et al., 2010).

Community psychology interventions

Community psychology is a branch of psychology that focuses on how individuals relate to society at large. It takes into account the broader social determinants of health and well-being, such as the impact of socioeconomic and resource inequalities on communities or the distress caused by the internalization of discrimination and powerlessness as a consequence of issues such as poverty, classism, sexism, racism, homophobia, or ableism (Levine, Perkins, & Perkins, 2004). Community psychologists go beyond an individual focus and integrate social, cultural, economic, political, environmental, and international influences to promote positive change, health, and empowerment (an example of a body that takes this approach is the Society for Community Research and Action).

Community psychologists work in schools and colleges, health and social care agencies, and public-policy and third-sector organizations. The approach encourages psychologists to work in partnership with marginalized communities and to facilitate interventions that empower and try to overcome these broader origins of distress. Emphasis is put on improving quality of access to resources, drawing on the strengths and assets of a community, creating policy and systems change, and raising people's consciousness of the wider social forces that have an impact on their well-being and the well-being of people around them (see Focus Point 16.6).

MAC-UK AND THE APPLICATION OF THE 'INTEGRATE' MODEL TO WORKING WITH YOUNG PEOPLE INVOLVED IN GANGS

MAC-UK is a charity organization that works with excluded young people aged 16–25. It aims to make evidence-based services more flexible, accessible, and relevant to the needs of young people in disadvantaged communities.

Applying the evidence-based 'Integrate' approach, MAC-UK practitioners engage with and work alongside a whole peer group of young people in their own community, through hanging out in places such as youth centres or local housing estates. Practitioners get to know young people over years to build trust, engaging in youth-led activities such as music creation, film making, sport, and trips. As collaborative relationships develop, staff use their clinical skills through 'Streetherapy' to offer support to young people with issues such as substance misuse, feelings of hopelessness or anger, trauma, low concentration, lack of confidence, low social skills development, lack of employability skills, and so forth. Ultimately, the aim is to help young people into other services they may want or need and to support them to discover a different life for themselves, by improving access to employment, education, and training.

Cultural and gender issues in psychological therapies

Cultural issues

So far in this chapter we have referred largely to generic interventions developed to target broad mental health problems. But can one size fit all? Mental health problems are a global phenomenon and treatments for them, including psychological therapies, must adapt to meet the needs of culturally diverse populations, both within and between countries (Sue, Zane, Hall, & Berger, 2009). Cultural competency requires psychological therapists to develop an awareness of their own cultural identity and that of their client, to acquire specific knowledge about the population they are working with, and to use this information to inform their use of translated, adapted, or culturally specific interventions likely to be of most benefit to that group. Interventions should be offered with skill and attunement to the individual client whatever their cultural background. Culturally adapted interventions appear to be more effective than generic approaches for adult populations (Griner & Smith, 2006), although further research is needed (Sue et al., 2009).

Gender issues

Common mental health problems such as anxiety and depression appear to be more common in women than men (Office for National Statistics, 2001), while alcohol and substance use problems are more common in men. Gender stereotypes may underlie some bias in the detection and treatment of mental health difficulties between genders. For example, even when presenting with identical symptoms, women are more likely to be diagnosed as depressed than men (Bertakis et al., 2001; Stoppe, Sandholzer, Huppertz, Duwe, & Staedt, 1999).

Gender biases are also evident in treatment seeking. Women are more likely to disclose and seek help for mental health problems in primary care, and they are more likely to be treated for a mental health problem than men. For example, women are more likely than men to be prescribed psychotropic medication even when demographic factors, socioeconomic factors, and diagnosis are taken into account (Simoni-Wastila, 2000). There is also a popular belief that women are more likely to benefit from psychological therapies than men, based on the idea that women are more relational and empathetic. However, the evidence to underpin this idea is scant and mixed findings are evident (Nadelson, Notman, & McCarthy, 2007).

TEST YOURSELF

1. What is behavioural activation, and what is it a recommended treatment for?
2. Can you describe three different ways of delivering psychological therapies?
3. How might gender stereotypes affect the treatment of mental health problems?

SECTION SUMMARY

- Social and environmental approaches to treatment consider the role of people's circumstances in their well-being.
- Having a supportive social network is believed to offer important protection against mental health problems and also to be a powerful promoter of recovery.
- Community psychology interventions integrate social, cultural, economic, political, environmental, and international influences to promote positive change, health, and empowerment.

- Wide cultural diversity means that therapists and researchers must develop strong cultural competency in the effective design and delivery of treatments for mental health problems.
- Gender stereotypes may underlie some bias in the detection and treatment of mental health difficulties between men and women.

BIOLOGICAL APPROACHES TO TREATMENT

LEARNING OBJECTIVE 16.5

Compare and contrast the use of different drug therapies and electroconvulsive therapy in the treatment of mental health problems.

While there is growing evidence that psychological interventions can be beneficial for many people experiencing mental health challenges, these may not be available to, or not preferred by, everyone seeking help. Pharmacological (or drug) treatments are often offered as an additional or alternative treatment option for people facing mental health challenges.

Some of the most commonly used types of drug treatments are antidepressant drugs (which are primarily used for the treatment of depression and mood disorders), anxiolytic drugs (which are used primarily to treat symptoms of anxiety and stress), and antipsychotic drugs (which are primarily used to treat symptoms of psychosis – for example, for people with a diagnosis of schizophrenia).

Antidepressant drugs

There are three main types of **antidepressant**: the tricyclics **monoamine oxidase inhibitors (MAOIs)**, **selective serotonin reuptake inhibitors (SSRIs)**, and **serotonin–norepinephrine reuptake inhibitors (SNRIs)**. It is thought antidepressants work by increasing levels of a group of chemicals in the brain called neurotransmitters. Certain neurotransmitters, such as serotonin and norepinephrine, are associated with variations in mood and emotion, although this process is not fully understood.

Antidepressant medications usually need to be taken regularly for 2–4 weeks before any benefit is felt, and a course of treatment usually lasts for around 6 months, although it may be longer for people with a history of previous episodes of depression. The Health and Social Care Information Centre recorded more than 50 million prescriptions of antidepressant drugs in England in 2012, with antidepressant use increasing since the 1980s across Europe (Gusmão et al., 2013). The Royal College of Psychiatrists (2015) estimates that 50–65% of people treated with antidepressant medication for depression see an improvement in their symptoms. Antidepressant medications are also sometimes used for the treatment of anxiety disorders such as obsessive compulsive disorder, generalized anxiety disorder, and post-traumatic stress disorder.

People taking antidepressant medication quite commonly experience side effects such as feeling sick, dry mouth, drowsiness, dizziness, diarrhoea or constipation, and loss of libido (sexual appetite). These unpleasant side effects alongside the delay in felt benefits of antidepressants lead many people to stop taking this medication. It is estimated that around one third of those who are prescribed antidepressants stop taking the drug within the first month.

While antidepressants are not thought to be addictive, sudden withdrawal of antidepressant medication is not recommended. At the end of a treatment period, medication use is often tapered (decreasing doses taken over a set period of time). This is because discontinuation effects of sudden withdrawal from medication have been reported, such as a rapid rebound of depressive symptoms, fatigue, irritability, anxiety, flu-like symptoms, and insomnia.

Antidepressant medications are not recommended as a first-line treatment for mild depression by NICE (2009), as there is evidence that they are only effective for people experiencing more severe symptoms (Fournier et al., 2010; Kirsch et al., 2008). While antidepressants can help to treat the symptoms of depression, they do not always address its causes. This is why it is recommended that they are usually used in combination with psychological therapy to treat more severe depression or other mental health conditions.

FOCUS POINT 16.7

SSRIS AND SUICIDE RISK

There has been a long-standing controversy about the possible link between selective serotonin reuptake inhibitors (SSRIs) and suicidality in some patients (Reeves & Ladner, 2010). Case studies describing increased agitation, worsening symptoms, and suicidality shortly following initiation of SSRIs have brought this issue to the attention of both the medical community and the world at large.

In 2009, a review by Stone and colleagues concluded that risk of suicidal acts and behaviour is age-related and specifically increases with the use of SSRIs or serotonin–norepinephrine reuptake inhibitors (SNRIs) in young people aged up to 25. This risk is greatest in the early stages of treatment and this may be because it can take 2 weeks or longer for these medications to have their antidepressant effects (Stone et al., 2009). Due to these risks, the following information is given in all packets of SSRIs and SNRIs in the United Kingdom, United States, and elsewhere:

> If you have thoughts of harming or killing yourself at anytime, contact your doctor or go to a hospital straight away. You may find it helpful to tell a relative or close friend that you are depressed or have an anxiety disorder and ask them to read this leaflet. You might ask them to tell you if they think your depression or anxiety is getting worse, or they are worried about changes in your behaviour.

You can read a summary of the study and news stories related to it at NHS Choices (2009).

Increased risk of suicidality is also found for children and adolescents taking antidepressant medication, and caution is advised in prescribing to this age group (Hetrick, McKenzie, Cox, Simmons, & Merry, 2012).

Anxiolytic drugs

If self-help and psychological therapies have not helped with anxiety, or if patients express a preference for medication, then doctors may prescribe two different types of medication to treat anxiety. The most common **anxiolytics** prescribed for the short-term management of anxiety symptoms are **benzodiazepines** (tranquillizers). While benzodiazepines can be effective in reducing symptoms of anxiety, they can be addictive; they have common side effects including drowsiness, clumsiness, slurred speech, and confusion; and they do not treat the causes of the anxiety symptoms.

Some medications, such as benzodiazepines, when taken regularly, can lead to physical dependence (addiction) quite quickly. Drug tolerance effects are also common, with increasingly large doses needed to get the same anxiety relief as before. When people become physically dependent on medication, it is difficult to stop taking it and they may experience unpleasant withdrawal effects if they do, which can encourage a return to taking the medication. Breaking this cycle of medication use can be difficult and unfortunately, because of this, many people continue to take this medication far beyond its intended treatment duration. For these reasons, benzodiazepines are only recommended to be used as a short-term measure during crises (NICE, 2011).

Longer-term medications are also used to treat anxiety problems such as generalized anxiety disorder and panic disorder in adults. These include SSRIs and SNRIs, which can be effective and are recommended by NICE for some people with these disorders (NICE, 2011).

Antipsychotic drugs

Antipsychotics can be helpful in reducing psychotic experiences and the distress associated with these experiences for some people, although approximately 40% of people are 'treatment resistant' and continue to experience these symptoms despite adequate medication. These medications are thought to work by changing the effects of chemicals in the brain including dopamine, serotonin, norepinephrine, and acetylcholine, although their effectiveness is often associated with their affinity for and impact on dopamine receptors. Current NICE guidelines suggest medication should be considered for all people with psychosis, and, where there is evidence of equal efficacy between 'typical' (older) and 'atypical' (newer) antipsychotics, side-effect profiles should govern treatment choice.

Taking any antipsychotic medication can be associated with unpleasant side effects including dry mouth, blurred vision, flushing, and constipation. Typical antipsychotics are also associated with movement disorders including tremor, stiffness, restlessness, and involuntary movements (known as 'extrapyramidal' side effects). Atypical antipsychotics are particularly associated with weight gain, changes in glucose and lipid metabolism, the risk of diabetes (metabolic side effects), and other hormonal changes.

A focus on physical health interventions for psychosis has emerged as a result of the strong and growing evidence for the physical health costs linked to antipsychotic medication, with people with psychosis dying up to 20 years earlier than the general population. The strongest evidence for interventions to counter these effects are for physical health programmes that combine exercise-based interventions with psychoeducation programmes to promote healthy eating.

Problems with drug treatments

All drugs have side effects, some of them unpleasant. Some drugs may also carry an associated risk. For example, lithium, which is used to treat bipolar disorder, can be toxic. Before starting medication, it is important that side effects and risks associated with a particular drug are communicated clearly, and that review appointments are scheduled to check progress and identify any difficulties with a prescribed medicine.

Offering drug treatments alone for mental health problems may also be problematic for other reasons. First, many people do not respond to drug treatment or do not recover fully using drug treatment alone. Second, long-term prescription of drugs for a psychopathology may lead sufferers to believe that their symptoms are unchangeable by any other means and that their daily functioning is dependent on them continuing to take their medication. This can prevent people from trying to understand their symptoms or learning to respond to them differently. Finally, there is some evidence that, while drug treatment of psychopathology may alleviate the immediate symptoms, it may worsen the long-term course of a disorder. For example, while antidepressant drugs may alleviate the immediate symptoms of depression, there is evidence that they may also increase vulnerability to relapse over the longer term (Fava, 2003).

Electroconvulsive therapy

Electroconvulsive therapy (ECT) involves sending an electric current through the brain to trigger a seizure and is delivered under general anaesthetic over a course of treatment episodes lasting several weeks. The aim of ECT, in most cases, is to relieve severe and complex depression that has not responded to other kinds of treatment, including medication and talking treatments. ECT can lead to memory loss, along with other side effects including drowsiness, confusion, headache, and feeling sick, and these costs must be balanced against potential benefits in making treatment decisions. NICE (2009) recommends that ECT be considered as a treatment choice where severe depression is life threatening and a rapid response is required. Read and Bentall (2010) present an alternative review and interpretation of the literature, which finds limited evidence of sustainable benefits from ECT and strong evidence of persistent amnesias and slight but significant increased risk of death as a consequence of ECT; these authors conclude that its use cannot be scientifically justified.

DISCUSSION POINT

Electroconvulsive therapy is a controversial therapy in many countries. Discuss the benefits and drawbacks of this therapy and give your opinions on its use.

SECTION SUMMARY

- Biological approaches to treating mental health problems include both drug treatments and other methods such as electroconvulsive therapy (ECT).
- Drug treatments are commonly used to treat the symptoms of a range of mental health problems including depression, anxiety, and psychosis.
- These drug treatments may be offered alone or in combination with psychological therapies.
- While several drug treatments may be helpful in treating mental health problems or reducing the distress associated with their symptoms, adverse side effects are also common.
- ECT is recommended by NICE as a treatment choice only for those with severe, life-threatening depression.

EVALUATING TREATMENTS FOR MENTAL HEALTH PROBLEMS

LEARNING OBJECTIVE 16.6

Evaluate the various therapies implemented in the treatment of mental health problems.

So far we have explored a number of different kinds of treatment for mental health problems, but how do we know if a treatment is effective? This may not be as simple as it sounds at first – different people have different ideas about what it means for a treatment to be effective, and measuring these outcomes and drawing confident conclusions about the causal effects of the interventions on measured outcomes is not always straightforward.

Different schools of thought can have quite different assumptions about what 'successful treatment' is. Psychodynamic and humanistic therapies consider insight and personal development to be optimal therapy outcomes, whereas cognitive and behavioural therapists are more likely to be looking for symptom reduction and personal goal achievement. Recovery-oriented practice promotes the idea that building a meaningful and satisfying life should be the primary treatment goal (Shepherd, Boardman, & Slade, 2008) (see Focus Point 16.8).

FOCUS POINT 16.8

RECOVERY-ORIENTED PRACTICE

Recovery is about building a meaningful and satisfying life, as defined by the person themselves, whether or not there are ongoing or recurring symptoms or problems.

(Shepherd, Boardman, & Slade, 2008, p. ii)

Recovery is personal, and people define and experience it for themselves. A discourse on recovery has been developed by people with lived experience of mental health challenges. They identify common features of recovery journeys: hope and the possibility of reaching personal goals and ambitions, taking back control of symptoms and life, developing valued roles and relationships, grieving what's been lost, finding meaning and purpose, and having the opportunity to do the things they value to build a life beyond illness.

Recovery is a philosophical orientation. Mental health practitioners cannot make someone recover although they can hinder or support the process. They can support someone's recovery as partners or coaches, by promoting self-management, valuing lived expertise, and supporting people to reach their personal life goals and improve their quality of life.

One example of a recovery-oriented service is Sussex Recovery College, which is a joint venture between Sussex Partnership NHS Foundation Trust and local voluntary-sector organizations (Meddings, Byrne, Barnicoat, Campbell, & Locks, 2014). It provides mental health, well-being, and recovery-focused education for people with mental health challenges, their friends and families, and staff. All courses are co-produced and co-facilitated by peer trainers with personal experience of mental health challenges alongside trainers whose expertise comes from professional training. Courses including mindfulness, managing anxiety, improving your sleep (using cognitive behavioural therapy), happiness, and understanding your diagnosis can support students to understand, self-manage, and recover from mental health challenges. People choose which courses to take from a prospectus and graduate with a certificate on completion. Evidence from the initial cohort suggests that the students were highly satisfied with the college and made significant progress towards their personal goals and improvements in recovery, well-being, and quality of life.

You can find out more about recovery at the website of **Implementing Recovery through Organisational Change (ImROC)**[5].

In the United Kingdom, NICE recommends treatments for specific mental health problems on the basis of their clinical and cost-effectiveness, which are estimated drawing on evidence from both research studies and clinical expertise.

Lambert (2013) suggests that the following questions are necessary in order to evaluate the benefits of psychological therapy:

1. Is it efficacious?
2. Do the benefits of therapy exceed placebo effects?
3. Do patients make changes that are clinically meaningful?
4. Do patients maintain their gains?
5. How much therapy is necessary?
6. Do some patients get worse?
7. Do the treatment effects generalize to routine care settings?

The same questions are relevant for pharmacological and other medical treatments, as well as for social and environmental interventions. We will now examine each of these questions in turn.

Is it efficacious?

What kind of evidence would you need to convince you that a treatment were effective? Would you accept the opinion of a doctor or therapist who offered that kind of treatment? Would it be enough to see evidence that a single person had benefited from the treatment, or would you want to see the treatment's effects generalized to a larger sample? Would it be good enough to know that this intervention was more effective than no treatment for that group of people, or would you want to know that the intervention was at least as effective as other interventions that might be available for that group of people (e.g. other kinds of psychological therapy, medication, or social intervention)? Would you be satisfied with evidence from just one large study of the treatment's effects, or would you want to see multiple studies by different researchers each independently supporting the intervention?

Each of these 'levels of evidence' forms a layer of an important hierarchy that is commonly used to evaluate the evidence base for psychological therapies (see Figure 16.2). Evidence from higher up the ladder in favour of the intervention provides stronger support for the treatment's efficacy.

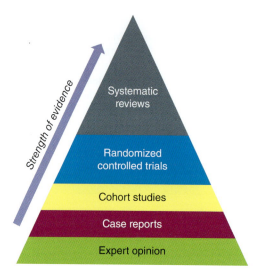

FIGURE 16.2 *Hierarchy of evidence.*

Source: Adapted and reprinted from Sackett, Straus, Richardson, Rosenberg, and Haynes (2000), with permission of Elsevier.

The development of the evidence base for a new psychological treatment typically ascends this evidence hierarchy, beginning with the conviction of one or more therapists as to the treatment's likely effects, followed by research into the intervention's effects first with one or more single individuals (or 'cases'), and, if these indicate positive effects, moving on to larger cohort studies (before–after designs), and then randomized controlled trials of the intervention may be conducted to test its efficacy in controlled conditions. When two or more randomized controlled trials have been conducted, evidence from these, alongside information from studies at other points of the hierarchy, can be considered in a **systematic review** – a kind of literature review with the aim of fully surveying all of the available research evidence relevant to the research question – to draw definitive conclusions about the likely benefits of the intervention. The conclusions of a systematic review may be supported by a **meta-analysis** – a statistical technique for combining the findings across multiple studies.

What are randomized controlled trials?

The current methodology of choice for assessing the effectiveness of therapies is the **randomized controlled trial (RCT)** (e.g. see Barker, Pistrang, & Elliott, 2002, pp. 153–159). This procedure compares the effectiveness of the treatment being assessed with a variety of control conditions. Participants in an RCT are assigned randomly to one of these conditions. Common control conditions include:

- a no-treatment or a **waiting-list control** group of participants who will receive no treatment (to control for the effects of **spontaneous remission**); this condition is often difficult to achieve because of the ethical issues involved in withholding treatment from clinically distressed individuals

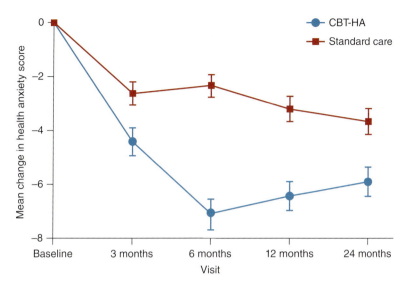

FIGURE 16.3 *Mean change in health anxiety score (± standard error) by treatment. CBT-HA = cognitive behavioural therapy for health anxiety.*

Source: Reprinted from Tyrer et al. (2014), with permission of Elsevier.

- an expectancy and relationship control group, to control for placebo effects (which are discussed in the following section) and for the beneficial effects of contact with a therapist
- a comparative treatment group, in which the original therapy can be compared with an alternative treatment that is known to have beneficial effects.

For the original therapy to be deemed effective, participants receiving that therapy must show greater improvement than those in both the no-treatment and the expectancy and relationship control conditions, and improvement that is at least equivalent to that exhibited by the comparative treatment group.

Figure 16.3 provides a schematic example of an RCT study comparing the effectiveness of CBT for health anxiety with standard care. It shows a significant difference in health anxiety change scores between groups and over time favouring the CBT condition.

What are meta-analyses?

Meta-analysis is a statistical technique for combining the findings from independent studies and it is most commonly used to assess the effectiveness of healthcare interventions by combining data from two or more RCTs (Crombie & Davies, 2009). By combining data from multiple studies, we can increase our confidence in the magnitude and generalizability of the treatment's effects.

Meta-analysis has been applied to the overarching questions about the benefits of psychological therapies. In Figure 16.4, you can see data from a number of studies all testing the same research hypotheses. Each row represents data from a separate study, and the large diamond at the bottom of the forest plot tells you about the overall effect. Here we can see that although individual studies comparing short-term psychodynamic psychotherapy (STPP) with other psychotherapies have found mixed results, the combined effect of these studies indicates that STPP is less efficacious than alternative interventions.

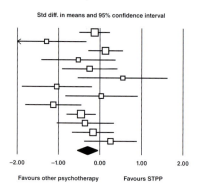

Study name	Subgroup within study	Comparison		Std diff. in means	Lower limit	Upper limit	P-value
Barkham, 1999	Blank	CBT	BDI	−0.13	−0.50	0.23	0.48
Carrington, 1979	Blank	CBT	Combined	−1.29	−2.25	−0.33	0.01
Cooper, 2003	Blank	Combined	EPDS	0.13	−0.28	0.55	0.54
Gallagher, 1982	Blank	Combined	Combined	−0.52	−1.42	0.37	0.25
Gilbert, 1982	Blank	CT	ZDS	−0.25	−0.92	0.42	0.47
Kornblith, 1983	Blank	Combined	Combined	0.55	−0.53	1.62	0.32
Liberman, 1981	Blank	BT	Combined	−1.04	−1.89	−0.19	0.02
Maina, 2005	Blank	ST	HAMD	0.03	−0.84	0.91	0.94
Morris, 1975	Combined	SMD	ZDS	−1.12	−1.81	−0.44	0.00
Shapiro, 1994	Combined	CBT	Combined	−0.45	−0.81	−0.10	0.01
Steuer, 1984	Blank	CBT	Combined	−0.35	−1.05	0.34	0.31
Thompson, 1987	Blank	Combined	Combined	−0.17	−0.67	0.34	0.52
Thyme, 2007	Blank	STPP-art	Combined	0.26	0.38	0.89	0.43
				−0.30	0.54	−0.06	0.02

FIGURE 16.4 *Three short-term psychodynamic psychotherapies versus other psychotherapies at post-treatment. BDI = Beck Depression Inventory; BT = behavioural therapy; CBT = cognitive behavioural therapy; CT = cognitive therapy; EPDS = Edinburgh Postnatal Depression Scale; HAMD = Hamilton Depression Rating Scale; SMD = Self-Instruction Method for Depression; ST = Supporting Therapy; Std diff. = standardized mean difference; STTP-art = Short-term Psychodynamic Psychotherapy–Art; ZDS = Zung Depression Scale. See original source for details of the 13 studies being compared.*
Source: Reprinted from Driessen et al. (2010), with permission of Elsevier.

THE DODO BIRD VERDICT

Source: John Tenniel's illustration for 'The Pool of Tears', 1865. An illustration from *Alice in Wonderland*.

Numerous important studies have suggested that, although psychotherapies are more effective in treating mental health problems than placebos and other control conditions, no psychotherapy is more effective than any other psychotherapy (Luborsky, Singer, & Luborsky, 1975; Smith, Glass, & Miller, 1980). As early as 1936, Saul Rosenzweig (1936/2010) labelled this effect the **Dodo Bird Verdict** after the bird in Lewis Carroll's *Alice's Adventures in Wonderland*. In that story, a number of animals had become wet and in order to dry themselves ran around the lake to see who could get dry first. No one measured how far they'd run or for how long; however, when asked who had won, the Dodo Bird said, 'Everybody has won and all must have prizes!'

Those who agree with the Dodo Bird Verdict claim that all psychotherapies are equally effective because they all contain important common factors that are shared across all psychotherapeutic interventions. This is known as the common factors theory, and Grencavage and Norcross (1990) identified up to 35 common factors across psychotherapies that influence therapeutic outcome. One of the most important common factors affecting outcome is the therapist–client relationship, known as the therapeutic alliance (Horvath, Del Re, Flückiger, & Symonds, 2011). Apart from the therapeutic alliance itself, specific therapist factors have also been identified as contributing to the success of therapy, such as positive, warm, and caring attitudes towards the client (Najavits & Strupp, 1994) as well as providing good feedback, helping clients to focus on and understand their own thoughts, attempting to promote autonomy and self-efficacy in clients, and helping clients with their existing relationships (Korchin & Sands, 1983).

However, there is also evidence that can be mustered in favour of the specific effects of different psychotherapies, and the Dodo Bird Verdict debate is consequently still very much alive (Siev & Chambless, 2009; Wampold, Imel, & Miller, 2009).

Do the benefits exceed placebo effects?

It has long been known that, if you give someone a pill that you tell them will have an effect on them, it typically will – even if it is just a sugar pill with no active ingredients. This effect is known as the **placebo effect** and it suggests that individuals will often get better because they expect to get better – even though the actual treatment that they have been given is effectively useless (Paul, 1966). Thus, it may be the case that many psychological treatments have beneficial effects simply because the client expects them to work – not because they are treatments that are effective in tackling the factors maintaining the psychopathology. However, comparative studies of placebo effects with actual structured psychotherapies strongly suggest that structured psychotherapies lead to greater improvement than placebo control conditions (Andrews & Harvey, 1981; Robinson, Berman, & Neimeyer, 1990).

We also know that people with psychological problems show some improvement in symptoms when they can simply talk about their problems in an unstructured way with either a professional therapist or a friend or relative (Lambert, Shapiro, & Bergin, 1986). This suggests that many forms of social support may have a therapeutic effect in and of themselves (Borkovec & Costello, 1993) and this factor must be taken into account when judging how effective a structured therapy is. One of the important things that we want to find out about therapies is not just whether they are effective in making people better but whether they make people better specifically because of the principles they contain.

Consequently, studies that attempt to evaluate the effectiveness of a therapy's principles also need to control for other factors, such as the amount of attention or empathy that the client is receiving from the therapist. One recently developed form of control condition for attention, understanding, and caring is known as **befriending**. This is a control condition designed to provide participants with approximately the same amount of therapist contact as the treatment conditions being tested, with sessions spaced at similar intervals. In the befriending condition the therapist aims to be empathetic and nondirective and does not attempt to tackle symptoms directly; the session is normally focused on the discussion of neutral topics such as hobbies, sport, and current affairs (Sensky et al., 2000).

DISCUSSION POINT

Discuss how the placebo effect works. Have you ever experienced it yourself? How did it affect you?

Do patients make changes that are clinically meaningful?

Now imagine that we have looked at the evidence for a psychological therapy and it appears to have performed well in an RCT, being significantly better than a well-designed control condition. So, 'it works!', right? Well, not necessarily. What if it were statistically better than no therapy but the real size of the benefit was hardly noticeable – for example, imagine a diet that could successfully help people to lose half a kilogram, but never more than that. Now this could be a real effect – a genuine measurable difference in weight between those on the diet and those not – but in real terms it is unlikely that this would meet the dieters' goals and it would have little impact on their appearance, health, or functioning. The same is true for psychological outcome measures: for an intervention to be considered beneficial, we would want to see it leading to a change that had a real impact on the individual and their loved ones, and lead to greater well-being and improved functioning.

So, how do we decide whether a treatment is having a large enough effect to be clinically meaningful? **Clinical significance** is one commonly used indicator. That is, we measure whether the participants exhibit recovery or change to the point where they no longer meet the criteria for clinical diagnosis (Jacobson & Truax, 1991).

While most structured interventions are more effective than **no-treatment control** conditions, a look at the **recovery rate** (the percentage of people who are no longer diagnosable once they have finished treatment) often suggests a less than perfect picture. Even for well-established psychological and pharmaceutical interventions, recovery rates for common mental health problems are normally between 50% and 70% (e.g. Baldwin, Woods, Lawson, & Taylor, 2011; Craske, Liao, Brown, & Vervliet, 2012; Hanrahan, Field, Jones, & Davey, 2013), suggesting that such interventions fail to 'cure' between 30% and 50% of those being treated. This probably testifies more to the complexity of many mental health problems and the factors that maintain psychopathology than the relative ineffectiveness of our current interventions. But clearly more needs to be done to develop interventions that will help larger proportions of sufferers to fully recover. See Davey (2012) for further discussion on this topic.

Do patients maintain their gains?

There is a significant body of evidence that psychological therapies can be effective in the short term, but what is the evidence of their longer-term effects? In order for us to consider a treatment to be truly effective, we would want to know to what extent its effects last over time. Do people who respond to the therapy stay well? What is the rate of relapse or recurrence of problems over time associated with this therapy in comparison to other therapies, or even in comparison to no treatment at all?

Smit et al. (2012) evaluated the long-term effects of psychoanalysis and long-term psychoanalytic psychotherapy in comparison to other treatments or no treatment at all and concluded that the recovery rate of various mental health problems was not greater for psychoanalysis and long-term psychoanalytic psychotherapy than for various control treatments, including treatment as usual. In the case of CBT, there is evidence of effectiveness in the long term against relapse and recurrence across a range of presenting difficulties (Butler et al., 2006). In the case of depression, several studies have concluded that CBT has better long-term effects than antidepressant medication (NICE, 2009).

How much therapy is necessary?

Different psychological therapy approaches advocate varying amounts of therapy that might be required to meet treatment goals. For example, long-term psychoanalytic therapies are often intended to last several years, while many cognitive behavioural therapies are designed to last between 16 and 24 sessions delivered over 6 months to 1 year. Some briefer therapies are designed to be delivered in just 6–8 weeks. The length of these interventions is based on a range of factors including the treatment goal, problem severity, chronicity, and complexity. However, relatively few studies have explored the idea of the optimal treatment 'dosage' to facilitate meaningful change (Hansen, Lambert, & Forman, 2002). A recent meta-analysis exploring the impact of the amount, frequency, and intensity of therapy for depression (Cuijpers, Huibers, Ebert, Koole, & Andersson, 2013) found no association between amount or duration of therapy and therapy outcomes for depression, but did find that two sessions a week appeared to be more effective than less frequent contact.

While some studies have found that more therapy is more effective (Shadish, Navarro, Matt, & Phillips, 2000), a classic meta-analysis (Howard, Kopta, Krause, & Orlinsky, 1986) identified a negatively accelerating improvement curve over the course of treatment length. Based on these findings the authors argued that, because about 75% of clients had shown some benefit after 26 sessions, and the increased rate of improvement would be relatively low over subsequent sessions, 26 sessions might be a 'rational time limit' (p. 163) for psychotherapy. However, more recent studies have challenged this account, suggesting that time limits for treatment uniform to all clients are unlikely to meet clients' differing needs.

Do some patients get worse?

In the case of pharmacological and other medical interventions, information about possible side effects or adverse reactions is usually a prominent feature of their packaging and marketing material. But no such warnings typically exist for psychological therapies. We must ask, can psychological therapies be harmful? Might symptoms

become worse over the course of therapy, or might new problems emerge as a consequence of psychological interventions? On closer inspection it seems logical that anything that is powerful enough to change the way we think and feel about ourselves
and the world could, if applied without care, lead to negative consequences (Barlow,
2010; Lilienfeld, 2007).

One example of this is critical incident stress debriefing (CISD). This is a therapeutic technique designed to help people immediately after experiencing a trauma
in their lives (such as a natural disaster or car accident). The common wisdom is that
counselling immediately after a trauma is likely to be beneficial to the victims. But
what the research has found is that CISD may actually impede natural recovery, at
least for some people (McNally, Bryant, & Ehlers, 2003).

Lilienfeld (2007) suggests an evidence-based list of potentially harmful therapies –
including CISD, recovered memory techniques, grief counselling for individuals with
normal bereavement reactions, and boot-camp interventions for conduct disorder –
and argues that, in order to take reasonable steps to avoid harm, psychologists need
to become more aware of the risks associated with some interventions.

Do the treatment effects generalize to routine care settings?

'Efficacy' refers to the extent to which an intervention can produce a beneficial outcome
under ideal circumstances. For example, an RCT where a strict protocol is adhered to
and only certain types of people are suitable for inclusion (e.g. people who have the
diagnosis of a single anxiety disorder and no other comorbid diagnoses – although having a comorbid diagnosis is in fact very common) is an efficacy trial.

'Effectiveness' refers to the extent to which an intervention produces beneficial
outcomes under ordinary day-to-day circumstances. This reflects 'real-life' conditions. An intervention may appear to work in an efficacy trial but be found to be less
effective or ineffective in ordinary day-to-day situations. In efficacy trials, there is
often careful monitoring throughout the trial; clients may be carefully selected and
have frequent contact with study personnel. These conditions are not necessarily met
in effectiveness trials or real-world healthcare contexts.

Trials of effectiveness often include a much broader spectrum of clients more
accurately reflecting the type of client who may come forward for treatment in a
routine care situation. Outcomes from effectiveness studies are often less supportive
of therapeutic interventions in real-world settings than in controlled research studies. Meta-analyses suggest that drop-out rates are higher in real-world studies (Swift
& Greenberg, 2012) and the effects of treatments may be inferior to those found in
RCTs for both individual and group treatments (Hans & Hiller, 2013).

Such effectiveness studies suggest that we should be cautious in drawing conclusions about the real-world effects of psychological therapies from efficacy studies, and
that these should be followed up with the scrutiny of **practice-based evidence** where
psychological interventions are implemented in routine care.

In addition to measures of the real-world effects of treatment methods, practice-
based evidence can, importantly, measure the acceptability of and preference for interventions in routine care. Acceptability and preference may be measured by self-report
of service users, carers, and health professionals and also through proxy measures such
as uptake, engagement, and drop-out from treatment. Some treatment methods that
are found to be highly effective in research studies may be acceptable only to a minority of service users in routine care, which may limit their impact in the real world.

Cost-effectiveness

Up to this point we have focused our attention on the 'clinical effectiveness' of psychological therapies – that is, the measurement of the effects of psychological therapies on target outcomes such as distress, maladaptive behaviours, and other symptoms. While such clinical benefits are likely to be of primary importance to the individual accessing the intervention, the feasibility of offering psychological therapies may to some extent be limited by their cost-effectiveness. Cost-effectiveness analysis considers the health benefits associated with an intervention in light of intervention costs. Healthcare costs are an increasingly important economic and political issue. The goal of cost-effectiveness research is to support healthcare service users, providers, and policymakers to make more rational decisions about clinical care and resource allocation (Cohen & Reynolds, 2008).

Cost-effectiveness is a fairly easy concept to grasp. If two interventions are demonstrated to have very similar outcomes but one of the interventions costs twice as much to administer as the other (e.g. because the treatment manual requires twice as many therapy sessions), then the latter intervention would be considered more cost-effective. Similarly, if two interventions have similar costs but the first one is twice as effective as the other, then the latter will be deemed less cost-effective (see Figure 16.5).

Direct treatment costs are not the only factor considered in cost-effectiveness studies. The potential cost savings associated with effective treatments may also be measured. These might include savings from additional healthcare provision that is no longer needed (e.g. if someone remains depression-free following a psychological therapy they are likely to make fewer visits to their GP), or savings in unemployment benefit if, following treatment, someone who has been unemployed is able to return to work. The argument that psychological therapies can be cost-effective has been critical to the UK government's investment in Improving Access to Psychological Therapies services (see Focus Point 16.1).

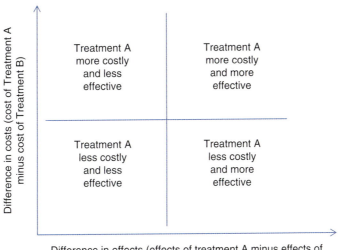

FIGURE 16.5 *A comparison of the cost-effectiveness of two hypothetical treatments (A and B).*

Qualitative research in treatment evaluation

So far this section has focused on quantitative evaluation of treatments for mental health problems, which may help us to answer the question of whether (or not) these treatments 'work'. It is important to note that qualitative research can be used to complement these quantitative methods, and to answer important questions regarding not just 'whether' they work but 'how' they work. Qualitative methods such as the 'change interview' can help researchers to explore the processes by which change occurs and to use this knowledge to develop interventions that include more of the ingredients that are helpful (and fewer that are not) (Elliott, 2010).

TEST YOURSELF

1. What do we need to know in order to evaluate the benefits of a psychological therapy?
2. What is 'cost-effectiveness' and how is this calculated in mental health?
3. What is the 'Dodo Bird Verdict' in relation to the effectiveness of psychological therapies?

SECTION SUMMARY

- In this section we have described some of the methods that have been developed to try to evaluate the effectiveness of treatments for mental health problems.
- Since the 1990s a large number of studies assessing the efficacy of therapies for mental health problems have been carried out and there is now good empirical evidence to support the effectiveness and internal validity of many of these therapies.
- It is important to consider not just the efficacy and safety of these interventions in RCTs but also their acceptability to those seeking treatment and their effectiveness and cost-effectiveness in routine care.

CONCLUSIONS AND FUTURE DIRECTIONS

LEARNING OBJECTIVE 16.7

Critically evaluate the methods employed in the treatment of mental health problems and possible future research and directions in the field.

In the past century, significant developments in the treatment of mental health problems have given rise to the development of healthcare guidelines and practices that recommend a range of treatments that may be effective for a significant proportion of those in need, meaning that many people who experience mental health problems recover and go on to lead healthy, happy, and fulfilling lives. For example, as discussed earlier in this chapter, recovery rates for common mental health problems (the percentage of people who are no longer diagnosable once they have finished treatment) are now normally between 50% and 70% (e.g. Baldwin et al., 2011; Craske et al., 2012; Hanrahan et al., 2013). However, not everyone who might benefit from treatment for mental health problems is able to access effective interventions (see Shafran & Craske, 2009), and as these recovery rates suggest as many as 30% to 50% of people may not benefit from the treatments that are currently available even when they are able to access them. Future directions for the treatment of mental health problems focus on these dual issues and aim at improving the effectiveness of treatments available – for example, the development of adapted and novel treatment approaches to meet the needs of people who do not want, or have not benefited from, current treatment methods and those who do benefit but remain at risk of relapse due to the recurrent nature of their difficulties. Current initiatives also seek to increase the reach of effective treatments to greater numbers of those who may benefit through investment in service development, training new staff groups to offer targeted interventions, and developing more cost-effective treatments, which may be briefer and/or include elements of self-help (e.g. see Focus Point 16.1).

SECTION SUMMARY

- As many as 30–50% of people may not benefit from the treatments that are currently available even when they are able to access them.

- Future directions for the treatment of mental health problems include improving the effectiveness of the available treatments.

- Current initiatives also seek to develop more cost-effective treatments, which may be briefer and/or include elements of self-help.

CHAPTER SUMMARY

This chapter has considered some of the issues fundamental to the appropriate treatment of mental health problems and how treatments and services are delivered and evaluated. We did this by first exploring the ways in which people might seek help for mental health problems, and the kinds of professionals and services with whom they might come into contact. We then considered the range of treatment options available to people and explored the variety of theoretical approaches underpinning such treatments, including biological, psychological, and social and environmental models of mental health. We closed the chapter by describing some of the methodologies that are currently used to assess and evaluate the effectiveness of treatment methods, and considered how treatment choices are made and how 'success' in the treatment of mental health problems is defined.

ESSAY QUESTIONS

1. Compare and contrast psychological and biological approaches to the treatment of mental health problems.

2. Describe the challenges of meeting mental health needs within traditional service settings and evaluate some of the methods used to address these challenges.

3. Imagine that you lead a national health service. How would you decide whether a mental health treatment should be offered (or not) to the population you serve? What are the key questions to consider when evaluating the evidence base?

KEY TERMS

- **acceptance and commitment therapy (ACT):** A third-wave cognitive behavioural intervention that adopts some aspects of mindfulness but that has developed more from the behaviour analysis (or Skinnerian) approach to understanding behaviour.
- **antidepressants:** Drugs used primarily for the treatment of depression and mood disorders. There are three main types of antidepressant medication: tricyclics, monoamine oxidase inhibitors, and selective serotonin and serotonin–norepinephrine reuptake inhibitors.
- **antipsychotics:** Drugs used primarily to treat symptoms of psychosis (e.g. for people with a diagnosis of schizophrenia). They can be helpful in reducing psychotic experiences and the distress associated with these experiences for some people, although approximately 40% of people are 'treatment resistant' and continue to experience these symptoms despite adequate medication.
- **anxiolytics:** These drugs are used primarily to treat symptoms of anxiety and stress. The most common prescriptions for the short-term management of anxiety symptoms are for benzodiazepines (tranquillizers).
- **aversion therapy:** A therapy involving attempts to condition an aversion to a stimulus or event to which the individual is inappropriately attracted. For example, aversion therapy has been most widely used in the treatment of addictive behaviours such as alcoholism, and in these procedures the taste of alcohol is paired with aversive outcomes (e.g. sickness-inducing drugs) in order to condition an aversive reaction to alcohol. Aversion therapy is no longer considered an acceptable treatment in the United Kingdom.
- **Beating the Blues:** A computerized CBT programme that helps the client to identify thinking errors, evaluate negative thoughts, and explore their core beliefs; it also provides help and advice on more adaptive thinking styles.
- **Beck's cognitive therapy:** A therapeutic intervention for depressed individuals involving an objective assessment of their beliefs and requiring them to evaluate the validity of their ideas about themselves, the world, and the future.
- **befriending:** A control condition designed to provide study participants with approximately the same amount of therapist contact as the treatment conditions being tested, with sessions spaced at similar intervals.
- **behaviour analysis:** Therapies based on learning principles of operant conditioning.
- **behaviour modification:** Therapies based on learning principles of classical conditioning.
- **behaviour therapy:** Therapeutic approaches based on classical and operant conditioning principles.

- **behavioural self-control:** The personal use of operant conditioning principles to change or control one's own behaviour.
- **benzodiazepines:** Commonly prescribed anxiolytic drugs. While benzodiazepines can be effective in reducing symptoms of anxiety, they can be addictive, have common side effects (including drowsiness, clumsiness, slurred speech, and confusion), and do not treat the cause of the anxiety symptoms.
- **client-centred therapy:** A Rogerian therapeutic approach that focuses on the individual's immediate conscious experience. Critical to this form of humanistic therapy is the creation of a therapeutic climate that allows the client to progress towards becoming a person who is independent, self-directed, and pursuing self-growth.
- **clinical significance:** The percentage of participants in a study who exhibit recovery or clinically significant change to the point where they no longer meet the criteria for a clinical diagnosis.
- **cognitive behavioural therapy (CBT):** An umbrella term for many different therapies based on the principle that how we think about a situation has a powerful effect on how we feel and how we act, and in turn that what we do can affect our thoughts and feelings.
- **conditioning:** A behavioural process whereby a response becomes more frequent or more predictable in a given environment as a result of reinforcement, with reinforcement typically being a stimulus or reward for a desired response.
- **continuing professional development (CPD):** The maintenance of knowledge and skills related to people's professional lives.
- **counselling:** A type of talking therapy that allows a person to talk about their problems and feelings in a confidential and dependable environment.
- **counterconditioning:** A behaviour therapy technique used to apply extinction principles whereby an unwanted behaviour is converted into a wanted behaviour by the association of positive actions with the stimulus.
- **Dodo Bird Verdict:** The claim, introduced by Saul Rosenzweig in 1936, that all psychotherapies, regardless of their specific components, produce equivalent outcomes.
- **dream analysis:** A psychoanalytic technique used to help an individual gain a sense of understanding of their symptoms, where unconscious conflicts are thought to reveal themselves in symbolic forms in dreams.
- **early intervention in psychosis:** An approach in which secondary-care teams try to detect and intervene early – and in a holistic manner – for young people with psychosis, incorporating a range of psychiatric, psychological, psychosocial, and vocational interventions.
- **empathy:** The ability to see another person's perspective and, for Rogers, the central important feature of any therapist–client relationship.
- **e-therapy:** The delivery and facilitation of communication and therapy using online methods.
- **evidence-based interventions:** Treatments whose efficacy has been proven through research using the scientific method.
- **exposure therapies:** Behaviour therapy techniques used to apply extinction principles whereby the patient is exposed to the feared object or context without any danger, in order to overcome their anxiety. Graded-exposure therapy is recommended by the National Institute for Health and Care Excellence for the treatment of anxiety disorders including phobias and post-traumatic stress disorder.
- **extinction:** The gradual weakening of a conditioned response that results in the behaviour decreasing or disappearing.
- **family therapy:** A therapeutic approach in which the therapist or family therapy team meets with those members of the family willing to participate in discussion about a topic or problem raised by one or more members of the family.
- **faulty learning:** A behaviourist approach that sees psychopathology as the result of maladaptive learning and believes that symptoms are acquired through simple conditioning processes.

- **FearFighter:** A computerized cognitive-behavioural-therapy-based package for phobic, panic, and anxiety disorders that helps clients identify specific problems, develop realistic treatment goals, and monitor achievement through graded exposure.
- **flooding:** Sometimes referred to as exposure therapy, flooding is a psychotherapeutic technique used to treat phobia and anxiety disorders by exposing the patient to their painful memories with the goal of reintegrating their repressed emotions with their current awareness.
- **free association:** A psychotherapeutic technique in which the client is encouraged to verbalize all thoughts, feelings, and images that come to mind, which helps to bring into awareness any unconscious conflicts or associations between thoughts and feelings.
- **functional analysis:** A therapeutic technique in which the therapist attempts to identify consistencies between problematic behaviours and their consequences – especially to try to discover whether there might be a consistent consequence that appears to be maintaining the behaviour by rewarding it.
- **group therapy:** The delivery of therapeutic intervention in a group setting. In group therapies, people can benefit not just from their relationship with the facilitator but also from their relationships with other members of the group.
- **holistic therapies:** A humanistic approach to therapy that emphasizes the need to consider the 'whole' person during therapy, not just their problems.
- **humanistic therapies:** Therapeutic approaches that emphasize a holistic, client-centred, and empathetic therapist–client relationship. Arguably the most successful of these is client-centred therapy (Rogers, 1961).
- **Improving Access to Psychological Therapies (IAPT):** Large-scale initiatives that offer a coordinated approach to primary care for adults with common mental health problems, such as anxiety and depression.
- **internet interventions:** Therapeutic interventions delivered online.
- **interpretation:** A psychoanalytic technique by which the psychoanalyst interprets information from a variety of sources to enable the client to identify important underlying conflicts.
- **meta-analysis:** A statistical technique for combining the findings from independent studies. It is most commonly used to assess the effectiveness of healthcare interventions by combining data from two or more randomized controlled trials.
- **mindfulness-based cognitive therapy (MCBT):** A therapeutic technique that incorporates mindfulness practice and principles with cognitive therapy.
- **monoamine oxidase inhibitors (MAOIs):** Together with selective serotonin and serotonin–norepinephrine reuptake inhibitors, one of the three main tricyclics used in the treatment of depression.
- **National Institute for Health and Care Excellence (NICE):** An independent organization in the United Kingdom that provides evidence-based national guidance on the most effective ways to prevent, diagnose, and treat disease and ill health.
- **no-treatment control:** Within the experimental paradigm, a group that is matched as closely as possible with an experimental group but is not exposed to any experimental treatment. The results are then compared to determine the changes that might have occurred because of the experimental treatment.
- **placebo effect:** A phenomenon in which a fake or inactive substance improves a patient's condition simply because the person has the expectation that it will.
- **practice-based evidence:** Evidence derived from naturalistic, real-world practice settings.
- **psychoanalysis:** Probably the most well-known form of psychodynamic therapy, based on the theoretical works of Sigmund Freud (1856–1939). Techniques including free association, transference, dream analysis, and interpretation are used to help the individual gain a sense of understanding of their symptoms.
- **psychodynamic therapies:** Therapeutic approaches that try to reveal unconscious conflicts that might be causing symptoms of psychopathology. Probably the most well-known form of

psychodynamic therapy is psychoanalysis, which is based on the theoretical works of Sigmund Freud (1856–1939).

- **psychological well-being practitioners:** A role held within Improving Access to Psychological Therapies services. These practitioners provide high-volume, low-intensity interventions for clients with mild to moderate mental health problems, and their work is usually based on a cognitive behavioural model.
- **randomized controlled trials (RCTs):** A type of scientific experiment that compares the effectiveness of the treatment being assessed with a variety of control conditions. Participants in an RCT are assigned randomly to one of these conditions.
- **rational emotive therapy:** Developed by Albert Ellis (1962), one of the first cognitive therapies to address the fact that the way in which people construe themselves, their life, and the world is likely to be a major determinant of their feelings.
- **recovery rate:** The percentage of people who demonstrate recovery or change to the point where they no longer meet the criteria for clinical diagnosis.
- **response shaping:** A procedure based on operant conditioning that can be used to encourage new behaviours that are not already occurring at a reasonable frequency.
- **selective serotonin reuptake inhibitors (SSRIs):** Together with monoamine oxidase inhibitors and serotonin–norepinephrine reuptake inhibitors, one of the three main tricyclics used in the treatment of depression.
- **self-help:** A self-administered intervention in which a person makes use of evidence-based books and manuals; self-help interventions can also be delivered by computer program, via an app, or in other multimedia formats.
- **serotonin–norepinephrine reuptake inhibitors (SNRIs):** Together with monoamine oxidase inhibitors and selective serotonin reuptake inhibitors, one of the three main tricyclics used in the treatment of depression.
- **spontaneous remission:** An unexpected improvement or cure from a disease or illness.
- **systematic desensitization:** A form of exposure therapy commonly used to treat fear, anxiety disorders, and phobias. Using this method, a person is gradually exposed to an anxiety-producing stimulus, such as an object or place.
- **systematic review:** A review of a clearly formulated question that uses systematic and explicit methods to identify, select, and critically appraise relevant research, and to collect and analyse data that are included in the review.
- **systems theory:** Systemic therapies work with the interactional patterns and relationship dynamics between people that may be associated with mental health difficulties.
- **teletherapy:** The delivery of therapeutic interventions by telephone or videoconference.
- **therapeutic alliance:** The therapist–client relationship, which is one of the most important factors affecting treatment adherence and outcome.
- **token economy:** An intervention, based on operant conditioning, that involves participants receiving tokens for engaging in desirable behaviours. These tokens can be exchanged for a variety of reinforcing or desired items.
- **transference:** A psychoanalytic phenomenon where the analyst is a target for emotional responses and the client behaves or feels towards the analyst as they would behave towards an important person in their life.
- **unconditional positive regard:** A humanistic approach in which the therapist agrees to value the client for who they are and to refrain from judging them.
- **waiting-list control:** Within the experimental paradigm, a group that is matched as closely as possible with an experimental group but is not exposed to any experimental treatment until after the active treatment group. Waiting-list control groups are often used when it would be unethical to deny participants access to treatment, provided the wait is still shorter than that for routine services.

NOTES

1. http://www.isanyoneelselikeme.org.uk/
2. http://www.commonwork.org/projects/grow2grow
3. http://www.baat.org/
4. http://interpersonalpsychotherapy.org
5. www.imroc.org

FURTHER RESOURCES

Barker, C., Pistrang, N. & Elliott R. (2015). *Research methods in clinical psychology* (3rd ed.). Chichester, UK: Wiley.

British Association for Behavioural & Cognitive Psychotherapies (n.d.). Retrieved 20 November 2017 from http://www.babcp.com

British Association of Art Therapists. (n.d.). Retrieved 20 November 2017 from http://www.baat.org

British Psychological Society. (n.d.). Division of Clinical Psychology. Retrieved 9 February 2018 from https://www1.bps.org.uk/networks-and-communities/member-microsite/division-clinical-psychology

Carr, A. (2012). *Clinical psychology*. Hove, UK: Routledge.

ClinPsy. (n.d.). Retrieved 20 November 2017 from http://www.clinpsy.org.uk

Davey, G. C. L. (2014). *Psychopathology* (2nd ed.). Chichester, UK: Wiley-Blackwell.

Implementing Recovery through Organisational Change. (n.d.). Retrieved 20 November 2017 from http://www.imroc.org

Interpersonal Therapy. (n.d.). Retrieved 9 February 2018 from https://www.interpersonalpsychotherapy.org

Marks, I., & Cavanagh, K. (2009). Computer-aided psychotherapy: State of the art and state of the science. *Annual Review of Clinical Psychology*, *5*, 121–141.

Marzillier, J. (2004). The myth of evidence-based psychotherapy. *The Psychologist*, *17*, 392–395.

National Institute for Health and Care Excellence. (n.d.). Retrieved 20 November 2017 from https://www.nice.org.uk

NHS. (n.d.). Adult Improving Access to Psychological Therapies programme. Retrieved 20 November 2017 from https://www.england.nhs.uk/mental-health/adults/iapt

Roth, A., & Fonagy, P. (2005). *What works for whom a critical review of psychotherapy research* (2nd ed.). New York, NY: Guilford Press.

Society for Psychotherapy Research. (n.d.). Retrieved 20 November 2017 from http://www.psychotherapyresearch.org

Society of Clinical Psychology. (n.d.). Psychological treatments. Retrieved 9 February 2018 from https://www.div12.org/psychological-treatments

UK Council for Psychotherapy. (n.d.). Retrieved 20 November 2017 from http://www.ukcp.org.uk

REFERENCES

Andrews, G., & Harvey, R. (1981). Does psychotherapy benefit neurotic patients? A reanalysis of the Smith, Glass and Miller data. *Archives of General Psychiatry*, *38*, 1203–1208.

Backhaus, A., Agha, Z., Maglione, M. L., Repp, A., Ross, B., Zuest, D., … Thorp, S. E. (2012). Videoconferencing psychotherapy: A systematic review. *Psychological Services*, *9*, 111–131.

Baldwin, D., Woods, R., Lawson, R., & Taylor, D. (2011). Efficacy of treatment for generalized anxiety disorder: Systematic review and meta-analysis. *British Medical Journal, 342*(mar11 1), d1199. doi:10.1136/bmj.d1199

Barazzone, N., Cavanagh, K., & Richards, D. A. (2012). Computerized cognitive behavioural therapy and the therapeutic alliance: A qualitative enquiry. *British Journal of Clinical Psychology, 51*, 396–417.

Barker, C., Pistrang, N., & Elliott, R. (2002). *Research methods in clinical psychology* (2nd ed.). Chichester, UK: Wiley.

Barlow, D. H. (2010). Negative effects from psychological treatments. *American Psychologist, 65*(1), 13–20.

Beattie, A., Shaw, A., Kaur, S., & Kessler, D. (2009). Primary-care patients' expectations and experiences of online cognitive behavioural therapy for depression: A qualitative study. *Health Expectations, 12*, 45–59.

Beavers, G. A., Iwata, B. A., & Lerman, D. C. (2013). Thirty years of research on the functional analysis of problem behavior. *Journal of Applied Behavior Analysis, 46*(1), 1–21.

Bennett-Levy, J., Richards, D., & Farrand, P. (2010). Low intensity CBT interventions: A revolution in mental health care. In J. Bennett-Levy, D. A. Richards, P. Farrand, H. Christensen, K. M. Griffiths, D. J. Kavanagh, … C. Williams. (Eds.), *Oxford guide to low intensity CBT interventions.* Oxford, UK: Oxford University Press.

Bertakis, K. D., Helms, L. J., Callahan, E. J., Azari, R., Leigh, P., & Robbins, J. A. (2001). Patient gender differences in the diagnosis of depression in primary care. *Journal of Women's Health and Gender-Based Medicine, 10*(7), 689–698.

Birchwood, M., Todd, P., & Jackson, C. (1998). Early intervention in psychosis. *British Journal of Psychiatry, 172*(Suppl. 33), 53–59.

Bishop, S. R., Lau, M., Shapiro, S., Carlson, L., Anderson, N. D., Carmody, J., … Devins, G. (2004). Mindfulness: A proposed operational definition. *Clinical Psychology Review, 11*, 230–241.

Blagys, M. D., & Hilsenroth, M. J. (2000). Distinctive activities of short-term psychodynamic-interpersonal psychotherapy: A review of the comparative psychotherapy process literature. *Clinical Psychology: Science and Practice, 7*, 167–188.

Borkovec, T. D., & Costello, E. (1993). Efficacy of applied relaxation and cognitive-behavioral therapy in the treatment of generalized anxiety disorder. *Journal of Consulting and Clinical Psychology, 61*, 611–619.

Brown, G. W., Adler, Z., & Bifulco, A. (1988). Life events, difficulties and recovery from chronic depression. *British Journal of Psychiatry, 152*, 487–498.

Brown, G. W., & Harris, T. O. (1978). *Social origins of depression: A study of psychiatric disorder in women.* London, UK: Tavistock.

Butler, A. C., Chapman, J. E., Forman, E. M., & Beck, A. T. (2006). The empirical status of cognitive-behavioral therapy: A review of meta-analyses. *Clinical Psychology Review, 26*, 17–31.

Cavanagh, K., Strauss, C., Forder, L., & Jones, F. W. (2014). Can mindfulness and acceptance be learnt by self-help? A systematic review and meta-analysis of mindfulness and acceptance-based self-help interventions. *Clinical Psychology Review, 34*(2), 118–129.

Cohen, D. J., & Reynolds, M. R. (2008). Interpreting the results of cost-effectiveness studies. *Journal of the American College of Cardiology, 52*, 2119–2126.

Conway, P., & Ginkell, A. (2014). Engaging with psychosis: A psychodynamic developmental approach to social dysfunction and withdrawal in psychosis. *Psychosis, 6*(4), 313–326.

Coull, G., & Morris, P. G. (2011). The clinical effectiveness of CBT-based guided self-help interventions for anxiety and depressive disorders: A systematic review. *Psychological Medicine, 41*(11), 2239–2252.

Craske, M. G., Liao, B., Brown, L., & Vervliet, B. (2012). Role of inhibition in exposure therapy. *Journal of Experimental Psychopathology, 3*, 322–345.

Crombie, I., & Davies, H. (2009). *What is meta-analysis?* London, UK: Hayward Medical Communications.

Cuijpers, P., Geraedts, A. S., Van Oppen, P., Andersson, G., Markowitz, J. C., & Van Straten, A. (2011). Interpersonal psychotherapy for depression: A meta-analysis. *American Journal of Psychiatry*, *168*(6), 581–592.

Cuijpers, P., Huibers, M., Ebert, D., Koole, S. L., & Andersson, G. (2013). How much psychotherapy is needed to treat depression? A metaregression analysis. *Journal of Affective Disorders*, *149*(1), 1–13.

Cuijpers, P., Van Straten, A., Andersson, G., & Van Oppen, P. (2008). Psychotherapy for depression in adults: A meta-analysis of comparative outcome studies. *Journal of Consulting and Clinical Psychology*, *76*(6), 909–922.

Cuijpers, P., Van Straten, A., & Warmerdam, L. (2007). Behavioral activation treatments of depression: A meta-analysis. *Clinical Psychology Review*, *27*(3), 318–326.

Dallos, R., & Draper, R. (2005). *Introduction to family therapy: Systemic theory and practice* (2nd ed.). Maidenhead, UK: Oxford University Press.

Davey, G. C. L. (1998). Learning theory. In C. E. Walker (Ed.), *Comprehensive clinical psychology: Foundations of clinical psychology* (Vol. *1*, pp. 391–421). Amsterdam, Netherlands: Elsevier.

Davey, G. C. L. (2012). The lost 40%. *Graham Davey's Blog*, 2 November. Retrieved 24 January 2018 from http://grahamdavey.blogspot.co.uk/2012/11/the-lost-40.html

Day, S. X., & Schneider, P. L. (2002). Psychotherapy using distance technology: A comparison of face-to-face, video, and audio treatment. *Journal of Counseling Psychology*, *49*, 499–503.

de Maat, S., de Jonghe, F., de Kraker, R., Leichsenring, F., Abbass, A., Luyten, P., ... Dekker, J. (2013). The current state of the empirical evidence for psychoanalysis: A meta-analytic approach. *Harvard Review of Psychiatry*, *21*(3), 107–137.

Department of Health. (2012). *IAPT three year report: The first million patients*. London, UK: Department of Health.

Dogg-Helgadottir, F., Menzies, R. G., Onslow, M., Packman, A., & O'Brian, S. (2009). Online CBT II: A phase I trial of a standalone, online CBT treatment program from social anxiety in stuttering. *Behaviour Change*, *26*, 254–270.

Driessen, E., Cuijpers, P., de Maat, S., Abbass, A. A., de Jonghe, F., & Dekker, J. J. (2010). The efficacy of short-term psychodynamic psychotherapy for depression: A meta-analysis. *Clinical Psychology Review*, *30*(1), 25–36.

Ekers, D., Richards, D., & Gilbody, S. (2008). A meta analysis of randomized trials of behavioural treatment of depression. *Psychological Medicine*, *38*(5), 611–623.

Elliott, R. (2010). Psychotherapy change process research: Realizing the promise. *Psychotherapy Research*, *20*(2), 123–135.

Elliott, R., Greenberg, L. S., Watson, J., Timulak, L., & Freire, E. (2013). Research on humanistic-experiential psychotherapies. In M. J. Lambert (Ed.), *Bergin and Garfield's handbook of psychotherapy and behavior change* (6th ed., pp. 495–538). New York, NY: Wiley.

Ellis, A. (1962). *Reason and emotion in psychotherapy*. New York, NY: Lyle Stuart.

Fava, G. A. (2003). Can long-term treatment with antidepressant drugs worsen the course of depression? *Journal of Clinical Psychiatry*, *64*, 123–133.

Fournier, J. C., DeRubeis, R. J., Hollon, S. D., Dimidjian, S., Amsterdam, J. D., Shelton, R. C., & Fawcett, J. (2010). Antidepressant drug effects and depression severity: A patient level meta-analysis. *Journal of the American Medical Association*, *303*, 47–53.

Frosh, S. (2012). *A brief introduction to psychoanalytic theory*. Basingstoke, UK: Palgrave Macmillan.

Gater, R., Waheed, W., Husain, N., Tomenson, B., Aseem, S., & Creed, F. (2010). Social intervention for British Pakistani women with depression: Randomized controlled trial. *British Journal of Psychiatry*, *197*(3), 227–233.

Gellatly, J., Bower, P., Hennessy, S., Richards, D., Gilbody, S., & Lovell, K. (2007). What makes self-help interventions effective in the management of depressive symptoms? Meta-analysis and meta-regression. *Psychological Medicine*, *37*(9), 1217–1228.

Greenwood, K. E., Berry, C., Labuschagne, K., Chandler, R., Peters, E., de Visser, R., ... Garety, P. (2015). Facilitating engagement and hope to protect against social disability: The Early Youth Engagement (EYE) project and beyond. *Schizophrenia Bulletin*, *41* (Suppl. 1), S174.

Grencavage, L. M., & Norcross, J. C. (1990). Where are the commonalities among the therapeutic common factors? *Professional Psychology: Research and Practice, 21*(5), 372–378.

Griner, D., & Smith, T. B. (2006). Culturally adapted mental health intervention: A meta-analytic review. *Psychotherapy: Theory, Research, Practice, Training, 43*(4), 531–548.

Grist, R., & Cavanagh, K. (2013). Computerized cognitive behavioural therapy for common mental health disorders, what works, for whom under what circumstances? A systematic review and meta-analysis. *Journal of Contemporary Psychotherapy, 43*(4), 243–251.

Gusmão, R., Quintão, S., McDaid, D., Arensman, E., Van Audenhove, C., Coffey, C., … Hegerl, U. (2013). Antidepressant utilization and suicide in Europe: An ecological multi-national study. *PLoS ONE, 8*(6), e66455.

Hanrahan, H., Field, A. P., Jones, F. W., & Davey, G. C. L. (2013). A meta-analysis of cognitive therapy for worry in generalized anxiety disorder. *Clinical Psychology Review, 33*, 120–132.

Hans, E., & Hiller, W. (2013). Effectiveness of and dropout from outpatient cognitive behavioral therapy for adult unipolar depression: A meta-analysis of nonrandomized effectiveness studies. *Journal of Consulting and Clinical Psychology, 81*(1), 75–88.

Hansen, N. B., Lambert, M. J., & Forman, E. M. (2002). The psychotherapy dose-response effect and its implications for treatment delivery services. *Clinical Psychology: Science and Practice, 9*(3), 329–343.

Hayes, S. C., Luoma, J. B., Bond, F. W., Masuda, A., & Lillis, J. (2006). Acceptance and commitment therapy: Model, processes and outcomes. *Behaviour Research and Therapy, 44*, 1–25.

Heather, N., Raistrick, D., & Godfrey, C. (2006). *A summary of the Review of the Effectiveness of Treatment for Alcohol Problems*. London, UK: National Treatment Agency for Substance Misuse.

Hetrick, S. E., McKenzie, J. E., Cox, G. R., Simmons, M. B., & Merry, S. N. (2012). Newer generation antidepressants for depressive disorders in children and adolescents. *Cochrane Database of Systematic Reviews, 11*. doi:10.1002/14651858.CD004851.pub3

Hollinghurst, S., Peters, T. J., Kaur, S., Wiles, N., Lewis, G., & Kessler, D. (2010). Cost-effectiveness of therapist-delivered online cognitive-behavioural therapy for depression: Randomised controlled trial. *British Journal of Psychiatry, 197*(4), 297–304.

Hollon, S. D., Stewart, M. O., & Strunk, D. (2006). Enduring effects for cognitive behavior therapy in the treatment of depression and anxiety. *Annual Review of Psychology, 57*, 285–315.

Horvath, A. O., Del Re, A. C., Flückiger, C., & Symonds, D. (2011). Alliance in individual psychotherapy. *Psychotherapy, 48*(1), 9–16.

Howard, K. I., Kopta, S. M., Krause, M. S., & Orlinsky, D. E. (1986). The dose–effect relationship in psychotherapy. *American Psychologist, 41*(2), 159–164.

Jacobson, N. S., & Truax, P. (1991). Clinical significance: A statistical approach to defining meaningful change in psychotherapy research. *Journal of Consulting and Clinical Psychology, 59*, 12–19.

Kabat-Zinn, J. (1994). *Wherever you go, there you are: Mindfulness meditation in everyday life*. New York, NY: Hyperion.

Kabat-Zinn, J. (2003). Mindfulness-based interventions in context: Past, present, and future. *Clinical Psychology: Science and Practice, 10*(2), 144–156.

Kessler, D., Lewis, G., Kaur, S., Wiles, N., King, M., Weich, S., … Peters, T. J. (2009). Therapist-delivered internet psychotherapy for depression in primary care: A randomised controlled trial. *Lancet, 374*(9690), 628–634.

Kirsch, I., Deacon, B. J., Huedo-Medina, T. B., Scoboria, A., Moore, T. J., & Johnson, B. T. (2008). Initial severity and antidepressant benefits: A meta-analysis of data submitted to the food and drug administration. *PLoS Medicine*, 26 February. doi:10.1371/journal.pmed.0050045

Klerman, G. L., Weissman, M. M., Rounsaville, B. J., & Chevron, E. S. (1984). *Interpersonal psychotherapy of depression*. New York, NY: Basic Books.

Kohn, R., Saxena, S., Levav, I., & Saraceno, B. (2004). The treatment gap in mental health care. *Bulletin of the World Health Organization, 82*, 858–866.

Korchin, S. J., & Sands, S. H. (1983). Principles common to all psychotherapies. In C. E. Walker (Ed.), *The handbook of clinical psychology: Theory, research, and practice* (pp. 270–299). Homewood, IL: Dow-Jones/Irwin,

Kuyken, W., Byford, S., Taylor, R. S., Watkins, E., Holden, E., White, K., … Teasdale, J. D. (2008). Mindfulness-based cognitive therapy to prevent relapse in recurrent depression. *Journal of Consulting and Clinical Psychology, 76*(6), 966–978.

Lambert, M. J. (2013). The efficacy and effectiveness of psychotherapy. In M. J. Lambert (Ed.), *Bergin and Garfield's handbook of psychotherapy and behavior change* (6th ed., pp. 169–218). New York, NY: Wiley.

Lambert, M. J., Shapiro, D. A., & Bergin, A. E. (1986). The effectiveness of psychotherapy. In S. L. Garfield & A. E. Bergin (Eds.), *Handbook of psychotherpay and behavior change* (3rd ed., pp. 157–212). New York, NY: Wiley.

Lemma, A., & Patrick, M. (Eds.). (2010). *Off the couch: Contemporary psychoanalytic application.* London, UK: Routledge.

Levine, M., Perkins, D. D., & Perkins, D. V. (2004). *Principles of community psychology: Perspectives and applications* (3rd ed.). New York, NY: Oxford University Press.

Lilienfeld, S. O. (2007). Psychological treatments that cause harm. *Perspectives on Psychological Science, 2*(1), 53–70.

London School of Economics. (2006). *The depression report: A new deal for depression and anxiety disorders.* London, UK: Centre for Economic Performances Mental Health Policy Group.

Luborsky, L. B., Singer, B., & Luborsky, L. (1975). Comparative studies of psychotherapies: Is it true that 'Everyone has won and all must have prizes'? *Archives of General Psychiatry, 32*, 995–1008.

Lutzker, J. R., & Martin, J. A. (1981). *Behavior change.* Monterey, CA: Brooks.

Ma, S. H., & Teasdale, J. D. (2004). Mindfulness-based cognitive therapy for depression: Replication and exploration of differential relapse prevention effects. *Journal of Consulting and Clinical Psychology, 72*(1), 31.

Markowitz, J. C., Svartberg, M., & Swartz, H. A. (1998). Is IPT time-limited psychodynamic psychotherapy? *Journal of Psychotherapy Practice and Research, 7*(3), 185.

Marshall, M., Lockwood, A., Lewis, S., & Fiander, M. (2004). Essential elements of an early intervention service for psychosis: The opinions of expert clinicians. *BMC Psychiatry, 4*(1), 17.

McGorry, P. D., Killackey, E., & Yung, A. (2008). Early intervention in psychosis: Concepts, evidence and future directions. *World Psychiatry, 7*(3), 148–156.

McNally, R. J., Bryant, R. A., & Ehlers, A. (2003). Does early psychological intervention promote recovery from posttraumatic stress? *Psychological Science in the Public Interest, 4*(2), 45–79.

Meddings, S., Byrne, D., Barnicoat, S., Campbell, E., & Locks, L. (2014). Co-delivered and co-produced: Creating a recovery college in partnership. *Journal of Mental Health Training, Education and Practice, 9*(1), 16–25.

Minuchin, P. (1985). Families and individual development: Provocations from the field of family therapy. *Child Development, 56*, 289–302.

Nadelson, C. C., Notman, M. T., & McCarthy, M. K. (2007). Gender issues in psychotherapy. In G. O. Gabbard, J. S. Beck, & J. Holmes (Eds.), *Oxford textbook of psychotherapy* (pp. 411–420). Oxford, UK: Oxford University Press.

Najavits, L. M., & Strupp, H. H. (1994). Differences in the effectiveness of psychodynamic therapies: A process-outcome study. *Psychotherapy, 31*(1), 114–123.

National Co-ordinating Centre for NHS Service Delivery and Organization. (2002). *Services to support carers of people with mental health problems.* London, UK: National Co-ordinating Centre for NHS Service Delivery and Organization.

National Institute for Health and Care Excellence. (2004a). *Eating disorders.* No. CG9. London, UK: National Institute for Health and Care Excellence.

National Institute for Health and Care Excellence. (2004b). *Depression: Management of depression in primary and secondary care.* No. CG23. London, UK: National Institute for Health and Care Excellence.

National Institute for Health and Care Excellence. (2009). *Depression in adults*. No. CG90. London, UK: National Institute for Health and Care Excellence.

National Institute for Health and Care Excellence. (2011). *Anxiety*. No. CG113. London, UK: National Institute for Health and Care Excellence.

National Institute for Health and Care Excellence. (2012). *Psychosis and schizophrenia in children and young people*. No. CG155. London, UK: National Institute for Health and Care Excellence.

National Institute for Health and Care Excellence. (2014). *Psychosis and schizophrenia in adults: Treatment and management*. No. CG178. London, UK: National Institute for Health and Care Excellence.

Newman, M. G., Szkodny, L. E., Llera, S. J., & Przeworski, A. (2011). A review of technology-assisted self-help and minimal contact therapies for anxiety and depression: Is human contact necessary for therapeutic efficacy? *Clinical Psychology Review, 31*, 89–103.

NHS Choices. (2009). Antidepressants and suicide risk. 12 August. Retrieved 24 January 2018 from https://www.nhs.uk/news/mental-health/antidepressants-and-suicide-risk

NHS Choices. (2016). Mindfulness. Retrieved 23 January 2018 from https://www.nhs.uk/conditions/stress-anxiety-depression/mindfulness/?

Nolen-Hoeksema, S. (2000). The role of rumination in depressive disorders and mixed anxiety/depressive symptoms. *Journal of Abnormal Psychology, 109*(3), 504–511.

O'Brien, M., Singleton, N., Bumpstead, R., & Office for National Statistics. (2001). *Psychiatric morbidity among adults living in private households, 2000*. London, UK: Stationery Office.

Office for National Statistics. (2001). *Psychiatric morbidity report*. London, UK: Office for National Statistics.

Öst, L.-G. (2008). Efficacy of the third wave of behavioural therapies: A systematic review and meta-analysis. *Behaviour Research and Therapy, 46*, 296–321.

Patel, V., Chowdhary, N., Rahman, A., & Verdeli, H. (2011). Improving access to psychological treatments: Lessons from developing countries. *Behaviour Research and Therapy, 49*, 523–528.

Paul, G. L. (1966). *Insight vs. desensitization in psychotherapy: An experiment in anxiety reduction*. Stanford, CA: Stanford University Press.

Radhakrishnan, M., Hammond, G., Jones, P. B., Watson, A., McMillan-Shields, F., & Lafortune, L. (2013). Cost of Improving Access to Psychological Therapies (IAPT) programme: An analysis of cost of session, treatment and recovery in selected primary care trusts in the east of England region. *Behaviour Research and Therapy, 51*, 37–45.

Read, J., & Bentall, R. (2010). The effectiveness of electroconvulsive therapy: A literature review. *Epidemiologia e psichiatria sociale, 19*(4), 333–347.

Reeves, R. R., & Ladner, M. E. (2010). Antidepressant-induced suicidality: An update. *CNS Neuroscience & Therapeutics, 16*(4), 227–234.

Retzlaff, R., von Sydow, K., Beher, S., Haun, M. W., & Schweitzer, J. (2013). The efficacy of systemic therapy for internalizing and other disorders of childhood and adolescence: A systematic review of 38 randomized trials. *Family Process, 52*(4), 619–652.

Richard, D. C. S., & Lauterbach, D. L. (2007). *Handbook of exposure therapies*. Amsterdam, Netherlands: Academic Press.

Richards, D., & Richardson, T. (2012). Computer-based psychological interventions for depression treatment: A systematic review and meta-analysis. *Clinical Psychology Review, 32*, 329–342.

Robinson, L. A., Berman, J. S., & Neimeyer, R. A. (1990). Psychotherapy for the treatment of depression: A comprehensive review of controlled outcome research. *Psychological Bulletin, 108*, 30–49.

Rochlen, A. B., Zack, J. S., & Speyer, C. (2004). Online therapy: Review of relevant definitions, debates, and current empirical support. *Journal of Clinical Psychology, 60*(3), 269–283.

Rogers, C. R. (1961). *Client-centered therapy*. Boston, MA: Houghton Mifflin.

Rosenzweig, S. (1936/2010). Some implicit common factors in diverse methods of psychotherapy. *American Journal of Orthopsychiatry, 6*, 412–415.

Royal College of Psychiatrists. (2015). Antidepressants. Retrieved 9 February 2018 from https://www.rcpsych.ac.uk/expertadvice/treatmentswellbeing/antidepressants.aspx

Sackett, D. L., Straus, S. E., Richardson, S., Rosenberg, W., & Haynes, R. B. (2000). *Evidence-based medicine: How to practice and teach EBM* (2nd ed.). Edinburgh, UK: Churchill Livingstone.

Segal, Z. V., Teasdale, J. D., Williams, J. M., & Gemar, M. C. (2002). The mindfulness-based cognitive therapy adherence scale: Inter-rater reliability, adherence to protocol and treatment distinctiveness. *Clinical Psychology & Psychotherapy, 9*(2), 131–138.

Sensky, T., Turkingon, D., Kingdon, D., Scott, J. L., Scott, J., Siddle, R., ... Barnes, T. R. E. (2000). A randomised controlled trial of cognitive-behavioral therapy for persistent symptoms in schizophrenia resistant to medication. *Archives of General Psychiatry, 57*, 165–172.

Shadish, W. R., Navarro, A. M., Matt, G. E., & Phillips, G. (2000). The effects of psychological therapies under clinically representative conditions: A meta-analysis. *Psychological Bulletin, 126*(4), 512–529.

Shafran, R., & Craske, M. (Eds.). (2009). Dissemination and implementation of cognitive behavioural therapy. Special issue, *Behaviour Research and Therapy, 47*(11), 901–994.

Shepherd, G., Boardman, J., & Slade, M. (2008). *Making recovery a reality*. London, UK: Sainsbury Centre for Mental Health.

Shore, J. H. (2013). Telepsychiatry: Videoconferencing in the delivery of psychiatric care. *Treatment in Psychiatry, 170*, 256–262.

Siev, J., & Chambless, D. L. (2009). The Dodo Bird, treatment technique, and disseminating empirically supported treatments. *Behavior Therapist, 32*, 69–75.

Simoni-Wastila, L. (2000). The use of abusable prescription drugs: The role of gender. *Journal of Women's Health and Gender-Based Medicine, 9*(3), 289–297.

Smit, Y., Huibers, M. J., Ioannidis, J. P., Van Dyck, R., Van Tilburg, W., & Arntz, A. (2012). The effectiveness of long-term psychoanalytic psychotherapy: A meta-analysis of randomized controlled trials. *Clinical Psychology Review, 32*, 81–92.

Smith, M. I., Glass, G. V., & Miller, T. I. (1980). *The benefits of psychotherapy*. Baltimore, MD: Johns Hopkins Press.

Stone, M., Laughren, T., Jones, M. L., Levenson, M., Holland, P. C., Hughes, A., ... Rochester, G. (2009). Risk of suicidality in clinical trials of antidepressants in adults: Analysis of proprietary data submitted to US Food and Drug Administration. *British Medical Journal, 339*(aug11 2), b2880. doi:10.1136/bmj.b2880

Stoppe, G., Sandholzer, H., Huppertz, C., Duwe, H., & Staedt, J. (1999). Gender differences in the recognition of depression in old age. *Maturitas, 32*(3), 205–212.

Sue, S., Zane, N., Hall, G. C. N., & Berger, L. K. (2009). The case for cultural competency in psychotherapeutic interventions. *Annual Review of Psychology, 60*, 525–548.

Swift, J. K., & Greenberg, R. P. (2012). Premature discontinuation in adult psychotherapy: A meta-analysis. *Journal of Consulting and Clinical Psychology, 80*(4), 547–559.

Thoresen, C. E., & Mahoney, M. J. (1974). *Behavioral self-control*. New York, NY: Holt, Rinehart and Winston.

Tolin, D. F. (2010). Is cognitive-behavioral therapy more effective than other therapies? Meta-analytic review. *Clinical Psychology Review, 30*, 710–720.

Tyrer, P., Cooper, S., Salkovskis, P., Crawford, M., Byford, S., Dupont, S., ... Barrett, B. (2014). Clinical and cost-effectiveness of cognitive behaviour therapy for health anxiety in medical patients: A multicentre randomised controlled trial. *The Lancet, 383*, 219–225.

von Sydow, K., Beher, S., Schweitzer, J., & Retzlaff, R. (2010). The efficacy of systemic therapy with adult patients: A meta-content analysis of 38 randomized controlled trials. *Family Process, 49*(4), 457–485.

Wampold, B. E., Imel, Z. E., & Miller, S. D. (2009). Barriers to the dissemination of empirically supported treatments: Matching evidence to messages. *Behavior Therapist, 32*, 144–155.

Whisman, M. A., Johnson, D. P., & Li, A. (2012). Couple-based interventions for depression. *Couple and Family Psychology: Research and Practice, 1*(3), 185–198.

Wolpe, J. (1958). *Psychotherapy by reciprocal inhibition*. Stanford, CA: Stanford University Press.

17 Social Development

Lance Slade, Mark Wright, and Robin Banerjee

INTRODUCTION

LEARNING OBJECTIVE 17.1

Understand the relevance of research on social development to society and everyday life.

On 6 August 2011, a police officer shot and killed 29-year-old Mark Duggan in Tottenham in the United Kingdom. What initially started out as a peaceful protest in response to the shooting later turned into rioting and looting, spreading throughout London and then into other areas of the country. By 16 August, when the rioting had come to an end, five people were dead and many others were injured as a direct result of violent acts. The events came to be known as the 'BlackBerry Riots' because people were using their mobile phones as well as Facebook and Twitter to organize some of the rioting.

The media, politicians, and political commentators offered a range of views about the riots and their possible causes. *The Sun* (2011) called it 'anarchy, pure and simple'; the *Daily Telegraph* (2011) reported that the sole intent was criminal and that the thugs needed to be taught the laws of the land the hard way. The Home Secretary, Theresa May, said that the riots were 'symptomatic of a wider malaise including worklessness, illiteracy, and drug abuse' and that 'everybody, no matter what their background or circumstances, has the freedom to choose between right and wrong' (BBC News, 2011). Former UK Prime Minister Tony Blair offered a different view in a newspaper article, saying that 'the big cause is the group of young, alienated, disaffected youth who are outside the social mainstream' (Blair, 2011). *The Guardian* ran stories with headlines including 'The Morality of Rioters', 'Don't Blame Our Parents, Say Rioters', 'Were the Riots About Race?'; 'The Women Who Rioted', and 'A Consumerist Feast Amid the Summer Riots'.

Amid the debates about the violence and criminality, many also pointed to a host of positive behaviours seen during and as a result of the riots. Local resident Pauline Pearce – later labelled 'the heroine of Hackney' – came out to chastise others for their behaviour. In the aftermath of the riots, thousands of users of social networking sites arranged clean-up operations of their local neighbourhoods, with hundreds of young people turning up with brooms to help with the clean-up.

The London riots thus provided countless examples of how young people are capable of participating in acts of violence and criminality as well as engaging in prosocial behaviour to protect and support their communities. In seeking to explain this behaviour, we might find ourselves delving into questions about the importance of various social influences such as parenting, peer relations, and the media. These social contexts in turn relate to psychological dynamics concerning the development of empathy, social understanding, self-control, identity, and morality. In this chapter, we examine what psychological research can tell us about the wide range of factors that play a role in how children and young people feel, think, and behave in social situations.

SECTION SUMMARY

- Events in everyday life challenge psychologists to provide explanations of the many different factors involved in how children and young people feel, think, and behave in social situations.

EARLY EMOTIONAL DEVELOPMENT AND TEMPERAMENT

LEARNING OBJECTIVE 17.2

Describe the development of emotion in early life and the role of temperament and plasticity in this development.

Emotions play a central role in our social experiences, and understanding the development of emotions is therefore a key starting point for understanding how we come to regulate our social behaviour and relationships. Drawing on a programme of cross-cultural research that involved presenting adults and children with photographs of different facial expressions, Paul Ekman (Ekman, 2003; Ekman & Friesen, 1971) identified what he believed to be six innate and universal emotions: happiness, sadness, anger, disgust, surprise, and fear. However, there has been heated debate about the extent to which these expressions are truly innate, the timing of their emergence during early development, and their connections with what infants actually feel. Is there a fundamental stability in the meaning of emotional expressions throughout the life course, or could it be, for example, that emotional expressions have different meanings in infants compared with adults and children (see Camras & Shutter, 2010)?

In fact, there are numerous perspectives on the nature of emotions and the mechanisms that drive the development of emotions in children. The **discrete emotions theory** suggests that there are several biologically determined emotional responses that are expressed and recognized universally (Izard, 2007). Other approaches, however, emphasize the social context to a much greater extent in the emergence of emotions. For example, when it comes to what is driving the development of emotional expressions, one view – in line with **social learning theory** – is that during the first few months of infancy, caregiver responses to infants lead to the matching of emotional expressions. Haviland and Lelwica (1987), for example, showed that 10-week-old infants adopted the appropriate matching facial expression when their mothers displayed an angry or sad face.

In a more complex way, **functionalist** approaches to emotion (e.g. Campos, Mumme, Kermoian, & Campos, 1994) emphasize the way in which emotions serve as a means of working towards relational goals: emotions are linked to 'action tendencies' such as escaping from dangerous situations (fear) or dealing with a conflict that has thwarted your plans (anger). Finally, the **dynamic systems perspective** emphasizes a more complex interplay – operating continually and in a bidirectional way – between children's developing brains, their bodily sensations and experiences, and social–environmental factors: children's emotional responses are said to be organized by the way in which socialization agents such as parents may promote 'linkages between specific appraisals, emotion-related goals, and culturally sanctioned means of achieving those goals, including the production of specific emotional facial expressions' (Camras & Shutter, 2010, p. 8).

Early emotional expressions

Regardless of the debates concerning the nature of emotions and the mechanisms involved in emotional development, it is widely accepted that expressions of emotional states are evident soon after birth, with a number of 'basic' emotional expressions observable in early infancy (see Figure 17.1).

Some researchers argue that there are initially just two global arousal states: attraction to pleasant stimuli and withdrawal from unpleasant stimuli, or positive and negative affect (Camras, Oster, Campos, & Bakeman, 2003). For example, Ganchrow, Steiner, and Daher (1983) showed that adult observers could judge which type of liquid was given to newborns from their facial expression; a slight smile was evident when the baby was given sweet liquid, in contrast to pursed lips when the baby was given a bitter liquid. However, distinctions between the kinds of 'basic' emotions described above have also been observed in early infancy.

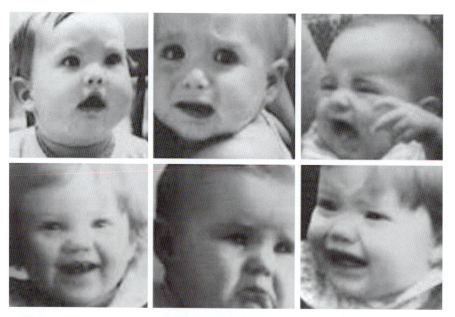

FIGURE 17.1 *Early emotional expressions. Izard, Huebner, Risser, and Dougherty (1980) found that people could reliably identify interest, joy, surprise, sadness, anger, disgust, contempt, and fear in infants' faces. How confident do you feel about reading emotions in babies' faces?*
Source: Izard, Huebner, Risser, and Dougherty (1980), American Psychological Association, reprinted with permission.

Among the first recognizable emotional expressions to appear is happiness, initially in the form of smiling. To begin with, infants produce instinctive, spontaneous 'smiles' in the absence of any external stimulation, and it is thus not clear whether these expressions reflect a 'happy' feeling state. Within their first few weeks of life, however, babies begin to smile in response to gentle stroking, rocking, and sounds – usually their mother's voice. By 6–10 weeks, the first 'social smiles' appear (LaFreniere, 2000; Lavelli & Fogel, 2005); infants begin to smile more often in the company of others than they do when alone. By 3–4 months, infants' smiles are produced most frequently in repetitive and contingent social interactions where social partners respond in systematically positive ways to their vocalizations and movements (Ellsworth, Muir, & Hains, 1993). Infants also begin to laugh, reflecting an increased sensitivity to behaviour such as an older sibling pulling a silly face (Sroufe, 1996). By the end of the first year, infants produce different smiles depending on the situation, such as a friendly smile for someone familiar or a nervous smile for someone they know less well (Messinger & Fogel, 2007), and these different smiles now appear to serve as intentional social signals.

A developmental trajectory in negative expressions is also evident. From birth, infants appear to show distress in response to unpleasant stimuli and situations. These emotional experiences are initially conveyed through crying in response to negative physiological sensations such as hunger or pain, but, as they get older, infants begin to display these emotions in response to a variety of social triggers. For example, infants can display a combination of sad and angry emotional expressions when interesting stimuli or contingent social interactions are withdrawn (e.g. when the caregiver maintains an expressionless 'still face' regardless of the infant's behaviour; Tronick, Als, Adamson, Wise, & Brazelton, 1978), possibly from as young as 6–10 weeks. Moreover, in the first 6 months, they begin to show signs of fear towards strangers (stranger anxiety), which coincides with the emergence of close attachment relations with caregivers (see the following section, on caregiver–child interactions).

Alongside the emergence of infants' own emotional *expressions*, there is a parallel development of emotion *recognition* and *understanding*. In a phenomenon known as **social referencing**, children draw on the emotional reactions of others to appraise uncertain situations. For example, in an adaptation of the visual cliff experiment (Sorce, Emde, Campos, & Klinnert, 1985), 1-year-old infants were placed on a Plexiglas table with a 'shallow' side, created by having a patterned material directly underneath, and a 'deep' side where the patterned material was some distance below the clear table-top, making it appear as though there were a deep drop. Most infants crossed over the 'cliff' if their mothers standing at the other end of the table expressed joy or interest, but not one crossed when their mothers expressed fear. The results seem to indicate that infants use their mother's emotional expressions as a source of information from which to appraise the danger of the situation.

Studies of emotional development show that changes in emotional experience are often linked to developments in other domains. Anger, for example, may emerge in response to instances where specific goals have been thwarted, indicating some sense in which infants are intentionally directing and controlling their behaviour in order to achieve certain goals. This increases throughout the second year, when infants come to direct their anger towards specific agents and causes (Mascolo & Fischer, 2007). The increase in self-awareness during the second year also seems to manifest itself in the emergence of **self-conscious emotions** such as shame, embarrassment, and pride. These differ from more basic emotions, such as anger and fear, in that they rely on the infant's developing sense of a unique 'self', separate from the world around them, allowing them to make self-evaluations. Kagan (1981), for example, observed that children in the second year of life may display **mastery smiles** upon successful achievement of a goal, such as reaching for and manipulating a new toy.

As children get older, more complex cognitive processes involving self-evaluations appear to be implicated in their emotional experiences. Embarrassment, for example, often results from a situation where a child feels that they have done something silly, usually in front of others, which they judge against a social standard of behaviour deemed appropriate for their age. However, it is important to remember that complex, self-conscious emotions could have roots in simple, low-level processes. For example, feelings of shyness are likely to have biological and temperamental origins (Jones, Schulkin, & Schmidt, 2014; Kagan, 1994), and facial expressions of 'coyness' can be triggered at a very young age (as early as 2–3 months) by attention from others (Reddy, 2000). A key question for future research is to track and understand the development of complex, self-conscious emotions from earlier and simpler emotions.

Temperament and plasticity

Any description of how emotions develop during infancy and early childhood must recognize that, at any given age, there are individual differences in children's emotional experiences and emotional responses to situations. In fact, individual differences in children's emotional activity are evident soon after birth, along with differences in motor behaviour, attentional reactivity, and self-regulation (Rothbart & Bates, 2006). These differences, which are considered to be genetically and biologically based and which show relative stability over time, are what psychologists refer to as **temperament** (Zentner & Shiner, 2012) and they have been shown to affect social behaviour right into adulthood (Caspi, 2000).

Children's temperamental differences can be identified and measured along a number of different dimensions, which can be examined individually or grouped together in specific ways. For example, Thomas, Chess, and Birch (1970) argued that infants show clear differences in nine biologically based characteristics:

1. level of motor *activity*
2. level of *approach versus withdrawal* when responding to new objects or people
3. *adaptability* to changes in the environment
4. general *mood*
5. *threshold of responsiveness* to stimuli
6. *intensity* of responses
7. extent of *distractibility* from what they are doing
8. *rhythmicity* of basic functions such as eating and sleeping
9. *attention span and persistence*.

By comparing infants' profiles across these characteristics, the authors identified three basic types of temperament. Infants who were negative in mood, high in their intensity, and low in adaptability, approach, and rhythmicity were said to have a **difficult temperament**, whereas those who were positive in mood and mild in their intensity, with high levels of rhythmicity, approach, and adaptability, were said to have an **easy temperament**. Infants with a **slow-to-warm-up temperament** were slightly negative in mood, mild in intensity, and low in adaptability, approach, and activity, and showed variable levels of rhythmicity.

More recent approaches have refined the characteristics and focused on basic underlying dimensions or factors rather than classifying types of infant. For example, Rothbart (e.g. Rothbart, 2007; Rothbart & Bates, 2006) has argued that temperament can best be understood in terms of three broad dimensions: **negative emotionality** (or reactivity), which involves high levels of anger/frustration, discomfort, fear, and sadness, and low levels of soothability; **effortful control**, which involves high levels of attentional control, inhibitory control, and perceptual sensitivity, and low levels of intensity pleasure; and **extraversion/surgency**, which involves high levels of activity and impulsivity, high-intensity pleasure, and low levels of shyness (Rothbart, Ahadi, Hershey, & Fisher, 2001).

Research has shown that both specific aspects and broad dimensions of temperament are directly linked to later social development (see Sanson, Hemphill, Yagmurlu, & McClowry, 2011). For example, children rated as difficult in temperament are more likely to engage in problem behaviour with their mothers at 2 years of age (Lee & Bates, 1985) and more likely to have problems with their peers (Szewczyk-Sokolowski, Bost, & Wainwright, 2005). More specifically, negative emotionality or reactivity has been linked to reactive aggression (aggressive responding to perceived provocation from others) in both North American (Vitaro, Barker, Boivin, Brendgen, & Tremblay, 2006) and Chinese (Xu, Farver, & Zhang, 2009) children. In addition, low levels of effortful control have been linked to antisocial and aggressive behaviour (Eisenberg et al., 2009), including violent criminality (Henry, Caspi, Moffitt, & Silva, 1996). Furthermore, negative reactivity and effortful control can also interact. For example, children who show high levels of negative emotion and poor levels of self-regulation have been shown to have the lowest levels of social skills and greater levels of peer problems (Eisenberg et al., 1993). Finally, it is important to note that the implications of temperament for social adjustment may vary by culture. For example, while inhibited behaviour in social situations tends to be associated with risks of social withdrawal in North America, children with such 'shyness–sensitivity' characteristics are often accepted and viewed positively by children and teachers in China (Chen, Rubin, & Li, 1995).

Temperament also moderates the effects of other factors, such as parenting and attachment. A substantial body of evidence shows that infants with difficult temperaments are at particularly high risk of negative social and emotional outcomes when they have been exposed to poor environments (e.g. insensitive parenting, poor childcare, and so on; Belsky & Rovine, 1988; Bradley & Corwyn, 2008). However, Belsky (1997, 2005) recognized that children with difficult temperaments, particularly during an early sensitive period, seem to do disproportionately *well* when they have experienced supportive environments. Thus, it seems that some infants may be especially sensitive or susceptible to positive as well as negative environmental influences (Belsky, 1997; Belsky, Bakermans-Kranenburg, & Van IJzendoorn, 2007; Ellis, Boyce, Belsky, Bakermans-Kranenburg, & Van IJzendoorn, 2011; Pluess & Belsky, 2011). Belsky (1997) initially proposed this **differential susceptibility hypothesis** to explain the variability reported in studies examining the effects of maternal sensitivity on attachment security, and went on to suggest that this could be applied across a range of environment–outcome effects.

Pluess and Belsky's (2010) analysis of a major longitudinal dataset showed that childcare quality rated as good (observed between 6 and 54 months) predicted fewer behaviour problems and less teacher–child conflict at 10 and 11 years of age for children assessed as having difficult temperaments in infancy, with the opposite pattern found when childcare was rated as poor. A similar pattern was found for the effect of parenting quality on the children's social skills. In contrast, neither childcare nor parenting quality predicted these outcomes for children who were not assessed as having difficult temperaments in infancy.

It has been argued by researchers (e.g. Ellis et al., 2011) that children with difficult temperaments are more susceptible to environmental influences because they are born with greater brain plasticity or neuroplasticity (i.e. the capability of neural pathways in the brain to change in response to environmental, emotional, and cognitive influences), which evidence has shown is crucial to learning (Fox, Calkins, & Bell, 1994; Galvan, 2010; Grossman & Johnson, 2007; see BrainHQ, 2018, for a simple summary). Belsky (1997, 2005) proposes that differential susceptibility may provide an evolutionary advantage as, in an uncertain world, having some children born less predisposed to respond to environmental influence on child rearing and others who will disproportionately thrive when environments are more favourable will maximize reproductive fitness. While research on the specific neurobiological processes underlying these patterns of differential susceptibility is ongoing, the research described above already makes a strong case for the importance of considering *interactions* between temperament and social environment: clearly, children may experience the same social environmental influences but respond in very different ways depending on their temperamental characteristics.

TEST YOURSELF

1. Describe the development of emotional expressions across the first years of an infant's life.
2. What is meant by temperament and why might this be important for a child's social and emotional development?

SECTION SUMMARY

- Emotions play a central role in our social experiences, and understanding the development of emotions is therefore a key starting point for understanding how we come to regulate our social behaviour and relationships.

- Basic emotional expressions appear soon after birth and infants quickly come to display a range of positive and negative expressions that indicate how they feel. These are precursors to more complex self-conscious emotions.

- Biologically based individual differences in infants' emotionality and effortful control are associated with a range of social and emotional outcomes right through to adulthood.

- Temperament also moderates the effects of other factors, explaining how children can respond differently to the same environmental experiences (e.g. parenting).

CAREGIVER–CHILD INTERACTIONS AND THE DEVELOPMENT OF ATTACHMENT

LEARNING OBJECTIVE 17.3

Describe the development, measurement, and consequences of attachment, as well as the consequence of maternal deprivation for the emotional and social development of a child.

All the developmental changes and individual differences described in the section above take place within a rich social context of relationships and interactions with other people. In this section, we consider the extensive body of research on how children come to communicate and interact with social partners. A particular focus is placed on the emergence of the attachment relationship between children and their caregivers.

Social communication in infancy

Compared with many other animal species, human infants are relatively helpless at birth: they cannot move their bodies to seek out food for themselves or escape from danger. However, they do come into the world with a number of inbuilt reflexes (e.g. grasping and sucking), and are also born with behaviours indicating they enter the world expecting a social partner. As we have seen, young infants cry and smile, and caregivers will usually respond by picking up the infant, providing physical care and nourishment, or giving positive emotional signals. Moreover, perhaps as a foundation for the patterns of social referencing described in the previous section, it seems that infants are 'preprogrammed' to recognize human faces (Bakti, Baron-Cohen, Wheelwright, Connellan, & Ahluwalia, 2000; Goren, Sarty, & Wu, 1975). Goren et al. (1975) showed newborn infants – with a median age of 9 minutes! – a face shape with features (eyes, nose, mouth) in the correct positions, compared with a face shape with scrambled features, or a blank face shape. Their eye and head movements in response to these stimuli indicated greater interest in the anatomically correct image of a face, indicating an inbuilt orientation to human faces. Morton and Johnson (1991) called this **conspec**, a primitive mechanism that draws infants' attention to members of the same species.

The responsiveness of infants to social partners can be seen in evidence of early imitation. A few weeks after birth, infants have been shown to mimic or match the facial expression of others. In a study conducted by Meltzoff and Moore (1997), adult experimenters made various facial expressions (tongue protrusion, open mouth, and protruded lips), and 12- to 21-week-old infants matched the experimenters' facial expression significantly more often than would occur by chance. More recent evidence has revealed that young infants' ability to imitate simple actions by manipulating parts of their body they cannot see can be explained by what are known as **mirror neurons**. These are brain cells that respond in a similar way whether we make a behavioural gesture ourselves or witness another person making the same or a similar gesture, such as smelling a noxious substance and pulling a face of disgust yourself or seeing someone else pull a face of disgust (Simpson, Murray, Paukner, & Ferrari, 2014).

By 2–4 months of age, infants' communicative interactions with social partners develop further, with the emergence of preverbal 'conversations' and laughter in the context of contingent responding by caregivers. For example, the soft vowel sounds (cooing) produced by infants may form part of a preverbal conversation with caregivers, whereby the infant coos, the caregiver coos back in a timely fashion, and so on. Infants appear to derive particular enjoyment from this form of contingent responding in reaction to their own vocalizations, and may come to expect that caregivers will be socially responsive. The sensitive, two-way communication whereby infant and caregiver match their emotional states in a rhythmic way is known as **interactional synchrony** (Isabella & Belsky, 1991). Laughter may often serve as a key marker of reciprocally positive social relations, whereby the infant's laughter elicits even more positive behaviour and warmth on the part of the social partner. In fact, research has shown that laughter triggers reward circuits in the brain, encouraging parental care and proximity (Mendes, Seidl-de-Moura, & Siqueira, 2009).

The importance of positive, reciprocal, and contingent interactions between infants and caregivers can be brought into sharp relief by instances where infants are unexpectedly faced with an unresponsive social partner. Their displeasure in these situations can be demonstrated using the **still-face paradigm** referred to earlier (Tronick et al., 1978). In this study, mothers interacted with their infants for around 3 minutes, after which they adopted a still face – remaining entirely unresponsive to the infant – before resuming normal interaction. Infants first responded to their mother's still face by pulling facial expressions, vocalizing, and moving their arms around, but then began to fuss, look away, and show visible signs of distress. The still-face paradigm has been criticized by some researchers for being too artificial, with arguments concerning whether caregivers ever really act in this way, but the importance of contingency in mother–infant interaction has been demonstrated in other studies. In one such study, mothers interacted with their infants via a monitor (Murray & Trevarthen, 1985). Initially, the mothers' behaviours were contingent on the infants' responses, but infants were then presented with video replays of their mothers from previous interactions, which were thus no longer contingent on their responses. The non-contingent interactions yielded similar results to the still-face paradigm. It thus appears that disruption to the interactional synchrony of infants and their caregivers is a stressful experience; in fact, there is evidence that such disruption during face-to-face interactions with mothers increases levels of the stress hormone, cortisol, in 4-month-olds (Crockett, Holmes, Granger, & Lyons-Ruth, 2013).

During the second half of an infant's first year, interactions with the caregiver become much more sophisticated. We begin to see **joint attention** between infants and caregivers, as they attend to the same object or event in the environment (Evans & Porter, 2009). As well as following the gaze of their parents to share the same attentional focus (e.g. when a parent draws the infant's attention to an interesting new toy), infants become capable of directing their caregivers' attention. This can include **proto-imperative pointing**, a gesture indicating to their social partner that they desire an object, and **proto-declarative pointing**, where the gesture is used to draw a social partner's attention to something they find interesting and want the partner to see too (Tomasello, Carpenter, & Liszkowski, 2007). And, as we saw in the previous section, infants develop the ability to use social referencing, reading the emotional reactions of others as nonverbal communicative gestures to help to inform their behaviour in ambiguous situations.

Forming a bond

Attachment refers to the close emotional bond formed between a child and caregiver during the first year of life (Bowlby, 1969; see also Ainsworth, 1979). The propensity to form this attachment relationship has been proposed to have a biological basis, one shared with other animals. According to attachment theory, infants are born with an **attachment behavioural system** that is activated by threat or separation and functions to elicit proximity seeking (Bowlby, 1969). Behaviours designed to bring about or maintain proximity to the caregiver provide not only physical security, through being close to the caregiver and able to benefit from their protection, but also psychological (or 'felt') security (Sroufe & Waters, 1977). When this kind of proximity has been achieved, the attachment figure can serve as a 'secure base' for the infant, from which they are able to explore the environment safely or to which they can return in times of threat (Ainsworth, Blehar, Waters, & Wall, 1978). However, as we will see later in this section, this is only likely to happen if infants have experienced their caregivers as consistently available, safe, and responsive in their interactions. If children experience inconsistent and unreliable care or rejection and hostility, they may fail to develop this sense of security and instead feel deeply anxious and distressed (Bowlby, 1969, 1973).

Attachment develops over a number of early phases (Bowlby, 1969). At first, up to around 2 months of age, infants show a range of social behaviours (crying, clinging, grasping, and gazing) that bring about social contact with others, but these are not directed at any specific person (*preattachment phase*). From around 2 to 7 months, this social responsiveness becomes more discriminating and focused on familiar caregivers (*attachment in the making phase*). This discrimination in the social signals emitted by babies builds on their much earlier capacity (within a few days of birth) to distinguish between the voice of their mother and the voices of strangers (Moon, Cooper, & Fifer, 1993). Then, from 7 months to around 2 years, in the *clear-cut attachment phase*, the specificity of the social connection between infants and their primary caregiver is crystallized: infants show clear evidence of attachment, such as protesting when an attachment figure leaves (separation anxiety), proximity seeking, and using the caregiver as a secure base.

For most infants, their first attachment is to their mother, but research has shown that infants will also form attachments to other caregivers, such as fathers and grandparents, as well as to siblings (Schaffer & Emerson, 1964). As such, there is no clear support for Bowlby's original claim for **monotropism**, the idea that infants have an inbuilt bias to form an exclusive attachment to one main figure (i.e. the mother). However, that said, research does point to qualitative differences in the nature of attachment relationships with different caregivers. For example, although sensitive interaction is important for fathers, as it is for mothers (Braungart-Rieker et al., 2014; Bretherton, 2010; Van IJzendoorn & De Wolff, 1997), fathers tend to engage in more challenging play with their infants, which is argued to be important for fostering exploratory behaviour (Grossman, Grossmann, Fremmer-Bombik, Kindler, & Scheuerer-Englisch, 2002).

By around 12 months, infants have developed an **internal working model (IWM)** of their experiences with their caregiver (Bowlby, 1969, 1973). IWMs are organized mental representations of the availability of caregivers and the likelihood of support, as well as general expectations about the interactions (Bretherton & Munholland, 1999). The notion that infants vary in their IWMs reminds us that, even though attachment in general may have a biological basis, the *quality* of the attachment relationship is dependent on the infant's environment, especially the experience with the caregiver. Specifically, reliable, positive, and sensitive caregiving should lead to an IWM of the caregiver as trustworthy and supportive (loving) and the self as worthy of that trust and care (lovable). Unpredictable, negative, and insensitive interaction, on the other hand, would lead to an IWM of the caregiver as untrustworthy and unsupportive and the self as not worthy of trust and support. Crucially, this model is thought by many psychologists to serve as a guide to future interaction with others throughout life. For example, an individual with a secure type of IWM may expect others – such as romantic partners – to be positive and supportive whereas an insecure individual's IWM could lead them to expect others to be negative or unsupportive (Dykas & Cassidy, 2011; Thompson, 2000).

Unreliable and aversive infant–caregiver interactions are thought to give rise to anxious and fearful feelings in the child that require responses (or 'secondary systems') to manage the distress (Main, 1990; Shaver & Mikulincer, 2002). For example, infants with intermittent and unreliable caregiving may anxiously cling to their caregivers and vigilantly monitor them for signs of being left or abandoned. This anxious attachment style thus appears to involve 'hyperactivation' of the attachment system in order to constantly monitor and/or elicit proximity of the attachment figure. In contrast, an infant whose attachment behaviours have been ignored or met with punishment may tend to avoid interpersonal interactions that might lead to such rejection. This avoidant attachment style involves deactivation of the attachment system to suppress and downplay proximity seeking or the emotions that might lead to proximity seeking. For example, a study of children with a very avoidant (dismissing) attachment style showed that they continued to expect rejection after playing a game involving social exclusion, unlike securely attached children (White, Wu, Borelli, Mayes, & Crowley, 2013). Taking into account the notion of the IWMs formed by infants on the basis of their early interactions with caregivers, these variations in attachment patterns can be seen as rational or adaptive strategies in response to problematic caregiving (Bowlby, 1969; Mikulincer & Shaver, 2005).

Numerous studies have suggested that variations in attachment style remain relatively stable both in the short term (Waters, 1978) and into adulthood (Waters, Merrick, Treboux, Crowell, & Albersheim, 2000). However, although the concept of an IWM would lead us to expect continuity in attachment behaviour to some extent, Bowlby (1980, 1988) did acknowledge that attachment styles are not immutable. Major traumatic life events – such as illness, divorce, or death of a caregiver; substance abuse by a caregiver; abuse of the child; and suchlike – that have a negative impact on the quality of caregiver–child interaction could result in alterations to the child's IWM. Certainly, longitudinal studies have shown that changes from **secure attachment** to insecure attachment are strongly linked to experiencing one or more negative life event (e.g. Waters et al., 2000). Likewise, movement from an insecure to a more secure style is possible given a change in the responsiveness and sensitivity of caregiving, such as that seen in parenting intervention studies or in a therapeutic relationship where the therapist is seen as providing a reliable secure base experience. Changes in significant relationships potentially allow a reappraisal of outdated working models of self and other (e.g. see Mallinckrodt, 2010).

Nonetheless, most researchers working in this area agree that attachment relationships play an important role in development throughout the lifespan. One substantial line of research concerns adults' mental representations of their attachment relationship with their own parents, and has revealed that differences in these representations are systematically linked to the way that they parent their own children (George, Kaplan, & Main, 1985; Van IJzendoorn, 1995). This raises the possibility of explaining the transmission of secure and insecure attachment patterns over multiple generations.

Measuring the attachment relationship

Individual differences in attachment can be measured using a wide range of approaches. For infants and children, these include observation in the laboratory (e.g. the so-called **strange situation** procedure; Ainsworth et al., 1978) and in the home (e.g. the Attachment Q-Sort; Waters & Deane, 1985; see also Van IJzendoorn, Vereijken, Bakermans-Kranenburg, & Riksen-Walraven, 2004), as well as responses to experimental tests (e.g. the Separation Anxiety Test [Shouldice & Stevenson-Hinde, 1992] and the MacArthur Story Stem Battery [Bretherton & Oppenheim, 2003]). For adults and adolescents, in-depth semistructured interviews (e.g. the Adult Attachment Interview [AAI]; George et al., 1985, 1996) and questionnaires (e.g. the Experience of Close Relationships Questionnaire; Brennan, Clark, & Shaver, 1998; Fraley, Waller, & Brennan, 2000) are dominant approaches (Crowell, Fraley, & Shaver, 2008).

The gold-standard measure for assessing attachment status in infant–caregiver dyads involves observation in a laboratory of a child's interaction with their primary caregiver (usually the mother) using the aforementioned strange situation (Ainsworth et al., 1978). At its core, this experimental procedure involves assessing a central aspect of attachment behaviour: the use of the caregiver or attachment figure as a secure base from which to explore and to which to return when in distress or under threat. Starting with the child's behaviour in the presence of their caregiver, the strange situation procedure gradually increases the emotional stress on the child through a structured sequence of episodes involving the children being (briefly) separated from and then reunited with their mother, as well as episodes involving an encounter with an unfamiliar adult. The experimental set-up and sequence of episodes is shown in Figure 17.2.

 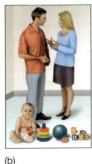 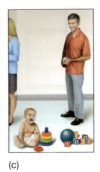  

(a)   (b)   (c)   (d)   (e)

FIGURE 17.2 *The strange situation procedure. (a) The baby plays while the mother is nearby. (b) A stranger enters the room, speaks to the mother, and approaches the child. (c) The mother leaves and the stranger remains in the room with the unhappy baby. (d) The mother returns and the stranger leaves. (e) The baby is reunited with the mother.*

Source: Comer, Ogden, and Furnham (2013). Reproduced with permission.

Ainsworth et al. (1978) noticed clear differences in how infants behaved with their mother (the extent to which they explored), how distressed they were when she left (**separation anxiety**), how they were with the stranger (their **stranger anxiety**), and especially how they were on her return. Based on such differences, infants were classified as secure (labelled Type B), **insecure–anxious avoidant** (labelled Type A), or **insecure–anxious resistant** (labelled Type C). A further category of **insecure–disorganized/disoriented** (labelled Type D) was included later (Main & Solomon, 1990).

As shown in Table 17.1, the variations in infant–caregiver attachment are thought to be linked to the parents' representations of their own attachment relationships earlier in life, as captured by the AAI (George et al., 1985, 1996; Main, Kaplan, & Cassidy, 1985). Rather than triggering attachment behaviours directly in a laboratory setting, the AAI involves interviewing a person in order to reveal their attachment-related state of mind (i.e. their IWM). This is accomplished by asking people to describe their early experiences with attachment figures and assessing the coherence (not the actual content) of their account. Whereas securely attached individuals (referred to as 'autonomous') are able to access and reflect on emotional

TABLE 17.1 *Attachment classifications in infancy and adulthood.*

Attachment classification	Infant behaviour in strange situation	Patterns in Adult Attachment Interview
Secure (Type B)	Explores environment and interacts with stranger in presence of caregiver (able to use caregiver as a secure base); upset when caregiver leaves, but comforted and reassured upon caregiver's return.	Autonomous: able to describe and reflect on childhood experiences in a coherent and emotionally balanced way.
Insecure–anxious avoidant (Type A)	Little use of the caregiver as a secure base; little emotion shown at caregiver leaving or returning; can include active ignoring or some approach behaviour and some ignoring.	Dismissing: tends to downplay or deny the importance of childhood memories and emotional experiences.
Insecure–anxious resistant (Type C)	Infant is clingy with caregiver and fails to explore the environment; great distress upon separation from the caregiver; ambivalent response to caregiver upon reunion, with efforts to gain comfort but also resistance to being soothed.	Preoccupied: still overwhelmed or overinvolved with experiences from childhood or their effects.
Insecure–disorganized/disoriented (Type D)	Lack of a consistent response to the strange situation, with evidence of disorientation and confused behaviours.	Unresolved/disorganized: confused or disoriented, particularly in relation to loss or trauma.

Note: Researchers have argued that working models of attachment serve as a basis for relationships throughout the lifespan. This includes evidence that attachment patterns are stable for individuals from infancy to young adulthood, over a 20-year period (Waters et al., 2000), and even that they can be transmitted across three generations (Benoit & Parker, 1994).

experiences in a balanced way, others tend to withdraw from or dismiss emotional experiences ('dismissing/avoidant') or seem overwhelmed or fixated on such experiences ('preoccupied').

Antecedents of attachment

In Ainsworth's original work using the strange situation, variations in attachment were found to be connected to differences in the levels of **maternal sensitivity** exhibited in interactions with infants. The term 'sensitivity' in this context indexes the degree to which a mother (or caregiver) is sensitive and responsive to her infant's signals and needs (such as responding appropriately to cries, behaving contingently in face-to-face interaction, and showing affection and tenderness; Ainsworth et al., 1978). A large number of studies have now shown that observational ratings of a mother's sensitivity when interacting with her infant strongly and consistently predict her infant's later attachment classification in the strange situation (Ainsworth et al., 1978; De Wolff & Van IJzendoorn, 1997). Further evidence comes from a meta-analysis (Bakermans-Kranenburg, Van IJzendoorn, & Juffer, 2003) of intervention studies that aimed specifically to enhance sensitive parenting – for example, through video recording the mother and infant interacting and giving feedback on their behaviour and reactions. These interventions have been shown to enhance both parental sensitivity and attachment security (Bakermans-Kranenburg et al., 2003). Importantly, the interventions that enhanced sensitivity the most also enhanced security the most, suggesting that maternal sensitivity is one of the key causal determinants of secure attachment. Other aspects of mother–infant interaction are also related to attachment security. In particular, both the ability to read the infant's behaviour in terms of underlying internal mental states – a tendency known as **mind-mindedness** (Meins, 2013; Meins, Fernyhough, Fradley, & Tuckey, 2001) – and early interactional synchrony involving coordinated and mutually rewarding interaction (Isabella, Belsky, & von Eye, 1989) have been found to strongly predict secure attachment. Furthermore, it seems likely that these kinds of parenting characteristics mediate the link between other social–contextual factors and attachment security. For example, community risk factors such as low socioeconomic status and family risk factors such as marital conflict might influence maternal sensitivity, which in turn affects attachment style (Bradley & Corwyn, 2002; Owen & Cox, 1997; Van IJzendoorn & Bakermans-Kranenburg, 2010).

Even though social influences have been found to be of great importance in shaping attachment relationships, child characteristics also appear to have an important role to play. We have seen already that child temperament predicts various aspects of adjustment, and attachment is no exception (Planalp & Braungart-Rieker, 2013). For example, Calkins and Fox (1992) have shown that infants' emotional reactivity (their distress when their pacifier was removed) when they were 2 days old was linked to later insecure attachment when they were aged 14 months. Beyond the main effects of temperament, we have already noted that a child's temperament may interact with social–environmental influences. In fact, temperament has been shown to moderate the effect of maternal sensitivity (Van den Boom, 1994). For example, Braungart-Rieker, Garwood, Powers, and Wang (2001) showed that, while mothers' sensitivity with their infants at 4 months predicted secure attachment at 1 year (as we would expect), maternal sensitivity was also related to temperamental differences in the infants' affect regulation: the more difficult the infants' temperament, the lower the maternal sensitivity. Thus, the effect of maternal sensitivity on attachment may be due at least in part to the infants' own temperament. Furthermore, temperament has been shown to moderate the effect of parenting interventions on attachment. In their study of the effects of a brief intervention designed to increase attachment security, Cassidy, Woodhouse, Sherman, Stupica, and Lejuez (2011) showed that highly irritable infants of mothers with a very avoidant (dismissing) attachment style were much more likely than moderately irritable infants to be classified as secure in the training condition, but much more likely to be classified as insecure in the no training condition. In other words, they responded disproportionately well to the positive condition and disproportionately poorly to the negative condition, consistent with the differential susceptibility hypothesis discussed earlier.

Consequences of attachment

As noted earlier, the concept of an IWM implies that the quality of the bond formed with our caregiver provides a powerful guide and model for our future social and emotional relationships (Bowlby, 1969). Consistent with this, research has shown that secure and insecure attachment styles predict a wide range of social, cognitive, and emotional outcomes. For example, securely attached children have consistently been shown to have better social relations with peers and a higher quality of friendship (Groh, et al., 2014; Schneider, Atkinson, & Tardif, 2001), and also demonstrate more constructive patterns of communication and problem solving (Frankel & Bates, 1990; Raikes & Thompson, 2008). In contrast, insecurely attached children and adolescents are much more likely to show internalizing symptoms (Brumariu & Kerns, 2010) and externalizing behaviour, particularly if they exhibit a disoriented–disorganized attachment pattern (Fearon, Bakermans-Kranenburg, Van IJzendoorn, Lapsley, & Roisman, 2010). Consistent with Bowlby's (1944) original observation of the link between disruption to attachment and delinquency, insecure attachment has also been associated with criminality, including violent offending (Hamill, Newman, Todd, & Peck, 2014). In contrast, securely attached children are better able to regulate their emotions (Thompson & Meyer, 2007) and show greater levels of self-esteem and confidence right into adulthood (Sroufe, 2005). Comparable links between attachment orientation and socio-emotional functioning have also been shown in adults (Fraley & Davis, 1997; Mikulincer & Florian, 1995; Simpson, Rholes, & Nelligan, 1992).

The links between attachment quality and socio-emotional outcomes are likely to be partly explained by variations in how social information is processed. Securely attached children have been shown to be better at understanding both basic emotions (Laible & Thompson, 1998; Ontai & Thompson, 2002) and more complex mental states, particularly of their mothers (Laranjo, Bernier, Meins, & Carlson, 2010). Likewise, insecure attachment has been linked to poorer emotional decoding in adults, as shown by both reaction time (Niedenthal, Brauer, Robin, & Innes-Ker, 2002) and brain-imaging studies (Zilber, Goldstein, & Mikulincer, 2007). In turn, these differences in processing emotional information could be responsible for variations in how securely and insecurely attached children and adults interact socially. For example, McElwain, Booth-LaForce, and Wu (2011) have shown that mothers with insecurely attached children tend to refer less to mental states in their conversations with their children, which in turn predicts their poorer friendship quality.

Maternal deprivation and disruption to attachment

The perceived importance of attachment in children's social development inevitably raises questions about what happens when attachment relationships are absent or disrupted. Bowlby (1953, 1969) himself formulated the 'maternal deprivation' hypothesis, proposing that being deprived of maternal contact during the critical period of 6 months to 3 years of age has strong, detrimental social and emotional effects on children. This idea was largely based on historical accounts of children placed in institutional care – for example, children raised in orphanages after World War II (Bowlby, 1953) – and might also be perceived to be supported by evidence from children in Romanian orphanages in the 1980s who showed severe developmental deficits (Rutter, 1998). Although there is little doubt that such extreme deprivation has strong negative effects on children's social and emotional development, the extent to which deprivation or disruption of attachment leads to irreversible damage to a child's socio-emotional development is a complicated question. As we have seen, major changes in life experience can lead to fundamental changes in the IWM and thus to significant shifts in attachment relationships, and this has been demonstrated even in the case of Romanian orphans, many of whom have been shown to display normal functioning following adoption (Rutter, Kreppner, & O'Connor, 2001). But perhaps most controversial of all has been the suggestion that any significant separation from the mother (or mother-substitute) – including mothers going out to work – is detrimental to a child's development.

The question of how non-parental care influences children's development is a high-profile concern for many societies. The US Census Bureau in 2011 reported that 62% of mothers in the United States with a birth in the previous year were in employment in 2008; in the United Kingdom, the Office for National Statistics (2013) reported that in April to June 2013 around 67% of women were in work. Numerous researchers have argued that there *are* potentially negative effects of early non-parental care, particularly day care, on children's development. Belsky and Rovine (1988), for example, found that infants who spent more than 20 hours per week in day care before the age of 1 were at greater risk of developing insecure attachments compared with those spending fewer than 20 hours a week in day care. Supporting this view, a survey by Baydar and Brooks-Gunn (1991) reported that parental employment in the first year had detrimental effects on infants' behavioural development, regardless of the parents' gender or socioeconomic status. More recent research examining the effects of universal childcare in Canada has shown that there may be detrimental effects in terms of behavioural and social development outcomes for children aged between 0 and 2 years (Kottelenberg & Lehrer, 2014).

However, despite these findings, there is now a large body of evidence suggesting that non-parental childcare per se is *not* detrimental to children's development. Instead, it is argued that many of the negative effects of non-parental care

are actually explained or moderated by a number of other factors (e.g. the quality and quantity of the non-parental care, parental sensitivity, the child's age and gender, family socioeconomic status, and genetic and temperamental factors). A large-scale longitudinal study by the National Institute of Child Health and Human Development (NICHD) in the United States has examined the effects of various kinds of childcare on children's development. In contrast with some of the earlier negative findings, this study has not revealed a main effect of day care on children's attachment security. Rather, it has shown a main effect of maternal sensitivity and responsiveness, and, when this was low *and* children spent long hours in poor-quality day care, there was significantly greater insecure attachment, particularly among boys (NICHD, 1997).

Later reports from the same longitudinal study examining day care's effects on social and behavioural outcomes have shown a more complex and mixed pattern of results. When controlling for a number of factors including gender, socioeconomic status, maternal sensitivity, and parenting quality, more hours in day care were related to increased behaviour problems (NICHD, 2002), more externalizing problems and adult–child conflict when children were aged 4.5 years (NICHD, 2003), and greater impulsivity and risk taking when children were aged 15 years (NICHD, 2011). Other studies, in contrast, have shown no evidence that day care is linked with greater behavioural problems. A large-scale Norwegian study by Zachrisson, Dearing, Lekhal, and Toppelberg (2013) with a sample of over 75,000 children showed no significant association between childcare and externalizing problems in 18-month-olds and 36-month-olds, and, in a sample of Canadian 2- and 3-year-olds, Borge, Rutter, Côté, and Tremblay (2004) found that aggression was actually *more* common in children looked after at home by their own mothers compared with those in childcare, though this was more true for those from high-risk families. This raises the possibility that, rather than being detrimental to children's development, childcare could actually be beneficial, particularly when the childcare is of good quality and children come from disadvantaged backgrounds.

Drawing a general conclusion about the impact of day care is therefore difficult because myriad social factors are involved (e.g. childcare quality and level of risk in the family environment). Moreover, we have already seen that the same social environment may have very different effects on children depending on their own temperamental characteristics (Pluess & Belsky, 2010). So, while there is some evidence to suggest that non-parental care *can* be detrimental for children's development, it would be wise to qualify this by noting that this becomes more likely when children attend non-parental care at a young age (particularly in their first year), when they spend long hours in poor-quality childcare, and when they have particular genetic and temperamental susceptibility to environmental influence.

DISCUSSION POINT

Discuss the key factors that affect the quality of attachment between a child and caregiver. Suggest some examples of issues that may affect the quality of the attachment relationship.

1. What social factors might influence the ways children behave in the 'strange situation'?
2. Identify the key evidence for and against the claim that non-parental daycare has a negative impact on children's development.

SECTION SUMMARY

- Children's attachments to their caregivers play an important role in development throughout the lifespan.

- Even though attachment in general may have a biological basis, the *quality* of the attachment relationship is dependent on the infant's environment, especially experiences with caregivers.

- A mother's sensitivity when interacting with her infant strongly and consistently predicts the later quality of attachment, as measured by the laboratory 'strange situation' task.

- Child characteristics such as temperament also appear to have an important role to play in influencing the quality of attachment.

- In turn, the quality of attachment has been associated with a wide variety of social outcomes.

- Concerns have been raised about the impact of non-parental day care on children's development, but the effects of such experiences depend on the quantity and quality of the childcare as well as the age, background, and temperamental susceptibility of the child.

SOCIAL UNDERSTANDING AND SELF-REGULATION

LEARNING OBJECTIVE 17.4

Discuss the roles of social understanding and self-regulation in the development of social behaviour.

Children's social behaviours are influenced not just by the interplay between emotions, temperament, and social experiences but also by the children's *understanding* of the social world, and by their capacity to control – or *regulate* – their own behaviours and emotions. Below, we explore the way in which children come to reason about the social world, and particularly their own and other people's mental states, before turning to questions about how children develop skills in controlling the way they behave as well as a variety of strategies for coping with uncomfortable emotions.

Theory of mind

Theory of mind (ToM) involves the ability to attribute mental states such as beliefs, desires, emotions, and intentions to yourself and to others in order to explain and predict behaviour (Premack & Woodruff, 1978; see Doherty, 2008, for an introduction and overview). Researchers have tracked the development of ToM through early understanding of a range of mental states. For example, infants will look more when a person's reaching behaviour is inconsistent with their goals (Woodward, 1998) and become frustrated when someone is *unwilling* to help and interact with them rather than just being *unable* to do so (Behne, Carpenter, Call, & Tomasello, 2005), indicating an appreciation of another's *intention*. They also begin to understand, by around 18 months, that people can have different *desires* from their own; one study suggested that children of this age have some preliminary understanding that people may have different preferences for food items (Repacholi & Gopnik, 1997). There is also clear improvement during the preschool period in children's understanding of basic *emotions* and their causes (Denham, Zoller, & Couchoud, 1994). Moreover, they appear to have some sensitivity to people's knowledge: researchers have shown that preschoolers will tend not to learn new words for objects from adults who appear unknowledgeable (such as being hesitant or not knowing about the object when labelling it), indicating the importance of *knowledge states* (Sabbagh & Baldwin, 2001).

But a crucial milestone in the development of ToM occurs when children gain an explicit understanding that someone can hold a mistaken (false) belief about the world, an ability that emerges around 4 years of age (Wellman, Cross, & Watson, 2001). This appears across a wide range of cultures (Callaghan et al., 2005), although there are some notable cultural variations (Hughes et al., 2014). The ability to pass **false-belief tasks** (see Focus Point 17.1) is thought to be particularly significant because it reflects a shift in reasoning about behaviours based on an understanding of *desires* (i.e. that people act according to what they want or like) to one involving reasoning about *beliefs* (that people act according to what they think, even if they are wrong or mistaken). This shift to **belief–desire reasoning** (Wellman, 1990) shows that a child is now able to think explicitly about how someone else *thinks about* something – in other words, to take and understand their *perspective* (Perner, 1991; Perner, Stummer, Sprung, & Doherty, 2002).

IMPLICIT AND EXPLICIT APPROACHES TO TESTING CHILDREN'S UNDERSTANDING OF FALSE BELIEF

Theory of mind (ToM) can be tested using false-belief tasks such as the unexpected transfer task (Baron-Cohen, Leslie, & Frith, 1985; Wimmer & Perner, 1983). This task involves a character (Sally) leaving an object (e.g. a marble) in one location and, while she is away, another character (Anne) unexpectedly moving the object to a new location. On Sally's return, the children being tested are asked a direct question – 'Where will Sally look for her marble first?' – and control questions to check they have followed the story. A child with mature belief–desire reasoning will understand that Sally will go to the location where she left the marble (because that is where she thinks it is) rather than the second location (where the marble actually is). Children pass these explicit (verbal) tasks around 4 years of age (Wellman et al., 2001).

Panel 1: **Sally** has a black box and **Ann** has a white box.

Panel 2: **Sally** has a marble. She puts the marble into her box.

Panel 3: **Sally** goes for a walk.

Panel 4: **Ann** takes the marble out of Sally's box and puts it into her box.

Panel 5: **Sally** comes back and wants to play with her marble.

Where will **Sally** look for her marble?

The unexpected transfer task.

Source: Byom and Mutlu (2013). Copyright © 2013 Byom and Mutlu.

More recent research, however, appears to show much earlier understanding of false belief in infants when looking time is used to measure understanding. For example, Onishi and Baillargeon (2005) used a nonverbal version of the Sally–Anne task, involving a violation-of-expectation design, to investigate false-belief understanding in 15-month-old infants. In some initial familiarization trials, infants see a female actor placing and then reaching for an object in either a yellow box or a green box. But, in the key false-belief trials, infants see a sequence of events where the actor could be expected to form and then act on her false belief.

In the following example, the actor first watches as the object is moved from the green box to the yellow box, but crucially is then absent when the object is moved back to the green box. When the actor returns, she is seen either reaching into the yellow box (consistent with where she falsely believes the object to be) or reaching into the green box (where the object actually is). Infants looked for reliably longer at the former rather than the latter, suggesting that they expected the actor to search in the yellow box on the basis of her false belief, and thus were surprised when she searched in the green box.

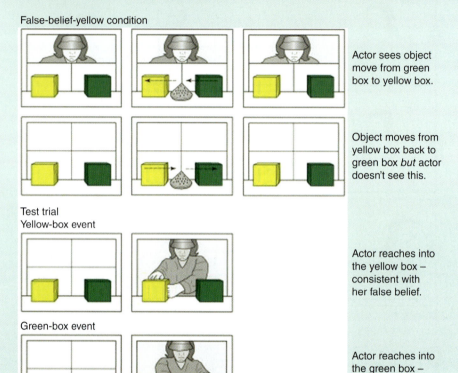

False-belief-yellow condition

Actor sees object move from green box to yellow box.

Object moves from yellow box back to green box *but* actor doesn't see this.

Test trial
Yellow-box event

Actor reaches into the yellow box – consistent with her false belief.

Green-box event

Actor reaches into the green box – not consistent with her false belief.

Source: Reprinted and adapted from Baillargeon, Scott, and He (2010). Copyright (2010), with permission from Elsevier.

More recent evidence suggests that infants as young as 7 months of age show such insight into false-belief understanding (Kovács, Téglás, & Endress, 2010). Moreover, like with explicit tasks, this early understanding is comparable across a range of cultures (Barrett et al., 2013).

These tasks can be said to be 'implicit' in the sense that looking time is an indirect measure of understanding. A crucial debate is whether the explicit and implicit measures are tapping the same conceptual understanding. For some researchers, who take a nativist position and argue that ToM ability is innate, this early understanding shown by looking time performance reflects the same understanding as that elicited in later standard tasks but without the cognitive (e.g. language) demands required for such explicit responding (Leslie, 2005; Scott, 2014) and as such is considered to reflect spontaneous understanding (He, Bolz, & Baillargeon, 2011; Luo & Baillargeon, 2010; Senju, 2012).

Other researchers, who take the constructivist position that the conceptual understanding of belief is constructed during the preschool years, argue that looking time performance reflects a much more basic or rudimentary type of understanding (Clements & Perner, 1994; Low & Perner, 2012) or even involves a separate system (Apperly & Butterfill, 2009). This understanding involves processing the actions of the agents in the stories in terms of their underlying regularity of behaviour (e.g. people will look in the last place they left an object) rather than understanding that is properly mentalistic (Perner & Ruffman, 2005; Ruffman, 2014).

Watch this video[1] of a series of theory-of-mind tests.

Theory of mind is considered to be crucial for everyday social interaction and communication (Waytz, Gray, Epley, & Wegner, 2010). Indeed, impairment in the development of this understanding is argued to account for the severe social problems in autism. Likewise, in typical development, ToM (as measured by false-belief performance; see Focus Point 17.1) has been linked with teacher ratings of social competence (Watson, Nixon, Wilson, & Capage, 1999), with cooperative behaviour and peer acceptance (e.g. Caputi, Lecce, Pagnin, & Banerjee, 2012), and with social behaviours that require perspective taking, such as maintaining connectedness with others when communicating with them (Slomkowski & Dunn, 1996). Interestingly, it has been pointed out there can also be a cost to such understanding, in that children with a more advanced ToM are more sensitive to teacher criticism of their work (Cutting & Dunn, 2002). Nonetheless, even this may not be a genuine cost in the long term: sensitivity to criticism has been shown to have a beneficial effect on later academic achievement (Lecce, Caputi, & Hughes, 2011).

It is important to recognize, however, that having a mature understanding of mental states may not be enough on its own to predict a given child's social behaviour. For example, while ToM predicts the amount of time children will spend observing a new, unfamiliar playmate, it does not predict whether or not they will actually engage with them (Moore, Bosacki, & Macgillivray, 2011). As noted by some researchers, little attention has been paid to children's own social motivation and it is likely that this is as important as their social cognitive abilities (Astington, 2001; Chevallier, Kohls, Troiani, Brodkin, & Schultz, 2012). For example, research on children's understanding of how they can control the impressions they make on others – also known as **self-presentation** – has shown that the ToM capabilities needed for this may be present by 6 years of age. Yet there is often a lag in children's reasoning about self-presentational behaviour, as the motivational importance of being evaluated by others tends to increase later in childhood, from around 8 years of age (Banerjee, 2002). Thus, as Astington (2003) observes, ToM may be *necessary* for certain social behaviours, but this does not mean it is always *sufficient*.

Furthermore, it is important to recognize that ToM itself continues to develop over a protracted timespan. Although much of the early work on ToM focused on development during the first 5 years of life, there is increasing recognition that children continue to develop their understanding of mental states throughout the school years, and perhaps beyond. This includes understanding recursive expansions of belief states (e.g. second-order reasoning such as 'he thinks that she thinks that...'; Perner & Wimmer, 1985) and the complex array of mental states involved in everyday social situations such as misunderstandings, unintentional insults, and the use of sarcasm and irony (e.g. Banerjee, Watling, & Caputi, 2011; Happé, 1994; Lecce, Bianco, Devine, Hughes, & Banerjee, 2014). Abilities to perform well on these kinds of tasks tend to emerge during the primary school years, and during this period children also come to recognize that two people who perceive the same stimulus may form different interpretations of it depending on their existing knowledge and preferences (e.g. Carpendale & Chandler, 1996).

Because ToM plays a crucial role in aspects of communication and interaction, it is important to understand the factors that facilitate its development. Both cognitive factors, such as children's developing verbal ability and language skills (Milligan,

Astington, & Dack, 2007), and social factors, such as social interaction within the family (Carpendale & Lewis, 2004), are thought to play important roles. Returning to our earlier discussion of parent–child interaction and caregivers' mind-mindedness, we can see how **mental-state talk** by mothers (i.e. conversations about thoughts, feelings, and desires) is likely to provide a powerful context within which children learn about the mind (De Rosnay & Hughes, 2006). Indeed, mothers' use of mental-state talk with their child is linked to advanced ToM in children who are typically developing (Ruffman, Perner, & Parkin, 1999), deaf (Moeller & Schnick, 2006), or autistic (Slaughter, Peterson, & Mackintosh, 2007). This can be understood with a **Vygotskian approach** (Vygotsky, 1978), whereby mothers use mental-state talk to scaffold children's emerging understanding (Taumoepeau & Ruffman, 2008; for a simple summary, see McLeod, 2014). Strong support for the idea that this facilitates children's understanding comes from longitudinal studies (e.g. Ensor, Devine, Marks, & Hughes, 2014; Meins et al., 2002). For example, in their study with preschool children, Ruffman, Slade, and Crowe (2002) showed that mothers' early use of mental-state talk consistently predicted children's later ToM – but not the other way around – across three time points (over and above any effects of socioeconomic status, age, language, and earlier ToM ability). The causal role of conversing with children about mental states appears to be significant for children's social and emotional development, predicting increased cooperation (Ruffman, Slade, Devitt, & Crowe, 2006) and reduced emotional and behavioural difficulties in at-risk, low-economic-status children (Meins, Centifanti, Fernyhough, & Fishburn, 2013). Furthermore, input from peer interaction may be critically important for continuing to develop the more advanced forms of ToM reasoning, such as understanding the subtleties of unintentional insults (e.g. Banerjee et al., 2011).

Emotion understanding and empathy

We noted above that a basic understanding of emotions is an important early step in children's understanding of the mind. This **emotion understanding** also continues to develop throughout childhood (Harris, 2008). At a young age, children begin to understand that people will have different emotional reactions to an event depending on their desires (e.g. that people will feel sad if they do not get what they want; Wellman & Wolley, 1990). Later, they come to appreciate complex ways in which our beliefs can influence our feelings. Imagine, for example, that someone is given their favourite drink can but is completely unaware that the can has been filled with a drink that they hate. How would that person feel? Harris, Johnson, Hutton, Andrews, and Cooke (1989) found that, as children increased in age between 3 and 6 years, they increasingly recognized that the person's emotional reaction would be dependent on their false belief about the contents of the can and that they would therefore feel happy. During the school years, they also come to reason in more complex ways about self-conscious emotions such as embarrassment (e.g. see Banerjee, 2002; Bennett, 1989), as well as about ambivalent or mixed emotions (e.g. that someone can feel both happy and sad at the same time – for instance, if they didn't win a prize but their friend did) (Harter & Buddin, 1987). Crucially, just as we have seen in the case of children's ToM, individual differences in emotion understanding have been found to be linked with children's social relationships and with subsequent developmental outcomes. For example, research by Ensor, Spencer, and Hughes (2011) suggests not only that parent–child relationships serve as an important platform for children's learning about emotions but also that such learning enables children to successfully navigate their social interactions with peers and other social partners during the school years. Indeed, mounting research points to the importance of children's emotion understanding for their classroom adjustment and academic profile (e.g. Denham, Bassett, Zinsser, & Wyatt, 2014).

The ability to reason about others' emotional states is an essential part of **empathy**. Researchers have argued that empathy involves both *understanding* others' feelings and *experiencing* affective reactions yourself when observing others' emotional states (e.g. feeling bad when someone else is hurt). Researchers have proposed that humans have a biological predisposition to respond emotionally to others (De Waal, 2006; Hoffman, 2000), with a rudimentary form of empathetic behaviour exhibited soon after birth, when infants cry in response to hearing another infant cry (Sagi & Hoffman, 1976). However, the development of empathy involves progressing from such simple 'emotional contagion' to a more mature understanding of others' feelings as well as prosocial intentions to comfort or otherwise alleviate others' negative emotions. These distinctions between affective, cognitive, and behavioural aspects of empathy are likely to be crucial for understanding differences in children's relationship and interaction patterns. For example, recent work has pointed to distinctive roles of cognitive and affective empathy in childhood conduct problems (Pasalich, Dadds, & Hawes, 2014).

DISCUSSION POINT

How do the parenting tips in **this article**[2] relate to what you have learned in this section about the development of empathy?

Self-regulation and executive function

Having a mature understanding of beliefs and emotions is undoubtedly an important platform for competent social interaction, but we need to have a great deal of self-control in order to act on our understanding. Researchers have emphasized the importance of **executive function** (**EF**) – involving working memory, inhibitory control, and cognitive flexibility – in children's capacity to control and regulate their own behaviour. These abilities emerge in the first years of life, with rudimentary abilities shown in infancy, and become stronger through to adolescence (Best & Miller, 2010), reflecting in large part the maturation of the prefrontal cortex (see Zelazo, Carlson, & Kesek, 2008).

A large number of developmentally sensitive tasks have been developed by psychologists to measure EF skills (e.g. Carlson, 2005). For example, the dimensional change card sort task (Frye, Zelazo, & Palfai, 1995) measures children's inhibitory and attentional control by seeing how well they are able to switch from sorting cards according to one rule (e.g. their colour) to sorting the same cards according to another (e.g. their shape). Some researchers make a distinction between 'hot' and 'cold' EF (e.g. Hongwanishkul, Happaney, Lee, & Zelazo, 2005). 'Cold' tasks, such as the dimensional change card sort task, tap more abstract reasoning and problem solving whereas 'hot' tasks, such as 'delay of gratification' measures (Mischel, Shoda, & Rodriguez, 1989), are also emotionally charged and personally meaningful (see Focus Point 17.2).

FOCUS POINT 17.2

DELAY IN GRATIFICATION

One marshmallow now, or two if you can wait! How do children respond to tasks where they need to resist temptation and wait for an even more desirable reward? Mischel's classic 'delay of gratification' paradigm drew attention to children's capacities for self-control. Crucially, Mischel et al. (1989) also reported that preschoolers who were able to delay gratification for longer in the laboratory tests were 'rated in adolescence by their parents as significantly more attentive and able to concentrate, competent, planful, and intelligent' (p. 936). They were also found to have higher academic achievement test scores. Skills in self-regulation are thus widely recognized as having a key role to play in children's development.

Skills in EF are thought to be critical for interacting successfully with social partners (see Hughes, 2011). In fact, deficits in EF development are thought to explain behavioural symptoms and associated social problems in disorders such as attention deficit hyperactivity disorder (ADHD) (e.g. see Tseng & Gau, 2013) and autism (see Hughes, 2002; Focus Point 17.3). Moreover, it seems highly possible that difficulties with self-control may underpin many social difficulties exhibited in typically developing children (e.g. see Morgan & Lilienfeld, 2000). Interestingly, Hughes, White, Sharpen, and Dunn (2000) showed that problems with EF control were a better predictor of antisocial behaviour than ToM ability. Indeed, the development of EF is strongly linked with the development of ToM ability itself (see Devine & Hughes, 2014). One view is that this is because the ability to express ToM understanding (whether in a false-belief task or in real-world situations) requires inhibiting one's own perspective (see Apperly, Samson, & Humphreys, 2009). As such, development of EF may also have an indirect effect on social behaviour via ToM understanding.

FOCUS POINT 17.3

DEVELOPING SOCIAL UNDERSTANDING AND SOCIAL COMPETENCE: INSIGHTS FROM AUTISM

Autism spectrum disorder (ASD) is a neurodevelopmental disorder characterized by impairments in social communication and interaction, and by restricted and repetitive behaviours (American Psychiatric Association, 2013; Lord & Jones, 2012; see also Frith, 2003). A dominant explanation at the cognitive level for the social impairment shown in autism is the mind-blindness (or theory-of-mind [ToM] deficit) hypothesis, which argues that people with ASD have impairments in representing mental states (Baron-Cohen, 1995). Clearly, making sense of people's behaviour and engaging in reciprocal social interaction is going to be difficult if we fail to appreciate the thoughts and feeling that underlie that behaviour (Frith, Happé, & Siddons, 1994).

Classic evidence for mind-blindness comes from a study by Baron-Cohen et al. (1985), who gave a false-belief test to a group of children with autism, a matched group with learning difficulties, and a group of typically developing 4-year-olds. Whereas the majority (around 85%) of children who were typically developing or had learning difficulties passed the task, only about 20% of the children with autism were able to correctly predict that Sally would look in the place where she thought her ball would be (rather than where it actually was). Given that these children passed the control questions (and so did not have problems following the story) and that children with learning difficulties generally passed, the problem seems to be a specific ASD difficulty with understanding mental states rather than understanding more generally.

Some have questioned the mind-blindness hypothesis because a small number of people with autism (particularly those with high-functioning ASDs) consistently pass ToM tasks, even though they still demonstrate significant social difficulties. If this deficit is not universal, it weakens the hypothesis' claim as an explanatory model (Rajendran & Mitchell, 2007). However, Senju, Southgate, White, and Frith (2009) have shown that, even when people with autism pass explicit verbal ToM tasks, they nonetheless do not look to the correct location in nonverbal tasks. This finding is consistent with the idea that people with autism may use a different way of solving explicit ToM tasks (Ruffman, Garnham, & Rideout, 2001) and also serves to underscore the importance of ToM as an explanation of the social impairments in autism (Senju, 2012).

Eyetracking is a very useful tool for investigating social impairments in autism as it allows researchers to examine how people with autism extract social information (Boraston & Blakemore, 2007). We saw earlier that young infants show a tendency to attend to faces, and it seems possible that this provides a platform for learning about the mind. However, eyetracking studies of autistic individuals show clear differences in their orientation to socially relevant information, such as faces (Riby & Hancock, 2008). In particular, people with autism show reduced attention to eyes compared to mouths (Klin, Jones, Schultz, Volkmar, & Cohen, 2002). While it is unclear whether this reflects an inability or unwillingness to process information from the eyes (Corden, Chilvers, & Skuse, 2008; Yoon & Vouloumanos, 2014), reduced looking to the eyes in toddlers with autism has been shown to predict level of social disability (Jones, Carr, & Klin, 2008).

When heatmaps are created of exactly where people are looking when they see a photograph, results show that, whereas people without autism tend to direct their attention to faces (picture on left), people with autism don't look as much to faces (picture on right).

(a)   (b)

Source: Reprinted from Riby and Hancock (2008). Copyright (2008), with permission from Elsevier.

Like ToM, EF abilities are influenced by social experiences, such as parenting style. For example, Bernier, Carlson, and Whipple (2010) showed that maternal sensitivity, mind-mindedness, and autonomy support when children were aged 12–15 months all predicted later EF ability, over and above any effects of general cognitive ability and maternal education. Importantly, the fact that EF development can be facilitated in this way has led some researchers to develop training programmes to promote children's executive control (e.g. see Diamond, Barnett, Thomas, & Munro, 2007). These seem to have powerful effects on children's behaviour and consequent achievement in school (Schmitt, McClelland, Tominey, & Acock, 2015).

The development of EF is closely linked with abilities to regulate and manage emotions (Carlson & Wang, 2007; Fox & Calkins, 2003). In the first few months, infants have a limited capacity to regulate their emotions, but, from around 3 to 6 months, behaviours such as thumb sucking and the seeking of a caregiver (Stifter & Braungart, 1995) demonstrate rudimentary efforts to manage emotions. Sensitive and contingent responding by caregivers is especially important in facilitating the development of early emotion regulation in the first year, and evidence has shown that a caregiver's failure to effectively regulate stressful events for infants can result in infants' reduced ability to manage their own emotions later on (Feldman, 2007). Even among older children, sensitive parenting has been shown to be associated with children's adaptive emotion regulation strategies (Morelen, Shaffer, & Suveg, 2014).

Infants' emotion regulation abilities increase through their first year along with increasing motor abilities (e.g. crawling and walking), which give them greater control over their environment, and by 2 years language becomes a key factor in helping them to regulate their emotions, as they are increasingly able to verbalize their feelings (e.g. Eisenberg et al., 2005). By 3 to 4 years, improved EF (e.g. being able to shift attention away from stressful stimuli) enables children to adopt more sophisticated strategies to deal with frustration, such as distraction from the emotion-eliciting event (Stansbury & Sigman, 2000). These skills have been associated with fewer externalizing problems and greater cooperation (Gilliom, Shaw, Beck, Schonberg, & Lukon, 2002).

As children move from early to middle childhood, their repertoire of cognitive and behavioural strategies increases, as they come to deal with more complex social and emotional challenges. Some strategies are oriented directly towards the source of stress (e.g. problem solving) whereas others focus on managing the associated emotions (e.g. seeking emotional support). These different strategies have been associated with a range of social and emotional developmental outcomes. For example, problem solving has been associated with more positive outcomes (e.g. reduced aggression and delinquency) whereas simply venting emotions is linked with more negative ones (for a review, see Fields & Prinz, 1997).

TEST YOURSELF

1. What does success on a false-belief task tell us about a child's theory-of-mind ability?
2. Describe how theory of mind, empathy, and executive function can be related to one another.

SECTION SUMMARY

- Children's social behaviours are influenced by their understanding of the social world and by their capacity to regulate their own behaviours and emotions.

- A theory of mind (ToM) allows children to attribute mental states such as beliefs, desires, emotions, and intentions to themselves and to others in order to explain and predict behaviour.

- ToM is considered to be crucial for everyday social interaction and communication, and impairment in the development of this understanding is thought to play a major role in the social problems of individuals with autism.

- ToM is thought to be influenced by children's developing verbal ability and language skills, as well as by social factors such as conversations about mental states within the family.

- Children also exhibit individual differences in emotion understanding and empathy, which, like ToM, have been linked with children's social relationships and with subsequent developmental outcomes.

- In addition, there are important developments in executive functions, which are the cognitive abilities involved in controlling our behaviour and mental processes, such as working memory and inhibitory control.

- These developments, which allow children to control the way they behave and even the way they feel, are linked to development in the prefrontal areas of the brain.

SOCIO-MORAL DEVELOPMENT

LEARNING OBJECTIVE 17.5

Describe how social and cognitive factors affect children's moral development.

We have already seen that children's understanding of the social world plays a key role in their social development, but one aspect of social life that deserves particular attention is the moral dimension. How do children come to reason about right and wrong, and to behave in ways that help versus harm others? These are key questions for researchers who study **moral development**, which concerns the rules and conventions regarding what people should do in their interactions with others (see Kurtines, Gewitz, & Lamb, 2014). Some have argued that the foundations of moral thought and behaviour appear very early in infancy. For example, as we will see later, even very young infants appear to prefer (i.e. will look longer towards) characters who act in a helpful, rather than hindering, way towards another (Hamlin, Wynn, & Bloom, 2010) and toddlers will direct positive behaviours towards those acting in a prosocial way (Hamlin, Wynn, Bloom, & Mahajan, 2011). In line with such evidence, some theorists have emphasized an innate basis, selected through evolution, for human morality. In other words, it is claimed that infants are born with the ability to automatically (or intuitively) process social situations in terms of basic moral dimensions, such as whether a situation involves harm. Although these capacities are developed by experience, they serve as an initial guide for that development (e.g. see Haidt & Joseph, 2007).

Notwithstanding the possibility of some innate foundations, most psychological research on moral development has focused on cognitive aspects of morality as well as the role played by sociocultural and emotional dimensions. In fact, one very straightforward account of moral development holds that children's moral behaviour and sense of right and wrong are transmitted to them by socialization agents such as parents, through processes of reinforcement (e.g. rewarding a child for morally 'right' behaviour) and modelling (e.g. exposing the child to prosocial behaviour). In a famous demonstration of how imitative learning can influence children's own moral behaviour, Bandura, Ross, and Ross's (1961) seminal experiments showed that young children could be influenced to behave in a highly aggressive way towards inflatable 'Bobo' dolls following exposure to adults who modelled this behaviour. Thus, social learning theory highlights the role of the social environment in shaping children's moral development. Using this framework, children would be expected to internalize and replicate the type of behaviour and judgement that is being modelled for them (Bandura & McDonald, 1963), particularly by parents.

On the other hand, much of the research on moral development since around the 1930s has concentrated on the way in which children's thinking about moral issues changes as they get older. The cognitive development approach argues that stage-like changes in moral reasoning and behaviour follow changes in underlying cognitive structures. This argument holds that moral development is primarily a consequence of a child's increasing cognitive capacities rather than an outcome of social relations. Greater cognitive capacity means more chance of finding complex and better solutions to moral problems, which in turn will inform moral behaviour (Kohlberg & Hersh, 1977).

Early work by Jean Piaget (1932) proposed that a key shift in moral understanding occurs when children move from the preoperational stage to the concrete operations stage, at around 7 years of age. Prior to this age, children were thought to lack the logical ability to understand how something can be represented (or seen) in different ways; in other words, they were thought to find it difficult to see things from other people's perspectives. Such **egocentrism** was thought by Piaget to compromise young children's ability to understand people's behaviour in terms of their beliefs and intentions. Instead, they were expected to focus only on external aspects or *outcomes* of the behaviour. In his classic example, children were asked who was more naughty – a boy who accidentally broke six cups while trying to help his mother in the kitchen or a boy who knocked over and broke one cup when trying to take some forbidden sweets from a high shelf while his mother was out. Piaget found that younger children evaluated the seriousness in terms of the outcome and felt that the boy who broke more cups was naughtier and deserved to be punished more (Piaget, 1932). Only older children, who were more adept at **perspective taking**, were able to take into account the different motives of the children and identify the second boy as naughtier.

Piaget's interviews with children about their experiences of playing marble games revealed some of the cognitive transformations that take place in children's concepts of rules: children appeared to move from a conception of rules as fixed and enforced in an absolute fashion by adults or some other higher authority (linked to a 'morality of constraint') to a concept of rules as arising from social consensus (linked to a 'morality of cooperation'). Piaget's emphasis on the role of perspective taking in moving to the latter, more subjective conceptualization of morality – where outcomes are not the only consideration – has been supported by more recent studies. For example, children who lack a ToM, as indicated by failing false-belief tasks, are less likely to appropriately assess the intentions of an accidental transgressor and are more likely to view their punishment as acceptable in comparison with those who have acquired this perspective-taking ability (Killen, Mulvey, Richardson, Jampol, & Woodward, 2011).

TABLE 17.2 *Kohlberg's stage model of moral development.*

Preconventional	**Stage 1 (obedience and punishment orientation)**	Tend to believe that rules are absolute, given by authority figures, and need to be obeyed (or transgression will rightly be punished).
	Stage 2 (individualistic and self-interest orientation)	Able to see things from others' point of view and in terms of fairness to some extent, but still tend to think about actions instrumentally in terms of how they benefit or serve their own interests.
Conventional	**Stage 3 (good boy/nice girl orientation)**	Aim to live up to social norms and expectations, with a focus on social approval, but can also take into account people's intentions and motives when forming judgements.
	Stage 4 (law and order orientation)	Move beyond the need for individual approval to understanding the needs of society and social order.
Postconventional	**Stage 5 (social contract orientation)**	Recognize that different societies may have different norms and expectations, and that rules and laws are created for people's mutual benefit.
	Stage 6 (universal ethical principle orientation)	Recognize that there are higher ethical principles that transcend any given set of societal rules or laws.

Kohlberg's (1969, 1976) theory extends Piaget's cognitive approach into adulthood. Like Piaget, Kohlberg analysed people's responses to hypothetical dilemmas, but he went beyond their moral judgements about those dilemmas and focused in particular on *how* people reasoned and justified their answers. Based on this, Kohlberg (1963) presented a detailed stage model of moral development. This development, shown in Table 17.2, was thought to start at the **preconventional** level, with a primary concern around the consequences of actions (e.g. punishments and rewards). During adolescence, moral reasoning was thought to progress to the **conventional** level, where reasoning is based on an acceptance of social rules and conventions, and moral behaviour is judged against these standards. Finally, in a small proportion of individuals, moral development may progress to the **postconventional** level, where it is understood that social conventions may need to challenged where they go against fundamental ethical principles.

Although Kohlberg's stage model is impressive in its scope, the assumption that the stages follow a fixed linear sequence, with higher stages indicating greater moral development, has been seen as highly problematic. One concern is that the same individual may apply different forms of reasoning in different social contexts. Moreover, the sequence of stages itself could reflect a particular, Western viewpoint that may not properly account for differences in moral reasoning across cultures (Shweder, Mahapatra, & Miller, 1987). For example, Haidt, Koller, and Dias (1993) have shown that Brazilian and US adults often make quite different judgements as to whether harmless but potentially disgusting or disrespectful actions (such as using a flag to clean one's toilet) are considered moral violations, suggesting that moral judgement draws quite heavily on cultural norms and expectations. In a similar way, others (e.g. Gilligan, 1982; Wark & Krebs, 1996) have laid an accusation of gender bias at the door of the Kohlbergian framework. The concern here is that Kohlberg's focus on reasoning about somewhat abstract notions of justice (e.g. in the 'law and order' orientation – Stage 4) reflects a more masculine perspective, whereas females are socialized to adopt a more caring orientation focused on interpersonal concerns (e.g. in the 'good boy/nice girl' orientation – Stage 3). While there is some doubt about whether men and women really do respond in systematically different ways to Kohlberg's dilemmas (Walker, 1984), these kinds of concerns do raise the important point that any approach to moral development needs to situate moral reasoning in the context of children's socialization experiences.

Distinguishing between social–conventional and moral rules

Contrary to early assumptions that young children have little capacity to reason about moral issues, research using **social domain approaches** to socio-moral understanding (e.g. Turiel, 1983) suggests that young children can make relatively sophisticated distinctions between different types of social rules. They recognize that social conventions (e.g. table manners, or saying please and thank you) are qualitatively different from rules involving moral imperatives (e.g. hitting others, stealing, or otherwise affecting people's rights and welfare). The latter are recognized as more serious and more universally and generalizably wrong (i.e. wrong even if there is no explicit rule). Even preschoolers may say that it is all right to talk in class if permission has been granted but that it is 'still not OK' to hit someone even when such behaviour is permitted (Smetana & Breages, 1990). This recognition of the distinction between moral and social–conventional domains is acknowledged across cultures (Song, Smetana, & Kim, 1987) and appears to be highly significant for adaptive social functioning. Indeed, failure to understand this distinction has been linked to aggressive and antisocial behaviour in children (Nucci & Herman, 1982) and psychopathic behaviour in adults (Blair, 1995).

Studies guided by this kind of approach to socio-moral development have illuminated the importance of the social environment for influencing children's cognition about moral situations and their behaviour. As discussed above, social learning approaches have highlighted the role of parents as key models for their children's acquisition of moral behaviour patterns. But parents' role in children's emerging cognition about social and moral rules can be understood not simply in terms of modelling behaviour but also in relation to key influences on children's social cognition. Indeed, it has long been recognized that reasoning with children following moral transgressions, rather than simply punishing them, may be a more effective model for promoting moral development. For example, Hoffman (1979) showed that parents who focused on getting their child to understand the consequences of their behaviour for others (what he called an 'inductive' style), rather just being warm and supportive or controlling and assertive, tended to have children who were more able to make their own mature moral judgements. These very meaningful parental responses are more likely to occur following transgressions in the moral rather than the conventional domain (Grusec & Goodnow, 1994). Consistent with this, Dunn, Brown, and Maguire (1995) showed that children's responses to various moral transgressions at 5 years of age were linked to the way their mothers controlled and resolved conflicts with them and their siblings, and also to the quality of the sibling relationship itself.

Moral emotions

If we accept that moral reasoning develops within a social context, we must also recognize the role played by emotions, since children's experience of interacting with others is frequently emotionally charged. Careful study reveals that the interplay of emotion and cognition in moral reasoning is complex and dynamic. We could argue that certain emotional reactions follow from moral reasoning – for example, feeling guilty after judging that we should have done more to help someone in need. But negative emotions such as anger and guilt might also serve as an antecedent to moral judgement by making us feel uncomfortable, which in turn alerts us to the moral salience of a situation (Decety, Michalska, & Kinzler, 2012; Tangney, Stuewig, & Mashek, 2007). For example, as Eisenberg (2000) notes, there is evidence to show that emotional responses such as anger and sadness – as might be felt by a young child whose favourite toy has been snatched away by another child – often prompt a consideration of the justice issues involved. Thus, our emotional responses could help to clarify the distinctive nature of moral (as opposed to social–conventional) violations.

The experience of moral emotions might also help us to clarify the basis for our judgements and behaviours in everyday situations. Painful or aversive self-conscious emotions such as guilt are thought to motivate changes in how we think and behave morally. In support of this, studies show that guilt is linked to lower levels of antisocial and risky behaviour, such as self-reported criminal behaviour and delinquency. Indeed guilt-proneness seems to serve as a protective factor against such behaviour (Tangney, Stuewig, & Martinez, 2014; Tangney et al., 2007). Furthermore, accurate processing of other people's emotions, as well as our own, may be a critical foundation for moral reasoning. For example, psychopaths are more likely to rate accidental harm as more morally permissible because they fail to take the victim's emotional experience into account (Young, Koenigs, Kruepke, & Newman, 2012). In a similar manner, while bullies may in general have a good understanding of mental states, they are often quite poor at linking emotions such as guilt and sympathy to their own and others' behaviour (e.g. see the study by Gasser & Keller, 2009).

Prosocial behaviour

Neither moral reasoning skills nor moral emotions in themselves can be assumed to lead to moral *behaviours*, yet we could argue that what ultimately matters for society is what people actually do. Fortunately, psychological research gives us a great deal of insight into the development of **prosocial behaviour**, which refers to a diverse group of voluntary behaviours that are intended to benefit another, such as helping, sharing, or comforting (Dunfield, Kuhlmeier, O'Connell, & Kelley, 2011; Grusec, Davidov, & Lundell, 2002). This contrasts with antisocial behaviour, which often involves harming others (e.g. aggression, stealing, disobedience, and suchlike), or showing no regard for others' welfare (Gardner, 1992). Children who engage in more prosocial behaviour are more likely to have good friendships (Sebanc, 2003), more likely to demonstrate positive social outcomes (Berndt, Hawkins, & Jiao, 1999), and less likely to have a negative impact on others. This significantly contrasts with the developmental outcomes associated with antisocial behaviour, particularly aggressive behaviour, which can lead to being less well liked (Burr, Ostrov, Jansen, Cullerton-Sen, & Crick, 2005), more negative social relationships (Moffitt, 1993;

Trentacosta & Shaw, 2009), poorer well-being of self and others (Hawker & Boulton, 2000; Nansel, Overpeck, Haynie, Ruan, & Scheidt, 2003), and having a negative effect on the wider environment, such as school (Mooij, Smeets, & De Wit, 2011) and neighbourhood (Egan, Bond, Kearns, & Tannahill, 2012).

Many factors are thought to contribute to the development of children's prosocial behaviour, including several already considered above: perspective taking, emotion understanding, cognitive skills, and parental influence. Evidence has shown that even infants in their first year of life can distinguish between prosocial and antisocial behaviour in the form of helping or hindering (Hamlin, Wynn, & Bloom, 2007). In Hamlin et al.'s (2007) study, 6- to 10-month-old infants watched a scene in which a shape (red circle) appeared to be climbing a hill and was either hindered (pushed down) or helped (pushed up) by another shape (e.g. a triangle or square). After viewing the scene, infants were presented with both shapes, and 100% of 6-month-olds reached for the shape that had 'helped', indicating a preference for the helper. It is not yet clear exactly what this signifies about children's deeper sense of morality, but it certainly seems clear that basic sensitivity to moral behaviour is present from a young age.

Indeed, from around 12 months of age, children themselves start to act prosocially in a range of situations, such as helping with housework and comforting others in distress (Hastings, Utendale, & Sullivan, 2007). Furthermore, from around 14 months of age, they respond to others' negative emotion and distress prosocially, using positive contact and verbal support (Zahn-Waxler, Robinson, & Emde, 1992). This marks the start of a transition from involuntary responses to distress (e.g. a simple 'emotion contagion') to voluntary prosocial responding. Some researchers have argued that this is linked with children's developing understanding of others' intentions and goals (Tomasello, Carpenter, Call, Behne, & Moll, 2005) and that it coincides with a clear understanding of self–other differentiation (Paulus, 2014). From 14 to 18 months, children demonstrate more advanced forms of prosocial behaviour, such as helping others to achieve instrumental goals by moving obstacles for them and retrieving objects that are beyond their reach (Warneken & Tomasello, 2006, 2007), and by 2 years of age children's prosocial responses to others in distress become more specific and nuanced. For example, they begin to provide verbal advice (e.g. 'be careful' or 'watch out'; Lamb & Zakhireh, 1997), with evidence that this kind of behaviour is facilitated by socialization processes such as parental talk about emotions (Brownell, Svetlova, Anderson, Nichols, & Drummond, 2013).

Research has shown that the frequency of prosocial behaviours increases from age 4 years onwards (Eisenberg & Fabes, 1998; Eisenberg, Fabes, & Spinrad, 2006), coinciding with developmental changes in social cognition, ToM understanding, and empathy. For example, Fehr, Bernhard, and Rockenbach (2008) showed that there was a strong increase in prosocial behaviour (anonymous sharing of sweets with another child) from 3 to 8 years of age. Other work has shown that prosocial behaviour at age 6 is predicted by earlier ToM understanding (Eggum et al., 2011) and associated with greater empathy (Farrant, Devine, Maybery, & Fletcher, 2012), although not all studies have found such increases (e.g. House, Henrich, Brosnan, & Silk, 2012). There is also evidence that these changes are reflected in children's behaviour towards others who act pro- versus antisocially. For example, in an experiment where preschoolers watched a puppet struggling to achieve goals and either being helped by a second or hindered by a third puppet, 4.5-year-old children almost always opted to give a greater reward to the helper (Kenward & Dahl, 2011).

Interestingly, findings have indicated either stability or decreases in prosocial behaviour from around 9–10 years through to early adulthood. For example, Flynn, Ehrenreich, Beron, and Underwood (2014) found that levels of children's teacher-rated prosocial behaviour (e.g. 'This child is helpful to peers') remained stable from 10 to 18 years, while research by Nantel-Vivier et al. (2009) showed that there was either no change or that there were decreases in levels of reported prosocial behaviour from 10 to 15 years, though this depended on who was reporting the behaviour – self-reported prosocial behaviour remained stable whereas teachers' and mothers' ratings of prosocial behaviour generally declined. Nantel-Vivier and colleagues (2009) argue that children are learning to focus their prosocial responding in more selective and differentiated ways. For example, they may act more prosocially with some people compared with others (Güroğlu, Van den Bos, & Crone, 2014). Further along the developmental trajectory, there is evidence for a subsequent increase in prosocial behaviour through to the age of 21 years (Luengo Kanacri et al., 2014), with relative stability through the 20s and early 30s (Eisenberg, Hofer, Sulik, & Liew, 2014). Nonetheless, it is important to remember that there are likely to be significant individual differences in these developmental trajectories. As well as the potential role played by the various dimensions of temperament discussed earlier, we will see later in this chapter that the family and the peer group are crucial contexts for understanding individual differences in children's prosocial behaviours.

TEST YOURSELF

1. What are the key features of social domain approaches to socio-moral development?
2. What factors influence the development of children's prosocial behaviour?

SECTION SUMMARY

- Research on moral development has focused on cognitive aspects of morality as well as the role played by sociocultural and emotional dimensions.

- Cognitive developmental theories have emphasized stage-like progressions in children's reasoning about moral rules, with development thought to be based on advances in perspective taking.

- More recent research using a social domain approach suggests that young children can make relatively sophisticated distinctions between different types of social rules, such as knowing the difference between moral violations and social–conventional violations.

- Social and emotional processes appear to play an important role in helping children to learn about these matters.

- The ability to detect and show a preference for prosocial behaviours develops in infancy.

- Prosocial behaviours increase during early childhood and are influenced by social and cognitive processes.

WHO AM I? THE DEVELOPMENT OF SELF AND IDENTITY

LEARNING OBJECTIVE 17.6

Identify the key stages in the development of self and identity, including the awareness of gender, ethnic, and national identity.

Just as children develop in their understanding of the social world, there is a significant developmental trajectory in their understanding of self. Our sense of identity or 'who we are' is complex and changes across childhood. At the simplest level, having a concept of self may be seen as requiring an ability to distinguish between self and not-self (i.e. what is part of me and what is not) but, as we will see below, explicit beliefs about the self become increasingly sophisticated and multifaceted as children get older.

Self-understanding

It was previously believed by some researchers that infants are unable to differentiate themselves from the environment (Mahler, Pine, & Bergman, 1975). For example, in the earliest phases of development within Mahler's separation/individuation theory, it is suggested that infants have a sense of omnipotence and are under the illusion that they and their mother are one. However, subsequent evidence has indicated that, even in the first few months of life, infants have a rudimentary sense that they are distinct and separate from others and the world around them. Rochat and Hespos (1997), for example, showed that newborn infants rooted (turned their head to suck) more frequently when an adult touched their cheek compared with when their own hand did, demonstrating a perceptual differentiation between the 'single touch' felt on their cheek from an external source (the adult's hand) and the 'double touch' felt when their own hand touched their cheek. It seems that infants' behaviours from birth onwards (e.g. kicking and crying) and the behaviours of others towards the infant (e.g. eye contact and smiles) provide important perceptual information to help them to distinguish the self from the environment. For example, Rochat and Morgan (1995) showed that infants as young as 3 months looked longer at a video image of their kicking legs from an observer's perspective (filmed from in front of the infant) compared with an image of their kicking legs viewed from their own perspective (filmed from behind the infant). This detection of discrepancies between the congruent versus incongruent visual outcomes of their own actions is thought to indicate early sensitivities that later allow infants to identify their own body as differentiated from the environment.

From around 18 months of age, children start to show explicit self-awareness. In the mirror self-recognition or 'rouge' test, infants are placed in front of a mirror after a dot of red dye has been surreptitiously smudged on their nose or forehead (Broesch, Callaghan, Henrich, Murphy, & Rochat, 2011; Lewis & Brooks-Gunn, 1979). Children under 18 months tend to either touch the mirror or try to interact with the image in the mirror, whereas many of the children between 18 and 24 months reach for the place on their *own* face where the red mark is on their reflection, indicating that they understand the image in the mirror is a reflection of themselves.

It has been proposed that sensitive and contingent caregiver–child interaction (see the earlier section 'Caregiver–Child Interactions and the Development of Attachment') serves to clarify the distinction between the self and the social world. For example, 18-month-olds who engaged in more joint attention with caregivers performed better on a task of self-recognition (Nichols, Fox, & Mundy, 2005). There is also evidence that cross-cultural differences exist in early self-recognition based on maternal-contingent responsiveness. German children whose mothers acted more contingently and engaged in more face-to-face communication recognized themselves in the mirror at an earlier age than Nso children from Cameroon, who were engaged in less of this kind of communication (Keller, Kärtner, Borke, Yovsi, & Kleis, 2005). It is thought that the cultural practice of fostering independence in German children compared with the fostering of interdependence in the Nso children also explains their earlier self-recognition.

Abilities in mirror self-recognition mark a shift towards a new concept of self, one where children can make themselves the object of their own thoughts as well as of their perceptions. At around 2 years, children also begin to use pronouns (e.g. 'I' and 'you'; Bates, 1990), engage in simple visual perspective taking (e.g. showing knowledge that an object is hidden from another person's view, even when it is in full view of the child; Moll & Tomasello, 2006), and demonstrate possessiveness (e.g. recognizing that an object is 'mine' as opposed to 'yours'; Levine, 1983). Mirror self-recognition is also implicated in the development of self-conscious emotions. For example, Lewis, Sullivan, Stanger, and Weiss (1989) have shown that embarrassed behavioural reactions (e.g. gaze aversion, coy smiles) are more evident in toddlers who pass the mirror self-recognition test.

After 2 years of age, children begin to develop a sense of a 'categorical self', initially referring mainly to their physical (e.g. gender, size, and age) and behavioural (e.g. activities) characteristics. During the preschool years, children begin to develop a sense of a 'social self', thinking about themselves as members of social categories and groups (playgroups, school, and suchlike) and referring to 'we' rather than just 'I' (Bennett & Sani, 2004). They also begin to develop a 'remembered self' or 'autobiographical memory' during this period, understanding that they are unique individuals with a life story. Research has shown that this sense of a continuing self is more developed in children whose mothers engage in highly elaborate reminiscing about past events (Fivush, 2007).

As children move into the early school years, they begin to develop a self-concept and a social identity that is more complex, using psychological and personality characteristics to describe themselves and others (e.g. 'Sometimes I feel shy', 'I am an honest person'; see Harter, 1998). By middle childhood, children are able to make complex social comparisons – for example, recognizing that they may be 'good at sports' compared with another child, but not as 'good at maths'. According to Damon and Hart (1982), children in early to middle childhood are in a process of trying to assimilate the different aspects of their self into a coherent whole, developing a 'theory' of their own personality. As children move into adolescence, the changes in physical and cognitive abilities are evident in their developing self-concept as more abstract thinking supports them in developing a more coherent sense of self, integrating a number of different identities and characteristics (Harter, 1998). However, this is also a time when youths often have to revise their identity and self-concept. Erikson's psycho-social model suggests that adolescents go through a phase of 'identity versus role confusion' in which they are attempting to forge a new sense of identity, which is simultaneously disrupted by impulses and rapid physical and cognitive changes that come with puberty (see Crain, 2010). As a consequence, adolescents may often 'try out' different identities encapsulated in particular peer groups and engage in behaviours that may be negative or risky (e.g. joining a gang or drug taking) in the search for a clear identity. See McLeod (2017) for a simple summary.

The social context plays a key role in how children conceive of the self, with researchers noting major cross-cultural variation in whether the self is emphasized as **independent versus interdependent**. For example, Markus and Kitayama (1991) reported the contrast between US culture, which fosters the development of a sense of individuality and independence, and Japanese culture, with its stronger focus on collective identity and interdependence. Moreover, in any culture, children come to appreciate how they can control the public self that they present to others. Efforts to engage in self-presentation, as we noted earlier, begin in early childhood but grow in importance as children become more focused on making the right impression on others, particularly in order to gain acceptance with peer groups (see Banerjee & Yuill, 1999; Watling & Banerjee, 2007a, 2007b).

Gender identity

One of the earliest categorical dimensions of self is the awareness of our sex. While sex differences in children's behaviour and activities may reflect biological and hormonal differences (Geary, 1998), the development of gender identity involves a great deal more (see Golombok & Fivush, 1994; Ruble, Martin, & Berenbaum, 2006). One approach already encountered, social learning theory, suggests that children learn about gender roles from socialization agents through modelling and reinforcement.

Examples of the differential treatment of boys and girls by adults can be seen with the classic 'Baby X' paradigm (Seavey, Katz, & Zalk, 1975), which involves observing how adults interact with an unfamiliar baby who is dressed and/or labelled as a girl or a boy. Although results across studies are somewhat mixed, some of the investigations using this kind of paradigm show that adults may respond to babies in systematically different ways depending on whether they are labelled as boys or girls (e.g. differences in levels and/or types of physical activity; encouraging play with gender-typed toys; using words such as 'big' and 'strong'; see Will, Self, & Datan, 1976). Differences seem to extend to subtle interpretations of emotional cues: in one variation of the paradigm, adults were more likely to interpret babies' crying (in response to a toy making a surprising movement and noise, for instance) as being angry (at the toy) if they believed the baby was a boy but sad if the baby was thought to be a girl (Condry & Condry, 1976).

Gender differences in socialization experiences are likely to continue throughout childhood. For example, researchers suggest that boys and girls often receive different conversational input from their parents, with some studies indicating that mothers tend to engage in more emotional talk – and do so in different ways – with girls than with boys (e.g. Aznar & Tenenbaum, 2014; Cervantes & Callanan, 1998; Fivush, Brotman, Buckner, & Goodman, 2000). Furthermore, in addition to being influenced by parents and other adults, children are thought to socialize each other in stereotypically gendered ways within peer interactions. For example, Maccoby (2002) argues that basic differences in the way boys and girls play and interact (e.g. boys in large-scale active games, away from an adult, contrasting with girls in more verbal or small-scale games, near an adult) play a key role in the socialization of masculine-typed and feminine-typed behaviours and attributes.

However, even though the social environment is likely to have a crucial role in shaping children's gender-related attributes, the development of a child's sense of identity as a boy or girl is thought to involve more complex cognitive processes. According to Kohlberg's (1966) **cognitive developmental account of gender development**, changes in conceptual understanding are crucial. By around 2 years of age, children are thought to have a basic understanding of the different gender categories (being a 'boy' or 'girl', 'mummy' or 'daddy' – **gender identity**), with an understanding that these categories are stable over time (**gender stability**) emerging at around 3 to 4 years. However, the Kohlbergian account suggested that a crucial developmental achievement is the understanding, at around 7 years of age, that gender remains constant even though people's appearance may change (**gender constancy**). This was seen as a key foundation for children's mature understanding of gender and their adoption of gender roles for behaviour (see Ruble et al., 2007).

More recent approaches have sought to synthesize social and cognitive approaches. For example, the **gender schema theory** (Martin & Halverson, 1981) argues that children's early experiences of gender are organized into 'schemas' and 'scripts', which provide general and specific information about each gender and associated behaviour. According to this kind of perspective, the social environment provides critical input to children as they actively seek information about what it means to be a boy or a girl. Thus, researchers have shown that social stereotypes regarding gender can have powerful consequences for developing youths' life choices. For example, one major line of research has examined how parent and teacher expectations regarding girls' versus boys' skills in mathematics play a key role in influencing children's own beliefs about gender and their own abilities, and in fact predict college and career choices (e.g. Bleeker & Jacobs, 2004; Eccles-Parsons, Adler, & Kaczala, 1982).

Yet, according to this kind of framework, children's cognitive models of gender can impose constraints in making sense of input from the social environment. For example, once stereotypes about gender roles are established in young children, they can have powerful effects on the way children process social information (e.g. distorting counter-stereotypical information to make the information consistent with the gender schema, such as mis-remembering a picture of a male nurse as a female; Liben & Signorella, 1993). It is only later in development that children become more flexible in their cognition about gender and can accommodate individual variations, such as a counter-stereotypical boy who likes playing with dolls. Thus, gender development appears to involve a complex interplay of social and cognitive developmental processes.

DISCUSSION POINT

Discuss what the Baby X paradigm can tell us about gender differences in socialization experiences.

Ethnic and national identity

In a world of multicultural nations and increasing international mobility, the way in which children come to develop a sense of ethnic and national identity also deserves attention as a key facet of the development of self. Ethnic identity can be described as the 'attitude towards and feeling of belonging to an ethnic group' (Marks, Szalacha, Lamarre, Boyd, & Coll, 2007, p. 501). Elements contributing to an ethnic identity include knowing that different ethnic groups exist (awareness), labelling groups and categorizing ourselves and others as belonging to a particular ethnic group (identification), feelings about our own and other ethnic groups (attitudes), and engagement in acts that are stereotypical of our group (behaviours).

Children begin to develop an ethnic awareness from around the age of 3–4 years and can differentiate between ethnic groups based on physical attributes such as skin colour. Systematic patterns of ethnic group attitudes also appear at this time. From around 4 years of age, children begin to show an in-group bias and out-group stereotyping, particularly when they belong to the dominant ethnic group (Aboud, 1988), suggesting that children at this age are beginning to identify with their own ethnic group. However, this differentiation tends to be based on overt physical characteristics, and evidence has shown that 5- to 7-year-olds are yet to appreciate that ethnic identity is constant – that it does not change across time or after superficial changes in appearance (Aboud, 1988).

From a cognitive developmental perspective, it may not be until key cognitive abilities develop at around 8 years of age that children begin to appreciate the qualities of individuals belonging to different ethnic groups, beyond superficial perceptions of physical attributes. For example, it has been reported that children's understanding of conservation (e.g. understanding that the amount of matter in a lump of clay remains the same despite changes in its shape) is positively correlated with their understanding of ethnic constancy (Aboud & Skerry, 1983; Semaj, 1980). On the other hand, this maturation of cognition is also negatively associated with their in-group preference and out-group stereotyping (Doyle & Aboud, 1995).

From around 12 years onwards, children begin to appreciate that differences between ethnic groups have symbolic characteristics, linked to attitudes and behaviours (e.g. religion and cultural practices), thus showing a more sophisticated understanding of ethnic identity. It is around this age, as they move into adolescence, that forming an ethnic identity becomes particularly important, especially for ethnic minority adolescents (Greig, 2003; Smith, 1991; St. Louis & Liem, 2005). Phinney (1989, 1993) suggested that older children and adolescents go through three stages of ethnic identity formation: 'unexamined identity' (pre-adolescence), in which there is little exploration of ethnic concepts and the values of the majority are more or less accepted; 'identity search' (early adolescence), in which individuals seek to understand what ethnicity means for the self; and 'achieved ethnic identity', in which they have a clear, confident sense of their own ethnicity and have dealt with any uncertainties. Successful progression through these stages to achieved identity status has been linked with a range of positive outcomes including higher self-esteem (Umaña-Taylor, Gonzales-Backen, & Guimond, 2009), more adaptive social and peer interactions, and better family functioning (Crocetti, Rubini, & Meeus, 2008; Phinney, 1989).

As well as ethnic identity, children develop a sense of belonging to a nation or state. This **national identity** can often be quite complex, as we saw in the 2014 Scottish independence referendum, where it was evident that people can feel Scottish, Scottish first and then British, British first and then Scottish, or equally Scottish, British, and European! Children's awareness of different national groups tends to emerge later than their awareness of different ethnic groups, with children having very little awareness of their own country or of other national groups (e.g. people being ' English' or 'American') before about 5 years of age (Piaget & Weil, 1951). From around 5 years onwards, children begin to refer to the name of their own country, and also begin to categorize themselves as belonging to their own national group (Barrett, 1996). Some studies have also found that children start to prefer their own national group over others from around 5 or 6 years (e.g. Bennett, Lyons, Sani, & Barrett, 1998), although other studies have suggested that this preference does not emerge until 7 years or later (e.g. Jaspers, Van de Geer, Tajfel, & Johnson, 1972; Middleton, Tajfel, & Johnson, 1970; for a simple summary, see ACT for Youth, 2018).

Although cognitive skills, such as the capacity to classify ourselves into multiple groups along various dimensions, are likely to play a key role in children's sense of ethnic and national identity (Aboud, 1988; Ocampo, Knight, & Bernal, 1997), social psychological approaches have emphasized a range of distinctive processes that are triggered when we categorize ourselves as a member of one group and not another. These processes in turn are believed to explain patterns of intergroup attitudes and behaviours in children as well as in adults. For example, according to **social identity theory** (Tajfel & Turner, 1979), in-group preference is motivated by a desire to seek a strong, positive social identity in order to maintain self-esteem (Brown, 2000). Therefore, people are expected to show a positive bias towards others from their own group, whom they perceive to be similar to themselves and as possessing positive traits, and a more negative bias towards out-group members, whom they perceive as having less favourable qualities. As a consequence of the importance of social identity, however, in-group members who are seen as having negative traits may be disliked *more* than out-group members because they pose a threat to the positive image of group members. Indeed, evidence has supported this idea in children, with Nesdale (1999) finding that 10- and 12-year-olds show less liking for an in-group member compared with an out-group member when they are both described as having negative qualities. These nuanced patterns in how children identify themselves as members of groups – and respond to people within and outside those groups – are likely to be crucial for understanding the development of complex social attitudes such as prejudice.

TEST YOURSELF

1. Describe the key changes in a child's understanding of self in relation to others.
2. How do social and cognitive factors influence the development of ethnic or national identity?

SECTION SUMMARY

- Soon after birth, infants show a rudimentary perceptual sense of self–world differentiation, and by 18 months they become explicitly self-aware, recognizing themselves in a mirror; they then go on to develop a more complex understanding of self in relation to others.

- Children learn about gender roles from socialization agents through modelling and reinforcement, but the development of a child's sense of identity as a boy or girl is thought to involve a more complex interplay of social and cognitive developmental processes.
- By 3 to 4 years of age, children are aware of ethnic differences based on superficial features.
- During early to middle childhood, children become aware of different national groups and come to appreciate the qualities of individuals beyond superficial differences before developing a more sophisticated understanding of ethnic and national identities from 12 years onwards.
- This process is likely to be influenced by children's cognitive development, but it is also dependent on children's view of themselves and others as members of social groups.

DEVELOPING IN A SOCIAL CONTEXT: FAMILY, PEERS, AND MEDIA

LEARNING OBJECTIVE 17.7

Compare and contrast the influences of family, peers, and media on the social development of children and adolescents.

We have already seen that interactions with caregivers provide a crucial context for children's social development. In this section, we expand our analysis to consider in more detail the roles played by various socialization agents in children's lives, starting with parenting patterns but then moving on to the dynamics within children's peer groups (particularly within the school context) and the broader media environment to which children are exposed. One conceptual approach that can help us to make sense of the complex and interrelated layers of social environmental influences on children's development is Bronfenbrenner's (1979) ecological systems theory. According to this theory, children grow and develop within complex social systems that are nested within several other wider social systems. These include the *microsystem*, which includes the interactions children have with their immediate social settings (e.g. family, friends, school); the *mesosystem*, which refers to how these settings interact (e.g. when children's parents meet with their teachers); the *exosystem*, which refers to surroundings that affect the children but with which they have little interaction (e.g. their parents' workplace); and the *macrosystem*, which refers to the values and attitudes of the wider culture (e.g. laws and customs).

Parenting

Parents are usually seen as the first and most important socialization guides for developing children. Thus, the techniques they use to rear their children may play a crucial role in shaping children's social development outcomes. Through the use of parental measures and extensive observations of preschool children and their families, Baum-rind (1971) identified three key dimensions of parenting: acceptance/involvement, control, and autonomy. *Acceptance/involvement* concerns the degree to which parenting is based on warmth and affection for children while also providing appropriate praise, encouragement, and interest in their activities. Parents low on this dimension tend to be cold and rejecting, with a greater tendency to be critical of or punish a child rather than provide affection and encouragement. *Control* describes the demands and expectations parents place on their children, aimed at fostering appropriate behavioural compliance. Parents low on control place few demands on their children regarding their behaviour and provide little structure for their activities. *Autonomy* describes the freedom parents grant their children based on their level of maturity, aimed at encouraging self-reliance.

Baumrind's (1971) dimensions have been used to describe distinct **parenting styles**, which have been presented by Maccoby and Martin (1983) in terms of a 2 × 2 matrix of responsiveness/warmth and demandingness/control (Figure 17.3). **Authoritative parenting** combines high acceptance and involvement with adaptive control techniques and granting of appropriate autonomy. Authoritative parents show warmth towards their children but are also firm in a non-punitive way, allowing open communication and negotiation with their children (Russell, Mize, & Bissaker, 2004). They grant their children autonomy in line with the child's readiness and maturity (Hart, Newell, & Olsen, 2003). **Authoritarian parenting** combines low acceptance and involvement with being high in coercive control and low in granting autonomy. This style of parenting is less warm and responsive, and parents are more likely to shout, use threats and punishments, give orders, and criticize their children. They expect compliance and obedience without negotiation and they make decisions for their children that they expect not to be questioned. They grant their children little autonomy, and when they do it is below what would be expected of the child's maturity level. **Permissive parenting** combines high acceptance and involvement with low control and high autonomy. These parents are warm and responsive but place few demands on their children, exercising little control, and thus tend to be overindulgent of their children. They grant autonomy, but this is often inappropriate and given before the child is sufficiently mature. **Uninvolved parenting** – a parenting style arising from Maccoby and Martin's (1983) two-dimensional

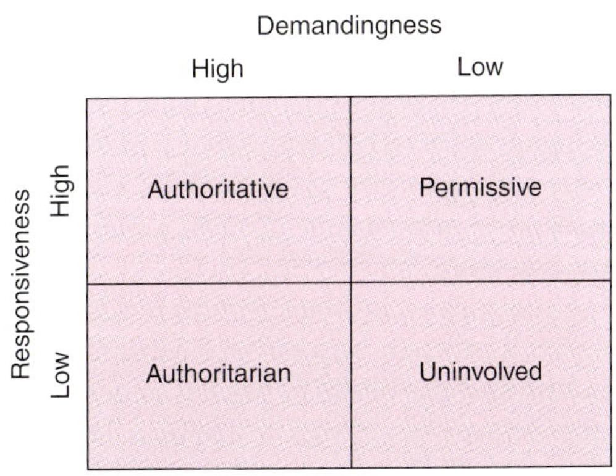

FIGURE 17.3 *Maccoby and Martin's (1983) two-dimensional model of parenting styles.*

Source: Maccoby and Martin (1983). Reproduced with permission.

framework – combines low acceptance and involvement with low control and high but inappropriate autonomy. These parents place few demands on their children while at the same time they lack warmth and are emotionally detached from their offspring; they show no interest or actively reject their children.

Differences in parenting style are understood to have a number of antecedents and consequences. Regarding the antecedents, Belsky's (1984) process model identifies a parent's psychological well-being (e.g. levels of depressive symptoms), personality (e.g. levels of trust), and quality of support from social relationships (e.g. marital relationships) as key determinants of parenting. In turn, the various parenting styles have been associated with a range of developmental consequences for children. Children raised with an authoritative parenting style tend to have the best developmental outcomes. They are more likely to be competent and self-reliant (Steinberg, Lamborn, Dornbusch, & Darling, 1992), socially responsible (Baumrind, 1991), keen to achieve (Gray & Steinberg, 1999), and cooperative (Baumrind, 1991). Children raised with an authoritarian parenting style, on the other hand, tend to be more anxious and/or angry (Baumrind, 1971), have low levels of psychosocial maturity (Mantzicopoulos & Oh-Hwang, 1998), are more likely to become bullies (Baldry & Farrington, 2000), have lower self-esteem (Martinez & Garcia, 2008), and display poorer moral reasoning (Boyes & Allen, 1993). In contrast, children raised with a permissive style of parenting tend to be more impulsive and aggressive (Nijhof & Engels, 2007), lack impulse control and self-reliance (Baumrind, 1971), lack social responsibility, and have poorer moral reasoning (Boyes & Allen, 1993). Lastly, evidence suggests that an uninvolved parenting style is most harmful to children. Children with uninvolved or neglecting parents tend to be more impulsive, are more antisocial, display greater anger and defiance, are less achievement oriented, and are more likely to become delinquent (Hoeve et al., 2009).

Despite the substantial body of empirical evidence linking parenting styles with various developmental outcomes, a number of critical limitations need to be recognized. First, it has been argued that much of the research is culturally biased because it has been based primarily on white, middle-class, Western families. For example, although some evidence has indicated that authoritarian parenting in Chinese samples can lead to anxiety, depression, and antisocial behaviour (Wang, Pomerantz, & Chen, 2007), in line with findings from Western samples, other studies have shown that the more authoritarian parenting styles common in China can also have positive outcomes, such as fostering high achievement (Chao, 1994; Chen & Kaplan, 2001). There is also evidence of subtle differential effects of parenting style on developmental outcomes, depending on ethnicity and gender. For example, Radziszewska, Richardson, Dent, and Flay (1996) found that African American boys with uninvolved parents scored higher on levels of depressive symptoms than white, Hispanic, and Asian children, whereas Asian girls with uninvolved parents scored higher on depressive symptoms than the other ethnic groups, reminding us of the importance of cultural context in social–emotional development.

In addition, much of the research focuses on parenting style without accounting for differences between mothers and fathers, with most developmental work on parenting focused on mothers because of challenges in recruiting fathers for research. Yet differences between maternal and paternal influences may be critical. Roopnarine, Krishnakumar, Metindogan, and Evans (2006), for example, found that increases in preschool children's literacy and maths skills were predicted by authoritative parenting in immigrant Caribbean families, but only with regard to fathers', not mothers', parenting style. Research also needs to address child-rearing patterns within the many different kinds of family structure found in contemporary society (e.g. single parent, step-parent, same-sex, and adoptive families; see Golombok, 2000).

A more profound challenge can be raised about the causal role of parenting styles in influencing child outcomes. The correlational nature of much of the research calls into question the direction of causal effect. For example, could it be that the temperament of the child elicits different parental practices, as well as the other way round? Longitudinal work by Rubin and colleagues, for instance, has shown that physiological and observed indicators of temperament predict parenting patterns 2 years later (Kennedy, Rubin, Hastings, & Maisel, 2004; Rubin, Nelson, Hastings, & Asendorpf, 1999). Also, small effect sizes in many of the large-scale studies (e.g. Lamborn, Mounts, Steinberg, & Dornbusch, 1991) call into question the robustness of the observed associations. Thus, rather than emphasizing parental influence, Harris's (1995, 2002) **group socialization theory** argues that genetic inheritance and children's wider social environment (e.g. peer groups) play a much greater role in children's social development than parenting styles.

Despite all of these criticisms, there is good reason to believe that the role of parenting in children's development is not insubstantial, even though it may be more complex than a one-way effect from parents to children. Collins, Maccoby, Steinberg, Hetherington, and Bornstein (2000) argue that the expression of genetic traits depends on environmental experiences including parental behaviours. Indeed, several lines of work show interactions between genetic factors and parenting experiences in children's behavioural and emotional characteristics: in one example, Sheese, Voelker, Rothbart, and Posner (2007) found that parenting quality – rated through observations of parent–child interaction – interacts with the presence of certain genetic features to predict patterns of sensation seeking in 18- to 21-month-olds.

Sibling interactions

Relationships with siblings are likely to be the longest-lasting ones we will have. These relationships are unique in that they involve interaction that can in some ways be parent-like (with the older sibling often having higher status and a degree of responsibility) and in other ways peer-like (involving reciprocal exchanges during play or conflict). As such, siblings can act as both teachers and playmates (Howe & Recchia, 2005). Sibling relationships are also characterized as being particularly emotionally disinhibited, often involving high degrees of warmth and intimacy but also conflict and rivalry, an ambivalence that is noticeable from the very start with the arrival of a new sibling (Dunn, 1985; Dunn & Kendrick, 1982) and continues into adulthood (Stocker, Lanthier, & Furman, 1997).

The quality of siblings' relationships with each other has been shown to be influenced by the children's temperament as well as by parenting patterns. For example, siblings whose mothers are rejecting towards them tend to be more aggressive with one another (MacKinnon-Lewis, Starnes, Volling, & Johnson, 1997). In turn, variations in sibling relationship quality appear to have important influences on children's developing social competence and well-being (Ripoll-Núñez & Carrillo,

2014). In general, children with warm sibling relationships tend to have higher levels of peer acceptance (Brody, 1998) and show greater prosocial (Pike, Coldwell, & Dunn, 2005) and teaching behaviours (Howe & Recchia, 2009). Early positive sibling relationships have also been shown to predict lower levels of internalizing and externalizing problems in later adolescence, with stronger effects being found when the siblings are brothers, closer in age, and younger generally (Buist, Deković, & Prinzie, 2013). Sibling relationship quality has also been shown to moderate or protect against negative life events (such as parental divorce) on social–emotional adjustment. In their longitudinal study, Gass, Jenkins, and Dunn (2007) showed that children with a positive affective relationship with their sibling were less likely to develop later internalizing symptoms if they had experienced stressful events, compared to those who had had more negative relationships. In fact, relationships high in conflict are linked to higher levels of peer aggression and lower levels of social competence (Volling & Blandon, 2003). Nonetheless, it is important to note that moderate levels of conflict within a generally positive relationship can promote constructive and effective ways of resolving conflict, which leads to more positive peer interaction and acceptance (Herrera & Dunn, 1997).

In fact, sibling relationships may have a particular role to play in shaping children's understanding of the social world. For example, evidence has shown that children's performance on false-belief tasks is positively associated with having more siblings. Potentially, the increased levels of social interaction afforded by the presence of siblings provide more opportunities for children to develop their mental-state understanding and practise perspective taking (Perner, Ruffman, & Leekam, 1994). Some have argued that it is particularly older siblings who are effective in this way (Ruffman, Perner, Naito, Parkin, & Clements, 1998). Older siblings are more likely than older peers to provide spontaneous and skilled assistance (Azmitia & Hesser, 1993) and more able to engage in more sophisticated pretend play involving role-play in which children can learn about different perspectives (Youngblade & Dunn, 1995). They also engage in mental-state talk with their younger siblings (Brown & Dunn, 1992), which – just like parental conversations – could help to scaffold children's understanding of the social world.

Peer relationships

Children's relationships with their peers are qualitatively different from their relationships with adults in terms of the relative status of the social partners: relationships with adults can be described as 'vertical' in terms of the power and knowledge differential between children and adults, whereas relationships with peers can be seen as 'horizontal' (Hartup, 1989). This quality of peer relationships provides important opportunities for children to appreciate and make sense of each other's perspective, as well as to develop skills in resolving differences, negotiating, and compromising (Rubin, Begle, & McDonald, 2012).

Interest in peers is evident in the first few months of an infant's life, with gaze being directed towards other infants, along with reaching and touching, in 3- to 4-month-olds (Hay, Nash, & Pedersen, 1983; Rubin, Bukowski, & Parker, 1998). By 6 months, infants become more aware of, and take a greater interest in, one another, with attention directed at each other in the form of peer-directed smiles and babbles (Rubin & Coplan, 1998). At around 12 months, this attention towards each other becomes more clearly recognized and reciprocated within sequences of imitative turn-taking (Vandell & Mueller, 1995). By 2 years of age, these reciprocal interactions become more regular, more coordinated, and increasingly sophisticated (e.g. copying specific words and actions), leading on to simple games such as hide-and-seek (Eckerman & Stein, 1990).

As children's awareness of self and social understanding develops in the toddler years, we see an increase in their peer play behaviours. Parten's (1932) seminal work identified six specific categories of play from observations of preschool children during natural play, with variations in how complex and social the play is: **solitary play** (playing alone); **onlooker** behaviour (watching others play); **unoccupied play** (watching others' interactions as well as events and objects of interest); **parallel play** (playing alongside other children using the same toys but with little, if any, interaction); **associative play** (playing alongside other children but exchanging play materials and/or conversing about each other's activity); and **cooperative play** (playing together towards joint goals, such as in pretend play, rule-based games, and building things together). Although these forms of play do not form a strict developmental progression, the final three are increasingly complex forms of social play, with parallel play more common among young toddlers and cooperative play becoming more common from the preschool period onwards (Howes & Matheson, 1992).

As children move through the early to middle school years, the dynamics of peer relationships begin to change, as children begin to interact in larger groups, new peer groups emerge, and adult supervision of peer interaction diminishes (Ellis, Rogoff, & Cromer, 1981). Gender differences also become apparent: from the age of 3 years, gender segregation can be observed in peer play and gender differences in the nature of group interaction begin to develop. Girls spend increasingly more time in dyadic interactions, often involving talking and sharing of thoughts and feelings, whereas boys spend more time in larger groups, often revolving around competitive activities such as sports (see Benenson, Apostoleris, & Parnass, 1997; Maccoby, 1998). In middle childhood, increasing concerns about acceptance by peers are evident (Parker & Gottman, 1989) and children become more selective in their choice of friends, with conformity to peer group norms becoming increasingly important. Indeed, many of their goal pursuits (e.g. wanting material goods and to 'look good') appear to be driven by a desire to fit in with, or stand out from, the peer group (Easterbrook, Wright, Dittmar, & Banerjee, 2014). During adolescence, this trend towards spending more time with the peer group continues, and intimacy and self-disclosure become important features of close friendships (Buhrmester, 1990). In fact, peer relationships now often supersede parental ones as a source of social support (Alder & Furman, 1988).

As peer groups become salient in children's social lives, individual differences in how much children are accepted or rejected by their peers become correspondingly prominent. Studies of **sociometric status** are based on children's rated liking of their peers, or on their nominations of others with whom they are most and least like to play (see Figure 17.4). Meta-analysis of research on sociometric status has shown that popular children have an array of competencies, such as greater social problem-solving skills (Newcomb, Bukowski, & Pattee, 1993). Popular children are also rated by peers as trustworthy, kind, cooperative, and sociable

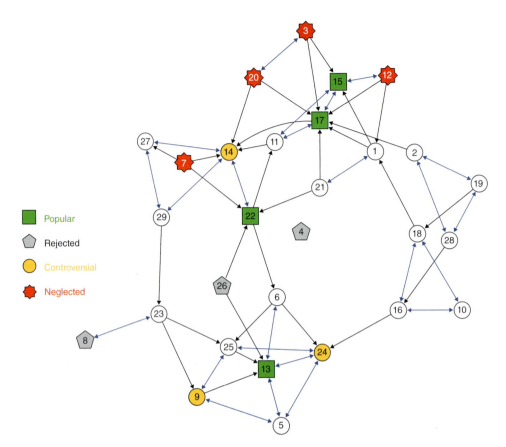

FIGURE 17.4 *Sociometric assessments of peer status. Asking children to nominate the classmates they most and least like to play with can enable researchers to create a visual representation of social relations within the class. The sociogram shown here depicts each child in the class as a node, with arrows indicating positive nominations. The colour-coding of the nodes is based on Coie and Dodge's (1983) approach to classifying peer status, using the numbers of most-like (ML) and least-like (LL) nominations received to identify four different status groups:* popular *(high level of social preference, with above-average ML and below-average LL),* rejected *(low level of social preference, with below-average ML and above-average LL),* controversial *(high level of social impact, with above-average ML and LL), and* neglected *(low level of social impact, with below-average ML and LL).*

(Cillessen & Mayeux, 2004). In contrast, rejected children are characterized by high levels of aggression and/or social withdrawal (Coie, Dodge, & Kupersmidt, 1990; Dodge, 1983; Newcomb et al., 1993). Peer acceptance is more generally associated with adaptive behaviour and hence is likely to lead to more positive outcomes, including greater school achievement (Kingery, Erdley, & Marshall, 2011), whereas peer rejection is associated with maladaptive behaviour and is likely to result in poorer outcomes, including both internalizing and externalizing problems (Ladd, 2006). Peer rejection is also associated with involvement in bullying, both as perpetrators and as victims (Boulton & Smith, 1994), and this too has become recognized as a significant risk factor for emotional difficulties and ongoing school adjustment problems (Scholte, Engels, Overbeek, de Kemp, & Haselager, 2007; see also Focus Point 17.4).

BULLYING: MORE THAN JUST A BULLY AND A VICTIM

There has been a major increase in research on peer victimization since the 1980s. This has coincided with a great rise in public attention to bullying in schools and the sometimes devastating consequences that bullying can have for young people's lives. More recently, this area of research and public interest has come to include a particular focus on cyberbullying, involving victimization of individuals through the internet and mobile phone technologies.

One important theme arising from the work on bullying is a growing recognition that this involves much more than simply the dyad of the bully and the victim. Key roles are played by the wider context of the members of the peer group as a whole (e.g. how do bystanders respond when they see victimization taking place?) and the broader ethos of the school community (e.g. how are supportive and respectful relationships prioritized within the school?). A research review specifically considered the many ways in which the peer group serves an important context for how and why bullying takes place (Salmivalli, 2010), and Ofsted (the UK national body for developing and evaluating standards in education and children's services) has produced a report on the role of school culture in bullying (Ofsted, 2012).

Not surprisingly, then, there is a very substantial literature on school-based initiatives to promote the social and emotional skills that underpin positive peer interaction, and to reduce the likelihood of antisocial behaviours. Moreover, because the classroom learning context is one that requires effective peer interaction (e.g. in the context of group work), it is noteworthy that 'social and emotional learning' programmes at school have in general been found to be successful not only in achieving social–relational goals but also in promoting academic achievement (Durlak, Weissberg, Dymnicki, Taylor, & Schellinger, 2011).

Media, television, and the internet

Beyond the immediate social encounters that children have with their families and their peers, a much wider set of sociocultural factors is likely to be at work in influencing children's behaviour, beliefs, feelings, and values. Increasing attention has been placed on the potential role of contemporary media and consumer culture in children's development. A report showed that 8- to 10-year-olds across the United States spent more time engaging with media in some form than any other waking activity – an average of 7.5 hours per day, or over 50 hours per week (Rideout, Foehr, & Roberts, 2010) – and, when accounting for the fact that children often 'multitask' (e.g. use their mobile phones while watching TV), it was calculated that they were exposed to over 10 hours of media content a day! This means that children are also being exposed to increasing levels of marketing and advertising (e.g. see Kunkel, 2001).

There is now a well-established body of literature linking media use to a range of social, emotional, and academic outcomes (for reviews, see Anderson et al., 2003; Napier, 2014; Strasburger, Wilson, & Jordan, 2014). For example, children's TV viewing has been associated with a number of negative social development outcomes, including increased attention problems and ADHD-like behaviours (Christakis, Zimmerman, DiGiuseppe, & McCarty, 2004; Nikkelen, Valkenburg, Huizinga, & Bushman, 2014; Zimmerman & Christakis, 2007), aggression and aggressive attitudes (Anderson et al., 2003; Eron, Huesmann, Lefkowitz, & Walder, 1972; Funk, Baldacci, Pasold, & Baumgardner, 2004), and materialistic values through the associated advertising exposure (Opree, Buijzen, Van Reijmersdal, & Valkenburg, 2013). Despite debates about the causal direction of these links, longitudinal studies have provided evidence indicating that TV viewing is indeed a likely cause of many of these negative outcomes. For example, Christakis et al. (2004) found that the amount of TV viewing between 1 and 3 years of age predicted later attention problems at age 7, and Eron et al. (1972) found that a preference for watching violent TV at age 9 was correlated with aggression at age 19, while there was no such correlation between aggression at 9 years and preference for TV violence at age 19. In a similar way, meta-analytic reviews of research on playing violent video games (Anderson, 2004; Anderson & Bushman, 2001) have found that it is associated with increased aggressive behaviour, aggressive thoughts and feelings, and decreased prosocial and helping behaviour.

Professor Dimitri Christakis shares his research and thoughts on media and children in **this 2011 TED Talk**[3].

How do we explain these effects of media on children's development? One of the most enduring explanations comes from Bandura's social learning theory (Bandura, 1965), which suggests that children may learn violent and aggressive behaviour through observing and imitating others, particularly when the behaviour is realistic, seems to be rewarded, and is carried out by role models. Other theories point to the role of the media in exerting a form of peer pressure by conveying the impression that certain behaviours are normative (e.g. everyone plays violent games) or in presenting adolescents and pre-adolescents with 'scripts' of how to behave in new or unfamiliar situations (see Huesmann, 1988). On the other hand, we must recognize that media effects are unlikely to be simplistic one-way impacts of media on children; similarly to our discussion of other social influences, Valkenburg and Peter's (2013) theory of media effects emphasizes how a range of factors can make certain children highly susceptible to negative media influences while other children remain fairly unaffected by media exposure.

FOCUS POINT 17.5

THE EFFECTS OF MEDIA EXPOSURE ON CHILDREN

How are children affected by exposure to media messages about popular culture? In the 'differential susceptibility to media effects model', Valkenburg and Peter (2013) show that this is not a simple matter of media exposure affecting all children in the same way or to the same degree. As shown in the diagram below, various factors are thought to play a role, including dispositional factors (e.g. differences relating to gender, temperament, and personality), developmental factors (e.g. cognitive and emotional changes that occur as children grow older), and social factors (e.g. differences in family, peer, and other sociocultural contexts).

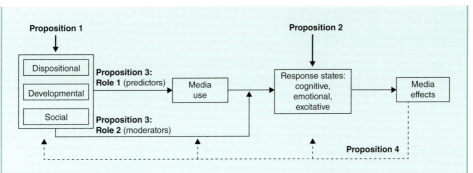

Proposition 1: Media effects depend on three types of differential susceptibility variables.
Proposition 2: Three media response states mediate the relationship between media use and effects.
Proposition 3: The differential susceptibility variables have two roles: they act as predictors and moderators.
Proposition 4: Media effects are transactional.

Source: Valkenberg and Peter (2013). Wiley. Reproduced with permission.

These factors not only influence *what* and *how much* media exposure occurs for a given child but also make some children more susceptible to the effects of that exposure than others, in terms of initial cognitive, emotional, and excitative (e.g. physiological arousal) responses and eventual outcomes such as aggressive behaviour or altered well-being. And the transactional, cyclical nature of the model implies that those outcomes in turn might influence the likelihood of future media exposure.

For example, the researchers note that watching violent television might have distinctive effects on a child growing up in a family where actual levels of physical violence are already high. Other research has shown that the development of materialistic values may be linked to experiences of peer rejection and perceptions of peer pressure (Banerjee & Dittmar, 2008). Could it be that such peer processes make some children more vulnerable to media messages that promote materialism, which in turn makes the children even more likely to access such media in the future? Learning more about such vicious cycles – and the intervention strategies that help to break them – is likely to be an important goal for future research.

Finally, we must not forget that, if the media can play a role in fostering negative behaviours in the ways described above, then it also has the potential to play a role in promoting positive developmental outcomes. In fact, numerous studies indicate that TV and media can have positive effects on children's development. For example, Calvert and Kotler (2003) found that educational programmes (e.g. *Sesame Street*) had positive social and emotional effects on children. In addition, Prot et al. (2014) found that greater use of prosocial media (TV and video games) was associated with more helping behaviour, while Coyne, Padilla-Walker, Fraser, Fellows, and Day (2014) revealed, through a combination of qualitative and quantitative methods, that collaborative and shared use of positive media can have a positive effect on families by bringing parents and adolescents together, helping them to connect by sparking discussion, and providing shared memories. Once again, then, research suggests that we need to consider a complex interplay between a wide range of factors when we seek to understand the impact of media and contemporary consumer culture on children's development.

DISCUSSION POINT

Discuss the benefits and drawbacks that have been researched in terms of children and media. Do you feel that the research has shown media to have an overall positive or negative influence on child development?

TEST YOURSELF

1. What parenting styles have been identified by psychologists? To what extent can any of these styles be considered the optimal way of parenting?
2. How might a child's relationship with their peers affect their socio-emotional development? How might we measure this?
3. What methodological approaches have been used to examine whether watching violent content on television causes children to become violent? What factors might influence the effect of this exposure?

SECTION SUMMARY

- Children are influenced by their experiences of social interaction within multiple contexts, including the family, peers, and the wider context of media and consumer culture.

- Different parenting styles based on dimensions of acceptance/warmth and control/demandingness are associated with a range of positive and negative outcomes for children.

- Siblings can act as both teachers and playmates, and variations in sibling relationship quality appear to have important influences on children's developing social competence and well-being.

- The quality of siblings' relationships with each other has been shown to be influenced by the children's temperament as well as by parenting patterns.

- Interest in peers is evident in an infant's first few months, and interactions with peers become increasingly complex during early childhood.

- As children move into middle childhood, peer acceptance and rejection become key concerns.

- School-based programmes can be helpful for reducing antisocial behaviour and bullying, and for promoting positive behaviour.

- Children are exposed to media more than ever before. There is a body of evidence linking children's use of media with a range of negative outcomes, but the impacts of media exposure are likely to depend on other social factors, developmental processes, and individual differences.

FUTURE DIRECTIONS

LEARNING OBJECTIVE 17.8

Critically evaluate possible future directions for research in social development.

Researchers have made great strides in understanding children's social development, but significant challenges remain. For example, extending our understanding of social, emotional, and cognitive development in the first few months of life requires more sophisticated and novel research techniques, such as the application of eyetracking and neuroimaging technology to infants. This kind of innovative work, which can provide greater insight into the mental life of young infants, not only would enhance our theoretical understanding of social development but also may ultimately give rise to new screening tools and intervention strategies for developmental disorders.

We also need to continue our progress with illuminating the dynamic and complex interactions between different levels of explanation for children's behaviour. Ongoing research will flesh out our knowledge of how specific gene–environment interactions influence social development, as well as how biological factors (e.g. the roles played by mirror neurons and oxytocin) may both drive and be affected by the environment in which they express themselves.

Research will also need to consider the rapid sociocultural changes occurring in an increasingly complex, multicultural, and globalized world. We will need to take into account how these changes, along with rapid advances in technology (e.g. children's interactions via social media), may influence identity, parenting, peer relations, values, and other issues examined in this chapter. This is likely to involve developments not only in research methodologies and techniques but also in the theoretical models we formulate in order to conceptualize children's social development.

SECTION SUMMARY

- We need to improve our understanding of development in the first few months after birth, and develop innovative methods to achieve this.
- We need to improve our understanding of the interactions between genes, biology, and environment that play a role in children's behaviour.
- We need to improve our understanding of the effects of sociocultural changes on children's development.

CHAPTER SUMMARY

This chapter has outlined the social and emotional development of children and adolescents. We started by thinking about the nature of emotions in childhood and the development of close relationships with caregivers. We then considered how children come to understand and reason about the social world and about moral dilemmas. Next, we reviewed research on how children come to develop a sense of self and identity and see ourselves as unique individuals who are also members of social groups. Finally, we investigated the influences of key social contexts, including family, friends, and the media. This chapter demonstrates that social development involves a complex and multidimensional interplay of attributes and experiences.

ESSAY QUESTIONS

1. What can the concept of 'differential susceptibility' tell us about the nature of parental, peer, and other social influences on development?
2. What factors influence a child's reasoning about either people's mental states or moral dilemmas?

KEY TERMS

- **associative play:** A pattern of play interaction that involves playing alongside other children and exchanging play materials and/or conversing about each other's activity.
- **attachment behavioural system:** Behaviours designed to bring about or maintain proximity to the attachment figure in times of distress or threat.
- **attachment:** A close emotional bond formed with a specific other; often used to describe the relationship between infants and their caregivers.
- **authoritarian parenting:** A style of parenting that combines low acceptance and involvement with being high in coercive control and low in granting autonomy.
- **authoritative parenting:** A style of parenting that combines high acceptance and involvement with adaptive control techniques and granting of appropriate autonomy.
- **belief–desire reasoning:** Children's conceptual understanding that people will act according to their desires (e.g. to get something they want) and beliefs (what they think or understand about something).
- **cognitive developmental account of gender development:** The theory that children's gender development results from changes in their underlying conceptual understanding of gender, such as when children acquire the conceptual understanding that gender will remain constant even if surface-level aspects of appearance (e.g. length of hair) change.
- **conspec:** A primitive mechanism that draws infants' attention to members of the same species.
- **conventional:** The level of moral reasoning in Kohlberg's theory where reasoning is based on an acceptance of social rules and conventions and moral behaviour is judged against these standards.
- **cooperative play:** A pattern of play in which children play together in a way designed to achieve joint goals; examples include pretend play, rule-based games, and building things together.
- **differential susceptibility hypothesis:** The idea that genetic differences between children, such as those linked to temperament, make children more or less susceptible to environmental influences: some children may do disproportionately well when they have

experienced positive and supportive environments but disproportionately badly in more negative environments, whereas other children may be generally less sensitive to the effects of their environment.

- **difficult temperament:** A description of infant temperament referring to those who are negative in mood, high in intensity, and low in adaptability, approach, and rhythmicity.
- **discrete emotions theory:** The proposition that there are several specific, biologically determined emotional responses that are expressed and recognized universally.
- **dynamic systems perspective:** A perspective that focuses on a complex interplay – operating continually and in a bidirectional way – between children's developing brains, their bodily sensations and experiences, and social–environmental factors.
- **easy temperament:** A description of infant temperament referring to those who are positive in mood and mild in intensity, with high levels of rhythmicity, approach, and adaptability.
- **effortful control:** The purposeful regulation of behaviour, cognition, emotion, and attention, including a capacity for inhibiting automatic responses.
- **egocentrism:** The inability to see or understand things from perspectives other than your own.
- **emotion understanding:** The ability to understand others' emotions, from simple recognition of happiness and sadness through to sophisticated insights into self-conscious emotions and emotional ambivalence.
- **empathy:** The ability to understand others' feelings and to experience affective reactions yourself in response to others' emotional states.
- **executive function (EF):** The capacity to control and regulate your thoughts and behaviour; linked to working memory, inhibitory control, planning, and cognitive flexibility.
- **extraversion/surgency:** A dimension of temperament that involves high levels of activity and impulsivity, high-intensity pleasure, and low levels of shyness.
- **false-belief tasks:** Tasks used to assess children's awareness and understanding of how someone thinks about something, involving situations where the belief (e.g. about the location or identity of an object) contrasts with the children's knowledge of reality.
- **functionalist:** An emphasis on the way in which emotions serve as a means of working towards relational goals: emotions are linked to 'action tendencies', such as escaping from dangerous situations (fear) or dealing with a conflict that has thwarted your plans (anger).
- **gender constancy:** An understanding children develop at around 7 years of age that gender remains constant even though people's appearance may change.
- **gender identity:** A basic understanding of the different gender categories (being a 'boy' or 'girl', 'mummy' or 'daddy') that children grasp at around 2 years of age.
- **gender schema theory:** A theory suggesting that information about gender is organized into 'schemas' and 'scripts', which shape children's reasoning about the behaviours and attributes associated with each gender.
- **gender stability:** An understanding that gender categories remain stable over time.
- **group socialization theory:** The idea that important socialization influences on children's attributes and personality take place not through dyadic relationships (e.g. with a parent) but through intragroup and intergroup processes (e.g. in peer groups).
- **independent versus interdependent:** The extent to which someone's sense of self is based on individuality and independence compared with collective identity and connections with others.
- **insecure–anxious avoidant:** An attachment style characterized by little use of the caregiver as a secure base and little emotional response to the caregiver's departure or reappearance.
- **insecure–anxious resistant:** An attachment style characterized by clinginess to the caregiver, great distress upon separation, and ambivalent/resistant responses upon reunion.
- **insecure–disorganized/disoriented:** An attachment style that reflects an incoherent and inconsistent mix of confused and disoriented behaviours, often associated with the greatest risk of later psychopathology.
- **interactional synchrony:** Sensitive two-way communication whereby infant and caregiver match their emotional states in a rhythmic and contingent way.

- **internal working model (IWM):** A cognitive model, or set of mental representations, that reflects an infant's experiences with, and expectations about, their caregiver; this is thought to serve as a guide or model for future interactions with people.
- **joint attention:** Where an infant and caregiver attend to the same object or event in the environment.
- **mastery smiles:** Smiles displayed by infants when they successfully achieve a goal.
- **maternal sensitivity:** A mother's (or caregiver's) ability to pick up on and respond appropriately to her infant's signals and needs.
- **mental-state talk:** Conversation and talk that involves references to your own or others' thoughts, feelings, desires, and intentions.
- **mind-mindedness:** The tendency to treat infants and children as independent beings with their own minds and to make sense of their behaviour in terms of underlying internal mental states.
- **mirror neurons:** Brain cells that respond in a similar way whether we make a behavioural gesture ourselves or witness another person making the same or a similar gesture.
- **monotropism:** The idea that infants have an inbuilt bias to form an exclusive attachment to one main figure (i.e. the mother).
- **moral development:** A term relating to how children come to reason about right and wrong, and to think and behave in accordance with rules and conventions regarding what people should do in their interactions with others.
- **national identity:** An individual's self-concept derived from their sense of belonging to a national group.
- **negative emotionality:** An aspect of temperament that involves high levels of anger and/or frustration, discomfort, fear, and sadness, and low levels of soothability.
- **onlooker:** A pattern of children's play interaction that involves simply watching other children play.
- **parallel play:** A pattern of children's play interaction that involves playing alongside other children using the same toys or materials but with little, if any, interaction.
- **parenting styles:** Styles of parenting based on dimensions of responsiveness/warmth, demandingness/control, and levels of autonomy granted to the child.
- **permissive parenting:** A parenting style that combines high acceptance and involvement with low control and high autonomy.
- **perspective taking:** The ability to see things from another person's point of view and to understand that others may see things differently from yourself.
- **postconventional:** The final level of Kohlberg's theory of moral development, which acknowledges that conventions may need to be challenged if they go against fundamental ethical principles.
- **preconventional:** The early stage of moral reasoning in Kohlberg's theory, where the primary concern is with the consequences of actions for yourself (e.g. punishment).
- **prosocial behaviour:** A diverse group of voluntary behaviours that are intended to benefit another, such as helping, sharing, or comforting.
- **proto-declarative pointing:** A gesture used to draw social partners' attention to something a child finds interesting and wants them to see too.
- **proto-imperative pointing:** A gesture used to indicate to social partners that a child desires an object.
- **secure attachment:** An attachment style characterized by infants' use of the caregiver as a secure base from which to explore or to which they can return in times of distress, including an ability to be soothed by reunion with the caregiver following a separation.
- **self-conscious emotions:** Emotions associated with an awareness of yourself as a social object, such as shame, embarrassment, and pride.
- **self-presentation:** The understanding of how you can control the impressions you make on others.
- **separation anxiety:** The experience of anxiety and distress when infants are separated from their attachment figure, often exhibited around 8 to 14 months of age.

- **slow-to-warm-up temperament:** A description of temperament referring to those who are slightly negative in mood, mild in intensity, and low in adaptability, approach, and activity, and who show variable levels of rhythmicity.
- **social domain approach:** An approach suggesting that children distinguish between various domains or types of social rules, enabling them to distinguish violations of moral rules (e.g. about not harming others) from transgressions of conventional rules (e.g. about saying please and thank you).
- **social identity theory:** A theory suggesting that we identify ourselves as members of social groups and that patterns of in-group versus out-group preference are motivated by a desire to seek a strong, positive social identity in order to maintain self-esteem.
- **social learning theory:** A theory suggesting that learning takes place through observing, internalizing, and replicating the behaviour of others.
- **social referencing:** Reading the emotional reactions of others as nonverbal communicative gestures to help to inform our behaviour in ambiguous situations.
- **sociometric status:** Peer status based on children's rated liking of their peers or on their nominations of peers with whom they most and least like to play.
- **solitary play:** A pattern of play in which the child is playing alone.
- **still-face paradigm:** An experimental procedure that demonstrates the importance of contingent caregiver interactions with infants, whereby the caregiver interacts with an infant for a short period of time before adopting a still face – remaining entirely unresponsive to the infant – before resuming normal interaction.
- **strange situation:** An experimental procedure for assessing individual differences in attachment, which involves observing infants in a laboratory setting and assessing the way they react to their caregiver in the context of exploring the environment and responding to separation and reunion.
- **stranger anxiety:** The distress infants feel on meeting new people, which becomes heightened at around 6 to 12 months.
- **temperament:** Biologically based and relatively stable differences in an infant's behavioural and emotional reactivity.
- **theory of mind (ToM):** The attribution of mental states such as beliefs, desires, emotions, and intentions to yourself and to others in order to explain and predict behaviour.
- **uninvolved parenting:** A style of parenting that combines low acceptance and involvement with low control and high but inappropriate autonomy.
- **unoccupied play:** A pattern of children's behaviour in which they are not involved in play but may be watching other children's interactions or other events and objects of interest.
- **Vygotskian approach:** A framework suggesting that children's cognitive development occurs through social interaction with more experienced and capable partners.

NOTES

1. https://www.youtube.com/watch?v=YGSj2zY2OEM
2. http://www.huffingtonpost.com/david-sack-md/empathy_b_1658984.html
3. https://www.youtube.com/watch?v=BoT7qH_uVNo

FURTHER RESOURCES

Braungart-Rieker, J. M., Garwood, M. M., Powers, B. P., & Wang, X. (2001). Parental sensitivity, infant affect, and affect regulation: Predictors of later attachment. *Child Development, 72*(1), 252–270.

Cillessen, A. H. N., & Mayeux, L. (2004). From censure to reinforcement: Developmental changes in the association between aggression and social status. *Child Development, 75*, 147–163.

Doherty, J. M. (2008). *Theory of mind: How children understand others' thoughts and feelings.* Hove, UK: Psychology Press.

Frith, U. (2003). *Autism: Explaining the enigma.* Oxford, UK: Blackwell.

Hamlin, J. K., Wynn, K., & Bloom, P. (2007). Social evaluation by preverbal infants. *Nature, 450* (7169), 557–559.

Hoffman, M. L. (2000). *Empathy and moral development: Implications for caring and justice.* Cambridge, UK: Cambridge University Press.

Hughes, C. (2011). *Social understanding and social lives: From toddlerhood through to the transition to school.* Hove, UK: Psychology Press.

Pluess, M., & Belsky, J. (2010). Differential susceptibility to parenting and quality child care. *Developmental Psychology, 46*(2), 379.

Rochat, P. (Ed.). (2014). *Early social cognition: Understanding others in the first months of life.* Mahwah, NJ: Psychology Press.

Ruffman, T., Slade, L., & Crowe, E. (2002). The relation between children's and mothers' mental state language and theory-of-mind understanding. *Child Development, 73*(3), 734–751.

Sanders, M. R. (2012). Development, evaluation, and multinational dissemination of the Triple P-Positive Parenting Program. *Annual Review of Clinical Psychology, 8,* 345–379.

Sroufe, L. A. (1996). *Emotional development.* Cambridge, UK: Cambridge University Press.

Watamura, S. E., Phillips, D. A., Morrissey, T. W., McCartney, K., & Bub, K. (2011). Double jeopardy: Poorer social-emotional outcomes for children in the NICHD SECCYD experiencing home and child-care environments that confer risk. *Child Development, 82*(1), 48–65.

REFERENCES

Aboud, F. (1988). *Children and prejudice.* Oxford, UK: Basil Blackwell.

Aboud, F. E., & Skerry, S. A. (1983). Self and ethnic concepts in relation to ethnic constancy. *Canadian Journal of Behavioural Science/Revue Canadienne des sciences du comportement, 15*(1), 14–26.

ACT for Youth. (2018). Ethnic and racial identity development. Retrieved 25 January 2018 from http://www.actforyouth.net/adolescence/identity/ethnic_racial.cfm

Ainsworth, M. D. S., Blehar, M. C., Waters, E., & Wall, S. (1978). *Patterns of attachment: A psychological study of the strange situation.* Hillsdale, NJ: Lawrence Erlbaum Associates.

Ainsworth, M. S. (1979). Infant–mother attachment. *American Psychologist, 34*(10), 932–937.

Alder, T. F., & Furman, W. (1988). A model for children's relationships and relationship dysfunctions. In S. Duck (Ed.), *Handbook of personal relationships: Theory, research, and interventions* (pp. 211–232). New York, NY: Wiley.

Anderson, C. A. (2004). An update on the effects of playing violent video games. *Journal of Adolescence, 27*(1), 113–122.

Anderson, C. A., Berkowitz, L., Donnerstein, E., Huesmann, L. R., Johnson, J., Linz, D., … Wartella, E. (2003). The influence of media violence on youth. *Psychological Science in the Public Interest, 4,* 81–110.

Anderson, C. A., & Bushman, B. J. (2001). Effects of violent video games on aggressive behavior, aggressive cognition, aggressive affect, physiological arousal, and prosocial behavior: A meta-analytic review of the scientific literature. *Psychological Science, 12*(5), 353–359.

American Psychiatric Association. (2013). *Diagnostic and statistical manual of mental disorders* (5th ed.). Washington, DC: American Psychiatric Association.

Apperly, I. A., & Butterfill, S. A. (2009). Do humans have two systems to track beliefs and belief-like states? *Psychological Review, 116*(4), 953–970.

Apperly, I. A., Samson, D., & Humphreys, G. W. (2009). Studies of adults can inform accounts of theory of mind development. *Developmental Psychology, 45*(1), 190–201.

Astington, J. W. (2001). The future of theory-of-mind research: Understanding motivational states, the role of language, and real-world consequences. *Child Development, 72*(3), 685–687.

Astington, J. W. (2003). Sometimes necessary, never sufficient: False-belief understanding and social competence. In B. Repacholi & V. Slaughter (Eds.), *Individual differences in theory of mind: Implications for typical and atypical development* (pp. 14–39). New York, NY: Psychology Press.

Azmitia, M., & Hesser, J. (1993). Why siblings are important agents of cognitive development: A comparison of siblings and peers. *Child Development, 64*, 430–444. doi:10.1111/j.1467-8624.1993.tb02919.x

Aznar, A., & Tenenbaum, H. R. (2014). Gender and age differences in parent–child emotion talk. *British Journal of Developmental Psychology, 33*(1), 148–155.

Baillargeon, R., Scott, R. M., & He, Z. (2010). False-belief understanding in infants. *Trends in Cognitive Sciences, 14*(3), 110–118.

Bakermans-Kranenburg, M. J., Van IJzendoorn, M. H., & Juffer, F. (2003). Less is more: Meta-analyses of sensitivity and attachment interventions in early childhood. *Psychological Bulletin, 129*(2), 195–215.

Bakti, A., Baron-Cohen, S., Wheelwright, S., Connellan, J., & Ahluwalia, J. (2000). Is there an innate gaze module? Evidence from human neonates. *Infant Behavioral Development, 23*, 223–229.

Baldry, A. C., & Farrington, D. P. (2000). Bullies and delinquents: Personal characteristics and parental styles. *Journal of Community & Applied Social Psychology, 10*(1), 17–31.

Bandura, A. (1965). Influence of models' reinforcement contingencies on the acquisition of imitative responses. *Journal of Personality and Social Psychology, 1*(6), 589–595.

Bandura, A., & McDonald, F. J. (1963). Influence of social reinforcement and the behavior of models in shaping children's moral judgment. *Journal of Abnormal and Social Psychology, 67*(3), 274–281.

Bandura, A., Ross, D., & Ross, S. A. (1961). Transmission of aggression through imitation of aggressive models. *Journal of Abnormal and Social Psychology, 63*(3), 575–582.

Banerjee, R. (2002). Individual differences in children's understanding of social evaluation concerns. *Infant and Child Development, 11*(3), 237–252.

Banerjee, R., & Dittmar, H. (2008). Individual differences in children's materialism: The role of peer relations. *Personality and Social Psychology Bulletin, 34*(1), 17–31.

Banerjee, R., Watling, D., & Caputi, M. (2011). Peer relations and the understanding of faux pas: Longitudinal evidence for bidirectional associations. *Child Development, 82*(6), 1887–1905.

Banerjee, R., & Yuill, N. (1999). Children's explanations for self-presentational behaviour. *European Journal of Social Psychology, 29*(1), 105–111.

Baron-Cohen, S. (1995). *Mindblindness: An essay on autism and theory of mind.* Cambridge, MA: MIT Press.

Baron-Cohen, S., Leslie, A. M., & Frith, U. (1985). Does the autistic child have a 'theory of mind'? *Cognition, 21*(1), 37–46.

Barrett, H. C., Broesch, T., Scott, R. M., He, Z., Baillargeon, R., Wu, D., … Laurence, S. (2013). Early false-belief understanding in traditional non-Western societies. *Proceedings of the Royal Society B: Biological Sciences, 280*, 1–6.

Barrett, M. (1996). English children's acquisition of a European identity. In G. Breakwell & E. Lyons (Eds.), *Changing European identities: Social psychological analysis of social change* (pp. 349–370). Oxford, UK: Butterworth-Heinemann.

Bates, E. (1990). Language about me and you: Pronominal reference and the emerging concept of self. In D. Cicchetti & M. Beeghly (Eds.), *The self in transition: Infancy to childhood* (pp. 165–182). Chicago, IL: University of Chicago Press.

Baumrind, D. (1971). Current patterns of parental authority. *Developmental Psychology, 4*(1, Pt. 2), 1–103.

Baumrind, D. (1991). The influence of parenting style on adolescent competence and substance use. *Journal of Early Adolescence, 11*(1), 56–95.

Baydar, N., & Brooks-Gunn, J. (1991). Effects of maternal employment and child-care arrangements on preschoolers' cognitive and behavioral outcomes: Evidence from the Children of the National Longitudinal Survey of Youth. *Developmental Psychology, 27*(6), 932–945.

BBC News. (2011). MPs debate England riots. Retrieved 20 November 2017 from http://news.bbc. co.uk/democracylive/hi/house_of_commons/newsid_9560000/9560113.stm

Behne, T., Carpenter, M., Call, J., & Tomasello, M. (2005). Unwilling versus unable: Infants' understanding of intentional action. *Developmental Psychology*, *41*(2), 328–337.

Belsky, J. (1984). The determinants of parenting: A process model. *Child Development*, *55*, 83–96.

Belsky, J. (1997). Theory testing, effect-size evaluation, and differential susceptibility to rearing influence: The case of mothering and attachment. *Child Development*, *68*(4), 598–600.

Belsky, J. (2005). Differential susceptibility to rearing influence. In B. J. Ellis & D. F. Bjorklund (Eds.), *Origins of the social mind: Evolutionary psychology and child development* (pp. 139–163). New York, NY: Guilford Press.

Belsky, J., Bakermans-Kranenburg, M. J., & Van IJzendoorn, M. H. (2007). For better and for worse: Differential susceptibility to environmental influences. *Current Directions in Psychological Science*, *16*(6), 300–304.

Belsky, J., & Rovine, M. (1988). Nonmaternal care in the first year of life and the security of infant–parent attachment. *Child Development*, *59*, 157–167.

Benenson, J. F., Apostoleris, N. H., & Parnass, J. (1997). Age and sex differences in dyadic and group interaction. *Developmental Psychology*, *33*(3), 538–543.

Bennett, M. (1989). Children's self-attribution of embarrassment. *British Journal of Developmental Psychology*, *7*, 207–217.

Bennett, M., Lyons, E., Sani, F., & Barrett, M. (1998). Children's subjective identification with the group and in-group favoritism. *Developmental Psychology*, *34*(5), 902–909.

Bennett, M., & Sani, F. (Eds.). (2004). *The development of the social self*. Hove, UK: Psychology Press.

Benoit, D., & Parker, K. C. (1994). Stability and transmission of attachment across three generations. *Child Development*, *65*(5), 1444–1456.

Berndt, T. J., Hawkins, J. A., & Jiao, Z. (1999). Influences of friends and friendships on adjustment to junior high school. *Merrill-Palmer Quarterly*, *45*, 13–41.

Bernier, A., Carlson, S. M., & Whipple, N. (2010). From external regulation to self-regulation: Early parenting precursors of young children's executive functioning. *Child Development*, *81*(1), 326–339.

Best, J. R., & Miller, P. H. (2010). A developmental perspective on executive function. *Child Development*, *81*(6), 1641–1660.

Blair, R. J. R. (1995). A cognitive developmental approach to morality: Investigating the psychopath. *Cognition*, *57*(1), 1–29.

Blair, T. (2011). Blaming a moral decline for the riots makes good headlines but bad policy. Retrieved 20 November 2017 from http://www.guardian.co.uk/commentisfree/2011/aug/20/ tony-blair-riots-crime-family

Bleeker, M. M., & Jacobs, J. E. (2004). Achievement in math and science: Do mothers' beliefs matter 12 years later? *Journal of Educational Psychology*, *96*(1), 97–109.

Boraston, Z., & Blakemore, S. J. (2007). The application of eye-tracking technology in the study of autism. *Journal of Physiology*, *581*, 893–898.

Borge, A. I., Rutter, M., Côté, S., & Tremblay, R. E. (2004). Early childcare and physical aggression: Differentiating social selection and social causation. *Journal of Child Psychology and Psychiatry*, *45*(2), 367–376.

Boulton, M. J., & Smith, P. K. (1994). Bully/victim problems in middle-school children: Stability, self-perceived competence, peer perceptions and peer acceptance. *British Journal of Developmental Psychology*, *12*(3), 315–329.

Bowlby, J. (1944). Forty-four juvenile thieves: Their characters and home life. *International Journal of Psychoanalysis*, *25*(19/52), 107–127.

Bowlby, J. (1953). *Childcare and the growth of love*. London, UK: Pelican Books.

Bowlby, J. (1969). *Attachment and loss: Vol. 1. Attachment*. New York, NY: Basic Books.

Bowlby, J. (1973). *Attachment and loss: Vol. 2. Separation: Anxiety and anger.* New York, NY: Basic Books.

Bowlby, J. (1980). *Attachment and loss: Vol. 3. Loss: Sadness and depression.* London, UK: Hogarth Press.

Bowlby, J. (1988). *A secure base: Parent–child attachment and healthy human development.* London, UK: Routledge.

Boyes, M. C., & Allen, S. G. (1993). Styles of parent–child interaction and moral reasoning in adolescence. *Merrill-Palmer Quarterly, 39,* 551–570.

Bradley, R. H., & Corwyn, R. F. (2002). Socioeconomic status and child development. *Annual Review of Psychology, 53*(1), 371–399.

Bradley, R. H., & Corwyn, R. F. (2008). Infant temperament, parenting, and externalizing behavior in first grade: A test of the differential susceptibility hypothesis. *Journal of Child Psychology and Psychiatry, 49*(2), 124–131.

BrainHQ. (2018). What is brain plasticity? Retrieved 25 January 2018 from https://www.brainhq.com/brain-resources/brain-plasticity/what-is-brain-plasticity

Braungart-Rieker, J. M., Garwood, M. M., Powers, B. P., & Wang, X. (2001). Parental sensitivity, infant affect, and affect regulation: Predictors of later attachment. *Child Development, 72*(1), 252–270.

Braungart-Rieker, J. M., Zentall, S., Lickenbrock, D. M., Ekas, N. V., Oshio, T., & Planalp, E. (2014). Attachment in the making: Mother and father sensitivity and infants' responses during the still-face paradigm. *Journal of Experimental Child Psychology, 125,* 63–84.

Brennan, K. A., Clark, C. L., & Shaver, P. R. (1998). Self-report measurement of adult attachment: An integrated overview. In J. A. Simpson & W. S. Rholes (Eds.), *Attachment theory and close relationships* (pp. 46–76). New York, NY: Basic Books.

Bretherton, I. (2010). Fathers in attachment theory and research: A review. *Early Child Development and Care, 180*(1/2), 9–23.

Bretherton, I., & Munholland, K. A. (1999). Internal working models in attachment relationships: A construct revisited. In J. Cassidy & P. R. Shaver (Eds.), *Handbook of attachment: Theory, research, and clinical applications* (pp. 89–111). New York, NY: Guilford Press.

Bretherton, I., & Oppenheim, D. (2003). The MacArthur Story Stem Battery: Development, administration, reliability, validity and reflections about meaning. In R. N. Emde, D. P. Wolf, & D. Oppenheim (Eds.), *Revealing the inner world of young children: The MacArthur Story Stem Battery and parent–child narratives* (pp. 50–80). New York, NY: Oxford University Press.

Brody, G. H. (1998). Sibling relationship quality: Its causes and consequences. *Annual Review of Psychology, 49*(1), 1–24.

Broesch, T. L., Callaghan, T., Henrich, J., Murphy, C., & Rochat, P. (2011). Cultural variations in children's mirror self-recognition. *Journal of Cross-Cultural Psychology, 40*(6), 1019–1031.

Bronfenbrenner, U. (1979). Contexts of child rearing: Problems and prospects. *American Psychologist, 34*(10), 844–850.

Brown, J. R., & Dunn, J. (1992). Talk with your mother or your sibling? Developmental changes in early family conversations about feelings. *Child Development, 63*(2), 336–349.

Brown, R. (2000). *Group processes.* Oxford, UK: Blackwell.

Brownell, C. A., Svetlova, M., Anderson, R., Nichols, S. R., & Drummond, J. (2013). Socialization of early prosocial behavior: Parents' talk about emotions is associated with sharing and helping in toddlers. *Infancy, 18*(1), 91–119.

Brumariu, L. E., & Kerns, K. A. (2010). Parent–child attachment and internalizing symptoms in childhood and adolescence: A review of empirical findings and future directions. *Development and Psychopathology, 22*(1), 177–203.

Buhrmester, D. (1990). Intimacy of friendship, interpersonal competence, and adjustment during preadolescence and adolescence. *Child Development, 61*(4), 1101–1111.

Buist, K. L., Deković, M., & Prinzie, P. (2013). Sibling relationship quality and psychopathology of children and adolescents: A meta-analysis. *Clinical Psychology Review*, *33*(1), 97–106.

Burr, J. E., Ostrov, J. M., Jansen, E. A., Cullerton-Sen, C., & Crick, N. R. (2005). Relational aggression and friendship during early childhood: 'I won't be your friend!' *Early Education and Development*, *16*(2), 161–184.

Byom, L. J., & Mutlu, B. (2013). Theory of mind: Mechanisms, methods, and new directions. *Frontiers in Human Neuroscience*, *7*, 413. doi:10.3389/fnhum.2013.00413

Calkins, S. D., & Fox, N. A. (1992). The relations among infant temperament, security of attachment, and behavioral inhibition at twenty-four months. *Child Development*, *63*(6), 1456–1472.

Callaghan, T., Rochat, P., Lillard, A., Claux, M. L., Odden, H., Itakura, S., … Singh, S. (2005). Synchrony in the onset of mental-state reasoning evidence from five cultures. *Psychological Science*, *16*(5), 378–384.

Calvert, S. L., & Kotler, J. A. (2003). Lessons from children's television: The impact of the Children's Television Act on children's learning. *Journal of Applied Developmental Psychology*, *24*(3), 275–335.

Campos, J. J., Mumme, D. L., Kermoian, R., & Campos, R. G. (1994). A functionalist perspective on the nature of emotion. *Monographs of the Society for Research in Child Development*, *59*(2/3), 284–303.

Camras, L. A., Oster, H., Campos, J. J., & Bakeman, R. (2003). Emotional facial expressions in European-American, Japanese, and Chinese infants. In P. Ekman, J. Campos, R. Davidson, & F. de Waal (Eds.), *Annals of the New York Academy of Sciences* (Vol. *1000*, pp. 135–151). New York, NY: New York Academy of Sciences.

Camras, L. A., & Shutter, J. M. (2010). Emotional facial expression in infancy. *Emotion Review*, *2*(2), 120–129.

Caputi, M., Lecce, S., Pagnin, A., & Banerjee, R. (2012). Longitudinal effects of theory of mind on later peer relations: The role of prosocial behavior. *Developmental Psychology*, *48*(1), 257–270.

Carlson, S. M. (2005). Developmentally sensitive measures of executive function in preschool children. *Developmental Neuropsychology*, *28*(2), 595–616.

Carlson, S. M., & Wang, T. S. (2007). Inhibitory control and emotion regulation in preschool children. *Cognitive Development*, *22*(4), 489–510.

Carpendale, J. I., & Chandler, M. J. (1996). On the distinction between false belief understanding and subscribing to an interpretive theory of mind. *Child Development*, *67*(4), 1686–1706.

Carpendale, J. I., & Lewis, C. (2004). Constructing an understanding of mind: The development of children's social understanding within social interaction. *Behavioral and Brain Sciences*, *27*(1), 79–96.

Caspi, A. (2000). The child is father of the man: Personality continuities from childhood to adulthood. *Journal of Personality and Social Psychology*, *78*(1), 158–172.

Cassidy, J., Woodhouse, S. S., Sherman, L. J., Stupica, B., & Lejuez, C. W. (2011). Enhancing infant attachment security: An examination of treatment efficacy and differential susceptibility. *Development and Psychopathology*, *23*(1), 131–148.

Cervantes, C. A., & Callanan, M. A. (1998). Labels and explanations in mother–child emotion talk: Age and gender differentiation. *Developmental Psychology*, *34*(1), 88–98.

Chao, R. K. (1994). Beyond parental control and authoritarian parenting style: Understanding Chinese parenting through the cultural notion of training. *Child Development*, *65*(4), 1111–1119.

Chen, X., Rubin, K. H., & Li, B. (1995). Social and school adjustment of shy and aggressive children in China. *Development and Psychopathology*, *7*(2), 337–349.

Chen, Z. Y., & Kaplan, H. B. (2001). Intergenerational transmission of constructive parenting. *Journal of Marriage and Family*, *63*(1), 17–31.

Chevallier, C., Kohls, G., Troiani, V., Brodkin, E. S., & Schultz, R. T. (2012). The social motivation theory of autism. *Trends in Cognitive Sciences*, *16*(4), 231–239.

Christakis, D. A., Zimmerman, F. J., DiGiuseppe, D. L., & McCarty, C. A. (2004). Early television exposure and subsequent attentional problems in children. *Pediatrics*, *113*(4), 708–713.

Cillessen, A. H. N., & Mayeux, L. (2004). From censure to reinforcement: Developmental changes in the association between aggression and social status. *Child Development*, *75*, 147–163.

Clements, W. A., & Perner, J. (1994). Implicit understanding of belief. *Cognitive Development*, *9*(4), 377–395.

Coie, J. D., & Dodge, K. A. (1983). Continuities and changes in children's social status: A five-year longitudinal study. *Merrill-Palmer Quarterly*, *29*, 261–282.

Coie, J. D., Dodge, K. A., & Kupersmidt. (1990). Peer status and aggression in boys' groups: Developmental and contextual analyses. *Child Development*, *61*, 1289–1309.

Collins, W. A., Maccoby, E. E., Steinberg, L., Hetherington, E. M., & Bornstein, M. H. (2000). Contemporary research on parenting: The case for nature and nurture. *American Psychologist*, *55*(2), 218–232.

Comer, R., Ogden, N., & Furnham, A. (2013). *Psychology*. Hoboken, NJ: Wiley.

Condry, J., & Condry, S. (1976). Sex differences: A study of the eye of the beholder. *Child Development*, *47*, 812–819.

Corden, B., Chilvers, R., & Skuse, D. (2008). Avoidance of emotionally arousing stimuli predicts social-perceptual impairment in Asperger's syndrome. *Neuropsychologia*, *46*, 137–147.

Coyne, S. M., Padilla-Walker, L. M., Fraser, A. M., Fellows, K., & Day, R. D. (2014). 'Media time = family time': Positive media use in families with adolescents. *Journal of Adolescent Research*, *29*(5), 663–688.

Crain, W. (2010). *Theories of development: Concepts and applications* (6th ed.). Upper Saddle River, NJ: Pearson.

Crocetti, E., Rubini, M., & Meeus, W. (2008). Capturing the dynamics of identity formation in various ethnic groups: Development and validation of a three-dimensional model. *Journal of Adolescence*, *31*(2), 207–222.

Crockett, E. E., Holmes, B. H., Granger, D. A., & Lyons-Ruth, K. (2013). Maternal disrupted communication during face-to-face interaction at 4 months: Relation to maternal and infant cortisol among at-risk families. *Infancy*, *18*, 1–24.

Crowell, J. A., Fraley, R. C., & Shaver, P. R. (2008). Measurement of individual differences in adolescent and adult attachment. In J. Cassidy & P. R. Shaver (Eds.), *Handbook of attachment: Theory, research and clinical applications* (2nd ed., pp. 599–634). New York, NY: Guilford Press.

Cutting, A. L., & Dunn, J. (2002). The cost of understanding other people: Social cognition predicts young children's sensitivity to criticism. *Journal of Child Psychology and Psychiatry*, *43*(7), 849–860.

Daily Telegraph. (2011, 9 August). The criminals who shame our nation. Retrieved 13 February 2018 from http://www.telegraph.co.uk/comment/telegraph-view/8691352/The-criminals-who-shame-our-nation.html

Damon, W., & Hart, D. (1982). The development of self-understanding from infancy through adolescence. *Child Development*, *53*(4), 841–864.

De Rosnay, M., & Hughes, C. (2006). Conversation and theory of mind: Do children talk their way to socio-cognitive understanding? *British Journal of Developmental Psychology*, *24*(1), 7–37.

De Waal, F. B. M. (2006). *Primates and philosophers: How morality evolved*. Princeton, NJ: Princeton University Press.

De Wolff, M. S., & Van IJzendoorn, M. H. (1997). Sensitivity and attachment: A meta-analysis on parental antecedents of infant attachment. *Child Development*, *68*(4), 571–591.

Decety, J., Michalska, K. J., & Kinzler, K. D. (2012). The contribution of emotion and cognition to moral sensitivity: A neurodevelopmental study. *Cerebral Cortex*, *22*(1), 209–220.

Denham, S. A., Bassett, H. H., Zinsser, K., & Wyatt, T. M. (2014). How preschoolers' social–emotional learning predicts their early school success: Developing theory-promoting, competency-based assessments. *Infant and Child Development*, *23*, 426–454.

Denham, S. A., Zoller, D., & Couchoud, E. A. (1994). Socialization of preschoolers' emotion understanding. *Developmental Psychology, 30*(6), 928–936.

Devine, R. T., & Hughes, C. (2014). Relations between false belief understanding and executive function in early childhood: A meta-analysis. *Child Development, 85*, 1777–1794.

Diamond, A., Barnett, W. S., Thomas, J., & Munro, S. (2007). Preschool program improves cognitive control. *Science, 318*(5855), 1387–1388.

Dodge, K. A. (1983). Behavioural antecedents of peer social status. *Child Development, 54*, 1386–1399.

Doherty, J. M. (2008). *Theory of mind: How children understand others' thoughts and feelings.* New York, NY: Psychology Press.

Doyle, A. B., & Aboud, F. E. (1995). A longitudinal study of white children's racial prejudice as a social-cognitive development. *Merrill-Palmer Quarterly, 41*, 209–228.

Dunfield, K., Kuhlmeier, V. A., O'Connell, L., & Kelley, E. (2011). Examining the diversity of prosocial behavior: Helping, sharing, and comforting in infancy. *Infancy, 16*(3), 227–247.

Dunn, J. (1985). *Sisters and brothers.* Cambridge, MA: Harvard University Press.

Dunn, J., Brown, J. R., & Maguire, M. (1995). The development of children's moral sensibility: Individual differences and emotion understanding. *Developmental Psychology, 31*(4), 649–659.

Dunn, J., & Kendrick, C. (1982). Siblings and their mothers: Developing relationships within the family. In M. E. Lamb & B. Sutton-Smith (Eds.), *Sibling relationships: Their nature and significance across the lifespan* (pp. 39–60). Hillsdale, NJ: Lawrence Erlbaum Associates.

Durlak, J. A., Weissberg, R. P., Dymnicki, A. B., Taylor, R. D., & Schellinger, K. B. (2011). The impact of enhancing students' social and emotional learning: A meta-analysis of school-based universal interventions. *Child Development, 82*(1), 405–432.

Dykas, M. J., & Cassidy, J. (2011). Attachment and the processing of social information across the life span: Theory and evidence. *Psychological Bulletin, 137*(1), 19–46.

Easterbrook, M. J., Wright, M. L., Dittmar, H., & Banerjee, R. (2014). Consumer culture ideals, extrinsic motivations, and well-being in children. *European Journal of Social Psychology, 44*(4), 349–359.

Eccles-Parsons, J. S., Adler, T. F., & Kaczala, C. M. (1982). Socialization of achievement attitudes and beliefs: Parental influences. *Child Development, 53*, 310–321.

Eckerman, C. O., & Stein, M. R. (1990). How imitation begets imitation and toddlers' generation of games. *Developmental Psychology, 26*(3), 370–378.

Egan, M., Bond, L., Kearns, A., & Tannahill, C. (2012). Is concern about young people's anti-social behaviour associated with poor health? Cross-sectional evidence from residents of deprived urban neighbourhoods. *BMC Public Health, 12*(1), 217.

Eggum, N. D., Eisenberg, N., Kao, K., Spinrad, T. L., Bolnick, R., Hofer, C., … Fabricius, W. V. (2011). Emotion understanding, theory of mind, and prosocial orientation: Relations over time in early childhood. *Journal of Positive Psychology, 6*(1), 4–16.

Eisenberg, N. (2000). Emotion, regulation, and moral development. *Annual Review of Psychology, 51*(1), 665–697.

Eisenberg, N., & Fabes, R. A. (1998). Prosocial development. In W. Damon (Ed.), *Handbook of child psychology: Social, emotional, and personality development* (Vol. 3, pp. 701–778). New York, NY: Wiley.

Eisenberg, N., Fabes, R. A., Bernzweig, J., Karbon, M., Poulin, R., & Hanish, L. (1993). The relations of emotionality and regulation to preschoolers' social skills and sociometric status. *Child Development, 64*(5), 1418–1438.

Eisenberg, N., Fabes, R. A., & Spinrad, T. L. (2006). Prosocial development. In N. Eisenberg (Ed.), *Handbook of child psychology: Vol. 3. Social, emotional, and personality development* (6th ed., pp. 646–718). Hoboken, NJ: Wiley.

Eisenberg, N., Hofer, C., Sulik, M. J., & Liew, J. (2014). The development of prosocial moral reasoning and a prosocial orientation in young adulthood: Concurrent and longitudinal correlates. *Developmental Psychology, 50*(1), 58–70.

Eisenberg, N., Sadovsky, A., Spinrad, T. L., Fabes, R. A., Losoya, S. H., Valiente, C., … Shepard, S. A. (2005). The relations of problem behavior status to children's negative emotionality, effortful control, and impulsivity: Concurrent relations and prediction of change. *Developmental Psychology*, *41*(1), 193–211.

Eisenberg, N., Valiente, C., Spinrad, T. L., Cumberland, A., Liew, J., Reiser, M., … Losoya, S. H. (2009). Longitudinal relations of children's effortful control, impulsivity, and negative emotionality to their externalizing, internalizing, and co-occurring behavior problems. *Developmental Psychology*, *45*(4), 988.

Ekman, P. (2003). *Emotions revealed*. New York, NY: Times Books.

Ekman, P., & Friesen, W. V. (1971). Constants across cultures in the face and emotion. *Journal of Personality and Social Psychology*, *17*, 124–129.

Ellis, B. J., Boyce, W. T., Belsky, J., Bakermans-Kranenburg, M. J., & Van IJzendoorn, M. H. (2011). Differential susceptibility to the environment: An evolutionary–neurodevelopmental theory. *Development and Psychopathology*, *23*(1), 7–28.

Ellis, S., Rogoff, B., & Cromer, C. C. (1981). Age segregation in children's social interactions. *Developmental Psychology*, *17*(4), 399–407.

Ellsworth, C. P., Muir, D. W., & Hains, S. M. (1993). Social competence and person-object differentiation: An analysis of the still-face effect. *Developmental Psychology*, *29*(1), 63–73.

Ensor, R., Devine, R. T., Marks, A., & Hughes, C. (2014). Mothers' cognitive references to 2-year-olds predict theory of mind at ages 6 and 10. *Child Development*, *85*(3), 1222–1235.

Ensor, R., Spencer, D., & Hughes, C. (2011). 'You feel sad?' Emotion understanding mediates effects of verbal ability and mother–child mutuality on prosocial behaviors: Findings from 2 years to 4 years. *Social Development*, *20*(1), 93–110.

Eron, L. D., Huesmann, L. R., Lefkowitz, M. M., & Walder, L. O. (1972). Does television violence cause aggression? *American Psychologist*, *27*(4), 253–263.

Evans, C. A., & Porter, C. L. (2009). The emergence of mother–infant co-regulation during the first year: Links to infants' developmental status and attachment. *Infant Behavior and Development*, *32*(2), 147–158.

Farrant, B. M., Devine, T. A. J., Maybery, M. T., & Fletcher, J. (2012). Empathy, perspective taking and prosocial behaviour: The importance of parenting practices. *Infant and Child Development*, *21*(2), 175–188.

Fearon, R. P., Bakermans-Kranenburg, M. J., Van IJzendoorn, M. H., Lapsley, A. M., & Roisman, G. I. (2010). The significance of insecure attachment and disorganization in the development of children's externalizing behavior: A meta-analytic study. *Child Development*, *81*(2), 435–456.

Fehr, E., Bernhard, H., & Rockenbach, B. (2008). Egalitarianism in young children. *Nature*, *454*(7208), 1079–1083.

Feldman, R. (2007). Parent–infant synchrony and the construction of shared timing: Physiological precursors, developmental outcomes, and risk conditions. *Journal of Child Psychology and Psychiatry*, *48*(3/4), 329–354.

Fields, L., & Prinz, R. J. (1997). Coping and adjustment during childhood and adolescence. *Clinical Psychology Review*, *17*, 937–976.

Fivush, R. (2007). Maternal reminiscing style and children's developing understanding of self and emotion. *Clinical Social Work Journal*, *35*(1), 37–46.

Fivush, R., Brotman, M. A., Buckner, J. P., & Goodman, S. H. (2000). Gender differences in parent–child emotion narratives. *Sex Roles*, *42*(3/4), 233–253.

Flynn, E., Ehrenreich, S. E., Beron, K. J., & Underwood, M. K. (2014). Prosocial behavior: Long-term trajectories and psychosocial outcomes. *Social Development*, *24*(3), 462–482. doi:10.1111/sode.12100

Fox, N. A., & Calkins, S. D. (2003). The development of self-control of emotion: Intrinsic and extrinsic influences. *Motivation and Emotion*, *27*(1), 7–26.

Fox, N. A., Calkins, S. D., & Bell, M. A. (1994). Neural plasticity and development in the first two years of life: Evidence from cognitive and socioemotional domains of research. *Development and Psychopathology*, 6(4), 677–696.

Fraley, R. C., & Davis, K. E. (1997). Attachment formation and transfer in young adults' close friendships and romantic relationships. *Personal Relationships*, 4(2), 131–144.

Fraley, R. C., Waller, N. G., & Brennan, K. A. (2000). An item response theory analysis of self-report measures of adult attachment. *Journal of Personality and Social Psychology*, 78(2), 350–365.

Frankel, K. A., & Bates, J. E. (1990). Mother–toddler problem solving: Antecedents in attachment, home behavior, and temperament. *Child Development*, 61(3), 810–819.

Frith, U. (2003). *Autism: Explaining the enigma*. Oxford, UK: Blackwell.

Frith, U., Happé, F., & Siddons, F. (1994). Autism and theory of mind in everyday life. *Social Development*, 3, 108–124.

Frye, D., Zelazo, P. D., & Palfai, T. (1995). Theory of mind and rule-based reasoning. *Cognitive Development*, 10(4), 483–527.

Funk, J. B., Baldacci, H. B., Pasold, T., & Baumgardner, J. (2004). Violence exposure in real-life, video games, television, movies, and the internet: Is there desensitization? *Journal of Adolescence*, 27(1), 23–39.

Galvan, A. (2010). Adolescent development of the reward system. *Frontiers in Human Neuroscience*, 4, 116–124.

Ganchrow, J. R., Steiner, J. E., & Daher, M. (1983). Neonatal facial expressions in response to different qualities and intensities of gustatory stimuli. *Infant Behavior and Development*, 6, 473–484.

Gardner, F. E. M. (1992). Parent–child interaction and conduct disorder. *Educational Psychology Review*, 4, 135–163.

Gass, K., Jenkins, J., & Dunn, J. (2007). Are sibling relationships protective? A longitudinal study. *Journal of Child Psychology and Psychiatry*, 48(2), 167–175.

Gasser, L., & Keller, M. (2009). Are the competent the morally good? Perspective taking and moral motivation of children involved in bullying. *Social Development*, 18, 798–816.

Geary, D. C. (1998). *Male, female: The evolution of human sex differences*. Washington, DC: American Psychological Association.

George, C., Kaplan, N., & Main, M. (1985). *Adult attachment interview (AAI)*. Unpublished manuscript, University of California at Berkeley.

George, C., Kaplan, N., & Main, M. (1996). *The attachment interview for adults*. Unpublished manuscript, University of California at Berkeley.

Gilligan, C. (1982). *In a different voice*. Cambridge, MA: Harvard University Press.

Gilliom, M., Shaw, D. S., Beck, J. E., Schonberg, M. A., & Lukon, J. L. (2002). Anger regulation in disadvantaged preschool boys: Strategies, antecedents, and the development of self-control. *Developmental Psychology*, 38(2), 225–235.

Golombok, S. (2000). *Parenting: What really counts?* London, UK: Psychology Press.

Golombok, S., & Fivush, R. (1994). *Gender development*. Cambridge, UK: Cambridge University Press.

Goren, C. C., Sarty, M., & Wu, P. Y. K. (1975). Visual following and pattern discrimination of face-like stimuli by newborn infants. *Pediatrics*, 56, 544–549.

Gray, M. R., & Steinberg, L. (1999). Unpacking authoritative parenting: Reassessing a multidimensional construct. *Journal of Marriage and the Family*, 61(3), 574–587.

Greig, R. (2003). Ethnic identity development: Implications for mental health in African-American and Hispanic adolescents. *Issues in Mental Health Nursing*, 24(3), 317–331.

Groh, A. M., Fearon, R. P., Bakermans-Kranenburg, M. J., Van IJzendoorn, M. H., Steele, R. D., & Roisman, G. I. (2014). The significance of attachment security for children's social competence with peers: A meta-analytic study. *Attachment & Human Development*, 16(2), 103–136.

Grossmann, K., Grossmann, K. E., Fremmer-Bombik, E., Kindler, H., & Scheuerer-Englisch, H. (2002). The uniqueness of the child–father attachment relationship: Fathers' sensitive and challenging play as a pivotal variable in a 16-year longitudinal study. *Social Development, 11*(3), 301–337.

Grossmann, T., & Johnson, M. H. (2007). The development of the social brain in human infancy. *European Journal of Neuroscience, 25*(4), 909–919.

Grusec, J. E., Davidov, M., & Lundell, L. (2002). Prosocial and helping behavior. In P. K. Smith & H. Craig (Eds.), *Blackwell handbook of childhood social development* (pp. 457–474). Malden, MA: Blackwell.

Grusec, J. E., & Goodnow, J. J. (1994). Impact of parental discipline methods on the child's internalization of values: A reconceptualization of current point of view. *Developmental Psychology, 30*(1), 4–19.

Güroğlu, B., Van den Bos, W., & Crone, E. A. (2014). Sharing and giving across adolescence: An experimental study examining the development of prosocial behavior. *Frontiers in Psychology, 5*, 291. doi:10.3389/fpsyg.2014.00291

Haidt, J., & Joseph, C. (2007). The moral mind: How 5 sets of innate moral intuitions guide the development of many culture-specific virtues, and perhaps even modules. In P. Carruthers, S. Laurence, & S. Stich (Eds.), *The innate mind* (Vol. 3, pp. 367–391). New York, NY: Oxford University Press.

Haidt, J., Koller, S. H., & Dias, M. G. (1993). Affect, culture, and morality, or is it wrong to eat your dog? *Journal of Personality and Social Psychology, 65*(4), 613–628.

Hamill, C. A., Newman, E., Todd, L., & Peck, D. (2014). Attachment and violent offending: A meta-analysis. *Aggression and Violent Behavior, 19*, 322–339.

Hamlin, J. K., Wynn, K., & Bloom, P. (2007). Social evaluation by preverbal infants. *Nature, 450*(7169), 557–559.

Hamlin, J. K., Wynn, K., & Bloom, P. (2010). Three-month-olds show a negativity bias in their social evaluations. *Developmental Science, 13*, 923–929.

Hamlin, J. K., Wynn, K., Bloom, P., & Mahajan, N. (2011). How infants and toddlers react to antisocial others. *Proceedings of the National Academy of Sciences of the United States of America, 108*(50), 19931–19936.

Happé, F. G. (1994). An advanced test of theory of mind: Understanding of story characters' thoughts and feelings by able autistic, mentally handicapped, and normal children and adults. *Journal of Autism and Developmental Disorders, 24*(2), 129–154.

Harris, J. R. (1995). Where is the child's environment? A group socialization theory of development. *Psychological Review, 102*(3), 458–489.

Harris, J. R. (2002). Beyond the nurture assumption: Testing hypotheses about the child's environment. In J. G. Borkowski, S. A. Ramey, & M. Bristol-Power (Eds.), *Parenting and the child's world: Influences on academic, intellectual, and social-emotional development* (pp. 3–20). Mahwah, NJ: Lawrence Erlbaum Associates.

Harris, P. L. (2008). Children's understanding of emotion. In M. Lewis, J. M. Haviland, & L. F. Barrett (Eds.), *Handbook of emotions* (3rd ed., pp. 320–33). New York, NY: Guilford Press.

Harris, P. L., Johnson, C. N., Hutton, D., Andrews, G., & Cooke, T. (1989). Young children's theory of mind and emotion. *Cognition and Emotion, 3*(4), 379–400.

Hart, C. H., Newell, L. D., & Olsen, S. F. (2003). Parenting skills and social-communicative competence in childhood. In J. O. Greene & B. R. Burleson (Eds.), *Handbook of communication and social interaction skills* (pp. 753–797). Mahwah, NJ: Lawrence Erlbaum Associates.

Harter, S. (1998). The development of self-representations. In W. Damon & N. Eisenberg (Eds.), *Handbook of child psychology: Vol. 3. Social, emotional, and personality development* (5th ed., pp. 553–617). Hoboken, NJ: John Wiley.

Harter, S., & Buddin, B. J. (1987). Children's understanding of the simultaneity of two emotions: A five-stage developmental acquisition sequence. *Developmental Psychology, 23*(3), 388–399.

Hartup, W. W. (1989). Social relationships and their developmental significance. *American Psychologist*, *44*(2), 120–126.

Hastings, P. D., Utendale, W. T., & Sullivan, C. (2007). The socialization of prosocial development. In J. E. Grusec & P. D. Hastings (Eds.), *Handbook of socialization: Theory and research* (pp. 638–664). New York, NY: Guilford Press.

Haviland, J. M., & Lelwica, M. (1987). The induced affect response: 10-week-old infants' responses to three emotion expressions. *Developmental Psychology*, *23*(1), 97–104.

Hawker, D. S., & Boulton, M. J. (2000). Twenty years' research on peer victimization and psychosocial maladjustment: A meta-analytic review of cross-sectional studies. *Journal of Child Psychology and Psychiatry*, *41*(4), 441–455.

Hay, D. F., Nash, A., & Pedersen, J. (1983). Interaction between six-month-old peers. *Child Development*, *54*, 557–562.

He, Z., Bolz, M., & Baillargeon, R. (2011). False-belief understanding in 2.5-year-olds: Evidence from violation-of-expectation change-of-location and unexpected-contents tasks. *Developmental Science*, *14*, 292–305. doi:10.1111/j.1467-7687.2010.00980.x

Henry, B., Caspi, A., Moffitt, T. E., & Silva, P. A. (1996). Temperamental and familial predictors of violent and nonviolent criminal convictions: Age 3 to age 18. *Developmental Psychology*, *32*(4), 614–623.

Herrera, C., & Dunn, J. (1997). Early experiences with family conflict: Implications for arguments with a close friend. *Developmental Psychology*, *33*(5), 869–881.

Hoeve, M., Dubas, J. S., Eichelsheim, V. I., Van der Laan, P. H., Smeenk, W., & Gerris, J. R. (2009). The relationship between parenting and delinquency: A meta-analysis. *Journal of Abnormal Child Psychology*, *37*(6), 749–775.

Hoffman, M. L. (1979). Development of moral thought, feeling, and behavior. *American Psychologist*, *34*(10), 958–966.

Hoffman, M. L. (2000). *Empathy and moral development: Implications for caring and justice*. Cambridge, UK: Cambridge University Press.

Hongwanishkul, D., Happaney, K. R., Lee, W. S., & Zelazo, P. D. (2005). Assessment of hot and cool executive function in young children: Age-related changes and individual differences. *Developmental Neuropsychology*, *28*(2), 617–644.

House, B. R., Henrich, J., Brosnan, S. F., & Silk, J. B. (2012). The ontogeny of human prosociality: Behavioral experiments with children aged 3 to 8. *Evolution and Human Behavior*, *33*(4), 291–308.

Howe, N., & Recchia, H. (2005). Playmates and teachers: Reciprocal and complementary interactions between siblings. *Journal of Family Psychology*, *19*(4), 497–502.

Howe, N., & Recchia, H. (2009). Individual differences in sibling teaching in early and middle childhood. *Early Education and Development*, *20*(1), 174–197.

Howes, C., & Matheson, C. C. (1992). Sequences in the development of competent play with peers: Social and social pretend play. *Developmental Psychology*, *28*(5), 961–974.

Huesmann, L. R. (1988). An information processing model for the development of aggression. *Aggressive Behaviour*, *14*, 13–24.

Hughes, C. (2002). Executive functions and development: Emerging themes. *Infant and Child Development*, *11*(2), 201–209.

Hughes, C. (2011). *Social understanding and social lives: From toddlerhood through to the transition to school*. Hove, UK: Psychology Press.

Hughes, C., Devine, R. T., Ensor, R., Koyasu, M., Mizokawa, A., & Lecce, S. (2014). Lost in translation? Comparing British, Japanese, and Italian children's theory-of-mind performance. *Child Development Research*, *2014*, 893492. doi:10.1155/2014/893492

Hughes, C., White, A., Sharpen, J., & Dunn, J. (2000). Antisocial, angry, and unsympathetic: 'Hard to manage' preschoolers' peer problems and possible cognitive influences. *Journal of Child Psychology and Psychiatry*, *41*(2), 169–179.

Isabella, R. A., & Belsky, J. (1991). Interactional synchrony and the origins of infant–mother attachment: A replication study. *Child Development*, 62(2), 373–384.

Isabella, R. A., Belsky, J., & von Eye, A. (1989). Origins of infant–mother attachment: An examination of interactional synchrony during the infant's first year. *Developmental Psychology*, 25(1), 12–21.

Izard, C. E. (2007). Basic emotions, natural kinds, emotion schemas, and a new paradigm. *Perspectives on Psychological Science*, 2, 260–280.

Izard, C. E., Huebner, R. R., Risser, D., & Dougherty, L. (1980). The young infant's ability to produce discrete emotion expressions. *Developmental Psychology*, 16(2), 132–140.

Jaspers, J., Van de Geer, J., Tajfel, H., & Johnson, N. (1972). On the development of national attitudes in children. *European Journal of Social Psychology*, 2, 347–369.

Jones, K. M., Schulkin, J., & Schmidt, L. A. (2014). Shyness: Subtypes, psychosocial correlates, and treatments interventions. *Psychology*, 5, 244–254.

Jones, W., Carr, K., & Klin, A. (2008). Absence of preferential looking to the eyes of approaching adults predicts level of social disability in 2-year-old toddlers with autism spectrum disorder. *Archives of General Psychiatry*, 65(8), 946–954.

Kagan, J. (1981). *The second year: The emergence of self-awareness.* Cambridge, MA: Harvard University Press.

Kagan, J. (1994). *Galen's prophecy: Temperament in human nature.* New York, NY: Basic Books.

Keller, H., Kärtner, J., Borke, J., Yovsi, R., & Kleis, A. (2005). Parenting styles and the development of the categorical self: A longitudinal study on mirror self-recognition in Cameroonian Nso and German families. *International Journal of Behavioral Development*, 29(6), 496–504.

Kennedy, A. E., Rubin, K. H., Hastings, P., & Maisel, B. (2004). Longitudinal relations between child vagal tone and parenting behavior: 2 to 4 years. *Developmental Psychobiology*, 45(1), 10–21.

Kenward, B., & Dahl, M. (2011). Preschoolers distribute scarce resources according to the moral valence of recipients' previous actions. *Developmental Psychology*, 47(4), 1054–1064.

Killen, M., Mulvey, K. L., Richardson, C., Jampol, N., & Woodward, A. (2011). The accidental transgressor: Morally-relevant theory of mind. *Cognition, 119*, 197–215.

Kingery, J. N., Erdley, C. A., & Marshall, K. C. (2011). Peer acceptance and friendship as predictors of early adolescents' adjustment across the middle school transition. *Merrill-Palmer Quarterly*, 57(3), 215–243.

Klin, A., Jones, W., Schultz, R., Volkmar, F., & Cohen, D. (2002). Visual fixation patterns during viewing of naturalistic social situations as predictors of social competence in individuals with autism. *Archives of General Psychiatry, 59*, 809–816.

Kohlberg, L. (1963). The development of children's orientations toward a moral order: I. Sequence in the development of moral thought. *Vita Humana, 6*, 11–33.

Kohlberg, L. (1966). A cognitive-developmental analysis of children's sex-role concepts and attitudes. In E. E. Maccoby (Ed.), *The development of sex differences* (pp. 82–172). Stanford, CA: Stanford University Press.

Kohlberg, L. (1969). *Stages in the development of moral thought and action.* New York, NY: Holt, Rinehart and Winston.

Kohlberg, L. (1976). Moral stages and moralization: The cognitive-developmental approach. In T. Lickona (Ed.), *Moral development and behavior: Theory, research, and social issues* (pp. 31–53). New York, NY: Holt, Rinehart and Winston.

Kohlberg, L., & Hersh, R. H. (1977). Moral development: A review of the theory. *Theory into Practice, 16*(2), 53–59.

Kottelenberg, M. J., & Lehrer, S. F. (2014). Do the perils of universal childcare depend on the child's age? *CESifo Economic Studies*, ifu006.

Kovács, Á. M., Téglás, E., & Endress, A. D. (2010). The social sense: Susceptibility to others' beliefs in human infants and adults. *Science, 330*(6012), 1830–1834.

Kunkel, D. (2001). Children and television advertising. In D. G. Singer & J. L. Singer (Eds.), *Handbook of children and the media* (pp. 375–393). Thousand Oaks, CA: SAGE.

Kurtines, W. M., Gewirtz, J., & Lamb, J. L. (Eds.). (2014). *Handbook of moral behavior and development: Vol. 1. Theory.* New York, NY: Psychology Press.

Ladd, G. W. (2006). Peer rejection, aggressive or withdrawn behaviour, and psychological maladjustment from ages 5 to 12: An examination of four predictive models. *Child Development, 77*, 822–846.

LaFreniere, P. J. (2000). *Emotional development: A biosocial perspective.* New York, NY: Wadsworth.

Laible, D. J., & Thompson, R. A. (1998). Attachment and emotional understanding in preschool children. *Developmental Psychology, 34*(5), 1038–1045.

Lamb, S., & Zakhireh, B. (1997). Toddlers' attention to the distress of peers in a daycare setting. *Early Education and Development, 8*(2), 105–118.

Lamborn, S. D., Mounts, N. S., Steinberg, L., & Dornbusch, S. M. (1991). Patterns of competence and adjustment among adolescents from authoritative, authoritarian, indulgent, and neglectful families. *Child Development, 62*(5), 1049–1065.

Laranjo, J., Bernier, A., Meins, E., & Carlson, S. M. (2010). Early manifestations of children's theory of mind: The roles of maternal mind-mindedness and infant security of attachment. *Infancy, 15*, 300–323. doi:10.1111/j.1532-7078.2009.00014.x

Lavelli, M., & Fogel, A. (2005). Developmental changes in the relationship between infant attention and emotion during early face-to-face communication: The 2-month transition. *Developmental Psychology, 41*, 265–280.

Lecce, S., Bianco, F., Devine, R. T., Hughes, C., & Banerjee, R. (2014). Promoting theory of mind during middle childhood: A training program. *Journal of Experimental Child Psychology, 126*, 52–67.

Lecce, S., Caputi, M., & Hughes, C. (2011). Does sensitivity to criticism mediate the relationship between theory of mind and academic achievement? *Journal of Experimental Child Psychology, 110*(3), 313–331.

Lee, C. L., & Bates, J. E. (1985). Mother–child interaction at age two years and perceived difficult temperament. *Child Development, 56*, 1314–1325.

Leslie, A. M. (2005). Developmental parallels in understanding minds and bodies. *Trends in Cognitive Sciences, 9*(10), 459–462.

Levine, L. E. (1983). Mine: Self-definition in 2-year-old boys. *Developmental Psychology, 19*(4), 544–549.

Lewis, M., & Brooks-Gunn, J. (1979). *Social cognition and the acquisition of self.* New York, NY: Plenum Press.

Lewis, M., Sullivan, M. W., Stanger, C., & Weiss, M. (1989). Self-development and self-conscious emotions. *Child Development, 60*, 146–156.

Liben, L. S., & Signorella, M. L. (1993). Gender-schematic processing in children: The role of initial interpretations of stimuli. *Developmental Psychology, 29*(1), 141–149.

Lord, C., & Jones, R. (2012). Annual research review: Re-thinking the classification of autism spectrum disorders. *Journal of Child Psychology and Psychiatry, 53*(5), 490–509.

Low, J., & Perner, J. (2012). Implicit and explicit theory of mind: State of the art. *British Journal of Developmental Psychology, 30*(1), 1–13.

Luengo Kanacri, B. P., Pastorelli, C., Eisenberg, N., Zuffianò, A., Castellani, V., & Caprara, G. V. (2014). Trajectories of prosocial behavior from adolescence to early adulthood: Associations with personality change. *Journal of Adolescence, 37*, 701–713.

Luo, Y., & Baillargeon, R. (2010). Toward a mentalistic account of early psychological reasoning. *Current Directions in Psychological Science, 19*(5), 301–307.

Maccoby, E. E. (1998). *The two sexes: Growing up apart, coming together.* Cambridge, MA: Harvard University Press.

Maccoby, E. E. (2002). Gender and group process: A developmental perspective. *Current Directions in Psychological Science, 11*, 54–58.

Maccoby, E. E., & Martin, J. A. (1983). Socialization in the context of the family. In E. M. Hetherington (Ed.), *Handbook of child psychology: Vol. 4. Socialization, personality and social development* (pp. 1–101). New York, NY: Wiley.

MacKinnon-Lewis, C., Starnes, R., Volling, B., & Johnson, S. (1997). Perceptions of parenting as predictors of boys' sibling and peer relations. *Developmental Psychology, 33*(6), 1024–1031.

Mahler, M. S., Pine, F., & Bergman, A. (1975). *The psychological birth of the human infant.* New York, NY: Basic Books.

Main, M. (1990). Cross-cultural studies of attachment organization: Recent studies, changing methodologies, and the concept of conditional strategies. *Human Development, 33*(1), 48–61.

Main, M., Kaplan, N., & Cassidy, J. (1985). Security in infancy, childhood and adulthood: A move to the level of representation. *Monographs of the Society for Research in Child Development, 50,* 66–104.

Main, M., & Solomon, J. (1990). Procedures for identifying infants as disorganized/disoriented during the Ainsworth Strange Situation. *Attachment in the Preschool Years: Theory, Research, and Intervention, 1,* 121–160.

Mallinckrodt, B. (2010). The psychotherapy relationship as attachment: Evidence and implications. *Journal of Social and Personal Relationships, 27*(2), 262–270.

Mantzicopoulos, P. Y., & Oh-Hwang, Y. (1998). The relationship of psychosocial maturity to parenting quality and intellectual ability for American and Korean adolescents. *Contemporary Educational Psychology, 23*(2), 195–206.

Marks, A. K., Szalacha, L. A., Lamarre, M., Boyd, M. J., & Coll, C. G. (2007). Emerging ethnic identity and interethnic group social preferences in middle childhood: Findings from the Children of Immigrants Development in Context (CIDC) study. *International Journal of Behavioral Development, 31*(5), 501–513.

Markus, H. R., & Kitayama, S. (1991). Culture and the self: Implications for cognition, emotion, and motivation. *Psychological Review, 98*(2), 224–253.

Martin, C. L., & Halverson, C. F., Jr. (1981). A schematic processing model of sex typing and stereotyping in children. *Child Development, 52,* 1119–1134.

Martinez, I., & Garcia, J. F. (2008). Internalization of values and self-esteem among Brazilian teenagers from authoritative, indulgent, authoritarian, and neglectful homes. *Adolescence, 43*(169), 13–29.

Mascolo, M. E., & Fischer, K. W. (2007). The codevelopment of self and sociomoral emotions during the toddler years. In C. A. Brownell & C. B. Kopp (Eds.), *Socioemotional development in the toddler years: Transitions and transformations* (pp. 66–99). New York, NY: Guilford Press.

McElwain, N. L., Booth-LaForce, C., & Wu, X. (2011). Infant–mother attachment and children's friendship quality: Maternal mental-state talk as an intervening mechanism. *Developmental Psychology, 47*(5), 1295–1311.

McLeod, S. (2014). Lev Vygotsky. *Simply Psychology.* Retrieved 25 January 2018 from https://www.simplypsychology.org/vygotsky.html

McLeod, S. (2017). Erik Erikson. *Simply Psychology.* Retrieved 25 January 2018 from https://www.simplypsychology.org/Erik-Erikson.html

Meins, E. (2013). Sensitive attunement to infants' internal states: Operationalizing the construct of mind-mindedness. *Attachment & Human Development, 15*(5/6), 524–544.

Meins, E., Centifanti, L. C. M., Fernyhough, C., & Fishburn, S. (2013). Maternal mind–mindedness and children's behavioral difficulties: Mitigating the impact of low socioeconomic status. *Journal of Abnormal Child Psychology, 41*(4), 543–553.

Meins, E., Fernyhough, C., Fradley, E., & Tuckey, M. (2001). Rethinking maternal sensitivity: Mothers' comments on infants' mental processes predict security of attachment at 12 months. *Journal of Child Psychology and Psychiatry, 42*(5), 637–648.

Meins, E., Fernyhough, C., Wainwright, R., Das Gupta, M., Fradley, E., & Tuckey, M. (2002). Maternal mind–mindedness and attachment security as predictors of theory of mind understanding. *Child Development, 7,* 1715–1726. doi:10.1111/1467-8624.00501

Meltzoff, A. N., & Moore, M. K. (1997). Explaining facial imitation: A theoretical model. *Early Development & Parenting, 6,* 179–192.

Mendes, D., Seidl-de-Moura, M. L., & Siqueira, J. D. (2009). The ontogenesis of smiling and its association with mothers' affective behaviors: A longitudinal study. *Infant Behavioral Development*, *32*, 445–453.

Messinger, D. S., & Fogel, A. (2007). The interactive development of social smiling. In R. Kail (Ed.), *Advances in child development and behavior* (Vol. *35*, pp. 327–366). Oxford, UK: Elsevier.

Middleton, M. R., Tajfel, H., & Johnson, N. B. (1970). Cognitive and affective aspects of children's national attitudes. *British Journal of Social and Clinical Psychology*, *9*(2), 122–134.

Mikulincer, M., & Florian, V. (1995). Appraisal of and coping with a real-life stressful situation: The contribution of attachment styles. *Personality and Social Psychology Bulletin*, *21*(4), 406–414.

Mikulincer, M., & Shaver, P. R. (2005). Attachment theory and emotions in close relationships: Exploring the attachment-related dynamics of emotional reactions to relational events. *Personal Relationships*, *12*, 149–168.

Milligan, K., Astington, J. W., & Dack, L. A. (2007). Language and theory of mind: Meta-analysis of the relation between language ability and false-belief understanding. *Child Development*, *78*(2), 622–646.

Mischel, W., Shoda, Y., & Rodriguez, M. I. (1989). Delay of gratification in children. *Science*, *244*(4907), 933–938.

Moeller, M. P., & Schick, B. (2006). Relations between maternal input and theory of mind understanding in deaf children. *Child Development*, *77*(3), 751–766.

Moffitt, T. E. (1993). Adolescence-limited and life-course-persistent antisocial behavior: A developmental taxonomy. *Psychological Review*, *100*(4), 674–701.

Moll, H., & Tomasello, M. (2006). Level 1 perspective-taking at 24 months of age. *British Journal of Developmental Psychology*, *24*(3), 603–613.

Mooij, T., Smeets, E., & De Wit, W. (2011). Multi-level aspects of social cohesion of secondary schools and pupils' feelings of safety. *British Journal of Educational Psychology*, *81*(3), 369–390.

Moon, C., Cooper, R. P., & Fifer, W. P. (1993). Two-day-olds prefer their native language. *Infant Behavior and Development*, *16*(4), 495–500.

Moore, C., Bosacki, S. L., & Macgillivray, S. (2011). Theory of mind and social interest in zero-acquaintance play situations. *Child Development*, *82*(4), 1163–1172.

Morelen, D., Shaffer, A., & Suveg, C. (2014). Maternal emotion regulation: Links to emotion parenting and child emotion regulation. *Journal of Family Issues*, 12 August. doi:10.1177/0192513X14546720

Morgan, A. B., & Lilienfeld, S. O. (2000). A meta-analytic review of the relation between antisocial behavior and neuropsychological measures of executive function. *Clinical Psychology Review*, *20*(1), 113–136.

Morton, J., & Johnson, M. (1991). CONSPEC and CONLEARN: A two-process theory of infant face recognition. *Psychological Review*, *98*, 164–181.

Murray, L., & Trevarthen, C. (1985). Emotional regulation of interactions between 2-month-olds and their mothers. In T. M. Field & N. A. Fox (Eds.), *Social perception in infants* (pp. 177–197). Norwood, NJ: Ablex.

Nansel, T. R., Overpeck, M. D., Haynie, D. L., Ruan, W. J., & Scheidt, P. C. (2003). Relationships between bullying and violence among US youth. *Archives of Pediatrics & Adolescent Medicine*, *157*(4), 348–353.

Nantel-Vivier, A., Kokko, K., Caprara, G. V., Pastorelli, C., Gerbino, M. G., Paciello, M., … Tremblay, R. E. (2009). Prosocial development from childhood to adolescence: A multi-informant perspective with Canadian and Italian longitudinal studies. *Journal of Child Psychology and Psychiatry*, *50*(5), 590–598.

Napier, C. (2014). How use of screen media affects the emotional development of infants. *Primary Health Care*, *24*(2), 18–25.

National Institute of Child Health and Human Development. (1997). The effects of infant child care on infant-mother attachment security: Results of the NICHD Study of Early Child Care. *Child Development*, *68*, 860–879.

National Institute of Child Health and Human Development. (2002). Early child care and children's development prior to school entry: Results from the NICHD Study of Early Child Care. *American Educational Research Journal*, *39*(1), 133–164.

National Institute of Child Health and Human Development. (2003). Does amount of time spent in child care predict socioemotional adjustment during the transition to kindergarten? *Child Development*, *74*(4), 976–1005.

National Institute of Child Health and Human Development. (2011). Do effects of early child care extend to age 15 years? Results from the NICHD study of early child care and youth development. *Child Development*, *81*(3), 737–756. doi:10.1111/j.1467-8624.2010.01431.x

Nesdale, D. (1999). Developmental changes in children's ethnic preferences and social cognitions. *Journal of Applied Developmental Psychology*, *20*(4), 501–519.

Newcomb, A. F., Bukowski, W. M., & Pattee, L. (1993). Children's peer relations: Meta-analytic review of popular, rejected, neglected, controversial, and average sociometric status. *Psychological Bulletin*, *113*(1), 99–128.

Nichols, K. E., Fox, N., & Mundy, P. (2005). Joint attention, self-recognition, and neurocognitive function in toddlers. *Infancy*, *7*(1), 35–51.

Niedenthal, P. M., Brauer, M., Robin, L., & Innes-Ker, Å. H. (2002). Adult attachment and the perception of facial expression of emotion. *Journal of Personality and Social Psychology*, *82*(3), 419–433.

Nijhof, K. S., & Engels, R. C. (2007). Parenting styles, coping strategies, and the expression of homesickness. *Journal of Adolescence*, *30*(5), 709–720.

Nikkelen, S. W., Valkenburg, P. M., Huizinga, M., & Bushman, B. J. (2014). Media use and ADHD-related behaviors in children and adolescents: A meta-analysis. *Developmental Psychology*, *50*(9), 2228–2241.

Nucci, L. P., & Herman, S. (1982). Behavioral disordered children's conceptions of moral, conventional, and personal issues. *Journal of Abnormal Child Psychology*, *10*(3), 411–425.

Ocampo, K. A., Knight, G. P., & Bernal, M. E. (1997). The development of cognitive abilities and social identities in children: The case of ethnic identity. *International Journal of Behavioral Development*, *21*(3), 479–500.

Office for National Statistics. (2013). *Full report: Women in the labour market*. Retrieved 20 November 2017 from http://www.ons.gov.uk/ons/rel/lmac/women-in-the-labour-market/2013/rpt—women-in-the-labour-market.html

Ofsted. (2012). *No place for bullying: How schools create a positive culture and prevent and tackle bullying*. Retrieved from http://www.ofsted.gov.uk/resources/no-place-for-bullying

Onishi, K. H., & Baillargeon, R. (2005). Do 15-month-old infants understand false beliefs? *Science*, *308*(5719), 255–258.

Ontai, L. L., & Thompson, R. A. (2002). Patterns of attachment and maternal discourse effects on children's emotion understanding from 3 to 5 years of age. *Social Development*, *11*(4), 433–450.

Opree, S. J., Buijzen, M., Van Reijmersdal, E. A., & Valkenburg, P. M. (2013). Children's advertising exposure, advertised product desire, and materialism: A longitudinal study. *Communication Research*, *41*(5), 717–735.

Owen, M. T., & Cox, M. J. (1997). Marital conflict and the development of infant–parent attachment relationships. *Journal of Family Psychology*, *11*(2), 152–164.

Parker, J. G., & Gottman, J. M. (1989). Social and emotional development in a relational context: Friendship interaction from early childhood to adolescence. In T. J. Berndt & G. W. Ladd (Eds.), *Peer relationships in child development* (pp. 95–131). New York, NY: Wiley.

Parten, M. B. (1932). Social participation among pre-school children. *Journal of Abnormal and Social Psychology*, *27*(3), 243–269.

Pasalich, D. S., Dadds, M. R., & Hawes, D. J. (2014). Cognitive and affective empathy in children with conduct problems: Additive and interactive effects of callous–unemotional traits and autism spectrum disorders symptoms. *Psychiatry Research*, *219*(3), 625–630.

Paulus, M. (2014). The emergence of prosocial behavior: Why do infants and toddlers help, comfort, and share? *Child Development Perspectives*, 8(2), 77–81.

Perner, J. (1991). *Understanding the representational mind: Learning, development, and conceptual change.* Cambridge, MA: MIT Press.

Perner, J., & Ruffman, T. (2005). Infants' insight into the mind: How deep? *Science, 308*(5719), 214–216.

Perner, J., Ruffman, T., & Leekam, S. R. (1994). Theory of mind is contagious: You catch it from your sibs. *Child Development, 65*(4), 1228–1238.

Perner, J., Stummer, S., Sprung, M., & Doherty, M. (2002). Theory of mind finds its Piagetian perspective: Why alternative naming comes with understanding belief. *Cognitive Development, 17*(3), 1451–1472.

Perner, J., & Wimmer, H. (1985). 'John *thinks* that Mary *thinks* that…': Attribution of second-order beliefs by 5- to 10-year-old children. *Journal of Experimental Child Psychology, 39*(3), 437–471.

Perry, P. (2014). Why we must take sibling bullying seriously. *The Guardian,* 9 September. Retrieved 25 January 2018 from http://www.theguardian.com/commentisfree/2014/sep/09/sibling-bullying-evidence-depression-parents

Phinney, J. S. (1989). Stages of ethnic identity development in minority group adolescents. *Journal of Early Adolescence, 9*, 34–49.

Phinney, J. S. (1993). A three-stage model of ethnic identity development in adolescence. In M. E. Bernal & G. P. Knight (Eds.), *Ethnic identity: Formation and transmission among Hispanics and other minorities* (pp. 61–79). Albany, NY: State University of New York Press.

Piaget, J. (1932). *The moral development of the child.* London, UK: Kegan Paul.

Piaget, J., & Weil, A. M. (1951). The development in children of the idea of the homeland and of relations with other countries. *International Social Science Bulletin, 3*(3), 561–578.

Pike, A., Coldwell, J., & Dunn, J. F. (2005). Sibling relationships in early/middle childhood: Links with individual adjustment. *Journal of Family Psychology, 19*(4), 523–532.

Planalp, E. M., & Braungart-Rieker, J. M. (2013). Temperamental precursors of infant attachment with mothers and fathers. *Infant Behavior and Development, 36*(4), 796–808.

Pluess, M., & Belsky, J. (2010). Differential susceptibility to parenting and quality child care. *Developmental Psychology, 46*(2), 379–390.

Pluess, M., & Belsky, J. (2011). Prenatal programming of postnatal plasticity? *Development and Psychopathology, 23*(1), 29–38.

Premack, D., & Woodruff, G. (1978). Does the chimpanzee have a theory of mind? *Behavioural and Brain Sciences, 1*, 515–526.

Prot, S., Gentile, D. A., Anderson, C. A., Suzuki, K., Swing, E., Lim, K. M., … Lam, B. C. P. (2014). Long-term relations among prosocial-media use, empathy, and prosocial behavior. *Psychological Science, 25*(2), 358–368.

Radziszewska, B., Richardson, J. L., Dent, C. W., & Flay, B. R. (1996). Parenting style and adolescent depressive symptoms, smoking, and academic achievement: Ethnic, gender, and SES differences. *Journal of Behavioral Medicine, 19*(3), 289–305.

Raikes, H. A., & Thompson, R. A. (2008). Attachment security and parenting quality predict children's problem-solving, attributions, and loneliness with peers. *Attachment & Human Development, 10*(3), 319–344.

Rajendran, G., & Mitchell, P. (2007). Cognitive theories of autism. *Developmental Review, 27*, 224–260.

Reddy, V. (2000). Coyness in early infancy. *Developmental Science, 3*, 186–192.

Repacholi, B. M., & Gopnik, A. (1997). Early reasoning about desires: Evidence from 14- and 18-month-olds. *Developmental Psychology, 33*(1), 12–21.

Riby, D. M., & Hancock, P. J. (2008). Viewing it differently: Social scene perception in Williams syndrome and autism. *Neuropsychologia, 46*(11), 2855–2860.

Rideout, V. J., Foehr, U. G., & Roberts, D. F. (2010). *Generation M²: Media in the lives of 8- to 18-year-olds*. Menlo Park, CA: Henry J. Kaiser Family Foundation.

Ripoll-Núñez, K., & Carrillo, S. (2014). Sibling relationships and children's social well-being. In A. Ben-Arieh, F. Casas, I. Frønes, & J. E. Korbin (Eds.), *Handbook of child well-being* (pp. 1817–1842). Dordrecht, Germany: Springer Reference.

Rochat, P., & Hespos, S. J. (1997). Differential rooting response by neonates: Evidence for an early sense of self. *Early Development and Parenting, 6*(34), 105–112.

Rochat, P., & Morgan, R. (1995). Spatial determinants in the perception of self-produced leg movements in 3- to 5-month-old infants. *Developmental Psychology, 31*(4), 626–636.

Roopnarine, J. L., Krishnakumar, A., Metindogan, A., & Evans, M. (2006). Links between parenting styles, parent–child academic interaction, parent–school interaction, and early academic skills and social behaviors in young children of English-speaking Caribbean immigrants. *Early Childhood Research Quarterly, 21*(2), 238–252.

Rothbart, M. K. (2007). Temperament, development, and personality. *Current Directions in Psychological Science, 16*(4), 207–212.

Rothbart, M. K., Ahadi, S. A., Hershey, K. L., & Fisher, P. (2001). Investigations of temperament at three to seven years: The Children's Behavior Questionnaire. *Child Development, 72*(5), 1394–1408.

Rothbart, M. K., & Bates, J. E. (2006). Temperament. In W. Damon, R. Lerner, & N. Eisenberg (Eds.), *Handbook of child psychology: Vol. 3. Social, emotional, and personality development* (6th ed., pp. 99–166). New York, NY: Wiley.

Rubin, K. H., Begle, A. S., & McDonald, K. L. (2012). Peer relations and social competence in childhood. In V. Anderson & M. H. Beauchamp (Eds.), *Developmental social neuroscience and childhood brain insult: Theory and practice* (pp. 23–44). New York, NY: Guilford Press.

Rubin, K. H., Bukowski, W. M., & Parker, J. G. (1998). Peer interactions, relationships, and groups. In N. Eisenberg (Ed.), *Handbook of child psychology: Vol. 3. Social, emotional, and personality development* (5th ed., pp. 619–700). New York, NY: Wiley.

Rubin, K. H., & Coplan, R. J. (1998). Social and nonsocial play in childhood: An individual differences perspective. In O. N. Saracho & B. Spodek (Eds.), *Multiple perspectives on play in early childhood education* (pp. 144–170). Albany, NY: State University of New York Press.

Rubin, K. H., Nelson, L. J., Hastings, P., & Asendorpf, J. (1999). The transaction between parents' perceptions of their children's shyness and their parenting styles. *International Journal of Behavioral Development, 23*(4), 937–957.

Ruble, D. N., Martin, C. L., & Berenbaum, S. A. (2006). Gender development. In N. Eisenberg, W. Damon, & R. M. Lerner (Eds.), *Handbook of child psychology: Social, emotional, and personality development* (pp. 858–932). Hoboken, NJ: Wiley.

Ruble, D. N., Taylor, L. J., Cyphers, L., Greulich, F. K., Lurye, L. E., & Shrout, P. E. (2007). The role of gender constancy in early gender development. *Child Development, 78*(4), 1121–1136.

Ruffman, T. (2014). To belief or not belief: Children's theory of mind. *Developmental Review, 34,* 265–293.

Ruffman, T., Garnham, W., & Rideout, P. (2001). Social understanding in autism: Eye gaze as a measure of core insights. *Journal of Child Psychology and Psychiatry, 42*(8), 1083–1094.

Ruffman, T., Perner, J., & Parkin, L. (1999). How parenting style affects false belief understanding. *Social Development, 8*(3), 395–411.

Ruffman, T., Perner, J., Naito, M., Parkin, L., & Clements, W. A. (1998). Older (but not younger) siblings facilitate false belief understanding. *Developmental Psychology, 34*(1), 161–174.

Ruffman, T., Slade, L., & Crowe, E. (2002). The relation between children's and mothers' mental state language and theory-of-mind understanding. *Child Development, 73*(3), 734–751.

Ruffman, T., Slade, L., Devitt, K., & Crowe, E. (2006). What mothers say and what they do: The relation between parenting, theory of mind, language and conflict/cooperation. *British Journal of Developmental Psychology, 24*(1), 105–124.

Russell, A., Mize, J., & Bissaker, K. (2004). Parent–child relationships. In P. K. Smith & C. H. Hart (Eds.), *Blackwell handbook of childhood social development* (pp. 204–222). Malden, MA: Blackwell.

Rutter, M. (1998). Developmental catch-up, and deficit, following adoption after severe global early privation. *Journal of Child Psychology and Psychiatry*, 39(4), 465–476.

Rutter, M. L., Kreppner, J. M., & O'Connor, T. G. (2001). Specificity and heterogeneity in children's responses to profound institutional privation. *British Journal of Psychiatry*, 179(2), 97–103.

Sabbagh, M. A., & Baldwin, D. A. (2001). Learning words from knowledgeable versus ignorant speakers: Links between preschoolers' theory of mind and semantic development. *Child Development*, 72(4), 1054–1070.

Sagi, A., & Hoffman, M. L. (1976). Empathic distress in the newborn. *Developmental Psychology*, 12(2), 175–176.

Salmivalli, C. (2010). Bullying and the peer group: A review. *Aggression and Violent Behavior*, 15(2), 112–120.

Sanson, A., Hemphill, S., Yagmurlu, B., & McClowry, S. G. (2011). Temperament and social development. In P. K. Smith & C. H. Hart (Eds.), *Wiley-Blackwell handbook of childhood social development* (2nd ed., pp. 227–245). Oxford, UK: Wiley-Blackwell.

Schaffer, H. R., & Emerson, P. E. (1964). The development of social attachments in infancy. *Monographs of the Society for Research in Child Development*, 29, 1–77.

Schmitt, S. A., McClelland, M. M., Tominey, S. L., & Acock, A. C. (2015). Strengthening school readiness for Head Start children: Evaluation of a self-regulation intervention. *Early Childhood Research Quarterly*, 30(Pt. A), 20–31.

Schneider, B. H., Atkinson, L., & Tardif, C. (2001). Child–parent attachment and children's peer relations: A quantitative review. *Developmental Psychology*, 37(1), 86–100.

Scholte, R. H. J., Engels, R. C. M. E., Overbeek, G., de Kemp, R. A. T., & Haselager, G. J. T. (2007). Stability in bullying and victimization and its association with social adjustment in childhood and adolescence. *Journal of Abnormal Child Psychology*, 35, 217–228.

Scott, R. M. (2014). Post hoc versus predictive accounts of children's theory of mind: A reply to Ruffman. *Developmental Review*, 3, 300–304.

Seavey, C. A., Katz, P. A., & Zalk, S. R. (1975). Baby X. *Sex Roles*, 1(2), 103–109.

Sebanc, A. M. (2003). The friendship features of preschool children: Links with prosocial behavior and aggression. *Social Development*, 12(2), 249–268.

Semaj, L. (1980). The development of racial evaluation and preference: A cognitive approach. *Journal of Black Psychology*, 6(2), 59–79.

Senju, A. (2012). Spontaneous theory of mind and its absence in autism spectrum disorders. *The Neuroscientist*, 18(2), 108–113.

Senju, A., Southgate, V., White, S., & Frith, U. (2009). Mindblind eyes: An absence of spontaneous theory of mind in Asperger's syndrome. *Science*, 325(5942), 883–885.

Shaver, P. R., & Mikulincer, M. (2002). Attachment-related psychodynamics. *Attachment & Human Development*, 4(2), 133–161.

Sheese, B. E., Voelker, P. M., Rothbart, M. K., & Posner, M. I. (2007). Parenting quality interacts with genetic variation in dopamine receptor D4 to influence temperament in early childhood. *Development and Psychopathology*, 19, 1039–1046.

Shouldice, A., & Stevenson-Hinde, J. (1992). Printed in Great Britain: Coping with security distress – The separation anxiety test and attachment classification at 4.5 years. *Journal of Child Psychology and Psychiatry*, 33, 331–348. doi:10.1111/j.1469-7610.1992.tb00870.x

Shweder, R. A., Mahapatra, M., & Miller, J. G. (1987). Culture and moral development. In J. Kagan & S. Lamb (Eds.), *The emergence of morality in young children* (pp. 1–83). Chicago, IL: University of Chicago Press.

Simpson, E. A., Murray, L., Paukner, A., & Ferrari, P. F. (2014). The mirror neuron system as revealed through neonatal imitation: Presence from birth, predictive power and evidence of plasticity. *Philosophical Transactions of the Royal Society B: Biological Sciences, 369*(1644), 1471–2970. doi:10.1098/rstb.2013.0289

Simpson, J. A., Rholes, W. S., & Nelligan, J. S. (1992). Support seeking and support giving within couples in an anxiety-provoking situation: The role of attachment styles. *Journal of Personality and Social Psychology, 62*(3), 434–446.

Slaughter, V., Peterson, C. C., & Mackintosh, E. (2007). Mind what mother says: Narrative input and theory of mind in typical children and those on the autism spectrum. *Child Development, 78*(3), 839–858.

Slomkowski, C., & Dunn, J. (1996). Young children's understanding of other people's beliefs and feelings and their connected communication with friends. *Developmental Psychology, 32*(3), 442–447.

Smetana, J. G., & Breages, J. L. (1990). The development of toddlers' moral and conventional judgements. *Merrill-Palmer Quarterly, 36*, 329–346.

Smith, E. J. (1991). Ethnic identity development: Toward the development of a theory within the context of majority/minority status. *Journal of Counseling & Development, 70*(1), 181–188.

Song, M. J., Smetana, J. G., & Kim, S. Y. (1987). Korean children's conceptions of moral and conventional transgressions. *Developmental Psychology, 23*(4), 577–582.

Sorce, J. F., Emde, R. N., Campos, J., & Klinnert, M. D. (1985). Maternal emotional signaling: Its effects on the visual cliff behavior of 1-year-olds. *Developmental Psychology, 21*, 195–200.

Sroufe, L. A. (1996). *Emotional development*. New York, NY: Cambridge University Press.

Sroufe, L. A. (2005). Attachment and development: A prospective, longitudinal study from birth to adulthood. *Attachment & Human Development, 7*(4), 349–367.

Sroufe, L. A., & Waters, E. (1977). Attachment as an organizational construct. *Child Development, 48*, 1184–1199.

St. Louis, G. R., & Liem, J. H. (2005). Ego identity, ethnic identity, and the psychosocial well-being of ethnic minority and majority college students. *Identity, 5*(3), 227–246.

Stansbury, K., & Sigman, M. (2000). Responses of preschoolers in two frustrating episodes: Emergence of complex strategies for emotion regulation. *Journal of Genetic Psychology, 161*(2), 182–202.

Steinberg, L., Lamborn, S. D., Dornbusch, S. M., & Darling, N. (1992). Impact of parenting practices on adolescent achievement: Authoritative parenting, school involvement, and encouragement to succeed. *Child Development, 63*(5), 1266–1281.

Stifter, C. A., & Braungart, J. M. (1995). The regulation of negative reactivity in infancy: Function and development. *Developmental Psychology, 31*(3), 448–455.

Stocker, C. M., Lanthier, R. P., & Furman, W. (1997). Sibling relationships in early adulthood. *Journal of Family Psychology, 11*(2), 210–221.

Strasburger, V. C., Wilson, B. J., & Jordan, A. B. (2014). *Children, adolescents, and the media*. Los Angeles, CA: SAGE.

Szewczyk-Sokolowski, M., Bost, K. K., & Wainwright, A. B. (2005). Attachment, temperament, and preschool children's peer acceptance. *Social Development, 14*(3), 379–397.

Tajfel, H., & Turner, J. C. (1979). An integrative theory of intergroup conflict. *Social Psychology of Intergroup Relations, 33*(47), 74.

Tangney, J. P., Stuewig, J., & Martinez, A. G. (2014). Two faces of shame: The roles of shame and guilt in predicting recidivism. *Psychological Science, 25*(3), 799–805.

Tangney, J. P., Stuewig, J., & Mashek, D. J. (2007). Moral emotions and moral behavior. *Annual Review of Psychology, 58*, 345–372.

Taumoepeau, M., & Ruffman, T. (2008). Stepping stones to others' minds: Maternal talk relates to child mental state language and emotion understanding at 15, 24, and 33 months. *Child Development, 79*(2), 284–302.

The Sun. (2011, 9 August). Be decisive. Retrieved 13 February 2018 from https://www.thesun.co.uk/archives/news/708796/be-decisive

Thomas, A., Chess, S., & Birch, H. G. (1970). The origin of personality. *Scientific American*, *223*(2), 102–109.

Thompson, R. A. (2000). The legacy of early attachments. *Child Development*, *71*(1), 145–152.

Thompson, R. A., & Meyer, S. (2007). Socialization of emotion regulation in the family. In J. J. Gross (Ed.), *Handbook of emotion regulation* (pp. 249–268). New York, NY: Guilford Press.

Tomasello, M., Carpenter, M., Call, J., Behne, T., & Moll, H. (2005). Understanding and sharing intentions: The origins of cultural cognition. *Behavioral and Brain Sciences*, *28*(5), 675–691.

Tomasello, M., Carpenter, M., & Liszkowski, U. (2007). A new look at infant pointing. *Child Development*, *78*(3), 705–722.

Trentacosta, C. J., & Shaw, D. S. (2009). Emotional self-regulation, peer rejection, and antisocial behavior: Developmental associations from early childhood to early adolescence. *Journal of Applied Developmental Psychology*, *30*(3), 356–365.

Tronick, E. Z., Als, H., Adamson, L., Wise, S., & Brazelton, T. B. (1978). The infant's response to entrapment between contradictory messages in face-to-face interaction. *Journal of the American Academy of Child Psychiatry*, *17*, 1–13.

Tseng, W. L., & Gau, S. S. F. (2013). Executive function as a mediator in the link between attention-deficit/hyperactivity disorder and social problems. *Journal of Child Psychology and Psychiatry*, *54*(9), 996–1004.

Turiel, E. (1983). *The development of social knowledge: Morality and convention*. Cambridge, UK: Cambridge University Press.

Umaña-Taylor, A. J., Gonzales-Backen, M. A., & Guimond, A. B. (2009). Latino adolescents' ethnic identity: Is there a developmental progression and does growth in ethnic identity predict growth in self-esteem? *Child Development*, *80*(2), 391–405.

US Census Bureau. (2011). Maternity leave and employment patterns of first-time mothers: 1961–2008. *Current Population Reports*, October. Retrieved 13 February 2018 from https://www.census.gov/prod/2011pubs/p70-128.pdf

Valkenburg, P. M., & Peter, J. (2013). The differential susceptibility to media effects model. *Journal of Communication*, *63*(2), 221–243.

Van den Boom, D. C. (1994). The influence of temperament and mothering on attachment and exploration: An experimental manipulation of sensitive responsiveness among lower-class mothers with irritable infants. *Child Development*, *65*(5), 1457–1477.

Van IJzendoorn, M. (1995). Adult attachment representations, parental responsiveness, and infant attachment: A meta-analysis on the predictive validity of the adult attachment interview. *Psychological Bulletin*, *117*(3), 387–403.

Van IJzendoorn, M. H., & Bakermans-Kranenburg, M. J. (2010). Invariance of adult attachment across gender, age, culture, and socioeconomic status? *Journal of Social and Personal Relationships*, *27*(2), 200–208.

Van IJzendoorn, M. H., & De Wolff, M. S. (1997), In search of the absent father: Meta-analyses of infant–father attachment – A rejoinder to our discussants. *Child Development*, *68*, 604–609. doi:10.1111/j.1467-8624.1997.tb04223.x

Van IJzendoorn, M. H., Vereijken, C. M. J. L., Bakermans-Kranenburg, M. J., & Riksen-Walraven, J. M. (2004). Assessing attachment security with the Attachment Q Sort: Meta-analytic evidence for the validity of the observer AQS. *Child Development*, *75*, 1188–1213. doi:10.1111/j.1467-8624.2004.00733

Vandell, D. L., & Mueller, E. C. (1995). Peer play and friendships during the first two years. In H. C. Foot, A. J. Chapman, & J. R. Smith (Eds.), *Friendship and social relations in children* (pp. 181–208). New Brunswick, NJ: Transaction.

Vitaro, F., Barker, E. D., Boivin, M., Brendgen, M., & Tremblay, R. E. (2006). Do early difficult temperament and harsh parenting differentially predict reactive and proactive aggression? *Journal of Abnormal Child Psychology*, *34*(5), 681–691.

Volling, B., & Blandon, A. Y. (2003). Positive indicators of sibling relationship quality: The sibling inventory of behavior. In K. A. Moore & L. H. Lippman (Eds.), *What do children need to flourish?* (pp. 203–219). New York, NY: Springer.

Vygotsky, L. S. (1978). *Mind in society.* Cambridge, MA: Harvard University Press.

Walker, L. J. (1984). Sex differences in the development of moral reasoning: A critical review. *Child Development, 55,* 677–691.

Wang, Q., Pomerantz, E. M., & Chen, H. (2007). The role of parents' control in early adolescents' psychological functioning: A longitudinal investigation in the United States and China. *Child Development, 78,* 1592–1610.

Wark, G. R., & Krebs, D. L. (1996). Gender and dilemma differences in real-life moral judgment. *Developmental Psychology, 32*(2), 220–230.

Warneken, F., & Tomasello, M. (2006). Altruistic helping in human infants and young chimpanzees. *Science, 311*(5765), 1301–1303.

Warneken, F., & Tomasello, M. (2007). Helping and cooperation at 14 months of age. *Infancy, 11*(3), 271–294.

Waters, E. (1978). The reliability and stability of individual differences in infant–mother attachment. *Child Development, 49,* 483–494.

Waters, E., & Deane, K. E. (1985). Defining and assessing individual differences in attachment relationships: Q-methodology and the organization of behavior in infancy and early childhood. *Monographs of the Society for Research in Child Development, 50,* 41–65.

Waters, E., Merrick, S., Treboux, D., Crowell, J., & Albersheim, L. (2000). Attachment security in infancy and early adulthood: A twenty-year longitudinal study. *Child Development, 71*(3), 684–689.

Watling, D., & Banerjee, R. (2007a). Children's differentiation between ingratiation and self-promotion. *Social Development, 16*(4), 758–776.

Watling, D., & Banerjee, R. (2007b). Children's understanding of modesty in front of peer and adult audiences. *Infant and Child Development, 16*(3), 227–236.

Watson, A. C., Nixon, C. L., Wilson, A., & Capage, L. (1999). Social interaction skills and theory of mind in young children. *Developmental Psychology, 35*(2), 386–391.

Waytz, A., Gray, K., Epley, N., & Wegner, D. M. (2010). Causes and consequences of mind perception. *Trends in Cognitive Sciences, 14*(8), 383–388.

Wellman, H. M. (1990). *The child's theory of mind.* Cambridge, MA: Bradford Books/MIT Press.

Wellman, H. M., & Woolley, J. D. (1990). From simple desires to ordinary beliefs: The early development of everyday psychology. *Cognition, 35*(3), 245–275.

Wellman, H. M., Cross, D., & Watson, J. (2001). Meta-analysis of theory-of-mind development: The truth about false belief. *Child Development, 72*(3), 655–684.

White, L. O., Wu, J., Borelli, J. L., Mayes, L. C., & Crowley, M. J. (2013). Play it again: Neural responses to reunion with excluders predicted by attachment patterns. *Developmental Science, 16,* 850–863. doi:10.1111/desc.12035

Will, J. A., Self, P. A., & Datan, N. (1976). Maternal behavior and perceived sex of infant. *American Journal of Orthopsychiatry, 46*(1), 135–139.

Wimmer, H., & Perner, J. (1983). Beliefs about beliefs: Representation and constraining function of wrong beliefs in young children's understanding of deception. *Cognition, 13*(1), 103–128.

Woodward, A. L. (1998). Infants selectively encode the goal object of an actor's reach. *Cognition, 69*(1), 1–34.

Xu, Y., Farver, J. A. M., & Zhang, Z. (2009). Temperament, harsh and indulgent parenting, and Chinese children's proactive and reactive aggression. *Child Development, 80*(1), 244–258.

Yoon, J., & Vouloumanos, A. (2014). When and how does autism begin? *Trends in Cognitive Sciences, 18*(6), 272–273.

Young, L., Koenigs, M., Kruepke, M., & Newman, J. P. (2012). Psychopathy increases perceived moral permissibility of accidents. *Journal of Abnormal Psychology, 121*(3), 659–667.

Youngblade, L. M., & Dunn, J. (1995). Individual differences in young children's pretend play with mother and sibling: Links to relationships and understanding of other people's feelings and beliefs. *Child Development, 66*(5), 1472–1492.

Zachrisson, H. D., Dearing, E., Lekhal, R., & Toppelberg, C. O. (2013). Little evidence that time in child care causes externalizing problems during early childhood in Norway. *Child Development, 84*(4), 1152–1170.

Zahn-Waxler, C., Robinson, J. L., & Emde, R. N. (1992). The development of empathy in twins. *Developmental Psychology, 28*(6), 1038–1047.

Zelazo, P. D., Carlson, S. M., & Kesek, A. (2008). The development of executive function in childhood. In C. A. Nelson & M. Luciana (Eds.), *Handbook of developmental cognitive neuroscience* (2nd ed., pp. 467–478). Cambridge, MA: MIT Press.

Zentner, M., & Shiner, R. L. (Eds.). (2012). *Handbook of temperament.* New York, NY: Guilford Press.

Zilber, A., Goldstein, A., & Mikulincer, M. (2007). Adult attachment orientations and the processing of emotional pictures–ERP correlates. *Personality and Individual Differences, 43*(7), 1898–1907.

Zimmerman, F. J., & Christakis, D. A. (2007). Associations between content types of early media exposure and subsequent attentional problems. *Pediatrics, 120*(5), 986–992.

18 Social Cognition and Attitudes

RUSSELL HUTTER, CHANTELLE WOOD, LUCY DAVIES, AND MARK CONNER

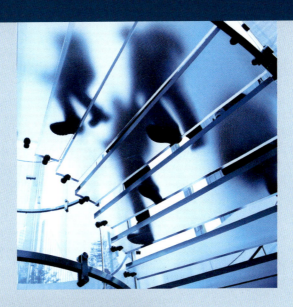

SOCIAL THINKING

LEARNING OBJECTIVE 18.1

Clearly describe what social thinking is and what is uniquely human about it.

What is social thinking? To help answer this question it might be easiest to think about how much time you devote to thinking about yourself and other people. Perhaps if you counted the number of social encounters you had in a single day, might that provide an answer? Or might the answer be found in the amount of time you spend on social media, such as Facebook? When alone, do you think about others? Do everyday activities such as a trip to the supermarket count, or simply walking through a crowded city street? How about a trip to the gym? Social psychologists view all of these activities and many, many more as social in nature. We are *social beings*, often living in large metropolitan areas, seeking out others of our species, in particular those who are similar to us: we are, at heart, quite self-obsessed!

Social cognition is a very broad area of social psychology that encompasses many approaches and perspectives. However, two main approaches are highly influential: (1) an approach reliant on methodologies and models derived from cognitive psychology – usually referred to as **social cognition** – and (2) a more motivationally oriented perspective, known as **social identity theory**. Let's think about each of these in turn.

First, the focus of the social cognition approach is not only on how social perceivers respond to social situations (social stimuli) but also on how people store (in memory) and think (or process) such information. It is heavily influenced by cognitive information-processing approaches, often adopting and modifying research methodologies from these. Social identity theory looks at intergroup behaviour from the perspective of shared identities. Social identity approaches originated with the work of Henri Tajfel (1919–1982), who is widely regarded as the father of social identity theory. Tajfel (originally Hersz Mordche) was born in Poland to a Jewish family and served in the French army during World War II, having originally moved to France to study chemistry. Following the war he returned home to discover many of his immediate family and friends had been exterminated during the Nazi occupation. His experiences influenced him so deeply, he switched his focus to social psychology. Social identity theorists believe that our self-concept is defined in terms of our *social identity* and our *personal identity*. According to this perspective, people have a preference for a positive **self-concept** instead of a negative one, and it is this motivation that drives much of our social behaviour. You will learn more about this approach in the section titled 'Self and Identity'.

Tajfel (1981a) strongly believed that social psychology must reject individualism and reductionism, not only as a matter of philosophy but also of good science. This emphasized his criticism of social psychology as addressing the individual as opposed to the social. He went on to explain that social psychological models appear to presume that we are describing and explaining the behaviour of randomly interacting individual persons, functioning in an unstructured, homogeneous social environment. In reality, however, people live and interact in a structured and complex social system that has fundamental psychological effects (Turner, 1996). While Tajfel originally helped to initiate cognitive approaches to social phenomena (which became dominant in the United States during the 1980s), he was later instrumental in rejecting what he saw as the excess of pure cognitive theory (Tajfel, 1981b). This is evident in Tajfel's dismissal of individual cognitive mechanisms (i.e. individuals' thought processes, rather than those of groups), which are unmodified for the social world and according to him cannot supply a satisfactory description of social psychological events (Turner, 1982). He strongly believed in putting the social context into social psychology.

While both social cognition and social identity perspectives have been hugely influential, what remains is that both are, despite Tajfel's criticism, concerned with the 'social'. But what is social? It can be difficult to formulate an all-encompassing definition, because what is social can change with time as our cultures develop. Thirty years ago who would have defined sitting in front of a computer as social? But today few could convincingly argue that internet-based social networking websites are not social. Therefore, we define social in this chapter as thoughts, feelings, and behaviours resulting from information about ourselves and others of our species.

Why have humans evolved to think socially?

Is social thinking uniquely human? Other seemingly unique human abilities (e.g. problem solving and tool use) have, on closer inspection, been found in animals. For example, the Behavioural Ecology Research Group at the University of Oxford has observed that crows can problem solve by fashioning and using tools (e.g. Wimpenny, Weir, Clayton, Rutz, & Kacelnik, 2009). What about social thinking? Some animals do display social cognition – particularly higher primates. The key difference is that, although higher primates can form mental representations and store information about others in a social network, they cannot convey them to others of their species at a high level (Dunbar, 2003). In humans this unique social cognitive ability is conveyed through language.

Another uniquely human attribute is our culture – cultures that can develop and change. High culture is reliant on advanced social cognitive ability (Dunbar, 2003). Human beings have therefore evolved the ability not only to form mental representations of ourselves and others (including groups) but also to communicate our thoughts, beliefs, and **attitudes** to one another – we have good social skills. Our societies are often very different today from the way we lived 200 years ago. Indeed, while we share 99% of our DNA with chimpanzees, their societies remain largely unchanged across time. Our brains are large at birth and grow to be 3.3 times larger on reaching adulthood; in comparison, chimpanzee brains increase proportionally by 2.5 times (DeSilva & Lesnik, 2008). Human brains need to develop considerably further to cope with the immense and complex processing required to think socially in our interconnected, changing cultures. Therefore, human culture is not innate – it is learned using high levels of processing ability.

Humans are interested in learning about one another because our societies require it. Is there evidence to suggest that advanced social thinking confers an evolutionary advantage? Well, some research suggests that Neanderthals became extinct in the face of competition from *Homo sapiens*, partially as a result of their poor social

FIGURE 18.1 *A Neanderthal skull (left) and an early modern human skull (right). The Neanderthal skull clearly shows large eye sockets, suggesting an evolutionary adaptation for poor lighting conditions. This adaptation would have required larger visual cortices in the brain.*
Source: John Reader / Science Photo Library. Reproduced with permission of Science Photo Library.

cognitive abilities (see e.g. Byrne & Whiten, 1988; Dunbar, 2003). Although Neanderthal brains were approximately equivalent in size to ours (perhaps even slightly larger), the Neanderthals appear to have evolved high visual and motor skills (to deal with poor lighting conditions, for example, in their native northern Europe) at the expense of social skills. This adaptation can be observed in the relatively large eye socket widths of Neanderthal skulls compared to humans skulls (Figure 18.1). This in turn would have required larger visual cortices (Pearce, Stringer, & Dunbar, 2013). Social skills allow the communication of ideas and, more importantly, the coordination of groups. These are key skills and attributes when hunting and foraging for food, and continue to be useful in contemporary human societies. Communicated ideas and information about others, as individuals or groups, can be stored in memory for use again. Indeed, social psychologists have long been intrigued by how we organize this vast array of information – our social memory.

Organizing social thinking

Broadly, the ways in which we organize perceptions of ourselves intuitively result from comparisons with others. Indeed, Moscovici (1976) notes that Festinger's (1954) **social comparison** notion was heavily influential on social identity theory. However, Floyd Allport (1890–1978), widely regarded as the founding father of modern experimental social psychology, took a different view (Katz, 1979). For Allport, because social psychology is a branch of psychology, it should be concerned with the behaviour and conscious processes of individuals (Allport, 1924). While Allport's views have been highly influential in experimental social psychology, his belief that it should focus on the *individual* (as opposed to the group) is not that taken by some approaches – most notably social identity theory (see the following section on 'Self and Identity'). Also, his belief in restricting social psychological study to conscious processes differs from those investigating cognition that is outside conscious awareness (see the later section on 'Automatic Processes in Social Cognition'). However, for many social psychologists, how we evaluate others, issues, or objects is shaped by **normative beliefs** and **subjective norms**. Behaviour is influenced by (significant) others – for example, family and peer groups (see the section on 'Attitudes and Attitude Change'). Again, this emphasizes a strong role for social thinking.

SECTION SUMMARY

- Social cognition is a broad area of social psychology encompassing a number of sometimes competing approaches and perspectives (e.g. social cognition and social identity theory).

- Humans have a uniquely highly developed social cognitive ability, which allows them to deal with their advanced cultures. Humans differ from some other hominids (e.g. Neanderthals) in possessing brains that have evolved highly in the ability to communicate ideas and coordinate groups.

- Perceptions of ourselves are influenced by social comparisons with others, according to some theorists (e.g. Festinger, 1954), while others have argued that social psychology should restrict itself to the behaviour and conscious processes of individuals (e.g. Allport, 1924).

SELF AND IDENTITY

LEARNING OBJECTIVE 18.2

Critically evaluate how our self and identity affect the way we think and behave.

The mystery of the self is a key interest to the modern human being – we yearn to know exactly who we are and what makes us tick. Likewise, the concept of the self is also a major focus of research in social psychology. In 2000, Abraham Tesser suggested that one in seven psychology papers relates to the self – the proportion today is likely to be considerably more.

The self-concept

In simple terms, the self-concept is the set of beliefs or knowledge that people have about themselves, such as the characteristics they possess (Baumeister, 1999). There is also general agreement that the self-concept is a multidimensional construct, composed of multiple aspects of the self and multiple identities. The prevailing view in social cognition is that these different components exist as **self-schemas** (Markus, 1977). Schemas are mental representations of knowledge about the world. Accordingly, self-schemas are the cognitive representations of the different identities and facets of the self that make up your self-concept. These self-schemas are dynamic and responsive to context, not only organizing and reflecting current experience and knowledge but also guiding information processing (Markus & Wurf, 1987).

So, what information do these self-schemas encompass? On an individual level, the characteristics for which we hold a self-schema differ, such that we are self-schematic (i.e. hold a schema) for aspects of the self that are important to us and that we are sure we possess, and self-aschematic (i.e. do not hold a schema) for those that are not (Markus, 1977). One of the authors of this chapter is quite proud (and certain) of her cooking skills, but not at all bothered about her apparent lack of skill at any form of sport. As a result, she can be considered self-schematic for cooking skills and self-aschematic for sporting ability.

On a broader level, there are many different theoretical approaches that define what general types of self-schemas the self may incorporate. Some approaches suggest that our self-concept contains information about who we want to be as well as who we are. Higgin's (1987) self-discrepancy theory, for example, suggests that the self-concept includes an actual self (who we are now), an ideal self (who we want to be), and an 'ought' self (who we think we should be).

However, human beings do not exist in a social void. As a result, many theories suggest that the self encompasses social as well as personal selves. The highly influential social identity theory (e.g. Tajfel & Turner, 1979) suggests that our self-concept encompasses multiple personal and social identities. Identities can be thought of as a type of self-knowledge that is socially constructed and concerned with roles or group memberships (Fiske, 2004). Baumeister (1999) alternatively defines an identity as 'a definition placed on the self' (p. 248). So, social identity approaches argue that we possess personal identities (which are composed of idiosyncratic characteristics and identities based on close personal relationships) and also social identities (which reflect our social group memberships). The existence of these social identities has substantial implications for our relations with and behaviour towards people who do or do not share our group memberships.

Other theoretical approaches organize the self slightly differently, distinguishing between interpersonal versus personal and intergroup selves. Brewer and Gardner (1996; see also Sedikides, Gaertner, & O'Mara, 2011), for example, conceptualize the self as encompassing a personal self (made up of unique traits that distinguish the self from others), a relational self (which contains knowledge about relationship roles and attributes that you share with key others), and a collective self (which contains knowledge about your group memberships and shared traits).

Regardless of the content of the self-schemas an individual possesses or the theoretical approach you take, it is clear that the self-concept is something that is formed over time rather than having always existed. So, how do we gain knowledge of the self, and just how accurate are our perceptions of who we are?

Pursuing self-knowledge

Burgeoning sales of self-help books suggest that the pursuit of self-knowledge and self-improvement is a major goal of modern humans. Indeed, research suggests that people who are able to report detailed knowledge of their 'true' self-concept see themselves as living a more meaningful existence (Schlegel, Hicks, King, & Arndt, 2011). Now we ask: how do we come by this knowledge of the self – how do we form our self-concept? There are a number of theoretical approaches that attempt to explain how we construct the self. We can think of these theoretical approaches as falling into two key categories: those that argue that we look to ourselves and our own behaviour to define who we are, and those that argue that we look to and compare ourselves with others. Bem's (1972) **self-perception theory**, for example, argues that because introspective knowledge of the self is rather sketchy, we learn about ourselves by a process of self-attribution. That is, we observe our own behaviour and the situation or context in which it occurs, and then infer the reasons behind that behaviour. For example, if I cook dinner every night, regardless of there being no inherent reward for doing so or social sanction if I do not, then I may attribute my culinary activities to an intrinsic love of cooking. On the other hand, Festinger's (1954) social comparison theory, as you can tell by the title, argues that people come to an understanding of the self by comparing that self with others. That is, how do I know that I'm a good cook unless I compare my own cooking skills with those of others?

However, the search for self-knowledge is unlikely to be as straightforward as it sounds. As Benjamin Franklin once quipped, 'There are three things extremely hard: steel, a diamond, and to know one's self' (Franklin, 1732/2004, p. 195). There are a number of core motives that influence how we search for knowledge about the self, some of which impede rather than aid our quest to find out about our true self. Social psychologists typically agree that there are three fundamental motives that affect how we seek and respond to information about the self: self-assessment, self-verification, and self-enhancement. The motive for self-assessment suggests that we are motived to reduce uncertainty about who we are by seeking accurate information about the self (Trope, 1986). In contrast, the motive for self-verification predicts that we seek information that confirms what we think we already know about ourselves (Swann, 1983). Finally, self-enhancement motives reflect the desire to seek out information that casts a positive light over the self while avoiding any negative aspersions (Sedikides, 1993). Some later theoretical approaches also argue for the operation of a fourth motive, self-improvement, which is concerned with seeking information that helps to 'better' or improve the self (Sedikides & Strube, 1997). Research by Sedikides (1993) suggests that the tendency to engage in self-enhancement is the strongest of the original three motives. Clearly, therefore, human beings aren't so much interested in knowing the truth about the self; they are more interested in knowing positive stuff about the self. This leads us on to our next topic in this chapter: **self-esteem**.

Self-esteem

Self-esteem is the evaluative component attached to your self-concept: it is the evaluation of your self-concept as generally positive or negative (Baumeister, Campbell, Krueger, & Vohs, 2003) or the attitude towards the self (Banaji & Prentice, 1994). Traditional views of self-esteem suggest that we get a sense of how we feel about the self through a conscious and introspective look at ourselves. Therefore, conventional measures of self-esteem tend to be **explicit measures**, a term used to describe self-report measures that directly ask how you feel about a particular topic or issue. In the case of explicit self-esteem measures, Rosenberg's (1965) 10-item scale, for example, asks participants to rate statements such as 'I feel that I am a person of worth, at least on an equal plane with others.' However, as we discussed above with relation to pursuing self-knowledge, people don't always have accurate introspective access to what they think or feel, and self-esteem is no different. As a result, **implicit measures** of self-esteem are becoming more popular. These measures indirectly tap into a form of self-esteem that is automatic and non-conscious, by looking at how people view objects connected with the self (Greenwald & Banaji, 1995). These implicit measures include tasks measuring preferences and liking for your own birth date or own initials (Koole, Dijksterhuis, & Van Knippenberg, 2001). Additionally, the **implicit association test** (Greenwald & Farnham, 2000), which is a popular measure of associations between concepts, has been adopted to measure self-esteem (you will learn more about the implicit association test when we talk about attitudes).

As the strength of self-enhancement biases demonstrates, human beings are somewhat fixated on maintaining a positive view of the self. In fact, we can conceptualize the self-enhancement motive as 'the desire to maintain, protect, and enhance one's self-esteem' (Leary, 2007, pp. 319–320). But why is self-esteem so important? One explanation for why we pursue self-esteem comes from 'terror management theory' (e.g. Greenberg, Pyszczynski, & Solomon, 1986). This theory is based on the assumption that, because we human beings are the intelligent and reflective creatures that we are, we are all painfully aware of our own mortality. Terror management theory argues that, in order to deal with this unsettling thought, we have developed a cultural 'anxiety buffer' composed of a cultural worldview and self-esteem. While the cultural worldview outlines what values and standards are important to society, self-esteem tells us whether we are living up to those values and standards, giving a sense of meaning and literal or symbolic immortality that should protect against the threat of death. Consistent with this theory, research has demonstrated that, when our mortality is made salient, self-esteem buffers against an increase in the accessibility of death-related thoughts (Harmon-Jones et al., 1997).

However, other theories have criticized this explanation for self-esteem. Leary and colleagues (see e.g. Leary, Tambor, Terdal, & Downs, 1995) instead argue that self-esteem acts as a 'sociometer' – a marker of how well we are accepted in society or our 'relational value' to others. In particular, the sociometer model maintains that self-esteem has evolved to signify how well we are meeting the innate human need to belong. Because behaviours that enhance self-esteem are likely to be those that are viewed positively by society, pursuing self-esteem not only helps us feel good but also helps us monitor and avoid social rejection. In short, the sociometer model argues that self-esteem is not an important construct in and of itself, but in its utility in monitoring and maintaining societal acceptance (Leary, 2005).

DISCUSSION POINT

Discuss why we pursue self-esteem. Can you add some examples from your own experience?

Self-awareness

When psychologists talk about **self-awareness**, they are referring to a concept that is not that different from how we might use the term in informal conversation. Most social psychologists define self-awareness as a state of self-focused attention, where individuals are cognizant of and able to reflect on the traits, feelings, behaviours and any other characteristics that the self encompasses (Duval & Wicklund, 1972; Morin, 2011). However, this term can also be used to refer to an awareness of the self as a unique being or object separate from the external environment (sometimes called subjective self-awareness; Sedikides & Skowronksi, 1997). We can therefore think of self-awareness as a transient state of self-focus that occurs in particular situations but also as a general ability (learned during development) to distinguish ourselves from the external environment.

The capacity for self-awareness is thought to develop in early childhood, around the age of 18 months. Classic research by Lewis and Brooks-Gunn (1978) examined the development of self-awareness in young children using a technique known as the rouge test or mirror test. In this test, the child is placed in front of a mirror with a small dot of rouge on their forehead. While children under the age of 12 months showed no recognition, children around 18 months old appeared to be aware that the person in the mirror was them, as indicated by their efforts to inspect the spot of rouge.

Although there are individual differences in the tendency for chronic self-awareness, known as self-consciousness (Fenigstein, Scheier, & Buss, 1975), human beings do not generally walk around in a prolonged state of self-awareness. Instead, awareness fluctuates over time, with acute increases prompted by situational factors. In empirical research, self-awareness is generally induced by the presence of objects that make the self salient, such as mirrors or cameras. Duval and Wicklund's (1972) seminal theory of objective self-awareness argues that, when self-aware, individuals tend to compare whichever aspect or part of the self is under focus with the relevant salient standard; that is, they compare their actual self with the relevant ideal or norm. Any discrepancy between these actual and ideal selves causes feelings of discomfort, which the individual then tries to lessen by actively attempting to reduce the discrepancy – for example, by changing their behaviour in line with the salient norm or by attempting to escape the situation that has prompted self-awareness.

More recently, a distinction has been made between **private self-awareness**, in which attention is directed at personal and inward aspects of the self, and **public self-awareness**, in which attention is instead directed at external aspects of the self as they appear to others (Carver & Scheier, 1981). Accordingly, people may adjust their behaviour in line with their personal internal attitudes when under conditions of high private self-awareness (e.g. in the presence of a mirror) but adjust their behaviour in line with salient social norms when under conditions of high public self-awareness (e.g. in the presence of an evaluative audience) (Froming, Walker, & Lopyan, 1982). Cialdini, Kallgren, and Reno (1991), for example, found that when participants were able to view themselves on a closed-circuit TV screen (prompting high private self-awareness), their littering behaviour tended to be more consistent with their own self-reported personal norms. That is, self-aware participants with a strong personal norm against littering littered less than participants who weren't self-aware. In another series of interesting experiments, Gervais and Norenzayan (2012) manipulated self-awareness by **priming** the concept of God in a scrambled sentence task, where participants unscrambled sentences that contained words related to God (e.g. 'sacred'). They argued that, for people who believe in God, increasing the salience of this omnipotent entity should invoke a state of public self-awareness. Indeed, not only did such participants, when primed with the concept of God, report greater levels of public self-awareness, but they also showed more socially desirable responding on a questionnaire – that is, they responded in line with social norms.

SECTION SUMMARY

- This section has demonstrated the major advances social psychologists have made in understanding the 'mystery of the self'.

- We have outlined how people represent their knowledge about the self, their self-concept, as self-schemas.

- However, research suggests that humans do not necessarily seek true information about the self, with self-enhancement motives more likely to guide the search for self-knowledge than self-assessment or self-verification motives.

- We also addressed how people feel about the self. We compared explanations suggesting that self-esteem has arisen from the need to manage our fear of mortality with those that suggest it forms a marker of our value to others.

- Finally, we talked about self-awareness, and how increased private or public self-awareness can have distinct effects on whether we behave in line with personal or social norms.

PERSON PERCEPTION 1: SOCIAL INFERENCE AND ATTRIBUTION

LEARNING OBJECTIVE 18.3

Clearly evaluate and describe how we understand others' behaviour and make inferences and attributions about their behaviour.

Social inference

Social inference refers to the way in which we process social information to form impressions of and make judgements about others. Social psychologists have gained a number of insights from their study of social inferences. For example, several social psychological theories make the distinction between social inferences based on careful, systematic processing of social information and the use of simple rules or **heuristics** (Brewer, 1988; Eagly & Chaiken, 1993). The former is slow and effortful; the latter is fast and automatic. Where we have the time and motivation to think carefully, it makes sense to methodically put together all the relevant information. For example, if you are trying to decide on a new flatmate, then it probably makes sense to carefully consider all the information you have about your potential 'roomie'. The phrase **naive scientist** has been used to describe this view of how we systematically assemble information to form impressions and make judgements. In a perfect world this would be the best way to proceed for most decisions, particularly those that are important. However, we do not have the time, the mental capacity, or the motivation to make all of our social inferences in this way – we act as **cognitive misers**. However, while the use of mental shortcuts is necessary in some cases, this can lead to poor decisions or biases when we inappropriately use heuristics or generalize too far. When considering which of these different techniques for processing social information is most appropriate under which circumstances, we become **motivated tacticians**.

HEURISTICS

'Heuristic', from the Greek word meaning 'to find or discover', refers to experience-based techniques for problem solving, learning, and discovery that give a solution not guaranteed to be optimal. Where an exhaustive search is impractical, heuristic methods are used to speed up the process of finding a satisfactory solution via mental shortcuts to ease the cognitive load of making a decision.

In social psychology, heuristics are simple, efficient rules that help to explain how people make decisions, come to judgements, and find solutions, typically when dealing with complex problems or incomplete information. These rules work well in most circumstances, but under certain conditions they lead to systematic errors or cognitive biases. Daniel Kahneman and Amos Tversky did much to explore the key heuristics in human decision making (see Pinker, 2014). These key heuristics apply not only to decision making but also to a wide range of topics in psychology (e.g. reasoning).

Cognitive heuristics are mental shortcuts based on our everyday experiences. Tversky and Kahneman (1974) identified three important heuristics. First, the *representative heuristic* assesses how similar a particular target is to a typical member of that category. If the target is perceived to be sufficiently similar to the category, we infer that it shares all the attributes of that category. For example, when we meet Tom for the first time and he is wearing a tracksuit and running shoes, we might infer that Tom shares all the attributes associated with the category 'sporty' (e.g. not interested in going out, not a deep thinker).

Second, the *availability heuristic* refers to the fact that events or associations that come readily to mind are considered to be more common and prevalent than they really are. Returning to Tom, we might overestimate the likelihood that he engages in other healthy behaviours, such as eating a low-fat diet or not smoking, just because he is wearing running shoes.

Third, *anchoring* and *adjustment* refer to the fact that impressions are tied to prior perceptions that form a starting point for future social inferences. For example, your first impression of Tom as sporty could act as an anchor in future judgements of him. This might mean that your view of Tom as sporty is difficult to shift despite lots of subsequent evidence to the contrary.

Although using heuristics can lead to inaccurate social inferences, motivated tacticians may find themselves using them regularly in the interests of speed or self-interest (i.e. when not having time to think carefully about what are perceived to be important decisions).

Attribution theories

Another aspect of social inference is trying to understand the causes of our own and others' behaviour. If we make appropriate social inferences about the causes of behaviour, we can better understand our world and respond to it appropriately to bring about the outcomes we desire. Individuals develop informal theories to explain and predict how people will behave – referred to as **attribution theories**. Heider (1958) drew attention to individuals' naive causal theories of human behaviour and pointed out the key features that these share. A key distinction is between internal (or dispositional) attributions, which implicate personal factors (e.g. personality, ability), and external (or situational) attributions, which implicate environmental factors (e.g. situations, social pressure). As we shall see, there is a tendency to assume that individuals' behaviour is caused by stable properties of people (i.e. to make internal attributions). A good example of this is a study by Scherer (1978), who found that people made assumptions about the personality traits of strangers simply based on hearing their voices on the telephone. This is an example of people making spontaneous trait inferences, which we discuss later in the section titled 'Automatic Processes in Social Cognition'.

Kelley (1967) developed a covariance model to help predict when individuals will make internal versus external attributions. He suggested that we use three types of information. First, we look at the *consistency* of the behaviour. Second, we look at the *distinctiveness* of the behaviour. Third, we look at the *consensus* of the behaviour. To take an example, imagine we are working on a group project with Sarah, who spends most of the time in the project smiling. Is Sarah smiling because she is a happy sort of person (i.e. an internal attribution) or is it the situation that makes her smile (i.e. an external attribution)? If consistency is low (e.g. Sarah only sometimes smiles in group projects) then we tend to look for alternative explanations. If, however, we have regularly seen Sarah smile when working on group projects, then consistency is high and we can look for further evidence to support an internal or an external attribution. An internal attribution will be likely when distinctiveness is low (e.g. Sarah smiles all the time) and consensus is low (e.g. no one else smiles in the group project). Alternatively, an external attribution will be likely when distinctiveness is high (e.g. Sarah only smiles in this situation) and consensus is high (e.g. everyone else smiles in the group project). Research shows that people can make attributions in this way, although they may not actually do so all the time (Kassin, 1979).

Another influential attribution theory is that developed by Weiner (1986). Weiner's work was particularly focused on the attributions we make about succeeding or failing on a task, and on three dimensions of causality: *locus*, *stability*, and *controllability*. Locus refers to whether the cause of success or failure is internal (the individual) or external (the situation); stability refers to whether the cause is stable or unstable; and controllability refers to whether future performance is under the actor's control or not. This combination of three factors, each with two levels, gives us a total of eight causes of success or failure (see Table 18.1). Imagine that your friend John is taking an exam and gets a really high mark. A range of attributions are open to you based on Weiner's work. For example, an attribution of the high scores to John's ability (he really is intelligent) is to an internal, stable, and uncontrollable cause. An attribution to John having worked really hard and put in lots of effort is to an internal, stable, controllable cause. An attribution of the high score to it being an easy exam is an external, stable, and uncontrollable cause.

TABLE 18.1 *Achievement attributions as a function of locus, stability, and controllability.*

	Internal		External	
	Stable	**Unstable**	**Stable**	**Unstable**
Controllable	Typical effort	Unusual effort	Consistent help from others	Unusual help from others
Uncontrollable	Ability	Mood	Task difficulty	Luck

Source: Weiner (1986).

Attribution biases

As is the case with social inferences based on heuristics, attributions can lead to various errors and biases. The best-known **attribution bias** is the 'fundamental attribution error' (also known as 'correspondence bias'). This refers to the tendency for people to attribute behaviour to stable personality dispositions (an internal attribution) even in the face of strong evidence for external causes (Ross, 1977). The classic demonstration was in a study by Jones and Harris (1967), in which students wrote speeches about the Cuban leader Fidel Castro that were either pro-Castro or anti-Castro. Participants unsurprisingly judged that those who had written pro-Castro speeches held pro-Castro attitudes whereas those who wrote anti-Castro speeches were anti-Castro. More surprisingly, participants made similar attributions even when they were told that the individuals were required to write either a pro-Castro or an anti-Castro speech. Despite the strong evidence for an external cause for the writers' behaviour, participants preferred to make a dispositional attribution. They were making a fundamental attribution error, just as we often do in everyday life. For example, when we see our friend John drop his mobile phone, we assume this is because John is clumsy, not that mobile phones are easy to let slip.

While we are more likely to focus on internal causes of behaviour when making attributions about others' behaviour, we are conversely more likely to attribute our own behaviour to external causes (e.g. the environment). There is considerable evidence to support this asymmetry in attributions (Jones & Nisbett, 1972), which is referred to as the 'actor–observer effect'. The most likely cause of the actor–observer effect is the salience of different types of information. When we are observing others, we tend to focus more on the person as opposed to the background of the situation. This makes the information about the person more salient than the information about the background. In contrast, when explaining our own behaviour, the situation and information about the situation become more salient than the person. A second explanation implicates asymmetry of information. That is, we know more about how we behave differently in different situations than we do about how others behave in different situations. The actor–observer effect becomes most apparent when we see the same behaviour from the point of view of actor and observer (e.g. when we watch a video of our own behaviour).

A further form of attributional bias is the 'false consensus effect'. This effect refers to the tendency to overestimate how typical our own behaviour is and assume that others behave in the same way. Ross, Greene, and House (1977) asked students whether they would walk around campus for 30 minutes wearing a sandwich board bearing the slogan 'Eat at Joe's'. While students who agreed estimated that 62% of their peers would also agree, those who did not agree estimated that 67% of their peers would also decline. False consensus arises because we like to believe that others see the world in a similar way to us, helping us to see our social world as stable and predictable. Social norming approaches attempt to change behaviours such as smoking by challenging the false consensus effect (Haines, Barker, & Rice, 2003). In this approach, we ask individuals and their peers for their thoughts in relation to smoking and their perceptions of what others think. We then feed back to individuals what people actually think as a way to challenge their false consensus (e.g. 'You thought 20% of your peers think smoking was acceptable; in fact only 5% of them actually think this').

SECTION SUMMARY

> **SECTION SUMMARY**

- In forming impressions of others, we can act like naive scientists and systematically assemble information to form impressions and make judgements.

- However, often we do not have the time or mental energy to do this and in these circumstances we use mental shortcuts or heuristics. For example, the availability heuristic refers to the fact that events or associations that come readily to mind are considered to be more common and prevalent than they really are.

- Social psychologists have also developed models of how we understand the causes of our own and others' behaviour. These are known as attribution theories.

- A key attribution is whether the cause of a behaviour is internal (i.e. something about the person) or external (i.e. something about the situation the behaviour is performed in).

- There are various biases in the attributions we make. For example, the fundamental attribution bias refers to the fact that we tend to overestimate the extent to which behaviour is caused by stable personality dispositions (i.e. an internal attribution bias).

PERSON PERCEPTION 2: SOCIAL COGNITION AND SOCIAL KNOWLEDGE

LEARNING OBJECTIVE 18.4

Clearly evaluate and describe both how we use social categorization and individuation to gain coherent impressions of others, and the associated disadvantages of categorial thinking.

Social categorization

In the previous section we saw how attribution theorists attempt to explain how we effortfully process social information in understanding others' actions and forming impressions. Ultimately attribution theories became quite unwieldy and overly complex. It is clear that human beings do not think like naive scientists much of the time when making inferences about others' actions. On the contrary, people often do resort to the use of time-saving cognitive heuristics. As we will discuss later, **stereotypes** can be viewed as a form of heuristic because they require little mental effort and are activated and applied automatically (Bodenhausen, 1990). A stereotype is formed using the most prototypical (representative) members of a category, or an averaging of traits of all members of a given group. They are generalizations that are often widely held by people (Hilton & von Hippel, 1996). Before we discuss stereotyping further, however, it is necessary to understand what precedes it: categorization.

How do we organize our social perception in a coherent fashion? Why do we need to organize our thoughts, memories, and perceptions? Faced as we are with a huge array of social information, our perceptual experience of the social world would be chaotic if we did not have methods or systems to organize it. Therefore, we often use a method to classify social stimuli called 'categorization'. Broadly speaking, categorization is the process by which we group like or associated things – whether that be objects, animals, or people. Defining categorization can be difficult because there are conflicting perspectives on how it actually works. However, according to McGarty (1999), 'Categorization is the process of understanding what something is by knowing what other things it is equivalent to, and what other things it is different from' (p. 1).

This is quite a flexible definition and is therefore useful in understanding how we categorize people – **social categorization**. Alternatively, conceptualizing things or people as 'all or nothing' (i.e. strict membership of one category or another) can cause problems because the human perceptual system can be fooled. For example, Leeper's (1935) 'ambiguous lady' (Figure 18.2) is an illusion in which it is possible to see an old woman or a young woman – the woman cannot be categorized as one or the other exclusively. Additionally, most categories (whether social in nature or not) have uncertain or **fuzzy boundaries** surrounding a **prototype**. Category or group membership cannot always be simply defined, therefore, because we rely on prototypes. For example, suppose your research methods class is taught in the first

FIGURE 18.2 *Leeper's ambiguous lady. Look closely at this picture – what do you see? It is possible to see either an old woman or a young woman. Try to look for both. Would you categorize this as a picture of an old or young person? Perceptual ambiguity like this shows that it is sometimes difficult to strictly categorize objects and – in the case of social cognition – people to mutually exclusive categories. It is, of course, very unlikely that you would ever meet someone like the ambiguous lady. However, there are more subtle examples of social categories where difficulty might occur in applying one social category to a person. Can you think of any?*
Source: William Ely Hill / public domain.

FIGURE 18.3 *A continuum of impression formation. The premise underlying the continuum model is that impressions vary in the degree to which they are based on categorical or individuating (i.e. individual attributes) information. Categorization and individuation lie at the extremes of a single continuum, but impressions can be made up of varying degrees of categorical and individuating information, depending on where a target person is perceived to sit on the continuum.*
Source: Reprinted from Fiske and Neuberg (1990). Copyright 1990, with permission from Elsevier.

5 weeks of the term by Dr Jones and several other lecturers. Because Dr Jones leads the teaching, she becomes your prototype of a research methods lecturer. However, in week 6 you discover that your social psychology classes will be taught by a cohort of lecturers – one of whom is Dr Jones. Therefore, you may well be slower to categorize Dr Jones as a social psychology lecturer because she is less representative and less prototypical. We refer to prototypes drawn from social categories as 'stereotypes'.

Categorization versus individuation

When is categorization not used? Fiske and Neuberg (1990) suggest that perception is based on a continuum from categorization through to **individuation** (Figure 18.3). Individuation refers to the ability to differentiate between group members based on their individual attributes. Individuation can occur when heuristic processing is difficult, such as when there is a poor fit between the person we are attempting to form an impression of and the activated category or categories. Encountering a counter-stereotypical bricklayer educated at Oxford, for example, could lead to difficulties in categorizing that person as a bricklayer (Hutter & Crisp, 2005). Because the fit between being a bricklayer and having an Oxford education is low, people tend to form more individuated impressions relative to when category fit is higher (e.g. when forming an impression of an Oxford-educated art critic).

Multiple categorization

Perceiving any person can potentially involve **multiple categorization** (Crisp, Ensari, Hewstone, & Miller, 2003). For example, we are all members of numerous social categories, including race, nationality, gender, and occupation. Forming an impression of a person when multiple social categories are salient can sometimes lead to conflicting expectations, especially when the categories are surprising or incongruent in nature (Hastie, Schroeder, & Weber, 1990; Kunda, Miller, & Claire, 1990). Perhaps a first encounter with a male midwife may lead us to ask ourselves, 'How did this person become a midwife?' (Figure 18.4).

It seems that people do engage in an **inconsistency resolution** process to resolve the poor fit between conflicting social categories, and this results in the application of new attributes not associated with the constituent stereotypes – these are referred to as **emergent attributes** (Hastie et al., 1990; Hutter & Crisp, 2005; Kunda et al., 1990). Emergent attributes facilitate the perception of incongruent category combinations and are likely to lead to individuation.

FIGURE 18.4 *How surprised would you be to discover that this person is a midwife?*

Source: Mihalec / Shutterstock.com.

Disadvantages of categorical thinking

So far we have seen that categorization provides a quick, easy path to perceptual structure in the social world. However, it is also a precursor of stereotyping. Categorization typically leads to heightened accessibility of stereotype-consistent information: Cohen (1981) showed participants a video of a woman having a birthday dinner and told them either that she was a librarian or that she was a waitress. Those participants told the woman was a waitress were more likely to recall later that she was drinking beer, while those told that she was a librarian were more likely to recall her wearing glasses. The associated stereotypes had biased their perceptions. The same biases apply for minority groups where undesirable traits come into play. Furthermore, people tend to recall positive information more readily about their **in-groups** (i.e. groups they are members of) and more negative information about **out-groups** (i.e. groups they are *not* members of) (Howard & Rothbart, 1980). You will learn more about why and when we stereotype in the next section. In addition, as you will read in the section on automaticity in social cognition, traits associated with stereotypes can also affect our behaviour in ways that lie outside conscious awareness, without active intention, and are uncontrollable (Bargh, Chen, & Burrows, 1996).

SECTION SUMMARY

- This section defined social categorization and individuation, two strategies through which we gain coherent impressions of others.
- Social categories are formed around a prototype, but the boundaries between categories are not always clearly defined (i.e. they are fuzzy boundaries).
- Furthermore, people are capable of perceiving more than one active category at the same time (multiple categorization).

- However, when active categories are incongruent, it creates conflicting expectations. This leads to a process involving inconsistency resolution, resulting in the application of emergent attributes that help to overcome the conflict and assist perception.
- Categorization can lead to negative side effects in the form of heightened accessibility of stereotype-consistent information.

STEREOTYPING

LEARNING OBJECTIVE 18.5

Discuss why and when we apply stereotypes to others.

The American journalist Walter Lippmann is commonly credited with the creation of the term 'stereotype' as psychologists use it today. Lippmann (1922) portrayed stereotypes as the pictures we carry inside our heads that help us to navigate the complex process of person perception and justify existing social hierarchies. As you will learn in this section, many of Lippmann's ideas regarding the functions and consequences of stereotyping have stood the test of time. However, we now tend to more formally define stereotypes as the collection of traits that society thinks is typical of members of a particular social group. While some groups are characterized by largely negative stereotypes (e.g. bankers are seen as greedy and careless), stereotypes can also be predominantly positive, or contain a mix of positive and negative traits (e.g. elderly people are seen as forgetful but caring).

Because stereotypes are a reflection of societal beliefs, they change as society does. The classic Princeton trilogy studies and their extensions have tracked stereotype change in Princeton University students over a period of almost 70 years, from Katz and Braly's initial survey in 1933 to Madon et al.'s follow-up in 2001. Madon et al. (2001) reported that, during this time, the content of the majority of ethnicity- and nationality-based stereotypes measured changed. The stereotype content model (Fiske, Cuddy, Glick, & Xu, 2002) suggests that the dynamic content of stereotypes can be classified along two key dimensions of warmth and competence, which arise from the group's status and potential for competition within society at that time. Specifically, low-status groups that do not compete for resources are seen as warm but incompetent, whereas high-status groups that do compete for resources are seen as cold but competent.

When social psychologists talk about stereotypes, we tend to distinguish between **stereotype activation** and **stereotype application** (Devine, 1989). Stereotype activation refers to the degree to which a stereotype is accessible in the mind (Kunda & Spencer, 2003) and is often measured by recording how quickly someone responds to a stereotypical trait after priming with the relevant social category cue. Activation of the stereotype of 'gay people', for example, would be inferred from a quicker response to a stereotypical trait following the word 'gay' relative to the word 'straight'. In contrast, stereotype application refers to the actual use of those activated stereotypes in judgements (Kunda & Spencer, 2003) – for example, when forming an impression. Other approaches to stereotyping use the distinction between implicit and explicit constructs that we've already talked about in this chapter, referring to stereotype activation as the activation of 'implicit stereotypes' (Blair, Ma, & Lenton, 2001).

Why do people stereotype?

Though it has been almost a century since Lippmann (1922) first credited stereotypes with 'economy of effort', stereotypes are still thought of as a tool that simplifies information processing and reduces **cognitive load** (Bodenhausen, Macrae, & Milne, 1998; Kunda & Spencer, 2003). As we discussed earlier, we can think of stereotypes as a judgemental heuristic – a mental shortcut for streamlining social perception (Bodenhausen & Wyer, 1985). In a classic series of studies, Macrae, Bodenhausen, Milne, and Jetten (1994) confirmed that stereotypes do help to conserve our cognitive capacity. In one study, participants were asked to form impressions of people presented on a computer screen while simultaneously monitoring an audio track describing the geography and economy of Indonesia. Participants in the experimental condition were given the name of each impression target (e.g. John) along with a social category label (e.g. skinhead) and characteristics that the individual was thought to possess, half of which were consistent with the relevant stereotype. Participants in the control condition were given the same names and character traits, but no social category labels. Macrae et al. (1994) found that participants given the social category labels not only showed better memory for the stereotypical traits but also had better knowledge of the geography of Indonesia relative to participants who had been given no labels. Because the stereotype made the process of impression formation so much easier, it left more cognitive resources to devote to the audio monitoring task.

Other approaches argue that stereotypes serve a justification function, to provide a rationale for why the world is the way it is. System justification theory (Jost & Banaji, 1994) argues that people like to believe that the systems underlying the world in which they live are fair and legitimate. Stereotypes can therefore act as a way of rationalizing any inequality that exists in the world. If you subscribe to the stereotype of women as weak and submissive, then the predominance of men in the upper echelons of the business world seems appropriate and fair. Furthermore, this theory argues that even disadvantaged groups may help to justify the existing social hierarchy. Consistent with this argument, Jost and Kay (2005) found that women exposed to stereotypes of women as communal endorsed the current state of gender relations and sex role division to a higher degree than those who were not exposed to these stereotypes – in fact, they showed equivalent levels of system justification to male participants.

Stereotype formation and maintenance

As stereotypes are constructs consisting of beliefs shared by society, it makes sense that one key way in which stereotypes can form is through socialization. We learn about the traits that society attributes to different social groups from our parents, our peers, and the wider world while we are still in childhood. However, we are prone to a number of cognitive biases that may also contribute to the development and persistence of stereotypes.

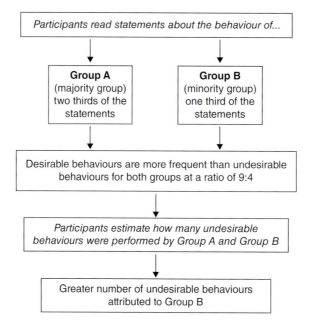

FIGURE 18.5 *Hamilton and Gifford's illusory correlation. Participants are presented with a number of statements describing positive and negative behaviours of members of Group A and Group B. As Group A is the majority group, two thirds of the statements describe the behaviour of members of this group, while only one third describe the behaviour of members of the minority (Group B). Accordingly, due to their relative infrequency, Group B behaviours are more distinctive than Group A behaviours. Within both groups, positive behaviours are reported more often than negative behaviours, at a ratio of 9:4. As a result, negative behaviours are more distinctive than positive behaviours. The combination of two distinctive events (being a member of a minority group and performing a negative behaviour) results in an illusory correlation between these events.*
Source: Reprinted from Hamilton and Gifford (1976). Copyright 1976, with permission of Elsevier.

One key cognitive factor involved in the formation and maintenance of stereotypes is known as the **illusory correlation** (Figure 18.5). Hamilton and Gifford (1976) suggest that, when two statistically infrequent events are paired, perceptions about the degree to which those events are correlated are inflated because of their distinctiveness, resulting in a false (or illusory) impression about the relationship between the two. If a member of a minority group (whose members are statistically seen relatively infrequently) is observed performing a negative behaviour (which is again statistically seen relatively infrequently), the distinctiveness of this co-occurrence results in better encoding of the information, and the degree to which the behaviour is characteristic of that minority group is therefore overestimated. This forms the basis for a negative stereotype.

Stereotypes may also be maintained by biases that affect which information we attend to and how we interpret it. Johnston and Macrae (1994) gave people a selection of questions and answers that ostensibly came from interviews of physics students but that actually differed in the degree to which they confirmed the stereotype of physics students. Interestingly, participants chose to view more stereotype-confirming than stereotype-disconfirming questions, accordingly disproportionately exposing themselves to information that confirmed their existing stereotypes. People are also subject to biases when interpreting the behaviour of the out-group. Pettigrew (1979) argued that we are prone to the **ultimate attribution error**, attributing negative or stereotypical behaviours to dispositional traits but positive or counter-stereotypical behaviours to situational causes – thus maintaining our stereotypical view of the out-group. In fact, we may even sustain a stereotypical view of our own social group in this way. Barrett and Bliss-Moreau (2009) found that, despite being given situational explanations for the emotional expressions depicted in a series of facial photographs, both male and female participants were more likely to attribute expressions to dispositional attributes (being an emotional person) when the photo depicted a female, and situational attributes (having a bad day) when the photo depicted a male.

In some cases, the expectancies that result from the above processes may also lead us to unintentionally behave in a way that encourages stereotype-consistent behaviour in others, thus further confirming our expectancies. This is known as a **self-fulfilling prophecy** (Snyder, Tanke, & Berscheid, 1977). Chen and Bargh (1997) found that participants who were subject to **subliminal priming** with the category of African Americans showed more hostile behaviour in a later interaction with a non-primed partner. Given that the trait of hostility is stereotypical of African Americans, it appears that priming this social category prompted stereotype-consistent behaviour. More interestingly, however, the non-primed partners of these participants showed similarly hostile behaviour in return. Given that these participants were not primed with the category of African Americans, their hostile behaviour was likely a direct response to the behaviour of the partner they were paired with. In short, the stereotypical expectancies of one partner unintentionally provoked stereotype-consistent behaviour in the other, further confirming initial expectancies. Awareness of stereotypes that may apply to our own social group can also have behavioural consequences.

FOCUS POINT 18.2

STEREOTYPE THREAT

Stereotype threat refers to the concern experienced by a person when there is a possibility that they may act in a way consistent with negative stereotypes (Steele & Aronson, 1995). Importantly, this threat has been found to result in actual decrements in performance on the stereotyped dimension. In the original demonstration of the effect, Steele and Aronson found that black participants performed worse than white participants on a test presented as a measure of their genuine verbal ability, but performed equally well when no reference was made to verbal ability. Since this seminal paper, the stereotype threat effect has been replicated in a range of social groups and domains, including men on measures of social sensitivity (Koenig & Eagly, 2005) and white psychology undergraduates on implicit measures of racial attitudes (Frantz, Cuddy, Burnett, Ray, & Hart, 2004).

 Claude Steele discusses stereotype threat in **this video**[1].

Perhaps even more alarming is the possibility that the effects of stereotype threat may extend beyond performance, impeding actual learning and future academic and career choices. Rydell, Rydell, and Boucher (2010) found that females subject to stereotype threat in the domain of maths showed attenuated learning of mathematical rules compared with females not exposed to threat. Davies, Spencer, Quinn, and Gerhardstein (2002) found that women exposed to gender-stereotypical television advertisements reported significantly less interest in pursuing qualifications or careers in fields involving quantitative skills (e.g. engineering, statistics, and physics). Clearly, therefore, stereotype threat has wide-reaching consequences and may even be a key contributor to the persisting under-representation of women in STEM (science, technology, engineering, and mathematics) careers.

WHAT CAUSES STEREOTYPE THREAT?

A number of processes have been proposed to underlie stereotype threat. However, there is mounting evidence that the limited nature of working memory plays a particularly central role. When under stereotype threat, people engage in suppression of stereotypes (Logel, Iserman, Davies, Quinn, & Spencer, 2009) and anxiety (Johns, Inzlicht, & Schmader, 2008). However, suppression is effortful and consumes cognitive resources, leaving less of this limited resource available for ensuring optimal task performance. Schmader and Johns (2003) found that female participants who expected to complete a maths task designed to evaluate gender norms subsequently performed worse on a test of working memory, relative to participants who were given a non-threatening explanation for the task. In addition, the degree of working memory depletion among these participants predicted their actual performance on the threatening maths task.

OVERCOMING STEREOTYPE THREAT

Given the substantial implications of stereotype threat, it is not surprising that a large amount of research is concerned with reducing the impact of threat on performance in the stereotyped domain. Some interventions focus on the impact of reframing or encouraging reappraisal of the threatening situation, and have found reduced stereotype threat effects when tests are reframed as a challenging learning experience (Alter, Aronson, Darley, Rodriguez, & Ruble, 2010) or when anxiety is presented as helpful rather than harmful to performance (Johns et al., 2008). Interventions encouraging de-emphasis of the threatened social identity or domain have been similarly successful. Ambady, Paik, Steele, Owen-Smith, and Mitchell (2004) found a reduction in stereotype threat when participants were given the opportunity to list negative and positive attributes that described their personal rather than social identity. Similarly, Cohen, Garcia, Apfel, and Master (2006) found that African American students given the opportunity to **self-affirm** by reflecting on important values outside the threatened domain at the beginning of term had significantly better end-of-term grades than students who didn't self-affirm. Impressively, this simple manipulation reduced the racial achievement gap by 40%.

When do people stereotype?

We have already talked about the function of stereotypes as an energy-saving device that helps to conserve our cognitive resources for other tasks. It should come as no surprise, therefore, that we are more likely to use stereotypes when our cognitive resources are taxed. Gilbert and Hixon (1991) found that participants only formed more stereotypical impressions of an Asian research assistant relative to a Caucasian research assistant if they formed these impressions while simultaneously completing a resource-consuming visual search task.

Research also suggests that stereotypes are more likely to be employed when there is a lack of information needed to make a more informed social judgement. Epley and Kruger (2005) led participants to believe that they would be interacting with an Asian American (stereotypically shy) or African American (stereotypically sociable) female by email or by telephone. Participants who interacted with their partner over the phone later rated them as equally sociable regardless of their purported racial identity. However, those who interacted over email rated their partner as more sociable if they thought they were African American as opposed to Asian American, indicating greater use of the stereotype. Because email removes many of the verbal and social cues that we use to tell us about people's characteristics, participants in this condition had to rely on stereotypes to make their judgements.

When we turn to the question of when stereotypes are *activated* (rather than applied), the answer becomes a little more complex. Early approaches suggested that the answer to this question was 'all the time'. Devine's (1989) highly influential dual-process model argued that, because stereotypes are well known, *activation* of stereotypes is automatic and unavoidable upon exposure to a member of a stereotyped group. Devine argued that it is only at the controlled level of processing that we choose whether or not we *apply* stereotypes in judgements. However, we now think that stereotype activation is more accurately viewed as *conditionally automatic*. If stereotypes really do exist to conserve cognitive resources, it would seem counterproductive if they were activated in situations when they are not relevant or useful. For example, Macrae, Bodenhausen, Milne, Thorn, and Castelli (1997) found that people were more likely to activate stereotypes when making socially meaningful decisions (e.g. whether photos depicted an animate or inanimate object) than non-social decisions (e.g. whether a white dot was present or absent on a photo), in which stereotype activation confers no obvious benefit.

In fact, human beings can be quite strategic about when they activate and use stereotypes. The concept of 'motivated stereotyping' suggests that we may be more (or less) likely to stereotype when it suits our particular purposes. Sinclair and Kunda (1999) found that participants who received negative feedback on a task from a black doctor tended to activate traits associated with the racial stereotype but inhibit those associated with the doctor stereotype. Participants who received positive feedback, however, showed the opposite pattern, inhibiting the racial stereotype and activating the doctor stereotype. Such results can be viewed in terms of self-enhancement – activating the black stereotype allowed the negative feedback given to the participant to be discounted more easily, while activating the doctor stereotype gave the positive feedback more legitimacy. Accordingly, when and whether a stereotype is activated may be determined by the perceiver's goals.

SECTION SUMMARY

- Due to its important real-life implications, stereotyping is a popular area of research in social psychology.
- Stereotypes help us to streamline information processing and can be used to justify existing social hierarchies.
- Cognitive biases, such as illusory correlations and the ultimate attribution error, contribute to the development and maintenance of stereotypes.
- It is important to differentiate between the two processes that make up the act of stereotyping (activation and application) and consider whether these are inevitable or guided by our goals.

ATTITUDES AND ATTITUDE CHANGE

LEARNING OBJECTIVE 18.6

Demonstrate a critical understanding of how our attitudes are formed and changed.

Defining attitudes

Attitudes are a key concept in social psychology. Back in 1935, Gordon Allport wrote that attitudes were 'probably the most distinctive and indispensable concept in contemporary American social psychology' (p. 198). Many social psychologists would consider this view to still apply today. Here are two widely used definitions of attitudes:

> [Attitude is] a learned disposition to respond in a consistently favorable or unfavorable manner with respect to a given object. (Fishbein & Ajzen, 1975, p. 6)
>
> Attitude is a psychological tendency that is expressed by evaluating a particular entity with some degree of favor or disfavor. (Eagly & Chaiken, 1993, p. 1)

Like other definitions of attitudes, these definitions describe three key features of attitudes. First, attitudes are motivating forces; they influence what we do. Second, attitudes are relatively enduring in nature; they are not like mood states, which last only a few minutes, but nor are they personality traits, which often last a lifetime. Third, attitudes are also evaluative in nature; they represent positive, negative, or neutral reactions to aspects of the world (what are often called 'attitude objects').

The concept of attitudes is widely used. One of the important features of attitudes is that they are an individual difference variable (i.e. they vary between people). For example, some of us really like cheese with a strong taste; others are not bothered one way or another; and some really dislike it. These differences are important because they can help to explain differences between people (e.g. differentiate those who buy piquant cheese). The concept of attitudes is so widely used across social psychology that whole subfields have grown up around studying different types of attitudes. For example, a great deal of prejudice research focuses on understanding the attitudes (usually negative) towards particular groups of individuals, while work on interpersonal attraction focuses on the attitudes we have towards specific others, and work on self-esteem focuses on attitudes towards ourselves. The focus of the attitude is usually referred to as the object or target and can include a very broad range of things from behaviours (e.g. playing tennis) to concrete objects (e.g. iPads) to people (e.g. Jane) to social policies (e.g. university tuition fees).

One popular model of attitudes, the 'ABC' or 'tripartite' model (Maio & Olson, 2000), distinguishes between three components: affective, behavioural, and cognitive. The affective component refers to feelings and emotions towards the attitude object or target (e.g. enjoying rock climbing). The behavioural component refers to action tendencies towards the attitude object or target (e.g. 'I plan to go rock climbing this weekend'). The cognitive component refers to ideas and beliefs about the attitude object or target (e.g. rock climbing requires skill; rock climbing is dangerous).

In the rest of this section, we look at how attitudes might be measured, the relationship between attitudes and behaviour, and how attitudes might be changed.

Measuring attitudes

One of the interesting features of attitudes is that we cannot directly observe someone's attitude. We have to infer an attitude from the relationship between stimuli that represent the attitude object (e.g. the object itself or a picture of the object) and the reaction to that object (e.g. responses to a questionnaire). So, for example, a positive attitude towards red clothes in our friend Judy might be inferred from regularly seeing Judy wear red clothes. Psychologists have devised various ways to measure attitudes.

The most popular means of measuring attitudes uses self-report questionnaires through which individuals rate their own attitudes. This method is valuable because individuals often have the most insight and knowledge about their own attitudes (e.g. Judy probably knows best about whether she has a positive attitude towards wearing red clothes). However, for some attitudes we may not want to rely on such self-reports because individuals do not have a good insight into their own attitudes or they are not inclined to tell us what those attitudes are (e.g. this might be the case if we hold a prejudicial attitude towards minority groups such as Asians). Psychologists have therefore come up with methods to try to assess such attitudes in ways that do not so heavily rely on self-reports, which can be faked.

Two of the most popular self-report measures of attitudes are semantic differentials and Likert scales. Semantic differential measures of attitudes are based on the work of Osgood and colleagues in the 1950s (Osgood, Suci, & Tannenbaum, 1957). This work suggests that three dimensions are tapped by our judgements of a broad range of objects: evaluation, potency or power, and activity. The evaluation dimension in particular appears to represent what is normally meant by attitudes and can be tapped by pairs of opposite words, also known as 'semantic differentials' (e.g. good–bad, pleasant–unpleasant, positive–negative). Since then, researchers have regularly used semantic differential items to measure attitude, where individuals are required to rate their attitude by placing it between pairs of words. For example, we might use the following to tap attitudes towards iPods:

An iPod is…

good	1 **2** 3 4 5 6 7	bad
pleasant	1 2 **3** 4 5 6 7	unpleasant
positive	1 2 3 **4** 5 6 7	negative

Taking an average rating across the three semantic differentials (of 2, 3, and 4) would give a rating of 3, which would equate to a slightly positive attitude towards iPods. Note that this form of measurement is called 'direct scaling' because it requires the individual to directly place themselves on an evaluative dimension to represent their attitude.

LIKERT SCALING FOR ATTITUDES

Likert scaling is an indirect form of measurement used to assess attitudes. Respondents are faced with a series of statements about an attitude object that are clearly positive or negative; respondents are then required to rate their degree of agreement or disagreement with each. A respondent's attitude is assumed to drive the response they give and the attitude score is derived from the responses to the questions. The statements need to be developed to represent the full range of views (from very positive to very negative) towards the attitude object.

For example, in relation to a Likert measure of attitudes towards an iPad we might have:

I enjoy using an iPad	Strongly agree	1	**2**	3	4	5	6	7	Strongly disagree
The iPad is a fantastically flexible device	Strongly agree	1	2	**3**	4	5	6	7	Strongly disagree
The iPad is too expensive	Strongly agree	1	2	3	4	5	**6**	7	Strongly disagree
I would choose a laptop over an iPad	Strongly agree	1	2	3	4	5	6	**7**	Strongly disagree

Here we would reverse the scores of the last two questions (convert 6 to 2 and 7 to 1) and then average across the items to give a mean score of 2, which would be a fairly strong positive attitude towards an iPad.

However, there are some attitudes that we may not want to measure using such self-report questions (e.g. when individuals have inadequate insight into their own attitudes or have prejudices that they are not inclined to tell us about). Psychologists have consequently come up with methods to try to assess such attitudes in ways that do not so heavily rely on self-report measures, which allow people to control what they report. Many non-self-report measures use the idea that attitudes will drive related behaviour and so measure relevant behaviour. So, for example, we might measure attitudes towards alcohol by looking at measures of how much alcohol people consume (e.g. via looking at till receipts or number of empty bottles of alcohol in the garbage).

Another interesting attitude measure is the lost-letter technique (Milgram, Mann, & Harter, 1965). In order to ascertain attitudes towards the Communist Party and the Nazi Party, this US study addressed a series of stamped envelopes to these two parties plus a medical group ('Medical Research Associates') or an individual ('Mr Walter Carnap'). The envelopes were then left near a postbox in full view and the researchers simply recorded how many letters were posted and made it back to the recipients (actually all a university address). This study showed that around 25% of letters to the Communist and Nazi parties made it back compared with around 70% for the medical group and the individual citizen. From this the researchers were able to conclude that people were equally negative about the Communist Party and Nazi Party.

Another type of non-self-report attitude measure that is becoming widely used is the aforementioned implicit association test (IAT) (Greenwald & Banaji, 1995). The basis of the IAT is that we find it easier to and are quicker at classifying things that are related in memory than things that are unrelated. For example, if the attitude object is Irish versus English (Greenwald, McGhee, & Schwartz, 1998) and we have a more positive implicit attitude towards Irish than English, then we will be quicker on tasks that require us to classify Irish names and positive words such as 'joyful' together than when we are required to classify English names and positive words

Sequence	1	2	3	4	5
Task description	Initial target–concept discrimination	Associated attribute discrimination	Initial combined task	Reversed target–concept discrimination	Reversed combined task

Task instructions	• Irish
	    English •
		• pleasant
		    unpleasant •
			• Irish
			• pleasant
			    English •
			    unpleasant •
				Irish •
				• English
					• Irish •
					• pleasant
					• English
					    unpleasant •

Sample stimuli	✓ Casey
	    Clark ✓
	✓ Duffy
	    Brown ✓
	    Richardson ✓
	✓ Fitzpatrick
	✓ Twoomey
		✓ diamond
		    disaster ✓
		✓ heaven
		    friend ✓
		    cancer ✓
		    rotten ✓
		✓ joyful
			✓ Driscoll
			✓ happy
			    Johnson ✓
			✓ joyful
			✓ Flanagan
			    abuse ✓
			    failure ✓
				✓ Clifford
				    Kelley ✓
				✓ Foster
				✓ Stevens
				    Duffy ✓
				✓ Johnson
				✓ Clark
					✓ loyal
					    Flanagan ✓
					    evil ✓
					✓ Clifford
					    Kelley ✓
					✓ Foster
					✓ lucky

FIGURE 18.6 *The implicit association test (IAT). This figure is an illustration of the IAT in relation to English and Irish names. In Task 1 and Task 4, individuals classify the names as Irish or English by pressing left and right keys. In Task 2, individuals classify words as pleasant or unpleasant. The key tasks are 3 and 5, where both names and words have to be classified. The IAT assumes that individuals who have more positive views of Irish names than English names will be faster at classifying when Irish and pleasant words share a response key (Task 3) than when Irish and unpleasant words share a key (Task 5). For individuals who are more positive about English names, the reverse pattern should hold (i.e. faster responses to Task 5 than to Task 3). The score on the IAT is a function of the differences in response times to Tasks 3 and 5.*

Source: Adapted from Greenwald, McGhee, and Schwartz (1998). American Psychological Association, adapted with permission.

such as 'joyful' together (Figure 18.6). The difference between consonant (Driscoll/joyful; Johnson/failure) and non-consonant (Driscoll/failure, Johnson/joyful) pairings forms the measure of attitudes in the IAT. It is very difficult for individuals to fake particular attitudes on such measures and consequently they have been found to be useful in relation to measuring attitudes towards sensitive topics such as race.

Attitudes and behaviour

One of the best-known studies in social psychology is an early attempt to examine the relationships between attitudes and behaviour (LaPiere, 1934). LaPiere was interested in prejudicial attitudes towards the Chinese and the impacts on discriminatory behaviours such as refusing service. To test this relationship he visited over 250 establishments (including hotels, diners, and restaurants) along with a Chinese couple, never once being refused service. LaPiere later wrote to each of the establishments asking, 'Will you accept members of the Chinese race as guests in your establishment?' Of the 128 replies he received, only one said 'yes'; nine said 'it depended on circumstances'; and 118 said 'no'. This seems like pretty convincing evidence of the lack of an attitude–behaviour relationship! Indeed, in a review of attitude–behaviour relationship studies like the LaPiere study, Wicker (1969) wrote, 'taken as a whole, these studies suggest that it is considerably more likely that attitudes will be unrelated or only very slightly related to overt behaviours than that attitudes will be closely related to actions' (p. 65). The striking nature of the findings by LaPiere and others has led to a persisting view that attitudes and behaviour are not related. This is in contrast with the views of most social psychologists, who note a moderate-sized relationship between appropriately measured attitudes and behaviours in relation to the same object. The key phrase here is 'appropriately measured'. If we return to LaPiere's study and look a little more closely, we can see some problems that affect this and many similar studies. First, note that LaPiere measured behaviour and *then* later attitudes, so he was perhaps testing the effect of behaviour on attitudes. Second, it seems unlikely that the people who provided the service in the establishments were the ones who responded to the letters. Third, the two measures were not well matched; that is, the behaviour measure was focused on being served while the attitude measure focused on being *accepted* as guests.

Attitudes towards behaviours

Social psychologists have provided a number of key insights into how to provide appropriate tests of the attitude–behaviour relationship. One such insight is the **principle of correspondence** developed by Ajzen and Fishbein (1977). They suggested that attitudes are held and behaviours performed in relation to principles corresponding to the acronym TACT:

- target at which the action is directed
- action being performed
- context in which the action is performed
- timeframe during which the action is performed.

Importantly, they suggested that only when both the attitude and the behaviour are measured in the same way in relation to each of these factors (i.e. they correspond) will attitudes predict behaviour. So, for example, say we want to predict Jane going to the Café Direct coffee bar (target and action) with her friend Helen (context) on Wednesday lunchtime (timeframe). Then we should assess Jane's attitude at the same level of specificity – that is, Jane's attitude to going to the Café Direct coffee bar with Helen on Wednesday lunchtime would be somewhere on a continuum from 'very bad' to 'very good'. Ajzen and Fishbein (1977) showed that, of the published studies on the attitude–behaviour relationship, only 4 out of 98 where correspondence was low or partial showed a strong relationship between attitudes and behaviour; however, among the studies with high correspondence, 35 out of 44 had strong attitude–behaviour relationships. McEachan, Conner, Taylor, and Lawton (2011) reported a medium-sized average attitude–behaviour relationship ($r = .31$) across 209 studies that used measures of attitudes and later measures of behaviour (i.e. prospective designs) that were matched based on the principle of correspondence.

Fishbein and Ajzen subsequently went on to develop a theory relating attitudes to behaviour and other constructs known as the 'theory of planned behaviour' (Ajzen, 1991; based on the earlier 'theory of reasoned action'; Fishbein & Ajzen, 1975). This remains one of the most influential accounts of how attitudes towards behaviours affect behaviour. It suggested that attitudes towards behaviour (i.e. an individual's overall evaluation of the behaviour) do not directly influence behaviour but do so through informing our intentions to act (i.e. an individual's conscious plan or decision to exert effort in order to engage in a particular behaviour). Intentions are also determined by two other factors: subjective norms (i.e. a person's beliefs about whether significant others think they should engage in the behaviour) and perceived behavioural control (i.e. a person's expectancy that performance of the

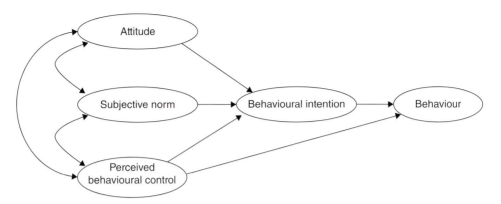

FIGURE 18.7 *The theory of planned behaviour. A model of how attitudes relate to behaviour.*

Source: Reprinted from Ajzen (1991). Copyright 1991, with permission from Elsevier.

behaviour is within their control, or confidence that they can perform the behaviour). Perceived behavioural control is assumed to influence both intentions and behaviour because we rarely intend to do things we know we cannot and because believing that we can succeed enhances effort and persistence and so makes successful performance more likely.

The theory of planned behaviour (TPB) (Figure 18.7) suggests that attitudes are just one of three key determinants of behaviour and that all other influences on behaviour first influence these components (i.e. a mediational model). The TPB has been widely applied across a range of behaviours with some degree of success (Armitage & Conner, 2001). Armitage and Conner (2001) reported that, across 154 applications of the TPB, intentions emerged as the strongest predictors of behaviour, while attitudes were the strongest predictors of intentions. The TPB suggests that the key predictors of intentions will vary as a function of the population and behaviour being studied and that identifying the key predictors can inform attempts to change these behaviours. For example, McEachan et al. (2011) reported the results for 237 prospective tests of the TPB. Interestingly, subjective norms were stronger predictors of intentions to engage in behaviours such as eating, while attitudes were stronger predictors of intentions to engage in behaviours such as physical activity. This would suggest the value of targeting subjective norms when trying to change eating behaviours and targeting attitudes when trying to change physical activity.

Attitudes towards objects

The TPB provides a largely rational account of how attitudes influence behaviour in that it rests on the assumption that we deliberate on our behaviour before deciding to act. Fazio (1990) has suggested that such deliberative models apply only to the extent that individuals have the motivation and opportunity to process the information; arrive at an attitude, a perceived norm, and a perceived behavioural control; and decide to act (intention). When motivation or opportunity to process information is lacking (e.g. when you are in a rush or distracted) then attitudes can influence behaviour through a more automatic route. Fazio suggested that under certain circumstances a behaviour can be produced spontaneously when an attitude is activated. Here activation simply means 'brought to mind' or 'brought to conscious attention'. Fazio suggested that attitudes can be automatically activated from memory by observation of the attitude object or cues associated with the object and that this will be

Complex processing only if motivation and opportunity permit

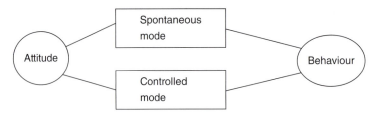

FIGURE 18.8 *The motivation and opportunity determine (MODE) processing model. The model describes how attitudes can influence behaviour through either a spontaneous mode (where automatic processes dominate) or a controlled mode (where deliberative processes dominate).*
Source: Reprinted from Fazio (1990). Copyright 1990, with permission from Elsevier.

particularly likely when the attitude is strong (i.e. is quickly reported or accessible). The MODE model (*m*otivation and *o*pportunity *de*termine how attitudes influence behaviour) is important in suggesting that action can be caused either through deliberative thought or in a more automatic manner (Figure 18.8).

The MODE model also emphasizes another important distinction. In the deliberative path, as described by models such as the TPB, the focus is on the *behaviour* (e.g. buying the iPad). In the automatic path, in contrast, the focus is on the *attitude towards the object* (e.g. the iPad itself). This reflects two important bodies of research on the attitude–behaviour relationship in social psychology. In the former tradition, researchers such as Fishbein (e.g. Ajzen & Fishbein, 1977) emphasize the need to match the measures of attitude to the thing (object) being predicted in terms of action, target, context, and timeframe in order to maximize the predictive power of attitudes (the principle of correspondence). Hence, if we wish to predict the purchase (action) of Tropicana orange juice (target) at the local supermarket (context) in the next week (timeframe), then our attitude measure should be framed at the same level of generality (e.g. my buying Tropicana orange juice at my local supermarket in the next week is: bad–good). In the latter tradition, researchers such as Fazio argue that such attitude measures are too specific to have widespread application (e.g. sometimes it is the object or target that is of interest rather than what we do with it) and in contrast emphasize the need to examine attitudes towards objects (e.g. orange juice is: bad–good). This tradition also emphasizes the importance of measuring how quickly such judgements can be made as a measure of the strength of an attitude rather than evaluation (e.g. judging an object as bad–good). The assumption is that attitudes that can be reported more quickly are more likely to influence behaviour because they can be automatically brought to mind in the presence of the attitude object or related cues. The classic demonstration of this effect is a study by Fazio and Williams (1986). They showed that attitudes towards objects were strong predictors of behaviour when individuals could quickly bring the attitude to mind but weaker predictors of behaviour when they were slow to bring the attitude to mind. The attitude object was the politician Ronald Reagan and the behaviour was voting for Reagan in the upcoming presidential election. Among those who were slower in reporting their reaction to Reagan, the correlation between the evaluation (i.e. attitude) of Reagan and voting for Reagan was $r = .66$ while among those with the faster reaction to Reagan the correlation was $r = .89$ (i.e. a stronger attitude–behaviour relationship). Other research shows that direct experience with the attitude object appears to be a key determinant of attitude accessibility.

These two traditions of work on the attitude–behaviour relationship have generally remained quite distinct. Fazio's (1990) MODE model represents one useful contribution to combining these two traditions and specifying when these different influences will dominate. So, when we have the motivation and opportunity to think things through, models such as the TPB (focusing on the attitude towards the behaviour) provide good descriptions of how attitudes (and other factors) influence behaviour. When motivation and/or opportunity are lacking then a simpler process best describes how attitudes towards the object influence behaviour (i.e. we tend to approach, support, or enhance attitude objects provided we have positive attitudes towards them).

Attitude change

We now turn to attitude change. Changing our attitudes in response to a persuasive message is something with which we are all familiar. But what factors influence the amount of attitude change? Social psychologists have looked at a range of factors that influence attitude change. We focus on cognitive dissonance theory and the elaboration likelihood model.

Cognitive dissonance theory

Cognitive dissonance theory (Festinger, 1957) claims that we are motivated to maintain a consistent view of the world because cognitive inconsistency creates dissonance, which is inherently unpleasant. This idea has inspired a whole area of social psychology research showing that getting individuals to act in a way that is inconsistent with their attitudes can change those attitudes and behaviour. This is assumed to happen because acting in a way that is not in accordance with our attitudes makes us feel uncomfortable. This feeling of discomfort is labelled **cognitive dissonance**. When we experience cognitive dissonance, we are motivated to reduce it by changing our attitudes to bring them more in line with our behaviour. For example, Zanna and Cooper (1974) showed that writing an essay that went against their views (i.e. counter-attitudinal) could lead individuals to change their attitudes in the direction of what was written in the essay. Importantly, this effect was strongest when individuals believed they had freely chosen to write the essay (i.e. taken responsibility for the action). The study also showed that the individual must experience some discomfort (i.e. dissonance), which they attribute to the behaviour (i.e. writing the essay), for the effect to occur. In Zanna and Cooper's study, participants were given a pill that would ostensibly make them either aroused or relaxed (it actually contained no active ingredients). In the aroused condition, the participants had a ready-made explanation for why they felt aroused (i.e. it was the pill) after writing the essay. In this case there was little attitude change after writing the essay because they thought changing their attitude was unlikely to reduce their feelings of discomfort. In contrast, in the condition where they expected the pill to make them feel relaxed, the effect of writing the essay on attitude change was even stronger. In this case, they could not explain their feeling of discomfort after writing the essay with reference to the pill (indeed, the pill should have been making them relaxed so writing the essay must have been the reason for their not feeling relaxed). The best way to reduce that discomfort or dissonance was to change their attitude to make it more in line with what they had written in the essay. This work shows that attitude change resulting from cognitive dissonance is most likely when people perceive negative consequences of the attitude-inconsistent action, when they take personal responsibility for the action, and when they attribute unpleasant arousal (i.e. dissonance) to the action.

Cognitive dissonance theory provides the basis for changing attitudes but obviously only applies to a very specific set of circumstances. What about the more common situation of attitude change in response to a persuasive message, such as that in a television or magazine advertisement?

The elaboration likelihood model

The elaboration likelihood model (Petty & Cacioppo, 1986) was developed to help account for the factors that explain attitude change in response to a persuasive message. One key factor is your reaction to the message – if your reactions to the message are mainly positive, then more attitude change will occur; if your reactions are negative or quite mixed, little or no attitude change will occur (Petty & Cacioppo, 1986). Social psychological models of attitude change suggest that there are two distinct routes to attitude change after reacting to a persuasive message. In one route, the information in the persuasive message is systematically and carefully considered and attitude change is determined by the extent to which the message produces mainly favourable thoughts about the message. Therefore, if after reading a message about the features of a new Blu-ray player you have mainly positive thoughts, then your attitude towards buying this Blu-ray player is likely to become more positive. This 'route' or way to persuasion is called the **central or systematic route**. It is what we traditionally think of as persuasion and requires quite a bit of mental effort. The second route to persuasion does not require such careful scrutiny of the message or detailed thought. Here attitude change depends on the presence of peripheral cues that prompt the use of heuristics. For example, one heuristic is that messages from an expert are more likely to be believed and lead to positive reactions to the message and subsequent attitude change independent of the message content. That is, if a message is known to come from an expert, it will generally produce more attitude change than a message from a non-expert. This route to persuasion is called the **peripheral or heuristic route** and requires little mental effort or detailed thought. Figure 18.9 sets out the two routes in the elaboration likelihood model, the factors influencing which route dominates, and the consequences of each route for attitude change.

Petty and Cacioppo (1986) argue that, because we receive so many messages, we do not have the motivation or ability to carefully process each one. Therefore, only for some messages will we have the motivation and ability to process systematically or centrally. For other messages, a lack of motivation or ability will force us to process them in a less effortful manner; here peripheral or heuristic processing will take place. Petty and Cacioppo refer to the amount of systematic processing devoted to a message as **cognitive elaboration** and, consequently, their model is known as the elaboration likelihood model. High elaboration is associated with central route (or effortful) processing of messages while low elaboration is associated with peripheral route (or effortless) processing. A very similar model, the heuristic–systematic model, labels these as the 'systematic' and 'heuristic' routes to persuasion (Chaiken, 1980).

Likelihood of elaboration is determined by both motivation and ability to think about persuasive messages. When we are highly motivated because the message is about an issue of interest to us, we are more likely to elaborate and so engage in central route processing (Petty & Cacioppo, 1986). Ability to think about a message is

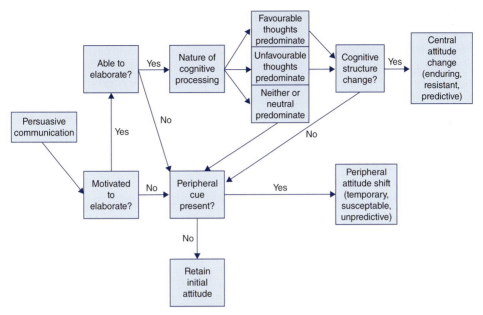

FIGURE 18.9 *A representation of the elaboration likelihood model. When an individual is motivated and able to elaborate, central route processing will occur. If central route processing happens, then attitude change will occur if the message produces mainly favourable (positive attitude change) or unfavourable (negative attitude change) thoughts. Attitude change through this route will produce attitudes that are strong (i.e. enduring, resistant to other change attempts, and predictive of behaviour). When an individual is not motivated or able to elaborate, then peripheral route processing will occur. If peripheral route processing happens, then attitude change will occur if a peripheral cue is present (e.g. the message is from an expert). Attitude change through this route will produce attitudes that are weak (i.e. more temporary, susceptible to other change attempts, and unpredictive of behaviour).*

Source: Adapted from Petty and Cacioppo (1986). Copyright 1986, with permission from Elsevier.

determined by factors such as not having time pressure or distraction, and again this increases the likelihood of elaboration (Petty & Cacioppo, 1986). When motivation or ability is low, then elaboration will be less likely and persuasion can occur mainly through the peripheral route. Central route processing involves greater cognitive elaboration and the strength of the arguments in the message is critical to the amount of persuasion that occurs (via making us think positive thoughts about the message). Here, therefore, the amount of attitude change is dependent on the arguments being strong. This is consistent with traditional views of how persuasion works: strong arguments will persuade us to change our views; weak arguments will be dismissed and have little impact on attitude change.

In contrast, peripheral route processing involves little systematic processing (low cognitive elaboration) and other characteristics of the message are more likely to determine whether or not it is persuasive. For example, people use simple rules or decision-making heuristics to evaluate messages (Chaiken, 1980). These include 'expertise = accuracy' (i.e. she's an expert so what she says must be right), 'consensus = correctness' (i.e. if so many people agree, they must be right), and 'length = strength' (i.e. there are lots of arguments for something so it must be true). Sometimes situational constraints force people into peripheral route processing. For example, the message may be presented quickly amid distractions, as is the case in many television advertisements. In addition, individual differences mean that some people are more or less likely than others to engage in systematic processing. For example, Chaiken (1980) identified people who agreed or disagreed with the length = strength heuristic (using agreement with questionnaire items such as 'the more reasons a person has for some point of view, the more likely he/she is to be correct'). These people were then presented with a message containing six arguments in favour of cross-course, end-of-year examinations for students. However, the message was described to participants as either containing ten or two arguments (although it always contained the same six arguments). The results showed that those who endorsed the length = strength heuristic were more likely to be persuaded when the message was described as having ten arguments than were those who did not endorse the heuristic. See Activity 18.1 for an exercise that you can complete on changing behaviours through persuasion.

ACTIVITY 18.1

CHANGING BEHAVIOURS THROUGH PERSUASION

1. Pick an important behaviour that you might want to change (e.g. increasing physical activity in young people).

2. Plan how you might develop an intervention to go about changing this behaviour by targeting attitudes towards this behaviour. Hint: focus on both how you might develop short but strong persuasive messages and how you might use peripheral cues to persuade. Focus on the attitude and the elaboration likelihood model in particular (you might find it useful to refer to Figure 18.9).

3. How might you go about evaluating the effectiveness of your attempts to change this behaviour? Hint: think about how you might develop measures of attitudes towards this behaviour that might be expected to change as a result of the intervention you develop.

SECTION SUMMARY

- Attitudes are motivating forces that are relatively enduring in nature and are evaluative in nature.

- Attitudes can be measured in a variety of ways, all of which require the individual to evaluate the attitude object on a positive-to-negative dimension.

- Attitudes are related to behaviour (i.e. we tend to approach attitude objects we evaluate positively) and predictive models have been developed to explain how attitudes and other factors guide related behaviour.

- The best way to change attitudes is an important area of research.

- Most modern views of attitude change suggest that attitude change can occur through two different routes.

- In one route (central route) the strength of the message is the key determinant of change; in the other (peripheral route), it is the presence of cues in the message that prompt the use of heuristics (e.g. if the message is from an expert, it is likely to be correct and we should change our attitudes accordingly). Only when motivation and opportunity permit will central route processing occur.

AUTOMATIC PROCESSES IN SOCIAL COGNITION

LEARNING OBJECTIVE 18.7

Describe the differences between automatic and controlled processes, particularly with regard to behavioural priming.

Experienced drivers will know the feeling of arriving at a familiar destination with very little memory of the numerous essential automotive actions enacted to safely make that journey. Similarly, much of our social life is driven by unconscious and **automatic processes**. The impact that automatic processes have in guiding our social cognition is so pervasive that we have already touched on it multiple times in this chapter, discussing a number of dual-process models that talk about the operation of automatic processes in comparison to their more controlled counterparts. For example, we touched on Devine's (1989) dual-process model of stereotyping, which argues that, while stereotype activation is automatic, stereotype application is under an individual's control. Similarly, you learned about the automatic (i.e. peripheral) and controlled (i.e. central) routes to persuasion in Petty and Cacioppo's (1986) elaboration likelihood model. But what exactly defines processing as automatic, and how is it distinct from a **controlled process**?

Automatic and controlled thinking

Schneider and Shiffrin (1977) define automatic processes as those that are activated (almost) with inevitability, without the need for attention or any form of control on the part of the actor. On the other hand, controlled processes are inherently dependent on active attention and control. More recently, Bargh (1994) has suggested that four key factors determine whether a process can be thought of as automatic as opposed to controlled: namely, lack of awareness, absence of intention, absence of control, and greater efficiency. However, the classification of automaticity is likely to be more complex than a simple dichotomy. As the examples in the previous paragraph demonstrate, it is clear that many social behaviours have both automatic and controlled components and features. Social psychologists therefore use Bargh's four criteria (which he called his 'four horsemen of automaticity') not as a strict benchmark for ultimate automaticity but to help us communicate what particular aspect of automaticity we are referring to when we say that a process or behaviour is automatic or controlled.

Awareness

Automatic processes are characterized by a lack of awareness of the operation of the process or, alternatively, its effects. Earlier, we talked about how Chen and Bargh (1997) found an effect of priming on the hostility of participants' behaviour. They used a subliminal prime – African Americans or Caucasians – by presenting participants with photos of African American or Caucasian faces at an exposure time that was too short to be consciously perceived. Because participants in this study were unaware of the prime, its influence on prompting hostile behaviour can be attributed to the operation of automatic processes.

Intention and control

Automatic processes are initiated without the deliberate intention of the individual and, relatedly, are seen as uncontrollable. Understandably, the prospect that many of our social actions are operating without our intention and beyond our control can be quite alarming, and it has considerable real-world relevance. In New York in 1999, a West African immigrant called Amidou Diallo was killed by a group of white police officers who mistook the wallet he withdrew from his pocket as a gun. This event prompted mass protests and demonstrations against racial profiling. Shortly afterwards, however, Payne (2001) found similar effects in the laboratory, demonstrating that, when participants were asked to respond under time pressure (as the police offers in the Diallo case would have been), they were more likely to incorrectly identify pictures of tools as guns after priming with an African American face as opposed to a Caucasian face.

Importantly, Payne (2001) also examined whether the processes responsible for these errors were intentional and controllable, or automatic and inescapable. Using a procedure known as process dissociation, Payne was able to separate out the influences of automatic and controlled processes by comparing responses on trials where an automatic bias and conscious decision would result in the same judgement (e.g. a picture of a gun following an African American prime) with those where judgements would be different (e.g. a picture of a tool following an African American prime). Using this procedure, Payne (2001) demonstrated that the effect of racial cues on weapons misidentification was due to automatic rather than controlled processing.

Efficiency

Finally, automatic processes should be efficient, sparing our cognitive resources. Indeed, one way in which researchers examine whether a process is operating automatically is to put participants under cognitive load. Winter, Uleman, and Cunniff (1985), for example, found that the tendency for people to make spontaneous trait inferences is not affected by cognitive load, suggesting that they operate automatically. On the other hand, more recent research by Wells, Skowronski, Crawford, Scherer, and Carlston (2011) found evidence that these inferences *are* interrupted by cognitive load, suggesting that some degree of controlled processing may be needed for their operation.

Behavioural priming

While there are many examples of automatic phenomena in social psychology, one in particular often catches people's attention and has been the subject of recent controversy. In 1996, Bargh, Chen, and Burrows demonstrated that participants primed with politeness-related words in a scrambled sentence task were less likely to subsequently interrupt a conversation between the experimenter and a confederate than if they were primed with rudeness-related words. In a second experiment, participants primed with words that were stereotypically associated with the elderly in a similar scrambled sentence task took longer to walk to the elevator after exiting the experiment compared with participants primed with neutral words.

Since this original demonstration of **behavioural priming**, a large body of research has replicated the effect across a range of contexts and behaviours. For example, research suggests that participants asked to imagine the typical behaviours and characteristics of professors later do better on a general knowledge test than participants who instead imagine the behaviours and characteristics of secretaries (Dijksterhuis & Van Knippenberg, 1998). You may also have spotted the similarities between behavioural priming and the self-fulfilling prophecy effect demonstrated by Chen and Bargh (1997). Chen and Bargh showed that participants primed with African American faces behaved in a more hostile (stereotypical) way than participants who were not primed. Other research has examined moderators of the effect. Macrae and Johnston (1998) demonstrated that behavioural priming effects can be overridden by situational cues and perceiver goals. They found that, while participants primed with help-related constructs in a scrambled sentence task were more likely to help an experimenter pick up her dropped pens than non-primed participants, this behavioural priming effect disappeared if the pens were covered in ink or if the participant was late for another experiment. More recent research suggests that behavioural priming effects can also be counteracted by using **implementation intentions** (Gollwitzer, Sheeran, Trötschel, & Webb, 2011).

Despite this large pool of research, some attempts to replicate behavioural priming effects have been unsuccessful (e.g. Doyen, Klein, Pichon, & Cleeremans, 2012; Shanks et al., 2013). This has been the catalyst for a heated debate as to whether behavioural priming effects are real or the result of methodological biases.

FOCUS POINT 18.3

THE REPLICATION CRISIS

Replication in psychology is more important than ever following reports of the suggested bias towards publishing significant findings (Asendorpf et al., 2013). Fanelli's (2012) review of published research found that psychology hypotheses are confirmed 92% of the time, a seemingly much higher rate than what should be expected, highlighting the potentially distorting effects of the **file-drawer problem**.

In particular, the social psychology research area of priming has come under fire for problems with replication. Psychologists attempting to replicate several popular priming effects have often failed (e.g. Doyen et al., 2012; Shanks et al., 2013). For instance, Shanks et al. (2013) attempted to replicate Dijksterhuis and Van Knippenberg's (1998) intelligence prime study across several experiments, where participants primed with the concept of 'professor' versus 'soccer hooligan' correctly answered more general knowledge questions. In contrast, Shanks and colleagues found no evidence that priming intelligence influenced participants' behaviour in any of their studies, and argued that priming effects do not stand up to scrutiny. However, there may have been problems with the replication studies themselves. Dijksterhuis (2013) criticized how Shanks et al. (2013) conducted the replication experiments, arguing that their experiments contained too few participants and that the participants varied too greatly in age (in one of Shanks' studies, the participants' ages ranged from 19 to 79 years).

In order to tackle problems rooted in the current culture of psychology, such as unreplicable findings, it is important to develop a range of systematic measures (see Asendorpf et al., 2013). Recommendations include establishing more rigorous testing in the peer-reviewed publication process. Emphasis should be placed on the quality instead of the quantity of publications, with universities moving away from rewarding researchers for the sheer number of their publications and towards considering their content and relevance (Asendorpf et al., 2013). This will help to reduce the pressure to publish significant and eye-catching results, which contributes to the file-drawer problem, whereby significant findings are published more often than null findings.

In addition, the **Open Science Framework** is a promising new project that offers researchers the opportunity to archive, share, and register research materials and data. Such collaborative efforts will help to provide greater data transparency and communication among psychology researchers. Indeed, researchers must work together to establish clear guidelines (Levelt Committee, 2012) that will improve the way social psychological research is conducted, thereby helping the discipline to return to being one of the leading areas of psychology (Asendorpf et al., 2013).

DISCUSSION POINT

Think of some examples of automatic and controlled thinking from your own experience and discuss how these may influence your behaviour.

TEST YOURSELF

1. What are Bargh's (1994) four horsemen of automaticity?
2. What is behavioural priming?

SECTION SUMMARY

- Many social behaviours operate automatically, without conscious intention or awareness, or the opportunity to control their operation.
- Automatic processes are beneficial in that they are efficient and do not overly tax our limited cognitive resources; this is essential given the complexity of our social world.
- However, as the case of Amidou Diallo demonstrates, automatic processes are a double-edged sword and may also have unwelcome consequences.

FUTURE DIRECTIONS

LEARNING OBJECTIVE 18.8

Critically evaluate possible future directions for research in social cognition and attitudes.

The research discussed in this chapter bears testament to the varied and valuable research conducted on social cognition and attitudes. However, the field faces a number of challenges to restore and improve its research culture (Levelt Committee, 2012) following the replication crisis. It is important that social psychologists conduct accurate and meaningful research rather than focusing exclusively on producing large numbers of eye-catching findings based on weak effects. Greater emphasis should also be placed on replication and transparency of results through projects such as the Open Science Framework. In the long term, new challenges for social psychology are continuing to arise from the emerging field of **social neuroscience**, which has the potential to make a substantial contribution to psychological research (Amodio, 2010). It is important that social cognition and attitudes research also develops further in new directions, including placing a greater emphasis on social *context*. For example, stereotypes and attitudes are too often considered as rigid cognitive structures lacking flexibility across situations (see Casper, Rothermund, & Wentura, 2010). At the start of the chapter we referred to Henri Tajfel's contention that social context should underpin social psychology – it is an important statement that may guide the future of research in social cognition and attitudes.

RESEARCH METHODS 18.2

THE RISE OF SOCIAL NEUROSCIENCE

Social psychologists and cognitive neuroscientists have started to work together. In recent years there has been a dramatic increase in the number of studies investigating the neural underpinnings of social behaviour (De Haan & Gunnar, 2009). Historically, the psychological and biological sciences were largely viewed as incompatible. However, the rise of social neuroscience, a new interdisciplinary field of research, has offered a fresh approach to understanding social cognition.

Social neuroscience uses three levels of analysis:

1. *the social level*, which focuses on motivational and social factors that influence behaviour and experience

2. *the cognitive level*, involving information-processing mechanisms

3. *the neural level*, which focuses on how brain mechanisms control cognitive-level processes (Ochsner & Lieberman, 2001).

Understanding how these three levels interact enables researchers to develop a bigger picture of complex psychological phenomena.

The development of new tools, such as **functional magnetic resonance imagining (fMRI)**, has enabled researchers to investigate human brain activity when engaging in social processing. For example, fMRI has been used to measure participants' brain activity when judging the sex of a target, thereby helping us to understand which parts of the brain are associated with social categorization (Cloutier, Turk, & Macrae, 2008). Therefore, despite being a relatively young field, social neuroscience is developing and advancing the way social psychological research is undertaken to understand human behaviour (Amodio, 2010).

SECTION SUMMARY

- Social cognition and attitudes research is wide and varied but faces challenges in the replication of findings and producing meaningful research.
- The recent focus on social neuroscience has opened up new areas in understanding how social, cognitive, and neural levels interact in producing social perception.

CHAPTER SUMMARY

This chapter has considered a wide range of theories that underpin social cognition and attitudes. Advanced culture depends on a highly developed social cognitive ability, and humans are unique in this respect (Dunbar, 2003). Clearly, the self-concept is at the heart of social thinking, consisting of information about not only who we are but also who we aim to be (Higgins, 1987). Social identity theorists have argued that multiple personal and social identities make up our self-concept (e.g. Tajfel & Turner, 1979). When attempting to understand the behaviour of others, we have the ability to switch from slow and effortful thinking to applying simple rules or heuristics. This switching depends on the requirements of the social situation (Brewer, 1988; Eagly & Chaiken, 1993). However, heuristic thinking is associated with a number of attributional biases or errors. The best known of these is the fundamental attribution error – a tendency to make internal attributions for others' behaviour based on stable personality dispositions, even when faced with contradictory evidence (Ross, 1977).

To organize information about others, we rely on a method called 'categorization', involving matching people's attributes to a category. Alternatively, we can form impressions based on an individual's unique attributes when categorization is difficult or impossible, and this is called 'individuation'. It is evident that categorization forms the basis for stereotyping, stereotypes being widely held generalizations about a particular group (Hilton & von Hippel, 1996). Because stereotypes rely on stored social categories, they are easily activated and require very little cognitive effort.

Attitudes are dispositions that people use to evaluate objects or entities (Eagly & Chaiken, 1993; Fishbein & Ajzen, 1975). According to the 'ABC' or 'tripartite' model (Maio & Olson, 2000), attitudes are made up of three components: affective, behavioural, and cognitive. Attitudes can, at times, be difficult to measure using traditional questionnaire-based responses when the topic of interest is socially sensitive (e.g. prejudice). Therefore, social psychologists have developed non-self-report measures, including the implicit association test (Greenwald & Banaji, 1995), that seemingly measure attitudes more accurately.

Cognitive dissonance theory (Festinger, 1957) is based on the premise of encouraging people to behave in ways that are inconsistent with their attitudes in order to modify those attitudes and alter behaviour, but cognitive dissonance theory only applies to specific circumstances. Attitude change following persuasive messages (e.g. advertisements) has been investigated using the elaboration likelihood model (Petty & Cacioppo, 1986). According to this model, persuasion follows two routes: the central route, requiring (controlled) cognitive effort, or the peripheral (automatic) route, which requires little effort. Finally, the distinction between automatic and controlled processing plays a significant role in many areas of social cognition and attitudes. These two processes are often differentiated using Bargh's (1994) four criteria – the 'four horsemen of automaticity': lack of awareness, absence of intention, absence of control, and greater efficiency.

ESSAY QUESTIONS

1. How do we organize our social thinking? Refer to relevant theories and perspectives.

2. Stereotype threat may be one factor underlying the under-representation of women in STEM (science, technology, engineering, and mathematics) fields. Explain why this may be the case and how we can remedy it.

3. Explain how we use social inference to try to understand the causes of our own and others' behaviour. Refer to relevant theories and perspectives.

KEY TERMS

- **attitudes:** Motivating forces that influence what we do and that are relatively enduring in nature. Attitudes are our evaluations of or feelings towards a particular object or target.
- **attribution bias:** Biases in our attribution theories developed to explain and predict other people's behaviour. For example, correspondence bias refers to our tendency to attribute others' behaviour to stable personality dispositions.
- **attribution theories:** Informal theories that we develop to explain and predict how other people will behave.
- **automatic processes:** Processes that are activated without intention or the need for conscious control. Automatic processes are also characterized by a lack of awareness and greater efficiency.
- **behavioural priming:** An automatic effect of priming on behaviour that occurs without awareness, such that behaviour is consistent with the activated construct.
- **central or systematic route:** Persuasion based on careful thought about the persuasive message.
- **cognitive dissonance:** An uncomfortable feeling generated when we act contrary to our attitudes.
- **cognitive elaboration:** The amount of message-relevant thinking we undertake when faced with a persuasive message.
- **cognitive load:** The degree to which current activities or tasks tax the limited capacity of working memory. Having participants engage in concurrent tasks is a common method for inducing high cognitive load.
- **cognitive miser:** A term referring to the tendency to be miserly in applying a systematic approach to dealing with the large number of social inferences we face each day (Nisbett & Ross, 1980). Where we can, we save time and our mental resources by using simple rules or heuristics to form impressions or make judgements in relation to others.
- **controlled process:** A process that is intentionally initiated and directed by the individual. In contrast to automatic processes, controlled processes are highly taxing on cognitive resources.
- **emergent attributes:** Attributes or traits used to form impressions that are independent of the activated categories. For example, when forming an impression of a female mechanic, the attribute 'butch' may be applied, but this attribute is unlikely to be used when describing a female or a mechanic independently.
- **explicit measures:** A class of measures that directly tap into a construct by asking people to report on it; an example is self-report questionnaires where individuals rate their own attitudes.
- **file-drawer problem:** The tendency to publish successful or significant findings and ignore failures (i.e. file them away).

- **functional magnetic resonance imagining (fMRI):** fMRI scanners measure blood flow to particular areas of the brain, potentially indicating which brain region is activated for specific social tasks.
- **fuzzy boundaries:** A term referring to the fact that categories tend to have unclear or uncertain boundaries because they are organized around the most prototypical exemplars (Rosch, 1978). Therefore, it is often unclear where categorical boundaries begin and end.
- **heuristics:** Shortcut methods by which inferences can be made that are accurate enough for perceivers to apply to the task at hand (e.g. impression formation).
- **illusory correlation:** The false perception of a relationship or correlation between two variables when none actually exists.
- **implementation intentions:** 'If–then' plans that specify a particular behaviour to be performed in a set situation; for example, 'If I see my psychology textbook, then I will sit down and read it.'
- **implicit association test (IAT):** A reaction-time test used to measure attitudes towards sensitive topics such as race in a way that is difficult to fake.
- **implicit measures:** A class of measures that indirectly and unobtrusively tap into a construct – for example, attitude implicit association tests, where individuals make speeded categorizations of stimuli.
- **inconsistency resolution:** The process by which a perceiver employs a mentally effortful search in their memory for stereotype-inconsistent material. Failure to find inconsistent material leads to a conscious, effortful process to reconcile the inconsistent material.
- **individuation:** The process of differentiating individuals from their group memberships based on a trait-by-trait approach or by using naive theories in order to understand how a person can be a member of a given category or categories.
- **in-groups:** Collections of people who share a group affiliation. The affiliation can be based on gender, race, religion, occupation, or a multitude of other categories. See also **out-groups**.
- **motivated tactician:** According to Fiske and Taylor (1991) 'a fully engaged thinker who has multiple cognitive strategies available and chooses among them based on goals, motives, and needs' (p. 13).
- **multiple categorization:** This occurs when two or more social categories are simultaneously active in a perceiver's thoughts when they are attempting to form an impression of a target person.
- **naive scientist:** According Heider (1958), people think like amateur or naive scientists when attempting to describe and understand the behaviour of others. This involves constructing an explanation (theory) for an observed effect (i.e. behaviour).
- **normative beliefs:** A person's perception about a given behaviour that is shaped by significant others, including friends, parents, and in-groups.
- **Open Science Framework:** An online project to allow the results of psychological studies to be uploaded and shared with others in an open and transparent manner.
- **out-groups:** Collections of people who do not share a group affiliation in terms of their gender, race, religion, occupation, or a multitude of other categories. See also **in-groups**.
- **peripheral or heuristic route:** A means of persuasion based not on careful thought about the persuasive message but rather on the presence of cues (e.g. the expert nature of the source).
- **priming:** A process whereby exposure to external cues activates a particular concept in the mind and makes it more accessible. The cues are referred to as 'primes' and may be deliberately manipulated (e.g. exposure to specific words or pictures) or naturally occurring.
- **principle of correspondence:** The idea that attitudes will predict behaviour when both are measured at the same level of specificity in relation to the target, action, context, and timeframe.
- **private self-awareness:** A state of self-awareness where personal and internal aspects of the self are salient.
- **prototype:** The most typical member, or an averaging of the features of all members, of a given category.

- **public self-awareness:** A state of self-awareness where public and external aspects of the self are salient.
- **replication:** In research, an observed effect is replicated when it is reproduced in a subsequent study. This reinforces the reliability and validity of observed effects, suggesting that they are genuine.
- **self-affirmation:** A process of affirming and reflecting on important personal values, which can help to reduce defensiveness to threatening information.
- **self-awareness:** A transient state of self-focused attention where you are aware of and able to reflect on aspects of your self. This is also known as objective self-awareness. Subjective self-awareness describes the general ability to distinguish ourselves from the environment around us.
- **self-concept:** The set of beliefs or knowledge that people have about themselves, such as the characteristics or traits that they possess. This may encompass both personal and social selves and identities.
- **self-esteem:** The evaluative or attitudinal component of your self-concept – that is, how you feel towards your self.
- **self-fulfilling prophecy:** The validation of beliefs and expectancies that occurs when our expectations lead us to unintentionally behave in a way that provokes expectancy-consistent behaviour in others.
- **self-perception theory:** A theory developed by Daryl Bem (1972) based on the premise that attitudes are developed through the observation of our own behaviour and our subsequent decisions about which attitude may have been causal in the behaviour.
- **self-schemas:** The cognitive representations of the various identities and facets of the self that make up your self-concept. We hold self-schemas for characteristics that are important to us and that we are sure we possess.
- **social categorization:** The allocation of a target person to category membership based on features, traits, or attributes they share with that category.
- **social cognition:** The International Social Cognition Network (2018) defines social cognition as follows: 'Social cognition is not a content area, but rather is an approach to understanding social psychology. It is a level of analysis that aims to understand social psychological phenomena by investigating the cognitive processes that underlie them.'
- **social comparison:** The idea that we define ourselves through comparison with others.
- **social identity theory:** A theory based on the premise that our self-concept is derived from both social and personal identity. Group affiliations determine social identity and this in turn influences our attitudes and behaviours in intergroup situations.
- **social neuroscience:** A relatively new area of investigation in which the focus is not only social representations and their associated processes but also the neural substrates involved.
- **stereotype activation:** The degree to which a stereotype is accessible or salient in the mind.
- **stereotype application:** The use of stereotypes in judgements or decisions about a member of the relevant social group – for example, when forming an impression.
- **stereotype threat:** The anxiety or threat experienced by a person when there is a possibility that they may act in a way that confirms negative stereotypes.
- **stereotype:** A set of traits, characteristics, and behaviours that a society thinks is typical of a particular group of people.
- **subjective norms:** The perception of social pressure to engage or not engage in a particular behaviour.
- **subliminal priming:** A form of priming where primes are presented outside conscious awareness – for example, by presenting them for too short a time to be consciously perceived, or presenting them in people's parafoveal visual field.
- **ultimate attribution error:** An attributional bias reflecting the tendency to attribute negative stereotypical behaviours performed by the out-group to dispositional traits, but positive counter-stereotypical behaviours to situational causes.

NOTE

1. https://www.youtube.com/watch?v=vvwvvbiwRkg

FURTHER RESOURCES

Ajzen, I. (1988). *Attitudes, personality, and behaviour*. Buckingham, UK: Open University Press.

Ajzen, I. (1991). The theory of planned behaviour. *Organizational Behaviour and Human Decision Processes, 50*, 179–211.

Baumeister, R. F., & Bushman, B. J. (2012). *Social psychology and human nature*. Belmont, CA: Wadsworth.

Doyen, S., Klein, O., Pichon, C. L., & Cleeremans, A. (2012). Behavioural priming: It's all in the mind, but whose mind? *PloS ONE, 7*(1), e29081.

Epley, N., & Kruger, J. (2005). When what you type isn't what they read: The perseverance of stereotypes and expectancies over e-mail. *Journal of Experimental Social Psychology, 41*(4), 414–422.

Fiske, S. T., & Neuberg, S. L. (1990). A continuum of impression formation from category based to individuating process: Influences of information and motivation on attention an interpretation. *Advances in Experimental Social Psychology, 23*, 1–74.

Fiske, S. T., & Taylor, S. E. (2013). *Social cognition: From brains to culture*. London, UK: SAGE Publications.

David, C., Funder, C. D., Levine, J. M., Mackie, D. M., Morf, C., Vazire. S., & West, S. G. (2013). Social psychology research and educational practice: Recommendations for improving the dependability of research in personality. *Personality and Social Psychology Review, 18*(1), 3–12.

Gervais, W. M., & Norenzayan, A. (2012). Like a camera in the sky? Thinking about God increases public self-awareness and socially desirable responding. *Journal of Experimental Social Psychology, 48*(1), 298–302.

Hutter, R. R. C., & Crisp, R. J. (2005). The composition of category conjunctions. *Personality and Social Psychology Bulletin, 31*, 647–657.

Macrae, C. N., & Johnston, L. (1998). Help, I need somebody: Automatic action and inaction. *Social Cognition, 16*(4), 400–417.

Tversky, A., & Kahneman, D. (1974). Judgement under uncertainty: Heuristics and biases. *Science, 185*, 1124–1131.

REFERENCES

Ajzen, I. (1991). The theory of planned behavior. *Organizational Behavior and Human Decision Processes, 50*, 179–211.

Ajzen, I., & Fishbein, M. (1977). Attitude–behavior relations: A theoretical analysis and review of empirical research. *Psychological Bulletin, 84*, 888–918.

Allport, F. H. (1924). *Social psychology*. Boston, MA: Houghton Mifflin.

Allport, G. W. (1935). Attitudes. In C. M. Murchison (Ed.), *Handbook of social psychology* (pp. 789–844). Worcester, MA: Clark University Press.

Alter, A. L., Aronson, J., Darley, J. M., Rodriguez, C., & Ruble, D. N. (2010). Rising to the threat: Reducing stereotype threat by reframing the threat as a challenge. *Journal of Experimental Social Psychology, 46*(1), 166–171.

Ambady, N., Paik, S. K., Steele, J., Owen-Smith, A., & Mitchell, J. P. (2004). Deflecting negative self-relevant stereotype activation: The effects of individuation. *Journal of Experimental Social Psychology, 40*(3), 401–408.

Amodio, D. M. (2010). Can neuroscience advance social psychological theory? Social neuroscience for the behavioural social psychologist. *Social Cognition, 28*(6), 695–716.

Armitage, C. J., & Conner, M. (2001). Efficacy of the theory of planned behaviour: A meta-analytic review. *British Journal of Social Psychology, 40*, 471–499.

Asendorpf, J. B., Conner, M., De Fruyt, F., De Houwer, J., Denissen, J. J. A., Fiedler, K., … Wicherts, J. M. (2013). Recommendations for increasing replicability in psychology. *European Journal of Personality, 27*, 108–119.

Banaji, M. R., & Prentice, D. A. (1994). The self in social contexts. *Annual Review of Psychology, 45*(1), 297–332.

Bargh, J. A. (1994). The four horsemen of automaticity: Awareness, intention, efficiency, and control in social cognition. In R. S. Wyer, Jr., & T. K. Srull (Eds.), *Handbook of social cognition* (2nd ed., Vol. 1, pp. 1–40). Hillsdale, NJ: Lawrence Erlbaum Associates.

Bargh, J. A., Chen, M., & Burrows, L. (1996). Automaticity of social behavior: Direct effects of trait construct and stereotype activation on action. *Journal of Personality and Social Psychology, 71*(2), 230–244.

Barrett, L. F., & Bliss-Moreau, E. (2009). She's emotional, he's having a bad day: Attributional explanations for emotion stereotypes. *Emotion, 9*(5), 649–658.

Baumeister, R. F. (1999). Self-concept, self-esteem, and identity. In V. Derlega, B. Winstead, & W. Jones (Eds.), *Personality: Contemporary theory and research* (2nd ed., pp. 339–375). Chicago, IL: Nelson-Hall.

Baumeister, R. F., Campbell, J. D., Krueger, J. I., & Vohs, K. D. (2003). Does high self-esteem cause better performance, interpersonal success, happiness, or healthier lifestyles? *Psychological Science in the Public Interest, 4*(1), 1–44.

Bem, D. J. (1972). Self-perception theory. In L. Berkowitz (Ed.), *Advances in experimental social psychology* (Vol. 6, pp. 1–62). New York, NY: Academic Press.

Blair, I. V., Ma, J. E., & Lenton, A. P. (2001). Imagining stereotypes away: The moderation of implicit stereotypes through mental imagery. *Journal of Personality and Social Psychology, 81*(5), 828–841.

Bodenhausen, G. V. (1990). Stereotypes as judgmental heuristics: Evidence of circadian variations in discrimination. *Psychological Science, 1*, 319–322.

Bodenhausen, G. V., & Wyer, R. S. (1985). Effects of stereotypes on decision making and information-processing strategies. *Journal of Personality and Social Psychology, 48*, 267–282.

Bodenhausen, G. V., Macrae, C., & Milne, A. B. (1998). Disregarding social stereotypes: Implications for memory, judgment, and behavior. In J. M. Golding & C. M. MacLeod (Eds.), *Intentional forgetting: Interdisciplinary approaches* (pp. 349–368). Mahwah, NJ: Lawrence Erlbaum Associates.

Brewer, M. B. (1988). A dual process model of impression formation. In T. K. Srull & R. S. Wyer (Eds.), *Advances in social cognition: A dual process model of impression formation* (Vol. 1, pp. 1–36). Hillsdale, NJ: Lawrence Erlbaum Associates.

Brewer, M. B., & Gardner, W. (1996). Who is this 'we'? Levels of collective identity and self representations. *Journal of Personality and Social Psychology, 71*(1), 83–93.

Byrne, R., & Whiten, A. (1988). *Machiavellian intelligence: Social expertise and the evolution of intellect in monkeys, apes, and humans.* Oxford, UK: Clarendon Press.

Carver, C. S., & Scheier, M. F. (1981). *Attention and self-regulation: A control theory approach to human behaviour.* New York, NY: Springer.

Casper, C., Rothermund, K., & Wentura, D. (2010). Automatic stereotype activation is context dependent. *Social Psychology, 41*, 131–136.

Chaiken, S. (1980). Heuristic versus systematic information processing and the use of source versus message cues in persuasion. *Journal of Personality and Social Psychology, 39*,(5) 752–766.

Chen, M., & Bargh, J. A. (1997). Nonconscious behavioral confirmation processes: The self-fulfilling consequences of automatic stereotype activation. *Journal of Experimental Social Psychology, 33*(5), 541–560.

Cialdini, R. B., Kallgren, C. A., & Reno, R. R. (1991). A focus theory of normative conduct: A theoretical refinement and reevaluation of the role of norms in human behavior. *Advances in Experimental Social Psychology, 24*, 201–234.

Cloutier, J., Turk, D., & Macrae, C. N. (2008). Extracting information from faces: The neural substrates of gaze detection and sex categorization. *Social Neuroscience, 3*, 69–78.

Cohen, C. E. (1981). Person categories and social perception: Testing some boundaries of the processing effects of prior knowledge. *Journal of Personality and Social Psychology, 40*, 441–452.

Cohen, G. L., Garcia, J., Apfel, N., & Master, A. (2006). Reducing the racial achievement gap: A social-psychological intervention. *Science, 313*, 1307–1310.

Crisp, R. J., Ensari, N., Hewstone, M., & Miller, N. (2003). A dual-route model of crossed categorization effects. In W. Stroebe & M. Hewstone (Eds.), *European review of social psychology* (Vol. 13, pp. 35–74). Hove, UK: Psychology Press.

Davies, P. G., Spencer, S. J., Quinn, D. M., & Gerhardstein, R. (2002). Consuming images: How television commercials that elicit stereotype threat can restrain women academically and professionally. *Personality and Social Psychology Bulletin, 28*(12), 1615–1628.

De Haan, M., & Gunnar, M. R. (2009). *Handbook of developmental social neuroscience*. New York, NY: Guilford Press.

DeSilva, J. M., & Lesnik, J. J. (2008). Brain size at birth throughout human evolution: A new method for estimating neonatal brain size in hominins. *Journal of Human Evolution, 55*, 1064–1074.

Devine, P. G. (1989). Stereotypes and prejudice: Their automatic and controlled components. *Journal of Personality and Social Psychology, 56*(1), 5–18.

Dijksterhuis, A. (2013, 25 April). Replication crisis or crisis in replication? A reinterpretation of Shanks et al. *PLoS ONE*. Retrieved 20 November 2017 from http://www.plosone.org/annotation/listThread.action?root=64751

Dijksterhuis, A., & Van Knippenberg, A. (1998). The relation between perception and behavior, or how to win a game of Trivial Pursuit. *Journal of Personality and Social Psychology, 74*, 865–877.

Doyen, S., Klein, O., Pichon, C. L., & Cleeremans, A. (2012). Behavioral priming: It's all in the mind, but whose mind? *PLoS ONE, 7*(1), e29081.

Dunbar, R. I. M. (2003). The social brain: Mind, language, and society in evolutionary perspective. *Annual Review of Anthropology, 32*, 163–181.

Duval, T. S., & Wicklund, R. A. (1972). *A theory of objective self-awareness*. New York, NY: Academic Press.

Eagly, A. H., & Chaiken, S. (1993). *The psychology of attitudes*. San Diego, CA: Harcourt Brace Jovanovich.

Epley, N., & Kruger, J. (2005). When what you type isn't what they read: The perseverance of stereotypes and expectancies over e-mail. *Journal of Experimental Social Psychology, 41*(4), 414–422.

Fanelli, D. (2012). Negative results are disappearing from most disciplines and countries. *Scientometrics, 90*, 891–904.

Fazio, R. H. (1990). Multiple processes by which attitudes guide behaviour: The MODE model as an integrative framework. In M. P. Zanna (Ed.), *Advances in experimental social psychology* (Vol. 23, pp. 75–109). San Diego, CA: Academic Press.

Fazio, R. H., & Williams, C. J. (1986). Attitude accessibility as a moderator of the attitude–perception and attitude–behavior relations: An investigation of the 1984 presidential election. *Journal of Personality and Social Psychology, 51*, 506–514.

Fenigstein, A., Scheier, M. F., & Buss, A. H. (1975). Public and private self-consciousness: Assessment and theory. *Journal of Consulting and Clinical Psychology, 43*(4), 522–527.

Festinger, L. (1954). A theory of social comparison processes. *Human Relations, 7*(2), 117–140.

Festinger, L. (1957). *A theory of cognitive dissonance*. Stanford, CA: Stanford University Press.

Fishbein, M., & Ajzen, I. (1975). *Belief, attitude, intention, and behavior*. Reading, MA: Addison-Wesley.

Fiske, S. T. (2004). *Social beings: A core motives approach to social psychology*. Hoboken, NJ: Wiley.

Fiske, S. T., Cuddy, A. J., Glick, P., & Xu, J. (2002). A model of (often mixed) stereotype content: Competence and warmth respectively follow from perceived status and competition. *Journal of Personality and Social Psychology, 82*(6), 878–902.

Fiske, S. T., & Taylor, S. E. (1991). *Social cognition* (2nd ed.). New York, NY: McGraw-Hill.

Fiske, S. T., & Neuberg, S. L. (1990). A continuum of impression formation, from category-based to individuating processes: Influences of information and motivation on attention and interpretation. In M. P. Zanna (Ed.), *Advances in experimental social psychology* (Vol. *23*, pp. 1–74). New York, NY: Academic Press.

Franklin, B. (1732/2004). *Poor Richard's almanack*. New York, NY: Barnes & Noble.

Frantz, C. M., Cuddy, A. J., Burnett, M., Ray, H., & Hart, A. (2004). A threat in the computer: The race implicit association test as a stereotype threat experience. *Personality and Social Psychology Bulletin, 30*(12), 1611–1624.

Froming, W. J., Walker, G. R., & Lopyan, K. J. (1982). Public and private self-awareness: When personal attitudes conflict with societal expectations. *Journal of Experimental Social Psychology, 18*(5), 476–487.

Gervais, W. M., & Norenzayan, A. (2012). Like a camera in the sky? Thinking about God increases public self-awareness and socially desirable responding. *Journal of Experimental Social Psychology, 48*(1), 298–302.

Gilbert, D. T., & Hixon, J. (1991). The trouble of thinking: Activation and application of stereotypic beliefs. *Journal of Personality and Social Psychology, 60*(4), 509–517.

Gollwitzer, P. M., Sheeran, P., Trötschel, R., & Webb, T. L. (2011). Self-regulation of priming effects on behavior. *Psychological Science, 22*(7), 901–907.

Greenberg, J., Pyszczynski, T., & Solomon, S. (1986). The causes and consequences of a need for self-esteem: A terror management theory. In R. F. Baumeister (Ed.), *Public self and private self* (pp. 189–212). New York, NY: Springer.

Greenwald, A. G., & Banaji, M. R. (1995). Implicit social cognition: Attitudes, self-esteem, and stereotypes. *Psychological Review, 102*, 4–27.

Greenwald, A. G., & Farnham, S. D. (2000). Using the implicit association test to measure self-esteem and self-concept. *Journal of Personality and Social Psychology, 79*(6), 1022–1038.

Greenwald, A. G., McGhee, D. E., & Schwartz, J. L. K. (1998). Measuring individual differences in implicit cognition: The implicit association test. *Journal of Personality and Social Psychology, 74*, 1464–1480.

Haines, M. P., Barker, G., & Rice, R. (2003). Using social norms to reduce alcohol and tobacco use in two midwestern high schools. In H. W. Perkins (Ed.), *The social norms approach to preventing school and college age substance abuse: A handbook for educators, counselors, and clinicians* (pp. 235–244). San Francisco, CA: Jossey-Bass.

Hamilton, D. L., & Gifford, R. K. (1976). Illusory correlation in interpersonal perception: A cognitive basis of stereotypic judgments. *Journal of Experimental Social Psychology, 12*(4), 392–407.

Harmon-Jones, E., Simon, L., Greenberg, J., Pyszczynski, T., Solomon, S., & McGregor, H. (1997). Terror management theory and self-esteem: Evidence that increased self-esteem reduced mortality salience effects. *Journal of Personality and Social Psychology, 72*(1), 24–36.

Hastie, R., Schroeder, C., & Weber, R. (1990). Creating complex social conjunction categories from simple categories. *Bulletin of the Psychonomic Society, 28*, 242–247.

Heider, F. (1958). *The psychology of interpersonal relations*. New York, NY: Wiley.

Higgins, E. T. (1987). Self-discrepancy theory: A theory relating self and affect. *Psychological Review, 94*, 319–340.

Hilton, J. L., & von Hippel, W. (1996). Stereotypes. *Annual Review of Psychology, 47*, 237–271.

Howard, J. W., & Rothbart, M. (1980). Social categorization and memory for in-group and out-group behavior. *Journal of Personality and Social Psychology, 38*, 301–310.

Hutter, R. R. C., & Crisp, R. J. (2005). The composition of category conjunctions. *Personality and Social Psychology Bulletin, 31*, 647–657.

International Social Cognition Network. (2018). What is social cognition? Retrieved 29 January 2018 from http://www.socialcognition.info/

Johns, M., Inzlicht, M., & Schmader, T. (2008). Stereotype threat and executive resource depletion: Examining the influence of emotion regulation. *Journal of Experimental Psychology, 137*(4), 691–705.

Johnston, L. C., & Macrae, C. N. (1994). Changing social stereotypes: The case of the information seeker. *European Journal of Social Psychology, 24*(5), 581–592.

Jones, E. E., & Harris, V. A. (1967). The attribution of attitudes. *Journal of Experimental Social Psychology*, *3*, 1–24.

Jones, E. E., & Nisbett, R. E. (1972). The actor and the observer: Divergent perceptions of the causes of behaviour. In E. E. Jones, D. E. Kanouse, H. H. Kelley, R. E. Nisbett, S. Valins, & B. Weiner (Eds.), *Attribution: Perceiving the cause of behaviour* (pp. 79–94). Morristown, NJ: General Learning Press.

Jost, J. T., & Banaji, M. R. (1994). The role of stereotyping in system-justification and the production of false consciousness. *British Journal of Social Psychology*, *33*(1), 1–27.

Jost, J. T., & Kay, A. C. (2005). Exposure to benevolent sexism and complementary gender stereotypes: Consequences for specific and diffuse forms of system justification. *Journal of Personality and Social Psychology*, *88*(3), 498–509.

Kassin, S. M. (1979). Consensus information, prediction and causal attribution: A review of the literature and issues. *Journal of Personality and Social Psychology*, *37*, 1699–1781.

Katz, D. (1979). Floyd H. Allport (1890–1978). *American Psychologist*, *34*, 351–353.

Katz, D., & Braly, K. (1933). Racial stereotypes of one hundred college students. *Journal of Abnormal and Social Psychology*, *28*(3), 280–290.

Kelley, H. H. (1967). Attribution theory in social psychology. In D. Levine (Ed.), *Nebraska Symposium on Motivation* (pp. 192–238). Lincoln, NE: University of Nebraska Press.

Koenig, A. M., & Eagly, A. H. (2005). Stereotype threat in men on a test of social sensitivity. *Sex Roles*, *52*(7/8), 489–496.

Koole, S. L., Dijksterhuis, A., & Van Knippenberg, A. (2001). What's in a name: Implicit self-esteem and the automatic self. *Journal of Personality and Social Psychology*, *80*(4), 669–685.

Kunda, Z., Miller, D. T., & Claire, T. (1990). Combining social concepts: The role of causal reasoning. *Cognitive Science*, *14*, 551–577.

Kunda, Z., & Spencer, S. J. (2003). When do stereotypes come to mind and when do they color judgment? A goal-based theoretical framework for stereotype activation and application. *Psychological Bulletin*, *129*(4), 522–544.

LaPiere, R. T. (1934). Attitudes vs action. *Social Forces*, *13*, 230–237.

Leary, M. R. (2005). Sociometer theory and the pursuit of relational value: Getting to the root of self-esteem. *European Review of Social Psychology*, *16*(1), 75–111.

Leary, M. R. (2007). Motivational and emotional aspects of the self. *Annual Review of Psychology*, *58*, 317–344.

Leary, M. R., Tambor, E. S., Terdal, S. K., & Downs, D. L. (1995). Self-esteem as an interpersonal monitor: The sociometer hypothesis. *Journal of Personality and Social Psychology*, *68*(3), 518–530.

Leeper, R. (1935). A study of a neglected portion of the field of learning: The development of sensory organization. *Journal of Genetic Psychology*, *46*, 41–75.

Levelt Committee. (2012). *Flawed science: The fraudulent research practices of social psychologist Diederik Stapel*. Retrieved 5 February 2017 from https://www.tilburguniversity.edu/upload/3ff904d7-547b-40ae-85fe-bea38e05a34a_Final%20report%20Flawed%20Science.pdf

Lewis, M., & Brooks-Gunn, J. (1978). Self-knowledge and emotional development. In M. Lewis & L. Rosenblum (Eds.), *The development of affect: The genesis of behavior* (Vol. 1, pp. 205–226). New York, NY: Plenum Press.

Lippmann, W. (1922). *Public opinion*. Oxford, UK: Harcourt Brace.

Logel, C., Iserman, E. C., Davies, P. G., Quinn, D. M., & Spencer, S. J. (2009). The perils of double consciousness: The role of thought suppression in stereotype threat. *Journal of Experimental Social Psychology*, *45*(2), 299–312.

Macrae, C. N., Bodenhausen, G. V., Milne, A. B., & Jetten, J. (1994). Out of mind but back in sight: Stereotypes on the rebound. *Journal of Personality and Social Psychology*, *67*(5), 808–817.

Macrae, C. N., Bodenhausen, G. V., Milne, A. B., Thorn, T. M., & Castelli, L. (1997). On the activation of social stereotypes: The moderating role of processing objectives. *Journal of Experimental Social Psychology*, *33*(5), 471–489.

Macrae, C. N., & Johnston, L. (1998). Help, I need somebody: Automatic action and inaction. *Social Cognition, 16*(4), 400–417.

Madon, S., Guyll, M., Aboufadel, K., Montiel, E., Smith, A., Palumbo, P., & Jussim, L. (2001). Ethnic and national stereotypes: The Princeton trilogy revisited and revised. *Personality and Social Psychology Bulletin, 27*(8), 996–1010.

Maio, G. R., & Olson, J. M. (Eds.). (2000). *Why we evaluate: Functions of attitudes*. Mahwah, NJ: Lawrence Erlbaum Associates.

Markus, H. (1977). Self-schemata and processing information about the self. *Journal of Personality and Social Psychology, 35*(2), 63–78.

Markus, H., & Wurf, E. (1987). The dynamic self-concept: A social psychological perspective. *Annual Review of Psychology, 38*(1), 299–337.

McEachan, R. R. C., Conner, M., Taylor, N. J., & Lawton, R. J. (2011). Prospective prediction of health-related behaviors with the theory of planned behavior: A meta-analysis. *Health Psychology Review, 5*, 97–144.

McGarty, C. (1999). *Categorization in social psychology*. London, UK: SAGE.

Milgram, S., Mann, L., & Harter, S. (1965). The lost-letter technique. *Public Opinion Quarterly, 29*, 437–438.

Morin, A. (2011). Self-awareness part 1: Definition, measures, effects, functions, and antecedents. *Social and Personality Psychology Compass, 5*(10), 807–823.

Moscovici, S. (1976). *Social influence and social change*. London, UK: Academic Press.

Nisbett, R. E., & Ross, L. (1980). *Human inference: Strategies and shortcomings of social judgment*. Englewood Cliffs, NJ: Prentice Hall.

Ochsner, K. N., & Lieberman, M. D. (2001). The emergence of social cognitive neuroscience. *American Psychologist, 56*(9), 717–734.

Osgood, C. E., Suci, G. J., & Tannenbaum, P. H. (1957). *The measurement of meaning*. Urbana, IL: University of Illinois Press.

Payne, B. K. (2001). Prejudice and perception: The role of automatic and controlled processes in misperceiving a weapon. *Journal of Personality Social Psychology, 81*, 181–192.

Pearce, E., Stringer, C., & Dunbar R. (2013). New insights into differences in brain organization between Neanderthals and anatomically modern humans. *Proceedings of the Royal Society B: Biological Sciences, 280*(1758), 20130168. doi:10.1098/rspb.2013.0168

Pettigrew, T. F. (1979). The ultimate attribution error: Extending Allport's cognitive analysis of prejudice. *Personality and Social Psychology Bulletin, 5*(4), 461–476.

Petty, R. E., & Cacioppo, J. T. (1986). The elaboration likelihood model of persuasion. In L. Berkowitz (Ed.), *Advances in experimental social psychology* (Vol. *19*, pp. 123–205). New York, NY: Academic Press.

Pinker, S. (2014). Daniel Kahneman changed the way we think about thinking. But what do other thinkers think of him? *The Observer*, 16 February. Retrieved 26 January 2018 from http://www.theguardian.com/science/2014/feb/16/daniel-kahneman-thinking-fast-and-slow-tributes

Rosch, E. (1978). Principles of categorization. In E. Rosch & B. B. Lloyd (Eds.), *Cognition and categorization* (pp. 27–48). Hillsdale, NJ: Lawrence Erlbaum Associates.

Rosenberg, M. (1965). *Society and the adolescent self-image*. Princeton, NJ: Princeton University Press.

Ross, L. (1977). The intuitive psychologist and his shortcomings. In L. Berkowitz (Ed.), *Advances in experimental social psychology* (Vol. *10*, pp. 174–220). New York, NY: Academic Press.

Ross, L., Greene, D., & House, P. (1977). The 'false consensus effect': An egocentric bias in social perception and attribution processes. *Journal of Experimental Social Psychology, 13*, 279–301.

Rydell, R. J., Rydell, M. T., & Boucher, K. L. (2010). The effect of negative performance stereotypes on learning. *Journal of Personality and Social Psychology, 99*(6), 883–896.

Scherer, K. R. (1978). Personality inference from voice quality: The loud voice of extraversion. *European Journal of Social Psychology, 8*, 467–488.

Schlegel, R. J., Hicks, J. A., King, L. A., & Arndt, J. (2011). Feeling like you know who you are: Perceived true self-knowledge and meaning in life. *Personality and Social Psychology Bulletin*, *37*(6), 745–756.

Schmader, T., & Johns, M. (2003). Converging evidence that stereotype threat reduces working memory capacity. *Journal of Personality and Social Psychology*, *85*(3), 440–452.

Schneider, W., & Shiffrin, R. M. (1977). Controlled and automatic human information processing: I. Detection, search, and attention. *Psychological Review*, *84*(1), 1–66.

Sedikides, C. (1993). Assessment, enhancement, and verification determinants of the self-evaluation process. *Journal of Personality and Social Psychology*, *65*(2), 317–338.

Sedikides, C., Gaertner, L., & O'Mara, E. M. (2011). Individual self, relational self, collective self: Hierarchical ordering of the tripartite self. *Psychological Studies*, *56*(1), 98–107.

Sedikides, C., & Skowronski, J. J. (1997). The symbolic self in evolutionary context. *Personality and Social Psychology Review*, *1*(1), 80–102.

Sedikides, C., & Strube, M. J. (1997). Self-evaluation: To thine own self be good, to thine own self be sure, to thine own self be true, and to thine own self be better. In M. P. Zanna (Ed.), *Advances in experimental social psychology* (Vol. *29*, pp. 209–269). New York, NY: Academic Press.

Shanks, D. R., Newell, B. R., Lee, E. H., Balakrishnan, D., Ekelund, L., Cenac, Z., ... Moore, C. (2013). Priming intelligent behavior: An elusive phenomenon. *PLoS ONE*, *8*(4), e56515.

Sinclair, L., & Kunda, Z. (1999). Reactions to a black professional: Motivated inhibition and activation of conflicting stereotypes. *Journal of Personality and Social Psychology*, *77*(5), 885–904.

Snyder, M., Tanke, E. D., & Berscheid, E. (1977). Social perception and interpersonal behavior: On the self-fulfilling nature of social stereotypes. *Journal of Personality and Social Psychology*, *35*(9), 656–666.

Steele, C. M., & Aronson, J. (1995). Stereotype threat and the intellectual test performance of African Americans. *Journal of Personality and Social Psychology*, *69*(5), 797–811.

Swann, W. B. (1983). Self-verification: Bringing social reality into harmony with the self. In J. Suls & A. G. Greenwald (Eds.), *Social psychological perspectives on the self* (Vol. *2*, pp. 33–66). Hillsdale, NJ: Lawrence Erlbaum Associates.

Tajfel, H. (1981a). *Human groups and social categories*. Cambridge, UK: Cambridge University Press.

Tajfel, H. (1981b). Social stereotypes and social groups. In J. C. Turner & H. Giles (Eds.), *Intergroup behaviour* (pp. 144–167). Oxford, UK: Blackwell.

Tajfel, H., & Turner, J. C. (1979). An integrative theory of intergroup conflict. In W. Austin & S. Worchel (Eds.), *The social psychology of intergroup relations* (pp. 33–48). Pacific Grove, CA: Brooks/Cole.

Tesser, A. (2000). On the confluence of self-esteem maintenance mechanisms. *Personality and Social Psychology Review*, *4*(4), 290–299.

Trope, Y. (1986). Self-enhancement and self-assessment in achievement behavior. In R. Sorrentino & E. T. Higgins (Eds.), *Handbook of motivation and cognition* (Vol. *2*, pp. 350–378). New York, NY: Guilford Press.

Turner, J. C. (1982). Towards a cognitive redefinition of the social group. In H. Tajfel (Ed.), *Social identity and intergroup relations* (pp. 15–40). Cambridge, UK: Cambridge University Press.

Turner, J. C. (1996). Fifty years' research on intergroup relations. Invited plenary paper presented to the symposium 'Social Psychology Over the Last 50 Years' at the 2nd Annual Meeting of the Society of Australasian Social Psychologists, Canberra, ACT, 2–5 May.

Tversky, A., & Kahneman, D. (1974). Judgement under uncertainty: Heuristics and biases. *Science*, *185*, 1124–1131.

Weiner, B. (1986). *An attributional theory of motivation and emotion*. New York, NY: Springer.

Wells, B. M., Skowronski, J. J., Crawford, M. T., Scherer, C. R., & Carlston, D. E. (2011). Inference making and linking both require thinking: Spontaneous trait inference and spontaneous trait transference both rely on working memory capacity. *Journal of Experimental Social Psychology*, *47*(6), 1116–1126.

Wicker, A. W. (1969). Attitudes versus actions: The relationship of verbal and overt behavioural responses to attitude objects. *Journal of Social Issues, 25*, 41–78.

Wimpenny, J. H., Weir A. A. S., Clayton, L., Rutz, C., & Kacelnik, A. (2009). Cognitive processes associated with sequential tool use in New Caledonian crows. *PLoS ONE, 4*(8), e6471.

Winter, L., Uleman, J. S., & Cunniff, C. (1985). How automatic are social judgments? *Journal of Personality and Social Psychology, 49*(4), 904–917.

Zanna, M. P., & Cooper, J. (1974). Dissonance and the pill: An attribution approach to studying the arousal properties of dissonance. *Journal of Personality and Social Psychology, 29*, 703–709.

19 Interpersonal, Group, and Intergroup Processes

RHIANNON N. TURNER

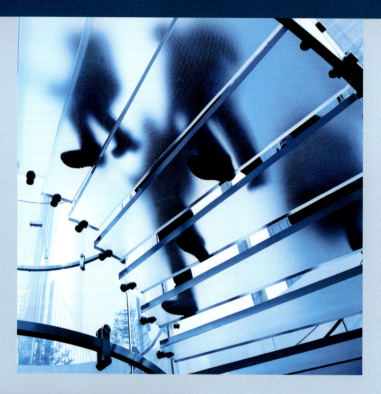

INTRODUCTION

LEARNING OBJECTIVE 19.1

Outline what social psychology is, and define three important aspects of it: interpersonal processes, group processes, and intergroup processes.

We humans are social beings: we spend much of our lives in the presence of others, and it is perhaps not surprising that those around us affect what we think and what we do. Social psychology has been defined as the 'attempt to understand and explain how the thoughts, feelings and behaviour of individuals are influenced by the actual, imagined or implied presence of others' (Allport, 1965, p. 3). This chapter examines three important aspects of social psychology. Research on *interpersonal processes* focuses on an association between two or more people – for example, acquaintances, friends, family members, and romantic partners. *Group processes* are what goes on inside a group – for example, the factors that ensure a group is productive and makes good decisions – and the processes by which group members influence others within the group. *Intergroup processes* are relations between different groups and include prejudice and discrimination. In this chapter, you will learn about all of these things.

SECTION SUMMARY

- Social psychology examines the social nature of human beings.
- Three things that social psychologists are interested in examining are the relationships between individuals, between members of a group, and between different groups.

INTERPERSONAL PROCESSES

LEARNING OBJECTIVE 19.2

Describe and explain the interpersonal processes behind friendship, romantic attractions, and romantic relationships.

Interpersonal processes play a major role in our lives. In the course of an average day you might, for example, chat to an acquaintance living in the same street as you, discuss an assignment with fellow students, chat on the phone with your parents, go for a coffee with friends, and meet up with a romantic partner. This is illustrative of the human tendency for **affiliation**, the desire to spend time with others. In this section, you will learn about three aspects of interpersonal relations: friendships, interpersonal attraction, and romantic relationships.

Friendship

When do the people with whom we affiliate become friends rather than mere acquaintances? What factors determine who we are drawn into friendships with, and what happens over time as a new friendship develops? Moreover, what factors determine the nature of our relationships with others in a world in which online communication interfaces, such as Facebook and Twitter, dominate?

Rory Varrato of Arizona State University discusses Friendship in the Age of Facebook in **this 2013 TED Talk**[1].

THE PSYCHOLOGICAL STUDY OF ONLINE COMMUNICATION

Source: Minerva Studio / Shutterstock.com.

Since the World Wide Web was made available for public access in 1992, a significant change has taken place regarding how and where we interact with our friends. While, not so long ago, face-to-face social engagements, phone calls, and letters were the main ways of keeping in touch, for the majority of us a significant proportion of our communication with our friends now takes place online. One of the most prominent ways in which we communicate online is via the social networking site Facebook, which has over 1 billion active users worldwide, more than one seventh of the world population (*Wall Street Journal*, 2012). Since the mid-2000s, research has begun to investigate Facebook and its relation to social behaviour. So, what do we know so far?

WHO SPENDS TIME ON FACEBOOK?

Individuals high in 'openness to experience', a personality trait that reflects creativity, intellectual curiosity, and a preference for variety (Goldberg, 1993), are especially likely to spend time on Facebook and have more friends on the site than do those with low openness to experience (Skues, Williams, & Wise, 2012). This might be because these individuals tend to have a broader range of interests and want to meet various types of people in order to widen their horizons, something that Facebook can help to facilitate.

Those with low self-esteem, and individuals who report feeling lonely, also spend more time on Facebook (Mehdizadeh, 2010; Skues et al., 2012). Facebook might help to compensate for these negative states by providing the opportunity for interactions and helping to build up social capital (Ellison, Stenfield, & Lampe, 2007).

WHAT ARE THE CONSEQUENCES OF FACEBOOK USE?

Use of Facebook has positive consequences for how people perceive the self. Gentile, Twenge, Freeman, and Campbell (2012) had participants spend 15 minutes either editing their Facebook profile or, in a control condition, undertaking a task on Google Maps. Those who edited their profile subsequently reported higher self-esteem. Given that a Facebook profile page typically represents a more polished 'version' of the self, editing their profile reminds people of positive, desirable aspects of themselves, enhancing self-esteem.

Facebook can be especially beneficial for those who have difficulty with face-to-face interactions. Campbell, Cumming, and Hughes (2006) found that online activities increase social support, skills, and networks for individuals with social apprehension, and provide the opportunity to develop and practise social skills that they might find difficult in offline encounters. Moreover, Indian and Grieve (2014) found that socially anxious individuals who received social support from Facebook reported increases in subjective well-being.

Some downsides to Facebook use have also been identified, especially for individuals with low self-esteem. Forest and Wood (2012) found that, while these individuals are drawn to Facebook in an attempt to enhance their self-esteem, their tendency to make negative, rather than positive, disclosures may actually make them less attractive to other Facebook users, making them more vulnerable to low self-esteem. Moreover, Clerkin, Smith, and Hames (2013) found that individuals who seek reassurance on Facebook – that is, they expect others to comment on their Facebook status and are disappointed when nobody does – have lower self-esteem, which in turn predicts greater perceptions that they do not belong and that they are a burden.

WHY DO PEOPLE USE FACEBOOK?

Nadkarni and Hofmann (2012) propose a 'dual-factor model of Facebook use'. Specifically, they argue that Facebook use is primarily motivated by two basic social needs: the need to belong and the need for self-presentation. As you will learn later in this section, people are highly dependent on social support from others (Baumeister & Leary, 1995) and being excluded from such support has a range of negative consequences (Baumeister & Tice, 1990). One way to ensure we feel supported is through online communication, which might in part explain why Facebook use – provided it is done in a positive manner – is associated with higher self-esteem. There is also evidence that humans are strongly motivated to perceive themselves, and be seen by others, in a positive light (Sedikides, 1993). Through our status updates and photos, we have a high degree of control over self-presentation and can present an idealized version of ourselves that makes us feel good about ourselves.

Whom do we become friends with?

Perhaps unsurprisingly, we tend to be friends with people whom we perceive to be similar to us. Kandel (1978) found that high school students' best friends were those who were similar to them in terms of sex, race, age, and school year. Similarity in attitudes and values is also important in promoting friendships. Newcomb (1961) had participants fill in questionnaires about their attitudes and values before they arrived at university. Although in their first few weeks of university participants preferred those who lived close to them, over time attraction was more closely related to similarity in their initial attitudes. Byrne and Nelson's (1965) experimental research revealed similar findings. They had participants complete attitude questionnaires before reading the same questionnaire, ostensibly completed by another participant but actually completed by the researcher to be either similar or dissimilar to the responses of the participant. The greater the proportion of similar attitudes participants thought they had with the other individual, the more they reported liking them.

So why do we like friends who are similar to us? Evolutionary psychologists argue that humans are unconsciously attracted to similar others because they share similar genes (see Ansari, 2014). By looking out for our friends, we may be increasing the probability that genes similar to our own will be passed on to future generations. Supporting this argument, there is evidence that friends have a tendency to be similar to one another in certain genetically determined characteristics (Rushton, 1989). An alternative social psychological explanation for why similarity breeds liking is a desire for *social comparison*. We like to compare ourselves to others because it offers social validity to important aspects of our self-concept. Clore (1976) argued that when someone agrees with our perceptions, our point of view is reinforced, which leads to greater liking. As a result, it makes sense that we prefer those who agree, rather than disagree, with our point of view.

People also tend to form friendships on the basis of *familiarity*, as a classic study by Festinger, Schachter, and Back (1950) illustrated. The researchers examined friendships among graduate students who had been randomly assigned to housing units in halls of residence at the Massachusetts Institute of Technology. They found that, despite the fact that the students did not know one another prior to moving in, two thirds of the residents' closest friends resided not only in the same building but also on the same floor as them. Moreover, residents were nearly twice as likely to name next-door neighbours as close friends than those living two doors away. Put simply, we are more likely to be friends with those who – because they live or work near to us – we encounter more frequently and are therefore more familiar with. The phenomenon whereby being exposed to someone or something repeatedly increases attraction, even if no information is provided about the object or person, is called the **mere exposure hypothesis** (Zajonc, 1968).

How do friendships develop over time?

What happens as a liking for someone we encounter develops into a friendship? According to **social penetration theory** (Altman & Taylor, 1973), self-disclosure, the imparting of personal information about yourself to another person, plays a crucial role in how friendships develop over time. As friends become closer, they gradually increase the breadth and intimacy of information they disclose to one another. This occurs reciprocally, with individuals matching one another's level of disclosure. Supporting this idea, Laurenceau, Barrett, and Pietromonaco (1998) found that, as the level of reciprocal self-disclosure increases during the early stages of friendship, so too does the level of intimacy in the relationship. However, if one individual discloses too slowly, the friendship partner could feel rejected, causing the relationship to falter. Conversely, if one individual discloses too much too soon, this can feel like an invasion of personal space and also result in the end of the friendship. Once the relationship has reached a high level of intimacy, the amount of self-disclosure levels off and is replaced by an exchange of support and understanding.

Although social penetration theory is an adequate description of many friendships, some friends 'click' straight away and immediately begin disclosing highly intimate information to one another, without the need for a gradual escalation in reciprocal self-disclosure (Berg, 1984). The theory also fails to distinguish between different types of disclosure. Hackenbracht and Gasper (2013) found that people prefer to listen to emotional rather than descriptive disclosures. This is because humans have a very powerful need to belong (Baumeister & Leary, 1995), and listening to someone talk about their emotions helps to promote this sense of belonging by making us feel a sense of social connection.

When friendships go wrong

As noted above, we have a powerful motivation to belong and therefore place a lot of importance on our friendships with others. So, what happens when we are excluded, rejected, or marginalized from desired relationships or social groups? Perhaps unsurprisingly, victims of exclusion experience a range of negative emotions. Williams, Cheung, and Choi (2000) had 1,486 participants from 62 countries play an online game. Participants were included in the game very frequently, quite frequently, rarely, or not at all. It emerged that the more that participants were excluded during the task, the more they experienced depressed mood and lower self-esteem.

There is also some evidence that being excluded can lead to antisocial behaviour. This is starkly illustrated by an extreme example: the Virginia Tech massacre in 2007. Seung-Hui Cho, a 23-year-old undergraduate, shot dead 32 of his fellow students before killing himself. In his suicide note, Cho wrote, 'You forced me into a corner and gave me only one option … you just loved to crucify me' (quoted in MacAskill, 2007). These words suggest that social exclusion was at least in part his justification for his actions. Leary, Kowalski, Smith, and Phillips (2003) conducted case studies of 15 school shootings between 1995 and 2001 to examine whether there is any truth in the argument made by media commentators that school shootings are often precipitated by social exclusion. They examined all available reports regarding each shooting and looked for evidence of teasing, ostracism, and rejection from a romantic relationship. In at least 12 of the 15 incidents, the perpetrator had been subjected to a pattern of malicious bullying, regularly being insulted, humiliated, and teased. The researchers also noted that, in many of the incidents, the victims included those who had been perpetrators of this exclusion. Rejection from romantic relationships, or unrequited love, was also a defining feature of half of the incidents. In only two of the shootings examined were there no histories of social rejection. Clearly these high-profile cases are extreme, and very unusual, outcomes. Nonetheless, empirical studies suggest that antisocial behaviours, including aggression, are a common consequence of social exclusion (e.g. Warburton, Williams, & Cairns, 2006).

Interpersonal attraction

Interpersonal attraction describes the desire to approach another individual, to seek them out for interaction. This section focuses specifically on three factors that help to explain when and why we become romantically attracted to another person: physical appearance, perceived similarity, and complementarity.

Physical appearance

When we meet someone for the first time, one of the first things we notice is their physical appearance. Although both men and women value physical attractiveness in a potential romantic partner, research suggests that physical appearance is especially important to men (Ford & Beach, 1951). Indeed, much of the research on this topic has focused on men's perceptions of women. But what makes a personal physically attractive? One factor that seems to be important is *body size*, although there are cultural differences in whether a larger or smaller size is seen as preferable. In one study, men in Ghana, West Africa, showed a preference for larger women than did men in the United States (Cogan, Bhalla, Sefa-Dedeh, & Rothblum, 1996). One explanation for this might be the relative availability of food in these two countries. Anderson, Crawford, Nadeau, and Lindberg (1992) found that where the availability of food is unpredictable, larger women are preferred, while where there is a reliable food supply, slim women are preferred. From an evolutionary perspective, this makes sense. Where food has, historically at least, been in short supply, women who carry extra weight are likely to remain healthy even during times of shortage and are therefore more likely to be fertile and produce offspring. *Body shape* is also important where perceptions of women are concerned. Evidence suggests that women with a small waist-to-hip ratio – a ratio of 0.7, for instance – are perceived as being especially physically attractive: in other words, men tend to have a preference for women with a classic 'hourglass' figure (Streeter & McBurney, 2003). There is also an evolutionary explanation for this: women with this figure are perceived as being fertile, in good health, and therefore especially likely to produce healthy offspring (Furnham, Moutafi, & Baguma, 2002).

There is evidence that people with a *symmetrical face* are perceived as more attractive (Figure 19.1). One explanation for this is that people perceive those with symmetrical faces as being healthier (Grammer & Thornhill, 1994) and there seems to be at least some truth to this perception: facial symmetry is a predictor of genetic quality and 'developmental stability', which refers to the body's ability to maintain good health by fighting off the impact of environmental stressors (Møller & Swaddle, 1997). From an evolutionary perspective, a healthy mate is attractive because they are more likely to survive long enough to produce healthy offspring. We also tend to prefer *average faces*. Langlois, Roggman, and Musselman (1994), for example, found that people preferred 'average' composite faces generated by a computer, created by combining a series of individual faces, to those individual faces that made up the composites. Again, perceptions of healthiness seem to play a role in explaining this. As with facial symmetry, people with average faces are perceived as healthier than those with distinctive faces, and there is some evidence to support this perception. Rhodes et al. (2001) found that facial distinctiveness ratings of 17-year-olds were associated with poor childhood health in males and poor current and adolescent health in females. However, an alternative explanation for these findings is the mere exposure effect, as discussed earlier in this chapter: average faces are more familiar to us and familiarity breeds attraction.

Perceived similarity and complementarity

In the same way that we tend to like friends who are similar to us, we are also attracted to romantic partners whom we perceived to be like us. Couples who are evenly matched in their appearance, social background, personality, interests, and

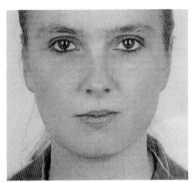 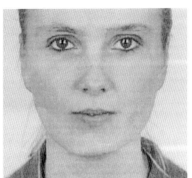

Normal version   More symmetrical version

FIGURE 19.1 *Normal and more symmetrical versions of a face. Research has shown that we tend to find symmetrical faces more attractive than less symmetrical faces. This might be because symmetrical individuals tend to have good genetic health and developmental stability, and may be perceived by potential partners as being more likely to successfully reproduce and pass on healthy genes to the next generation.*
Source: Reprinted from Jones et al. (2001). Copyright 2001, with permission from Elsevier.

leisure activities are more likely to be attracted to one another. In fact, a longitudinal study of married couples over 21 years revealed that spouses become increasingly similar over time in terms of both attitudes and mental abilities (Gruber-Baldini, Schaie, & Willis, 1995). There is also evidence that people tend to prefer those who are similar in physical attractiveness to them (Berscheid, Dion, Walster, & Walster, 1971). According to the 'matching hypothesis', this is because we estimate that they will have a similar opinion about us, reducing the risk of our being rejected (Garcia & Khersonsky, 1997). However, it is important to acknowledge that there is still an overriding tendency for people to prefer physically attractive others, even if they are not especially attractive themselves (Berscheid et al., 1971). It may therefore be that less attractive individuals are simply being realistic and, despite preferring highly attractive potential partners, they choose to pursue a more realistic target.

Despite this preference for similar others, there is also evidence that on certain criteria we are attracted to those with characteristics that *complement*, rather than mirror, our own. Put another way, we find others attractive when they hold a trait that we value but do not possess ourselves. Townsend and Levy (1990) asked students to evaluate strangers who varied in physical attractiveness and social status. Men showed a preference for highly attractive but low-status women. In contrast, women found that high-status men who were only moderately attractive were as appealing as highly attractive but only moderate-status men. Thus, women can trade looks for status and men can trade status for looks, but the reverse is not true. These results can be explained in terms of a **looks-for-status exchange**. Men are attracted to young women because female youth signifies beauty, while women are attracted to older men because age is likely to be accompanied by higher social status. However, it is clear that, as society changes and gender equality gradually increases, perceptions of what is attractive are starting to change, and the looks-for-status exchange is becoming less relevant. A content analysis of personal ads in a Spanish newspaper revealed that, although the looks-for-status exchange predictions still applied overall, women under the age of 40 sought physical attractiveness rather than socioeconomic status in men (Gil-Burmann, Peláez, & Sánchez, 2002). Meanwhile, Strassberg and Holty (2003) posted several versions of a 'female seeking male' ad online and found that, when the woman was described as successful and ambitious, this generated 50% more responses than the next most popular ad, which described the woman as attractive and slim.

Romantic relationships

Above we explored how romantic attraction develops. In this section, we consider what happens when that attraction is reciprocated and develops into love and romantic relationships. We explore what love is and how it arises, the factors that determine whether a relationship is a success, and what happens when a relationship fails.

What is love?

Love is of great interest to psychologists. However, it has typically been regarded as something mysterious and unfathomable, and there is no clear agreement on how love should be defined. We might argue that it is simply a stronger form of the bond that arises between two friends. However, psychologists generally argue that love and liking are qualitatively different from one another. Lamm and Wiesmann (1997), for example, proposed that 'liking' is the desire to interact with another person, while 'love' also involves trust and being excited by another person. Love can be divided into two types: passionate and compassionate.

Passionate love is a state of intense longing for another person and is experienced during the early stages of a romantic relationship. Neuropsychologists have found that the experience of passionate love is associated with changes in brain chemistry (in particular an increase in the powerful stimulant dopamine), which lead to a sense of physiological arousal. There is also evidence that people in love who are given brain scans show increased activity in the caudate nucleus area (near the centre of the brain), an area associated with reward and pleasure, when they are shown photos of their partners, but not when they are shown photos of their friends (Fisher, 2004). Aron, Paris, and Aron (1995) found that people in love report a range of positive experiences, including an increase in self-efficacy and self-esteem.

So when does passionate love arise? According to Hatfield and Walster's (1981) **three-factor theory of love**, three conditions must be met. First, it is necessary for an individual to understand what love is and have the expectation that at some point they will fall in love. In other words, whether or not a person falls in love depends on whether they are from a culture that believes in the concept of love. Second, it is necessary to meet someone who fits your expectations of what makes an appropriate partner – for example, someone attractive and of the preferred sex. Third, when thinking about or being in the presence of this potential partner, the individual must experience a state of physiological arousal, which they then attribute to the potential partner. Clearly, though, these three factors together are not the only reason we fall in love: as noted earlier, physical attraction, perceived similarity, and complementarity, among other things, also play roles. While passionate love captures the early stages of a new relationship, this phase – characterized by uncertainty, euphoria, and a focus on the new partner to the exclusion of almost everything else – cannot be maintained in the long term.

Inevitably, these heightened feelings of passionate love fade and, in long-term relationships, are replaced by a less passionate but more enduring **compassionate love** (Hatfield, 1988), the persistent affection we feel for someone with whom our life is deeply entwined. This shift makes evolutionary sense. In the early stages of a relationship, the sexual mating system, the goal of which is to sexually reproduce and pass on genes to the next generation, is dominant. In the later stages of a relationship, however, the attachment system, the goal of which is to establish and maintain a strong emotional bond between two people, is more important. Parents who love each other are more likely to stay together to raise their children, and this will ensure offspring are better provided for and more likely to survive childhood.

Relationship satisfaction and commitment

Once people are in an established romantic relationship, what determines whether or not the relationship will be happy? Several theories and factors have been proposed to explain relationship satisfaction. According to **social exchange theory** (Thibaut & Kelley, 1959), people keep track of what they contribute to a relationship and what their partner contributes. This can include material contributions, such as money and food, and non-material contributions, such as affection, support, and interesting conversation. The theory argues that people make a cost–benefit analysis in order to determine how satisfying a relationship is. If the benefits outweigh the costs, the relationship will inevitably be seen as more satisfying than if the costs outweigh the benefits.

Equity theory extends social exchange theory by focusing specifically on what happens when a relationship is seen as equal or unequal. The theory proposes that people in close relationships expect an equal exchange in terms of love, emotional and financial support, and doing household tasks. Inequity leads to negative emotions, but the type of emotion will vary depending on the direction of the inequity: a person in a relationship will experience guilt if they receive more from the relationship than they give but resentment if they give more to the relationship than they receive. Buunk and VanYperen (1991) found that, while those in equal relationships tended to be satisfied, those who received less than they gave were least satisfied in the relationship, followed by those who received more than they gave.

Another factor thought to be crucial in explaining satisfaction in a relationship is the degree to which it is characterized by intimacy. Reis and Patrick (1996) argued that intimate, and therefore satisfied, relationships are characterized by three things. First, our partner should be *caring*, displaying a kindness and concern for us. Second, they should be *understanding*, holding an accurate perception of our feelings, needs, beliefs, and life circumstances. Swann, de la Ronde, and Hixon (1994), for example, found that married people were most satisfied with their relationship when their partner perceived them in line with their self-perceptions. Third, we should receive *validation* from our partner; that is, they should be able to communicate their acknowledgement and support for our point of view.

So, what factors determine whether a relationship will last? It would not be unreasonable to assume that an increase in satisfaction would strongly predict *relationship commitment*, the desire or intention to continue an interpersonal relationship. However, this relationship is not always as strong as we might expect. We can probably all think of people who seem unhappy with their partner but nonetheless remain in the relationship. According to Rusbult's (1983) **investment model**, this is because while *high satisfaction* in a relationship has an impact on commitment, two further factors also play a role. *Investment size* is important; couples in a relationship become increasingly intertwined. They invest time and effort in each other, make sacrifices, develop mutual friends and shared memories, and have shared activities and possessions. The greater the investment, the more committed people tend to be in a relationship. The *perceived quality of alternatives* to the present relationship also plays a role; for example, is there an alternative partner who might be preferable? If the quality of alternatives is low, we are more likely to commit to a relationship.

Clearly, the presence of an attractive alternative may threaten the stability of an existing romantic relationship. However, research suggests that, when we are in a successful relationship, we engage in strategies to ward off the lure of these alternatives. Karremans and Verwijmeren (2008) had male and female heterosexual participants, half of whom were in a romantic relationship, complete a task with an attractive confederate of the opposite sex. These interactions were videotaped and were rated for how much the participant mimicked the behaviour of the confederate. It emerged that participants who were in a relationship mimicked the behaviour of their interaction partner to a lesser extent than participants who were currently single. Participants who were especially close to their romantic partner were especially unlikely to engage in mimicry. Although mimicry seems to be unconscious, it serves an important social function, creating a smoother, more pleasant interaction, and induces liking from one's interaction partner. By mimicking less, people who were happy in their relationship reduced their chance of a successful interaction and thus protected their current relationship from the risk posed by an attractive alternative.

Relationship breakdown

What happens when satisfaction and commitment are low; when an individual is unhappy in their relationship and is considering terminating it? According to Rusbult and Zembrodt (1983), a partner may react in a positive or negative, or an active or passive way, resulting in four possible reactions. If a partner wants to save the relationship, they may react with *loyalty*, passively waiting for the relationship to improve, or *voice behaviour*, by actively working at the relationship. If, on the other hand, a partner thinks the relationship is truly over, they may respond with *neglect*, passively letting the relationship deteriorate, or *exit behaviour*, choosing to end the relationship.

Unsurprisingly, the end of a relationship can be a very difficult time, especially when there was a lot invested in it or when a partner did not choose to end the relationship. This raises two questions: how do people react and does time heal? Sbarra and Emery (2005) found that, following a breakup, feelings of anger dissipate very quickly, typically within 18 days, but sadness declines relatively slowly, taking at least a month to dissipate. Lucas (2005) examined data from an 18-year-long panel study of 30,000 Germans in order to examine how life satisfaction was affected in the years prior to and following a divorce. He found that life satisfaction dropped considerably as people moved closer to the point at which they got divorced. While their life satisfaction began to increase again following the divorce, it did not return to pre-divorce levels of satisfaction.

On a positive note, however, people do seem to overestimate the negative impact that a breakup will have on them. Eastwick, Finkel, Krishnamurti, and Loewenstein (2008) had college students who were in a romantic relationship complete a questionnaire every other week for 9 months, in which they reported whether they were still in the relationship. If they reported that the relationship had ended, they were asked to indicate their current level of distress, whereas those who were still in the same relationship were asked to indicate how distressed they thought they would feel 2 weeks, 4 weeks, 8 weeks, and 12 weeks following the breakup if their own relationship had ended. Among participants whose relationship ended during the first 6 months of the study, predicted distress (assessed 2 weeks before the breakup) was compared with the actual distress respondents felt. While participants were accurate at predicting how quickly their levels of distress would reduce (predicted and actual levels of distress reduced at about the same rate), they significantly overestimated *how* distressed they would feel. However, this overestimation was driven by people who were in love with their partner just prior to the breakup. Those who were not in love were actually very accurate at predicting both the trajectory and intensity of their distress in the weeks following the breakup, perhaps because they were able to make judgements from a cooler, more rational, and more dispassionate state than those who were in love. In sum, when we feel sad after a breakup with a loved one, we must take comfort in the fact that we will feel less distress over the coming weeks than we expect.

DISCUSSION POINT

Discuss what psychological theories and research can tell us about how friendships develop over time.

SECTION SUMMARY

- This section has focused on friendships, romantic attraction, and romantic relationships.
- Research suggests that we are typically friends with individuals who are similar to ourselves and who are familiar to us.
- Social penetration theory proposes that new friends gradually escalate the breadth and intimacy of information they disclose to one another, which increases mutual liking and trust.
- However, when we are excluded from friendships, this can result in depressed mood, lower self-esteem, and aggression.
- Research has also examined when we are romantically attracted to someone. A slim body (in Western societies, at least), a small waist-to-hip ratio, and a symmetrical, average face are all considered attractive, as are similarities to us in personality, attitudes, and physical looks.
- After attraction develops into a relationship, people seem to be satisfied when the benefits outweigh the costs in the relationship, when we put in and take out an equal amount from it, and when the relationship is characterized by intimacy.
- Satisfaction is not the only predictor of whether we will stay in a relationship. The more we have invested in a relationship and the poorer the perceived quality of alternatives, the less likely we are to leave.
- If we *do* end a relationship, it can take some time for our levels of happiness to recover but, typically, we overestimate how painful a breakup will be.

GROUP PROCESSES

LEARNING OBJECTIVE 19.3

Describe how the presence of others can affect our productivity, judgements, and behaviours, and explain the psychological processes underlying these effects.

A group can be defined as a collection of individuals, but a group has more **entitativity** – is more 'group-like' – to the extent that members are *similar* to one another, share a *common goal*, are *interconnected* with one another or *cohesive*, and *interact* with one another (Lickel et al., 2000). Groups can be based on intimacy (e.g. family, a friendship group), tasks (e.g. work colleagues, student body), and social categories (e.g. gender, ethnicity, nationality), or looser associations (e.g. participants in the same study, same hair colour). This section will primarily focus on loosely associated groups and task groups. We begin by talking about the effect of the presence of others on group productivity. Next, you will learn about how group members influence one another, either by changing attitudes or by encouraging conformity or obedience. Finally, the role of groups in explaining aggressive behaviour will be examined.

Group productivity

You can probably think of times when you have had to perform in front of others, whether it was describing a concept to the rest of your tutorial group, giving a presentation, or taking part in a sporting event where your team-mates were depending on you. But are audiences a help or a hindrance?

Social facilitation and inhibition

Early research found evidence for **social facilitation**, a tendency for people to perform better when in front of an audience (an effect originally observed by Allport, 1920; see also Triplett, 1897). However, there is also evidence that sometimes an audience can lead to **social inhibition** – that is, worse performance when we are being watched. So what determines which of these effects will occur? Research seems to suggest that, while the presence of others increases performance on simple tasks (e.g. running, eating), it inhibits performance on more complex tasks (e.g. solving maths problems). The question is, *why* does performance depend on task complexity?

According to **drive theory**, the mere presence of others increases physiological arousal (Zajonc, 1965). From an evolutionary standpoint, it makes sense for people to experience a heightened sense of physiological readiness when others are present, because others could represent either a threat to survival or an opportunity to reproduce. The theory proposes that physiological arousal enhances the performance of dominant, well-learned response tendencies. The presence of a crowd at the finishing line of a race may, by increasing physiological arousal, result in a runner experiencing a last-minute burst of energy to finish in a faster time. However, physiological arousal can be detrimental to performance on a complex task. This is because such arousal is associated with a narrowed focus of attention and an overreliance on automatic processes and heuristics as we try to simultaneously deal with both the arousal and the task at hand. This shift can lead to errors in information processing and, therefore, worse performance (e.g. see Kahneman, 1973). However, other psychologists argue that it is **evaluation apprehension**, concern about being evaluated by others, rather than the mere presence of others, that causes physiological arousal in the presence of others (Cottrell, Wack, Sekerak, & Rittle, 1968).

Social loafing

The research discussed above focuses on what happens to an individual's performance when in front of an audience. But how does working in a team affect our performance? Latané, Williams, and Harkins (1979) investigated this. Six blindfolded participants had to sit in a semicircle wearing headphones that played a recording of people shouting into their ears. Participants were asked to shout as loudly as possible while listening to the shouts coming through into their headphones. In one condition, participants were told that they were shouting alone, while in a second condition they were told that they were shouting with five other people. In fact, only the participant was shouting in any one trial. The researchers found that participants who believed they were shouting in a group shouted with less intensity than participants who believed they were shouting alone. The phenomenon whereby people in teams put in less effort than those working alone is called **social loafing** (Karau & Williams, 1995). It seems to occur because, when working in a team, people individually feel less personally responsible for any task at hand. As they are in a group, their contribution is lost in the crowd, and so it matters less how much effort they put in. This phenomenon is called **diffusion of responsibility** (Comer, 1995).

Social influence

Social influence refers to the way in which our thoughts, feelings, and behaviours change when in the presence of others. People are influenced by those around them in one of two ways. **Conformity** occurs when people change their attitudes or behaviour due to an implicit social norm, whereas **obedience** is attitude or behaviour change in response to a direct, or explicit, order. This section also covers majority influence, when a large proportion of group members influences others, and minority influence, when a small proportion of group members can influence the rest.

Conformity

One of the earliest social psychology studies examined social influence. Sherif (1935) invited participants to take part in a study that was ostensibly about visual perception. They were led to a room, which was pitch black except for a small dot of light on a wall, and were asked to make judgements about how far the dot moved along the wall. In reality, the dot was not moving at all. However, because of a perceptual illusion called the autokinetic effect, the dot appeared to move around because the room was dark and there was no other point of reference. First, participants made these judgements individually, with no one else present. Then participants undertook the same task but in the presence of several other participants. Sherif found that, when participants made their judgement alone, there was variation in their estimates of the distance moved. However, when participants made the judgement in the presence of others, they tended to converge, each making a similar estimate. Sherif argued that a group norm had formed to which participants conformed. Interestingly, participants denied that their judgements had been influenced by their fellow participants, demonstrating that this norm was implicit, outside their awareness. One explanation for this effect is that when people are uncertain about how to respond in a situation, they conform to a group norm as a way of gaining information.

Deutsch and Gerard (1955) called this phenomenon 'informational influence'. Supporting this idea, Sherif (1935) found that the level of uncertainty in the task increased the rate at which people converged on a common response. However, there are other situations in which we are very certain about how we think or feel, yet we still adhere to the attitude of the group, even if we privately do not agree with it. A classic experiment conducted by Solomon Asch in 1951 demonstrated this.

Asch (1951) invited participants to take part in a visual perception study in the presence of five other people whom they believed to be participants but who were in fact confederates: actors following a script given to them by the experimenter. Unlike Sherif's study, where the task was difficult and participants were uncertain, the task here was very easy. Participants were presented with a standard line and three comparison lines, two of which were clearly a different length from the standard line and one of which was clearly exactly the same length. Across a series of trials, each of the six participants was asked, one at a time, to call out which of the three comparison lines was the same length as the standard line. The experiment was always arranged so that four confederates called out their response first, followed by the naive participant, followed by a final confederate. These confederates unanimously gave an *incorrect* answer, picking the wrong line despite it being very obvious that this was incorrect. Asch found that, when this visual perception task was undertaken with no other people present, only 1% of people gave the wrong answer. However, when confederates unanimously gave an incorrect response, participants gave an incorrect response in 37% of trials (and 76% of participants conformed in at least one of the trials). These findings suggest that, at times, people conform to a social norm even when they privately hold a different attitude.

This begs the question, why did participants in Asch's study agree with someone whose answer was clearly incorrect? In this situation, it may be that **social norms**, commonly held attitudes among group members, dictated how participants responded. More specifically, participants may have gone along with the attitudes of others in order to gain acceptance from the group, something Deutsch and Gerard (1955) called 'normative influence'. We want to be included and find being excluded or ignored very unpleasant. To avoid these negative consequences, we are sometimes motivated to go along with the group norm in public, even if privately we disagree.

When social influence goes wrong

In addition to changing the attitudes of an individual, research suggests that the presence of others can change the attitudes of the group *as a whole*. **Group polarization** is the phenomenon whereby, after a period of discussion, the initial attitude held by a group becomes exaggerated or polarized, especially where important issues are concerned (Kerr, 1992). Why does this occur? Well, as noted above, group members are motivated to publicly express attitudes that match the social norm of the group. Because of this, when the group engages in a discussion, the members are likely to all converge around the same perspective. In encountering more arguments that support the initial position, and in the absence of contradictory, counternormative arguments, they are even more persuaded by this initial position, exaggerating the consensus further. When pushed to its extreme, group polarization can lead to **groupthink** (Janis, 1982), which refers to group decision making in which, in their desire to achieve consensus, the group suffers from failures in mental efficiency, closed-mindedness, and an overestimation of its competence in making a decision. Groupthink is especially likely to occur when the group is highly cohesive (and therefore especially susceptible to the influence group norms) and when the situation is threatening or stressful – for example, if the group is making a decision with far-reaching and potentially catastrophic consequences.

Groupthink can be identified as a possible cause of poor decision making in one example event. In June 2012, the Pennsylvania State University assistant football coach, Jerry Sandusky, was found guilty of 48 counts of sexual abuse against children dating from 1994 to 2009 and was imprisoned for a minimum of 30 years (BBC News, 2011a). An independent investigation by former FBI investigator Louis Freeh revealed that the university president, vice-president, athletic director, and head coach had all known about allegations of abuses as early as 1998 yet had covered up the incidences, failing to disclose them to the authorities. Groupthink might help to explain why these apparently dedicated, competent university leaders made an appalling decision with dire consequences for the children involved (Cohen & DeBenedet, 2012). The individuals involved in the cover-up were highly cohesive, working closely together to run a successful, well-regarded university. The situation was highly stressful: the consequence of the scandal emerging would have been catastrophic for the image of the university. Moreover, there may have also been pressure to conform to the group norm (to project a positive image of the university) rather than to be true to their morals and values (to protect vulnerable children). Given the illegality of the decision being made by the group (to cover up the abuse), the group would not have consulted outsiders, resulting in a closed-minded decision-making process. Indeed, emails between the group members showed that they had decided it was more 'humane' to cover up the allegations than report them to the police.

Minority influence

The research discussed above focused on how the majority in a group can influence the minority. However, social psychologists have also found evidence to suggest that, sometimes, minorities can change the attitudes and behaviours of majorities. This was demonstrated in a study conducted by Moscovici, Lage, and Naffrechoux (1969). Participants were asked to undertake an easy visual perception task in the presence of five other participants: they had to judge whether a series of slides, which were clearly blue in colour, were either green or blue. Unlike in Asch's (1951) study, in this case the group taking part was composed of four genuine participants and just two confederates. The confederates gave their answers first, both stating that the slide was green. In other words, a minority in the group gave an *incorrect* answer. It emerged that, compared with participants who completed this task alone and always gave a correct answer, 8% of participants completing the task in a group were influenced by the minority and also gave the incorrect answer. Moscovici and colleagues created two further conditions in which the confederates gave the wrong answer either consistently (every time) or inconsistently (just some of the time). It emerged that this minority influence *only* occurred when the confederates consistently gave the wrong answer. When the confederates were inconsistent, very few of the participants went along with the wrong answer (see Figure 19.2).

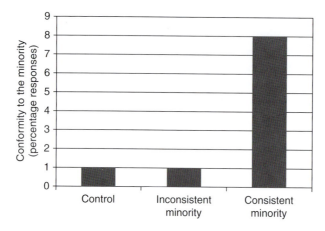

FIGURE 19.2 *Effect of the presence of a consistent or inconsistent minority on conformity among participants.*

Source: Based on Moscovici and Naffrechoux (1969).

Clearly, in this research, only a relatively small proportion of participants were influenced by the minority. However, these findings do suggest that, under the right circumstances, the minority *can* influence the majority in a group. So, why does this occur? We might expect that, given the positive consequences of conforming (social acceptance, having information from the majority of group members on which to base a decision) and the negative consequences of failing to conform to the majority (social exclusion), the minority would never have any influence. However, when someone consistently and confidently maintains an opinion that is in the minority *despite* these potentially negative consequences, this gives their argument real credibility. After all, why would anyone take these social risks if they didn't truly believe in their argument? This credibility can, in some cases, result in the majority shifting their perception towards the minority viewpoint.

Now we need to ask, how does minority influence compare to the majority influence – or conformity – discussed earlier on? Moscovici (1980) argued that they work rather differently. As majority influence is driven primarily by normative concerns, there is unlikely to be deep thought about the issue. Instead, people will *publicly* adopt the viewpoint without necessarily agreeing in private. In contrast, someone consistently and confidently sticking to an attitude that goes against the rest of the group is pretty surprising and unexpected. As a result, people are more likely to consider in some depth why the minority is expressing this viewpoint. When attitudes shift as a result of minority influence, they are therefore more likely to be adopted *privately*, but not necessarily in public because of fears of exclusion from the group.

Aggression

In our discussion of group processes so far, we have considered how the presence of others can make us more or less productive and can influence our attitudes and behaviours in various ways. Here we move on to talk in more detail about the dark side of groups: the fact that being in a group can at times cause us to act with

aggression: verbal or physical acts intended to cause harm to people or property. While acts of extreme aggression – such as murder, assault, sexual abuse, and terrorism – are committed by a small minority, most people would probably admit to feeling angry or aggressive from time to time. Here we will consider two types of aggression – following orders to cause harm and behaving aggressively in a crowd – and the psychological processes thought to explain why they take place.

Obedience

The Holocaust, the systematic and state-sponsored genocide of 6 million Jews during World War II, is an example of aggression at its most extreme and horrifying. Between 1933, when Adolf Hitler became Chancellor of Germany, and the end of the war in 1945, two thirds of the Jews living in Europe were killed. Many others, including gay people, Poles, Slavs, Russians, mentally disabled people, and communists, were also killed in large numbers. While the Holocaust was instigated and supervised by senior members of the Nazi party, many people working for government ministries, the police, the SS, and the Gestapo were involved in rounding up, transporting, and systematically killing victims. Milgram (1963) was interested in what factors might explain why these individuals followed such horrific orders, and he conducted a laboratory study to investigate.

Participants were invited to take part in a study concerning the effects of punishment on learning, although this was just a cover story. The participant entered the laboratory ostensibly with a second participant who was in fact a confederate. The experimenter then allocated them to one of two roles, supposedly on a random basis. However, in reality the participant was always assigned to be the 'teacher' and the confederate the 'learner'. The learner was asked to learn pairs of words and the teacher was instructed to give the learner an electric shock if they made a mistake, with the intensity of the shock increasing each time a mistake was made. In order to ensure that the participants truly believed they would be giving electric shocks, each participant was given a real 15 volt electric shock as an example of what would happen in the study. However, for the rest of the study, no electric shocks were really administered to the confederate.

During the study, the confederate made a number of deliberate mistakes. At each point, an increased intensity of shock was given and the confederate's reaction became increasingly distressed. At 150 volts, the learner cried out, 'Experimenter! That's all! Get me out of here. My heart's starting to bother me now. I refuse to go on!' At 300 volts the learner screamed in agony at each shock and from 330 volts there was silence, as if the confederate were no longer conscious. The participant had the option of continuing up to 450 volts. Milgram was interested in how far participants would go in the experiment. Would they refuse to continue on hearing the discomfort of the learner? Psychiatrists he spoke to prior to the study predicted that only 0.1% of participants would obey the experimenter completely. However, the reality was very different. At 210 volts, even after the learner had complained about his heart, not one participant refused to go on, and only a tiny minority even questioned the experimenter. At 315 volts, when the learner was screaming in agony and apparently on the verge of unconsciousness, only 22% refused to continue. Finally, 65% of participants obeyed the experimenter right up to the maximum shock of 450 volts.

What do these findings mean? Do they show that humans are so immoral that they will cause extreme harm to others just because they are told to? Milgram argued that people who commit extreme acts of aggression at the instruction of a higher authority are not inherently evil. Instead, he proposed that anyone could potentially be influenced by an authority figure to behave aggressively if certain conditions are in place. Milgram argued that, in most societies, there is a general *cultural norm* to obey authority. People are generally rewarded for obeying authority and expect authority figures to be trustworthy and legitimate. In addition, in his experiment the requests to obey increasingly immoral acts were *gradual*. People were led into shocking at potentially lethal levels over a relatively long time so that before they knew it they were administering apparently lethal shocks. Third, Milgram argued that there is a shift in *agency*, so that people no longer regard themselves as personally responsible but attribute responsibility (agency) to others in the context, a phenomenon known as diffusion of responsibility (see Focus Point 19.2).

Professor Philip Zimbardo talks about how obedience can lead ordinary people to do terrible things in **this video**[2].

DISCUSSION POINT

Discuss the main elements of conformity and obedience, and how they compare to one another.

FOCUS POINT 19.2

TEN STEPS TO EVIL

Most of us would probably like to think of human beings as inherently good. Indeed, we can probably all think of examples of nice things we, and those around us, do on a daily basis: looking after our family, helping our friends, doing voluntary work, and so on. But, at the same time, a quick perusal of any newspaper or news website will reveal examples of harmful human behaviour that most of us struggle to understand, such as terrorism, murder, assault, and domestic violence. So how can we make sense of these things? Drawing on Milgram's early work, Zimbardo (2008) argued that a series of situational and systemic factors can seduce an ordinary individual into the harmful behaviours that are often described in the media as 'evil'. The following 10, he argues, are especially important.

1. Get the individual to agree to some form of contractual obligation. Even if this is verbal rather than written, or is not legally binding, having 'signed up' for something, it will be more difficult for individuals to ignore instructions.

2. Give the individual a specific role to play; tell them that this role is important and valuable.

3. Present basic rules to the individual, such as 'any instruction you are given must be obeyed'. This may seem to make sense on first glance but in fact can be used to justify mindless compliance.

4. Use semantic framing to take the focus away from the harmful act; for example, rather than telling an individual who is about to engage in a terrorist act and that they will be harming people, tell them that they will be committing an act of great good in terms of protecting the culture and values of the terrorist group.

5. Provide opportunities for the individual to engage in diffusion of responsibility. For example, in Milgram's obedience studies, participants who were giving electric shocks were told that the experimenter would take responsibility for anything that happened.

6. Start with a small act of harm. Once the door is open, it will be easier for more consequential acts of harm to be undertaken.

7. Gradually escalate the harm: each slightly more harmful act will seem little different from the previous act. Without realizing what has happened, the individual will be engaging in real harm.

8. The authority figure should become increasingly less reasonable and more demanding in their behaviour. The individual will initially have been compliant, but they will later be confused because we expect consistency from authority figures and friends. By this time, however, the individual will be in a pattern of compliant behaviour that it is difficult to back out of.

9. Make it difficult for the individual to leave the situation. Allow them to verbally complain but insist on behavioural compliance; this makes people feel better about what they are doing, as they have at least expressed concerns.

10. Give a desirable, essential outcome of the harmful behaviour that justifies the use of any means to achieve it. Terrorist groups, for example, might use the threat to their religion, ideology, or politics as a justification for their actions, while an interrogator working for their country's secret service might argue that using torture to get information out of terrorists is crucial in order to eliminate threats to national security.

What is so concerning about these steps is how they entail normal social psychological processes, such as adopting the norms and roles of the group we belong to. But, on a more positive note, Zimbardo (2008) argued that understanding the social psychological processes that can lead to extreme acts of harm might be enough to withstand those impulses.

Crowd behaviour

On 6 August 2011, there was a protest in Tottenham, London, about the shooting by police of a local man, Mark Duggan. This quickly escalated, with violent clashes between protesters and the police; the destruction of cars, homes, and businesses; and looting of the damaged properties. Over the following days, the riots spread to other areas of London, and then to other cities, including Birmingham, Bristol, and Manchester. By 15 August, over 3,000 people had been arrested in connection with the riots and there was an estimated £200 million worth of damage caused (BBC News, 2011b). How can these events be explained? Politicians, the media, and the general public were divided. Some commentators focused blame on the individuals involved: these were just criminal individuals from broken homes – hooligans taking opportunity of a tense situation to go out and cause havoc. Others talked of the breakdown of social morality in society and of a 'broken Britain'. However, relatively large numbers were involved in the riots. Were all of these people really innately immoral and aggressive?

An alternative explanation offered was that frustration at perceived racism and classism from the authorities, in combination with difficult economic conditions, might have played a role in the escalation of violence. According to the **frustration–aggression hypothesis** (Dollard, Doob, Miller, Mowrer, & Sears, 1939), aggression is caused by frustration at a particular person or event. If aggression cannot be directly targeted at the cause of the frustration because the person is too physically or socially powerful, or because the cause is a situation rather than a person, it may be redirected onto a more realistic target. In the case of the riots, those frustrated at perceived injustice would have been unable to directly attack the government. Moreover, as the frustration was at a complex situation rather than one individual, the aggression was redirected to more realistic targets such as vehicles, homes, and business.

Psychologists also argue that a unique combination of factors come into play when people are in a large group or a crowd, and this might explain the aggression that occurred. First, being crowded is likely to lead to an increase in physiological arousal and feelings of stress, irritation, and frustration, such that the threshold for aggression is lowered. Second, when people are part of a crowd, or acting as a member of a larger group, they are less likely to see themselves as idiosyncratic individuals and more likely to see themselves as relatively anonymous group members. This process of **deindividuation** leads individuals to see themselves as less identifiable and less accountable for their behaviour than normal. As a result, the social norms that normally inhibit them from behaving aggressively are no longer so applicable. However, despite significant evidence for the role of deindividuation in producing aggression, some social psychologists oppose the idea. According to the **emergent norm theory**, people behave aggressively when they are in a group not because they *ignore* the societal norm of non-violence but because they *adhere* to a different group norm of aggression that may arise in a particular circumstance (Reicher, Spears, & Postmes, 1995). When some members of a group start to behave aggressively, other members are likely to adhere to this behaviour if they perceive it to be normative.

TEST YOURSELF

What factors determine whether or not we behave aggressively?

SECTION SUMMARY

- The presence of others can influence our productivity, judgements, and levels of aggression.

- Research suggests that on simple tasks we perform better in the presence of others but on complex tasks we perform worse; these effects are driven by physiological arousal and evaluation apprehension.

- Research on social loafing suggests that, when we are working in a team, we put in less effort than when we are working alone because we experience a diffusion of responsibility.

- Research on conformity suggests that, in order to conform to group norms, we tend to go along with the attitudes of other group members, even if we know them to be wrong.

- At its most extreme, conformity can lead to groupthink and, thereby, faulty decision making caused by an excessive adherence to group norms.

- Despite this, minorities can also be influential in a group, provided that they are confident and consistent.

- Research on obedience has shown that people often obey authority figures, even when the orders they are obeying might harm others.

- Being in a crowd may also lead to aggression because of the resultant frustration and deindividuation.

INTERGROUP PROCESSES

LEARNING OBJECTIVE 19.4

Compare and contrast explanations for the causes of prejudice, as well as interventions developed by social psychologists to reduce prejudice.

In this section, we will consider how different groups react to, and interact with, one another. In particular, we will examine intergroup prejudice and what can be done to alleviate it. We begin by defining a few key terms that are used frequently in research in this area. An 'in-group' is a social category to which you belong. Other people who share your category membership are 'in-group members'. 'Out-groups' are social categories to which you do not belong, and people who are members of those categories are 'out-group members'. In this section we will also consider **intergroup bias**, the preference people often show for in-groups over out-groups. We will also discuss **prejudice**, a negative attitude or feeling held towards members of an out-group, and **discrimination**, which is negative behaviour, associated with prejudiced attitudes, towards an out-group member.

Prejudice

Although prejudice has undoubtedly reduced in the past century, and what was once considered acceptable is now seen as violating the egalitarian norms of society, prejudice is still a problem in society and can manifest itself in a number of different ways. Overweight individuals are subject to weight stigma – stereotyped as lazy, socially inept, unhappy, ugly, and stupid (Puhl & Brownell, 2001). People with a mental health condition also experience prejudice: in a survey by the UK Department of Health (2014), 16% of respondents believed that those with a mental illness should be excluded from public office, while 71% of women believed that individuals who had at any point been a patient in a mental health hospital could not be trusted as babysitters. Two of the most investigated forms of prejudice are racism and sexism, which we will now discuss in more detail.

Racism

Psychologists have identified two different types of racism. Old-fashioned racism is the blatant expression of negative and unfair stereotypes of others based on their category membership – for example, perceiving African Americans as aggressive (Devine, 1989) and of low intelligence (Steele & Aronson, 1995). Over time, the blatant expression of such views has reduced significantly and we now have societal norms that largely prohibit the open expression of racism. Nonetheless, the Office for National Statistics (2013) estimated there to have been 185,000 racial or religiously motivated hate crimes in England and Wales in 2012 and 2013, demonstrating that some people still hold openly negative views of racial and religious out-groups.

In addition, psychologists argue that there is a second form of racism that people do not admit to, namely **aversive racism**. Gaertner and Dovidio (1986) argued that aversive racists hold two conflicting sets of views. On the one hand, they hold egalitarian values, believing that all people should be treated equally in society, regardless of ethnicity or other social group memberships. But, at the same time, they have been exposed to negative stereotypes that exist in society about minority ethnic groups. As a result of this conflict, aversive racists experience negative emotions about members of other groups, such as uneasiness, fear, and discomfort. As a consequence of this, these individuals may not publicly express (or even hold) racist attitudes, but may nonetheless subtly discriminate against ethnic minority groups.

Sexism

As with racism, sexism can be divided into two types that have been investigated by psychologists. Typically, research on sexism has focused on prejudice towards women, although, in principle, it could just as well apply to prejudice towards men. 'Hostile sexism' refers to the perception of women as holding a range of stereotypical and negative traits, such as being inferior, incompetent, irrational, and weak. However, not all sexist attitudes are negative. 'Benevolent sexism' refers to attitudes that are very positive on the surface but deep down reflect a view of women as inferior to men (Glick & Fiske, 1996). It has three components: 'paternalism', the view that women are less powerful and therefore deserve men's protection; 'gender differentiation', the exaggeration of differences between men (powerful, dominant) and women (warm, emotionally sensitive); and 'heterosexual intimacy', the emphasis on women as objects of beauty and as targets of romantic attraction. Benevolent sexists therefore view women positively *provided* they conform to traditional stereotypes. Abrams, Viki, Masser, and Bohner (2003) found that the higher men scored in benevolent sexism, the more likely they were to blame a woman who was raped in her home by an acquaintance (but not a victim of stranger rape), perhaps because, by taking a man home with her, the woman supposedly violated a traditional view of women as chaste and pure.

Although these two forms of sexism seem quite different, research in fact suggests that it is possible to possess both hostile and benevolent attitudes at the same time. Glick, Diebold, Bailey-Werner, and Zhu (1997) found that men high in 'ambivalent sexism' had polarized views of women that fell into the two types of sexism. Men high in ambivalent sexism who were asked to think about a woman transcending traditional roles (e.g. a career woman) reported negative feelings such as fear and envy. These negative feelings were correlated with hostile sexism but *not* with benevolent sexism. Men high in ambivalent sexism who thought about a woman in a traditional role (e.g. a homemaker) reported positive feelings (warmth, trust), which were correlated with a measure of benevolent sexism but *not* hostile sexism.

Causes of prejudice

Above we have discussed just two of the many types of prejudice that can arise. But why are people prejudiced in the first place? Numerous theories have been developed by social psychologists to try to answer this question. Some focus on characteristics of the prejudiced individual while others focus on the social context in which people find themselves. Both of these sources of prejudice are discussed below.

Personality theories

Some of the earliest studies on prejudice and its causes were conducted by Adorno, Frenkel-Brunswick, Levinson, and Stanford (e.g. 1950). Using the ideas of Sigmund

Freud as a basis, they argued that some people are brought up in a way that gives rise to the development of an **authoritarian personality**, a tendency to express prejudice towards a whole range of minority groups, particularly those perceived as lower status or weak in society. Specifically, they argued that these individuals are reared by very strict parents who do not allow them the opportunity to express the aggression that Freud argued naturally arises in humans. This aggression builds up and is later transferred elsewhere, particularly onto 'easy targets', such as minority groups, who are already in a less powerful position in society and are therefore more easily denigrated.

Supporting this theory, Adorno and colleagues (1950) created an F-scale (with the 'F' standing for fascism), which correlates with participants' levels of prejudice. The study was, however, flawed: the sample was predominately white, male, and middle class, making it impossible to generalize the findings to wider society. Moreover, the F-scale failed to predict racism in South Africa in the 1950s (Pettigrew, 1958) despite a high prevalence of prejudice there. This suggested that other factors must have been explaining prejudice instead.

Sidanius, Pratto, and colleagues (Pratto, Sidanius, Stallworth, & Malle, 1994; Sidanius, 1993) proposed a different personality theory of prejudice. They argued that people vary according to something called **social dominance orientation (SDO)**, which reflects the degree to which people desire a hierarchy of inequality in society. Put simply, those high in SDO believe that some groups are better than others and that it is necessary for society to have high- and low-status groups. The theory argues that these individuals are especially likely to support hierarchy-legitimizing myths – myths that dominant groups use to explain why they deserve their perceived superiority. Examples of this would be making internal attributions for wealth and success (e.g. 'Our group is rich and powerful because we tend to be higher in intelligence and harder working') and notions of fate (e.g. 'God placed us in the high-status group – things are meant to be this way').

There is considerable evidence to support this theory: SDO has been found to predict sexism, nationalism, and ethnic prejudice against a range of minority groups and among samples from a range of countries including Canada, China, Israel, Mexico, New Zealand, Taiwan, and the United States. There is also evidence that people high in SDO support the suspension of civil liberties and are opposed to immigration and gay rights (Pratto et al., 1994). But there is a limitation to any theory that attributes prejudice to personality traits: such theories cannot adequately explain why levels of prejudice vary over time or between different contexts. While it is clear that individuals vary in their level of prejudice, it is also important to understand variations between contexts. It is to theories that focus on the social context that we now turn.

Situational theories

Muzafer Sherif and his colleagues pioneered research into the situational causes of prejudice in the 1950s (Sherif & Sherif, 1953; Sherif, White, & Harvey, 1955). To examine how intergroup conflict arises and how it can be alleviated, they organized a field study at a summer camp at Robbers Cave State Park, near Oklahoma City in the United States. The camp was attended by 20 white, middle-class, 11- to 12-year-old boys who were there to take part in outdoor pursuits. Sherif and his colleagues orchestrated three stages during which they observed the behaviour of the boys. In the first stage, boys arriving at the camp were divided into two groups. They quickly became cohesive, coming up with group names (the Eagles and Rattlers) and putting down members of the other group. In the next stage, the groups competed in a series of games, such as baseball and tug-of-war, with the successful team winning a prize. At this point Sherif noticed a dramatic increase in conflict between the two groups, with each group derogating the other, burning the other's flags, and ransacking each other's cabins. Finally, to reduce conflict, a cooperative goal was introduced: the boys' bus appeared to break down on their way back to the camp and only by working *together* to push-start the bus would they achieve the goal of getting the bus going again. This task reduced conflict and increased liking between the members of the two groups. See Socially Psyched (n.d.) for more about this experiment.

These findings contributed to the development of the **realistic group conflict theory** (Levine & Campbell, 1972), which proposed that conflict and prejudice between groups was the result of competition for scarce resources. In the case of Sherif's study, conflict increased when the groups were competing for a prize that only one group could win. However, this theory cannot explain why, even *before* any competition for resources, the groups began to compare themselves to, and even derogate, each other. Understanding why this might happen was the focus of research by Henri Tajfel and his colleagues.

Tajfel, Billig, Bundy, and Flament (1971) showed participants, on arrival at the laboratory, a number of slides of abstract paintings by two artists, Paul Klee and Wassily Kandinsky, and asked them to indicate which pictures they preferred. They were told that they had been assigned to either the 'Klee' or the 'Kandinsky' group based on their preferences, but in reality participants were randomly assigned to conditions. Next, participants were required to allocate points, which represented money, to people in the two groups. The points were allocated via a series of decision matrices on which participants indicated with a cross through one column how much an anonymous in-group member and an anonymous out-group member should receive. There were a number of options available; for example, the participant could give the in-group member and out-group member the same amount of money, give the in-group member more than the out-group member, or vice versa. Importantly, allocation was completely anonymous and, because participants could not allocate points to themselves, there was no element of self-interest.

Aside from their apparent painting preference, participants knew nothing about the group members or any of their characteristics. The group had no shared history and no real meaning. For this reason, this type of study became known as the **minimal group paradigm**. The *only* thing that participants knew about the people to whom they were allocating points was whether they were an in-group member or an out-group member. Nonetheless, Tajfel and colleagues observed a persistent tendency for participants to allocate more points to people in their own group compared with people in other groups. Put another way, it seems that simply knowing that someone is in the same group as you is sufficient to elicit intergroup bias. This finding is important because it suggests that there is a psychological component to prejudice beyond any economic, political, or historical factor. Interestingly, research examining brain activity after assignment to minimal groups has found that people are also better, at a neurological level, at visually encoding information about the faces of in-group members than those of out-group members (Ratner & Amodio, 2013).

To explain how 'mere categorization' can lead to intergroup bias, Tajfel and his colleague John Turner (Tajfel & Turner, 1979) developed **social identity theory**. According to this approach, people's identity can be divided into two components: our *personal identity*, which refers to idiosyncratic components of the self, such as our personality traits, values, and beliefs, and our *social identity*, which refers to the numerous groups to which we belong. The theory goes on to argue that people prefer to feel good about themselves: to have a positive self-concept or high self-esteem. One potential source of self-esteem is the social groups to which we belong. If our social groups are seen as being of high status and positively valued, then by extension we, as members of such groups, can also view ourselves positively (Abrams & Hogg, 1990). However, in order to achieve a positive self-esteem through our group, it is crucial that we see our group in a positive light. In order to achieve this, we are motivated to do what we can to increase the status of our own group relative to others. According to this theory, then, people give more money to in-group members than out-group members, even though they will not personally benefit, because this will make the in-group better off (and therefore of a higher status) than the out-group. This will increase the value of the group and, in turn, our own self-esteem (e.g. Rubin & Hewstone, 1998).

DISCUSSION POINT

Discuss factors that might explain why people are sometimes prejudiced towards other groups. Have you ever witnessed or experienced prejudice towards specific groups?

Reducing prejudice

There are far-reaching consequences for people who experience prejudice and discrimination. In a meta-analysis of 134 studies, Pascoe and Smart (2009) found a significant negative effect of perceived discrimination on both physical and mental health. Reminding a stigmatized individual of the discrimination they face can also result in self-defeating behaviours. Major, Hunger, Bunyan, and Miller (2014) reminded women of weight stigma by having them read a news article on the subject or, in a control condition, had them read an article on a different subject. They were then placed in a room that contained sweets and snacks. Overweight participants in the weight-stigma condition subsequently consumed more calories and reported feeling that they had less control over their weight, while the manipulation had no effect on non-overweight women. Given these sorts of consequences, it is more important than ever that we develop interventions to alleviate prejudice. Below, we examine three approaches to reducing prejudice that have been developed by psychologists.

The intergroup contact approach

According to the **contact hypothesis**, contact between members of different social groups will lead to more positive attitudes towards others (Allport, 1954). However, the theory cautions that the contact must have certain qualities in order for it to have positive consequences. First, there must be institutional support for the contact; for example, government policy, schools, and workplaces should support the integration of different groups. Second, contact must occur under conditions of equal status. If a minority group has contact with the majority group as a subordinate then this is likely to perpetuate negative stereotypes of inferiority. Third, contact must involve cooperation to achieve a common goal. This was neatly illustrated by Sherif and Sherif's (1953) summer camp study described above.

Intergroup contact has been studied extensively since the mid-20th century, with many hundreds of studies testing its basic principles. So, how effective is contact at reducing prejudice? A meta-analysis, which examined 515 contact studies, was conducted by Pettigrew and Tropp (2006) and found that contact had a robust negative effect on prejudice. Contact that met the qualities noted above was especially effective, but even contact that did not meet these criteria was still effective in reducing prejudice. Given the strength of these findings, it is perhaps unsurprising that intergroup contact is now one of the most widely used psychological interventions for the reduction of prejudice and the improvement of intergroup relations (Oskamp & Jones, 2000).

Nonetheless, contact research has been subject to criticism. Some theorists have questioned whether the effects of contact will always generalize beyond the immediate situation to other situations and from the individuals involved in the contact to the entire out-group. For instance, if a white person and a black person have a friendly, positive interaction with one another, although they will likely develop a positive opinion of one another, how can we be sure (1) that they would be nice to members of the other ethnic group in other situations and (2) that they would have a more positive attitude towards the other ethnic group *in general*? Contact may also lead to 'subtyping' of individuals involved in the contact away from the group representation. The white person in the previous example may, for example, decide that, although they like the black person they met, this person is unusual, an 'exception to the rule', and therefore cannot be considered representative of black people in general. However, it is now generally agreed that, provided that the contact is positive *and* those involved remain aware of their respective group memberships, contact is likely to be effective at generalizing from the contact situation to the out-group as a whole (Brown & Hewstone, 2005).

Another limitation is that contact can only be used as an intervention to reduce prejudice when group members have the *opportunity* for contact in the first place. That is, unless an individual lives in the same community, attends the same school, or works in the same place as out-group members, they will not be able to form friendships with them. As a result, this approach may not be useful in segregated settings. In addition, there is evidence that, even when people live in diverse settings and the opportunities for contact do exist, people have a tendency to self-segregate (e.g. Aboud & Sankar, 2007; Graham & Cohen, 1997), forming relationships primarily with people from the same group as themselves. This may occur for a number of reasons. First, as noted earlier in the chapter, we like people who are similar to ourselves and may assume people in the same social group as us share similar characteristics. Second, people may avoid intergroup contact because they experience 'intergroup anxiety'. This is the negative emotional arousal that can arise when anticipating an intergroup encounter because they fear behaving in an incompetent or offensive manner, or being rejected by an out-group member (Stephan & Stephan, 1985).

Now we must ask, how can we get around these concerns? Research on 'indirect contact' may provide a solution. Indirect contact refers to interventions that are based on the principles of contact theory but don't involve any direct, face-to-face interaction. As a result, they can be used in segregated settings and may be less anxiety inducing while still having some of the benefits of direct contact.

Wright, Aron, McLaughlin-Volpe, and Ropp (1997) showed that *just the knowledge* that other people in your group have friends in the out-group can reduce intergroup bias, a phenomenon referred to as **extended contact**. To test this idea, participants were divided into two small groups, which then competed with one another in a series of tasks. This increased intergroup bias. Next, two participants, one from each group, worked together on a task that had previously been shown to create high levels of interpersonal closeness among pairs of strangers in a short period of time. They then returned to their groups to share their experience of intergroup contact. This led to a significant reduction in intergroup bias among group members, even though they did not personally interact with an out-group member.

Extended contact has been successfully applied with children in educational contexts. Non-disabled children who read stories about a friendship between a non-disabled and a disabled child subsequently showed more positive attitudes towards disabled children (Cameron & Rutland, 2006). Extended contact works by reducing intergroup anxiety (Paolini, Hewstone, Cairns, & Voci, 2004; Turner, Hewstone, Voci, & Vonofakou, 2008). Knowing an in-group member who has experienced positive contact with an out-group member shows us that contact with the other group might not be so bad; perhaps we won't be rejected or say something inappropriate. Supporting this idea, West and Turner (2014) found that observing an intergroup encounter reduced anticipatory stress (e.g. an increase in heart rate) among participants who had been told they were about to meet an out-group member.

A second type of indirect contact, **imagined contact**, is the mental simulation of a social interaction with an out-group member (Crisp & Turner, 2009). Mentally simulating a positive contact experience activates concepts normally associated with successful interactions with members of other groups. These can include feeling more comfortable and less apprehensive about the prospect of future contact with the group, and this reduced anxiety should reduce negative out-group attitudes. When people imagine intergroup contact, they also engage in conscious processes that parallel the processes involved in actual intergroup contact. They may, for example, actively think about what they would learn about the out-group member and how they would feel during the interaction. This will provide them with a clear script regarding how to behave in an intergroup context, which may help to reduce the anxiety often experienced when anticipating contact.

To test this idea, Turner, Crisp, and Lambert (2007) asked young participants to spend a minute imagining a positive interaction with an older adult. Participants in a control condition were asked to imagine an outdoor scene instead. After writing down what they had imagined, participants were told about a future study in which they would be asked to interact with either an older person or a young person, and were asked to indicate how keen they would be to take part in these two interactions. While participants in the control condition were biased in favour of young people, preferring to interact with a young person rather than an older person, those who had previously imagined interacting with an older person were equally happy to interact with an older person or a young person. Imagined contact has subsequently been shown to improve attitudes towards a variety of target groups, including ethnic minorities and religious groups (for a review, see Crisp & Turner, 2012).

Although both direct and indirect forms of contact can reduce prejudice, there are some differences between the two approaches. Indirect forms of contact are more versatile because they are not reliant on opportunity for contact, which means they can be used to improve attitudes even in segregated settings (e.g. Turner, Hewstone, & Voci, 2007). They are easier to implement from a practical point of view and are likely to be less expensive and time consuming because they can be done in the classroom without having to physically bring two groups together. On the other hand, attitudes based on direct experience are thought to be longer-lasting and more powerful than attitudes based on indirect experiences (Stangor, Sullivan, & Ford, 1991). Research comparing actual and extended contact, for example, typically shows actual contact to have the stronger impact on prejudice (Paolini et al., 2004). These findings suggest that, when no opportunities exist, indirect contact will work best, but, when opportunities are present, direct-contact interventions will be more useful. However, indirect interventions might also be used as a precursor to direct contact, helping to prepare people for such encounters by reducing high initial anxiety levels (Crisp & Turner, 2009, 2012). For another take on indirect contact, see Focus Point 19.3.

FOCUS POINT 19.3

USING ONLINE CONTACT IN THE CLASSROOM TO REDUCE PREJUDICE

White and Abu-Rayya (2012) developed and tested a novel intervention that they called electronic contact, or e-contact. Like extended and imagined contact, e-contact is a form of indirect contact because in-group and out-group members never physically meet or see one another. Instead, they interact using a synchronous internet text-only chat tool.

White and Abu-Rayya tested e-contact between 104 Christians and 116 Muslims attending religiously segregated high schools in Australia. Pairs of Christian children took part in a classroom project on environmental issues with pairs of Muslim children. Each week for 9 weeks, the group of four children (two Christian and two Muslim) worked on the project together using the online chat tool for sessions lasting 45 minutes. The task encompassed the characteristics originally proposed by Allport's (1954) contact hypothesis that are thought to make contact especially effective at reducing prejudice. The children were working together as equal participants on a cooperative task in order to achieve a common goal – namely, producing a poster about environmental issues. As this was a classroom activity incorporated into the curriculum, there was also institutional support for the contact. To make the intervention even more effective, the respective religious group memberships of the participants *and* the shared group membership (that the children were all Australian) were emphasized during the programme. Emphasizing a common in-group identity is known to have benefits for intergroup relations, but, by emphasizing the unique group memberships of those involved, any positive effects are likely to be generalized to the out-group as a whole (e.g. Brown & Hewstone, 2005) and are likely to avoid any threat to group distinctiveness that can be caused by emphasizing a common in-group. This strategy is referred to as holding a dual identity (Gaertner & Dovidio, 2000).

To test the effectiveness of the programme, children completed measures of inter-group bias and intergroup anxiety before the start of the intervention, 2 weeks after the programme ended, and 6 months later. The same measures were taken from a group of control children, who undertook the same programme but with children from the same religious group as them.

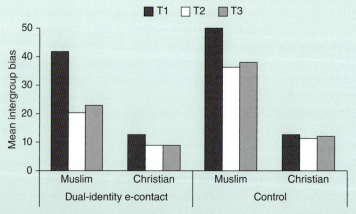

Source: Reprinted from White and Abu-Rayya (2012). Copyright 2012, with permission from Elsevier.

While there was no change in intergroup bias and intergroup anxiety over time in the control condition, children who took part in the programme showed a significant reduction in intergroup bias and intergroup anxiety between the pre-test and the 2-week post-test. More encouragingly, levels of bias and anxiety remained lower 6 months later, suggesting that the programme had a long-term effect on children's intergroup attitudes.

While many prejudice-reduction interventions used in the classroom are based on teachers' intuition, these findings highlight the value of developing interventions based on social psychological theory and research, and applying them in an educational setting.

Changing social categorization

Earlier, we introduced the minimal group paradigm and how merely categorizing people as in-group or out-group members is sufficient to generate intergroup bias (Tajfel et al., 1971). Turning this idea on its head, social psychologists have asked whether strategies that *change* the way we categorize people might help to reduce intergroup bias and prejudice.

Gaertner and Dovidio (2000) proposed that, rather than people seeing themselves as in-group or out-group members, if people realize that they all belong to one overarching group, this might reduce intergroup bias. According to their **common in-group identity model**, if individuals from two separate groups come to perceive themselves as members of just one inclusive group, the initial groups will be eliminated and everyone within the inclusive group will be perceived as in-group members and will therefore be liked equally. To test this idea, Gaertner, Mann, Murrell, and Dovidio (1989) assigned participants to one of two groups (A and B). They then seated them around a table to complete a task, but how they were seated varied depending on the condition. In the *two-groups condition*, members of group A were seated on one side of the table and members of group B on the other. Participants wore a name badge that reflected their group membership. In the *common in-group condition*, the members of the two groups were seated alternately around the table, so that each member of group A was seated next to two members of group B and the two groups were fully integrated. The participants were also each given a badge with the same name on to reflect their common group membership. Supporting the theory, it emerged that participants showed significantly less intergroup bias in the common in-group condition than in the two-groups condition.

Despite the advantages of encouraging a common in-group identity, Hewstone (1996) questioned whether recategorization can overcome powerful ethnic and racial categorizations on more than a temporary basis, or work where there is intense intergroup conflict. We cannot, for example, imagine Catholics and Protestants in Northern Ireland relinquishing their religious group membership – an important aspect of their identity – to be known simply as 'Northern Irish'. Indeed, research has shown that categorizing people from two groups into one overarching group can actually lead to an increase in intergroup bias among people for high in-group identifiers – individuals for whom a group membership is very important (Crisp, Stone, & Hall, 2006).

A third approach to reducing prejudice, the **multiple categorization approach**, is based on encouraging people to use *many* different ways of categorizing people, rather than thinking about others all the time in terms of simple social categorizations. To test this idea, Crisp, Hewstone, and Rubin (2001) asked university students to think about a number of different categorizations that they could use to describe someone from a rival university, other than their university membership. Compared with a control condition where participants did not engage in this task, participants subsequently had lower levels of intergroup bias (favouritism for their own university over the rival university).

So, why does multiple categorization reduce intergroup bias? It is thought that, when the social context is simple – that is, we perceive people in terms of just one or two groups – it is easy to use those group memberships to form judgements of the out-group, resulting in intergroup bias. However, when the social context becomes increasingly complex and we realize someone can be categorized in a whole host of different ways, it is very difficult to use group-related information to form judgements. It might be easy to form perceptions of an 'Asian woman', for example, but, if the perceiver thinks of that same individual as a 'single, atheist, educated, female, Asian scientist', this is simply too difficult to process using group memberships. In this situation, the perceiver may be forced to seek alternative ways of forming an impression of a person. Theories of impression formation (Brewer, 1988; Fiske & Neuberg, 1990) suggest that, although people tend to use categories to process information, where there is a poor fit between the category and the target, there is a shift towards an individuated mode of processing: seeing the individual in terms of their individual traits rather than the group to which they belong.

SECTION SUMMARY

- This section introduced intergroup processes.
- Prejudice can manifest itself in many forms (e.g. weight and mental health stigma) but much research has focused on racism and sexism.
- Research suggests that our personality characteristics (whether we have an authoritarian personality or are high in social dominance), alongside situational factors such as a scarcity of resources and social categorization, can help to explain why we display intergroup biases and prejudice.
- Social psychologists have developed numerous means of reducing prejudice. Contact between members of different groups, under the right conditions, reduces prejudice.
- Even using contact in an indirect manner – learning about others' contact experiences, and imagining a positive intergroup encounter – has benefits for intergroup relations.
- Changing the way we categorize can help too: emphasizing an overarching group that members of both groups belong to or encouraging people to categorize along many different dimension – rendering categories useless as a way of forming judgements – both help to reduce intergroup bias.

FUTURE DIRECTIONS

LEARNING OBJECTIVE 19.5

Critically evaluate possible future directions for research in interpersonal, group, and intergroup processes.

The interests of social psychologists are constantly changing and developing in order to understand a fast-paced and ever-changing social world. A key focus of research in the next decade will be how technological developments affect our communication with others, in terms of our friendships and romantic relationships (interpersonal processes), our work team (group processes), and our interactions with and perceptions of members of other social groups (intergroup processes). There are now believed to be over 3 billion internet users worldwide (World Internet User Statistics, 2014), and more than 80% of these users access the internet via a smartphone (Smart Insights, 2015). Given our increasing reliance on these technologies, social psychologists have already begun to examine the role they play in influencing our social behaviour, but this will increasingly come into the spotlight in coming years.

Romantic relationships now often begin over internet dating websites and phone dating apps such as Tinder. Researchers will be interested in understanding how this influences our choice of romantic partners. Are there core similarities in the predictors of attraction in online and traditional dating, or does the use of technology affect what is perceived as important? With regard to group processes, increasingly work meetings occur online via Skype (for example) rather than face to face. Does the online nature of these interactions affect group behaviour and, in turn, work productivity and creativity? Finally, can online intergroup encounters – for example, e-contact, described earlier in the chapter (White & Abu-Rayya, 2012) – have as powerful an impact as face-to-face contact? And, in a world in which we increasingly interact with others online, how can we best harness online communication to improve intergroup relations?

Another key area of pursuit for social psychologists in the coming years will involve working at the interface of different disciplines. Rather than focusing purely on psychology to understand social phenomena, we can learn from and develop exciting new approaches by working with academics in other fields. For example, intergroup processes researchers and educationalists can work together to develop school-based interventions that not only improve intergroup relations but also improve educational outcomes. Similarly, interpersonal relations researchers might work with computer scientists to develop new smartphone apps that can be used by people to improve their success in dating. By working with researchers from other disciplines, the fields of interpersonal, group, and intergroup relations can be considerably enriched.

ACTIVITY 19.1

DEVELOP YOUR OWN PREJUDICE-REDUCTION INTERVENTION

In this chapter, we have discussed some of the theories devised by social psychologists to explain why prejudice arises and how it might be reduced. Using your knowledge of these theories, come up with your own intervention that could be used in an educational setting to reduce prejudice.

When coming up with your intervention, you might want to consider the following:

- Look at theories on the situational causes of prejudice. Can you turn these on their head? If a particular situation increases prejudice, can you reverse the situation to reduce prejudice?

- Look at the personality approaches to prejudice. Will your intervention work for people with a prejudiced personality? Can you think of ways to make your intervention more effective for these individuals?

- Look at the theories and research on intergroup contact, indirect contact, and changing social categorization. Based on the evidence, which of these might be most effective? Might different strategies be used in combination to reduce prejudice or would an intervention based on just one theory work best?

SECTION SUMMARY

- A key focus of research in the next decade will be how technological developments will affect social psychological processes.

- Examining the psychological processes involved in widely used online dating websites and smartphone apps will become increasingly important.

- The use of online methods to reduce prejudice and discrimination, for example encouraging e-contact between groups, is a valuable line of research.

- Perhaps some of the most exciting findings in social psychology will emerge through its integration with other disciplines; for example, social psychologists and computer scientists might work together to create optimal dating apps.

CHAPTER SUMMARY

In this chapter, we considered some of the key theories and studies on interpersonal, group, and intergroup processes. We started by examining interpersonal relations, exploring who we like to be friends with (similar others who we see often), how friendships develop (through an escalation of self-disclosure), what determines romantic attraction (physical features such as body shape and facial features, in addition to perceived similarity), and what determines a successful relationship (equity, a good cost–benefit analysis, and intimacy). We then moved on to group processes and developed our understanding of how our productivity is affected by the presence of others, how group norms can lead to conformity in judgements and attitudes, how the minority can affect our views, and how obedience to authority figures as well as frustration and deindividuation in a crowd can lead to aggression. Finally, we considered intergroup processes, discovering some of the ways in which prejudice can manifest itself and outlining what factors might predict prejudiced attitudes. These include holding certain personality traits, such as being high in authoritarianism or a social dominance orientation, and experiencing certain situations, such as a perceived lack of resources. We also examined some of the ways in which social psychologists have tried to reduce prejudice, including experiences of intergroup contact, either direct or indirect, and changing the way in which we categorize the people around us.

ESSAY QUESTIONS

1. Which is more important in understanding romantic attraction: physical characteristics or attitudes and values?

2. Does the presence of others affect our behaviour for the better or for the worse?

3. Compare and contrast direct and indirect contact as ways of reducing prejudice.

KEY TERMS

- **affiliation:** A social link formed between two or more individuals.
- **aggression:** Verbal or physical acts intended to cause harm to someone or something.
- **authoritarian personality:** The theory that people who have overly strict parents during childhood have a tendency to derogate and show hostility towards minority groups.
- **aversive racism:** A conflict between modern egalitarian values and negative emotions towards out-group members, resulting in negative emotions such as uneasiness, fear, and discomfort.
- **common in-group identity model:** The theory that recategorizing members of two groups into one overarching, superordinate group will reduce intergroup bias.
- **compassionate love:** The less intense but more enduring type of love that characterizes long-term relationships, once passionate love has waned.
- **conformity:** Attitude or behaviour change in the presence of others, in response to a social norm.
- **contact hypothesis:** The premise that, under conditions of cooperation, common goals, equal status, and institutional support, contact between members of two different groups should lead to more positive attitudes towards the other group.
- **deindividuation:** The process by which people lose their identity as an idiosyncratic individual and come to perceive themselves as an anonymous – and therefore less accountable – group member.
- **diffusion of responsibility:** The tendency perceivers have to assume less personal responsibility for something in the presence of others, who might take personal responsibility for the situation instead.
- **discrimination:** The negative behaviour towards an out-group member that is associated with prejudiced attitudes.
- **drive theory:** Zajonc (1965) proposed that the mere presence of others increases physiological arousal, which, in turn, enhances the performance of automatic response tendencies.
- **emergent norm theory:** The proposal that people may adhere to a novel group norm that may arise in a particular circumstance.
- **entitativity:** The extent to which a collection of individuals is perceived as 'group-like'. A group has entitativity if it is cohesive, interconnected, and similar, and if it shares common goals and involves physical interaction.

- **equity theory:** Based on social exchange theory, this theory proposes that a relationship is most likely to be successful when each partner believes their ratio of inputs to outputs is equal.
- **evaluation apprehension:** Concern about being evaluated by others. People who are more publicly self-aware tend to be more nervous at the prospect of a negative evaluation from those around them.
- **extended contact:** A form of indirect contact whereby just knowing that other people in your group have friends in an out-group can reduce prejudice, even when you yourself have had no direct contact with the out-group.
- **frustration–aggression hypothesis:** The idea that aggression is a direct consequence of feelings of frustration that people experience. The theory been used to explain hate crimes during times of economic difficulty.
- **group polarization:** A shift in attitude towards an extreme version of the initial social norm that can occur when people are making a decision as a group.
- **groupthink:** An extreme form of group polarization that can lead to groups making poor decisions.
- **imagined contact:** A form of indirect contact in which people are encouraged to imagine a positive social interaction with a member or members of an out-group.
- **intergroup bias:** The tendency we have to evaluate in-group members more positively than out-group members.
- **investment model:** A theory that proposes that people will be committed to a relationship to the extent that they have high satisfaction, low perceived quality of alternatives, and a high level of investment.
- **looks-for-status exchange:** The idea that youth and beauty tend to be more important determinants of attractiveness in women than status, whereas status and power are more important than physical attributes in men.
- **mere exposure hypothesis:** The idea that the more exposure we have to a stimulus, whether it is an object or a person, the more positive is our attitude towards it.
- **minimal group paradigm:** A classic experimental context in which groups are formed on an ad hoc basis, with no obvious reason to compete with one another.
- **multiple categorization approach:** An approach to reducing prejudice based on encouraging people to use many different ways of categorizing people, rather than thinking about others all the time in terms of simple social categorizations.
- **obedience:** Attitude or behaviour change in response to an explicit order.
- **passionate love:** The intense longing for another person that is experienced during the early stages of a romantic relationship.
- **prejudice:** A negative attitude or feeling held towards members of an out-group.
- **realistic group conflict theory:** The theory that conflict between groups results from competition for scarce resources.
- **social dominance orientation (SDO):** An attitude held by people who favour intergroup hierarchies, believing that high-status groups deserve their dominance over low-status groups.
- **social exchange theory:** According to this theory, a key characteristic of social relationships is the exchange of valuable 'goods', whether material or emotional.
- **social facilitation:** The tendency for people to perform better when in front of an audience.
- **social identity theory:** A theory that proposes that when our membership in a particular group is salient, it is our social self rather than our personal self that guides our self-concept, attitudes, and behaviour.
- **social inhibition:** The tendency for people to perform worse when they are being watched.
- **social loafing:** The tendency for individuals to reduce the amount of effort they put in as group size increases.
- **social norms:** Attitudes and behaviours that are commonly held in a particular group and that hold a powerful influence over the attitudes and behaviours of group members.

- **social penetration theory:** The proposal that the way in which friendships initially develop – and break down – is dependent upon reciprocal self-disclosure.
- **three-factor theory of love:** This theory argues that three conditions must be met to fall in love: (1) understanding and accepting the concept of love, (2) meeting a suitable potential lover, and (3) attributing physiological arousal to the presence of the potential lover.

NOTES

1. http://ed.ted.com/on/lDgf2zQ4
2. http://www.youtube.com/watch?v=8g1MJeHYlE0

FURTHER RESOURCES

Brown, R. (2010). *Prejudice: It's social psychology.* Malden, MA: Wiley-Blackwell.

Crisp, R. J., & Turner, R. N. (2009). Can imagined interactions produce positive perceptions? Reducing prejudice through simulated social contact. *American Psychologist, 64*, 231–240.

Fugere, M. A., Leszczynski, J. P., & Cousins, A. J. (2015). *The social psychology of attraction and romantic relationships.* London, UK: Palgrave.

Karremans, J. C., & Verwijmeren, T. (2008). Mimicking attractive opposite-sex others: The role of romantic relationship status. *Personality and Social Psychology Bulletin, 34*, 939–950.

Levine, J. M. (Ed.). (2013). *Group processes.* New York, NY: Psychology Press.

Spielman, S. S., & McDonald, G. (2016). Nice guys finish first when presented second: Responsive daters are evaluated more positively following exposure to non-responsive daters. *Journal of Experimental Social Psychology, 64*, 99–105.

Sprecher, S., Treger, S., Wondra, J. D., Hilaire, N., & Wallpe, K. (2013). Taking turns: Reciprocal self-disclosure promotes liking in initial interactions. *Journal of Experimental Social Psychology, 49*, 860–866.

Stott, C., & Drury, J. (2016). Contemporary understanding of riots: Classic crowd behaviour psychology, ideology, and the social identity approach. *Public Understanding of Science, 26*, 2–14.

Vezzali, L., Stathi, S., Giovannini, D., Capozza, D., & Trifiletti, E. (2014). The greatest magic of Harry Potter: Reducing prejudice. *Journal of Applied Social Psychology, 45*, 105–121.

Wagner, U., Tropp, L. R., Finchilescu, G., & Tredoux, C. (Eds.) (2008). *Improving intergroup relations: Building on the legacy of Thomas F. Pettigrew.* Malden, MA: Blackwell.

White, F. A., & Abu-Rayya, H. M. (2012). A dual identity-electronic contact (DIEC) experiment promoting short- and long-term intergroup harmony. *Journal of Experimental Social Psychology, 48*, 597–608.

REFERENCES

Aboud, F. E., & Sankar, J. (2007). Friendship and identity in a language-integrated school. *International Journal of Behavioral Development, 31*, 445–453.

Abrams, D., & Hogg, M. A. (1990). *Social identity theory: Constructive and critical advances.* London, UK: Harvester Wheatsheaf.

Abrams, D., Viki, G. T., Masser, B., & Bohner, G. (2003). Perceptions of stranger and acquaintance rape: The role of benevolent and hostile sexism in victim blame and rape proclivity. *Journal of Personality and Social Psychology, 84*, 111–125.

Adorno, T. W., Frenkel-Brunswick, E., Levinson, D. J., & Stanford, R. N. (1950). *The authoritarian personality*. New York, NY: Harper & Row.

Allport, F. H. (1920). The influence of the group upon association and thought. *Journal of Experimental Psychology, 3*, 159–182.

Allport, G. W. (1954). *The nature of prejudice*. Reading, MA: Addison-Wesley.

Allport, G. W. (1965). *Letters from Jenny*. New York, NY: Harcourt Brace College Publishers.

Altman, I., & Taylor, D. A. (1973). *Social penetration: The development of interpersonal relationships*. New York, NY: Holt, Rinehart and Winston.

Anderson, J. L., Crawford, C. B., Nadeau, J., & Lindberg, T. (1992). Was the Duchess of Windsor right? A cross-cultural review of the socioecology of ideals of the female body shape. *Ethology and Sociology, 13*, 197–227.

Ansari A. (2014). We're genetically linked to our friends. *CNN*, 15 July. Retrieved 26 January 2018 from http://edition.cnn.com/2014/07/14/health/friends-genetic-link

Aron, A., Paris, M., & Aron, E. N. (1995). Falling in love: Prospective studies of self-concept change. *Journal of Personality and Social Psychology, 69*, 1102–1112.

Asch, S. E. (1951). Effects of group pressure upon the modification and distortion of judgments. In H. Guetzkow (Ed.), *Groups, leadership and men: Research in human relations* (pp. 177–190). Pittsburgh, PA: Carnegie Press.

Baumeister, R. F., & Leary, M. R. (1995). The need to belong: Desire for interpersonal attachments as a fundamental human motivation. *Psychological Bulletin, 117*, 497–529.

Baumeister, R. F., & Tice, D. M. (1990). Anxiety and social exclusion. *Journal of Social and Clinical Psychology, 9*, 165–195.

BBC News. (2011a). Jerry Sandusky regrets showers with boys at Penn State. Retrieved 14 November 2014 from http://www.bbc.co.uk/news/world-us-canada-15730317

BBC News. (2011b). English riots: Maps and timeline. Retrieved 18 January 2014 from http://www.bbc.co.uk/news/uk-10321233

Berg, J. H. (1984). The development of friendships between roommates. *Journal of Personality and Social Psychology, 46*, 346–356.

Berscheid, E., Dion, K., Walster, E., & Walster, W. G. (1971). Physical attractiveness and dating choice: A test of the matching hypothesis. *Journal of Experimental Social Psychology, 7*, 173–189.

Brewer, M. B. (1988). A dual process model of impression formation. In T. K. Srull & R. S. Wyer (Eds.), *Advances in social cognition* (Vol. 1, pp. 1–36). Hillsdale, NJ: Lawrence Erlbaum Associates.

Brown, R., & Hewstone, H. (2005). An integrative theory of intergroup contact. In M. P. Zanna (Ed.), *Advances in experimental social psychology* (Vol. 37, pp. 255–343). San Diego, CA: Academic Press.

Buunk, B. P., & VanYperen, N. W. (1991). Referential comparisons, relational comparisons and exchange orientation: Their relation to marital satisfaction. *Personality and Social Psychology Bulletin, 17*, 710–718.

Byrne, D., & Nelson, D. (1965). Attraction as a linear function of proportion of positive reinforcements. *Journal of Personality and Social Psychology, 1*, 659–663.

Cameron, L., & Rutland, A. (2006). Extended contact through story reading in school: Reducing children's prejudice towards the disabled. *Journal of Social Issues, 62*, 469–488.

Campbell, A., Cumming, S., & Hughes, I. (2006). Internet use by the socially fearful: Addiction or therapy? *Cyberpsychology and Behavior, 9*, 69–81.

Clerkin, E. M., Smith, A. R., & Hames, J. L. (2013). The interpersonal effects of Facebook reassurance seeking. *Journal of Affective Disorders, 151*, 525–530.

Clore, G. L. (1976). Interpersonal attraction: An overview. In J. W. Thibaut, J. T. Spence, & R. T. Carson (Eds.), *Contemporary topics in social psychology* (pp. 135–175). Morristown, NJ: General Learning Press.

Cogan, J. C., Bhalla, S. K., Sefa-Dedeh, A., & Rothblum, E. D. (1996). A comparison study of United States and African students on perceptions of obesity and thinness. *Journal of Cross-Cultural Psychology, 27*, 98–113.

Cohen, L. J., & DeBenedet, A. T. (2012). Penn State cover-up: Groupthink in action. *Time Ideas*, 17 July. Retrieved 8 February 2014 from http://ideas.time.com/2012/07/17/penn-state-cover-up-group-think-in-action

Comer, D. R. (1995). A model of social loafing in real work groups. *Human Relations*, 48, 647–667.

Cottrell, N. B., Wack, D. L., Sekerak, G. J., & Rittle, R. H. (1968). Social facilitation of dominant responses by the presence of an audience and the mere presence of others. *Journal of Personality and Social Psychology*, 9, 245–250.

Crisp, R. J., Hewstone, M., & Rubin, M. (2001). Does multiple categorization reduce intergroup bias? *Personality and Social Psychology Bulletin*, 27, 76–89.

Crisp, R. J., Stone, C. H., & Hall, N. R. (2006). Recategorization and subgroup identification: Predicting and preventing threats from common ingroups. *Personality and Social Psychology Bulletin*, 32, 230–243.

Crisp, R. J., & Turner, R. N. (2009). Can imagined interactions produce positive perceptions? Reducing prejudice through simulated social contact. *American Psychologist*, 64, 231–240.

Crisp, R. J., & Turner, R. N. (2012). The imagined contact hypothesis. In M. P. Zanna & J. Olson (Eds.), *Advances in experimental social psychology* (Vol. 46, pp. 125–182). Orlando, FL: Academic Press.

Department of Health. (2014). *Attitudes to mental illness 2014*. Retrieved 8 February 2018 from https://www.time-to-change.org.uk/sites/default/files/Attitudes_to_mental_illness_2014_report_final_0.pdf

Deutsch, M., & Gerard, H. B. (1955). A study of normative and informational influences upon individual judgment. *Journal of Abnormal and Social Psychology*, 51, 629–636.

Devine, P. G. (1989). Stereotypes and prejudice: Their automatic and controlled components. *Journal of Personality and Social Psychology*, 56, 5–18.

Dollard, J., Doob, L. W., Miller, N. E., Mowrer, O. H., & Sears, R. R. (1939). *Frustration and aggression*. New Haven, CT: Yale University Press.

Eastwick, P. W., Finkel, E. J., Krishnamurti, T., & Loewenstein, G. (2008). Mispredicting distress following romantic breakup: Revealing the time course of the affective forecasting error. *Journal of Experimental Social Psychology*, 44, 800–807.

Ellison, N. B., Stenfield, C., & Lampe, C. (2007). The benefits of Facebook friends: Social capital and college students' use of online social network sites. *Journal of Computer Mediated Communication*, 12, 1143–1168.

Festinger, L., Schachter, S., & Back, K. (1950). *Social pressures in informal groups: A study of human factors in housing*. New York, NY: Harper.

Fisher, H. (2004). *Why we love: The nature and chemistry of romantic love*. New York, NY: Holt.

Fiske, S. T., & Neuberg, S. L. (1990). A continuum of impression formation, from category-based to individuating processes: Influences of information and motivation on attention and interpretation. In L. Berkowitz (Ed.), *Advances in experimental social psychology* (Vol. 23, pp. 1–74). New York, NY: Academic Press.

Ford, C. S., & Beach, F. A. (1951). *Patterns of sexual behavior*. New York, NY: Harper.

Forest, A. L., & Wood, J. V. (2012). When social networking is not working: Individuals with low self-esteem recognize but do not reap the benefits of self-disclosure on Facebook. *Psychological Science*, 23, 295–302.

Furnham, A., Moutafi, J., & Baguma, P. (2002). A cross-cultural study of the role of weight and waist-to-hip ratio on female attractiveness. *Personality and Individual Differences*, 32, 729–745.

Gaertner, S. L., & Dovidio, J. F. (1986). The aversive form of racism. In J. F. Dovidio & S. L. Gaertner (Eds.), *Prejudice, discrimination, and racism* (pp. 61–89). Orlando, FL: Academic Press.

Gaertner, S. L., & Dovidio, J. F. (2000). *Reducing intergroup bias: The common ingroup identity model*. New York, NY: Psychology Press.

Gaertner, S. L., Mann, J. A., Murrell, A. J., & Dovidio, J. F. (1989). Reducing intergroup bias: The benefits of recategorization. *Journal of Personality and Social Psychology*, 57, 239–249.

Garcia, S. D., & Khersonsky, D. (1997). 'They are a lovely couple': Further examination of perceptions of couple attractiveness. *Journal of Social Behaviour and Personality*, 12, 367–380.

Gentile, B., Twenge, J., Freeman, E. C., & Campbell, W. K. (2012). The effect of social networking websites on positive self-views: An experimental investigation. *Computers in Human Behavior, 28,* 1929–1933.

Gil-Burmann, C., Peláez, F., & Sánchez, S. (2002). Mate choice differences according to sex and age: An analysis of personal advertisements in Spanish newspapers. *Human Nature, 13,* 493–508.

Glick, P., & Fiske, S. T. (1996). The ambivalent sexism inventory: Differentiating hostile and benevolent sexism. *Journal of Personality and Social Psychology, 70,* 491–492.

Glick, P., Diebold, J., Bailey-Werner, B., & Zhu, L. (1997). The two faces of Adam: Ambivalent sexism and polarized attitudes towards women. *Personality and Social Psychology Bulletin, 23,* 1323–1334.

Goldberg, L. R. (1993). The structure of phenotypic personality traits. *American Psychologist, 48,* 26–34.

Graham, J. A., & Cohen, R. (1997). Race and sex as factors in children's sociometric ratings and friendship choices. *Social Development, 6,* 355–372.

Grammer, K., & Thornhill, R. (1994). Human (*Homo sapiens*) facial attractiveness and sexual selection: The role of symmetry and averageness. *Journal of Comparative Psychology, 108,* 233–242.

Gruber-Baldini, A. L., Schaie, K. W., & Willis, S. L. (1995). Similarity in married couples: A longitudinal study of mental abilities and rigidity–flexibility. *Journal of Personality and Social Psychology, 69,* 191–203.

Hackenbracht, J., & Gasper, K. (2013). I'm all ears: The need to belong motivates listening to emotional disclosure. *Journal of Experimental Social Psychology, 49,* 915–921.

Hatfield, E. (1988). Passionate and compassionate love. In R. J. Sternberg & M. L. Barnes (Eds.), *The psychology of love* (pp. 191–217). New Haven, CT: Yale University Press.

Hatfield, E., & Walster, G. W. (1981). *A new look at love.* Reading, MA: Addison-Wesley.

Hewstone, M. (1996). Contact and categorization: Social psychological interventions to change intergroup relations. In C. N. Macrae, C. Stangor, & M. Hewstone (Eds.), *Stereotypes and stereotyping* (pp. 323–368). New York, NY: Guilford Press.

Indian, M., & Grieve, R. (2014). When Facebook is easier than face-to-face: Social support derived from Facebook in socially anxious individuals. *Personality and Individual Differences, 59,* 102–106.

Janis, I. (1982). *Groupthink* (2nd ed.). Boston, MA: Houghton Mifflin.

Jones, B. C., Little, A. C., Penton-Voak, I. S., Tiddeman, B. P., Burt, D. M., & Perrett, D. I. (2001). Facial symmetry and judgements of apparent health support for a 'good genes' explanation of the attractiveness–symmetry relationship. *Evolution and Human Behavior, 22,* 417–429.

Kahneman, D. (1973). *Attention and effort.* Englewood Cliffs, NJ: Prentice Hall.

Kandel, D. B. (1978). Similarity in real-life adolescent friendship pairs. *Journal of Personality and Social Psychology, 36,* 306–312.

Karau, S. J., & Williams, K. D. (1995). Social loafing, research findings, implications, and future directions. *Current Directions in Psychological Science, 4,* 134–140.

Karremans, J. C., & Verwijmeren, T. (2008). Mimicking attractive opposite-sex others: The role of romantic relationship status. *Personality and Social Psychology Bulletin, 34,* 939–950.

Kerr, N. L. (1992). Norms in social dilemmas. In D. Schroeder (Ed.), *Social dilemmas: Psychological perspectives.* New York, NY: Praeger.

Lamm, H., & Weismann, U. (1997). Subjective attributes of attraction: How people categorize their liking, their love, and their being in love. *Personal Relationships, 4,* 271–284.

Langlois, J. H., Roggman, L. A., & Musselman, L. (1994). What is average and what is not average about attractive faces? *Psychological Science, 5,* 214–220.

Latané, B., Williams, K., & Harkins, S. (1979). Many hands make light the work: The causes and consequences of social loafing. *Journal of Personality and Social Psychology, 37,* 822–832.

Laurenceau, J. P., Barrett, L. F., & Pietromonaco, P. R. (1998). Intimacy as an interpersonal process: The importance of self-disclosure, partner disclosure, and perceived partner responsiveness in interpersonal exchanges. *Journal of Personality and Social Psychology, 74,* 1238–1251.

Leary, M. R., Kowalski, R. M., Smith, L., & Phillips, S. (2003). Teasing, rejection and violence: Case studies of the school shootings. *Aggressive Behavior, 29*, 202–214.

Levine, R. A., & Campbell, D. T. (1972). *Ethnocentrism: Theories of conflict, attitudes and group behavior.* New York, NY: Wiley.

Lickel, B., Hamilton, D. L., Lewis, A., Sherman, S. J., Wierczorkowska, G., & Uhles, A. N. (2000). Varieties of groups and the perception of group entitativity. *Journal of Personality and Social Psychology, 78*, 223–246.

Lucas, R. E. (2005). Time does not heal all wounds. A longitudinal study of reaction and adaptation to divorce. *Psychological Science, 16*, 945–950.

MacAskill, E. (2007). Families rebuke NBC for broadcast of killer's rant. *The Guardian*, 20 April. Retrieved 23 January 2014 from http://www.theguardian.com/media/2007/apr/20/1

Major, B., Hunger, J. M., Bunyan, D. P., & Miller, C. T. (2014). The ironic effects of weight stigma. *Journal of Experimental Social Psychology, 51*, 74–80.

Mehdizadeh, S. (2010). Self-presentation 2.0: Narcissism and self-esteem on Facebook. *Cyberpsychology, Behaviour, and Social Networking, 13*, 357–363.

Milgram, S. (1963). Behavioral study of obedience. *Journal of Abnormal and Social Psychology, 67*, 371–378.

Møller, A. P., & Swaddle, J. P. (1997). *Asymmetry, developmental stability and evolution.* Oxford, UK: Oxford University Press.

Moscovici, S. (1980). Toward a theory of conversion behavior. In L. Berkowitz (Ed.), *Advances in experimental social psychology* (Vol. 13, pp. 209–239). New York, NY: Academic Press.

Moscovici, S., Lage, E., & Naffrechoux, M. (1969). Influence in a consistent minority on the responses of a majority in a color perception task. *Sociometry, 32*, 365–379.

Nadkarni, A., & Hofmann, S. G. (2012). Why do people use Facebook? *Personality and Individual Differences, 53*, 243–249.

Newcomb, T. M. (1961). *The acquaintance process.* New York, NY: Holt, Rinehart and Winston.

Office for National Statistics. (2013). *An overview of hate crime in England and Wales.* Retrieved 19 January 2014 from https://www.gov.uk/government/uploads/system/uploads/attachment_data/file/266358/hate-crime-2013.pdf

Oskamp, S., & Jones, J. M. (2000). Promising practice in reducing prejudice: A report from the President's Initiative on Race. In S. Oskamp (Ed.), *Reducing prejudice and discrimination* (pp. 319–334). Mahwah, NJ: Lawrence Erlbaum Associates.

Paolini, S., Hewstone, M., Cairns, E., & Voci, A. (2004). Effects of direct and indirect cross-group friendships on judgements of Catholic and Protestants in Northern Ireland: The mediating role of an anxiety-reduction mechanism. *Personality and Social Psychology Bulletin, 30*, 770–786.

Pascoe, E. A., & Smart, R. L. (2009). Perceived discrimination and health: A meta-analytic review. *Psychological Bulletin, 135*, 531–554.

Pettigrew, T. F. (1958). Personality and socio-cultural factors in intergroup attitudes: A cross-national comparison. *Journal of Conflict Resolution, 2*, 29–42.

Pettigrew, T. F., & Tropp, L. R. (2006). A meta-analytic test of intergroup contact theory. *Journal of Personality and Social Psychology, 90*, 751–783.

Pratto, F., Sidanius, J., Stallworth, L. M., & Malle, B. F. (1994). Social dominance orientation: A personality variable predicting social and political attitudes. *Journal of Personality and Social Psychology, 67*, 741–763.

Puhl, R. M., & Brownell, K. (2001). Bias, discrimination, and obesity. *Obesity Research, 9*, 788–805.

Ratner, K. G., & Amodio, D. M. (2013). Seeing 'us vs. them': Minimal group effects on the neural encoding of faces. *Journal of Experimental Social Psychology, 49*, 298–301.

Reicher, S. D., Spears, R., & Postmes, T. (1995). A social identity model of deindividuation phenomena. *European Review of Social Psychology, 6*, 161–198.

Reis, H. T., & Patrick, B. C. (1996). Attachment and intimacy: Component processes. In E. T. Higgins & A. W. Kruglanski (Eds.), *Social psychology: Handbook of basic principles* (pp. 523–563). New York, NY: Guilford Press.

Rhodes, G., Zebrowitz, L. A., Clark, A., Kalick, S. M., Hightower, A., & McKay, R. (2001). Do facial averageness and symmetry signal health? *Evolution and Human Behavior, 22,* 31–46.

Rubin, M., & Hewstone, M. (1998). Social identity theory's self-esteem hypothesis: A review and some suggestions for clarification. *Personality and Social Psychology Review, 2,* 40–62.

Rusbult, C. E. (1983). A longitudinal test of the investment model: The development (and deterioration) of satisfaction and commitment in heterosexual involvements. *Journal of Personality and Social Psychology, 45,* 101–117.

Rusbult, C. E., & Zembrodt, I. M. (1983). Responses to dissatisfaction in romantic involvements: A multi-dimensional scaling analysis. *Journal of Experimental Social Psychology, 19,* 274–293.

Rushton, J. P. (1989). Genetic similarity in male friendships. *Ethology and Sociobiology, 10,* 361–373.

Sbarra, D. A., & Emery, R. E. (2005). The emotional sequelae of nonmarital relationship dissolution: Analysis of change and intraindividual variability over time. *Personal Relationships, 12*(2), 213–232.

Sedikides, C. (1993). Assessment, enhancement, and verification determinants of the self-evaluation process. *Journal of Personality and Social Psychology, 65,* 317–338.

Sherif, M. (1935). A study of some social factors in perception. *Archives of Psychology, 27,* 1–60.

Sherif, M., & Sherif, C. W. (1953). *Groups in harmony and tension: An integration of studies of intergroup relations.* Oxford, UK: Harper & Brothers.

Sherif, M., White, B. J., & Harvey, O. J. (1955). Status in experimentally produced groups. *American Journal of Sociology, 60,* 370–379.

Sidanius, J. (1993). The psychology of group conflict and the dynamics of oppression: A social dominance perspective. In S. Iyengar & W. McGuire (Eds.), *Explorations in political psychology* (pp. 183–219). Durham, NC: Duke University Press.

Skues, J. L., Williams, B., & Wise, L. (2012). The effects of personality traits, self-esteem, loneliness, and narcissism on Facebook among university students. *Computers in Human Behavior, 28,* 2414–2419.

Smart Insights. (2015). Digital marketing statistics 2015. Retrieved 21 May 2015 from http://www.smartinsights.com/marketplace-analysis/customer-analysis/digital-marketing-statistics-sources

Socially Psyched. (n.d.). Robbers Cave experiment. Retrieved 26 January 2018 from https://www.dowellwebtools.com/tools/lp/Bo/psyched/15/Robbers_Cave_Experiment

Stangor, C., Sullivan, L. A., & Ford, T. E. (1991). Affective and cognitive determinants of prejudice. *Social Cognition, 9,* 359–380.

Steele, C. M., & Aronson, J. (1995). Stereotype threat and the intellectual test performance of African Americans. *Journal of Personality and Social Psychology, 69,* 797–811.

Stephan, W. G., & Stephan, C. W. (1985). Intergroup anxiety. *Journal of Social Issues, 41,* 157–176.

Strassberg, D. S., & Holty, S. (2003). An experimental study of women's internet personal ads. *Archives of Sexual Behavior, 32,* 253–260.

Streeter, S. A., & McBurney, D. H. (2003). Waist–hip ratio and attractiveness: New evidence and a critique of a critical test. *Evolution and Human Behavior, 24,* 88–98.

Swann, W. B., Jr., de la Ronde, C., & Hixon, J. G. (1994). Authenticity and positive strivings in marriage and courtship. *Journal of Personality and Social Psychology, 66,* 857–869.

Tajfel, H., Billig, M., Bundy, R., & Flament, C. (1971). Social categorization and intergroup behaviour. *European Journal of Social Psychology, 1,* 149–178.

Tajfel, H., & Turner, J. C. (1979). An integrative theory of intergroup conflict: The social identity theory of intergroup behaviour. In W. G. Austin & S. Worchel (Eds.), *The social psychology of intergroup relations* (pp. 33–47). Monterey, CA: Brooks/Cole.

Thibaut, J. W., & Kelley, H. H. (1959). *The social psychology of groups.* New York, NY: Wiley.

Townsend, J. M., & Levy, G. D. (1990). Effects of potential partners' physical attractiveness and socioeconomic status on sexuality and partner selection. *Archives of Sexual Behaviour, 19,* 149–164.

Triplett, N. (1897). The dynamogenic factors in pacemaking and competition. *American Journal of Psychology, 9*, 507–533.

Turner, R. N., Crisp, R. J., & Lambert, E. (2007). Imagining intergroup contact can improve intergroup attitudes. *Group Processes and Intergroup Relations, 10*, 427–441.

Turner, R. N., Hewstone, M., & Voci, A. (2007). Reducing explicit and implicit prejudice via direct and extended contact: The mediating role of self-disclosure and intergroup anxiety. *Journal of Personality and Social Psychology, 93*, 369–388.

Turner, R. N., Hewstone, M., Voci, A., & Vonofakou, C. (2008). A test of the extended intergroup contact hypothesis: The mediating role of intergroup anxiety, perceived ingroup and outgroup norms, and inclusion of the outgroup in the self. *Journal of Personality and Social Psychology, 95*, 843–860.

Wall Street Journal. (2012, 4 October). Facebook: One billion and counting. Retrieved 8 February 2018 from https://www.wsj.com/articles/SB10000872396390044363540457803616402738612

Warburton, W. A., Williams, K. D., & Cairns, D. R. (2006). When ostracism leads to aggression: The moderating effect of control deprivation. *Journal of Experimental Social Psychology, 42*, 213–220.

West, K., & Turner, R. N. (2014). Using extended contact to improve physiological responses and behavior towards people with schizophrenia. *Journal of Experimental Social Psychology, 50*, 57–64.

White, F. A., & Abu-Rayya, H. M. (2012). A dual identity-electronic contact (DIEC) experiment promoting short- and long-term intergroup harmony. *Journal of Experimental Social Psychology, 48*, 597–608.

Williams, K. D., Cheung, C. K. T., & Choi, W. (2000). Cyberostracism: Effects of being ignored over the internet. *Journal of Personality and Social Psychology, 79*, 748–762.

World Internet User Statistics. (2014). Retrieved 21 May 2015 from http://www.internetworldstats.com/stats.htm

Wright, S. C., Aron, A., McLaughlin-Volpe, T., & Ropp, S. A. (1997). The extended contact effect: Knowledge of cross-group friendships and prejudice. *Journal of Personality and Social Psychology, 73*, 73–90.

Zajonc, R. B. (1965). Social facilitation. *Science, 149*, 269–274.

Zajonc, R. B. (1968). Attitudinal effects of mere exposure. *Journal of Personality and Social Psychology, 9*, 1–27.

Zimbardo, P. G. (2008). *Jonestown (the situational of evil) revisited*. Retrieved 7 November 2013 from http://thesituationist.wordpress.com/2008/11/17/jonestown-the-situation-of-evil-revisited

Index

Psychology, First Edition. Edited by Graham Davey.
© 2019 John Wiley & Sons, Ltd. Published 2019 by John Wiley & Sons, Ltd.